For my wise and strong grandmothers, Monica and Grace,
my loving parents, Monica and Pierre,
and my darling family, Michael, Stella and Amber

Karen Martini

COOK

Hardie Grant

BOOKS

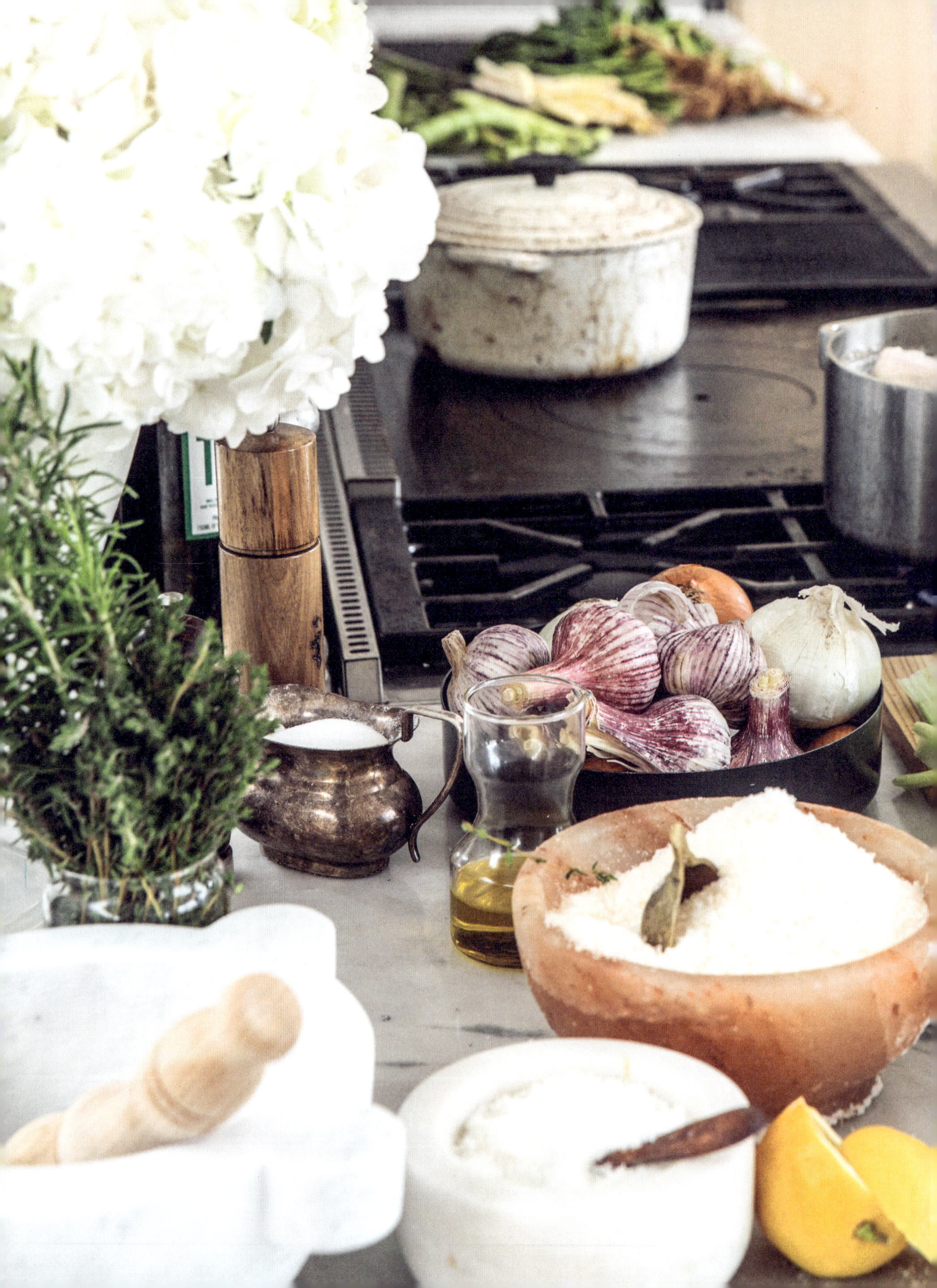

Contents

Introduction 4
Essentials 6
Equipment 34
A few notes on using this book 42

Stocks 45

Sauces & dressings 61

Stock reductions 64
Dairy 69
Emulsions 74
Vinaigrettes & herb-based sauces 82
Asian sauces 93

Pasta 107

Risotto 143

Seafood 153

Fish 154
Crustaceans 194
Shellfish 204
Cephalopods 216

Chicken 225

Duck & quail 255

Duck 256
Quail 268

Beef & veal 271

Beef 272
Veal 294

Lamb 299

Pork 321

Eggs & dairy 347

Grains, pulses, seeds & nuts 367

Vegetables 397

Asian greens 398
Asparagus 404
Avocado 408
Beetroot 416
Borlotti beans 422
Broad beans 428
Green beans 434
Broccoli, broccolini & cime di rape 440
Cabbage & brussels sprouts 446

Capsicum 458
Carrot 466
Cauliflower 474
Celeriac 480
Celery 486
Chilli 492
Corn 496
Cucumber 504
Eggplant 514
Fennel 524
Globe artichoke 532
Jerusalem artichoke 540
Kohlrabi 546
Leafy vegetables & salad leaves 550
Mushroom 568
Okra 578
Olives 584
Onion & leek 592
Parsnip 604
Peas 608
Potato & sweet potato 616
Pumpkin 628
Radish, daikon & turnip 636
Rhubarb 644
Tomato 652
Zucchini 666

Fruit 677

Apple 678
Berries 686
Citrus 690
Fig 700
Pear 708
Quince 712
Stone fruit 718

Sweet baking & desserts 727

Cakes, cupcakes & muffins 731
Biscuits, slices & sweet buns 754
Pancakes, doughnuts, scones & crumpets 768
Puddings & other desserts 776
Sweet essentials & snacks 786
Icings, fillings, syrups, sauces & glazes 792

Pastry 809

Sweet 812
Savoury 828

Savoury baking & breads 835

Index 860
Acknowledgements 908
About the author 912

Introduction

This is a big book. Vast even. It's a book about my experience, about how I cook, about what I like to eat, and about how I understand food. Even at 900-odd pages, it is not exhaustive. And that's okay. A book like this can never be truly definitive, but hopefully it is interesting, informative, helpful – inspiring, even.

When we were planning this book, the list of recipes was terrifyingly long, almost unmanageably so, and still there were more recipes that could have been added. It's astonishing how much is in your head once you start to unpack it. And unpack it we did, drawing out all my favourites from childhood through to today, making use of all the real estate we could – not even the margins were safe!

I have a strong fascination with many different cuisines, and I also like to carve my own path. So, this book could never have been a guide to all the cuisines that I adore. It could never begin to capture Thai food like David Thompson has, or Lebanese food like Greg and Lucy Malouf, or the cuisines of the Levant like Yotam Ottolenghi. I could go on.

This book houses my best recipes from the simple to the elaborate, roaming broadly and for all skill levels and occasions. It is a deeply personal book, crammed full of favourite recipes, ones learnt from my family, ones that have been inspired by meals made for me, both professional and homely, ones that have featured on my restaurant menus over the years, and plenty of classics. They are recipes that I constantly tweak and refine, and they have all been carefully tested and honed for the home cook.

But this is more than just a book of recipes; rather it is an approach to food that reflects my ever-keen interest in the richly diverse world of food, in taking it all in and viewing it through my own lens. And I want you to view these recipes through your lens, too. Throughout the book I give variations, simplifications and amplifications for the recipes, as well as lots of pairing advice. Cook the recipes, understand them, then make them your own.

Writing this book was a long process, much longer than I thought it would be. I should say, making this book was a long process. Documenting recipes (in words and images), and stories and details on produce and techniques was one thing, but the countless hours of testing and tweaking, of fine-tuning new recipes and revisiting old ones was something else altogether. It was all-consuming.

One thing that was easy, though, was the title. It was put forward early on, agreed to, and we never questioned it once. *COOK*. All caps, if you please!

I'm a chef, yes, but a chef is always a cook at heart. It's where we start and it's who we are at home, cooking for family and friends. Even in a restaurant, that spirit is present in the best of chefs, that sense of generosity, that connectedness to who they're feeding. The title is also an encouragement, a gentle one, if you like, or an exhortation. 'Cook! Please cook.'

Cooking can be such a joy, and it's one to be shared. That's something I hope to do with this book. Not to just share recipes, but to share a love of produce, an appreciation for food that is grown, raised and reared well. To encourage us all to treat our produce with respect, and to pause and understand our impact, to be humane, to not waste.

Even though I was classically trained at a young age and have cooked for more than thirty years professionally, when I am cooking at home I feel my family stretching out before and after me. I feel the hand of my Meme, her deft touch and innate understanding of flavour, and I take great pleasure in cooking with my girls, not just showing them how to make this or that, but also passing on the love of the process just as much as the result.

I grew up cooking with my mother and grandmothers. The first dishes I grappled with were simple – ratatouille, lasagne, crumbed schnitzel, stuffed capsicums – passed down over time, cooked without fuss but with a real understanding of flavour, of detail. It was addictive. Crafting something from raw ingredients, investing in the process, caring every step of the way. And then I got to eat!

I was drawn to my parents' garden from a young age. We lived on a large block in suburban Melbourne. They made the most of the space, planting what they could grow: a small patch, some herbs and vegetables, and a handful of fruit trees. Collecting firewood, pulling carrots from the ground, and grabbing low-slung oranges from the tree were regular chores, as was feeding the chickens.

It was simple, but that connection from the ground to the plate is such an important one. It's one we need to get back to. We can't all grow what we need, but we're all better cooks for being connected to what grows.

It is perhaps unavoidable that an Australian book of this scope will bring Stephanie Alexander to mind. Stephanie's influence has been immense. The purity of her cooking and gift for communication was a beacon in my early years, and it has left a great impression. While mine is necessarily a different book, a chronicle of a different journey, our two major works share an undeniable kinship. And that's something that makes me very proud. Nothing would make me happier than to see well-thumbed copies of both books nestled against each other on a cook's shelf.

This book is about the love of cooking. It is a book flushed with my own history and what I have learnt from so many brilliant cooks, both celebrated and humble. It is a book that will hopefully age well, too, as the principles and flavours are timeless. It is a book that I hope will help those tentative about cooking to become more confident, and one that I hope will add colour and texture for those more experienced. As the title says: *COOK*.

Essentials

Acidulated water

Simply water with a good squeeze of lemon juice, this stops vegetables from browning after being peeled or cut.

Ajwain seeds

Originally from Northern India and Iran, ajwain seeds have a peppery thyme-like flavour that works well in vegetable and fish curries, as well as root vegetables and pumpkin.

Aleppo pepper

Aleppo peppers, also called halaby peppers, are traditionally grown in the Middle East. When ripe, they blush to an intensely deep red, retaining that vibrancy when dried and broken into flakes or ground to a powder. They have a gentle but meaningful heat and sweet fruity flavour with caramel notes. I love using aleppo pepper with eggs or fish, to finish a soup or braise, with beans, to sprinkle over dips or scatter over freshly cooked Pitta bread (p. 854).

Aleppo chilli salt. This chilli salt is great as a finishing seasoning on eggs, grilled vegetables, baked rice dishes or with fresh curd cheeses, among other things. Add 2 tablespoons ground aleppo pepper and 1½ tablespoons salt flakes to a bowl and combine by crushing the flakes a little. Store in an airtight container for up to 1 month.

Amaranth

There are several species of amaranth that are cultivated for food, with both the seeds and leaves being edible. The leaves can be stir-fried, boiled or steamed, while the dried seeds are a pseudocereal. The seeds are very nutritious and can be boiled and used in salads, soups and stews. Amaranth seeds do not contain gluten and can be ground to a flour or flaked, and they're often used to make porridge or in muesli. Amaranth is related to quinoa.

Amchur

Ground unripe mango, amchur powder is used as a souring agent for curries, pickles, relishes and dressings.

Anchovies

A plump pink anchovy is a wondrous thing, but an oxidised brownish-grey one can be woeful. Once opened, they will deteriorate, so it's best to keep them refrigerated and always under oil. They will still oxidise, but not as rapidly. A top-quality anchovy, such as Ortiz or Cuca, is marvellous eaten as is or draped over some chargrilled bread, so I tend to use a tin that will fulfil my immediate cooking needs along with providing a pre-dinner snack.

Anise seeds

Unrelated to fennel or star anise, anise seeds have a similar aniseed flavour that I liken to sweet liquorice, and are more akin to fennel than star anise. The tiny green-brown seeds are used widely across the Middle East and Mediterranean for sweet and savoury dishes. I use them for pastries and biscuits, root vegetables and seafood braises.

Arame

Arame is a species of kelp that is dried and used in Japanese cooking. It is dark in colour and comes in strands, which are rehydrated before use. It has a mild and gently sweet flavour profile.

Artichoke hearts

These are handy for a quick snack with some salami, olives, cheese and the like, or as a component of a more formal antipasti selection. They can be sliced and stuffed into a sandwich with mozzarella or provolone and mortadella or salami, added to a Lamb ragù (p. 535) or quick pasta sauce, or used in place of freshly cooked artichokes in most dishes. Find a brand you like, as they're not all equal.

Asafoetida

Used in Ayurvedic cooking as a replacement for garlic and onion, asafoetida powder is the dried root of a type of fennel. It has a pungently sulphurous smell reminiscent of fermented garlic. It can make you wince if you inhale it too deeply. Try not to. But it does add a welcome savoury touch to curries and braises, just use very sparingly. Asafoetida is also used in Ayurvedic medicine, and it is supposed to quell flatulence when added to leguminous dishes.

Bacon See p. 326

Baharat

A Middle Eastern spice blend, baharat is commonly built around paprika, black pepper, coriander seeds, cumin, cinnamon, green cardamom and nutmeg, but there are many regional variations. It is somewhat like the garam masala of the Middle East, being an incredibly versatile mix that adds a warm depth of flavour to all manner of dishes, from dusting koftas to braises, rice dishes, salads, in marinades. Finely grind 1½ tablespoons black peppercorns, 1½ tablespoons coriander seeds, 2 teaspoons cardamom seeds, 2 teaspoons cumin seeds, two allspice berries and two star anise in a mortar or with a spice grinder, then combine with 2½ tablespoons sweet paprika, 1½ tablespoons ground cloves, 2 teaspoons ground cinnamon and 2 teaspoons freshly grated nutmeg. Store in an airtight container for up to 2 months.

Baking powder (baking soda)

A combination of bicarbonate of soda (see p. 8) and an acid, baking powder only requires dissolving into a batter/mix to become active.

Barberries

A small scarlet berry sold dried with a little moisture in the fruit, barberries are extremely tart and fruity, tasting a little like sweet tamarind. I love to use them cooked in rice and cold in grain salads and dressings. I sometimes add them too my Apple pie (p. 818) for the acidic tang against the sweetness, as well as for the little pop of colour. Barberries are also excellent in spiced chicken dishes.

Barley

Most barley available is pearled barley, where the bran has been removed. Unlike rice, barley has plenty of nutrients in the kernel, so while stripping off the bran does remove vitamins and minerals, it isn't reduced to basic carbohydrates. Hulled barley has the inedible outer husk removed, with most of the bran intact, so it is more nutritious, but it does take a lot longer to cook and has a different textural feel. I like the nutty quality of barley, whether pearl or hulled, and I do like the slightly chewy and slippery quality of pearled barley. Black barley is becoming increasingly available. It is an ancient grain, which naturally has no outer hull and needs no further refinement. It is highly nutritious and has a distinctive texture and nutty flavour, not to mention its dramatic visual appeal.

Basil, Greek

Perennial Greek basil is a great addition to the garden, being a hardy plant that produces fragrant leaves all year round, though they tend to die back a bit in colder conditions. The scent is similar to sweet basil, with less anise, while the leaves are smaller and hardier. It's not something that you'd make pesto from, but Greek basil can be used to make aromatic herb oils and dressings, or just add it to braises, soups and sauces.

Basil, holy

It's not uncommon to hear holy basil and Thai basil being used synonymously, but they are not the same. Holy basil is also called tulsi, which is thought to have originated on the subcontinent, where it is used for cooking, Ayurvedic medicine and to make tea. Holy basil is also used in South-East Asian cuisines where a number of varieties are used, perhaps the most famous of which is Thai holy basil – which is no doubt where the confusion comes in. Holy basil is not common in Australian markets. It has a spicy flavour profile with some heat.

Basil, sweet

Sweet basil is sold year-round, often grown hydroponically, but there is nothing like a bunch of sun-kissed summer basil. It's worth tasting the leaves before using, especially when making something like Pesto (p. 90), as plants going to seed can be bitter, with the anise tones quite pungent. Basil is best added towards the end of cooking to capture its fresh flavour, but I will also add whole sprigs of basil to sauces, then remove once the sauce is cooked, finishing with some fresh leaves. And it's always best torn or cut just before using, as it can oxidise and turn black. I never chop basil, only ever tear or chiffonade (slice into fine strips), as it tends to accelerate that oxidation. Whatever you do, prepare your basil just before using or protect it with oil, such as with a pesto. Also, never store basil wet, as it will blacken quickly. Sweet basil also comes in a purple cultivar, which is somewhere between classic sweet basil and Thai basil. Dried basil has a different flavour altogether, and it's not something I use. Basil has a celebrated affinity with tomatoes, but also pairs beautifully with other vegetables that peak at the same time, such as eggplants (aubergines) and capsicums (bell peppers).

Basil, Thai

Thai basil is similar in appearance to sweet basil, but with purple stems and purple accents to the leaves. It has a similar flavour, but it is more pungently spicy and clove-like with the anise notes turned up. It's a wonderfully aromatic herb for salads and stir-fries, or to finish soups and curries.

Bay leaves

I'm a big fan of bay leaves, but less so the dried ones. Plucked fresh from the tree, the flavour is superb. I use them in a bouquet garni, or just drop them in soups and braises, and will often roast pork or fish directly on top of a small branch. Bay is also easy to grow at home, but they can grow to be quite big trees, so if you don't have the space, a large pot is best.

Beans, adzuki

Common to East Asia, adzuki beans are responsible for red bean paste, which is used widely for sweets in Japan and China, but the beans can be used in soups, salads and stews. They are quite compact, with a mild nutty flavour and a gentle sweetness.

Beans, black turtle

Strikingly black with a white strip where they attach to the pod, black turtle beans are full-flavoured beans that work well in spicy braises.

Beans, borlotti (cranberry)

I tend to use fresh borlotti beans in season, but the dried beans are nearly as good, cooking to a rich and creamy consistency. They are ideal for soups, stews and braises.

Beans, cannellini

A beloved legume in central Italy, cannellini beans are a medium-sized white bean that have a creamy but light texture. They take up flavours well and can be perfumed with herbs such as rosemary in the cooking water. They are excellent in soups and work beautifully in salads, marrying well with things such as preserved tuna, tomatoes, shaved onion and olive oil.

Beans, fava

Dried broad beans, known as fava beans, have a mealy texture when cooked and can be mashed with lots of olive oil and lemon to make a pleasing dip.

Beans, gigante

A large white bean, gigante beans are a staple of Greek cuisine, most famously used to make Gigantes plaki (p. 380).

Beans, great northern

A white bean that sits in between cannellini and haricot (navy) beans in size, great northern beans have a similar creamy texture and flavour to cannellini beans.

Beans, haricot (navy)

Small white legumes, these are best known for their contribution to baked beans. They are not hugely flavoursome.

Beans, kidney

Most associated with chilli con carne and its ilk, as well as being pivotal in three-bean mix, red kidney beans have a slightly powdery texture and distinctive flavour. They work well in spicy dishes.

Beans, mung

Green mung beans are used in Indian cooking either whole (sabut moong) or split (moong dal), and they are commonly sprouted for mung bean sprouts.

Biber salçasi

A Turkish paste made from red peppers and chillies, biber salçasi comes in mild and hot versions. It can be used to flavour all manner of dishes, from Cabbage rolls (p. 451) and stuffed vegetables and Lebanese talami bread (p. 852), to soups, braises, dressings and marinades.

Bicarbonate of soda (baking soda)

An alkaline leavening agent, bicarbonate of soda requires an acid to become active, releasing carbon dioxide, which gives cakes and the like their rise.

Bonito flakes See katsuobushi (p. 17)

Bottarga

Made from the roe sac of grey mullet that has been cured in salt and dried until firm, bottarga is most associated with Sardinian cuisine, but the Sicilians make a version from tuna roe: bottarga di tonno. The process is linked back to Byzantium, with similar products produced across Europe, the Middle East and parts of Asia, notably Japan and Korea. In Sardinia, bottarga is often shaved or grated over pasta (see p. 123) or served with crostini and olive oil. It has a wonderfully distinctive oceanic flavour, packed with umami.

Bouquet garni

You can make your bouquet out of any herbs you like, but parsley, thyme and bay are the basics, with rosemary and orange rind sometimes included depending on what you're cooking. The little bundle is trussed with kitchen twine and dropped in the pot. If using rosemary, it is a handy way to stop all the needles ending up in the dish.

Bread improver

This is something that I use for one recipe only, a Classic dinner knot roll (p. 846) that I used to make as an apprentice at Tansy's. Bread improver is a combination of yeast and some enzymes to make bread light and fluffy.

Brik pastry

Similar to filo, brik is a fine pastry from North Africa, which is often wrapped into a parcel with egg, tuna, herbs and Harissa (p. 92) (and many other combinations), then deep-fried until golden and crisp. The pastry can also be rolled into cigars with sweet or savoury fillings and fried.

Buckwheat

A pseudocereal, buckwheat is a seed that is increasing in popularity, no doubt due to the fact that it contains no gluten (the name is as deceptive as 'glutinous rice'). In Italy, it is a staple in Lombardy where it is used to make pasta, perhaps most famously for pizzoccheri. It is more prevalent in Eastern Europe, though, where it is called kasha, with a porridge-like dish of buckwheat also known by that name. Buckwheat is also the key ingredient in soba noodles, though wheat flour is sometimes used. Buckwheat can be used in salads or in place of brown rice, and it can be toasted before boiling for a richer flavour. I always wash buckwheat first and skim well while cooking, as the purplish scum that forms can be bitter. Draining and rinsing will also prevent bitterness.

Bulgur wheat

Parboiled cracked wheat, bulgur wheat is most famously associated with tabouleh, but is used in many dishes in the Middle East, from salads and pilaf-like dishes to stews. Bulgur comes in different grades of coarseness, and instructions for cooking vary, but you can generally cover with warm water and soak until swollen for 20–30 minutes. Regular cracked wheat is not parboiled, so it will need to be cooked until tender.

Burrata See mozzarella (p. 20)

Butter

I generally buy unsalted butter, then season with the salt of my choice. The choices then are really between regular butter and cultured butter, with the latter traditionally fermented, though a culture is generally added to modern versions. Cultured butter has a more intense flavour. Whichever type I buy, I try to ensure that it is organic and made from grass-fed cow's milk/cream.

Capers and caperberries

Capers are the emerging buds on a caper bush, while caperberries are the fruit produced after the buds flower. Capers come in different sizes, but they are all rather petite compared to caperberries, which look like an olive with one end tapering into a gently curled stem. The berry contains crunchy but quite edible seeds. Both can be pickled in vinegar or brine, or packed in salt. For those salt-packed, soak in water for 15 minutes to remove excess salt and they are ready to go. You can then store in a little salty water or pour some white-wine vinegar over the top. Caperberries can be eaten whole or sliced, and can be served with things like Gravlax (pp. 167, 171), terrines (pp. 327–8) and cured meats, while capers are essential for making Tartare (pp. 77, 279) and Puttanesca sauce (p. 117), and are brilliant in a Burnt butter sauce (p. 73) for fish, or with egg salad.

Caraway seeds

Perhaps mainly known for their use in traditional European rye loaves, caraway is a much more versatile, if underused, spice. It's great in sauerkraut and vinegary pickles, pairs beautifully with braised cabbage and roasted vegetables, particularly carrots, and adds an extra dimension to roast pork or braised beef. I like it both in bread and crackers or on pretzels with salt. It is also lovely with orange in sweet baking, and it's a must in my fresh Harissa (p. 92) and Zhoug (p. 87), along with braised Tunisian-style vegetables. Caraway seeds look a little like cumin, with warm pepper, fennel, woody and earthy notes and a sweet orange-like twist.

Cardamom, brown

Not to be confused with green cardamom (see above right) and its distinctly floral notes, brown cardamom has a smoky, eucalypt, woody and peppery flavour. The pods are much larger, roughly ridged, and somewhat predictably brown, while the seeds are dark brown to almost black. Brown cardamom is commonly used in subcontinental and Chinese cooking, and it is an essential element of a good master stock.

Cardamom, green

The fibrous husks of green cardamom pods (or true cardamom) hide the tiny aromatic seeds, which have a pungently floral, eucalypt/camphor and clove perfume that can be used to flavour anything from curries to desserts, also being excellent in marmalade. If I need a reasonable amount, I will smash the pods in a mortar, then sift through a coarse strainer to catch the seeds. I never buy ground cardamom, as the volatile oils quickly lose their pungency.

Cassia bark

Resembling cinnamon in both flavour and appearance, cassia is somewhat more robust and pungent. Although used to flavour 'cinnamon' doughnuts and the like in commercial bakeries (it is also called baker's cinnamon), I think cassia is best used in curries and savoury Indonesian and Chinese dishes. It has a warm woody scent, like cinnamon, but with a hint of anise and menthol as well as a tinge of bitterness. It comes either ground or in pieces.

Cayenne pepper

A chilli powder made from dried cayenne chillies, cayenne pepper is relatively hot and can be used whenever chilli powder is called for.

Celery salt

Use celery salt on sashimi-style tuna or kingfish, crisp sweet potato chips, Pan con tomate (p. 656) or in a virgin or bloody mary. Spread the leaves from a head of celery out on a large baking tray and dehydrate in a 90°C (195°F) fan-forced oven for about 2 hours until brittle. Add 1 heaped teaspoon black peppercorns and 1 tablespoon celery seeds to a spice grinder and blitz, then add the dried celery leaves and pulse. Add 40 g (1½ oz/⅓ cup) salt flakes and pulse to a coarse powder. Store in an airtight container for up to 2 months – it won't spoil, but it will lose its potency.

Celery seeds

Celery seeds are not actually derived from what we know as celery, rather a wild version. The seeds are tiny, with a woody celery note paired with anise. I adore them. I use them in my Thai-style chilli jam (p. 96) and various pickles and chutneys.

Cheddar

Generic cheddar-style cheese has its place, but if I'm cooking with it, I want some of the characteristic tang and umami depth. It's worth investing a little more to make those muffins or that cheesy bake really sing.

Chervil

Related to parsley, chervil is a delicate feathery herb of fine flavour with a gentle anise note. It's not readily available, but it works well with white fish and other seafood, as well as smoked fish, caviar, eggs and tender young vegetables. It is one of the four components of fines herbes, and essential in classic French cookery.

Chia

Chia seeds will absorb a large amount of liquid, swelling and forming a jelly-like cushioning. This property makes them a handy natural thickener to make puddings or to add to bircher muesli. Unswollen, the seeds have quite a charming nuttiness that can be used in seed mixes, granola and muesli bars.

Chickpeas

There are two main types of chickpeas: kabuli and desi. Kabuli chickpeas are larger than desi, paler in colour and are used for hummus and the like. Desi chickpeas are a staple of Indian cuisine, with the darker, tougher skin removed and the chickpeas split to make chana dal or ground into gram flour.

Chilli sauce

I make my own Fermented cooked chilli sauce (p. 97), but I always keep some hot sauce on hand, generally red and green Tabasco, which add a consistent dose of heat, as well as sriracha (see p. 29) for spiking dipping sauces, fried eggs, dumplings, etc. If you have dietary preferences or restrictions, always check store-bought hot sauce for gluten and anchovies.

Chillies, dried

I have a vibrant collection of dried chilli products, from paprika (see p. 23), cayenne (see p. 9), gochugaru (see p. 16) and aleppo pepper (see p. 6), along with other chilli powders of varying strengths and flavour profiles, both bought and home-made, to a range of dried Mexican chillies. Dried chilli flakes are also always on my bench for spicing up a pasta, sprinkling over some grilled sardines or adding to a marinade or braise. It is also a good idea to have dried Thai chillies, which are traditionally used for curry pastes (soak first and remove the seeds), though I typically use fresh ones. While this book is not the place to venture deeply into Mexican chillies, they really are marvellous things. It does get confusing, as the names are often different when dried, with poblano chillies called ancho and jalapeños known as chipotle, for example. The wonderful thing about them is the flavours they develop when dried. Some remain red, resembling their fresh counterpart more clearly, while those that become quite dark, almost black, tend to have a range of engaging flavours, notably tasting of raisins, dates, bitter chocolate and coffee, sometimes with no or very little heat. They need to be rehydrated in boiling water before use, with the bitter seeds discarded. You can also toast the whole chillies in a frying pan before soaking, which is said to unlock more flavour. The soaked flesh can be used in salsas or braises, or made into a paste, much as dried cayenne peppers, or similar, can be used to make Harissa (p. 92). You can also buy dried pasilla powder, which has some of the darker flavour notes with modest heat. Another dried chilli worth investigating is Kashmiri, which you can buy whole or as a powder. The latter adds a mild fruity heat, along with an intense red

colour. Sweet and smoky Spanish ñora peppers can also be bought dried. They work well in Spanish-style dishes with beans and pork, or anytime you are after a smoky depth in a soup or braise. Once rehydrated, scrape the flesh from the skin to use.

Chinese five-spice

Chinese five-spice is a warm but intense spice mix widely used in Chinese cooking. In a mortar and pestle or spice grinder, finely grind 1 tablespoon sichuan peppercorns, ten cloves, one cinnamon stick, 2 tablespoons fennel seeds and six star anise, then sift. Sometimes ground ginger, nutmeg and anise seeds are swapped in for one or other of the ingredients. Use it sparingly, as it's quite heady. Store in an airtight container for up to 3 months.

Chinese five-spice salt. Combine 2 teaspoons Chinese five-spice with 2 tablespoons salt flakes, crushing the salt flakes a little in the process. Sprinkle over roasted or fried chicken or fried quail, and on fried eggplant (aubergine) or over tofu with pickles.

Chives

Chives are like delicately onion-scented grass, and I love them. It's a herb that seems to have fallen out of favour of late, and that perhaps has a little to do with getting them in good condition. A bunch of parsley is a robust thing, but not so much a bunch of chives. They should never be wet or they will become slimy quickly, so dry them thoroughly before storing or chopping. I love them with scrambled eggs and omelettes, with crème fraîche, sour cream, yoghurt, beetroot, smoked fish and potatoes, amongst other things. Slice them in a bundle with a sharp knife.

Chives, garlic

Garlic chives are fabulous, but they're not for the timid. They pack an oniony garlic kick, but they tend to mellow a lot once cooked. They are great in stir-fries and soups, steamed with fish, or snipped into a prawn

(shrimp) or chicken dumpling mix or in a pork gyoza with Chinese cabbage (wombok).

Chocolate

For cooking, I use couverture chocolate. It's been processed to a fine grade and has a high proportion of cocoa butter with deeper flavour and better texture than standard cooking chocolate. It tempers to a glossy sheen and sharp snap more readily. Having said that, I use whatever I have on hand, and it's not always fancy. I generally use dark chocolate when baking, and often bitter dark chocolate, as I want that flavour intensity. The higher the cocoa content in chocolate, the darker and more bitter it will be. The lower the cocoa, generally the higher the sugar. Brands will vary in respect to classifying their chocolate, with dark chocolate as low as 40 per cent, but if you want a proper dark chocolate impact, aim for more than 60 per cent. Milk chocolate contains milk solids, and I rarely cook with it, while white chocolate is not really chocolate; it is made up of cocoa butter, sugar, milk solids and lecithin.

Cinnamon

Cassia's refined cousin, cinnamon is significantly more expensive than its rustic counterpart, but the refinement of the sweetly warm and woody scent is simply irreplaceable in sweet dishes and for use in Middle Eastern spice blends. Cinnamon also has a natural sweetness, where cassia can be bitter – I sprinkle cinnamon over yoghurt and/or granola for a sweet lift. It is wonderful in cream or milky desserts or for flavouring poached fruit, and is great with chocolate or on pumpkin before roasting. I also use it with chilli and black pepper to season beef and lamb before roasting.

Citric acid powder

Often used in Middle Eastern savoury pastries, adding a zesty lift.

Clarified butter See p. 360

Cloves

Cloves are markedly pungent with a medicinal/antiseptic note that can easily overpower a dish, but judiciously used in conjunction with other spices they can add lifted top notes to both sweet and savoury dishes. They are the flower buds of the clove tree, which turn a deep reddish dark brown when dried. I find the aroma extremely warming; it's a sweet earthy flavour that lingers beautifully. I use cloves in cakes, curries, pickles and spice mixes. They also work well with oranges, pears and apples, and with preserved lemon.

Cocoa powder

You can buy cocoa powder in its raw form or as Dutch cocoa powder. The latter has had its acidity reduced with an alkaline agent, which reduces the bitterness. Dutch cocoa will dissolve more readily and yield a deeper colour, but be careful interchanging the two in recipes as the acidity difference can influence the finished dish.

Coconut, desiccated

I generally use shaved or shredded dried coconut, even for Lamingtons (p. 749), but desiccated coconut is a handy way to add coconut flavour in a compact way. I use it to perfume a no-bake biscuit base (p. 738), for example.

Coconut flakes

I use dried coconut for baking, biscuits and the like, as well as to sprinkle over muesli and desserts.

Coconut milk/cream

I always have a few tins or tetra packs of coconut milk in the pantry for curries (pp. 238, 266, 633), tapioca desserts (see p. 780) or panna cottas (see p. 783). Coconut cream simply has less water than coconut milk, with a higher fat content and thicker texture. It should be used when you want more flavour and less liquid, but it can be thinned out and used as you would coconut milk. Find a brand(s) that you are happy with – you may prefer some over others for different applications. Note that some recipes call for 'cracking' the milk or cream, which is where it is heated until the oil separates and is then used to fry curry paste, etc. Many products, especially in tetra packs, will have stabilisers added and will be near impossible to crack, but they have a refined consistency that can be perfect for desserts or soupier dishes.

Coconut, powdered

I have only recently discovered powdered coconut milk, which is lovely added to rice cooked by the absorption method with a pinch of salt to make a quick coconut rice – sometimes I throw in a makrut lime leaf, too.

Coriander (cilantro)

A polarising herb, coriander is loved and loathed. People that love coriander and those that hate it aren't tasting the same thing, with a smaller percentage (this varies depending on heritage, but 10–20 per cent is a rough average) being genetically disposed to tasting an unpleasant soapy character, while the rest taste the peppery citrus notes only. Thankfully, I am in the latter group – it is essential to me in so many cuisines: Mexican, Indian, South-East Asian, Middle Eastern … it seems many people only use coriander leaves, but the roots and the base of the stems are very aromatic and fantastic in curry pastes. They can also be finely chopped and fried off in any dish that is using coriander as a flavour, adding an integral aromatic lift and freshness. The stems are also marvellous, full of flavour and with a textural quality that works beautifully chopped in salads or sauces, such as a Mexican salsa. Wash coriander very well, changing the water once, as it carries the most grit of any herb, but you especially need to thoroughly wash the roots, getting any grit out of the stem base, and you can also scrape off the fine lateral roots, but they will blitz up when making a paste or just chop finely before frying.

Coriander & black pepper salt. This salt is perfect for seasoning stir-fried beef, roasted root vegetables, pork or fish. Blitz 5 tablespoons coriander seeds, 2 tablespoons salt flakes and 2½ tablespoons freshly ground black pepper in a spice grinder, or pound using a mortar and pestle to a coarse powder. Store in an airtight container.

Coriander, onion & citrus sauce. I often make a simple sauce of finely chopped coriander leaves and stalks, grated garlic and shaved red or white salad onion that has been soaked in iced water to remove some astringency, then drained and dried, along with chopped lemon or lime segments and salt and pepper. It's great with spiced grilled fish or meat, or spoon over roasted eggplant (aubergine) or slow-roasted or grilled tomatoes on a bed of yoghurt. Try adding yoghurt for a sauce to serve with roasted pumpkin (winter squash) or sweet potato, or toss through warm lentils, freekeh, barley or quinoa for a delicious grain salad, finishing with a splash of fruity extra-virgin olive oil.

Coriander seeds

With distinct sweet citrus notes, coriander seeds are essential to so many spice blends, such as Ras el hanout (p. 25), Baharat (p. 6), Garam masala (p. 15) and Dukkah (p. 13). They add a lemony lift and feature across Indian, South-East Asian and Middle Eastern cuisines. I use ground coriander in many curries, and I also really like them lightly toasted, then ground with salt and pepper, loosened with olive oil and spooned over fresh mozzarella or ricotta, boiled eggs, potatoes, pan-fried fish, prawns (shrimp) or calamari, or on bread.

Cornflour (cornstarch)

In Australia, cornflour is often made from wheat, and it is sometimes labelled 'wheaten cornflour'. In the US, cornflour is made from corn (maize). Both products are used as thickening agents, and both are much more effective than regular flour. Make a slurry with the cornflour and some water before adding to the pot, as it can clump. It will thicken as it heats towards the boil, with the fine grains swelling with liquid. This reaction won't happen with a cold liquid.

Cotechino See p. 326

Couscous

Made from semolina rolled into small balls, I prefer to cook couscous using the instructions on p. 537. The old way is to steam it over a broth slowly, removing and separating and aerating the grains before returning to the steamer several times. (Also see Moghrabieh, p. 20.)

Cream

The nomenclature around cream can be very confusing, and it changes country by country. Cooking cream is relatively low-fat (around 17 per cent) and thin in texture, and it's not something I use. It's not to be confused with pouring (single/light) cream, which is also called pure cream in Australia or just cream. Thickened (whipping) cream has gelatine added and a fat content of 35 per cent. Pure cream will vary in fat from 35 per cent up to 45 per cent. The gelatine in thickened cream makes it easy to dollop, and helps stabilise the mix when whipped. I usually add a little higher fat pure cream, which stabilises it further. Double cream has a higher fat content again, above 45 per cent, but some versions use thickeners to simulate the texture of genuine double cream, so read the ingredients. You can also buy clotted cream, which is closer to 60 per cent fat, but why not make your own (see p. 800)?

Cream of tartar

Potassium bitartrate is used to stabilise whipped eggs and cream and acts as an anti-caking agent. It is an acidic powder, so can be used to activate bicarbonate of soda (baking soda).

Crème fraîche

A cultured cream, crème fraîche is similar to sour cream, but richer, more luscious and less tart. It should be made from pure cream, meaning it will have a high fat content and be thick. I love it for both sweet and savoury applications, with its gentle tartness ideal when regular cream is too cloying.

Cumin

Perhaps the spice most associated with subcontinental curries, as well as being a pervasive spice in Middle Eastern cooking, cumin is also essential to Mexican as well as North African cuisine. Cumin has its own distinct aroma that is not served well by a description. Black cumin is a different beast again, with a smoky, earthy flavour – it is often confused with nigella. Cumin is a stunning spice that lingers on the palate and marries other spices together perfectly. I buy both whole seeds and ground cumin; I go through so much, freshness is not really an issue. I also like the texture of whole seeds in spice mixes where I'm using ground cumin.

Curry leaves

Curry leaves are one of the most stunning herbs, with a wholly unique pungent flavour, which touches on citrus, anise and pepper. They have a great affinity with tomato and coconut. You can buy them both fresh and dried, but there is no comparing the two. Freshly dried curry leaves have some merit, but the flavour soon wanes. I like to use the fresh leaves in the last 15 minutes or so of cooking a curry to retain their heady aroma. They are also lovely fried until crisp in ghee or oil and used to finish dishes. They will usually come on the stem, and they're best stored in a sealed bag with as much air as possible forced out. They will keep in the crisper for a couple of weeks like this, or freeze. Use them when bright green, not brown.

Curry powder

An incredibly broad category, curry powders vary significantly in composition, though cumin, coriander, turmeric, black pepper, fennel seeds, mustard seeds, fenugreek, dried chilli and ground ginger are common ingredients. It is actually a colonial invention, or rather one of colonial times – a means of replicating curry spicing in one powder, often being somewhat more varied in flavour than garam masala. Curry powders from Malaysia and Japan, for example, have their own distinct profiles. I have a fondness for Malaysian versions, but find the ones that you like – it does make for a handy shortcut, as intended.

Dashi powder

This is simply a dashi stock powder and it's the easiest way to make Dashi (p. 53), if not the best. It's something I keep on hand when time is poor.

Dill

I find dill's intense minty caraway-like scent utterly engaging, and beyond the classic uses for Pickles (p. 505), Gravlax (pp. 169, 171) and Tartare (p. 77), it is also marvellous in Böreks with cheese & greens (p. 852), with eggs, smoked fish, potatoes, beetroot (beet) and smoked beef bresaola, as well as added to white sauces, vinaigrettes and butter sauces. I also love dill chopped and combined with shredded left-over meat from a roast chicken, with kewpie or Master olive oil mayonnaise (p. 74), finely shredded white salad onion, a splash of green Tabasco, salt and freshly ground pepper, then pushed into a well-buttered soft ciabatta roll or white bread sandwich with some finely sliced cucumber.

Dill seeds

Dill seeds have a more robust flavour than the fronds, with additional light anise and caraway-like notes. Often used as a pickling spice or in chutneys.

Dried fruit

I keep dried fruit on hand, as I use it in both sweet and savoury dishes. Currants rehydrated in vinegar make a lovely addition to salads, while they're also ideal for Sicilian-style in saor dishes that play off sweet-and-sour flavours, perhaps most famously with sardines (see p. 124). I keep dark raisins, dried muscatels for cheese and both golden and green sultanas, as well as dried Australian apricots and Turkish apricots, with the former chewier and more intense. Barberries (see p. 7) are a bracingly sour addition to grain salads, while goji berries and dried cranberries can provide a less-tart alternative. I always buy dried fruit and nuts from shops with a high turnover, generally Middle Eastern grocers. If you're familiar with the smell of rancid vegetable oil, then you've likely encountered the same aroma on sultanas or raisins. This is because vegetable oil is sometimes used as a coating on dried fruit to stop it clumping together. Increasingly, palm oil is being used, which is one of the most environmentally destructive products in the world. So, if packaged, check the ingredients, or ask your supplier. Above all, trust your senses – if it smells bad, it's going to taste bad. Rice flour is the more acceptable alternative from where I stand.

Dried limes See p. 692

Dried scallops (conpoy)

Dried scallops are used in many Cantonese dishes, from congee to stir-fries, but I mainly use them in XO sauce (p. 98). They have a rich and earthy flavour that's meaty and almost sweet, with plenty of umami. I prefer to use the larger Japanese dried scallops.

Duck fat

You can buy duck fat in tubs, or gather your own after roasting a duck (see p. 258) or by cooking down fatty trimmings and skin, then straining carefully. It is a fabulously flavourful cooking medium, essential for confit duck and stunning for roasting potatoes. The fat will refrigerate well for about 6 months.

Dukkah

A spice and nut mix of Egyptian origin, dukkah is typically eaten by dipping soft bread first in oil and then in the mix. It is also excellent with haloumi or Labneh (p. 362), or sprinkled over fried eggs. The version I like to make employs both ground and whole

spices, adding texture and a more complete flavour expression.

Dukkah, Tunisian

Combine 75 g (2¾ oz/1 cup) chopped pistachio kernels, 75 g (2¾ oz) toasted and crushed blanched almonds, 2 tablespoons sesame seeds, 1½ tablespoons ground coriander, 1½ tablespoons coriander seeds, lightly crushed, 1¼ tablespoons nigella seeds, 1 tablespoon ground cumin, 1 tablespoon cumin seeds, 1 tablespoon caraway seeds, ½ tablespoon turmeric powder, ½ teaspoon chilli powder, ½ teaspoon ground black pepper and two pinches each of ground cardamom and lightly ground saffron threads. Store in an airtight container in the fridge for up to 3 months.

Edamame

Edamame are young soybeans, typically sold frozen in their pods. They can be steamed, boiled or microwaved for a few minutes until vibrant in colour and tender. A sprinkle of sea salt and they're a great snack, or they can be added to salads, rice bowls or Chawanmushi (p. 356). Frozen beans have been par-cooked, but it's worth noting that you should never eat raw soybeans, as they can be toxic.

Eggs

When glazing pastry with egg wash, add a pinch of salt to the beaten eggs to break down the proteins and make for a more even application. For a deeper glaze, use only yolks. Always glaze before cutting any air vents, otherwise the wash will pool in the cuts.

Whenever you are crumbing anything for frying, like Schnitzel (p. 345) or Crumbed lamb cutlets (p.310), you can always use left-over whisked egg whites instead of whole eggs.

Farro

Also called emmer and often confused with spelt, farro is an ancient grain that can be sold as a whole grain, pearled or as flour. It is very low in gluten, nutty

in flavour, a little like brown rice, and releases starch when cooked while holding its shape and bite, so can be added to soups and braises to add flavour and texture as well as to thicken.

Fennel

The ferny fronds of wild and Florence fennel can be used as herbs, lending dishes their distinct anise flavour. Sadly, most fennel bulbs have had the greenery lopped off, but I always pick the ones with the most and use it to finish whatever I am cooking. Wild fennel grows in spring and summer. The flowers and fronds are both edible, as is the pollen, which can be dried and used as a seasoning, and the seeds, either used 'wet' or dried for a punchier spice hit.

Fennel seeds

Fennel seeds are a favourite of mine. I'm obsessed with the warm anise flavour that also has a hint of pepper, and they release a refreshing menthol flavour when chewed. They are a natural flavour enhancer for all kinds of dishes, imparting their scent without dominating. Like coriander seeds, they provide an excellent base to spice blends, imparting their own character and helping other spice flavours mesh. I pound them with black pepper and garlic (see p. 529) and use the paste to stir-fry. I also sometimes fry them at the start of a ragù or chilli con carne, as they add a little lift to the sauce that cuts through the acidic tomato. I also use in minestrone and marinades for fish. Everything tastes a little better with a touch of fennel.

Fenugreek

The seeds of the fenugreek plant are a pungent spice, while the leaves are an equally impactful herb. As fresh leaves, the flavour is mild and I use them in salads or to dress seafood dishes but, once dried, their flavour becomes somewhat intense. Called kasoori methi, dried fenugreek leaves are used to perfume curries both at the start and towards the end of cooking. They are more subtle in flavour than the seeds.

Fenugreek seeds

Fenugreek seeds are much like the dried leaves, though stronger in flavour, being a particularly aromatic spice. They are best popped in oil like mustard seeds to release their full flavour. They have a nutty and slightly bitter taste with a sweet curry flavour, tasting a little like cumin (see p. 12). Add them to curries, soups, braises, pickles and chutneys.

Fermented black beans See p. 100

Feta

I keep a couple of types of feta as staples. A firm, crumbly Greek sheep's and/or goat's feta in brine is essential, which I use for salads, pies (pp. 564, 631) and pastries (pp. 829, 831, 833), while I also love soft Persian-style feta, either in plain oil or marinated with herbs and garlic. It's delicious spread on grilled Sourdough bread (p. 847), added to omelettes and salads, or for adding to an antipasti spread.

Fish sauce

Fish sauce is an acquired taste, to be sure. But they're not all created equal. Indeed, although they are all pungent, there is a refinement to the best versions that sets them apart. The best Thai versions are made from salt and anchovies, and that's it. So, if you can source one of the top brands (Red Boat is my favourite) then stick with it, as there are many more versions that are pungent in all the wrong ways. Vietnamese fish sauce, or nuoc mam, is typically lighter and less pungent, though still has all that salty umami-laced character that we're chasing.

Flour, chestnut

Predictably nutty, chestnut flour is milled from dried chestnuts and can be used to add depth of flavour to pasta, cakes and baked goods. You can buy whole dried chestnuts, then mill your own. But be warned: they are incredibly hard and will come out the victor if using lesser equipment. Chestnut flour is much more perishable than other flours, with a rancid flavour developing with time, so milling your own will be a better guarantee of freshness. It is best stored in the freezer to preserve the integrity of the oils.

Flour, chickpea (gram/besan)

Made from milled desi chickpeas, besan/gram flour is used widely on the subcontinent, including for pakoras, pappadums, bhajis and the like, and it is also used as a thickening agent in some dishes. Chickpea flour is employed to make a kind of savoury pancake/torta in Liguria, Tuscany and Sardinia. It has no gluten and is high in protein and fibre.

Flour, rice

Rice flour generally comes in two forms: ground from standard medium- or long-grain rice, or from glutinous rice. The former is labelled rice flour, while the latter will be labelled glutinous or sweet rice flour (though it is not sweet and doesn't contain gluten). Both can be used for baking and making noodles or dumpling skins. Rice flour is often used in gluten-free baking, and it is also employed as a thickening agent.

Flour, rye

Rye flour is something that I'm never without, as even a small amount in a Sourdough bread (p. 847) loaf increases flavour, moistness and extends the longevity of the loaf. Note that rye takes up more liquid, so the more rye you add, the more liquid you will need.

Flour, wheat

You can get by using plain (all-purpose) flour for many tasks, but it is best to use specific flours for baking and making pasta. The higher the protein content of a flour the more gluten it contains, making for greater elasticity and a more robust texture. High-protein flours (often labelled baker's flour) are ideal for making bread and pizza, while soft, low-protein flours are better for cakes, where a light texture is favoured. Plain flour sits in the middle. I also add semolina (made from durum wheat) to my pasta and pizza doughs, which adds extra bite (pp. 111, 131, 856). I favour unbleached white flour for pizza and bread, and use 'Tipo 00' grade (referring to the fineness of the milling) for pasta and pizza. Self-raising flour is soft wheat flour combined with baking powder. If caught without, combine 100 g (3½ oz) plain (all-purpose) flour and 1 teaspoon baking powder. I use wholemeal (whole-wheat) flour for Sourdough bread (p. 847) loaves, with up to about one-third of the total flour content working well. Spelt flour can also be used as you would wholemeal (whole-wheat). It is not gluten free, and it has a high protein content, so suits sourdough baking or biscuit or cracker mixes.

Fontina

A cheese traditionally from Valle d'Aosta in Italy's north-west, fontina is a semi-soft cow's milk cheese that has a reasonably pungent earthy and nutty flavour. It is firm enough to be sliced and is a supreme melting cheese, making it ideal for toasted sandwiches and piadini.

Freekeh

Made from green wheat, freekeh is a wholegrain where the young grains are harvested, roasted and dried. It is highly nutritious and cooks relatively quickly (see p. 371). It can be sold as a wholegrain or cracked into smaller pieces, which makes it quicker to cook. Use freekeh for grain salads, buttered as a side or in a braise.

Fried shallots

You can make your own fried shallots (see p. 600), but they are readily available at Asian grocers. I like to make them myself, as the flavour of the oil is a lot cleaner and fresher. But convenience wins sometimes, and I love the texture and flavour sprinkled over dishes much more than I am opposed to using bought ones.

Furikake

Traditionally a seasoning for rice, furikake can be used to add a salty umami lift to all manner of dishes. There are also many different types, with things like katsuobushi (see p. 17), nori, dried shiso and sesame employed.

Galangal

Related to ginger, galangal is a very firm and fibrous rhizome. It has its own unique floral and woody aroma, with a bitterness that adds additional complexity to South-East Asian curries, sauces and relishes. There was a time when ginger was often commonly noted as an alternative to galangal in recipes, but they really are very different, with the results often still successful but not comparable. Galangal is now generally available at Asian grocers, and it can be frozen.

Garam masala

A ubiquitous spice mix in Indian cuisine, garam masala is used both at the start of cooking and towards the end to boost flavours. It is different to curry powder, an eighteenth century invention, in that it has fewer spices, though there are countless regional variations. To a frying pan, add four fresh bay leaves, three cinnamon sticks, 2¼ tablespoons coriander seeds, 2 tablespoons cumin seeds, 1¼ tablespoons cloves, 1 tablespoon green cardamom pods, 1 tablespoon black peppercorns, 2 teaspoons fennel seeds, two star anise and four blades of mace. Toast over a medium heat for about 4 minutes, shaking the pan frequently, until fragrant. Cool the spices, then grind to a fine powder in a mortar or spice grinder, then sieve to remove any husks. Store in an airtight container for up to 3 months.

Garlic

My kitchen is never without garlic, and I'm fussy about what I use. The heads need to be properly cured/dried until they have dry, papery skin and are firm when squeezed. If not, there's a good chance they're going mouldy.

That off flavour, even if the soft parts are cut away, can permeate the cloves. Wet garlic (not yet cured) has a milder flavour and needs to be used more swiftly or dried. Spring garlic resembles spring onions (scallions) with the bulb not yet developed. It is milder again and can be used raw in salads and the like. Wet garlic can be sliced across the head and used raw or cooked. There are many different garlic cultivars and I prefer those with a purply-pink blush to the skin. I generally like the flavour of purple garlic, but white and purple are interchangeable. It's also best to choose heads that haven't started to sprout, as the green shoot can be bitter. You can plant them, however. Around mid-autumn push the sprouting cloves into the garden, sprout-end up, and water in. They will shoot up fairly quickly, sit through winter, then start to form a bulb in spring/summer, being ready in November to December (in the southern hemisphere). Selecting larger cloves to plant is preferable, as they will tend to produce heads with larger cloves. You can plant them quite closely, then thin out in spring, giving you a harvest of marvellous spring garlic, while making room for the bulbs to grow and separate into cloves. There are two broad types of garlic, softneck and hardneck, with the former collapsing as the garlic reaches maturity, with yellowing foliage on either type indicating it's time to harvest. You can also harvest the curly scapes from hardneck garlic in summer, as you can the young flowers, which have a subtle garlic flavour. Once harvested, hang the garlic in a dry place to cure, with the skin becoming papery and the cloves firming up. I always buy local garlic, or an organic import if the local stuff isn't available. I never buy vibrantly white imports and chopped garlic in a jar. The former is typically bleached with chlorine, and the latter is dreadful, in my opinion. It has a certain unpleasant flavour that you can taste in any dish. I would always prefer to omit garlic than use that. Black garlic is also something that features in my kitchen. The whole bulbs are slowly cooked for about a month at a relatively low temperature

and with controlled humidity until the cloves turn black. The result is quite an extraordinary product, with the garlic flavour transformed into deeply caramelised, malty and umami-rich tones. It can be used to flavour dressings and sauces, and is especially good stirred into a jus to serve with poultry – it is also visually dramatic. You can make black garlic at home, but most recipes require you to leave a slow cooker on for a month ... it's hard to see how this can be justified, practically or environmentally

Garlic powder

I keep this on hand to add to dry rib rubs and marinades or to spice flour for frying.

Gelatine

I only ever buy gelatine in sheet/leaf form, as powdered gelatine can have an off-putting flavour, is liable to clump and can be cloudy when set. The sheets come in varying strengths: titanium, bronze, silver, gold and platinum. These sheets have various bloom strengths, but they also come in varying weights to equalise that strength difference – the same weights of platinum and titanium do not have the same gelling properties. I stick with gold-strength, which is a good all-purpose type. I favour Alba or Gelita. Leaf gelatine needs to be bloomed in cold water for about 5 minutes before squeezing out the excess liquid and adding the gelatine to the warm liquid to be set. Don't boil any liquid once the gelatine has been added or the gelling properties will be lost.

Ghee See p. 159

Ginger, fresh

Fresh ginger falls into two categories: young and old. Young ginger is pale in colour with barely evident skin. It is sweeter and juicier than older ginger and doesn't need peeling. The older rhizomes develop a thicker skin, which generally needs to be peeled, and are more fibrous. They're also a bit hotter, so quantities used may need to be adjusted depending on age.

Ginger, ground

Ground ginger is simply ginger root that has been dried and ground to a powder. It has similar ginger freshness and heat but a warmer more caramelised flavour. I use it frequently in baking for biscuits and spiced cakes as well as Gingerbread (p. 757).

Ginger, pickled

Most would be familiar with pink pickled ginger that is typically served with sushi, which generally owes its hue to dye. Young ginger naturally has pinkish tips, which can account for the colour, but this is rare in practise. The dye is not harmful, but I favour a more natural product and either buy white pickled ginger or the naturally pink version. Beyond sushi and sashimi, pickled ginger is also good with deep-fried things and shaved in salads or mixed with other pickles for a salad to eat with rice or cold noodles.

Glucose

I use liquid glucose in sorbets, as it won't crystallise once frozen like regular sugar can. You can also use trimoline/invert sugar.

Goat's curd

I love fresh curd cheeses, especially goat's curd with its silky richness and distinctive flavour. I always have some in my fridge. I use it to dollop onto salads, spread on bruschetta or drop into an omelette.

Gochugaru

Korean chilli powder or flakes are all called gochugaru, though the heat and the flavour will vary depending on the chillies used, from mild to wildly hot, and from fruity to smoky and deeply flavoured.

Gochujang

Usually made from gochugaru, fermented soybeans, glutinous rice and salt, and sometimes along with sugar, gochujang is a pillar of Korean cuisine. It is a unique chilli condiment, with often fiery heat accompanied by fermented umami notes. It can be added to dishes or diluted with soy, vinegar and/or water to make a bracingly hot condiment or dressing with things like ginger, garlic and sesame oil.

Gomashio

Gomashio is a classic and versatile Japanese seasoning that can be used to sprinkle over just about anything, from rice bowls and salads to cooked vegetable and meat dishes. You can buy it pre-made, but I don't see why you would. Making it yourself is no trouble, and you can ensure that the sesame is in the best condition. Grind 3 tablespoons lightly toasted sesame seeds with 2 teaspoons salt flakes in a mortar to make a moist salt. Store in an airtight container for up to 1 month.

Grana Padano See Parmigiano Reggiano (p. 24)

Greek spice mix

This is a spice mix I use to recreate a memory of souvlaki in Greece (see p. 312) with barbecued lamb skewers, but it's also great for skewered pork, chicken or beef, or rub on lamb chops before barbecuing. Combine 1 tablespoon sumac, 2 teaspoons ground black pepper, 1 teaspoon ground allspice, 1 teaspoon onion powder and 1 teaspoon salt flakes, crushing the salt flakes a little as you go. Store in an airtight container for up to 2 weeks.

Gremolata

Gremolata is classically used on osso buco, and gives hearty braises and slow-roasted dishes a charming lift of freshness just before serving. It is also excellent on a tray bake of chicken pieces, or similar. Finely grate the zest of one lemon and combine with half a bunch of flat-leaf (Italian) parsley leaves that have been roughly torn (you can chop if you prefer, but I prefer the texture). Season with salt and pepper and loosen with some extra-virgin olive oil.

Gruyère

Both Gruyère and Comté cheeses are made using the same methods, but on different sides of the border: Comté in the Jura, France, and Gruyère from Gruyère, Switzerland. Both cheeses are firm and super-rich in umami. I like to keep either on hand for sandwiches and for various melting purposes. Both can be expensive, so pick a higher grade for serving in a cheese selection, and something more economical for sandwich and melting duties.

Haloumi

A brined cheese made from sheep's and goat's milk, haloumi has a firm-ish and squeaky texture. Best known as a Cypriot cheese, it has been made throughout the Levant and Mediterranean for centuries. It yields to heat less quickly than most cheeses, making it an ideal candidate for pan-frying or grilling.

Harissa

Ubiquitous in North Africa, harissa is a hot chilli paste made from roasted or rehydrated dried chillies blended with spices and garlic, and loosened with oil. The spices employed vary, but cumin, caraway and coriander seeds are commonly used. You can make your own fresh version (see p. 92), or buy it in a jar or tube. The commercial version will be quite hot and concentrated, making it ideal to use in marinades, or to add to a braise or tagine, while the fresh version is ideal as a condiment or to finish a dish.

Herbs

Also see individual herbs.

Herbs have always played an integral role in my cooking, from my training days finely chopping parsley, chervil, tarragon and chives for fines herbes to later embracing them by the handful in all manner of recipes. Although herbs were always an essential part of classical cooking, the reality is that they used to be underutilised, especially in the home. My grandparents used to grow all their own herbs, as they were not so readily available. Even parsley – and it was always curly parsley – was primarily used to decorate plates, usually loitering uneaten after the meals had been finished.

Much has changed. You would have to really push things to put too many fresh herbs in a dish now. A big grain salad can easily swallow a bunch of parsley or coriander (cilantro), probably both, and be vastly the better for it. Naturally, stronger herbs like tarragon and rosemary need to be used a little more prudently, but you still want them to have a meaningful impact. Don't skimp. There should be a sense of generosity. To me, a meal prepared without fresh herbs is missing an essential vitality – okay, there are exceptions to this, but the general sentiment holds true.

Growing herbs is something we should all do. Space will limit some of us, but we can all grow something, whether it's a pot of rosemary or a garden full of fragrant plants. Many woody herbs are extremely hardy, and things like parsley grow abundantly and happily self-seed. I am far from a committed gardener, but I do have a successful living – thriving even – herb collection.

Buying three or four herbs for a dish can get expensive, and you can often be left with ones you won't use. So often, we just use less, or skip this or that herb. Growing your own also means that you can have seasonal herbs at their best. You also have access to the flowers, which make stunningly pretty and aromatic additions to salads and for finishing dishes.

Having said all that, I certainly buy herbs, and lots of them. I couldn't possibly grow enough parsley or coriander (cilantro) to satisfy my needs. However, I always try to buy from the market, rather than the supermarket.

If buying herbs, buy in bountiful bunches that are vibrant in colour and fragrant. I never wash mint before storing as it can go black, as can basil, but I usually store soft herbs in just-damp paper towel in a sealed bag or airtight container in the crisper. Always wash and thoroughly dry soft herbs before chopping or using whole (a salad spinner can come in handy). There was an old method that used to be employed in professional kitchens where you'd chop herbs, then wrap in a tea towel (dish towel) and wring out excess water, but you ended up wicking out flavour, too. If your herbs have begun to wilt, pick the leaves and add to a bowl of water until they perk up.

An exquisite herb salad. Pick a bunch of parsley and gather handfuls of other herbs, such as mint, chervil and tarragon, with some batons of chives. Wash and dry them all well. Add to a bowl with some small nasturtium leaves, flowers and wild rocket. Season with salt flakes, add a good squeeze of lemon and a generous drizzle of extra-virgin olive oil. Toss to dress well and serve with steak, grilled, roasted or cured fish or roasted bone marrow.

Hoisin sauce

Perhaps most famously used to sauce the pancakes for Peking duck, hoisin is a thick, dark sauce made from fermented soybeans, garlic, sesame, ginger, five-spice and anise (see p. 96). It is often used as a condiment or glaze for duck, quail and pork.

Honey

Whether acacia, manuka or leatherwood, I love a heady floral honey, though sometimes the flavour is too strong for some applications. Honey is sugar, sure, but it is also high in antioxidants and has been linked to lowering cholesterol and improving cardiovascular health. It is also anti-inflammatory and antimicrobial. Many baking recipes can have the sugar switched out for honey, sweetening still, but enriching the flavour immeasurably. The commercial value of honey has led to unethical hive management practices as well as adulteration of the final product. This can be through added sugar syrup, to blending a quality honey with a cheaper version to pad it out. Cheaper honeys can come from anywhere in the world, with unethical practices that can see the honey containing dangerous levels of toxins and antibiotics. There is also a significant industry in making completely fake honey and passing it off as the real thing. Buying from trusted sources is key.

Horseradish

Freshly grated horseradish is one of my favourite things, but it is not always available. You can buy prepared horseradish in jars, but I always look for those with little or no added sugar.

Jamón

Spanish jamón serrano differs from Italian prosciutto in that it is typically aged for longer, resulting in a firmer texture. In Spain, the bone is typically left in, so is sliced by hand. The bone must be removed by law in Australia, so will typically be sliced mechanically. The finest iteration is Jamón Ibérico de Bellota, which must be made from black-hooved Ibérico pigs fed acorns (bellota), which gives the ham its distinctive flavour. It is one of the world's most extraordinary foodstuffs, and the price matches the reputation.

Juniper berries

Known as the principal botanical used to flavour gin, juniper berries are also an excellent flavouring for cured oily fish or with beef, lamb, pork, venison and duck. The blue-black berries should be a little dimpled and moist to touch; they should never be dry. They have a peppery resinous pine quality, are savoury and a little spicy.

Kaffir lime leaves See Makrut lime leaves (p. 19)

Kaiserfleisch See p. 325

Katsuobushi

Cooked, smoked then cured through fermentation, katsuobushi is traditionally made from skipjack tuna fillets. It is often sold as flakes, though you can shave it yourself (there's a specialised tool for this). The flakes are generally marketed as bonito flakes – bonito is a type of fish that resembles skipjack, but they are unrelated. Katsuobushi is another weapon in Japanese cuisine's remarkable umami arsenal, and along with kombu (see p. 18) forms the basis of Dashi (p. 53).

Kecap manis

An Indonesian sweet soy sauce, kecap manis is thick and syrupy, with deep molasses-like tones. It has a big flavour impact in a dish without overloading it with salt, while the sweeter profile pairs well and balances heat from chilli.

Kefalograviera

Either made from sheep's milk or sheep's and goat's milk, kefalograviera is a salty hard cheese that comes from three regions on the Greek mainland. It is most famously fried in a pan and served with lemon or a drizzle of honey and wild thyme or oregano. That dish is almost ubiquitously called saganaki, and for many that's what they call the cheese, though the name refers to the pan, and it can reference many appetisers served this way.

Kenchur

Classified as a member of the galangal family, kenchur is quite different to the rhizome associated with Thai food. A key component of Indonesian cuisine, it is used in a similar way to ginger and galangal, as an aromatic component of a curry paste. It is not something I have come across fresh where I live, but you can buy it in ground form.

Koji

Aspergillus oryzae is a fungus that is responsible for such things as sake, soy sauce, miso, shochu, mirin and the like. Through fermentation, it transforms grains (and often sweet potatoes) into umami wonderlands.

Kombu

Kombu is dried kelp, and it is used widely in Japanese cuisine, imparting a distinctive flavour and plenty of umami. It is a key ingredient in Dashi (p. 53). There are several types of kombu, but I've never encountered a broad selection locally, so use what is available. It's important to wipe the kombu before using as there can be grit on the outside, but do so with a dry cloth and be gentle. The white powdery coating is where much of the glutamine lives, hence much of the umami. It's also important never to boil kombu, as it can impart bitterness.

Lardo See p. 326

Legumes, tinned

It's hard to argue against the convenience of tinned legumes, but the flavour is always somewhat flat. Hummus made from tinned chickpeas will be serviceable but nowhere near as creamy or flavoursome as one made with dried chickpeas. In a braise or soup, tinned legumes do a credible job. I tend to use tinned butter beans most frequently, as the flavour is quite good. The key with any tinned bean is to drain and rinse well; I find the liquid to have a somewhat objectionable character, the magical properties of aquafaba (see p. 348) notwithstanding.

Lemongrass

Lemongrass is a large genus of plants that have an intense citrus scent with floral and herbal overtones. It can be used for both sweet and savoury and is also made into tea. The lemongrass stems can be bruised with the back of a knife, with the softer top tied in a knot, then dropped in curries or to perfume rice, or the paler heart can be sliced and fried at the start of cooking or whizzed or ground into a paste.

Lemon myrtle

Perhaps the most recognised native Australian herb, lemon myrtle has a gentle fragrance that is a cross between lemongrass and the green note of lemon you smell in lemon verbena, with a little menthol thrown in. The leaves, flowers and fruit can be used, but I have used the leaves most often. Fresh lemon myrtle is hard to source, and is often sold powdered or as dried leaves, though it loses pungency quickly. I have used it in custards and slices or as a tea, or added it to a spice mix with pepper to go on roasted poultry.

Lemon verbena

Native to South America, lemon verbena is a flowering plant that has long and pointy rough-textured leaves. They have a strong lemony green and floral scent.

I like to use the leaves fresh, but they can also be dried and used for tea. I add lemon verbena to poaching liquor for fruit, to infuse in an anglaise along with vanilla to make panna cotta, or to perfume a rice pudding.

Lentils, beluga (black)

Named for their resemblance to caviar, beluga lentils are a small, glossy black lentil that are shaped like a slightly flattened sphere. They are quick to cook but hold their shape well. They have an intensely earthy and nutty flavour and are excellent for salads. Beluga lentils are not to be confused with urad dal, which are sometimes called black lentils but are actually related to mung beans and break down more readily when cooked.

Lentils, brown

The workhorse lentil, brown lentils come in a range of cultivars with size varying across them. They are earthy in flavour and retain their form reasonably well, though not as well as puy or beluga lentils. They work well in soups, braises and curries, including for dal. Somewhat more specialised are Castelluccio brown lentils from Umbria, Italy, which hold their shape very well and are ideal for salads with herbs and vinaigrette, but they also cook down well with their distinct nutty and earthy tones adding exceptional flavour to soups and braises.

Lentils, green

The most famous green lentil is the puy lentil, which is traditionally grown in central France in Le Puy-en-Velay near the Loire River. The Le Puy name is legally protected, but they are grown elsewhere now, including very successfully in Australia, where they are typically sold as French green lentils. They hold their shape well when cooked, so they're ideal for salads or as a side dish buttered or served warm in a vinaigrette with lots of herbs. They also work well in soups and stews where you want them to remain intact. There are green lentils with similar properties to puy lentils, though none quite so refined, being larger and holding their form less resolutely.

Lentils, red

Standard red lentils or masoor dal (sold split and whole) are generally more carrot-like in colour and they cook quickly, breaking down readily. If you want a lentil to hold its form, these are the last ones to use. That makes them perfect for dal, though, where they yield into the liquid, effortlessly puréeing themselves. They are also useful for thickening other curries, with a small handful adding earthy flavour and filling out the sauce. Persian red lentils are a little different, though, holding their shape well, they are suitable for salads.

Mace

Mace blades are the dried coatings of nutmeg. Mace has a similar flavour to nutmeg, and it can be used in sweet and savoury dishes.

Mahleb seeds

The kernel of a small wild black cherry, tan-coloured mahleb seeds have the aroma of sweet cherry and almond, a bit like marzipan, but a little bitter in the aftertaste. I buy the whole seeds, then grind them myself, as the potency is lost very quickly. But use sparingly, as they are very intense. Mahleb seeds are used in Middle Eastern pastries

and breads, and I use them in a Sweet spice mix for baked goods (p. 792).

Makrut lime leaves

The leaves of makrut (commonly known as kaffir) lime trees are incredibly fragrant and used to perfume South-East Asian curries and salads. I add them to curry pastes, as well as to the sauce as it cooks, infusing flavour at the start and adding a brighter punch towards the end. The citric lift is utterly distinctive and quite mesmerising. They come as double leaves on a stem and are shiny and quite tough. Torn or crumpled and dropped into a curry, they lend their fragrance but don't soften much, so are not eaten. With the stem removed, they can be very finely sliced or chopped to provide a textural element in salads or when finishing dishes. Makrut lime leaves are also wonderful in desserts, such as perfuming a Coconut panna cotta (see p. 783). I often drop one or two in jasmine rice just before cooking by the absorption method. They keep well in the crisper in a sealed bag with the air forced out, or you can freeze them, and while they will lose some of their visual lustre, they are still aromatic and can be used in curries.

Maple syrup

Maple syrup used for the table is all classified as A-grade, but the intensity of colour and flavour is officially graded in four groups, from pale and delicate to very dark and strong. I use it as an alternative sweetener, with its own distinct woody vanillin caramel flavour, for things like making granola or muffins, to sweeten icing, and sometimes in dressings and marinades. Pancakes, though, account for the bulk of my maple syrup usage. Always buy the real stuff, and refrigerate after opening.

Marjoram

Oregano and marjoram are closely related and look similar, but marjoram's sweeter in scent and flavour, with a gently floral and lemony perfume. I sometimes

slice it and scatter over bruschetta with burrata and oil, or over grilled zucchini (courgette) with feta. It is also fabulous in summer on a crudo of white fish dressed with lemon, capers and peppery oil, or in an omelette or frittata.

Mayonnaise

Firstly, make your own mayonnaise (pp. 74–5). But it is handy to have a quality mayonnaise on hand for sandwiches or to spike with chilli or load up with chopped capers, pickles and herbs for a quick tartare. Kewpie mayonnaise is also one that I use at times. It is made from egg yolks, rather than whole egg like other commercial mayo, and it has a decent sprinkling of MSG (621), upping its umami appeal. That may put some people off, but the bad reputation that MSG has is not deserved, with studies showing no ill-effects, aside from a very small percentage of people reacting when given doses at levels that would never be present in foods. Kewpie is great for squeezing little blobs onto Japanese-themed canapés, for Japanese meatballs (p. 251), to make Sesame dressing (p. 94), to serve with a poké bowl (see p. 415) or anoint a bun to take some fried fish or chicken.

Milk

Organic milk is generally not madly expensive, unless you compare it to the absurdly cheap prices offered at supermarkets, which can only mean a miserable deal for farmers. I use milk to make simple cheeses (see p. 362), desserts (pp. 782–3), smoothies and occasionally to add to a ragù (see p. 283), and I always buy full-cream (whole) milk. The only other question is whether to buy homogenised or unhomogenised milk. The process of homogenisation reduces the particle size of the fat, distributing it evenly through the milk. It's a mechanical process, but some believe that the smaller size poses a health risk – this is not backed up with causal evidence. Unhomogenised milk will form a cream layer on top, which is how I remember milk growing up, and it will not last quite as long.

Mint

Mint provides such a stimulating burst of freshness in dishes. I think it is often underused, as that profile can seem a strong one, but when used in concert with other herbs, it plays a critical role, and it works across cuisines, from the Mediterranean to the subcontinent, Middle East and Asia. I love it, both fresh and dried, in Tzatziki (p. 507) and Raita (p. 98), as well as fresh leaves torn into slaws, or salads with coriander (cilantro) and parsley – try making a tabouleh with half mint and half parsley – or combined with coriander, Thai basil and Vietnamese mint to dress spicy dishes or toss through a vermicelli salad, or even simpler, a salad of shaved white onion and mint with a little salt works well with big flavoured oily fish, like salmon, mackerel, tuna or sardines. I even like old-school mint sauce (see p. 82), which just managed to rescue the perennially overcooked lamb of my childhood. Mint grows like a weed, so a couple of pots should be enough, but it does need water.

Mint, Vietnamese

Also called hot mint and Vietnamese coriander, Vietnamese mint is not in the mint family at all, with it said to resemble mint in flavour and appearance. I find that to be drawing a long bow on both fronts, with the slender pointed leaves having a dark purplish 'v' on them, and the flavour genuinely unique. It does have a lifted cleansing quality that is reminiscent of mint, but it's paired with a peppery heat, and the flavour is more different than similar. It is ubiquitous in herb plates in Vietnamese cuisine to add to dishes like pho and to add to a lettuce cup before wrapping around spring rolls. Vietnamese mint is also great in vermicelli and other similar salads.

Mirin

A Japanese rice wine for cooking, mirin has an alcohol content of about 14 per cent and an elevated level of sweetness. It is used in sauces and marinades, adding sweetness and plenty of umami from the koji fermentation.

Miso

Miso comes in countless variants, but in general terms they range from mild and sweet to deeply coloured, salty and intense. Most miso is made from rice, soybeans and salt, with koji employed to ferment the natural sugars (miso can also be made from other grains and legumes, so check the label if you are gluten intolerant). The longer the miso is fermented, the darker it becomes and the more savoury. Fermented for a shorter time, white miso or shiro miso (which has fewer soybeans, replaced with more rice, or barley) is sweeter due to the carbohydrates still present. The pale colour is due to the low soybean content. Red miso or aka miso is a very broad category, ranging from yellow to almost black. Often, the term yellow miso is applied to any milder, sweeter miso with a yellow hue, but most of these are technically red miso, with genuine yellow miso coming from the Shinshu province. In practical terms, yellow-coloured miso does fit in the middle in terms of its flavour profile. The other general category is awase miso, which just means that it is a mix of miso types, creating a unique whole.

Mixed spice

As the name suggests, mixed spice is a blend of spices, generally cinnamon, ginger, cloves, nutmeg, mace and coriander, though cassia and allspice can feature, too. It is generally used for baking.

Mizithra

A cheese made throughout Greece but most associated with Crete, mizithra can be made from sheep's or goat's milk, or a combination. Whey from cheese- or yoghurt-making is used to sour milk and create curds, which are strained to make a fresh cheese similar to ricotta. That cheese is more a local thing given its perishability, so you're most likely to encounter a hard salted version similar to ricotta salata, which can be very salty and crumbly. The fresh version has sweet and savoury applications, while the aged version is grated over pasta, soups and stews.

Moghrabieh

Also called pearl or giant couscous, moghrabieh is a staple of Lebanese cooking, even if its name points to North Africa (as in from the Maghreb). It is essentially just large couscous, durum wheat semolina rolled (traditionally by hand) into balls. It is cooked by boiling in salted water for about 15 minutes until tender but with a little bite. The term 'pearl couscous' is often associated with Israeli couscous or ptitim. Moghrabieh is a traditional preparation, where ptitim is a modern creation (perhaps in imitation), engineered to manage the period of economic hardship in Israel in the 1950s.

Mozzarella

Proper mozzarella is made from buffalo milk, and originates in southern Italy, though it is now made all over the country. Fior di latte is the cow's milk version, though most cheese sold as mozzarella around the world is made with cow's milk, with only the name mozzarella di bufala guaranteeing buffalo milk, and the legally controlled Mozzarella di Bufala Campana PDO ensuring that it comes from the traditional southern Italian zones (although a perishable cheese, it is frequently airfreighted around the world). Whatever the milk employed, the fresh cheese will be quite white, have a high moisture content and be milky in flavour. It is best eaten sooner and at room temperature, or it can be drained and used on pizza (most famously margherita). That firm yellow cheese that is often called mozzarella and used on pizza is a different thing altogether, with low moisture content and mild flavour.

Morcilla See p. 325

Mustard

Dijon and a wholegrain preparation accommodate most needs, from dressings to mayonnaise to accompanying a steak, but a little hot English doesn't hurt, especially on something like a roast beef and cheddar sandwich, and a squirt of American mustard is useful if you're partial to hot dogs. There are countless variations of mustard, with Germany alone accounting for a dizzying array of regional styles, while you'll no doubt find an even greater range across farmers' markets. I largely head down the classic line, and also make my own from time to time. Paler mustard seeds are less hot than darker ones, so you can tweak the mix to your preference. I find that home-made mustard only improves with time, which I believe is due to it lacto-fermenting, and it will not readily spoil.

Mustard seeds

Naturally, mustard seeds are ground to make mustard, but they also feature heavily in the curries of the subcontinent. They come in brown, black and yellow hues that vary in heat and intensity, with yellow being the mildest. The seeds can also be popped in hot oil and then used to dress a finished curry, or fried at the start to release their pungent and nutty flavour. I frequently add them to pickling liquids.

Wholegrain mustard. To make your own, blitz 2 tablespoons mustard seeds, 1 tablespoon brown mustard seeds, 2 teaspoons mustard powder, two allspice berries, 1½ teaspoons salt flakes and 1 teaspoon green peppercorns in a spice grinder to a coarse paste. Tip into a bowl and combine with 1 teaspoon nigella seeds, 125 ml (4 fl oz/½ cup) white-wine vinegar and 2 teaspoons soft brown sugar, stirring to combine and dissolve the sugar. Transfer to a sterilised jar, seal and store at room temperature for 10 days to develop the flavour, then store in the fridge for up to 2 years.

Nduja See p. 325

Nigella seeds

Jet-black nigella seeds are the classic topping for Turkish bread. They have a slightly sharp, vaguely ferrous character. They are sometimes inaccurately referred to as black cumin, and there is a suggestion of cumin to the flavour, with peppery notes. I use them to top pastries and breads, and also add them to the mix when I make wholegrain mustard (see below left).

Noodles

I generally keep a range of noodles on hand, from soba, udon and ramen for broths and stir-fried dishes, to rice stick and rice vermicelli for salads and rice paper rolls. It's best to follow the instructions on the packet, as they will vary, but most cooked noodles will benefit from being refreshed in iced water before being heated in the final dish, or served cold. This will stop the cooking and also help to keep the strands separate, rather than clumping. Dried ramen noodles are especially handy for a quick meal. I usually cook them in chicken stock with some miso paste, then throw in some greens and crack in an egg at the end. They're also good stir-fried after boiling with some sesame soy dressing (see p. 94), chopped spring onion (scallion) and sliced chilli.

Nori sheets

Essential for making sushi rolls, nori sheets are also a versatile ingredient to add that distinctive seaweed flavour to many dishes. Snip them with scissors over a broth, noodles, salad, tempura or a rice bowl, or blitz to a powder with salt to make a seasoning mix (see p. 187). Nori can also be added to sauces, such as for a Japanese-themed tartare (pp. 77, 187).

Nut meal

You can make a meal/flour out of most nuts, although almond is the most common. Nut meals can be used to make flourless cakes or to add more flavour to those containing flour. Almond meal is also used to make Frangipane (p. 796). It's better to make your own nut meals, rather than pre-milled versions. You can use a blender to do this, or a Thermomix does an excellent job. Once milled, the nuts are exposed to oxygen, so they will deteriorate quickly and become prone to rancid flavours. So, just process what you need, and if you have any left over, store it in the freezer.

Nutmeg

Nutmeg is a classic sweet spice that adds warming flavours to sweets and baked goods. It also has a savoury role, adding complexity and warmth to the flavours of anything from a Béchamel (p. 70) to a Ragù (p. 336). Nutmeg's sweet flavour pairs well with cream or custard, and I also use it in curry pastes. I'm a fan of it with silverbeet (Swiss chard) or spinach finished with butter or cream; roasted carrots tossed in a little maple syrup and some nutmeg grated over the top is also delicious. I always finely grate nutmeg as I need it, as the flavour is so much better and a little bit will go a long way.

Nuts

I use a lot of nuts for snacking and in salads, desserts, baking, stuffing, on muesli … for all manner of things. I always buy them raw, then roast as required. It doesn't take long (see p. 371) and enhances the flavour superbly. The key is to buy them from somewhere that has a high turnover. I favour Middle Eastern grocers. They can then be stored in jars or airtight containers in a cool, dark place, but I prefer to freeze if keeping for more than a few weeks, as the oils can become rancid.

Oats

Aside from making porridge and bircher, I use oats to make muesli/granola and to add to muesli bars, cookies and the like, and they are essential for Anzac biscuits. Steel-cut oats are chewy and nutty and take longer to cook, while rolled oats are steamed and rolled, which makes them quicker to cook with a more consistent result. Instant oats are pre-cooked and flatter than rolled oats. I don't use them.

Oil, avocado

Avocado oil has a high smoke point and is mild in flavour, making it an ideal frying oil, and its gentle buttery flavour works well in salad dressings or mayonnaise. It has similar healthful properties to olive oil, but ensure that it has been processed by mechanical means, as some undergo industrial chemical processes.

Oil, coconut

Coconut oil is excellent for frying, remaining very stable at higher temperatures. It also has a good flavour profile for many curries, stir-fries or for some baking applications. I buy the unrefined versions, as the others have been heavily processed. Unrefined coconut oil will solidify readily at room temperature, but it will liquefy with gentle heat. It is also quite strongly flavoured, so be sure you want a coconut flavour in whatever you're cooking. The refined versions are colourless and almost odourless with a high smoke point.

Oil, nut

Unlike vegetable and seed oils, most nut oils are processed through simple mechanical means. They are not terribly stable and should generally be used in a short period to avoid rancidity. I use nut oils for their flavour, with a little walnut, macadamia or hazelnut oil in a salad dressing a wondrous thing. Buy in small, dark bottles and store in the fridge.

Oil, olive

There is much contention about which oils and fats are good for you, but to me it's simple. Use the most natural product. Seed oils are highly industrialised products, requiring solvents and multiple processes to render them usable. Additionally, canola, a rapeseed cultivar, is almost exclusively genetically modified. These polyunsaturated oils are also quite unstable chemically and prone to oxidation and rancidity, both over time and when heated. Extra-virgin olive oil is rich in antioxidants that preserve it better over time, as well as when heated. It can also be heated to a level that will accommodate all cooking methods. And while some of these antioxidants will be lost at higher temperatures while 'protecting' the oil, many remain. I use a lighter oil when deep-frying, but I don't deep-fry often. I will often shallow-fry in EVOO, though, and the flavour is fantastic.

In Australia, we're spoiled with great local olive oil, and it's becoming more accessibly priced, too. Most olive oils made here are extra-virgin, made with olives pressed shortly after harvest, ensuring freshness. All oil will go rancid over time, and it is always better when it is freshest. And while the production date, which is preferable to a best before date, will give you an idea of freshness, your senses are the best guide. Taste your oil as is, or use a piece of bread to soak up a good slick of it. It should have a bright and zesty profile (the flavours will vary with peppery, floral, grassy, green and even tropical characters, depending on the varieties used) with no rancid notes. Rancidity is tricky to describe, but once you're familiar with the taste of properly fresh oil, a rancid one will stand out in sharp relief. The other key to good, fresh oil is a decent level of bitterness, which indicates a high level of biophenols (natural antioxidants). Once you're sold on EVOO, this bitterness is quite compelling, but don't worry about it translating negatively to your food. The combination of richness, freshness and structure given by a good EVOO at the start and the end of cooking is unmatched.

I would never buy something called 'light/mild olive oil'. But I would buy 'light/mild extra-virgin olive oil'. The former is a product of refining, while the latter is produced with olive varieties that have a milder flavour profile. It's something that you could use in mayonnaise, as a robust EVOO can be too pungent in that kind of concentration. Colour is not a reliable indicator of quality, with some pale oils exceeding deeply coloured ones. As always, taste. Products simply labelled 'olive oil' have undergone industrial refining processes to get to market. They are sometimes blended with some EVOO, or can just be standalone refined oils. Beware words like, 'traditional', 'light', 'classic', 'pure', 'original', etc. on the packaging if they are not accompanied by 'extra-virgin'.

I always have a range of EVOOs at home, and they have different profiles. Some I use for general cooking, while other oils are reserved for dressing and finishing. For example, big bitey, peppery oils go well with roasted or charred flavours and stand up to a perky tapenade (pp. 584, 587, 590) or Mezzanotte paste (p. 588), and fruitier styles that are lighter in flavour are perfect for finishing and dressing vegetables and salads, as well as raw and cooked fish and seafood. Those dressing oils are usually bought in smaller bottles, and often for not insignificant cost, but a quality EVOO for general cooking is best bought in a larger tin.

Oil, peanut

Peanut is a general cooking oil with a high smoke point, but like all highly polyunsaturated oils, it's prone to rancidity.

Oil, pumpkin seed (pepita)

With a very distinctive deeply nutty flavour and deep-green hue, pumpkin seed (pepita) oil is something I use sparingly in dressings or to drizzle over roasted vegetables. Like all seed and nut oils, it is prone to oxidation, so store in the fridge.

Oil, sesame

Sesame oil is very much a less-is-more oil, with it being particularly strong in flavour. So, not a cooking oil as such, but rather an oil used for flavouring. Often a few drops will do the trick.

Oil, vegetable and seed

I use industrial vegetable and seed oils as little as possible. Extra-virgin olive oil is my go-to, and I find the aroma of vegetable oil quite off-putting. There is also mounting evidence that they are not as good for you as once thought, and I just avoid heavily processed food in any form. I do like grapeseed oil, and you can buy cold-extracted versions, rather than those made with solvents. The gentle flavour is perfect for when olive oil is too strong (mayonnaise, etc.). Rice bran oil is a handy oil for frying with a neutral flavour, and it has a high smoke point, making it good for wok frying and the like. Like all polyunsaturated oils, I use it sparingly. You can also buy cold-pressed sunflower and safflower oils, which are significantly preferable to those made with solvents, but they are pricey. However, they are handy if you need a more neutral flavour in a dressing. If you are buying vegetable or seed oils, there are high-oleic oils now on the market. Those oils have less of the unstable polyunsaturated fats and more monounsaturated fats, making them naturally more stable and healthier. They're both GMO.

Olives

It's a lovely thing to cure your own olives (see p. 585), but it's not always practical. I always buy olives whole rather than pitted. I think they taste better, and I don't like the look of an olive that has had the pit mechanically removed – even with a hand pitter. I like them torn or cracked. I always have some top-quality Spanish queen green olives, some kalamata, tiny wild olives, briny green manzanillas for the occasional martini ... Buy olives from a deli where you can taste first or work out which jarred brands you prefer.

Orange-blossom water

This fragrant liquid is made from the distilled oil extracted from flowers of the bitter orange tree, or Seville orange as it is commonly called. It is traditionally used in North Africa as a perfume or freshening salve, but it is better known as a flavouring used in sweets. My grandmother Grace used to enjoy orange-blossom water added to her black tea.

Oregano

Oregano is easy enough to grow and, while I use dried Greek oregano (rigani) more frequently, fresh common oregano works well when finely chopped and added to a vinaigrette, perhaps with roasted garlic, to dress roasted Dutch carrots or blanched green beans. It has an affinity with lamb and can be used in marinades or added to tomato sugo and used for pasta and pizza. I also use it to make fresh Salmoriglio (p. 83).

Oregano, Greek (rigani)

Dried rigani is something that I use a lot, and that says a lot considering my general preference for fresh herbs over dried. In fact, I rarely use any dried herbs, except dried mint, Mexican oregano, fenugreek leaves ... that's about it, but rigani is marvellous stuff and I use it more than fresh oregano. The Greek variant of oregano grows wild (it is often sold as wild oregano) in upright bushes and is gathered into bundles at its peak when the leaves are the most intense, then dried. Unlike many herbs, rigani remains intensely scented once dried, and it is marvellous with lamb, in braises or in marinades with garlic and pepper for grilling chicken. Sprinkle the leaves over a large piece of feta with shaved onion and black olives, then douse with extra-virgin olive oil, or add to a bowl of chopped tomato and cucumber with some shaved radish or diced capsicum (bell pepper) dressed with oil and vinegar to eat with grilled meats or schnitzel. Rigani generally comes with a plastic bag on the stems, and you can snip a corner off the bag and rub the stems together with your hands, dispensing the leaves through the opening. It's best to pick any fine stems out, as they can be a little sharp. If you're more organised, you can take it all out of the packet and rub the leaves off into a large bowl, then store in a jar.

Oregano, Mexican

Unrelated to the more familiar Mediterranean oregano, Mexican oregano is in the verbena family, with citrus and aniseed notes. It is a herb that can be used both fresh and dried, but I've never encountered it fresh in my neck of the woods. Don't be tempted to substitute with regular oregano in Mexican dishes.

Oyster sauce

Oyster sauce is a handy way to quickly flavour stir-fried greens, mushrooms, beef or noodles, or to add flavour to dumpling fillings (see p. 500). Its brooding flavour and gentle sweetness make for a simple way to boost a dish, but make sure you're using a good one. I avoid those labelled 'oyster-flavoured', though vegan versions obviously have their place.

Pancetta See p. 325

Pandan leaf

Pandan has a sweet and mossy/grassy flavour with a hint of vanilla, but it's quite unlike anything else. It is used for both sweet and savoury applications. You can buy fresh or frozen pandan leaves from Asian grocers, which can be knotted and used to infuse rice (see p. 384). You can also buy an extract that is handy when making desserts (see p. 744).

Panko

For lighter, less-oily crumbing, panko is ideal. It also makes for a very crunchy result. It doesn't need to be confined to Japanese dishes, with it working equally well for other crumbing/breading tasks.

Paprika

Paprika is made from ground dried peppers, and comes in a broad range of styles, from those that seem to have only colour as an attribute to those that are significantly spicy. The two broad categories are Hungarian and Spanish paprika. Perhaps most famously used in goulash, Hungarian paprika comes in a raft of grades, from sweet paprika that has an earthy capsicum (bell pepper) flavour to very hot versions. I look for paprika that has a bright colour and no bitterness, using it in braises, stuffings, curries, with vegetables and for sausages. The most common Spanish paprika or pimentón has been made from peppers dried over wood fires, creating an elevated smoky profile, which come in sweet (dulce), spicy (agridulce) and hot (picante) versions. It is the emblematic spice of Spain, and is used in so many dishes, from making chorizo to seafood and vegetable dishes. Just be wary, as the flavour is very strong and can easily dominate. Also, buy in modest amounts as it will fade in potency and become disagreeably dusty.

Parmigiano Reggiano/Grana Padano

Parmigiano Reggiano is the king of cheeses. An amazing table cheese on its own – perhaps with some sliced pear or fig – it is also a supreme cheese to use in a luxury risotto or pasta. Some believe grating it is a sin, but a simple bowl of egg noodles, truffle, butter and Reggiano is sublime, as is a Risotto funghi (see p. 149) or polenta with Mushroom ragù (p. 576) with Reggiano shaved over, and its intensity is beautiful in salads, shaved against peppery rocket or bitter radicchio, for example. Parmigiano Reggiano and Grana Padano are made in a similar way, with semi-skimmed unpasteurised cow's milk from the evening milking mixed with whole milk from the morning milking, but Reggiano uses animal rennet and is aged for a minimum of 12 months, up to 36 months. The older the wheel, the more intense the flavour, and more crystalline and granular the texture. Grana Padano is aged for a minimum of eight months and is made across northern Italy, while Parmigiano Reggiano is made only in certain areas of Emilia-Romagna. However, a lesser Reggiano will be trumped by a longer-matured quality Grana. Never throw out parmesan rinds, as they contain so much flavour. Use them to add

richness to soups and braises, or they can be infused into oil with rosemary and garlic (see p. 26).

Parsley

An essential herb, I use an extraordinary amount of parsley. It adds a burst of freshness to so many things. Parsley is so universal, complementing egg, vegetable, chicken, fish, beef and grain dishes, as well as emulsion sauces and oil-based sauces. For me parsley is not a thing to be used sparingly, whether finely chopped to add to a sauce or as handfuls of picked leaves to add to a salad. It also does the heavy lifting in sauces like Salsa verde (p. 86) and Persillade (p. 86) and is wonderful in a flavoured butter (see p. 73) for fish or steak. It's also the way I finish so many dishes, whether a soup, stew or pasta, with Linguine vongole (p. 127) just not quite right without it. I always buy the flat-leaf type (continental, Italian, call it what you will). Parsley is very easy to grow, and it will self-seed readily. Don't discard the stems, as they are full of flavour and the texture when chopped can be quite engaging in a salad or salsa, and they can be fried off with a sofrito, adding depth of flavour to soups and braises. The stalks should also be kept for stocks.

Passata (puréed tomatoes)

Passata is simply cooked, strained and puréed tomato, which can be added to sauces, stews and braises. It's more concentrated, and naturally smoother, than tinned tomatoes and will not need to be cooked as long, but it depends on the texture you want in the finished dish. Sometimes a combination works well.

Pasta, dried

I keep a good range of dried pasta at home, from tiny risoni for soups and seafood stews to oversized rigatoni, with all manner of long and short pasta in the middle. It doesn't keep forever, so I don't overstock, but the variety is important when cooking different sauces. Cheap dried pasta is okay now

and then when pushed, but it is worlds away from real dried pasta (pp. 108–9).

Pecorino

A sheep's milk cheese, pecorino comes in many forms, though the best known is pecorino romano. As the name suggests, it is a Roman cheese, but most of the production is now in Sardinia, where they also make a range of local pecorino types. Aged less, it is a milder cheese suitable for the table; aged longer, it is best for grating, as well as for a cheese course. Aged pecorino romano is sharp, tangy and salty. It is the classic cheese for those iconic Roman pasta dishes Spaghetti carbonara (see p. 119), Cacio e pepe (p. 120) and Amatriciana (p. 121), though I often use it in combination with Parmigiano Reggiano.

Peppercorns

The same vine (*Piper nigrum*) is responsible for green, white, black and some pink peppercorns. Dried pink peppercorns are from a different plant entirely, well two plants, trees from both Peru and Brazil. For black pepper, the unripe berries are sun-dried, which switches on an enzyme that turns them black and produces their characteristic flavour. To keep them green, they are generally brined, or they can be boiled and dried. Green pepper is suitable for dressings and sauces for beef, and for using in pâtés, terrines and pickles. True pink peppercorns are the ripe berry and are sold brined. White pepper is made from ripe berries that have had the outer husk removed, then are dried. White pepper is somewhat hotter with a lingering dry pepper flavour. I use white pepper in white sauces, butter sauces, Asian pastes, stir-fries, hot pots, noodles, dressings and for pasta. Black pepper is a constant companion, going into much of my savoury cooking.

Quatre épices. 1½ tablespoons ground white pepper, 1½ tablespoons ground allspice, 2 teaspoons ground cinnamon, 2 teaspoons ground cloves and 2 teaspoons finely grated fresh nutmeg. Store in an airtight container for up to 1 month.

Pickles

I make plenty of pickles for snacking, sandwiches, burgers, falafel wraps, salads and to serve with charcuterie, amongst other things, but I also generally have some bought ones, too. A proper polski ogórki or crisp American-style dill pickle is always a resident in my fridge, as are cornichons, which I cannot do without if serving terrine, rillettes and the like. Pickled cucumber of one sort or another is essential for making tartare sauce (see p. 77). I also always have pickled jalapeños in the fridge, which I use sliced in tacos and wraps and dice to add to sauces, dressings and salads.

Polenta

Both yellow and white polenta are traditional in Italy, with the latter a specialty of the Veneto region and having a finer flavour. They are both coarse cornmeal and can be bought in instant or classic iterations. Instant is fine at a pinch, but the traditional slow-cooked method (see p. 383) reigns supreme.

Pomegranates

Pomegranates keep exceedingly well in the fridge, a month easily and up to two. And even when they look a little shrivelled, they can still yield fine seeds and juice. The old trick to extract the seeds is to cut the fruit in half, then tap the back of each half with a wooden spoon over a bowl. You may need to dig out any stubborn seeds, and ensure you remove any part of the membrane that holds the seeds in, as it's bitter.

Pomegranate molasses

This sweet and super-tart syrup is made from pomegranate juice that has been boiled until reduced. It can be added to Middle Eastern-leaning dressings, braising liquids, marinades or to drizzle over a dish to finish.

Ponzu

A sauce used in marinades, dressings, dipping sauces and to finish dishes, ponzu is made from rice vinegar and mirin that have been infused with kombu (see p. 18) and katsuobushi (see p. 17), then spiked with citrus, commonly yuzu. Ponzu shoyu contains soy sauce.

Poppy seeds

Tiny, blue-tinged poppy seeds have a distinctive and slightly nutty flavour. I use them primarily for topping breads and pastries. They have a high amount of oil and will turn rancid if stored too long, so only buy small amounts and store in the fridge or freezer.

Porcini, dried

Dried porcini mushrooms or ceps are a very handy pantry staple, which can be used to make an umami-packed risotto (see p. 150) or added to all manner of dishes to boost flavour. Fresh porcini are magnificent, but dried porcini are also superb, with the drying process creating a different side to the fungi, with a nutty, woody, earthy and sweet caramel scent. Always reconstitute them in hot stock or water for 15 minutes, then lift them from the soaking water so as to not collect any foreign matter – they're collected wild. Strain the liquid through a fine-mesh sieve (never discard the water, as it is precious) before using with the chopped flesh. You can also blitz dried porcini to a powder and use as a flavour booster or to finish a dish, say a risotto or an omelette with fontina.

Potato starch

A fine white powder, potato starch can thicken sauces at a lower temperature and does so with brilliant clarity.Boiling will lose its binding properties. Make a slurry with water before adding to a dish to avoid clumping. It is also used in baking, especially gluten-free.

Prosciutto

Prosciutto is made in many Italian regions, with the PDO status awarded to ten localised products in northern and central Italy. The rules and results vary among these, but the principle is the same. The hind legs of pigs are salt cured, then washed and air dried before being coated in lard to encourage even curing. The total curing time for what is perhaps the most famous prosciutto, Prosciutto di Parma from Emilia-Romagna (though Prosciutto di San Daniele from Friuli is similarly revered), is no less than 400 days, though some legs are aged for up to 36 months.

Provolone

Made in the same way (pasta filata) as mozzarella, provolone is a firm-ish cow's milk cheese that comes in both piccante and dolce versions. The former is aged for longer and employs goat enzymes, which make it a sharply flavoured cheese, while the dolce uses calf enzymes and is aged for a shorter period. Both are fashioned into distinctive shapes: large, trussed cylinders; melon/pear-shapes, also trussed; a tapered cylinder; and a smaller version where the curd is stretched into a topknot so it can be hung, creating a teardrop shape.

Quinoa

A plant native to South America, quinoa is related to amaranth, with highly nutritious seeds. It comes in a variety of hues from white to red to black, all having a distinctive earthy and nutty flavour. It can be cooked by absorption, but it is just as readily boiled and drained. I like a little chew left in it, as it can become claggy rather than fluffy. Quinoa will often come pre-washed, as the seeds are naturally coated with saponin, which deters birds. Saponin is quite bitter, so I always recommend washing it even if pre-washed.

Ras el hanout

There is a no one recipe for ras el hanout. The Arabic name reflects it being the top or best spice blend, with each merchant having their own proprietorial blend. Most mixes, though, will be of a vibrant colour, with paprika and turmeric common inclusions. Ginger, coriander, cumin, cinnamon, fennel, cardamon, nutmeg/mace and allspice are also fairly safe bets, with cayenne pepper and chilli often adding the heat, though not all blends are hot. A given mix could have ten or twelve spices, or double or triple that. Find one you like or make your own. Lightly toast 1 tablespoon cumin seeds, 3 teaspoons coriander seeds, 3 teaspoons fennel seeds, 2 teaspoons allspice berries, fourteen cardamom pods, seeds removed, and 1½ teaspoons black peppercorns in a dry frying pan over a medium heat until fragrant, about 2 minutes. Grind the spices using a mortar and pestle or spice grinder to a fine powder, then sieve to remove any husks. Combine with 3 teaspoons sweet paprika, 2½ teaspoons ground turmeric, 2 teaspoons ground cinnamon, 1½ teaspoons cayenne pepper and 2 teaspoons salt flakes. Store in an airtight container for up to 3 months. Ras el hanout is great to have as an all-rounder to add oomph to a dish. Use it in sausage rolls and cheese pies, or add to flour to fry fillets or darnes of fish. Use to season beetroot (beet) before roasting or add to cooked potato to make a potato and cheese pastry, or to Zucchini & haloumi fritters (p. 673). Ras el hanout is also excellent to use when roasting or braising chicken or lamb.

Rice, basmati

Basmati rice is very versatile, with long grains that hold their shape and don't stick together. It is what I use for most subcontinental curries as well as for Middle Eastern dishes, and it's not unusual for me to serve it with South-East Asian curries. I also sometimes use brown basmati rice.

Rice, black

Black rice is a wholegrain rice that can be used for sweet and savoury applications. There are several different cultivars, with some glutinous and often used to make desserts. The dark colour is typically a very deep purple, which is more evident once cooked. That colour is a sign that it is jam-packed with antioxidants, so it is often touted as a superfood.

Rice, bomba

A short-grain rice from eastern Spain, bomba absorbs a lot of liquid while retaining its shape. Along with calasparra rice, it is ideal for paella or croquetas.

Rice, brown

Brown rice is wholegrain rice with the bran and germ intact. It takes longer to cook, but it is far more nutritious, with the stripped-back grains of white rice essentially just carbohydrate. Ideally soak brown rice overnight in water with a little vinegar or lemon juice to make it more digestible.

Rice, glutinous

Also called sticky rice when cooked, glutinous rice is used in savoury and sweet dishes in South-East Asia and the subcontinent. It is often cooked in a banana leaf, becoming a deliciously dense and sticky mass. I also use glutinous rice to grind to a rough powder for Thai-style salads (p. 384). There is no gluten in glutinous rice.

Rice, jasmine

Fragrant jasmine rice is my preference for South-East Asian and Chinese-themed dishes. It has a long grain and a pleasingly sticky finish when cooked.

Rice, koshihikari

A short-grained rice, koshihikari is a relatively modern cultivar but it is Japan's most common rice. It is perfect for sushi and for donburi (rice bowl) dishes.

Rice, risotto

I prefer to use carnaroli and vialone nano (see p. 144) for risotto.

Rice, wild

Wild rice is unrelated to other forms of rice, rather just sharing a vague similarity in grain shape and size, though they are typically longer and finer as well as ranging from pale brown to quite black in colour. Three of the four species of aquatic plants whose seeds yield wild rice are native to North America, while the fourth is from China.

Ricotta See p. 362

Rosemary

Often described as thriving on neglect, rosemary is as hardy as they come, and you will find it growing everywhere. A short stroll will generally uncover an easily (and legally) accessible bush, and if not, then growing it yourself is incredibly easy. Don't forget the flowers, as they have a lovely rosemary scent but are soft and fine, so can be used for more delicate cold dishes. Rosemary automatically has me thinking of consuming large amounts of roasted pork or lamb smothered and slow-roasted in garlic and rosemary. I use rosemary for scenting roasted potatoes (see p. 626), or tossed with finely sliced potato to top a pizza with a base of mozzarella and taleggio. Rosemary is a robust herb and can take heat, but it's best not to push that resilience too far. Rosemary added to potatoes at the start of roasting will likely have lost its charm after a long hot roast; added a bit later, it will keep its aroma. Rosemary can also be thrown on a fire when barbecuing, adding fragrant notes to whatever you're grilling, and a sprig makes an aromatic basting brush, or strip off most of the leaves and use sturdy sprigs as skewers for grilling.

Rosemary & bay salt. Use this sparingly over freshly pork, lamb or chicken, or sprinkle over whole roasted fish such as snapper or flathead. This is also a great seasoning for chips tossed with feta, or roasted pumpkin or potatoes. Chop three large fresh bay leaves and the needles from two rosemary sprigs, then grind in a mortar to a slightly damp green powder. Add 1½ tablespoons salt flakes and grind to combine. You could also add some finely grated lemon zest. Keep in an airtight container for up to 2 weeks.

Rosemary, garlic & parmesan oil. Throw a few sprigs of rosemary, some parmesan rinds and a few garlic cloves into a saucepan and cover with extra-virgin olive oil. Gently warm to about 40°C (104°F) for 30 minutes (a Thermomix is ideal for this, but you can take on and off a very low heat, just be sure not to actually fry anything), then turn off the heat and set aside overnight to infuse. Use as a flavoured oil to dip fresh Focaccia (p. 845) into; toss fresh young broad beans or blanched romano beans in the oil with pepper; dress a rocket (arugula) salad with shaved pear and parmesan; or toss with shaved raw cabbage or brussels sprouts with grated parmesan, ground chill and a touch of lemon.

Rosewater

Like orange-blossom water, rosewater is an aromatic floral essence that can be used to scent foods, primarily sweets and desserts.

Saba, vincotto and mosto cotto

The three names are Italian regional terms for much the same thing: wine grape juice/must that has been boiled into a syrup. It's also the first step used to make balsamic, but skipping the fermentation, acetification and lengthy ageing processes. While it is naturally sweet, with all the sugar concentrated, the acid is also concentrated, giving it freshness. It can be used like balsamic, drizzled over dishes to finish, and it can also be paired with umami-rich cheese like Parmigiano Reggiano, or drizzled over fruit-based desserts or ice cream.

Saffron

The king of spices, or rather the queen, as saffron is produced from drying the stigma (female organ) of the saffron crocus, not, as is often cited, the stamen (the male organ). It is wildly expensive, but the yields are painfully small (something like 100 g/3½ oz per acre), and the work incredibly hard. I have harvested it myself, and it is back-breaking work. Although expensive, it is a magical and unique spice imparting a distinctive earthy golden hue and medicinal, honeyed and woody flavour that has a sweet earthy finish – there is nothing like it.

The flavour is extracted in warm liquid, either by soaking first and adding the threads and water or dropping the threads or powder directly into the pot. I use saffron in rice dishes, fish stews, dressings, to flavour mayonnaise, in an a la grecque cooking liquid to poach seafood and vegetables, and it can also be infused in cream, milk or butter for desserts and pastry.

Sage

Another herb that should be in everyone's garden, sage requires little attention and one bush will produce more than enough leaves for most households. A perennial, sage produces most abundantly in spring and summer, with purple flowers appearing around the start of summer that are quite edible, too. I'm particularly fond of young sage leaves that are soft and intensely flavoured. Sage leaves can be used in braises, sauces and soups, and they are marvellous fried in butter (see p. 73) to serve with Egg pasta dough (p. 111) or with pumpkin, or fry until crisp and drop on dishes as a garnish. On my first trip to Tuscany, I had sage leaves lightly battered with an anchovy and fried until crisp. Such a simple combination, but the flavours were exquisite. Sage pairs exceptionally with rosemary and is required for saltimbocca (pp. 268, 702) and Porchetta (p. 338) and it is excellent in stuffing.

Sake

Japanese rice wine comes in myriad forms, and is as complex as the world of wine made from grapes. I use inexpensive sake for cooking, as I do wine. You can buy cooking sake, but note that it will contain salt to make it saleable without a liquor licence. For cooking purposes, sake is used in sauces, stocks and marinades.

Salt

I take great interest in salt. Some will tell you that salt is salt: sodium chloride and that's that. And in a way that's true, but the seasoning function of salt is not the only important

element. Table salt has been processed to strip away everything except for the salty bit, taking out minerals and other subtle flavouring elements characteristic of where it is sourced from. These elements are subtle but important to me, and the loss of minerals may not be significant to human health, but with much farmland long stripped of minerals due to intensive farming, I'm happy to get all I can naturally. Plus, unrefined salt simply results in a more complex flavour profile in a finished dish. I also find generic table salt to be quite tough on the palate, almost burning it, while a good sea salt will be gentle, almost sweet. I use sea salt flakes a lot. They are easily ground in your fingers for a finer result, but the crunch of the fine flakes is also lovely as a finishing touch. I have a large collection of salts, from French fleur de sel to celtic sea salt to local Murray River pink salt to Himalayan salt to … well, so many. I also use smoked salt occasionally, as well as black lava salt, which is somewhat dramatic in appearance – be sure to season as a finishing touch at the last moment, as the colour will weep. I use finer sea salt for brines and pickles, as well as seasoning water for pasta and blanching vegetables. I use rock salt, which is unrefined, for curing, such as with gravlax (pp. 169, 171). Seasoning is one of the fundamental skills for cooking well, and tweaking the salt just before serving can elevate a dish. Under-seasoned food is flat, but be careful, as you can go too far. This is something to be especially wary of with a reduction sauce, braise or ragù, as to properly concentrate the flavour, you will also concentrate the salt, so work with a light hand until the final flourish. Having said that, it's also important to season as you cook, because you can't always adjust effectively at the end: season but under-season, then correct at the end. It's also critical to note that when I give a volume measure for salt flakes the equivalent volume in a finer salt will be significantly more by weight. In some cases, this could be 70 per cent more. That's a big difference.

Sansho pepper

Closely related to sichuan pepper, sansho pepper is made from the berries of the Japanese prickly ash tree, native to Japan and Korea. The crushed berries are a component of shichi-mi togarashi (often just called togarashi). Some ground mixes of sansho will contain both the leaves and seeds. The flavour is similar to sichuan pepper in its citrus-like profile and numbing effect, but it has spicier peppery notes.

Sardines, tinned

I always have a few tins of sardines on hand, and preferably under olive oil. I'll drain that oil off and use a better one, but the impact on the flesh in the tin is far better than those in water. I use them for pasta sauce, or drain the tin, then toss with finely shaved shallot, parsley, olive oil, vinegar, chilli flakes, plenty of pepper, a squeeze of lemon and maybe some capers, then pile onto grilled bread as a snack.

Savoury

A typical component of herbes de Provence (with rosemary, thyme, oregano …), savoury is a herb in the mint family that comes in both winter and summer versions. Summer savoury is seen as the superior of the two, with more delicate flavour and less bitterness. The flavour is often described as being peppery with flashes of oregano, marjoram and mint. It is used widely in Europe, but you need to grow your own in Australia.

Scamorza

A southern Italian cow's milk cheese made with stretched curds, scamorza is somewhat like a low-moisture mozzarella-type cheese. Fashioned in a bowl with a topknot so it can be hung, scamorza has a yellowish hue and more flavour than commercial dry 'mozzarella'. It is an excellent melting cheese, so can be used for pizza and baked pasta dishes. It also comes smoked version (scamorza affumicata).

Sesame seeds

I prefer white sesame seeds to black. The latter are called for in some Asian and Middle Eastern recipes, but I find them less versatile, and they become quite bitter when toasted. A slight bitterness is evident in the white seeds, but I find the balance appealing. I always have them on hand for sprinkling over baked goods, stir-fries and salads, or to grind and sprinkle over all manner of things to add a nutty, toasty boost. Store in an airtight container somewhere cool and dark.

Shaoxing cooking wine

There are essentially two types of Chinese cooking wine; both are rice wines, with one a clear and mild version, while the other, Shaoxing cooking wine, has a mahogany hue and is an aged version with deeper and richer flavours. I generally use Shaoxing wine, but the paler version is often recommended for more delicate dishes.

Shiso (perilla)

Shiso is in the mint family, and it has a fresh brightness that fits with that connection, but its flavour is quite bold, individual and hard to pin down. Shiso comes in both a green and purple-red version, with the latter used in Japan to both flavour and colour, such as with umeboshi. The green version is more commonly used fresh and can be shredded in salads or the leaves are often battered for tempura.

Shiitake mushrooms, dried

The dried porcini of Asian cooking, if you will, dried shiitakes add a deep flavour and umami boost to dishes. They can be reconstituted in hot water and chopped or used whole, sans stem, in soups, stews, stir-fries, hotpots, or spring roll or dumpling fillings. They can also be used to flavour a stock or master stock (use the stems here, too, as they have plenty of flavour). As with dried porcini, ensure you use the soaking water, as it is full of flavour.

Shoyu

Japanese soy sauces come in a broad range of styles, with shoyu the overarching term. They all taste recognisably different to Chinese soy sauce, and should not be used interchangeably. The most common is koikuchi shoyu, which is used as an all-round sauce for cooking and as a condiment; usukuchi shoyu is paler but a little saltier; tamari shoyu is perhaps the best known, and typically does not contain any wheat; saishikomi shoyu is darker, richer and sweeter; while shiro shoyu is quite pale and sweet.

Shrimp, dried

Dried shrimp add a pungent briny fish flavour, which adds depth to curries and relishes, and are great for making sauces and chilli pastes. Choose small brightly coloured specimens that are not rock hard. Soak for 20 minutes in warm water before using, then pound in a mortar before cooking. They can also be blitzed in a high-speed blender to make a floss to then garnish salad and rice dishes.

Shrimp paste

Shrimp paste or belachan is made from fermented shrimp or other sea creatures, such as anchovies. You can buy it in jars or tubs, or a firmer version set into blocks. It is used widely in Thai cooking, as well as across South-East Asia. The looser jarred versions can be used directly, while it is advised to toast the firmer version. This can be done by wrapping in foil and placing in a dry pan or the oven for about 5 minutes. Shrimp paste is very pungent and can be a bit off-putting at first, like fish sauce, but it adds so much depth and complexity to dishes, so please don't be deterred.

Sichuan pepper

Sichuan pepper has a curious tingling, numbing effect on the tongue, while the flavour is citric with a warm peppery profile. I use it in rice dishes, dressings and oils, and also for a seasoning to sprinkle on wontons or pickles. The husks are used, with the black seeds hard and flavourless. A light toasting enhances the flavour, then grind a little and use as is, or grind more and sieve to a fine powder.

Sichuan pepper salt. Use this simple seasoning for fried quail (see p. 269), on pork dumplings (see p. 342), noodle salads, stir-fries and Asian omelettes (see p. 353). Heat 1 tablespoon sichuan peppercorns and 3 tablespoons salt flakes in a dry frying pan over a medium heat until the peppercorns pop, about 3 minutes, then grind in a mortar or spice grinder. Pass through a fine-mesh sieve to remove any husks, then store in an airtight container for up to 2 months.

Sichuan pepper & mandarin salt. To make the mandarin powder, dehydrate the peel of three mandarins on a baking tray in a 100°C (210°F) fan-forced oven for 2–3 hours until brittle. Using a spice grinder or mortar and pestle, grind the peel to a fine powder. Toast 3 tablespoons sichuan peppercorns in a dry frying pan over a medium heat until they pop, about 3 minutes. Grind 1 tablespoon fennel seeds and peppercorns to a powder, then combine with 2½ tablespoons salt flakes, ½ teaspoon Chinese five-spice and 1 tablespoon mandarin powder, crushing the salt flakes a little. Store in an airtight container for up to 1 month.

Sorrel

Available in a couple of cultivars, sorrel has a lemony flavour and attendant acidic bite. You can buy red-veined sorrel as larger leaves or micro-herbs, or in the more classic, green-leafed type, which looks a little like spinach but with an intense lemony flavour (see p. 552). It's also very easy to grow.

Soy sauce

In addition to Japanese soy sauce (shoyu) and sweet Indonesian soy (kecap manis). I always have a Chinese light soy and dark soy. Light soy is good as more of a seasoning, while dark soy adds deeper caramel notes to a dish and is more fitting for marinades or glazes.

Speck See p. 325

Split peas

Split peas are dried garden peas, coming in both green and yellow types. The green version is what is used to make classic pea and ham soup, while the yellow version is used to make the Greek dip fava. Split pigeon peas (toor dal) are also yellow and are commonly used in Indian cooking.

Squid ink

You can buy squid ink in jars, but I find small sachets the most convenient form. They keep well and you can use just what you need. It can be used to make dramatically black sauces (pp. 76, 89) or fresh pasta (see p. 128), both of which will have a distinctive briny umami quality.

Sriracha

The original sriracha was developed from a family recipe in the Thai coastal town of Si Racha. What most of us know as sriracha is not a traditional preparation, but rather an invention of David Tran in 1980 and manufactured in California. That familiar squeeze bottle with the rooster logo has become one of the world's most famous condiments, but it is somewhat simpler than the real deal, leaning more on heat than complexity. Whichever version you can get, sriracha is a very handy fiery chilli sauce that can be used to spike mayonnaise and the like, or just used as a condiment.

Star anise

Unsurprisingly, star anise is star shaped and anise flavoured, but its profile is quite different from anise and fennel seeds. The woody liquorice character is darker and more brooding, with the flavours knitting well into poached fruits and many Asian dishes, especially with beef, pork and duck, and it loves soy. It is also good with pears, plums, persimmons, apples and custard. Star anise is also integral to Chinese five-spice (see p. 10) and a good master stock. When ground, star

anise is very pungent, but the whole spice, or a point or two of a star, can subtly flavour a dish when fried off at the start and left to infuse. It's best to remove before serving, though, as they remain stubbornly hard.

Stock cubes/powder

I always endorse making your own stock whether it is a carefully constructed affair or one whipped up out of a left-over chicken carcass (see p. 49), but there are some excellent stock cubes/powders on the market, and they're often vegan – I would rather stay away from meat products of hard-to-establish origin (you can buy organic chicken cubes, though they're not readily available). Stock cubes add umami notes, which add a lift that water will not. Just don't be too heavy handed, as the flavour can overwhelm. I keep a range at home, from basic vegetable and chicken (often sans actual chicken) to dashi and miso powders.

Sugar, brown

Regular brown sugar, demerara and raw sugar are unrefined sugars, with the molasses content accounting for the colour and deeper flavour. Once refined, you have white sugar. It's important to note, though, that most commercial brown sugars are in fact refined white sugar that has molasses added back. This makes it easier to control colour and consistency, but don't be lured into thinking these are more natural due to their hue. I don't use the larger brown sugar crystals much, as they don't dissolve readily, but I do use demerara or raw sugar sometimes to decorate baked goods, as they add a pleasing crunch. I use soft brown sugar most often, as it dissolves and disperses readily. I will use it when I want to add rich caramelised base notes. Soft brown sugar will typically be available in lighter and darker versions. Rapadura is unrefined brown sugar, so it contains trace vitamins and minerals and less sucrose than refined sugar. Muscovado is also a partially refined sugar available in various grades of darkness, with the darkest adding deep toffee notes. Its soft texture also yields very moist results when baking. If available, use muscovado over generic soft brown sugar, as the flavour is superior.

Sugar, palm

Palm sugar is a traditional sweetener used in South-East Asian cooking, both sweet and savoury. It can be made from a variety of palm trees, with the flavour varying but the uses the same. I tend to favour the lighter coloured and flavoured ones from Thailand and Indonesia over the darker Malaysian versions. Palm sugar comes in hard blocks/discs (sometimes called jaggery, though the term applies to blocks of cane sugar, too), which can be grated, shaved with a knife or pounded in a mortar and pestle. If stored for a long time, these blocks can become extremely hard, though still usable. Store in an airtight container in the pantry. There is some confusion between the environmental impacts of palm oil and palm sugar, but palm sugar is seen as a positive industry, as wild trees are tapped rather than land being cleared for plantations.

Sugar, rock

Crystallised refined sugar, rock sugar, as the name suggests, comes in irregular lumps. It is used in Chinese cooking to add sweetness and a shiny gloss to sauces and glazes, for both sweet and savoury dishes.

Sugar, white

Refined white sugar is not something I use a lot, but its neutral flavour is best for many baking applications or to make custard and sauces where the caramelised flavour of brown sugar would jar. Caster (superfine) sugar is my go-to. It is simply white sugar ground to a finer grade, which makes it dissolve easily, especially for baking or when working with cold liquids like in a Thai dressing. Finer again than caster sugar, icing (confectioners') sugar is ideal for making icing. It is also used for dusting cakes and desserts just before serving (dusting too early will see it soaked up by any moisture, such as on a lemon tart). The easiest way to dust is to add some icing sugar to a fine-mesh sieve, then tap the edge to sift the sugar in a fine mist. Be aware that most shops will sell pure icing sugar and icing sugar mixture, which has cornflour in it as an anti-caking agent. I prefer to use the pure version. Snow sugar is icing sugar that doesn't melt. It's made from dextrose with a coating of oil (palm oil is commonly used, which you should never use, unless verified sustainable) and titanium dioxide to make it brilliantly white. It won't melt on warm dishes and will not be absorbed by moisture on a tart or the like.

Sumac

There are many species of sumac, with the small berry-like fruit (or drupes) of a few used to make the spice. Sumac berries generally appear in strikingly red clusters, with that vibrant colour deepening to richly saturated reddish brown when dried. The drupes are then ground to a slightly moist rough powder. The flavour is fruity and lemony, but it is not an overly aromatic spice, rather one about the tangy sharpness and gentle flavour on the palate. Like all spices, sumac should be used as fresh as possible, but it can lose its vital vibrancy somewhat quickly, so only buy in small amounts, or use a lot! Sumac can be used before and after cooking. Mix sumac with salt and black pepper for a marvellous pre-grill rub for lamb or chicken, which it is especially good with. It's a key ingredient in Za'atar (p. 33) and is lovely with tomatoes. I use sumac to finish dishes a lot, whether sprinkled over salads, dips or grilled meats, perhaps cooked lamb skewers anointed with yoghurt and finished with sumac and coriander.

Roasted tomatoes with sumac & cumin. Halve some ripe tomatoes and place in a baking dish or roasting tray, cut side up, then sprinkle over some sumac, salt flakes and ground cumin. Slow roast at 120°C (250°F) fan-forced for 2½ hours. Sprinkle over some thyme and crumbled feta and serve as is with some bread or with grilled meats. They also work well dropped on a grain salad to serve.

Tahini

Most of us know tahini as the brown paste made from hulled white sesame seeds, but it also comes in a black version, which is made from unhulled black seeds. The flavour of the latter is deeper with caramelised notes. From the paler iteration, I make a lot of Tahini dip/sauce (p. 71) to drizzle over a number of sweet and savoury dishes. Tahini is also essential for such things as hummus and baba ghanoush. Although larger tubs are more economical, be mindful of your needs, as the oils can become rancid and it will develop a bitterness over time. Storing opened containers in the fridge slows this down, but it does become thick so may need to be brought to room temperature and stirred well before use.

Taleggio

A semi-soft washed-rind cow's milk cheese from Lombardy, Italy, Taleggio is a marvellously pungent cheese that is brilliant for a cheese board, but also wonderful cooked. I drop cubes into a risotto see (pp. 148, 151) just at the end of cooking so that they ooze but still hold their form, and it's great with finely sliced potato and rosemary on a bianco pizza base (pp. 856–7).

Tamarind

Tamarind trees are native to Africa but grow in many tropical regions. They produce an elongated, brittle, bulging pod. Inside the pod, the seeds are encased with a pulpy, fibrous flesh, which is distinctly flavoured and both sweet and eye-wateringly sour. The flesh can be used fresh or bought in jars or compressed blocks. The jars are easiest to use, while the blocks need to be soaked in hot water. The flesh will start to pull apart and it is the strained liquid that you use. Tamarind is often used in curries, chutneys and sauces.

Tapioca

Tapioca is the starch of the cassava root, which is used as a flour and a thickener. The starch is often used to thicken coconut milk for desserts. Tapioca has little nutritional value, its contribution almost entirely textural. If cooking with tapioca balls, rinse well after cooking to stop clumping.

Tarragon, French

I adore French tarragon. It is a must for Béarnaise (p. 79), is great added to tartare sauce or salad dressings, is amazing when roasting chicken or making pot au feu, and enhances flavour of beans and carrots. French tarragon is at its finest in spring, with the leaves dainty and the anise flavour insistent but delicate. For those avid gardeners, beware tarragon seeds, as these will all be Russian tarragon; French tarragon is only grown from cuttings, with the few viable seeds it may produce reverting to wild ancestry once germinated. Russian tarragon is sometimes sold as French tarragon, but the flavour is intense and a little peppery and it is coarsely textured.

Tarragon, winter/Mexican

Winter tarragon is unrelated to Russian or French tarragon, being, instead, closely related to marigolds. It is robust and edgy with a powerful anise flavour, which the yellow flowers have as well. Winter tarragon leaves have a thick vein, so you need to chop them finely, or pick the more tender new growth.

Thyme

I am very effective at killing plants under my guardianship, but thyme, along with rosemary, sage and sorrel, seem to be immune to even my worst periods of neglect. I use thyme a lot in sauces, stocks (it's a must in a delicate fish stock), braises, marinades and mushroom and vegetable dishes, and it has a striking synergy with chicken. I will strip the leaves off the stems for a marinade or if pushing under chicken skin with butter before roasting, but I'll usually throw them in the pot for most other applications, then fish the

stalks out later. Thyme can also be infused into oil (see p. 165) to make an aromatic addition to a vinaigrette or to dress green beans, peas, spinach, mushrooms or new potatoes.

Thyme, lemon

Combining the flavour of thyme with an intense lemon character, I find lemon thyme best used very sparingly, or perhaps not at all.

Tofu

I mainly use silken tofu, firm tofu and fried tofu puffs. The latter can be used in soups, braises and stir-fries, while firm tofu will hold its shape when cooked for stir-fries and the like. Silken tofu will melt into silky curds, such as for Mapo-style tofu (p. 436), unless coated with potato starch and deep-fried for agedashi tofu, where it will hold its shape before the coating is broached.

Togarashi

Shichi-mi togarashi is a spice mix based on chilli (togarashi), along with sansho pepper, nori, sesame, poppy seeds, orange peel and ginger. There are variations in ingredients and ratios, but the name roughly translates as 'seven-flavour chilli', so seven ingredients is key, as is the chilli. Ichi-mi togarashi is one-flavour chilli, so just ground chilli.

Tomato paste (concentrated purée)

It's worth buying concentrated tomato paste in larger tins and freezing it in small portions. The cost is significantly better, and it freezes with no loss of quality. Tomato paste is an ideal way of adding intense tomato flavour to a dish without the bulk of tomato flesh, or to boost and concentrate tinned tomatoes or passata. Be wary, though – adding too much can make a dish taste heavy and conserve-like with sharp acidity.

Tomatoes, tinned

I always stock up on quality tinned tomatoes. I tend to stick to a few brands that I know reliably preserve only intense sun-ripened fruit. One thing to look out for is acidity regulator.

This is usually citric acid, which is fairly benign in itself, but can have a rather disastrous effect on the tomatoes and your dish. It is used as a preservative, but given that tomatoes can be quite acidic anyway, it can be too much. I don't mind adding a pinch of sugar to tomatoes when necessary, fresh or tinned, but baulk at having to add sugar to balance the added acidity.

Tom yum paste

Having a quality Thai tom yum paste on hand is a quick way to add an instant punchy lemongrass and tamarind flavour to sauces, broths and curries. It's a very handy shortcut, and can be used to make the classic sweet-and-sour soup.

Trimoline/invert sugar

Equal parts fructose and glucose, invert sugar is often used by bakers, pastry chefs and confectioners, as the syrup disperses readily and won't form crystals when chilled, which makes it useful for sorbets and the like (though I often use liquid glucose). It is also said to improve the colour and longevity of baked goods.

Turmeric, fresh

Fresh turmeric is becoming increasingly available, and while the per kilo price can seem alarming, the amount required in most dishes makes the cost negligible. Dried turmeric has its place, but the earthy flavour of fresh turmeric is a wondrous thing. It also freezes well, so it's worth buying up when the price is best.

Turmeric, ground

I buy fresh turmeric when I can, as the flavour is so much better, but the dried stuff does the job. Both have the characteristic earthy aroma and orangey yellow hue, and both will stain skin and clothes if you're not careful. Ground turmeric is an essential ingredient in curry powder, and it can add an earthy underpinning to a dish, plus it adds such wonderful colour, too. It is also used to get a vibrant hue in mustard or to colour pickles.

Tuna, tinned/jarred

Quality preserved tuna is quite the delicacy, and really elevates a niçoise salad (see p. 438), but it's important to know what you're buying. Greenpeace.org is a good source of information but, at the time of writing, skipjack is the preferred species, with bluefin and yellowfin tuna threatened. Fishing methods are also key, with bycatch a significant concern with tuna fishing. Do your research and buy prudently.

Umeboshi

Often translated as preserved plums, umeboshi are made from Japanese ume fruit, which are in the prunus family, but are not plums as such. They are salted and fermented, resulting in a preserved fruit that is exceedingly sour, from both the citric acid of the fruit and the lactic acid of the fermentation.

Vanilla

The scent of real vanilla is sweet and floral, a very dreamy aroma used to perfume baked goods, biscuits and pastries, poaching liquids and sauces. The pods are dark brown to black with tons of tiny black seeds inside. Both the pods and seeds are aromatic, with the seeds typically scraped into custards and the like, while the pod is removed once its job is done. If not using the pods in a recipe, store them in a jar of sugar, which will take on the flavour. You are not supposed to store pods that have been used to flavour milk or cream, but I do, simply washing and drying well first. However, I also often use the whole pod these days, slicing into fine splinters and leaving in the dish, as it is all edible. Vanilla pods will deteriorate with exposure to light and air. If they are dry and brittle, chances are they won't have great flavour. To store, place in a sealed bag, squeezing out as much air as possible, then store in a jar or airtight container in the fridge or a cool, dry place. They will keep for 6 months to more than a year like this, depending on how fresh they were to begin with. Ideally, only store small amounts. Vanilla paste is something that I always keep, too, as

the flavour is great and it's convenient. Vanilla extract can be used instead, but I would never buy vanilla essence. It's an artificial simulation of vanilla that tastes as ordinary as that sounds.

Verjuice/verjus

Verjuice is simply the unfermented juice of unripe grapes, which can be used to add acid to a dish without the intensity of vinegar and with a different flavour profile to wine. It can be used as is in a dressing or sauce, or cooked with, and it also adds a balanced sweetness, which enriches without becoming cloying.

Vine leaves

Brined vine leaves will either come in a jar or vacuum pack. They generally need to be rinsed and dried before use, as they can be very salty otherwise.

Vinegar

I have quite the collection of vinegars. Different varieties of wine vinegars, both red and white, as well as those built on wine appellations, notably, Champagne and sherry, with the latter near-to indispensable. I use apple-cider vinegar for many general applications, from salads to pickling, as I do brown and white rice vinegars, which have pleasing umami notes. It's worth spending the extra on good vinegar, as the flavour has a big impact on your cooking. Decent vinegar is not that expensive, unless you're talking about balsamic. Most people know balsamic as the thin dark vinegar that is readily available at the supermarket. This is a commercial product that uses caramel with an everyday vinegar to mimic real balsamic. The real stuff – or Aceto balsamico Tradizionale di Modena/ Reggio Emilia – is only made from Trebbiano and Lambrusco varieties, with the grape must (juice) boiled until a syrup, that is then fermented very slowly before being converted to vinegar. As liquid evaporates over the years, the vinegar is rehomed in ever-smaller barrels, with twelve years the minimum age, and twenty-five years

plus for extravecchio (extra old). The result is an incredibly flavourful and thick syrup, with a sweet-and-sour profile. Real balsamic is not for making salad dressings, rather I will serve it with some chunks of exceptional Parmigiano Reggiano and hand-rolled Grissini (p. 856) to kick off dinner, or drizzle a little over perfectly ripe tomatoes with burrata or buffalo mozzarella, or to finish a special risotto (see p. 148) or pasta (see p. 132). There is a middle-range balsamic called condimento for more everyday applications, such as dressings. Aceto balsamico di Modena IGP is the designation used if from Modena, but condiment balsamic can be made outside of the area, too. These vinegars generally fall short of the standards of traditional balsamic, and may have caramel and other vinegars added to build the flavour and colour profile, but some can be of very high standard. Black vinegar is often referred to as Chinese balsamic, with the ageing process adding complexity in a similar way, bestowing it with deep umami character. Chinese black vinegar is based on a wholegrain fermentation, though, and has a malty and darkly spiced presentation. Chinkiang (also spelt zhenjiang) vinegar is a type of rice-based black vinegar that is used primarily in dumpling dipping sauces; it is less intense than black vinegars made from other grains. Vinegar will deteriorate, so buy only what you will use in 6–12 months, and keep the bottles tightly sealed out of direct light, somewhere cool. Proper balsamic should still be stored somewhere dark and cool, but it is somewhat less affected by the ravages of time.

Wakame

A type of kelp, wakame typically comes dried. Once rehydrated, it is quite finely textured with a mild flavour. It is used in many dishes, but perhaps most recognisably so in miso soup.

Wasabi

If you're lucky enough to be able to source fresh wasabi (Japanese horseradish), then it is at its best when freshly grated, but it can be reconstituted from a powder or bought in a tube already mixed. It is naturally used to serve alongside sushi and sashimi, but can also be used to spike mayonnaise or other sauces, adding a hot, peppery and mustardy bite.

Wasabi tobiko

Tobiko is flying fish roe, which is used for sushi and other applications. They can be served as is or flavoured and coloured, such as with wasabi tobiko, with the eggs bright green and hot.

Water chestnuts

The tuber of a fresh-water vegetable, I love the texture and gently individual flavour of water chestnuts. I use them diced to add to fillings for dumplings, sang choi bao and stir-fries. They come tinned, frozen or vacuum-packed.

White anchovies

Unlike regular anchovies under oil, white anchovies (boquerones) are cured for only a short time, rather than many months, before being marinated in oil and vinegar, and often with garlic and herbs. They have a vinegary tang and a much milder flavour.

Wine

Do not sacrifice fine bottles to the pot. The maxim for me is that the wine should be pleasant, if unremarkable, and it's important to consider the impact of different varieties/styles on your dish, as some wines can be too heavy, while others too acidic. For savoury cooking, wine needs to be dry, as any sweetness will concentrate once reduced to become cloying. If cooking with red wine, rich, full reds work well when making intense red wine sauces or beef braises, but I like to use savoury reds, like Sangiovese or Nebbiolo, for red wine risotto, and I even use Chianti in a granita with raspberries (see p. 784). Match lighter reds to the style of the dish, with Pinot Noir, Gamay and the like working well with lighter proteins, and even matching well with fish in a sauce such as Beurre rouge (p. 69). You can also be more generous with red wine, with a ragù happily taking a bottle, where a bottle of white wine would generally make it unpleasantly acidic. But that acidity is your friend, too. It adds so much pep and complexity to seafood and poultry dishes when used judiciously (I generally lean towards bright acidic whites, like Riesling, Semillon or light Pinot Grigio/Gris, for seafood, but slightly richer ones, like Chardonnay or richer Grigio/Gris, work well with chicken). It also needs to be reduced to have the best gains. The term often used is to 'cook off the alcohol', but this is not quite how it works, with the alcohol not being discretely evaporated to leave all the flavour behind, but you can certainly smell a change from a raw winey-ness to a general sense of harmony. As always, use your senses. If I'm using wine in a ragù, I will reduce it to pretty much dry before adding any other liquid, where in a braise, the wine is used as a braising liquid, then reduced afterwards to make a sauce.

Xanthan gum

A thickener and stabiliser, xanthan gum is used widely in processed foods, but can also be useful for the home cook, especially in gluten-free baking to imitate some of the elastic properties of gluten.

Yeast

Dried yeast is a handy thing, but it's important that it is still active. Excess heat or exposure to air will render it less effective, if not completely ineffective. Mostly, it will come in packets with sachets of 7 g (¼ oz) each, but you can also buy it in larger vacuum-packed bags. The individual sachets proffer a level of confidence, but they have failed me before while still in date. I find it best to keep any dried yeast in the fridge or freezer in an airtight container, which will also generally keep it beyond the expiry date. Fresh yeast is less readily available, and more perishable, so it must be refrigerated or frozen. As a general rule, use half the amount of dried yeast to fresh yeast.

Yoghurt

I buy various types of natural yoghurt, but it's always full-fat, organic and never sweetened, and I stay away from those thickened with milk solids. Thinner yoghurt is ideal for muesli (see p. 394) or fresh or poached fruit (pp. 710–1, 714, 723–4), while thick yoghurt is best to make things such as Tzatziki (p. 507) or to mix through flavourings or combine with mayonnaise, lightening the oily feel and adding a sour tang, to dress a potato salad or the like. You can thicken yoghurt further by draining it through a few layers of muslin (cheesecloth) in a sieve over a bowl or a tub in the fridge – don't do this with thinner yoghurts, though, as the yield will be miserable. How long this takes depends on how thick you want it, but if taken to the extreme you will end up with Labneh (p. 362).

Za'atar

Za'atar refers to both a wild herb of the Middle East and a mix containing it along with other dried herbs and sesame seeds. The herb is the same as biblical hyssop and is also often called Lebanese oregano or wild thyme. The blend is what most of us will come across, but be aware that many don't actually contain za'atar, instead being made of oregano, thyme, marjoram and other similar herbs. Za'atar blends are best stirred into oil and served with or cooked on top of Arab-style breads and pastries. Use it as is on feta or fried haloumi, to season lamb, poultry and vegetables before grilling or roasting, or use to top Arabic breads, pastries or man'oushe. To make, combine 150 g (5½ oz) toasted and crushed blanched almonds (optional), 50 g (1¾ oz) dried za'atar, wild thyme or regular dried thyme, 1½ tablespoons sumac, 2 tablespoons sesame seeds, 1 tablespoon ground cumin, 1 teaspoon cumin seeds, 1 teaspoon ground aleppo pepper (optional), ½ teaspoon ground black pepper and a pinch of ground cardamom. Store in an airtight container for up to 2 weeks.

Equipment

A properly equipped kitchen is essential to cooking efficiently and well. That doesn't mean you need to be elaborately kitted out, just armed with quality essentials. You really don't need a lot, but buy well, as good equipment will last a lifetime. I'm not one for gadgets. I like classic equipment, and I have a blushingly deep crush on copper cookware, but I also own a Thermomix (see p. 41). This is a list of essential – and some not so essential – kitchen tools that will have you ready in the kitchen.

Apple corer

These are very handy if you're cooking apples or want to cut apples into rings to caramelise (see p. 769). They're cheap, readily available and worth the little space they occupy.

Bain marie

Although it no doubt conjures up images of canteen food kept hot for too long, a bain marie is a handy way to cook at an even temperature, which is especially important when making terrines (see p. 328) or parfait/pâté (pp. 233, 327) or setting delicate desserts in the oven. It is simply a water bath, which can be achieved in a roasting tin or high-sided ceramic dish. Be sure to use hot water, otherwise it will skew cooking times and likely yield an inconsistent result.

Baking dishes & cazuelas

I have a collection of ceramic baking dishes, all of them presentable enough to grace the table, as it's rare that a dish cooked in one would not be served this way. Glazed clay cazuelas are even more versatile, as you can cook in them directly on the stovetop and they retain heat very well, so a bubbling dish of garlic prawns (shrimp) can finish cooking at the table. Cazuelas just need to be seasoned first. Soak in water overnight, then dry, coat with oil and place in the oven for an hour at about 150°C (300°F) fan-forced. If not seasoned properly, they will crack. Cazuelas are also somewhat handsome tableware, and I use variously sized ones for plating up dishes both hot and cold.

Baking paper/silicone mats

Non-stick baking paper is invaluable in the kitchen, and not just for lining cake tins and trays for biscuits. It's also a sure way of stopping roast vegetables sticking to the tray. But before you start peeling off reams and reams of the stuff, consider its disposable nature. Baking paper is typically coated with silicone, which won't readily degrade in landfill. More environmentally friendly options are biodegradable/compostable papers, or silicone mats. Yes, silicone again, but they last incredibly well, and they can be recycled or downcycled – you just need to make sure a recycler does this, as dropping them in a council bin is likely not the answer.

Baking trays/sheets

While you can only probably get two to three trays in a standard oven at any one time, it is always useful to have more on hand. It just makes it easier if you need to roll out and rest pastry or the like, as it's easy to move around as you need the space, or to take in and out of the fridge if resting. They're also good for holding fresh pasta, gnocchi or dumplings and easy to take to the pot to cook. And they're ideal for crisping potatoes or roasting vegetables. I also use heavy cast-iron baking sheets (they have no lip), which hold plenty of heat and don't buckle in the oven. They can also stand in quite well for a pizza stone.

Banneton

These cane (they can be plastic, too, but cane is best) baskets are used to prove bread before baking. They create an ideal humid environment, and they stop the shaped bread spreading. They come in various sizes and shapes for everything from baguettes to large rounds. They will also typically come with a lining cloth, which you can use heavily dusted with flour, or you can place the bread directly in the basket, dusted with flour again. There is more chance of the dough sticking without the liner, but they do yield a very professional-looking pattern of rings on the loaf. Once used a few times, the cane will build up a layer of flour that will stop any sticking issues. Dust off and remove any dough that may have become stuck, but then just allow to dry out and store in a dry place.

Blender

A sturdy blender that operates at a high speed is ideal for making purées and smoothies (or blended cocktails, if that's your thing), as food processors never do the job quite as well.

Blowtorch

This may not seem the most essential piece of kit, but they are relatively cheap and will make short work of caramelising a Crème brûlée (p. 780), which is much harder to achieve with a domestic griller.

Bowls

Nesting stainless-steel bowls are an absolute must. They are unbreakable and incredibly useful. It's good to have a range from large down to quite petite to start with, then you can up the stocks of the ones you use the most. I use them for everything, from washing and prepping to mixing batter and making sauces. Some recipes call for a glass bowl to melt chocolate or make a sauce such as hollandaise, but I prefer steel, as you can adjust the temperature quickly, where glass bowls will hold the heat. Some steep-sided, heavy ceramic mixing bowls are also a good idea, as they will stay put when you are whisking a mayonnaise or similar. Old-fashioned pudding bowls are perfect, and you can also make old-fashioned puddings in them.

Box grater

A box grater should last a long, long time. I find the more expensive ones tend to be made of a combination of plastic and steel, and they are more prone to failure over time. Sturdy steel ones are generally very economical and are hard to damage.

Cake, muffin & tart tins

Springform cake tins are the easiest option, as it makes unmoulding cakes fuss-free. Mostly, 20–23 cm (8–9 in) tins will be your workhorses, but it's good to also have a high-sided one for cheesecakes, and a 20 cm (8 in) square tin (equivalent to a 23 cm/9 in round tin) or two. A couple of 20 × 30 cm (8 × 12 in) brownie tins are also important if you're partial to baking. I use a 20 × 40 cm (8 × 15¾ in) tin for larger celebration cakes or lamingtons. For tarts, I have a range of fluted, loose-bottomed tart tins, but 20–24 cm (8–9½ in) is probably the most useful range. To make smaller tarts, 8–10 cm (3¼–4 in) tins work well, and you'd need ten to twelve of those. I also use tart rings, which have no base, so you fill directly onto a lined baking sheet, then lift off once baked. Muffin trays come in a variety of sizes, but I tend to use the larger-holed trays. A large and a medium tray is a safe bet. If you want to make Madeleines (p. 736), then you'll need a madeleine pan (see p. 37). For friands, a friand tin is required, not for anything other than achieving the classic oval shape – you can use a muffin tin, of course. A couple of loaf (bar) tins fill out the basic needs; start with ones about 22 cm–25 cm (8¾ in–10 in) long and 11–12 cm (4¼–4¾ in) wide.

Cast iron, seasoning

Unfinished cast-iron cookware will develop a non-stick surface if properly seasoned. Often this is done in the factory prior to sale but not always. Seasoning will naturally develop over time, but the surface does need to be treated prior to use. Simply wash with soap and water, dry thoroughly, then coat the cooking surface very lightly with oil. Flip upside-down on an oven shelf, with a tray underneath to catch any oil, and bake at about 200°C (400°F) for about an hour. Cool in the oven before using. You can repeat this process to build up a better coating. That initial seasoning will build over time as oils polymerise and layer into the surface. It is often advised to not clean with soap and water, but once the protective layer is well established this should not be a major issue, as long as you're not scrubbing hard or soaking. Acidic foods can cause havoc with cast-iron cookware, but this is usually when the seasoning layer is developing. Once established, this is not such a concern.

Cherry/olive pitter

This is the kind of thing you buy when you need it, rather than being prepared for an unexpected abundance of cherries. Naturally, I use mine infrequently, but it's invaluable when I do need it. I rarely use them for olives, though, unless stuffing them, say with slivers of pickled peppers or a superior anchovy to skewer and have as a snack or to lodge in a martini. I like to squash olives to break the flesh, then tear them in half or pieces to add to a sauce or the like. I prefer the natural shape here, but that's entirely personal.

Chopping boards

A heavy hardwood chopping board is a core workstation in my kitchen. I prefer wood to plastic for most uses, but I do have some plastic boards that will sit on top of my main board, with a tea towel (dish towel) in between, for preparing poultry, meat and fish. It's not that plastic boards are safer (the cuts in a plastic board can more readily harbour pathogens, where wood tends to have a smoother finish as it wears), but they can be scrubbed and sanitised more easily, or run through the dishwasher. Hardwood boards are best, as they are less likely to crack or be nicked, and I like the weight, with the boards staying put when working. To deep-clean a wooden chopping board, rub lots of table salt and a little water into the wood thoroughly with a scourer. Allow to sit for 30 minutes, then scour off. I do this every couple of months.

Colander

I like to use a large steel colander, as it is good to have some extra space to rough up potatoes by tossing them to create frayed edges, which will crisp up marvellously in the oven.

Crepe pan

Essential? No. But if you want to make perfect Crepes (p. 771), then you really need a properly flat pan with low sides. I think it's worth it, but then I do rather like crepes.

Dariole moulds

These are used for setting panna cottas (pp. 707, 781, 783) or the like, and they can be bought in metal or plastic versions. The plastic ones work quite well, as they are flexible and make breaking the surface tension seal quite easy, but pulling the edge away with your fingertip works fine if using metal, or just dip in hot water briskly. You can buy various sizes, but 125 ml (4 fl oz/½ cup) is a good standard capacity.

Dough knife/scraper

This is not an absolutely essential piece of equipment, but it's very, very handy. You can buy simple plastic ones, though a good steel one with a wooden handle is worth the investment if you bake a lot. They can be used to bring a dough or pastry together, scraping up all the residue, and are excellent for handling sticky doughs. They are also invaluable when making gnocchi, helping to chop through and begin to incorporate the potato and flour, and you can also use the blade to cut the snakes into dumplings.

Dutch/French oven

After a basic set of saucepans (see p. 39) and frying pans (see right), a wide, heavy-based saucepan such as a Dutch or French oven should be something that every cook invests in. It can be either a well-seasoned cast-iron Dutch oven or the slicker enamelled cast iron of a French oven, both being excellent for slow cooking on the stovetop or in the oven. I would advise buying the enamelled versions, as they are much easier to maintain and the surface is not compromised by acidic ingredients (see 'seasoning cast iron', p. 35), making them more versatile.

Fish grill

If barbecuing fish often, these simple devices are invaluable. They consist of two pieces of grill or mesh that are hinged, with a handle and clasp to fasten the sides together. It stops the fish skin sticking to the barbecue grill, and it makes cooking lots of small fish at once a breeze. They are also very effective for barbecuing vegetables such as spring onions, baby leeks and Dutch carrots.

Food mill

These are wonderful for making super-smooth mash, they're ideal for gnocchi, and they will mill a passata while kindly trapping the skins and seeds. They can be used to puree any cooked vegetables, so can effectively stand in for a blender if needed.

Food processor

You can do a lot with a food processor, though a lot of the attachments go unused in my kitchen. Food processors are great for making things such as Pesto (p. 90) and Salsa verde (p. 86) and pasta dough (pp. 111, 128, 131) – just don't run them for long stints as the blades can heat up and you will lose your sauce's freshness. They're also perfect for making Mayonnaise (pp. 74–5) in larger quantities, for mixing pasta dough or for grating a lot of vegetables. Where they fall down is with small quantities, but the bowl attachment that comes with a stick blender does the trick there.

Frying pans

It's ideal to have frying pans in various sizes, with a larger one with high sides (making it good for shallow-frying) and a clear lid, ideally, which is handy for Pot-sticker dumplings (p. 500), among other things. A cast-iron skillet, or two, is also a worthwhile investment. They're incredibly durable and the way they retain heat makes them ideal for certain types of cooking; they are perfect for searing meat well, as lighter weight pans lose a lot of heat once you add meat or fish, and they are also great for hotcakes/pancakes. Cast iron is not responsive, though, so anything where you need to adjust the heat quickly and in a nuanced way is not advised. Copper pans have the opposite properties, with the metal conducting and shedding heat quickly. Copper is eye-wateringly expensive, though, and stainless-steel frying pans do the job just fine – most have a layer of copper or similarly conductive metal in the base to simulate the performance of more luxe options. The next question is whether to buy non-stick or not. They certainly work well, for a time at least. Teflon and similar coatings can degrade quickly at high temperatures, producing gasses that can be harmful. How harmful is not well established, but it's enough to put me off. I also often want a pan super-hot, and I'm not going to change the way I cook because of a pan's surface. As well, the coating ends up

scratching off over time, making the pans essentially disposable, the cheap versions even more so. That's not how it should be, so I invest in quality non-stick pans in four sizes and rotate them when they start to wear out.

If you want to cook with little or no butter or olive oil, then ... well, you're talking to the wrong person. A properly clean pan (any residue, no matter how small, can become an anchor point for sticking), properly hot oil and sealing until a crust forms will stop things from sticking. Butter also has marvellous non-stick properties, but naturally this depends on the heat, with clarified butter/ghee best for high-heat cooking.

Griddle pan

These are very handy, but please buy a heavy cast-iron one. I also prefer the flatter ones, without high sides, as they are more versatile with larger or awkward items. Also, avoid the non-stick versions. Most synthetic non-stick cookware will start to degrade and release chemicals at high heats, and if there's any piece of cookware that you want to get blisteringly hot, it's a griddle pan. Before cooking, I will put the pan over a high heat for at least 5 minutes. Needless to say, a good extractor and perhaps an open window or two are called for, but if you want to emulate the heat from a chargrill, then you need it hot, really hot.

Kitchen spoons

Metal kitchen spoons are ever useful, both solid and perforated. A couple of each is ideal.

Knife sharpening stone & steel

It's good to get in the practice of running your knife over a stone regularly. It's easy to leave that first sharpen until the factory-keenness has long since gone, and bringing back a proper edge can be quite laborious. Sharpen your knives before they are dull, and it will make the process less of a chore. It's worth investing in a quality stone with a coarse side and a fine side. The finer side should be about 1000 grit while the other will be around 300–400. If you look after your knives, you should rarely use the coarse side, but no-one's perfect. When sharpening, it takes a little practice to get the angle right, but many stones come with guides that attach to the back of a knife to provide a perfect angle. It also takes a little patience to bring out the best edge and to ensure that edge is consistent from tip to heel. I use a diamond steel, too, which is an easy and quick way to refine the edge on your knife. Unlike a diamond steel, a regular steel won't sharpen your knife as such, but it makes it more effective by straightening out the edge. This is particularly useful after sharpening, when metal debris is often present on the edge, and it makes a noticeable difference after the knife has been in use.

Knives

You can get by with a simple selection of knives, but a decent quality chef's knife is a must. A 20 cm (8 in) knife is the perfect all-purpose blade, and it's worth spending extra on a proper one. Take a moment and stop yourself being drawn in by that block of knives at the same price as one blade. You don't need them all, and half a dozen dull knives will never trump one keen blade. A good bread/serrated knife is also essential, and not just for bread, but for cutting cakes in half to fill, or to trim pineapple, watermelon and the like. A paring knife and a small, serrated version are also necessary, and they're economical. The paring knife is useful for, well, paring and peeling, while the serrated one is handy for slicing through things such as super-ripe tomatoes, especially when your chef's knife is a little dull. Which, of course, will never happen, as you'll look after it, have it sharpened regularly, or do it yourself (see left). We're all guilty of letting our knives go blunt, but try to stay on top of it, as it will make things so much easier, more enjoyable and the results will be better. It's also safer. Sounds odd, but a dull knife is more likely to stick or slip. A sharp knife will do what you ask of it – just pay attention. There are many

more knives you can add. I have an affection for Japanese blades, which take a little getting used to, as many have a bevel on one edge only, like a chisel, but they are beautiful to use, once familiar, and they hold an edge wonderfully well. But that's a personal choice. If I were to add another knife to the arsenal, it would be a 17 cm (6¾ in) fine-bladed cleaver, which is great for chopping, shredding and cutting through soft bones, such as in chicken or young pork. You can also use the flat edge to crush garlic or lift things into the pan/wok.

Ladles

I recommend a few sizes of ladles, with larger ones useful for stock or soup and small ones for basting or saucing dishes.

Madeleine pan

To recreate that most Proustian little cake, you absolutely need a madeleine pan, with its distinctive scalloped recesses. But you don't need it for anything else. In fact, it really has no-other uses, except to shape another batter or chocolate into a madeleine shape, which feels a little blasphemous.

Mandoline

A Japanese mandoline is an essential part of a professional kitchen, and I think they're invaluable at home, too. They make short work of shredding, finely shaving and julienning. The only caveat is caution, as the blade is ruthlessly sharp, and it does not discriminate between vegetables and fingers. Use the guard … well, I say that, but I never do. I just use abundant caution, then slow my process as the vegetable dwindles, being even more abundantly cautious. You won't slice it all, but you can eat that last bit, and we all need to eat more vegetables. Officially, though, my advice is to use the guard.

Measuring cups & spoons

I typically weigh ingredients when precision is required, but spoon and

cup measures are very handy for those recipes with a bit of latitude. I have many sets of measuring spoons, but one needs to be wary of tablespoon measures. Australia, as I understand it, is the only country that uses 20 ml (¾ fl oz/4 teaspoon) tablespoons, rather than 15 ml (½ fl oz/three teaspoon) tablespoons. And because I have always worked with this measure, I believe that it is the morally superior size (a view that is entirely unsupportable, but there you have it). This variation may not matter in some recipes, but it can make a real difference for baking recipes and, if it is for multiple tablespoons, that variation can blow out somewhat. It always pays to verify the measure used in the cookbook you are working from. Standard cup measures can differ, too. In the US, there are two cup sizes, which is quite unhelpful, even if they are similar in size (237 ml/8 fl oz for the 'customary' and 240 ml/8 fl oz for the 'legal' cup), while the rest of the world uses the metric cup, which is 250 ml (8½ fl oz). Naturally, this time I side with the majority. The only other hiccup would be using an old UK recipe, where cup sizes are 285 ml 9½ fl oz) or thereabouts. It's also worth having a glass measuring jug or two, which are ideal for larger volumes when you don't need to be precise to the gram/ml by weighing. I favour ones with ribbed measures, rather than just painted, as paint can wear off.

Meat mincer (grinder)

This is specialised, but if you're making your own terrines or sausages then it's worth having a good one. You can buy dedicated mincers, but if you own a stand mixer, then a mincing attachment is the best bet. If using an electric mincer of any sort, ensure that you are feeding through smaller pieces, as overloading will make the machine work harder and can result in overheating, which can mar the mince and damage the machine.

Microplane

It would be extreme to say that when these little tools came along they revolutionised cooking, but they certainly had a big impact. Being able to grate ultra-fine citrus zest without catching any of the white pith is a real bonus, as is being able to quickly grate ginger, garlic, horseradish, nuts and chocolate. A slightly coarser mesh is wonderful for Parmesan or other hard cheeses, too, with the fine snow of cheese melting into a sauce effortlessly.

Microwave

A microwave is not something that I have used very often, but they are useful for melting butter and chocolate, and in the professional kitchen they are an important tool for the dessert section to heat components. Of course, none of this mounts a good case for owning one. I have no doubt that they can be very useful for convenience reheating, but they are entirely dispensable for me.

Mortar & pestle

I have several of these. I do love them and their primal quality, both visual and practical. I have a large stone one from Thailand that I use all the time. It's brutal and very effective for pesto or a curry paste, but then I also have small ones, which are entirely useless for such jobs but so handy to have on the bench to make a quick spice salt by grinding salt flakes and toasted coriander seeds, cumin, carraway or the like, or to smash some garlic with salt to start a dressing or marinade or to make a quick pesto.

Muslin (cheesecloth)

A super-light open-weave cloth, muslin is handy to strain yoghurt to thicken or to make Labneh (p. 362), or you can use it to tie up lemon pips or cracked cherry pips to thicken a jam. You will generally need to use a few layers to stop curds pushing through the weave.

Oyster knife/shucker

I'm a huge advocate for opening your own oysters (see p. 208). It's not hard, and the rewards are immense. I favour the narrow-bladed shuckers.

The broad flat-bladed knives with a guard feel a little clumsy to me, but that is, I'm sure, very much down to personal preferences.

Oven

In general, I always cook with the fan on, as I find the heat more even, but if you don't have that functionality, add about 20°C (35°F) to the temperature given, but beyond that you'll need to adjust based on local conditions. No time given in any recipe should ever be seen as set and forget. And cooking well is never like that. Watch, smell and listen. These are your best guides. If your oven is quite old, an oven thermometer is worth buying. They're economical and will be a better guide to the true temperature of the oven than an old thermostat.

Palette knife

A spatula can be used for icing cakes, but a couple of sizes of steel palette knives will make that process much easier and yield a finer result. An offset palette knife is also a worthwhile investment. They make it easier to smooth icing and ice awkward areas as well as to smooth out things like praline, or a tuile batter (p. 788). They can also be used to lift fragile warm biscuits off a baking tray.

Pasta machine

You can buy a decent benchtop pasta machine for a relatively modest price, and they should last a lifetime if treated properly. They can also be used to roll dough for things such as cannoli (see p. 820), or to get a uniform finish on crackers (see p. 838–40). The key is to never force the mechanism with a dough that is too thick and/or stiff. Always roll out the dough so that it can pass through the widest setting with relative ease. You can also buy attachments that fit on a stand mixer, but I like the manual act of turning the crank – it's somewhat cathartic. Pasta machines should not be washed, as you will interfere with the greasing of the gears. Simply dust off and store. Mine goes back in the box it came in.

Pastry brush

A pastry brush with natural bristles is best for glazing and egg washing. I have a fancy rubber one that is easier to clean and will last a long time, but it is a clumsy affair and not suited to brushing delicate pastry.

Pie dish

Metal, ceramic or enamel all work equally well for a pie dish. To start, I would opt for one at least 23 cm (9 in) across and 4–5 cm (1½–2 in) deep.

Piping (icing) bag

While I don't want to advocate using disposable items, I do find disposable piping bags very useful. You can buy them on a roll, and biodegradable ones are readily available. They are easy to fill. If I have two or three elements that will be piped, I find it easiest to have them ready to go in the fridge in the bags.

Pizza stone

This is key to baking pizza in a domestic oven, as they hold heat very well, giving the dough the best chance to puff up and cook quickly. A cast-iron baking sheet does a decent job, too. Whatever you are using, heat in the oven for a good 30 minutes before baking.

Plastic wrap

Professional kitchens churn through an astonishing amount of plastic wrap. It is convenient and effective, but its days should be numbered, along with all plastic. At home, I found myself mirroring that professional approach. Then I took pause, and now I barely use it. Throughout the book I have tried to limit its use, and if I do use plastic it is generally reused. I use plastic bags to rest doughs and pastry, then wash and store them for next time, and a shower cap used to cover the bowl of a stand mixer works a treat – and can be used countless times. There are still times when I use plastic wrap, as I have found the results are superior, but by all means find a more creative solution.

Reactive cookware

Iron, copper, aluminium and steel (not stainless steel, but like the steel used to make woks) are all reactive materials, which means they can leach out their metals when in contact with acidic or alkaline foods. This is rarely an issue with copper, as most pans have a stainless-steel lining (or tin if very old), but it can lend a metallic edge to the dish at times. A well-seasoned iron or steel pan will not react, as the protective coating built over time will not be affected by either acidic or alkaline solutions. The other issue with reactive metals is that they can discolour some foods. I find it easiest to avoid aluminium and make sure anything reactive is well seasoned (see 'seasoning cast iron, p. 35).

Rice cooker

I don't have one. I like cooking rice the old-fashioned way (see p. 372), and I'm convinced the results are better, as the rice seems to hold its shape a little better – that may or may not be true. To remove my bias for a moment, these are very economical and generally foolproof. They also keep the rice warm, so timing is not an issue, and you can use them as a steamer. They are a bit disposable, though (not to mention rather bulky) and I know the pot I cook my rice in will last a lifetime.

Roasting tins

Deep enamel or stainless-steel roasting tins can be used for roasts and as a bain marie in the oven for parfait/pâté (pp. 233, 327), terrines (see p. 328), set custard desserts (pp. 500, 698–9) and similar. A couple of large ones that will just fit in the oven are ideal for large joints of meat, while a few smaller ones can handle other tasks.

Rolling pins

I have two types: a standard, heavy cylindrical one, and a French-style tapered one. The tapered one is good for delicate work with pastry, as you can apply pressure where needed by pivoting off the central point, while the other is good for any heavier work.

I don't use rolling pins that spin on a central rod with handles. It's very hard to get a feel for what you're doing with these, and they seem unnecessarily complicated to me. If you're in the habit of making your own dumplings or tortillas, then a small rolling pin is also a good idea (though a tortilla press is far easier for the latter).

Salad spinner

Salad leaves need to be properly dry before they are dressed or chopped, and a salad spinner is by far the easiest method of achieving this. They are also great for drying herbs, as too much water on the leaves will negatively skew a pesto or salad. The only downside is that they're bulky, so not ideal if storage space is light on.

Saucepans

A decent set of saucepans is an important part of any kitchen. A stockpot is maybe not the first thing you would buy, but an 8–10 litre (270–338 fl oz) saucepan is essential for cooking pasta and the like, and it will handle moderately sized stocks. If making a serious stock, such as a Brown beef stock (p. 55), making a good quantity just makes sense, as it takes some time and it can be reduced and frozen, so a 20 litre (676 fl oz) pot becomes more practical. A 6 litre (202 fl oz) and a 4 litre (135 fl oz/16 cup) pot will do lots of the heavy lifting, while a couple of 2 litre (68 fl oz/8 cup) pans with long handles are good for smaller jobs and holding sauces. A couple of 1 litre (34 fl oz/4 cup) pans will likely get less of a workout, but they're invaluable for smaller quantities. Another pan I would really recommend is a wide heavy-based pan that is only about 12 cm (4¾ in) tall but about 30 cm (12 in) wide. The extra surface area helps to keep the pan and its contents nice and hot, which is ideal if searing or browning at the start of cooking, and it's also excellent for caramelising onions and vegetables, with the low sides making it easy to access and stir through without leaving anything to catch. All my saucepans are stainless steel, except for a few copper ones that are more of an indulgence. I don't use aluminium, but they do heat effectively and evenly, and they are much more economical. Just be aware that aluminium can react with acidic ingredients and can discolour some foods.

Scales

A good set of digital scales is a must. Being able to measure down to the gram is a great advantage when baking, precisely measuring small portions to achieve the best and most consistent results. Good sprung scales are effective for most weights, but I find them troublesome when measuring below 10 g (¼ oz). Digital scales are not expensive, and they don't take up much space.

Scissors

Heavy-duty snips are invaluable in a kitchen. From cutting through poultry rib bones to trimming fish fins/tails, to cutting through lobster or marron shells to snipping woody stems from cime di rape and the like, they're a versatile way to cut where a knife would be awkward or hazardous.

Sieves

A couple of sizes of fine-mesh sieves are handy for draining finer items such as lentils and quinoa after washing and cooking. They are also good for draining yoghurt to thicken – just line with muslin (cheesecloth) first, as the solids will press through the mesh otherwise. They are also good for straining custards or tart fillings for a super-smooth result, or to pass a sauce or coulis to remove any seeds or other matter. It's good to include a fine conical sieve in your collection, as it makes pushing through sauces easier and directs them more accurately into your vessel. Professionally, a steel conical sieve (or chinois) is employed to pass sauces, with the sturdiness and shape ideal for using a ladle to force the liquid out. Most people won't need to go this industrial, but they are a very practical tool.

Skewers

I have a quiver full of skewers, from plain steel ones to those with more decorative handles for grilling meat and vegetables. Metal skewers are also handy for testing cakes or the doneness of meat (feel the warmth of the tip after you've inserted it for a few seconds). I generally avoid using disposable ones unless I'm entertaining on a larger scale, and then bamboo skewers do the trick. These should be soaked in water for about half an hour if using on a grill to stop them from burning.

Spatulas

Flexible spatulas are immensely useful for mixing and smoothing, and they are invaluable for getting every last bit of batter or the like from the bowl. But they're also handy to cook with, with many chefs using them to stir risotto or make scrambled eggs and omelettes. I'm a bit of a traditionalist with my wooden spoon for risotto, but a spatula is a great way to ensure you drag the rice out of the corners of the pan, especially if making smaller amounts. Just ensure that the spatula is heat-tolerant, with food-grade silicone regarded as the best option. I'd also recommend buying a stainless-steel fish spatula. They have a long blade with perforated slots and the tip is typically on a bias, making it easy to slide underneath delicate fish without damaging it. It's also excellent for fritters, burgers and anything else that needs to be flipped or removed from a pan. This can also stand in for the more regular egg flip/slice, but you'll need a sturdy steel wok spatula for stir-frying.

Spice grinder

A small electric spice grinder is handy and effective, blitzing toasted spices to a powder in no time. I'll generally use a mortar and pestle (see p. 38) for small quantities, but an electric grinder is best for medium to large jobs.

Stand mixer

A good stand mixer is not a casual investment, but mine has paid for itself many times over. They are great for mixing and kneading, as well as whisking, whipping and beating, but they're also adaptable, with attachments for rolling pasta, mincing (grinding) meats, milling vegetables, such as tomatoes for passata, slicing, coring, spiralising, juicing, milling and sifting.

Steamers

A bamboo steamer or two is an inconsequential investment, and they perform their function marvellously well. You can pop them on a saucepan or use in a wok, and they're made from one of the most abundantly renewable materials there is. Just remember that many items will need to sit on something (from a piece of baking paper to a torn piece of cabbage leaf) to stop them from sticking.

Sterilised jars

There are a few methods to sterilise jars before bottling jams or preserves, none of which are particularly complex. Whichever method you use, start with jars that have been freshly washed in warm soapy water and rinsed.

Either place the jars and lids/seals in a large saucepan of water, bring to the boil and simmer for 10 minutes, or simmer the lids/seals in a saucepan, then place the jars upright in the oven on a baking tray for about 10 minutes at 160°C (320°F), then turn off the heat.

I don't often use the oven method, but instead enlist the dishwasher by running the clean jars and lids through the hottest cycle, without detergent. I do this when that batch of preserves has nearly finished cooking, leaving the jars and lids/seals in the dishwasher or hot water until ready to jar.

Whichever of these methods you use, you can then 'hot bottle' – put the hot preserve straight into hot jars.

With the hot preserve going into hot jars, then being sealed with hot lids, you will create a vacuum as it cools, sucking the lid down and creating a seal. This is a bit of a cheat's method, but it works well for me. Some argue that the seal isn't always effective enough, but I've never had a problem when everything is genuinely hot and you work reasonably quickly.

To ensure a more reliable seal – which is more important with lower-sugar preserves – fill and seal the hot jars and stand them upright in a pot of simmering water, with the water level at least a few centimetres (about an inch) above the lids. Bring the water to the boil and 'heat process' the jars for 10 minutes, then remove from the water and stand to cool. The lids will suck down, indicating a seal.

If any lids haven't sealed, either refrigerate the preserve and use reasonably promptly, or replace the lid(s) and process again. Keep in mind that while you can reuse lids to a degree, they will need to be replaced at some point. Always discard any that have damage to the seal, or any signs of rust.

Stick blender

If you're in the habit of making puréed soups or sauces, a stick blender is a must. Transferring soup in batches to a blender is a messy affair, while blitzing it in the pot is simple and the clean-up is effortless. You can also thicken a chunky soup by blending a portion in the pot before stirring through. They usually come with small food processor bowl attachments, which are ideal for making a small amount of, say, Pesto (p. 90) or Salsa verde (p. 86). They are also good for blending small amounts or combining sauces in the plastic cylinder that they come with. Most also now have potato mashers, which don't turn potatoes into the gluey mess that food processors do.

Tape measure/ruler

It's very handy to have some form of measuring device in your kitchen drawers, especially when working with pastry, and I often give dimensions in those recipes, so a quick check on progress is a good path to success – plus, double-checking the size of a cake tin or the like is a good idea.

Tea towels (dish towels)

In a professional kitchen, things grind to a halt without tea towels. Well, that's not quite true, as the show always goes on, but they're essential for handling hot things, drying hands, covering proving doughs (not the same ones you dry your hands with, mind you), to clean and dry benches down, to clean up spills … It's no different at home, and I always make sure I've got a stack when I'm cooking for a crowd.

Terrine mould

This is a specialised piece of equipment, and a loaf tin can stand in on most occasions, but there is something rather nice about an enamelled cast-iron terrine mould (perhaps it's that specificity that I find appealing, a bit like the charm of a fish kettle) and they do perform particularly well when used in a bain marie, providing even heat.

Thermometers

I was trained to cook by feel, and I still do just that, but a probe/meat thermometer is very handy. It's also invaluable with larger pieces of meat. Judging the right cooking degree in a large joint can be tricky. A bit of variation in some meats is not always a big problem if you don't err too far either way, but sometimes you really want to be precise. It can also help you to become more used to cooking by feel, employing it as a guide but then being observant about how the meat feels and looks. I'd advocate against just relying on the gauge, becoming disconnected from the process. As well, a temperature of 90°C (195°F). inside any cake or loaf will guarantee it ready. You'll also need a sugar thermometer if you need to get sugar to a certain temperature for making Italian meringue (p. 807), for example, and most will measure across a range to use as a basic thermometer to measure less volcanic liquids.

Thermomix

I use this when I need a precise temperature control over a longer period of time, such as when infusing an oil (see p. 165), or if I want to mill a specialty flour, or create an especially silky purée, fine spice salt or a super-quick curry paste or pesto. I find it exceptionally good at these tasks, but do I use it to make risotto or a ragù? Certainly not. And that's no offence meant to those who do, it's just not for me. I love the romance and nuance of stirring a pot.

Tongs

A couple of pairs of quality stainless-steel tongs is essential kit for me. I despise rubber-capped tongs. While the intent is to be less abrasive on the food that you're handling, I find the opposite is true, as you can't 'feel' what you're gripping nearly as well. Anything that is likely damaged with tongs shouldn't be handled with them anyway, but for flipping meat or lifting pasta out of the cooking water, for example, tongs are invaluable. Tweezer tongs are also handy and very chef-like for plating up or arranging delicate garnishes on plates or cakes.

Tortilla press

This is a simple gadget that effectively and evenly flattens a ball of dough into a tortilla. One of these is well worth the small cost if you're in the habit of making your own tortillas.

Vegetable peeler

Although vegetable peelers come in many fancy forms, I am a fan of the old-school plastic type that my mother and grandmothers used to use. They're still readily available and economical, and they're very effective. Steel swivel peelers are also excellent and sturdy.

Whisks

You can get by with one whisk, but a couple are better. Making a one-egg mayonnaise with a large whisk is not ideal, nor is whipping egg whites with a compact one. So, a small–medium one and a large one is best.

Wok

There are all sorts of fancy woks, from non-stick to cast iron, but I'm a fan of the traditional fine-gauge Chinese woks. They work very well if you have an intense flame to cook on, and they are very economical. The issue mainly is most domestic heat sources simply aren't hot enough. If you have a wok burner on your stove, and many modern stoves do, then they should work just fine. Otherwise, you could buy a cast-iron wok, which will build and retain heat very effectively. The downside is that you can't toss the food, as they're too heavy, but if the heat is not ideal, then keeping constant contact with the flame is best anyway. Electric woks can get very hot – and they make very good steamers – but you can't toss with those either. As for non-stick woks, I wouldn't venture there. Properly seasoned, a traditional wok is non-stick, and the kind of heat required to cook properly in a wok will degrade the non-stick coating and potentially be toxic. To season a steel wok, wash inside and out with a metal scourer and hot soapy water to remove the machine oil coating that protects it from rusting. Place over a gas burner on medium–high for 4 minutes to dry and heat through. Remove from the heat and rub the inside and outside of the wok with a paper towel that has been dabbed in a little neutral oil. Place over a medium heat, rotating to evenly heat for about 5 minutes. The wok will change colour all over. Remove from the heat and wipe with oiled paper towel inside and out. The wok is now ready for use, and frequent cooking will improve the non-stick qualities.

Wooden spoons

I have many of these, but always reach first for a couple of favourites. I like them fairly heavy with a broad bowl and a comfortable, moulded stem. Those narrow-bowled spoons with a simple turned handle of consistent width leave me a little cold. I also favour one with a flat blade at the end, so you can really pull caramelisation off the pan, plus it also helps with things that are liable to catch.

A few notes on using this book

Dietary requirements

If a recipe meets certain dietary requirements, you'll find its symbol next to the recipe title.

GF   gluten-free

V   vegetarian

VG   vegan

Staples

Some ingredients lists will include a section for staples. These are ingredients needed simply for things like seasoning, greasing and dusting.

BTR   knob of butter

EVOO   extra-virgin olive oil

FLR   flour for dusting

ISGR   icing sugar, for a dusting

LMN   squeeze or wedge of lemon

OIL   neutral-flavoured oil

S&P   salt flakes and freshly ground black pepper

S&WP   salt flakes and freshly ground white pepper

SGR   sugar, for a pinch of sugar with yeast etc.

VNGR   vinegar, for things like poaching eggs

Special equipment

If a recipe calls for non-standard equipment that is key to the success of the recipe, it will be listed in the special equipment section at the end of the ingredients list.

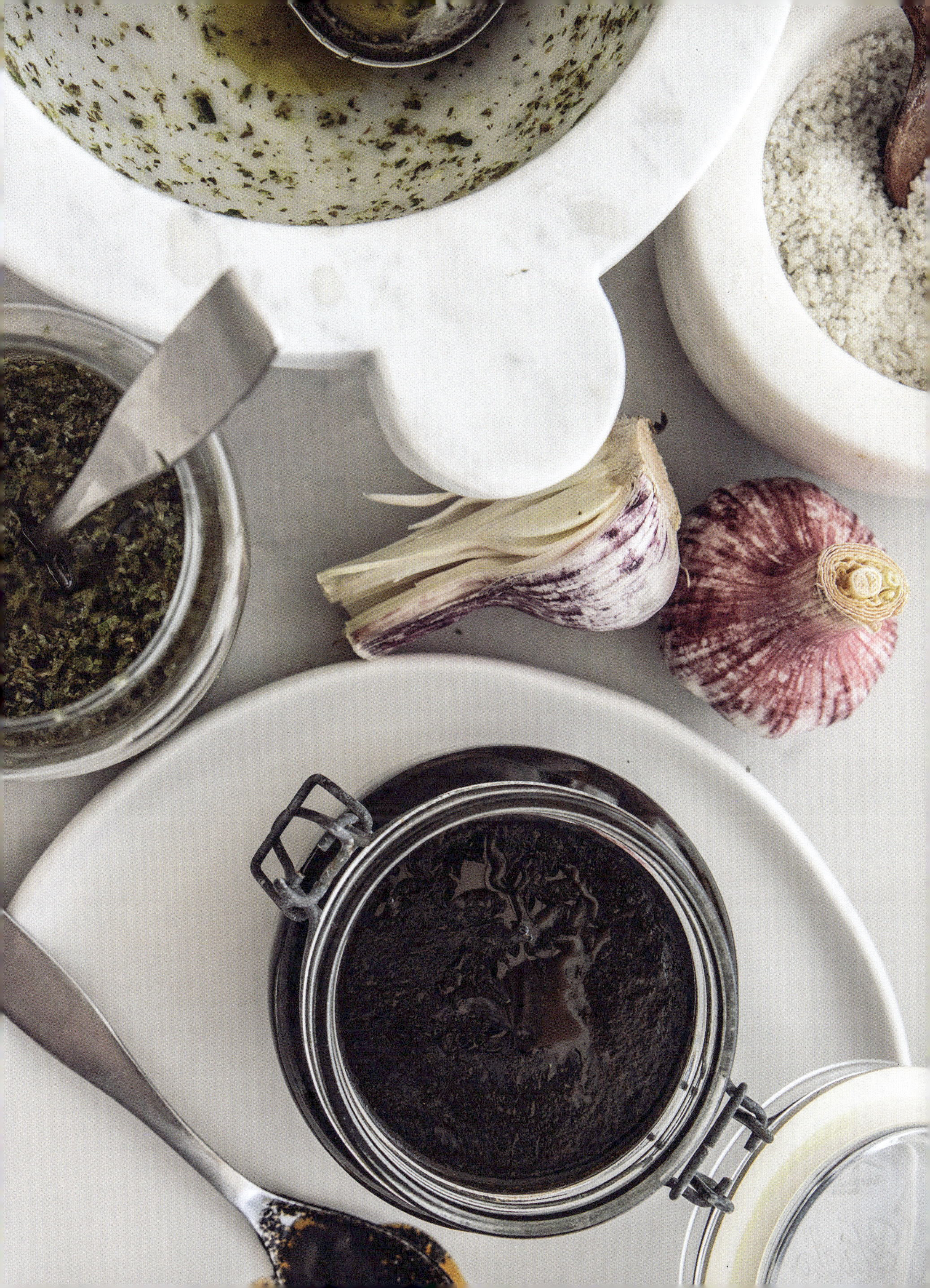

Also see

Stock-based sauces **64-8**

White poached chicken with soy stock **230**

Quick & simple duck stock **266**

Braised lamb neck & barley broth **308-9**

Braised fresh borlotti beans in lemon & cumin stock **426**

Stocks

Stocks

Few things will elevate your cooking like stock. And a carefully made, well-flavoured stock can be truly transformative. Stocks deepen flavour, add complexity, amplify umami, they enrich, and they can thicken and gloss, providing both texture and body. Stocks are clear champions in some dishes, but play quiet roles in so many others. While a bowl of pho is defined by its broth, a ragù bolognese does not require stock to be delicious, but is immeasurably better when made with it. I always have home-made stock on hand. Always. And you should too.

Stocks are essential to any professional kitchen, but they are not the preserve of restaurants. While they are used in many refined ways, stocks are an ancient fundament of cooking, essentially healthful elixirs derived from the need to make the most of a hunt. Those traditional broths were long regarded as nutrient-rich, restorative and fortifying, as well as delicious – a fact we have sadly lost touch with in a food world that has become so portioned and packaged. Thankfully, this is all changing.

Stock is one of the foundations of good cooking. And that foundation needs to be strong. A quality stock, home-made or store-bought, will enhance the depth and complexity of flavour in a dish, as well as enriching the mouthfeel. A commercial, mass-made stock will do neither of these things, and often it will contain a level of salt that precludes you from reducing it down in any meaningful way, because the salt will become acridly dominant as the liquid is concentrated. Once reduced, the flavour will also concentrate, and if this flavour starts out wrong to begin with, it's going to be much worse once intensified. I would always use water over a mass-market stock, and in fact would prefer a quality bouillon cube to add some level of umami and detail to simpler dishes. That said, there are better commercial stocks on the market these days, but please taste them first before using them in a dish.

Ideally, just get in the practice of making stock yourself, because it really isn't complicated. Fish and vegetable stocks are ready in no time, and while meat stocks take considerably longer, they require little attention once skimmed (see p. 48) and gently simmering. Stocks are also very economical, consisting largely of 'waste' material. Well, that's how bones and the like are often seen, which is a great shame. In reality, all those bones are full of flavour potential, along with essential minerals and vitamins, which just need to be unlocked. A good chicken stock, for instance, is rich in collagen, which turns into gelatine, which adds texture and luscious viscosity to dishes, as well as offering health benefits for our joints, skin, hair and nails. Seeing bones as waste reflects a wasteful attitude, and doesn't give due respect to the animal from whence it came.

I always save chicken bones, whether it's a backbone removed when butterflying a chicken, or the left-over carcass from a roasted bird. If I've stuffed a lemon in the cavity of a roasted bird, this gets discarded, but the rest either gets frozen or thrown in a pot to make a quick stock on the spot. If it's lucky, the pot will also get a few extra garlic cloves, an onion split in half and a bay leaf or a handful of fresh herbs, such as parsley or oregano; then it gets topped with water and left to simmer for an hour or two. I have to admit it probably doesn't even get skimmed, simply strained and stashed in the fridge. If there's a left-over roasted chicken leg, I'll just pick off the meat and use it and the stock to make a soup with some vegetables and perhaps a handful of barley. It couldn't be simpler.

This kind of stock never usually makes it into the freezer (though you could freeze it), as I'll use it for general cooking over the next few days, or as a light meal, especially in winter. I might just simmer some dark leafy greens in it, then finish with lemon juice, or stir a beaten egg through, too. It's delicious as is with generous seasoning and a piece of toasted Sourdough bread (p. 847) on the side, which sometimes I butter, and sometimes I drizzle with oil and rub with a cut garlic clove and tomato, and top with ricotta, feta or goat's cheese. The stock will also easily go in quite a different direction with some miso paste and silken tofu stirred through and a boiled egg on the side.

This approach to making stock applies to any bones, whether bacon or ham bones, a left-over duck carcass (see p. 266) or bones left over from a lamb or other roast. Just roast any uncooked bones; the bigger the bones, the longer they need to be cooked. If you're planning on cooking a boned lamb leg, ask your butcher to bone it for you and give you the bone as well, and you'll have another meal in the making. A reasonably meaty bone, such as a joint, is also ideal. Roast these with onion, carrot and a halved garlic bulb, then drain off the fat and simmer with water and a bay leaf or two and some fresh thyme, if you have it. Simmer for 6–8 hours, then skim off the fat (see p. 48) and use as is, or reduce into a glacé (see p. 55), which is simple to do and will make the most amazing base for a lamb stew, braise, soup or pie.

Sometimes you'll end up with a 'stock' when preparing another dish. If poaching a ham hock (see p. 324), keep any left-over poaching liquid and use it for soups, braises and the like; I always throw in some basic stock elements, such as onion, carrot, celery, leek, garlic and bay leaves, but it's perfectly fine without any of these, too. The hock stock will have a meaty, smoky character and a nice level of viscosity. Just be careful if reducing it heavily, as it will be saltier than a regular stock. If you keep aside a little of the hock meat from the other dish, you can make a basic risotto (see p. 148) using the hock stock, adding the meat and a big handful of peas just before it's ready, then finishing as usual with parmesan, butter and plenty of black pepper.

If you're cooking mussels and not using the liquor, you can strain and freeze it to boost the sauce of a seafood pasta, stew or soup. If you're poaching a whole chicken (see p. 230), you'll end up with a light stock, which can be reduced, or used to lift the intensity of a dedicated chicken stock. In short, think twice before discarding a cooking liquid: if it tastes good, if it has flavour, then it has a use. Just always consider the salt level, as this will concentrate if the liquid is boiled down.

If you're preparing a dedicated stock from scratch, it makes sense to make a larger batch and freeze it in usable portions. I use a lot of stock, so I'll freeze it in larger amounts and use any thawed leftovers within a day or so. You can freeze stock in small containers or ice-cube trays, then unmould the frozen stock into a container or freezer bag for convenient portions to add flavour, depth and texture and really elevate your cooking. Use a few cubes to make a gravy out of pan juices with a slab of butter whisked in to finish, or add to a pasta to build a sauce.

Stock essentials

Stockpots

It's worth investing in a stockpot or two, as making meat or vegetable stocks in larger volumes (with several on the go at the same time) is not much more work, and means you'll have plenty on hand. It's also important that your pot can accommodate all the ingredients comfortably, rather than being jammed in. A 10–12 litre (338–405 ¾ fl oz/40–48 cup) stockpot is essential.

Cooking

Stocks should barely be simmering, with the liquid quivering rather than bubbling. This isn't always easy to achieve at home. Depending on your stove, it may be hard to keep the temperature low enough. In a larger pot with more liquid this is easier to control, although it may take a bit of tinkering to get the heat right. If you're having trouble getting it low enough, a slow bubbling at the side of the pot is acceptable. If the liquid level drops over a long extraction, you'll need to top the pot up with water to just cover the bones and aromatics.

Skimming

It is very important to skim stocks (except vegetable ones) to remove fat and impurities. If you don't remove the fat, it tends to cook through the stock as it boils. Skimming is especially important in the early stages, with frequent skimming necessary, but keep checking periodically for the whole cooking time, and also when reheating. By skimming frequently, you'll be removing fat, but also proteins that can set into the stock, especially if it simmers or boils, which can result in a murky stock, with a less pure and refined flavour. Stocks should never be stirred, as any agitation will tend to make the stock cloudy, potentially muddying the flavour; this is especially important towards the end of cooking.

You can simmer some stocks for a shorter time, though you won't get the same flavour development. However, be wary of cooking them for longer than the specified times, as you can end up with a dull result. This is especially true for vegetable and seafood stocks; unless making a bone broth, chicken stock can also be taken too far.

Once the stock is cooked, letting it settle will give you the clearest result; just ladle the last of the stock out, rather than trying to pour it off. For a more refined result, strain the stock through a fine-mesh sieve or through a few layers of muslin (cheesecloth). If reducing a meat-based stock, cool it until the fat forms a layer on top, so it can be easily removed. This isn't necessary for a vegetable or fish stock, though any impurities should be skimmed. All stock can be reduced to a more concentrated state, which will deliver more flavour, as well as saving space in the fridge and freezer. The stock can then be thinned out with water if a lighter stock is required, or if it needs to be reduced during cooking, such as with risotto.

Cooling

Always let stocks cool down a bit before refrigerating or freezing to protect the other food in your fridge. Putting several litres of hot stock in the fridge will raise the fridge temperature substantially and for quite some time, especially being in an enclosed container, which will trap the steam and heat even more. Dividing the stock into smaller portions and leaving it uncovered on the bench for half an hour will generally be enough. A chef's trick for larger batches is to prop one side of the container off the ground to allow airflow underneath (usually done in a cool room). You can also stand the containers in cold or iced water to speed things along.

Storing in the fridge

To ensure that stocks keep in the fridge, make sure the temperature is stable. A full fridge with the door constantly opening will compromise the longevity of any foodstuff, and stock is no exception, with fish and meat stock more susceptible than vegetable stock. Always store stock in sealed containers in the back of the fridge, where it remains the coldest. Fish stocks will keep for around 3 days, and meat-based stocks for up to 4 days.

Freezing

If you're not planning on using your stock within a few days, freeze it immediately to preserve its freshness. A frozen fish or vegetable stock will retain its integrity for up to 3 months, and a meat-based stock up to 6 months. Stocks frozen for too long are not harmful but will pick up less desirable flavours and lose their vibrancy, so the flavour will start to deteriorate. Freeze in sizes that are useful to you, and always leave a little 'headspace' in your containers, as the stock will expand as it freezes. Always clearly mark and date your stocks, as it's easy to forget stock you have months down the track, and naturally it's best to use the oldest stock first. I always boil and skim (see left) frozen stocks before use.

A note on vegetables

There seems to be a common view that you can throw any old bits of vegetables and trimmings into a stock – but old vegetables will taste a lot like, well, old vegetables. And a pile of trimmings can often muddy clarity of flavour. That's not to say you can't keep fennel stalks or pale green leek tops to use for stock, but the deep green ends of leeks, mature celery leaves, vegetable peelings, soft or blemished vegetables, mushroom stalks (unless making stock for a mushroom dish) and the like are best sent to the compost pile.

The flavour you prefer in your stock is entirely up to you, of course, but making pure versions is the best place to start, so you become familiar with the classic flavour profiles. Please make sure your vegetables are well washed, as any dirt will impart its own signature. A good stock will have a pure, complex, but defined character; it should never be muddy or indistinct.

Beef or veal stock

Using some jointed bones will yield more collagen and flavour, making for a richer and more luscious stock. Given that we're trying to extract as much as possible, it's worth making the effort to get the best bones you can; organic, grass-fed beef bones are generally available for a small cost. Take the time to roast them for about 45 minutes at 180°C (350°F) fan-forced until deeply coloured, but never burnt, and thoroughly caramelise your vegetables, too. You also want to make sure you get all the sticky caramelised bits (but as little fat as possible) from the roasting tins, so always deglaze with a splash of wine (or chicken stock or even water) and scrape up all the flavour-packed residue. These early steps establish the intensity and character of the finished stock, so a little attention here is time well spent.

Chicken stock from a left-over roast

If all you had was a left-over chicken carcass from a roast, then you simmered it in water for an hour or so, you'd have a flavourful stock. It wouldn't have the intensity of the other stocks detailed later in this chapter, but it's super simple and still excellent. I'll always throw in some other aromatics to make the flavour more intense – a quartered onion, roughly chopped carrot and celery, a few garlic cloves, fennel stalks, leek tops, whatever stock staples I have on hand. I tend to cut the vegetables up a bit more than if I'm making a dedicated stock, as this

one won't cook for as long. You also won't get quite the collagen/gelatine-loaded result, but stirring in any roasting juices will certainly add lustre. I'll then pop in a bay leaf, a few sprigs of fresh thyme and/or oregano if I have them, parsley stalks (don't throw these out; just secure with a rubber band or twine and keep in your crisper for a stock), some peppercorns and a pinch of salt. Bring to a gentle simmer and cook for 40 minutes, or up to 2 hours. The stock won't require much skimming, if any; simply strain before using. This stock can be made while you start preparing a risotto, and it'll be ready to go when you're ready to cook. You can ladle hot stock straight from the pot into your risotto as needed, using a fine-mesh sieve to catch any debris – then, when your risotto is ready, you can keep cooking any left-over stock for longer to extract all the goodness. (You can top this up with a little more water, but there's only so much more you'll get from the bones, so you'll get a much lighter result.)

Chicken stock from raw bones

You can use any combination of chicken frames, necks, wings and/or even some feet (which increase the collagen/gelatine content), but chicken wings – often the most neglected and wasted part of the bird – are the route to the most intensely golden and deeply flavoursome stock. After simmering for 3–4 hours, any left-over bits of chicken meat and vegetables (minus the onion) can be put to good use in the dog's dinner bowl, with a little broth to up the goodness.

If using chicken wings, maximise the flavour by chopping them into three, four or more pieces first. Use the heel of a heavy knife to cleave through the bone; simply cutting through the joints, although substantially easier, will not yield the same flavoursome result. Roasting the wings first until golden, for about 30 minutes at 200°C (400°F)

fan-forced, will give you more edges to caramelise, and the flavour and collagen extraction seems so much more effective, especially if cooking the stock for a shorter time when you're in a bit of hurry. When roasting chicken for stock, line the roasting tin with a sheet of baking paper to make it much easier to remove all the sticky caramelised bits to stir into the stock, adding real depth of flavour.

Fish stock

It is important to use the freshest bones and heads possible; buying fish on the bone and having it filleted for you (or doing it yourself) is the best way to ensure this, so find a good fishmonger. Use your eyes and nose here: any bones/heads should have a marine aroma, rather than being overtly 'fishy', as should the whole shop. If the fish on display is bright and vibrant, and the eyes of whole fish are clear, you're on the right track. Remember that you'll be extracting and amplifying the flavour of anything you buy, so make sure you want to do that. Lastly, avoid oily fish, such as salmon or ocean trout, as they are too strongly flavoured to yield a desirable result. Instead, ask for the bones and heads of white fish (snapper, blue eye, flathead).

Make your fish stock as soon as possible, and always on the same day. Be sure to remove any innards that may have been left behind, as well as the gills, and wash thoroughly under cold water. Using a heavy knife, crack through the backbone several times, which will make it easier to fit the fish in your pot, but most importantly it will help to extract as much flavour as quickly as possible, which is vital over the short cooking time of a fish stock. This is why I always slice the vegetables quite finely, too. I'll also add plenty of fresh fennel when it's in season, as it enhances and complements the flavour of any seafood stock like no other herb or vegetable.

While I will freeze bones for a meat-based stock, I would never do so for a fish stock, as capturing that fleeting freshness is vital. Having said that, freezing raw crustacean shells and heads – prawns (shrimp), lobster, crayfish – works quite successfully. As with chicken bones, you can just keep adding to these in the freezer, then make a stock when you have enough. You can of course then freeze the stock, too.

Quick duck stock

Sometimes I might buy a roast duck for rice paper rolls or Peking duck pancakes, and occasionally I roast one myself. The carcass can be turned into a rich stock using the method described for the Left-over chicken soup (p. 252), but will require the full 2 hours to extract enough flavour. You'll be rewarded with a versatile, full-flavoured stock for soups and braises.

Quick prawn (shrimp) stock

When preparing raw prawns (shrimp) for another dish, keep the shells and heads to turn into a quick but intensely flavoured stock. Cook the heads and shells in olive oil over a medium heat, crushing the heads with a wooden spoon to extract all the juices. After about 10 minutes, once cooked and fragrant, push them to one side and add a little more oil, then fry a few sliced garlic cloves, half a sliced onion, a little sliced fennel and/or celery and a teaspoon of fennel seeds for a few minutes. If you have some, splash in some wine and reduce until the winey smells have cooked off, cover with water and simmer for 20 minutes, then just allow to settle and finely strain. You won't have a lot of stock, but it can be used as the flavourful base of a pasta sauce, or to bolster the broth of a seafood stew, or to supplement chicken stock if you're making a prawn risotto (p. 149).

Classic white vegetable stock ⒼⒻ Ⓥ ⓋⒼ

This is a gentle infusion of 'white' vegetables, making a very pure and light stock. Use this as an all-round stock when a vegetable stock is called for, or as a replacement for meat stock in soups, braises, sauces or the like.
Makes about 2.5 litres (85 fl oz/10 cups)

100 ml (3½ fl oz) extra-virgin olive oil
3 white onions, peeled and cut into 6 wedges each
3 leeks, white part only, sliced lengthways, then cut into 3 cm (1¼ in) pieces
1 celery heart, plus the surrounding inner stalks and leaves, quartered

lengthways, then cut into 3–4 cm (1¼–1½) pieces
1 large fennel bulb, quartered
1 kg (2 lb 3 oz) white button mushrooms, halved
2 garlic bulbs, cut in half crossways
½ bunch of thyme
8 bay leaves
1½ tablespoons white peppercorns

2 teaspoons fennel seeds
750 ml (25½ fl oz/3 cups) white wine
3 litres (101 fl oz/12 cups) cold water
2 teaspoons salt flakes
2 bunches of parsley stalks, or 1 bunch of flat-leaf (Italian) parsley

Heat the oil in a stockpot over a medium heat. Add the vegetables, garlic, thyme and bay leaves, then cook until softened but not coloured, about 10 minutes. Add the peppercorns, fennel seeds and wine, then simmer until the liquid has reduced by half.

Cover with the water and add the salt. Bring to the boil, then reduce to a gentle simmer and cook for 30 minutes. Add the parsley stalks and simmer for 10 minutes, then turn off the heat and stand for 20 minutes before straining through a fine-mesh sieve.

Robust vegetable fumet ⒼⒻ Ⓥ ⓋⒼ

This is a heartier stock than the one above, with the sweetness and full flavour of the carrot, the warmth of ginger and a lacing of spice taking it in a more robust direction. All stocks should be cooked gently, but think of this one as being like brewing tea: it's an infusion, and by letting it steep you extract pure, defined flavours. If you cook it for longer or more aggressively, the flavours will be overly 'cooked' and indistinct. Done correctly this will be pretty clear and very fragrant, perfect for soups, braises and sauces. **Makes about 3 litres (101 fl oz/12 cups)**

2 white onions, finely sliced
½ leek, white part only, finely sliced
3 carrots, finely sliced
4 celery stalks, finely sliced
1 fennel bulb, finely sliced
6 garlic cloves, sliced

1 thumb-sized piece of fresh ginger, sliced
6 thyme sprigs
3 star anise
2 bay leaves
2 teaspoons salt flakes
2 teaspoons coriander seeds

1 teaspoon fennel seeds
1 teaspoon white peppercorns
3.5 litres (118 fl oz/ 14 cups) water
6 tarragon sprigs
6 flat-leaf (Italian) parsley sprigs

Add all the ingredients except the tarragon and parsley to a stockpot and cover with the water. Bring to the boil, then reduce the heat and simmer, uncovered, for 10 minutes.

Turn off the heat and add the tarragon and parsley. Seal with a tight-fitting lid and steep for 30 minutes, then strain through a fine-mesh sieve.

Crustacean stock (GF)

Deliciously full-bodied and fragrant, this stock, once seasoned, is almost a standalone soup. It is an ideal base for intensely flavoured seafood dishes.
Makes about 1.5 litres (51 fl oz/6 cups)

3 blue swimmer crabs, or sweet small crabs
6 large prawn (shrimp) heads and shells
60 ml (2 fl oz/ ¼ cup) extra-virgin olive oil
60 g (2 oz/¼ oz) butter
1½ onions, finely sliced
1 leek, white part only, finely sliced
4 celery stalks, finely sliced

8 garlic cloves, finely sliced
½ fennel bulb, finely sliced
2 teaspoons coriander seeds
2 teaspoons fennel seeds
4 tomatoes, diced
1 tablespoon tomato paste (concentrated purée)
1 bird's eye chilli, split lengthways
10 thyme sprigs
½ bunch of parsley stalks

1 bay leaf
2 teaspoons white peppercorns
2 teaspoons caster (superfine) sugar
1½ teaspoons salt flakes
500 ml (17 fl oz/2 cups) white wine
3.5 litres (118 fl oz/14 cups) Fish stock (below)

Preheat the oven to 160°C (320°F) fan-forced.

Turn the crabs over and lift the V-shaped flap on the belly, then pull it towards you to remove the top shell. Break off the legs, then remove and discard the dead man's fingers (see p. 198) and eyes, and tip out the 'mustard'; don't worry if some sticks to the shell, as it will add flavour. Cut the body in half down the middle, then press most of the meat from the shell. Remove any good-sized morsels from the legs and claws (and use in a quick pasta or risotto, pp. 125, 149), but make sure you leave some meat behind (the fiddly bits), as this is what makes a great stock.

Spread the crab shells and prawn heads and shells on a baking tray and roast for 35 minutes.

Heat the oil and butter in a wide-based saucepan over a medium heat. Add the onion, leek, celery and garlic, then cook until softened but not coloured, about 5 minutes. Add the fennel and cook until softened, about 5 minutes.

Stir in the coriander and fennel seeds and cook for a couple of minutes. Add the tomato, tomato paste, chilli, thyme, parsley stalks, bay leaf, peppercorns, sugar and salt, and cook for 2 minutes.

Tip in the roasted heads and shells, with any juices from the tray, and stir them through. Add the wine and reduce by two-thirds. Add the stock and bring to a simmer, then simmer gently for 20 minutes, skimming frequently.

Turn off the heat and allow to stand for 20 minutes, then strain through a fine-mesh sieve into a clean saucepan. Reduce the stock by half over a medium heat, skimming frequently.

Make it different
With herbs. Perfume the stock further by throwing in a bunch of basil or tarragon after it has reduced. Stand for 10 minutes to infuse, then strain.

Fish stock (GF)

I would never buy fish stock. It is neither difficult nor time consuming to make, and the results are very rewarding. If necessary, chicken stock can often be used in its place. **Makes about 3 litres (101 fl oz/12 cups)**

Pair with

Use as a broth for ravioli or cannelloni.

Reduce and use in a sauce for seafood.

Use as the stock for a Crab, prawn or bug tail risotto (p. 149), finishing with cooked crabmeat, and soft herbs such as chervil, parsley or tarragon.

Crustacean essence (GF)

Reduce the Crustacean stock (left) right down to just under 400 ml (13½ fl oz) to make an intense sauce. Whisk in a little peppery olive oil and a tiny squeeze of lemon juice. Use to dress a seafood salad served with crisp leaves or pearl couscous.

Crustacean vinaigrette (GF)

Start reducing 1 litre (34 fl oz/4 cups) Crustacean stock (left) in a saucepan over a medium heat. Meanwhile, halve, core and peel 3 large ripe tomatoes and scoop the seeds and jelly into the reducing stock. Cut the tomato flesh into 5 mm (¼ in) dice and set aside. Once the stock has reduced to about 200 ml (7 fl oz) or a little less, cool at room temperature. While still warm, add the tomato, 2½ tablespoons lemon juice and 150 ml (5 fl oz) extra-virgin olive oil and whisk to emulsify. Season with salt and pepper and serve straight away. Makes about 400 ml (13½ fl oz). Delicious with Crab cannelloni (p. 135).

Pair with

Use as the base for fish soups and stews, risotto (see p. 149) or a Fish pie (p. 188).

Dashi GF

Wipe a 10 cm (4 in) piece of dried kombu with a dry cloth, but don't scrape off any white powder on the surface, as it is the amino acid glutamine, which is responsible for much of the umami. Add the kombu and 1.5 litres (51 fl oz/6 cups) cold water to a saucepan over a low heat. Bring the water barely to a simmer and infuse gently for 10 minutes. Don't boil, as it can make the stock bitter. Remove and discard the kombu. Bring to the boil, then add 15 g (½ oz) katsuobushi (bonito flakes) and 15 g (½ oz) niboshi (dried baby sardines) (you can omit the niboshi, but you'll need to double the quantity of katsuobushi). Immediately turn off the heat and leave to stand for a couple of minutes. Strain through a fine-mesh sieve, allowing the stock to filter through gradually. Gently squeeze the solids so you don't extract bitterness. Use immediately, or refrigerate for no more than 2–3 days. Makes about 1.5 litres (51 fl oz/6 cups). Use to make brothy soups or in Japanese-inspired dipping sauces. You can also use dashi in place of water when cooking rice by the absorption method (p. 372).

60 g (2 oz/¼ cup) butter
50 ml (1¾ fl oz) extra-virgin olive oil
1 onion, finely sliced
1 small garlic bulb, cut in half crossways
2 celery stalks, finely sliced

½ fennel bulb, finely sliced, plus any fronds
500 ml (17 fl oz/2 cups) dry white wine
2 kg (4 lb 6 oz) white fish bones and heads (see p. 49)

3.5 litres (118 fl oz/14 cups) cold water, approximately
½ bunch of parsley stalks
3 thyme sprigs
1 bay leaf
1 tablespoon white peppercorns

Heat the butter and oil in a large, heavy-based saucepan over a medium heat. Add the onion, garlic, celery and fennel and sweat until softened but not coloured, about 5 minutes. Add the wine and reduce by two-thirds.

Add the fish bones and heads and cook for about 5 minutes. Add the cold water to just cover, along with the remaining ingredients, then bring to a very slow simmer, skimming frequently. Reduce the heat so it is just below a simmer, with the water barely moving. Simmer gently for 20 minutes, skimming frequently.

Turn off the heat and allow to stand for 20 minutes, then strain through a fine-mesh sieve into a clean saucepan. Reduce the stock by half over a medium heat, skimming frequently.

Chicken bone broth GF

This is a deeply flavoured and nutrient-rich broth, with incredible gelling properties from both the long extraction and the use of chicken feet. The idea is to draw all the minerals from the bones, which will crumble between your fingers once cooked. It can be used like any other stock, but it has a meaty intensity and sticky mouthfeel, so is best for more robust dishes, or to be drunk as a broth. It can just be seasoned and sipped, but I especially love it with some cavolo nero or silverbeet (Swiss chard) and some buttered sourdough toast. When my girls were little, I used to simmer tiny pasta in this broth, then reduce the stock and finish with butter and parmesan. **Makes about 4.5 litres (152 fl oz/18 cups)**

3 kg (6 lb 10 oz) chicken wings, necks or frames (a mix is ideal)
4 chicken feet, or 1 pork trotter, split
1½ tablespoons apple-cider vinegar

2 large onions, skin on, cut in half
3 celery stalks, cut on angle
1 carrot, sliced lengthways
2 garlic bulbs, cut in half crossways
½ bunch of thyme

4 bay leaves
1 bunch of parsley stalks
20 white peppercorns
1 teaspoon sea salt

Add all the chicken bits to a large stockpot and cover with cold water. Add the vinegar and bring to a simmer over a medium heat, skimming frequently as the impurities rise, which will take about 20 minutes.

Add the remaining ingredients, turn the heat down to the lowest setting possible and cook for 8–12 hours, topping up with water as necessary.

Turn off the heat and allow to stand for 20 minutes, then strain through a fine-mesh sieve.

Make it different

With chicken giblets. Adding a handful or two of chicken giblets will intensify the flavour.

Roasting the chicken and vegetables before adding to the pot will add an even deeper golden hue.

Golden chicken stock GF

Chicken wings are ideal for stock. You get all that extra flavour from the skin and meat, and the joints are loaded with collagen, which is transformed into luscious gelatine. Roasting them first gives this stock its golden hue and rich umami-laced flavour. Carrying more depth and richness than the White chicken stock below, this is still versatile, ideal for adding a savoury punch of flavour. Try adding this to a ragù instead of water for a huge boost of flavour and a silky texture. It's also great in a Crab, prawn or bug tail risotto (p. 149) for unmatched richness that won't intrude on the flavour of the seafood. **Makes about 5 litres (170 fl oz/20 cups)**

3.5 kg (7 lb 12 oz) chicken wings, cut into 3–4 pieces through the bone	2 large onions, skin on, cut in half	½ bunch of thyme
	2 garlic bulbs, cut in half crossways	4 bay leaves
6 celery stalks, cut on an angle into 4 cm (1½ in) pieces	6 litres (204 fl oz/24 cups) cold water	1 bunch of parsley stalks
1 carrot, cut on an angle into 4 cm (1½ in) pieces	½ bunch of oregano	1 tablespoon white peppercorns

Preheat the oven to 200°C (400°F).

Line two baking trays with baking paper and spread the chicken pieces on them, leaving as much space between them as possible. Roast for about 30 minutes, until golden.

Tip the roasted wings into a large stockpot, along with all the juices and any sticky caramelised bits on the baking paper. Add the celery, carrot, onion and garlic, and top with the water. Bring to a simmer over a medium heat, skimming frequently as the impurities rise, about 20 minutes.

Add the herbs and peppercorns and simmer gently for 2½ hours.

Turn off the heat and allow to stand for 20 minutes, then strain through a fine-mesh sieve.

Make it different

Roasting the vegetables until lightly caramelised before adding them to the stock will add depth and enrich the flavour.

White chicken stock GF

This is the stock I make for all-round use. It has a lighter and cleaner flavour than a stock made with roasted chicken wings, which makes it very versatile as a base for dishes such as soups, braises and risotto to support bolder flavours, or to highlight more delicate ones without dominating. **Makes 5–6 litres (170–204 fl oz/20–24 cups)**

4 chicken frames, cut in half, or 10 wings, or 1 kg (2 lb 3 oz) chicken necks	5 garlic cloves, skin on, smashed	4 thyme sprigs
	1 large onion, skin on, quartered	1 bay leaf
3 celery stalks, cut into 4 cm (1½ in) pieces	½ bunch of parsley stalks	1 tablespoon white peppercorns

Add the chicken frames to a large stockpot and cover with cold water. Bring to a simmer, skimming frequently. Add the remaining ingredients and bring back to a very gentle simmer. Cook for 4 hours, skimming and topping up with water as necessary.

Turn off the heat and allow to stand for 20 minutes, then strain through a fine-mesh sieve.

Double chicken stock GF

This is simply made by using White chicken stock (below) rather than water in the Golden chicken stock recipe (left). You can use this whenever Golden chicken stock is asked for.

Chinese chicken stock GF

This very simple, light and delicate stock is lovely as a base for noodle soups and Chinese or South-East Asian dishes. Rinse a whole 1.4 kg (3 lb 1 oz) chicken and dry with paper towel. Cut into eight pieces, place in a large saucepan and cover with 3.5 litres (118 fl oz/ 14 cups) water. Add 1 teaspoon white peppercorns, 2 peeled garlic cloves, 3 slices fresh ginger, about 3 mm (⅛ in) thick, and the green and white parts of 2 spring onions (scallions). Bring to a simmer over a high heat, then reduce the heat to medium and start to skim off any impurities. Simmer for 30 minutes, skimming frequently. Turn the heat down as low as you can and cook for 1½ hours. Stand for 3 minutes, then strain through a fine-mesh sieve. Makes about 3 litres (101 fl oz/12 cups) stock. The meat can be shredded and used for salads, broths or cold noodle dishes, but will be very lean and delicately flavoured, as the broth will have taken much of the fat and collagen out.

Brown beef glacé GF

Simply simmer down your Brown beef stock (right) over a medium heat until reduced by two-thirds, skimming as you go. This can then be used as the base of sauces, or to add a flavour punch when finishing a Beurre rouge (p. 69), braised brisket (see p. 291) or any braised beef (see p. 285). The glacé is also perfect to freeze, as an ice-cube's worth will go a long way – either used concentrated, to bolster a lighter stock, or dilute back into a broth with water.

Stracciatella soup

This is a dish that is so easily conjured from a few kitchen staples, and one I make often when we've been away and the pickings at home are lean, or for a fortifying snack when I'm feeling under the weather. It's as simple as whisking up an egg or two or three with a generous grating of parmesan, a pinch of flour (not essential, but it helps to stabilise the eggs), a good pinch of salt and plenty of pepper, then stirring it through simmering Golden chicken stock (opposite) until it sets into 'broken' strands. That's at its simplest, though I'll often cook some tiny pasta in the stock first – and a handful of chopped parsley never goes astray.

Brown beef stock GF

This intensely flavoured stock can be used as the foundation for red-wine sauces, braises, French onion soup and the like, or in rich beef dishes such as beef bourguignon. Veal and beef bones can be used interchangeably, and a combination is fine, too. It may seem excessive to use chicken stock to make beef stock, but the depth of flavour cannot be achieved otherwise – and if you are already going to the trouble of making a stock like this, the end result is well worth it. **Makes about 4 litres (135 fl oz/16 cups)**

- 5 kg (11 lb) beef or veal neck, shin or knuckle bones
- 3 brown onions, skin on, quartered
- 3 carrots, cut into large chunks on an angle
- 2 garlic bulbs, cut in half crossways
- 4 celery stalks, quartered lengthways
- 1 leek, white part only, cut in half lengthways
- 100 g (3½ oz) tomato paste (concentrated purée)
- 200 ml (7 fl oz) red wine
- 1 pig's trotter, split (get your butcher to do this)
- 6 litres (204 fl oz/24 cups) White chicken stock (p. 54), or water
- 6 thyme sprigs
- 2 bay leaves
- 8 white peppercorns

Preheat the oven to 180°C (350°F) fan-forced.

Evenly spread the bones out on two large roasting trays and roast them for about 45 minutes, turning halfway through, until a deep brown. Do not allow the bones to burn, as this can make the stock bitter.

Transfer the bones to a large stockpot. Drain and discard the fat from the trays. Spread the onion and carrot on the trays and roast for 10 minutes. Add the garlic, celery and leek, then roast until turning golden, about 15 minutes. Tip all the vegetables onto one tray. Add the tomato paste and mix through to coat, then roast for 10 minutes. Meanwhile, pour some wine onto the other tray and deglaze it over a medium heat, scraping until all the residue comes away from the surface, then set aside.

Once roasted, tip the vegetables into the pot, then tip the liquid from the deglazed tray onto the other tray, along with the remaining wine. Boil over a medium heat for 2–3 minutes, scraping all the residue from the tray, then tip it into the pot. Add the trotter and stock. Bring to a simmer, skimming off the fat and impurities as they rise, 10–15 minutes.

Add the herbs and peppercorns, then simmer very gently for 6–8 hours, skimming from time to time. You won't need to top the water up here, as the stock should be simmering so slowly that it should barely be reducing.

Once ready, turn off the heat and stand for 20 minutes to settle. To avoid stirring up any sediment, use a jug to strain the stock through a fine-mesh sieve, then chill. Remove the fat once it solidifies on top of the liquid.

The stock can be used as is, or reduced to intensify the flavour and texture.

Make it different
The un-reduced stock can also be clarified with a protein 'raft' in the same way as in the Oxtail consommé (p. 56), which will leave you with a brilliantly clear amber liquid. This can be seasoned and used as a broth for filled pasta, dumplings or poached vegetables with braised meat.

Oxtail consommé ⓖⓕ

This is so superb to eat, and especially rewarding to make. A consommé is a show of skill for a chef, a crystal-clear amber broth that conceals a deep resource of flavour. This is technical and very classical cooking, but for those so inclined it is a stunning method to master. The clarification is achieved through using a high-protein 'raft' to filter out any impurities. The raft starts as a minced paste of meat, vegetables and egg whites, which is stirred into the stock while gently heating. As the mixture cooks, it will set into a 'raft' that floats to the surface of the broth. Over time, the impurities are forced up as the stock is heated and are filtered out by this raft, leaving behind a brilliantly clear liquid. This method can be employed with any deeply flavoured stock. Just be aware that the raft also adds flavour, so it can be fine-tuned to support the flavour profile of the stock – fish instead of chicken, or other aromatics and so on. **Makes about 1.5 litres (51 fl oz/6 cups)**

Pair with

My favourite use for this consommé is with filled pasta (see p. 113) or dumplings (see p. 500).

Use the unclarified stock and picked meat to make an amazing Oxtail risotto finished with chervil and black truffle (p. 148).

Add the meat to a Beurre rouge (p. 69) just before serving, and spoon over seared beef (see p. 292).

Reduce the stock and toss with crushed chestnuts, oxtail and pappardelle pasta (see p. 112), then serve with good parmesan and chopped parsley.

2 kg (4 lb 6 oz) oxtail (larger mid-tail pieces are best), fat trimmed
50 ml (1¾ fl oz) grapeseed oil
5 litres (170 fl oz/20 cups) Double chicken stock (p. 54)
1 teaspoon salt

Marinade
750 ml (25½ fl oz/3 cups) red wine
200 ml (7 fl oz) dry sherry

2 brown onions, skin on, each cut into 6 wedges
2 garlic bulbs, cut in half crossways
2 celery stalks, sliced 2 cm (¾ in) thick
1 carrot, sliced 2 cm (¾ in) thick
2 bay leaves
2 star anise
8 juniper berries
1 teaspoon white peppercorns

Raft
200 g (7 oz) chicken breast
½ celery stalk, roughly chopped
1 bunch of parsley stalks
4 thyme sprigs, leaves stripped
1 teaspoon white peppercorns
1 teaspoon salt flakes
6 egg whites (about 200 g/ 7 oz)

Staples
S&P

Add the oxtail and the marinade ingredients to a bowl or container. Toss through to coat all the oxtail pieces, then refrigerate overnight.

Preheat the oven to 165°C (330°F) fan-forced.

Strain off and reserve the oxtail marinating liquid. Separate the oxtail from the aromatics, then pat both dry with paper towel and set aside.

Heat the oil in a large, heavy-based saucepan over a medium heat. Working in batches, add the oxtail, season with salt, then brown all over; it will become quite dark as the wine sugars caramelise. Set the browned oxtail aside, then add the aromatics to the pan and cook until softened, about 10 minutes.

Return the oxtail to the pan, sitting the pieces cut side up, so they fit snugly in the base. Pour the reserved marinade over and reduce the liquid by half. Add the stock (if it doesn't all fit, use any residual to top up as it reduces) and bring to a simmer. Reduce the heat to low, then cook gently for 4 hours, until the connective tissue is very soft. It's very important to regularly skim for impurities.

Once cooked, cool for 30 minutes, then gently lift the oxtail from the liquid. Using a fork, remove the meat and connective tissue from the bones, discarding any hard or gristly bits. Dress the meat with 100 ml (3½ fl oz) or so of the broth (to stop it drying out) and the salt. Check the meat very carefully for bone, as it's easy to miss fragments. The meat can be used to fill pasta to serve in the consommé (see p. 113).

Beef pho GF

Finely slice the cooked brisket from the Pho broth (right). Finely slice 300 g (10½ oz) raw sirloin steak across the grain. Reheat the Pho broth and stir in 80 g (2¾ oz) grated palm sugar (jaggery) and 3 tablespoons fish sauce; keep hot. Soak 1 kg (2 lb 3 oz) dried flat pho noodles (rice stick noodles) in hot water for 20 minutes until soft, or briefly heat the same quantity of fresh noodles in boiling water. Arrange the noodles in four to six deep serving bowls and add the brisket, topped with the sirloin. Top with finely sliced white onion and lots of spring onion (scallion), cut into batons, and a little white pepper. Ladle the hot pho broth over. Add lime juice and sliced chillies to taste, followed by plenty of bean sprouts and Vietnamese mint, Thai basil, coriander (cilantro) and/or mint. Serve immediately.

Strain the broth through a fine-mesh sieve, then skim again. Chill completely, then remove the solid layer of fat from the top.

To make the raft, blitz the chicken, celery, herbs, pepper and salt in a food processor until finely chopped, then tip into a bowl. Blitz the egg whites until starting to foam, then tip them over the chicken mixture and combine.

Add the cold broth to a wide-based saucepan over a medium heat. Whisk the raft into the broth, then stir with a wooden spoon until just simmering. It's important that none of the raft sticks to the base of the pan, so make sure you scrape thoroughly with the spoon. Once simmering, turn the heat down as low as possible. The raft will set and float to the top of the broth. After about 10 minutes, make a hole in the raft to check the clarity of the consommé with a ladle. It will take about 40 minutes to fully clarify the consommé, but just keep an eye on it: the liquid should be very gently moving with the heat, but not simmering.

Once you're happy with the clarity, ladle the consommé out through the hole in the raft; for an ultra-clear result, strain it through a fine-mesh sieve or a strainer lined with muslin (cheesecloth) or a coffee filter. The last bit of stock in the pan will be less brilliant in clarity, so you can either filter it and use in the consommé, or add to another dish for a dose of flavour.

Make it faster

If your focus is on flavour and the meat itself, you can skip the clarification step entirely and just strain the broth. It's less fancy, but just as delicious.

Pho broth GF

Pho is something I crave, especially if I'm feeling worse for wear. Whenever jetlagged, rundown or just plain tired, I head for my long-time favourite Vietnamese restaurant for a nourishing bowl of beef pho. For me, it will need a seasoning tweak, a squeeze of lemon and a good spike of fresh chilli, but absolutely essential is a big handful of fresh herbs and bean sprouts – I always have to ask for more. Truth is, I'm unlikely to make this pho if I'm in the condition that makes me crave it in the first place, but it's far more than a physical and emotional curative: the depth of flavour you get in what looks like a relatively light broth is stunning. As with the Shoyu ramen broth (p. 58), the intensity and warmth of flavour and full-bodied feel is achieved by cooking with both bones and meat. The charring of the onions and ginger may seem unusual, but it adds a background smokiness to the finished dish that is vital. The blanching of the bones and meat is also important to achieve clarity, by removing any blood and some fat. The broth will freeze like any stock, so it can be kept on hand for emergencies. **Makes about 4 litres (135 fl oz/16 cups)**

2 brown onions, skin on, cut in half	800 g (1 lb 12 oz) brisket	1½ tablespoons fennel seeds
15 cm (6 in) piece of fresh ginger, sliced 3 cm (1¼ in) thick	6 litres (204 fl oz/24 cups) water	1½ tablespoons black peppercorns
	1 garlic bulb, cut in half crossways	2 tablespoons salt flakes
800 g (1 lb 12 oz) cut beef bone pieces (knuckle, if possible)	10 cm (4 in) piece of cassia bark	
1.5 kg (3 lb 5 oz) beef shin (osso buco cut)	5 star anise	
	2 tablespoons coriander seeds	

Blacken the onion and ginger over the flame of a gas burner, or under a hot grill (broiler) for about 15 minutes.

Add the beef bones, shin and brisket to a stockpot and cover with cold water. Bring to the boil and cook vigorously for 3 minutes. Discard the water and rinse the bones and meat with warm water.

Wipe out the pan, return the bones and meat, then cover with the water. Bring to a simmer over a medium heat, skimming frequently as the impurities rise, which will take about 20 minutes.

Add the charred onion and ginger, along with the garlic, spices and salt, then cook for 1½ hours, until the brisket is cooked (slightly chewy but not tough). Remove the brisket and submerge it in cold water for 5 minutes, then drain and refrigerate.

Cook the broth for a further 2 hours, then strain through a fine-mesh sieve and chill, removing the fat once it sets on top.

Shoyu ramen broth

Ramen is a dish obsessed over like few others, with infinite variations and devotees intractable in their divided opinions. It is one of Japan's most malleable classics, with none of the rigidity of much of its traditional cuisine. You need broth. You need noodles. You need seasoning. You need toppings. But the rules beyond that are bent in all manner of interesting directions – and perhaps it owes much of its popularity to this flexibility. The key to any good ramen is a great broth, and key to this is cooking the meat in the stock, which adds a depth of flavour and warmth that bones alone can't achieve. The tare is what defines the finished soup – the seasoning that becomes the background flavour profile. I have used soy (shoyu) here, but the tare could be miso paste or shio (salt). This broth is beautiful to have on hand for a quick soup or to enhance Japanese-leaning soups and braises; if you are using it in a ramen (see right), adorn it in any way you see fit – remember, there are no rules.

Makes about 4 litres (135 fl oz/16 cups)

800 g (1 lb 12 oz) pork shoulder, or scotch, rolled and tied
2 tablespoons grapeseed oil

Broth
4.5 litres (152 fl oz/18 cups) water
50 g (1¾ oz) dried kombu
4 chicken wings, each cut into 3–4 pieces, through the bone

150 g (5½ oz) double-smoked bacon rashers
2 carrots, split lengthways
4 French shallots, skin on, cut in half
3 large garlic cloves, skin on, smashed
4 dried shiitake mushrooms
80 g (2¾ oz) fresh ginger, cut into rough chunks

30 g (1 oz) katsuobushi (bonito flakes)

Tare
80 ml (2½ fl oz/⅓ cup) aged soy sauce
2 tablespoons mirin
2 tablespoons sake

Staples
S&WP

Pair with

If not taking this broth down the full ramen route, the pork can be sliced and used for a salad with handfuls of Asian herbs, chilli and bean sprouts. It can also be pushed into crusty rolls for a fabulous bánh mi.

It's also delicious with Spiced sesame and peanut dressing (p. 94) in a salad or sandwich.

The broth itself is delicious as is, but can also be used as the base of soups or braises. You could use miso paste instead of the shoyu tare, and serve with silken tofu, wakame and sliced spring onion (scallion), or other ingredients that take your fancy.

Ramen

To a medium saucepan of boiling water, add 800 g (1 lb 12 oz) dried ramen noodles and cook for 3–4 minutes, then drain and set aside. Divide the noodles among six bowls and arrange some pork slices on top. Cover with hot Shoyu ramen broth, then top with spring onion/ scallion (white and pale green bits, finely sliced on an angle), finely sliced pickled bamboo shoots, sliced shiitake mushrooms, bean sprouts and 4 soft-boiled eggs, cut in half. Sprinkle with black sesame seeds and serve immediately with togarashi, chilli oil and torn roasted nori.

For the broth, boil the water in a large saucepan, then add the kombu. Turn off the heat and leave to stand for 1 hour.

Heat a large frying pan over a medium heat. Rub the pork shoulder with the oil and season with salt and white pepper, then brown evenly all over, about 10–12 minutes.

Add the pork and remaining broth ingredients to the kombu stock. Bring to the boil and immediately reduce the heat. Simmer for 10 minutes, skimming frequently, then cover and simmer gently for about 1 hour, until the pork is tender.

Remove the pork from the liquid and set aside to cool slightly. Strain through a fine-mesh sieve.

Once the pork is cool to the touch, wrap tightly in three layers of plastic wrap and refrigerate until firm, about 1½–2 hours. Then unwrap and slice finely and use in a Ramen (left), or in other dishes (see 'Pair with' suggestions, opposite).

Combine the tare ingredients in a small bowl, then add to a large saucepan with the broth. Simmer very slowly for 20 minutes and use as required; without the tare and pork, the broth can also be frozen.

Also see

Simple tomato sugo, Puttanesca sauce 116–7

Mignonette dressing for oysters 207

Roasted plum & hoisin sauce 263

Pomegranate dressing 314

Buttermilk dressing 361

Umeboshi & sesame dressing 410

Tahini & yoghurt dressing 478–9

Sweet & sour tamarind sauce 611

Quick apple sauce for roasts 684

Sauces & dressings

Sauces & dressings

In a classical kitchen, the role of a saucier is a lofty one. And so it should be. The responsibility for preparing and balancing a range of sauces to finish dishes – bringing together flavours, enriching and enhancing everything on the plate – is not to be taken lightly. A clumsy sauce will sully the good work on the protein and vegetable components, while a good sauce will elevate the produce and the technique. A saucier can make or break a restaurant, and many of those sauces take significant time, with quick alternatives not easily whipped up when things go awry.

Scary, hey. But for those of you not considering working in a high-pressure role in a classical kitchen, please relax. Sauces and dressings are the things that make your cooking special, but they don't have to be complicated and they shouldn't cause you any real stress. Building and refining flavour in more complex reductions is really quite a pleasing and addictive process, but a quick sauce is equally satisfying, turning a pan-fried piece of fish or meat into a restaurant-grade meal.

Having a well-stocked pantry is important, and gives you so many options for sauces and dressings. And when I say well-stocked, I don't mean to excess. Oils and things like fish sauce deteriorate, so be sensible about quantity but aim for plenty of variety. For me, that means various types of soy, from light to dark and thick, along with mirin, rice vinegar, oyster sauce and the like, and I have a specific grinder locked and loaded with toasted sesame seeds.

I have a formidable array of vinegars, from lusciously thick and devilishly expensive real balsamic to apple-cider vinegar, with almost everything in between, including varietal wine vinegars (chardonnay being a bit of a favourite) as well as regional ones (Champagne and sherry seeing most use) and a few flavoured ones, tarragon being the hero. I also go long on oils, including several nut oils, which are marvellous on salads, but they're fragile, so small bottles are the go. I use a huge amount of extra-virgin olive oil, but I always have a little army of smaller ultra-premium bottles that each have their own distinctive character. It's these that I use to essentially sauce things like raw fish or a carpaccio of beef, or they go into vinaigrettes and dressings. These preparations rely on the oil and vinegar quality, so don't skimp. The same is true for butter and other dairy, as well as eggs used for mayonnaise. Buy the best you can for best results.

Some sauces just take time, such as making a reduction from stock or braising juice, or something like XO sauce (p. 98). Having stock in the freezer is a must for me, which can certainly save time, and you can freeze reduced meaty sauce bases, just warm and whisk in butter to finish, adjusting the seasoning as necessary.

I make large batches of things that keep well, such as plum sauce (pp. 263, 725), Black bean sauce (p. 100), chilli sauce (see p. 97) or XO sauce (p. 98), as you can turn out very sophisticated dishes with minimal effort. I also tend to make more than I need of things that will keep for a week or so, giving some shape and direction to the week's meals. If you've also made and bottled your own passata and have some flavoured butters in the freezer (pp. 72–3), then you're well positioned to make some fabulous dishes quite simply.

Sauces can also be made quickly on the stove. A pan that has just been used to cook meat or fish is generally full of flavourful juices, which you can also add any resting juices to. Use a splash of stock (this is where it's handy to have stocks frozen in small quantities – ice cubes or the like) and/or

wine used to deglaze and pull off any caramelised morsels, then bubble away to reduce and thicken before adding a big knob of butter, whisking or stirring in to combine. You can add some capers if you like and/or a squeeze of lemon, then check the seasoning and spoon over your protein, which will be nicely rested once the sauce is finished. It really is so simple.

I tend not to make vinaigrette in large batches, as the acid level changes over time. Enough for a few days is good, kept in a jar in the fridge. It's something I use every day, mostly, so it's handy to be able to just shake the jar and dress some leaves or shaved raw vegetables when time is tight. A drizzle of oil and a splash of vinegar or a squeeze of lemon over that salad with some salt and pepper and a quick toss through does the job, too. If you whisk the two together you will get a more emulsified dressing, but it's not necessary. Don't always be constrained by 'correct' technique, just taste a little and aim for a pleasing acid balance and good seasoning, and don't overdress – you can then always adjust the balance and quantity.

Mayonnaise is something you can also make and store (pp. 74–5) – it takes about five minutes, is very handy to have on hand, and is vastly superior to anything you can buy in a jar. I find that I tend to make it for a specific dish, deliberately making more than I need, then the leftovers get used up through the week: on sandwiches or for a quick potato salad, or I spike it with Fermented cooked chilli sauce (p. 97) or whip up a quick tartare, which may have all the trimmings (see p. 77), or it might just have some capers, a chopped cornichon or two and whatever soft herbs I have on hand. Don't be worried about missing an ingredient or two, as it will taste great either way.

There are some sauces that I would never store, as they quickly lose their vibrancy. Anything that has a strong citrus focus, like Nuoc cham (p. 93), suffers quickly, with the acidity seemingly dropping off and the flavours losing their pep. That said, sauces that need the pop of fresh citrus can be refreshed. Something like a Thai chilli sauce (see p. 97) or a Satay sauce (p. 104) just needs to be refreshed with a little more lime. I also check for seasoning with refrigerated sauces, as sometimes they just need a little extra salt. Butter-heavy sauces are also ones that I like to make as close as possible to serving.

When making reduced sauces, such as from a red-wine braising stock for beef cheeks (see p. 285), I like to reintroduce some of the core flavours before reducing. This usually means a splash more wine and a handful of herbs, such as thyme, which just freshens and intensifies the flavours.

As I've said, sauces don't have to be complicated or intimidating to make, but they are an essential tool for the cook, a vital part of the DNA of making your food truly sing. As with anything, a little practice will make the basics instinctive, while the complicated will start to look more than achievable. The world of sauces and dressings is a vast one – and there are many other recipes throughout the book – but this chapter is devoted to many of my go-to saucing options, the ones that I use frequently in any given year.

Stock reductions

Velouté (GF)

Firstly, this is not a classic velouté. One of French cuisine's five 'mother sauces', velouté is quite an old-fashioned sauce, which is basically stock thickened with a roux – or a Béchamel (p. 70) with stock, if you like. A traditional velouté is something I'll use with chicken stock to make a sauce for a chicken pie or the like, but I'm not a fan of flour-thickened sauces for fish, as I find them heavy and flat. I do, however, like the texture and the idea of the sauce, so I have fiddled with a classic here. I believe this version delivers the principle in an elegant and light way, perfect for showcasing seafood of any type. It has a lovely briny tang, with aromatic vegetable undertones, and lustre and silkiness from the cream. This sauce can also be made ahead of time and will hold well in the fridge for a few days. **Makes about 500 ml (17 fl oz/2 cups)**

Pair with

Seafood! This is great with just about any cooked sea creature.

Stir it through sea urchins just before serving, or use it to dress a fillet of fish and finish with a few pearls of salmon or trout roe.

Add some smoked bacon or speck to the reduction and serve with just-opened clams (vongole) or mussels (minus the cooking liquor, which you can add to a stock – see p. 47).

20 g (¾ oz) butter
5 French shallots, finely sliced
2 pale inner celery stalks and leaves, finely sliced
8 small white mushrooms (champignons), finely sliced

10 white peppercorns
2 thyme sprigs
100 ml (3½ fl oz) dry vermouth (Noilly Prat is my ideal here)
200 ml (7 fl oz) white wine

300 ml (10 fl oz) Fish stock (p. 52)
300 ml (10 fl oz) thick (double/heavy) cream

Staples
S&WP

Melt the butter in a medium saucepan over a medium heat. Add the shallot, celery and mushroom, season with salt and sweat until softened but not coloured, about 8 minutes. Add the peppercorns, thyme, vermouth and wine and simmer until reduced and syrupy, about 5 minutes.

Stir in the stock and simmer until reduced by two-thirds, about 8 minutes. Add the cream and simmer until the sauce coats the back of a spoon, about 5 minutes. Strain and adjust the seasoning as necessary.

The velouté will keep for up to 3 days in the fridge; just warm through when needed. Foaming with a stick blender just before serving is a nice touch, too.

Make it different

This sauce is complete as is, but is also a great foil for other flavours. You can do so much with it – just add delicate flavours at the end, and robust ones early.

Herbed velouté. (GF) Add soft herbs such as chopped parsley, sorrel, chives or tarragon, or stir in some watercress or parsley purée, and serve with pan-fried scallops, salmon or ocean trout.

Spiced velouté. (GF) Add spices such as fenugreek or curry powder to the reduction with the peppercorns, stir some Fermented cooked chilli sauce (p. 97) through the finished sauce and serve with mussels.

Prawn velouté. (GF) Prawn (shrimp) heads sweated out with the shallot will turn the velouté in a deeply flavoured bisque-like direction.

Sauce diable ⓖ

This is a very snazzy onion sauce, employing both the sweetness of shallots and caramelised notes from the blackened onions, balanced with a spike of white pepper and a zippy backbone of vinegar. Blackening the onions might feel odd at first, but it adds a depth and colour to this sauce that you can't achieve otherwise. This recipe makes a fair bit, but it's very versatile – and trust me, you'll appreciate the surplus. **Serves 10–12; makes about 600 ml (20½ fl oz)**

Pair with

This makes humble sausages and mash absolutely captivating. Some grilled Italian pork and fennel sausages atop a creamy mash, drowned with plenty of this ... well, it's heavenly.

Serve with Petit salé aux lentilles (p. 334), or a well-charred steak.

It also works well with poultry, such as grilled quail or poussin.

Try it with offal such as liver, kidneys or sweetbreads.

A thick piece of well-toasted Sourdough bread (p. 847) topped with gruyère and then doused with this gravy is marvellous (perhaps as a cook's snack after the sauce is made and before dinner is served).

Fast red-wine sauce for meat ⓖ

After cooking meat, don't waste any pan or resting juices, or those caramelised bits left behind in a roasting tin. Instead, pour off any fat and make a delicious sauce from them. (If the pan's contents are looking burnt, however, it's best not to use them.) Fry 2 smashed garlic cloves in a little butter in a frying pan until lightly golden, then add a large glass of dry red wine (about 200 ml/7 fl oz) and a sprig of thyme, rosemary or sage, and reduce over a medium heat by just under half. Add 100 ml (3½ fl oz) chicken or beef stock and any meat resting juices or pan scrapings, then reduce by half over a high heat. Finish by swirling in a few knobs of cold butter, which will gloss and thicken the sauce. Season with salt and pepper, then spoon the sauce over whatever meat you're serving.

130 g (4½ oz) cold butter, cut into 1 cm (½ in) dice
10 French shallots, finely sliced into rings
5 thyme sprigs, leaves stripped
¼ teaspoon ground white pepper, or cayenne pepper

Stock
1 kg (2 lb 3 oz) chicken wings, cut into 3–4 pieces each, through the bone
2 large brown onions, skin on, quartered
100 g (3½ oz) butter
80 g (2¾ oz/⅓ cup, firmly packed) brown sugar

125 ml (4 fl oz/½ cup) sherry vinegar
1.2 litres (41 fl oz) Golden chicken stock (p. 54)
2 teaspoons white peppercorns, crushed
2 thyme sprigs
1 bay leaf

Staples
S&P

Preheat the oven to 200°C (400°F) fan-forced. Line a baking tray with baking paper.

For the stock, spread the chicken pieces on the baking tray, leaving space in between for air to circulate (use two trays if necessary). Roast for about 30 minutes, until deeply golden, then set aside.

Meanwhile, add the onion quarters, cut side down, to a large frying pan over a high heat. Cook for about 10 minutes on each side, until blackened.

Melt the butter in a large saucepan over a medium heat. Add the charred onion pieces and cook for about 3 minutes, squashing with a wooden spoon as you do. Add the sugar and cook for 2–3 minutes, stirring constantly, until you have a toffee-like caramel.

Add the chicken pieces to the pan with the caramel, then drain and discard the fat from the baking tray before scraping any of the sticky bits from the baking paper into the pan. Add the vinegar, then simmer without stirring for 2 minutes (stirring can make the sauce murky). Add the stock, peppercorns and herbs and simmer for 45 minutes.

Remove from the heat and leave to settle for 5 minutes, then strain through a fine-mesh sieve. Cool the stock until the fat starts to congeal on top, then skim the fat off.

To finish the sauce, melt 30 g (1 oz) of the butter in a saucepan over a medium heat. Add the shallot and cook until softened but only slightly coloured, about 5 minutes. Stir in the thyme and pepper, then add the strained stock. Reduce the mixture for about 10 minutes, until slightly thickened into a sauce consistency, then whisk in the remaining cold butter until emulsified. Adjust the seasoning as necessary.

The sauce will keep well covered in the fridge for up to 10 days, or can be frozen for up to 6 months.

Roasted garlic jus with tarragon ⓖⒻ

This is a very fancy gravy – rich, creamy and packed with flavour. The velvety consistency, deep bass notes of roasted garlic and the anise-tinged scent of tarragon make this a perfect match for roast poultry. **Makes 450–500 ml (15–17 fl oz/2 cups)**

Pair with

Built with chicken in mind, this jus is just as superb with a simply roasted whole bird (see p. 229) as it is with seared chicken of any kind, roasted chicken leg quarters or chicken supremes.

Also great with duck and quail.

2 garlic bulbs
4 thyme sprigs
1 bay leaf
100 ml (3½ fl oz) white wine
100 ml (3½ fl oz) verjuice

1 litre (34 fl oz/4 cups)
    Double chicken stock
    (p. 54)
150 ml (5 fl oz) pouring
    (single/light) cream

6 tarragon sprigs
Staples
EVOO, S&WP

Preheat the oven to 180°C (350°F) fan-forced.

Place the garlic bulbs on a piece of foil and drizzle with oil. Wrap up and roast for 40 minutes, then remove from the oven. Once cool enough to handle, cut in half crossways.

Add the garlic halves to a saucepan, squeezing out some of the pulp along the way. Add the thyme, bay leaf, wine and verjuice and simmer for about 5 minutes, until reduced by two-thirds. Add the stock and simmer very gently for 20–30 minutes, skimming as necessary, until reduced by two-thirds; doing this slowly means the garlic will infuse properly.

Strain the reduced stock into a clean saucepan and season with salt and white pepper. Add the cream and tarragon, then simmer for 5 minutes. Strain and use straight away, or refrigerate for up to 10 days; the jus can also be frozen for up to 1 month.

Mustard sauce ⓖⒻ

Roux-based sauces can be a bit old-fashioned and heavy, but they certainly have their place – especially when accompanying quite robust flavours and textures but less so when saucing more delicate dishes. Bolstered with umami-laced Golden chicken stock and spiked with mustard and horseradish, this sauce makes perfect use of a roux for thickening. **Makes about 300 ml (10 fl oz)**

Pair with

Perfect for meaty dishes such as cotechino, corned beef or braised brisket, roast beef, sausages, polpette and rissoles.

Also great with chips.

30 g (1 oz) butter
1½ tablespoons plain
    (all-purpose) flour
300 ml (10 fl oz) Golden
    chicken stock (p. 54), hot
2 tablespoons dijon mustard
1 tablespoon crème fraîche

1 heaped teaspoon mustard
    powder
1 teaspoon finely grated
    fresh horseradish,
    or unsweetened prepared
    horseradish

Staples
S&P

Melt the butter in a small saucepan over a medium heat. Once foaming, stir in the flour and cook, stirring constantly, for 5 minutes, until the raw flavour has cooked out and the roux has darkened.

Whisk in the stock in a steady stream, then cook for about 5 minutes, whisking constantly, until thickened into a smooth sauce. Stir in the remaining ingredients and season with salt and pepper to taste.

If not using straight away, simply stir again before serving, or you could keep a cartouche on top and gently reheat for serving.

Quick prawn essence GF

This is a very quick prawn (shrimp) sauce, mirroring the flavours and intensity of a Crustacean stock (p. 52) without the fuss. If you get into the habit of freezing small bags of raw prawn heads and shells (from the last time you peeled fresh prawns) for seafood stocks, you'll be able to whip up this flavoursome essence in about 20 minutes. You can use it to boost all kinds of seafood dishes, or as a sauce on its own, or take it a step further and make an intense dressing or simple bisque. If you don't have any chicken stock on hand, you can simply use water, although the finished essence won't have quite the same depth of flavour.

Makes about 200 ml (7 fl oz)

Pair with

The prawn essence is great for finishing seafood dishes such as risottos, pastas, curries or soups.

Use as a dipping sauce for seafood dumplings (see p. 500).

Use a spoonful to dress a crab or prawn omelette (see p. 352).

Quick creamy seafood sauce or bisque GF

Heat the Quick prawn essence (right), stir in 300 ml (10 fl oz) pouring (single/light) cream, then bring to a simmer. Season to taste, and serve as a creamy sauce for cooked seafood – or add some cooked prawns or flaked crabmeat, top with croutons and serve as a soup.

---

80 ml (2½ fl oz/⅓ cup) extra-virgin olive oil
6 large prawn (shrimp) heads and shells
3 large garlic cloves, smashed
1 teaspoon fennel seeds

150 ml (5 fl oz) white wine
500 ml (17 fl oz/2 cups) Golden chicken stock (p. 54)
1 handful of parsley leaves, or stalks

1 teaspoon caster (superfine) sugar
1 red bird's eye chilli, split lengthways

Staples
S&P

Heat the oil in a large, deep-sided frying pan over a medium heat. Add the prawn heads (but not the shells), garlic and fennel seeds, season with salt and pepper and stir, crushing the prawn heads to extract all the juices. Fry for 5 minutes, until golden, then add the prawn shells and fry for another 2–3 minutes, until golden.

Add the wine and cook until reduced by half. Add the stock, parsley, sugar and chilli and simmer vigorously for 5 minutes, then reduce the heat and simmer gently for another 5 minutes.

Strain through a fine-mesh sieve and season as needed. The essence is best used straight away.

Make it different

Prawn dressing. GF To make a prawn dressing, reduce the prawn essence to 100 ml (3½ fl oz), to further intensify its flavour, and leave to cool. Whisk in 60 ml (2 fl oz/¼ cup) lemon juice and 80 ml (2½ fl oz/⅓ cup) extra-virgin olive oil, season to taste and use to dress any cooked seafood. Toss with freshly cooked prawns, calamari or scallops and serve on warm potato with shaved fennel, or couscous with chopped chilli and a burst of fresh herbs such as mint, coriander (cilantro) or parsley. Toss with mussels or clams (vongole), or spoon over a seared fish fillet.

A quick Bordelaise sauce with bone marrow & roasted shallots ⓖⓕ

This is a classic French sauce for beef – super-rich and glossy, and unapologetically traditional. Its title gives away its origin, with the Bordeaux region lending both its name and its most famed product: its Cabernet-based wines, so a similar wine is best here. Sometimes Bordelaise is made with bone marrow in the sauce, and sometimes the bone marrow is served alongside, but I find the version below particularly compelling. I actually made it on television in an improvised roadside setup in Bordeaux, roasting the shallots and marrow at a nearby château (as you do). It was challenging to film, but the result was divine. Do try this at home – before you try it roadside, that is. Just remember that the marrow needs to be roasted to warm through, so ideally it should come out of the oven just as the beef you are serving it with has finished resting.

Serves 4

Pair with

Beef – just about any cut, grilled, roasted, pan-seared … A good grating of fresh horseradish over the sauced meat when serving tastes wonderful; skip the jarred stuff, unless you can find one that contains no sugar.

500 ml (17 fl oz/ 2 cups) Brown beef stock (p. 55), or any good-quality meat stock
15 French shallots, 12 whole with the skins on, 3 finely chopped
1 tablespoon extra-virgin olive oil

150 g (5½ oz) cold butter, diced
4 garlic cloves, sliced
5 thyme sprigs
1 bay leaf
350 ml (12 fl oz) Cabernet Sauvignon (Bordeaux, if you want to be authentic)

4 × 2.5 cm (1 in) thick pieces of bone marrow in the bone (ask your butcher to cut these for you)
1 handful of flat-leaf (Italian) parsley leaves, torn

Staples
EVOO, S&P

Preheat the oven to 180°C (350°F) fan-forced. In a saucepan, heat the stock over a medium heat for about 10 minutes, until reduced to 300 ml (10 fl oz). Keep the stock hot.

Place the whole shallots on a piece of foil, season with salt and pepper and drizzle with a little oil. Fold into a parcel and bake for 30 minutes, until soft. Set the roasted shallots aside in the foil to keep warm.

While the shallots are roasting, start making the sauce. Add the oil and 30 g (1 oz) of the butter to a saucepan over a medium heat. Add the chopped fresh shallot and garlic and sauté for 3–5 minutes, until softened. Add the thyme, bay leaf and wine, then reduce the wine by two-thirds, about 6–8 minutes. Now add the stock and simmer for 6–8 minutes, until reduced by two-thirds.

At this point, have whatever beef you are serving resting, ready for serving. Place the bone marrow rings on a baking tray and roast for 6–8 minutes to warm through, while you finish off the sauce.

Slowly add the remaining butter to the sauce, whisking until thickened and glossy. Remove from the heat and season to taste.

To serve, place the marrow bones to the side of the beef you are serving. Squeeze the roasted shallots from their skins onto the meat, spoon the sauce over the top and scatter with parsley.

Dairy

Beurre blanc GF V

This sauce is about as classic as it gets, its reputation virtually undented by shifts in food fashion. Okay, maybe the butter police have railed against it, but I pay no notice. Done well, this is a sublime accompaniment to seafood and vegetable dishes. **Serves 4–6; makes about 250 ml (8½ fl oz/1 cup)**

Pair with

This sauce is so good spooned over freshly cooked vegetables: asparagus, broad beans, peas, artichokes, broccolini, cauliflower …

Try it as an alternative to Hollandaise (p. 79) on coddled eggs (p. 357 or 359) or poached eggs (see p. 351), with ham or ham hock meat (see p. 324).

The sauce also accompanies pretty much any cooked seafood, from scallops to whole fish.

It's also perfect with a good old-fashioned vol-au-vent filled with seafood.

For a real indulgence, spoon over warmed oysters with a little fresh horseradish and caviar or other fish roe.

4 French shallots,
  finely sliced into rounds
300 ml (10 fl oz) white wine
2 tablespoons white-wine
  vinegar

8 white peppercorns
1 tablespoon cream
  (35% fat)
250 g (9 oz/1 cup) cold
  unsalted butter, diced

Staples
LMN, S&P

In a saucepan, reduce the shallot, wine, vinegar and peppercorns over a medium heat until you have a syrupy liquid, about 50 ml (1¾ fl oz) in volume. Stir in the cream, which helps to stabilise the sauce, then start adding the butter slowly while whisking. Once all the butter is added and the sauce has emulsified, season with salt and squeeze in lemon juice to taste. Strain through a fine-mesh sieve. You can use the sauce immediately, or keep somewhere warm until needed, stirring again just before serving.

Make it different

While perfect in its own right, a beurre blanc can be tweaked just before serving. At the last moment, stir in shredded sorrel, chopped chives, chervil or summer tarragon, some soaked saffron threads, or a pinch or two of curry powder, depending on what you are using it with.

Beurre rouge GF V

Unsurprisingly, this is the red wine version of beurre blanc. The method and the ingredients are the same, except for the wine. Choose a full-flavoured red, and make sure it is quite drinkable. I'd never suggest putting an expensive wine in a sauce (though I've been known to do it), but do make sure that the palate is agreeable, bright and clean, because you'll be reducing the wine heavily, thereby concentrating its flavours. The red wine will give the finished sauce a deeper colour. **Serves 4–6; makes about 250 ml (8½ fl oz/1 cup)**

Pair with

Beurre rouge is classically served with meatier and richer types of fish, such as salmon and trout, or smoked fish.

Try it with braised lentils (see p. 387), bacon and a poached egg.

Use it to sauce a poached egg on garlic-rubbed toast, for a simpler version of the classic oeufs en meurette of Burgundy.

4 French shallots, finely
  sliced into rounds
400 ml (13½ fl oz) red wine
2 tablespoons red-wine
  vinegar

8 white peppercorns
1 tablespoon cream
  (35% fat)
250 g (9 oz/1 cup) cold
  unsalted butter, diced

Staples
LMN, S&P

In a saucepan, reduce the shallot, wine, vinegar and peppercorns over a medium heat until you have a syrupy liquid, about 50 ml (1¾ fl oz) in volume. Stir in the cream, which helps to stabilise the sauce, then start adding the butter slowly while whisking. Once all the butter is added and the sauce has emulsified, season with salt and squeeze in lemon juice to taste. Strain through a fine-mesh sieve. You can use the sauce immediately, or keep somewhere warm until needed, stirring again just before serving.

Bread sauce ⓥ

Bread sauce: now that's about as uninspiring a name as you're likely to come across. And indeed, done badly, bread sauce could create a lifelong prejudice. This is not a traditional version, though the bread and dairy base is similar. Instead of cream I use crème fraîche, which adds a pleasing sour tang, and spike it with mustard and fresh horseradish. Always go for a good full-cream (whole)milk. **Serves 10; makes about 800 ml (27 fl oz)**

375 ml (12½ fl oz/1½ cups) full-cream (whole) milk
1 French shallot, sliced
1 large garlic clove, finely sliced
1 bay leaf

250 g (9 oz) crustless white Sourdough bread (p. 847), diced
300 g (10½ oz) crème fraîche, at room temperature
60 g (2 oz) fresh horseradish, finely grated, or

unsweetened preserved horseradish
3 teaspoons dijon mustard
½ teaspoon hot English mustard

Staples
LMN, S&P

Add the milk, shallot, garlic and bay leaf to a saucepan and bring to a simmer over a medium heat. Add the bread and stir in to moisten, then simmer for 1 minute. Remove from the heat and stand for a couple of minutes to soften the bread. Remove the bay leaf, then purée with a stick blender until the sauce is as smooth as possible. Stir the remaining ingredients through. Season with salt and pepper, then squeeze in lemon juice to taste. Serve immediately.

Make it different

Without mustard & horseradish. If you're after a more traditional feel, you can omit the mustard and horseradish, or adjust their quantity to taste.

With onion. Add two whole white onions that have been baked until very soft and purée with the bread after soaking to make a smooth onion and bread sauce.

With cloves and nutmeg. A classic addition; just be sure to remove any cloves before blitzing.

Pair with

Bread sauce is classically served with roasted fowl, often at Christmas, but this version is also perfect with roast beef.

Horseradish cream dressing ⒼⒻ ⓥ

Combine 2½ tablespoons finely grated <u>horseradish</u>, 125 ml (4 fl oz/½ cup) <u>pouring (single/light) cream</u>, the juice of 1 <u>lemon</u> and 1 tablespoon <u>extra-virgin olive oil</u>. Season with <u>salt</u> and <u>pepper</u> and combine. Makes about 250 ml (8½ fl oz/1 cup). This dressing is best used on the day. Great with seared steak, roast chicken, a grain or lentil salad and boiled potatoes.

Béchamel ⓥ

Béchamel is one of the five 'mother sauces' of classical French cuisine – though the Italians would say the French have borrowed from their besciamella, which is integral to that most emblematic of Italian dishes: lasagne. Either way, in its most basic form, béchamel is simply a white sauce with milk thickened by a roux – a cooked paste of butter and flour. Adding cheese is a diversion from the French mother sauce, but it's probably the most likely direction anyone would take it; simply omit if you are using the sauce for something cheese would jar with, such as seafood. Once you have the hang of it, you can make a simple béchamel by feel. Just melt some butter and add enough flour to bring it together into a thick paste. Cook until the raw smell of the flour has gone, then whisk in some milk, and keep adding and whisking in more milk as the sauce thickens to the desired consistency. Simple really. Using warm milk is always recommended, but cold milk will work just fine as long as you whisk well to break up any lumps. **Makes about 1.5 litres (51 fl oz/6 cups), enough for 1 large tray of lasagne; recipe can be halved**

Pair with

Cauliflower cheese (p. 479).

Mac & cheese (p. 120).

Lasagne (p. 136).

Baked pasta (see p. 138).

Use as the base for a cheese soufflé (see p. 357).

Toss an extra-cheesy version through cooked silverbeet (Swiss chard) or spinach, or pour over cooked leeks or cauliflower, then scatter over breadcrumbs and bake until golden.

Simple seafood pie sauce

Omit the cheese, and use just enough Béchamel (left) to bind a mixture of cooked sliced potato, peas, poached or pan-fried fish and chopped cooked prawns (shrimp). Mix in plenty of chopped parsley and a good squeeze of lemon. Season generously and tip into a pie dish. Top with Classic puff pastry (p. 822), glaze the pastry with milk and/or egg wash (see p. 13) and bake at 200°C (400°F) fan-forced until the pastry is puffed and golden, about 20 minutes.

1.2 litres (41 fl oz) full-cream (whole) milk
300 ml (10 fl oz) pouring (single/light) cream
2 bay leaves
100 g (3½ oz) unsalted butter
100 g (3½ oz/⅔ cup) plain (all-purpose) flour
120 g (4½ oz) Grana Padano, grated
¼ whole nutmeg, finely grated

Staples
S&WP

Add the milk, cream and bay leaves to a saucepan over a medium heat. Bring to just under the boil, then remove from the heat.

Melt the butter in a saucepan over a medium heat. Stir the flour through and cook for about 2 minutes, until the roux comes off the bottom of the pan in a mass and the raw flour aroma has gone; this is important, as the sauce will taste floury otherwise.

Gradually whisk in the hot milk until incorporated and smooth. Whisk continuously until just starting to boil; the sauce will have thickened considerably. If you're not adding cheese, the béchamel is now ready to use.

Whisk in the Grana Padano and nutmeg, then season with salt and white pepper. Use the béchamel while still hot, or store in the fridge for up to 5 days in an airtight container, with plastic wrap or baking paper sitting directly on top to stop a skin forming, then reheat very gently on the stove.

Make it different

With cheese. Double the cheese or add different types, such as cheddar or gruyère, to make Mac and cheese (p. 120) or a vegetable gratin (see p. 537).

For Moussaka (p. 310). After whisking in the cheese and nutmeg, fold in two well-whisked eggs.

With mustard & parsley. Spike the base béchamel with a few spoons of mustard and a handful of chopped parsley to serve with corned beef.

Tahini dip/sauce GF V

This dip-style sauce is creamy and nutty, freshened with the sharp tang of yoghurt and lemon. It's something I always have in the fridge, ready to scoop up with crudités or pitta bread for a quick snack, or to drizzle over salads, roasted lamb, eggs – almost anything that can take a Middle Eastern accent. I love it on scrambled or poached eggs for breakfast. **Makes about 500 ml (17 fl oz/2 cups)**

Pair with

Crudités or pitta bread (see p. 854).

Falafel (p. 432).

Fritters (see p. 664).

Koftas (pp. 249, 309).

Scrambled, boiled or poached eggs.

Grilled or pan-fried fish.

Spiced roasted lamb leg (see p. 311), back strap or cutlets.

Grilled or roasted chicken or quail.

Baked kingfish, ocean trout or salmon.

1 garlic clove, finely grated
1½ teaspoons salt flakes
juice of 1 lemon
250 g (9 oz/1 cup) thick plain yoghurt
150 g (5 oz) tahini
2½ tablespoons extra-virgin olive oil

In a bowl, smear the garlic and salt into a paste with the back of a spoon, then mix in the lemon juice. Add the remaining ingredients and combine until smooth. If it's too thick, thin it down with water.

The sauce will keep in the fridge for about a week.

Cafe de Paris butter ⓖ

This is quite a classic, though not actually a French one. Cafe de Paris does seem to be an oddly literal name for a cafe in Paris, or anywhere else in France for that matter – though they certainly do exist there. The venue in question was, and still is, in Geneva, Switzerland. The original recipe was developed in the early 1940s to sauce entrecôte (sirloin, porterhouse), and remains a closely guarded secret. So, to be fair, this is an interpretation of an interpretation of the original. The original is also served more as a sauce, while I prefer the butter to melt on the hot steak. This recipe makes a fairly large amount, but given the longish ingredients list, it's worth making in a meaningful quantity and freezing.

Makes 20 portions

2 French shallots, finely diced
2 garlic cloves, finely grated
1 bunch of flat-leaf (Italian) parsley, leaves finely chopped
4 thyme sprigs, leaves chopped
4 tarragon sprigs, leaves chopped

zest of ½ lemon, plus the juice of 1 lemon
6 anchovies
2 tablespoons small capers
2 tablespoons tomato sauce (ketchup)
2 tablespoons worcestershire sauce
1 tablespoon dijon mustard

2 teaspoons salt flakes
1 teaspoon freshly ground black pepper
¼ teaspoon sweet paprika
¼ teaspoon curry powder
2 pinches of cayenne pepper
500 g (1 lb 2 oz) unsalted butter, softened at room temperature

Combine all the ingredients except the butter in a bowl. Cover and refrigerate overnight.

The next day, using a stand mixer fitted with a whisk attachment, beat the butter for 4–5 minutes on medium speed.

Meanwhile, add the marinated ingredients to a blender and blitz to a smooth paste.

Fold the herb and spice paste into the whipped butter. Shape the butter into three logs, about 4 cm (1½ in) thick, on lengths of plastic wrap. Roll up tightly, twisting the ends to compress each log into even cylinders, then chill or freeze until required. The flavoured butter will keep for 2 weeks in the fridge, or 3 months in the freezer.

To use, slice the butter into discs and place on cooked and rested steaks, then flash briefly in a hot oven or under a hot grill (broiler) until the butter is just starting to melt.

Pair with

Beef! The piquant flavours of this butter were designed for beef, and go best with it. Sirloin is the original choice, but it will enhance any steak.

Sliced grilled lamb.

Roasted or grilled field mushroom.

Grilled or boiled white or green asparagus.

Salt-roasted celeriac 'steaks'.

Nasturtium & miso butter ⓖ Ⓥ ⓥⓖ

Add 50 g (1¾ oz/1⅔ cups) chopped picked watercress, 20 small nasturtium leaves (spray-free ones), 2 tablespoons white miso paste, 1 tablespoon grapeseed oil, ½ teaspoon salt flakes and ½ teaspoon ground white pepper to a blender and blitz to a purée. Add 200 g (7 oz) butter and blitz thoroughly until smooth. Use as is, or chill until firm. This butter will keep for a few days in the fridge, but it's best used fresh. Makes about 300 g (10½ oz). Use to sauce cooked fish, to melt on minute steak, or to smother on fresh rye bread with hot-smoked trout.

Parsley & lemon butter GF V

So simple and versatile, this flavoured butter is perfect to have in the freezer to add flavour to meat, fish and vegetables at the last minute. You can let it melt on the hot finished dish, help it along by flashing under a hot grill (broiler), or quickly toss in a pan with vegetables, prawns (shrimp) and the like – but please don't cook it as such, as you want the lemon flavour punchy and fresh.

Makes 12 portions

350 g (12½ oz) unsalted butter, softened at room temperature
1½ lemons

1½ bunches of flat-leaf (Italian) parsley, leaves finely chopped

1 teaspoon cayenne pepper, or ground aleppo pepper
Staples
S&P

Using a stand mixer fitted with a whisk attachment, beat the butter for 4–5 minutes on medium speed.

Finely grate the zest of the lemons directly into the bowl, then squeeze the lemons and add the juice as well. Season with salt and pepper, add the parsley and cayenne pepper and combine well.

Shape the butter into a 4 cm (1½ in) thick log on plastic wrap. Roll up tightly, then twist the ends to compress the log into an even cylinder. Chill until firm, or freeze. This butter will keep for 2 weeks in the fridge, or 3 months in the freezer.

Pair with

Melt onto grilled or seared meats.

Toss with cooked green vegetables, such as asparagus, or pour over mushroom, pumpkin (winter squash) or sweet potato.

Top a hot baked potato with a thick disc.

Melt in the pan to finish cooked fish, prawns (shrimp) or scallops.

Burnt butter sauce with lemon, capers & parsley GF V

Melt 180 g (6½ oz) unsalted butter in a frying pan over a medium heat. It will foam, then subside and start to turn light brown with a distinctly nutty aroma. Add 1½ tablespoons small capers and fry for a minute or so. Season with salt and pepper, then stir in the juice of 1 lemon and the finely chopped leaves of 5 sprigs flat-leaf (Italian) parsley. Let the butter bubble for about 15 seconds, then remove from the heat and use immediately. Makes about 200 ml (7 fl oz), or enough for 6. Spoon over cooked seafood, drizzle over cooked leeks, beans or asparagus, or coat a hero-filled pasta (especially if it's seafood-based).

Burnt butter sauce with lemon, sage & toasted walnuts GF V

Melt 180 g (6½ oz) unsalted butter in a frying pan over a medium heat. It will foam, then subside and start to turn a light brown with a distinctly nutty aroma. Add 20 sage leaves and 50 g (1¾ oz) walnuts, then fry until the sage leaves are crisp, 1–2 minutes. Season with salt and pepper, then stir in the juice of 1 lemon. Let it bubble for about 15 seconds, then remove from the heat and use immediately. This is great with white meats.

Emulsions

Master olive oil mayonnaise GF V

Mayonnaise seems to have an aura of difficulty around it. Sure, there's something magical, mystical even, about emulsifications, as there is with fermentation (involved in making sourdough, sauerkraut, etc.), but the principles are really quite simple. While this recipe may seem very precise, making a quick mayonnaise doesn't require anything but a grip on the technique and observation. Many cooks suggest ensuring the egg yolks are at room temperature, but I've made many a mayonnaise with cold eggs, and you can always warm the bowl with hot water, if you like. The real key is to add the oil very slowly at the start. An emulsification is where two liquids that normally repel each other are combined by suspending one 'inside' the other. In the case of a vinaigrette, this suspension is temporary, but an egg has properties that make that bond stable – so once that emulsification has been established and the mayonnaise starts to thicken, it is very unlikely to split. Indeed, some cavalier oil additions towards the end of the whisking will likely have no ill-effects at all. This is my staple mayonnaise, one I make in larger batches for all manner of applications. I like the flavour and richness extra-virgin olive oil adds, but for some people it is too dominant on its own, so for a more neutral result you can increase the grapeseed oil and add the olive oil to taste. This recipe can be halved, or proportionally fractioned up or down. Smaller quantities are best whisked by hand (which arguably yields the best result), whereas larger amounts can be hard to work manually. **Makes 850 g (1 lb 14 oz)**

4 egg yolks	350 ml (12 fl oz) extra-virgin	60 ml (2 fl oz/ ¼ cup) lemon
1½ tablespoons dijon mustard	olive oil	juice
1½ tablespoons white-wine	350 ml (12 fl oz) grapeseed	**Staples**
vinegar	oil	S&P

Add the egg yolks, mustard and vinegar to a food processor, season with salt and process until combined. Slowly drizzle the olive and grapeseed oils through the feeder while processing; as the mixture emulsifies and thickens, you can pick up the speed of the oil a little. Once all the oil is incorporated and the mayonnaise is quite thick, follow with the lemon juice. Adjust the seasoning and acid to taste.

Use straight away, or refrigerate in an airtight container, with plastic wrap or baking paper sitting directly on top of the mayonnaise to stop a skin forming; it will keep for up to 10 days.

Make it faster

For a mayo on the fly, simply add an egg yolk to a mixing bowl (a heavy, high-sided one is best, so it won't move around so much as you whisk, and the emulsion will be contained in a smaller area). Add a dollop of mustard, a splash of vinegar and some salt. Whisk until combined, then start to drizzle in a little oil while whisking. This is easiest if you have an oil bottle with a spout, but you can always stop and start, ensuring that you have whisked in all the oil before adding more. Once the emulsification is established, keep whisking in more oil until quite thick. Add some lemon juice to sharpen the flavour and season to taste. Super simple, and just so quick!

Pair with

Use on any kind of sandwich or roll, in salads and as a base sauce.

Tuna mayonnaise GF

Using a mortar and pestle, finely grind 2 teaspoons fennel seeds. Add 1 garlic clove and grind to a paste with a little bit of salt. Transfer to a food processor. Drain a 185 g (6½ oz) tin tuna in oil, add to the food processor and blitz until crumb-like in texture. Add 160 g (5½ oz/ ⅔ cup) Master olive oil mayonnaise (left) and blitz until smooth. If necessary, add a little more mayonnaise to achieve a thick sauce-like consistency. Mix in the juice of ½ lemon, then season as needed with salt and pepper. The mayonnaise will keep in an airtight container in the fridge for up to 3 days. Makes about 500 g (1 lb 2 oz/2 cups).

Oat milk mayonnaise GF V VG

In a high-speed blender, combine 80 ml (2½ fl oz/⅓ cup) oat milk, 2½ teaspoons apple-cider vinegar, 2 teaspoons dijon mustard, 1½ teaspoons caster (superfine) sugar and 1 teaspoon salt flakes. With the motor running, drizzle in 250 ml (8½ fl oz/1 cup) grapeseed oil. This will make a thick mayo – to thin it slightly, add a splash of hot water. This will keep in an airtight container in fridge for up to 10 days. Makes about 300 g (10½ oz).

Sesame mayonnaise (GF) (V)

Finely grind 2 teaspoons toasted sesame seeds using a mortar and pestle. Add to 250 g (9 oz/1 cup) Whole-egg mayonnaise (right), along with 2 teaspoons rice-wine vinegar and ½ teaspoon sesame oil.

Pair with

This is a good all-round mayo for sandwiches, slaws and potato salad (see p. 624), or whenever a lighter flavour is preferred.

Saffron mayonnaise (GF) (V)

Soak 3 pinches saffron threads in 1 tablespoon boiling water for 5–10 minutes, until the colour has been liberated. Using a mortar and pestle, grind a small garlic clove with the saffron threads (reserving the soaking water), into a smooth paste. Combine the garlic paste with 250 g (9 oz/1 cup) Master olive oil mayonnaise (oppsoite) and the saffron soaking water. Squeeze in lemon juice to taste, then season as needed with salt and pepper. Use straight away, or refrigerate in an airtight container, with plastic wrap or baking paper sitting directly on top of the mayonnaise to stop a skin forming; it will keep for up to 3 days. This is ideal with seafood and makes about 250 g (9 oz/1 cup).

Pair with

Kohlrabi, cabbage & beetroot slaw (p. 548).

Use as a dressing for salads, or as a sauce in a bánh mì (see p. 332) or the like.

Use in wraps or sandwiches.

Spike with sriracha or Fermented cooked chilli sauce (p. 97) and use as a dipping sauce.

Fix it

Sometimes, mayonnaise does split – usually because the yolks were flooded with too much oil at the start, so the bonds that provide the emulsification aren't able to form. This is easy to spot, as the mayo will be thin, with no 'resistance'. To fix it, whisk another egg yolk by hand in a clean bowl, then whisk in oil as you normally would, until the mixture is stiffening. Continue adding the split liquid and any remaining oil (plus extra as needed) until the mayo is the desired consistency. (If making a larger quantity, you can transfer to a food processor once stable.)

Whole-egg mayonnaise (GF) (V)

This is a more neutral, lighter-style mayonnaise than the one opposite. Using a whole egg as well as a few egg yolks makes it less rich, as does the lower ratio of olive oil. With this mayonnaise, it is important to add vinegar only at the end, or the egg white will 'cook' in the acid, and the texture will be compromised.
Makes 550 g (1 lb 3 oz/2¼ cups)

2 egg yolks	300 ml (10 fl oz)	3 teaspoons white-wine
1 egg	grapeseed oil	vinegar
25 g (1 oz) dijon mustard	100 ml (3½ fl oz) extra-virgin	3 teaspoons lemon juice
(about 5 teaspoons)	olive oil	**Staples**
		S&P

Add the egg yolks, egg and mustard to a food processor, season with salt and pepper and process until combined. Slowly drizzle the grapeseed and olive oils through the feeder while processing. Add a small drizzle of cold water every now and then to help stabilise the mixture. Once all the oil has been incorporated, blend in the vinegar and lemon juice. Adjust the acid and season with salt and pepper to taste.

Use straight away, or refrigerate in an airtight container with plastic wrap or baking paper sitting directly on top of the mayonnaise to stop a skin forming; it will keep for up to 10 days.

Make it different
With sweetness. If you're fond of the sweetness of commercial mayonnaise (we all have our vices), add a few teaspoons of sugar at the start.

Tofu 'mayonnaise' (GF) (V) (VG)

This mayonnaise-like dressing is thick and luscious, with sweet and savoury notes playing against each other. It works beautifully with raw vegetables, and can be used to replace mayonnaise in any dish where it is called for.
Makes about 500 g (1 lb 2 oz/2 cups)

250 g (9 oz) silken tofu	2 tablespoons apple-cider	1 tablespoon umeboshi paste
80 ml (2½ fl oz/⅓ cup)	vinegar	(optional)
grapeseed oil	2 tablespoons crunchy	1 tablespoon dijon mustard
3 tablespoons maple syrup,	peanut butter	2 teaspoons white miso
or honey		paste

Blitz all the ingredients in a blender until smooth. The mayonnaise will keep in an airtight container in the fridge for several days.

Aïoli (GF) (V)

This is a version of the classic garlic mayonnaise from Provence – not to be confused with allioli, which is Catalan. The latter is a hard-won emulsification of garlic and olive oil, while the former employs egg yolk to form the sauce. Originally the French version was closer to the Catalan one, but the mayonnaise-like aïoli dominates today. This recipe can easily be doubled, in which case it can be made in a small food processor (just finely grate the garlic first), but the texture is not as fine as when made by hand. **Makes about 300 g (10½ oz)**

2 small garlic cloves
½ teaspoon salt flakes
2 egg yolks

150 ml (5 fl oz) extra-virgin olive oil
100 ml (3½ fl oz) grapeseed oil

Staples
LMN, S&P

Using a mortar and pestle, crush the garlic and salt into a smooth paste. Add to a bowl with the egg yolk and whisk to combine. Whisking constantly, start adding the olive and grapeseed oils gradually. As the mixture emulsifies and thickens, you can pick up the speed of the oil a little. Once all the oil is incorporated and the aïoli is quite thick, add lemon juice to taste; if it is too thick, dilute with a little water. Season with salt and pepper to taste.

Use straight away, or refrigerate in an airtight container with plastic wrap or baking paper sitting directly on top of the aïoli to stop a skin forming; it will keep for up to 10 days.

Make it different
Spicy aïoli. (GF) (V) For a spicy version, add 1½ teaspoons smoked paprika to the garlic and salt, then proceed with the recipe. Finish with 1 tablespoon sriracha or hot sauce, such as Tabasco, to taste.

Pair with

In Provence, aïoli is served with a platter of cooked vegetables, potatoes, hard-boiled eggs, and snails or simply cooked seafood under the name aïoli garni.

Aïoli enhances most seafood dishes, especially simply cooked fish fillets and shellfish; also try it with toasted Sourdough bread (p. 847) and tinned sardines, mussels or anchovies. It is a classic accompaniment for seafood soups and stews such as Bouillabaisse (p. 214). Dollop directly into the soup, or smear on toasted baguette and dunk.

It works extremely well with croquetas (see p. 190).

Black aïoli (GF)

Gloriously black, rich and briny, and punchy in both colour and flavour, this is definitely a show-off sauce. It is somewhat messy to make, but is delicious and makes a big impact. **Serves 12; makes about 350 g (12½ oz)**

pulp from 1 roasted garlic bulb (see p. 66)
3 teaspoons dijon mustard
½ teaspoon sweet smoked paprika
20 ml (¾ fl oz) squid ink

2 egg yolks
150 ml (5 fl oz) grapeseed oil
150 ml (5 fl oz) extra-virgin olive oil
1 tablespoon red-wine vinegar

juice of 1 lemon
hot green jalapeño sauce, such as green Tabasco, to taste

Staples
S&P

In a blender or food processor, combine the garlic, mustard, paprika, squid ink and egg yolks. Slowly add half the grapeseed and olive oils while processing. Add the vinegar and half the lemon juice, then drizzle in the remaining oils until you have a thick emulsion. Add the remaining lemon juice to taste. Add a good shake of jalapeño sauce, and season to taste with salt and pepper. If it's too thick, mix in a little water.

Use straight away, or refrigerate in an airtight container with plastic wrap or baking paper sitting directly on top of the aïoli to stop a skin forming; it will keep for up to 3 days.

Make it different
With cured meat. To dress it up even more, gently fry some nduja or chopped raw chorizo in a small frying pan over a medium heat. When golden, tip onto paper towel to drain, then crumble over a plate of aïoli and Calamari fritti (p. 223) or frutti di mare.

Pair with

Croquetas (see p. 190).

Arancini (see p. 148).

Calamari fritti (p. 223).

Cooked crayfish, scallops or bug (flat-head lobster).

Marie Rose sauce (cocktail sauce)

A pioneering British celebrity chef, a tenuous link to a shipwreck and a Frenchified affectation are the players in this little sauce. The idea of mixing mayonnaise and tomato sauce is attributed to Fanny Cradock, back in the 1960s – but how Henry VIII's ill-fated flagship *Mary Rose*, sunk in 1545, became the eponym, and how it ended up with a French distortion to the name (probably a little insensitively, given the ship was sunk by the French) is unclear. What is known, however, is that this was an immensely popular sauce for seafood from the 1960s to the 1980s, especially on a prawn (shrimp) cocktail. These days it may be considered a little unfashionable, but it's still delicious with chilled seafood, making it a great fridge staple for the warmer months. **Serves 8–10; makes about 280 ml (9½ fl oz)**

250 g (9 oz/1 cup) Master olive oil mayonnaise (p. 74)
1 tablespoon tomato sauce (ketchup)
3 teaspoons lemon juice

2 teaspoons hot sauce, such as Tabasco
1 teaspoon worcestershire sauce

½ teaspoon caster (superfine) sugar
½ teaspoon ground white pepper

Combine all the ingredients in a bowl, then chill for about 1 hour before using, for the sauce to stiffen. It will keep in an airtight container in the fridge for up to 3 days.

Make it different

To jazz this sauce up further, add 2 tablespoons plain yoghurt, two chopped anchovies, along with an extra 1 tablespoon tomato sauce, 2 teaspoons worcestershire sauce, 2 teaspoons hot sauce, half a finely grated garlic clove, 1 teaspoon caster (superfine) sugar and 2 teaspoons grated horseradish.

Italian tartare ⓖ

A thick, gutsy take on tartare, this is punchy, rich and flavoursome with a generous pickle content. And why Italian? Well perhaps the link is a bit tenuous, but it has accompanied my Calamari fritti (p. 223) for over two decades on my menus – so let's say it is Italian by association. **Makes about 650 g (1 lb 7 oz)**

1 garlic clove
2 teaspoons salt flakes
1½ tablespoons dijon mustard
400 g (14 oz) Master olive oil mayonnaise (p. 74)
2 large handfuls of flat-leaf (Italian) parsley leaves, finely chopped
2 large handfuls of dill, finely chopped

4 tablespoons finely chopped cornichons
2½ tablespoons tiny capers, drained
2½ tablespoons finely chopped pickled onions/ shallots, or pickled cocktail onions
2 anchovies, very finely chopped

2 teaspoons caster (superfine) sugar

Staples
LMN, S&P

Using a mortar and pestle, grind the garlic and salt into a paste, then mix in the mustard and plenty of pepper. Combine with the remaining ingredients in a bowl, adding lemon juice to taste.

This tartare will keep in the fridge for up to 3 days, or up to 10 days if you add the fresh herbs just before each use.

Pair with

Prawn cocktail (see p. 413).

Use as a dipping sauce for any hot or chilled seafood: cooked prawns (shrimp), boiled crab, lobster tails, fish and chips …

Great in sandwiches or rolls – say a brioche bun with avocado, shredded iceberg lettuce, Chinese cabbage (wombok) or watercress, and cooked prawns (shrimp), lobster or the like.

Nori tartare ⓖ ⓥ

Rehydrate 4 nori sheets in boiling water for 5 minutes. Drain, slice very finely and mix together with 230 g (8 oz) Master olive oil mayonnaise (p. 74), 3 tablespoons chopped gherkins (pickles) or Chinese pickles (p. 640), 4 finely sliced spring onions (scallions; white part only), a small handful of chopped dill fronds, chopped, a small handful of shredded shiso leaves, 1 tablespoon dijon mustard, 2 teaspoons umeboshi purée or 1 chopped umeboshi plum and 1 teaspoon sesame oil. This tartare is best used fresh, but will keep for several days in the fridge. Makes about 350 g (12½ oz).

Pair with

This is divine with almost anything fried, but it especially sings with seafood.

Simply crumbed fish.

Calamari fritti (p. 223).

Beer-battered flathead & twice-cooked potato cakes (p. 187).

Croquetas (see p. 190).

Vegetable fritters (see p. 673).

Stuffed zucchini flowers (p. 668).

Sauce gribiche (GF) (V)

This classic sauce is essentially a mayonnaise made with cooked egg yolks, which is then spun into a sort of tartare with the cooked egg whites, capers, cornichons and herbs. You will sometimes see the name used where chopped eggs are bound with regular mayonnaise, or it might be an oily vinaigrette with chopped egg mixed through it. All angles are quite delicious.

Makes about 450 g (1 lb)

3 eggs
2 teaspoons dijon mustard
185 ml (6 fl oz/¾ cup) extra-virgin olive oil
2 teaspoons white-wine vinegar

2 handfuls of mixed parsley, chervil and tarragon, chopped
6 cornichons, finely diced
15 tiny capers, rinsed and squeezed dry, chopped

Staples
S&P

Cook the eggs in a saucepan of simmering water for 8 minutes, then refresh in iced water. Peel the eggs once cool. Separate the egg yolks and whites. Chop the whites very finely and set aside.

In a bowl, mash the egg yolks and the mustard into a smooth paste. While whisking or beating with a fork, slowly pour in the oil until emulsified. Add the vinegar and combine. Add the egg whites and remaining ingredients and mix well.

Season with salt and pepper and serve at room temperature. The gribiche is best used straight away. It will keep for a day or two in the fridge, but will lose its bright, rich colour reasonably quickly.

Pair with

This sauce is wonderful with a seared fish fillet, crabmeat, prawns (shrimp), or simply crumbed fish ... and any of these wedged into a fresh baguette with plenty of gribiche and some shredded cos (romaine) lettuce is a delight.

It is equally good with cold meats, such as sliced roast pork, and adds a nice sharp accent to tongue.

Pair with cooked green vegetables, such as beans or asparagus.

Use to dress a potato salad (see p. 624).

Make a salad with tinned tuna, chickpeas toasted in a pan and tossed with Baharat (p. 6) or aleppo pepper, and blanched kale dressed with lemon juice, then generously spoon the gribiche over.

Anchoïade (GF)

Anchoïade is a traditional Provençal sauce made from anchovies, olive oil, capers and garlic, which are pounded to a paste in a mortar. It is used for dipping crudités in, or smearing on bread as an appetiser. This version employs mayonnaise instead of olive oil, which is certainly not traditional, but the applications are the same. Use the best anchovies you can here. **Serves 6–8; makes about 250 g (9 oz)**

10 anchovies
2 tablespoons small capers, drained
pulp from 1 roasted garlic bulb (see p. 66)

½ garlic clove, finely grated
2 red or green bird's eye chillies, finely sliced
6 tarragon or oregano sprigs, leaves chopped

250 g (9 oz) Master olive oil mayonnaise (p. 74)
1 hard-boiled egg

Staples
S&P

In a blender, process the anchovies, capers, roasted and raw garlic, chilli and herbs to a smooth paste. Add the mayonnaise, season with lots of pepper and blend. The anchoïade will keep in an airtight container in the fridge for up to 3 days. Serve with the boiled egg finely grated over the top.

Pair with

Use to sauce grilled asparagus or broccolini, paired with soft-boiled eggs.

Try it as a sauce-like dip for tender new-season spring or summer vegetables: broad beans, sugar-snap peas, Dutch carrots, fennel, radishes, asparagus, spring onions (scallions), celery, kohlrabi, pickled or fresh cucumbers, baby zucchini (courgettes) with blossoms ...

Serve as a condiment with crumbed fish, grilled tuna or kingfish or Tuna niçoise (p. 438).

Freshly made flatbread (see p. 852).

Hollandaise GF V

Pair with

A very versatile sauce, hollandaise can be used to dress seafood and grilled or roasted meats.

Eggs of any kind are generally improved by adding a splash of hollandaise. Eggs Benedict (with ham) and Eggs Florentine (with spinach) are probably the most famous uses for hollandaise, but it is also particularly good with cured trout or salmon (see p. 163).

Hollandaise is a beautiful sauce for green vegetables such as asparagus, broad beans, green beans and broccolini.

Hollandaise is one of those sauces that people dine out on – usually at breakfast or brunch these days, given it has become a decadent cafe staple on account of how wonderful it is with eggs … especially with some ham or bacon as well. Eggs Benedict lives on! Hollandaise is one of the five 'mother sauces' of French cuisine, forming the basis of béarnaise and, less famously, choron, paloise and maltaise sauces. And though it is one of those sauces that can intimidate a cook, it's really not that complicated. You can even make the reduction (the first step in the method) in a larger quantity to have on hand, which means you can whip up a hollandaise sauce quite quickly. A splash of reduction, an egg yolk, some salt and enough clarified butter to bring the sauce to a ribbon stage and you're done. **Serves 6–8; makes about 500 ml (17 fl oz/2 cups)**

4 French shallots, finely sliced
6 parsley stalks
250 ml (8½ fl oz/1 cup) white-wine vinegar
20 white peppercorns, lightly crushed

2½ tablespoons white wine
2½ tablespoons water
4 egg yolks
juice of 1 lemon
2 pinches of cayenne pepper

500 g (1 lb 2 oz) Clarified butter (p. 360), warmed to around body temperature
Staples
S&P

In a small saucepan, bring the shallot, parsley stalks, vinegar and peppercorns to the boil over a medium heat. Cook until the liquid is heavily reduced, about 5–8 minutes, then add the wine and water. Bring to a simmer and cook for 3 minutes, then strain the remaining liquid. This is your reduction.

Add the egg yolks, lemon juice, cayenne pepper and a good pinch of salt to a steel or glass bowl. Whisk until combined, then gradually whisk in the reduction until you have a frothy mix of yolks. Whisk for a couple more minutes to aerate, then place the bowl over a saucepan of gently simmering water. Don't let the water boil or the bowl touch the water, or the mixture may curdle.

Whisking constantly, add the butter in a slow, steady stream. Once all the butter has been added, you will have a thick emulsion that trails off the whisk in thick ribbons. Season to taste with salt.

The hollandaise will keep for about 2 hours in a bain marie (see p. 34) at about 60°C (140°F), or in a vacuum flask.

Make it different

Béarnaise sauce. GF V Add several tarragon stalks to the vinegar before boiling, reducing and infusing, then prepare the sauce as above. To finish, add about 40 very finely chopped tarragon leaves to the sauce just as you serve, not before. Béarnaise has the same uses as hollandaise – but is especially wonderful with grilled steak (and ideally French fries).

Choron. GF V A choron is hollandaise flavoured with tomato. You can add the tomato as a purée, or as a splash of tomato sauce (ketchup) and some diced fresh tomato. Try it with pan-fried fish, crabmeat, crayfish, lobster or prawns (shrimp); some prefer to pair it with steak.

Paloise sauce. GF V Add finely chopped mint leaves to the hollandaise just before serving. Paloise is perfect with roasted or grilled lamb.

Maltaise sauce. GF V Add some blood orange zest and juice to the hollandaise just before serving. Serve with spring's first flush of asparagus.

Rouille GF V

Rouille is de rigueur with bouillabaisse, but somewhat oddly it doesn't seem to have a definitive traditional recipe. Its name means 'rust' in French, in reference to its colour – but some versions use capsicums (bell peppers), others use saffron or paprika, while some use tomato paste (concentrated purée) to obtain that hue. Many recipes call for breadcrumbs, some use potatoes; some employ fish stock, and others no liquid at all. Some use mayonnaise, and others omit eggs altogether. This is my version. **Makes about 600 g (1 lb 5 oz)**

3 red capsicums
  (bell peppers)
3 egg yolks
1 garlic clove, finely grated

125 ml (4 fl oz/½ cup)
  extra-virgin olive oil
100 ml (3½ fl oz)
  grapeseed oil

Staples
EVOO, S&P

Preheat the oven to 180°C (350°F) fan-forced.

Lightly oil the capsicums on a baking tray, then roast for about 35 minutes, until tender and blistering. Stand in a covered bowl to steam for about 10 minutes, then remove the cores and seeds and slip off the skins. Blot the moisture off the flesh with paper towel until quite dry, then chop.

In a blender, blitz the egg yolks, garlic and a couple of pinches of salt. Add the chopped capsicum, then gradually add the olive and grapeseed oils while puréeing, to form a thick sauce. Season to taste with salt and pepper. The rouille will keep in an airtight container in the fridge for up to 3 days.

Make it faster

Preserved roasted capsicums or peppers will work just as well here. You could also replace the egg yolks and oils with 280 g (10 oz) Master olive oil mayonnaise (p. 74).

Pair with

Bouillabaisse (p. 214).

Rouille also goes well with soups; especially tomato (pp. 461, 665) or potato-based soups (pp. 519, 544). It would also pair well with Spiced green soup (p. 381). Either dollop into the soup, or smother over toasted Sourdough bread (p. 847) and serve on the side.

Smear on toast and top with crabmeat, tinned sardines, or roasted capsicum (bell pepper) and hard-boiled egg.

Dollop on roasted potatoes (p. 626) or boiled eggs.

Serve with fish and chips.

Lemon emulsion GF V VG

This is such a basic dressing, but I find it invaluable to anoint all manner of things, whether just a bowl of leaves fresh from the garden or some sparklingly fresh seafood, raw or seared. Naturally, this relies on the pristine quality of its components: just-squeezed lemon juice, good salt flakes and the best extra-virgin olive oil you have. Use this ratio to make as much as you need.

80 ml (2½ fl oz/⅓ cup)
  extra-virgin olive oil
50 ml (1¾ fl oz) lemon juice

Staples
S&P

Whisk the oil and lemon juice together until emulsified, then season with salt and pepper to taste. Use immediately.

Make it a meal

Drizzle over some buffalo ricotta, scatter on a handful of crushed toasted hazelnuts with thyme flowers and/or leaves, and grate over a little lemon zest just before serving with steak or on grilled bread. Some freshly cooked green beans would also work well.

Toss with roasted capsicum (bell pepper), torn parsley and a little grated garlic, then drape over grilled bread with ricotta, or serve with lamb chops.

Pair with

Dress green salad leaves for a simple salad.

For a quick Italian-style salad with pasta or steak, toss rocket (arugula) leaves and radicchio with the emulsion, then finish with grated or shaved Grana Padano.

Dress finely shaved or shredded vegetables, such as fennel, raw asparagus or cucumber, for a crunchy and fresh salad.

Use to dress sliced ripe tomato and finely sliced raw onion.

Toss with finely shaved cabbage and finely grated Grana Padano.

Drizzle over seared rare tuna, salmon or ocean trout, and finish with a handful of herbs, such as dill or mint.

Pour this dressing over sliced raw scallops, tuna or kingfish.

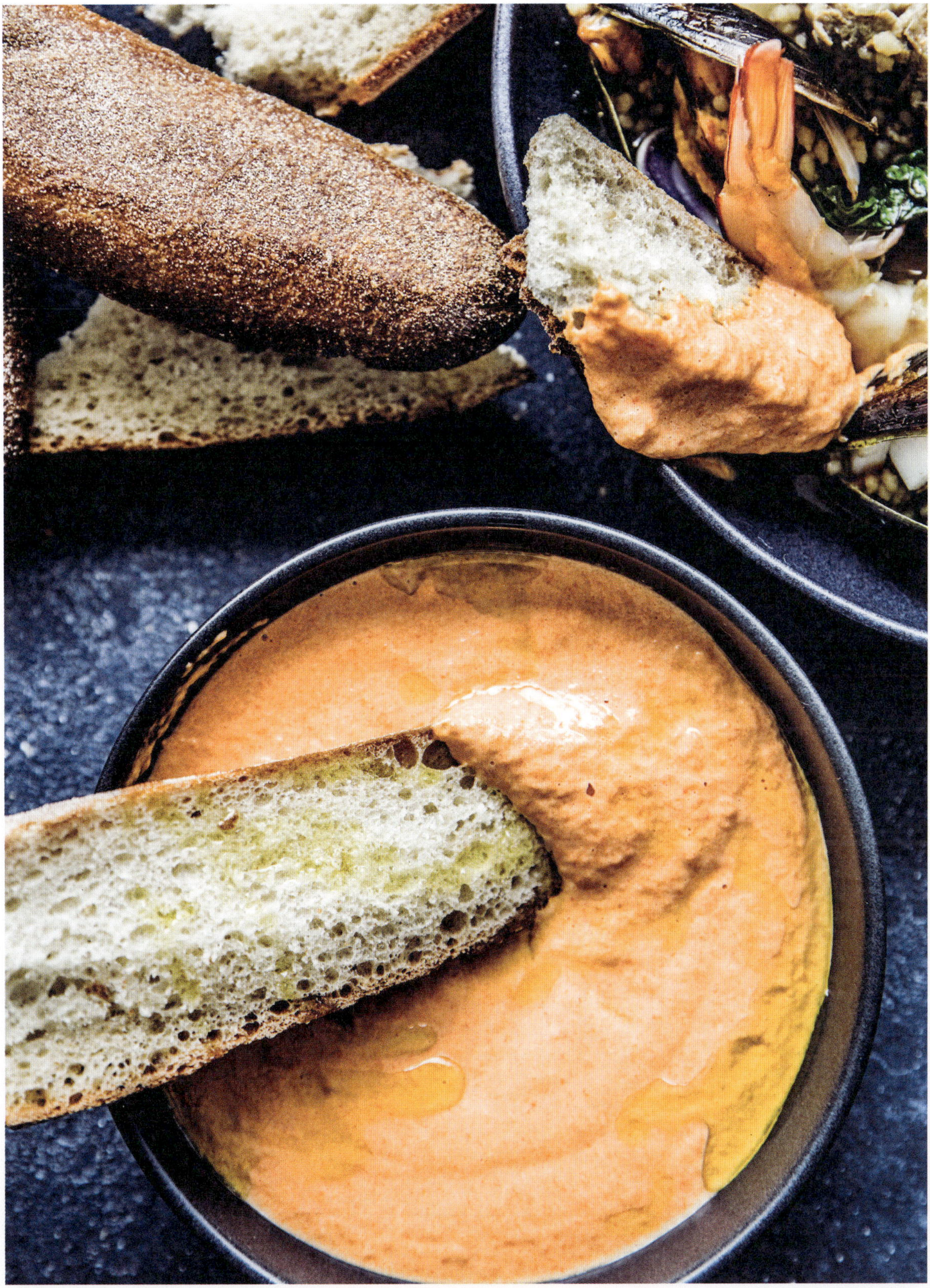

Vinaigrettes & herb-based sauces

Sauce vierge GF V VG

This captures that shift from heavier classical French cooking to bright, natural flavours. In truth, this is more vinaigrette than sauce, with an application of gentle heat used to simply infuse the flavours into the oil rather than actually cook anything. Classically, sauce vierge would have less spice and herbs, but I love the added complexity. **Serves 8–10; makes about 300 ml (10 fl oz)**

2 teaspoons fennel seeds
2 teaspoons coriander seeds
250 ml (8½ fl oz/1 cup) extra-virgin olive oil
1 large tomato, peeled see (p. 655), seeded and finely diced
½ small shallot, finely diced

3 garlic cloves, very finely sliced
½ bunch of flat-leaf (Italian) parsley, leaves finely sliced
20 small basil leaves
10 large basil leaves, central vein removed, thickly sliced

1 large handful of fennel fronds, roughly chopped
3 tablespoons lemon juice

Staples
S&P

Working in separate batches, toast the fennel seeds and coriander seeds in a dry frying pan over a medium heat for a minute or so, until slightly coloured and fragrant. Roughly grind the seeds using a mortar and pestle and set aside.

Gently warm the oil in a small saucepan to about 40°C (105°F). Remove from the heat and add the ground spices, tomato, onion and garlic. Season with salt and pepper and set aside for 15 minutes.

Add the remaining ingredients and stir gently, then adjust the seasoning as necessary. Use at room temperature on the day of making.

Make it different
With herbs. Basil is beautiful in this, but chervil or summer tarragon would work wonderfully, too.

Pair with

This is fabulous with fish, whether a pan-fried fillet, or a baked or grilled whole specimen.

Serve with cooked asparagus, or tender green beans.

Spoon over poached or soft-boiled eggs.

Fresh mint sauce GF V VG

Pick the leaves from ½ bunch mint. Bring 150 ml (5 fl oz) white-wine vinegar, 150 g (5½ oz) caster (superfine) sugar and the mint stems to the boil in a small saucepan, stirring to ensure the sugar has dissolved. Set aside to cool. Blanch the picked mint leaves in a saucepan of boiling water for 10 seconds, then refresh in cold water. Drain and squeeze out any excess water, then finely slice and add to the syrup. Serve immediately. Makes about 300 ml (10 fl oz).

Tomato, pomegranate & sumac dressing GF V VG

This is so punchy and bright. The combination is probably made famous by Australian–Lebanese chef Greg Malouf's salad of tomato and pomegranate, which he devised independently before encountering a similar version in Istanbul. A stunning dressing for fish, meat and poultry. **Makes about 500 ml (17 fl oz/2 cups)**

2 large ripe tomatoes, finely diced
2 French shallots, finely sliced
1 garlic clove, crushed and finely chopped

125 ml (4 fl oz/½ cup) extra-virgin olive oil
2½ tablespoons red-wine vinegar
2½ tablespoons pomegranate molasses

1 tablespoon ground sumac
1 teaspoon ground cumin
1 pomegranate, seeds reserved

Staples
S&P

Pair with

Slow-roasted lamb shoulder (p. 304) or grilled lamb cutlets.

Salt-baked fish (p. 175), baked whole fish or seared fish fillets.

Simple grilled chicken skewers.

Fried or grilled quail.

Combine all the ingredients, except the pomegranate seeds, in a medium bowl. Season with salt and pepper and set aside for a few minutes for the flavours to merge. Stir the pomegranate seeds through and serve.

Make it different

With chilli. I like this dressing spiked with a finely chopped red bird's eye chilli.

With rosewater. Romance it with a slug of rosewater for a lovely dressing for chicken or quail.

Bagna cauda GF

Bagna cauda is a classic dipping sauce from Piedmont in Italy's north-west. It is traditionally kept warm in a terracotta pot over a flame and used as a dip for crudités. It's like a fondue in terms of how it is classically served. It can also be used as a sauce to dress vegetables or salads. **Makes about 300 ml (10 fl oz)**

Pair with

Salads such as Tuna niçoise (p. 438) and Broad bean & pea salad with nasturtium leaves (p. 431).

Use as a sauce for vegetable dishes, or serve the traditional way, with fresh crudités: Dutch carrots, soft lettuces, whole radishes, celery heart, fennel, lightly blanched beans or sugar-snap peas, spring onions (scallions) or salad onions …

Quartered hard-boiled eggs are a great match, too.

Pile fresh red capsicum (bell pepper) cheeks around a bowl of bagna cauda with bread and chunks of Parmigiano Reggiano.

Serve spooned over torn fresh mozzarella, with plenty of Sourdough bread (p. 847).

Toss with shaved raw globe artichoke and plenty of fresh lemon to accompany grilled fish.

80 g (2¾ oz) anchovies, chopped
3 garlic cloves, finely grated

125 ml (4 fl oz/½ cup) extra-virgin olive oil
80 g (2¾ oz) unsalted butter, at room temperature

Staples
S&P

Gently warm the anchovies, garlic and some of the oil in a small saucepan over a low heat. Once the anchovies have dissolved, add the remaining oil and let it just bubble, then take the pan off the heat. Stir the butter through until melted and combined. Add plenty of pepper and some salt – even though the anchovies are salty, this sauce needs a good saline punch. The bagna cauda is best served on the day of making; it is not to be stored.

Salmoriglio GF V VG

Salmoriglio is a classic dressing from both Sicily and Calabria, in Italy's south. In Sicily, it is made from wild oregano and the region's legendary lemons, and is just so aromatic. Vibrancy of flavour is critical here, so use this to dress dishes once cooked. **Makes about 450 ml (15 fl oz)**

Pair with

Use to dress grilled meat, poultry and vegetables.

Use to dress seafood, such as grilled skewered squid.

Spoon over grilled haloumi just before serving.

Toss with hot cooked spaghetti and chopped prawns (shrimp).

2 garlic cloves, finely grated
2 teaspoons salt flakes
½ bunch marjoram, picked
2 tablespoons dried Sicilian oregano

¼ bunch of flat-leaf (Italian) parsley, leaves finely chopped
150 ml (5 fl oz) lemon juice (from about 3 lemons)

200 ml (7 fl oz) extra-virgin olive oil
2 tablespoons hot water

Staples
S&P

In a mortar and pestle, grind the garlic and salt to a paste. Add the herbs and grind further to a paste, then mix in the lemon juice.

Heat the oil to about 40°C (105°F), then combine with the hot water. Gradually whisk it into the lemon juice mixture until emulsified, then season with pepper.

Salmoriglio is best used fresh; use any leftovers to boost the flavour of soups, braises and the like.

Smoky tomato dressing GF

Blackening the tomatoes in the pan may seem unusual, but it adds gently smoky notes, rather than burnt ones, with the tomatoes also intensifying in flavour but still retaining their sweet freshness. The fish sauce knits into these flavours, upping the umami without skewing the sauce in another direction, with the briny capers, slick of olive oil and tang of raw red onion firmly pulling it towards the Mediterranean. **Makes about 500 ml (17 fl oz/2 cups)**

400 g (14 oz) ripe but tart full-flavoured tomatoes (such as black Russians), halved
4 French shallots, very finely sliced

150 ml (5 fl oz) extra-virgin olive oil
100 ml (3½ fl oz) white-wine vinegar
2 teaspoons tiny capers, drained

2½ teaspoons caster (superfine) sugar
2½ tablespoons fish sauce
1 teaspoon fennel seeds, ground

Sear the tomatoes, cut side down, in a frying pan over a medium heat for 7–10 minutes, until the flesh is blackened on the cut side and the flesh has softened.

Remove the tomatoes from the pan and discard the skins. Add the flesh to a bowl and mash a little. Add the other ingredients and combine well, then set aside for 5 minutes before using.

This dressing is best used on the day.

Salsa romesco GF V VG

Romesco sauce is a classic condiment for seafood from Tarragona, Catalonia. This is also famously served with charred calçots (which resemble a rather fat spring onion or scallion) at a ritual-like feast called a calçotada – a convivial community-minded affair typically accompanied by plenty of wine. Sometimes, especially when served with calçots, the sauce is thickened with bread and is called salsa salvitxada. Either way, the flavour of romesco is vibrant, deeply flavoured and nutty, with a garlic punch. **Makes about 350 ml (12 fl oz)**

3 large, densely fleshed tomatoes, such as roma (plum)
2 red capsicums (bell peppers)
1 large garlic bulb, cloves separated

150 g (5½ oz/1 cup) blanched almonds
100 g (3½ oz/¾ cup) hazelnuts, toasted
2 teaspoons sweet smoked paprika

100 ml (3½ fl oz) extra-virgin olive oil
2½ tablespoons sherry vinegar

Staples
EVOO, S&P

Preheat the oven to 180°C (350°F) fan-forced.

Add the tomatoes, capsicums and garlic, reserving one clove, to a roasting tin that fits them snugly. Drizzle with a little oil and roast for 45 minutes. Once cooked, cover with foil and set aside to cool for 30 minutes, then slip the skins off the tomatoes and the capsicums. Remove the seeds and cores from the capsicums. Squeeze the pulpy flesh out of each garlic clove and set aside.

Toast the almonds in a dry frying pan over a medium heat until well covered in scorch marks, about 10 minutes.

Peel the reserved garlic clove and blitz into rough crumbs in a food processor with the almonds and hazelnuts. Add the roasted capsicums, tomatoes and garlic, and the paprika, season with salt and

Pair with
Grilled calamari (p. 223).

Pan-seared or grilled fish.

Grilled scallops or prawns (shrimp).

Grilled haloumi.

Grilled chicken.

Burrata.

Bruschetta (p. 655).

Green peppercorn sauce for steak GF V

Once your steaks have been cooked and are resting, tip out the fat from the pan, leaving any caramelised crusty residue. Add 30 g (1 oz) butter over a medium heat. Once foaming, add 1 finely grated garlic clove and cook for 10 seconds. Add 1 tablespoon fresh or brined green peppercorns, crushing some with the back of a spoon to release some flavour, then add 4 thyme sprigs and swirl around in the pan. Add 1 tablespoon cognac or brandy and simmer for 30 seconds. Stir 3 tablespoons dijon mustard through, then 100 ml (3½ fl oz) pouring (single/light) cream, and leave to simmer while you move the steaks to serving plates. Season the sauce with salt, simmer for a moment longer, then spoon over the steaks to serve.

Pair with
Barbecued or grilled seafood.

Fried baccalà.

Chargrilled vegetables.

Grilled par-boiled potato slices, grilled onions and seared steak.

Barbecued chicken.

Dollop on a salad with chicory (witlof/endive), curly endive (frisée), hard-boiled eggs, and seared tuna, swordfish or mackerel.

Smear on toasted Sourdough bread (p. 847) with manchego or haloumi, or white anchovies.

pepper and blitz. Slowly add the oil until you have a very smooth paste. Mix in the vinegar and adjust the seasoning as necessary. The salsa will keep for a day in the fridge; serve at room temperature.

Make it different

With ñora peppers. While regular red capsicums (bell peppers) yield an excellent result and are readily available, for a slightly more authentic result, use ñora peppers, if you can find them. Ñora peppers are a squat, heart-shaped capsicum with a sweetly intense flavour and a gentle suggestion of heat. Use fresh ones instead of the capsicum, or add two ñora peppers to this recipe; simply rehydrate them in boiling water first.

Chimichurri GF V VG

Here is Argentina's classic accompaniment to grilled meat. And given the place asado (barbecue grilling) holds in Argentine cuisine, you can understand why chimichurri has its own distinct and fiercely defended identity. The basis is parsley, oregano (sometimes dried), garlic, chilli, vinegar and oil, making it a salsa verde, or green sauce of sorts – just don't call it that in the presence of an Argentine! Some versions are light on the chilli, but I prefer it with a decent spike of heat, some chopped shallot and a little paprika. **Serves 8–10; makes about 200 g (7 oz)**

150 ml (5 fl oz) extra-virgin olive oil

½ bunch of flat-leaf (Italian) parsley, leaves finely chopped

8 oregano sprigs, leaves finely chopped

2 red bird's eye chillies, finely diced

3 tablespoons finely diced French shallots, or chopped spring onions/scallions

3 garlic cloves, finely grated juice of ½ large lemon

2½ tablespoons red-wine vinegar

½ teaspoon smoked paprika (optional)

Staples
S&P

Combine all the ingredients in a bowl, mixing well. You can let the mixture sit for 5 minutes, for the flavours to mingle a little, but ideally it should be served at its vibrant best.

Make it different

Dial down the heat with milder chillies, or omit the seeds if you're really sensitive. And if no fresh chillies are available, use 1 teaspoon (or to taste) of chilli flakes or chilli powder; I like ground aleppo pepper.

Pair with

Serve with grilled meat and poultry, or with robust seafood such as tuna or mackerel.

Although chimichurri is typically used when serving, you can marinate meat in it, or use it to baste meat towards the end of cooking.

Tomato essence GF V VG

In a large bowl, combine 2.5 kg (5½ lb) roughly chopped very ripe <u>tomatoes</u>, 100 ml (3½ fl oz) <u>white wine</u>, 3 finely sliced <u>French shallots</u>, the leaves from 3 <u>tarragon sprigs</u>, 1 <u>garlic clove</u>, 3 tablespoons <u>sherry vinegar</u>, 1 tablespoon <u>salt flakes</u> and 1 teaspoon <u>caster (superfine) sugar</u>. Cover and set aside to marinate for 1 hour. Working in batches, pulse the mixture roughly in a food processor. Tip into a bowl, cover and refrigerate for 4 hours. Line a sieve with muslin (cheesecloth), then suspend over a large bowl to catch the juices. Tip the mixture into the sieve and leave the mixture to strain. This should take about 2 hours in a warm environment, or a little longer if cooler. The liquid should be quite clear, with any sediment settling to the bottom of the bowl. Pour the essence off the sediment, or use a ladle. Use on the day of making. Makes about 450 ml (15 fl oz). Serve as a palate-teaser, warm or cold; combine with a splash of extra-virgin olive oil for a superb dressing for seafood; or turn into a vinaigrette with more vinegar, some oil and finely grated garlic.

Salsa verde GF V VG

Available herbs, and personal whim, often take the ever-mutable salsa verde in different directions. Unlike the Mexican version, which is based on tomatillos and chillies, this one draws inspiration from the Italian iteration, which normally contains anchovies. You can, of course, add three or four anchovies; another option is to lay white anchovies on a steak, for example, and spoon the sauce over the top. This recipe is easily doubled. **Makes about 300 g (10½ oz)**

125 ml (4 fl oz/½ cup) extra-virgin olive oil
3 handfuls of flat-leaf (Italian) parsley leaves, finely chopped
3 handfuls of mint leaves, finely chopped

1 handful of tarragon leaves, finely chopped
3 French shallots, very finely diced
1 garlic clove, finely grated
3 tablespoons small capers, chopped

Staples
S&P

Add all the ingredients to a medium bowl and season generously with salt and pepper. Mix well to combine, then stand for 10–15 minutes for the flavours to develop and meld. The salsa verde is best used fresh, at room temperature.

Make it different
With horseradish. Spike the salsa with freshly grated horseradish to taste.

Pair with
This is excellent spooned over fish, steak and other grilled meats and poultry, and works well in combination with mustard, too.

Persillade GF V VG

In a small bowl, combine 100 ml (3½ fl oz) extra-virgin olive oil, ½ bunch flat-leaf (Italian) parsley, finely sliced (chiffonaded), 2 finely grated garlic cloves and 2 teaspoons toasted and ground fennel seeds. Season to taste. Makes about 250 ml (8½ fl oz/1 cup). The persillade is best used on the day. Add to pan-fried seafood at the last minute, or use to dress beef cheeks, roasted carrots or boiled potatoes.

Rustic salsa verde with potato GF

This is somewhere between a salsa and a salad, with the potato giving the sauce a chunky texture and robust feel. The flavours suit all the classic applications of salsa verde, but the presentation is, charmingly, more rustic. It is heavenly over just about anything, with its chunky feel and flavour-packed profile delicious enough to simply pile on top of toasted Sourdough bread (p. 847). **Serves 10**

3 kipfler (fingerling) potatoes
2 long green chillies, seeds removed, very finely sliced
½ bunch of flat-leaf (Italian) parsley, leaves picked
½ bunch of mint, leaves picked

6 tarragon sprigs, leaves picked
1 large garlic clove, finely grated
zest and juice of ½ lemon
250 ml (8½ fl oz/1 cup) extra-virgin olive oil
8 cornichons, sliced

6 anchovies, finely chopped
2 tablespoons small capers, chopped
1½ tablespoons sherry vinegar

Staples
S&P

Cook the potatoes in boiling salted water for about 15–20 minutes, until quite tender. Drain and cool to room temperature, then peel and cut into 1 cm (½ in) dice – or you can crumble them in your hands for a more rustic feel.

'Chiffonade' half the parsley and mint leaves by stacking them on top of each other, then slicing finely into long thin strips. Roughly tear the remaining parsley, mint and tarragon.

Combine the garlic, lemon zest and oil in a large bowl with a pinch of salt, then add the herbs, potato, cornichons, anchovies and capers. Season with lots of black pepper and mix to combine. Set aside at room temperature for 10–15 minutes for the flavours to develop and meld.

Mix the lemon juice and vinegar through, adjust the seasoning as necessary and serve.

Pair with
This dish will accompany all types of seafood: roasted scallops, poached baccalà, grilled prawns (shrimp), Moreton Bay bugs, grilled calamari, grilled or seared tuna, snapper, salmon …

It also works beautifully with grilled meats and poultry.

Herb & chilli oil GF V VG

Using a mortar and pestle, pound 2 roughly chopped long red chillies, 1 garlic clove and 1 teaspoon salt flakes to a paste. Add 60 ml (2 fl oz/¼ cup) extra-virgin olive oil, the sliced leaves from ½ bunch flat-leaf (Italian) parsley and 5 chopped mint sprigs and grind into a paste. Stir in the same amount of oil again along with 1 long green chilli, sliced into rounds. Serve at room temperature. Makes about 180 ml (6 fl oz).

Make it different

You can omit the potato, if you like, and make a smoother sauce. Increase the parsley by half, or add a few handfuls of picked watercress and blitz in a blender until smooth; it is best served the same day.

Zhoug (GF) (V) (VG)

Originally from Yemen, zhoug is appreciated throughout much of the Arabic world, with the fiery combination of chillies and herbs a versatile condiment for meat, fish and vegetable dishes. There are several versions, but perhaps the most familiar, and my favourite, employs green chillies, coriander (cilantro) and parsley, spiced with cumin and cardamom. **Makes about 250 ml (8½ fl oz/1 cup)**

3 garlic cloves, finely grated
4 cardamom pods, seeds removed and ground
2 teaspoons caraway seeds, toasted
2 teaspoons cumin seeds
2 teaspoons salt flakes

1 tablespoon finely chopped preserved lemon
1 bunch coriander (cilantro), leaves and fine stems picked, plus 5 cleaned roots
½ bunch of parsley, leaves picked

10 red bird's eye chillies, finely chopped

Staples
EVOO

Using a mortar and pestle, pound the garlic, spices, salt and preserved lemon with a little oil. Gradually add the herbs and chilli, while pounding into a paste. (Alternatively, once the spices and garlic are ground, transfer to a blender and blitz to a paste.)

Add enough oil to loosen, then serve. Zhoug is best used fresh, but it will keep for a day or so in the fridge if the sauce is topped with oil to cover.

Wholegrain mustard & maple dressing (GF) (V) (VG)

There's a lovely interplay of sharpness and sweetness to this dressing, meaning it stands up to some quite robust flavours, and is also a great foil for bitter leaves. It's worth investing in real maple syrup for its superior flavour; the imitation stuff has artificial additives and tastes more confected. **Makes about 300 ml (10 fl oz)**

2 garlic cloves, finely grated
2 tablespoons wholegrain mustard
1 tablespoon dijon mustard
½ teaspoon salt flakes
125 ml (4 fl oz/½ cup) extra-virgin olive oil

2 red Asian shallots, very finely sliced
3 tablespoons red-wine vinegar, or sherry vinegar
2 tablespoons maple syrup, or honey
juice of ½ lemon

Staples
S&P

In a bowl, mash the garlic, mustards and salt together using the back of a spoon (or use a mortar and pestle). Add the remaining ingredients with 1 tablespoon water and a grind of pepper, then beat with a fork until emulsified. Season to taste with salt and pepper. The dressing will keep in an airtight container in the fridge for about 5 days.

Pair with

Grilled lamb or chicken.

Grilled or baked fish.

Falafel (p. 432).

Braised or grilled vegetables.

Koftas (pp. 249, 309).

Tabouleh (V) (VG)

Add 1 tablespoon Baharat (p. 6) and 100 g (3½ oz) fine bulgur wheat to a medium bowl and cover with boiling water. Set aside for 10 minutes. Add the bulgur, the finely chopped leaves and stems from 1 bunch of flat-leaf (Italian) parsley, 4 large tomatoes and 1 large white onion cut into 5 mm (¼ in) dice to a large bowl and combine. Add 100 ml (3½ fl oz) extra-virgin olive oil, 80 ml (2½ fl oz/⅓ cup) lemon juice, season with salt and pepper and toss to combine well. Serve or chill. This will keep for 2 days in the fridge. Serves 4–6.

Pair with

This dressing has a natural affinity with bitter leaves, such as radicchio, curly endive (frisée), chicory (witlof/endive), dandelion and the like.

It's also great on charred broccoli, roasted cabbage, celeriac, parsnip and brussels sprouts.

Use it to dress wedges of iceberg lettuce and serve with grilled pork sausages or chicken.

Bois Boudran sauce

The story goes that the luminary French chef Michel Roux Snr invented this sauce while working as a personal chef for the Rothschild family. On the surface, it looks very much like a scramble using a few fresh ingredients and some pantry-dwellers – a piece of improvisation rather than something planned out. But there's certainly nothing wrong with that. Indeed, it has turned out to be the triple Michelin–starred chef's most famous sauce, ketchup and all. This is a lively and very flavoursome dressing, which I think has a natural synergy with roasted poultry, but is also excellent with steak and fish.

Serves 10; makes about 600 ml (20½ fl oz)

4 large, ripe oxheart tomatoes, peeled (see p. 655), seeded and finely diced (450 g/1 lb chopped weight)

150 ml (5 fl oz) extra-virgin olive oil

70 g (2½ oz) finely diced French shallots (about 5 shallots)

2 garlic cloves, finely diced

½ bunch of chervil, leaves roughly chopped

¼ bunch of chives, very finely snipped

12 tarragon sprigs, leaves picked

2 tablespoons sherry vinegar

2½ tablespoons tomato sauce (ketchup)

1½ tablespoons worcestershire sauce

1 tablespoon white-wine vinegar

hot sauce, such as Tabasco, to taste

Staples
S&P

Combine all the ingredients in a bowl, adding hot sauce and black pepper to taste. Set aside at room temperature for at least 20 minutes for the flavours to meld. Adjust the seasoning to taste. This sauce is best used fresh; use any leftovers to boost the flavour of soups, braises and the like.

Pair with

Use with all poultry, roasted or grilled.

Spoon half the sauce over some roasted jointed or split chickens laid out on a tray. Set aside for 20 minutes to take up the flavours. Transfer to a serving dish and drizzle with all the tray juices and the remaining sauce.

Serve with strongly flavoured fish, such as tuna, swordfish and sardines, or with grilled prawns (shrimp) or scallops.

Spoon over sliced rested steak just before serving.

Stir through cooked rice or grains to use as a side dish, or the basis of a salad.

French-style vinaigrette (GF)(V)(VG)

This is my go-to basic vinaigrette, which I use on salads and any mixed leaves to complete any meal, be it a steak, a roasted bird, a braise, a pasta or a vegetable tart. You can keep the dressing in the fridge for a few days to have on hand – just bring back to room temperature before emulsifying again, as the oil may solidify. **Makes about 250 ml (8½ fl oz/1 cup)**

1 large garlic clove, finely grated

1 tablespoon dijon mustard

1 tablespoon salt flakes

125 ml (4 fl oz/½ cup) extra-virgin olive oil

juice of ½ lemon

1½ tablespoons white-wine vinegar (I use chardonnay vinegar)

1 tablespoon water

2 pinches of caster (superfine) sugar

Staples
S&P

In a bowl, mash the garlic, mustard and salt together using the back of a spoon (or use a mortar and pestle). Add the remaining ingredients and a grind of pepper and beat with a fork until emulsified. Season to taste with salt and pepper. The vinaigrette will keep in an airtight container in the fridge for up to a week.

Make it a meal

Add a splash of walnut or hazelnut oil and serve with apple or pear in a salad of bitter leaves with toasted nuts and a blue cheese such as gorgonzola or Roquefort.

Pair with

Just about any salad! Try it on a mix of iceberg, oak leaf lettuce, picked watercress, chicory (witlof/endive), fluffy chervil sprigs, snipped chives and a handful of yellow celery leaves (from the heart).

Basic vinaigrette lentils (p. 385).

Nero vinaigrette (GF)

This is a dramatic sauce: glossy obsidian in appearance and just as intense in flavour, a sauce to be used sparingly to dress seafood dishes, particularly cephalopods. Cooking the garlic slowly from cold adds so much to the depth, with the deeply resonant bass note of toasted garlic laying the foundation for the other flavours. **Makes about 400 ml (13½ fl oz)**

150 ml (5 fl oz) extra-virgin olive oil
10 large garlic cloves, sliced
2 celery hearts with leaves, finely sliced
1½ tablespoons toasted coriander seeds, ground
1 tablespoon toasted fennel seeds, ground
5 saffron threads
6 confit tomatoes, or 10 semi-dried tomatoes soaked in boiling water for 15 minutes, then drained and finely chopped
300 ml (10 fl oz) water
100 ml (3½ fl oz) sherry vinegar
20 ml (¾ fl oz) squid ink
1 tablespoon dried Greek oregano (rigani)
1½ teaspoons chilli flakes
juice of ½ lemon
1½ teaspoons salt flakes

Add the oil and garlic to a small frying pan. Place over a medium heat. Cook from cold until the garlic is lightly golden, about 6 minutes. Add the celery and cook for 5 minutes, until softened. Stir the coriander, fennel and saffron through, then pour into a bowl and cool for 5 minutes.

Transfer the garlic mixture to a saucepan with the remaining ingredients. Bring to a simmer over a medium heat and cook for 5 minutes.

Transfer to a blender and blitz very well until smooth, then pass through a fine-mesh sieve. The vinaigrette will keep in the fridge for 3 days.

Pair with

Seared sardines.

Dot the sauce on a serving plate with grilled or pan-fried seafood. I particularly like it with grilled and sliced calamari tossed with yellow celery leaves and parsley. Octopus and cuttlefish are lovely, too, as are prawns (shrimp). You could also serve with pan-seared fish, such as red mullet or flathead with the skin on.

Green goddess dressing (V) (VG)

This is my version of the famous dressing, omitting the mayonnaise or dairy for a more greens-driven version. In fact, this is far removed from the classic, but it's a stunning verdant sauce to serve with anything from the barbecue: grilled vegetables, meat, poultry or fish, or serve with ricotta or another fresh cheese. In a high-speed blender, blitz the leaves from ½ bunch <u>mint</u>, the leaves from ½ bunch <u>flat-leaf (Italian) parsley</u>, ½ bunch roughly chopped <u>watercress or spinach</u>, 90 ml (3 fl oz) <u>extra-virgin olive oil</u>, 25 ml (¾ fl oz) <u>white-wine vinegar</u>, 25 ml (¾ fl oz) <u>light soy sauce</u>, 1 tablespoon <u>dijon mustard</u>, 1 chopped <u>large green chilli</u> and ½ tablespoon <u>honey</u>. Strain through a fine-mesh sieve. Makes about 250 ml (8½ fl oz/1 cup).

New potatoes with green goddess dressing (GF) (V)

Boil 1.5 kg (3 lb 5 oz) small <u>new potatoes</u> with 10 <u>mint</u> stalks (the gentle flavour penetrates the thin skins), then drain and toss in the <u>Green goddess dressing</u> (above). Serve on top of <u>Labneh</u> (p. 362), finishing with 1 tablespoon <u>pink peppercorns</u>, sliced <u>caperberries</u> and torn mint leaves scattered over the top.

Pesto **GF** **V**

This is one of those amazing ingredient combinations that just defies its naked simplicity. Everything you use here must be of exemplary quality: beautifully fresh and unblemished basil leaves, aromatic extra-virgin olive oil, and of course 'real' parmesan – I have listed Grana Padano, but I'll use Parmigiano Reggiano if I have it, as it is nuttier and more intense in flavour. You can also halve this recipe. **Makes about 650 g (1 lb 7 oz/2½ cups)**

300 g (10½ oz) basil leaves, roughly chopped
3 garlic cloves, sliced
250 ml (8½ fl oz/1 cup) extra-virgin olive oil

80 g (2¾ oz/½ cup) pine nuts
200 g (7 oz/2 cups) finely grated Grana Padano

Staples
S&P

Add a handful of basil and the garlic to a food processor and blitz to a rough paste. Keep adding handfuls of basil and pulse – if you add too much at once it is hard for the blades to do their job. Season with salt and pepper, add the oil and pulse until just mixed. Add the pine nuts and parmesan and pulse until combined, then blitz to the desired consistency. I like my pesto quite textured, but you can blitz until smooth if you like. Just be wary of running the blades for too long, as they can heat up and dull the result.

Season again and use immediately, or transfer to an airtight jar, pour a layer of olive oil on top to stop oxidation, and refrigerate until needed. Re-cover any remaining pesto with oil before storing again; it's also best to wipe down the inside of the jar, or the exposed pesto will go black. If you do this carefully, the pesto can last for weeks. You can also freeze pesto quite successfully.

Make it different
While the machine-made version is perfectly delicious, pesto made using a mortar and pestle is in many ways superior – somehow, its more rustic texture elevates it. If you have the time and inclination, your extra efforts will be amply rewarded.

Pair with

Genovese salad (p. 624).

Toss through any type of cooked dried pasta (also see pp. 131, 137). You could also add cooked diced potato, well-cooked chopped green beans, extra basil leaves and toasted pine nuts to serve.

Smear over bruschetta and top with sliced tomato and torn fresh mozzarella.

Drizzle over ripe sliced tomatoes.

At the table, add a dollop to finish a minestrone or a classic French soupe au pistou – a light, brothy vegetable soup with spring vegetables cooked until just tender.

Chermoula **GF** **V** **VG**

Consisting of chopped herbs and spices in oil, chermoula is an essential element of North African cooking. Like harissa, it can be used in cooking or at the table. This version evolved out of a trip to Morocco some years ago.
Makes about 200 g (7 oz)

½ bunch of flat-leaf (Italian) parsley
½ bunch of coriander (cilantro)
6 small garlic cloves, finely grated

30 g (1 oz) fresh turmeric (size of an index finger), peeled and finely grated, or 1 teaspoon ground turmeric
1½ tablespoons sweet paprika

2 teaspoons ground cumin
2 teaspoons ground coriander
2 teaspoons salt flakes
juice of 1 lemon

Staples
EVOO, S&P

Roughly pick the parsley and coriander leaves, along with the finer stems. Chop until reasonably fine, but still with some texture, then combine in a medium bowl with the garlic, turmeric, spices, salt and a good grind of pepper. Add a splash of water and enough oil to loosen, then stir the lemon juice through. Adjust the seasoning as necessary. Chermoula is best used fresh; use any leftovers to boost the flavour of soups, braises and the like.

Pair with

Classically a wonderful marinade or dressing for seafood, chermoula is also delicious with vegetables, meat and poultry.

Stir through dishes to add a fragrant lift at the end of cooking, or serve alongside as a condiment.

Spoon over prawns or fillets of fish and roast or braise covered.

Top to bottom: Green harissa (p. 92); Pesto

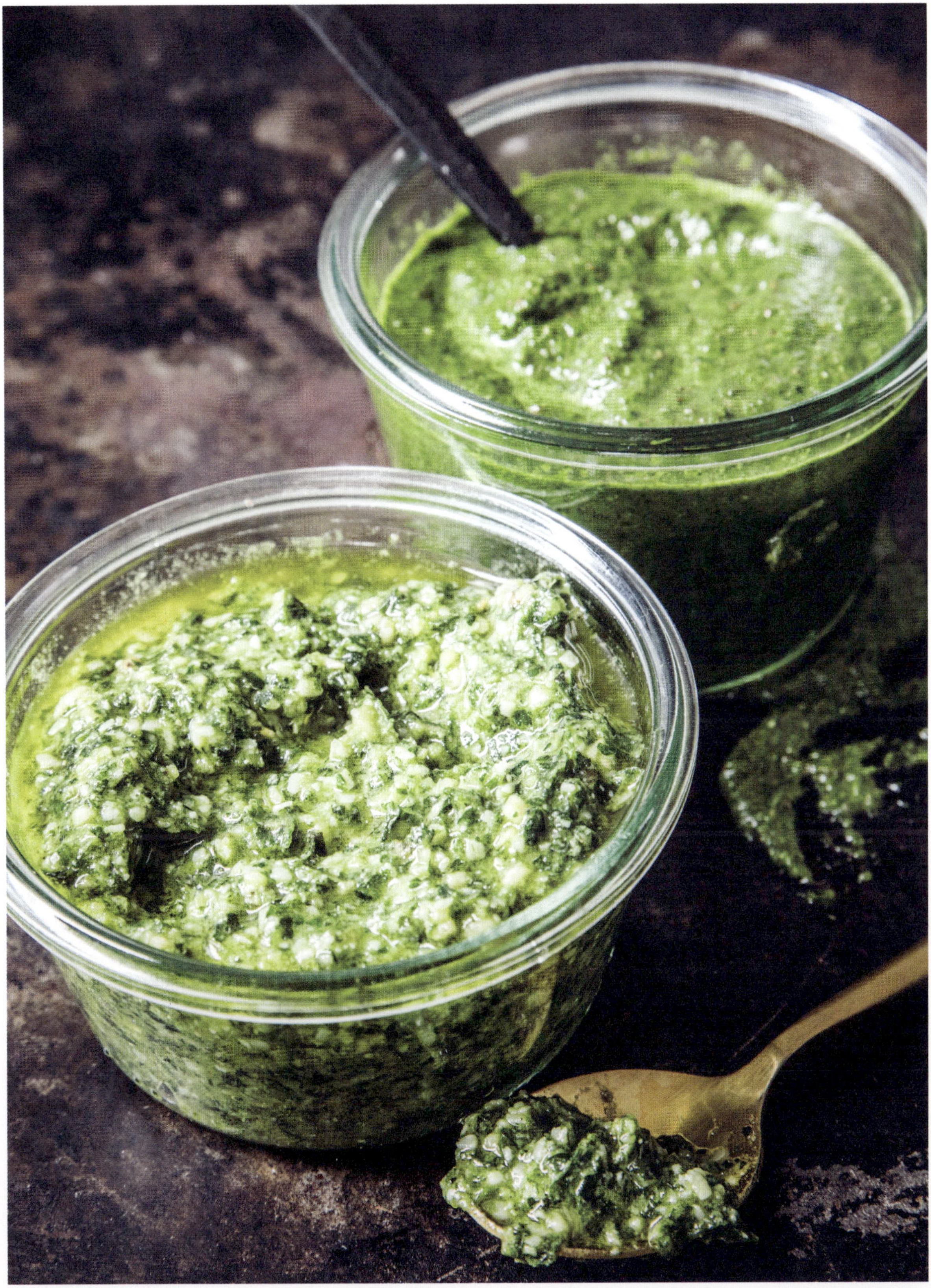

Harissa ㉓ⓋⓋⓖ

Harissa is enjoyed across North Africa, and recipes vary considerably, though the basic principle of a spiced chilli paste remains recognisable. I use fresh chillies and capsicum (bell pepper), but harissa is often traditionally made with rehydrated dried chillies. This version here has a fresher feel and is especially good as a condiment, while the more concentrated commercial versions are less suited for the table, and are better used in cooking. **Makes about 300 g (10½ oz)**

1 large red capsicum (bell pepper)
8 long red chillies
1 garlic bulb
3 teaspoons cumin seeds
3 teaspoons caraway seeds

2 bullet chillies, finely chopped
100 ml (3½ fl oz) tomato passata (puréed tomatoes)
2½ tablespoons extra-virgin olive oil

1 tablespoon tomato paste (concentrated purée)
1 tablespoon salt flakes
2 teaspoons caster (superfine) sugar

Staples
EVOO, S&P

Preheat the oven to 160°C (320°F) fan-forced.

Add the capsicum, chillies and garlic bulb to a baking tray and drizzle with oil. Roast for 20 minutes, then remove the chillies and place in a bowl, cover tightly and stand for 10 minutes. Continue roasting the garlic and capsicum for a further 10 minutes. Once cooked, place the capsicum in the bowl and cover again. Stand for 10 minutes, then peel and core the chillies and capsicum and scrape out the seeds. Set the garlic bulb aside.

Toast the cumin and caraway seeds in a small frying pan over a medium heat for about 1 minute, until fragrant and lightly coloured. Grind to a powder using a mortar and pestle or spice grinder.

Cut the top off the garlic bulb and squeeze the pulp into a food processor. Add the capsicum and chilli flesh, ground spices and remaining ingredients and process until smooth. Loosen with more oil if desired, and season to taste with salt and pepper. The harissa will keep in an airtight container in the fridge for up to 5 days.

Pair with

Almost anything, as they do in northern Africa. Serve as a condiment with tagines, couscous, braises, soups, grilled meat, poultry, fish, vegetables, or even loosened with olive oil as a dip for pitta bread (see p. 854).

Spread over grilled or roasted whole fish.

Use as a marinade or rub for meat or poultry before roasting or grilling.

Add to the pan when sautéing onion and garlic to add spice and heat to Middle Eastern–themed dishes.

Green harissa ㉓ⓋⓋⓖ

As with the red harissa above, this can be used broadly as a condiment or in cooking – but rather than the spicy roasted flavours, this harissa has a bright, vibrant profile, with the fresh green chillies and coriander adding fragrant herbal notes, along with some spice and heat. If you'd like to tone down the heat, simply remove the chilli seeds. **Makes about 500 g (1 lb 2 oz/2 cups)**

2½ teaspoons caraway seeds
2 teaspoons cumin seeds
2 teaspoons coriander seeds
200 g (7 oz) long green chillies (about 10), chopped
100 ml (3½ fl oz) extra-virgin olive oil

100 g (3½ oz) baby English spinach leaves, chopped
½ bunch of coriander (cilantro), leaves and stems chopped
2 garlic cloves, finely sliced

1 tablespoon caster (superfine) sugar
2 teaspoons salt flakes
2½ tablespoons water

Staples
S&P

Toast the caraway, cumin and coriander seeds in a small frying pan over a medium heat for about 2 minutes, until fragrant and lightly coloured. Grind the toasted seeds to a powder using a mortar and pestle or spice grinder.

Add the spices to a blender, along with the remaining ingredients, and blitz to a smooth paste. The harissa will keep in an airtight container in the fridge for 5–7 days.

Pair with

Spoon over a simple buttered rice pilaff with yoghurt.

Use as a marinade for grilled chicken, pork skewers or fish.

Drizzle over grilled lamb, beef or seafood just before serving.

Add a generous dollop to a pan of steamed mussels or pan-fried prawns (shrimp) and toss for a minute or so before serving.

Spoon over baked eggs or shakshuka.

Asian sauces

Nuoc cham

Pair with

Drizzle over a rice noodle salad or chilled seafood salad.

Serve as a dipping sauce with rice paper rolls, spring rolls or dumplings (see pp. 231, 342, 500).

Use to dress grilled or fried seafood, poultry or meat.

A great all-rounder for dressing and dipping, nuoc cham is a classic Vietnamese sauce of lime, fish sauce, lemongrass, chilli and sugar. Like its Thai counterpart prik nam pla (chopped bird's eye chillies with grated garlic, fish sauce, lime juice and a pinch of sugar, combined raw and used immediately), its success relies on a balance between sweet, salty, hot and sour – though the perception of that balance is entirely personal, so you may prefer it less or more hot, sweet, or salty. **Makes about 625 ml (21 fl oz/2½ cups)**

120 ml (4 fl oz) fish sauce
3½ tablespoons finely grated palm sugar (jaggery), or caster (superfine) sugar
300 ml (10 fl oz) water

2 small garlic cloves, smashed
juice of 3 limes
4 red bird's eye chillies, finely chopped

1 lemongrass stem, white part only, finely chopped
80 ml (2½ fl oz/3 cups) rice vinegar

Add the fish sauce, sugar, water and garlic to a small bowl and stir to dissolve the sugar. Add the remaining ingredients and leave to infuse for 5 minutes. Adjust with more lime, sugar, chilli or fish sauce to taste and serve.

The sauce will keep in a clean airtight jar in the fridge for up to a week.

Sichuan pepper & chilli dressing Ⓥ ⓋⒼ

Pair with

This is a versatile condiment for soups, noodles and dumplings (see pp. 231, 342, 500). Try it with Chicken & corn soup (p. 502), Tuna poké bowl (p. 415), Fried rice with wood ear fungus & cashews (p. 402), Soba noodle salad (p. 410) or Charred broccoli ramen (p. 444).

Use it to dress side dishes such as steamed Chinese cabbage (wombok) or lightly pickled vegetables (see p. 470).

Serve with steamed fish (see p. 162) or poached chicken (see p. 230).

I find this pungent, spicy sauce quite addictive, and use it on anything from dumplings to soups. **Makes about 250 ml (8½ fl oz/1 cup)**

125 ml (4 fl oz/½ cup) grapeseed oil
2 teaspoons chilli flakes
2 tablespoons light soy sauce

2 tablespoons hot water
1½ tablespoons rice vinegar
2 teaspoons caster (superfine) sugar

1 teaspoon Sichuan pepper salt (p. 29)

Heat the oil in a small saucepan over a high heat until shimmering, 2–3 minutes. Place the chilli flakes in a heatproof bowl, pour the oil over and stir to combine. Leave to steep for 30 minutes.

Strain the steeped oil into a bowl, discarding the chilli flakes, then stir the remaining ingredients through.

The dressing will keep in an airtight jar in the fridge for about 7 days.

Crispy garlic & soy vinegar dressing Ⓥ Ⓥᴳ

The crispy garlic here is divine, adding texture and flavour to this basic soy dressing. **Makes about 200 ml (7 fl oz)**

60 ml (2 fl oz/¼ cup) neutral oil, such as grapeseed or rice-bran

5 garlic cloves, chopped

1 heaped teaspoon chilli flakes

90 ml (3 fl oz) light soy sauce, or Enhanced soy sauce (p. 101)

60 ml (2 fl oz/¼ cup) rice vinegar

1 tablespoon lime juice

In a small saucepan, heat the oil over a medium heat. Add the garlic and fry until golden, about 2 minutes. Remove from the heat and add the chilli flakes. Set aside to infuse and cool. Stir in the remaining ingredients and serve. The dressing will keep for 2 days.

Pair with

This is the best pairing for Pork, wombok & ginger dumplings (p. 500).

Spoon over steamed greens or simply cooked seafood or fish.

Great with noodles.

Sesame dressing

If you frequently cook Asian-themed dishes, here's a very handy umami-packed sauce to have at your disposal. Use it to dress salads and sides, or as a dipping sauce. It keeps quite well, too. **Makes about 450 ml (15 fl oz)**

150 g (5½ oz/1 cup) toasted sesame seeds

150 g (5½ oz) kewpie mayonnaise

100 ml (3½ fl oz) water

2½ tablespoons light soy sauce

2½ tablespoons mirin

2 teaspoons fish sauce

2 teaspoons white miso paste

1 teaspoon sesame oil

Blitz all the ingredients in a blender until smooth. The dressing will keep in an airtight jar in the fridge for about 2 weeks.

Pair with

Toss the dressing through warm or chilled noodles.

Spoon over freshly cooked snow peas (mangetout) or asparagus, sautéed mushrooms, raw or cooked spinach, or roasted eggplant (aubergine) halves.

Toss with firm tofu stir-fried with fresh ginger, then add edamame beans and plenty of herbs such as coriander (cilantro), mint and Thai basil before serving.

Use as a dipping sauce for crumbed seafood or vegetables.

Spiced sesame & peanut dressing Ⓖᶠ Ⓥ

This sauce is spicy and nutty with a creamy texture, perfect to accompany roast chicken and pork, or freshly steamed greens, either hot or cold. **Makes about 350 ml (12 fl oz)**

90 g (3 oz/⅓ cup) smooth peanut butter

90 g (3 oz/⅓ cup) sour cream

90 g (3 oz/⅓ cup) mayonnaise (pp. 74–5)

2½ tablespoons sesame seeds, toasted

1 tablespoon tahini

3 teaspoons chilli sauce (such as sriracha), or Fermented cooked chilli sauce (p. 97)

2 teaspoons hot English mustard

2 teaspoons salt flakes

2 teaspoons caster (superfine) sugar, or brown sugar

1½ garlic cloves, finely grated

juice of 2 limes

Blitz all the ingredients in a blender until very smooth. The dressing will keep in an airtight container in the fridge for up to 7 days.

Pair with

Crispy pork belly salad (p. 331).

Left-over ramen pork (see p. 58) or for a Bánh mì (p. 332).

Use to dress a slaw-style salad with Asian herbs and pickles.

Serve as a last-minute dressing or condiment with spiced roast pork or chicken.

Use as a dipping sauce for fried chicken, or barbecued pork ribs.

Spoon over noodles, rice or Congee (p. 383), or steamed greens.

Peanut & ginger dressing

This is texturally exciting, with the crunch of toasted peanuts, the freshness of spring onion (scallion) and a hint of heat. A favourite. **Makes 300 ml (10 fl oz)**

125 ml (4 fl oz/½ cup) light soy sauce
8 spring onions (scallions), white bits and half the green, finely sliced
80 ml (2½ fl oz/⅓ cup) oyster sauce

80 ml (2½ fl oz/⅓ cup) brown-rice vinegar
5 cm (2 inch) piece of fresh ginger, peeled and finely diced
½ teaspoon chilli powder
½ teaspoon sesame oil

½ teaspoon finely ground white pepper
½ teaspoon caster (superfine) sugar
3 tablespoons chopped toasted peanuts

Combine all the ingredients, except the peanuts, in a bowl. Scatter the peanuts over the top to serve.

Pair with

This is a must with wontons (pp. 231, 342) and pot-sticker dumplings (see p. 500).

Spoon over udon or ramen noodles.

Serve on Congee (p. 383).

Great with poached chicken, roast pork and deep-fried tofu.

Try it with Chicken & corn soup (p. 502), Tuna poké bowl (p. 415), Fried rice with wood ear fungus & cashews (p. 402), Soba noodle salad (p. 410) or Charred broccoli ramen (p. 444).

Ginger & spring onion sauce 🅥 🆅🅶

This vibrant sauce is a versatile condiment for fish or chicken dishes. **Makes about 250 ml (8½ fl oz/1 cup)**

10 spring onions (scallions), white and green parts finely sliced

10 cm (4 in) piece of fresh ginger, peeled and finely diced
80 ml (2½ fl oz/⅓ cup) grapeseed oil

2 tablespoons light soy sauce
2 teaspoons sherry vinegar
1 teaspoon salt flakes

Combine all the ingredients in a small bowl, then set aside for 10 minutes before using. This sauce is best used same day.

Pair with

Bo ssäm (p. 341).

Steamed fish.

Dumplings (see pp. 231, 342, 500).

White-poached chicken (p. 230).

Use as a condiment for udon or ramen noodle dishes and soups.

Spoon over a simple omelette (see p. 352).

Spoon over freshly shucked (see p. 208) or steamed oysters.

Ginger, soy & gochujang sauce 🅥 🆅🅶

This is a punchy, fresh and spicy sauce, with earthy layers of umami. It's something that I often serve with chicken poached in a simple Chinese broth or master stock, but it's so versatile and can be used for noodles, broths, salads or a bánh mì. It's a completely stunning and addictive sauce. **Makes about 250 ml (8½ fl oz/1 cup)**

4 cm (1½ in) piece of fresh ginger, peeled and sliced
2 spring onions (scallions), white part only, sliced
2 garlic cloves, peeled

3 coriander (cilantro) roots with some stem, finely chopped
3 tablespoons gochujang paste

2½ tablespoons Enhanced soy sauce (p. 101), or light soy sauce
1½ teaspoons sesame oil
1 teaspoon ground white pepper
juice of 1 lime or lemon

Using a mortar and pestle, pound the ginger, spring onion, garlic and coriander to a rough paste. Add the remaining ingredients and combine.

This sauce is best used on the day, but will keep refrigerated until the next day.

Pair with

Chinese-style roast chicken (p. 243).

White-poached chicken (p. 230).

A cold chicken or roasted pork salad with glass noodles (see p. 240), and Thai basil.

Fried rice (p. 610).

Dumplings (see pp. 231, 342, 500).

Bánh mì (p. 332).

Use as a condiment for a chicken broth with noodles.

Thai-style chilli jam

Here's my take on the classic Thai chilli jam, nam prik pao. More sauce-like than jammy, but with the hallmark sweet, sour, hot and salty profile and syrupy richness, mine uses celery seeds, which add a beautifully pungent aromatic note, a crunchy textural component and some pleasing bitterness to accent the sweetness. **Makes about 400 ml (13½ fl oz)**

4 garlic cloves, sliced

2 teaspoons salt flakes

15 red bird's eye chillies, sliced

2 heaped tablespoons small dried shrimp

350 g (12½ oz/1½ cups) caster (superfine) sugar

320 ml (11 fl oz) white-wine vinegar, or brown-rice vinegar

2 tablespoons celery seeds

2 teaspoons ground white pepper

3½ tablespoons fish sauce

Using a mortar and pestle, pound the garlic and salt to a smooth paste. Add the chilli and pound to a rough paste, then tip into a small saucepan.

Add the dried shrimp to the mortar and pound until starting to look fluffy. Add to a pan with the sugar, vinegar, celery seeds and pepper, then simmer over a medium heat until slightly syrupy, 5–8 minutes.

Stir in the fish sauce and simmer for 1 minute, then pour into an airtight jar and cool completely before using. The sauce will keep in the fridge for at least 1 month once opened, or up to 1 year sealed.

Pair with

Use as a condiment on pretty much anything you like!

With a good squeeze of lime and some fresh coriander (cilantro) it can be used to sauce steamed fish, fried or roasted chicken or quail, and skewers of pork, chicken or beef.

Drizzle it over steamed eggplant (aubergine), stir-fried greens or soft-boiled eggs.

Coconut hoisin dipping sauce V VG

Combine 150 ml (5 fl oz) coconut cream and 80 ml (2½ fl oz/⅓ cup) Wholesome hoisin sauce (below) in a bowl. Garnish with crushed peanuts or fried Asian shallots, along with shredded mint and/or coriander (cilantro). Makes 230 ml (8 fl oz) and works well with rice paper rolls of any kind.

Wholesome hoisin sauce V VG

Simmer 12 pitted prunes in hot water for 5 minutes, let it stand for 5 minutes and then strain and set aside. In a small saucepan, bring 150 ml (5 fl oz) tomato passata (puréed tomatoes) to the boil. Add the prunes, 100 ml (3½ fl oz) rice vinegar, 2 tablespoons fish sauce or smoky soy sauce, 2 tablespoons tamari, 1 teaspoon Chinese five-spice and 1 teaspoon ground white pepper and cook over a medium heat for 5 minutes, then set aside to cool. Blitz the cooled sauce in a food processor until smooth, then transfer to a jar and refrigerate. Makes about 300 ml (12 fl oz) and will keep for up to 2 weeks in the fridge. Pair with Bánh mì (p. 332), Shiitake, tofu & cashew san choy bau (p. 555), roast pork, duck, quail or chicken.

Gochujang chilli sauce (V)(VG)

I love the umami-funky-ferment quality of the Korean red chilli paste gochujang, which adds so much depth and complexity to this sauce, not to mention a decent dose of heat. **Makes about 400 ml (13½ fl oz)**

10 cm (4 in) piece of young fresh ginger, peeled and finely grated
2 garlic cloves, finely grated
150 g (5½ oz) gochujang (about 5 tablespoons)

100 ml (3½ fl oz) brown or white rice vinegar, plus extra to taste
3 tablespoons white miso paste
2 tablespoons maple syrup

1½ tablespoons grapeseed oil
1½ tablespoons toasted sesame seeds
3 teaspoons sesame oil
1 tablespoon water

Combine all the ingredients, except the water, in a small saucepan over a medium heat, stirring until you have a smooth paste. Simmer for 2 minutes, then remove from the heat and cool a little. Add a little more vinegar to sharpen the flavour, and the water to bring it to a pouring consistency.

Keeps in an airtight jar in the fridge for 1 month, but the brightness of the ginger and garlic will diminish.

Fermented cooked chilli sauce (GF)(V)(VG)

Pair with

Serve as a condiment whenever a little heat is needed.

Stir through Mayonnaise (pp. 74–5) to go in a hamburger or sandwich.

Add to a soy dressing (see p. 94) to serve with dumplings (see pp. 231, 342, 500).

Toss through a stir-fry with beef or mussels.

Add to a broth, pasta or braise.

Add to the pot when steaming open mussels (see p. 205); for 1 kg (2 lb 3 oz) mussels/clams, add 2 teaspoons Fermented cooked chilli sauce, along with 100 ml (3½ fl oz) white wine.

This is a gently fermented then cooked chilli paste where you can use whichever type of red chillies you like – or even a mix. **Makes about 800 ml (27 fl oz)**

2 kg (4 lb 6 oz) red chillies, stems removed
60 g (2 oz) fine sea salt, approximately

4 garlic cloves, peeled and finely grated
500 ml (17 fl oz/2 cups) white-wine vinegar, or apple-cider vinegar

2 tablespoons white sugar

Roughly chop the chillies, then blitz in a food processor. Weigh the chilli pulp, then add 3% of the weight in salt. Add the garlic and stir thoroughly.

Transfer to jars or a container with a lid and stand at room temperature for about 3 days, until there is a light bubbling to the paste, then refrigerate until cold, about 3 hours.

Add the chilli paste, vinegar and sugar to a blender and blitz until smooth. Tip into a saucepan and simmer, stirring regularly, until it thickens and comes away from the sides of the pan and brightens in colour, about 10 minutes.

Once at the desired consistency, transfer to sterilised jars (see p. 40) and store in the fridge. The sauce will keep for up to a year.

Raita ⒼⒻ Ⓥ

When making subcontinental curries, I like to make my own Naan (p. 855) if I have time, but I always make raita. Diced or grated cucumber often finds its way into that raita, but I do love this version, with a spike of freshness from the ginger and sharpness from the raw onion pairing with cooling yoghurt to balance out the fiery tendencies of some curries. **Serves 4–6**

1 white onion, finely sliced
4 cm (1½ in) piece of fresh
 ginger, finely diced

2 handfuls of coriander
 (cilantro) leaves, chopped
juice of ½ lemon or lime

250 g (9 oz/1 cup) thick plain
 yoghurt
2 teaspoons nigella seeds
½ teaspoon salt flakes

Combine all the ingredients in a bowl. The raita is best used same day.

Pair with

Spiced grilled or fried fish.

Lamb rogan josh (p. 317).

Lamb & eggplant karahi curry (p. 318).

Crab, pea & potato samosas (p. 611).

Naan (p. 855).

XO sauce

XO has become a rather emblematic sauce, though its history is relatively short. Named after the XO quality designate for Cognac (meaning 'extra old'), the sauce was developed in Hong Kong in the 1980s with prestige in mind, with many pointing to The Peninsula Hotel as its birthplace. The sauce has its foundations in dried shrimp, dried scallops and chilli, and is cooked out until quite relish-like; beyond that there are nowadays endless variations. As the name suggests, this is a decadent sauce, which requires careful cooking and a little time, but its deeply mysterious flavour and flush of sweetly laced heat is incredibly addictive. You can use it as a condiment, but it's also a brilliant ready-to-go base for stir-fried seafood, pork or vegetables. **Makes about 500 ml (17 fl oz/2 cups)**

100 g (3½ oz) dried shrimp
100 g (3½ oz) dried scallops
400 ml (13½ fl oz) grapeseed
 oil
5 small dried red chillies
6 red Asian shallots, chopped
100 g (3½ oz) fresh ginger,
 peeled and finely chopped

100 g (3½ oz) garlic, sliced
250 g (9 oz) speck, or bacon,
 finely diced
5 long red chillies, chopped
5 red bird's eye chillies,
 chopped
90 g (3 oz) brown sugar

125 ml (4 fl oz/½ cup) light
 soy sauce
125 ml (4 fl oz/½ cup)
 shaoxing rice wine
2 teaspoons ground
 white pepper

Soak the dried shrimp and scallops in boiling water for 1 hour. Drain, then blitz in a food processor.

Heat the oil in a saucepan over a medium heat. Add the dried chillies and fry for 1 minute, then remove and chop once cool enough to handle.

Add the shallot, ginger and garlic to the pan and cook until golden, 8–10 minutes. Add the speck and cook for about 5 minutes until golden and rendered. Add all the fresh chilli and the shrimp and scallop paste, then cook for 20 minutes over a medium–low heat, stirring frequently to stop the mixture catching. It will become molten and quite deeply coloured.

Remove from the heat and stir in the sugar to caramelise in the residual heat. Stir in the chopped dried chillies and remaining ingredients and cook over a low heat for 15 minutes.

Blitz the mixture in a food processor, then transfer to a clean airtight jar and refrigerate. The XO will keep for up to 3 months.

Pair with

Stir-fried clams with XO (p. 211).

Stir-fried greens & shiitake with XO sauce (p. 401).

Use as a base to stir-fry greens, seafood and pork.

Use as a condiment at the table, or spoon over cooked proteins, vegetables and dumplings (see p. 500).

Tempura dipping sauce

In a saucepan, bring a 20 cm (8 in) piece of kombu and 350 ml (12 fl oz) water to a simmer over a medium heat. Add 2 tablespoons katsuobushi (bonito flakes), remove from the heat and stand for 5 minutes to infuse. Strain the liquid and return to the pan with 125 ml (4 fl oz/½ cup) Japanese soy sauce, 125 ml (4 fl oz/½ cup) mirin and a peeled and julienned thumb-sized piece of fresh ginger. Bring to the boil, then immediately remove from the heat. Add a peeled and finely grated 12 cm (4¾ in) piece of daikon and allow to cool completely before using. If you like, just before serving, sprinkle with toasted and ground sesame seeds. Makes 500 ml (17 fl oz/2 cups).

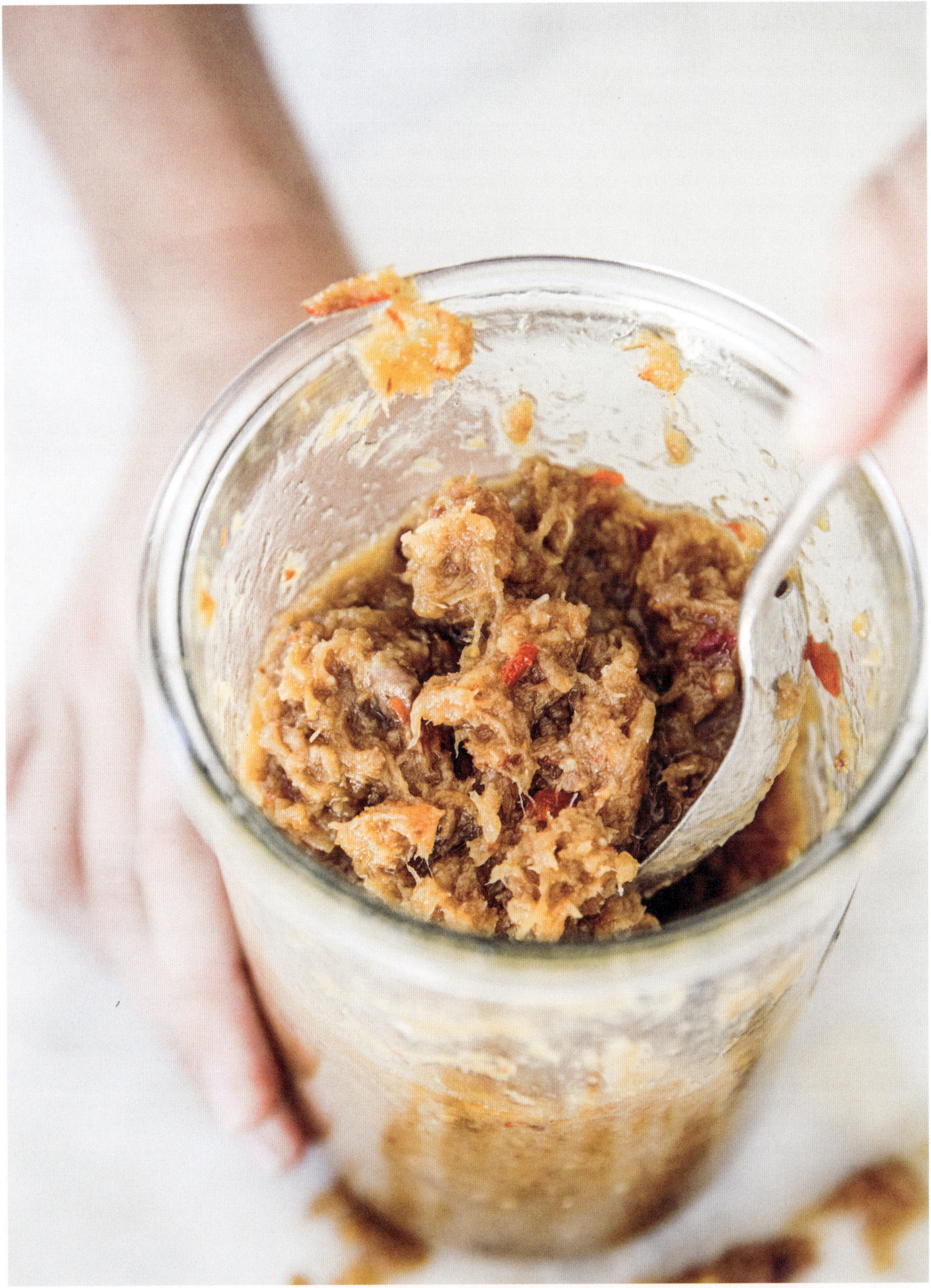

Black bean & ginger sauce Ⓥ ⓥⓖ

What we call 'Chinese black beans' are actually fermented black soy beans (douchi), which are used extensively in Chinese cuisine, their pungent fermented flavour adding depth to all manner of dishes. The method of preserving soy beans by salting and fermenting is an ancient one. The fermenting agent is *Aspergillus oryzae*, or what the Japanese call koji. This version is more luscious and a bit wetter than anything you might buy in a jar, and can be used as a flavour addition, or as a standalone sauce. If using as a sauce, allow 250–300 ml (8½–10 fl oz) for 500 g (1 lb 2 oz) of protein. **Makes about 900 ml (30½ fl oz)**

100 ml (3½ fl oz) grapeseed oil
12 garlic cloves, finely grated
120 g (4½ oz) young fresh ginger, peeled and finely diced
14 spring onions (scallions), white part only, sliced
2 red bird's eye chillies, sliced into rings

250 g (9 oz) fermented black beans, rinsed lightly under hot water
500 ml (17 fl oz/2 cups) Classic white vegetable stock (p. 51)
200 ml (7 fl oz) shaoxing rice wine
200 ml (7 fl oz) rice vinegar

3 tablespoons light soy sauce
2 tablespoons brown sugar
3 teaspoons ground white pepper
2 star anise
2½ tablespoons cornflour (cornstarch), dissolved in a little cold water

Heat the oil in a saucepan over a medium heat. Add the garlic, ginger, spring onion and chilli and cook until softened and starting to caramelise, about 5 minutes. Add the beans and stock, then simmer for about 15 minutes, until the liquid has reduced by half.

Stir in the rice wine, vinegar, soy sauce, sugar, pepper and star anise, then simmer gently for 10 minutes. Add the cornflour slurry and stir until thickened.

The sauce will keep in an airtight container in the fridge for up to 3 weeks.

Pair with

Add chilli and black vinegar to make a dipping sauce for dumplings (see p. 500).

Add a spoonful to a stir-fry – it works well with other strong flavours, particularly garlic, onion and chilli.

Add to a braise for pork belly ribs or beef.

Use as a sauce with fried shiitake mushrooms, garlic, chilli and spring onion (scallion) for beef, chicken, pork or fish.

Pan-sear a fish fillet, skin side down, flip when the skin is golden and pour in some of the sauce. Once the fish is cooked, serve it on rice with the sauce poured over, topped with fresh coriander (cilantro).

Sweet & sour sauce with pineapple Ⓥ ⓥⓖ

At its core, this is complete nostalgia. This sauce brings back plenty of happy childhood memories for me, with some grown-up refinement. **Makes about 750 ml (25½ fl oz/3 cups)**

200 ml (7 fl oz) brown-rice vinegar
150 ml (5 fl oz) shaoxing rice wine
125 g (4½ oz) caster (superfine) sugar
1½ teaspoons salt flakes
4 garlic cloves, finely grated

10 cm (4 in) piece of fresh ginger, peeled and julienned
1 red bird's eye chilli, finely sliced
2 star anise
150 g (5½ oz/1 cup) pineapple pieces (fresh or tinned)

½ yellow capsicum (bell pepper), diced
1 tomato, finely diced
3 tablespoons light soy sauce
1 tablespoon cornflour (cornstarch), dissolved in a little cold water
1 teaspoon pink peppercorns

In a saucepan, bring the vinegar, rice wine, sugar and salt to the boil over a high heat, stirring to dissolve the sugar. Add the garlic, ginger, chilli and star anise, reduce the heat and simmer for 10 minutes.

Add the pineapple, capsicum and tomato and simmer for 5 minutes. Stir in the soy sauce and cornflour slurry, bring to a simmer and stir until thickened. Stir in the peppercorns.

Use the sauce hot or cold. It will keep for up to 1 month in an airtight container in the fridge.

Pair with

Fried wontons (see p. 342).

Grilled pork chop or pork loin, or diced roasted pork belly or serve with Roasted rack of pork (p. 340).

Use to sauce stir-fried pork or chicken.

You could use this as a sauce for a pan-fried ham steak.

Teriyaki sauce V VG

You can buy teriyaki sauce quite readily, but don't; they're almost always too sweet and very monotone in flavour. A good teriyaki sauce is a thing of wonder, though, and just so versatile, whether used as a marinade, or as a glaze to finish a grilled or pan-fried dish. **Makes about 900 ml (30½ fl oz)**

40 g (1½ oz) fresh ginger, peeled and sliced
3 garlic cloves, smashed and peeled
280 ml (9½ fl oz) light soy sauce

200 ml (7 fl oz) sake
200 ml (7 fl oz) mirin
125 ml (4 fl oz/½ cup) freshly squeezed orange juice
80 g (2¾ oz) caster (superfine) sugar

2½ teaspoons sriracha sauce

Combine all the ingredients in a saucepan. Simmer over a medium heat for 1 minute, then remove from the heat and chill.

When ready to use, strain out the garlic and ginger. The sauce will keep for up to 3 months in the fridge.

Make it different
If you want a sauce with more body, mix 1 tablespoon cornflour (cornstarch) and 1 tablespoon cold water until smooth. Just as the sauce comes to the simmer, stir in well to combine. Chill and strain.

Pair with

Teriyaki pork belly parcels with shiitake mushrooms, spring onion (scallion) and togarashi (see p. 31).

Use as a marinade or finishing glaze for pork, beef, chicken, seafood, tofu, mushrooms or vegetables.

Enhanced soy sauce

While this version dials up the umami, it can be used whenever soy sauce is called for. Combine 500 ml (17 fl oz/2 cups) light soy sauce, 100 ml (3½ fl oz) mirin, 2½ tablespoons sake, 2 teaspoons caster (superfine) sugar, 5 g (⅛ oz) katsuobushi (bonito flakes) and 10 g (¼ oz) dried shiitake or porcini mushrooms in a saucepan. Simmer over a medium heat for 1 minute, then turn off the heat. Leave to steep for 1 hour, then strain and transfer to a bottle. Best kept in the fridge; the sauce will last for weeks. Makes 650 ml (22 fl oz), and will make the simplest meal special. Especially good with steamed noodles with fish or chicken.

Pair with

Use to dress meat, fish, oysters and vegetables, or as a dipping sauce for tempura (pp. 187, 580) or dumplings (see pp. 231, 342, 500).

Fresh ponzu

Ponzu is a citrus-based condiment (often with soy sauce) that is used for dressings, marinades and as a dipping sauce. The original leans heavily on yuzu, a citrus fruit that looks a bit like a small bumpy grapefruit and is a hybrid between a mandarin and a tart Chinese lemon-like fruit called ichang papeda. While Japan has embraced the yuzu, it is originally from China. Yuzu is not always easy to find, so I have improvised and used a mix of more accessible citrus fruits to achieve a similar result. You can sweeten the finished sauce with mirin to taste, which is quite traditional. **Makes about 600 ml (20½ fl oz)**

4 oranges
2 lemons
2 limes
1 grapefruit

600 ml (20½ fl oz) Japanese light soy sauce
5 × 10 cm (2 × 4 in) piece of kombu

15 g (½ oz) katsuobushi (bonito flakes)

Wash all the citrus thoroughly, then slice the oranges, lemons and limes into very fine rounds, and the grapefruit into very fine half-moons. Add to a bowl with the soy sauce, kombu and bonito, mixing together gently, then infuse overnight in the fridge.

The next day, strain the mixture through a fine-mesh sieve, pressing gently to extract as much liquid as possible without actually squeezing the fruit. Discard the solids.

The ponzu will keep in an airtight container in the fridge for up to 1 month.

Goma dare (sesame dressing) ⒼⒻ Ⓥ ⓋⒼ

This fabulously rich and nutty Japanese sauce can be used with all manner of hot and chilled dishes, from vegetables, tofu and noodles to pork, beef, chicken and fish. **Makes about 600 ml (20½ fl oz)**

125 ml (4 fl oz/½ cup) tamari
100 g (3½ oz/⅔ cup) sesame
  seeds, lightly toasted (see
  p. 371)
80 ml (2½ fl oz/⅓ cup) rice
  vinegar

juice of ½ lemon
3 tablespoons mirin
3 tablespoons caster
  (superfine) sugar
2½ tablespoons water
2 tablespoons sesame oil

2 tablespoons sake
1 tablespoon tahini

Blitz all the ingredients in a blender. The dressing will keep in an airtight container in the fridge for up to 7 days.

Pair with

Horenso gomaae (p. 561).

Use to dress cooked or raw vegetables.

Spoon over fish, chicken or pork.

Toss through hot or chilled noodles.

Serve with fried tofu or chilled silken tofu.

Serve alongside grilled skewers of meat, pork, prawns (shrimp), poultry or vegetables.

Soy, sesame & apple vinaigrette Ⓥ ⓋⒼ

I picked up this recipe while holidaying with a Japanese friend, taking mental notes of ingredients and ratios as she quickly threw the vinaigrette together. So, I guess I pinched it, really! Like most recipes acquired this way, this is naturally steps away from hers, but the principle of the apple taking up the dressing and adding its own sweet tartness is the same. The quantity here is sufficient to dress a salad for six, but can also be scaled down.
Makes about 185 ml (6 fl oz/¾ cup)

3 tablespoons light soy
  sauce, or tamari
2 tablespoons brown-rice
  vinegar

1 tablespoon extra-virgin
  olive oil
3 teaspoons caster
  (superfine) sugar

½ teaspoon sesame seeds
1 green apple, peeled and
  finely grated

Combine the soy sauce, vinegar, oil, sugar and sesame seeds in a bowl, then toss the apple through. Use immediately.

Pair with

Use as a dressing for a Japanese-inspired salad of raw vegetables and leaves. A great combination is finely shredded daikon, carrot, cabbage, sliced cherry tomatoes, snow peas (mangetout), sugar-snap peas, oak leaf lettuce and edamame.

Toasted sesame & miso dressing Ⓥ ⓋⒼ

This dressing has a lovely rich nuttiness that is perfect with blanched or grilled greens, tofu or fish. **Makes about 250 ml (8½ fl oz/1 cup)**

80 g (2¾ oz/½ cup) sesame
  seeds
3 tablespoons mirin
80 g (2¾ oz) white or brown
  miso paste

80 ml (2½ fl oz/⅓ cup)
  brown-rice vinegar
1 tablespoon raw sugar

100 ml (3½ fl oz) Dashi
  (p. 53), Vegetable stock
  (p. 51), or water

Toast the sesame seeds in a small frying pan over a medium heat until golden, about 3 minutes.

Using a small food processor or mortar and pestle, blitz or pound the sesame seeds into a paste. Add the mirin, miso paste, vinegar and sugar, then gradually work in the stock.

The dressing will be creamy and on the runny side. It will keep in the fridge for 2 weeks.

Pair with

Spoon over freshly cooked greens that still have a bit of crunch, or drizzle over wilted spinach.

Pair with bitter leaves such as chicory (witlof/endive) or radicchio.

Use to dress grains and sprouts.

Spoon over grilled fish.

Serve with grilled corn or asparagus and shiitake mushrooms.

Spoon over crispy fried tofu.

Spring onion oil (GF) (V) (VG)

Use this very simple but deeply flavoured oil as a condiment or a finishing dressing. **Makes about 150 ml (5 fl oz)**

Pair with

Spoon over sliced raw fish, or cooked oily fish such as trout, salmon or mackerel.

Use as a condiment for ramen noodles or White-poached chicken (p. 230).

Use as a finishing oil for noodle dishes, soups, braises and dumplings (see pp. 231, 342, 500).

5 spring onions (scallions), white and pale green parts finely chopped	2 tablespoons finely grated fresh ginger ½ teaspoon salt flakes	1 teaspoon sesame oil 70 ml (2¼ fl oz) grapeseed oil

Using a mortar and pestle, grind the spring onion, ginger and salt together, then add the sesame oil and grind until you have a rough paste.

Heat the grapeseed oil in a small saucepan until smoking. Pour the oil over the paste and stir through. Stand for at least 5 minutes before using; it will pick up more flavour if left longer.

The oil will keep in an airtight container in the fridge for up to 7 days.

Chilli & ginger dumpling dipping sauce (V) (VG)

This is my go-to dumpling dipping sauce for seafood, pork, chicken or vegetable dumplings. **Makes 125 ml (4 fl oz/½ cup)**

Pair with

Pork & prawn wontons (p. 342).

Prawn, corn & shiitake pot-sticker dumplings (p. 500).

Pork, wombok & ginger dumplings (see p. 500).

1 tablespoon julienned fresh ginger 1 long red chilli, finely sliced	3 tablespoons light soy sauce 1 tablespoon rice vinegar	1 teaspoon caster (superfine) sugar ½ teaspoon sesame oil

Combine all the ingredients in a small bowl. Best used on the day.

Soy vinaigrette (V) (VG)

Here's a super-versatile dressing to have in your repertoire. It's big on flavour but couldn't be simpler. **Makes about 250 ml (8½ fl oz/1 cup)**

Pair with

Dumplings (see pp. 231, 342, 500).

Noodles.

Use to finish cooked green vegetables, fish, meat, poultry or rice, and to dress Asian salads.

Tamari-boosted all-round vinaigrette (GF) (V) (VG)

Combine 60 ml (2 fl oz/¼ cup) extra-virgin olive oil and 1 tablespoon each of red- or white-wine vinegar, tamari and lemon juice. Use to dress greens, leaves or herbs of any type. Add crunchy seeds if you like.

125 ml (4 fl oz/½ cup) rice vinegar	100 ml (3½ fl oz) light soy sauce	2 teaspoons sesame oil

Mix the ingredients until well combined. The vinaigrette will keep in an airtight container in the fridge for up to 2 weeks.

Make it different

Dial up the heat and flavour by adding a finely grated thumb-sized piece of fresh ginger, a finely chopped red bird's eye chilli, and togarashi and lemon juice to taste.

Satay sauce

Satay is an Indonesian dish of grilled skewered proteins served with condiments. This is a slightly easier satay sauce than other recipes you might find, and readily achievable with a well-stocked pantry. Well, that's how this one came about, as my family – me excluded, of course – has an extremely annoying habit of opening new jars of peanut butter when there is already one open. One day, I found five jars with modest yet meaningful amounts of peanut butter in them, so this version of satay sauce was born.

Makes about 500 ml (17 fl oz/2 cups)

½ white onion, finely diced
3 garlic cloves, finely sliced
1½ lemongrass stems, white part only, finely sliced
3 red bird's eye chillies, finely chopped
40 g (1½ oz) fresh galangal, or ginger, peeled and chopped

2 teaspoons coriander seeds
½ teaspoon shrimp paste
1½ tablespoons coconut oil
40 g (1½ oz) grated palm sugar (jaggery), or brown sugar, plus extra as needed
1½ teaspoons ground white pepper

2 teaspoons kecap manis
3 teaspoons fish sauce, plus extra as needed
250 g (9 oz/1 cup) crunchy peanut butter
250 ml (8½ fl oz/1 cup) coconut milk
juice of 1 lime

Blitz the onion, garlic, lemongrass, chilli, galangal and coriander seeds in a food processor, then add the shrimp paste and blitz again until smooth.

Heat the coconut oil in a saucepan over a medium heat, then add the paste and fry for about 4 minutes, until fragrant.

Stir in the sugar, pepper, kecap manis, fish sauce, peanut butter and coconut milk to combine, then bring to a simmer. Reduce the heat to low and simmer for 5 minutes to make a smooth sauce. If too stiff, add a little water to thin out.

Adjust with more fish sauce and sugar if needed. Add the lime juice just before serving warm.

This sauce will keep for about a week in the fridge. Reheat and freshen with more lime juice just before serving.

Pair with

Skewers of meat, seafood such as prawns (shrimp), vegetables, tofu, tempeh – grilled hot (preferably over a real fire) to get a little char and gentle smokiness, served with lime wedges.

Balinese-style chicken skewers (below).

Use as a dressing for salads such as Gado gado (p. 478).

Use as a dipping sauce for rice paper rolls or raw vegetables.

Steamed rice.

Balinese-style chicken skewers

Make a marinade by combining the following in a large bowl: 3 finely chopped garlic cloves, ½ lemongrass stem (white part only), finely sliced, 1 tablespoon grapeseed oil, 1 tablespoon kecap manis, 1 tablespoon grated palm sugar (jaggery), 1 tablespoon light soy sauce, 1 tablespoon fish sauce, 1 tablespoon roughly ground coriander seeds, 2 teaspoons ground white pepper and ½ teaspoon ground turmeric. Cut 800 g (1 lb 12 oz) boneless chicken thighs into 3 cm (1¼ in) dice, then toss in the marinade. Marinate in the fridge for 2 hours, or overnight depending on how strong you want the flavours. When ready to cook, heat a barbecue chargrill plate on medium–high. Thread the chicken pieces onto the skewers (if using bamboo skewers, soak them in water first, for at least 15 minutes). Grill for about 3–5 minutes on each side, until charred and cooked through. Serve warm, with 1 × quantity Satay sauce (p. 104) on the side.

Thai caramel sauce for fish

Pair with

This sauce is designed for fish, but is just as good on fried or grilled chicken, or spooned over deep-fried or steamed eggplant (aubergine).

You can also eat it on its own over steamed rice and greens.

This is classically sweet, salty, sour and hot, as Thai sauces typically are, but there's a level of richness and depth of flavour in the caramel that makes it engagingly spicy and somewhat decadent. It can be used to dress almost any fish, whole or fillets, pan-fried, baked or grilled. Just support the dish with a salad showcasing an array of herbs – Thai basil, coriander (cilantro), mint, Vietnamese mint. **Makes about 500 ml (17 fl oz/2 cups)**

300 g (10½ oz) caster (superfine) sugar
100 ml (3½ fl oz) water
400 g (14 oz) cherry tomatoes, cut in half
2 garlic cloves, smashed

12 red bird's eye chillies, finely sliced
2 lemongrass stems, white part only, sliced on a steep angle

2½ tablespoons tom yum paste
8 small dried shrimp
6 lime leaves
2½ tablespoons fish sauce
juice of 3 limes

Add the sugar and water to a saucepan. Bring to a simmer over a medium heat and cook, without stirring, until the mixture turns a medium–dark caramel, 6–8 minutes.

Remove from the heat and stir the tomatoes through. The caramel will seize a little, but just put the pan back on the heat and add the garlic, chilli, lemongrass, tom yum paste, shrimp and lime leaves, then stir to combine. Once simmering, add the fish sauce and simmer until the tomatoes start to soften, 2–3 minutes.

Set aside to cool a little, then stir in the lime juice. (If you add the lime while it's still very hot, it will cook the lime flavour and you'll lose the vital freshness.)

This sauce is best served straightaway, but it will keep in the fridge for several days if necessary. Gently reheat to use, refreshing with more lime juice before serving.

Also see

Linguine with prawns & broad beans **433**

Orecchiette with broccoli & cime di rape **444**

Pasta alla Norma **521**

Malloreddus with prawns & fennel **526**

Pasta with fresh tomato sauce **658**

Gnocchi with leek & gorgonzola **602**

Genovese salad **624**

Zucchini & pesto pasta **674**

Pasta

Pasta

Pasta was the fast food of my youth. As soon as I could, at about eleven or twelve years old, I would chop an onion and a little garlic, fry them in oil, add tinned tomatoes and simmer for just as long as it took the pasta to cook: spaghetti, spirali or penne with a handful of grated parmesan tossed through. It was either that or ratatouille I was making.

Some of my earliest memories are of loitering in the kitchen and sneakily pulling the sheets of pasta stuck to tea towels (dish towels) laid out on benches as my mother was making lasagne or cannelloni with ricotta, tomato and peas. When I started cooking seriously, I was given a pasta machine. On the weekends, I'd make rolled egg pasta for pappardelle and ricotta ravioli. I was more obsessed with the rolling of the dough than making sauces, as pasta tossed simply with butter and parmesan, or sugo with fresh basil and olives, was so good. And that's all the rest of the family wanted to eat.

Over time, I realised that the pasta is always king, and it should never be swamped and lost. But more than that, it was also important to understand the essential relationship between the sauce and the pasta, that they need to unite before serving. Sauce is not just a coating. Done properly, the sauce is absorbed into the pasta and clings to it. The addition of some pasta cooking water helps this, with its starchy content and flavour contributing to the sauce, thickening and emulsifying it.

I use three general types of pasta. First and foremost dried pasta, and that's not just for convenience; it is unmatched with certain sauces. Then, if I'm making my own, I use either a simple dough of semolina and flour, water and salt (p. 131), or an egg-based dough enriched with extra yolks (p. 111). The former is for making pasta more typical of southern and central Italy, while the latter is more classically from the north. Generalise about Italy at your peril, of course – but it's not a bad way to think about some of the classic sauces; oily, tomato-based sauces and salty, sharp ingredients such as olives, anchovies, capers, guanciale or pancetta are a better fit for dried pasta or a simple semolina dough, while those that lean more on butter or dairy are more suited to an egg dough. And ragù, well ragù is made everywhere, but if you insist on calling that ragù a bolognese, then tradition dictates pairing it with a wide-ribbon egg pasta – though, in truth, ridged short pasta or gnocchi are both fabulous with that most famous of meat sauces.

In the north of Italy, the flour traditionally employed was softer, with lower protein, while the durum wheat from the south is hard and loaded with protein. Wheat flour has several proteins, but the major one is gluten, or more accurately glutenin and gliadin, which make up about 80 per cent of the protein content of flour. Although gluten has a fairly bad reputation, it's responsible for so many of the qualities we love. It helps give pasta its bite and uniquely elastic textural chew, and is responsible for the structure in bread. When wet, it forms longer molecular chains, which are stronger and more elastic the higher the gluten content. Those expertly airy loaves of sourdough with their glassy crusts are the product of high-protein flours – and a whole lot of skill.

This explains why, traditionally, the soft wheat flour of northern Italy required the binding agent of eggs in pasta, while in the south it did not. Naturally, the egg content of the best egg pasta is not solely built around the need for a binding agent, with an alarming amount of yolks going into the best golden pasta. Indeed, that necessity has been extrapolated into an artform. Today, durum wheat, which is the hardest of wheat varieties, is grown right across Italy, though the best is still said to come from the south. Durum wheat is not easy to grind into a fine flour – though it can be – and is generally milled into a sandy grain made from the middle or endosperm of the wheat, called semolina.

Italy is awash with pasta types, and often very similar shapes carry very different names. Whenever I think I have come across most of them, after having cooked obsessively for over three decades, a few more will pop into view, making me feel quite uneducated on the matter. I will leave the chronicling of this to some brilliant fanatics who are already on the job.

Spaghetti is one of my favourite dried pasta shapes – but not for bolognese. It is best for slick, oil-based and tomato-based sauces, but nothing too chunky, as everything slides off; you need sauces that cling, such as carbonara, puttanesca (see p. 117) and aglio e olio (pp. 122–3). And the same for spaghettini. It is slightly finer than spaghetti, so the sauces should always be a little finer for the sauce to sit comfortably with the pasta. Bucatini is a fat tubular pasta with a hole all the way down the middle, and bigoli is equally chunky but sans hole, while fusilli lunghi is like spaghetti with a corkscrew twist.

Dried short tubes – penne, maccheroni, rigatoni – trap chunky sauces, while the fancier shapes that I like are farfalle, fusilli, orecchiette and strozzapreti, which can be bought dried and also made with a simple semolina dough. And then there is pastina, tiny pasta of various shapes – orzo, stelline, risoni, farfalline – which are used in soups or for children, cooked in broth and tossed in butter and cheese, and sometimes served with seafood stews or broth-like dishes.

When buying imported dried pasta, 100 per cent Italian durum wheat is the first thing I look for, then it's the use of bronze extruding dies. Mass-produced commercial pasta is extruded through non-stick dies, creating a glassy exterior, which is perfect if you want your sauce to slide straight off. I do not. Traditional bronze extruding dies make for a rougher surface, which helps the sauce cling to the pasta. When dried, this pasta will also sometimes have a powdery coating when handled, as opposed to the glossy sheen of generic pasta. With mass-produced pasta, the transfer of starch to the cooking water isn't as effective either, so the water isn't as good at bringing sauce and pasta together. In other words, the elements that are meant to meld in the finished dish stay separate.

In Italy, durum wheat is mandated by law in the production of dried pasta, but it doesn't have to be Italian wheat. And, naturally, not all Italian wheat is created equal. It's good to become familiar with brands that yield better results, and you will inevitably pay a premium for the best ones. That premium is justified, though, as the finest makers employ the best wheat, use traditional production methods and dry the pasta slowly, which improves both the flavour and the texture of the cooked pasta.

Although it has become a cheap mass-produced food, the slow-food properties of artisanal pasta need to be understood and respected. And when you consider the oft-repeated mantra that a bowl of pasta is about the pasta first and the sauce second, then it is not the place to skimp. In the best pasta, the nutty flavour of the durum wheat is quite apparent, as is the inherent quality of the ingredients and their production methods. And while the skilful cook always unifies sauce and pasta, good pasta always retains its distinct identity. Buy quality, support the preservation of traditional ways and reap the – significant – rewards.

Preparing pasta

When cooking pasta, dried or fresh, a lot of water is needed so that it returns to a rapid boil quickly and the pasta doesn't clump, creating uneven cooking conditions. The water also needs to be well salted. Poorly seasoned pasta water will leave your dish dull and flat, but well-seasoned water will bring out the flavour of the pasta itself and enhance the dish immeasurably. It's often said the water should be salty like the ocean, and I was even taught that it should taste like the Mediterranean. Now that's specific. The Mediterranean is actually quite a salty body of water at 3.8 per cent salinity, or thereabouts, but I think the reference had more to do with evoking an Italian context. Either way, closer to 1 per cent or a little more is enough, so not nearly as salty as any ocean, let alone the Mediterranean, but still quite salty. I never measure it, however, just season the water generously by feel.

There are also a couple of persistent myths that perhaps are worth addressing. There is no need to add salt just as the water boils, as some insist for consistency or to increase the boil. Coarse salt added at the start and left to sit on the base of the pot can pit stainless steel cookware, but it doesn't affect the actual cooking – so if using heavy salt crystals or rock salt, it's best to add these once the water is boiling to dissolve quickly to protect your pot, but not for any culinary reason. The other myth is probably long dispelled, but just in case: adding oil to the water to stop the pasta sticking serves absolutely no function.

When cooking dried pasta, taking a minute or so off the prescribed time is a good idea, then taste for doneness. Naturally, we're looking for the pasta to be al dente – with some bite – but I almost always finish pasta in the sauce on the stovetop, unless tossing with Pesto (p. 90), a crab and herb sauce (see p. 125) or the like. So, the pasta being marginally underdone is ideal, as it will continue to cook to the right degree while the sauce is taken up and reduces a little to get the right balance.

Once your timing is refined, it's easiest to either use tongs (for long pasta) or a sieve or large slotted spoon (for short pasta) to transfer the pasta to the sauce. This will bring enough cooking water with it to add some starch to thicken and emulsify the sauce as you toss, and you can always ladle a little more, if required. Naturally, you can also drain the pasta and simply reserve some of the water to use. Whichever method, when you first add the pasta, the sauce may seem a little separate, even a little watery, but soon enough, as you toss – or fold with a spoon or tongs – the sauce will start to cling and look glossy. A little oil or butter can help here, too.

While egg pasta may have traditionally employed softer flours, durum wheat – often ground to '00' fineness – is commonly used, and gives the pasta characteristic bite. I find this component of durum wheat to be key, so when making pasta I use a mix of standard '00' wheat flour and fine semolina (ground from durum flour), which provides both bite and a silky texture. In fact, semolina combined with plain (all-purpose) flour will yield a fine result, too, but I wouldn't use a low-protein soft cake flour. I try to source semolina ground as finely as possible, which always has a yellow hue. Australia now produces world-class durum semolina, but it is currently less available than Italian imports, so I use either one. (Our production of world-class dried pasta is still lagging – but, as with olive oil, that's hopefully only a matter of time.)

When making egg pasta, you will always have some scraps – offcuts too small to make ribbons from, or quite a bit of waste from cutting out ravioli or tortellini, especially if being ultra-precise. None of this should ever be wasted. I'll usually cook the scraps then and there, toss them in butter – or a ragù I have bubbling away – and top with a cloud of finely grated parmesan and a good grind of pepper. There's usually a small crowd by then, or a small crowd of small people to be precise, and little bowls are devoured and mopped clean with bread. If there's enough, I'll dry the pasta scraps on a tray in the pantry, then add to a plain chicken or vegetable stock, Left-over chicken & barley broth (p. 252), Chicken noodle broth (p. 253) instead of the noodles, or Stracciatella soup (p. 55), or cook off and toss in sugo for a snack during the week.

A note on cheese

Like the pasta itself, the cheese you use with your pasta is crucial. Parmigiano Reggiano is expensive, and many would object to it being used on pasta, deferring to the simpler and less expensive Grana Padano, but I like to use it when its intensity and nutty umami depth is required. A very simple pasta benefits from the flavour, as does one where indulgence is the theme, such as with truffles (see p. 119). It's really up to you and your budget.

Keep in mind, too, that not all Grana and Parmigiano is created equal, with better examples of the former exceeding lesser examples of the latter, and lesser examples of Grana undeserving of the name and the mark of approval. Use your senses, not the name. Taste, and buy accordingly.

Pecorino Romano is another cheese you can use, but it has a tangier, more robust and more assertive character. I tend not to use it often, though it can work with more southern-style pastas with wilted bitter greens and the like – and many would regard an Amatriciana (p. 121) or Cacio e pepe (p. 120) to be imposters made with anything other than Pecorino Romano.

A cucina povera alternative to cheese, Pangrattato (p. 123) is not cheese at all but rather fried breadcrumbs. It is wonderful on pasta dishes with oil-based sauces, or with seafood dishes where cheese would clash.

Egg pasta dough ⓥ

This is my ideal all-round egg-pasta dough, which I use for all kinds of applications: lasagne, cannelloni, tagliatelle, pappardelle and any filled pasta. A mix of '00' flour and semolina gives it a silkiness as well as a pleasing bite tension. Many recipes call for more yolks, and less (or no) whole egg, and while I can admire the deeply coloured yolk-rich result, I don't find it necessary. Plus, I shudder at the waste of discarding all those egg whites. After all, there are only so many meringues you can make, and so many egg-white omelettes you can suffer through. Naturally, egg whites can be frozen, but if, like me, your pasta-to-meringue consumption ratio is heavily tilted to the former, then this is a piece of self-deception, simply delaying the waste. I only ever make this dough in a food processor, as I'm always in a hurry, but the classic method will naturally work, too. **Serves 6–8**

350 g (12½ oz/2⅓ cups) plain (all-purpose) '00' flour
300 g (10½ oz) fine semolina, plus extra for dusting

½ teaspoon salt flakes
5 × 70 g (2½ oz) eggs, plus 4 egg yolks (310 g/11 oz total weight)

1 tablespoon extra-virgin olive oil

Special equipment
Pasta machine (recommended)

To make in a food processor
Add the dry ingredients to the food processor. In a jug, beat the eggs, egg yolks and oil with a fork, then, with the machine running, pour into the feed tube of the processor in a continuous stream. After about 1 minute, once the mixture comes together like very wet sand, turn the dough out onto the bench and press together into a ball. Seal in an airtight container and rest at room temperature for about 45 minutes.

To make by hand

Combine the dry ingredients on the bench, making a well in the centre. Add the eggs, egg yolks and oil to the well. Break the yolks up, then gradually bring the flour into the egg mixture with your fingers. Once incorporated into a dough (you may need to moisten your hands to bring the last of it together), knead with the heel of your hand by pressing the dough down and away from you, then pulling back over itself. Knead for about 10 minutes, rotating the dough as you do, until springy and firm. Seal in an airtight container and rest on the bench for 45 minutes.

To roll out the dough

This will probably offend some traditionalists (though I've probably already accomplished that by using a food processor), but I always use a pasta machine to roll the dough. It's what I've always used professionally, and it's what I use at home. Maybe my days with a textured wooden board and long rolling pin will come, but a pasta machine is a great way to get an excellent and very consistent result. But if you're experienced, there is nothing stopping you using this basic recipe for rolling by hand.

Cut the rested dough into four even pieces, then flatten out one piece as much as possible with your hands. Set the pasta machine so that the rollers are at their widest setting, then pass the dough through the machine. Don't force it – roll it out flatter with a rolling pin, if needed, to make it fit more easily. Fold the rolled pasta in two, then feed through again, leading with the folded edge, before feeding through once more. The action of rolling strengthens the gluten, and the dough will shrink back a little. Repeat with the other pieces of dough, laying the sheets flat on the bench. Cover the rolled dough with slightly damp tea towels (dish towels).

Reduce the thickness by two turns of the dial, then repeat the process again twice for each piece of dough. This process of folding and rolling is called laminating, and it strengthens and smooths the dough.

Turn the dial down one more setting and feed each piece through without folding. Cutting the sheets in half now can make the next stage a little easier to handle. Turn down the dial with each pass so the pasta becomes thinner, smoother and longer, being careful to support the sheets as they lengthen, to avoid breaking or sticking together.

Once the pasta is the desired thickness, sprinkle with a fine dusting of semolina to stop the pasta sticking together. You want the pasta sheets to be 2–3 mm (⅛–⅙ in) thick if making long pasta such as linguine, fettuccine, pappardelle or tagliatelle, and 1–2 mm (⅙ in) thick if using the sheets for lasagne or a filled pasta such as ravioli or tortellini. Stack the sheets overlapping, rather than directly on top of each other. Cover with damp tea towels to stop the sheets drying out, and cut to the desired shape immediately.

To make linguine or fettuccine

Roll the pasta sheets 2–3 mm (⅛–⅙ in) thick. Cut into 30 cm (12 in) lengths and run through the appropriate setting on the pasta cutter attachment. (The pasta machine will have two sets of roller cutters. Run the sheets through the finer cutter for linguine, or through the wider setting for fettuccine.) Gently pull the pasta strands apart and either hang them over a suspended dowel (or pasta hanger, if you have one), or dust with semolina and transfer to a tray, spreading them out so they're not piled up.

To make pappardelle or tagliatelle

Roll the pasta sheets 2–3 mm (⅛–⅙ in) thick. Cut into 30 cm (12 in) lengths and dust with a little semolina. Stack the sheets four high, then cut into 2–3 cm (¾/1¼ in) widths for pappardelle, or 8 mm–1.5 cm (⅓–½ in) for tagliatelle. You can fold the sheets over to make the cutting easier, but I prefer to cut them flat. Gently pull the pasta strands apart and either hang them over a suspended dowel (or pasta hanger, if you have one), or dust with semolina and transfer to a tray, spreading them out so they're not piled up.

To store long pasta: Dry the pasta strands for 1 hour after cutting. Divide the pasta into parcels of about 150 g (5½ oz) and roll the strands around your hand to make loose bundles. Place on a tray, cover with a tea towel and refrigerate. The pasta will keep for 3 days like this.

Alternatively, you can dry the strands on a drying rack or dowel for 3–4 hours, until firm enough to slide off the rack. Once firm, pile on a tray, cover with a tea towel and store in the pantry or cupboard. The pasta will last for 5–7 days, depending on humidity. It would potentially keep for longer, but I find it gets brittle after a while, and tends to break into pieces – which is not what you want after going to all that trouble.

To cook long pasta: Cook in plenty of boiling salted water for 3–3½ minutes until al dente. Lift directly from the water into the pan with your sauce, with the cooking water thickening and glossing.

To make large ravioli

Roll the pasta sheets 1–2 mm (⅛ in) thick. Cut into strips 10 cm (4 in) wide. Brush half of one piece with beaten egg white, then place 1 tablespoon of your chosen filling on top of the egg wash in the middle. Fold the top over and press the pasta together all around the filling, pushing the air out with your fingers. Seal firmly, then cut along the three joined edges with a fluted pastry cutter or sharp knife, leaving an even pasta border around the filling. Repeat with the remaining pasta and filling.

To make small ravioli (agnolotti)

Roll the pasta sheets 1–2 mm (⅛ in) thick. Lay out a 40 cm (15¾ in) length of pasta sheet on the bench. Brush half the length with beaten egg white, then dot 1½ teaspoons of filling at regular 4.5 cm (1¾ in) intervals all the way up the length of the sheet. Fold the top over and press the pasta together all around the filling, pushing the air out with your fingers. Cut the long joined edge with a pastry cutter or sharp knife, then cut to separate the ravioli. Repeat until all the pasta and filling is used.

To store ravioli. The ravioli can be refrigerated on a tray dusted with semolina until ready to use. They will keep for a day or so, but are best cooked as soon as possible. See below for information on freezing filled pasta.

To cook ravioli. Cook in plenty of boiling salted water for 2½–3 minutes for small parcels, and about 4 minutes for larger ones. If cooking from frozen (see below), add about 3 minutes to the cooking time.

To make tortellini or tortelloni

Roll the pasta sheets 1–2 mm (⅛ in) thick. Use a round pasta cutter or pastry cutter to cut as many circles out of your rolled pasta sheets as you can. Tortellini are the smaller of the two types – little pasta dumplings where the tips of the filled and folded pasta are brought together to form a ring shape – though the method for making them is the same. Tortellini are best for intensely flavoured meat fillings and perfect for serving in broth, while the larger tortelloni are typically filled with things such as spinach and cheese or pumpkin (winter squash) – although those fillings work well in tortellini, too. The only rule I adhere to is to not use intense meat fillings for large filled pasta. For tortelloni, I typically use an 8–10 cm (3¼–4 in) cutter but up to 12 cm (4¾ in) also works; I scale down to 5 cm (2 in) for very small tortellini. Lightly brush one edge of each round with egg white. For an 8–10 cm (3¼–4 in) round, pipe or spoon 1 tablespoon of filling into the middle; for a 5 cm (2 in) round, use 1½ teaspoons of filling. Fold the pasta over so that the edges meet, pressing together to seal, squeezing out any air. You will now have a semicircle of pasta with the centre filled. With the straight edge facing you, bring the opposing tips (where the straight edge meets the curved one) together, being careful not to split the pasta as you do. Overlap the ends and press together to secure, then place on a tray dusted with semolina. Repeat with the remaining pasta rounds and filling, covering with a tea towel to stop them drying out while you finish forming the rest.

To cook tortellini & tortelloni. Cook tortellini in plenty of boiling salted water for 2–3 minutes, and tortelloni for about 4 minutes, before adding them to your serving sauce. They can also be refrigerated on a tray dusted with semolina until ready to use. They will keep for a day or so but are best cooked as soon as possible and then reheated in sauce if necessary.

To freeze filled pasta. I'm not big on freezing filled pasta, especially larger ones, as they can crack. You would need to set them out on trays dusted with semolina and then, once frozen, wrap individually with plastic wrap (not ideal) to protect against chipping and freezer burn. It's better to freeze small ravioli or tortellini, as they fare substantially better. After being frozen on trays, they can be batched into convenient serving portions in airtight containers or freezer bags. Cook from frozen, adding about 3 minutes to the cooking time.

Tortelloni with pumpkin, sage & mustard fruits, with burnt butter sauce ⓥ

This is a version of the classic pumpkin filling from the north of Italy, with a balance of both sweet and savoury richness. Roasting the pumpkin yields a richer, drier and more full-flavoured filling, perfumed gently with warm spices. The mustard fruits can be omitted, but they dial up that savoury sweetness and add a gentle heat that is superb with the pumpkin. **Serves 6–8**

1.5 kg (3 lb 5 oz) jap or kent pumpkin (winter squash), skin on, cut into thick wedges

2 teaspoons ground cinnamon

2½ tablespoons extra-virgin olive oil

2 garlic cloves, finely grated

½ bunch of sage, leaves finely chopped

1½ teaspoons ground allspice

100 g (3½ oz) parmesan, finely grated

25 g (1 oz/⅓ cup) fresh breadcrumbs

50 g (1¾ oz) mustard fruits, very finely chopped

1 teaspoon salt flakes

1 × quantity Egg pasta sheets (p. 111)

2 × quantities Burnt butter sauce with lemon, capers & parsley (p. 73)

Staples
EVOO, S&P

Preheat the oven to 170°C (340°F) fan-forced. Line a baking tray with baking paper.

Coat the pumpkin with oil, season with salt and pepper, then rub half the cinnamon over. Lay the wedges on the baking tray and roast for about 60 minutes, until tender. Set aside to cool, then scoop the flesh from the skin into a bowl. Mash with a fork, then drain in a colander for 30 minutes, until quite dry. The mixture should weigh 800–900 g (1 lb 12 oz–2 lb).

Heat the oil in a small frying pan over a medium heat. Fry the garlic, sage, allspice and remaining cinnamon until fragrant, about 1 minute. Tip the mixture into the mashed pumpkin, along with the parmesan, breadcrumbs and mustard fruits. Combine well, adjusting the seasoning as needed. If you'd like a super-smooth filling, blitz the mixture in a blender or food processor.

Chill for 1 hour, then transfer to a piping (icing) bag fitted with a large nozzle. Chill again until needed.

Shape and fill the tortelloni as directed (see p. 113).

Cook the pasta in boiling salted water for about 4 minutes while making the sauce. Lift the tortelloni from the water directly into the pan of sauce, toss through to coat and serve immediately.

Roast meat tortellini

This is a superb way to use up leftovers from a roast, with meat, root vegetables and any gnarly caramelised bits all contributing to the mix and to its success. Any roast will do, whether lamb, pork, beef or chicken, just as long as it has a northern Mediterranean accent and it's slow-cooked or pink, as rare meat will not yield the right result. This is one of those dishes where it's wise to plan for some roast leftovers by over-catering a little. A filling like this is suitable for smaller filled pasta, such as tortellini or agnolotti, as it is too intensely flavoured for large parcels. And as the flavour is more intense, keep the accompanying sauce simple or the broth light. Tiny hand-made pasta parcels may be a labour of love, but they taste like heaven to me. **Serves 6–8 (Makes about 45 tortellini or agnolotti)**

Mortadella agnolotti

Fry 350 g (12½ oz) minced (ground) veal or pork in a splash of oil over a medium heat until caramelised, about 10 minutes. Season with salt and pepper and set aside to cool. (Alternatively, you could use 250 g/9 oz roasted left-over meat). In a food processor, blitz the meat, 150 g (5½ oz) mortadella cut into 1 cm (½ in) dice and 1 egg white to a fine paste. Add 100 g (3½ oz/1 cup) finely grated Grana Padano, 100 g (3½ oz/1¼ cups) fresh breadcrumbs, 2 teaspoons dried oregano, ½ teaspoon ground black pepper and ¼ nutmeg, finely grated, or 1 teaspoon ground nutmeg and pulse until combined. Tip into a bowl and adjust the seasoning as needed. Transfer the mixture to a piping (icing) bag fitted with a 1 cm (½ in) nozzle, or use two teaspoons to portion. Don't chill unless using later, as the mixture will firm up and be hard to handle. Using 1 × quantity Egg pasta sheets (p. 111), shape and fill the agnolotti as directed (see p. 113). Cook the agnolotti in plenty of boiling salted water for 2½–3 minutes. Serve with your choice of sauce. Serves 6–8 (makes about 45 tortellini or agnolotti).

Pair with

Alfredo sauce (see p. 119).

Simple tomato sugo (p. 116).

Roasted tomato passata (p. 660).

Serve in a seasoned broth made with Golden chicken stock (p. 54).

Agnolotti del plin

This is one of Piedmont's most famous dishes, with the small parcels – meat-filled ravioli, essentially – pinched (plin means 'pinch' in the local dialect) together along the cut edges, forming a small pocket. The fillings vary greatly, with the sauce typically simply melted butter or a little sauce made from braising stock.

1 × quantity Egg pasta sheets (p. 111)

Roast meat filling
400 g (14 oz) left-over roasted meat, with any caramelised bits from the roasting tin, and some root vegetables

1 egg white
100 g (3½ oz/1 cup) finely grated Grana Padano
100 g (3½ oz/1¼ cups) fresh breadcrumbs
½ teaspoon ground black pepper

¼ nutmeg, finely grated, or 1 teaspoon ground nutmeg
1 tablespoon extra-virgin olive oil
4 flat-leaf (Italian) parsley sprigs, leaves finely chopped, or 1½ teaspoons dried oregano

For the filling, blitz the meat and egg white into a fine paste using a food processor. Add the parmesan, breadcrumbs, pepper, nutmeg and oil and pulse until combined. Tip into a bowl and mix the parsley through. If your roast was properly seasoned, then this mixture will be too, but check to be sure – it should taste like a fabulous roast dinner.

Transfer the mixture to a piping (icing) bag fitted with a 1 cm (½ in) nozzle, or use two teaspoons to portion. Don't chill unless using later, as the mixture will firm up and be hard to handle.

Shape and fill the tortellini as directed (see p. 113).

Cook the tortellini in plenty of boiling salted water for 2½–3 minutes. Serve with your choice of sauce.

Mushroom tortellini (V)

Pair with

Alfredo sauce (see p. 119).

Simple tomato sugo (p. 116).

Roasted tomato passata (p. 660).

Burnt butter sauce with lemon, sage & toasted walnuts (p. 73).

Serve in a seasoned broth made with Golden chicken stock (p. 54).

This is a simple duxelles recipe enhanced with cream. You could use a mix of any meaty, fleshy mushrooms – with 100 g (3½ oz) fresh porcini (you can buy them frozen these days) a wonderful addition. I have also experimented with using some shiitake in the mix, which works well, so long as it's not the dominant flavour. Use this filling with smaller pastas. **Serves 6–8 (Makes about 45 tortellini or agnolotti)**

1 × quantity Egg pasta sheets (p. 111)

Mushroom filling
50 g (1¾ oz) butter
2½ tablespoons extra-virgin olive oil
5 French shallots, finely diced

4 garlic cloves, finely diced
400 g (14 oz) field or pine mushrooms (or a mix), finely diced
3 thyme sprigs, leaves stripped
3 teaspoons Porcini powder (p. 570)

150 ml (5 fl oz) white wine
2 tablespoons thick (double/heavy) cream

Staples
S&P

For the filling, heat the butter and oil in a frying pan over a medium heat. Sweat the shallot and garlic for 5 minutes without colouring. Add the mushrooms, thyme and porcini powder, season with salt and pepper, and fry until softened and looking quite dry, about 10 minutes.

Stir in the wine and cook until dry, about 5 minutes. Add the cream and cook until the mixture has reduced and is quite sticky, about 2 minutes.

Set aside to cool, then use two teaspoons to portion.

Shape and fill the tortellini as directed (see p. 113).

Cook the tortellini in plenty of boiling salted water for 2½–3 minutes. Serve with your choice of sauce.

Make it different
You could make large tortellini using a half quantity of the Ricotta and goat's cheese filling (see p. 117), with the whole mushroom mixture folded in. Serve with a butter and chopped parsley sauce with plenty of parmesan.

Ricotta & spinach ravioli Ⓥ

This classic ricotta and spinach filling can be used just as effectively for large or small filled pasta. **Serves 6 (Makes about 30 large ravioli)**

1 × quantity Egg pasta
  sheets (p. 111)
Ricotta & spinach filling
450 g (1 lb) English spinach,
  washed well

375 g (13 oz/1½ cups) ricotta
150 g (5½ oz/1½ cups)
  finely grated Parmigiano
  Reggiano
2 eggs, lightly beaten

3 basil or mint sprigs, leaves
  chopped
¼ nutmeg, finely grated, or
  1 teaspoon ground nutmeg

Staples
S&P

Pair with

*Melted butter, parmesan
and pepper.*

*Burnt butter sauce with lemon,
sage & toasted walnuts (p. 73).*

Simple tomato sugo (below).

*Roasted tomato passata
(p. 660).*

Puttanesca sauce (opposite).

For the filling, heat a large frying pan over a high heat. Add the spinach and a small splash of water. Cover and cook for 3 minutes, then drain in a colander. Press out any excess water, then chop roughly.

Add the spinach to a bowl, along with the remaining filling ingredients. Season with salt and pepper and combine well.

Transfer the mixture to a piping (icing) bag fitted with a 1 cm (½ in) nozzle. Chill for 30 minutes before using.

Shape and fill the ravioli as directed (see p. 113).

Cook the ravioli in plenty of boiling salted water for 2½–3 minutes for small parcels, and about 4 minutes for larger ones. Serve with your choice of sauce.

Simple tomato sugo Ⓥ ⓋⒼ

Passata is the simplest tomato sauce, being cooked sieved tomatoes, typically just with salt. A tomato sugo (Napoli) ups things a little with the addition of oil, garlic and some herbs. Some cooks add onion, but I prefer its simplicity without. I generally tweak the acidity with a little sugar, though this is not necessary if using a home-made passata made from oozingly ripe summer tomatoes. Most commercial passata or tinned tomatoes – especially if they have had citric acid added (appearing as 'acidity regulator' on the label), which sadly is most of them – need the sharpness clipped with a little sweetness. Cooking for 45 minutes is enough to reduce and concentrate the flavours; cooking down even further is ideal for a pizza sauce, but it becomes too conserve-like for most other applications. **Makes 650 ml (22 fl oz)**

150 ml (5 fl oz) extra-virgin
  olive oil
3 large garlic cloves, sliced
1.2 litres (41 fl oz) tomato
  passata (puréed tomatoes),
  3 × 400 g (14 oz) tins diced

tomatoes, or 16 roma
  (plum) tomatoes, skinned
  and sliced with seeds in
2 teaspoons dried oregano,
  or 2 basil sprigs
2 fresh bay leaves

2 teaspoons caster
  (superfine) sugar

Staples
S&P

Pair with

*Use this sugo whenever you
need a simple tomato sauce –
either as a standalone pasta
sauce with basil and a dollop of
ricotta on top, a base for another
pasta sauce such as Puttanesca
(opposite), or to dress a cheese
ravioli (opposite) or Ricotta
& spinach ravioli (above) to
highlight the filling.*

*Use a reduced version to top
pizza (see p. 857).*

*At the end of cooking, add
500 ml (17 fl oz/2 cups) White
chicken stock (p. 54) for a sauce
to cook meatballs in (see p. 337).*

*Spoon onto crumbed chicken
or veal schnitzel.*

*Use to sauce an Eggplant
parmigiana (p. 522) or Summer
vegetable lasagne (p. 136).*

*Add to a pot of mussels (see
p. 204) while they steam open.*

Heat the oil in a saucepan over a medium heat. Fry the garlic until fragrant, 1–2 minutes. Stir in the remaining ingredients (if using basil, throw in the whole stalks and fish them out at the end).

Season with salt and pepper and simmer slowly for 45 minutes to 1 hour, depending on how reduced you want the sauce. This is personal preference and also depends on what the application is. For pasta, I would cook the sauce for around 45 minutes, and for pizza just over an hour.

Ricotta & goat's cheese ravioli (V)

To make a ricotta & goat's cheese filling, combine 400 g (14 oz) ricotta and 2 lightly beaten eggs in a large bowl. Add 100 g (3½ oz/1 cup) grated Parmigiano Reggiano and ¼ nutmeg, finely grated, or 1 teaspoon ground nutmeg, season with salt and pepper and combine. Crumble in 150 g (5½ oz/1 cup) soft goat's milk or sheep's milk feta and combine – but not too smoothly. Transfer the mixture to a piping (icing) bag fitted with a 1 cm (½ in) nozzle. Chill for 30 minutes before using with 1 × quantity Egg pasta sheets (p. 111). Shape and fill the ravioli as directed (see p. 113). Cook the ravioli in plenty of boiling salted water for 2½–3 minutes for small parcels, and about 4 minutes for larger ones. Serves 6 (makes about 30 large ravioli). Great with melted butter, parmesan and pepper, Burnt butter sauce with lemon, sage & toasted walnuts (p. 73), Simple tomato sugo (opposite), Roasted tomato passata (p. 660) and Puttanesca sauce (right).

Spaghetti puttanesca

The origins of this pasta sauce are oft discussed yet rarely agreed on. That it is from the south – Campania perhaps, or maybe Sicily – is not in dispute. That it is some culinary specialty of prostitutes in the bordellos of Naples seems tenuous at best, while other claims seem credible enough, if entirely unprovable – although it's hard to imagine there is one single instance of combining anchovies, olives, capers, tomatoes and herbs to make a sauce for pasta. Such is the affinity of those ingredients, more than one cook surely stumbled over versions of it, and the similarity of that name to the Italian word for prostitute (though the somewhat vulgar but more accurate translation of puttana is 'whore') seems to be a conflation. Either way, this is one of my favourite pasta sauces, and it can be magicked out of a depleted pantry, which is something I do often. Don't be afraid with the quantity of oil here, as the sauce demands it, and it will be the poorer for skimping. **Serves 4–6**

600 g (1 lb 5 oz) dried spaghetti, bigoli, bucatini or pennette
100 g (3½ oz/1 cup) finely grated Grana Padano

Puttanesca sauce
250 ml (8½ fl oz/1 cup) extra-virgin olive oil

1 onion, very finely diced
8 garlic cloves, finely sliced
100 g (3½ oz) anchovies, finely chopped
150 g (5½ oz) black olives, pitted and chopped
80 g (2¾ oz) small capers
2 tablespoons dried oregano

2 teaspoons chilli flakes
1 teaspoon ground black pepper
200 ml (7 fl oz) white wine
1.2 litres (41 fl oz) tomato passata (puréed tomatoes)

For the sauce, heat the oil in a wide-based saucepan over a medium heat. Cook the onion and garlic until transparent and a little golden, about 5 minutes. Add the anchovies and fry until dissolved, about 2 minutes. Stir in the olives, capers, oregano, chilli flakes and pepper, then cook for about 3 minutes. Stir in the wine and reduce by half. Add the passata and simmer gently for 10 minutes.

Meanwhile, cook the pasta in plenty of boiling salted water according to the packet instructions until al dente.

Tong the pasta directly into the sauce. Toss and cook for a minute or so, adding a little pasta water if needed.

Toss all the parmesan through and cook for 2 minutes, tossing until the sauce clings to the pasta, then serve.

Fettuccine alfredo ⓥ

The sauce, much like carbonara (see below), has been dogged by an association with cream. But like proper carbonara, fettuccine alfredo does not employ cream. The sauce is basically a central tenet of pasta cookery stripped back to its barest essentials, with pasta water, cheese and butter emulsifying to make the silkiest of sauces – but the triumph of simplicity here is a true wonder. Cook 300 g (10½ oz) dried or fresh fettuccine (see p. 112) in plenty of boiling salted water until al dente – 3–3½ minutes for fresh pasta and 8–10 minutes for dried (check the packet instructions). Drain, reserving 100 ml (3½ fl oz) of the cooking water. Melt 120 g (4½ oz) unsalted butter in a large frying pan over a low heat. As it starts to soften, season with salt and pepper, then add the pasta and reserved cooking water. Toss once, then toss 100 g (3½ oz/1 cup) finely grated Parmigiano Reggiano through to melt and become creamy. Keep tossing until the pasta has a silky coating of sauce, then serve immediately. Serves 2.

Tagliatelle with egg, truffle & Parmigiano Reggiano ⓥ

Truffles are wonderful with fresh pasta, with the heat from the noodles lifting the unique fragrance in a heady cloud. Truffles are also amazing with eggs. The cheese needs to be very finely grated for this mesmerising dish, as it needs to melt into the sauce completely. Before eating, cut the egg to mix the yolk and truffle through the pasta. **Serves 4**

4 eggs
100 g (3½ oz) butter
5 garlic cloves, finely sliced
150 ml (5 fl oz) white wine
350 ml (12 fl oz) pouring (single/light) cream

½ quantity egg tagliatelle (see p. 112)
150 g (5½ oz/1½ cups) very finely grated Parmigiano Reggiano, plus extra to serve

black truffle, or white truffle (as much as your budget permits)

Staples
EVOO, S&P

In a large frying pan, fry the eggs in a generous amount of oil over a medium heat for 3–4 minutes.

While the eggs are cooking, heat half the butter and a splash of oil in a large frying pan over a medium heat. Add the garlic, season with salt and cook until turning golden, about 2 minutes. Add the wine and reduce by half. Add the cream, season with pepper and reduce by one-third.

Meanwhile, cook the pasta in boiling salted water for 3–3½ minutes.

Add the remaining butter to the sauce, then tong the pasta straight from the pot and toss through. Add the cheese and toss through to melt.

Plate the pasta. Top each serve with an egg, then shave the truffle over. Drizzle with oil, season with salt and, if you like, grate over extra Parmigiano Reggiano. Serve immediately.

Spaghetti carbonara

Carbonara is potentially the most bastardised and ardently defended pasta dish there is. I will sidestep discussing the culinary crimes committed under the carbonara banner, as they have been covered exhaustively and will continue to be. I'd rather talk about what it is rather than what it isn't. The central tenet of carbonara is a sauce composed of egg and rendered fat from some kind of cured pork; I use flat pancetta or guanciale. The eggs cook gently in the heat of the pasta, not on the stove, and emulsify into a silky, glossy coating for the pasta. Plenty of cheese and ample pepper are the other key ingredients. You'll encounter fierce opposition from some about adding garlic, but I still do. Some will be offended by the parsley, but that doesn't put me off. Others will be appalled at the use of whole eggs, rather than yolks, but they sauce the dish beautifully, and I'm not about to waste egg white from the beautiful, pasture-raised eggs that I pay very good money for. Some will dispute the use of Parmigiano Reggiano, rather than Pecorino Romano (it is a Roman dish, after all) – but, for me, its nutty luxury can't be beaten. And then there are the pasta varieties. Spaghetti appears to be traditional, though macaroni mounts a formidable case. And, in truth, a fresh or dried egg pasta, tagliatelle or fettuccine, also works wonderfully. Do as you will, just please do not add cream. **Serves 4**

Tagliatelle with egg, truffle & Parmigiano Reggiano

5 eggs
150 g (5½ oz/1½ cups) finely grated Parmigiano Reggiano or Pecorino Romano

6 flat-leaf (Italian) parsley sprigs, leaves finely chopped
600 g (1 lb 5 oz) dried spaghetti, or fresh or dried tagliatelle or fettuccine

250 g (9 oz) guanciale or flat pancetta, cut into 5 mm (¼ in) thick lardons
3 garlic cloves, finely sliced

Staples
EVOO, S&P

Add the eggs, cheese, parsley and about twenty grinds of black pepper to a large bowl. Whisk well.

Cook the pasta in plenty of boiling salted water until al dente.

Meanwhile, heat a good splash of oil in a large frying pan over a medium–high heat. Fry the guanciale until golden and crisp, about 3 minutes. Turn the heat to low and add the garlic. Cook until fragrant and lightly golden. Season with salt and pepper, take off the heat and add a couple of tablespoons of the pasta cooking water to stop the garlic burning.

Tong the cooked pasta from the water directly into the frying pan, over a medium heat. Toss through until any pasta water has been absorbed and the pasta is coated, rather than sitting in liquid.

Remove from the heat, then add the egg mixture and toss to combine. The sauce will thicken with the residual heat of the pasta. Don't be tempted to return to the stove, or there's a danger of scrambling the egg. Serve immediately.

Mac & cheese

Mac and cheese is a beloved dish, and one people seem obsessed with refining, making it ever more explosively cheese-laden and complex. I'm making no grand claims here, but the (optional) inclusion of bonito in the mix is somewhat of a secret weapon, giving the cheese sauce a supercharged level of umami. **Serves 4**

800 ml (27 fl oz) full-cream (whole) milk
15 g (½ oz) katsuobushi (bonito flakes)
500 g (1 lb 2 oz) dried macaroni, or fresh or bought gnocchi
60 g (2 oz/¼ cup) butter
1 onion, finely diced

5 garlic cloves, finely sliced
60 g (2 oz) plain (all-purpose) flour
1½ tablespoons dijon mustard
100 ml (3½ fl oz) pouring (single/light) cream
100 g (3½ oz/1 cup) finely grated Grana Padano

150 g (5½ oz) aged sharp cheddar or gruyère, coarsely grated
4 spring onions (scallions), white part only, finely sliced
2 handfuls of fresh breadcrumbs

Staples
S&P

Preheat the oven to 180°C (350°F) fan-forced.

Add the milk and bonito to a small saucepan and heat until just under a simmer. Turn off the heat and leave to infuse for 15 minutes, then strain. Keep the milk warm.

Cook the pasta in plenty of boiling salted water until al dente, then drain and add to a large bowl.

Meanwhile, add the butter to a saucepan over a medium heat. Add the onion and garlic, season with salt and pepper and cook until softened, about 4 minutes. Stir the flour through and cook out the raw flavour for 1–2 minutes. Whisk in the warm infused milk to combine. Add the mustard and cook, whisking, for about 2 minutes, until thickened and smooth. Stir in the cream, cheeses and spring onion until combined. Adjust the seasoning.

Tip the sauce into the bowl of pasta and combine.

Tip the mixture into a baking dish, top with the breadcrumbs and bake for about 20 minutes, until the sauce is golden and bubbling.

Make it vegetarian **V**
Simply omit the katsuobushi.

Cacio e pepe **V**

This is another Roman classic. Cacio e pepe simply translates as cheese and pepper. And that's pretty much it. Crack 1½ teaspoons black peppercorns in a mortar, or using the base of a clean pan. Combine 80 g (2¾ oz) finely grated pecorino, and 50 g (1¾ oz/½ cup) finely grated Parmigiano Reggiano in a bowl. Cook 300 g (10½ oz) dried chitarra/tonnarelli, bucatini or spaghetti in plenty of boiling salted water a few minutes less than directed, until very al dente. Meanwhile, add the pepper to a frying pan over a medium heat. Toast until fragrant, about 1½ minutes. Lift the pasta out of the water with tongs and add directly to the frying pan with about 180 ml (6 fl oz) of the pasta cooking water. Simmer the pasta in the pan, agitating with tongs, and tossing every 15 seconds or so. Meanwhile, add 80 ml (2½ fl oz/⅓ cup) of the pasta water to the cheese and mix with a spatula into a smooth paste, the consistency of room-temperature butter. When the liquid in the frying pan is glossy and coating the pasta, check to see that the pasta is al dente. If not, add a little more cooking water. When the pasta is done, add the cheese paste and toss rapidly to coat, loosening with a little more pasta water if needed. Serve immediately, finishing with a little more pepper for good measure. Serves 2.

Pair with

Dressed leaves, with or without a chargrilled rib-eye steak (see p. 278).

If you want to take this to a ridiculous level and demand supreme luxury from your comfort food, shave a black truffle over once cooked.

Bucatini amatriciana

For the sauce, heat 60 ml (2 fl oz/¼ cup) extra-virgin olive oil in a deep frying pan over a medium heat. Cut 150 g (5½ oz) guanciale or flat pancetta into 5 mm (¼ in) dice until golden and translucent, about 3 minutes. Add ¼ onion, finely sliced, and 4 finely sliced garlic cloves and fry until softened, about 5 minutes. Stir in 2 teaspoons dried oregano and 1½ teaspoons chilli flakes, then add 150 ml (5 fl oz) white wine and reduce by half. Add 400 g (14 oz) tomato passata (puréed tomatoes) or Simple tomato sugo (p. 116) and 1 teaspoon tomato paste (concentrated purée) and simmer for 15 minutes. Meanwhile, cook 500 g (1 lb 2 oz) dried bucatini, spaghetti or penne in boiling salted water according to the packet instructions, until al dente. Add the pasta to the sauce with about 100 ml (3½ fl oz) of the pasta cooking water and toss. Cook the sauce a little longer until it clings to the pasta. Add 60 g (2 oz) finely grated Pecorino Romano or Grana Padano and toss to combine. Serve with an extra 40 g (1½ oz) cheese on the side. Serves 4.

Casarecce with osso buco

While risotto alla milanese is the traditional accompaniment for osso buco, making saffron risotto on top of the osso buco isn't always going to fit one's schedule. This is a simpler family-friendly way to serve it. **Serves 4–6**

1 × quantity Osso buco (p. 296)
500 g (1 lb 2 oz) dried short pasta, such as casarecce, conchiglie, penne, macaroni or casarecce

80 g (2¾ oz) butter
2 handfuls of flat-leaf (Italian) parsley leaves, or basil leaves, torn, plus extra to garnish
zest and juice of 1 lemon

150 g (5½ oz/1½ cups) finely grated Grana Padano
150 g (5½ oz) fresh ricotta

Make the osso buco as directed and keep it warm in the saucepan.

Cook the pasta in plenty of boiling salted water according to the packet instructions, until al dente. Drain.

Remove the osso buco pieces from the saucepan while you add the pasta and mix it through the sauce. Add the butter, parsley, lemon zest and juice, and half the Grana Padano, and season as needed.

Return the osso buco to the sauce. Take the whole pot to the table, along with the remaining Grana Padano, herbs and ricotta to serve.

Green aglio e olio Ⓥ

This sauce uses the principle of aglio e olio, with a deeply toasted garlic flavour infusing the oil-based sauce, anointed with a vibrantly green purée. **Serves 4–6**

150 ml (5 fl oz) extra-virgin olive oil

4 garlic cloves, peeled and halved

1 bird's eye chilli, sliced into rings

200 g (7 oz) silverbeet (Swiss chard), cavolo nero or kale leaves, without stalks, torn into small pieces

150 g (5½ oz) baby English spinach (or use half rocket/arugula)

¼ bunch of flat-leaf (Italian) parsley, leaves picked

120 g (4½ oz) Parmigiano Reggiano or Pecorino Romano, finely grated

500 g (1 lb 2 oz) dried short pasta, such as penne, strozzapreti, casarecce, orecchiette or stracci, or fresh tagliatelle (see p. 112) or paccheri

Staples
S&P

Add the oil and garlic to a small saucepan over a medium heat and cook until golden, about 6 minutes. Take off the heat, then add the chilli.

Cook the silverbeet, spinach and parsley in a saucepan of boiling salted water for 2½ minutes, then drain briefly and chop roughly. Blitz in a blender, then add the oil, garlic and chilli with a few tablespoons of water and blitz until smooth, adding a little more water if needed to make a smooth sauce. Stir through the cheese, then season with salt and pepper.

Cook the pasta in boiling salted water according to the packet instructions, until al dente. Drain, reserving a little of the pasta water.

Heat the sauce in a large saucepan over a medium heat. Add the pasta to the pan with a splash of the reserved pasta water and toss through until the sauce clings to the pasta. Serve immediately.

Make it different

With crunch. Sprinkle on some toasted walnuts or pine nuts to finish, or Pangrattato (opposite).

With cheese. Add torn burrata or stracciatella, or dollop with ricotta, and finish with chilli flakes.

With another pasta. Instead of short pasta, serve the warmed sauce with ricotta gnocchi, Ricotta & goat's cheese ravioli (p. 117), Ricotta & spinach ravioli (p. 116) or fresh pappardelle.

Toasted anchovy crumbs

Spread 150 g (5½ oz) fresh white breadcrumbs on a baking tray and toast for 5 minutes in a preheated 170°C (340°F) fan-forced oven. Heat 100 ml (3½ fl oz) extra-virgin olive oil in a medium frying pan over a medium heat. Fry 8 finely sliced French shallots and 2 finely diced garlic cloves until softened, about 4 minutes. Add 6 finely chopped anchovies and stir to dissolve, 1–2 minutes. Stir the breadcrumbs through and toast them for about 3 minutes. Season with pepper and toss in a bowl with ¼ teaspoon chilli powder and the grated zest of ½ lemon and toss together. Sprinkle over simply cooked pasta tossed in butter, or Spaghetti with spinach & lemon (p. 124), boiled potatoes with Buttermilk dressing (p. 361), braised cavolo nero, cime di rape or broccolini with a good squeeze of lemon, or over ricotta, simply cooked fish or mussels opened in wine and cream.

Pangrattato Ⓥ

Famously called 'poor man's parmesan', pangrattato is used to finish pasta and other dishes, but it really has its own special place, with the salty crunch of fried breadcrumbs (the literal translation of pangrattato is 'breadcrumbs') adding a stellar dimension. It is often thought of as a parmesan substitute, but I do love using both on pasta together, one adding textural crunch, and the other enriching. Heat 2 tablespoons extra-virgin olive oil and 30 g (1 oz) butter in a frying pan over a high heat. Add 1 cup (80 g/2¾ oz) freshly blitzed breadcrumbs (made from stale bread) to the pan; you can also add a sliced garlic clove or two. Season with salt and pepper and cook for 5–8 minutes, tossing frequently until crisp and light golden, then tip onto a plate to cool. Pangrattato is also wonderful sprinkled over wilted greens, or blanched broccolini that has been tossed with oil, garlic and chill, then finished with lemon.

Spaghetti aglio e olio

Spaghetti aglio e olio, named for its principal ingredients, garlic and oil, is without complication and is a good degree less technical than that other famous twin-noun pasta, Cacio e pepe (p. 120). I take it a little further with chicken stock and anchovies – just because I want to, and it's delicious, but omit them if you like. The two ingredients that aren't in the recipe title that I can't do without, however, are chilli and parsley. But that's up to you, too. **Serves 4**

500 g (1 lb 2 oz) dried
  spaghetti
180 ml (6 fl oz) extra-virgin
  olive oil
4 large garlic cloves, finely
  sliced

2 red bird's eye chillies,
  finely sliced
4 anchovies, chopped
200 ml (7 fl oz) Golden
  chicken stock (p. 54), hot

½ bunch of parsley, very
  finely chopped

Staples
EVOO, S&P

Cook the pasta in plenty of boiling salted water according to the packet instructions, until al dente.

Meanwhile, add the oil to a wide saucepan over a medium heat. Cook the garlic, chilli and anchovies until the garlic is golden and fragrant, and the anchovies dissolve, about 2 minutes. Add the stock and parsley, then simmer for 2 minutes.

Tong the pasta directly into the pan, along with a splash of the pasta water. Cook for a couple of minutes, tossing frequently. Once the sauce is clinging nicely, gloss with an extra splash of oil and serve immediately.

Make it different
With mint & broad beans. When adding the stock, toss in some fresh mint and two large handfuls of double-podded broad beans, roughly chopped.

With prawns. Prawns (shrimp) are a perfect match for the garlicky sauce. Cut eight deveined prawn cutlets into 1 cm (½ in) pieces and add to the pan once the anchovies have dissolved. Season with salt and pepper, then proceed with the recipe.

Make it vegan Ⓥ Ⓖ
Leave out the anchovies. Instead of chicken stock, add 1½ tablespoons white miso or brown-rice miso mixed with 200 ml (7 fl oz) hot water.

Tagliatelle with lemon cream Ⓥ

Bottarga – salt-cured mullet roe – is such an amazing thing, capturing the briny quality of the sea with a seemingly endless resource of umami. It works so well with the richness of cream, with the lift of lemon a balancing foil. This is certainly a starter-style pasta, being far too intense in larger portions. **Serves 4**

3 tablespoons extra-virgin
  olive oil
3 garlic cloves, finely sliced
100 ml (3½ fl oz) wine white
150 ml (5 fl oz) pouring
  (single/light) cream

2 thyme sprigs, leaves picked
½ quantity egg tagliatelle
  (see p. 112), or 500 g
  (1 lb 2 oz) dried spaghetti
80 g (2¾ oz) butter, diced
zest and juice of ½ lemon

100 g (3½ oz) bottarga,
  Grana Padano, or
  2 handfuls spinach,
  finely shredded

Staples
S&P

Heat the oil in a large frying pan over a medium heat. Fry the garlic until turning golden, about 2 minutes. Add the wine and reduce by half. Stir in the cream, thyme and a good grinding of pepper, then simmer for 2 minutes to reduce and thicken slightly.

Meanwhile, cook the pasta in boiling salted water until al dente.

Once the sauce has reduced, tong the pasta straight from the pot with a small amount of the pasta water to loosen the sauce. Add the butter, lemon zest and lemon juice, then toss through. Finely grate in a little bottarga or Grana Padano, or add the spinach, and toss.

Plate the pasta, grate the remaining bottarga over and serve immediately.

Make it different

With caviar. Top each serve with caviar or salmon roe.

With capers. Thoroughly dry 50 g (1¾ oz) tiny capers using paper towel, then fry in oil for about 3 minutes. Drain on paper towel to crisp, then scatter over the pasta after adding the bottarga, cheese or spinach.

Spaghetti with sardines, currants & pine nuts

These flavours are just so southern Italian, with the interplay of sweet and sour such a critical component of the cuisine. The pangrattato adds such textural detail and flavour to the intense sauce. The splash of cream may seem unusual but it disappears, leaving behind a richness and silkiness. **Serves 4**

2 handfuls of currants
80 ml (2½ fl oz/⅓ cup) sherry vinegar
500 g (1 lb 2 oz) dried spaghetti
80 ml (2½ fl oz/⅓ cup) extra-virgin olive oil
4 large garlic cloves, finely sliced

2 red bird's eye chillies, finely sliced
150 ml (5 fl oz) Golden chicken stock (p. 54)
100 ml (3½ fl oz) pouring (single/light) cream
100 g (3½ oz/⅔ cup) pine nuts, toasted
2 × 120 g (4½ oz) tins sardines in olive oil, drained

2 handfuls of pale-yellow celery leaves, torn
4 flat-leaf (Italian) parsley sprigs, leaves and stalks finely chopped
1 × quantity Pangrattato (p. 123)

Staples
EVOO, S&P

Add the currants and vinegar to a small saucepan, bring to the boil and take off the heat. Set aside for the currants to plump up.

Cook the pasta in plenty of boiling salted water according to the packet instructions, until al dente.

Meanwhile, heat the oil in a wide-based saucepan over a medium heat. Fry the garlic and chilli until fragrant and lightly coloured, about 2 minutes. Add the currants and residual vinegar, season with salt and pepper and cook for about 1 minute.

Add the stock and cream and bring to a simmer. Cook for about 30 seconds, then tong the pasta directly into the pan, along with a splash of the pasta water. Add the pine nuts and sardines, breaking the fish up a little. Simmer in the sauce for a minute or so, tossing through a few times, and adding more pasta water as needed to loosen.

Once the sauce is clinging nicely, gloss with an extra splash of oil, toss the celery leaves and parsley through and serve immediately, with the pangrattato sprinkled over the top.

Spaghetti with spinach, lemon & pangrattato ⓥ

Cook 250 g (9 oz) dried spaghetti in boiling salted water according to the packet instructions, until al dente. Towards the end of cooking, add 50 ml (1¾ fl oz) extra-virgin olive oil to a large frying pan over a medium heat. Fry 4 finely sliced garlic cloves until fragrant, 1–2 minutes. Add 100 g (3½ oz) chopped English spinach leaves, a handful of torn flat-leaf (Italian) parsley leaves, the zest of 1 lemon and ½ teaspoon chilli flakes, season with salt and pepper, then stir through to wilt and warm, about 1 minute. Lift the cooked spaghetti out of the water with tongs, taking a little pasta water with it, then toss through in the pan; if it's a little dry, splash in a little more of the cooking water. Toss until the sauce is emulsified and clings to the spaghetti, then toss through the juice of 1 lemon, a large handful of Pangrattato (p. 123) and another 50 ml (1¾ fl oz) oil. Season and serve with lots of grated parmesan. Serves 2. You could enhance this dish further by adding anchovies or tinned sardines to the pan after frying the garlic. You could also add 2 tablespoons mascarpone or 80 ml (2½ fl oz/⅓ cup) pouring (single/light) cream when adding the lemon juice and remaining oil, then toss through in the pan until the sauce is clinging to the pasta.

Pennette with tuna, tomatoes & mascarpone

Heat 125 ml (4 fl oz/½ cup) extra-virgin olive oil in a wide saucepan over a medium heat. Add 3 red onions, finely sliced into half-moons, 4 large finely grated garlic cloves and 15 halved cherry tomatoes, season with salt and pepper and cook until very soft, about 10 minutes. Add 1 teaspoon each of chilli seeds and fennel seeds and cook for about 2 minutes; the onion should be meltingly soft. Add a 185 g (6½ oz) tin tuna in oil, the zest and juice of 1 lemon and stir through quickly, then take off the heat, stirring through and breaking up the tuna. Meanwhile, cook 500 g (1 lb 2 oz) dried pennette or other short pasta in boiling salted water according to the packet instructions, until al dente. Lift the cooked pasta out of the water and add to the sauce, taking some of the pasta water with it, along with 2 tablespoons mascarpone. (If draining the pasta, reserve some of the water and add a splash to loosen.) Stir or toss through over a medium heat until the sauce has emulsified and is clinging to the pasta, then add ½ radicchio or a bunch of parsley, finely sliced, and toss to wilt. Adjust the seasoning and drizzle with more oil if necessary, then serve. Serves 4. You could also replace the tuna with a small tin of best-quality anchovies, melting them into the onions once cooked. Instead of radicchio, you could use the pale hearts of curly endive (frisée) or picked watercress.

Spaghettini with crab, lemon, herbs & chilli

This is such a lovely and bright combination, with no cooking of the sauce required. It's all about the heat of the pasta warming the crab and gently wilting the vibrant riot of herbs. Superior olive oil, the zing of lemon and punch of chilli complete the picture, with the short marination and a little pasta water dragged across with the pasta bringing everything together. **Serves 4**

200 ml (7 fl oz) extra-virgin olive oil
2 small garlic cloves, finely grated
2 long green chillies, finely sliced into rings
zest and juice of 2 lemons
300 g (10½ oz) cooked crabmeat

½ bunch of chervil, leaves and fine stems roughly chopped
6 dill sprigs, fronds finely chopped
6 flat-leaf (Italian) parsley sprigs, leaves finely sliced
½ bunch of chives, finely snipped

2 handfuls of curly endive (frisée), finely chopped
500 g (1 lb 2 oz) dried spaghettini
80 g (2¾ oz) unsalted butter, finely diced

Staples
S&P

Add the oil, garlic, chilli, lemon zest and lemon juice to a large bowl (stainless steel is best to take on the heat of the pasta, rather than cooling it down). Season with salt and pepper and combine. Flake the crabmeat in and submerge it under the oil. Add the herbs and endive to the side of the bowl, so they're not in the oil mix. Marinate the crabmeat for 5 minutes or so while the pasta cooks.

Cook the pasta in plenty of boiling salted water according to the packet instructions, until al dente.

Tong the pasta directly into the bowl, taking a little pasta water with it. Drop the butter on top of the pasta, grind in plenty of pepper, then toss through the sauce quite vigorously, to soften the herbs and emulsify the sauce. Adjust the seasoning as needed and serve immediately, in warmed bowls.

Linguine vongole

I crave this on a regular basis, and order it whenever I can in Italy. It was a dish my dear grandmother Grace would always ask me to cook for her. It was her favourite pasta, and it's my father's favourite, too. You can add me to that list, though I have too many darlings to be truly monogamous. The simple combination of briny clams, garlic, chilli, wine, parsley and oil is revelatory enough, but the inclusion of anchovies and a little chicken stock just adds so much weight and intensity, without intruding on the core flavours. The sauce should be wet and luscious, but not oily, glossing the pasta but pooling a little in the bowl, invitingly whispering for good bread. **Serves 4**

500 g (1 lb 2 oz) dried linguine
125 ml (4 fl oz/½ cup)
  extra-virgin olive oil
4 large garlic cloves, finely
  sliced
5 anchovies
2 red bird's eye chillies,
  finely sliced into rounds

1.5 kg (3 lb 5 oz) clams
  (vongole), or pipis, surf
  clams or the like
150 ml (5 fl oz) white wine
250 ml (8½ fl oz/1 cup)
  Golden chicken stock
  (p. 54)

½ bunch of flat-leaf (Italian)
  parsley, leaves very finely
  chopped

Staples
S&P

Cook the pasta in boiling salted water until just before al dente.

Meanwhile, heat a large wide saucepan over a high heat. Add half the oil. Cook the garlic, anchovies and chilli for about 2 minutes, to colour the garlic and dissolve the anchovies.

Carefully add the clams to the pan, without damaging the shells. Cook until they start to open, about 2 minutes. Pour in the wine, being careful not to flame the pan. Simmer for 2 minutes, then lift the open clams into a bowl.

Add the stock and parsley to the pan, then tong in the cooked pasta directly from the pot.
Simmer the pasta in the sauce for 2 minutes, tossing through, then return the clams and any juices. Add the remaining oil and toss until the sauce is glossy and clinging to the pasta, adding a little pasta water if needed. The sauce should be glossy and a little wet.

Serve immediately.

Squid ink pasta

This is the most dramatic of pastas: jet black and infused with the briny tang of the ocean, making it an ideal pairing with seafood. **Serves 8–10**

500 g (1 lb 2 oz/3⅓ cups) '00' flour
150 g (5½ oz) fine semolina
2 teaspoons salt flakes
6 eggs

2 × 20 g (¾ oz) sachets of squid ink (or ink sacs reserved by your fishmonger)

1 tablespoon extra-virgin olive oil

Add the dry ingredients to a food processor. In a jug, whisk the eggs, squid ink and oil to combine. Pour the egg mixture in while processing. Once a dough forms, tip onto a bench and bring together, then proceed as per the Egg pasta recipe (p. 111), cutting into linguine (see p. 112) or tagliatelle (see p. 112) once rolled.

Pair with

Use in any seafood pasta – including Sea urchin linguini with roasted tomato (below).

Sea urchin linguini with roasted tomato passata & butter

This is a special occasion pasta, prepared wholly from scratch by a confident cook. Take the trouble to make the pasta, and do also make the Roasted tomato passata (p. 660), as the details matter here. I wouldn't bother making this with commercial passata, no matter how artisan its credentials. Sea urchin has a gently buttery and briny quality, which is stunning with the roasted tomato flavour, spike of chilli and savoury richness of the squid ink pasta. It's also a strikingly dramatic dish visually. As said, this is special occasion stuff. **Serves 4**

3 tablespoons extra-virgin olive oil
4 garlic cloves, sliced
200 ml (7 fl oz) Roasted tomato passata (p. 660)

2 red bird's eye chillies, finely sliced
14 sea urchin lobes
140 g (5 oz) butter, diced

400 g (14 oz) Squid ink linguine (above)
8 basil leaves

Staples
LMN, S&P

Heat the oil in a frying pan over a medium heat. Fry the garlic until turning golden, about 2 minutes. Add the passata and chilli and cook for a couple of minutes, then pull off the heat and add the sea urchin and butter. Stand, don't stir. Season with salt and pepper.

Meanwhile, cook the pasta in boiling salted water for 3–3½ minutes, then tong directly into the pan, placing it back over a medium heat. Toss through for a minute, adding the basil – you just want to warm but not really cook the urchin.

Squeeze in some lemon and serve immediately.

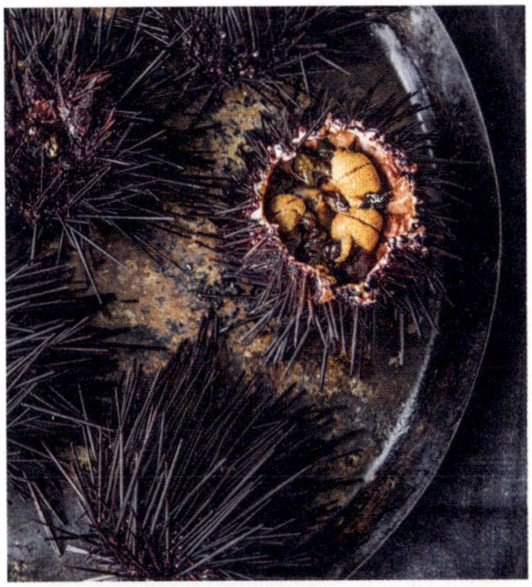
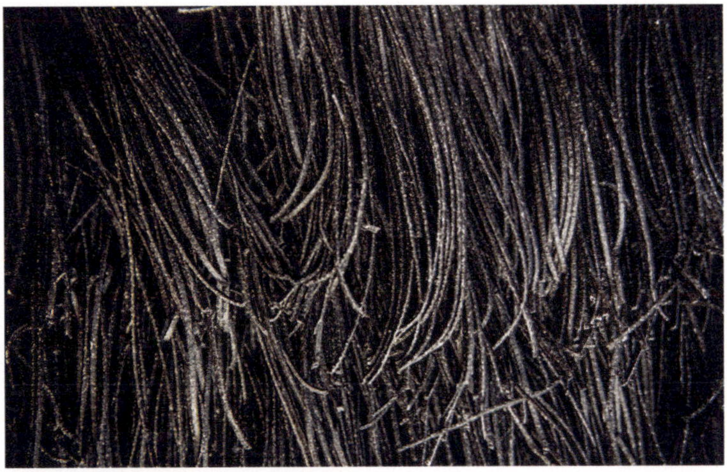
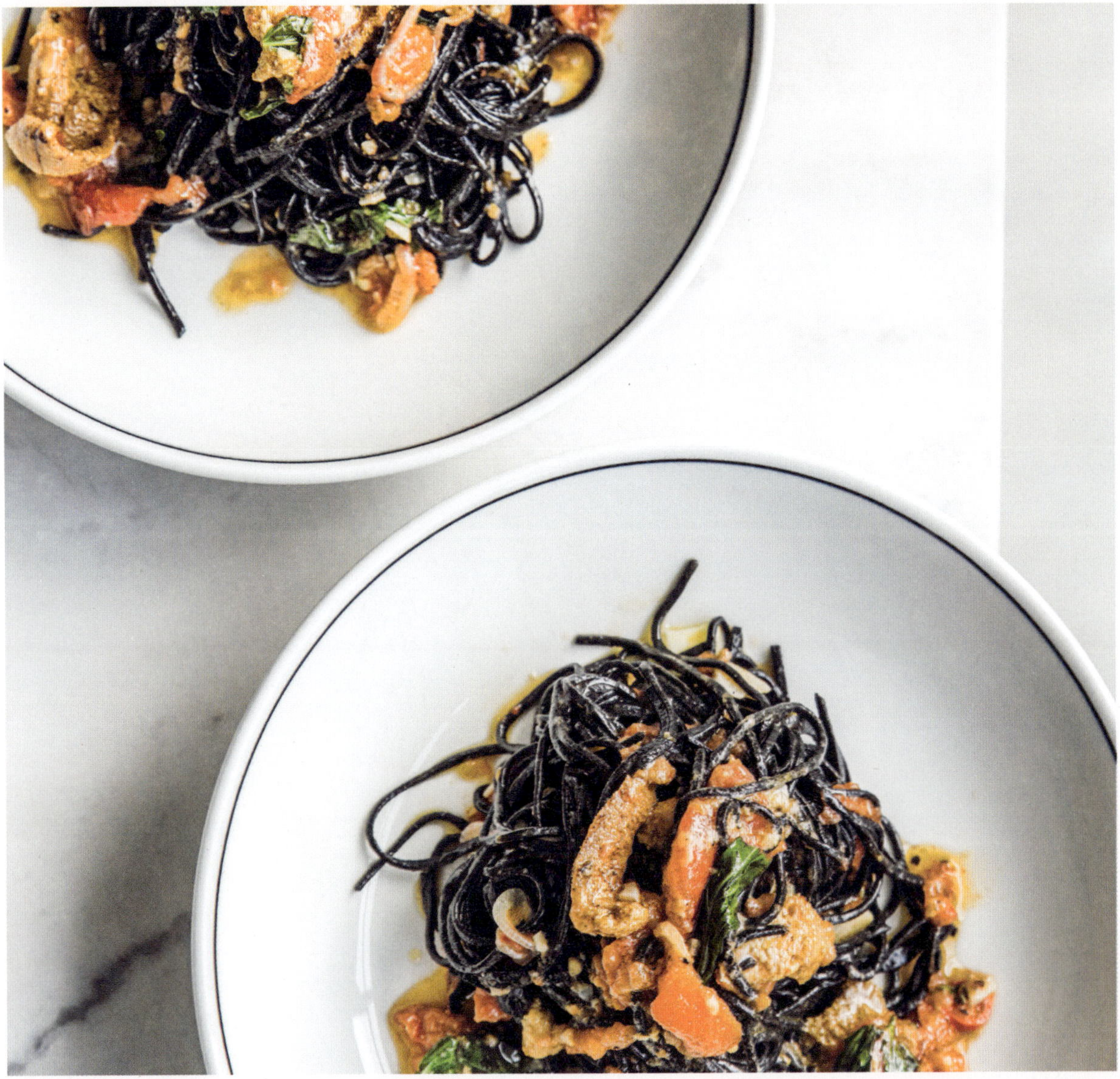

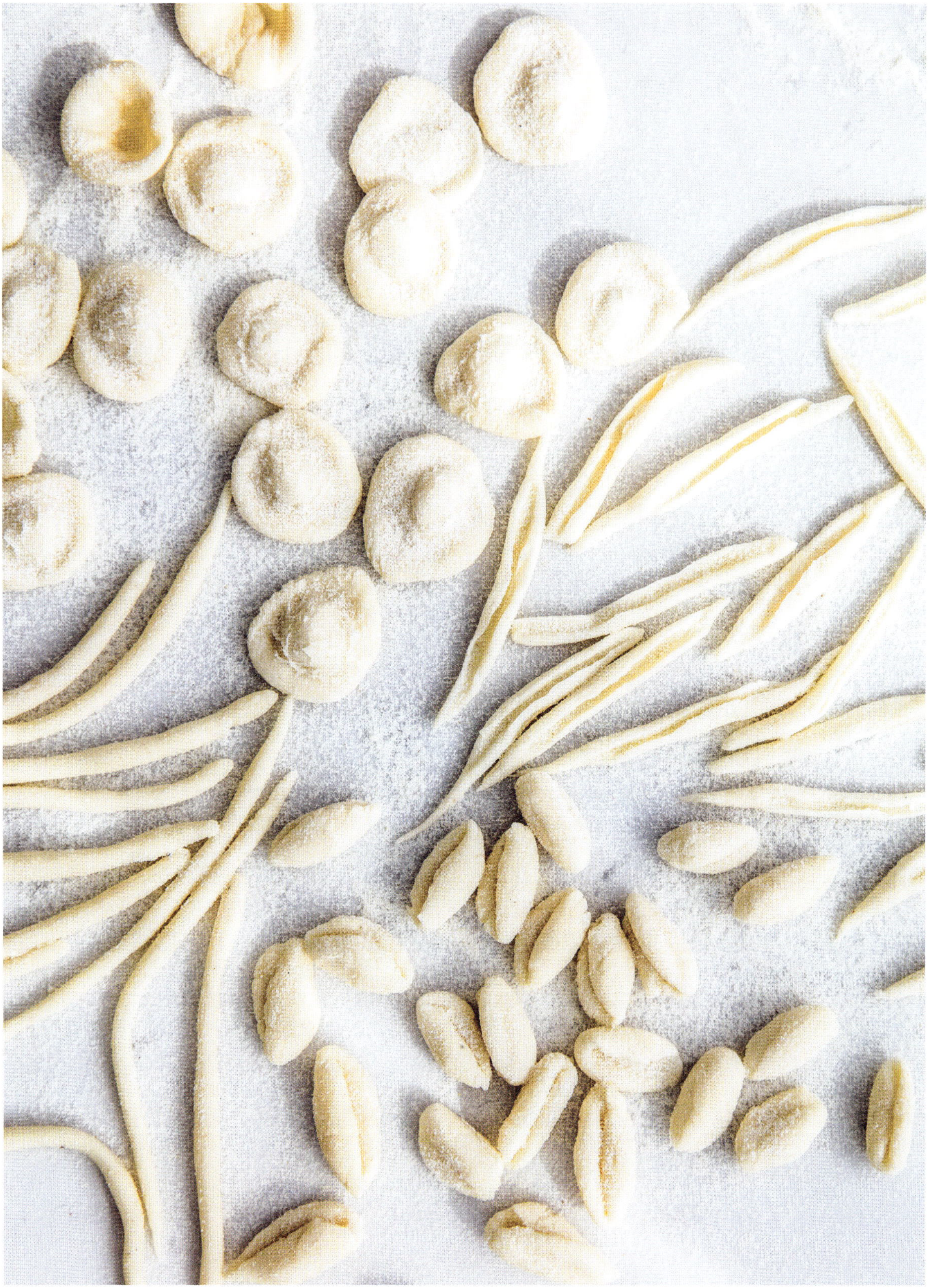

Semolina dough for orecchiette, pici & gnocchi sardi Ⓥ Ⓥ🄶

Pair with

Octopus braised in rosé (p. 219).

Osso buco (p. 296).

Pesto (p. 90).

Green aglio e olio (p 122).

Roasted tomato passata (p. 660).

Any ragù (pp. 259, 283, 335, 336, 535, 576).

Simple tomato sugo (p. 116) with ricotta and basil.

Pasta alla Norma (p. 521).

Eggplant, oregano, balsamic & ricotta (see p. 132).

Tomato, mint & anchovy sauce (p. 132).

This is the simplest of doughs, and it can be made just with semolina, though the proportions are slightly different – 420 g (15 oz) fine semolina to 250 ml (8½ fl oz/1 cup) boiling water – with the semolina absorbing much more water than flour. This version is much easier to work, and it doesn't dry out as readily and crack, which is especially helpful when you're getting your bearings with shaping. The semolina creates a toothsome bite, with a distinctive chew to the texture (and even more so in a straight semolina dough). It is quite unlike egg pasta and bought dried pasta, and I tend to serve it with more southern Italian sauces with oil and tomato the key ingredients. I am sticking to ones that are easy enough to master, but don't feel limited by the examples below, as the dough is a versatile one. **Serves 4**

350 g (12½ oz) fine semolina, plus extra for dusting

200 g (7 oz/1⅓ cups) '00' flour
½ teaspoon salt flakes

250–270 ml (8½–9 fl oz/1 cup) boiling water

Combine the dry ingredients in a bowl, then pour in the water. Combine with a spoon, then tip onto the bench and start to work the dough. It will naturally be quite hot, but it's important to work while it is warm. Knead until you have a knobbly, pliable dough, about 5 minutes, adding a little more semolina if sticky. Roll into a log and cover with a tea towel (dish towel) for 5 minutes to relax. Clean the bench, then cut the dough into six even pieces.

To make orecchiette
Roll one portion into a 1.5 cm (½ in) thick snake, then cut into 1.5 cm (½ in) pieces. Place your index finger at the tip of a table knife and press it flat into the top of a cut side of one of the pieces, then drag it back towards you so the pasta rolls back over the tip of the knife, making a rough cup shape (see the photograph opposite). Once formed, turned the pasta inside out to reveal the rough side made by the knife, which will help the pasta cling. Toss onto a tray dusted with a little semolina, then repeat for the remaining dough. Cook for 5–6 minutes in boiling salted water.

To make cavatelli & gnocchi sardi
Cavatelli and gnocchi sardi (malloreddus, a.k.a. Sardinian gnocchi) are very similar in shape, with the dough rolled over a grooved paddle to curl over itself, yielding a cuff of dough with a ridged exterior. Traditionally, gnocchi sardi are often flavoured and coloured with saffron, but you can skip this and then call them whatever you will. If using saffron, add ½ teaspoon saffron powder (or three saffron threads, ground and steeped in a little boiling water for 3 minutes) to the boiling water before making the dough. Once the dough has been rolled into snakes, cut off 1 cm (½ in) pieces. Using a grooved pasta paddle or butter paddle, press in the centre of one of the pieces with a downward action so that it curls back over your thumb. Repeat for all the dough.

To make pici
Cut the pasta snakes into 4 cm (1½ in) lengths, then roll on the bench with the palm of your hand to make long noodles that taper to a point at each end. Don't try to make them perfect – the variation between them is part of the charm.

To make strozzapreti
Take your pici, push a wooden skewer into the centre and roll over it with the palm of your hand. Remove the skewer to leave an uneven groove in the length of the noodle.

Orecchiette with tomato, mint & anchovy sauce

A celebration of summer and Sicilian flavours, this is possibly my favourite sauce with home-made semolina pasta (p. 131), with the fresh and dried mint immediately distinguishing it from the basil and tomato combination we're so familiar with. Decadently ripe summer tomatoes are laced with peppery olive oil and anchovies, spiked with capers, caperberries and a lift of dried chilli – it has to be dried – with a dollop of the freshest ricotta to finish. **Serves 4**

1 × quantity Orecchiette or
   gnocchi sardi (see p. 131)
150 g (5½ oz) fresh ricotta
50 g (1¾ oz/½ cup) grated
   Parmigiano Reggiano or
   Pecorino Romano

**Tomato, mint &
anchovy sauce**
125 ml (4 fl oz/½ cup)
   extra-virgin olive oil
5 garlic cloves
6 large anchovies
5 ripe, densely fleshed
   tomatoes (oxhearts, ideally),
   roughly diced

1 tablespoon small capers
8 caperberries, with stems
1 teaspoon dried mint
1 teaspoon chilli flakes
2 large handfuls of mint, torn

Staples
S&P

For the sauce, heat the oil in a large frying pan over a medium heat. Fry the garlic until lightly golden and fragrant, about 2 minutes. Stir in the anchovies until dissolved, 1–2 minutes. Add the tomato, season with salt and pepper and cook until collapsing, about 5 minutes. Add the capers, caperberries, dried mint and chilli, and cook until a saucy consistency, about 2 minutes.

Meanwhile, cook the pasta in plenty of boiling salted water for 4–5 minutes.

Using a sieve or slotted spoon, lift the pasta from the pan directly into the sauce, adding a little extra cooking water. Cook in the sauce for a minute or two, tossing to coat.

Once the sauce is clinging to the pasta, remove from the heat and toss the fresh mint through.

Serve with the ricotta and Parmigiano over the top.

Orecchiette with eggplant, oregano, balsamic & ricotta ⓥ

Often, eggplant (aubergine) pasta goes in a heavier and more rustic direction, and charmingly so, but I also love this route that takes southern Italian flavours down a more refined path. Boiling the eggplant first yields a finer, lighter result, with a finishing touch of balsamic vinegar lacing the eggplant and ricotta with acidity and moreish sweetness. **Serves 4**

3 large eggplants
   (aubergines), peeled in
   stripes and cut into 3 cm
   (1¼ in) dice
100 ml (3½ fl oz) extra-virgin
   olive oil
4 garlic cloves, sliced
2 tablespoons tiny capers
4 anchovies

2 teaspoons chilli flakes
4 oregano sprigs, leaves
   picked, or 1½ tablespoons
   dried oregano
200 ml (7 fl oz) dry white
   wine
100 ml (3½ fl oz) balsamic
   vinegar (or 50 ml/1¾ fl oz
   if using the good stuff)

500 g (1 lb 2 oz) dried or
   fresh Orecchiette (p. 131)
80 g (2¾ oz) Grana Padano,
   finely grated
300 g (10½ oz) ricotta

Staples
EVOO, S&P

Cook the eggplant in boiling salted water for 10 minutes. Drain well, then gently press out any excess moisture.

Heat the oil in a wide-based saucepan over a medium heat. Cook the garlic, capers, anchovies, chilli flakes and oregano until the anchovies have dissolved and the mix is fragrant, about 2 minutes. Stir the eggplant through and season with pepper. Add the wine and cook until almost dry. Drizzle with half the vinegar and cook for a couple of minutes, until the eggplant takes up the vinegar.

Meanwhile, cook the pasta in plenty of boiling salted water until al dente.

Lift the pasta with a sieve or slotted spoon, directly into the pan, adding a little extra cooking water. Cook in the sauce for a minute or two, tossing to coat. Once the sauce is clinging to the pasta, stir the parmesan through and add a little extra oil if needed.

Serve with the ricotta crumbled over and drizzled with the remaining vinegar to finish.

Spinach, ricotta & feta cannelloni with mint passata sauce Ⓥ

There are few things I find more comforting than baked pasta, and this one provides all the essential comfort. What is a very simple sugo-based dish takes on a new dimension with a little dill mixed with the spinach, and a final flourish of smoked mozzarella. For a more classic version, swap the dill for basil, and use mozzarella sans smoke. **Serves 6**

24 dried cannelloni shells
250 g (9 oz) smoked or plain
  mozzarella, sliced
50 g (1¾ oz/½ cup) finely
  grated Grana Padano

Mint passata sauce
125 ml (4 fl oz/½ cup)
  extra-virgin olive oil
4 large garlic cloves, finely
  sliced

700 ml (23½ fl oz) tomato
  passata (puréed tomatoes)
400 g (14 oz) tin diced
  tomatoes
250 ml (8½ fl oz/1 cup) water
1 tablespoon sugar
2 teaspoons dried mint

Spinach, ricotta & feta filling
450 g (1 lb) English spinach
375 g (13 oz) ricotta

2 eggs, lightly beaten
200 g (7 oz) bocconcini,
  finely diced
150 g (5½ oz/1 cup) firm feta,
  crumbled
100 g (3½ oz/1 cup) finely
  grated Grana Padano
3 dill sprigs, fronds chopped
½ large nutmeg, finely grated

Staples
EVOO, S&P

For the passata sauce, heat the oil in a saucepan over a medium heat. Fry the garlic until fragrant and just changing colour. Stir in the passata, tomato and water, then simmer for 15 minutes over a low heat. Add the sugar and dried mint, season with salt and pepper and take off the heat.

Meanwhile, preheat the oven to 180°C (350°F) fan-forced.

For the filling, heat a large frying pan over a high heat. Add the spinach and a small splash of water. Cover and cook for 3 minutes, then drain in a colander. Press out any excess water, then chop roughly.

Combine the ricotta and eggs in a large bowl. Add the spinach, remaining cheeses, dill and nutmeg, season with salt and pepper and combine. Transfer the mixture to a piping (icing) bag fitted with a large nozzle, then pipe into the cannelloni shells.

Spread half the passata sauce across a 24 cm × 30 cm (9½ ×12 in) baking dish. Arrange the cannelloni on top of the sauce in one layer, then spoon the remaining sauce over. Scatter with the mozzarella and parmesan, then drizzle with extra oil. Cover with baking paper, then foil.

Bake for 45 minutes, then uncover and bake for another 10 minutes, until golden.

Orecchiette with eggplant, oregano, balsamic & ricotta

Crab cannelloni with crustacean dressing

Pair with

Serve as a starter or light meal with dressed leaves.

This is an old menu favourite of mine, an indulgent dish that I cooked professionally on and off for many years. While not a traditional recipe, it is unashamedly a restaurant recipe, a true labour of love, and a very striking dish to put in front of loved ones and guests alike. The silky pasta envelops an even silkier crabmeat-flecked filling, infused with an intensely flavoured crustacean vinaigrette, with more crabmeat spooned over the top, and finished with a scattering of fried basil and caramelised guanciale. Impressive stuff. **Serves 6**

1 × quantity Egg pasta dough (p. 111)

150 g (5½ oz) guanciale, cut into 5 mm (¼ in) dice

oil, for shallow-frying

5 basil sprigs, leaves picked, small ones separated

60 g (2 oz/¼ cup) unsalted butter, diced

60 g (2 oz) parmesan, finely grated

400–500 ml (13½–17 fl oz/ 2 cups) Crustacean vinaigrette (p. 52)

250 g (9 oz) cooked crabmeat

Crab & ricotta filling

2½ tablespoons extra-virgin olive oil

60 g (2 oz/¼ cup) unsalted butter

4 French shallots, finely diced

4 garlic cloves, finely chopped

2 red bird's eye chillies, finely chopped

300 g (10½ oz) cooked crabmeat

650 g (1 lb 7 oz) drained ricotta

120 g (4½ oz) parmesan, finely grated

1 egg and 2 egg yolks, lightly beaten

fresh fenugreek, or fresh or fried basil, to serve

Staples
EVOO, S&P

For the filling, heat the oil and butter in a frying pan over a medium heat. Cook the shallot and garlic until just turning golden, about 5 minutes. Add the chilli and fry for 1 minute. Stir in the crabmeat, just to heat through, then tip into a bowl and cool for 5 minutes. Once cooled, add the ricotta, parmesan and egg mixture, season with salt and pepper and mix until well combined. Transfer to a piping (icing) bag fitted with a 1.5 cm (½ in) nozzle and refrigerate.

Roll the pasta into sheets (see p. 111), then cut into 40 cm (15¾ in) lengths. You will need eight 40 cm (15¾ in) sheets (two are spare for any that tear). Cook them in ample boiling salted water for 2 minutes, two sheets at a time. Lift out carefully (the pasta will be slippery to handle) and refresh in iced water, then drain off, shaking off any water. Coat with a little oil and press flat, layering between baking paper. Don't stress if one or two break or get punctured; toss them straight in butter, season, heap with parmesan and enjoy.

Cut the cooked pasta sheets into 20 cm (8 in) lengths; they will lengthen once cooked. There will be some scraps – eat these, or dry them and use for soup. If you have excess sheets, just cut into pappardelle (see p. 112) or the like and use or dry for later.

Preheat the oven to 200°C (400°F) fan-forced. Line a baking tray with baking paper.

Fry the guanciale in a dry frying pan over a high heat, tossing frequently until translucent, about 6 minutes. Drain and set aside to crisp up, then lightly crush using a mortar and pestle.

Heat about 2 cm (¾ in) of oil in a saucepan over a high heat. Fry the large basil leaves in batches of five for 20 seconds, then drain in one layer. They will crisp as they cool.

Lay the pasta sheets out flat. Pipe about 2½ tablespoons of the filling along the long edge of each sheet. Roll up the pasta tightly to make the cannelloni. Place each on the baking tray, seam side down, in sets of two touching. Divide the butter and parmesan between each set. Bake for 10 minutes, then turn on the oven grill (broiler) until browned, about 3 minutes.

Just before serving, heat the crustacean vinaigrette in a small frying pan until just simmering. Add the crabmeat and warm through briefly, then stir the small basil leaves through and take off the heat.

Plate the cannelloni in sets of two, then spoon the dressing and crabmeat over. Finish with the guanciale and fenugreek or basil, and serve immediately.

Summer vegetable lasagne Ⓥ

This lasagne is exuberantly flavoured with the vegetables that scream summer to me: capsicum (bell pepper), eggplant (aubergine), zucchini (courgette) and tomato. They're also the ratatouille vegetables, but really they are just a classic southern Mediterranean combination, with the long hot days cramming them full of sun-kissed flavour. The key here is roasting the vegetables first, which wicks out a lot of the water, concentrating them and making this just so much more intense and flavourful. **Serves 6–8**

3 large red capsicums (bell peppers), cut into 2 cm (¾ in) dice
3 zucchini (courgettes), cut into 2 cm (¾ in) dice
2 large eggplants (aubergines), peeled in stripes and cut into 2 cm (¾ in) dice
100 ml (3½ fl oz) extra-virgin olive oil

2 teaspoons dried oregano
4 large garlic cloves, sliced
1 × quantity Béchamel (p. 70), warmed
500 g (1 lb 2 oz) fresh pasta sheets (see p. 111), or instant lasagne
200 g (7 oz) ricotta
200 g (7 oz) baby bocconcini, torn

250 g (9 oz) scamorza or firm mozzarella, finely sliced
100 g (3½ oz/1 cup) finely grated Grana Padano
½ bunch of basil, leaves picked and torn
800 ml (27 fl oz) Simple tomato sugo (p. 116)

Staples
EVOO, S&P

Preheat the oven to 170°C (340°F) fan-forced.

Add the capsicum and zucchini to one high-sided baking dish, and the eggplant to another. Drizzle the oil over the vegetables, with more of it on the eggplant. Sprinkle with the oregano and garlic, season with salt and pepper and roast for 50 minutes, stirring every 15 minutes or so. Once the vegetables have collapsed, tip into a large bowl and combine.

Spoon a thin layer of béchamel into a 25 × 30 cm (10 × 12 in) baking dish. Top with a layer of pasta. Follow with another layer of béchamel, half the ricotta and bocconcini, one-third of the scamorza, a generous scattering of parmesan and half the basil. Season with salt and pepper and drizzle with a little oil.

Add another layer of pasta, followed by half the sugo and half the roasted vegetables.

Top with more pasta, then repeat the béchamel, cheese and basil layer. Add another layer of pasta, followed by the remaining sugo and vegetables.

Finish with the last of the pasta. Top with the remaining béchamel, scamorza and parmesan.

Cover with baking paper, then foil. Bake for 45 minutes, then uncover and bake for a further 20 minutes, until golden.

Preparing gnocchi

For many, making gnocchi is one of those seemingly impenetrable techniques. It takes a little practice, a little time to understand the texture – when a little more flour is necessary, when a little less – but it is not complicated. Just do it, then do it again. You'll get better at it, and quicker at it, and you'll learn to love it, as it is such a satisfying thing to make. That sense of specialisation with gnocchi brings with it all sorts of 'absolute' rules. The truth is, there is not one absolute way to make gnocchi. Indeed, if you watch it being made traditionally across Italy, there is a wide variation in the types of potatoes used, from starchy ones to waxy ones; some cooks peel only after boiling, some before; some employ egg, others do not. In other words, the method is not that precise.

Lasagne

Preheat the oven to 170°C (340°F) fan-forced. Warm 1.5–2 litres (51–68 fl oz/ 6–8 cups) Ragù (pp. 283, 335, 336, 576). Prepare 500 g (1 lb 2 oz) fresh pasta sheets or instant lasagne, 1 × quantity Béchamel (p. 70), 200 g (7 oz) ricotta, 200 g (7 oz) torn baby bocconcini, 250 g (9 oz) firm finely sliced mozzarella or scamorza, 100 g (3½ oz/1 cup) finely grated Grana Padano and ½ bunch basil, leaves picked and torn. Spoon a layer of ragù into a 30 × 40 cm (12 × 15¾ in) baking dish and top with a layer of pasta. Follow with a layer of béchamel, half the ricotta and bocconcini, one-third of the mozzarella, a generous scattering of parmesan and half the basil. Season with salt and pepper and drizzle a little oil over. Add another layer of pasta, followed by half the remaining ragù. Top with more pasta, then repeat the béchamel, cheese and basil layer. Add another layer of pasta, followed by the remaining ragù, then the last of the pasta. Top with the remaining béchamel and parmesan. Cover with baking paper, then foil. Bake for 45 minutes. (At this point, you could cool the lasagne and freeze for another day. Simply defrost and cook, uncovered, for about 30 minutes.) Remove the baking paper and foil and bake for a further 20 minutes, until golden. Serves 6–8. For a Roman touch, finely chop 6 firmly boiled eggs (see p. 351) and add to the middle ragù layer with about 8 slices of rolled pancetta.

Different types of potatoes do work, though waxier potatoes tend to be less successful – in my opinion, of course. Desiree potatoes, which are somewhere in the middle of being waxy or starchy, and are readily available, make wonderful gnocchi. Is there a holy grail potato that trumps them? Probably, but desiree potatoes have excellent flavour, achieve the right texture and are easy to work. Too waxy and the dough can get sticky; too floury and binding into a cohesive dough can be tricky – but it will work with an experienced hand, and the result will be light and fluffy.

It *is* important, though, to work with a hot and dry dough. And chefs go to all sorts of lengths to improve recipes by infinitesimal degrees. In the restaurant, we bake whole potatoes on rock salt to achieve a super-dry and light mash, but the yield is very variable, so it's a dough you make by feel, after much practice. You can also boil potatoes whole, then peel, and they will tend to be drier. It works just as well to peel the potatoes first, cut into evenly sized pieces so they cook evenly, then boil until properly tender and drain well – or drain then add to the dry pot over the heat to expel any moisture. As said, it doesn't need to be an over-complicated process.

Either way, once you have passed the potato through a food mill or ricer, work the flour in immediately. The heat encourages the starch and gluten to bind, meaning the dough will come together quickly. If you work the dough too much, the gluten bonds will strengthen and the gnocchi will be tough, so it's best to work quickly with a light hand (don't panic, just don't go and have a cup of tea) is best. How much flour the mash takes up will depend on the starch and water content of the potato and this will always vary, so I add the minimum flour I might need, then add more if it's not coming together or is sticky. It's a feel thing, and you'll understand by doing.

Many people add egg with the flour. I do not. I just don't think it's necessary, and I find it makes gnocchi less light and airy. Perhaps eggs were used in some Italian regions due to the available potatoes, or low protein levels in the flour. I'm not sure.

Once rolled and shaped, cook the gnocchi in boiling water straight away, in batches if needed. Once they float, after 30 seconds or so, they're done. Dressed with oil, they'll hold well in a low oven, or you can refresh them in iced water and refrigerate for later. If you're super organised, just lift them straight into the sauce you have bubbling on the stove.

Classic potato gnocchi Ⓥ ⓋⒼ

Pair with

Roasted tomato passata (p. 660).

Any ragù (pp. 259, 283, 335, 336, 535, 576).

Use in Gnocchi with leek & gorgonzola (p. 602).

Use in Pan-seared potato gnocchi with scallops, mushrooms & lemon (p. 140).

Pan-fry the drained hot gnocchi in olive oil, finishing with a little butter cooked until brown, and serve with saltimbocca (pp. 268, 702) or roast duck (pp. 258, 264) – or toss with parsley and a little lemon juice and serve with seared fish.

1 kg (2 lb 3 oz) desiree potatoes, or other all-purpose or starchy potatoes, peeled and cut into evenly sized pieces; you will need a peeled weight of 900 g (2 lb) potatoes

1 tablespoon sea salt
4 litres (135 fl oz/16 cups) water
300 g (10½ oz/2 cups) '00' flour, plus extra for dusting

Special equipment
Potato ricer or food mill

Staples
EVOO, BTR, FLR

Add the potato, salt and water to a large saucepan and bring to the boil. Cook until the potato is very tender and almost falls apart when tested with a knife, then drain very well. Stand for 2 minutes to steam off some moisture, or return to the dry pan over a medium heat for a minute or so.

Meanwhile, put a large saucepan of salted water on to boil, so you can cook the gnocchi as soon as they're shaped. Preheat the oven to 100°C (210°F).

Pass the hot cooked potato through a ricer, onto a clean bench. Sift the flour over the top, then chop in with a pastry scraper/cutter or large knife, to make incorporating and handling the hot dough easier. Mix to an even dough, a little like soft playdough, adding extra flour as needed. Knead about five times to a smooth, feathery dough. Dust again with a little flour and shape into a fat log. Cover with a tea towel.

Cut the dough into six pieces, then roll into snakes about 1.5 cm (½ in) thick. Very lightly dust with flour, then cut into 2 cm (¾ in) pieces. You can line up the snakes and cut two or three at once, if you like. You can cut the gnocchi straight or on an angle, then leave as is, pinch into a little cushion or roll over the back of a fork or pasta paddle to add ridges to trap the sauce. If shaping all the dough at once – rather than cooking a batch while shaping the next lot of gnocchi – transfer to a floured tray and cover with a tea towel.

Drop the gnocchi into the pot of boiling water, gently lifting them from the base of the pan with a slotted spoon so they don't stick. Once they float, cook for about 30 seconds (about 3 minutes total), but don't let the water boil again or they will swell too much. Lift out with a slotted spoon or strainer, drain briefly, then add to a large baking dish with a little oil or butter to coat, then keep warm in the oven, for an hour at the most. Repeat for the remaining gnocchi.

Once all are cooked, add the gnocchi to your sauce. Toss carefully, or combine with a metal spoon. Don't use a blunt object, such as a wooden spoon, as you will mash the dumplings; just run the blade of the spoon against the side of the pan, turning the gnocchi over to coat – or gently toss if you have the knack.

If you want to cook the gnocchi ahead of time, as soon as you lift them from the cooking water, dunk them in iced/cold water until cool, about 2 minutes. Drain, coat with oil or butter, then spread out in a large airtight container and refrigerate. They will store for 2–3 days like this. To serve, refresh for 2 minutes in simmering water before adding to your sauce.

Gnocchi alla romana ⓥ

This is quite an ancient dish, somewhat resembling set polenta – semolina enriched with butter and parmesan and set with eggs. The cooking process is similar to traditional polenta, too, albeit quicker. Once cut and baked, with a dusting of cheese, these dumplings are radiantly golden, with a crunchy exterior that reveals a fluffy, buttery interior. The dumplings are not pasta as such, serving more as an accompaniment to vegetable and meat dishes, but they can be baked with cheese, such as gorgonzola or taleggio, and served as a meal with some sharply dressed bitter leaves. **Serves 8**

1 litre (34 fl oz/4 cups) full-cream (whole) milk
300 g (10½ oz) fine semolina
2 eggs, lightly beaten

100 g (3½ oz) unsalted butter
100 g (3½ oz/1 cup) Grana Padano, finely grated

Staples
BTR, EVOO, S&P

Bring the milk to the boil in a saucepan over a medium heat, then rain in the semolina, continually whisking until smooth. Cook for about 8 minutes, until it's a smooth paste. Remove from the heat and whisk in the eggs, half the butter and about 60 g (2 oz) of the cheese. Stir through until well combined, then season with salt and pepper.

Oil a 20 × 30 cm (8 × 12 in) baking dish, then tip in the mixture, smoothing out evenly with a spatula. Refrigerate for 1 hour, until firm.

Preheat the oven to 200°C (400°F) fan-forced.

Cut the gnocchi into squares, then arrange on a lined baking tray with space between each piece, as they will swell. Alternatively, cut out 4 cm (1½ in) rounds with a pastry cutter, and layer the gnocchi like fallen dominoes in a buttered baking dish.

Sprinkle with the remaining cheese and bake for about 25 minutes, until the edges are golden. Serve.

The gnocchi will keep in an airtight container in the fridge for 3 days. Reheat in a moderate oven to serve.

Pair with

This is a great accompaniment to saltimbocca (pp. 268, 702).

Their pure, uncomplicated flavour and texture can really go with any braise or roast, such as Abbacchio al forno (p. 315), roast duck (pp. 258, 264) or Porchetta (p. 338).

Serve as a starter with salads, or braised vegetables such as fennel, artichokes and peas.

Dress the gnocchi with gorgonzola and parmesan, then bake until golden. Serve scattered with walnuts, and shredded radicchio dressed with oil and balsamic vinegar.

Spoon Béchamel (p. 70) over the gnocchi, sprinkle with grated parmesan and bake as a side for crumbed chicken, veal schnitzel, pork schnitzel (p. 345) or steak.

Classic potato gnocchi

Pan-seared potato gnocchi with scallops, mushrooms & lemon

This is a busy dish to cook, but it's well worth the brief moment of stress. Just familiarise yourself with the method, as there'll be no time to read and absorb the next step in the heat of battle. And have everything on hand. Also, have your guests seated and ready to go – none of this ambling to the table, finishing conversations, lingering over that martini. The cooking will be over in a flash, and the result is spectacular. **Serves 4**

Pair with

A simple leafy salad.

300 g (10½ oz) large scallops (roe on), or bug (flat-head lobster) tails
250 g (9 oz) king brown mushrooms, sliced lengthways 5 mm (¼ in) thick, then halved lengthways
4 garlic cloves, finely sliced

600 g (1 lb 5 oz) cooked Classic potato gnocchi (p. 137)
80 g (2¾ oz) butter
5 thyme sprigs, leaves stripped
½ teaspoon chilli powder
80 ml (2½ fl oz/⅓ cup) white wine

200 ml (7 fl oz) Golden chicken stock (p. 54)
80 ml (2½ fl oz/⅓ cup) pouring (single/light) cream
juice of 1 lemon

Staples
EVOO, S&P

Have a large saucepan of simmering water ready to refresh the gnocchi (unless they've been freshly cooked and are being kept warm in a low oven).

Season the scallops with salt and pepper and coat with oil. Set aside.

Heat a large frying pan over a high heat for 2 minutes. Add a good splash of oil, then the mushrooms and garlic. Season with salt and pepper and sauté until softened, about 3 minutes. Tip into a large bowl.

Meanwhile, refresh the gnocchi in the pot of simmering water for 2 minutes.

Drain the gnocchi and tip on top of the mushrooms.

Wipe the pan out and place back over a high heat for 2 minutes. Spread the scallops out in the pan. Sear on one side for 2 minutes, then add half the butter, the thyme and chilli powder. Once the butter has melted, toss the scallops once, then immediately tip from the pan into a separate bowl.

Add the gnocchi and mushrooms to the pan. Add the wine, which will reduce quickly, then add the stock and boil for 1 minute.

Add the cream and remaining butter, bring to a simmer and reduce a little, until the sauce clings to the gnocchi.

Season with salt and pepper, return the scallops, add the lemon juice and toss to combine. Serve immediately.

Ricotta & semolina gnocchi

These dumplings are delicate to make, and so light, with a gentle crust of semolina enveloping a pillowy interior of milky ricotta. They need the simplest of sauces, so as not to overpower the delicate flavour or distract from the unique texture. And it's important to use properly fresh ricotta. **Serves 4–6**

700 g (1 lb 9 oz) fresh ricotta
100 g (3½ oz/⅔ cup) '00' flour

1 egg
1 teaspoon salt flakes

zest and juice ¼ lemon
300 g (10½ oz) fine semolina

Line a sieve with paper towel. Add the ricotta and drain for 30 minutes.

Tip the ricotta into a bowl. Add the flour, egg, salt, lemon zest and lemon juice and combine well. Transfer to a piping (icing) bag fitted with a 2 cm (¾ in) nozzle.

Scatter the semolina evenly in a large tray. Pipe the ricotta mixture onto the tray in long straight lines. Carefully roll the ricotta 'tubes' in the semolina to coat. Refrigerate, uncovered, for 2 hours.

Cut the ricotta into 2.5 cm (1 in) pieces and coat well in the semolina. Refrigerate overnight. The moisture will be absorbed by the semolina, forming a crust on the outside.

The next day, roll the gnocchi in the excess semolina in the tray to coat well, covering any moisture spots. Refrigerate for 1 hour.

Cook the gnocchi in simmering salted water for 3½ minutes, until they float to the surface. Don't boil the gnocchi, as they are delicate and will swell too much, and the coating will rupture.

Drain, then carefully toss in your warm chosen sauce and serve.

Pair with

Burnt butter, sage & walnut sauce (p. 73).

Green aglio e olio (p. 122).

Burnt butter sauce with lemon, capers & parsley (p. 73). Delicious additions to this sauce are a handful of French tarragon, 80 g (2¾ oz/½ cup) toasted pine nuts and 80 g (2¾ oz) currants that have been soaked in hot water for 30 minutes, then drained.

Toss in melted or browned butter, season with salt and pepper and serve with Twice-roasted duck (p. 264) with a jus (see p. 66) and pickled grapes (see p. 630).

Ricotta & spinach gnudi Ⓥ

In a food processor, blitz 500 g (1 lb 2 oz) well-drained full-fat ricotta, 1 large egg, 120 g (4½ oz/1¼ cups) grated parmesan, 1 teaspoon nutmeg and salt and pepper until smooth. Transfer to a bowl and add 500 g (1 lb 2 oz) drained cooked spinach (make sure it's well chopped – you can use frozen) and 160 g (5½ oz) plain (all-purpose flour). Thoroughly combine, then roll into balls of about 3 cm (1¼ in). Lay them out on a tray dusted with flour and chill for 1 hour or overnight. Cook in simmering salted water for 3½ minutes, until they float to the surface. Don't boil the gnudi, as they are delicate and will swell too much, and the coating will rupture. Drain, then carefully toss in your warm chosen sauce and serve. Serves 6.

Ricotta & semolina gnocchi with Roasted tomato passata (p. 660)

Also see

Stocks 45

Barley 'risotto' with mushrooms & speck 572

Risi e bisi 613

Pumpkin, rosemary & taleggio risotto 632

Risotto

Risotto

There seems to be a lot of fearfulness about risotto. A sense that it is difficult, fraught with pitfalls: that it is a dish for experts. This is all nonsense of course. Risotto is not hard to make, though a poorly executed one can certainly be a thing of woe. There are general rules, but they're not as rigid as one might think, and they are not hard to follow. In fact, the core rules describe the same arc as most fundaments of cooking: use the right ingredients, the best ingredients (though these can certainly be humble), keep it simple, pay attention and taste. Always taste.

Risotto, as is inherent in its name, is all about the rice – but it is also, in fact, equally about stock. The quality of those two ingredients is the heartbeat of a fine risotto. The best rice will not transform a poor stock, or vice versa, and a simple Risotto bianco (p. 148) made with Golden chicken stock (p. 54) and quality rice – and yes, butter and good parmesan – is truly a thing of beauty, requiring only seasoning to sing.

The 'wetness' of your finished risotto is a matter of preference, and indeed you will find much dispute on this across Italy – as there is about so many ultrafine culinary details. The term all'onda is often cited to describe a correct rendering of stock to rice, with the expression referring to the risotto rippling in small waves like the surface of the ocean – or a lagoon perhaps, as it is often attributed as a Venetian term. The Venetians in particular favour a looser risotto, though they are justifiably famous for seafood risotto, which demands a luscious looseness to complement the delicacy of seafood.

The northern regions of Lombardy, Piedmont and the Veneto are Italy's rice hubs, with a huge selection of rice varieties now produced. The nineteenth century saw an exploration of crossbreeding cultivars to achieve different outcomes. Rice has been cultivated there since at least the fifteenth century, with risotto the cornerstone of Italian rice use, though it finds its way into soups as well, perhaps most famously in the ultra-loose risotto-like Risi e bisi (p. 613). While historically a very northern thing, you will find risotto right across Italy, and it is equally embedded in traditions in central and southern Italy.

We often think about Italian food traditions as being ancient, protected by intractable guardians over countless generations, a line of nonnas filing back into the mists of time, turning out the same dish. But that's not really true. The traditions run deep, true, and family secrets are passed down from one generation to the next, but the Italians are adaptable. To think of Italian food and not think of tomatoes is almost impossible, but the Italians guarded their traditions long before tomatoes arrived, and before potatoes, too. Granted, a near-500-year history of tomato cultivation is not a blip, but the point is that not all Italian traditions are quite as primordial as we often think. Natural cooks – and Italy has its fair share – always tinker. It's in their nature. Even in a land as fiercely wedded to tradition as Italy, cooking is never static. Once you have grasped the basics of risotto, as with pasta, adhere to tradition, if you will, or tinker as much as it pleases you.

When I first started cooking, you needed to track down a specialty Italian grocer to find the right rice, and it was always arborio. My first risotto memories are of making mushroom risotto, and arancini balls with the leftovers. Today, arborio is widely available in supermarkets, and it is grown quite successfully in Australia, but I'm now more likely to use carnaroli or vialone nano rice. Both are relatively modern cultivars with distinct properties. Arborio releases a lot of starch from its outer layer, yielding a quite creamy, slightly sticky result, but it can be heavy and stodgy if not handled well. Vialone nano has short, stubby grains and takes on lots of liquid, making for a very tasty risotto. Either type works well with robust flavours, such as mushrooms, sausage and sage, or in a red wine risotto, say. Carnaroli grains are longer and finer, both absorbing liquid and releasing good amounts of starch. It's what I prefer for a seafood or delicate vegetable risotto, or something super simple like a saffron risotto.

EXTRA SELECTION
100% CARNAROLI
PRODUCT OF ITALY
30-12 2021
L. 190594

Exclusively selected and distrib
by

ENOTECA
SILENO
GASTRONOMIA DAL 1953

Ancient Renowned Rice Mill

FERRON ®

Isola della Scala
Since 1650

ISOLA DELLA SCALA
• VERONA •

Carnaroli
The Risotto R

Preparing a risotto

Risotto is a dish of focused attention. And I think this is where some of its mystique stems – that it requires constant attention for about 20 minutes. I'm not sure why this is seen as such an ordeal, as most of us are required to concentrate for longer periods all the time. And the attention required is not taxing. You just need to keep the rice in motion more often than not, keeping the grains in contact with liquid and stopping anything from catching. Truth is, you can add slightly larger applications of stock and stir less frequently in the earlier stages, if you like. There are champions of no-stir methods, and both will yield good results, done properly – but I like to stir. And I also appreciate the singular catharsis of crafting a risotto bent over a favourite copper pot or the like. But then I do like to cook.

The method you take is personal. This is my approach.

Firstly, your sublime home-made stock needs to be hot on the stove. You could use a superior bought stock, but if you intend on using a supermarket broth, your time is better spent otherwise. The stock reduces and absorbs as you cook, so the flavour of the stock will largely determine the flavour of the finished dish, no matter what else you add. Your stock can be a quick one or long-simmered, but it needs to be well flavoured – so even if you don't have the ideal amount, start your risotto right.

If I'm cooking with prawns (shrimp), I'll fry off the heads in olive oil until darkened in colour and releasing their juices, then cover with water or a light fish or chicken stock and simmer for about 20 minutes with some aromatic vegetables and whatever herbs I have on hand (see p. 50). Similarly, a left-over roast chicken stock (see p. 49) or duck stock (see p. 50) or the broth from cooking a ham hock (see p. 324) does the job; just watch your seasoning with the latter. I keep stock on hand for making risotto on the fly, so I'll often make a quick stock and freeze it for later, wasting nothing. And I'm always thankful I have. If using clams (vongole) or mussels, I'll steam them with a little wine until just opened, then add the strained juices to whatever stock I have. If rehydrating dried wild mushrooms in water, I always add the umami-rich water to the rice or to the stock.

Keep the stock in a saucepan on a very low heat with a ladle at the ready. If I've made a quick stock from a left-over roast bird or the like, I'll just poise a fine-mesh sieve on the simmering stockpot, then ladle the broth through the sieve into the risotto pan, to extract all the goodness and flavour from the bones right up to the last. If ever you run out of stock, hot water from a kettle can be used to finish a risotto or to top up your dwindling stock.

Cook the risotto in a wide, heavy-based saucepan. You want even heat distribution, and space is important to agitate the rice and whip in the butter and cheese at the end. Very large amounts of risotto make this hard, so should be avoided – as should small quantities. The soffritto is where the cooking starts, as it so often does, with onion or French shallots (I prefer the flavour and delicacy of texture of the latter) – and garlic, though it is often not traditional. The onion or shallots need to be finely diced, never larger than a grain of rice, and sweated down in butter or oil, or both, until very soft and just starting to colour. If the garlic burns or the onion catches, you're better off starting again. You'll never rid the rice of the flavour of burnt garlic – it's a curse – and the onion will fleck the risotto, rather than melting away and surrendering to the broth, as it should – a lesser fault, but not ideal, nonetheless. Rushing the soffritto can also leave the onion visible and crunchy in the finished dish, which again is far from desirable.

Once the onion has softened, the rice can be added, but if I'm using robust ingredients, such as pancetta, that can handle (and will benefit from) longer cooking, I'll fry these first until coloured before adding the rice. Or, if I haven't already made stock from them, I'll sometimes throw prawn (shrimp) heads in now, if I have them. Similarly, if I'm using dried porcini, the soaked and chopped mushrooms will go in at this stage.

Once the rice is added, the real stirring starts. The aim here is to coat all the grains with fat and slightly toast the rice, so that it is hot to touch, stirring all the time for a couple of minutes.

Then the wine goes in. It will sizzle, as the mix will be hotter than it looks, and the wine will reduce until it's gone ... stirring, stirring. Now the stock, a ladle or two, stirring until it is mostly absorbed, then another one or two ... stirring, stirring ...

The rice will be cooked in somewhere between 15–20 minutes – and when I say cooked, I mean al dente, still with a little chalky bite. If you press a grain between your fingers, the outer layer will yield to the pressure and reveal a thin white inner, which may be whole, or broken into two or three pieces. If that white core is gone or barely present, you've gone too far. It's also always best to be conservative with your stock applications towards the end, as you can't reverse a heavy hand at this point, meaning a soupy or overcooked result, or both. I like the rice to have a noticeable bite, but you can take it further if you prefer – just don't lose that texture, and remember that it will still cook a little as it sits before serving.

In my opinion, stiff risotto is not something one should aspire to making. When risotto is plated, and you tap the plate – yes, classically often a plate, not a bowl, though I usually use shallow bowls – on the bench, it should level out rather than hold its form, with ripples in the liquid. In general, I will leave the risotto a bit wetter for seafood, though not soupy.

The risotto should focus on a hero flavour, which might just be a beautifully flavoured stock – but as with pasta, the rice should be given equal billing and not be swamped with too much or too many embellishments. Even when you serve a risotto with another dish, such as Risotto alla Milanese (p. 148) with Osso buco (p. 296), it is not a sideshow.

Usually when I make risotto, hero ingredients will have been blanched, seared, sautéed, puréed or roasted to a certain point, to get the best from that ingredient. When cooking seafood, I always sear it first in a hot pan to half-cook and get some caramelisation, then add at the end to warm through and finish cooking. Cooking solely in the risotto gives seafood a boiled character, which I very much dislike.

If I'm adding something like pumpkin (winter squash) to a risotto, I will always roast it first, reducing the water content, concentrating the flavour and adding caramelised notes. It will also hold its shape better. Steaming or boiling the pumpkin first will result in a bland, soapy character, a lack of flavour focus, and the pumpkin will likely break up into a purée. Similarly, I may blanch and refresh asparagus or pan-fry it first, then add it towards the end of cooking, whereas the pumpkin will go in about two-thirds of the way through cooking – it just depends on the robustness of the ingredient. If using something like braised oxtail or a ham hock, I will add it about the same time as I would pumpkin, but seared prawns (shrimp) or opened clams (vongole) will go in at the end to finish cooking in the residual heat.

The final stage, which is very important, is known as mantecatura in Italian. Oddly, the word seems to be derived from the Spanish word for butter, and refers to the process of beating in cold butter and parmesan (or generally just butter with some extra-virgin olive oil for a seafood risotto) to create a creamy texture. This is done off the heat and, depending on the delicacy of the ingredients in the risotto, can be performed quite vigorously to properly emulsify. Then the risotto rests for 2 minutes before serving, so the rice will take up the cheese and stock a little more, and the risotto will thicken.

I have naturally given quantities for rice in all the recipes, though I never measure it myself. The same goes for the stock. I have what I have, and I will bolster it sometimes as described earlier. I generally add a handful of rice per person, and one for the pot. This is certainly not one of the rules of risotto; it's just what I've always done. A general allowance of 100 g (3½ oz) uncooked rice per person and 400–500 ml (13½–17 fl oz/2 cups) stock for each portion is a good basic guide.

Aside from the quality of the stock and rice, use the best cheese you can. It's indulgent, but I like to use Parmigiano Reggiano, which makes a real difference when the risotto is very simple. Good Grana Padano is also fine, or use a mix. I also make sure I have a little extra Parmigiano to snack on while the risotto comes together, spoon in one hand, glass of wine in the other. It helps with the catharsis. Cheese is not classically used in a seafood risotto, but a little can be used to enrich it without clashing. Sometimes, instead of (or as well as) some cheese, I use an enriching swirl of crème fraîche or a dollop of mascarpone in a seafood risotto, to up the creaminess.

Risotto bianco GF V

This is the foundation recipe for risotto, with all manner of potential additions making it distinctly different. It is, however, quite lovely as it is, especially if you splurge on good Parmigiano Reggiano – though Grana Padano will yield a fine result, too. **Serves 4–6**

2 litres (68 fl oz/8 cups)
  Golden chicken stock
  (p. 54), or Classic white
  vegetable stock (p. 51)
2½ tablespoons extra-virgin
  olive oil

5 French shallots, or 1 onion,
  finely diced
3 garlic cloves, finely sliced
1 fresh bay leaf
500 g (1 lb 2 oz) carnaroli,
  vialone nano or arborio rice
200 ml (7 fl oz) white wine

120 g (4½ oz) unsalted butter,
  diced
180 g (6 oz) Parmigiano
  Reggiano, finely grated

Staples
S&P

Heat the stock in a saucepan and keep hot over a low heat.

Heat the oil in a wide, heavy-based saucepan over a medium heat. Add the shallot, garlic and bay leaf, season lightly with salt, then sweat until softened but not caramelised, about 5 minutes.

Add the rice, stirring constantly until the grains are hot to the touch, about 2 minutes, then add the wine. Stir until the wine has reduced to almost nothing, then start adding a ladleful or two of stock. Stir until almost dry again, then repeat. Cook until the rice is al dente, 15–20 minutes. If you run out of stock, use hot water from the kettle.

Turn off the heat and add the butter and parmesan. Whip the risotto quite vigorously with your spoon until creamy. Adjust the seasoning if needed, adding a little more stock if too stiff.

Stand for 2 minutes before serving.

Make it different

Risotto bianco with brown butter, hazelnuts, lemon & ricotta. GF V This is an easy way to turn a risotto bianco into a somewhat fancy dish. Add half the butter to the risotto with the parmesan, then melt the remaining butter in a small frying pan over a medium heat. Once starting to foam, add 60 g (2 oz) chopped roasted hazelnuts and season with salt and pepper. Cook until the butter is golden brown, about 2 minutes, then take off the heat and squeeze in half a lemon. Plate the risotto and top each serve with a small blob of ricotta – about 100 g (3½ oz) for the whole recipe. Spoon the burnt butter and hazelnuts over and finish by drizzling with a little quality balsamic vinegar.

Risotto alla Milanese. This is the traditional accompaniment to Osso buco (p. 296). It is simply a risotto bianco delightfully stained with saffron. Follow the basic recipe, but infuse eight saffron threads into the stock over a very low heat for 20 minutes before cooking. Serve the osso buco spooned over the side of the risotto. You can take it even further by grilling split marrow bones under the oven grill (broiler) until hot and to serve alongside the osso buco, or you can scoop out the marrow and drop on top. Finish with a gremolata (pp. 16, 296).

Oxtail risotto. GF Use a well-skimmed oxtail broth (see p. 56) – no need to clarify it – to make a risotto with the same method, adding the picked oxtail meat after about 10 minutes of cooking. Just before serving, stir through a few handfuls of chopped parsley or chervil, and maybe black truffle.

Ham hock & pea risotto. GF Use the broth from cooking a ham hock (see p. 324) instead of (or combined with) some chicken stock. Add the chopped or flaked ham after about 10 minutes of cooking. Finish with a few handfuls of blanched peas just before starting the mantecatura.

Ham hock, rosemary & taleggio risotto. GF Use the broth from cooking a ham hock (see p. 324), infused with four rosemary sprigs for about 10 minutes over a low heat. Add the chopped or flaked ham after about 10 minutes of cooking. Use half the quantity of Parmigiano Reggiano, and finish with 150 g (5½ oz) chilled taleggio cut into 1 cm (½ in) dice and stirred through after finishing the mantecatura. The idea is that the cheese will melt but still be visible in dissolving chunks when plated.

Arancini

Use well-chilled left-over risotto scooped into heaped tablespoons (about 50 g/ 1¾ oz) and add a small dice of soft scamorza or fresh mozzarella-style cheese to the centre. Roll into a firm ball and chill. To crumb the arancini, roll them in plain (all-purpose) flour, then in a bowl of beaten egg (or left-over egg whites) and, finally, roll them in fine Japanese panko crumbs. (If the crumbs are coarse, blitz them in a food processor until fine.) Chill the crumbed arancini in the fridge while you heat the oil to 175°C (345°F). Deep-fry the arancini for 4–5 minutes, until golden brown, then serve hot.

Sausage & sage risotto. Remove the skins from five Italian pork and fennel sausages, then crumble the meat into your pan with a little oil. Cook until browned, then remove from the pan. Add some more oil and make the Risotto bianco (opposite) as normal, adding half a bunch of finely chopped sage leaves with the rice. Return the sausage meat after the rice has been cooking for about 5 minutes, then proceed with the recipe.

Spring vegetable risotto. (GF) (V) Trim and slice a bunch of asparagus. Cut three small zucchini (courgettes) into 1 cm (½ in) dice. Fry the vegies in your pan with a little oil for 2–3 minutes over a high heat, seasoning with salt and pepper. Remove from the pan and proceed with the recipe (opposite), adding the greens back in for the last minute of cooking, along with a few handfuls of peas and some torn zucchini blossoms, before finishing with the cheese and butter.

Risotto funghi. (GF) (V) Stir in the Mushroom ragù (p. 576) halfway through cooking.

Crab, prawn or bug tail risotto. (GF) The basic technique is the same for any seafood risotto (see p. 149), but I always like to reinforce the stock with the main ingredients, which might mean frying or roasting prawn (shrimp) heads or crab shells, then infusing them in a light Fish stock (p. 52) or Golden chicken stock (p. 54) for 20 minutes. Sear the meat in the pan, then set aside. Make the risotto as normal, dropping the seafood in before starting the mantecatura. I would omit the cheese, but add a good slurp of peppery olive oil.

Risotto with ricotta, spinach & verjuice-braised leek. (GF) (V) This recipe is wonderful with spinach; it is also an ideal way to use fine young cime di rape if you can find it at the market. Or, even better, if you grow cime di rape, pick off and use the fine leaves, stems and flowering heads (the thick stems are too woody). Either way, it's an elegant way to finish off a simple risotto. Heat a splash of olive oil in a frying pan over a medium heat. Add three trimmed leeks and gently brown all over. Season with salt and pepper, then add 250 ml (8½ fl oz/1 cup) verjuice and 200 ml (7 fl oz) water. Simmer for about 10 minutes, until the leeks are tender and the liquid has evaporated. Cut the leeks into 3 cm (1¼ in) thick rounds and set aside. Meanwhile, cook 300 g (10½ oz) chopped English spinach leaves – or cime di rape leaves and fine stalks, cut into 3 cm (1¼ in) pieces – in a good splash of water with a pinch of salt. After about 5 minutes, once the spinach has wilted and the water has evaporated, add a splash of oil and keep warm. Add the leek and spinach before finishing the risotto with the cheese and butter. Crumble 200 g (7 oz) ricotta over the plated risotto and drizzle with a little peppery olive oil.

Risotto nero with cuttlefish (GF)

This is a very dramatic risotto, a real showstopper. The black rice sits in vivid contrast to the white cuttlefish, with an engulfing fragrance of briny seafood, toasted garlic, peppery oil, bright lemon and parsley. It's also a risotto best avoided by those on a first date, as that ink does tend to stain teeth (temporarily) and cloth in equal measure. **Serves 6**

2 litres (68 fl oz/8 cups) light Fish stock (p. 52), or White chicken stock (p. 54)
100 ml (3½ fl oz) extra-virgin olive oil
5 French shallots, or 1 onion, finely diced
4 garlic cloves, finely sliced
1 fresh bay leaf
500 g (1 lb 2 oz) carnaroli rice
200 ml (7 fl oz) white wine
7 × 4 g (⅛ oz) sachets of cuttlefish ink)

100 g (3½ oz) unsalted butter, diced
60 g (2 oz) Grana Padano, grated
zest and juice of ¼ lemon

Cuttlefish
125 ml (4 fl oz/½ cup) extra-virgin olive oil
600 g (1 lb 5 oz) cleaned, small cuttlefish with tentacles (or start from 1.2 kg/2 lb 10 oz whole), cut into 1 cm (½ in) rings

3 garlic cloves, finely sliced
1½ teaspoons chilli flakes
6 flat-leaf (Italian) parsley sprigs, leaves roughly torn
juice of ½ lemon

Staples
S&P

Heat the stock in a saucepan and keep hot over a low heat.

Heat half the oil in a wide, heavy-based saucepan over a medium heat. Add the shallot, garlic and bay leaf, season lightly with salt, then sweat until softened but not caramelised, about 5 minutes.

Add the rice, stirring constantly until the grains are hot to the touch, about 2 minutes, then add the wine. Stir until the wine has reduced to almost nothing, then start adding a ladleful or two of stock. Stir until almost dry again, then repeat. After about 10 minutes, stir the ink through and continue with the applications of stock and stirring.

Cook until the rice is al dente, another 5–10 minutes.

Turn off the heat and add the butter, parmesan and remaining oil. Whip the risotto quite vigorously with your spoon until creamy.

Add the lemon zest and juice, and adjust the seasoning if needed. Add a little more stock if too stiff, then let the risotto stand while you cook the cuttlefish.

For the cuttlefish, heat a large frying pan over a high heat. Add half the oil and cook the cuttlefish, stirring for 1–2 minutes. Add the garlic, season well with salt and pepper, then add the chilli flakes and cook for another 30 seconds or so, until the cuttlefish is just cooked and fragrant. Stir in the parsley, then the lemon juice and remaining oil.

Plate the risotto, then spoon the cuttlefish over – or stir the cuttlefish through the risotto just once, which will help retain its brilliant whiteness. Serve immediately.

Simple porcini risotto 🅖🅕

This is essentially the same as the Risotto bianco (p. 148), except with rehydrated dried porcini mushrooms, and a stock infused with bay leaves (rosemary and thyme would work well also) and boosted with the mushroom-soaking liquor. It is the launching place for a few other variations, with wild and cultivated mushrooms natural additions. I like to keep the porcini very fine, so that it melds into the luscious, silky rice – it's all about the rice, after all. **Serves 4–6**

2 litres (68 fl oz/8 cups) Golden chicken stock (p. 54), or at least 1 litre (34 fl oz/4 cups) stock and 1 litre (34 fl oz/4 cups) water
10 g (¼ oz) dried porcini mushrooms
2 fresh bay leaves

2½ tablespoons extra-virgin olive oil
5 French shallots, or 1 onion, finely diced
3 garlic cloves, finely chopped
500 g (1 lb 2 oz) carnaroli, vialone nano or arborio rice

200 ml (7 fl oz) white wine
120 g (4½ oz) butter
180 g (6 oz) Parmigiano Reggiano, finely grated, plus extra to serve

Staples
S&P

Heat the stock in a saucepan over a low heat.

Soak the porcini in 100 ml (3½ fl oz) boiling water for 10 minutes, then pour the liquid into the stock, leaving any sediment in the bowl, as it can be gritty. Finely chop the mushrooms and set aside.

Add the bay leaves to the stock and boil for 3 minutes, then turn to the lowest heat to keep warm.

Heat the oil in a wide, heavy-based saucepan over a medium heat. Add the shallot and garlic, season lightly with salt, then sweat until softened but not caramelised, about 5 minutes.

Add the chopped porcini and rice, stirring constantly until the grains are hot to the touch, about 2 minutes, then add the wine. Stir until the wine has reduced to almost nothing, then start adding a ladleful or two of stock. Stir until almost dry again, then repeat. Cook until the rice is al dente, 15–20 minutes. If you run out of stock, use hot water from the kettle.

Turn off the heat and add the butter and parmesan. Whip the risotto quite vigorously with your spoon until creamy. Adjust the seasoning if needed, adding a little more stock if too stiff.

Stand for 2 minutes before serving.

Porcini & asparagus risotto

Make it different

Porcini, rosemary & taleggio risotto. ⓖⓕ Instead of bay leaves, add a few rosemary sprigs to the stock and infuse for 10 minutes. Make the risotto as opposite, finishing with 150 g (5½ oz) chilled taleggio cut into 1 cm (½ in) dice and added after the mantecatura. Stir through until just starting to melt, then serve immediately, so the chunks of cheese are still visible.

Porcini & asparagus risotto. ⓖⓕ Trim and slice a bunch of asparagus. Fry them in your pan with a little oil for a minute or two over a high heat, seasoning with salt and pepper. Remove from the pan and proceed with the recipe, adding the asparagus again in the last minute, before finishing with the cheese and butter.

Mushroom risotto. ⓖⓕ Take 500 g (1 lb 2 oz) sliced fresh mushrooms, such as champignons, Swiss browns, pine mushrooms and/or slippery jacks. (Fresh porcini would be just wonderful, or use frozen ones.) Fry them in 80 ml (2½ fl oz/⅓ cup) oil and 50 g (1¾ oz) butter, season well with salt and pepper, toss in some chopped parsley and finish with a squeeze of lemon. Stir the mushrooms into the rice just before the mantecatura – or spoon over your plated porcini risotto. Or, if you have any left-over Mushroom ragù (p. 576), use that instead for a supremely satisfying version.

Also see

Crustacean stock, Fish stock **52–3**

Linguine vongole **127**

Crab cannelloni **135**

Risotto nero with cuttlefish **149–50**

Pork & prawn wontons with chilli & sichuan pepper dipping sauce **342**

Fluffy prawn & crab omelette with prawn essence & watercress **355**

Tuna niçoise **438–9**

Sour fish & mussel curry with celery hearts & kang kong **488–9**

Fried sardines with tomato & fig **705**

Seafood

Fish

Besides its integral health benefits, seafood is something I enjoy almost more than anything else. However, I have met lots of people who have had negative experiences with eating and cooking fish, and this saddens me very much.

Buying properly fresh fish and cooking it simply is a pleasure that I hope I can even convince those most adamantly opposed to try. Many people's distaste for fish is coloured by exposure to produce that was not sparklingly fresh at its best. Fishy fish. And that's not how it should be.

While fish consumption is on the increase, many seem to focus on a very narrow band of what's available. I know people who only eat farmed salmon, and many who would raise an eyebrow at the notion that seafood is seasonal. Yes it's true, there *are* better times to be eating one species over another. Sometimes this has a direct quality parallel, especially with something like oysters (see p. 206), and sometimes it has sustainability and cost implications.

Fishing outside of season will deplete fish stocks before they've had a chance to spawn; but when carefully managed, those stocks will be plentiful, with ongoing sustainable management possible. The abundant nature of those stocks, as with a fruit or vegetable in season, will also mean the prices will be better. As always, ask questions. That well-priced squid or snapper might not be a cheap import, but be priced well due to being locally fished in peak season – an ideal situation, and some of the best and freshest seafood you'll ever eat.

In Australia, the cooler months are the best time for many types of fish and seafood. The flavour is brighter and also richer, due to extra fat just below the skin. The fillets are also generally thicker, as the fish are well nourished at that time, so their texture and flavour are far superior. There are also generally more species available in the cold seas. Remember, a fish eaten in the height of its season will always taste best.

Fish is one of the few wild foods we can have on our dinner tables regularly. But the sustainability of fishery stocks is a complicated issue. Australia has some of the best standards in the world – but unfortunately most commercial fishing operations result in a significant amount of bycatch, which can be small or non-commercial fish, and might also include other marine species, while dredging and trawling nets can also strip an ecosystem of vital plant life and coral.

Even the term 'longline' – which, for me, conjures up an image of smaller-scale fishing – is far from problem-free. Indeed, 'long' is the operative word, with thousands of baited hooks across kilometres of line. Yes, kilometres – with the average length of line nearly 50 kilometres (31 miles), and sometimes double that. The bycatch for longlines can also include dolphins, seals and turtles, as well as seabirds.

Having said that, a longline might only have twenty-five hooks, with fishermen being able to monitor and release any unintended catch. As a term, though, it more often than not refers to industrial fishing practices, with a significant amount of collateral damage.

Whatever the methods, large-scale fishing operations – as well as endemic pollution – have led to the depletion of global fish stocks, with aquaculture often touted as the solution, rather than imposing genuinely sustainable practices.

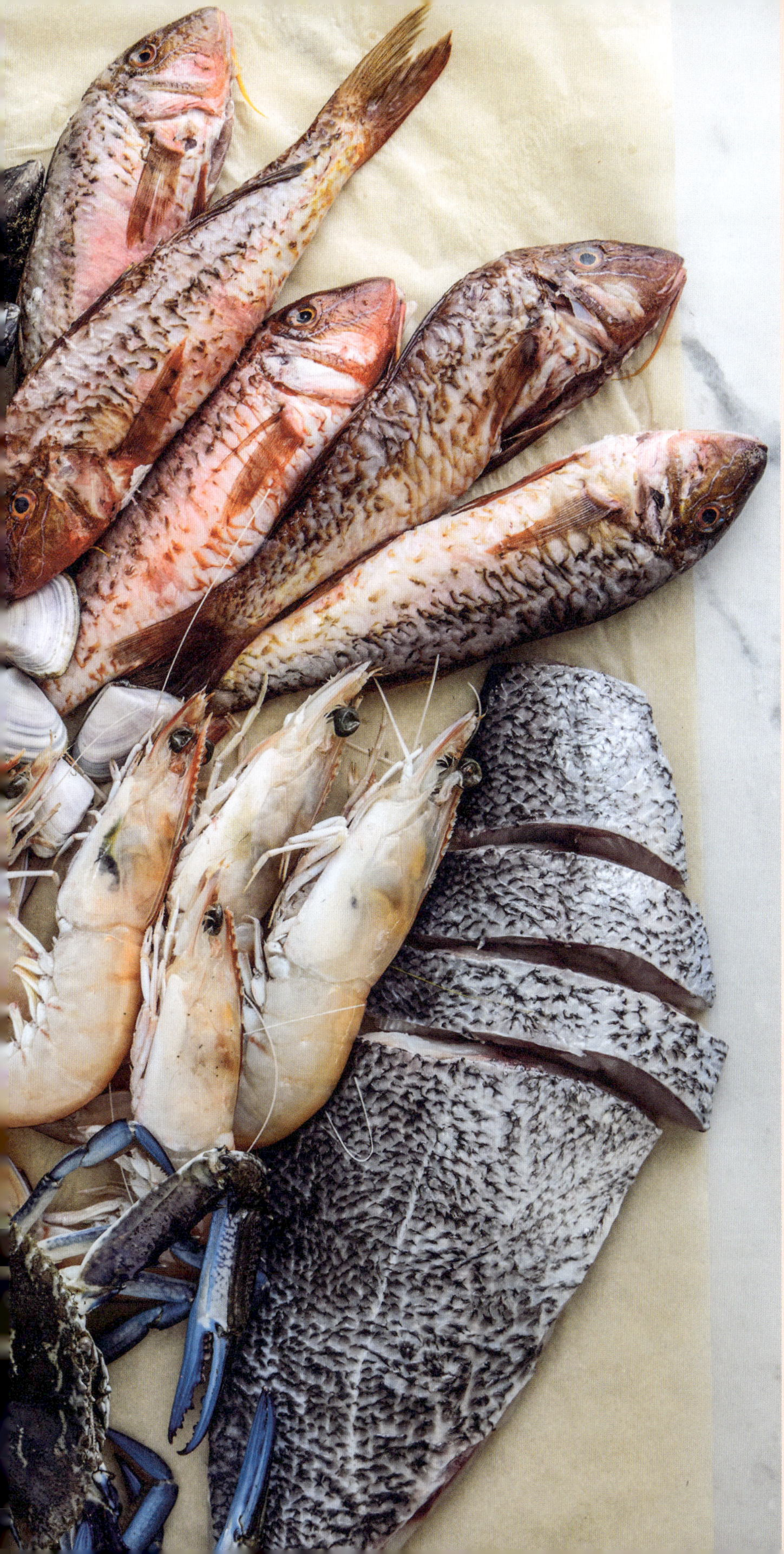

Aquaculture is an answer to overfishing but also a big part of the problem, sadly. Most farmed fish are fed pellets that contain a good portion of wild fish. And those fish, which rightly or wrongly have next to no commercial value, are caught in the most industrial of ways – not to mention the vast amount of fish and krill caught to supply fish oil for supplements. There's an economic edge to growing high-value fish in a contained way, but unless it is underpinned by a philosophy of sustainability, then it is simply factory farming, with the sea still being ravaged for feed.

Then there are wider welfare and localised sustainability issues to be considered. While looking at a salmon may not elicit the same emotive response from us that a calf, lamb or piglet might, cramming a large number of fish into a cramped sea pen is not ethical, or humane. Additionally, as highlighted by scandals in Tasmania, overstocked aquaculture operations deplete the water of oxygen, which kills other marine life, as well as generating problems associated with excessive phosphorous and nitrogen in the ecosystem, as well as faecal waste and water turbidity.

This problem is a global one, too, with farmed fish eclipsing the global output of beef. Much of this farming is in Asia, and much of it is not regulated at all. Akin to the destruction of ancient forests for grazing land, many marine ecosystems have been poisoned to farm all manner of sea creatures, with much of it destined for export markets. These environments are hazardous to what's being farmed, as well as to everything nearby, with pesticides and antibiotics sometimes used to ensure the survival of enough creatures to be viable. On a welfare level, it's as grim a picture as battery hens or crated veal, and significantly more devastating on an environmental level.

The global demand for fish is not one that can be satisfied with wild fish, so aquaculture is essential for the future. But that model naturally needs to be sustainable. There certainly are sustainable and ethically managed aquaculture operations all around the world, but, oddly, the idea of traceability seems to be less of a prominent issue with fish than it is for, say, beef or pork. Thankfully that is changing, with my local fishmongers now selling only ethically caught, traceable wild fish, and sustainable, responsibly farmed fish.

While the Australian fishing industry is tightly – if imperfectly – regulated, we should all make an effort to ask questions and do a little research, to make sure we buy local seafood and support local fishers, not cheap imported products.

It might be a bit harder to get an answer from some fishmongers about the origin of much of their produce, given that most buy via a wholesale market, but please try. They might at least know what kind of scale a lot of their seafood is fished on. It might be as simple as small local boats or larger trawlers, or from a fish farm, but that tells you more than enough to start making some choices. And most good fishmongers will know much more than this about some of their catch, with a high degree of traceability possible. If they don't know much more than that, then do some research. Don't buy anonymous fish with price as the only guide.

I have said it about almost every creature that we consume, and perhaps I may be labouring the point, but it can't be stressed enough: buy ethically reared or caught produce, eat less of it, eat all of it, use the bones for stock, and savour it for the luxury it should be. The impacts on our global environment if we continue down the same path of fishing and farming will have dire environmental consequences that most of us will see in our lifetimes. But if we all take some small steps, then the future will be a brighter one.

While I use more recognisable fish for many of the recipes here, don't be constrained by them, as there are many species that are largely ignored by shoppers. These are often economical choices, and often delicious – far, far more so than industrially farmed salmon (which are usually made orange from dye in their food, by the way). Your fishmonger will always be the best resource for exploring other species. They will have the knowledge about what's best on the day, and usually advice on how to cook it, or which fish will suit a recipe that you want to cook – especially if you regularly present asking questions.

Naturally, fish is best fresh, mounting an even better case for fishing from small boats and local sourcing. Larger boats often go out for days, and even weeks at a time, super-chilling or freezing their catch onboard. Freshly caught fish brought straight to market is the ideal scenario. Often, those fish won't be the glamorous species that you might be chasing, but they'll often be much fresher, much tastier and much cheaper.

Choose a trader with a large variety of whole fish on display, which usually means they're filleting everything in-house. And while I do buy fillets from trusted sources, more often than not I will buy whole fish, then either cook them whole, or have them filleted, or fillet them myself, using the bones and heads for a simple stock (see p. 52) that can be used in the dish, or frozen for later. (When making stocks, use only the bones and heads from white-fleshed fish; snapper is ideal. Bones and heads from oily fish, such as salmon or mackerel, aren't right for stock.)

When buying whole fish, look for a shiny mucus-like coating, which is a protective layer that is more apparent when it is freshly caught, with time and washing diminishing it. The eyes should be perfectly clear, bulbous and shiny, the gills should be bright red, healthy-looking and clear of mucus, and the fish – whole or fillets – should never smell fishy in any way. You are looking for a minerally ocean smell. Fillets should never be limp or dull in appearance; rather, they should be glossy, firm and perky. If you pay attention, you'll begin to spot the differences in a flash.

More fish than you realise has been frozen, generally on larger boats, then thawed by fishmongers prior to sale. The efficiency of the process causes much less damage than your home freezer would, but it still does cause some quality degradation. In some instances, freezing is a quality option due to the time involved with the logistics from catching to bringing to market, but it is not ideal, and some operations and equipment will yield better results than others. Again, ask questions and use your senses.

Preparing fish

As a rule, I always suggest fish should be consumed the day of purchase, or at the least by the following day. Especially if filleted, fish will start to deteriorate very quickly, and more so when water is introduced in the process. Fresh water will introduce bacteria that will degrade the quality rapidly, so storing it dry with air circulating is best and, if a fillet, always skin up – this will also dry out the skin, making it easier to crisp up in the pan.

Most fishmongers will fillet with a lot of water to wash away the entrails and make their job easier, but this is not ideal. If you are getting your fishmonger to fillet for you, ask them to do so with as little water as possible, as water washes away the essential oils, and also increases the temperature of the fish, which decreases shelf life.

I remember learning this the hard way early in my career. I had kilograms of sardines to fillet alongside another apprentice, for a special dish on that night's menu. We did so in record time, using lots of clean water to rinse the sardines and the guts away. But, of course, we had washed all the flavour away, and the fillets were waterlogged, and would be tasteless, and not special at all, we were told. It may seem extreme, but the sardines were all binned, and that night's dinner service was a very hard affair, with a special missing, and a pall of gloom hanging over the kitchen.

From that day on, I have always essentially dry-filleted fish, wiping anything unwanted away with a cloth, and only using minimal water to sponge away entrails, which can have a bitter note.

Always take fish from the fridge before cooking to come up in temperature a little, just as you would any other protein. Cooking fridge-cold fish will shock the proteins and the flesh will cook unevenly, with some overcooked parts almost guaranteed. It's also important to rest fish for a few minutes before serving, which is as much about finishing the cooking as it is about relaxing the flesh. If your fish, be it a fillet or a whole specimen, is fully cooked when you take it from the heat, it will overcook as it rests. Fish should be cooked to about 75–80 per cent done, with the residual heat finishing the job. When aiming for fully cooked fish, as opposed to a rare or medium tuna steak, for example, you still want to only just cook it through in that resting phase.

Simple pan-frying

Finer fillets of fish, such as flathead, whiting, garfish, gurnard, snapper or dory, are ideal to simply pan-fry. Dusted in a thin layer of flour, fried in olive oil until golden, then served simply with a good squeeze of lemon is one of my favourite ways to eat fish. It's a homely midweek approach, and one my girls loved when they were little, learning to appreciate the pure favour of beautifully fresh fish. This is a time when I will buy fillets, and some of the fish mentioned are almost always filleted anyway. As always, tell your fishmonger what your plans are, and they'll tell you what's best on the day. If possible, opt for fillets with the skin on – although the method below is fine without, too.

Rest about six small fish fillets out of the fridge for 20 minutes. Put a large cast-iron pan over a high heat and glug in about 5 mm (¼ in) of olive oil. Meanwhile, in a freezer bag or similar (I always wash and reuse these), add 2 tablespoons plain (all-purpose) flour (or a mix of plain and rice flour), 2 teaspoons salt flakes and half a dozen grinds of black pepper; I sometimes add a teaspoon ground cumin, depending on what I'm serving the fish with. A shake to mix, then in goes the fish. Gently shake the fish around to achieve a light coating, then once the oil is hot (about 3 minutes), add the fillets to the pan, skin side down, or the side where the skin was. Naturally the cooking time will vary a little depending on the fillets, but 2½ minutes on the skin side is a decent target (you'll get a feel for it), then flip and cook for 1 minute before transferring to a warm plate. A squeeze of lemon and straight to the table, where you'll have your salads waiting. The fish will finish cooking on the plate for 1 or 2 minutes as it rests, but that all happens while you serve up and gather the flock. As you hone your timing, watch out for white protein oozing from the fish. It's a sign you're overcooking it, so pull back a bit next time.

Sometimes, for a Thai influence, I will toss the fillets in 1½ tablespoons fish sauce and stand for 20 minutes, then dust with rice flour and fry the same way, or deep-fry at 180°C (350°F) for 3 minutes. Serve with Thai caramel (p. 105), a spicy mayonnaise (see p. 620) or some Fermented cooked chilli sauce (p. 97), and a herb salad and/or some wilted greens.

Pan-frying for crisp skin

As with chicken, so much fish is sold without the skin, which in both cases disturbs me no end. For those who love fish, crispy skin can become something of an obsession, and there's more to it than being some technical barometer of a cook's abilities or a preoccupation with crunchy things. There is so much flavour and character in the fats just under the skin, and cooking them properly celebrates the full flavour of the fish. The skin also protects the flesh while it cooks. It's an aesthetic triumph and it's often crunchy, of course. But even if it's not crunchy, you'll find when you remove it that it has done its job in protecting the flesh and absorbing the cooking fat.

Some fish varieties yield better results than others. Bream, mahi-mahi, snapper, mackerel, john dory, turbot, red mullet, mulloway, murray cod, kingfish, salmon and blue-eye trevalla all have ideal skin for cooking to a stunning crust – though there are many more, and the species will naturally depend on the waters they are fished from.

There are simple techniques to ensure a consistently fine result. The right heat, enough of the right fat, and good contact with the pan are also key to the process. A fish weight is a very handy tool to ensure even contact and cooking, but you can also place a piece of baking paper on the fillet and weigh it down with a small pan. Similarly, you can press down with your hand as the fish overcomes the shock of the heat to make good contact, but a weight is a good investment if you're planning to cook more fish – and you are!

When cooking fish at home, I feel people can be a bit nervous about getting a pan hot enough – which impacts your ability to sear anything well – and also fall into the trap of overcrowding. I get it, you've only got so much space, so many pans, but there's no point trying to jam four fillets into a small pan. The fish will stew, and the skin will never crisp up. Even if you use a particularly large frying pan, an average domestic burner won't stand a chance of heating it evenly. Stick to a frying pan – something heavy-based, ideally – that will accommodate two fillets very comfortably and receive even heat from the burner. Four fillets? Two pans.

I often fry in olive oil (always extra-virgin), and often add a knob of butter towards the end to caramelise and add flavour. Ghee is excellent for pan-frying fish, and many other things too. Ghee is clarified butter that has been cooked until the milk solids caramelise, giving it a nutty character. Those solids are then strained out, meaning you get the flavour but no solids that would otherwise burn when frying – meaning ghee has a very high smoke point. It's great for frying fish, achieving a very crisp and glassy skin to contrast with the pearly flesh. Work out which ghee works best for you. Some Indian ghee can have a sour character to it, as buffalo milk is often used; it may be ideal for a curry, but may be too strong for fish. I use quite a pure one made with butter from grass-fed cows.

If frying two 200 g (7 oz) fillets (of any of the fish mentioned opposite), leave them on the bench for at least 20 minutes, skin up and uncovered. I've found that a light coating of rice flour on the skin yields a perfect result every time. You'd never know it was there, and it crisps and caramelises the skin beautifully. Naturally, also season the skin well with salt flakes. Put a heavy-based frying pan over a medium–high heat, then add about 3 tablespoons ghee. Once the fat is translucent and there's a heat haze to it, carefully lay the fish in the pan, skin side down. Weigh down with a fish weight or another pan – about 1 kg (2 lb 3 oz) is good – and cook undisturbed for 2 minutes. Move the fillets a little – the skin will have sealed – to pick up more contact heat from the pan. Cook a thicker fillet for 3–4 minutes (less for a thinner, flatter fillet of the same weight), until the top of the fish is warm to the touch. Remove the weight and flip, seal for just 10 seconds or so, then transfer to a warm plate. Remember that we're cooking to 75–80 per cent of doneness only, with the residual heat finishing the job. By the time you've busied yourself with finishing sauces and sides, or dressing plates and the like, that fish will be ready.

If you want to slice the pan-fried fillets, rest them on a board for 2 minutes, then flip and slice with a sharp knife. (If you try to cut through the skin first, it will resist, and you will squash that perfectly cooked flesh.) Firm, tightly fleshed fish are best for slicing like this, such as Spanish mackerel, salmon, kingfish and mahi-mahi.

I serve pan-seared fish simply with lemon – or mayonnaise (pp. 74–5) with Fermented cooked chilli sauce (p. 97) stirred through, or with some saffron, ground fennel, chopped lemon, and maybe chives or tarragon folded in. A simple Burnt butter sauce with lemon, sage & toasted walnuts (p. 73) or a Beurre blanc (p. 69) are also wonderful.

Deep-frying

While deep-fried fish with a crisp salty batter is probably the most universally loved and eaten style, it's not something many of us do at home. To do it properly (see p. 187), you need a lot of oil, and it can be a bit messy – but then it's not always easy to get super-fresh fish from a local fish and chip shop, so it's often worth the effort. There's certainly something special about breaking the fish open with the flesh piping hot and delicate, having essentially steamed in the batter. This kind of cooking cries out for a dip in a tartare (see p. 77) or other mayonnaise-based sauce (pp. 74–8), or a good splash of vinegar. Even if I've outsourced the frying to a trusted fish and chip shop, I'll always double down on home-made sauces.

While frying a lot of fish and chips for a crowd is beyond most, crumbed fish fried for a fish burger is far more manageable, and it's something I have a real weakness for. Dredge 140 g (5 oz) fillets in rice flour, then coat with whisked egg, and finally crumb with panko or breadcrumbs. About 2½ minutes in 180°C (350°F) oil will be enough. A good season while hot, a quick drain, then wedge into brioche buns with soft butter lettuce, pickled onions and tartare and you're good to go – or try it with a Japanese angle (see p. 191).

Some of the fish I like to fry, whether battered or crumbed, are snapper, gurnard, mullet, leather jackets, sardines, whiting, garfish, flathead, dory, mahi-mahi, rockling, gummy shark, sprats, whitebait, ocean trout and salmon.

Baking & roasting

Baking or roasting a whole fish, or a side of large fish, is something I do a lot, especially to feed a group. Baking a whole specimen is a particular favourite, maintaining moisture and sealing in maximum flavour, while baking in a salt crust (see p. 175) or in a sealed parcel (see p. 178) gently steams the flesh, which is ideal for finely textured fish.

When roasting or baking, I often opt for fish with a high fat content. Whole or sides of salmon or ocean trout (see p. 181) bake well, as do whole rainbow trout, coral trout, john dory, murray cod, turbot and bass grouper. Two all-time favourites are whole rock flathead and black bream.

Unless you're employing a more rustic wet-roasting method (paragraph below), having a rack that fits inside your roasting tin is a great investment. By elevating the fish, you'll allow the heat to penetrate from all angles, giving a more consistent result.

I also use an Italian/Spanish wet-roasting method for large, whole fish such as turbot or john dory. A fish of about 3.5 kg (7 lb 11 oz) will feed four to six. This method is great if you have a wood-fired oven in the backyard; otherwise, crank your oven to 250°C (480°F) fan-forced, or as high as it will go. Season the cavity with salt and pepper, then sit the fish on a bed of very finely sliced potatoes, with some onion, garlic, lemon slices, dried oregano and a sprinkling of smoked paprika. Pour over 100 ml (3½ fl oz) white wine, 100 ml (3½ fl oz) White chicken stock (p. 54) and a generous amount of oil, then season heavily with salt and pepper. Cover with baking paper, then foil, and roast for 15 minutes. Uncover and roast for another 30 minutes or so, until the skin is blistered and crispy. Rest for 10 minutes and serve from the tray, with a salad and bread. It's messy, but gloriously delicious.

Barbecuing & grilling

My family are big on beach holidays, and there's nothing better than securing some of the day's local catch – sardines, octopus, prawns (shrimp), sea bass, calamari, swordfish – and barbecuing it. The aroma of fish skin blistering and fat sizzling as it cooks over real coals is one of my favoured scents in summer – or any time of the year, really. While you can of course use a gas-fired grill, I rarely do. If I'm barbecuing a whole fish, or have taken the time to braise octopus to then grill, I want that intoxicating grill flavour and aroma, and lighting a fire to get red coals doesn't seem like too much work.

However, there is nothing different about the cooking process, so do what works for you. If using coals, it will take a little practice to get the heat right, but you're looking for a fire that has burned down to even, glowing coals with no large flames, just the occasional flicker.

Great fish for grilling are those with a high fat content or a high gelatinous content, such as flounder, turbot, sole, mullet, red mullet, mackerel, tommy ruff, bonito, sardines, cod, tuna and swordfish. Whiting, garfish and snapper don't have a high fat content, but I particularly love their flavour off the grill.

Fish sticks to the grill easily, and you don't get a second chance to cook the skin when it's stuck on the grill. There are a couple of important factors here, with a little patience and care required. Firstly, the barbecue grill bars need to be spotlessly clean. Any burnt-on residue, even if quite minor, will adhere to the skin and will cause it to rip, as will moving the fish too early. Once the skin has been properly sealed, it will come away cleanly. If you rush it, the skin will rip, and probably take some flesh with it. Ensure the heat is evenly medium–hot, and that the fish is not fridge-cold.

A handy tool is a fish grilling basket, which will enclose a whole fish, making turning simpler, especially for larger specimens. The flat versions are also excellent for very small fish or fillets, such as sardines. Sandwiching a number of them together in a grill is ideal, as you can turn them all at once – a great advantage when you only have quite a narrow time frame to sear the skin without overcooking. Whatever fish you are cooking, ensure you liberally oil the grill before using.

Lately, once I've seared the first side and flipped it over, I've taken to using an atomiser to spray the fish with lightly salted water, made with 1 tablespoon salt flakes dissolved in 300 ml (10 fl oz) water. Then I also spray the fish lightly on the other side as it comes off the grill, just before resting. Sometimes I use fish sauce, or seasoned rice vinegar or stock, depending on what I'm cooking. Essentially, the spray is a form of basting, which adds moisture, imparts flavour and helps the skin to blister. It's such a simple and economical trick, but it's a real game-changer.

The one thing you'll never find near my barbecue are barbecue tongs. I'm not really sure what they're intended for, as they are so brutal, but certainly keep them well away from fish, with kitchen tongs preferred. If you're not using a grilling basket, use two sets of tongs to flip a whole fish, supporting the tail end with one and the head with the other.

Timing is something you simply need to practise. As a guide, a well-oiled and seasoned plate-sized snapper of about 450 g (1 lb) will take about 9 minutes each side. Remember you want to cook the fish to 75–80 per cent doneness before resting; a temperature of 60°C (140°F) at the thickest point just prior to coming off the grill is ideal. You can also look inside the cavity, where the spine should not look raw or translucent. Once off the grill, I will brush the fish with some good oil and season with salt and pepper before resting on a warm plate for 5 minutes.

Wet-grilling

There is another method that I use, which I learned from Thai fishermen barbecuing on the beach. Soaking the fish with its scales on in a salt slurry before grilling stops the skin sticking to the grill bars, which is handy when you're working with a fluctuating temperature, as is often the case at home. You won't get crispy charred skin, but you still get all the barbecued flavour. I used this method in Ibiza to grill fennel-stuffed lubina on a parrilla grill, peeling the skin back to reveal the steamed flaky flesh, laced with smoky notes.

It's a technique I would use on larger fish, anything over 600 g (1 lb 5 oz) or so. Snapper and sea bass are particularly good using this method.

Make a slurry from 200 g (7 oz) sea salt and 600 ml (20½ fl oz) water, then immerse the fish – which should be gutted with the gills removed, but have the scales intact. Soak for 30 minutes, or an hour for large fish, turning it halfway through. Remove from the slurry and grill. For a 1.2 kg (2 lb 10 oz) snapper, cook for 15 minutes over a hot grill (hotter than if not soaking in the slurry, as the salt protects the skin, but more heat is needed to penetrate the flesh properly). Flip and cook for another 15 minutes, then rest for 10 minutes before peeling back the salt-crusted skin.

Poaching & steaming

Poaching is an easy, healthy way of cooking fish, with a very delicate and pure result. You can add all sorts of aromatics to the poaching liquid to enhance the flavour. For me, a fish that yields large flakes is ideal for poaching, with that texture enhanced by the method. Blue-eye trevalla is my ultimate, but kingfish, ocean trout, murray cod, hapuka, mackerel, snapper, turbot and gurnard are also favourites.

To poach four 180–200 g (6½–7 oz) fillets of blue-eye (or another thick fish fillet), bring a wide saucepan of water to a simmer with a little sliced celery, onion, fennel seeds and maybe some parsley stalks and peppercorns. Add about 1½ tablespoons fine sea salt and simmer for 5 minutes to infuse. Meanwhile, space the fillets out on a heatproof plate that will easily fit in the saucepan. Turn the heat off, then immediately submerge the plate and fish. If the fish is not fully submerged, tip in some boiling water. Cover the pan and stand for 10 minutes, then lift the fillets out with a slotted spoon. Rest on a warm plate for 5 minutes to finish cooking. Serve with a little splash of the poaching liquid, a drizzle of good oil and some salt flakes and fresh pepper. The flesh should have a delicate texture, with the centre a little translucent.

Steaming is also a beautifully delicate way to cook fish, whether fillets or whole. Place 180–200 g (6½–7 oz) fish fillets on a heatproof plate, then into a steamer basket, and set over a wok or saucepan filled with about 5 cm (2 in) water on a high heat. Blue-eye fillets will take about 6 minutes, then 5 minutes to rest and finish cooking on a warm plate. If using fine fillets, such as whiting or garfish, they're best rolled and skewered first. A 1 kg (2 lb 3 oz) whole fish, scored in 4 cm (1½ in) intervals about 1 cm (½ in) deep, will take about 14 minutes to steam, then a rest for 5 minutes or so to finish the job. Serve with a punchy dipping sauce or make a Simple coconut soup–style sauce (right).

Simple coconut soup–style sauce for steamed fish (GF)

In a medium saucepan, combine 1 litre (34 fl oz/4 cups) coconut milk, 1½ tablespoons fish sauce and 2 teaspoons caster (superfine) sugar. Slice a 6 cm (2½ in) piece of fresh ginger, then add to the pan with 4 bruised makrut lime leaves and 2 red bird's eye chillies, split lengthways. Add 1 lemongrass stem, pale part only, bruised and halved lengthways. Simmer over a medium heat for about 10 minutes to reduce and infuse. Once reduced by about one-third, stand for 10 minutes, then strain. Serve spooned over steamed fish fillets, or flakes lifted from a whole steamed fish, with rice or noodles and greens on the side.

Preparing raw & cured fish

While some still baulk at the idea, raw fish is a sublime treat. Naturally, the art of sushi and sashimi is a hard-won skill, but that doesn't mean you can't enjoy raw or lightly cured fish at home. Good fishmongers will sell sashimi-grade fish, and using a properly sharp knife and ensuring you cut the flesh cleanly across the grain is enough for an excellent experience at home.

Tuna, salmon and kingfish are probably the easiest to slice; you want the slices about 4 mm (¼ in) thick. Blue mackerel, snapper, sea bream and sea bass are also not too tricky to slice, and lovely. Serve any of these simply with Ponzu (p. 101), Enhanced soy sauce (p. 101), or with a little flavoured salt and a squeeze of lemon or a dash of verjuice, Harissa (p. 92) or a green hot sauce (such as green Tabasco).

If dressing raw fish with a vinaigrette or citrus emulsion – as in a crudo dish (pp. 164, 165, 510) – the acid will start to 'cook' the fish, changing the texture, so a dressed crudo is best served and consumed immediately. This is a process that is taken further when making a ceviche, with lime juice, along with coconut and chilli, used to 'cook' the proteins and turn them milky quite quickly. I find orange and mandarin juice a little more subtle, along with verjuice or lacto-fermenting liquids, such as the brine from pickles or kimchi liquor, with the acidity level a lot lower and therefore gentler on the proteins. You can experiment with any of these, as well as adding herbs, seasonings and a drizzle of oil. How far you take the curing/cooking is really up to you, so taste and judge.

I also use citrus juices, along with salt and sugar, to make gravlax (pp. 169, 171), which is my favourite way to enjoy salmon or ocean trout. Smoked salmon, or cured salmon or trout, has been on my menus in one way or another for as long as I can recall, and I always cure a side of fish for Christmas and most large celebrations. Unless it's an exemplary example, however – which is rare where I come from – I am no great fan of commercially smoked salmon, which can be very overpowering, the flavours lingering longer than welcome. A home-cured version (see p. 169) is vastly superior and alarmingly simple to achieve – and it's one of those dishes people can't believe you did yourself.

I will also sometimes brine fish quickly (see p. 168), which will partially cure it, before slicing and dressing. Hot-smoked fish, mainly freshwater trout, is also something I like to have on hand to add to a salad (see p. 385) or a pie (see p. 188), or to serve alongside other salads, perhaps with some crème fraîche spiked with horseradish and dill. The other cured fish that I use reasonably often – besides anchovies, bottarga (see p. 8) and the like – is salt cod or baccalà, whether for baccalà mantecato or a fritter.

Snapper crudo with a lemon emulsion & horseradish ⓖ

Given the delicate freshness of a dish like this, spiked with heat from a cloud of finely grated horseradish, you'd be forgiven for thinking this was a summer recipe. But, like the wintery mineral purity of a cold-water oyster, snapper is best in the cooler months, as is fresh horseradish, and lemons, too. This is perfectly lovely in summer as well; just use fresh radish, micro mustard cress or watercress instead of the horseradish – no jarred preparations, please. **Serves 4–6**

Pair with

Eat as is, or serve with Lavoche (p. 840) or similar.

1 × 400 g (14 oz) fillet of snapper, tuna or kingfish, skin, bones and bloodline removed

3 tablespoons extra-virgin olive oil

35 ml (1¼ fl oz) lemon juice

8 cm (3¼ in) piece of fresh horseradish

1½ tablespoons diced pickled onion (see p. 594)

Staples
S&P

Slice the fish 4 mm (¼ in) thick across the grain. Lay the slices flat on a serving plate.

Whisk the oil and lemon juice until emulsified.

Season the fish well with salt, then smear the emulsion all over. Finely grate the horseradish over, scatter with the pickled onion and serve.

Kingfish crudo with chilli, ginger & coriander ⓖ

Fragrant with ginger and coriander (cilantro), this crudo dressing has a gentle but assertive flush of heat. **Serves 4**

1 × 400 g (14 oz) fillet of kingfish, snapper, tuna or mackerel, skin, bones and bloodline removed

1 jalapeño chilli, or 2 long green chillies, seeds removed, finely sliced

3 cm (1¼ in) piece of fresh ginger, peeled and finely diced

5 coriander seeds

10 coriander (cilantro) leaves

1½ tablespoons extra-virgin olive oil

25 ml (1 fl oz) lemon or lime juice

Staples
S&P

Slice the fish 4 mm (¼ in) thick across the grain. Lay the slices flat on a serving plate.

Add the chilli, ginger, coriander seeds and leaves to a mortar and grind to a rough paste. Add the oil and citrus juice, season with salt and pepper and grind to combine.

Spoon the dressing over the fish and serve immediately.

Snapper crudo with finger lime, fennel, chilli & a burnt butter dressing (GF)

This combination of rich and nutty brown butter with the zesty punch of finger limes and lime leaves against the pearly freshness of raw fish is something of a revelation. **Serves 4–6**

150 g (5½ oz) unsalted butter
2½ tablespoons extra-virgin olive oil
600 g (1 lb 5 oz) snapper or rock flathead, skin and bones removed
3 spring onions (scallions), white part only, finely sliced

2 long green chillies, seeds removed, very finely diced
2 slices of Pickled fennel (p. 531), finely diced, or finely diced fresh fennel or tiny pickled cocktail onions
5 finger limes, split, or 2 large peeled limes, with the flesh finely diced

3 makrut lime leaves, very finely shredded
a handful of picked watercress or mustard cress (optional)

Staples
S&P

Melt the butter in a small saucepan over a medium heat. Cook until golden brown with a nutty aroma, about 8 minutes. Pour into a small bowl, leaving the burnt milk solids in the pan. Add the oil to the butter, then season lightly with salt and combine. Set aside and keep warm – if it cools too much, it will set when you dress the plate.

Slice the fish 4 mm (¼ in) across the grain. Lay the slices on individual plates, overlapping slightly. Season well with salt and pepper, then sprinkle with the spring onion, chilli and fennel. Push out the finger lime pearls onto the fish, then scatter over the lime leaves and cress, if using.

Dress with the warm dressing (reheat gently if necessary) and serve immediately.

Herb oil for fish (GF) (V) (VG)

Pair with

Drizzle over raw fish, such as kingfish or tuna.

Drizzle over cured sardines or cured mackerel.

Drizzle over cooked scallops in the shell, or grilled or roasted prawns (shrimp), along with a squeeze of lemon.

The herb oil could also be used on fresh cheese, such as ricotta or goat's cheese, and served with bread.

Dressing seasoned raw fish with flavoured olive oil is a beautiful way to showcase and accent the delicate flesh. You will need a high-speed blender that heats precisely, such as a Thermomix. **Makes 250 ml (8½ oz/1 cup)**

125 ml (4 fl oz/½ cup) extra-virgin olive oil
125 ml (4 fl oz/½ cup) grapeseed oil

Herbs (choose one)
50 g (1¾ oz) thyme or rosemary, leaves picked and chopped
50 g (1¾ oz) bay leaves
50 g (1¾ oz) fresh curry leaves

100 g (3½ oz) makrut lime leaves, fig leaves or lemon verbena leaves, thick veins removed, leaves chopped
125 g (4½ oz) fennel tops

Add all the oil and your chosen herb to the Thermomix. Set the temperature to 85°C (185°F) and blitz on high speed for 2 minutes, then on medium speed for 8 minutes.

Strain the mixture through a paper filter (such as a coffee filter), into a container in an ice bath. It will take some time to strain through.

To use, bring to room temperature naturally, freezing any left-over oil to retain the bright freshness.

Kingfish kibbeh nayyeh

A very popular dish of the Levant, kibbeh has many different forms, but the central tenet is that it is a dish of ground meat – usually lamb or beef – and grain with spices. Kibbeh nayyeh is the raw version: a tartare, if you like. Over the years I have made several versions employing fish instead of red meat. The robust, sweet flavour and fabulous mouthfeel of kingfish is ideal, but salmon and ocean trout are fine alternatives. Naturally, sashimi-grade fish is needed here, and it's important to keep everything cold while making this dish.

Serves 4–6

4 tablespoons salmon roe
3 coriander (cilantro) sprigs, leaves picked
2 dill or mint sprigs, leaves picked
6 small radishes, with some vibrant greenery left on
2 handfuls of fresh fenugreek leaves, or mizuna, mâche (lamb's lettuce/corn salad), curly endive (frisée) or picked watercress
sumac, to serve
1 lemon, cut into wedges or cheeks

soft pitta breads (see p. 854), to serve

Kingfish kibbeh
50 g (1¾ oz) cracked freekeh, medium bulgur wheat or black barley
400 g (14 oz) kingfish, salmon or ocean trout, skin, bones and bloodline removed, well chilled
2 red Asian shallots, or 1 small white onion, finely diced

2 long green chillies, seeds removed, finely diced
zest and juice of ½ lemon
3 tablespoons extra-virgin olive oil
1 heaped teaspoon ground sumac
½ teaspoon ground allspice
1 teaspoon celery seeds
1½ teaspoons salt flakes

Staples
EVOO, S&P

For the kibbeh, if using freekeh, boil for 15–20 minutes, until tender, then drain well and cool, spreading the freekeh out on a plate to dry out. If using bulgur, soak in hot water just to cover, then stand until cool.

Carefully cut the fish into 3 mm (⅛ in) dice (or as small as possible), then add to a chilled bowl. Add the remaining kibbeh ingredients and combine, adjusting the seasoning as needed. Pile the kibbeh onto a serving plate, then spread out with a spatula. Cover with plastic wrap, pressing it onto the kibbeh, then chill for 10 minutes.

To serve, unwrap, then spoon on the caviar and scatter over the coriander and dill. Arrange the radishes and fenugreek around the edge. Drizzle with a little oil, sprinkle with sumac and serve with the lemon and pitta breads.

Make it faster
Instead of pairing it with home-made fresh soft pitta (see p. 854), toast some bought pitta breads in a 170°C (340°F) fan-forced oven for 10 minutes, then cool.

Make it different
With egg. Three soft-boiled eggs (see p. 351) sprinkled with Dukkah (p. 13) could also garnish this dish, with an incision made so the yolk runs a little, saucing the kibbeh.

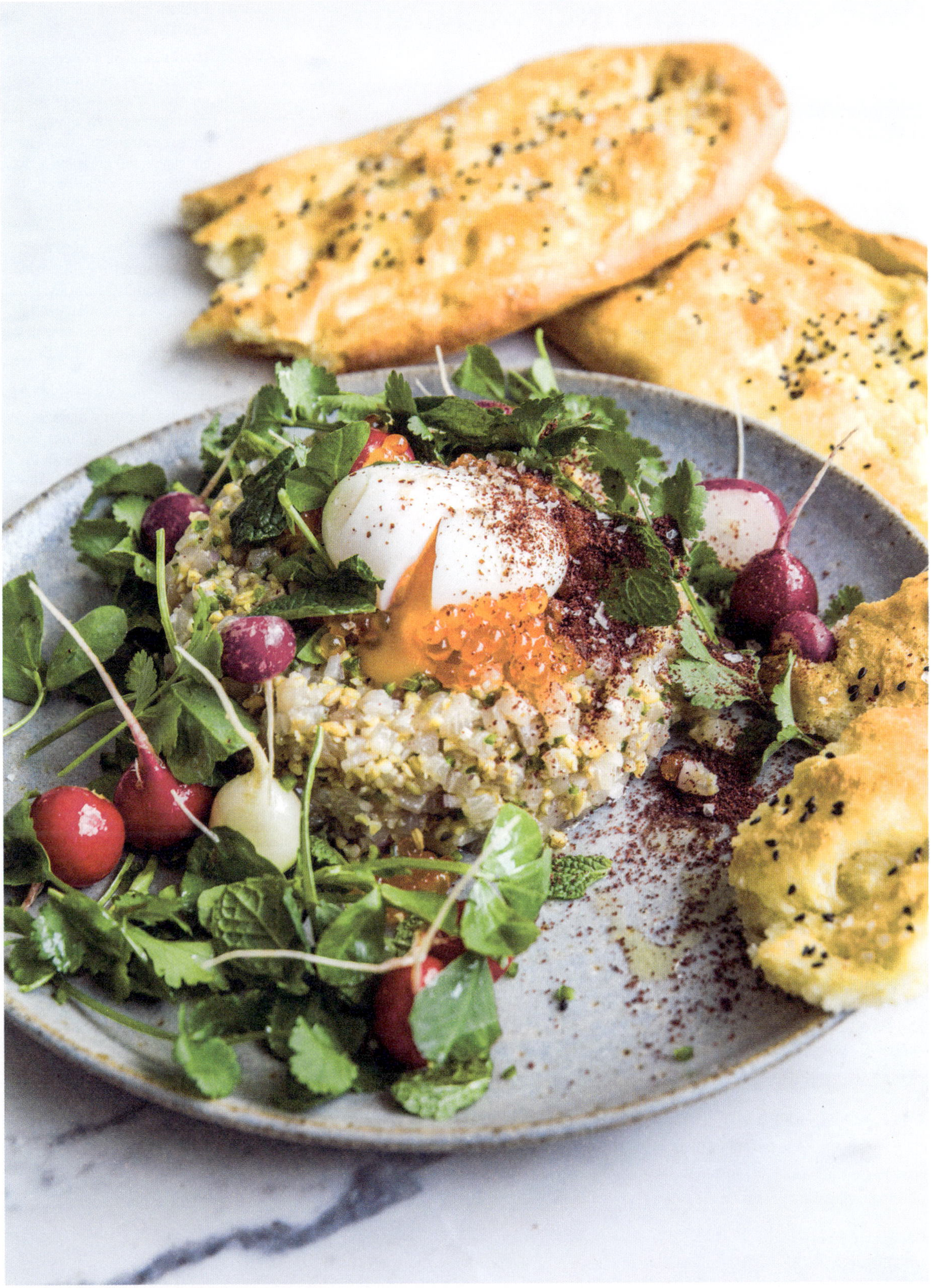

Quick-cured ocean trout with finger lime & coriander GF

This super-quick method firms the fish flesh slightly, skewing the flavour and texture to somewhere between raw and cured. **Serves 4–6**

1 × 400 g (14 oz) thick end fillet of ocean trout, kingfish, salmon or mackerel, skin, bones and bloodline removed
2 tablespoons salmon roe
3 finger limes, split, or 1 large peeled lime, with the flesh finely diced

20 rye or Spiced seed crackers (p. 839), Lavoche (p. 840) or sliced ficelle, toasted until crisp

Brine
150 g (5½ oz) fine sea salt
110 g (4 oz/½ cup) caster (superfine) sugar
1 litre (34 fl oz/4 cups) water

Lemon & coriander coating
2 teaspoons ground coriander
1 teaspoon freshly ground white pepper
zest of 1 lemon

Staples
EVOO

For the brine, dissolve the salt and sugar in the water by stirring. You can heat to fully dissolve if necessary, but make sure you cool completely before using. Submerge the fish in the brine and stand for 20 minutes, then remove and pat dry.

Combine the coating ingredients in a shallow bowl. Locate the side of the fish fillet that was nearest the bones when you removed them; lightly brush only that side of the fish with oil, then lay in the mixture to coat. Wrap tightly in plastic wrap and refrigerate for 30 minutes, or up to 5 hours.

To serve, slice the fish 4 mm (¼ in) thick across the grain and lay the slices on a serving plate. Dress the caviar with a little oil, then spoon over the fish. Push the finger lime pearls out onto the fish. Serve with the crackers on the side of the plate, or you can plate as canapés, if preferred.

Make it different
Serve as a starter. Use four slices per person, and a little salad of finely shaved fennel, apple and radish with a makrut lime dressing (see p. 165).

Cured kingfish with crema fresca, lime & spiced seed crackers GF

This is an elegant way to serve the cured kingfish (see p. 164), either as a refined starter or canapé (just top a cracker with a slice of fish and dress). **Serves 6**

½ fennel bulb
24 slices of cured kingfish (see p. 164)
90 g (3 oz/⅓ cup) Crema fresca (p. 364), or crème fraîche

1 lime, peeled, segmented and diced
juice of ½ lime
80 ml (2½ fl oz/⅓ cup) extra-virgin olive oil
6 Kale chips (p. 551)

6 Spiced seed crackers (p. 839), Grissini (p. 856), or baguette slices

Special equipment
Mandoline

Using a mandoline, finely slice the fennel lengthways, to 1 mm (¹⁄₁₆ in) thick.

Plate four slices of fish per serve, then top with some fennel, a dollop of crema fresca and some lime.

Beat the lime juice and oil until emulsified, then spoon over the top. Finish by topping with the kale and laying the crackers on the side.

Make it different
With finger lime. Use two finger limes instead of lime. Push the pearls onto the fish to finish.

Citrus-cured sardines GF

Cut the head off a sardine, then slice open the belly and pull out the entrails with your finger. Press the fish open, then pull the backbone out from the head end, lifting out the spine and ribs, snapping off at the end to leave the tail intact. Run your finger across the flesh to make sure you've removed all the bones, then cut the fillet in half down the middle and lay, skin side down, in a ceramic dish. Repeat with 11 more sardines. Season the fillets well with salt and pepper. Finely slice ½ lemon, then cover the fillets with the slices and marinate on the bench for 15 minutes. Very finely slice 1 garlic clove into twelve slices, then lay a garlic slice on each fillet. Drizzle with extra-virgin olive oil and serve, or cover and refrigerate until ready to serve. The sardines will hold for 24 hours like this. Finely slice 1 white salad onion, then soak the slices in water, drain and dry. To serve four, use six fillets per plate, top with some oil from the dish and a few onion slices, sprinkle with a little chilli powder or paprika and splash on a little sherry vinegar. Flood the plate with some more oil and scatter over oregano flowers or thyme leaves. If keeping for more than 24 hours, sprinkle the sardines with a little more vinegar and some chilli powder. They will keep for a couple of days, but they will cure further and yield a different texture.

Citrus-cured gravlax ⒢Ⓕ

This is my go-to gravlax recipe, one I've been using for decades. It may seem a big thing to cure a piece of fish like this, but the core principle – and the manner of preparation – is all so simple, with the citrus curing and perfuming, and the salt and sugar drawing out moisture. You can also just use salt and sugar, as long as there's enough to cover the outside of the fish well; adding other flavours such as spices or vermouth is simply up to you. Over time, you will also work out how cured you like it, with some people preferring a light cure of less than ten hours, and others taking it as far as twenty-four hours for a firmer result. Again, that's up to you. Just be sure to use fish in immaculate condition, as curing highlights the fish's quality, but it won't compensate for a lack of it.

Serves 15–20 (more for canapés)

1.2–1.4 kg (2 lb 10 oz–3 lb 1 oz) side of ocean trout or salmon, skin on, bones removed
2 tablespoons dijon mustard
1 bunch of dill, fronds finely chopped

Citrus cure
200 g (7 oz) rock salt
150 g (5½ oz/⅔ cup oz) caster (superfine) sugar
zest and juice of 1 lemon
zest and juice of 1 orange

In a bowl, mix the cure ingredients into an even slurry.

In a ceramic dish or tray, lay out two overlapping lengths of plastic wrap that will be large enough to wrap the fish, pressing the overlapping section together to join. Spoon one-third of the cure evenly down the length of the dish and place the fish, skin side down, on top. Spoon the rest of the cure over the flesh and spread out evenly. Pull the plastic wrap over the fish, pressing the cure into an even layer and sealing as tightly as you can.

Refrigerate for 12 hours, then lift the fish out of the slurry and wipe clean with damp paper towel.

Brush the flesh with a fine layer of mustard, then press on the dill. Wrap tightly in fresh plastic wrap, then press the flesh against the bench to help the dill stick. Refrigerate for another hour before slicing.

The gravlax will keep for about 10 days, tightly wrapped and refrigerated.

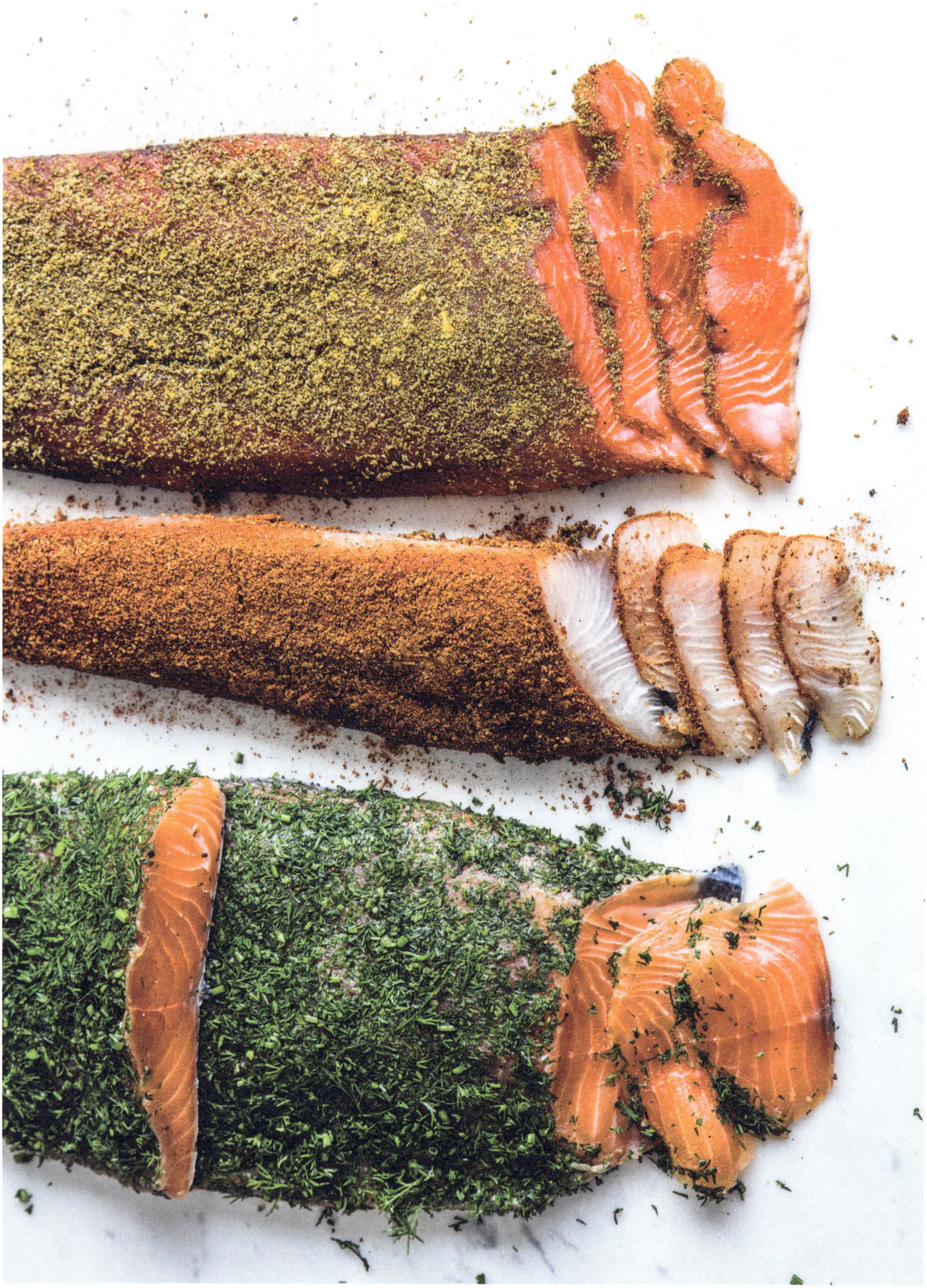

Gravlax with treacle, fennel & pepper ⓖⓕ

This cure has sweeter characteristics than the Citrus-cured gravlax (p. 169), with a peppery and anise-laced undertone that works particularly well with rye or pumpernickel bread. **Serves 15–20 (more for canapés)**

1.2–1.4 kg (2 lb 10 oz–3 lb 1 oz) side of ocean trout or salmon, skin on, bones removed
2 tablespoons fennel seeds
2 tablespoons fennel pollen
2 teaspoons freshly ground black pepper

2 tablespoons dijon mustard

Treacle, fennel & pepper cure
150 g (5½ oz) rock salt
150 g (5½ oz) treacle
50 g (1¾ oz) golden syrup, or light treacle

2 tablespoons mustard powder
1 tablespoon fennel seeds, lightly ground
1½ tablespoons white peppercorns, lightly ground
zest and juice of 2 lemons

In a bowl, mix the cure ingredients into an even slurry.

In a ceramic dish or tray, lay two overlapping lengths of plastic wrap that will be large enough to wrap the fish. Press the overlapping section together to join. Spoon one-third of the cure evenly down the length of the dish and top with the fish, skin side down. Evenly spread the rest of the cure over the flesh. Pull the plastic wrap over the fish, pressing the cure into an even layer and sealing tightly.

Refrigerate for 12 hours, then lift the fish out of the slurry and wipe clean with damp paper towel.

Finely grind the fennel seeds, pollen and pepper using a mortar and pestle. Lightly coat the flesh of the fish with mustard, then dust with the fennel mixture. Wrap the fish in plastic wrap, then chill for another 30 minutes before slicing.

The gravlax will keep for about 10 days, tightly wrapped and refrigerated.

Cured kingfish with fennel, paprika & pepper ⓖⓕ

Pair with

This dish is quite intensely flavoured, so it doesn't need much. Serve it as a starter, with other small morsels.

Serve on Rye crackers (p. 838) with crème fraîche and a slice of hard-boiled egg.

Dress with a little rosemary, bay leaf or thyme oil (see p. 165).

With its dense and rich flesh, kingfish really takes to a good cure. Dishes using this preparation have been on my menus for years. **Serves 15–20**

1.5 kg (3 lb 5 oz) side of kingfish, skin on, bones removed
3 teaspoons fennel seeds
2 teaspoons black peppercorns

3 teaspoons smoked sweet paprika

Lemon & peppercorn cure
160 g (5½ oz) coarse sea salt
100 g (3½ oz) caster (superfine) sugar

zest and juice of 1 large lemon
1 bay leaf
1 teaspoon black peppercorns, lightly crushed

Combine the cure ingredients in a ceramic dish, then add the fish. Cover the fish evenly, so that it's sitting on a bed of the cure, with the rest covering the top. Refrigerate for 10 hours, turning and recoating evenly after about 6 hours.

Once cured, lift out the fish and wipe down with slightly dampened paper towel. Cut the fish in half lengthways.

Finely grind the peppercorns and fennel seeds using a mortar and pestle. Grind in the paprika to combine, then sift. Press the spice mix evenly onto the flesh side of the fish, then wrap tightly in plastic wrap. Refrigerate for at least 1 hour to set the spices into the fish.

The fish will keep for a week, as long it is wrapped well after using. To serve, slice about 3 mm (⅛ in) thick across the grain.

Top to bottom: Gravlax with treacle, fennel & pepper (above); Cured kingfish with fennel, paprika & pepper (right); Citrus-cured gravlax (p. 169)

Rockling with Thai caramel sauce & herbs

Hot and fragrant Thai caramel is marvellous with fish. A quick cook under a hot grill, a vibrant salad and rice is all that's needed for a stunning meal. **Serves 6**

Pair with

Steamed jasmine rice.

oil, for shallow-frying
6 stems of curry leaves
½ bunch of mint, leaves
  picked
½ bunch of Thai basil
  (optional), leaves picked
3 Lebanese (short)
  cucumbers, peeled and

sliced on an angle 3 cm
  (1¼ in) thick
1.2 kg (2 lb 10 oz) rockling,
  snapper or blue-eye trevalla
  fillets, skin off, bones
  removed, cut into 120–150 g
  (4½–5½ oz) pieces

1 × quantity Thai caramel
  (p. 105), hot to serve
5 snake beans, chopped
  (optional)

Staples
S&P

Heat 2 cm (¾ in) of oil in a small frying pan for 3 minutes over a medium heat. Fry the curry leaves, on their stems, for 2 minutes, until translucent, then drain on paper towel – they will become crunchy.

Preheat the oven grill (broiler) on high. Line a baking tray with baking paper.

Meanwhile, combine the herbs and cucumber in a bowl.

Season the fish pieces with salt and pepper, then lay them on the baking tray. Grill (broil) for about 6 minutes, then set aside to rest for 2 minutes to finish cooking.

Plate the fish. Spoon over the caramel. Scatter with the herb salad, finish with the curry leaves and snake beans, if using, and serve.

Side of salmon with walnuts, tahini, mint & pomegranate molasses GF

This is a simple way of cooking a whole side of salmon or ocean trout. Wrapping the fish in baking paper and foil allows it to gently steam, resulting in flesh that's delightfully vibrant pink in colour, rich and unctuous, which marries so well with the spiced nutty topping. A dinner party dish that pleases every time. **Serves 6**

Pair with

Kohlrabi & cucumber salad (p. 549).

Grilled asparagus.

Byzantine salad (p. 379).

Mejadra (p. 385).

900 g (2 lb) thick end fillet of
  salmon or ocean trout, skin
  on, bones removed
150 g (5½ oz/1¼ cups)
  walnuts, toasted and finely
  chopped
2 teaspoons cumin seeds,
  toasted and roughly ground

2 teaspoons ground fennel
2 teaspoons ground sumac
1 bunch of mint, half the
  leaves finely shredded,
  half left whole
4 spring onions (scallions),
  white and some of the
  green, finely sliced

1 × quantity Tahini dip/sauce
  (p. 71)
1 pomegranate, seeds
  reserved
2½ tablespoons
  pomegranate molasses

Staples
EVOO, S&P

Preheat the oven to 200°C (400°F) fan-forced. Coat the salmon with oil and season. Lay a double length of foil and baking paper on tray to fit the salmon and cover and seal the fish tightly, folding in the edges. Bake for 15 minutes, then remove from the oven and rest for 10 minutes.

Meanwhile, add the walnuts, cumin seeds, fennel and sumac to a bowl. Drizzle in about 2 teaspoons of oil, season and combine. Toss the shredded mint and spring onion through.

Unwrap the salmon and transfer to a serving plate. Smear the tahini sauce over the fish, to coat about 3 mm (⅛ in) thick, putting the rest in a bowl to serve on the side. Sprinkle the walnut mixture evenly across the fish. Scatter with the pomegranate seeds and mint leaves. Drizzle the pomegranate molasses over and serve.

Rockling with Thai caramel
sauce & herbs

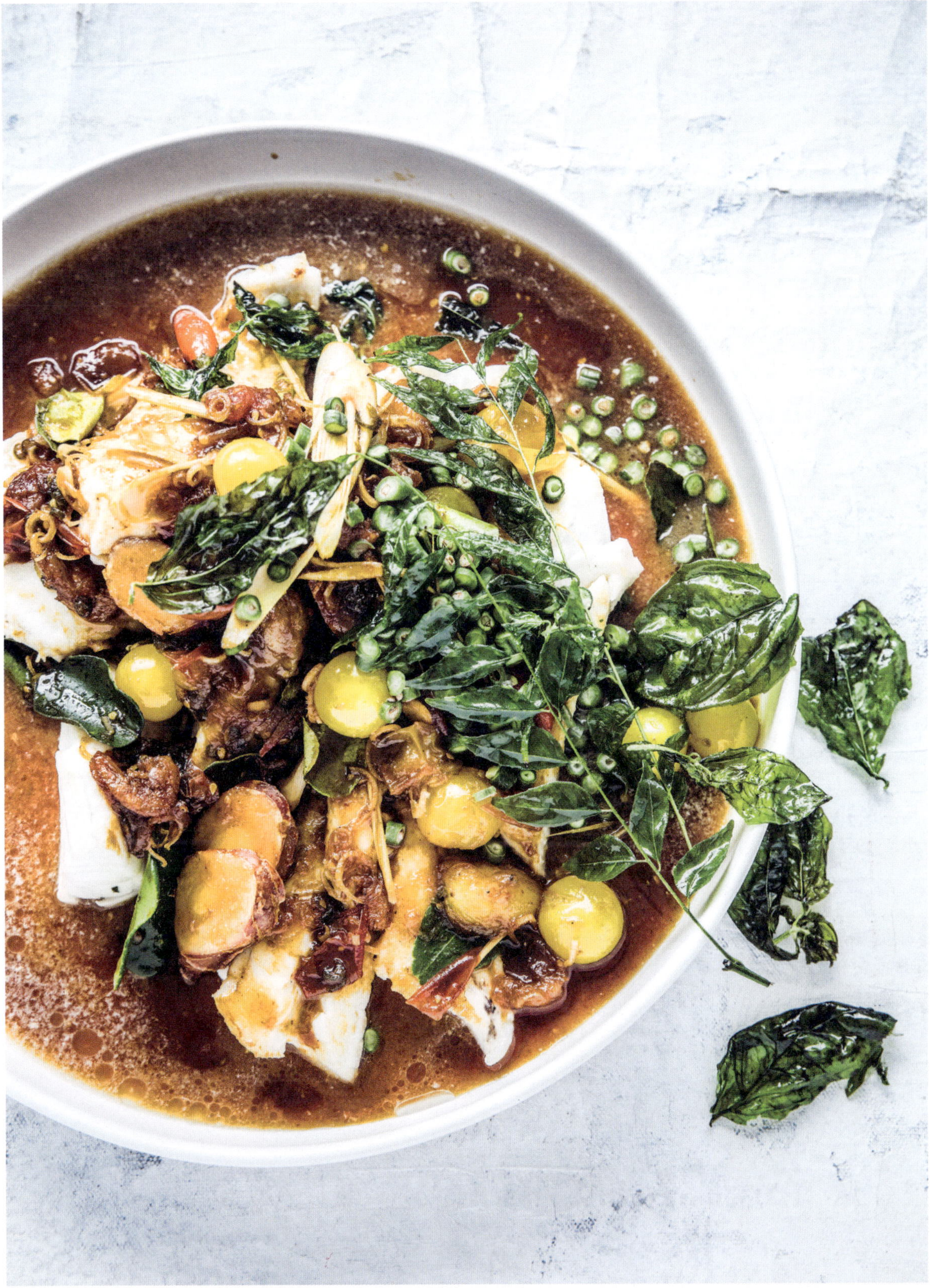

Ocean trout & smoked trout rillettes (GF)

This is a lovely starter in place of the usual charcuterie suspects, or alongside them – the more the merrier, I say. **Serves 8–10 as a starter**

600 g (1 lb 5 oz) ocean trout fillet, without skin, bones or bloodline
150 g (5½ oz) unsalted butter, at room temperature
120 g (4½ oz) plain yoghurt
3 egg yolks

3 tablespoons extra-virgin olive oil
1 tablespoon ground sumac
1½ teaspoons ground allspice
150 g (5½ oz) hot-smoked trout fillet, bones and bloodline removed

juice of 1 large lemon
4 spring onions (scallions), white and pale green parts, very finely sliced

Staples
S&P

Bring a large, deep frying pan of salted water to the boil. Lower the fresh ocean trout fillet into the water and reduce to a simmer. Poach for 2 minutes, then turn off the heat and stand for 5 minutes. Transfer the fillet to a colander and cover with a plate.

Using an electric stand mixer, whisk the butter and yoghurt on medium–high speed for 2 minutes. Add the egg yolks, oil and spices. Season with salt and pepper and whisk into a smooth and glossy paste.

Uncover the poached fish, then flake the flesh into a bowl, along with the smoked trout. Set aside to cool to room temperature.

Add the cooled fish to the butter mixture, along with the lemon juice and half the spring onion. Gently fold to combine, then adjust the seasoning to taste.

Tip into a serving dish and top with the remaining spring onion to serve. Best at room temperature, and especially good just made.

Pair with

Pile onto a slice of grilled brioche or Sourdough bread (p. 847).

Sesame milk buns or challah.

Mini tarts, made with Pâte brisée (p. 829).

Serve with some crackers – Lavoche (p. 840), Rye crackers (p. 838), Spiced seed crackers (p. 839) or the like.

For a canapé, pile onto crostini, dot with salmon roe and shower with snipped chives.

Serve with a few tablespoons salmon roe on top, and pane croccante on the side.

Fish soup with spiced rouille & croûtes

This is modelled on classic Mediterranean dishes where fish too inferior to be sold at market were cooked down with aromatics, then pushed through a sieve to make a flavourful soup. The fancy versions of fish soup (pp. 201, 214), with whole prawns (shrimp), scampi, crab claws, scallops and the like are wondrous – but so is this somewhat thriftier version. **Serves 6**

100 ml (3½ fl oz) extra-virgin olive oil
1 onion, finely sliced
5 garlic cloves, sliced
2 celery stalks, finely sliced
1½ fennel bulbs, finely sliced
1 leek, white part only, finely sliced
1 × 1 kg (2 lb 3 oz) whole gurnard or sand or grey mullet, filleted (use the bones for the stock)
6 raw prawns (shrimp), peeled (use the heads and shells for the stock)

2 teaspoons fennel seeds
10 saffron threads
1 fresh bay leaf
zest of ½ orange, and juice of 1 orange
1 long red chilli, chopped
3 tablespoons tomato paste (concentrated purée)
1½ tablespoons white miso paste
3 tablespoons pastis
150 ml (5 fl oz) white wine
400 g (14 oz) tin diced tomatoes

2.5 litres (85 fl oz/10 cups) Fish stock (p. 52 – use the bones and prawn/shrimp peelings)
½ teaspoon cayenne pepper
1 × quantity Rouille (p. 80)

Croûtes
2 small baguettes, sliced
1 garlic clove

Staples
EVOO, S&P

Heat the oil in a wide, heavy-based saucepan over a medium heat. Cook the onion, garlic and celery until softened, about 5 minutes. Add the fennel and leek, then cook over a low heat for about 15 minutes, to soften without any colour. Add the fish, prawns, fennel seeds, saffron, bay leaf, orange zest and chilli. Stir through for a minute or so.

Stir in the tomato paste, miso paste, pastis, orange juice and wine, then simmer for 4 minutes. Stir in the tomatoes and stock and simmer for 30 minutes.

Meanwhile, for the croûtes, toast the bread slices, or fry in oil, until crisp. Rub with the whole garlic clove and set aside.

Once the soup has finished cooking, remove the bay leaf and blitz in batches in a blender. Pass through a robust coarse-mesh sieve (you can use a food mill with the large-holed plate), pressing quite firmly to push a little of the solids through. Add the cayenne to the soup, season with salt and to stir to combine well. Add a little extra water (100–200 ml/3½–7 fl oz) if the soup is too thick.

Serve the soup with a drizzle of oil on top, with the croûtes and rouille on the side.

Salt-baked fish GF

This is a lovely dish for entertaining, with a little bit of theatre when it comes to cracking the salt crust open. The wow comes in the eating, though, with the pure flesh delicately steamed in its own juices and perfumed with lemon and herbs. Besides the fish listed below, you can use this versatile method on all kinds of varieties, including whole salmon, ocean trout, coral trout, sea bass and barramundi. **Serves 6–10**

Pair with

Dressed leaves and fresh Sourdough bread (p. 847).

Tartare sauce (see p. 77).

Salmoriglio (p. 83).

Salsa verde (p. 86).

Smoky tomato dressing (p. 84).

1 × 1.7–2 kg (3 lb 12 oz–4 lb 6 oz) whole snapper, turbot, bass grouper or murray cod, gills and scales removed

1 lemon, sliced into 5 mm (¼ in) thick rounds
4 flat-leaf (Italian) parsley sprigs, or fennel or wild fennel tops
3 egg whites

200 ml (7 fl oz) water
3 tablespoons fennel seeds
3.5 kg (7 lb 12 oz) rock salt

Special equipment
Probe thermometer

Preheat the oven to 190°C (375°F) fan-forced. Line a large baking tray with baking paper.

Stuff the cavity of the fish with the lemon and parsley.

Whisk the egg whites, water and fennel seeds in a large bowl, then add the salt and combine well. Add one-third of the mixture to the baking tray, on the diagonal. Make an indentation to take the fish, then lay the fish on top. Cover with the rest of the salt mixture, creating an even coating, about 2 cm (¾ in) thick. Pat flat to seal the fish in.

Bake for about 35 minutes, until a thermometer inserted in the thickest part of the fish, near the head, reads 45°C (115°F). Set aside on the bench for 45 minutes to finish cooking in the residual heat.

To serve, crack the crust and remove the salt in large pieces. Once liberated, lift the fish to a serving plate. This is made easier by leaving the scales on, but ensure you support the whole fish while you move it. Peel the skin back and scrape away any of the dark bloodline. Flake the fish, starting at the head end, and serve with your favourite sauces.

Roasted flounder with charred fennel GF

Roasted flounder is just superb, and it's a great fish for those less used to picking over a whole specimen, with the bones lifting away easily. Dory and mirror dory roast equally well, so it's hard to pick a favourite. And simply dressed charred fennel is the perfect accompaniment for either. Speaking of fennel, I love using a handful of bronze fennel fronds to stuff the fish with, subtly perfuming the flesh with sweetly anise tones. Bronze fennel is something I grow in my backyard, and though it has no bulb, the purplish mist of the fronds is visually enticing. I often find the fronds left on most fennel bulbs at the market a little too scant. **Serves 2**

Pair with

Fresh Harissa (p. 92) would be lovely with this, as would Smoky tomato dressing (p. 84).

a handful of fennel tops
(from the salad)
2 × 450 g (1 lb) whole
flounder or dory
80 ml (2½ fl oz/⅓ cup) white
wine

Charred fennel salad
2 French shallots, finely
sliced
2 tablespoons white-wine
vinegar
1½ tablespoons extra-virgin
olive oil
1 teaspoon caster (superfine)
sugar

1 teaspoon salt flakes
½ fennel bulb, fronds picked
and reserved, the bulb
sliced 4 mm (¼ in) thick
crossways

Staples
EVOO, LMN, S&P

Preheat the oven to 200°C (400°F) fan-forced. Line a shallow, heavy-based roasting tin with baking paper.

For the salad, add the shallot, vinegar, oil, sugar and salt to a bowl. Add a few grinds of pepper and toss to combine.

Season the fennel slices with salt and pepper, then dress with a splash of oil and toss to coat.

Drizzle some oil in the roasting tin. Stuff the fennel tops into the fish, then lay them in the tin. Season the fish with salt and pepper, then drizzle generously with oil and pour the wine over. Season with a little more salt and roast for 8 minutes, then turn the oven grill (broiler) on high and grill for 8 minutes.

Meanwhile, heat a heavy-based frying pan for 3 minutes, then spread the fennel slices in a thin layer in the pan. Cook until charred, about 2 minutes, then turn and cook for another minute. Add straight to the bowl with the shallot dressing and toss to coat. Stand for at least 5 minutes before serving.

Once cooked, rest the fish for 5 minutes. Squeeze over some lemon and transfer to plates, drizzling with the roasting juices. Serve with the salad on the side.

Steamed whole fish with spring onion, ginger & sesame

Pair with

Serve on a bed of blanched greens and/or shiitake mushrooms, with rice on the side.

This is a very simple way to cook a large fish as a centrepiece. Murray cod, coral trout, red emperor, turbot, rainbow trout and barramundi are all wonderful choices. **Serves 4–6**

1.3–1.4 kg (2 lb 14 oz–3 lb 1 oz) whole fish, such as murray cod or rainbow trout, left at room temperature for at least 30 minutes before cooking
200 ml (7 fl oz) shaoxing rice wine
2 tablespoons finely shredded fresh ginger
120 ml (4 fl oz) neutral-flavoured oil

5 spring onions (scallions), white and most of green parts, finely sliced on an angle

Soy stock sauce
150 ml (5 fl oz) light soy sauce
150 ml (5 fl oz) Golden chicken stock (p. 54), or White chicken stock (p. 54)

4 cm (1½ in) piece of fresh ginger, peeled and finely grated
2 large garlic cloves, finely grated
3 teaspoons caster (superfine) sugar
½ teaspoon ground white pepper
½ teaspoon sesame oil

Preheat the oven to 220°C (430°F) fan-forced.

Make a trivet in the base of a roasting tin using a pair of crossed chopsticks. Place the fish on top, ensuring it is elevated off the base. Pour the rice wine over, then scatter with the ginger. Cover with baking paper, then foil to seal. Bake for 30 minutes, then remove from the oven and rest for 5 minutes, covered.

Meanwhile, warm the sauce ingredients in a small saucepan.

Carefully lift the fish onto a warm serving plate. Scatter with the spring onion.

Heat the oil in a small saucepan over a high heat. Pour the oil over when it begins to smoke, and follow with the sauce. Serve.

Make it different
With fish fillets. This method of scalding the fish with the hot oil can also be done on a smaller scale with steamed fillets (see p. 162); you can spoon the same sauce over, too.

Use the stock sauce to dress prawns (shrimp), steamed quartered crabs, lobster or other fish

Fish & mussels en papillote ⒼⒻ

This is a lovely way to cook fish. And opening the individual seafood parcels at the table is such a thrilling moment, with the most glorious waft of scented steam rising up to greet your guests. It's also a fabulous dinner-party dish, and not just for the theatre, of which I am a confessed advocate, but also for the ease, as there's nothing complicated about it. You can have the parcels ready to go, to pop in the oven when ready. Just ensure that everything that goes into the parcel is well seasoned, and the fish is properly sealed, with the oven and resting finishing the job. And don't get ahead of yourself too much, as you don't want to refrigerate the parcels once made. A little work right before your guests arrive will result in a serenely delicious evening. **Serves 4**

1 fennel bulb, fronds reserved
125 ml (4 fl oz/½ cup) white wine
20 mussels, scrubbed, beards removed
6 large garlic cloves, finely sliced
3 tablespoons extra-virgin olive oil

4 × 180 g (6½ oz) fillets of bass grouper, blue-eye trevalla or hapuka, skin on
3 boiled or baked boiling (waxy) potatoes (such as kipfler), broken roughly
2 handfuls of fennel fronds and/or flat-leaf (Italian) parsley leaves, torn

1 large lemon, sliced
2 tablespoons small capers
150 g (5½ oz) crème fraîche
1 egg white, lightly whisked

Staples
EVOO, LMN, S&P

Cook the whole fennel bulb in simmering salted water for 30 minutes. Drain and chill to firm up, then cut lengthways, yielding four slices about 1.5 cm (½ in) thick.

Meanwhile, preheat the oven to 220°C (430°F) fan-forced. Cut four lengths of baking paper into 45 cm (18 in) lengths.

Heat the wine in a large saucepan over a high heat. Add the mussels, cover and cook for a few minutes, then uncover and lift out the mussels as they open. Once all are cooked, remove any stray beards, then remove the top shells from all but four, leaving those whole for presentation. Reduce the mussel liquor to about 80 ml (2½ fl oz/⅓ cup), then strain.

Add the garlic cloves and oil to a small frying pan over a high heat and fry until lightly golden, 4–5 minutes. Remove from the heat and immediately add the mussel liquor to stop the garlic burning.

Heat a large frying pan over a high heat for 2–3 minutes. Season the fish with salt and pepper and coat with oil, then fry, on the skin side only, for 3 minutes. Transfer each fillet to a sheet of baking paper, skin side up, so they sit in the middle of one half of each sheet.

Slip a slice of fennel and some potato under each fillet, then season with salt. Stuff some fennel fronds and/or parsley next to the fish, and a slice of lemon on top. Add the mussels, then sprinkle with the capers and fried garlic, with the oily liquid. Spoon the crème fraîche over and squeeze on some lemon.

Brush the egg white on the paper around each fillet, then fold the top over to meet the other end. Roll the edges tightly in on themselves from one end to the other, to form a calzone-like parcel. Lay the parcels on a baking tray with a little space in between, as the air will need air to circulate around them.

Bake for about 12 minutes, then rest unopened for 2 minutes on serving plates. Cut open with scissors at the table.

Make it different
Snapper en papillote. ⒼⒻ Use this technique for a plate-sized snapper, about 450 g (1 lb) to serve one person, but bake for about 20 minutes before resting for 5 minutes.

You can also use other types of fish, including other shellfish, though the timing will naturally vary.

Whole snapper pan-fried with bay & garlic (GF)

Pair with

A salad and/or seasonal greens.

This is a wonderful way to cook plate-sized snapper, an easy dinner for two. The smell is quite intoxicating, and the sauce is stunning in its simplicity. **Serves 2**

2 × 450 g (1 lb) snapper, cleaned and scaled
3 tablespoons extra-virgin olive oil

4 garlic cloves, skin on, smashed
1 lemon, sliced into rounds
6 fresh bay leaves

125 ml (4 fl oz/½ cup) white wine
80 g (2¾ oz) unsalted butter

Staples
S&P

Preheat the oven to 200°C (400°F) fan-forced.

Bring the snapper close to room temperature before cooking.

Dry the fish. Make an incision, about 1 cm (½ in) deep, down the length of each fish, along the spine to the tail, on both sides.

Heat a large ovenproof frying pan over a high heat. Season the fish with salt and pepper. If you like, place a piece of baking paper in the pan (to stop the fish sticking), then add the oil, followed by the fish. Cook for 3 minutes on one side, then turn the fish over. Add the garlic, lemon and bay leaves, cook for 2 minutes, then add the wine and simmer for 30 seconds.

Top each fish with half the butter, then transfer the pan to the oven. Cook for 8 minutes, then remove from the oven and rest for 2 minutes in the pan to finish cooking.

To serve, transfer the fish to plates and drizzle with the pan juices.

Whole snapper baked with cumin, lemon, bay & green harissa (GF)

Pair with

Couscous or a grain salad (pp. 378–9).

Cooking a large fish can be daunting, but this method is a blissfully simple way to feed a full table of guests. **Serves 6–8**

1 × 2 kg (4 lb 6 oz) whole snapper, cleaned and scaled
2 lemons, 1 sliced into rounds
6 fresh bay leaves – on the branch, if possible

3 garlic cloves, peeled
1 tablespoon ground cumin
2 teaspoons cumin seeds
Green harissa (p. 92), to serve

Yoghurt & lemon sauce
300 g (10½ oz) plain yoghurt
juice of ½ lemon
½ teaspoon salt flakes

Staples
EVOO, S&P

Preheat the oven to 220°C (430°F) fan-forced.

Lay out two lengths of foil, so that they overlap in the middle, then fold to join. Place another piece of foil down to cover the overlap. Top with two layers of overlapping baking paper, then place the fish on top. Squeeze the whole lemon over the fish and inside the cavity. Tuck the lemon slices and bay leaves into the cavity. Finely grate the garlic over the fish. Season with salt and pepper, sprinkle with all the cumin, then drizzle generously with oil. Wrap the fish with the baking paper and foil, folding to seal.

Place the fish on a baking tray and bake for 40 minutes.

Meanwhile, combine the yoghurt sauce ingredients in a small bowl.

Remove the baking tray from the oven and turn the oven grill (broiler) on high. Unwrap the parcel to just expose the fish, then grill (broil) for 10 minutes to colour slightly.

Rest for 10 minutes before serving with the harissa and yoghurt sauce on the side.

Taramasalata

With olives and warm pitta bread, I could eat this every day. I first tasted taramasalata when I was about thirteen. I went to secondary school in Richmond, Melbourne, and when everyone brought a plate to share for special occasions, taramasalata was right there alongside the chicken sandwiches. I was a convert. We've become accustomed to this dip being luridly pink, but this is somewhat of a deception, with the carp or cod roe traditionally employed naturally rendering it more beige. I guess this was seen as unappetising, but it doesn't look that way to me. You may eat with your eyes, as they say, but the knowledge of how delicious something is certainly helps to shape how delicious it looks. **Serves 10**

125 g (4½ oz) white bread, crusts removed
150 g (5½ oz) cured white fish roe
½ white onion, chopped

½ small garlic clove, finely grated
juice of 2 lemons
300 ml (10 fl oz) neutral oil
100 ml (3½ fl oz) extra-virgin olive oil

80 ml (2½ fl oz/⅓ cup) warm water
salmon roe, to serve (optional)

Soak the bread in water for 5 minutes, then squeeze most of the water out with your hands.

In a food processor, blitz the bread, roe, onion, garlic and half the lemon juice into a smooth paste. Gradually add some of the oils while processing, then a little lemon juice, then the oils again, alternating until smooth. Drizzle in the warm water while processing, which will give a fluffy texture.

Serve with the salmon roe spooned over, if using. The taramasalata will keep refrigerated in an airtight container for up to 10 days.

Pair with

Fresh pitta bread (see p. 854), olives and other meze.

Cut crudités from cucumber, celery heart, raw white and green asparagus, baby carrots, radishes, small green beans, chicory (witlof/endive) and the like. Stand them in a clear serving bowl with crushed ice in the base, with the taramasalata on the side.

Smother on toast, then top with a soft fried egg.

Serve as a sauce for a Prawn cocktail (p. 413).

Serve alongside barbecued seafood.

Simit/koulouri.

Serving tarama with beer-battered fish and chips (p. 187) is a revelation.

Swordfish with beurre rouge ⓖⓕ

When buying swordfish, always look for pearly white flesh, with bright red blood lines. With its densely flaked flesh, swordfish lends itself to so many flavours, from strong Mediterranean ones to Asian curries. It also works so well with a rich butter sauce spiked with red wine, with mash to mop up all the juices – such a wintery fish dish. **Serves 4**

1 white salad onion, finely sliced, soaked in cold water, then drained and dried
4 × 200 g (7 oz) swordfish or tuna fillets

5 mint sprigs, leaves torn
5 flat-leaf (Italian) parsley sprigs, leaves torn
2 teaspoons small capers
1 × quantity Classic potato mash (p. 625), hot to serve

1 × quantity Beurre rouge (p. 69), hot to serve

Staples
EVOO, S&P

Soak the onion in cold water for about 10 minutes. Drain and dry, then set aside.

Heat a large frying pan or chargrill pan over a high heat for several minutes, until very hot.

Season the fish fillets with salt and pepper and oil lightly. Cook on one side for 3½ minutes, then flip and cook on the other side for 3 minutes, to cook to medium.

Meanwhile, toss the onion, herbs and capers with a little oil and a pinch of salt.

Plate each fish fillet with a generous dollop of mash, then spoon over some beurre rouge sauce. Crown the fish with the salad so it spills off to the side. Serve immediately.

Tunisian grilled smashed sardines on toast

Pair with

Sriracha or Fermented cooked chilli sauce (p. 97).

This is a recipe from my grandmother Grace, who enjoyed sardines very much. This is how her mother made them in Tunis, and I still make this recipe for my father occasionally, as he loves them too. **Serves 6**

2 garlic cloves, peeled
2 teaspoons salt flakes
2 teaspoons cumin seeds
1 teaspoon caraway seeds
½ teaspoon freshly ground black pepper

1 tablespoon extra-virgin olive oil
12 whole sardines, cleaned, heads removed
1 handful of flat-leaf (Italian) parsley leaves, chopped

6 slices of Sourdough bread (p. 847)

Staples
BTR, LMN, S&P

Preheat a barbecue or the oven grill (broiler) on medium.

Using a mortar and pestle, roughly grind the garlic, salt, cumin, caraway and pepper. Add the oil and grind to a rough paste.

Rub the paste into the sardines and grill for about 2 minutes each side, until cooked. Transfer to a plate.

Squash a sardine a little with a fork, then open out the fish to expose the backbone. Pull the spine out from the head end, which should remove the ribs, too – but check to be sure. Repeat for all the fish, then add the flesh to a bowl and break up with a fork. Add the parsley and a squeeze of lemon, then combine. Adjust the seasoning as needed.

Meanwhile, toast the bread, making sure there is some softness in the middle, then butter generously. Pile on the sardine mixture and serve.

Fish marinated with white miso

Misozuke is a traditional Japanese miso-marinating and pickling method that is used for both vegetables and seafood, especially oil-rich fish such as salmon, ocean trout, cobia, mackerel and kingfish; I like blue-eye trevalla served this way also. Marinating fish in miso gives you a sweetly pleasing and very satisfying umami character, which makes the fish even richer and fuller in its natural flavour. **Serves 4**

Pair with

Short-grain rice dressed with vinegar and mirin (see p. 372), and wilted greens.

Pickled daikon & mint salad (p. 304).

4 × 200 g (7 oz) fish fillets, skin on, bones removed
oil, for shallow-frying
8 cm (3¼ in) piece of fresh ginger, peeled and julienned

1½ tablespoons toasted white sesame seeds
300 g (10½ oz) peeled daikon, julienned
2 limes, cut into cheeks or wedges

White miso marinade
120 g (4½ oz) white miso paste
3 tablespoons mirin
2 tablespoons sake
1 teaspoon sesame oil

Combine the marinade ingredients in a bowl, then rub all over the fish. Refrigerate in an airtight container overnight, or for at least 2 hours.

When ready to cook, fry the ginger in 4 cm (1½ in) of oil for 4 minutes, until lightly golden, then drain on paper towel. The ginger will crisp up as it cools.

Heat the oven grill (broiler) on high. Line a baking tray with baking paper.

Wipe most of the marinade off the fish with paper towel, then cover the skin with the sesame seeds. Lay on the baking tray, skin side up. Grill (broil) for 5 minutes, then rest for 2 minutes.

Serve with the daikon, garnished with the fried ginger, with lime on the side.

Make it different
With shiitake mushroom. Add eight trimmed shiitake mushrooms to the marinade. Once marinated, wipe most of the marinade off the mushrooms and grill them alongside the fish.

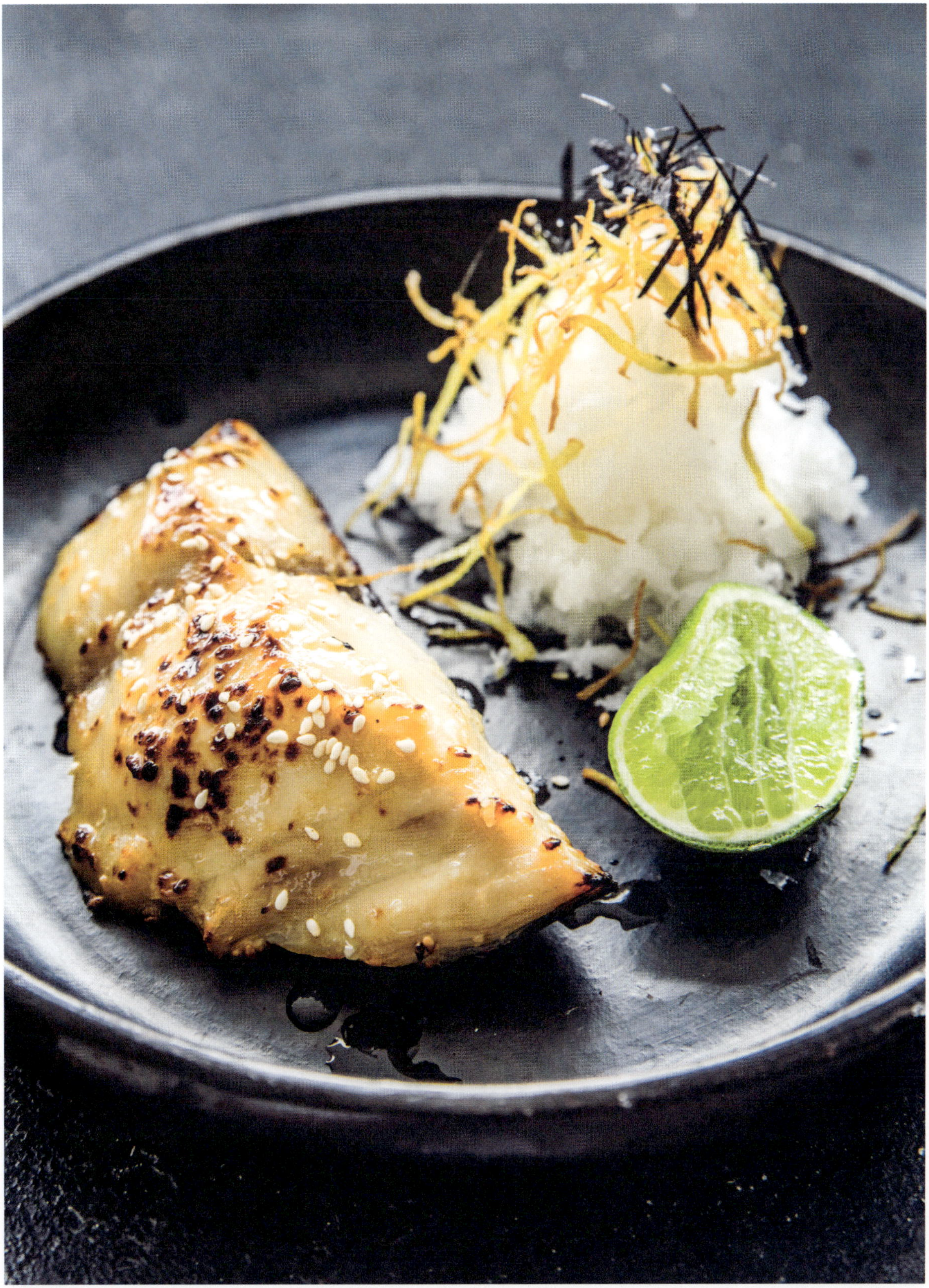

Beer-battered flathead & twice-cooked potato cakes

The batter I use here is a mix between a tempura batter and a traditional beer batter, with the flavour of the latter and the brittle crispness of the former. To get good results, though, it is important to coat the fish with only the lightest dusting of flour, then dip in the batter and fry in clean oil. The ideal temperature for this batter is 180°C (350°F), so it's important not to crowd the pan or deep-fryer, as you will lower the heat too much and the oil won't return to the right temperature quickly enough. For most domestic fryers, about four items is the limit. You can always keep the cooked items warm in a low oven, but if you cram the fryer the batter will take up too much oil and become heavy. Also, don't try to fry in a smaller amount of oil. This is proper deep-frying, and you need the volume of evenly hot oil to get a great result. **Serves 4 as a starter, 2 as a meal**

oil, for deep-frying (see p. 22)
4 × 150 g (5½ oz) rock
 flathead fillets, skin on
1 quantity Nori tartare (p. 77)
Potato cakes
300 g (10½ oz) rock salt
4 large boiling (waxy)
 potatoes (such as Dutch

cream, nicola or desiree),
 scrubbed
Nori salt
4 nori sheets, torn
2 tablespoons salt flakes
Tempura beer batter
250 g (9 oz/1⅔ cups) plain
 (all-purpose) flour

250 g (9 oz/2 cups) cornflour
 (cornstarch)
1 tablespoon salt flakes
375 ml (12½ fl oz/1½ cups)
 beer
250 ml (8½ fl oz/1 cup)
 mineral water
Staples
FLR

Preheat the oven to 190°C (375°F) fan-forced.

For the potato cakes, spread the rock salt on a baking tray, then nestle the potatoes into the salt and bake for 50 minutes. Cool to room temperature.

For the nori salt, blitz the nori in a high-speed blender, then combine with the salt.

For the batter, combine the flours and salt in a large bowl. Combine the beer and mineral water, make a well in the dry ingredients, then gradually whisk in the liquid until smooth.

Heat 20 cm (8 in) of oil in wide heavy-based saucepan or in a deep-fryer until 180°C (350°F).

Meanwhile, heat the oven to 100°C (210°F) fan-forced.

Slice the potatoes into rounds 3.5 cm (1½ in) thick. Working and cooking in batches, dust the potato rounds with flour, shaking off any excess, then submerge in the batter. Fry for 3–4 minutes, until golden. Drain, season with the nori salt and keep warm on a baking tray in the oven.

Working in batches if needed, dust the fish in flour, shaking off any excess, then coat in the batter; I like to batter the flesh but leave the skin mostly exposed for effect, but that's entirely up to you. Lower into the oil and cook until golden, about 3 minutes.

Season with the nori salt and drain, then serve immediately, with the potato cakes and nori tartare.

Make it different
Classic fish & potato cakes. Skip all the nori and simply serve the fish and potato cakes with salt and vinegar, or a more classic tartare (see p. 77).

Deep-fried red mullet with celery & olive salad

The best fried fish I have ever had was outside the marine barracks in Athens. It's an understated place on a corner, where they fry the day's catch in huge flat pans of olive oil. This is my homage. I love red mullet cooked this way, with the flesh reminding me a little of lobster. **Serves 6**

oil, for deep-frying (olive oil is best; see p. 22)
100 g (3½ oz/⅔ cup) plain (all-purpose) flour
100 g (3½ oz) fine semolina
6 × 200–300 g (7–10½ oz) whole red mullet, sand whiting or leatherjacket, cleaned
2 lemons, cut into wedges

Celery & olive salad
1 celery heart, leaves picked, stems finely sliced

4 spring onions (scallions), white part only, finely sliced
1 lemon, finely sliced, each slice cut into 8 triangles
2 large handfuls of flat-leaf (Italian) parsley leaves, roughly torn
1 handful of mint leaves, torn
5 dill sprigs, fronds chopped
5 fresh fenugreek sprigs, leaves picked, or a handful of rocket (arugula)

4 slices pickled cocktail onions, finely chopped (optional)
14 black olives, squashed to pit, then torn
10 large green olives, squashed to pit, then torn
2 teaspoons small capers
2½ tablespoons extra-virgin olive oil

Staples
LMN, S&P

Add all the salad ingredients to a large bowl, squeeze in some lemon and toss to combine.

Heat 20 cm (8 in) of oil in a heavy-based saucepan or deep-fryer until 170°C (340°F).

Combine the flour and semolina. Working in two batches, heavily dust the fish with the flour mixture and fry for about 5 minutes. Drain on paper towel, seasoning with salt and pepper as soon as they come out of the oil.

Serve the fish immediately, with the salad, and extra lemon on the side.

Fish pie

I make many versions of fish pie, from the humble to the decidedly fancy, but this is just about my favourite template. The sauce is so velvety, while the hot-smoked fish adds a warming note. I can't help adding some prawns (shrimp), as I love them in pies like this – but it can simply be made with fish. **Serves 6**

75 g (2¾ oz) unsalted butter
1 onion, diced
5 garlic cloves, sliced
1 fennel bulb, cut into 1 cm (½ in) dice
350 g (12½ oz) all-purpose potatoes (such as desiree), peeled and finely diced
800 ml (27 fl oz) Fish stock (p. 52), or Golden chicken stock (p. 54), hot
200 ml (7 fl oz) pouring (single/light) cream

200 g (7 oz) smoked trout, flesh flaked
6 spring onions (scallions), white part only, cut into 3 cm (1¼ in) lengths
4 flat-leaf (Italian) parsley sprigs, leaves chopped
4 dill sprigs, fronds chopped
zest and juice of 1 lemon
600 g (1 lb 5 oz) small flathead fillets, or any boneless white-fleshed fish

300 g (10½ oz) raw prawn (shrimp) cutlets, sliced in half lengthways
375 g (13 oz) piece of puff pastry (or make your own, p. 822, or use Rough puff, p. 823), rolled and chilled
1 egg, beaten

Staples
EVOO, S&P

Pair with

A leafy salad.

Just-cooked crab meat or scallops (you can even decorate the pastry with the shells if using the latter).

Preheat the oven to 200°C (400°F) fan-forced.

Melt the butter in a heavy-based saucepan over a medium heat. Cook the onion and garlic until softened, about 3 minutes. Add the fennel and potato, season with salt and pepper and cook for 3 minutes, stirring constantly. Pour in the stock and cream, bring to a simmer and cook for 20 minutes, until the potato is tender.

Once cooked, blitz with a stick blender until smooth, then strain into a bowl. Add the trout, spring onion, herbs, lemon zest and lemon juice, season and set aside.

Heat a large frying pan over a high heat for a few minutes. Toss the fish and prawns in a little oil, then sear in three batches, seasoning as you go, for a minute or so, to just colour but not cook through. Drain, then place in a 28 cm (11 in) pie dish (or use individual pie dishes). Pour the sauce over the top.

Cut the pastry the same shape as your dish, but with a 3 cm (1¼ in) overhang. Brush the top edges of the dish with beaten egg, then drop the pastry on top. Decorate with any pastry scraps and cut some slits to release steam. Brush the pastry with egg.

Bake for about 25 minutes, until the pastry is golden and the mixture is bubbling. Serve hot, garnishing with the shells if desired.

Croquetas with smoked eel & manchego

I fell in love with smoked eel in my early days of cooking. The texture and flavour are such distinctive pleasures, adding so much to these croquetas, with a textural contribution from the rice, and the manchego adding melting richness. If I ever open a tapas bar, these will be the first things on the menu. **Makes 30**

30 g (1 oz) unsalted butter
1 leek, white part only,
 finely diced
700 ml (23½ fl oz) full-cream
 (whole) milk
300 ml (10 fl oz) Fish stock
 (p. 52)
2 garlic cloves, peeled
2 fresh bay leaves
100 ml (3½ fl oz) extra-virgin
 olive oil

125 g (4½ oz) plain
 (all-purpose) flour
100 g (3½ oz) bomba rice,
 freshly cooked using the
 absorption method (see
 p. 372)
300 g (10½ oz) smoked eel,
 cut into 5 mm (¼ in) dice
100 g (3½ oz) manchego, cut
 into 5 mm (¼ in) dice
½ teaspoon ground white
 pepper

oil, for deep-frying (see p. 22)
Aïoli (see p. 76), to serve

To crumb
200 g (7 oz/1⅓ cups) plain
 (all-purpose) flour
3 eggs, beaten
400 g (14 oz/4 cups) dried
 breadcrumbs

Staples
S&WP

Melt the butter in a small saucepan over a medium heat. Add the leek, season with salt and cook until softened with a little colour, about 5 minutes. Set aside.

In a saucepan, heat the milk, stock, garlic and bay leaves to just under a simmer. Remove from the heat and set aside for 15 minutes to infuse, then strain into a saucepan or jug.

Add the oil and flour to a saucepan over a medium heat. Stir until lightly golden, about 3 minutes, then remove from the heat. Whisk in 250 ml (8½ fl oz/1 cup) of the milk mixture until smooth. Cook again for 1 minute, then gradually whisk in the remaining milk mixture until incorporated. Cook for about 5 minutes, until thickened and a smooth, silky consistency.

Stir the rice through, then the eel, leek, manchego and white pepper. Remove from the heat and adjust the seasoning as needed.

Tip the mixture into a lined 20 cm (8 in) square tray, smoothing it out. Cover with plastic wrap and refrigerate for at least 6 hours or overnight.

Tip the mixture onto a chopping board, cut into thirty evenly sized pieces, and mould into barrel shapes. Chill on a tray for a further 30 minutes.

To crumb the croquetas, coat them in the flour, then dip in egg, then coat with the breadcrumbs. These can be frozen at this point and thawed at room temperature for about 20 minutes before frying; otherwise, chill on a tray for a final 30 minutes.

Heat 20 cm (8 in) of oil in a wide heavy-based saucepan or deep-fryer until 170°C (340°F).

Working in batches (making sure the oil comes back up to temperature before frying the next batch), cook the croquetas for 5 minutes, rotating to colour evenly.

Drain briefly, season and serve immediately, with aioli on the side.

Fish cakes with parsley

These delicate, luscious fish and crab cakes are delicious with Aïoli (p. 76) as a tapas course, or finger food for a crowd – or you could serve them with a few dressed leaves as a light meal. **Serves 4–6**

Pair with

*Aioli (p. 76) or tartare
(see p. 77), and some simply
dressed leaves.*

600 g (1 lb 5 oz) flathead,
blue-eye trevalla or gurnard
fillets, skin and bones
removed
350 g (12½ oz) rock salt
500 g (1 lb 2 oz) all-purpose
potatoes (such as desiree),
peeled and cut into 3 cm
(1¼ in) dice
300 ml (10 fl oz) full-cream
(whole) milk

1 garlic clove, sliced
2 fresh bay leaves
1 teaspoon white
peppercorns
3 egg yolks
oil, for deep-frying (see p. 22)
lemon wedges, to serve

Parsley & lemon paste
6 flat-leaf (Italian) parsley
sprigs, leaves chopped

zest of ½ lemon
½ garlic clove
½ teaspoon salt flakes

To crumb
3 eggs, whisked
300 g (10½ oz/5 cups) panko
breadcrumbs

Staples
FLR, S&P

Surround the fish with the rock salt in a non-reactive container. Refrigerate for 1 hour, then shake off the excess salt.

Boil the potato from cold in salted water until tender, about 20 minutes. Drain, pass through a ricer or food mill into a large bowl, then cool for 5 minutes.

Meanwhile, in a saucepan, bring the milk, garlic, bay leaves and peppercorns to a simmer over a medium heat. Add the fish and simmer for 2 minutes, then turn off the heat and stand for 3 minutes to finish poaching. Remove the fish from the liquid and stand in a colander.

Grind the parsley paste ingredients together using a mortar and pestle, then tip into a bowl. Flake in the poached fish and combine.

Fold the fish mixture through the cooled potato. Season with pepper, then fold the egg yolks through. Refrigerate for 15 minutes to firm up.

Heat 5 cm (2 in) of oil in a wide heavy-based saucepan or deep-fryer until 170°C (340°F).

Shape the chilled fish mixture into 5 cm (2 in) long torpedo shapes, about 80 g (2¾ oz) each. Dust in flour, then coat in the whisked eggs, then the panko, crumbing well.

Working in batches, carefully lower the cakes into the oil and cook for 3–4 minutes, until golden, then drain on paper towel.

Serve immediately, with lemon wedges and a sauce of your choice.

Sesame-crumbed ocean trout with nori mayo in a brioche bun

I am particularly fond of a fried fish sandwich, with this version skewing things in a Japanese direction. This is also a great way to feed a crowd – once set up, you can have these coming out of the kitchen in a near-constant flow. **Serves 6**

oil, for deep-frying (see p. 22)
200 g (7 oz/3⅓ cups) panko
breadcrumbs
80 g (2¾ oz/½ cup) sesame
seeds
1 teaspoon ground white
pepper
1 × 800 g (1 lb 12 oz)
mid-section of ocean
trout, salmon or gummy
shark fillet, skin and bones

removed, cut crossways
into 6 pieces
2 eggs, lightly beaten
6 long brioche rolls
6 iceberg lettuce leaves,
finely sliced
2 tablespoons drained and
finely sliced pickled white
ginger
2 limes, cut into cheeks or
wedges

Miso & nori mayonnaise
2 roasted nori sheets,
soaked in cold water for
5 minutes
250 ml (8½ fl oz/1 cup)
Master olive oil mayonnaise
(p. 74)
3 teaspoons white miso
paste

Staples
FLR, S&P

Preheat the oven to 160°C (320°F) fan-forced.

To make the mayonnaise, squeeze the excess water out of the nori and chop finely. Add to a small bowl with the mayonnaise and miso, mixing well.

Heat about 10 cm (4 in) of oil in a wide-heavy-based saucepan over a medium heat until 175°C (345°F).

Meanwhile, combine the panko, sesame seeds and white pepper in a shallow bowl. Dust the fish pieces with flour, dip in the beaten eggs, then coat with the sesame crumbs.

Slice the buns open, but not all the way through. Lightly toast in the oven for a couple of minutes while you fry the fish.

Working in two batches, carefully lower the fish into the hot oil and cook for about 2½ minutes, rotating to cook evenly. Drain on paper towel, seasoning with salt and pepper as they come out of the oil.

To assemble, spoon a generous amount of the nori mayonnaise on the bottom half of each bun. Top with some lettuce, a piece of crumbed fish, some pickled ginger, more lettuce and a little more mayonnaise.

Serve immediately, with the lime cheeks to squeeze over.

Thai fish cakes

There's something addictive about the texture of these, and they take up the dipping sauce beautifully. This recipe looks daunting, but it's quite simple once the ingredients have been gathered. The flavour intensifies, so they can be made earlier in the day, or even the day before, and then fried as needed. The duck or pork fat is optional, but it is the secret for a gold-standard fish cake. **Makes about 20**

Pair with

This is just about the best way to kick off a Thai banquet!

The fish cakes can be dressed up with coriander, mustard cress or mustard leaf lettuce, makrut lime leaves, cucumber and snake beans, or just served with the dipping sauce.

500 g (1 lb 2 oz) skinless white fish such as perch, ling or snapper, cut into thick chunks
2 egg whites
2 red bird's eye chillies, finely sliced into rounds
1 lemongrass stem, white part only, very finely sliced
2 tablespoons cornflour (cornstarch), or rice flour
1½ tablespoons duck or pork fat, or left-over bacon fat (optional)
1½ tablespoons tom yum paste, or red curry paste
1½ tablespoons fish sauce

1½ tablespoons caster (superfine) sugar
150 g (5½ oz) raw prawn (shrimp) meat, finely chopped
4 snake beans, very finely sliced
8 makrut lime leaves, finely sliced
oil, for deep-frying (see p. 22)
lime cheeks or wedges, to serve
fried curry leaves (see p. 581), to garnish (optional)

Chilli cucumber dipping sauce
150 g (5½ oz/⅔ cup) caster (superfine) sugar

1 tablespoon salt flakes
100 ml (3½ fl oz) white vinegar
100 ml (3½ fl oz) water
8 red bird's eye chillies, finely sliced
1 tablespoon fish sauce
2 red Asian shallots, finely diced
1 Lebanese (short) cucumber, quartered lengthways and sliced, or cut into 'pearls' with a melon baller
juice of 1½ limes
5 coriander (cilantro) sprigs, leaves and fine stems roughly chopped

Blitz the fish in a food processor, then add the egg whites and blitz until combined. Add the chilli, lemongrass, cornflour, duck fat (if using), tom yum paste, fish sauce and sugar. Process until smooth and combined, stopping to scrape down the sides as needed.

Transfer the mixture to a bowl and stir the prawn meat through, then thoroughly mix the snake beans and lime leaves through. Shape into walnut-sized patties and flatten into 1 cm (½ in) thick discs. Refrigerate until needed.

For the dipping sauce, bring the sugar, salt, vinegar and water to the boil in a small saucepan. Boil for 3 minutes, then remove from the heat. Add the chilli, then cool for 10 minutes before adding the other ingredients. Stir well and set aside for about 10 minutes for the flavours to mesh.

Heat 8 cm (3¼ in) of oil in a deep heavy-based frying pan or deep-fryer until 180°C (350°F).

Fry the fish cakes for about 4 minutes, until just golden, turning to colour evenly, then drain briefly on paper towel.

Serve the fish cakes warm, garnished with fried curry leaves if desired, with the dipping sauce and lime cheeks or wedges on the side.

Crustaceans

I have a deep love for all seafood, but it would not be entirely unfair to characterise my interest in crustaceans as obsessive. When I'm at a good fishmonger's, prawns (shrimp) in particular tend to sharpen my focus and result in me buying too much – but then there are never too many prawns. I also adore more expensive items such as lobster and crayfish, as well as all manner of crabs, though the preparation needed makes them more inconsistent features of my home menu – though a feature, nonetheless. The wonderful thing about all crustaceans, beyond their sweet and divinely textured flesh, is that the shells and heads, and any juices they contain, make marvellous stock, brilliant for boosting a fish broth for a stew, or being roasted and cooked into a deeply scented stock or sauce.

Prawns

Prawns (shrimp) hatch in their millions in Australia's deeper northern waters, then move into estuaries and inlets along the coast to feed, scavenging off the seabed and eating a varied diet, before eventually heading back out to sea to spawn, with the cycle starting again. Prawns are caught by trawlers running otter nets, which skim above the seafloor. Most of those prawns are either frozen or cooked on the boat, or both. These methods result in very good outcomes, with quickly frozen prawns – raw or cooked – retaining their integrity well.

Australia's prawn industry is highly managed and world class, but it's not without its problems. Prawns themselves are abundant, and there is no imminent risk of overfishing, but there is a risk to other species.

Prawns are necessarily trawled, and trawling catches all manner of things, so there is a still a lot of waste, with non-commercial fish caught and killed in vast numbers – even in areas with mandatory bycatch reduction measures in place.

The obvious solution to this is aquaculture, and our farmed prawn industry is certainly world-leading. Aquaculture also means you can now readily source prawns that have not been frozen, which was virtually impossible not so long ago. In general, farmed Australian prawns are the best option environmentally, and the quality is very high.

I never buy imported prawns, as there is no way to establish the fishing or farming practices used, and indeed if they have been caught wild or farmed. Unregulated aquaculture operations are often significantly damaging to the environment, and antibiotics and other medications are often used, which can involve health risks from consuming them. Unless the provenance and practices can be verified, on no level is it worth buying imported prawns. Unless, of course, cost is more important ... and I hope it's not. I'd prefer to eat glorious local mussels if I couldn't afford prawns.

King prawns are the most commonly available. They actually consist of three main species: eastern, western and red spot king prawns, all of which are often sold simply as 'king' prawns. Tiger prawns, which are predictably striped and quite dramatic looking, are the most commonly farmed species. In general, king and tiger prawns are interchangeable, with sweet firm flesh when cooked. Both are ideal for grilling (see p. 202), as you can source quite large specimens, meaning you can get good grill flavour without overcooking; both are also excellent for frying, to roast in the shell (see right), and to use in pastas and soups.

Endeavour prawns are less common and less dramatic in size or appearance than king and tiger prawns, but their flavour is prized. I find banana prawns of less reliable quality, as they become somewhat mushy if not in sparkling condition, but you *can* buy quality farmed banana prawns – again, just talk to your fishmonger. They're an excellent prawn for peeling and stir-frying.

Pair with

Prawns are similar to lobster in terms of complementary flavours (see p. 196). They are also enhanced by soy sauce, rice wine, honey, cumin and mint, and pair well with avocado, corn and nori.

Prawns a la plancha GF

A plancha is a flat grill commonly used in Spain. Most of us don't have one of those, me included, so this is a fairly simple way to replicate the same cooking effect using your oven. This dish is also an excellent example of why cooking prawns in their shells is so rewarding, adding another level of superb flavour. Spread 500 g (1 lb 2 oz) rock salt on a heavy heatproof tray – one that won't buckle as it gets hot. Preheat the oven to 240°C (465°F) fan-forced, then heat the tray and salt for 15 minutes. The salt will now be blisteringly hot. On top of the salt, place 10 large, whole king prawns (shrimp) that have been deveined (see opposite), pressing them in slightly, then roast for about 10 minutes. Remove from the oven and set the tray aside for 1 minute, then pick off the prawns with tongs. Serve with lemon and Spicy aïoli (p. 76). These are best hot.

Instead of discarding prawn heads or using for stock, make a flavoursome dust that enhances the flavour of soups or wontons, or sprinkle over fried rice, noodles, pasta, seafood risotto or salads. Totally dehydrate the heads of 12 raw prawns spread out on lined a tray for 3–4 hours in a 100°C (210°F) oven. They are ready when brittle and completely dry. Blitz the cooled prawn heads to a fine powder in a blender on high. Store in an airtight container in the fridge for around a month.

School prawns are generally only about 10 cm (4 in) long and can be fried and eaten whole. I have eaten immaculately fresh ones raw, too. On one holiday, I came across the sweetest tiny school prawns in Brunswick Heads on the north coast of New South Wales. They were amazing peeled and served raw with extra-virgin olive oil, finely shaved celery heart (with the leaves torn), some finely diced green chilli, salt flakes, black pepper and a squeeze of lemon just before eating. They were truly magnificent, and a memorable summer experience.

Schoolies are also perfect fried whole. Drain well of any water, then dust lightly in semolina and flour (as for Calamari fritti, p. 223) and deep-fry at 180°C (350°F) for 2 minutes. Eat immediately with lemon, and mayonnaise (pp. 74–5) as is, or spiked with Fermented cooked chilli sauce (p. 97).

Buying & storing prawns

When buying prawns, look for translucent shells with vibrantly coloured tails, and without any discolouration or blackness around the head or legs. They should be firm, with a sweet iodine sea smell, and they should be removed from the bag you bought them in as soon as you get home.

Whether buying whole raw or cooked prawns, they are very delicate and should be consumed as soon as possible. The best way to store cooked prawns is buried in salted ice. Add 2 teaspoons salt to 500 g (1 lb 2 oz) ice and toss to coat, then tuck the prawns into the ice in a container in the fridge until needed, a few days at the most. If keeping raw prawns for more than 24 hours, submerge them in an iced water slurry, with 35 g (1¼ oz) salt for every 1 litre (34 fl oz/4 cups) water. This slurry is also a good way to thaw raw prawns. Leave them like this in the fridge overnight, and it will stop the heads going black. Prawn cutlets are best kept wrapped tightly in plastic, then placed in a container over ice, as they can become waterlogged otherwise.

Peeling & deveining prawns

You can peel prawns simply enough by holding the shell at the legs and stripping it off. The head will also twist off, but I generally like to leave the head on, as it's full of flavour and will contribute to a dish, whether in a pan or on the grill. If you do decide to peel, or the recipe calls for it, save those heads and shells for a wonderful Crustacean stock or Crustacean essence (p. 52).

To devein but leave the shell on, curl the prawn in its natural arc, opening a space along the back between the shell sections. Slip a skewer between the shell plates and pick out the digestive tract; you should then be able to pull it out in one or two pieces. To devein a peeled prawn, lay the prawn on its side, then use a paring knife to lightly slice all along the back, then remove the intestinal tract.

Butterflying prawns

When cutting into the back of the prawns to remove the intestinal tract, make that cut deeper, and they will curl up when cooked. The shells can be slippery, which can make things a bit tricky; a handy trick is to put the uncooked prawns in the freezer for 30 minutes to semi-freeze and firm up. They will then be naturally easier to hold, which will make slicing into the shell easier and less hazardous.

Skewering prawns

You can skewer peeled prawns for grilling through the tail end, then again towards the top end, so they sit in the curl they will naturally take once cooked – or, to extend it out straight for grilling, slide a skewer through the length of a peeled prawn, or a semi-peeled prawn with the tail and head on.

To boil prawns

Boiling your own raw prawns is so much better than buying them already cooked, and it's something I would always do if making a Prawn cocktail (p. 413) or the like. For four people, you will need twenty prawns, 6 litres (204 fl oz/24 cups) water and about 300 g (10½ oz) salt. With the heavily salted water at a rolling boil, cook the prawns for 2½–3 minutes, then lift them from the water and plunge into iced water to refresh for 5 minutes, before draining well. The timing will vary depending on size, so you may need to allow a few extra prawns and test one when it's getting close to cooked.

Lobster

Lobster is the richest and most indulgent of crustaceans. Its delicate, sweet flesh is best enhanced gently and with simple ingredients, so the sweet flavour can be appreciated. Lobster thermidor did not make the shortlist for this book (much to the horror of my mother, I am sure). The boozy swamp of cream cheese crowned with a crust of grilled cheese is just about the last thing I would ever do to a lobster.

In Australia, we confuse things somewhat by commonly referring to rock lobsters as crayfish, which they are not. Try telling that to an Australian, though; I use the term myself. Crayfish are freshwater creatures, lobsters saltwater ones. In Australia, our most famous real crayfish is the common dam-dweller, the yabby, while marron inhabit moving fresh waterways in Western Australia, and redclaw those in Queensland and the Northern Territory. These can all be treated like lobster in terms of cooking and applications, though they vary considerably in size, so cooking times need to be adjusted accordingly. There is also a less well-known species in Tasmania that happens to be the world's largest crayfish – and indeed the world's largest freshwater invertebrate – but, sadly, overfishing is threatening their existence. Don't eat them.

For the cook, rock lobsters and lobsters are differentiated by their claws: lobsters have them, rock lobsters do not. In southern waters, rock lobsters are what you're liable to catch, while in the northern hemisphere, lobsters with forbidding pincers are the norm. In the end, though, the creatures and their applications are essentially the same. For Australian cooks, the choice will likely be between an eastern, western, tropical or southern rock lobster; I prefer the latter. They are generally larger, and I find them to have a fuller and more intense flavour. In general, rock lobsters are abundant and are caught in a targeted way, with little impact on the environment – but stocks of the southern rock species are thought to have been taxed a little more than the others. The current information will always vary, so always do a little research first. In Australia, a great place to start is the sustainable seafood guide on the GoodFish website at goodfish.org.au.

To humanely kill a lobster

A quick, humane end is the only way to dispatch any sentient creature. The simplest and most gentle method is to wrap the lobster in a new bin liner (they can leak a dark liquid, which you won't want to drip everywhere) and place in the freezer for 30–45 minutes. This will put the lobster to sleep, and it will also help the flesh relax and be tender.

Splitting a raw lobster for roasting

Remove the lobster from the freezer and lay it on a board, legs down. Hold the head with a tea towel (dish towel) and pierce the middle of the tail with a large knife. Push the knife through the shell to the board, then cut down to split the tail in half. Turn the knife around and cut through the head while holding the tail, yielding two halves.

Remove the digestive tract and discard (as with a prawn/shrimp), then remove the green tomalley (the liver and pancreas, essentially) from the head and reserve.

Use a paring knife to gently loosen the flesh from the tail, so it's easier to remove once cooked. Place the two lobster halves on a baking tray, flesh side up, with the tomalley sitting on top. Spoon generously with melted butter, season with salt and pepper, then roast in a preheated 220°C (430°F) oven for 7 minutes (for a 1.2 kg/2 lb 10 oz rock lobster).

Once cooked, scatter with chopped parsley or pulled tarragon, and some fried capers, then serve with lemon.

By the way, don't throw away the head; raw or cooked, it has a good application, too. Chop it into four to six pieces before roasting for about 25 minutes at 180°C (350°F) fan-forced, then add to a Crustacean stock (p. 52) as you would prawn or crab shells.

Pair with

Lobster just loves butter, cream, Crema fresca (p. 364), eggs and mayonnaise (pp. 74–5). Scent with parsley, coriander (cilantro), chives, chervil, fenugreek, tarragon, thyme and bay leaf, and pair with peppery leaves like watercress. Match lobster with fennel, cucumber, celery, potato, peas, tomato and spring onion (scallion). Cook lobster with aromatics such as ginger, garlic and shallots, and spike with chilli, pepper or a hot sauce such as Tabasco. Lobster is brightened by gentle acidity, whether lime, lemon, white wine or verjuice, and its decadence is enhanced with even more decadence by shaving some fresh truffle over.

Cooking a whole lobster

As a guide, a 1.2 kg (2 lb 10 oz) rock lobster will yield about 400–450 g (14 oz–1 lb) flesh. If serving roasted, you'd serve a half lobster for each person, but in a salad or the like, a lobster could stretch to feed six or more.

The general rule I use when boiling a lobster is to allow 10 minutes per 500 g (1 lb 2 oz).
It's important to ensure there's *plenty* of water, and that the water is well salted – I go to full seawater level, at 35 g (1¼ oz) salt per 1 litre (34 fl oz/4 cups) – and that the water is at a rolling boil before cooking. In most domestic settings, it's hard to get the water back to a boil quickly once the lobster is added, so cover the pot and wait with it until you can feel it coming back up to a simmer, then start your timer and take the lid off.

Once cooked, lift the lobster out with tongs and place on a tray to cool. Leave for at least 45 minutes, and up to 2 hours, before breaking down. If you rush this resting and cooling, you risk the meat being not fully cooked, or bleeding out the juices and flavour onto your board. The meat needs to first finish cooking in the residual heat, then it needs to reabsorb the juices and set. Additionally, lobster tastes better at room temperature.

If preparing well ahead of time, chill the cooked lobster at around the 1½ hour mark, then bring back to temperature on the bench before using.

Breaking down a lobster

Whether you have cooked it yourself, or bought it cooked from a trusted supplier, a lobster is easy enough to break down. Remove the tail from the body by twisting it away in one piece. Use scissors to cut along the underside of the tail, where it joins the heavy top shell on both sides, then remove the bottom membrane. Gently work the tail out in one piece. (You can use this same technique to remove a raw tail if you want to pan-fry it as one piece, or cut into medallions). Tear the legs and feelers from the head, then crack at the joints to remove the flesh. Split the head in half, then pick out the flesh – you may need a lobster pick or similar for this.

The meat is now ready to be used in salads (see p. 200). You can also stir the tomalley into your dressing or some mayonnaise to serve alongside. One of the finest ways to eat lobster cooked like this is in a brioche or milk bread bun, with shaved iceberg lettuce and/or watercress and mayonnaise (pp. 74–5).

To chop the lobster for stir-frying or a seafood broth

Remove the legs and feelers using a firm blow with a cleaver or heavy knife. Flatten the tail out and insert a sharp knife where the tail and head meet, cutting the connecting membrane. Rotate the tail from the body, then cut through the shell, using the segments as a guide, to produce even medallions with the shell on. Split the head in two, standing it on one end to do so. You can now add these pieces to a broth or stir-fry.

Crab

Crabs are relatively plentiful, and are caught in a way that has minimal environmental impact, so they're typically a deliciously ethical option. Blue swimmers are the most commonly available crab in Australia. They are vibrantly blue when raw, and reddish orange when cooked. The flesh is easy to extract, and is moist and full-flavoured, with a sweet, grassy note. The meat has a fine-textured flake, which is great in pasta, salads, fish cakes, spring rolls and dumplings.

Spanner crab is a very sweet crab that has a delicate scallop-like flavour, with a slippery, fine and tight texture. They are bright orange–red, and predominantly caught in Queensland. They are great for salads, omelettes, stir-fries and noodle and rice dishes.

Both blue swimmer and spanner crabs are wonderful, but mud crab, I believe, is king.

Mud crabs live in tidal flats in tropical and subtropical environments. The flavour of the meat is just so distinctive and delicate, with umami notes of shiitake and a smoky sweetness. Mud crabs yield much of their flesh from their formidable claws and the back of the body, and the meat is juicy and broad-flaked. Chilli crab (p. 199) is such a wondrous dish, and even better if you can source live mud crabs for it.

I have actually hunted for mud crabs in the mangroves on Bardi Jawi country, at the Kooljaman wilderness camp at Cape Leveque, in the Kimberley region of Western Australia. With an indigenous elder as my guide, it was a revelatory way to see that magical part of the world, and to learn about Bardi Jawi culture from the current custodians. Barefoot on the muddy sand in the mangroves – which happen to be home to a whole lot of other wildlife, such as birds and crocodiles! – soldier crabs marched in front of us, snapping at toes here and there. In the end, I was down on my belly, pushing a long pole with a large hook into what seemed like a very small hole. Tap, tap ... until you hear a shell-like sound, I was told, then twist and hook the mud crab out. And they don't come out with their claws strapped – they come out fighting and snapping! Quickly covered with a hessian bag, they were flung into a bucket ... and then we hauled our bounty out of the mangroves, over a dune and to the water's edge. Making sure no crocs were about, we made a driftwood fire on the beach and cooked the crabs on a grill fashioned from chicken wire. Cooled rapidly in seawater-soaked hessian, we tore the crabs open and feasted. I had brought along a fancy dipping sauce, but there was no way a mud crab this fresh needed anything else to showcase its exceptional flesh, with the umami savoury notes of shiitake, and the smoky sweetness the crab naturally has. Weighing roughly 700 g (1 lb 9 oz), each crab yielded about 180 g (6½ oz) of the most marvellous flesh.

Choosing & preparing crabs

Always select crabs that are heavy for their size. If buying them live, they should never be blowing bubbles, as this is a sign of distress. Blue swimmer crabs are rarely sold live, so ensure they are properly fresh. If a recipe calls for crabmeat, you can also buy very high-quality vacuum-packed spanner or blue swimmer meat, which is a convenience I am often guilty of when making an omelette (see p. 353) or dumplings (see p. 500), for example.

Much like lobster (see p. 196), chill live crabs in the freezer for 30–45 minutes before cooking, which will put them to sleep. Cook them very much the same way as lobster, 8 minutes for every 500 g (1 lb 2 oz), then cool in iced water for a few minutes. Drain well. Either use immediately, refrigerate for no more than 24 hours, or break the crabs down and pick the meat, which will last in an airtight container in the fridge for about 2 days.

Breaking down a crab

Flip the crab over, then lift up the triangular flap that's on the belly, which will pull back and take off the whole top shell. Remove the gills ('dead man's fingers') and discard. Using a large sharp knife or meat cleaver, cut the crab in half lengthways. You can then quarter the crab or break it down further, depending on its size. Crack the legs and claws with the back of the knife to make it easier to access the meat. You can now pick the meat if cooked, or add the pieces to a broth (see p. 214) or stir-fry (see p. 199) if raw. The 'mustard' and juices in the head can also be added to a dressing or sauce.

Pair with

Crab pairs with what lobster does (see p. 196), as well as tamarind, oyster sauce, soy sauce. It's exceptionally good with Thai flavours, including lime, makrut lime leaf, chilli, sweet chilli black and white pepper and fenugreek.

Crab cakes

Pair with

Fermented cooked chilli sauce (p. 97).

A fresh salsa of a finely chopped green chilli (including the seeds), a peeled and diced lime, six finely chopped sprigs of coriander, dill or parsley and salt to taste.

These delightfully light and flavoursome morsels are loaded with crabmeat, and bound together by crushed crackers. The better the crab, the better the cakes will taste. **Makes 12–14**

450 g (1 lb) cooked crabmeat
150 g (5½ oz) water crackers or other dry-style salted cracker, crushed to a rough powder
5 spring onions (scallions), very finely sliced
5 dill or flat-leaf (Italian) parsley sprigs, finely chopped
4 eggs, lightly beaten

3 tablespoons Master olive oil mayonnaise (p. 74), or kewpie mayonnaise
1½ tablespoons sour cream
1 tablespoon dijon mustard
zest and juice of ½ lemon
2 teaspoons worcestershire sauce
1½ teaspoons hot sauce, such as Tabasco
½ teaspoon cayenne pepper
1 teaspoon salt flakes

150 g (5½ oz) fine semolina
150 ml (5½ fl oz) Clarified butter (see p. 360), or extra-virgin olive oil mayonnaise (pp. 74–5) spiked with extra lemon juice, to serve
100 g (3½ oz) watercress or rocket (arugula), to serve

Staples
S&P

Gently combine the crabmeat, cracker crumbs, spring onion and dill in a bowl.

In another bowl, combine the eggs, mayonnaise, sour cream, mustard, lemon zest and juice, worcestershire and hot sauce, cayenne pepper and salt. Grind in plenty of pepper, then add to the crab mixture and carefully mix through, ensuring you leave chunks of meat.

Refrigerate for at least 1 hour or overnight, to soften the crackers.

When ready to cook, preheat the oven to 120°C (250°F) fan-forced.

Shape the mixture into twelve to fourteen patties, then roll in the semolina to coat.

Heat the clarified butter in a large frying pan over a high heat for 4 minutes. Cook the crab cakes in batches, frying for 3 minutes on each side until crisp and golden.

Serve the warm crab cakes with mayonnaise, scattering the watercress over to finish.

Chilli crab

Pair with

Steamed rice and greens, finger bowls and plenty of napkins – it's messy!

It's important to have everything on hand and ready to go when cooking this dish, as you need to be at the wok the whole time. The other key is heat – so get the wok blisteringly hot before starting, and prepare the crabs swiftly so they stay warm. Don't be tempted to increase the quantities, as you will drop the temperature too much and get an uneven result. **Serves 2**

3 × 300 g (10½ oz) raw blue swimmer crabs
3 tablespoons coconut oil, or grapeseed oil
4 red Asian shallots, finely sliced
3 garlic cloves, sliced
2 long red chillies, julienned

1 bird's eye chilli, finely sliced
5 makrut lime leaves, split
125 ml (4 fl oz/½ cup) White chicken stock (p. 54)
150 ml (5 fl oz) Thai-style chilli jam (p. 96), or Fermented cooked chilli sauce (p. 97)

3 tablespoons oyster sauce
2 tablespoons fish sauce
4 spring onions (scallions), white part only, cut into 3 cm (1¼ in) batons
2 handfuls of Thai basil or coriander (cilantro) leaves

Steam the crabs for about 3 minutes in a steamer basket. Prepare the crabs while still hot – pull the tab on the underside and peel off the top shell, then remove the dead man's fingers (see p. 198). Cut the crabs in quarters through the middle, then crack the claws with the back of a knife. Clean the crabs, retaining any mustard and juice from the top shell to add to the sauce.

Heat a large wok over a high heat until very hot. Add the oil, then the shallot and garlic and stir-fry until golden, about 1 minute. Add the fresh chillies and lime leaves and fry for 30 seconds.

Add the stock, chilli jam, oyster sauce, fish sauce and any crab mustard and liquid. Bring to a quick simmer, then add the crab and stir-fry, tossing in the sauce for 4 minutes.

Add the spring onion, toss for about 30 seconds, then toss the herbs through. Serve immediately, piled up with the sauce poured over.

Lobster salad à la russe GF

I learned how to make this salad with my grandmother Grace, but I have toyed with it over the years, pushing it in a decidedly luxurious direction. Sometimes I make this with seared bug meat, crabmeat or peeled cooked prawns (shrimp) but lobster is my preferred option. For best results, buy a live lobster and cook it yourself (see p. 197), although a cooked one will do fine. Most of the work can be done ahead of time, leaving the assembly to a few moments before serving. Just don't do it so far ahead that you need to chill everything, as refrigerating will dull the flavour. **Serves 6–8**

1 × 1.6 kg (3½ lb) freshly cooked lobster (see p. 197)
5 creamy yellow-fleshed potatoes (such as Dutch cream, royal blue or kipfler/fingerling)
2 carrots
1 celeriac
1 large turnip
80 g (2¾ oz/½ cup) podded fresh peas

1 bunch of white asparagus, trimmed
3 hard-boiled eggs, finely chopped
50 g (1¾ oz) salmon roe (optional)
2 chicory (witlof/endive), sliced 3 cm (1¼ in) thick on an angle
½ bunch of chives, finely snipped

1 celery heart, yellow leaves reserved, heart finely sliced

Lemon garlic mayonnaise
250 g (9 oz/1 cup) Master olive oil mayonnaise (p. 74)
120 g (4½ oz) Greek-style yoghurt
1 large garlic clove, finely grated
juice of 1 lemon

Staples
EVOO, LMN, S&P

Break down the lobster (see p. 197), crack the legs and remove the flesh. Split the head, then remove and dice any meat in the head. Scrape out the mustard in the head and set it aside in a separate bowl. Reserving the shells for presentation, chop the leg and head meat, place in a large bowl, dress with oil and a squeeze of lemon, then set aside at room temperature. Set the tail aside separately.

For the dressing, add all the lemon garlic mayonnaise ingredients to the reserved crayfish mustard. Season with salt and pepper and combine.

Peel the potatoes, carrots, celeriac and turnip and cut into 1 cm (½ in) dice. Cook the potato from cold in salted water until tender, 5–8 minutes, then drain well.

Meanwhile, cook the carrot, celeriac and turnip in boiling salted water until tender, 5–7 minutes, adding the peas for the last 30 seconds. Drain well.

Cook the asparagus in boiling salted water until tender, about 3 minutes, then drain and slice on an angle.

Add all the cooked vegetables, except the asparagus, to the bowl with the chopped lobster meat. Add three-quarters of the dressing and adjust the seasoning as needed. Fill the lobster shells with the mixture and arrange on a serving plate.

Slice the tail into six pieces and dress with the remaining dressing. Spread the slices on top of the salad. Top with the asparagus and egg, then spoon over the salmon roe, if using.

Add the witlof, chives and celery heart and leaves to a bowl. Squeeze in some lemon, drizzle with oil, then season and toss to coat. Sprinkle over the top of the salad, and serve with lemon on the side.

Watermelon & prawn salad with citrus & chilli relish GF

For this Thai-style appetiser, cut the flesh from ¼ watermelon into 5 mm (¼ in) dice. Slice 12 cooked peeled prawns (shrimp) across the middle, about 5 mm (¼ in) thick. Add to a large bowl with the watermelon and chill for 30 minutes. Add 1 × quantity Citrus & chilli relish (see p. 358) and toss to combine. Serve with prawn crackers or large savoury rice crackers.

Tom yum goong

This classic hot and sour soup is a well-loved staple of Thai cuisine, and it's not so hard to pull together at home – just make sure you buy an authentically punchy tom yum paste. **Serves 4–6**

1 litre (34 fl oz/4 cups) Golden chicken stock (p. 54)
1 teaspoon salt flakes
1 tablespoon grated palm sugar (jaggery)
3 tablespoons tom yum paste
1 tablespoon tomato paste (concentrated purée)
250 g (9 oz) cherry tomatoes
1 lemongrass stem, white part only, finely chopped

6 makrut lime leaves, roughly torn
4 × 3 mm (⅛ in) thick slices of fresh galangal
2 × 3 mm (⅛ in) thick slices of fresh ginger
2 red bird's eye chillies, split lengthways
150 g (5½ oz) oyster mushrooms, trimmed and sliced
100 g (3½ oz) enoki mushrooms, trimmed

12 raw prawns (shrimp), peeled and deveined; keep the heads and tails on if you like
1 Lebanese (short) cucumber, peeled, halved lengthways, seeded and sliced on an angle
3 tablespoons lime juice
2 tablespoons fish sauce
½ bunch of Thai basil

Bring the stock to a boil in a large saucepan, then turn the heat down to a simmer. Add the salt, sugar, tom yum paste, tomato paste and tomatoes. Simmer until the tomatoes soften, about 5 minutes.

Add the lemongrass, lime leaves, galangal, ginger and chillies and bring to a simmer, then stir in the mushrooms and prawns. Simmer until the prawns are just cooked, 2–3 minutes.

Add the cucumber, then remove from the heat and stir in the lime juice and fish sauce.

Divide between serving bowls, top with Thai basil and serve immediately.

Barbecued prawns ⒼⒻ

I like to grill large, meaty prawns (shrimp), as these have enough contact with the grill to impart some flavour without overcooking. When cooking in the shell like this, that flavour is enhanced, and more so if using real coals. Even if using gas – making sure it is properly hot – the flavour that develops through the shell and the split head of the prawn is simply mesmerising. Remember that it's best to take the prawns off the grill just before they're completely cooked, as they'll finish cooking by the time you've plated up; otherwise, they can be powdery.

Serves 6–8 as a starter

16 very large raw king
  prawns (shrimp)

Staples
EVOO, LMN, S&P

To make butterflying the prawns quick and easy, put the raw prawns in the freezer for 30 minutes to semi-freeze and firm up. They won't be as slippery, making them easier to hold when it comes to slicing into the shells.

Meanwhile, preheat the barbecue on high. If cooking over coals, which is ideal, burn the fire down to medium–hot coals with no flames.

Using a sharp serrated knife, butterfly the prawns by slicing through the back of the shell lengthways, including the head, until you can open them out flat; you could also cut the shell with a pair of kitchen scissors, then open the tail out with a knife. Remove the intestinal tract and wipe out the heads with paper towel if you feel the need – I actually like this part cooked. Brush the prawns with oil and season lightly with salt and pepper.

Grill the prawns, flesh side down, for 1 minute, until just turning opaque. Flip and grill on the shell until still just slightly undercooked, about 3 minutes.

Remove the prawns from the barbecue. Season again with salt and plenty of pepper, and drizzle with oil and a squeeze of lemon. Serve hot.

Make it different
Skewer raw prawn cutlets and barbecue them for a couple of minutes on each side.

Butter-poached prawns

This is a delightfully messy dish. The prawns gently cook in the browned butter, with the prawn juices imparting so much flavour to the sauce, while the butter seems to seep into the flesh, making the prawns velvety and stunningly tasty. Don't waste a drop of the sauce. It's marvellous to sop up with bread – or the whole lot can be tossed through cooked pasta or used to finish a risotto. **Serves 4**

8 raw king or large tiger prawns
  (shrimp), shells on, deveined
  with a skewer (see p. 195)
250 g (9 oz/1 cup) unsalted
  butter

2 garlic cloves, smashed
2 fresh bay leaves
1½ tablespoons Enhanced
  soy sauce (p. 101), or light
  soy sauce

bread, to serve

Staples
LMN, S&P

Using kitchen scissors, cut along the underside of the shell of each prawn and through the base of the head, forcing it open slightly. Try not to cut the flesh too much as you do this. (When the prawns cook, the shell will curl back and make it easier to peel when eating – but you'll get all that flavour from the heads and shell while they cook.) Season the prawns with salt and pepper and set aside.

Caramelised barbecued prawns ⒼⒻ

Brush the Barbecued prawns (left) with coconut cream prior to grilling; it will caramelise the prawn meat slightly.

Barbecued prawns with gochujang, sesame & lime

When the Barbecued prawns (left) come off the grill, brush well with Gochujang chilli sauce (p. 97), then arrange on a platter. Squeeze over some lime and sprinkle with 3 sliced spring onions (scallions) and 1 tablespoon toasted sesame seeds. Serve immediately.

Barbecued prawns with taramasalata & salmon caviar

Arrange the Barbecued prawns (left), on a platter. Season with salt and pepper, drizzle with olive oil and squeeze on some lemon. Dollop on some Taramasalata (p. 182), then scatter on a few tablespoons of salmon roe. Serve with warm soft pitta breads (see p. 854).

Barbecued prawns with smoky tomato dressing

Arrange the Barbecued prawns (above left), on a platter. Season with salt and pepper, drizzle with olive oil and squeeze on some lemon. Spoon some Smoky tomato dressing (p. 84) over, then serve the remaining dressing on the side, with lots of torn Sourdough bread (p. 847).

Barbecued prawns with salsa verde ⒼⒻ

Arrange the Barbecued prawns (above left), on a platter. Season with salt and pepper, drizzle with olive oil and squeeze on some lemon. Spoon some Salsa verde (p. 86) over, then serve the remaining salsa verde on the side, with lots of torn Sourdough bread (p. 847).

Peel the cooked prawns, leaving the heads on. Add them at the end when making a risotto (see p. 149) using Fish stock (p. 52) or Crustacean stock (p. 52) – or drop on top of a Risotto nero (p. 149) with some of the buttery juices spooned over.

Dress some freshly cooked short pasta, such as gnocchi sardi (see p. 131) with the juices and toss the peeled prawns through with a good squeeze of lemon. A few handfuls of chopped parsley and a sprinkling of chilli flakes would also be a nice touch.

Peel and slice the prawns (or Moreton Bay bug meat; see below) and serve in a salad with warm boiled potatoes, watercress, chicory (witlof/endive), and a simple Lemon emulsion (p. 80) with small capers.

A note on Moreton Bay bugs

What is commonly called a flat-head lobster around the world, Australians know as Moreton Bay bug. It is named after a bay in Queensland, but fished all across the waters of Queensland, the Northern Territory and the northern half of Western Australia. The term actually refers to two species from the genus *Thenus*, one a bay dweller and the other a reef dweller. In a culinary and a commercial sense the two species are the same. The term 'Balmain bug', also named after an Australian location, covers four species of fan lobster, which frequent the cooler waters of southern Queensland and New South Wales, as well as more southerly waters. Whatever the type, bugs are all similar in size and application, with all the meat found in the body.

Add the butter, garlic and bay leaves to a deep frying pan over a medium heat. Cook until the butter is light brown, about 8 minutes. Remove from the heat, then stir in the soy. Arrange the prawns so they're all sitting on the base of the pan. Return to the heat and cook for 3 minutes, then remove from the heat and stand for 3 minutes to finish cooking in the residual heat.

Remove the prawns from the sauce and arrange on a warm serving plate. Spoon the buttery juices over and serve hot, with plenty of lemon and bread on the side.

Make it different

Butter-poached Moreton bay bugs. Use Moreton Bay bug meat (see below) instead. Remove the meat from the shell, season lightly and cook for 1½ minutes, then set aside and rest in the butter for the same time before serving.

Prawns with cannellini beans & truffle ⓖⒻ

Here, the prawn juices flavour the beans, along with lots of lemon juice and good olive oil. The salad adds a welcome crispness and gentle bitterness, with the shaved truffle making it that bit more special – it's also tasty without. **Serves 4–6**

200 g (7 oz/1 cup) dried
  cannellini beans, soaked
  overnight (see p. 370)
1 fresh bay leaf
150 ml (5 fl oz) extra-virgin
  olive oil
4 French shallots, finely diced
2 garlic cloves, finely
  chopped
100 ml (3½ fl oz) lemon juice
12 raw king prawns (shrimp),
  peeled and deveined,
  heads on

1 chicory (witlof/endive),
  sliced on an angle 1 cm
  (½ in) thick
1 fennel bulb, fronds
  reserved, bulb finely shaved
1 celery heart, leaves
  reserved, heart finely sliced
½ bunch of chives, finely
  snipped
20 g (¾ oz) fresh truffle; if
  unavailable, increase the
  truffle paste in the dressing
  to 30 g (1 oz)

Truffle dressing
1 roasted garlic bulb (see
  p. 66)
80 ml (2½ fl oz/⅓ cup)
  extra-virgin olive oil
2 tablespoons black or white
  truffle paste
1½ tablespoons lemon juice

Staples
S&P

Drain the beans, then place in a saucepan with the bay leaf. Cover with ample lightly salted water. Bring to the boil, then simmer for about 45 minutes, until tender. Drain, reserving 250 ml (8½ fl oz/1 cup) of the cooking water.

For the dressing, squeeze the garlic flesh from the bulb, into a small bowl. Add the remaining ingredients, season with salt and pepper and combine.

Heat 100 ml (3½ fl oz) of the oil in a frying pan over a medium heat. Cook the shallot and garlic until golden, about 4 minutes. Add the beans, season and toss through to combine.

Remove from the heat and add the lemon juice and 125 ml (4 fl oz/½ cup) of the reserved bean cooking water. Mash in one-third of the beans to thicken, then set aside somewhere warm.

Heat a large frying pan over a high heat for 3 minutes. Season the prawns and dress with the remaining oil. Sear for 1½ minutes on each side, then press down on the heads to release some juices. Add the remaining beans and heat through for a minute or so, swirling the pan to combine, then remove from the heat and divide between serving plates.

Combine the witlof, fennel and celery, and the fennel and celery fronds. Dress with a tablespoon of the truffle dressing. Arrange to the side of each pile of beans and prawns. Spoon the truffle dressing over, sprinkle with the chives, finish with shavings of truffle over the top if using, and serve.

Make it different

Bruschetta of prawns, cannellini beans & truffle. This also works well on bruschetta. Grill fat slices of Sourdough bread (p. 847), then top with the beans and fried sliced prawns, crowning with the salad.

Shellfish

Shellfish are plentiful, often economical, typically environmentally sound, and they're also extremely good for you. The farming of shellfish has little to no negative impact on the surrounding environment, with no feed required, and they function as a filter, in fact, purifying the water around them (hence the need to eat them from pristine locations). Shellfish are of course also stunningly delicious, carrying the scents of the sea like no other, whether raw or cooked – from the cold, briny lash of a pristine winter oyster, to clams (vongole) sprung open in a hot pan in a shallow bath of wine laced with garlic and chilli, ready for an al dente linguine. And there's an upside to that virulent marine pest that is the sea urchin: their roe is rightly prized, and just happens to be an essay in gastronomic marine complexity – so eat those sea urchins in the millions and do your bit for marine biodiversity.

Mussels

Australian blue mussels (or black mussels) are cheap, plentiful, sustainable, very good for you and completely delicious. Well-managed mussel farms have little to no negative impact on local ecosystems, with no feed required beyond what they filter from the water, much like oysters. We should all be eating more of them.

However, I never buy imported mussels. I'm sure New Zealand green lips are amazing in New Zealand, but they're not by the time they get here, having been cooked by law and becoming quite rubbery. Local blue mussels are stunning, and I see no reason to use anything else. They are also available year round, but the peak season from February to June sees them in their plumpest condition.

Like the persistent myth that pork needs to be cooked through (it doesn't – truly), it seems many people still believe mussels that don't open are hazardous. In truth, it is the mussels that have opened *before* cooking that may pose a problem, as they are dead, and who knows how long for – while the ones that resist the sauna in your pan are merely a little resistant to being dispatched. Persist a bit longer, but some may never open, so don't risk overcooking them. Simply pluck them out, then pop them open by inserting a knife between the shells. If they look and smell fine, then they will be.

Like all bivalves, mussels should either be closed, or the adductor mussel should clamp the shells shut when you apply gentle pressure. They should also have an ocean-fresh briny aroma and not smell fishy in any way.

Preparing mussels

Mussels need to be scrubbed before cooking, though these days that is usually done before you buy them. However, they will usually have a 'beard' – which hangs out of the shell towards the point – that needs to be removed. Grasp the beard and drag it down towards the point to pull it away. Don't do this the other way, as you can damage the flesh. You don't always get all of it, so it's best to check once they open to remove any stray beards in the shells.

The simplest way to cook mussels is to do so in their own juices. Heat a large saucepan over a high heat for 6 minutes, then add 1 kg (2 lb 3 oz) cleaned mussels. Cover with the lid, then shake the pan around a little and cook for 3 minutes. Take the lid off and start picking out the open mussels with tongs, adding them to a strainer over a bowl to catch all the juices. Mussels don't take long to cook,

Pair with

Mussels pair well with olive oil, white wine, garlic, chilli, thyme, bay, parsley, jamón, chorizo, fennel, tomato and potato.

Moules frites (GF)

To make the classic Belgian mussel dish, moules frites, bring 125 ml (4 fl oz/½ cup) white wine to a simmer in a large saucepan over a high heat, then add 1 kg (2 lb 3 oz) mussels. Cover and cook for 2 minutes, shaking the pan a few times, then drop in 150 g (5½ oz) unsalted butter. Cover and cook, shaking now and then, for 2 minutes. Check to see they're all open, then tip into a big bowl and serve with French fries. You can also add sliced onion or herbs such as oregano and thyme with the wine.

Moules frites meets South-East Asia (GF)

To take classic moules frites in a different direction, add makrut lime leaves, sliced fresh ginger or galangal and lemongrass to the wine, let the mussels steam open, then at the end throw in lots of herbs, such as Thai basil, coriander (cilantro) and/or Vietnamese mint. Serve spooned over steamed rice.

but you do want the flesh to set, so don't take them out too early – but equally, don't leave them too long, or they will be rubbery. Picking them out like this is the best way to get a consistent result.

Once they're all cooked, pick out any stray beards, then strain the juices into a clean pan (there'll be a lot of grit and debris in the bottom). You can then reduce the juice until it tastes good – it'll be salty, so don't go too far – then whisk in a few tablespoons of good olive oil and pour over the mussels in a bowl and eat with plenty of bread. Or whisk about 150 g (5½ oz) butter into the juices, with about four sliced spring onions (scallions), reduce for a few minutes, then toss through the mussels and eat just like that.

Mussels cooked simply like that can then be used in other dishes, such as pasta with garlic, tomato (the Roasted tomato passata on p. 660 would be ideal), chilli flakes and basil or parsley, or added to a fish stew or the like. And don't forget to add the juices to the sauce – but remember they're salty, so hold off on seasoning until the end. The mussels would also be lovely tossed with freekeh or barley with plenty of chopped herbs, such as dill, mint, coriander (cilantro) and/or parsley. You could also add cooked mussels, with their brine, to risotto at the last minute, or add cooked mussels to a pot of beurre noisette with garlic, thyme and Fermented cooked chilli sauce (p. 97) and serve on toast with its juices.

Once steamed as above, you can also whip off all the top shells from the mussels, whisk a couple of grated garlic cloves into the reduced juices and oil, then spoon it over the mussels on their half shells on a baking tray. Top with fresh breadcrumbs and chopped parsley, then pop under a very hot grill (broiler) for a couple of minutes to toast the crumbs before serving.

Clams & pipis

Pair with

Clams and pipis like white wine, oil, cream and butter, parsley, saffron, paprika, garlic, shallots, chilli, tomato, white beans (such as navy or cannellini), jamón and sausage such as nduja and chorizo.

Vongole and pipis are the most available clams in Australia, and while some will bristle at calling pipis clams, their uses are the same, and 'clam' is simply a generic term, rather than a technical one.

Vongole have heavy, ridged, oval shells, while pipis have somewhat lighter shells that are more triangular. 'Vongole' is simply the Italian word for clam, but the term is now used in Australia specifically for what used to be called sand cockles. There is a lower yield of meat in vongole to pipis, but I find vongole meat to be sweeter. The flavour of pipis is clean and fresh with an iodine sea note, with the meat cream coloured and fleshy. Both can be used in the same sort of dishes, such as Linguine vongole (p. 127).

Surf clams are less commonly available, as are strawberry clams, which are both generally larger, with a meatier texture and a nutty, buttery flavour. They are both well worth seeking out. Diamond clams and storm clams come via New Zealand, so they are pre-cooked as per quarantine regulations, and are also on the large side, with a relatively high meat yield. Larger clams can be steamed open and used as you would mussels.

Preparing clams & pipis

All clams need to be purged of sand before eating. This is often done for you before you buy them – but if not, a quick soak in salt water will fix that. Some years ago, I went digging in tidal flats in New Zealand for tuatua, which are like large pipis (they are related), and we would have been eating more sand than meat if we'd cooked those straight away. A 30-minute soak in salt water – 1 tablespoon salt to 1 litre (34 fl oz/4 cups) water – then drain and repeat twice, and they were grit free. It's a simple technique you can apply to any clam or pipi.

As with any bivalve (oysters, mussels, scallops), clams and pipis are sold live (unless imported) – or they should be. So, you're looking for shells that are closed, or that close when touched. Open shells that don't respond defensively and close are dead, and should not be eaten. Use your good sense here, as a clean-smelling specimen is unlikely to cause an issue.

As with mussels, clams and pipis that don't open once cooked can be pried open and checked. Again, use your nose, as almost all of these will be stubborn rather than bad.

Scallops

In Australia, two types of scallops are generally available, known as the 'commercial' scallop and the 'saucer' scallop. The latter is found in the warmer waters of Queensland, the Northern Territory and Western Australia's top end, while the former is found in New South Wales and southern Australian waters. Both can be farmed or caught wild, though fishmongers don't always make that distinction.

I always try to opt for hand-dived scallops, whatever the type, as dredging methods can be ecologically damaging. Scallops are dredged by dragging the seafloor with a metal cage that filters the sand and ensnares the scallops, which is unsurprisingly destructive to other bottom-dwelling creatures and plants.

Australian commercial scallops are creamy beige in colour, turning a milky white and becoming more opaque when cooked. They are usually sold with the orange roe attached. The saucer scallop tends to be whiter in colour, and the roe, which is grey in colour, is always removed before sale. If possible, buy the scallops live, as you might an oyster, then have them shucked and cleaned by your fishmonger. The roe, or coral, on commercial scallops is something I always leave on, as I really like the flavour, but it is certainly a different textural experience, and not for everyone.

If buying out of the shell, avoid scallops that have been frozen, as they can become soft and flabby once thawed (though one exception is Canadian scallops, a great product). Frozen scallops are often treated with sodium tripolyphosphate, which will preserve them after harvesting – but it also helps them take up and retain water, and is often used to increase the weight and therefore the price of the meat. That moisture will shed once you cook them, and the scallops will tend to be rubbery, even if not overcooked. Raw scallops should be 'dry', with scallops sitting in a pool of water at the fishmonger best avoided. If you need to wash scallops for some reason, do so in a brine, then dry off. Naturally, a wet scallop will never caramelise in a hot pan.

Scallops have a caramel sweetness combined with a fresh iodine flavour when cooked, and they should have a soft centre, with the opaque exterior giving way to a milky translucency in the very middle. If they're firm and bouncy, they're overcooked. And they're easy to overcook.

Scallops really only take 30 seconds or so on each side, so you need to hit them with a lot of heat to stand any chance of caramelising them. Heating a cast-iron pan over a high heat for several minutes should do the trick. Oil the scallops, lightly season with salt and pepper, and add to the pan one at a time, in a pattern, so you can flip them in the same order, so they cook for the same time.

The other way is to grill them, but again you need to get the oven grill (broiler) as hot as possible. This method is best for scallops in the shell, and they will take about 2 minutes.

Once cooked by either method, they can be served with lemon, salt flakes and some butter, either plain or flavoured (see p. 73) with herbs. Try dolloping on some Salsa verde (p. 86), or Beurre blanc (p. 69) with salmon roe and snipped chives. Spring onion oil (p. 103) are also fabulous.

Pair with

Pair scallops with pork, chorizo and jamón.

Oysters

The first oysters I enjoyed were probably smoked from a tin. And I'm not too proud to admit I still enjoy them on a Savoy cracker with lemon. The all-you-can-eat oyster bar was a favourite place to visit for my father, who just adores oysters. When I started cooking, it was quite a regular thing on his birthday – and particularly Father's Day – to buy him a dozen oysters and to shuck them for him. Father's Day was a better time of year to be eating oysters, though, as his birthday is in December when the oysters start to spawn, and their texture becomes somewhat unpleasant.

In Australia, we have two general types of native oysters, and only one that is readily available. The rock oyster (or Sydney rock oyster), which is an estuarial oyster, grows prolifically in the wild and is farmed in New South Wales, as well as further north in Queensland. The Pacific oyster, which is an introduced species, is farmed in the cooler southern waters; they also thrive in the wild, somewhat

Pair with

Lemon, shallots, spring onion (scallion), chardonnay vinegar, soy, ginger, chilli, pepper, horseradish, black bean, spinach, watercress, breadcrumbs, bacon sausage, cream and parmesan.

problematically. There is also growing interest in farming the native angasi oysters that once dominated the southern waters.

A thriving oyster industry in the nineteenth century saw most of our local naturally occurring oyster beds wiped out, both for the oyster meat and the shells, which were crushed to extract lime to be used in mortar for the building industry. Farming took the place of wild sourcing, with both rock and angasi oysters cultivated. In 1947, Pacific oysters – long a farmed species in Japan – were introduced.

Pacific oysters, delicious as they may be, are a marine pest, dominating the most suitable environments and out-competing the angasi. Pacific oysters produce a huge amount of spawn, releasing them to latch onto anything remotely solid, from large rocks to pebbles and even bits of shell in the sand, while angasi oysters grow their spats in the shells before releasing them, putting them at an evolutionary disadvantage – being all but wiped out by Pacific oysters.

Thankfully, angasi oysters are on the comeback trail, with dedicated farms specialising in growing them. Additionally, farming of Pacific oysters is tightly controlled to avoid their spread from farming operations, but this is more a control measure to stop their occupation further north, rather than having any serious impact on their numbers in southern waters.

The angasi is a large, flat oyster with a heavy shell. Meaty and intense, with a distinctive flavour, they tend not to keep as well as rock oysters, and less well again than Pacifics – but unless you're buying oysters in bulk, that shouldn't pose a problem. The angasi is related to the fabled French Belon oysters from Brittany – they're a wonderful delicacy and should be celebrated.

A rock oyster has a much smaller, finer and somewhat more irregular shell than the angasi, with a slightly deeper cup that cradles the muscle, which helps it keep a little better. All oysters will open to try to feed once harvested, but the angasi is more likely to lose its little pool of seawater due to its relatively flat shell.

I find rock oysters to be more complex in flavour, often slightly ferrous, and much sweeter than a Pacific oyster, due to their environments and respective diets, as well as the species.

The Pacific is a deep-cupped oyster that tastes fresh, salty and mineral. They're very straight-up in terms of flavour: uncomplicated, though still delicious. They were the first fresh oyster I ever tried, and they're a good one to school the uninitiated. They're also my preferred oyster for cooking, which admittedly I don't do a lot. The Pacific, depending on its grade, will generally have a good amount of flesh, which is a little more important if cooking, though quite irrelevant if not – larger is not better with oysters. They are excellent steamed for a few minutes with soy and ginger, then finished with spring onion (scallion) and soy; I also crumb and fry them to serve with a Watercress & potato soup (p. 558), as well as grill them (see p. 210). The key is to warm the oyster rather than cooking it through, so you retain the briny flavour.

The true joy of an oyster is eating it raw and alive, engaging with all the briny mineral qualities that make it so special. And for the oyster aficionado, there is great pleasure in the subtleties between oysters from different locations. Like the idea of terroir in wine, oysters capture some of the essence of their environment and transmit that when you eat them. The salinity will vary, as it does in different bodies of water, and the flavour will be affected by their localised diet and mineral composition. Oysters are quite exciting, really – but you have to have them at their best.

Buying & storing oysters

When selecting oysters, it's really a matter of finding the farms you like and talking to your fishmonger about what's good. I encourage you to open your own oysters, and to buy them unwashed if you can. As soon as the outside shell is washed, they tend not to last as long. This is not a huge issue if you're opening them in a day or two, but you can keep live oysters in perfect condition in moist, cool conditions for some time. They should feel relatively heavy in the hand, being full of liquid. Generally, I would never buy Pacific oysters in the warmer months, as they spawn in the warmer waters and become creamy in all the wrong ways. (There is an exception to this: triploid oysters, which are bred to produce non-creamy oysters in summer.) Native oysters, on the other hand, can be perfect in summer, depending on where they grow – as always, talk to your fishmonger.

It's best to keep all oysters sitting with their top shells as level as possible, as they will retain more of their brine this way when they open and close. Kept this way, a live oyster can last for up to a week. The key is that they should still be alive when you want to eat them. If a shell has popped open, this doesn't mean the oyster is dead – but it may be the case. If you apply a little gentle pressure to the top shell and it reacts and closes, the oyster is still alive. If it stays open, discard it. Also, use your nose, as you can have live oysters that are quite unpleasantly pungent. Oysters should smell like the sea and nothing much else. Sometimes a freshly opened oyster may have slightly funky aquatic smell from the lip of the shell where it seals, but this aroma should blow off quickly. If not … in the bin.

Shucking an oyster

A fresh oyster is a thing of wonder, and it's worth learning to open oysters yourself. I would never buy an opened oyster, unless it had been opened in front of me, and I would eat it then and there. As soon as they're opened, oysters deteriorate. Buying trays of opened oysters, then serving them the next day, as is so often done at Christmas, does no justice to the oyster, and the risk of food poisoning is also more of an issue – especially if they're sitting on that table in the sun for several hours.

There are different types of oyster shuckers, but the best – for me – have a relatively fine blade and point. I find large flat blades unwieldy and liable to splinter shells and generally make a hash of the job. Do not use a knife for this process, or a screwdriver, as this can be quite dangerous.

All oysters have a hinge with a muscle that cantilevers the top shell open to be able to feed. That hinge is where the shell ends in something like a point, while the muscle adductor is on the right side, about halfway up the oysters if you hold the oyster with the point facing you. Take a tea towel (dish towel) and roll up the end a little so that you can support the pointed end, with the flat of the shell facing up. Take the tip of the shucker and insert it between the top and bottom shells at the pointed end. Fold the tea towel over and put your left hand (if you're right-handed) over the shaft of the shucker (it's safer if you slip), then apply some gentle pressure through the length of the shucker to push the tip between the shells. Don't push aggressively, just gently wiggle the blade to find a point of less resistance. You'll get used to this. It's not about force, just a gentle coaxing wiggle and a bit of forward pressure. Once you can feel it yield and the blade pushes in a little, stop or you will pierce the flesh. Grab the handle of the shucker and twist the blade a little to pop the top slightly, then run the blade around the inside of the oyster on that slight angle so the edge runs against the top shell, which will cut the muscle. Once cut, the shell will come straight off. Check the oyster for any shell fragments, which can be flicked out with the tip of the shucker, then … well, eat this one – it's your first, after all.

Once shucked, place the oysters on a bed of salt or ice so that they stay upright and retain all their briny juices – this is a key part to enjoying fresh oysters. Serve immediately, with lemon, and perhaps a Mignonette dressing (p. 207).

Oysters with fire ice ⒼⒻ

For the fire ice, cut 1.5 kg (3 lb 5 oz) very ripe tomatoes into 2 cm (¾ in) dice. In a large heatproof bowl, toss the tomato with 5 finely sliced red bird's eye chillies, 3 teaspoons salt flakes and 2 teaspoons caster (superfine) sugar. Tightly seal the bowl with foil, then set over a pan of just-simmering water for 2 hours, ensuring the bowl doesn't touch the water. Strain the tomato mixture through a very fine-mesh sieve into a bowl; you should have 350–450 ml (12–15 fl oz) of tomato water. Soak 3 leaves gold-strength gelatine in cold water for about 5 minutes. Warm about 100 ml (3½ fl oz) of the tomato water in a small saucepan. Squeeze the excess water out of the gelatine, then stir into the warmed tomato water to dissolve. Combine with the remaining tomato water, strain into a shallow container and freeze for 3–4 hours, until solid. Just before serving, scrape the fire ice with a fork to make ice shards, then scatter over the oysters. Great served with a pile of rye bread, butter and watercress sandwiches, alongside a little pile of freshly cooked potato chips (some quality bought ones would be fine, too). Serves 6–12.

Oysters with fire ice

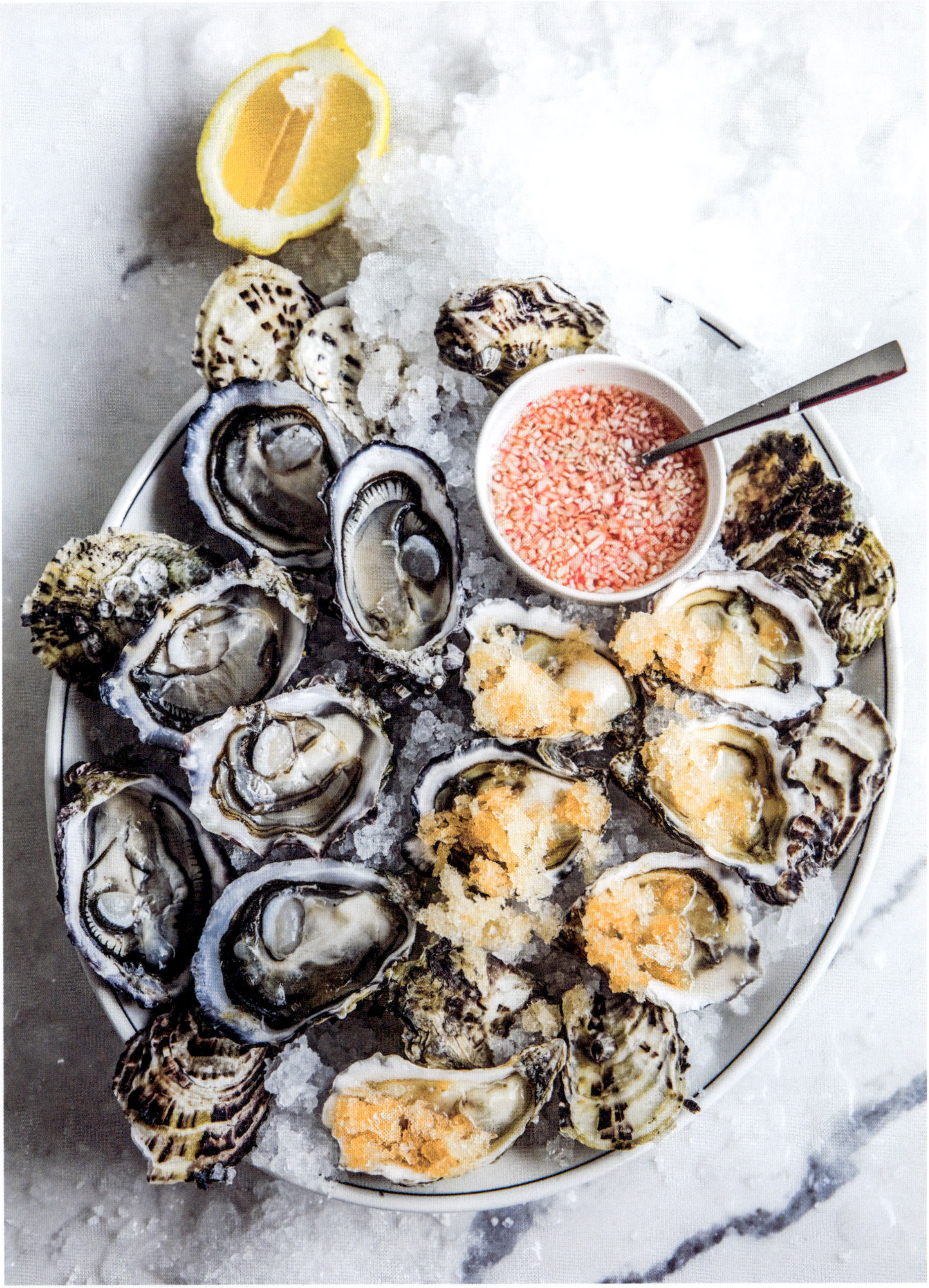

Grilled oysters with horseradish

Hand these around at a cocktail party, or serve as a starter. The pepperiness of fresh horseradish is superb, and plays well against the salty richness of the oysters. I prefer Pacific oysters here, as the cup is deeper and the flavour uncomplicated; a more ferrous, characterful oyster may clash. **Serves 4–6**

1.5 kg (3 lb 5 oz) table salt
2 dozen Pacific oysters, just-shucked (see p. 208)
125 ml (4 fl oz/½ cup) pouring (single/light) cream
35 g (1¼ oz/⅓ cup) finely grated Parmigiano Reggiano

60 g (2 oz) fresh horseradish root, peeled and finely grated, plus extra to serve
60 g (2 oz/¼ cup) unsalted butter, finely diced and chilled

25 g (1 oz/⅓ cup) fresh white breadcrumbs
lemon cheeks or wedges, to serve

Staples
S&P

Preheat the oven grill (broiler) on high.

Add the salt to a bowl with enough water to make a very stiff paste.

Check the oysters for any bits of shell, then use some of the salt paste to make beds to stand the oysters upright in, on a baking tray, nestling them into the salt. Prepare a serving platter or plates with the remaining salt, ready for the cooked oysters.

In a small bowl, combine the cream, parmesan and horseradish with some freshly ground pepper. Spoon onto the oysters, then top each with the butter and more pepper. Finish by sprinkling the breadcrumbs over. Place the tray under the grill and cook until the topping is golden, about 2½ minutes.

Transfer the oysters to the serving plate, grate over some extra horseradish and serve with the lemon.

Make it different
Grilled scallops with horseradish & Parmigiano Reggiano. Instead of oysters, use cleaned scallops.

With bacon. Cut five streaky bacon rashers (slices) into batons. Pan-fry over a high heat until crisp. Spoon over the cooked oysters.

Crumbed scallops

Top cleaned scallops in the shell with a sprinkling of breadcrumbs and butter. Cook in a 220°C (430°F) fan-forced oven for 2½ minutes, then remove from the oven and spoon over your choice of dressing. For a starter, allow two or three scallops per person.

Seared scallops with chorizo & apple

This is a sophisticated little starter, with the flavours of apple, chorizo and caramelised seared scallops just so very complementary. **Serves 4**

1 large granny smith apple, skin on, finely julienned
1 hot dry chorizo sausage, cut into 4 cm (1½ in) long batons

16 large scallops in the shell, cleaned (with or without roe)
2 tablespoons Master olive oil mayonnaise (p. 74)

4 mint sprigs, leaves torn
lemon cheeks or wedges, to serve

Staples
LMN, S&P

Preheat the oven to 160°C (320°F) fan-forced.

Toss the apple in a small bowl with a squeeze of lemon and a little salt.

In a frying pan over a medium heat, fry the chorizo until coloured and crisp, about 5 minutes. Remove from the heat and keep warm.

Remove the scallops from their shells, then warm eight of the shells in the oven for 5 minutes.

Heat a large frying pan over a high heat for 3 minutes. Oil the scallops and lightly season with salt and pepper. Once the pan is very hot, place the scallops in the pan, sitting separate from each other. Cook for only 30 seconds each side, then lift out. They will turn white and take on a little colour, but be quite soft to touch. It helps to be systematic when cooking these, so you know which ones to turn first, otherwise the result can be quite uneven. Some cooks work clockwise around the pan, others left to right in lines. It doesn't matter – just make sure the first scallop you put in the pan is the first you flip, and the first you remove, and so on.

Place two scallops in each warmed shell. Top with a teaspoon of mayonnaise, then the chorizo, then the apple, and finally the mint. Serve with lemon.

Clams with jamón, garlic & butterbeans (GF)

A balance of simple ingredients, with clams and their divine juices the stars. **Serves 4**

2 French shallots, finely
  sliced
3 garlic cloves, finely sliced
1 kg (2 lb 3 oz) clams
  (vongole, diamond or
  strawberry clams), or pipis
  or mussels

2 fresh bay leaves
300 ml (10 fl oz) white wine
400 g (14 oz) tin butterbeans,
  drained and rinsed (or cook
  your own, see p. 371)
120 g (4½ oz) jamón, cut into
  5 mm (¼ in) dice

80 g (2¾ oz) unsalted butter
¼ bunch of flat-leaf (Italian)
  parsley, finely chopped

Staples
EVOO, LMN, S&P

Heat a good splash of oil in a wide heavy-based saucepan over a high heat. Cook the shallot and garlic until just softened, about 2 minutes. Add the clams and bay leaves, swirl in the pan to coat in the oil for 1 minute, then add the wine. Cover and steam until the clams just open, about 2 minutes.

Add the beans, jamón, butter and parsley, then simmer for about 3 minutes, until you have a good sauce consistency. Grind in some pepper, drizzle in a little oil, squeeze in some lemon and serve.

Make it different

With broad beans or chickpeas. In spring, this is lovely with double-podded broad beans instead of butterbeans. You could also use cooked chickpeas.

With Fino sherry. A similar dish is famously made along the coast of Spain, using Fino sherry instead of wine. Follow the recipe up to adding the wine, then add 125 ml (4 fl oz/½ cup) Fino or Manzanilla sherry instead. Once cooked, finish the clams with the butter and oil, then dust the plate with sweet smoked paprika before serving with plenty of bread – plain, or grilled and rubbed with garlic and oil.

Clams in white-wine sauce

A classic that just needs plenty of bread and some crisp white wine. **Serves 2–4**

1 kg (2 lb 3 oz) clams
150 ml (5 fl oz) white wine
60 g (2 oz/¼ cup) unsalted
  butter
4 French shallots, finely
  chopped

4 garlic cloves, finely sliced
3 teaspoons plain
  (all-purpose) flour
150 ml (5 fl oz) full-cream
  (whole) milk

6 flat-leaf (Italian) parsley
  sprigs, leaves finely
  chopped
2 teaspoons crème fraîche

Staples
S&P

Heat a large heavy-based saucepan over a high heat for a few minutes, then add the clams and wine. Cover and steam until the clams open, about 2 minutes. Strain the liquid through a fine-mesh sieve, into a bowl, and set the clams aside somewhere warm.

Melt the butter in a frying pan over a medium heat. Sweat the shallot and garlic until softened but not coloured, about 3 minutes. Add the flour and stir to coat, then whisk in the milk and clam liquor. Bring to a simmer and cook for 2 minutes, whisking to incorporate and thicken the sauce.

Whisk in the parsley, crème fraîche and plenty of pepper to combine. Pour over the clams and serve.

Pair with

Ample bread: torn chunks of Sourdough bread (p. 847), or grilled slices rubbed with garlic and then anointed with olive oil.

Stir-fried clams with XO sauce

Add a splash of shaoxing rice wine to a hot wok, then add 1 kg (2 lb 3 oz) clams. Stir-fry for about 2 minutes. Clear a little space in the wok, fry 3 tablespoons XO sauce (p. 98) in the wok for a minute or so, then toss the clams through to coat. Once the clams have opened, finish with a little more rice wine, makrut lime leaves and, if desired, some sliced spring onion (scallion) and chilli. Toss through and serve with steamed rice.

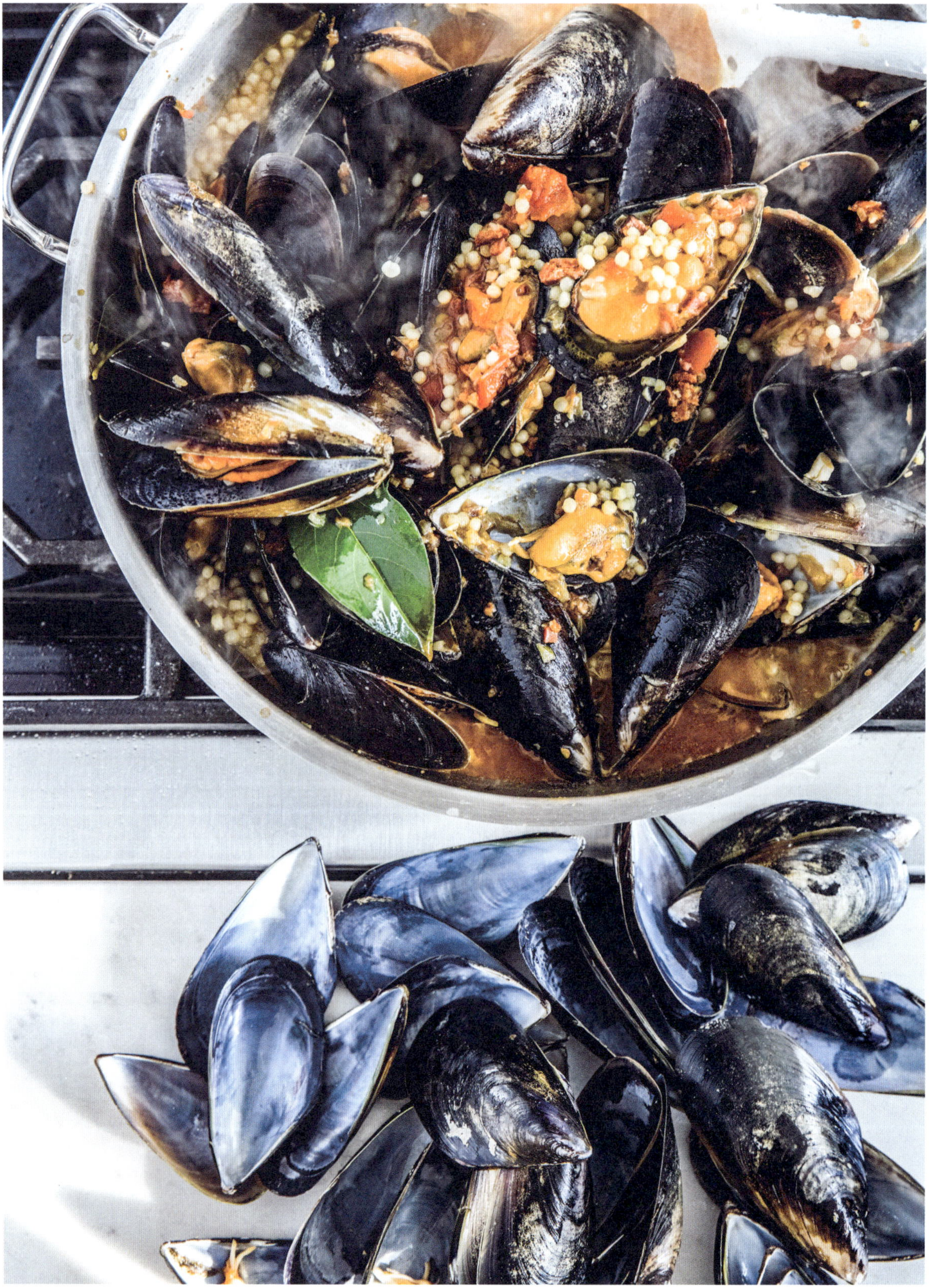

Mussels with chorizo, tomato & white wine

Pair with

Bread, lots of bread …

Mussels with garlic, black pepper & fennel seeds GF

In a large, heavy-based saucepan, fry 1 × quantity Fennel, black pepper & garlic paste (p. 529) in about 125 ml (4 fl oz/½ cup) good olive oil, over a high heat. Once fragrant with golden garlic notes, add 2 kg (4 lb 6 oz) cleaned mussels and stir through vigorously. Add 350 ml (12 fl oz) white wine, cover and cook for about 3 minutes, shaking the pan frequently, then stir through and start to pick out the open mussels, into a sieve over a bowl. Strain the cooking liquid, then add back to the pan with any juices that have drained off the mussels. Add 80 ml (2½ fl oz/⅓ cup) pouring (single/light) cream to the pan and a few handfuls of torn parsley leaves, then reduce by about half. While it reduces, remove most of the top shells from the mussels and pick out any stray beards, then add the mussels to a serving bowl. Once reduced, tip the sauce over the mussels and serve with plenty of bread.

I've been making this dish almost as long as I can recall. Engagingly rustic, it's a step up from the simplest versions of mussels with a tomato-based sauce, but has a real edge of sophistication from the chorizo, saffron and slippery pearl couscous. I love mussels in the colder months, like I do so much seafood, when they taste sweeter and more pure. Black mussels are wonderful in this, but you could use larger clams instead. **Serves 6–8 as a starter**

250 g (9 oz) dry spicy chorizo sausage, finely diced
6 French shallots, finely diced
4 garlic cloves, finely diced
4 red bird's eye chillies, finely sliced into rings
2 fresh bay leaves

5 saffron threads
250 ml (8½ fl oz/1 cup) Roasted tomato passata (p. 660), or jarred passata
150 g (5½ oz) pearl couscous, fregola or pastina
300 ml (10 fl oz) white wine

2 kg (4 lb 6 oz) black mussels, scrubbed, beards removed
2 handfuls of flat-leaf (Italian) parsley leaves

Staples
EVOO, S&P

Heat a good splash of oil in a large heavy-based saucepan over a medium heat. Fry the chorizo until starting to brown, about 3 minutes. Add the shallot, garlic, chilli, bay leaves and saffron. Cook until softened, about 5 minutes, then add the passata and cook for 5 minutes on a medium–low heat to thicken a little. Remove from the heat.

Cook the couscous in boiling salted water until tender, then drain and lightly coat with oil.

Heat a large saucepan over a high heat for a couple of minutes, then add the wine. Add half the mussels, cover and cook until they steam open, about 4 minutes. Lift out the mussels with tongs or a slotted spoon, then add the remaining mussels to the pan. Once cooked, remove the mussels and strain the liquor through a fine-mesh sieve, into a bowl. Remove any stray beards from the mussels and most of the top shells, leaving some whole for effect.

Clean out the pan, as there may be grit left behind. Tip in the chorizo mixture and reserved mussel liquor over a high heat, then add the mussels, parsley and couscous and bring to a simmer. Drizzle in some oil, and a splash of water if it is looking dry. Check for salt, season with pepper and serve immediately.

Bouillabaisse-style stew

Winter is my favourite time for a feast like this, with seafood at its best, and the hearty, brothy nature of the dish just so apt for the season. There are many approaches to making a fish soup, from blitzed versions passed through a sieve (see p. 174) that are big on flavour and light on extravagance, to those that go big on both. This one is in the latter camp: an intensely flavoured broth crammed full of so many delights of the sea. It is modelled on a recipe I used to cook at the Melbourne Wine Room when we first opened. That one included potato, and while I've turned the dial up on the seafood a little, the spirit is the same. It's important to have everything prepared when making this stew, as it all happens rather quickly. And if you feel like economising on the work and not searing the seafood … please don't. Getting your pan properly hot, then searing everything, changes the flavours, with the final dish having caramelised accents, rather than tasting boiled. I wouldn't do it any other way. **Serves 6–8**

1 × 400 g (14 oz) fillet of thick white-fleshed fish (blue-eye trevalla, hapuka, cod), skin on, cut into 3 cm (1¼ in) × 4 cm (1½ in) pieces

4 small red mullet, cleaned (or gurnard fillets, or double the white fish above)

10 king prawns (shrimp), heads on, but peeled and deveined

2 small squid, cleaned (300 g/10½ oz cleaned weight), cut into 3 cm (1¼ in) thick rings

300 ml (10 fl oz) white wine

20 black mussels, scrubbed, beards removed

500 g (1 lb 2 oz) clams (diamond clams, strawberry clams, vongole), or pipis

100 ml (3½ fl oz) extra-virgin olive oil

6 French shallots, finely diced

6 garlic cloves, sliced

1 fennel bulb, cut into 5 mm (¼ in) dice

2 red bird's eye chillies, split lengthways

2½ teaspoons fennel seeds

8 saffron threads

1½ tablespoons tomato paste (concentrated purée)

4 large ripe tomatoes, peeled (see p. 655) and cut into

large chunks – or 300 ml (10 fl oz) Roasted tomato passata (p. 660)

1.5 litres (51 fl oz/6 cups) Crustacean stock (p. 52), or 3 litres (101 fl oz/12 cups) Fish stock (p. 52), reduced by half

100 g (3½ oz) fregola or pastina

2 raw blue swimmer crabs or sand crabs, cleaned and quartered (see p. 198)

8 scallops in the shell, cleaned

15 basil leaves

1 × quantity Rouille (p. 80)

Staples
EVOO, S&P

Pair with

Grilled slices of Sourdough bread (p. 847) rubbed with garlic and drizzled with oil.

Mussels with garlic & tomato ⒼⒻ

Simpler still than the Mussels with garlic, black pepper & fennel seeds recipe (p. 213), fry 5 sliced garlic cloves in the oil until golden. Add 2 chopped fresh tomatoes, or 80 ml (2½ fl oz/⅓ cup) Roasted tomato passata (p. 660), and heat through. Add the mussels and wine and cook covered for about 3 minutes, shaking the pan frequently. Then strain the liquor and return to the pan. Tear in a handful of basil leaves, then pour the liquor over the mussels and finish with some oil. This is particularly good with grilled garlicky bread, drizzled with olive oil.

Heat a deep heavy-based frying pan over a high heat for several minutes. Separately coat the white fish, mullet, prawns and squid with oil and season with salt and pepper.

Sear the fish pieces, skin side down, for 1 minute, then remove from the pan. Sear the mullet on one side for 1 minute, then remove from the pan. Sear the prawns for about 30 seconds on each side, then remove. Add the squid and sear for 30 seconds, stir through for 30 seconds to seal any raw edges, then remove from the pan.

Add half the wine to the pan, then the mussels and clams. Steam open for about 3 minutes, uncovered, picking out the shells as they open. Strain the liquid from the pan through a fine-mesh sieve and reserve. Remove the top shells from the mussels.

Add the oil to a wide heavy-based saucepan over a medium heat. Add the shallot, garlic, fennel and chilli, season and cook for about 15 minutes, until golden. Stir the fennel seeds, saffron and tomato paste through and cook for 3 minutes to slightly caramelise the tomato paste. Add the tomatoes and cook to soften, about 5 minutes.

Add the remaining wine, with the reserved mussel liquor. Reduce for 2 minutes, then add the stock and bring to the boil. Add the pasta and cook for a few minutes to intensify the broth and mostly cook the pasta.

Add the crab and cook for 3 minutes, then add the scallops and seared seafood, with any resting juices. Bring to a simmer, then cook for 2 minutes. Don't stir the pot, as it's all very delicate, and you don't want to break the fish up. Adjust the seasoning as needed. Push the basil leaves into the broth and drizzle on some oil.

To serve, pick out the fish and transfer to shallow bowls first, then spoon over the other seafood and broth. Serve immediately, with the rouille on the side.

Cephalopods

Cephalopods are molluscs, being part of a very large family that includes clams, oysters, scallops, mussels and snails – both aquatic and terrestrial – along with squid, octopus and cuttlefish. The last three are in the cephalopod class, but, over time, their shells have become internalised – such as the cuttlebones that you'll often find on a beach, like small chalky surfboards – with only the impressively shelled nautilus still wearing its body armour.

While I have no personal experience with cooking nautilus, I have significant affection for the culinary pleasures of squid, octopus and cuttlefish – with the aroma of any of them being grilled over coals one of my all-time favourite scents. The cooking time is key, with cuttlefish and squid needing a quick or long cook, while octopus needs a little more attention to achieve tenderness – but it's well worth the trouble.

Squid & cuttlefish

Southern reef squid (also known as southern calamari) is something we should eat more of, both because of its deliciousness and because harvesting it is sustainable and has a low environmental impact. Southern reef squid and the commonly sold arrow squid (or Gould's squid) are fast-growing creatures that appear not to have suffered from overfishing, in Australian waters at least. Additionally, the catch methods are low impact, rather than indiscriminate trawling. Imported squid, though, is linked to overfishing and high mortality in non-targeted species. Don't buy it.

I will buy southern reef squid ahead of arrow/Gould's squid, as I find the flavour and texture finer and sweeter. In the cooler months, squid are abundant and easily caught. It's obviously a great time to buy them – local, plentiful, environmentally sound, healthy, economical, fresh and delicious. As always, by asking a few questions of your fishmonger, you'll be buying and eating the best, spending the least, caring for the environment and local businesses, and safeguarding our future.

Cuttlefish are similar to squid in their environmental impact, being quick to repopulate their ranks. However, most cuttlefish are actually caught incidentally, as there is less of a market for them, and some of the fishing operations that provide the bulk of cuttlefish aren't as well monitored in terms of their primary catch, namely prawns (shrimp). Ask questions, and your fishmonger can likely steer you in the right direction. Cuttlefish are generally interchangeable with squid, though they have a thicker wall to the main body tube, so if deep-frying (see p. 223) select smaller, finer specimens, while larger ones will work well in Fish soup (p. 174).

Preparing squid & cuttlefish

Whatever you do, don't buy those frozen and unnaturally white prepared tubes – most of it is bleached, and probably imported. It's best to buy squid and cuttlefish whole and ask your fishmonger to clean them for you, keeping the tentacles, and asking them to leave the 'wings' on. They are not hard to clean as such, but it can be a little time consuming and messy if you're not used to it – which doesn't mean you shouldn't get used to it, of course.

To clean squid and cuttlefish, you'll find the innards will mostly come out as you pull the head from the tube, with the rest easily fished out, along with the cartilaginous backbone. Cut away the tentacles from just near the eyes, then pop out the tough beak. You can then divide the tentacles into sets of two a piece, and also cut into manageable lengths, if required. The tube will have a thin skin on it, which can just be grasped at the edge and peeled off. I always leave the 'wings' on. They taste perfectly delicious, and I think they are generally removed for some misguided aesthetic consideration.

You can now marinate and grill or slice as needed. If you want to achieve that cross-hatched curled-up look, slice the tube open down one side, then score partway through the inside face on a diagonal, then the opposite diagonal. You can then slice into strips or tickets, and the squid or cuttlefish will curl as it cooks, with the pattern on the outside.

Squid and cuttlefish need to be braised for a long time if they're not cooked quickly. In general, I prefer the swift method, whether that's pan-fried or dusted in semolina and flash-fried (see p. 223), then served with a peppery salad and a generous splodge of Italian tartare (p. 77) or a suite of sauces (pp. 76, 78, 86, 92, 93, 182) – or marinated in smashed garlic, fresh oregano, chopped chilli and a slick of good oil, then grilled (see p. 218) on either side to just cook and take on some char. A squeeze of lemon, some salad and a good bit of bread for the juices, and I'm very, very happy.

You can also oil a whole cleaned squid or cuttlefish and season with salt and pepper. Either thread the tentacles onto the full tube and grill whole, or grill the tentacles and tube separately. Slice and toss in a bowl with Salsa verde (p. 86) or fresh Harissa (p. 92) before serving – or toss in Chermoula (p. 90) before grilling, then serve with fresh pitta breads (see p. 854), dips and a chopped tomato and cucumber salad.

Octopus

Like squid and cuttlefish, octopus grows quickly, and the local wild population appears to be at very healthy levels. In general, targeted octopus fishing has very little, if any, environmental impact and is sustainable, with little bycatch; indeed, octopuses are occasionally snared in rock lobster pots, which is the only meaningful bycatch from lobster fishing. However, octopuses are also sometimes snared by other fishing methods, particularly in northern waters where prawn (shrimp) trawling is focused – along with many other species of sea creatures. This is the reality of prawn trawling, and it should be considered when shopping.

You're unlikely to see octopus sold by any metric other than size, but there are several species caught in Australian waters. I've always preferred those from South Australia and Western Australia, with the meat always reminding me of lobster. It's only recently that I discovered how much their diet affects the flavour of the meat, and it seems like those octopuses like lobster – as do I! If not buying baby octopus, one or two tentacles might be enough when they're particularly large; sometimes you'll find a mid-sized specimen where you can cook the whole creature.

Most octopus you buy will have been frozen, and this is done as much for preservation as it is for texture. Freezing denatures the protein somewhat, resulting in more tender flesh. That's rarely the end of the story, though, with an improperly prepared octopus woefully leathery and barely edible – a fate no creature should lose its life for.

Preparing octopus

Octopus will often be already prepared before purchasing, but it's best to rub the skin with coarse salt to strip off any sliminess. The suckers can also harbour small stones and debris, so check them before cooking.

There are many methods of tenderising octopus, from bashing on rocks, to spinning in a cement mixer, to hanging from a clothesline and beating with a stick, to cooking with a cork or tea leaves (both all about the tannins, it seems), to salting … In general, though, marinating and slow-cooking does the trick (see p. 219), and then a flash on a hot grill will reheat and add some char (see p. 218).

If I'm preparing small octopus, then I generally braise and serve in a sauce, or I braise them in a simple stock of aromatics and wine until tender, then pickle in vinegar with some fresh herbs and chilli.

Chargrilled octopus

The lengths taken to tenderise octopus (see p. 217) are legendary, with all manner of hostilities unleashed on the cephalopod. I have tested many processes without – thankfully – having to venture onto a building site or into the laundry. These are my preferred methods at home, with the final grilling and plating quick, so it's one of those things that can be served somewhat serenely, but to great effect. If you're curious about the addition of soy in this essentially Mediterranean recipe, it enhances the natural flavour of the octopus and dials up the umami without bending the profile in a jarring direction. You can skip the dressing altogether, if you like, and just serve with a drizzle of quality oil and a good squeeze of lemon. **Serves 4–6**

Pair with

Serve as an appetiser or antipasto with Taramasalata (p. 182), olives and fresh pitta breads (see p. 854).

2 large octopus tentacles, about 2 kg (4 lb 6 oz) in total
coarse salt, for rubbing

White wine & lemon marinade
100 ml (3½ fl oz) white wine
juice of 1 lemon
3 garlic cloves, skin on, smashed

2½ tablespoons extra-virgin olive oil
1 teaspoon black peppercorns, cracked

Lemon & oregano dressing
juice of 1 lemon
2 garlic cloves, smashed
2½ tablespoons extra-virgin olive oil

1½ tablespoons light soy sauce
2 teaspoons dried Greek oregano (rigani)

Staples
S&P

Rub the tentacles with a couple of handfuls of coarse salt for a few minutes to clean and massage away any sea sliminess. Check the suckers for any embedded debris, then rinse thoroughly. Use tongs to lower the tentacles into unsalted boiling water for 20 seconds, then plunge into iced water until chilled. Repeat the process three times.

Combine the marinade ingredients and use to coat the tentacles, then cover and marinate overnight. (If you have a steam setting on your oven, you can skip this marinating step. Instead, steam the tentacles for 12 minutes on 50 per cent, then chill on a clean tray in the fridge for 2 hours or more.)

Once the octopus is marinated, heat the barbecue on high – or ideally, light a fire and let it burn down to even, hot coals.

Lay out four 70 cm (28 in) long sheets of foil, fanning and overlapping like a hand of cards, then put a fifth sheet on top. Lay a sheet of baking paper on top of that, then curl the octopus tentacles together on top of each other. Spoon on half the marinade, then fold the paper over to cover the octopus, folding the edges together. Follow with the foil, folding the edges over at least three times to seal tightly, making an airtight parcel.

Grill the parcel for about 5 minutes over a high heat until it balloons, then reduce the heat to medium. If cooking over coals, move to a cooler part of the grill and cook for 20 minutes. (Alternatively, you can place the parcel in a 200°C/400°F fan-forced oven for 10 minutes, then reduce the heat to 160°C/320°F fan-forced and cook for 35 minutes.)

Once cooked, remove the octopus from the parcel. Grill over a high heat, or on the hot part of the grill, for about 5 minutes, rotating to colour and char all over.

Meanwhile, add the dressing ingredients to a large bowl, season with pepper and combine.

Drop the charred tentacles in the dressing and coat well. Take to the table and slice into 3 cm (1¼ in) pieces to serve.

Braised baby octopus with red wine, oregano, paprika & cherry tomatoes (GF)

Pair with

Serve on top of fresh ricotta with chopped parsley.

Serve with freshly cooked Focaccia (p. 845) and black olives as antipasti.

Pair with Baked beans with mustard seeds, vinegar & tomato (p. 390).

I don't ever grill small octopuses – hence the two braise recipes here – as I think they're best braised to render them tender and flavoursome, which also perfumes the sauce beautifully. Enjoy this hot or cold. **Serves 6 as antipasti**

500 g (1 lb 2 oz) cleaned baby octopus

70 ml (2¼ fl oz) extra-virgin olive oil

5 French shallots, sliced into thirds

3 garlic cloves, sliced

2 red bird's eye chillies, split lengthways

2 teaspoons tomato paste (concentrated purée)

1 tablespoon dried Greek oregano (rigani)

1 fresh bay leaf

½ teaspoon smoked paprika

½ teaspoon fennel seeds

½ teaspoon cumin seeds

300 ml (10 fl oz) red wine

500 ml (17 fl oz/2 cups) Golden chicken stock (p. 54)

200 ml (7 fl oz) tomato passata (puréed tomatoes)

250 g (9 oz) cherry tomatoes, peeled (see p. 655)

1½ tablespoons sherry vinegar

1 teaspoon caster (superfine) sugar

Staples
S&P

Blanch the octopus for 1 minute in boiling salted water.

Heat the oil in a large heavy-based saucepan over a medium heat. Cook the shallot, garlic and chilli until caramelised, about 10 minutes.

Add the octopus, tomato paste, herbs and spices, season with salt and pepper, then stir through to coat. Cook for 2 minutes, then add the wine and simmer for 5 minutes.

Stir in the stock and passata and bring to a simmer. Turn the heat down to low and braise, uncovered, for about 30 minutes.

Once the octopus is tender, add the remaining ingredients, then simmer for 5 minutes. Adjust the seasoning as needed and serve hot or cold.

Octopus braised in rosé & tomato with radicchio & bottarga (GF)

Pair with

Serve as is, with plenty of good bread.

Cook hand-made semolina pasta (p. 131) or shell pasta until a little underdone, then finish in the sauce for a minute or two before plating and dressing with the radicchio and bottarga.

Serve on wet Polenta (p. 383).

Once braised, the octopus is blushed with a delightful shade of pink and scented with fennel and oregano, then crowned with torn radicchio and finely grated bottarga. Serve as an antipasto, or toss with fresh semolina pasta (p. 131), with its charming chewiness a perfect match. **Serves 6 as a starter**

1.5 kg (3 lb 5 oz) medium–large cleaned octopuses, with heads (about 3 octopuses)

coarse salt, for rubbing

150 ml (5 fl oz) extra-virgin olive oil

2 large onions, sliced

4 garlic cloves, sliced

400 g (14 oz) very ripe tomatoes, peeled (see p. 655) and roughly diced

450 ml (15 fl oz) rosé

1 tablespoon dried Greek oregano (rigani)

500 ml (17 fl oz/2 cups) Golden chicken stock (p. 54)

2 teaspoons fennel seeds

1 teaspoon chilli flakes

1 head of radicchio, roughly torn into 3 cm (1¼ in) pieces

3 tablespoons finely grated bottarga

Staples
EVOO, LMN, S&P

Rub the tentacles with a couple of handfuls of coarse salt for a few minutes to clean and massage away any sea sliminess. Check the suckers for any embedded debris, then rinse thoroughly. Use tongs to lower the tentacles into unsalted boiling water for 20 seconds, then plunge into iced water until chilled. Repeat the process three times. Trim the heads of the octopuses, cleaning out anything inside. Cut the heads into 2 cm (¾ in) dice, and slice the tentacles into 3 cm (1¼ in) pieces.

Heat 100 ml (3½ fl oz) of the oil in a wide heavy-based saucepan over a medium heat. Cook the onion and garlic until softened and starting to take on colour, about 5 minutes. Add the octopus pieces and cook for about 3 minutes. Stir in the tomatoes, wine and oregano, season with salt and pepper and simmer for 3 minutes, then add the stock and bring to a simmer. Turn down the heat and simmer gently for about 1½ hours.

When the liquid has reduced by three-quarters, add the fennel seeds and chilli and simmer for 5 minutes. Stir the remaining oil through and turn off the heat.

Dress the radicchio with a squeeze of lemon and some oil, season and toss. Serve on top of the octopus, with the bottarga scattered over.

Blanched calamari with tuna sauce & olives GF

This salad borrows a technique from South-East Asia. I was inspired by blanched squid, tenderly just cooked in a hot and spicy dressing with a bounty of herbs. The flavour was amazing, but it was the tenderness that had me hooked. This version strongly veers in an Italian direction, borrowing and reworking a tonnato sauce – more famously used for the veal dish Vitello tonnato (p. 297) – which is marvellous here with olives and a spike of fresh green chilli. It's important that your saucepan is quite large, so when you add the squid is starts boiling again almost immediately, as it's a very quick, hot blanch. If you drop the temperature too much, it either won't cook in time, or you'll have to cook for longer and your squid will likely stew and be tough. **Serves 4–6**

Pair with
Plenty of bread, to mop up every last bit of that sauce.

1 red or white onion, peeled
700 g (1 lb 9 oz) cleaned small squid, wings on, tentacles cut into pairs
1 × quantity Tuna mayonnaise (p. 74)
2 lemons, segmented and diced (squeeze and reserve the juice from the membranes)
1 tablespoon small capers
2 long green chillies, finely sliced into rounds
10 semi-dried or Kalamata olives, pitted and torn
1 handful of mint leaves and fennel fronds (optional)
2 teaspoons fennel seeds, roughly ground, or fennel pollen

Staples
EVOO, S&P

Special equipment
Mandoline

Using a mandoline, finely slice the onion into rounds, then soak in cold water for 15 minutes.

Meanwhile, bring a large heavy-based saucepan of salted water to a rolling boil. Blanch the squid (in batches if needed, to maintain the heat) for 40 seconds. Refresh in cold water and drain very well. Finely slice the hoods crossways.

Spoon the tuna mayonnaise onto a serving plate, then arrange the squid over the top. Pat the onion dry and scatter over the squid. Top with the lemon segments and juice, capers, chilli and olives. Scatter the herbs and fennel seeds over, season with salt and pepper and drizzle generously with oil before serving.

Blanched calamari with tuna sauce & olives

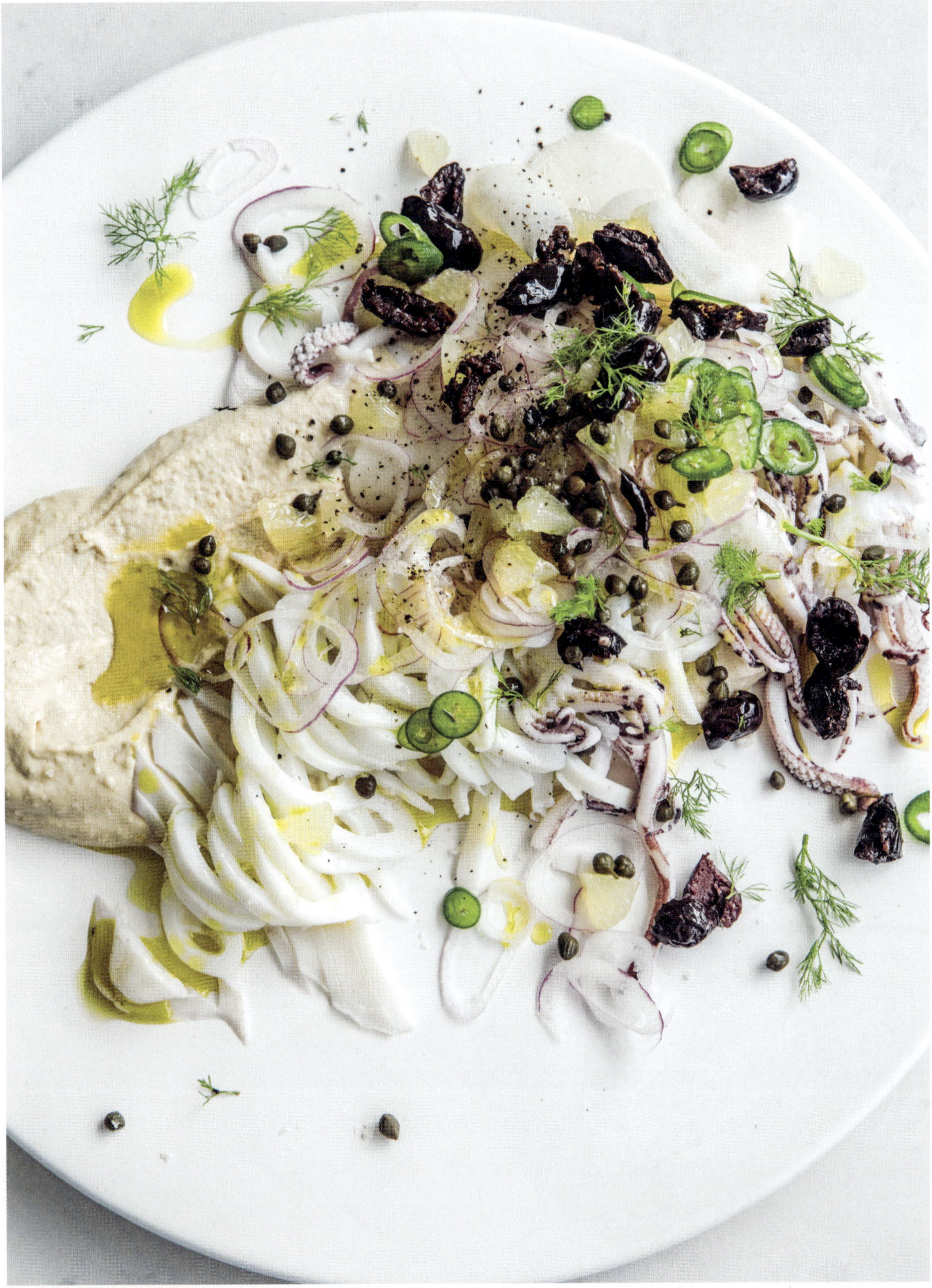

Calamari fritti

Pair with

Nori tartare (p. 77).

Italian tartare (p. 77).

Saffron mayonnaise (p. 75).

Black aïoli (p.76).

Sichuan pepper & mandarin salt (p. 29).

Serve on a bed of rocket (arugula), lettuce and/or curly endive (frisée) for some extra freshness, and to turn a snack into a starter or light meal.

Calamari fritti is such a triumph of simplicity. For me, it's the quintessential summer dish – especially after coming straight from the beach after a long day lounging, swimming and reading. It's also an immensely popular one, which I've served as simple restaurant and wine bar fare for many years. Tilt this in any direction with your choice of sauce, and dress it up with some leaves to make a light meal. **Serves 6 as a starter**

oil, for deep-frying (see p. 22)
120 g (4½ oz/1 cup) fine semolina
100 g (3½ oz/⅔ cup) plain (all-purpose) flour

1 kg (2 lb 3 oz) cleaned squid, wings on, tubes cut into rings, tentacles cut into pairs

Staples
LMN, S&P

Heat 8–10 cm (3¼–4 in) of oil in a wide, deep-sided frying pan over a high heat for 4 minutes; it should be about 180°C (350°F).

Combine the semolina and flour, then dust the squid in a coarse-mesh sieve, shaking to remove any excess. Test one piece in the oil to see if it sizzles straight away. If so, fry the squid in two batches for 3 minutes each, bringing the oil back up to temperature between each batch.

Drain on paper towel and immediately season well with salt.

Serve with lemon, and your choice of sauce (see Pair with).

Grilled calamari with smoky tomato dressing

Pair with

Stir the residual dressing through just-cooked freekeh or barley and serve with the calamari.

Try the grilled calamari with other sharp, vinegary sauces (see pp. 82, 83, 84, 86) or Green tomato salsa (p. 664).

I find the smell of squid being barbecued – especially over real coals – so unique and tantalising. Don't bother making this if you're buying prepared squid hoods, as you need the tentacles to add flavour and character, with everything cooking and charring and tasting a little different. The charred squid is particularly good with the sharp, smoky tomato dressing, but you can use the same 'burning' trick (see p. 84) with some of your other favourite sauces, especially those with sharp, vinegary overtones. Or you could simply serve the calamari with good olive oil, a generous seasoning of salt and pepper and a squeeze of lemon. **Serves 4–6**

1 kg (2 lb 3 oz) cleaned squid, wings on
1 lemon, cut in half

1 × quantity Smoky tomato dressing (p. 84)

Staples
EVOO, S&P

Special equipment
Metal skewers

Pierce one edge of each squid tube with a skewer, and thread through a couple of times down the length. Attach the tentacles to the ends of the skewers.

Heat the barbecue on high – or ideally, cook over a bed of hot coals.

Oil the squid, then season with salt and pepper. Grill for about 5 minutes on the first side, weighing the squid down with a pan or pot to get better contact with the grill, then flip and cook only for 1 minute on the other side. At the same time, grill the lemon, cut side down, until charred.

Remove the skewers and slice across the body in 1 cm (½ in) intervals, transferring the squid in its natural form to a serving plate. Drizzle with some of the dressing and serve with the charred lemon. Serve with the remaining dressing on the side.

Also see

Golden chicken stock, White chicken stock **54**

Balinese-style chicken skewers **104**

Udon noodles with chicken, shiitake, bok choy, miso & kimchi **402**

Chicken, corn & noodle soup **502-3**

Oven-baked poussins with tomato, sherry, fennel & olives **590-1**

Chicken, leek & mushroom pie **603**

Chicken

Chicken

Chicken is such a versatile protein. It is adaptable to all cooking methods, and receptive to pretty much all flavours, from creamy to violently spicy.

For me, one of the most comforting meals is a simple roasted chicken, and it is something I cook most weeks (or my partner, Michael, does – delegation is important). But that bird needs to be a fine specimen, pasture raised and fed a natural diet of seeds and grains, plus plenty of worms and bugs. That bird needs to reach maturity slowly and naturally, and it needs to get plenty of exercise and fresh air. The meat will be creamy in colour, rather than white, and it will be full of flavour – quite unlike the bland intensively farmed ones that have become all too common. It will also be nutritionally superior, with even the bones richer in minerals, making for a more nourishing stock.

Chicken raised this way costs more, and often quite a lot more, so I can understand people baulking at the price, but the rewards are immense. It is also worth stepping back and considering the economies that are woven into intensive farming to achieve low market prices. A chicken that costs less than $10 – and sometimes two for $10 on special – can hardly have had much of a life, squeezed into cramped cages and fattened as quickly as possible on foods that often are not part of its natural diet. Once they are slaughtered, processed, packaged and sent to the supermarket to be sold at a profit, it's quite shocking how low the prices are. And it's an equation that should make us pause.

As well as diminishing chicken into an industrial protein, these intensive farming efficiencies have grave animal welfare ramifications, and wider moral and environmental ones, too. In 1960, Australians ate 4.2 kg (9 lb) of chicken per annum, rising to an astonishing 47.4 kg (104 lb) per annum in 2018/19. Chicken has become a ubiquitous meat – and often, sadly, a somewhat bland and anonymous one, stripped of skin, fat and any real flavour.

Selective breeding and intensive farming can bring a chicken from unhatched egg to full weight in about thirty-five days. In Australia, chickens destined for the mass market will spend their entire short life in a barn, without ever going outside to forage. It is worth noting that hormones are not used in the Australian chicken meat industry, and antibiotics are used only for disease control and treatment, and not for growth stimulation. However, given the close living conditions, as well as the selective breeding that has produced birds with endemic health issues and suppressed immune systems, it is common – if not inevitable – for antibiotics to be administered by a veterinarian.

A mix of grains is fed to intensively farmed chickens, which typically will include canola seed and soybean meal, often from a proportion of GM crops. Once of size, chickens are slaughtered, mechanically plucked and dipped in a bleach/peroxide solution to kill any of the nastiness that thrives in the sometimes squalid conditions – including endemic faecal contamination from the intense stocking – then packaged for sale.

While general standards of animal welfare are much higher here in Australia than in many other countries, I still find this an exceedingly grim picture, and one that we need to change. It is hard for a small-scale farmer currently, but with the right systems in place, the right breeds, and the consumer understanding that doing things right comes at a cost, chickens can be raised responsibly, with access to natural pasture and sunlight. And it's also possible to do this at a reasonable enough price, if the rewards of environmental and animal welfare are considered.

Make chicken, like all meat, a treat, and use every bit of it. Roast the bird, use left-over meat for a salad or for sandwiches, then extract all the nutrients from the left-over carcass in a stock (see p. 49) for a quick soup or risotto, or to bolster a braise. We'll fix a lot by living more like this, and if you can appreciate the specialness of it and not expect to eat it all the time, then it won't blow the budget. Properly raised birds will also instruct us on what real chicken tastes like – so far removed from the bland, chalky meat that is commonplace. If it tastes special, then it will be treated that way.

It's a pleasure to see the increase in responsible, transparent farming of chickens that has occurred of late, with ethical, pasture-raised farming of birds for meat and eggs. Rather than large flocks of

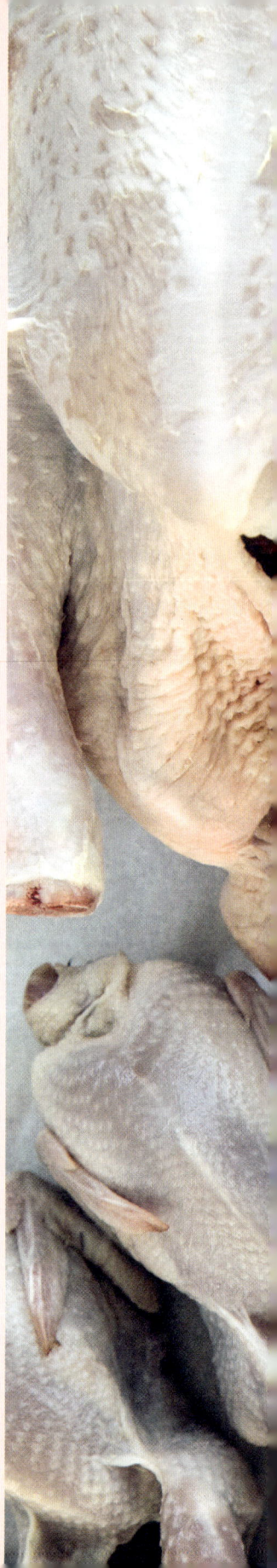

Pair with

Chicken is a meat that doesn't really clash with anything much, but here are some of my favourite matches. Pair with dairy, such as cream, butter, yoghurt and crème fraîche. Try soft herbs such as tarragon, parsley, dill, coriander (cilantro), chives, basil and chervil, and hard herbs such as rosemary, thyme, oregano, bay, marjoram and sage. Pair with chilli, spring onions (scallions), shallots, garlic, onion, ginger, celery, carrots, citrus, potatoes, fennel, tomatoes and peas. Chicken takes to so many spices, but some of my go-to ones are fennel, coriander seed, cumin, black pepper, sichuan pepper, star anise, paprika, cinnamon, cloves and mustard. Mushrooms are also a wonderful match with chicken, but I do love pine mushrooms and porcini in particular. Also, soy sauce, all types of vinegar (wine, red and white), bacon, pancetta, chorizo, speck, capers, verjuice, coconut cream … so many things.

so-called free-range birds endlessly depleting the same tracts of land, it's particularly gratifying to see the rotation of animals through farmland, allowing them fresh pasture to forage for worms and bugs and then move on. It's good for the birds, good for the land, good for us.

Progressive activist farmers such as Joel Salatin have helped to reshape this notion of bare-earth poultry farming – and farming in general – with a focus on the land having a living, biologically active soil rich in microorganisms. Indeed, with mixed farming, various animals can be rotated through pasture – each gaining benefit, while adding nutrition back to the soil – then be moved on before depleting or damaging the local systems. Then the pasture is rested to recover, or another herd or flock that will benefit from or complement the one prior will pass through, and so on.

There is another layer of complexity, though, and that is the availability of breeds that are suited to ethical farming. Chickens have been genetically selected to overeat, and to grow muscle and fat quicker than their systems can sustain. Australian meat chickens are generally from two strains, Ross and Cobb, and their health can become precarious around the time they reach slaughter weight and before they reach sexual maturity. They are not heat tolerant, resulting in exposure-related fatalities, and will favour grain over foraging as they default to the easy option. As it stands, ethical egg farming is an easier option, as laying breeds with broad genetic diversity are more generally available – but there is no question that sensitive, ethical farming, no matter the breed, is the better choice.

The key when buying chicken is traceability: knowing exactly where that bird came from. Most farmers pursuing a better product will be very open about their farming practices, proclaiming stocking densities (free-range eggs must have the density displayed on the packaging, but no such requirement exists for meat poultry), and detailing methods on their packaging or websites. They're usually proud of their processes. Ambiguous or opaque claims are best treated with suspicion. Thankfully, non-government bodies have sought to provide consumer assurance through regulation programs for pasture-raised animals – such as PROOF (Pasture Raised On Open Fields) – much like organic certification for farmers. It is a positive step.

Happily, more and more farmers are pursuing better outcomes for the birds they raise, as well as better products. Milking Yard Farm in Trentham, Victoria, is the finest example I have yet come across. They raise Sommerlad chickens, which have been selectively bred by Michael Sommerlad since 2001. A poultry breeder all his life, Sommerlad recognised the deficiencies in the commercial approach, as well as the ethical dilemmas, and developed his birds based on breeding across heritage Australian breeds. His birds have been crossbred to be heat tolerant, to grow slowly, developing strong bones, and to favour natural behaviours such as foraging, as well as be resistant to the common diseases of Australian poultry.

The Sommerlad birds at Milking Yard Farm are comparable in flavour to those that I have tasted in Europe. Especially in France, traditions for maximising the quality of chickens – most famously with Bresse chickens (with their own appellation control, no less) – have long been celebrated. May we see more of that approach here. It is an exciting and gratifying return to older, slower, kinder and more flavoursome ways.

Preparing chicken

Whatever the source, always choose fresh chicken over frozen, where possible. If buying a frozen bird, defrost it in the fridge out of any packaging on a rack or on paper towel to absorb any juices. Whether thawed or fresh, rinse the bird, including the cavity, then thoroughly dry inside and out. Never cook meat that isn't fully defrosted. The skin will never brown and crisp properly, as it needs to be thoroughly dry to do so. Plus, there is a real danger of the meat not cooking properly, leading to disappointment at the least, and a hazardous situation at the worst. Eating raw or undercooked chicken can cause salmonella poisoning, as a range of salmonella bacteria are frequently found in chicken meat. Fully cooking will negate any problems, but that doesn't mean you need to overcook a bird to be safe; just bring it up to the correct temperature. Naturally, this means raw chicken needs to be handled carefully, with separate boards employed, and knives and utensils washed after use.

A simple roast chicken (GF)

Remove a rinsed and dried 1.6 kg (3½ oz) chicken from the fridge at least 30 minutes before cooking. Rub with oil or brush with lots of melted butter, then season very well with salt and pepper. Place on a 'trivet' of very thickly sliced onion or fennel in a roasting tin, or suspend on a rack. Pour 2–3 cm (¾–1¼ in) of boiling water into the roasting tin, then roast at 200°C (400°F) fan-forced for 1 hour. Mostly I will roast breast-up the whole time, or sometimes I will start on one side for 20 minutes, then on the other for 20 minutes more, then breast-up to finish, which gives a more evenly golden result. To test, insert a skewer into the thickest part of the thigh; the juices should run clear. Or use a probe thermometer, making sure you don't touch the bone. A temperature of 70°C (160°F) is ideal, as it will come up to about 74°C (165°F) once rested. Tip the bird, with the main cavity pointing upwards and the breast down, which allows the juices to recirculate while the meat relaxes, for 10–15 minutes. When ready to serve, discard the trivet vegetables (if using), and scrape any caramelised bits in the tin into the juices and strain into a small saucepan. Bring to a simmer, reducing if thin, then finish with a big knob of butter. Serve with the carved chicken. You could, of course, stuff butter and thyme or tarragon under the skin (see right) and/or fill the cavity with herbs, garlic and lemon, but this is stunning done simply, too.

Sometimes buying a cut, rather than a whole bird, is desirable, but often the skin is removed when the birds are broken down. Skin, along with the subcutaneous fat, adds so much flavour to a dish, though it is not always required in a recipe. If thighs are called for, chicken chops are a good option (as are drumsticks), being bone-in thighs with the skin still attached. Boning is a simple enough process. Flip the chop over and run a knife along both edges of the thigh bone, cutting along and around it until you can gently pull it away from the flesh. You get the skin-on meat, along with some bones that you can pop into the freezer to add to a stockpot later. However, filleted thighs quickly marinated with garlic, herbs, oil, salt and pepper and barbecued on a hot grill make for a super-simple, quick and tasty meal – so sometimes convenience wins out.

If I'm not buying a whole chicken, I will generally buy thighs/chops. I sometimes buy leg quarters (marylands), mainly if I'm frying chicken (see p. 230), but they're also an economical and tasty cut for roasting. Occasionally, I will buy chicken breasts to poach (see p. 230) for a salad. Thighs have a good meat yield and are flavoursome, and the fat and connective tissue content keeps them moist and succulent. They can be cooked quickly, or braised or stewed, making them ideal for curries.

If making a stock, I will of course use any bones saved from deboning or filleting, or left over from a roast, and will buy frames, necks and sometimes feet, which add plenty of collagen (becoming gelatine). As with the rest of the bird, I like to know exactly where the feet have come from – perhaps especially so! I also buy minced (ground) chicken for things like dumplings, but always opt for thigh mince, and ideally have it minced fresh with a little skin and fat – lean mince is a woeful thing.

Whole chickens are sold by size, with a size 14 being a 1.4 kg (3 lb 1 oz) chicken, size 16 a 1.6 kg (3½ lb) chicken, and so on. Young chickens are called 'poussin' and are generally in the 500–700 g (1 lb 2 oz–1 lb 9 oz) range. Sometimes the term 'spatchcock' is used interchangeably with 'poussin', which is no doubt connected to restaurants commonly spatchcocking poussins!

To spatchcock is to remove the backbone and butterfly the bird, whether a poussin, a more mature chicken, a quail, duck or game bird. It is a handy technique, especially if grilling, and speeds up the cooking process considerably. Lay the bird on a board, breast side up. Insert a knife in the main cavity so that it pokes out the neck cavity, then cut through the rib bones on both sides and remove the backbone (keep it for stock). Open the bird flat on your board, pressing down hard on the breast to flatten it out. Depending on size and heat, a spatchcocked chicken will cook in 35–40 minutes.

To cut a chicken into four once flattened, flip over to expose the inside breast bone, insert a knife in the top and apply pressure to cut in half exactly down the middle. Flip over the two halves and cleanly cut the skin between breast and leg on each. You now have four pieces. To make eight, cut the breast, skin side up, on an angle to the wing. Then, skin side down, cut the leg on the seam through the joint to remove the drumstick from the thigh. Repeat.

The various parts of a chicken will cook at different rates and with quite different results. Overcooking the breast will result in dry meat, whereas the thighs, drumsticks and wings are far more forgiving. If roasting a whole bird, you can push butter under the skin to baste the breast meat while it cooks; this will lubricate the meat, and makes for amazing pan juices. Starting at the main cavity, push your fingers between the flesh and the skin, carefully lifting the skin off without tearing it. You should be able to fairly easily separate it from the breast, and even from the drumsticks if you like. You can then insert sliced seasoned butter, garlic and herbs, such as thyme, before roasting.

For a moist result, it is best to cook a whole bird until just done, or barely underdone, at about 70°C (160°F) – the safe temperature is officially 74°C (165°F) – as it will finish cooking those last few degrees as it rests. Or, you can give yourself a little more leeway by brining prior to roasting. Immersing the bird (or pork or lamb) in salted water first for a few hours, or even days, will push water and salt into the flesh, resulting in succulent and perfectly seasoned meat. This is effective for poussin (see p. 229) or a large chicken (see p. 245), though the former will give considerably quicker results. Whether brining or not, to ensure crisp skin, refrigerate the dried chicken uncovered before roasting, as the low humidity of the fridge will dehydrate the skin very effectively – a few hours works well, but overnight is best. And always bring a whole chicken closer to room temperature before cooking by leaving it on the bench for at least 30 minutes. It will cook more evenly, and rather than taking the chill off the bird, the heat in the oven can get to work on caramelising that skin.

White-poached chicken

Such a faultless technique for cooking chicken – the bird gently poaches in the simple stock, finishing cooking as the liquid cools, which results in all the flavour and moisture being retained in the flesh. This can be served warm, or the chicken can be chilled in the broth and served cold. **Serves 4–6**

1 × 1.6 kg (3½ lb) chicken
Soy stock
3 litres (101 fl oz/12 cups)
  water

100 ml (3½ fl oz) soy sauce
4 spring onions (scallions)
4 garlic cloves

5 cm (2 in) piece of fresh
  ginger, sliced
3 star anise

Remove the chicken from the fridge about 30 minutes before cooking.

Add the stock ingredients to a large, heavy-based saucepan (cast-iron is ideal) and bring to a simmer over a medium heat. Simmer for 5 minutes, then add the chicken, breast side down, allowing the cavity to fill with water. Simmer for 12 minutes (or 14 minutes for a 1.8 kg/4 lb bird), then turn off the heat and cover. Stand for 2 hours (or 2½ hours for a 1.8 kg/4 lb bird) at room temperature, to cook gently in the residual heat. Resist the urge to lift the lid, as the heat will escape. Patience is required.

Serve warm, or chill in the broth. To carve the chicken, lay it on a chopping board, breast side up. Insert a knife in the main cavity so that it pokes out the neck cavity, then cut through the rib bones on both sides and remove the backbone (keep this for stock). Flip over and cut along both sides of the sternum, through the breastbone, yielding two halves. Cut between the legs and body, detaching each leg at the hip joint. Separate the legs from the thighs at the joint with the heel of your knife. Cut the wings and drumettes from the breasts in one piece, then cut through at the joints to separate into two pieces each. Cut each breast into four pieces, crossways through the bone.

Arrange the chicken on a serving plate, reassembling the halves. Ladle over a little broth, then spoon over your choice of sauce (see 'Pair with', right).

Pair with

Ginger, soy & gochujang sauce (p. 95), soy sauce with a splash of sesame oil and Fermented cooked chilli sauce (p. 97), or ginger and Spring onion oil (p. 103).

Serve with cucumber on the side, plain noodles and some coriander (cilantro).

Rice, Spiced Chinese pickles (p. 640), stir-fried greens (pp. 400, 401) and fresh coriander (cilantro).

Shred for a salad, or use whenever poached chicken with Japanese or Chinese flavours is called for.

The broth can be used for Congee (p. 383) or a soup, or frozen in smaller portions and used in stir-fries when a stock is called for.

Simple fried buttermilk chicken

You can go to a lot of trouble to make fried buttermilk chicken, but this is a super simple route and the result is superb. By cooking the chicken first, you don't need to fry then re-fry, or risk the chicken not cooking through once the crust is perfectly golden – and you also get a light chicken stock as well. The thick and tangily acidic buttermilk holds on to the flour, making for a deliciously crunchy spiced crust. **Serves 6**

12 bone-in chicken chops, skin on, slashed along the bone on the underside
350 ml (12 fl oz) buttermilk
oil, for deep-frying (see p. 22)
Brine
1 litre (34 fl oz/4 cups) water
80 ml (2½ fl oz/⅓ cup) white-wine vinegar, or chardonnay vinegar
30 g (1 oz) soft brown sugar

1 white onion, finely sliced
2 garlic cloves, smashed
10 allspice berries
8 fresh bay leaves
2 teaspoons salt flakes
Spiced dusting flour
3 teaspoons white peppercorns
3 tablespoons coriander seeds

1½ teaspoons smoked sweet paprika
1 tablespoon salt flakes
150 g (5½ oz/1¼ cup) rice flour
150 g (5½ oz) cornflour (cornstarch)
¾ tablespoon baking powder
Staples
S&P

Pair with

Serve in a seeded or brioche bun with slaw (p. 448) and a mayonnaise mixed with Fermented cooked chilli sauce (p. 97) or green chilli.

Pure corn purée (p. 499).

Chips.

Shaved white cabbage and super-thin shavings of celeriac seasoned with caster (superfine) sugar, rice vinegar and extra-virgin olive oil.

A mix of coriander, (cilantro) fried mint and mustard seeds.

Sweet Zuni-style pickles (p. 668) made with jalapeños.

Corn purée (499).

In a large saucepan, bring all of the brine ingredients to a simmer, then turn off the heat place in the fridge until chilled.

Add the chicken to the brine and marinate for 8 hours.

For the spiced flour, grind the peppercorns and coriander in a mortar and pestle. Add the paprika and salt, then stir the spice mix through the flours and baking powder. Set aside.

Strain the liquid from the chicken. Dry the brine off the chicken pieces, then dip the chicken in the buttermilk and shake the excess off. Coat with the spiced flour, shake off the excess, then rest on a lined tray for 10 minutes.

Heat about 10 cm (4 in) of oil in a wide saucepan until 170°C (340°F).

Dust the chicken in the spiced flour again to cover any damp spots. Fry in batches, so as not to crowd the pan, until deeply golden, about 6 minutes. Serve as you cook, or keep the chicken warm in a low oven and serve all at once.

Make it different

You can make this with boneless chicken thighs marinated in brine, with the skin on (you need the skin for flavour and the crust). Cut each thigh into four pieces. Season and soak in the buttermilk for 30 minutes, then dust in the spiced flour mix. Stand for 15 minutes, then dust again. Shallow-fry, skin side down, in a mix of clarified butter and olive oil for 8 minutes, then flip over and cook for 5 minutes. Drain, season and serve hot, with slaw and mayonnaise.

Chicken & ginger wontons with peanuts

Pair with

Peanut & ginger dressing (p. 95).

Unless expert with chopsticks – and I am not – you're likely to chase these slippery, silky wontons around the plate a little, but the pursuit is well worth it. This is a stunning weekend treat, either as a starter or a standalone brunch, lunch or supper. You can, of course, buy minced (ground) chicken thighs for this, but being able to include skin and fat in the mince makes all the difference to the result. Fillet some thigh chops yourself (see p. 229), or ask your poultry supplier to fillet and mince them for you. **Makes 30–36 wontons**

30–36 square wonton wrappers
50 g (1¾ oz/⅓ cup) chopped roasted salted peanuts

Wonton filling
500 g (1 lb 2 oz) boneless chicken thighs, skin on

5 spring onions (scallions), white bits and half the green, finely sliced
3 tablespoons very finely diced fresh ginger
1 tablespoon shaoxing rice wine

1 tablespoon light soy sauce
1 tablespoon oyster sauce
1 teaspoon sesame oil
1 teaspoon caster (superfine) sugar
½ teaspoon ground white pepper

For the filling, remove one-third of the skin from the chicken (saving it for stock), then dice the meat with a sharp knife as finely as you can. Chill in the freezer for 30 minutes, then pulse to a rough mince in a food processor. Combine with the other filling ingredients, then refrigerate for 5 minutes or so.

Place a rounded teaspoon of the filling mixture on a wonton wrapper, then dampen the top edge and sides with a wet finger. Fold in half to form a rectangle, then press together firmly. Take the two corners on the folded edge and bring them together to overlap, wetting the edge and pressing firmly to stick.

Cook the wontons in batches in simmering water for about 2½ minutes; remove one and test by cutting in half to check if it is cooked. Once cooked, lift the wontons from the water with a slotted lifter and drain a little.

Place in a serving dish and spoon the sauce over straight away. Serve sprinkled with the peanuts.

Chilli con pollo with chorizo & beans

This a variant on chilli con carne, with a lighter result, although the chicken thighs add a surprising richness and lusciousness to the braise that you just won't get with another cut. You can serve this with rice, but it's a fantastic centrepiece for a feast of tacos. **Serves 4–6**

100 ml (3½ fl oz) extra-virgin olive oil
150 g (5½ oz) chorizo
1 onion, finely diced
6 garlic cloves, sliced
2 red capsicums (bell peppers), finely diced
4 celery stalks, finely diced
1 kg (2 lb 3 oz) boneless chicken thighs, preferably with the skin on, cut in six
1½ tablespoons coriander seeds, roughly ground

1 tablespoon fennel seeds
1 tablespoon dried oregano
1 teaspoon sweet smoked paprika
1 teaspoon ground black pepper
3 large tomatoes, diced
2½ tablespoons unsweetened (Dutch) cocoa powder
2½ tablespoons red-wine vinegar, or sherry vinegar
2 tablespoons brown sugar

500 ml (17 fl oz/2 cups) White chicken stock (p. 54)
500 ml (17 fl oz/2 cups) water
3 handfuls of freshly podded borlotti (cranberry) beans, or 400 g (14 oz) tin cannellini or kidney beans, drained

Staples
S&P

Pair with

Serve with tortillas or rice, and a salad of shredded iceberg lettuce, dill and coriander (cilantro) dressed with olive oil and white-wine vinegar. Have some grated cheddar, yoghurt or sour cream, and a hot sauce or Fermented cooked chilli sauce (p. 97) or pickled jalapeños (see p. 494) on the side. A few split finger limes are a lovely addition, but some lime cheeks or wedges do the trick, too.

Heat a little of the oil in a frying pan over a medium heat. Add the chorizo and fry until a little golden, about 3 minutes. Set aside. Add the chicken and cook for 10 minutes, then set aside.

Heat the remaining oil in a wide saucepan over a high heat. Cook the onion and garlic until softened, about 3 minutes. Add the capsicum and celery, then cook until starting to soften and caramelise, about 10 minutes.

Add the chorizo and chicken, browning the chicken for about 5 minutes. Stir in the spices and tomato and cook to soften the tomato.

Season well with salt and pepper, then add the cocoa, vinegar and sugar. Stir them through, then add the stock and water. Simmer quite hard, stirring regularly, for 10 minutes.

Add the beans, reduce the heat and simmer for 50 minutes to reduce the sauce. Shred the chicken a little in the pan with two forks before serving.

Chicken liver parfait (GF)

Parfait means 'perfect' in French, and according to the *Larousse Gastronomique* it is exclusively applied to desserts. Pâté, a term most associate with a spreadable charcuterie often made from livers, is technically a pie of sorts, with a pastry crust and a rich filling. Pâté en terrine covers familiar bacon-wrapped rustic terrines as well as the smoother forcemeat ones, which we – and most of the French – call pâté, while pâté en croûte is a pâté en terrine wrapped in pastry rather than bacon. Parfait, as I was always taught, was when livers (or other forcemeat) was pushed through a fine-mesh sieve, resulting in a seamless, silky texture – a parfait pâté, if you will. Clear? Well, either way, this is by far the best way to make pâté. Use the best livers you can find, preferably organic. **Makes about 800 g (1 lb 12 oz)**

Pair with

Crostini, pane croccante, Lavoche (p. 840) or grilled Sourdough bread (p. 847).

Pickled shallots & currants with parsley & cornichons (p. 596).

Quince jelly (p. 717), or currants or sultanas (golden raisins) warmed in vinegar or brandy to plump up.

Freshly pickled grapes (see p. 630) or sliced figs.

Sprinkle Seasoned pistachio dust (p. 376) over the plated parfait, or on top of parfait smeared over crostini.

A note on livers

Always buy fresh livers – look for bright colour and firm texture. Rinse in water, then trim away the connective tissue along with any discoloured parts, including anything greenish, which may be bile. Once cleaned, the livers can be soaked in milk as described (right).

600 g (1 lb 5 oz) trimmed chicken livers, or duck livers
400 ml (13½ fl oz) full-cream (whole) milk
2 French shallots, finely diced
1 garlic clove, chopped
150 ml (5 fl oz) port, madeira or brandy (an equal mix of all three is ideal)

2 eggs
1 egg yolk
200 g (7 oz) Clarified butter (p. 360)
1 fresh bay leaf
¼ nutmeg, finely grated
½ teaspoon ground white pepper
½ teaspoon ground allspice
2 teaspoons salt flakes

To decorate & seal
a handful of thyme leaves
150 g (5½ oz) Clarified butter (p. 360), melted

Staples
EVOO, S&P

Special equipment
Thermometer

Cover the livers with the milk in a bowl or container and refrigerate overnight, or for at least 3 hours. Drain, then dry on paper towel.

Heat a little oil in a small saucepan over a medium heat. Add the shallot and garlic, season with salt and cook until softened, about 3 minutes. Add the spirit(s) and reduce to a glaze of about 2 tablespoons.

Add the eggs, yolk and spirit reduction to a bowl, beat to combine, then add the livers. Marinate for 1 hour at room temperature.

Preheat the oven to 110°C (230°F) fan-forced. Line a 1.2 litre (41 fl oz) terrine mould or small non-stick loaf (bar) tin with baking paper, or use unlined individual ceramic dishes or ramekins.

Add the clarified butter and bay leaf to a small saucepan and heat to 30°C (85°F).

Add the liver mixture, spices and salt flakes to a blender. Remove the bay leaf from the warm clarified butter and add it in a slow stream as you blitz. Once smooth, strain the mixture through a fine-mesh sieve into the prepared mould(s). Cover tightly with baking paper, then foil, and transfer to a roasting tin. Pour hot water into the roasting tin, to come halfway up the mould(s).

Transfer to the oven and bake for 25 minutes. The parfait should set like jelly, with a slight wobble. If still loose, continue to cook, checking at five-minute intervals.

Stand the parfait in the water bath at room temperature for 2 hours, then refrigerate for an hour or so.

Once cold, sprinkle some thyme leaves over the top, then pour the melted clarified butter over to seal the surface and stop the parfait discolouring, then refrigerate again. It will keep for 4–5 days.

Chicken livers with witlof & radicchio fatoush salad, currants & sumac

While eating liver pâté would rarely raise an eyebrow, the idea of eating chicken livers seems to be an unassailable hurdle for many people. But it's a hurdle worth clearing. Poorly sourced or poorly cooked livers could no doubt generate unshakeable disgust – but pristinely fresh livers, cooked until pink and accompanied by sweet and bitter accents to complement their richness and unique slippery texture, are a thing of wonder. Don't expect immediate converts, but when wooing liver haters, source the livers carefully from an organic supplier who understands what you're using them for. It will make all the difference. **Serves 4**

400 g (14 oz) trimmed chicken livers (see p. 233)
400 ml (13½ fl oz) full-cream (whole) milk
1 small white onion, finely sliced into rounds or half-moons
3 small pitta breads (see p. 854), cut into large triangles
2 tablespoons red-wine vinegar

3 tablespoons currants
juice of ½ lemon
2 heaped tablespoons ground sumac, plus extra to serve
100 ml (3½ fl oz) extra-virgin olive oil
1 small dense head of radicchio, leaves roughly shredded or torn

1 red or white chicory (witlof/endive), sliced on an angle 1 cm (½ in) thick
15 mint leaves, torn
100 g (3½ oz) butter
3 tablespoons pomegranate molasses

Staples
EVOO, S&P

Add the livers to a bowl, cover with the milk and stand for about 30 minutes. Soak the onion slices in cold water.

Meanwhile, preheat the oven to 180°C (350°F) fan-forced. Open the pitta triangles out into diamonds, spread out on a baking tray, and drizzle with oil. Bake for about 5 minutes until crisp, then cool.

Add the vinegar and currants to a small saucepan, bring to the boil, then take off the heat. Set aside to plump up for about 10 minutes.

Drain the onion and pat dry, then add to a large bowl with the soaked currants, along with any residual vinegar. Add the lemon juice, sumac and oil, season with salt and pepper, then combine.

Combine the radicchio, witlof and mint in another bowl.

Heat a large frying pan over a high heat until very hot. Drain the livers and pat dry with paper towel. Coat with oil, season generously with salt and pepper and fry for about 1½ minutes on each side – do this in batches so that the livers stay separate and fry properly, rather than stew. They should be firm but still pink in the middle. With the last batch, add the butter and cook until nut brown, about 2 minutes.

Return all the livers to the pan and toss through for a few seconds, then tip into the bowl with the onion. Add about half the pomegranate molasses and toss through.

Arrange the pitta on plates, then follow with the radicchio mix. Pile the liver mixture on top of the leaves. Drizzle with the remaining pomegranate molasses and sprinkle on a little extra sumac. Serve immediately.

Stir-fried chicken thighs with kecap manis, curry leaves & black pepper (GF)

Cut 600 g (1 lb 5 oz) boneless chicken thighs into 3 cm (1¼ in) dice. Heat a wok or large frying pan over a high heat for about 5 minutes, until very hot. Add 40 ml (1¼ fl oz) grapeseed oil, then spread out the chicken in the wok, so it is all in contact with the surface. Cook for 4 minutes, until caramelised. Season with salt, then flip and cook for 4 minutes on the other side. Don't move it around, or you won't get enough colour and flavour. Remove the chicken from the wok, leaving the oil behind. Add 20 curry leaves and toss in the oil for about 1 minute, until they change colour. Remove from the wok and set aside. Add another 40 ml (1¼ fl oz) oil, an onion, finely sliced lengthways into half-moons, and 4 finely sliced garlic cloves and stir-fry until golden, about 4 minutes. Return the chicken, with 2 teaspoons freshly ground black pepper, 2½ tablespoons kecap manis and half the curry leaves. Toss to coat well, then squeeze in the juice of 1 lime. Serve with the remaining curry leaves on top. Serves 4. Serve with steamed rice and greens.

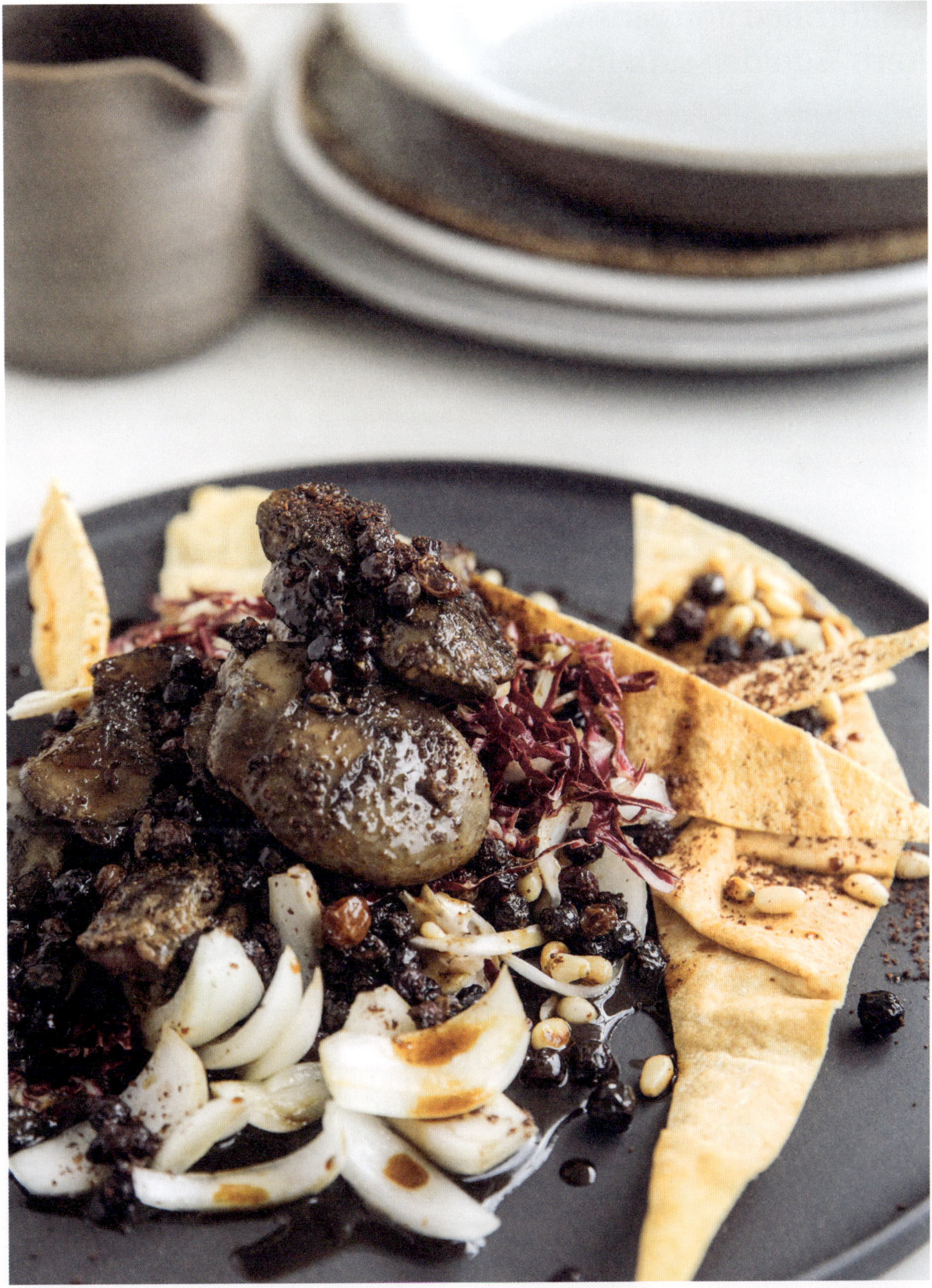

Chargrilled poussins with a lemon, chilli, herb & golden sultana salad (GF)

The spiced marinade, combined with a good char on the sweet and succulent poussins, which are then crowned with the punchy salad of herbs, chillies and sweet golden sultanas, is ever so delicious. If you have the opportunity to cook the birds over real coals, the flavour from the charcoal makes such a huge difference. A gas barbecue also yields a fine result – just ensure good colour from the grill. You could also use quails in this recipe. **Serves 6 as a main, or 12 as a starter**

Pair with

Baked buttered rice (see p. 384), with almonds or couscous.

Labneh (p. 362).

Charred fennel salad with tarragon (p. 528).

White or brown rice.

- 6 × 600 g (1 lb 5 oz) poussins, trimmed, backbones removed, and flattened (see p. 229)
- 2 tablespoons golden sultanas (golden raisins)
- 2 tablespoons white-wine vinegar
- 1 tablespoon ground aleppo pepper, plus extra to serve

- 1 bunch of coriander (cilantro), leaves picked
- 1 bunch of flat-leaf (Italian) parsley, leaves picked
- ½ bunch of dill, fronds picked
- 1 lemon, zested, peeled and segmented

Dijon, cumin & lemon marinade
- 1½ tablespoons extra-virgin olive oil

- 1 lemon, juiced
- 4 garlic cloves, finely grated
- 2 tablespoons dijon mustard
- 2 tablespoons ground cumin
- 2 teaspoons ground cinnamon
- 1 tablespoon salt flakes
- 1½ teaspoon black pepper
- 2 teaspoons brown sugar
- 1 teaspoon chilli powder

Add the marinade ingredients to a large bowl and combine well. Add the birds and toss until well coated. Refrigerate for at least 1 hour and for up to 12 hours.

Remove the birds from the fridge 30 minutes prior to cooking. Heat a barbecue on high, or burn a fire down to evenly hot coals.

Add the sultanas, vinegar and aleppo pepper to a small saucepan and bring to the boil. Take off the heat and set aside.

Grill the birds for about 8 minutes on each side, until just cooked through and well charred. Rest for 5 minutes on a tray before transferring to a serving platter. Serve whole, or cut in half or into quarters. Reserve the resting juices.

Add the herbs, plumped sultanas and any residual vinegar to a bowl, along with the lemon segments, half the zest and any juice. Add the resting juices from the poussins and toss, then scatter over the birds.

Sprinkle with a little more aleppo pepper and serve.

Make it different
With orange. Substitute the lemon for orange.

Sweet & spicy Thai chicken drumettes

It's all about the marinade here, which only really needs an hour to work its magic – but overnight is even better. Well, actually it's all about the marinade *and* the sweet chilli sauce, which is much better if you make your own, though a good commercial one can be used, perhaps spiked with a little lime juice and fresh chilli, as they can be a little sweet and flat. These are perfect for entertaining – just don't skimp on the napkins. **Makes about 30**

Simple honey, soy & ginger drumettes

Preheat the oven to 180°C (350°F) fan-forced. Add 1.5 kg (3 lb 5 oz) chicken drumettes, 200 ml (7 fl oz) shaoxing rice wine or water, 150 ml (5 fl oz) honey, 100 ml (3½ fl oz) light soy sauce, 100 ml (3½ fl oz) oyster sauce, a 6 cm (2½ in) piece of fresh ginger, peeled and finely grated, 4 finely grated garlic cloves, 2 tablespoons sesame seeds and 1½ teaspoons Chinese five-spice to a large flameproof baking dish, stir and bring to a simmer over a medium heat. Transfer to the oven and roast for 30 minutes. Increase the oven temperature to 200°C (400°F) fan-forced and bake for another 10 minutes, until the drumettes are browned and the sauce is sticky. Transfer the chicken to a serving plate and drizzle the juices over the top. Scatter with extra sesame seeds before serving. Makes about 16. This recipe also works with drumsticks or thigh – just increase the cooking time by about 10 minutes.

2 kg (4 lb 6 oz) chicken drumettes (about 30)
250 ml (8½ fl oz/1 cup) Thai-style chilli jam (p. 96), plus extra to serve
4 spring onions (scallions), white bits and most of the green, finely sliced
¼ bunch of coriander (cilantro), leaves and fine stems picked

2 tablespoons black or white sesame seeds
2 limes, cut into wedges

Lemongrass & ginger marinade
3 lemongrass stems, pale part only, finely chopped
5 cm (2 in) piece of fresh ginger, peeled and finely chopped
6 coriander (cilantro) roots and stems, chopped

3 garlic cloves, chopped
3 long red chillies, chopped
3 makrut lime leaves, finely sliced
100 ml (3½ fl oz) fish sauce
3 tablespoons grated palm sugar (jaggery), or 2½ tablespoons brown sugar
2 tablespoons grapeseed oil
3 teaspoons Chinese five-spice

For the marinade, blitz all the ingredients to a rough paste. Coat the chicken in the marinade and refrigerate for 1 hour or overnight.

Preheat the oven to 200°C (400°F) fan-forced. Line two baking trays with baking paper.

Spread the chicken over the baking trays with all the residual marinade. Roast for 25 minutes, turning the oven temperature up to 220°C (430°F) fan-forced for the last 10 minutes, to colour well.

Toss the chicken in a bowl with half the chilli sauce, then pile on a serving plate. Sprinkle with the spring onion, coriander and sesame seeds. Serve with the lime wedges and remaining chilli sauce on the side.

Make it different
This recipe works with drumsticks – just increase the cooking time by about 10 minutes.

Korean-style fried chicken

In my opinion, Korean fried chicken is vastly superior to the kind with which it shares an acronym – far, far better. Don't worry if the batter clumps a little when coating, as those bits will fry into crunchy outcrops that take up the sauce readily and are quite delicious. That balance between crunch and saucy coating is key, so dress the chicken quickly and eat immediately. If serving in batches as you cook, just divide the sauce evenly between the batches. **Makes 32 pieces**

oil, for deep-frying (see p. 22)
16 chicken wings, drumettes and wings separated, wing tips left on
100 g (3½ oz) glutinous rice flour
1 × quantity Gochujang chilli sauce (p. 97)

3 tablespoons toasted sesame seeds
4 spring onions (scallions), finely sliced

Rice flour batter
3 egg whites
200 ml (7 fl oz) water
3 teaspoons salt flakes

150 g (5½ oz) glutinous rice flour
100 g (3½ oz) potato starch
2 teaspoons ground black pepper
1 teaspoon bicarbonate of soda (baking soda)

Preheat the oven to 100°C (210°F) fan-forced.

Heat 15 cm (6 in) of oil in a large saucepan until 170°C (340°F).

For the batter, whisk the egg whites in a large bowl until foaming, then whisk in the water and salt. Sift in the remaining ingredients, then mix into a smooth batter.

Dust the chicken in the rice flour and add to the batter. Toss through until well coated.

Fry the chicken in four batches for 7 minutes each. Drain on paper towel and set aside, keeping the batches separate.

Once all the chicken has been cooked, starting with the first batch you cooked, fry again for 7 minutes. Drain again and keep warm in the oven.

Once all the chicken has been cooked a second time, toss in a large bowl with the sauce until thoroughly coated.

Tip onto a serving plate, sprinkle with the sesame seeds and spring onion and serve immediately.

Chicken coconut curry with makrut lime leaf, lemongrass & turmeric

This is a super-fragrant and vibrant curry with earthy bass notes of turmeric. The silky richness of coconut cream is perfect with the succulent thigh meat. I haven't met anyone who doesn't love this curry. Doubling the paste is a good idea as it freezes well, making a repeat appearance incredibly simple – I'm always thankful for the forethought, and the extra effort is minimal. **Serves 6–8**

Pair with

Steamed rice, fried shallots (see p. 600) and greens.

12 chicken thigh chops, skin on
800 ml (27 fl oz) coconut cream
400 ml (13½ fl oz) water
4 makrut lime leaves
250 g (9 oz) cherry tomatoes
1 lime

Curry paste
3 lemongrass stems, pale part only, finely sliced
12 makrut lime leaves, sliced
50 g (1¾ oz) piece of fresh turmeric, peeled and finely sliced, or 3 teaspoons ground
5 garlic cloves, chopped
5 French shallots, sliced
4 red bird's eye chillies, split lengthways
3 tablespoons finely grated palm sugar (jaggery), or

2½ tablespoons brown sugar
3 tablespoons fish sauce
2½ tablespoons rice vinegar
2 tablespoons coconut oil
1 heaped tablespoon vegetable or chicken stock (bouillon) powder
3 teaspoons ground white pepper

In a blender, blitz all the curry paste ingredients to a smooth paste.

Place a chicken chop on a chopping board, skin side down. To help the thighs cook faster and more evenly, run a knife along both edges of the thigh bone, cutting along and around it until you can gently pull it away from the flesh, but don't remove the bone. Repeat for the other chops.

Add the curry paste to a large saucepan and fry over a medium heat until fragrant and changing colour, about 4 minutes. Add the chicken and stir through to coat. Cook for 5 minutes, then add the coconut cream, water and lime leaves. Bring to a simmer and add the tomatoes. Simmer for 45 minutes, until the chicken is very tender.

Squeeze in some lime juice and serve.

Chicken fricassee with Dutch creams, speck & tarragon ⒢

Pair with

Simply dressed salad leaves.

Memories play such a big part with food, for better or worse. For me, this dish snaps memories into sharp focus of being a 17-year-old getting to grips with being a contributing member of a proper classical kitchen. It's a dish that Tansy's Flemish head chef, Marc Bouten, used to make. The first time I tasted it, the timeless combination of tarragon and chicken floored me, but it was more than that. The craft of building flavour through carefully caramelising the chicken until golden at the start, tweaking with the acid of the vinegar, then reducing until the sauce was glossy and thickened, and the vinegar had mellowed but still provided definition, was just a beautiful snapshot of the cook's art viewed through the portal of a very simple dish. **Serves 4–6**

150 g (5½ oz) unsmoked pancetta, guanciale or speck, cut into 5 mm (¼ in) batons

1 × 1.6 kg (3½ lb) chicken, cut into 8 pieces (see p. 229), or 8 chicken chops (skin on)

8 small French shallots, peeled and cut in half

6 garlic cloves, skin on, smashed

3 large, creamy yellow-fleshed potatoes (such as Dutch cream or royal blue), peeled and cut into 2 cm (¾ in) rounds

100 ml (3½ fl oz) chardonnay vinegar

750 ml (25½ fl oz/3 cups) Golden chicken stock (p. 54)

5 tarragon, or thyme, sprigs

3 fresh bay leaves

Staples
EVOO, S&P

Preheat the oven to 180°C (350°F) fan-forced.

Heat a wide-based flameproof casserole dish over a medium heat. Add a splash of oil and half the pancetta, then fry until lightly browned, about 3 minutes. Season the chicken well with salt and pepper. Add half the chicken to the dish, brown well all over, then remove, along with the pancetta.

Repeat with the remaining pancetta and chicken and set aside with the first batch.

Cook the shallot and garlic in the same dish, with a little more oil if needed, until starting to brown, about 4 minutes. Remove and set aside with the chicken.

Add the potatoes to the dish, season and cook until starting to brown, about 4 minutes. Return the chicken, pancetta and shallot mixture, then add the vinegar. Stir well, picking up and stirring in any caramelisation with your spoon. Simmer for 1 minute, then add the stock, tarragon and bay leaves and bring to a simmer.

Cover, transfer to the oven and bake for 25 minutes.

Remove the chicken from the dish and reduce the liquid on the stovetop, to a lightly thickened, saucy consistency. The potatoes will take a little longer than the chicken, so just remove them once tender.

Return the chicken and potatoes to the dish and take straight to the table, or arrange on serving plates and ladle the sauce over.

Make it different

With porcini. Soak 15 g (½ oz) dried porcini mushrooms in boiling water to cover for 15 minutes. Add the chopped porcini with the shallots, and the mushroom soaking liquid with the stock.

With cream. Adding a few spoonfuls of cream or crème fraîche when reducing the sauce will make it even more intense and luxurious.

Prawn & poached chicken vermicelli salad

Thai and Vietnamese salads are always ultra-bright, zapping you with an intense vibrancy of flavour, sour lime, exhilarating herbs and dressings laced with heat and sweetness. They're my ideal hot summer's day lunch or afternoon snack, especially when I don't think I can eat anything. I have poached a breast here, but you could easily use shredded left-over roasted bird, or leave the chicken out entirely. The sweet mango dressed in fish sauce and lime is a real hero for me here. **Serves** 4

2 large chicken breasts, about 250 g (9 oz)
fish sauce, for seasoning
2 large ripe but firm mangoes
2 long red chillies, finely chopped
1 lime, plus lime cheeks to serve
400 g (14 oz) bean thread noodles or rice vermicelli
1 tablespoon extra-virgin olive oil
8 cooked king prawns (shrimp), peeled and sliced in half lengthways

1 × quantity Nuoc cham (p. 93)
50 g (1¾ oz/⅓ cup) small salted roasted red-skinned peanuts

Cucumber, celery heart & herb salad
2 Lebanese (short) cucumbers, semi-peeled in stripes and sliced 5 mm (¼ in) thick
2 limes, segmented and cut into small triangles
1 celery heart, leaves picked, sliced

2 handfuls of snow peas (mangetout), finely sliced
2 handfuls of Vietnamese mint leaves
2 handfuls of Thai basil leaves
2 handfuls of snow pea (mangetout) sprouts, or pea shoots
2 long green chillies, sliced

Add enough water to just cover the chicken (but don't add the chicken yet) to a saucepan, with a splash of fish sauce. Bring to a simmer over a medium heat, then add the chicken. Reduce the heat to low and poach, with the water not moving, for 10 minutes. Turn off the heat and stand for 10 minutes. Remove the chicken, then rest for a few minutes before slicing.

Meanwhile, slice the cheeks off the mangoes. Cut the flesh into a checkerboard pattern, then cut each cheek into quarters. Dress on the serving plate to catch all the juices – sprinkle with the red chilli, splash on some fish sauce and squeeze the juice of a lime over.

Cook the noodles as per the packet instructions, then refresh in cold water and cut into shorter lengths.

Add the noodles to a bowl with the oil and 1½ tablespoons fish sauce, then toss to combine. Pile on the serving plate, then arrange the chicken and prawns next to the noodles.

Add the salad ingredients to a bowl. Dress with a little of the nuoc cham and toss. Pile the salad next to the noodles and chicken. Spoon the nuoc cham generously over everything, then scatter the peanuts over. Serve with any remaining nuoc cham, and the lime cheeks on the side.

Make it different
The poaching technique used here can be used whenever you need poached chicken, with the water seasoned with salt rather than fish sauce, depending on the application.

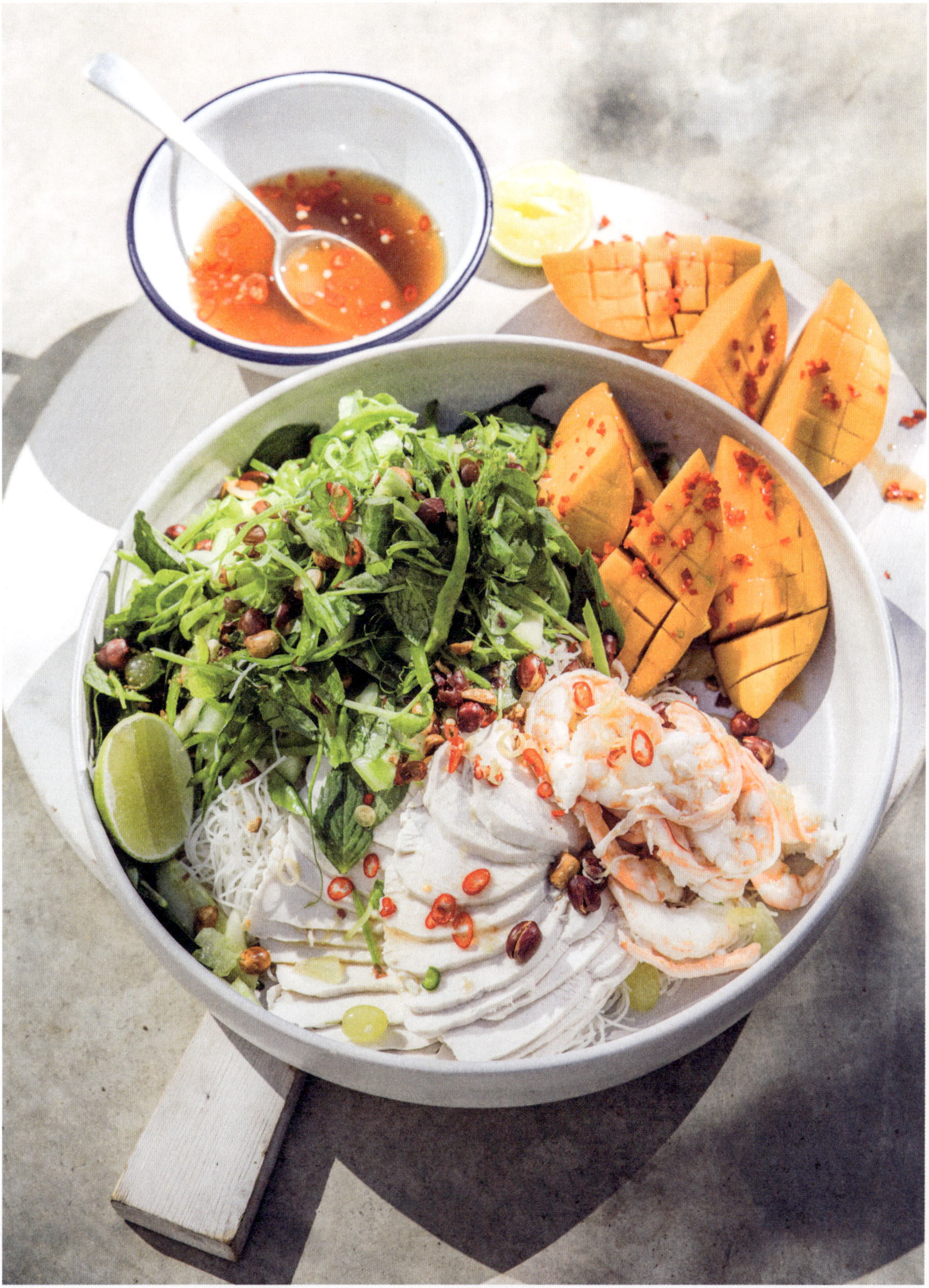

Crispy sweet-chilli chicken with wombok, Thai basil & peanuts

The secret to this dish is rendering the fat from the chicken skin while crisping it up and building deeply intense flavours, which will fill the house with the most amazing aroma of caramelised chicken. And the crispy, crunchy result, dressed with chilli sauce, peanuts, lime and a bounty of herbs, is just a stunning combination. Do not attempt this dish with skinless chicken. **Serves 6**

Pair with

Steamed jasmine rice and greens. A few giant prawn (shrimp) crackers wouldn't go astray, either.

8 chicken thigh chops, skin on
2½ tablespoons Thai-style chilli jam (p. 96)
2 handfuls of Thai basil leaves
2 handfuls of coriander (cilantro) leaves

2 long red chillies, sliced on an angle
2 red Asian shallots, sliced
3 tablespoons fried shallots (see p. 600)
3 tablespoons toasted peanuts, crushed

juice of 1 lime, plus lime cheeks to garnish
1 tablespoon fish sauce
½ wombok (Chinese cabbage), cut into wedges

Staples
S&P

Heat a large frying pan over a high heat for about 4 minutes, until very hot. Season the chicken with salt and add to the dry pan, skin side down. Turn the heat down to medium and cook for 8 minutes, until the chicken is deeply golden and the skin is very crisp. Flip the chops over, cover with a piece of baking paper and weigh down with a saucepan or another frying pan. Cook for 6 minutes, then remove the top pan and paper, flip the chicken again and cook for a few more minutes. Absorb the fat with paper towel. Drizzle with the chilli sauce, toss, then turn off the heat and stand for 5–10 minutes.

Add the herbs, chilli, sliced shallots, half the fried shallots and half the peanuts to a bowl. Dress with the lime juice and fish sauce, then toss to combine.

Arrange the wombok on a serving plate and pile the salad on top, finishing with the remaining fried shallots and peanuts. Pile the chicken next to the salad, drizzling all the pan juices over the top. Serve with lime cheeks.

Iraqi chicken with tomato & cardamom rice GF

My friend Allona has cooked this dish for me quite often, and I just love the fragrantly exotic quality of what is essentially a simple tray-baked chicken. The rice is stained red from the tomato and so delicately perfumed, with a crisply crunchy crust. So simple, yet so beautiful. Superb dolloped with tart yoghurt, this makes a perfect midweek meal, and is wonderful as part of a more involved spread. **Serves 4–6**

3 tablespoons extra-virgin olive oil
1 × 1.6 kg (3½ lb) chicken, cut into 8 pieces (p. 229), or 6–8 chicken chops (skin on)
80 g (2¾ oz) butter
1 onion, finely diced
4 garlic cloves, finely sliced

400 g (14 oz/2 cups) basmati rice
10 cardamom pods, bruised
400 g (14 oz) tin diced tomatoes, or 6 ripe tomatoes, diced
60 g (2 oz) tomato paste (concentrated purée)

800 ml (27 fl oz) White chicken stock (p. 54)
zest of ½ lemon
5 dill or coriander (cilantro) sprigs, picked
200 g (7 oz) plain yoghurt

Staples
S&P

Preheat the oven to 180°C (350°F) fan-forced.

Heat the oil in a wide flameproof casserole dish. Brown the chicken pieces all over, about 8 minutes, seasoning with salt and pepper as you go. Remove the chicken and set aside.

Add the butter and cook the onion and garlic until starting to brown, about 10 minutes. Add the rice and cardamom, season and cook for 3 minutes to heat the rice. Add the tomato, tomato paste and stock, then stir through to coat. Bring to a simmer and turn off the heat.

Sprinkle the lemon zest over, then lay the chicken pieces on top. Cover with baking paper, then foil. Transfer to the oven and bake for 30 minutes, then uncover and bake for a further 15–20 minutes, until golden.

Once cooked, place the dish over a high heat to crust the rice, about 3 minutes. Scatter with the herbs, squeeze over the zested lemon and serve the yoghurt on the side.

Roast chicken with coriander seeds, thyme & tomato (GF)

A gently spiced dry marinade adds a surprising warmth and intensity to what is otherwise a very simple tray-baked chicken. Another key step is finishing with the vinegar, which really brightens and enhances the cooking and resting juices.
Serves 4

1 × 1.6 kg (3½ lb) chicken, cut into 8 pieces (see p. 229), or 8 chicken chops (skin on)
3 tablespoons coriander seeds
2 teaspoons black peppercorns

8 garlic cloves, skin on
2 tablespoons salt flakes
1 teaspoon chilli flakes
6 thyme sprigs
250 g (9 oz) cherry tomatoes, cut in half and squashed a little

2 tablespoons extra-virgin olive oil
1 tablespoon sherry vinegar, or red-wine vinegar

Add the chicken pieces to a large plastic sealed bag (I wash and reuse mine, rather than contributing to the overuse of plastic).

Semi-grind the coriander seeds and peppercorns using a mortar and pestle. Add the garlic, salt and chilli flakes and crush to a paste.

Transfer the spice mix to the bag along with the thyme, tomatoes and oil, seal the bag and massage into the chicken. Marinate for 30 minutes at room temperature – or refrigerate for longer, ideally overnight.

Preheat the oven to 220°C (430°F) fan-forced.

Tip the chicken into a 25 × 40 cm (10 × 15¾ in) baking dish (or one that fits the chicken snugly), skin side up. Roast for about 50 minutes, until golden.

Drizzle the vinegar over the cooked chicken and rest, uncovered, for 5 minutes. Serve with the pan juices spooned over the top.

Pair with

Classic potato mash (p. 625) and a simple leaf salad.

Chinese-style roasted chicken

A fragrant, Chinese-style roasted chicken is very achievable at home. Combine 2 tablespoons salt flakes and 1 teaspoon Chinese five-spice (p. 10), then rub all over a rinsed and dried 1.6 kg (3½ lb) chicken, including inside the cavity. Separate the skin from the breasts (see p. 229) and distribute 3 finely sliced garlic cloves across the flesh. Stuff the cavity with 4 crushed garlic cloves, 2 roughly chopped spring onions (scallions), greens and all. Slice a 5 cm (2 in) piece of fresh ginger and add that, too. Rub the outside of the bird with 2 teaspoons sesame oil, place on a rack over a roasting tin and roast as per the simple method on p. 229. Once cooked, add the juices to a small saucepan with 2 tablespoons light soy sauce, bring to a simmer, then strain. Serve the chicken and sauce with rice and Asian greens (see p. 398).

Dry-fried chicken GF

Cut a slash across 10 skin-on chicken chops, about 1 cm (½ in) deep. Make a marinade by combining the following in a large bowl: 45 ml (1½ fl oz) extra-virgin olive oil, 2 finely grated garlic cloves, 2½ tablespoons malt vinegar, 1 tablespoon vegetable stock (bouillon) powder, 1 tablespoon brown sugar, 1 tablespoon salt flakes and 1½ teaspoons ground turmeric. Add the chicken pieces and toss to thoroughly coat. Marinate overnight if possible, or for as long as you can, removing from the fridge an hour before cooking. Preheat the oven to 180°C (350°F) fan-forced. Mix 3 tablespoons cornflour (cornstarch) or potato starch into the marinade until combined, coating the chicken thoroughly. Spread the chicken pieces on a lined baking tray. Roast for 45 minutes, then rest for 5 minutes before serving. Serves 4–6.

Brined roast chicken, Greek-style, with magic smashed potatoes GF

The emblematically Greek flavours of lemon and oregano are the ones I use most at home for both chicken and lamb, among other things. Taking the time to boil and squash the potatoes makes such a difference, as you expose the fluffy interior, allowing all those ragged edges to become golden and crisp, while the skins become so glassy and crunchy. **Serves 4–6 as a main**

300 g (10½ oz) fine salt
3.5 litres (118 fl oz/14 cups) water
1 × 1.6 kg (3½ lb) chicken
8 large, creamy yellow-fleshed potatoes (such as Dutch cream), scrubbed

2½ tablespoons dried Greek oregano (rigani)
1 onion, sliced 2.5 cm (1 in) thick
2 lemons, sliced
1 garlic bulb, skin on, cloves separated and smashed

Staples
EVOO, S&P

Dissolve the salt in the water, heating if necessary, but cool before adding the chicken. Immerse the chicken in the brine, making sure the cavity fills with the water. Weigh the chicken down with a plate to keep it submerged, then refrigerate overnight or for 12 hours.

Once brined, drain and dry well. Refrigerating the chicken uncovered for a few hours or another day will yield very crisp skin, or just pat dry thoroughly and stand at room temperature.

Preheat the oven to 200°C (400°F) fan-forced.

Meanwhile, add the potatoes to a saucepan of cold salted water. Bring to the boil and cook for 20–25 minutes, until tender. Drain, then squash the potatoes so they split and flatten.

Rub the chicken with oil. Sprinkle half the oregano over and season with pepper. Arrange the onion in a roasting tin, to make a trivet, and crown with the chicken. Surround with the potatoes, lemon and garlic. Season the potatoes, scatter with the remaining oregano and drizzle with oil. Roast for 1 hour 10 minutes.

Rest the chicken for 15 minutes before serving.

Make it faster
You can skip the brining altogether and roast the chicken as is.

Make it different
Boost the brine with drained sauerkraut, Kimchi (p. 455), olives or any other pickling liquid. Just replace 600 ml (20½ fl oz) of the water with whatever pickling liquid you have, then halve the salt in the recipe.

Roasted lemongrass & turmeric chicken steaks

This is a supremely versatile Vietnamese-inspired chicken dish, which can be used in myriad ways. **Serves 8**

8 chicken chops, skin on, boned (see p. 229)

Lemongrass & turmeric marinade

2 lemongrass stems, finely sliced on a steep angle

20 g (¾ oz) piece of fresh turmeric (about 6 cm/2½ in), peeled and finely grated

2 red bird's eye chillies, split lengthways

2½ tablespoons fish sauce

2 tablespoons rice vinegar

2 heaped tablespoons brown sugar

1 heaped tablespoon vegetable stock (bouillon) powder

2 teaspoons ground white pepper

Combine the marinade ingredients in a bowl, stirring to dissolve the sugar, then spread half out evenly in a shallow dish or storage container. Lay the chicken on top, then spread the remaining marinade over the chicken. Ideally refrigerate overnight, but a few hours will still be worthwhile.

When ready to cook, preheat the oven to 200°C (400°F) fan-forced.

Spread the chicken chops in a roasting tin, reserving the marinade for basting, and cook for 40 minutes. Baste halfway through, then pour over the marinade.

Set aside to rest for 5 minutes, basting a few times, then serve.

Make it different

With another protein. Quails or boned poussins are equally good cooked this way – as are pork loin steaks or pork scotch steaks.

Pair with

Serve with rice, with some finely shaved wombok (Chinese cabbage) and crushed peanuts over the top, and your favourite condiments on the side – a little Fermented cooked chilli sauce (p. 97) mixed with the pan juices makes a good accompaniment.

Use the sliced chicken in a bánh mì with coriander (cilantro), cucumber, chilli, pickles and a drizzle of cooking juices.

Slice and serve cold in a wrap or sandwich.

Slice finely and toss through a salad with vegetables, pickles, and herbs such as coriander (cilantro), Vietnamese mint and/or Thai basil.

Shred and add to a rice noodle salad or ramen soup (pp. 58–9).

Roast chicken & black barley salad

This is a merging of roast chicken and side salads, or perhaps the deconstruction of a chicken salad. Either way, there's something about the way the cooking juices merge with the salad components that makes an awful lot of sense to me. Roast any of your favourite vegetables as well as, or instead of, the carrots. **Serves 4**

1 × 1.6 kg (3½ lb) chicken

⅓ bunch of thyme

½ lemon

150 g (5½ oz) unsalted butter, at room temperature

2 large red onions, skin on, thickly sliced

6 garlic cloves, skin on, bruised

6 carrots, halved lengthways

Black barley salad

250 g (9 oz) black barley

2 tablespoons sherry vinegar

2 tablespoons extra-virgin olive oil

50 g (1¾ oz) toasted hazelnuts

1 baby cos (romaine) lettuce, cut in half lengthways, then sliced in three

5 dill sprigs, fronds picked

5 flat-leaf (Italian) parsley sprigs, leaves picked

½ red onion, finely sliced

Staples

EVOO, LMN, S&P

Preheat the oven to 200°C (400°F) fan-forced.

Pat the chicken dry inside and out with paper towel. Stuff the cavity with the thyme, lemon and 30 g (1 oz) of the butter. Gently separate the skin from the breasts, then distribute the remaining butter under the skin. Season the skin with salt and pepper and coat with oil.

Arrange the onion slices in a baking dish, then sit the chicken on top. Scatter the garlic and carrot around the chicken. Drizzle the carrot with oil and season.

Roast the chicken for 1 hour 10 minutes, then remove from the oven and rest loosely under foil for 20 minutes.

Meanwhile, for the salad, add the barley to a large saucepan of cold water, bring to the boil, then simmer for 15–20 minutes, until just tender. Drain well, then add to a bowl.

Once the chicken has rested, strain the pan juices into a jug. Dress the barley with half the pan juices, the vinegar and the oil. Season and toss, then pile on the side of a serving plate.

Cut the chicken into eight to ten pieces, or tear into large pieces. Take the garlic cloves from the baking dish and squeeze the garlic flesh from their skins into a bowl. Add the cooked onion slices and half the toasted hazelnuts, squeeze in some lemon juice and stir through.

Toss the lettuce, herbs and finely sliced onion in another bowl. Dress with most of the remaining pan juices and squeeze over a little lemon.

Pile the leaves next to the barley, arranging the hazelnut mixture and roasted carrot next to the leaves. Pile the chicken to the side. Scatter the remaining nuts over and drizzle with the remaining pan juices.

Lebanese skewered chicken with cumin, lemon, black pepper & garlic

Pair with

A chopped tomato and cucumber salad or Beetroot tabouleh (p. 419).

Garlic, cumin, lemon and black pepper are a great fall back for chicken, and an easy way to pack it with plenty of flavour. The addition of haloumi and capsicum (bell pepper) is a simple way to elevate the dish. This recipe has a strong Lebanese and Turkish influence. **Serves 6**

900 g (2 lb) boneless chicken thighs, cut into 3 cm (1¼ in) dice
2 green capsicums (bell peppers), cut into 3 cm (1¼ in) dice
200 g (7 oz) haloumi, cut into 2 cm (¾ in) dice
1 lemon, cut in half

pitta (see p. 854) breads, to serve
plain yoghurt, to serve

Cumin & lemon marinade
80 ml (2½ fl oz/⅓ cup) extra-virgin olive oil
2 garlic cloves, finely grated

1 tablespoon cumin seeds, lightly ground
juice and zest of 1 lemon

Staples
S&P

Special equipment
12 metal skewers

Preheat a barbecue on high.

Add the marinade ingredients to a large bowl, season with salt and pepper and combine. Add the chicken and toss to coat.

Skewer the chicken alternately with the capsicum and haloumi. Grill for about 4 minutes on each side, until cooked through.

Meanwhile, grill the lemon halves until charred, and grill the pitta breads to warm through.

Serve the grilled chicken in the pitta breads with a dollop of yoghurt, and the charred lemon squeezed over.

Roast chicken & black barley salad

Syrian chicken with ginger, lemon & saffron ⓖⒻ

This is a dish I've been cooking for years, and it has developed a life of its own. The spices develop such a deep flavour profile, and there's a lovely sweetness from the currants and honey. And even with that list of ingredients, it's simple and quick to cook. **Serves 4**

Pair with

Couscous or rice, to soak up all the juices.

Baked buttered rice (p. 384).

Labneh (p. 362).

2 teaspoons salt flakes
2 teaspoons ground cumin
2 teaspoons ground cinnamon
1 teaspoon ground black pepper
1 teaspoon ground turmeric
1.6 kg (3½ lb) chicken, cut into 8 pieces (p. 229), or 8 chicken chops (skin on)
100 ml (3½ fl oz) extra-virgin olive oil

2 onions, thickly sliced
100 g (3½ oz) fresh ginger, peeled and cut into matchsticks
5 garlic cloves, peeled and smashed
2 red bird's eye chillies, split lengthways
2 tomatoes, coarsely chopped
2 pinches of saffron threads
½ teaspoon cumin seeds

5 thyme sprigs, leaves picked
zest and juice of 1 lemon
2 tablespoons honey
100 g (3½ oz/⅔ cup) currants
2 tablespoons vegetable stock (bouillon) powder
½ bunch of coriander (cilantro), leaves picked

Combine the salt and ground spices in a bowl. Add the chicken pieces and toss to coat.

Heat the oil in a large heavy-based saucepan over a high heat. Add the chicken and brown on all sides, about 8 minutes. Remove the chicken from the pan, leaving the oil behind.

Cook the onion, ginger, garlic and chilli until softened, about 3 minutes. Add the tomato, saffron, cumin seeds and thyme and cook for 2 minutes. Return the chicken to the pan and add the lemon zest and juice, honey, currants, stock powder and enough water to just cover the chicken. Cover and simmer over a medium heat for 10 minutes, then uncover and simmer for 10–15 minutes, until the chicken is tender and the sauce slightly reduced. Stir in the coriander just before serving.

Butter chicken ⓖⒻ

This version of butter chicken is lively and fragrant, with a nutty undertone. Its mildly spicy and buttery nature have made it a firm family favourite in my house. **Serves 6-8**

Pair with

Basmati rice and Naan (p. 855), and perhaps some dal (pp. 387–9) and poppadoms.

juice of 2 limes
1 tablespoon salt flakes
2 teaspoons chilli powder
1.6 kg (3½ lb) boneless chicken thighs, each cut in half
100 g (3½ oz/1 cup) ground almonds
2½ tablespoons Garam masala (p. 15)
2½ tablespoons ground coriander
3½ tablespoons ground cumin
1 teaspoon ground turmeric

250 g (9 oz/1 cup) plain yoghurt
3 tablespoons extra-virgin olive oil
2 red capsicums (bell peppers), cut into 4 cm (1½ in) dice
2 onions, finely sliced
10 garlic cloves, finely chopped
5 cm (2 in) piece of fresh ginger, peeled and finely chopped
1 bay leaf
400 ml (13½ fl oz) tomato passata (puréed tomatoes)

2 tablespoons tomato paste (concentrated purée)
700 ml litres (23½ fl oz) White chicken stock (p. 54)
1 tablespoon fenugreek seeds (optional)
2 long red chillies, split lengthways
60 g (2 oz/½ cup) unsalted butter
½ bunch of coriander (cilantro), leaves and fine stems picked

Staples
S&P

Combine the lime juice, salt and chilli powder in a large bowl. Add the chicken and mix to thoroughly coat.

Heat a dry frying pan over a medium heat. Add the ground almonds and toast for 2 minutes, then add the garam masala, tossing the pan frequently until fragrant, about 30 seconds. Turn off the heat, add the ground coriander, cumin and turmeric and toss to combine. Combine half the spice mix with the yoghurt and add to the chicken. Mix through to coat, then set aside to marinate for 1 hour.

Heat the oil in a large saucepan over a medium heat. Add the capsicum, onion, garlic, ginger, bay leaf and the remaining spice mix. Season with salt and fry until the onion is golden, about 8 minutes. Add the chicken and marinade and cook for about 5 minutes.

Stir in the passata, tomato paste, stock, fenugreek seeds and chilli, then simmer gently for 40–50 minutes, until the chicken is tender and the sauce has reduced by half. Adjust the seasoning as needed, then transfer to a serving dish.

Melt the butter in a small saucepan and cook until just turning nut brown. Pour over the chicken, then top with the coriander and serve.

Chicken & corn koftas with avocado & coriander

These super-bright and light rissoles make great snacks and finger food for entertaining, or can be served as a main with salad or slaw and rice. They're also delicious cold, so any leftovers are great for a packed lunch. **Makes 10–12**

Short cut

In place of the charred corn, use 200 g (7 oz/1 cup) cooked corn kernels.

Pair with

A green salad or slaw (see p. 448), with Baked buttered rice (p. 384) on the side.

Pop into warm tortillas or soft buns with a spicy mayo (see p. 620), or some sour cream and Fermented cooked chilli sauce (p. 97).

2 corn cobs
1 large onion, finely diced
2 large garlic cloves, finely grated
3 teaspoons ground cumin
1 teaspoon smoked paprika
1 teaspoon chilli powder

80 g (2¾ oz/1 cup) fresh breadcrumbs
500 g (1 lb 2 oz) minced (ground) chicken thighs
1 handful of coriander (cilantro) leaves, chopped, plus extra leaves to serve

1 egg, lightly whisked
½ teaspoon salt
2 ripe avocados
1 lime

Staples
EVOO, S&P

Brush the corn with oil, season with salt and grill until tender and charred, 6–8 minutes, turning regularly. Once cool enough to handle, shave the kernels off the cob using a large knife.

Preheat the oven to 180°C (350°F) fan-forced. Line a baking tray with baking paper. Preheat a chargrill pan on high until very hot.

Heat a splash of oil in a medium frying pan over a medium heat. Add the onion, garlic, cumin, paprika and chilli powder and fry until the onion has softened, about 3 minutes.

Tip the onion mixture into a large bowl, along with the corn kernels, breadcrumbs, chicken, chopped coriander, egg, salt and a generous grind of black pepper. Mix with your hands until well combined, then lightly oil your hands and roll the mixture into egg-sized balls.

Heat a large frying pan over a medium heat. Add a splash of oil and cook the koftas in batches, flattening them a little as they cook, for 2–3 minutes on each side until golden.

Transfer to the baking tray and bake for 6–8 minutes, until just cooked through.

Dice the avocado and spread out on a serving platter. Squeeze the lime over and season with salt and pepper. Pile the koftas on top, scatter with the coriander leaves and serve.

Persian roast chicken on buttered rice with quince paste & bay leaves GF

This is a version of a baked chicken and rice dish that has featured on my restaurant menus over the years. I just love the spiced buttery rice, which becomes infused with all the cooking and resting juices from the chicken. And while it may seem unusual, the quince paste melts into the rice, adding a delightful touch of perfumed sweetness. You could naturally skip the brining step, but a little forward planning does really elevate the result. **Serves 4–6**

300 g (10½ oz) fine salt
3.5 litres (118 fl oz/14 cups) cold water
1 × 1.6 kg (3½ lb) chicken
350 g (12½ oz/1¾ cups) basmati rice
160 g (5½ oz) butter

2 large white onions, sliced into half-moons 1 cm (½ in) thick
5 garlic cloves, finely sliced
1 tablespoon cumin seeds
80 g (2¾ oz) Quince paste (p. 717), cut into 3 cm (1¼ in) dice

1 litre (34 fl oz/4 cups) Golden chicken stock (p. 54)
3 fresh bay leaves
1 lemon, with half the zest peeled

Staples
S&P

Dissolve the salt in the water, heating if necessary, but cool before adding the chicken. Immerse the chicken in the brine, making sure the cavity fills with water. Weigh the chicken down with a plate to keep it submerged, then refrigerate for 4 hours, or ideally overnight. Once brined, drain and dry well.

Preheat the oven to 200°C (400°F) fan-forced.

Add the rice to a 20 cm × 30 cm (8 in × 12 in) baking dish or enamel tray.

Melt half the butter in a large deep frying pan over a medium heat. Add the chicken, breast side down, and sear for about 5 minutes to brown, then rotate the bird to sear all sides for a few minutes on each side. Place on the rice, breast side up.

Add the remaining butter to the pan, then the onion, garlic and cumin seeds, and cook until softened and lightly coloured, about 6 minutes. Don't let the pan get too hot, as you don't want the butter to burn. Season generously with salt and pepper, then spread the mixture on top of the rice, spooning all the residual butter over the chicken. Season the bird well with pepper, then randomly push the quince paste into the rice.

Return the pan to the heat and add the stock. Bring to a simmer and stir to deglaze the pan, then pour over the rice.

Push two bay leaves into the rice, then stuff the other one into the cavity of the chicken, with the lemon zest. Squeeze the lemon juice over the rice. Cover with baking paper, then foil.

Roast for 40 minutes, then uncover and bake for about 25 minutes, until the chicken is golden.

Rest the chicken uncovered for 15 minutes, before carving in the dish, so the rice catches all the juices.

Pair with

A leafy salad with spinach and some yoghurt sauce (see p. 558) with chopped mint stirred through, or your favourite spicy sauce.

Roast carrots.

Brussels sprouts.

Roast chicken with butter & dill GF

Smash 4 garlic cloves and 1½ tablespoons salt flakes to a paste in a mortar, then add 150 g (5½ oz) of soft unsalted butter and combine. Mix in a bunch of dill that has been picked and finely chopped and grind in plenty of black pepper. Separate the skin from the breast and thighs of a 1.4–1.6 kg (3 lb 1 oz–3½ lb) chicken gently with your hands (see p. 229) and spread the butter mix across the flesh. Insert a cut lemon into the cavity and season the skin with sweet paprika and salt flakes. Set the bird on top of thickly sliced onions in a roasting tray, cover with foil and roast at 200°C (400°F) fan-forced for 30 minutes, then uncover and roast for 30 minutes to brown. Rest for 20 minutes lightly covered with foil, then carve, serving with the buttery juices. You can also toss boiled potatoes in the juices and serve with roasted carrots and buttered peas, or grilled zucchini (courgette) tossed with soft feta.

Japanese-style chicken meatballs

These meatballs draw on Japanese flavours, but are not actually based on a classic dish as such – just a cook playing around. They are quite delicious and very versatile, though. Serve as finger food or a starter, drop in a broth, or serve with rice and other Japanese (or Japanese-inspired) dishes. **Makes 20**

Pair with

Steamed Japanese rice, Chawanmushi (p. 356) and Pressed spinach with sesame (p. 561).

Skip the mayo and add the meatballs to a miso broth, or to a chicken broth with udon noodles and greens.

750 g (1 lb 11 oz) ground (minced) chicken thighs
6 cm (2½ in) piece of fresh ginger, peeled and finely grated
2 garlic cloves, finely grated
1½ tablespoons soy sauce
1 tablespoon miso paste
1 tablespoon maple syrup

80 g (2¾ oz/1⅓ cups) panko breadcrumbs
½ teaspoons salt flakes
½ teaspoons ground white pepper
1 egg
10 shiitake mushrooms, stems removed

50 g (1¾ oz/⅓ cup) sesame seeds
3 tablespoons kewpie mayonnaise
3 nori sheets, finely shredded
togarashi, to serve

Staples
EVOO

Preheat the oven to 200°C (400°F). Line a baking tray with baking paper.

Add the chicken to a food processor, along with the ginger, garlic, soy sauce, miso paste, maple syrup, panko, salt and pepper. Blitz for 30 seconds, then add the egg and blitz for another 30 seconds or so, until well combined.

Add the shiitake mushrooms, cap side down, to a large frying pan over a medium–high heat. Dry roast for 10 minutes, then slice finely and mix the shiitake through the chicken mixture by hand.

Spread the sesame seeds on a plate or tray. Lightly oil your hands and roll the chicken mixture into meatballs the size of golf balls (or smaller if serving as a finger food). Roll them in the sesame seeds and place on the baking tray.

Drizzle some oil over and bake for 10 minutes, then remove from the oven and rest for 2 minutes to finish cooking.

Spoon a small dollop of mayo on a serving plate, place a chicken ball on top of the mayo, then top with another small dollop of mayo. Top with nori, sprinkle with togarashi and serve.

Left-over chicken, barley & vegetable soup

This is the soup – or endlessly different versions of it – I make when I have a little left-over chicken on a picked-over roast. Truth is, I always try to keep a leg intact, as I do love this soup, and drumstick and thigh meat are best. Treat this recipe as a base to add whatever you like. Brown rice works instead of barley, use cavolo nero or kale instead of silverbeet (Swiss chard), toss in some frozen peas at the end, a sprinkling of smoked paprika tilts the profile … The key is that it's a chicken-flavoured broth with grains, plenty of vegetables and the occasional piece of chicken. **Serves 8–10**

120 g (4½ oz) pearled barley
1 large onion, finely diced
4 large garlic cloves, finely sliced
4 celery stalks, cut lengthways in three, then finely sliced
2 leeks, white part only, sliced into rounds
2 carrots, cut into 5 mm (¼ in) dice
½ fennel bulb, cut into rough 3 cm (1¼ in) dice
2 teaspoons ground cumin

2 teaspoons ground fennel
2 fresh bay leaves
½ bunch of silverbeet (Swiss chard), sliced 1 cm (½ in) across, including most of the stem
2 handfuls of green beans, cut into 2 cm (¾ in) lengths
2 zucchini (courgettes), cut into 1 cm (½ in) dice

Stock
1 left-over roast chicken carcass, preferably with a leg intact

5 black peppercorns
4 garlic cloves, skin on, smashed
1 large brown onion, skin on, quartered
1 fresh bay leaf
1 vegetable stock (bouillon) cube, crumbled

Staples
EVOO, S&P

To make the stock, pick all the meat left on the carcass and the leg. Chop the meat into small dice and set aside. Place the bones, skin and any jelly and fat into a large pot with the remaining ingredients and cover with cold water. Bring to a simmer and cook for 30 minutes.

Strain off the liquid and discard the bones and aromatics; you should have about 1.5–2 litres (51–68 fl oz/6–8 cups) stock.

Simmer the barley in salted water for 10 minutes, then drain.

Heat a good splash of oil in a large saucepan over a medium heat. Add the onion and garlic and cook until softened, about 4 minutes. Add the celery, leek, carrot and fennel and cook over a lowish heat for about 20 minutes, until caramelised.

Stir in the spices, add the bay leaves, silverbeet and barley, season with salt and pepper and cook for about 10 minutes. Add the beans, zucchini and stock, then bring to a simmer. Cook for 20 minutes, adding water if needed.

Stir the reserved chicken meat through, simmer for a minute or so, adjust the seasoning as needed and serve.

Roast chicken with spiced yoghurt crust (GF)

In a blender, blitz 1 roughly chopped onion, 5 roughly chopped garlic cloves, a 5 cm (2 in) piece of fresh ginger, peeled and roughly chopped, 1 tablespoon extra-virgin olive oil and 2 teaspoons salt flakes to a smooth paste. Add to a saucepan and fry over a medium heat until golden, about 10 minutes. Tip into a bowl, then stir in the zest and juice of 1 lime. Add 200 g (7 oz) plain yoghurt, 2 teaspoons Garam masala (p. 15), 2 teaspoons ground cumin and 1 teaspoon ground black or white pepper and combine. Smear the paste all over 1 × 1.6 kg (3 lb 8 oz) chicken, inside and out. Marinate, uncovered, in the fridge for at least 1 hour or overnight. Make sure the bird sits at room temperature for 30 minutes before cooking. Preheat the oven to 200°C (400°F) fan-forced. Roast the chicken on a rack in a roasting tin (or in the roasting tin on a 'trivet' of thickly sliced onions) for 1 hour 10 minutes. Rest, uncovered, for 15 minutes before serving. Serves 4–6.

Chicken noodle broth with porcini polpette

There are a few unusual turns in this recipe, with shiitake mushrooms bolstering the porcini flavour in the polpette and unleashing their umami stores, and a little maple syrup adding the slightest sweetness and a whole lot of depth – but at its heart it is a nourishing bowl of chicken noodle soup with meatballs.
Serves 4

10 shiitake mushrooms, stems removed
2 litres (68 fl oz/8 cups) Golden or Double chicken stock (p. 54)
200 g (7 oz) dried long pasta, or two bundles of instant ramen noodles (about 95 g/3 oz each)
½ bunch of flat-leaf (Italian) parsley, leaves finely chopped

Polpette
750 g (1 lb 11 oz) minced (ground) chicken
80 g (2¾ oz/1⅓ cups) panko breadcrumbs
80 g (2¾ oz) parmesan, finely grated
2 tablespoons Porcini powder (p. 570)
2 garlic cloves, finely grated
1 tablespoon maple syrup

2 teaspoons chicken stock (bouillon) powder
½ teaspoon salt flakes
½ teaspoon ground white pepper
1 egg
Staples
EVOO, S&P

Add the shiitake mushrooms, cap side down, to a large frying pan over a medium–high heat. Dry roast for 10 minutes, then slice finely and set aside.

Meanwhile, bring the stock to a simmer in a large saucepan.

For the polpette, add the chicken to a food processor, along with the panko, parmesan, porcini powder, garlic, maple syrup, stock powder, salt and pepper. Blitz for 30 seconds, then add the egg and blitz for another 30 seconds or so, until well combined. Mix the shiitake through by hand. Lightly oil your hands and roll the mixture into meatballs the size of golf balls.

Heat a little oil in a frying pan over a high heat. Add the meatballs in batches, rolling around to seal on all sides, 3–4 minutes.

Break the pasta into the simmering broth and add the meatballs. Cook until the pasta is cooked, about 8 minutes.

Stir in the parsley, season with salt and pepper and serve.

Make it different
With greens. Add a handful of peas or baby English spinach leaves to warm through just before serving.

To make a more substantial meal, double the size of the meatballs, pan-sear until browned, then roast on a lined tray at 200°C (400°F) for about 10 minutes. Serve as a main course for four people, with Classic potato mash (p. 625) or buttered risoni pasta; the roasted polpette are also delicious cold, sliced and layered in a sandwich or roll.

Also see

Duck liver parfait **233**

Roasted lemongrass & turmeric quail steaks **246**

Duck rillettes with sherry **330**

Cassoulet **391**

Roasted potatoes with thyme **626**

Duck & Quail

Duck

For most Australians, duck is very much a special occasion meat, and one typically consumed in a restaurant – the most likely route either being via barbecued Peking duck pancakes, in a Thai duck curry, or perhaps a confit duck salad or pan-seared duck breast in a French-leaning restaurant. Cooking duck at home is undoubtedly a big ask for many, but it is not too much of a stretch. It can get a little messy roasting a whole duck, with blastingly high heat best to get super-crisp and golden skin, and the high fat content resulting in a bit of oven spatter – but don't let that put you off.

Pekin (or Peking) and a crossbred Aylesbury-Pekin are the most common ducks reared for meat, both in Australia and around the world. Australia's duck meat industry is somewhat fledgling, dominated by two companies, which also work with a network of smaller farms. There are some smaller quality operators in the mix, but it is currently a very small part of the picture.

Muscovy ducks used to be more prevalent, and they can still be sourced, but a longer incubation time before hatching ducklings, coupled with slow growth to full weight, has seen their numbers decline. They are originally from Central and South America, and were introduced to Europe in the 1500s. They produce a leaner, darker meat, which is prized by some, though their low fat content makes it less forgiving for the cook.

A result of ancient Chinese selective breeding, the Pekin is white with an orange bill and grows to slaughter weight quickly, in about six weeks. The meat yield is high, though not as high as the male Muscovy duck, which can weigh almost double that of a Pekin (and a female Muscovy) at maturity – though it takes twice the time to get there. Pekins can also be reliable egg layers, though Indian Runner and Khaki Campbell are the preferred commercial laying breeds.

Aylesbury ducks are originally from Aylesbury in Buckinghamshire, England, and are the classic English table duck, though subsequent crossbreeding with Pekin ducks has seen the breed decline. They are similar to Pekins but can grow to a significant size. The pale and mild but beautifully flavoured meat from a purebred Aylesbury – relatively rare these days – is a favourite of mine.

Unless you have located a free-range supplier, all commercial ducks are housed in barns. Ducks simply cannot be farmed in the same intensive way that chickens can – so, thankfully, the stocking is about one-quarter of the density. The industry maintains that rearing inside is essential to controlling predation from foxes and the like, as well as avoiding diseases from migratory birds. Naturally, there are farmers who combat these issues in other ways, including employing the services of Maremma guard dogs, which is a common practice for ethical poultry farming. The dogs form a bond with the flock and have strong protective instincts.

In Victoria, Great Ocean Ducks has been leading the charge for free-range birds, proving that the obstacles described by the mainstream industry are surmountable. They raise both Aylesbury and Pekin ducks on a naturally scrounged diet supplemented by grain and quite a bit of fruit, notably strawberries. Their market is largely top restaurants, with the farming costs suiting high-end dining far better than supermarket shelves. As it stands, the cost of these birds isn't excessive for the quality, all things considered, and the rewards, as with properly raised chickens, are great. Besides, duck is already a special occasion meat; let's not make it an anonymous protein.

Ducks have a larger frame, thicker skin, more fat and less meat than chickens, meaning they will always be relatively more expensive, but the meat is intense and flavourful, with a little going a long way. That fat is also important, as it will render out when roasting, and is a wonderful asset for making duck confit, or roasting or frying potatoes and the like – the flavour and the crunch is incomparable. For those worried about fat for health reasons, it also has a couple of positives, with a relatively high level of monounsaturated fat and linoleic acid. It's not quite olive oil, but it's not as distant as you might think.

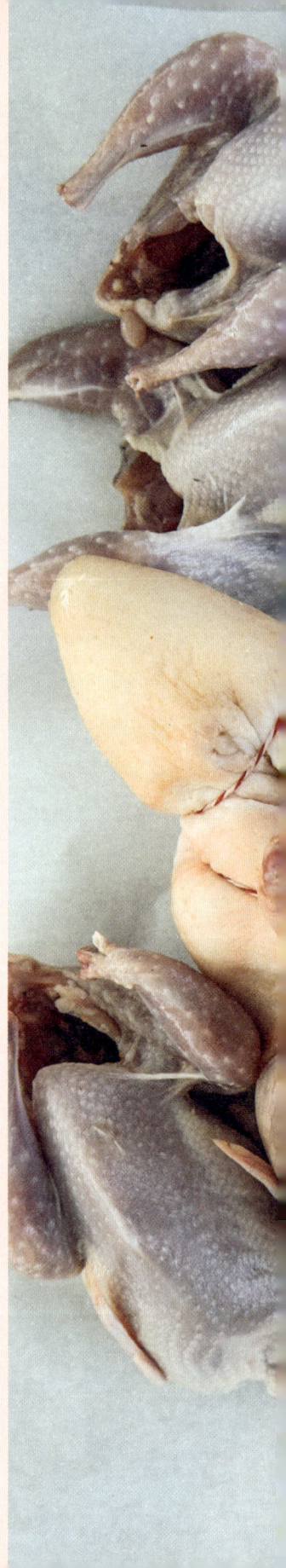

Pair with

The richness of duck pairs well with sweetness, though acidity is important also. Try duck with orange, cumquat, mandarin, cherries, plums, figs, honey, currants, barberries, brown sugar, maple syrup, pomegranate molasses, verjuice and sherry vinegar. Duck loves deep and salty flavours, such as soy sauce, kecap manis and hoisin sauce. Allspice, cinnamon, star anise, fennel seeds, cumin, baharat, white and green peppercorns and sichuan peppercorns are all wonderful spices with duck, and sage, thyme, bay leaves and coriander (cilantro) are ideal herbs. Pair with onion, spring onion (scallion), garlic, ginger, chilli, cabbage, carrot, radish, turnip, rhubarb, pumpkin (winter squash), bitter leaves, eggplant (aubergine), and mushrooms such as porcini, pine and shiitake. Almonds, pistachios, chestnuts and pine nuts all work, as do olives, lentils, couscous and freekeh.

Preparing duck

Ducks need to be slaughtered at a reasonable level of maturity to ensure there is enough meat, which will typically see a dressed bird weighing in at 2–2.5 kg (4 lb 6 oz–5½ lb). I wouldn't buy a bird under 2 kg (4 lb 6 oz) unless it came on the advice from a quality farmer or supplier.

I will often buy duck leg quarters (marylands), which are perfect for a confit (see p. 260), curry (see p. 266) or ragù (opposite). I also sometimes buy duck fat for a confit (if I don't have enough saved), and duck livers in lieu of chicken livers, to make pâté or parfait (pp. 233, 327).

When buying a whole duck, ask your supplier to pop the thigh bones out of the hip sockets and remove the wishbone. This is not essential, but it will make the bird easier to carve after cooking.

Remove the duck from its wrapping and drain off any liquid, then pat dry. Always trim away any excess fat from the neck and inside the cavity; you can render the fat to use later.

Add the fat to a pan with a splash of water and slowly warm over a low heat until liquified and clear. Strain and refrigerate, or you can freeze it. Also, be sure to save any fat after roasting, straining it before storing.

Prick the duck around the legs and neck with a knife for the fat to render out while cooking, then refrigerate on a rack over a tray or bowl for a day or two, if possible. Don't cover the bird, as you want to dry out the skin. Always remove the bird from the fridge 45 minutes before roasting.

Take a Chinese barbecued duck and …

On the cheat side, buying a Chinese barbecued duck is an easy route to making tasty bao buns or pancakes (see p. 457), or to add to a salad with rice noodles and plenty of herbs, or to shred into a soup (see p. 265), with the frame contributing to a simple home-made Duck stock (p. 266).

Roast duck & pan sauce GF

This roasting method will give you a beautifully moist result, with some pan juices to drizzle over the duck or to turn into a simple sauce.
Serves 2 generously, or 4 elegantly

1 × 2.2–2.5 kg (5–5½ lb) duck
2 teaspoons ground allspice
3 celery stalks
1 onion, thickly sliced

80 ml (2½ fl oz/⅓ cup) white-wine vinegar, or sherry vinegar
500 ml (17 fl oz/2 cups) water

50 ml (1¾ fl oz) Golden chicken stock (p. 54)
1 thyme sprig

Staples
EVOO, S&P

Trim any excess fat from the neck and inside the cavity of the duck and save it for roasting potatoes (see p. 626). Prick the skin around the legs and the neck.

Ideally, refrigerate the duck, uncovered, for a couple of days to dry out the skin. Remove from the fridge at least 45 minutes before roasting.

Preheat the oven to 220°C (430°F) fan-forced.

Dry the cavity of the duck. Rub inside and out with oil, season generously with salt and pepper, then rub the allspice over. Position the duck in a roasting tin, on top of the celery stalks and onion. Add the vinegar and water to the tin. Cover with baking paper, then foil, and roast for 40 minutes.

Uncover the tray, and reduce the oven temperature to 180°C (350°F) fan-forced. Roast for a further 1 hour, basting the duck with the pan juices a few times after the 30-minute mark.

Turn the temperature up to 220°C (430°F) fan-forced and roast for 20 minutes to crisp the skin.

Remove from the oven and rest for 20 minutes, loosely covered with foil.

Tip the juices from the cavity into the roasting tin and keep the duck warm. Strain the juices and skim off most of the fat, reserving the fat for roasting potatoes.

Add the juices, stock and thyme to a saucepan and bring to the boil. Add a tablespoon of the reserved duck fat and boil to emulsify. Once thickened and glossy, adjust the seasoning and keep warm.

Pair with

Roasted quince & chestnuts (p. 716).

Roasted rhubarb, blood plum & ginger chutney (p. 646).

Pickled cherries (see p. 566).

Gnocchi alla romana (p. 138).

Classic potato mash (p. 625) or celeriac mash.

Wombok, daikon, shiitake & tofu salad (p. 450).

Roasted beetroot (beet) or pumpkin salad (see p. 630).

Crispy eggplant with spiced caramel & fried Thai basil (p. 522).

Chicory (witlof/endive) and bitter leaf salad with a citrus or pomegranate dressing.

Roasted potatoes, and Honey & thyme gastrique (see p. 265).

Braised fresh borlotti beans (p. 432) and sautéed mushrooms.

Roasted parsnips with maple syrup (see p. 607).

To carve the duck, cut the skin between one of the legs and the body, pulling back the leg to expose the joint. Run your knife through the middle of the ball joint, cutting any skin and meat to separate the leg – it should come away easily. Now cut the drumstick from the thigh, at the joint. Repeat for the other leg. Cut the wings away from the breast. You can then slice the breast on the crown, carving down on an angle, or remove the breast and slice. This is easy enough to do by locating your knife between the breasts, against the protruding keel of sternum, then running your knife along the breastbone and down the rib cage to cut it free. Repeat for the other side.

Slice the meat and serve with the sauce.

Make it different

I also like to fill the cavity with some smashed garlic cloves and hard herbs, such as thyme, sage or bay leaves. Slices of citrus – orange, mandarin or lemon – are also good. If you stuff the duck with citrus, add the zest from half an orange when emulsifying the pan juices to make the sauce.

Duck, celeriac & verjuice ragù ⓖⓕ

Duck legs make such a luxurious and indulgent ragù, and it's quite easy to achieve a deeply complex result in much less time than with beef and/or pork. In fact, cooking for too long will do it a disservice, with the meat becoming stringy. The sweetness and acidity of verjuice and earthiness of celeriac are ideal pairings with the duck, making for a very satisfying meal served with pasta, which I always crown with a salad of shredded radicchio dressed in balsamic vinegar – it's a must. **Serves 6–8**

Pair with

Polenta (p. 383), Classic potato mash (p. 625) or Gnocchi alla romana (p. 138).

Short pasta (gnocchi sardi [see p. 131], pennette, giant rigatoni) or fresh pappardelle (see p. 112), with plenty of Parmigiano Reggiano on the side. I also always serve this with a salad of finely shredded radicchio dressed with good balsamic or saba and extra-virgin olive oil, scattered over each bowl of pasta. The bitter, acidic and sweet notes are perfect with the duck. If you are serving the ragù through pasta, cut the meat into largish chunks, leaving the skin on, after you remove it from the pan.

8 duck leg quarters (marylands)
315 g (11 oz/1 cup) rock salt
3 tablespoons extra-virgin olive oil
60 g (2 oz/½ cup) butter
2 onions, finely diced
1 leek, white part only, sliced into 2 cm (¾ in) rounds

8 garlic cloves, sliced
½ celeriac, peeled and cut into 1 cm (½ in) dice
2 carrots, cut into rough 1 cm (½ in) dice
½ bunch of thyme, leaves stripped
2 fresh bay leaves
1½ teaspoons ground allspice

500 ml (17 fl oz/2 cups) verjuice
250 ml (8½ fl oz/1 cup) white wine
1.5 litres (51 fl oz/6 cups) Golden chicken stock (p. 54)

Staples
S&P

Coat the duck pieces with the rock salt and set aside for 30 minutes.

Preheat the oven to 200°C (400°F) fan-forced.

Wipe the salt from the duck with damp paper towel. Arrange a rack over a roasting tin and roast the duck legs, skin side up, for 30 minutes, or until golden.

Heat the oil and butter in a wide-based saucepan over a medium heat. Add the onion, leek and garlic, season with salt and pepper and cook until softened, about 5 minutes. Add the celeriac and carrot and cook for about 15 minutes, until caramelised.

Stir the thyme, bay leaves and allspice through. Add the duck, verjuice and wine and simmer for 5 minutes.

Add the stock and simmer very gently for 50 minutes, or just before the meat falls off the bone.

Remove the duck from the pan. Reduce the liquid to a sauce consistency, then return the duck meat to the pan. Adjust the seasoning to taste and serve.

Duck leg confit GF

Confit is an old French method of cooking and preserving meat, with the meat typically salted then cooked in fat (usually from the same animal, but not always) for a long time at a low temperature. The resulting meat is incredibly tender, and will keep exceptionally well under the fat. Traditionally, the meat was layered into pottery crock pots and sealed with more fat – often with lard, which is less permeable than duck fat and will maintain a better barrier – before being stored in a cool cellar. In the right conditions, the meat could be kept for many months. These days, confit is a delicacy whose properties of longevity are almost irrelevant now, with the prize of flavour and texture being the main motivation. Duck legs are an ideal candidate for a confit, with the meat becoming so rich and tender – and, once heated, the skin crisps to a glorious crackle. You can halve the recipe, but during the cooler months I do find it great having these on hand (which is where the longevity comes in) for all sorts of dishes. Always serve hot or warm, crisping up the skin first. **Makes 12**

2 teaspoons black
  peppercorns
4 juniper berries
1 cinnamon stick
2 bay leaves
15 thyme sprigs

500 g (1 lb 2 oz) rock salt
  (or allow about 40 g/1½ oz
  per duck leg)
12 duck leg quarters
  (marylands)

1 garlic bulb, skin on, cloves
  separated and roughly
  crushed
1 kg (2 lb 3 oz) duck fat,
  melted

Staples
EVOO

Pair with

Cassoulet (p. 391).

Braised silverbeet (Swiss chard) or cavolo nero (see p. 555).

Classic potato mash (p. 625) and Beurre rouge (p. 69).

Use in a Spiced duck with pickled watermelon (p. 262).

Serve on a bed of braised lentils (see p. 387), or chickpeas (using the same lentil dressing).

Sauté brussels sprouts with pancetta or kaiserfleisch (see p. 325), top with confit duck and spoon over some simple Duck sauce (p. 262) or chicken jus (see p. 66). Some pickled grapes (see p. 630) would also be lovely with this.

Use in a bisteeya, the Moroccan pie.

Shred into Fried rice (p. 610).

Crispy reheated confit duck meat over a salad of bitter leaves.

Using a mortar and pestle, roughly crush the peppercorns, juniper, cinnamon stick, bay leaves and half the thyme, then rub into the salt in a large bowl. Toss the duck legs through the salt mix, then layer into a non-reactive dish, distributing the salt in between and over the top to completely coat.

Refrigerate for 5 hours, then remove the legs one by one, rinsing off the salt and patting dry.

Preheat the oven to 110°C (230°F) fan-forced.

Scatter the garlic and remaining thyme in a roasting tin. Add the duck fat and let it melt in the oven. Submerge the duck in one layer, topping up with oil as necessary to cover the legs. Cover with baking paper, then foil. Cook for about 5 hours, until the meat is falling from the bone.

Stand the duck in the dish until cool enough to handle, then transfer to a storage container. Cover with the fat and let it set in the fridge.

The duck will keep for up to 4 weeks if completely covered with fat, and any strained residual fat will keep for up to 3 months to reuse for confit, or to roast or fry potatoes in. (You can also remove the thigh bones by twisting them out, then refrigerate the legs on a tray, wrapped in plastic wrap, for about a week. They can then be heated up and served as is, making them easy to handle on the plate.)

To serve, reheat the duck in a 180°C (350°F) fan-forced oven, skin side up, on a lined tray, until crisp, 10–15 minutes. Drain off and reserve the excess fat (for potatoes, of course) before serving.

Make it different

With spices. This recipe is very traditional as far as flavours go. Experiment with other spices, such as cumin, coriander or fennel seeds, or cinnamon and orange rind.

Swap half the duck fat for extra-virgin olive oil.

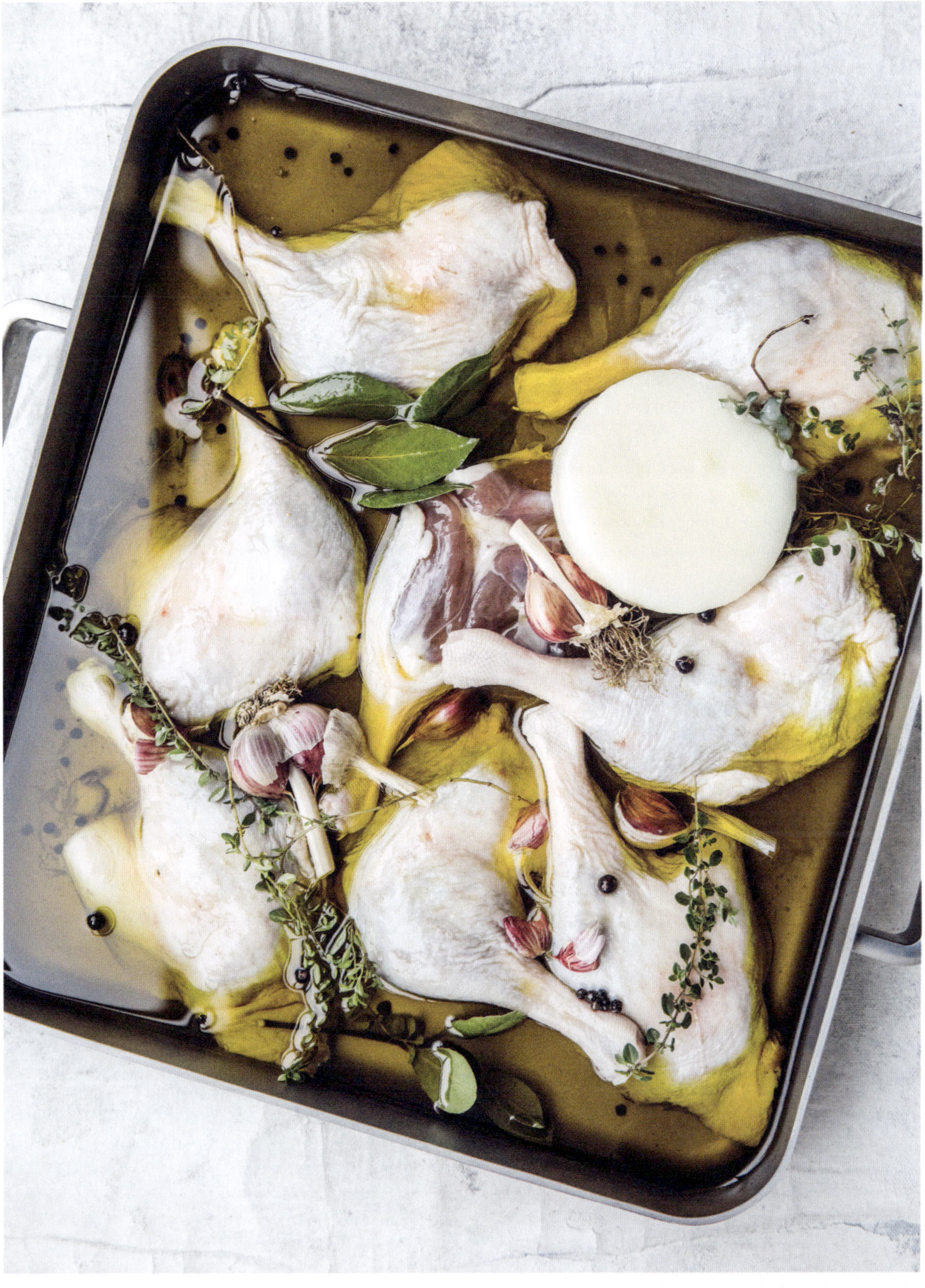

Spiced duck with pickled watermelon

Exotic and captivating, this salad is certainly in the entertaining realm. With pops of herbs, heat, and sweet and sour notes, the contrast between the pickled and fresh watermelon and the crisp, salty duck is a revelation. A perfect starter on a hot day. **Serves 4**

¼ seedless watermelon, 500 g (1 lb 2 oz) rind removed
60 ml (2 fl oz/¼ cup) gin or 1 pastis
2 teaspoons caster (superfine) sugar
150 g (5½ oz/1 cup) tapioca flour
2 tablespoons Baharat (p. 6)
oil, for shallow-frying

4 confit duck legs (see p. 260)
1 egg white, whisked
1 white onion, finely sliced
2 limes, flesh diced
2 handfuls of mint leaves
2 handfuls of pomegranate seeds
4 small ripe heirloom tomatoes, sliced
80 g (2¾ oz) very green pistachio nut kernels

Pomegranate dressing
juice of 2 limes
3 tablespoons pomegranate molasses
2 tablespoons extra-virgin olive oil
1 teaspoon caster (superfine) sugar

Staples
S&P

Trim the rind off the watermelon and slice the flesh into 3 cm (1¼ in) cubes. Transfer to a tray and sprinkle over the gin, sugar and some salt. Chill for 1 hour.

In a shallow bowl, combine the tapioca flour and baharat.

Combine the dressing ingredients in a small bowl.

Dust the confit leg in the spiced flour mix, dip it in the egg white, then in the flour mix again. Heat 10 cm (4 in) of oil in a deep frying pan until it reaches 170°C (340°F) – it will sizzle when you add the duck. Fry the duck two legs at a time until very crisp, about 5 minutes on each side. Drain.

Mix the white onion, diced lime, mint leaves and pomegranate seeds together.

Drain the pickled watermelon, then arrange it, along with the fresh watermelon, on a serving plate with the tomato. Spoon over a little dressing, top with the fried duck, then some more dressing. Add the onion mix and finish by sprinkling over the pistachio nuts.

Simple duck sauce (GF)

If twice-roasting ducks (see p. 264), you can turn the frames into a reasonably quick but intensely flavoured duck sauce. Chop each duck frame into four pieces with a heavy knife and add to a roasting tin with a quartered onion, and a carrot and 2 celery stalks chopped into 2 cm (¾ in) pieces. Roast for 30 minutes at 200°C (400°F). Transfer to a saucepan with a few smashed garlic cloves, a couple of peppercorns and some herbs such as rosemary, thyme, tarragon or sage. Pour in chicken stock – ideally a Double chicken stock (p. 54), but whatever you have – to just cover, then simmer for 30 minutes. Strain into a saucepan and reduce by two-thirds. Whisk in 100 g (3½ oz) unsalted butter to thicken the stock, then check the seasoning and serve spooned over the warmed duck.

Pan-seared duck breasts ⓖⒻ

You can use this universal method whenever you need a pink duck breast with crisp skin – whichever flavour direction you take it. **Serves 4–6**

Pair with

Pancakes or bao buns with Roasted plum & hoisin sauce (below).

Simple duck sauce (opposite).

Roasted quince & chestnuts (p. 716).

Roasted rhubarb, blood plum & ginger chutney (p. 646).

Pickled cherries (see p. 566).

Gnocchi alla romana (p. 138).

Classic potato mash (p. 625) or celeriac mash.

Salted orange, cacao nibs & coffee (see p. 264).

Wombok, daikon, shiitake & tofu salad (p. 450).

Crispy eggplant with spiced caramel & fried Thai basil (p. 522).

Chicory (witlof/endive) and bitter leaf salad with a citrus or pomegranate dressing.

Roasted potatoes, and Honey & thyme gastrique (p. 265).

Braised fresh borlotti beans in lemon & cumin stock (p. 426) and sautéed mushrooms.

Roasted parsnips with maple syrup (see p. 606).

4 × 150–180 g (5½–6½ oz)
duck breasts

Staples
EVOO, S&P

Remove the duck breasts from the fridge 30 minutes before cooking. Score the skin in a crisscross pattern, season well with salt and pepper and rub with oil.

Heat a large frying pan over a medium heat. Add the duck, skin side down. Cook for about 10 minutes to render the fat and crisp up the skin, turning the heat down a little if necessary to stop it burning. Flip the breasts over and quickly seal the other side for about 2 minutes.

Transfer to a warm plate, lightly cover with foil and rest for 10 minutes.

Serve whole, or sliced on a slight angle.

Seared duck breast with roasted plum & hoisin sauce for pancakes or bao

Whether it be Peking duck pancakes, or a bao stuffed with roasted duck meat, cucumber and a sauce of some kind, duck's rich intensity makes it perfect for flavour-packed parcels made to be eaten in a couple of bites. Aside from the sauce, which can be substituted with quality hoisin, this is a simple way to deliver a very satisfactory result using pan-seared breasts. Left-over roast duck – or bought barbecued duck – will also work wonderfully. So will confit duck, if you have some lurking in the fridge. **Serves 8–10**

4 × 150–180 g (5½–6½ oz)
duck breasts
bao buns or Kimchi pancakes
(p. 457), to serve
2 Lebanese (short)
cucumbers, cut into 6 cm
(2½ in) batons
1 bunch of fine spring onions
(scallions), cut into 6 cm
(2½ in) batons

½ bunch of coriander
(cilantro), fine stems and
leaves picked

**Roasted plum & hoisin
sauce**
16 blood plums, stones
removed, flesh cut into
quarters
8 cm (3¼ in) piece of fresh
ginger, finely chopped

200 g (7 oz) brown sugar
200 ml (7 fl oz) sherry vinegar,
or red-wine vinegar
125 ml (4 fl oz/½ cup) hoisin
sauce
2 star anise
1 tablespoon salt flakes
2 teaspoons white
peppercorns, finely ground

Staples
EVOO, S&P

Preheat the oven to 200°C (400°F) fan-forced.

Add all the plum sauce ingredients to a ceramic baking dish that will fit everything in one snug layer. Toss well, stand for 15 minutes, then roast for 25 minutes, stirring after about 10 minutes. The plums will soften and start to melt into a sauce. Cool undisturbed and use at room temperature.

Season the duck breasts, then pan-sear (see above), slicing each into 6–8 pieces after resting.

Serve each bao or pancake with a slice of duck, some cucumber, spring onion, coriander and a spoonful of the plum sauce.

Make it different
With duck. Crisp up four confit duck legs in the oven (see p. 260), then shred and use instead of the sliced breast – or use left-over Twice-roasted duck (p. 264) or bought barbecued duck.

Twice-roasted duck GF

While duck breast is beautiful served pink, roasting a whole bird yields incredibly tender flesh, with deeply burnished crispy skin. It can be done well ahead of time, with the duck halves flashed in the oven to finish. **Serves 2–4**

1 × 2.2 kg (4 lb 13 oz) duck
1½ tablespoons salt flakes

2 teaspoons ground white pepper
2 teaspoons ground allspice

1 tablespoon extra-virgin olive oil

Trim any excess fat from the neck and inside the cavity of the duck and save it for roasting potatoes (see p. 626). Prick the skin around the legs and the neck.

Ideally, refrigerate the duck, uncovered, for a couple of days to dry out the skin. Remove from the fridge at least 30 minutes before roasting.

Preheat the oven to 220°C (430°F) fan-forced. Line a baking tray with baking paper.

Using a mortar and pestle, finely grind the salt, pepper and allspice together. Add the oil and combine.

Rub the salt mix all over the duck, inside and out. Prick the neck and legs with a knife. Place on a rack (or on a 'trivet' of onion and/or celery) in a roasting tin. Roast for 1 hour 10 minutes.

Remove from the oven and rest for 30 minutes.

Score the skin in two lines down each side along the back of the duck – this is so the skin comes away cleanly when you remove the meat, rather than tearing. Turn the bird over. Cut along the keel of the breastbone, working your knife along the rib cage, to cut away the breast and wing as cleanly as possible. Slide the knife down the rib cage and cut away the leg at the thigh joint, yielding one complete side with the skin intact.

Lay the half duck, skin side up, on the baking tray, then repeat for the other side.

Either stand at room temperature until ready to roast, or cover and refrigerate for up to 5 days.

To serve, preheat the oven to 230°C (445°F) fan-forced. Roast for 15–20 minutes, until the duck halves are hot and the skin is crisp. You can turn on the oven grill (broiler) if needed to finish crisping, but watch closely.

Serve generously as a half duck, or cut the legs from the breast and portion, with some sliced breast and leg for each person.

Any fat from the baking tray and the roasting tin can be strained and saved for roasting potatoes.

Pair with

Duck sauce (p 262).

Roasted quince & chestnuts (p. 716).

Roasted rhubarb, blood plum & ginger chutney (p. 646).

Pickled cherries (see p. 566).

Gnocchi alla romana (p. 138).

Classic potato mash (p. 628) or celeriac mash.

Salted orange, cacao nibs & coffee (see below).

Wombok, daikon, shiitake & tofu salad (p. 450).

Roasted beetroot (beet) or pumpkin salad (see p. 630).

Crispy eggplant with spiced caramel & fried Thai basil (p. 522).

Chicory (witlof/endive) and bitter leaf salad with a citrus or pomegranate dressing.

Roasted potatoes, and Honey & thyme gastrique (p. 265).

Braised fresh borlotti beans in lemon & cumin stock (p. 426) and sautéed mushrooms.

Roasted parsnips with maple syrup (p. 606).

Twice-roasted duck with salted orange, cacao nibs & coffee GF

Duck and orange are a classic combination. Here is an updated examination of that coupling, bringing in the equally complementary notes of cocoa and coffee. This is a special occasion dish, and one that relies on using two duck frames to make a successful sauce – so don't be tempted to halve the quantities. **Serves 6–8**

2 × 2.2 kg (4 lb 13 oz) Twice-roasted ducks (above), roasted and halved, carcasses reserved
1 litre (34 fl oz/4 cups) Golden chicken stock (p. 54)
2 garlic cloves

3 thyme sprigs
1 fresh bay leaf
2 tablespoons freshly ground coffee beans
4 oranges
2½ tablespoons extra-virgin olive oil

1½ tablespoons sherry vinegar
watercress sprigs, to serve
2 tablespoons crushed cacao nibs

Staples
S&P

Pair with

Celeriac mash, roasted beetroot (beet) or Dauphinoise potatoes (p. 627).

Any simply cooked greens.

A bitter leaf salad.

Scorched honey & thyme gastrique for duck 🆖

Serve this gastrique-style sauce with roasted (see p. 258) or Twice-roasted duck (opposite) or pan-seared breasts (see p. 263). Add 4 tablespoons honey to a saucepan over a high heat. Cook for 1½–2½ minutes, until the honey is 125°C (257°F) and a dark caramel colour. Stir in 80 ml (2½ fl oz/⅓ cup) sherry vinegar and 1 tablespoon water. Add 1 teaspoon cracked white peppercorns and 4 thyme sprigs and simmer for 2 minutes over a medium heat. Stir in 700 ml (23½ fl oz) Duck stock (p. 266) and let it reduce by half, then stir in 60 g (2 oz/ ¼ cup) unsalted butter, which will gloss and thicken the sauce. Season with salt and pepper and serve straight away, or keep warm until needed. Makes about 400 ml (13½ fl oz).

Slow-roasted duck with baharat & pomegranate molasses 🆖

Dry a trimmed duck then rub with salt and 1½ tablespoons Baharat (p. 6). Place the duck in a heavy ovenproof pot and drop in a whole bulb of garlic, 6 small to medium carrots and parsnips and a few fresh bay leaves. Drizzle with 3 tablespoons each of sherry vinegar and pomegranate molasses and 150 ml (5 fl oz) water or White chicken stock (p. 54). Cover with the lid. Cook in a 150°C (300°F) fan-forced oven for 3 hours, skimming off some of the fat halfway through. Increase the heat to 220°C (430°F) and cook for a further 20 minutes uncovered to colour the duck. Once cooked, serve the duck with the juices spooned over, along with couscous, fresh pomegranate seeds, Tabouleh (p. 419) and fresh Pitta bread (see p. 854) on the side. Labneh (p. 362) mixed with dried mint and lemon juice would also be a lovely addition.

Preheat the oven to 200°C (400°F) fan-forced.

Chop the duck carcasses and spread out on a baking tray. Roast for about 15 minutes, until coloured.

Add the bones to a saucepan with the stock, garlic, thyme, bay leaf and coffee. Peel the rind off half an orange and add to the pan. Simmer for 45 minutes to 1 hour, until intensely aromatic.

Meanwhile, peel and slice three of the oranges. Season the slices with salt and pepper and chill until needed. Juice the remaining orange and set aside.

Strain the stock and add to a saucepan with the orange juice. Reduce to about 150 ml (5 fl oz), then set aside to cool for 5 minutes before adding the oil and vinegar to make a vinaigrette. Adjust the seasoning to taste.

Preheat the oven to 230°C (445°F) fan-forced.

Roast the duck halves for 15–20 minutes, until they are hot and the skin is crisp. You can turn on the oven grill (broiler) if needed to finish crisping, but watch closely.

Gently warm the duck vinaigrette over a low heat.

Slice the duck into pieces. Arrange the orange slices on serving plates and top with the duck. Drop on a handful of watercress, sprinkle with the cacao nibs, drizzle the vinaigrette over and serve.

Roast duck, crab & tapioca soup

This soup is as much about texture as it is flavour. The fungus is crunchy and slippery, while the tapioca gives the soup a velvety mouthfeel. It's luxurious, too, with the twin powers of two pretty fancy proteins in crab and duck. Delicious with Fermented cooked chilli sauce (p. 97). **Serves 4–6**

65 g (2¼ oz/⅓ cup) large sago (tapioca) pearls, rinsed
1 litre (34 fl oz/4 cups) Golden chicken stock (p. 54), or Duck stock (p. 266)
120 g (4½ oz) fresh wood ear fungus, sliced
4 shiitake mushrooms, trimmed and sliced
3 tablespoons soy sauce

2 tablespoons oyster sauce
2 tablespoons tamarind paste (in a jar, not from a block)
1 tablespoon palm sugar (jaggery)
½ roast duck, meat removed, breast sliced and leg finely chopped
250 g (9 oz) cooked crabmeat
2 handfuls of micro cress

5 coriander (cilantro) sprigs, leaves finely shredded
4 spring onions (scallions), white part only, sliced
½ teaspoon ground white pepper
2 tablespoons crisp fried garlic or shallots (see p. 600)
½ teaspoon sesame oil
1 lime

Whisk the sago into a large saucepan of boiling, lightly salted water. Simmer for 30 minutes, stirring regularly, then drain.

Bring the stock to the boil in a saucepan. Add the wood ear, shiitake, soy and oyster sauce, tamarind, sugar, sago and duck leg meat. Bring to a simmer, then turn the heat to low.

Divide the crab and breast meat between bowls. Top with the cress, coriander, spring onion, pepper and garlic, then spoon the hot soup over. Drizzle with the sesame oil, squeeze in the lime and serve immediately.

Make it different
With confit duck. Instead of roast duck, use two confit duck legs, crisped and shredded (see p. 260).

Red duck curry with lychee & fried basil salad

Thai curries are complex, layered and deeply flavoured. Aside from the classic sweet, sour, hot and salty balance, there are myriad flavours combining into a beguiling, wildly aromatic whole. I love Thai food: the way the unbelievable intensity of pretty much everything marries with an extraordinary clarity of detail. This is very much a special occasion dish, built for a feast – and worth every bit of effort. This is something I make when I have the time, rather than rushing it or skimping on any ingredients. If anything, I might double the curry paste and freeze it for another time, but that's as far as I go with shortcuts. **Serves 10–12**

12 duck leg quarters
   (marylands)
500 ml (17 fl oz/2 cups)
   coconut cream
300 g (10½ oz) peeled fresh
   ginger, julienned
2 tablespoons coriander
   seeds
180 g (6½ oz) palm sugar
   (jaggery)
12 apple eggplants
   (aubergines), quartered – or
   use 300 g (10½ oz) pea
   eggplants, or 2 regular
   eggplants (skin on, diced)
1.5 litres (51 fl oz/6 cups)
   Golden chicken stock
   (p. 54)
500 ml (17 fl oz/2 cups)
   coconut milk
125 ml (4 fl oz/½ cup) fish
   sauce, plus extra to serve
6 long red chillies, seeded
   and finely julienned
4 limes, plus extra to serve

Red curry paste
3 tablespoons shrimp paste
80 g (2¾ oz) peeled fresh
   galangal, finely chopped
12 red Asian shallots,
   chopped
10 garlic cloves, chopped
10–12 red bird's eye chillies,
   sliced (you will need
   180 g/6½ oz)
8 dried long red chillies,
   soaked for 15 minutes in
   boiling water, then drained
   and chopped
12 coriander (cilantro) roots,
   cleaned well, plus all the
   stems from 1 bunch, finely
   chopped
12 makrut lime leaves, vein
   removed, finely chopped
5 lemongrass stems, white
   part only, finely sliced
1½ tablespoons salt flakes
1 nutmeg, freshly grated, or
   1½ tablespoons ground

nutmeg – but it's much
   better to grate it fresh
3 teaspoons ground white
   pepper
250 ml (8½ fl oz/1 cup) water
2½ tablespoons coriander
   seeds, ground

Lychee & fried basil salad
oil, for shallow-frying
1 bunch of Thai basil,
   leaves picked
1 bunch of coriander
   (cilantro), picked (use the
   stems and roots in the
   paste)
5 makrut lime leaves, very
   finely shredded
20 lychees, peeled, halved
   and pitted

Staples
S&WP

Pair with

Wedges of wombok (Chinese cabbage), trimmed snake (yard-long) beans and chilled sliced cucumber, with steamed jasmine rice and a sprinkling of crushed toasted glutinous rice (p. 384).

Quick & simple duck stock GF

Once a duck has been roasted – even if you've simply bought a Chinese barbecued duck – don't discard the bones. Save them for stock! Using a heavy knife or cleaver, chop through the duck carcass, which will speed up the extraction from the bones considerably. You can freeze the carcass like this for later, if you're short on time, otherwise roast it in a hot oven for about 15 minutes, until colouring up, then drop into a saucepan. Add some onion, cut into quarters, along with some garlic, celery, leek tops, whatever you have; just be sure to cut the vegetables up a little, as the cooking is relatively quick. Add some fresh bay leaves, thyme and parsley stalks, if you have them, plus a few peppercorns. Cover with White chicken stock (p. 54) (or water, but stock is best if making a sauce). Simmer for 45 minutes to 1 hour, then strain. Use in a braise, soup, risotto or ragù – or reduce by half and make a sauce by beating in butter (or boil in a little duck fat to emulsify, see p. 262). The stock can also make a quick meal: stir some miso paste into the hot broth and add some cooked noodles and wilted greens; tofu and seaweed would be a nice addition, too.

Preheat the oven to 200°C (400°F) fan-forced. Line a baking tray with baking paper.

Trim any excess fat from the duck legs and season with salt and white pepper. Roast on the baking tray for 35 minutes. Pour off the duck fat and reserve for roasting potatoes and the like. Scrape any caramelised bits from the paper and reserve with the duck, to add to the curry.

To make the curry paste, wrap the shrimp paste in a square of foil and flatten. Add to a dry frying pan over a medium heat and cook until it smells pungent, about 4 minutes, turning halfway through.

Remove the shrimp paste from the foil and add to a blender. Add all the remaining curry paste ingredients and blitz to a smooth paste.

Add the coconut cream to a large saucepan over a medium heat. Cook until it cracks (the oil separates), or until it starts to darken and caramelise, about 8 minutes. Add the curry paste and half the ginger, then fry for about 10 minutes, until the water has evaporated and the paste is fragrant and has darkened a little.

Quick herb salad GF V

Pick and wash the leaves from 3 sprigs dill, 3 handfuls coriander (cilantro) and 4 handfuls parsley, and chill with 80 g (2¾ oz) washed baby spinach leaves. Toast 100 g (3½ oz) whole almonds in 60 g (2 oz) butter in a frying pan over a medium heat until golden brown, about 5 minutes. Lift the almonds from the pan and allow to cool, reserving any residual butter, then roughly chop the almonds. Add the warm reserved butter to 50 ml (1¾ fl oz) each of lemon juice and extra-virgin olive oil. Season with salt and pepper. Combine the spinach and herbs with the almonds and dress with the lemon dressing.

Duck bresaola GF

Make a curing mix by combining 100 g (3½ oz/¾ cup) sea salt, 40 g (1½ oz) brown sugar, 10 roughly crushed white peppercorns, 4 juniper berries, a handful of thyme or sage leaves and 1 teaspoon chilli flakes. Rub over the duck in a non-reactive dish. Refrigerate, uncovered, for 48 hours, turning the duck every 12 hours. Wipe the cure from the duck with a damp towel. Tie the breasts with kitchen twine and either hang in a large jar(s) from a chopstick (this method is ideal, as they won't get knocked about), or hang over a tray. Cure in the fridge for 3–4 weeks, until firm. Wrap in a cloth and refrigerate. The bresaola will keep for about 2 months.

Add the coriander seeds and sugar and stir until caramelised, about 5 minutes. Add the eggplant and stir through the paste to coat.

Stir in the stock, coconut milk and fish sauce. Bring to a simmer, then cook gently for 20 minutes. The flavours should mature a little; taste and balance with more sugar, chilli or fish sauce as needed.

Add the duck legs, with any of their caramel and juices, plus the chilli and remaining ginger. Simmer for a further 15 minutes, then turn off the heat and stand. The duck will cook a little more as it stands, taking it to the point where it is coming away from the bone. If it goes too far, the meat will start to shred.

Heat 2 cm (¾ in) of oil in a frying pan over a high heat for 4 minutes. Flash-fry the basil leaves for 20 seconds, then drain. The leaves will change colour in the oil and become crisp as they cool.

Combine the fried basil, coriander and lime leaves, then toss with the lychees. Add a little extra fish sauce and the juice of 1½ limes.

Squeeze the remaining 1½ limes into the curry and serve with the lychee and fried basil salad on top and extra lime on the side.

Quail

I love game birds. The delicate yet robust flavours they deliver are superb, but they sit in a specialised area, both for sourcing and cooking. While squab (pigeon) is something you can find on occasion, I still rarely cook a game bird – aside from quails, which are relatively inexpensive and readily available. The flesh is tender, mildly meaty, delicately textured and quite distinctly different to chicken or duck.

'Quail' is a very general term, with many different species falling loosely into New World and Old World groups, and both belonging to different scientific families. There are even Australian native quail species, with the stubble quail the most common. In terms of farming, Japanese quail are the most commonly raised species, reaching maturity quickly for slaughter, as well as laying consistently for egg production.

Quail is the most farmed game bird in Australia – and, sadly, it is not always well farmed, with birds stuffed into cramped cages and never seeing the world outside their sheds. While chicken farming has its issues, there is at least a growing level of transparency around the industry, while quail farming methods are still somewhat opaque. Suffice to say, cruel intensive farming does occur with quails around the world, and unless we are shown otherwise, we must assume the worst.

Having said that, there are excellent small farms producing spectacular quail in environmentally sustainable and ethical ways. The best quail I have eaten are raised on the New South Wales Central Coast by Brendan Sheldrick (one of Neil Perry's ex-head chefs) and Leanne Crofts of Eugowra Game Birds (they also raise pheasant, partridge and guinea fowl). They stock Japanese quail, but apparently from a select breeding strain. Whatever the merits of that genetic lineage, there is little doubt in my mind that the way the pair lovingly pasture-raise the birds is largely responsible for the supremely delicious meat, which is deep in colour, with a delicate yet rich flavour.

Preparing quails

Quails are easily prepared and can be bought whole, butterflied or boned. I will naturally opt for fresh birds, but properly thawed frozen quails are totally fine, too. Quail can be roasted whole in a hot oven, or you can remove the rib bones with your fingers and stuff them for a pot roast. Partially deboned quails (with the legs and wingettes attached) can be marinated and grilled, or pan-fried as is, or wrapped in prosciutto for Saltimbocca (below). Quail is best cooked with a blush of pink in the breast, though you can also slow-cook the birds in duck fat for rillettes (see p. 330), or to fold through a Mushroom ragù (p. 576) and serve with gnocchi (pp. 131, 137) or pasta. Quail can also generally be used in poussin recipes (pp. 236, 590), but just consider the size difference when assessing the timing.

Quail saltimbocca with caramelised pears GF

Quail is ideal for saltimbocca, with the boned birds cooking to a golden hue quickly, while keeping a blush of colour in the breast. The meat also stands up nicely to the intense flavours of the pears, sage and prosciutto. **Serves 4**

Pair with

Scent quails with sage, coriander (cilantro), thyme, parsley and bay leaves, and spice with cumin, chilli, black and white pepper, anise, juniper, sichuan pepper, Chinese five-spice, coriander seed and cinnamon. Team up with onion, spring onion (scallion), garlic, ginger, cabbage, brussels sprouts, spinach, peas, and porcini and pine mushrooms, as well as citrus, plums, figs, sultanas (golden raisins), grapes and currants. Quail can handle rich, sweet and/or acidic foils, such as saba, vincotto, vinegar (including balsamic), fortified wine, pomegranate molasses, honey and soy sauce. Cured meats such as prosciutto, pancetta, bacon and speck work well with quail, as do butter and cream. Also match with freekeh, lentils, chestnuts, rice and pine nuts.

Pair with

Gnocchi alla romana (p. 138).

Classic potato mash (p. 625).

Polenta (p. 383).

4 butterflied jumbo quails, with wing and leg bones intact
4 slices of prosciutto
4 large sage leaves
120 g (4½ oz) butter

2 beurre bosc pears, peeled, cored and cut into 8 wedges each
100 g (3½ oz) brown sugar
100 ml (3½ fl oz) sherry vinegar

200 ml (7 fl oz) white wine
2 handfuls of rocket (arugula), or curly endive (frisée)

Staples
EVOO, S&P

Special equipment
Strong, sharp toothpicks

Wrap the quails in a strip of prosciutto, from the top of the breast around, securing with a toothpick through a sage leaf on the skin side.

Melt 80 g (2¾ oz) of the butter in a frying pan over a medium heat. Add the pear wedges and sugar, season generously with salt and pepper and toss. Once the sugar starts to caramelise, about 4 minutes, add the vinegar, then simmer until the liquid has fully reduced, about 3 minutes. Set aside, but keep warm.

Heat a large frying pan over a high heat for 3 minutes, until very hot. Rub the quails with oil and season. Sear, breast side down, until golden, about 4 minutes. Add the remaining butter and let it melt, then flip the quails over. Add the wine and let it reduce for 2 minutes.

Add the pears and bring to the boil, then remove the quails and lay on a serving plate. Toss the pears through the sauce until hot and glossy; adjust the seasoning to taste.

Scatter the leaves over the quails, and spoon the pears and sauce over and serve.

Spicy fried quail with sichuan pepper salt

Pair with

Lime wedges and shredded wombok (Chinese cabbage), or iceberg lettuce and Thai-style chilli jam (p. 96).

This is a version of a dish that I have eaten countless times – not infrequently for supper after a busy service, but these days I'm more inclined to make this for the family at a far more civilised hour. Marinating the quails in the kecap manis is a must, imbuing them with an underlying sweet soy flavour. **Serves 6**

2½ tablespoons kecap manis
1½ teaspoons sesame oil
6 quails, cut in half, with the backbones, ribs and necks removed
oil, for deep-frying (see p. 22)
4 large garlic cloves, skin on, smashed

2 long green chillies, sliced on an angle
4 spring onions (scallions), white and green parts, finely sliced
sichuan pepper salt (p. 29), to serve

Spice coating
80 g (2¾ oz) tapioca starch
1 tablespoon ground coriander
2 teaspoons chilli powder
½ teaspoon Chinese five-spice

Staples
S&P

Combine the kecap manis and 1 teaspoon of the sesame oil in a large bowl. Add the quails and toss to coat. Marinate at room temperature for at least 1 hour, or preferably refrigerate overnight.

Add the spice coating ingredients to a large bowl and combine well. Set aside.

Heat a good splash of the frying oil in a wok over a high heat. Fry the garlic and chilli until lightly coloured and fragrant, about 30 seconds. Add to a large bowl with the spring onion and remaining ½ teaspoon sesame oil, season with salt and toss together.

Wipe the wok out (or use a large saucepan). Heat another 10 cm (4 in) of oil until 180°C (350°F).

Working in two batches, dust the quail well in the spice coating mix and deep-fry for about 3 minutes, until a deep golden brown. Toss with most of the fried garlic mixture and season with a little sichuan salt.

Pile the quail onto a serving plate and serve garnished with the remaining garlic mixture.

Also see

Oxtail consommé **56**

Beef pho **57**

Roast meat tortellini **114–5**

Veal & pork polpette with savoy cabbage, taleggio & truffled pecorino **337**

Borscht **418**

Martini family stuffed capsicums **464–5**

Veal saltimbocca with fresh figs **702–3**

Beef & Veal

Beef

While the quality of lamb in Australia has been reliably high, beef has suffered somewhat over the years, transitioning from a traditional approach where meat from older animals and dry-ageing were common, to one favouring lean meat from young animals that are hung for no longer than they take to sell. The global war on fat saw yearling beef being promoted as the preferred option – the less fat, the better – and proclaimed as a mark of quality. Indeed, many butchers only sold virtually fat-free yearling beef for quite some time, and many still do.

A yearling is a young animal, male or female, up to 18 months of age, without permanent incisor teeth. The meat is pale pink, the intramuscular fat is rarely well developed, if at all, and the flavour is typically somewhat bland, and often with a pasty and powdery texture when cooked – which is one of the reasons I don't cook with it at home or professionally. Mature beef, ideally from an animal closer to three years of age, will develop a strong beefy flavour, and the fibres of the meat will be more structured but also more yielding if the animal was raised well and the meat properly dry-aged.

I also believe grass-fed beef tastes better, with animals grazing on naturally lush pastures the ideal scenario. Rich, fertile pasture also encourages high levels of omega-3 fatty acids in the meat, which is optimal from a health perspective, and the flavour is simply superior to my palate. Cattle don't naturally feed on corn and soy (there's a GM flag there, too), and the inclusion of these grains in their diets is used to fatten them before slaughter. A diet centred on these foods is essentially an unhealthy one for them – a junk food diet, if you like.

Then there is the absurdity of growing crops – with all the energy, water and time, as well as the pesticides and herbicides involved – to feed an animal that naturally eats grass, is healthier eating it, and in turn yields healthier meat.

Grain-feeding and finishing can increase intramuscular fat, which reaches its apotheosis in the rearing of wagyu cattle, where the diets are meticulously structured to achieve a high level of marbling. The intramuscular fat of wagyu can actually be high in monounsaturated fat and high in omega-3 fatty acids, while young cattle fattened for the mass market with grain and soy will tend to be low in omega-3 fatty acids and have more total fat than grass-fed meat. In general, grass-fed beef will have significantly more omega-3s than grain-fed beef. Our modern diets have distorted the balance of essential fatty acids in our bodies, with omega-6 generally in much higher concentrations than omega-3. A 1:1 ratio, or closer to it, is seen as more akin to how humans evolved, with the inflammatory effects of omega-6 in high doses thought to contribute to chronic diseases. Returning closer to that balance naturally – not through supplements – can be achieved by eating grass-fed meat and wild-caught seafood.

Whatever the composition of the fat, grain-fed cattle will tend to have fat that is whiter, while grass-fed beef will have fat with more of a yellow hue, especially in older animals. That colour difference is due to carotenes – which give vegetables such as carrots their colour – absorbed from grazing on natural pasture. Carotenes are health-giving antioxidants, and another good reason for choosing grass-fed beef.

Australia's largest feedlot can house almost 80,000 cattle at one time, while in the United States the largest feedlot company can feed about 1 million head of cattle across eleven sites. That's a lot of beef, a lot of grain, and a lot of greenhouse gases. Animals fed like this will reach maturity much more quickly and will actually expel less methane than grass-fed cattle – both due to their feed and because they don't live as long – but I don't in any way see this as an environmental solution.

Methane is a potent greenhouse gas, much more so than carbon dioxide. But methane is a short-lived gas, breaking down into carbon dioxide and water after about a decade. In an ideal agricultural model, that carbon is absorbed by plants, creating a balanced system. The fossil fuel industry produces a vast amount of methane and carbon dioxide with no natural system to remove it from the atmosphere, unlike best-practice agriculture. Additionally, there have been some very successful trials using kelp supplements to stop methane production in cows.

Properly managed organic pasture can be carbon neutral or, in fact, carbon negative. A soil rich in micro-organisms essentially feeds off the carbon dioxide that has been consumed by plants during photosynthesis. That process converts carbon dioxide and water into carbohydrates, with some stored and some leaching into the soil, which is consumed by those micro-organisms, meaning the process removes carbon from the atmosphere and encourages microbial life. If that pasture is allowed to recover and be lush, and not become denuded from overgrazing, then the carbon emissions from cattle can be more than offset.

That pasture also needs to be managed without chemicals, as pesticides and herbicides are like antibiotics for the soil, killing all the good along with the – perceived – bad. So, sourcing your meat carefully has rewards well beyond what's on your plate. That relationship to the land used and its supportive capacity is critical. A local system with a 'closed loop' approach is an ideal model that will lay a sustainable foundation for the future.

The argument advocating for feedlots based on the lower emissions per head of cattle is misguided – except if we don't ever intend to actually solve the problem, but simply reduce some of the impact. For me, mitigation at the source is essential. It's not just about reducing those emissions – it's about negating them and being sustainable. Choosing to buy your beef from a farmer who understands this is a simple way to play your part.

When you talk to farmers who are seeking the best outcome for both meat quality and animal welfare – for any livestock – the subject of abattoirs is a thorny one. Sadly, a farmer can raise their cattle to the highest standards in a low-stress natural environment, only to have to transport those animals long distances to an abattoir, and sometimes one that is out of keeping with their best practices. As well as giving rise to significant animal welfare concerns, those stresses have impacts on the meat quality.

Stressed animals will convert glycogen to lactic acid, which will result in meat with a mahogany hue. The industry refers to this as 'dark cutting' meat, and it is the product of stressful situations, and should be avoided. The meat holds more water and has a higher pH, making it more perishable, and also likely to shed water when cooked. It is an indication of stress and/or poor nutrition, and it will never occur under best-practice conditions. Don't buy it.

On-farm processing is one logical answer to reducing the stresses that arise during transportation to an abattoir, but this is a regulated process that is beyond most farmers. Another solution is to use a mobile processing facility. Provenir is one such Australian company that partners with farmers who champion high-welfare practices, and manages their slaughter and butchery. May we see more companies like this. Abattoirs may not be a part of the process that many of us want to talk about, but by being blind to it we risk tacitly endorsing inhumane practices.

I like to think that attitudes are changing, and there is now a stronger demand for quality meat. As more consumers choose to eat a smaller amount of quality meat over a large amount of low-grade, tasteless mass-market meat, cattle breeders and farmers are stepping up their methods and practices to deliver a superior product – with many of the processes better for the animals, better for the environment and better for us.

There are many breeds of cattle raised in Australia. When you include dairy cattle, it's thought to be around 100, with various adaptions to wildly different conditions across the country – though much of the beef sold here is not marketed by type. Angus and Black Angus are the most commonly declared breeds sold as a premium product – even in prominent fast-food establishments – while

Belted Galloway, Scottish Highland, Limousin and Chianina, for example, are somewhat more rarefied. Chianina is one of the oldest breeds of cattle, said to date back to the Bronze Age. It has actually been raised here for decades but typically as stock for crossbreeding, because while they can significantly improve the genetic strain, they are very slow maturing and not commercially attractive unless a significant premium is attached to the beef.

Generally, I find that the most critical determiners for quality are the age of an animal, as well as careful, ethical rearing and slaughter, and proper ageing of the meat. For example, older ex-dairy cows produce marvellous meat, rich and intense, with intramuscular marbling and deep yellow fat. Naturally, it depends on where and how these cows were raised. In areas where rainfall is high, natural grazing is more common, and if sensitive farming practices are employed, the meat can be extraordinary.

With increasing numbers of quality-conscious consumers, interest in specific breeds will naturally rise, but the decision to mature cattle beyond reaching a target weight – especially if rearing slow-growing cattle – is not an easy financial one to take. I have eaten meat from specialised breeds that has been poor due to the young age at slaughter, which is a great shame. I understand the demand, cost and pressures on patience that motivate the decision to come to market early, but it can result in an expensive and unsatisfactory outcome for the consumer. As always, work with your butcher or supplier to get exactly what you're after.

Ageing beef is essential to developing full flavour and tenderness. And dry-ageing is by far my preferred method. Meat can be wet-aged in vacuum packs, but it often develops a flavour that can be somewhat off-putting. Dry-ageing also develops a distinctive character – one I find utterly compelling.

Dry-ageing meat is an involved and technical process, with temperature and humidity maintained to very tight thresholds. During the ageing process there is some moisture loss, but this stops once a crust has formed over the meat – either a whole or half carcass, or a primal cut – meaning that the succulence of the meat is retained. As the meat ages, with two weeks being the very bare minimum, naturally occurring enzymes soften the muscle fibres and tenderise the meat, while with longer ageing, the fat develops a distinctive flavour due to the oxidative exposure. There is a little waste to dry-ageing, as the hard outer crust needs to be cut away, but the rewards are immense. Grass-fed beef aged for thirty, sixty or even 120 days will be expensive, but it is an extraordinary delicacy and one to be savoured.

My favourite steak cut is from the ribs, or cube roll. A rib-eye steak or rib cutlet, with the bone – or scotch fillet, without – is the most flavoursome piece of meat for me, and it also has a marvellous fat content. With the bone left on, the flavour is incredible. My butcher leaves much of the meat attached to that bone, because while flaying the bones back to a French-trimmed white may look fancy, there's an awful lot of delicious, succulent, fat-laced meat running along that bone – especially if it's been dry-aged. Plus, the tender heart of the rib-eye – the 'eye' itself – is protectively wrapped in arguably the tastiest and most tender piece of beef of all: the rib cap, or spinalis dorsi. That muscle, which cradles the bottom of the steak, and partially separates in a distinct strip when cooked, remains ultra-tender even though it cooks more than the eye, and it has the most amazingly intense beefy flavour. Some butchers and chefs chasing a luxury cut will take the whole muscle off the rib rack and cook it alone, but to me, this does a disservice to the rest of the rack. Leave it on and enjoy the morsel you get with each steak. Bone in or out, this is my first choice cut for grilling. You can also roast a standing rib rack for the ultimate roast dinner.

Behind the ribs, towards the back of the animal, lies the next best steak cut for me – the sirloin or porterhouse, which can also be roasted whole. Behind that is the T-bone, which carries a sirloin on one side of the bone and fillet on the other. The T-bone is the emblematic cut for the Tuscan classic Bistecca alla fiorentina (p. 278), and always from white Chianina cattle, although my homage to that great dish employs rib-eye. It is also a great cut for barbecuing, but it's so often cut far too thin, which makes it very hard to do the quite different cuts on either side of the central bone justice while getting adequate colour on the meat. A properly cut T-bone for bistecca alla fiorentina is an

Beef loves onion, shallot, leek, spring onion (scallion), garlic, ginger, horseradish, celery, celeriac, potato, parsnip, tomato, capsicum (bell pepper), chilli, eggplant (aubergine), spinach, chicory (witlof/endive), rocket (arugula), chicory (witlof/endive), radicchio, mushrooms, walnuts, sesame seeds, chestnuts and pine nuts. Pair it with bay leaves, thyme, rosemary, tarragon and coriander (cilantro), and spice with star anise, cumin, cardamom, cassia, paprika and all kinds of pepper. Beef adores peppery olive oil as much as it does butter, cream, sour cream and crème fraîche. Fermented foods such as pickled cucumber, pickled onion, sauerkraut, Kimchi (p. 455), olives and cured meats are great complementary flavours. Beef also takes to miso, sake, molasses, pomegranate molasses, mustard, soy sauce, fish sauce, vinegar, red wine, sweet sherry and port.

imposing thing, and it will spend a decent amount of time on the grill standing on its end, with the heat radiating through the bone.

Rump steak is naturally at the rear of the animal. It doesn't generally have a lot of intramuscular fat (unless wagyu, of course), but it is a flavourful and generally economical cut, good for barbecuing or pan-frying. The rump cap, however, is a little more sought after. It is a very prized cut (called picanha in Brazil, and one of the most revered cuts there), with a commanding layer of fat and wonderful flavour. It can be barbecued, or pan-seared and roasted.

Hanger is a steak cut that has become immensely popular, which is tricky, as there's not much to go around. I always called this cut a bavette, though flank steak seems to be the butcher's term in this country. The skirt steak is similar, with both giving more flavour rewards (which are considerable) than tenderness ones.

The eye fillet was traditionally seen as the prized luxury cut, but that's really only valid to those who prize tenderness over flavour. I do enjoy good eye fillet – usually raw in a carpaccio (see p. 280) or tartare (see p. 279), though it can be cooked as a whole or part fillet (pp. 285, 286) very effectively. For me, the cuts with more fat and interesting texture, rather than melt-in-your mouth tenderness, are vastly superior. It seems people like to elevate this notion of 'melt in the mouth' as a pinnacle. It's not. Some things should melt, and others not. Texture is important, not a lack of it. And flavour is even more important.

Chuck is from the neck and shoulder area, and is a fantastic braising cut. It also makes superb minced (ground) meat for slow cooking in a ragù and the like. There is so much connective tissue in chuck, which melts into a sauce, giving it a luscious richness. Just behind the chuck is the blade, which is another fine braising or mince cut (I often use a mix of blade and chuck), and it also yields the flat-iron steak – also known as a butler's steak – which is another of those much-pursued cuts that account for a tiny portion of the beast. Nonetheless, it is a very flavourful and quite tender steak once the tough central sinew has been removed; ask your butcher to do this, if they haven't already. Beef shin is also great for braising, whether off the bone, or cut crossways for Osso buco (p. 296) – ideally from a younger animal or veal.

People are fanatical about brisket, with it seemingly the cornerstone of the American barbecue. Cooked well, it is incredibly moist and flavoursome, but it requires long and slow cooking (see p. 291). In the United States, a part of the brisket is used to make pastrami, which is corned, coated in spices, hot-smoked, then steamed to serve. The whole brisket is also corned to be simmered for corned beef. In Australia, more likely than not, corned beef will come from the silverside, at the other end of the beast. It's a tough cut that needs brining and slow simmering to be tender. I tend to prefer corned beef from the eye round or girello, which is a cut near the hind leg, but corned silverside and brisket also grace my table.

Beef short ribs will generally come as individual ribs, or cut across the bones as asado. Either way, long cooking is required. They can be roasted in a marinade (see p. 290), or sealed first in a pan and then braised for a few hours, until tender, in the same way you might braise beef cheeks (see p. 285). Cheeks are an especially luscious cut when braised, having a fine-grained and gelatinous (in a good way) texture with intense flavour. Oxtail is also incredible braised, with a unique flavour. There's a little work involved, but once cooked in broth and the meat picked, it makes the most sublime consommé (see p. 56) with tortellini (see p. 113).

Preparing beef

The general rule with steak cuts is the leaner the meat, the rarer it should be cooked.

So, eye fillet can be sealed and essentially served warm. A little greater application of heat is fine, too – but it really should be on the rarer side. With the connective tissue in a rib-eye steak, a degree of medium-rare or even closer to medium is best, for me, though a properly aged piece of meat will not require cooking to dissolve any of those more rugged pockets of tissue. While I accept that how you like your steak is personal, it is simply a fact that by cooking it more, the flavour of the meat will be compromised and eventually lost when thoroughly cooked. If that steak has been carefully selected from an older animal, then dry-aged for an extended period, all that care and craft has been lost as well.

As with all meat or poultry, bring beef closer to room temperature before cooking. A cold piece of meat will alter the cooking time and take time to warm up before it starts to seal and brown properly, meaning it will tend to stew a little first. A large piece of meat will take longer to reach a better temperature, with an hour or two best for a very large piece, and it will throw temperatures off if using a probe thermometer, especially if attempting to cook to rare or medium-rare. You'll be okay if going to well-done – but please don't do that.

Taking the chill off is also as true for minced (ground) meat as it is a steak. Adding cold mince to make a ragù or the like can lead to a poor result. I often crumble mince into the pan a bit at a time – especially if there's a soffritto already in there – so that it has a chance to brown without crowding the pan. A large mass of cold mince will compete with the heat in the pan, and the meat will release water and won't brown quickly – meaning it will boil in that liquid before the moisture is cooked off, then finally brown up, leaving a dry and often powdery result. It's not ideal. Either add it slowly, or take the mince from the fridge 30 minutes before cooking, flattening it out in the bag to warm up evenly.

Take a steak from the fridge 30–60 minutes before cooking, depending on the thickness, and pat dry with paper towel. A wet surface will also have to be boiled off before the meat will brown, and you need all that precious time to caramelise the crust. As with drying poultry or pork skin, a steak can also be left uncovered in the fridge to dry out for a day or two before cooking, which improves the result even more. Just remember to flip the meat over and wipe the underside, as it will be moist. And a thick steak can be stood on its side, to allow both sides to dry out more evenly. (If it lays flat, one side will dry nicely, but the other will be wet.)

Give it a rest

Resting steaks or a roast is also critically important, and needs to be factored into your timing. Spending good money on an amazing piece of meat that you've carefully cooked only to compromise it at the last moment is a tragedy. No, that's not overly dramatic. Plan, and be patient. And tell the hungry ones around you to be patient, too. As it rests, the meat will relax, and the juices will redistribute, after having been forced to the centre, away from the heat. After proper resting, the juices will be reabsorbed. If cut too early, those juices will be lost: all that careful rearing, ageing and fastidious cooking just spilling out onto your board. You get to keep the dry meat, but that's little solace. I think I've made my point.

An old rule of thumb is to rest for about half the time it took to cook a steak or the like. It's a decent guide, but it depends a bit on how you're cooking that meat. An eye fillet slow-cooked at 100°C (210°F) to an even medium-rare should not be rested for half the cooking time, unless you want it quite cold.

A note on probe thermometers

There are many probe thermometers available these days that are easy to use and run with an app where you can set and control temperatures. These apps also tell you how long your meat will take to cook.

All meat will keep cooking while resting – some a little, some quite a bit. So, the process of resting is actually an arc in which the cooking is completed, with the internal temperature continuing to rise, then coming back down as the meat rests and stabilises. The larger the piece of meat, the longer this process will be. I would always rest a roast, loosely covered with foil, for at least 20 minutes, and at least 30 minutes if a bit larger. But it isn't just about weight. The shape – and whether it has a bone or not – is just as relevant to the cooking and resting time. It will take longer for the heat to reach the centre of a standing rib rack than it would a side of porterhouse, even if the porterhouse weighs more. It can be tricky to judge, which is where a thermometer is useful.

I never use a thermometer when cooking steaks (although you can), but it is a very useful tool when roasting. It can be very hard to judge the temperature degree of a large roast by feel. If working with consistent weights, and ensuring the meat is brought to temperature before cooking, times will generally be very reliable, but a good probe thermometer will take a bit of guesswork out of the process. As a general guide, when removing from the oven – remember it will cook more while resting – I work with 35°C (95°F) for rare, 45°C (115°F) for medium-rare, 55°C (130°F) for medium, 65°C (150°F) for 'Oh, no, I forgot the meat!', and 75°C (165°F) for 'Pasta, anyone? (well done).

Cooking the perfect steak

Ideally, I grill a large steak on the barbecue over real coals. At home, we will light a fire on the weekend, and take the time to do it properly. But that's not possible or practical most of the time. Professionally, I had the luxury of a charcoal-fired grill for many years (I say luxury due to the superior result – but it's hard work, and maintaining chef's whites when working with charcoal is a nightmare). You can certainly get a good result in a pan, but you need to be ready for a lot of smoke. A good extraction fan is your friend here, but popping open a window and door to create some airflow might also be necessary. For best results, use a heavy cast-iron pan, and only work with one steak at a time (or two, once you're practised). To get a good crust and not overcook the meat, those steaks need to be thick, so work with pieces of meat – scotch fillet for me – that weigh 550–650 g (1 lb 3–1 lb 7 oz) without the bone. Cooking on the bone is great, but it's not that easy to manage in a pan, and you don't always get good contact with the meat and pan surface. It can certainly be done, but it's easier to get your skills up sans bone.

To cook a 550–650 g (1 lb 3 oz–1 lb 7 oz) scotch fillet steak. Remove the meat from the fridge 1 hour before cooking. Preheat the pan over a high heat for 5 minutes. Season the steak generously with fine sea salt or salt flakes and ground white pepper (or black pepper – I've always used white pepper, and I've forgotten why). Have four thyme sprigs, 50 g (1¾ oz) unsalted butter and two smashed garlic cloves, with the skin on, at the ready. Once hot, lay the steak in the pan. Cook on one side for 4–5 minutes, depending on thickness, then flip and cook for 6 minutes. Add the garlic, butter and thyme and start spooning the butter over the steak. Once melted, take off the heat, tilt the pan and continuously baste the steak with the butter for 2 minutes. Remove the steak from the pan and rest on a chopping board for 8 minutes, loosely covered with foil. Set the pan aside. Once rested, you can serve the steak with the buttery juices spooned over, and some Béarnaise (p. 79). I also like to serve it by drizzling some of the butter from the pan over toasted Sourdough bread (p. 847), coating it with dijon mustard and a layer of very finely diced French shallots. I then slice the steak across the grain and arrange on the toast, then top with a salad of parsley and watercress, and maybe some tiny capers, before spooning any residual buttery juices over, serving a few baby radishes and a lemon cheek on the side.

Bistecca alla fiorentina GF

At the Melbourne Wine Room, the salt-crusted rib-eye steak was the cornerstone of the menu. It was a nod to the world-famous Tuscan bistecca alla fiorentina, though a T-bone is the traditional cut, and we were not able to reliably get Chianina beef back in the day. But we did do the meat justice back then by lighting a charcoal fire every day, as opposed to the all-too-common gas grill, which never attains the same char, and can leave a flavour taint rather than the positive flavour dimension added by a 'real' fire. The best peppery oil, a lemon cheek, a large splodge of dijon mustard and a signature horseradish and celeriac condiment completed the plate at the MWR, and it's exactly how I have it now, too. **Serves 4–6**

Pair with

A potato salad (see p. 624) or grain salad (pp. 378–9) and some dressed leaves.

Harissa roast capsicum salad with goat's cheese (p. 462).

Chips.

2 × 700–750 g (1 lb 9 oz–1 lb 11 oz) dry-aged rib-eye steaks
3 tablespoons white peppercorns, coarsely ground

100 g (3½ oz/¾ cup) fleur de sel, or coarse sea salt
1 × quantity Celeriac & mustard condiment for steak (p. 485)
dijon mustard, to serve

Staples
EVOO, LMN

Remove the steaks from the fridge 1 hour before cooking.

Light a fire using wood or charcoal, then let the flames die down until you have an even bed of hot coals, with the occasional flicker of small flames. (You can also use a gas barbecue, of course.)

Lightly coat the steaks in oil. Season with a light coating of the ground white pepper. Just before you cook, generously pack the sea salt on both sides. Don't do this ahead of time, or the steaks will 'weep' and you will lose moisture and flavour. The coating will seem heavy, but it protects the meat and stops the fat burning over the intense heat.

Lay the steaks on the hottest part of the grill, but don't allow them to flame. If they do, move them where they don't, so you don't ruin the flavour of the steaks. Cook for 4 minutes on each side, then rest in a warm place for 6 minutes.

Return the steaks to the grill and cook for 3 minutes on each for medium-rare, which I think is ideal for this cut, but adjust the cooking time to your liking. Please don't cook much more, though, as you will only lose flavour and texture.

The steaks don't need to rest as much now because of the initial cooking and resting, but pause before slicing while you ready the condiments or gather diners.

Serve as is for two – if outrageously hungry – or cut off the bone, then cut each steak into six or seven slices on an angle, reassembling on the plate with the bone. Drizzle with oil and serve with condiments and lemon on the side. Don't forget to gnaw on the bone, too, as some of the best morsels are there.

Traditional French steak tartare

This is a traditional steak tartare. It's a dish that polarises a little, with both raw egg and raw meat being off-putting to some – although the high seasoning and flavouring would probably be much more palatable than many adverse to the idea might realise. But it's not a dish you push on people. It's one you come to over time. With the right guests, it's a superb dinner-party starter, with a good deal of table theatre – something I don't mind. The balance of seasoning and chilli heat in this are entirely personal, so tweak and adjust as you see fit, but always ensure you start with a beautiful piece of meat, and ideally one that hasn't been vacuum-packed, as the wet-ageing character can be a little prominent. **Serves 6–10 as a starter**

1 × 900 g (2 lb) beef eye fillet
3 egg yolks
40 g (1½ oz) small capers
40 g (1½ oz) cornichons, finely diced
40 g (1½ oz) finely diced French shallots
3 tablespoons finely chopped parsley

baguette toasts, to serve
yellow leaves from 1 celery heart

Cognac dijon dressing
80 g (2¾ oz) dijon mustard
80 ml (2½ fl oz/⅓ cup) tomato ketchup
2 tablespoons extra-virgin olive oil

1½ tablespoons worcestershire sauce
1 tablespoon Cognac, or brandy
6 drops of hot sauce (such as red Tabasco)

Staples
EVOO, S&P

Trim any sinew or silver skin from the beef and slice lengthways about 5 mm (¼ in) thick. Cut those slices into 5 mm (¼ in) strips, then dice. Take your time and do this carefully to achieve an even result. Chill the beef.

Combine the dressing ingredients in a small bowl and season with salt and pepper. Refrigerate if not using immediately; it's important to keep everything chilled.

When ready to serve, add the beef to a chilled bowl with the dressing and toss to coat. Pile onto a serving plate in a mound and top with the egg yolks. Around the beef, make little mounds of the capers, cornichon, shallot and parsley. Finish with a drizzle of oil.

Serve with the baguette toasts and celery leaves on the side. Present the tartare at the table like that, and then combine everything for that bit of theatre.

Make it different

With chips. Instead of – or as well as – the baguette, serve with pommes frites or freshly fried potato chips, or even some quality plain potato crisps. Watercress is also a nice addition.

With lettuce. Separate the leaves of a head of chicory (witlof/endive) or butter lettuce and use as cups for the tartare.

With tarragon. Try this with chopped tarragon as well as the parsley.

With horseradish. Fresh horseradish grated over the top of the just-mixed tartare takes the dish to another level.

With truffles. Serve with truffled shaved over the top.

Beef carpaccio

Beef carpaccio, of one type or another, has been on my menus as long as I can recall. Thinly sliced prime eye fillet with shavings of Parmigiano Reggiano, a handful of rocket (arugula), a slick of the best peppery olive oil, a generous seasoning of salt flakes and freshly ground pepper, with a hand-rolled grissini set across the plate and a lemon cheek on the side, is a wonderful way to start a meal. From that base, you can add things like fried capers, pickles, watercress, fried shallots, fresh horseradish … whatever works for you. Just don't overload the plate, as it's all about the meat – both the flavour and the texture. As with steak tartare, this is best made with meat that hasn't been vacuum-packed. **Serves 4–6**

500 g (1 lb 2 oz) centre cut eye fillet, trimmed
¼ bunch of flat-leaf (Italian) parsley, leaves finely sliced
6 tiny pickled onions, sliced in rings

2 tablespoons fried shallots (see p. 600)
80 g (2¾ oz) Parmigiano Reggiano
1 × quantity Lemon emulsion (p. 80)

Grissini (p. 856), to serve
Staples
S&P

Roll the beef tightly in plastic wrap, then chill in the freezer for 30 minutes to firm up, to make it easier to cut. Don't freeze it, though.

Once firm, unwrap the beef and slice 2–3 mm (⅛–⅙ in) thick, laying the pieces on a serving plate as they're cut, with the slices overlapping a little.

Season the beef very well with salt and pepper, then top with the parsley, onion and shallots. Using a vegetable peeler, shave the Parmigiano over, then spoon the emulsion over.

Serve a couple of grissini across each plate if serving individually, or stand them in a tumbler if making a platter.

Make it different

With Jerusalem artichokes. Peel and julienne four Jerusalem artichokes, then immediately dress in the seasoned lemon emulsion. Scatter over the seasoned beef before adding the remaining ingredients.

With broad beans. Toss a large handful of chopped double-podded broad beans and the parsley in the emulsion, then spoon over the seasoned beef before adding the other ingredients.

With truffle. Shave over fresh black or white truffle just before serving.

A nod to Harry's Bar original carpaccio

A nod to the iconic carpaccio of Venice's Harry's Bar – home of the undisputed original. There, the 'universal sauce' – as it is known – is a simple affair, apparently consisting of mayonnaise, lemon juice, worcestershire sauce and milk, though there's undoubtedly a secret element. This version is a little more complex. As said, it's a nod, not an imitation. Combine a half portion of the Cognac dijon dressing (p. 279) with 150 g (5½ oz) home-made mayonnaise (pp. 74–5). If you like, add it to a squeeze bottle or piping (icing) bag fitted with a fine nozzle. Slice and plate 500 g (1 lb 2 oz) centre cut eye fillet, trimmed, drizzle with a little oil, then pipe or smear on the sauce. Finely grate 80 g (2¾ oz) Parmigiano Reggiano over the top. Add about 50 g (1¾ oz) rocket (arugula) or curly endive (frisée) and a few pickled cocktail onions and serve immediately, with lemon cheeks or wedges and Grissini (p. 856).

A nod to Harry's Bar original carpaccio

Grilled minute steak with soy & sesame mushrooms

Preheat the barbecue on high. Place 4 × 180 g (6½ oz) scotch fillet steaks between two pieces of plastic wrap and beat with a mallet, rolling pin or bottle to just under 1 cm (½ in) thick. Oil and season 5 large field mushrooms and grill for 3–4 minutes on each side. Meanwhile, make a marinade by combining the following in a bowl: 2 tablespoons oyster sauce, 2 tablespoons light soy sauce, 2 tablespoons extra-virgin olive oil, ½ teaspoon sesame oil, 8 cm (3¼ in) piece of fresh ginger, peeled and finely grated, 2 small finely grated garlic cloves and the juice of ½ lemon. Trim and separate 150 g (5½ oz) enoki mushrooms, slice 10 champignons, finely slice 2 long red chillies on an angle and finely slice 6 spring onions (scallions) (white and some green parts). To the marinade, add the enoki mushrooms, champignons, chilli and most of the spring onion and toss through. Set aside to marinate and soften. Slice the grilled mushrooms, then toss through the marinated raw mushrooms. Season and lightly oil the steaks, then cook on the hottest part of the grill for 1½ minutes each side. Rest for a couple of minutes, then pour the resting juices into the mushroom bowl. Slice the steaks on an angle and arrange on serving plates. Spoon the mushrooms and dressing over, sprinkle with 2 large handfuls coriander (cilantro) leaves and the remaining spring onion and serve immediately. Serves 4–6.

Cured beef with black onion spice & parmesan

I make this as a centrepiece appetiser, something for one of those major holiday days devoted to eating and drinking, or just because eating and drinking feel like they need to be celebrated. It's something to be snacked on with a glass of wine or aperitivo in those exciting first moments when your guests are caught up in the wafting aromas of all the fabulous food to come. Treat it like a plate of salumi, or portion all the elements onto small slices of charred bread to make balancing that drink a little bit easier; it also makes a lovely individually plated light starter. **Serves 12–16 as an appetiser**

900 g (2 lb) mid-section eye fillet, trimmed
50 g (1¾ oz/⅓ cup) pistachio kernels, roughly chopped
4 handfuls of rocket (arugula), or watercress
120 g (4½ oz) Parmigiano Reggiano
charred Sourdough bread (p. 847) and/or Grissini (p. 856), to serve

Horseradish cream dressing (p. 70), to serve
Crema fresca (p. 364), to serve
pickled cocktail onions, to serve

Gin & allspice cure
120 g (4½ oz) brown sugar
100 g (3½ oz) sea salt
80 ml (2½ fl oz/⅓ cup) vermouth or gin
3 teaspoons roughly ground black peppercorns

10 allspice berries, roughly ground

Black onion spice
1½ bunches of spring onions (scallions), made into ash (see p. 602)
2 teaspoons finely ground fennel seeds
1 teaspoon finely ground black pepper

Staples
EVOO, LMN, S&P

Combine the cure ingredients in a bowl. Lay out two overlapping layers of plastic wrap large enough to wrap the beef. Spoon half the cure over the plastic. Lay the beef on top, then top with the remaining cure and tightly wrap. Place the beef in a deep dish, top with a tray that fits inside, then weigh down with some tins of food. Refrigerate for 6 hours, turning the beef over about halfway through.

Once cured, unwrap the beef, clean off the cure and pat dry with paper towel.

Combine the black onion spice ingredients in a bowl, then spread out on a lined baking tray. Roll the beef in the mix to coat completely, then roll tightly in plastic wrap. Refrigerate for about 20 minutes, until firm.

Carefully slice the beef 2–3 mm (⅛–⅙ in) thick. Trying not to handle it too much, lay the slices on a serving plate.

Spoon the horseradish dressing and crema fresca over the beef. Scatter the pistachios and rocket around. Grate or shave the Parmigiano over, then finish with the cocktail onions and a drizzle of oil. Serve with lemon and charred sourdough and/or grissini.

Ragù alla bolognese GF

Pair with

Pappardelle (p. 112), rigatoni, penne or Gnocchi (pp. 131, 137).

Stir in a handful of frozen peas before serving.

1 × quantity semolina pasta in pici shape (see p. 131).

Roasted scotch fillet GF

A large piece of scotch fillet also slow-roasts wonderfully, and it's perfect for a large gathering, with a 2.5 kg (5½ lb) piece feeding eight to ten, along with sides and salad, or course. Strip the leaves from 5 or 6 rosemary or thyme sprigs and chop finely. Combine with 150 ml (5 fl oz) olive oil, 2 tablespoons dijon mustard, 4 smashed garlic cloves and 80 ml (2½ fl oz/⅓ cup) balsamic vinegar, saba, vincotto or even sherry vinegar. Season the meat with salt and pepper, and rub two-thirds of the marinade over. Marinate at room temperature for 2 hours or overnight. Bring to room temperature for 1 hour, then transfer to a rack over a roasting tin and cook in a preheated 110°C (230°F) fan-forced oven for 2½–3 hours, until the internal temperature is 55°C (135°F) for medium-rare. Pour the reserved marinade over the meat, cover loosely with foil and rest for 20 minutes before slicing. Serve with the resting juices poured over the meat. A Beurre rouge (p. 69) or Horseradish cream (p. 70) would work well here, along with some Salt-roasted shallots (p. 595) and Classic potato mash (p. 625) and your favourite vegetables.

Firstly, this is an inauthentic recipe. It is a corruption adjusted over time. A real bolognese would not have garlic in it, nor chicken, and red wine would never be suggested as an option. But rightly or wrongly, 'bolognese' has become a byword for a meat ragù. Of the many versions that I make, this is the one I make the most. It is based on one my grandmother Grace used to cook, although she always added peas as well. It's also a lighter version, with the pork, chicken and milk contributing to that effect. I'm not sure how chicken made it into the original recipe. I suspect Grace used chicken livers (a not uncommon practice to get depth of flavour) – but one day there were none available and minced (ground) chicken occupied that position, never to be replaced. The thigh meat does contribute texture – and, well, it works – so they have remained in my version, too (though you could also replace the chicken with pork mince).

Like any meat ragù, this improves over a day or two, or more. So, if I'm freezing some, I will do so once it has matured a little. Frying mince separately may seem cumbersome, but it allows you to colour the meat without it boiling in its own juices – and it makes a big difference. **Serves 10**

50 g (1¾ oz) unsalted butter	300 g (10½ oz) minced (ground) pork	1 sprig of rosemary
150 ml (5 fl oz) extra-virgin olive oil	900 g (2 lb) minced (ground) beef	½ nutmeg, finely grated
2 onions, finely diced	200 g (7 oz) tomato paste (concentrated purée)	1 teaspoon chilli flakes
6 garlic cloves, finely sliced	200 ml (7 fl oz) milk	2 × 400 g (14 oz) tins diced tomatoes
3 celery stalks, very finely sliced	300 ml (10 fl oz) red or white wine	1.2 litres (41 fl oz) White chicken stock (p. 54)
100 g (3½ oz) pancetta, finely diced	2 fresh bay leaves	**Staples**
300 g (10½ oz) minced (ground) chicken thighs	2 sage sprigs, leaves chopped	*S&P*

Heat the butter and 100 ml (3½ fl oz) of the oil in a large heavy-based saucepan over a medium heat. Cook the onion and garlic until softened, about 5 minutes. Add the celery and cook for about 15 minutes, until caramelised.

Add the pancetta and fry for a minute or two, then add the chicken and pork mince, bit by bit, crumbling it in and stirring through as the meat browns.

Meanwhile, heat the remaining oil in a large frying pan over a medium heat. Add the beef mince and cook until browned, about 10 minutes – add a bit at a time if there's a danger of crowding the pan at the start.

Once the meat is browned in both pans, add the beef to the main pan and stir it through. Add the tomato paste and stir through for a couple of minutes, then add the milk and simmer for 3 minutes. Stir in the wine and simmer for 5 minutes.

Once the liquid has almost gone, stir in the bay leaves, sage, rosemary, nutmeg and chilli flakes and season lightly with salt and pepper. Stir in the tomatoes and stock, then bring to a simmer. Turn the heat down to low and cook for about 2 hours, stirring occasionally.

Once the sauce has reduced and the flavours intensified, adjust the seasoning as needed. I like to stir the ragù through freshly cooked pasta, and finish it with fresh ricotta or freshly grated Parmigiano Reggiano.

Make it vegan VG
For a vegan option, see the Vegetable bolognese on p. 576.

Boeuf bourguignon

This is classic winter food, with the braising cuts of beef giving up their collagen to gloss and thicken this hearty stew, while the meat slowly yields to become collapsingly tender. The time taken to properly caramelise the beef, and then to braise it, and the addition of porcini mushrooms (and importantly, their soaking water) – as well as the bacon, the bundle of orange peel and herbs, the seeming excess of onion and garlic, a nearly full bottle of wine, and the best stock you can lay your hands on – all conspire to make this dish deeply complex and utterly comforting. So, please don't skimp on ingredients or technique. **Serves 6**

15 g (½ oz) dried porcini mushrooms
2 fresh bay leaves
¼ bunch of thyme
1 rosemary sprig
4 parsley stalks
2 strips of orange peel
200 g (7 oz) thick-cut streaky bacon, cut into 2 cm (¾ in) dice

10 garlic cloves, smashed and peeled
2 onions, diced, or 18 French shallots, peeled and left whole
60 g (2 oz) plain (all-purpose) flour
1.5 kg (3 lb 5 oz) chuck steak, oyster blade and/or shin, cut into 6 cm (2½ in) dice

1 tablespoon tomato paste (concentrated purée)
600 ml (20½ fl oz) red wine
800 ml (27 fl oz) Beef stock (p. 55), or Golden chicken stock (p. 54), warmed
80 g (2¾ oz) unsalted butter
250 g (9 oz) champignon mushrooms, cut in half

Staples
EVOO, S&P

Preheat the oven to 165°C (330°F) fan-forced.

Cover the porcini mushrooms with boiling water. Leave to rehydrate for 10 minutes, then strain off and reserve the liquid. Chop the porcini finely and set aside.

Tie the bay leaves, thyme, rosemary, parsley stalks and orange peel together with kitchen twine, by winding it all down the length and tying securely into a bouquet garni. Set aside.

Heat a large, flameproof casserole dish over a medium heat. Add a glug of oil and the bacon and cook until browned, about 6 minutes. Lift the bacon out and set aside.

Add another good splash of oil and cook the onion and garlic until golden, about 10 minutes. Lift out, leaving most of the oil behind, and set aside separate from the bacon.

Add some more oil, then scatter the flour over the beef, tossing to coat. Cook the beef in three batches over a medium–high heat, seasoning with salt and pepper, until well caramelised, about 6 minutes per batch. Once cooked, tip the fat out of the pan and return the bacon, onion and porcini to the pan with the beef. Add the tomato paste and cook to darken slightly, about 3 minutes.

Return the onion and garlic, then add the bouquet garni. Pour in the wine and reduce by about half, about 5 minutes. Pour in the stock and reserved porcini water, and bring to a simmer.

Press a piece of baking paper on top of the braise to cover. Put the lid on and braise in the oven for 2½ hours.

Towards the end of cooking, melt the butter in a frying pan over a high heat, then add the champignons. Season with salt and pepper and sauté for about 2 minutes to soften.

Remove the baking paper from the braise and add the mushrooms to the stew. Cover with the lid and braise for a further 30 minutes.

Adjust the seasoning as needed, then serve, or cool and refrigerate overnight, as the flavours only improve on standing. Reheat, uncovered, in a 180°C (350°F) fan-forced oven for 30 minutes.

Pair with

Classic potato mash (p. 625).

Boiled potatoes tossed in butter and chopped parsley.

Glazed turnips or carrots.

Boeuf bourguignon cobbler

Prepare a batch of Classic scone dough (p. 772) and roll into balls. Arrange on top of the fully cooked Boeuf bourguignon (left) braise, leaving a 1 cm (½ in) gap between each ball. Cook, uncovered, in a 200°C (400°F) fan-forced oven for about 20–30 minutes, until the scones have risen and are lightly browned on top.

Boeuf bourguignon pie

Filling a deep 23 cm (9 in) pie dish with the warm cooked Boeuf bourguignon (left) braise. Brush the edge of the dish with an egg wash (see p. 13). Top with a 400 g (14 oz) piece of Classic puff pastry (p. 822) or Rough puff pastry (p. 823), rolled 4–5 mm (¼ in) thick, and cut to fit with a 2 cm (¾ in) overhang. From the excess pastry, cut out pieces to decorate the pie. Brush the pastry with more of the egg wash, add the decorations, then egg-wash them as well. Bake for 25–30 minutes at 200°C (400°F) fan-forced, until the pastry is richly golden and puffed. Serve with a green salad or buttered peas.

Italian-style braised beef GF

Pair with

Serve over Polenta (p. 383) or pasta – or with potato mash or Gnocchi alla romana (p. 138) on the side.

Slow-roasted eye fillet GF

Cooking eye fillet very slowly will yield an evenly cooked and extra-tender piece of meat. Not that eye fillet needs to be more tender, but even, slow cooking to a perfect degree is the ideal way to maximise the texture and delicate flavour. You can simply season a 1.2–1.3 kg (2 lb 10 oz–2 lb 14 oz) trussed centre-cut eye fillet with salt and pepper before cooking, or season and coat with 1 tablespoon dijon mustard, vincotto, saba or balsamic vinegar, then marinate on the bench for an hour with 5 sprigs of thyme or rosemary, 3 smashed garlic cloves and a drizzle of olive oil. Sear the meat all over for about 8–10 minutes to evenly colour, then place on a rack in a roasting tin and cook in a preheated 110°C (230°F) fan-forced oven for 2–2½ hours, until the internal temperature is about 45°C (115°F) for medium-rare. Rest, loosely covered with foil, for 10 minutes, then serve with your favourite trimmings.

Sophisticated yet robust, this is a braise that verges on a ragù. Indeed, it can happily be served with mash or polenta, or be tossed through with pasta – either as is, or with the meat shredded a little. **Serves 6**

1.2 kg (2 lb 10 oz) beef shin, rib meat or cheeks, cut into 6 cm (2½ in) dice
150 g (5½ oz) pancetta, cut into 5 mm (¼ in) dice
2 onions, finely diced
6 garlic cloves, chopped
2 celery stalks, finely diced

2 carrots, finely diced
3 tablespoons tomato paste (concentrated purée)
1 tablespoon fennel seeds
3 teaspoons ground allspice
3 rosemary sprigs
4 sage sprigs, leaves picked
1 tablespoon dried oregano

2 fresh bay leaves
500 ml (17 fl oz/2 cups) red wine
1.5 litres (51 fl oz/6 cups) Brown beef stock (p. 55), or White chicken stock (p. 54)

Staples
EVOO, FLR, S&P

Season the beef with salt and pepper and very lightly dust with flour.

Heat a good splash of oil in a heavy-based casserole dish over a medium heat. Add the beef in batches, seasoning with more salt, and searing on all sides until well browned and crusted, 2–3 minutes per side. Don't rush this step. Set the seared beef aside.

Pour off the oil and wipe out the pot, but leave in any caramelisation unless it's burnt.

Add the pancetta and another splash of oil to the pot. Cook over a medium heat until a little brown, about 5 minutes. Add the onion, garlic, celery and carrot and cook until caramelised, about 15 minutes.

Season with salt and pepper, then stir in the tomato paste and cook for 3 minutes. Add the fennel seeds, allspice, herbs and bay leaves.

Stir the beef back in until coated, then add the wine, scraping up any residual caramelisation. Reduce the liquid by half, then stir in the stock and bring to a simmer.

Reduce the heat to low, partially cover and cook for about 2 hours, until the meat is tender and the sauce reduced. (You can also braise the beef in a preheated 150°C/300°F fan-forced oven for 2 hours, with the lid ajar.)

Adjust the seasoning and serve.

Pedro Ximénez–braised beef cheeks with celeriac & parsnip purée & persillade GF

This is an involved, luxurious and deeply rewarding dish: a depth-of-winter-with-time-on-your-hands kind of recipe. This is all about building deep flavour slowly, then highlighting key aromatics by reintroducing them to the sauce when you finish it. This is important when making complex flavoured sauces like this, as you want those bass notes from the slow cooking, but you also want to recapture some of the vibrant character that was dulled in the process. Take your time and enjoy making this. **Serves 6–8**

175 g (6 oz) butter

2.5 kg (5½ lb) trimmed beef cheeks (6 large cheeks), or beef ribs (6–8)

2 onions, roughly diced

1 large garlic bulb, skin on, cloves separated and smashed

2 carrots, roughly diced

4 celery stalks, sliced

2 leeks, white part only, sliced into 2 cm (¾ in) rings

3 teaspoons fennel seeds

2 cinnamon sticks

4 star anise

3 fresh bay leaves

10 thyme sprigs

200 ml (7 fl oz) Pedro Ximénez sherry

750 ml (25 fl oz/3 cups) full-bodied red wine

1 litre (34 fl oz/4 cups) Brown beef stock (p. 55), or Double chicken stock (p. 54)

1 × quantity Persillade (p. 86)

Celeriac & parsnip purée

1 large celeriac, peeled and cut into small chunks

(650 g/1 lb 7 oz trimmed weight)

4 parsnips, peeled, cored and cut into small chunks (350 g/12½ oz trimmed weight)

3 garlic cloves

500 ml (17 fl oz/2 cups) full-cream (whole) milk

100 g (3½ oz) butter

100 ml (3½ fl oz) pouring (single/light) cream

Staples

EVOO, FLR, S&WP

Preheat the oven to 160°C (320°F) fan-forced.

Add a knob of the butter and a good splash of oil to a large heavy-based casserole dish over a medium heat. Season the beef well with salt and white pepper and coat with flour, shaking the excess off. Brown all over, gradually adding more butter as you go, but reserving 70 g (2½ oz) for finishing the sauce. You want a nice deep crust on the cheeks, but be careful not to burn them. Remove from the pan and set aside.

Wipe out the pot and add a splash of oil over a medium heat. Cook the onion, garlic, carrot, celery and leek until sticky and nicely caramelised, 15–20 minutes.

Stir in the fennel seeds, cinnamon sticks and three of the star anise, along with the bay leaves and eight of the thyme sprigs. Pour in half the sherry and 650 ml (22 fl oz) of the wine. Return the beef cheeks so that they're nestled snugly in one layer, then cover with the stock.

Bring to a simmer and skim off any impurities, then cover and braise in the oven for 3 hours.

Uncover and set aside for 20 minutes, before carefully lifting the cheeks out of the liquid and onto a plate. Cover with plastic wrap and chill for 2 hours, which will firm up the meat and make it easy to slice.

Strain the braising liquid into a jug and chill for about 30 minutes, until a fat layer forms. Remove the fat layer. Reserve two ladlefuls of the liquid and add the rest to a saucepan over a medium heat. Stir in the remaining wine, sherry, thyme and star anise and reduce by at least two-thirds.

For the purée, add the celeriac and parsnip to a saucepan with the garlic, milk and a couple of pinches of salt. Top up with enough water to just cover. Cut a cartouche to fit the pan, then cook over a very low heat for about 1 hour, until the vegetables are very tender. Drain, then transfer to a blender. Gradually adding the butter and cream, blend into a smooth purée. Season with salt and white pepper and keep warm.

Pour the reserved braising liquid into a deep-sided frying pan. Slice each beef cheek in half, add to the pan, then gently reheat over a medium heat for 2–3 minutes.

Strain the thyme and star anise from the other pan of sauce, then reheat the sauce. Stir in the remaining 70 g (2½ oz) of butter until glossy. Adjust the seasoning as needed.

To serve, spoon some purée onto each plate, then add the beef cheeks, draining off any of the braising liquid first. Spoon the remaining sauce over the cheeks and finish with some persillade, with any residual sauce served on the side.

Classic roasted eye fillet (GF)

Rest a 1.2–1.3 kg (2 lb 6 oz–2 lb 9 oz) trussed centre-cut eye fillet at room temperature. Season with salt and lots of pepper, then coat with olive oil. Sear the fillet in a large frying pan over a medium heat until browned all over, 8–10 minutes. Transfer to a rack in a roasting tin, or place atop a 'trivet' of onions, cut into three rings each, and roast at 200°C (400°F) fan-forced for 18–20 minutes, until the internal temperature is 45°C (115°F) for medium-rare. Rest for 15 minutes before slicing and serving with roasted root vegetables and Classic potato mash (p. 625) and with seasonal greens. Some quality dijon mustard and/or a Beurre rouge (p. 69) or Horseradish cream (p. 70) would not go astray.

Roasted eye fillet with Japanese seasonings

Use the same roasting method as the classic roasted eye fillet (above), but make a coating mix by combining 2 tablespoons finely grated fresh ginger, 2 tablespoons red miso paste, 2 tablespoons light soy sauce, 1 tablespoon mustard powder and 1 tablespoon caster (superfine) sugar. Season the beef with salt and white pepper, then coat with the ginger mixture. Either sear after the meat has warmed at room temperature, or marinate for a few hours, or even overnight. Roast as normal. Serve with rice, wilted greens, wilted asparagus and/or shiitake mushrooms, and some pickled daikon (see p. 304) or the like.

Vine leaf beef & bone marrow pie GF

Pair with

Labneh (p. 362) and Dukkah (p. 13).

Tahini dip/sauce (p. 71) or plain yoghurt, and a grain salad (pp. 378–9) or wild rice salad (p. 378).

Quick herb salad (p. 267).

Braised zucchini with fresh tomato & herbs (p. 671).

Grilled eggplant with tahini, pomegranate & mint (p. 516).

Shaved brussels sprouts with roasted king brown mushrooms, manchego & maple dressing (p. 453).

This is inspired by a fabulously rich and fragrant pie from Yotam Ottolenghi's *Nopi* cookbook. Well-caramelised celeriac provides a lovely rounded flavour base for minced beef and lamb, enhanced with currants, pine nuts, rice, dried herbs and gentle spices, then studded with bone marrow and swaddled in brined vine leaves before being baked. A truly stunning dish. You'll probably need to order the bone marrow ahead, from a good butcher, and you'll find the jarred or vacuum-packed vine leaves in Mediterranean delicatessens. **Serves 6–8**

40 g (1½ oz) currants
80 ml (2½ fl oz/⅓ cup) red-wine vinegar
125 ml (4 fl oz/½ cup) extra-virgin olive oil
6 French shallots, finely diced
4 garlic cloves, finely chopped
500 g (1 lb 2 oz) trimmed celeriac, finely diced
1½ teaspoons ground cinnamon
2 teaspoons ground allspice

½ teaspoon ground black pepper
2 teaspoons dried Greek oregano (rigani)
1½ teaspoons dried mint
2 tomatoes, coarsely grated
150 g (5½ oz) arborio rice
40 g (1½ oz/¼ cup) pine nuts, toasted
350 g (12½ oz) minced (ground) beef
150 g (5½ oz) minced (ground) lamb
1 tablespoon salt flakes

200 g (7 oz) brined vine leaves, rinsed and dried
100 g (3½ oz) bone marrow, cut into 2 cm (¾ in) pieces
600 ml (20½ fl oz) Veal stock (p. 55, the Brown beef stock made with veal bones), or Double chicken stock (p. 54)
350 g (12½ oz) plain yoghurt

Staples
S&P

In a small saucepan, simmer the currants in the vinegar for a few minutes, then set aside to plump for 10 minutes.

Meanwhile, heat the oil in a large, deep frying pan over a medium heat. Cook the shallot and garlic until softened, about 5 minutes. Add the celeriac, season with salt and pepper and cook for 30 minutes over a low heat to caramelise.

Stir in the spices, oregano, mint and tomato. Cook for 5 minutes, then add the rice, pine nuts and the vinegary currants and stir through to coat.

Tip into a large bowl and cool for 5 minutes. Add the beef, lamb and salt and very thoroughly mix together.

Line the base of a 28 cm (11 in) ovenproof frying pan with a circle of baking paper. Line the pan well with overlapping vine leaves, shiny side down. Tip the filling into the pan, pressing firmly to flatten, then stud with the marrow, pushing it into the mix. Cover the top with an overlapping layer of leaves, tucking down the sides to cover completely. Refrigerate for 30 minutes to firm up.

Preheat the oven to 200°C (400°F) fan-forced.

Heat the stock and pour over the pie. Place the frying pan over a medium heat and simmer for 10 minutes.

Cover with a plate, transfer to the oven and bake for 45 minutes, until most of the stock is absorbed.

Remove from the oven and rest for 15 minutes, until the remaining stock is absorbed.

Once rested, carefully invert the pie onto a plate. Cut into six to eight wedges and serve with dollops of plain yoghurt.

Maltagliata of beef with rocket, fine kale & ricotta

Maltagliati is a type of roughly cut pasta, with the name – mal tagliati – translating as 'badly cut'. Originally, these irregular tickets of pasta were no doubt scraps from making other pasta types, such as ravioli or tortellini. I am probably guilty of mangling the language somewhat, but maltagliata was the term I applied to a beef dish I created when we opened mr. wolf in 2004. The beef was roughly cut, pan-fried and served on a rocket (arugula) and radicchio salad with fresh ricotta, and a sauce made in the pan with ample balsamic vinegar. It's still on the menu more than fifteen years later, and the name – whatever disservice I have done to the language – has stuck. **Serves 4**

½ iceberg lettuce, torn into bite-sized pieces
3 handfuls of mature rocket (arugula) leaves
3 handfuls of young Russian red kale, or curly endive (frisée), young cavolo nero or radicchio
4 radishes, finely sliced

4 flat-leaf (Italian) parsley sprigs, leaves torn
2 handfuls of basil leaves
125 ml (4 fl oz/½ cup) extra-virgin olive oil
150 ml (5 fl oz) balsamic vinegar
700 g (1 lb 9 oz) rump steak, sliced 1 cm (½ in) thick

150 g (5½ oz/1 cup) plain (all-purpose) flour
½ red or white salad onion, finely sliced
250 g (9 oz/1 cup) ricotta
50 g (1¾ oz/⅓ cup) pine nuts, toasted

Staples
EVOO, S&P

Arrange the lettuce, rocket, kale, radish, half the parsley and half the basil on a serving plate. Drizzle with a little of the oil and a splash of the vinegar, then season with salt and pepper.

Heat a heavy-based pan over a medium heat. Add 80 ml (2½ fl oz/⅓ cup) of the oil and heat for 2 minutes. When hot, toss the beef in the flour, shaking off any excess, then add to the pan. Turn the heat up to high and fry without moving for 2 minutes. Season with salt and pepper, then flip the meat over and cook for another minute, seasoning again.

Remove from the heat and add the remaining vinegar, swirling to combine. Add the onion and remaining oil, and a little more if needed, and swirl to combine.

Tong the beef onto the salad, pouring the pan sauces over everything. Top with the ricotta, pine nuts and remaining herbs and serve immediately.

Beef & pork loaf with haloumi, pistachio & pomegranate molasses

I endured many loaves of anonymous meat as a child, and I never really saw a career in professional cooking as a crusade to righting that particular wrong. Cooking for television or writing recipes for other media does, however, sometimes push you down laneways you had previously thought too dark. And while sometimes you get mugged, other times there are some very happy surprises. This is very much in the serendipitous camp – spicy and textural, with the salty squeak of haloumi and crunch of pistachios, and topped with a sweetly tart glaze of pomegranate molasses. This loaf is delicious hot, and makes equally wonderful picnic fare served cold in warmer weather. **Serves 6**

Roasted standing rib rack (GF)

Bring a standing rib rack to room temperature for 2 hours. A six-point rack weighing about 3.5 kg (7 lb 12 oz) will feed six to eight, while a four-point rack will feed four or five (ask your butcher to remove the chine bone). Season with salt and black pepper and rub with oil, then season in a large frying pan over a medium heat, browning all surfaces. This will take about 20 minutes. Transfer to a rack over a roasting tin, or set on a 'trivet' of thickly cut onions. Roast in a preheated 180°C (350°F) fan-forced oven for about 45 minutes for a four-point rack, or 1¼ hours for a six-point rack – we're looking for an internal temperature of around 45°C (115°F) for medium-rare. Rest, loosely covered with foil, for 30 minutes for the smaller roast, and 35–40 minutes for the larger roast. Slice and serve with your favourite condiments and trimmings. Or, for a slow-roast option, season and rub the room temperature rib rack with oil. Roast in a preheated 95°C (200°F) oven for 4 hours, rotating the tray every 45 minutes. It will reach an internal temperature of 53°C (127°F) for rare–medium rare. Carve the meat from the bone and slice the meat.

Pair with

Classic potato mash (p. 625) with a leafy salad, green beans, peas or braised silverbeet (Swiss chard).

Slice finely and serve in sandwiches with cheese and chutney or relish.

Serve a thick slice on some mash, topped with a fried egg, with relish on the side.

Finely slice any left-over loaf, drizzle with oil and pomegranate molasses, and serve with a dip, pickles, olives and flatbread.

Left-over corned beef, egg & cabbage salad with smoked salt (GF)

Cut 200 g (7 oz) Corned beef (p. 289) into matchsticks, then add to a large bowl along with 300 g (10½ oz) finely shaved savoy cabbage, 80 g (2¾ oz) finely grated Grana Padano, 2 finely diced dill pickles, 3 tablespoons mayonnaise (pp. 74–5), 1 tablespoon sour cream, yoghurt or crème fraîche, 2 handfuls flat-leaf (Italian) parsley, chopped and 2 teaspoons ground aleppo pepper or a few pinches of cayenne pepper. Season with smoked salt and combine. Pile onto a serving plate, then slice 2 hard-boiled eggs and lay them on the side. Season with a little more salt and serve. Serves 2–4.

Pair with

Mustard kipfler potatoes (p. 622), Eggplant & tomato kasundi (p. 520), Salsa verde (p. 86), in a sandwich with Jerusalem artichoke pickle (p. 545) or freshly grated horseradish.

Corned beef with herb & mustard sauce

Make a roux from 25 g (1 oz) butter and 25 g (1 oz) flour in a small saucepan over a medium heat. Add 300 ml (10 fl oz) of the hot poaching stock from the corned beef recipe (right), plus 200 ml (7 fl oz) cream or milk and spike with 1½ tablespoons dijon or English mustard. Finish with a few handfuls of chopped fresh herbs (parsley, chervil, tarragon) or watercress. Spoon over the warm corned beef and serve with horseradish and mash.

---

1 onion, finely chopped
6 garlic cloves, finely chopped
3 teaspoons ground cinnamon
3 teaspoons chilli flakes
350 g (12½ oz) minced (ground) pork
450 g (1 lb) minced (ground) beef

2 eggs, lightly beaten
120 g (4 oz/1½ cups) fresh breadcrumbs
1 tablespoon salt flakes
2 teaspoons Baharat (p. 6) (optional)
½ bunch of oregano, leaves coarsely chopped

175 g (6 oz) haloumi, cut into 1 cm (½ in) dice
100 g (3½ oz/⅔ cup) pistachio kernels
2 tablespoons pomegranate molasses

Staples
BTR, EVOO, S&P

Preheat the oven to 180°C (350°F) fan-forced. Grease a 25 cm (10 in) loaf (bar) tin or ovenproof dish.

Heat a good splash of oil in a large frying pan over a medium heat. Cook the onion and garlic until softened, about 3 minutes. Stir in the cinnamon and chilli flakes, season with salt and pepper and remove from the heat.

Working in two batches, add the onion mixture, pork, beef, eggs, breadcrumbs, salt and baharat, if using (it's not essential, but it will brighten the spice notes), to a food processor and process until well combined. Tip the batches into a bowl and thoroughly combine, then mix the oregano and haloumi through.

Spoon the mixture into the loaf tin, smoothing the surface flat. Top with the pistachios, pressing them into the mix. Cover with baking paper, then foil.

Bake for 40 minutes, then uncover, glaze with the pomegranate molasses and bake for a further 20 minutes.

Rest briefly before turning out, slicing and serving hot, or serving cold.

Corned beef (GF)

Corned beef is one of the dishes my mother made extremely well, usually with mashed potato and peas, and more often than not in the cooler months. I do also remember enjoying a hideously sweet, yellow chutney with it as well. That piece of beef would typically have been silverside, a cut that really needs to be corned to give positive returns – in my experience at least. I'm perfectly happy with corned silverside, but always opt for corned girello, if you can get it. Corned beef is also marvellous the next day, especially in a sandwich with cheddar and a good chutney (see p. 520). **Serves 4–6**

1 × 1.5 kg (3 lb 5 oz) corned beef girello or silverside, rinsed

2 celery stalks, cut into large dice
1 carrot, cut into large dice
1 onion, cut into large dice

½ bunch of parsley stalks
2 fresh bay leaves
1 teaspoon black peppercorns

Add the beef to a large saucepan and cover with cold water. Bring to a simmer, then drain.

Add the beef to a large clean saucepan with the remaining ingredients. Cover well with fresh water and bring to a simmer, then gently simmer so the water just ticks for about 2½ hours, until tender – or 50 minutes per 500 g (1 lb 2 oz) if the beef is a different weight.

(The beef can also be cooked in a preheated 160°C/320°F fan-forced oven for the same length of time – either covered with baking paper and foil, or in a lidded casserole dish.)

When ready to serve, slice thickly and keep warm in some of the liquid.

The leftovers can be kept in the liquid in the fridge for up to 5 days. Either slice and serve cold, or gently warm them in the liquid.

Slow dry-roasted spiced asado ribs ⓖⓕ

This is quite a long cook, but it's such an amazing result, making for delicious, sticky, spicy and very messy eating. You can dial up the quantity to serve a crowd, giving you plenty of time to prepare a flotilla of side dishes and accompaniments. **Serves 4–6**

3 kg (6 lb 10 oz) asado beef ribs (6 pieces)

Seasoning powder
2 teaspoons fennel seeds
2 teaspoons coriander seeds
2 teaspoons chicken stock (bouillon) powder
2 teaspoons garlic powder
1 tablespoon brown sugar
2 teaspoons sweet paprika

1½ teaspoons cayenne pepper
1 teaspoon black peppercorns
1 teaspoon smoked paprika
½ teaspoon celery seeds

Dry marinade spices
3 fresh bay leaves, chopped
2 tablespoons coriander seeds
2 tablespoons fennel seeds

2 teaspoons black peppercorns
2¼ teaspoons garlic powder
2 tablespoons brown sugar
2 tablespoons salt flakes

Wet marinade
100 ml (3½ fl oz) malt vinegar, or apple-cider vinegar or white-wine vinegar
100 ml (3½ fl oz) maple syrup
90 g (3 oz/⅓ cup) dijon mustard

Pair with

Serve with a simple cabbage slaw, pickled cucumbers, sour cream, Fried onion rings (p. 594) or fried onions and buttered soft buns.

Barbecued whole corn (p. 498).

Green lettuce leaves dressed in French-style vinaigrette (p. 88).

Whole baked potato or sweet potato.

Baked buttered rice (p. 384) cooked with dried oregano.

The seasoning powder can also be sprinkled on all types of roasted or grilled meats, fried chicken wings, grilled firm tofu or roasted pork ribs.

Preheat the oven to 230°C (445°F) fan-forced. Place a large pan of water in the base of the oven.

For the seasoning powder, blitz all the spices in a spice grinder, or finely grind them in a mortar. Set aside.

For the marinade spices, blitz the bay leaves, coriander seeds, fennel seeds, peppercorns and garlic powder in a spice grinder, then combine in a bowl with the sugar and salt.

Combine the wet marinade ingredients on a large tray. Add the ribs and toss to coat.

Lay out a double layer of foil, then top with a 60 cm (2 foot) length of baking paper. Pour some of the wet marinade on the paper, then top with 1½ tablespoons of the dry marinade spices. Place two of the well-coated ribs, fat side down, on the paper, then sprinkle another 1½ tablespoons of the marinade spices on top. Wrap the ribs with the baking paper, then the foil. Do this as tightly as you can, sealing well.

Repeat for the remaining ribs, ending up with three parcels.

Place the parcels on a baking tray, fat side down, and roast for 1¾ hours.

Turn the oven temperature down to 140°C (285°F) and cook for 2 hours, until very tender.

Once the ribs are cooked, open the parcels and carefully flip the ribs, with the meat facing up and exposed.

Return for a final 20 minutes at 200°C (400°F) to colour. Once dark, remove from the oven and baste with the juices, if any, in the foil.

Transfer the ribs to a serving plate, cutting between the bones or leaving them whole, with the meat facing up. Sprinkle with the seasoning mix and serve.

Asian brisket with vinegared blood plums

Pair with

Short-grain rice, and shaved cabbage simply dressed with white-wine vinegar, olive oil, salt and a little sugar.

Sautéed Asian greens (pp. 400, 401).

Kimchi (p. 455) and Kimchi pancakes (p. 457).

Sweet potatoes simply roasted in their skins, then peeled and lightly fork-mashed with butter.

Pile on a nest of cold soba noodles, dress with some of the pan juices and serve with crisp, cold lettuce piled high with mint and coriander.

Brown rice, cooked with the absorption method (see p. 372).

Japanese mixed rice & grains (p. 382).

There's quite a bundle of ingredients in this, but zero technical complexity. All those spices, vegetables and various liquids get unceremoniously tipped into the tray with the brisket, then the oven does all the work. The result is simply spectacular, with fork-tender meat laced with punchy Asian flavours. It's a bit of a showstopper. **Serves 6–8**

1.5 litres (51 fl oz/6 cups) water
2 tablespoons sea salt
1 × 1.7 kg (3 lb 12 oz) brisket
5 blood plums
100 ml (3½ fl oz) apple-cider vinegar

Braising ingredients
250 ml (8½ fl oz/1 cup) White chicken stock (p. 54)
3 tomatoes, sliced

2 French shallots, sliced
2 celery stalks, chopped
15 cm (6 in) piece of fresh ginger, peeled and sliced
2 long red chillies, split lengthways
3 tablespoons oyster sauce
3 tablespoons light soy sauce
2 tablespoons rice vinegar, or apple-cider vinegar

2 tablespoons coriander seeds
2 tablespoons sichuan peppercorns
2 tablespoons brown sugar
1 tablespoon salt flakes
3 teaspoons white peppercorns
3 teaspoons sesame oil
4 star anise

Staples
OIL, S&P

Add the water and salt to a large saucepan and heat to dissolve the salt. Once cooled, immerse the brisket in the brine and refrigerate overnight.

When ready to cook, preheat the oven to 150°C (300°F) fan-forced.

Remove the brisket from the brine and dry thoroughly. Coat with oil and brown very well in a large frying pan over a medium heat, about 5 minutes each side.

Add the brisket to a roasting tin with all the braising ingredients. Cover with baking paper, then foil, sealing well. Transfer to the oven and braise for 3 hours.

Uncover, turn the oven temperature up to 200°C (400°F) and cook for a further 30 minutes to brown the brisket.

Meanwhile, cut the plums in half, remove the stones and cut each half into six wedges. Add to a bowl with the vinegar and several pinches of salt. Toss gently, then stand for 10 minutes.

Carefully lift the cooked brisket from the roasting tin and slice. Return to the roasting tin and spoon the pan juices over. Scatter the plums over the top. Serve directly from the roasting tin, at the table.

Chow mein-style beef with wombok

This is based on a dish my mother used to cook in the 1980s – an interpretation of Chinese food viewed through a distinctly Western lens. We used to love it, caring little about authenticity back then. I have tweaked the recipe plenty, but it is still a midweek hero in my house. **Serves 4**

3 bundles of instant ramen, or udon, noodles (about 95 g/3¼ oz each)
125 ml (4 fl oz/½ cup) oyster sauce
80 ml (2½ fl oz/⅓ cup) light soy sauce
2 teaspoons sesame oil
125 ml (4 fl oz/½ cup) hot water
500 g (1 lb 2 oz) minced (ground) beef

3 teaspoons curry powder
1 teaspoon chilli powder
1 large onion, sliced into half-moons from root to tip
5 garlic cloves, finely grated
12 cm (4¾ in) piece of fresh ginger, peeled and diced
2 long green chillies, sliced
600 g (1 lb 5 oz) wombok (Chinese cabbage), core removed, finely sliced

80 g (2¾ oz/½ cup) frozen peas, thawed under hot water
10 green beans, finely sliced into rounds
6 spring onions (scallions), white and most of the green parts, sliced on an angle
100 g (3½ oz) bean sprouts

Staples
EVOO

Cook the noodles in boiling water for 1½ minutes, then refresh in cold water. Drain, snip with scissors into shorter lengths and coat with a little oil. Set aside.

Combine the oyster sauce, soy sauce, sesame oil and water in a small bowl.

Heat a wok or large frying pan over a high heat until very hot. Add a good splash of oil and the beef and stir-fry for about 5 minutes, until browned. Add the curry powder and chilli powder and stir through quickly to coat, then tip into a bowl.

Add another good splash of oil and the onion, garlic, ginger and chilli and stir-fry for about 2 minutes, until fragrant and softened. Stir the cabbage through. Add the oyster sauce mixture and cook for about 3 minutes, until the cabbage is just softened.

Stir the peas, beans and spring onion through, then the noodles and bean sprouts. If the mixture is looking dry, add a splash more hot water; taste and add more soy sauce if needed salt. Serve hot.

Make it different

With another protein. Instead of beef, use minced pork or chicken or firm tofu.

With vermicelli. Some fried dried vermicelli noodles make a tasty garnish and a crunchy contrast.

Make it vegan

Use crumbled firm tofu instead of the beef, and a vegan oyster sauce.

Beef rendang

While we think of rendang as a curry, it is classically a lot drier than what most would expect. Originating in Indonesia, rendangs are traditionally cooked to quite a dry state, effectively preserving the meat, which is said to hold for weeks at room temperature. I make no such claims about this version, and, indeed, this is somewhat wetter. I like sauce, what can I say. It's worth seeking out a quality Indonesian or Malaysian curry powder, which typically have pronounced cardamom and cinnamon notes. Another vital note is to cook until the sauce oils out and splits – it's funny how faults in one cuisine can be viewed as the opposite in another. **Serves 6**

Seared beef with bean thread noodles, beans, wood ear fungus & gochujang

Soak 100 g (3½ oz) bean thread (glass) noodles in cold water for 15 minutes, then drain and snip into rough 5 cm (2 in) lengths with scissors. Meanwhile, slice a 250 g (9 oz) scotch or porterhouse steak 5 mm (¼ in) thick, then marinate the beef in 1 tablespoon kecap manis and 1 teaspoon ground white pepper for 15 minutes. Add 1½ tablespoons grapeseed oil to a very hot wok or frying pan over a high heat. Stir-fry the beef until just cooked through, about 4 minutes. Remove and set aside. Add another 1½ tablespoons oil to the wok and fry 2 finely sliced garlic cloves and a peeled and finely sliced 3 cm (1¼ in) piece of fresh ginger for a minute until fragrant. Cut ½ white salad onion into 5 mm (¼ in) rings and cut 12 green beans into 2 cm (¾ in) batons, then stir-fry for about 3 minutes to colour slightly. Add 50 g (1¾ oz) finely sliced shiitake mushrooms (stems removed), 50 g (1¾ oz) wood ear fungus and 4 spring onions (scallions) cut into 3 cm (1¼ in) batons and stir-fry for about 1½ minutes. Add 150 ml (5 fl oz) White chicken stock (p. 54), Pho broth (p. 57) or water and 1 heaped tablespoon gochujang chilli paste diluted with 2 tablespoons boiling water, then add the noodles and toss quickly to heat through. Toss the beef through at the last minute. Serve with ½ bunch coriander (cilantro), fine stems chopped, and bean sprouts scattered over the top. Serves 2.

Pair with

Steamed basmati rice and smashed chunks of chilled cucumber & sesame salad (p. 507).

Korean sesame grilled beef with sake, ginger & soy marinade

To make the marinade, combine 80 g (2¾ oz) peeled and finely grated fresh ginger, 3 finely grated garlic cloves, 2 tablespoons caster (superfine) sugar, 3 tablespoons light soy sauce, 3 tablespoons cooking sake, 2 tablespoons mirin, 2 tablespoons sesame seeds and 1 teaspoon sesame oil. Slice a 600 g (1 lb 5 oz) beef scotch fillet, rump or hanger steak into longish pieces about 5 mm (¼ in) thick. Lay the meat flat in a container or on a small tray and cover with the marinade. Leave to marinate for at least 20 minutes, ideally an hour. Preheat a barbecue on high. Put ⅛ cabbage, cut into a wedge, on a chopping board. Cut across into 4 cm (1½ in) slices, stand them on a large serving plate and push them over like fallen dominoes. Season with the 1 teaspoon salt flakes and 2 teaspoons caster (superfine) sugar. Stand for 10 minutes, then spoon the sesame dressing over and sprinkle with 1½ tablespoons toasted and lightly ground sesame seeds. Grill the meat for a total of 2½ minutes, flipping halfway. If you like, you could also grill a selection of vegetables, such as broccoli, red capsicum (bell pepper), white onion, shiitake mushroom and spring onion (scallion), until just undercooked. Plate the meat and serve with the plate of vegetables, with the sauce on the side. Serves 4.

130 g (4½ oz/1⅓ cups) coconut flakes
80 ml (2½ fl oz/⅓ cup) extra-virgin olive oil
1.5 kg (3 lb 5 oz) beef chuck, rump, shin or oyster blade, cut into 5 cm (2 in) cubes
2 heaped teaspoons shrimp paste
2 tablespoons Indonesian or Malaysian curry powder
800 ml (27 fl oz) water
800 ml (27 fl oz) coconut cream
2½ tablespoons brown sugar
6 makrut lime leaves

2½ tablespoons kecap manis
juice of 1 lime
6 coriander (cilantro) sprigs, leaves and fine stems picked
50 g (1¾ oz/⅓ cup) roasted red-skinned peanuts, or salted beer nuts

Rendang paste

1½ large red onions, roughly diced
6 large garlic cloves, roughly diced
3 lemongrass stems, pale part only, finely sliced
10 cm (4 in) piece of fresh turmeric, peeled and finely sliced
10 cm (4 in) piece of fresh ginger, peeled and finely sliced
10 cm (4 in) piece of fresh galangal, peeled and finely sliced
10 red bird's eye chillies, roughly chopped
3 tablespoons water
2½ teaspoons salt flakes

Toast the coconut flakes in a dry frying pan over a high heat, tossing frequently, until brown, about 6 minutes. Tip into a bowl, reserving 30 g (1 oz/½ cup) of the coconut flakes for serving.

In a blender, blitz the rending paste ingredients to a smooth paste.

Add the oil to a large saucepan and fry the paste over a medium heat until fragrant and changing colour, about 8 minutes. Add the beef and turn the heat up to high. Stir the beef until well coated and cook until seared all over, about 6 minutes. Stir in the shrimp paste and curry powder and fry for 2 minutes. Add the toasted coconut flakes, water, coconut cream, sugar and lime leaves.

Simmer over a low heat for 2 hours, until the beef is tender and the sauce splits.

Stir the kecap manis through. Squeeze the lime juice over. Serve scattered with the coriander, peanuts and remaining toasted coconut flakes.

Veal

Veal is an uncomfortable topic for many, and for good reason. The reality is that veal is mainly a by-product of the dairy industry. As with laying hens, the males are 'waste' for the industry, either sold for a pittance and slaughtered at a few days of age and used in low-cost products, or raised as 'rose veal' on specialised farms.

Also, the process of raising calves to produce milk-white and ultra-tender meat can be a cruel one. Too young and the meat will be pale, mild and tender, but there will be little of it; once there is enough meat present, that meat is darker, stronger in flavour and less tender. The methods developed to maintain colour, taste and texture are well documented, but they mainly involve restricting movement – sometimes in crates – as well as deprivation of light and iron. The horrific practice of 'crating' has apparently never been used in Australia and is now illegal in many countries.

There is an RSPCA approval standard for dairy veal in this country, but no farms had signed up to the charter at the time of writing. Thankfully, some farmers are raising veal in a considered way. White Rocks Veal in Western Australia has become the leading supplier of pale, largely milk-fed veal from the 'waste' bull calves from their dairy farm, with the animals raised to 6–8 months in large, open barns, rather than slaughtered at 2–3 months, as is traditional. While some will still take a dim view of dispatching such a young animal, raising the animals humanely onsite is a significantly less grim option than transporting five-day-old calves long distances for sale and slaughter.

There are also farms raising calves specifically for veal, either from dairy herds or beef cattle, sometimes with the meat a little darker due to the calves grazing prior to slaughter, increasing the iron content of their meat. There are several farms producing veal in a humane and sustainable way, and the best of them are selling their products at a significant premium. As with everything, know what you're buying and make good choices.

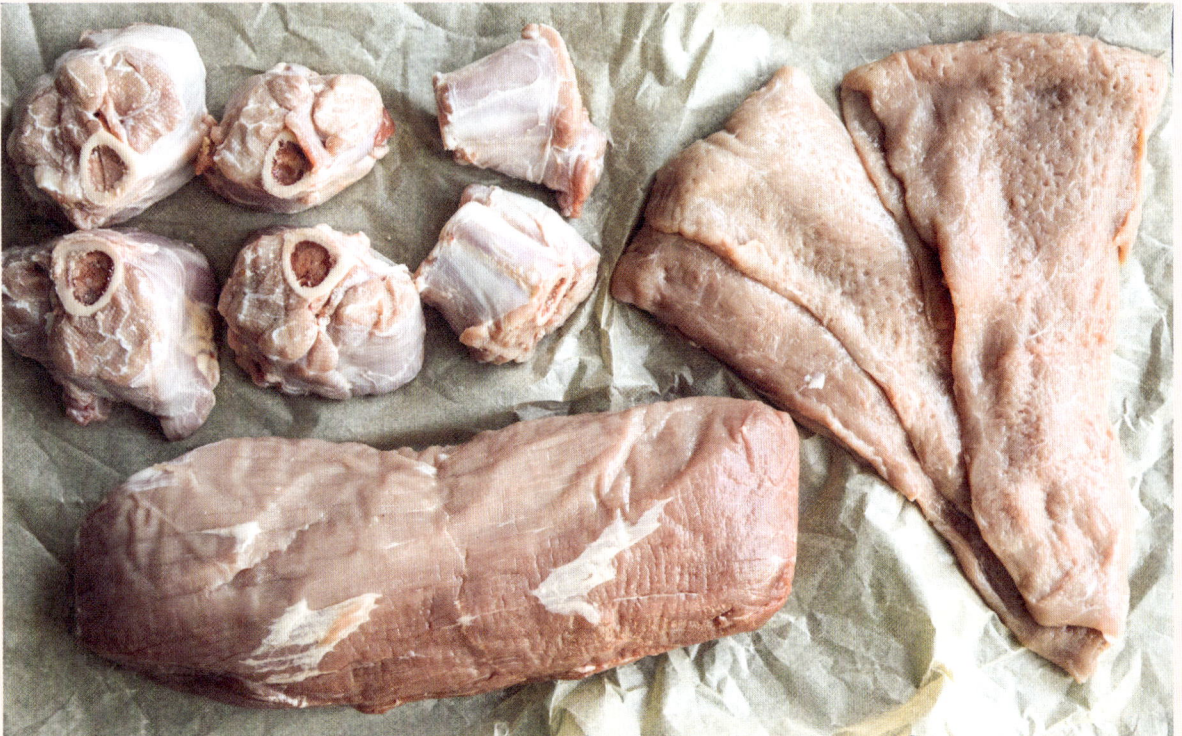

Veal scallopini with guanciale, oyster mushrooms & thyme GF

Pair with

A salad and Classic potato mash (p. 625).

Simply cooked greens.

Back in the day, veal scallopini was one of the ubiquitous 'fancy' dishes in Italian restaurants – the sort in which tables were graced with candles thrust into empty Chianti bottles as claims to authenticity. Given most people probably gorged on garlic bread, pizza and pasta, veal scallopini – or almost anything from the secondi section of the menu – was special occasion stuff, ordered when a sense of continental sophistication was desired. It was always bathed in a rich and creamy sauce, and always came with an abundance of sautéed button mushrooms. I have pushed the refresh button on that memory, using some crispy pork bits and roasted oyster mushrooms, with a touch of sweetness from vincotto. **Serves 4**

150 g (5½ oz) oyster mushrooms, or sliced king browns
4 × 150 g (5½ oz) veal round steaks or loins
120 g (4½ oz) guanciale, or pancetta, cut into 5 mm (¼ in) dice

2 French shallots, finely sliced
2 garlic cloves, finely sliced
5 thyme sprigs, leaves stripped
150 ml (5 fl oz) white wine
30 ml (1 fl oz) vincotto, or quality balsamic vinegar
60 g (2 oz/¼ cup) butter

Staples
EVOO, FLR, S&P

Preheat the oven to 180°C (350°F) fan-forced.

Coat the mushrooms with oil, season with salt and pepper, spread out on a baking tray and roast for 15 minutes.

Lay the veal steaks between sheets of baking paper. Flatten slightly using a meat mallet, rolling pin, or the flat side of a knife, then dust with flour.

Heat a large frying pan over a medium–high heat. Fry the guanciale until the fat renders and it is golden and crisp, about 5 minutes. Lift from the pan, into a large bowl, leaving the fat behind.

Add a few tablespoons of oil to the pan. Cook the shallot and garlic until softened and a little golden, about 2 minutes. Add the thyme and roasted mushrooms and cook for 1 minute, then tip onto the guanciale.

Place the pan back over a high heat. Add a splash of oil, then the veal. Season with salt and pepper and cook for 45 seconds on each side, until browning. Tip the mushrooms and guanciale mix onto the veal. Add the wine and vincotto and simmer for 1 minute, then lift the veal out onto serving plates.

Add the butter to the pan, swirling around to melt and combine, then spoon it over the veal and serve immediately.

Make it different
With fermented garlic. To really up the complexity in the sauce, replace the garlic with three sliced cloves of fermented black garlic.

Veal osso buco with white wine & gremolata

Osso buco, with a saffron-hued risotto alla milanese, is Milan's emblematic dish, and one of Italy's enduring classics. Braised cross-cut veal shin has been spun into countless versions, and in Australia is most commonly a hearty affair, often employing red wine, with lots of tomato and chunky vegetables. The true osso buco of Milan, or Lombardy in general, while still hearty, is a considerably more delicate expression, with the sticky braising liquid more bianco in hue, lightened with the bright herbal and citric punch of gremolata. You can see how well this would marry with a beautifully simple risotto scented with saffron. That's not to say that the darker, more robust versions aren't delicious, just less traditional – and usually due to the available meat. In Europe, sourcing pale veal shin is more common, whereas in Australia you are more likely to be buying shin from an older animal, and the meat is darker and beefier, and marries better with more tomato and red wine. This version leans into the original more heavily. Serve as is with Polenta (p. 383) or mash, or toss through pasta (see p. 121) – or go all in by also making Risotto alla milanese (p. 148) enriched with bone marrow. **Serves 6**

Pair with

Risotto alla milanese (p. 148).

Wet Polenta (p. 383) enriched with parmesan or Classic potato mash (p. 625).

Toss with pasta in the pot (see p. 121).

- 6 garlic cloves, peeled and sliced
- 3 rosemary sprigs, leaves finely chopped
- ½ bunch of sage, leaves finely chopped
- 1 tablespoon salt flakes
- 2 teaspoons ground white pepper
- 125 ml (4 fl oz/½ cup) extra-virgin olive oil
- 1.5 kg (3 lb 5 oz) small veal osso buco, about 4 cm (1½ in) thick

- 40 g (1½ oz) plain (all-purpose) flour
- 60 g (2 oz/¼ cup) butter
- 100 g (3½ oz) pancetta, finely diced
- 2 onions, finely diced
- 1 carrot, very finely diced
- 4 pale inner celery stalks, finely sliced
- 2 fresh bay leaves
- 1½ tablespoons tomato paste (concentrated purée)
- 350 ml (12 fl oz) white wine

- 1.5 litres (51 fl oz/6 cups) Golden chicken stock (p. 54)

Gremolata
- ½ bunch of flat-leaf (Italian) parsley, finely chopped
- zest of 1 lemon
- 1 garlic clove, finely grated
- 1 tablespoon extra-virgin olive oil

Staples
EVOO, S&P

Using a mortar and pestle, grind the garlic, rosemary, sage, salt flakes and white pepper into a rough paste. Stir in 2½ tablespoons of the oil, then smear all over the veal. Dust with the flour to coat.

Heat the butter and remaining oil in a large heavy-based saucepan over a medium heat. Fry the pancetta until golden, about 5 minutes. Remove from the pan and set aside.

Working in batches so as not to crowd the pan, brown the veal evenly, about 2 minutes each side. Do this watchfully – you don't want to burn anything, as it will form the basis for deeper flavour in the sauce, but it is equally important to get good colour on the meat. Remove from the pan and set aside.

Add another splash of oil to the pan. Cook the onion, carrot, celery and bay leaves until soft and golden, about 10 minutes. Stir the tomato paste through, then return the veal and pancetta.

Add the wine and simmer for 5 minutes, then pour in the stock and simmer for another 5 minutes. Reduce the heat to medium–low and simmer for about 40 minutes.

Near serving time, combine the gremolata ingredients in a small bowl and season with salt and pepper.

Once the meat is tender and about to fall off the bone, take the pan off the heat. You want to be able to serve the pieces whole, so don't take it any further.

Serve with the gremolata sprinkled over.

Vitello tonnato

Pair with

Enjoy in a baguette, sauce, garnishes and all.

Serve with Roman-style fried artichokes and shaved parmesan.

For a landlocked region, it seems a little odd that tuna is crucial to one of Piedmont's most famous dishes – vitello tonnato. No doubt trade with neighbouring Liguria – that crescent-shaped region that arcs over the Italian Riviera – would have had an influence. For the dish, slices of poached (sometimes roasted) cold veal are dressed in an emulsion of tuna and oil with capers and sometimes anchovies; that emulsion is often now a mayonnaise of sorts. As with so many classic preparations, this is a dish that has evolved over the years, so it's hard to say one thing or the other is right or traditional. I do like the richness of chopped egg in this rendition of tonnato sauce, which is my favourite. Some recipes call for the sauce to be spooned over the veal, then for it to sit for several hours, or even overnight– but I find this version best assembled when serving. I like to dress this with peppery rocket or watercress, little Ligurian olives, a scattering of capers and lemon segments and a slick of the finest oil, with some hand-rolled grissini on the side. **Serves 6–8**

1.5 kg (3 lb 5 oz) veal girello, or veal round, topside or loin
1 handful of small Ligurian olives
1 tablespoon tiny capers, drained
1 lemon, segmented and cut into small triangles
4 flat-leaf (Italian) parsley sprigs, leaves picked
3 handfuls of rocket (arugula), or picked watercress
6–8 Grissini (p. 856)

Poaching stock
1 onion, finely sliced
1 garlic bulb, cut in half crossways
1 carrot, finely sliced
2 celery stalks, finely sliced
100 ml (3½ fl oz) white wine
100 ml (3½ fl oz) white-wine vinegar
5 cloves
3 teaspoons fennel seeds
2 teaspoons black peppercorns
2 fresh bay leaves
½ bunch of flat-leaf (Italian) parsley

Tonnato sauce
3 × 175 g (6 oz) tins tuna under oil, drained
6 hard-boiled eggs, chopped
80 ml (2½ fl oz/⅓ cup) extra-virgin olive oil
50 ml (1¾ oz) lemon juice (from about ½ lemon)
2½ tablespoons small capers

Staples
EVOO, S&P

Special equipment
Probe thermometer

Heat a splash of oil in a wide saucepan over a medium heat. Add the veal and lightly seal all over, about 8 minutes. Remove from the pan and set aside.

To make the poaching stock, cook the onion, garlic, carrot and celery in the same pan until softened, about 8 minutes. Return the veal to the pan. Add the wine, vinegar, spices and bay leaves and bring to a simmer, then add just enough water to cover. Simmer on a very low heat for 15 minutes, then add the parsley and turn off the heat. Stand the veal in the stock until it reaches an internal temperature of 50°C (120°F), then set aside in the stock for 30 minutes, before removing and chilling. There should be a rosy hue to the flesh when sliced. Strain the stock and use to store any left-over veal in.

To make the tonnato sauce, add all the ingredients and a good grinding of pepper to a food processor and blend until smooth. Adjust the seasoning as needed, adding a little veal poaching liquor if it's too stiff.

Slice the chilled veal about 3–4 mm (⅛–¼ in) thick and lay on a serving platter or plates. Spread the sauce over the veal, then scatter the olives, capers, lemon and parsley over. Arrange the rocket leaves around the edges. Drizzle with oil, grind some pepper over and finish with the grissini.

Also see

Cabbage rolls with lamb, rice, pine nuts & dill **451**

Harira **461**

Pasties **469–70**

Baked lamb-stuffed eggplant **520–1**

Braised lamb, artichokes, lemon & cinnamon with couscous **537**

Lebanese peas with lamb **614**

Lamb navarin **643**

Spiced lamb shanks with rhubarb, honey & fried vine leaves **647**

Lamb

Lamb

When I was growing up, lamb was something we ate often, mainly as a Sunday roast. Usually, it was a lamb leg studded with rosemary and garlic, accompanied by roast potatoes and a cheesy cauliflower gratin. I was always asked to make the mint sauce (see p. 82), from vinegar, sugar and fresh mint from the garden. The dressing was very sharp and sweet at the same time, which was perfect for the somewhat overcooked lamb. I think it's best to roast a leg of lamb quite hot and serve it pink, or to cook it long and slow and have the meat meltingly tender – but our timing tended to be right in the middle of these desirable extremes.

Lamb has so taken over the category of meat from sheep that its elders – hogget and mutton – have become something of a footnote. The peak body that governs lamb in Australia was actually called the Sheepmeat Council of Australia before recently adopting the slightly more elegant title Sheep Producers Australia. But lamb has its own marketing body, and is certainly synonymous with meat coming from sheep for most of us, with even the word 'mutton' a quaint curio from an earlier time, and 'hogget' a little-known one.

Lamb becomes hogget – also known as two-tooth – when the first permanent tooth appears. Officially, everything that isn't lamb is regarded as mutton, though a young hogget is quite a different prospect to a two- or three-year-old sheep. Grading before slaughter will determine the age category, and the price, with mutton not achieving the premium price that lamb can attract. However, the definition of a lamb was changed subtly in 2019, bringing it in line with New Zealand: 'Young sheep under 12 months of age, or which do not have any permanent incisor teeth in wear.'

This change meant that sheep that were essentially lambs could still be brought to slaughter weight and sold at a premium, without losing their value by being reclassified as mutton. This has no doubt been a great boon to farmers, with little or no negative impact on consumers, but it tends to reinforce the notion that hogget and mutton are inferior meat. I must admit I have much more experience cooking lamb, but hogget and mutton are not inferior, just different, with the flavour intensifying with age.

The flavour can be off-putting for some when sheep get relatively mature, but for those who appreciate intense flavour, slow-roasted mutton can be quite the revelation, with it also being the preferred protein for many subcontinental curries. It is also a better end for an animal that has no doubt produced a lot of wool in its life – making more considered use of the whole animal, given no-one is raising sheep to sell solely as mature mutton.

While it is no doubt possible to improve most of our methods of livestock management and welfare, mainstream sheep farming is worlds away from the problems associated with intensive pig and poultry farming. Sheep mature naturally on pasture, but that doesn't make it a problem-free industry. Increasingly, feedlots are being employed to 'finish' lambs on a diet of hay, lupin and grain. It is a way of getting a lamb up to slaughter weight in a controlled and quick way. And while feedlots aren't exactly battery-hen cages, they are heavily stocked environments, with thousands of animals in often hot and exposed conditions.

Pair with

Lamb takes to spices well. Some of my favourite matches are cumin, allspice, pepper, cinnamon, sumac, aleppo pepper, saffron and chilli, while oregano, mint, coriander (cilantro), thyme and rosemary are ideal herbs. Pair with onion, garlic, eggplant (aubergine), carrot, fennel, tomato, cucumber, kohlrabi, potatoes, peas, broad beans, green beans, spinach and lemon. Lamb's richness also matches up well to sweetness, with dates, pomegranate, pomegranate molasses, quince and honey all working beautifully. Yoghurt (p. 365), Labneh (p. 362), haloumi, feta and olives are all excellent pairings, as are preserved lemon, miso and soy sauce.

I believe it is important to ensure the lamb you buy is solely fed on grass, being aware that grass-fed animals can be fed supplemental grain, or finished on grain, and still be called 'grass fed', due to lack of regulation. As always, it is up to the consumer to be proactive. Terms like 'grass fed' or 'free range' or pictures of verdant fields or some kind of eco-like gesture in the packaging are not enough. But we need to be honest with ourselves. Almost all farmers who are making deliberate steps towards farming more ethically, with both local and broader environmental considerations, want to share that fact and back up their claims. Ambiguous packaging gestures will fool the less considered consumer, as they are designed to, but as a thoughtful shopper, buying such products is simply self-deception.

There are many breeds of sheep in Australia, some solely for wool production, some for meat, and some for both. Many are crossbreeds with some Merino lineage, selectively bred over time to enhance wool or meat production and to be adapted to Australian conditions. When buying lamb, it is rare to have the breed declared, unless you are buying from a specialised farm.

Increasingly, Suffolk and White Suffolk are being raised in considered ways, with the meat presented as a prime product, as it should be. Dorper is another breed that discerning shoppers would probably have come across. A South African breed (a cross between Dorset Horn and Blackhead Persian), Dorpers are well adapted to the similarly varied conditions of mainland Australia. They are a 'shedding' breed, so they don't require shearing, or the painful and highly contentious practice of 'mulesing' to stop flystrike, and they produce a good yield of very high-quality meat.

Perhaps Australia's best lamb comes from organic Dorper sheep grazing on saltbush in South Australia. Mineral-rich saltbush is nutritious – and not just for sheep – and imbues the meat with a distinctive flavour, as well as fine intramuscular fat, making saltbush lamb a real culinary treasure of this country. Plus, the Dorper's very makeup as a shedding sheep makes painful practices to avoid flystrike unnecessary, meaning they have an ethical advantage from the beginning.

Preparing lamb

I adore lamb cutlets or a roasted rack with the fat left on and well rendered, but shoulder is my favourite and most-cooked cut. It is marvellous slow roasted on the bone (see p. 307) or fully boned (see p. 304), and it makes for a wonderful curry (see p. 317). It's a working cut with lots of connective tissue and flavour-giving fat. Cooking very slowly over a long period, either in the oven or as a braise, or cooking a bit hotter and a bit quicker, though still relatively slowly, both produce wonderful results, with shoulder an exceptionally forgiving cut.

Cuts from the forequarter – bone-in shoulder with shank attached, square-cut shoulder sans shank, forequarter rack, forequarter chops and boned shoulder, whether butterflied or rolled – are all best slow-cooked, whether roasted or braised, melting away the toughness and leaving the meat incredibly tender. Shanks also require slow cooking, yielding some of the most distinctive meat, with intense flavour and a slippery, supple texture. Shanks can be used for braises, pies or curries. I always seal and colour shanks well in oil and butter before braising, which contributes a lot to the intensity and complexity of flavour in the finished dish.

Lamb leg, for me, is best roasted fiercely and served pink. It can certainly be slow-cooked, but I do find that some of the muscles of the leg can sometimes produce stringy and dry results, while the shoulder will be universally tender and delicious. Having said that, a properly marinated leg can produce superb results (see p. 311). Meat from the leg, apart from the shank, is best cooked around medium-rare, as it will become tough and lose flavour cooked much further. Leg can be bought bone-in, butterflied, boned and rolled, or cut into mini roasts or steaks. I also buy boned leg to dice and barbecue on skewers (see p. 312). Lamb steaks are simply a cross-section of the leg and are an excellent alternative to a beef steak for barbecuing or searing in a hot pan.

Other candidates for shorter cooking times, whether roasting, grilling or pan-frying, are the rump, chump chops, loin and rack, while the neck and ribs require longer cooking. The tenderloin (fillet) is a particularly lean cut, free of connective tissue and fat; it can just be seasoned and sealed on both sides for a couple of minutes, then rested and sliced for a sandwich or salad. Lamb backstrap, from near the spine, is similarly lean, but thicker than a fillet, and will take about 5 minutes each side to cook, with a five-minute rest, and is also ideal for a salad (see p. 314).

The problem with lamb chops, as with so many pre-cut steaks, is that they're cut too thin. Getting anything like a reasonable char on them without overcooking the meat is near impossible, with both an unappetisingly grey and overcooked result likely. A good butcher will recognise this and cut them accordingly, but it is alarmingly rare. If you have a good relationship with your butcher, which is always something worth cultivating, ask them to cut the chops for you. Double cutlets or double loin chops are preferable, and they will both take about 6 minutes a side on a hot barbecue. A thick forequarter chop will be closer to 5 minutes a side for pink lamb and an engagingly charred exterior.

The neck will come either as a cross-section, a neck chop (from closer to the shoulder) or neck fillet. All need slow cooking to break down the connective tissue. I use neck cuts for braises (see p. 316) and soups (see p. 308). Lamb ribs, from the belly and breast, have very flavourful meat and layers of fat and connective tissue. They require slow cooking and can be braised (see p. 304) or steamed, or braised or hot-smoked and then grilled.

I very rarely buy diced lamb, preferring to cut it myself. Typically, most butchers dice the meat too small, and I prefer to control how much fat accompanies it, with most butchers trimming too much away, sensitive to the wider community's fear of fat. Also, as soon as you cut meat of any kind, the cut surface will start to oxidise. More surface area, more oxidation. Minced (ground) lamb, with some fat – I would never buy lean mince of any kind – can be used to make a wonderfully flavourful Ragù (p. 535), using lamb rather than beef, white wine rather than red, and herbs such as rosemary, sage, oregano and bay leaves; some diced pancetta or guanciale would be good at the start, too. I also use minced lamb for Koftas (p. 309), Moussaka (p. 310), Shepherd's pie (p. 319) or a Merguez-style sausage (p. 308). And they may have fallen out of favour, but lamb's brains (see p. 308) are quite delicious – and, of course, we should be eating as much as possible of the animals that grace our tables.

Slow-roasted boned lamb shoulder GF

This popular recipe is cooked often in my house, as it's set and forget. The result from cooking this way is somewhat similar to spit-roasted lamb, the full-flavoured meat falling apart with lots of crisp and crunchy edges. **Serves 6**

5 garlic cloves, sliced
2 tablespoons salt flakes
1 tablespoon black peppercorns
1 tablespoon dried Greek oregano (rigani)

2 tablespoons extra-virgin olive oil
1.8 kg (4 lb) semi-boned or boned lamb shoulder
300 ml (10 fl oz) water

80 ml (2½ fl oz/⅓ cup) white-wine vinegar

Staples
LMN

Preheat the oven to 130°C (265°F) fan-forced.

Using a mortar and pestle, grind the garlic, salt and peppercorns to a rough paste. Add the oregano and oil, mix well, then rub into the meat.

Place the lamb in a roasting tin, then pour in the water and vinegar. Cover with foil, then baking paper, and roast for 3 hours.

Increase the oven temperature to 220°C (430°F) fan-forced and turn on the oven grill (broiler). Uncover the lamb and brown under the grill for about 15 minutes, until the surface is crisp.

Roughly break or pull apart the meat and arrange on a large serving plate. Using a large spoon, skim off some of the fat from the pan juices, then ladle some of the juices over the meat. Serve with lemon.

Pair with

Kohlrabi & cucumber salad (p. 549).

Yoghurt, cucumber & mint salad/dip (p. 508).

Rainbow chard & chickpea salad (p. 556).

Horta-style greens (p. 552).

Pumpkin & feta pie (p. 631).

Beetroot dip (see p. 420) or pumpkin dip (see p. 632).

Grain salad (pp. 378–80).

Lamb ribs braised with treacle & dark ale

Lamb ribs are so deeply flavoured and work perfectly with the dark ale, treacle and miso, and the healthy glug of apple-cider vinegar cuts the fattiness. The flavour return is substantial for the relatively short prep and cook time, with the braising liquid cooking down to a sticky glaze – and no need to marinate first. **Serves 10**

20 meaty lamb ribs
2 tablespoons white miso paste
1 tablespoon salt flakes
2 teaspoons chilli powder

3½ tablespoons treacle, or honey or maple syrup
250 ml (8½ fl oz/1 cup) dark ale (any flavourful beer will work)

150 ml (5 fl oz) apple-cider vinegar, plus extra for dressing
1 bunch of red radishes, cut in half, with some stalk left on

Preheat the oven to 180°C (350°F) fan-forced.

Add the ribs, miso paste, salt and chilli powder to a large baking dish and toss to coat. Pour the treacle, beer and vinegar over. Cover with baking paper, then foil, sealing well. Bake for 1 hour.

Uncover the ribs and cook for a further 30 minutes, until dark and crispy but with some juices still left in the tray. You can colour the ribs more by turning on the oven grill (broiler) for a few minutes, but watch carefully.

Arrange the ribs on a serving plate with the radishes. Serve.

Make it different
With hazelnuts. For texture and flavour, sprinkle over 80 g (2¾ oz) toasted and chopped hazelnuts.

If ribs are too fatty for you, cover them with water and bring to a simmer, then drain and proceed with the recipe. You can also steam them for about 20 minutes before braising.

Pair with

Fermented cooked chilli sauce (p. 97).

Add some wilted greens and rice to make this more of a meal.

Pickled daikon & mint salad (below).

Baked potato.

Pickled daikon & mint salad GF V VG

Finely slice ½ daikon (white radish), then, in a bowl, toss with 1 tablespoon caster (superfine) sugar and 2 teaspoons salt flakes. Set aside for 30 minutes. When ready to serve, drain the liquid from the daikon, then add the torn leaves from 4 mint sprigs and 100 g (3½ oz) mâche (lamb's lettuce/corn salad). Dress with a little apple-cider vinegar and extra-virgin olive oil, then toss and serve.

Sticky spiced honey lamb shanks **GF**

Pair with

Freekeh, couscous or Classic potato mash (p. 625) with seasonal greens.

Roasted lamb rack **GF**

Lamb rack is expensive, but from well-sourced lamb, it's a wonderful luxury to indulge in. I will usually buy a rack with the bones French-trimmed, but I always prefer the cap of fat left on. To cook a rack with four or five points, score the fat deeply in a crisscross fashion and season generously all over. Rub with extra-virgin olive oil and pan-fry, fat side down, over a medium heat for about 6 minutes, until golden. This will render the fat crispy. Flip and seal on the other side for a minute. Transfer to a baking tray and roast at 200°C (400°F) fan-forced for 10–12 minutes, then rest for about 6 minutes. I then like to cut the racks in half, into double cutlets. Serve with Smashed broad beans (see p. 432), and potatoes roasted with garlic and rosemary.

The deep intensity of lamb shanks marries so well with warm spices and a spike of chilli, with the sweetness of honey, shallots and sultanas knitting subtly into the sticky richness after the long, slow braising. **Serves 4–6**

100 ml (3½ fl oz) extra-virgin olive oil
6 French-trimmed lamb shanks
12 French shallots, peeled
10 garlic cloves, peeled and crushed
2 red bird's eye chillies, split lengthways

4 oregano sprigs
1 tablespoon cumin seeds
1 cinnamon stick
3½ tablespoons honey
2½ tablespoons red-wine vinegar
1 tablespoon tomato paste (concentrated purée)

1.6 litres (54 fl oz) White chicken stock (p. 54), or 800 ml (27 fl oz) water
100 g (3½ oz) sultanas (golden raisins)

Staples
S&P

Heat half the oil in a large flameproof casserole dish over a medium heat. Working in two batches, brown the shanks all over, about 2½ minutes each side. Season with salt and pepper as you seal. Remove the shanks and set aside.

Add the shallots, garlic, chillies, oregano, cumin seeds and cinnamon stick to the dish. Cook, stirring now and then, until the shallots are turning golden, about 15 minutes. Return the shanks and add the honey, vinegar and tomato paste. Stir to coat, then add the stock and sultanas. Bring to a simmer and cook for 10 minutes.

Meanwhile, preheat the oven to 170°C (340°F) fan-forced.

When the shanks have finished simmering, put the lid on and transfer to the oven to braise for 2 hours.

Once the meat is just starting to pull from the bone, remove the shanks, allowing the liquid to drain back into the dish. Arrange the shanks in a baking dish with a little space between each. Reduce the sauce by one-third, then whisk in the remaining oil. Pour the sauce over the shanks so that it comes a bit over halfway up – reduce first if necessary.

Turn the oven up to 220°C (430°F) fan-forced and roast the shanks for 15 minutes to colour.

Make it a meal
Add a couple of sweet potatoes, cut into 3 cm (1¼ in) discs halfway through cooking.

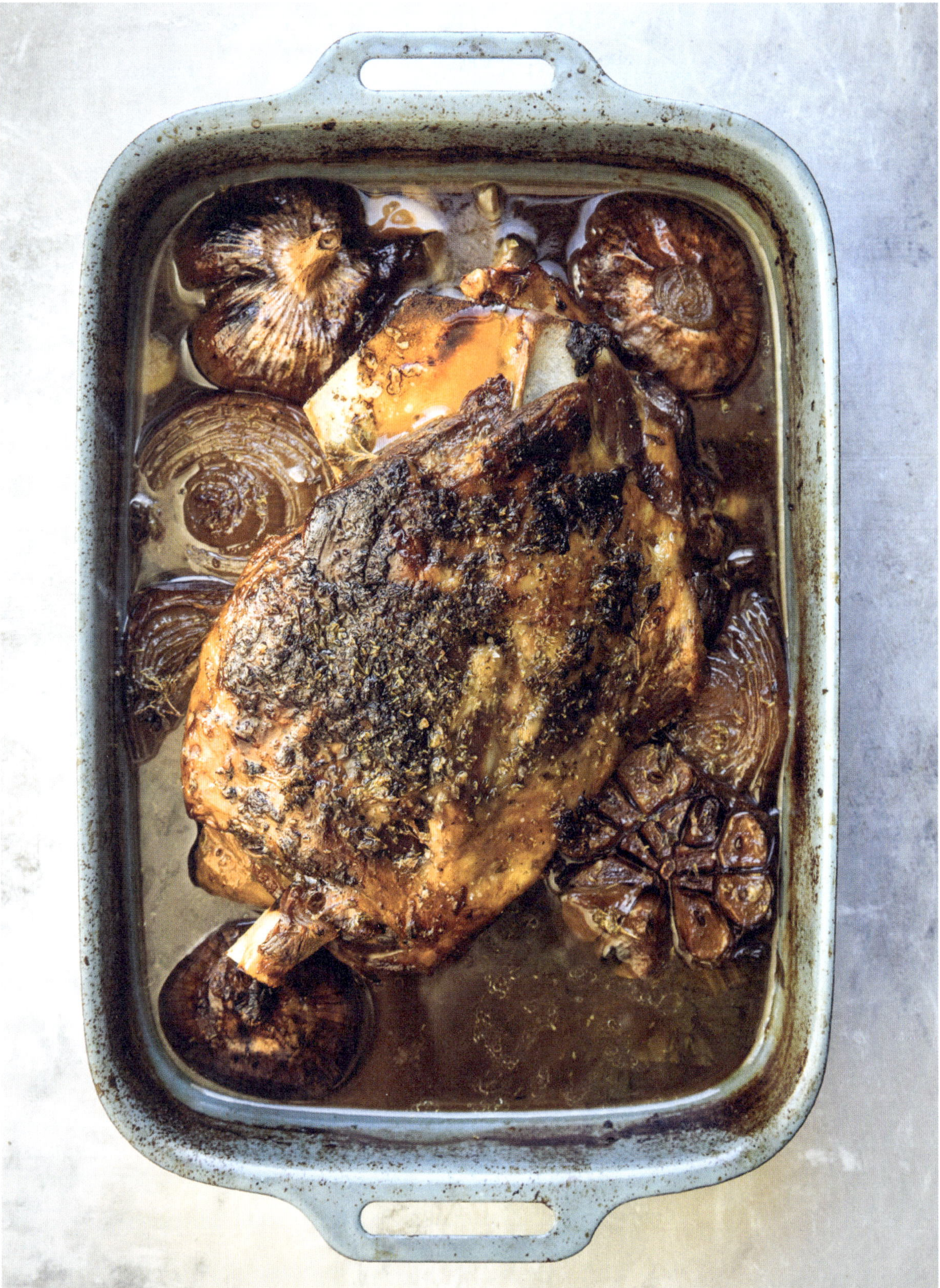

Brined lamb shoulder GF

Short cut

If you want to skip the brining step, simply roast for an extra hour.

Pair with

Kohlrabi & cucumber salad (p. 549).

Yoghurt, cucumber & mint salad (p. 508).

Rainbow chard & chickpea salad (p. 556).

Horta-style greens (p. 552).

Pumpkin & feta pie (p. 631).

Beetroot dip (see p. 420) or pumpkin dip (see p. 632).

Grain salad (pp. 378–80).

Cooking a bone-in lamb shoulder is very rewarding, with both the presentation and the flavour quite spectacular. And brining elevates it to something extraordinary. On the surface, lamb shoulder seems the least likely contender for brining, as it is typically a method employed to make drier cuts more moist. Lamb shoulder is anything but dry – but brining just makes it doubly delicious, with a deep savoury flavour imparted to the meat, and the luscious texture quite incomparable. A bone-in shoulder is also hard to season properly, but the brine solves that, penetrating the meat and perfectly salting it. The sugar adds a richness without being sweet per se, and aids in burnishing the crust to a stunningly crispy intensity. Hungry? **Serves 6**

3 kg (6 lb 10 oz) bone-in lamb shoulder
2 onions, skin on, each cut into 3 rings
3 celery stalks
juice of 2 lemons
2 tablespoons dried Greek oregano (rigani)
1 garlic bulb, cut in half crossways

500 ml (17 fl oz/2 cups) Golden chicken stock (p. 54)
300 ml (10 fl oz) water
80 ml (2½ fl oz/⅓ cup) white-wine vinegar

Brine
3 litres (101 fl oz/12 cups) water
500 g (1 lb 2 oz) sea salt

350 g (12½ oz/1½ cups) caster (superfine) sugar
40 g (1½ oz) black peppercorns, cracked
1 garlic bulb, cut in half crossways
3 fresh bay leaves
1 litre (34 fl oz/4 cups) cold water, or 1 kg (2 lb 3 oz) ice

Heat the brine ingredients in a large saucepan over a high heat. Stir until the salt and sugar have completely dissolved, then remove from the heat. Add the cold water or, for a quicker result, the ice, and cool to room temperature.

Once the brine has cooled, add the lamb, then refrigerate overnight to brine, or for at least 10 hours.

When you're ready to cook, preheat the oven to 130°C (265°F) fan-forced.

Remove the lamb from the brine and pat dry. Arrange the onion and celery in a large roasting tin, to form a 'trivet', then place the lamb on top. Pour the lemon juice over and sprinkle with the oregano. Add the garlic to the tin and pour in the stock, water and vinegar.

Cover with baking paper, then foil, and roast for 5½ hours.

Once the meat is very tender, uncover the lamb and turn the oven up to 200°C (400°F) fan-forced. Cook for 30 minutes to brown the meat, basting regularly with the pan juices.

Once darkened, with crisp edges, remove the lamb from the oven and set aside to rest. Tip the juices into a small saucepan, skimming off most of the fat, and reduce by half over a high heat.

Transfer the lamb to a large serving plate, with some of the lamb pulled from the bone, then pour the juices over the top. Heaven.

Crispy lamb's brains, pancetta & feta, with curly endive & mint (GF)

No matter how much nose-to-tail eating is championed, offal is still not widely embraced. Mention eating brains to people and you'll get some pretty visceral responses, but I have had surprising success over the years with lamb's brains on restaurant menus. Versions of this dish were a regular feature at the Melbourne Wine Room, with the unique texture and flavour a lovely combination with the feta, pancetta, spike of vinegar and wiry freshness of curly endive (frisée). **Serves 4 as a starter**

4 lamb's brains
oil, for deep-frying (see p. 22)
12 slices of flat pancetta
150 g (5½ oz) firm Greek-
    style feta, cut into 12 slices
2 egg whites, whisked
2 tablespoons plain yoghurt
2 handfuls of curly endive
    (frisée), torn

4 mint sprigs, leaves torn
2 tablespoons white-wine
    vinegar
1 teaspoon aleppo pepper
Poaching liquid
1 litre (34 fl oz/4 cups) water
1 onion, finely sliced
1 garlic clove, finely sliced

1 celery stalk, finely sliced
1 fresh bay leaf
½ teaspoon salt flakes
½ teaspoon black
    peppercorns

Staples
EVOO, FLR, LMN, S&P

Cover the brains in water and stand overnight in the fridge.

In a small saucepan, bring the poaching liquid ingredients to a simmer over a medium heat. Carefully add the brains to the pan. Reduce the heat to low and poach for 5 minutes, then turn off the heat and cool to room temperature.

Once cooled, carefully lift the brains out of the liquid and add to a bowl or container. Strain the poaching liquid over the brains and refrigerate for 3 hours.

When ready to cook, heat 8 cm (3¼ in) of oil in a large saucepan or deep-fryer until 180°C (350°F).

Drain the brains and dry on paper towel. Slice each brain into three even pieces. Lay each piece on a slice of pancetta, top with a slice of feta, then roll up. Dredge the parcels in flour, then the egg whites, then coat again in flour. Fry in batches of six until golden, about 6 minutes, turning to cook evenly.

Meanwhile, smear the yoghurt on a serving plate. Dress the curly endive (frisée) and mint with the vinegar and an equal amount of oil, season with salt and pepper and arrange on the plate.

Season the fritters with salt and arrange on the yoghurt, then dust with the aleppo pepper and squeeze over some lemon. Serve immediately.

Braised lamb neck & barley broth

I grew up with lamb broth as a cool weather staple. This version is inspired by my mother's recipe. She would keep it very simple – a basic Irish broth – but I've added some spice, as I particularly like cumin's savoury notes with lamb. I also like to add a good squeeze of lemon at the end, which is a very Greek approach to finishing a broth, and one that really sharpens the flavours, combats the fatty richness of the lamb and highlights the spices. **Serves 8**

Skinless merguez-style sausages (GF)

Cut a 900 g (2 lb) lamb shoulder into 2 cm (¾ in) dice, then chill in the freezer until firm but not frozen. Meanwhile, toast 1 tablespoon cumin seeds, 3 teaspoons fennel seeds and 3 teaspoons coriander seeds in a dry frying pan over a medium heat, agitating to toast evenly until fragrant and darkened, about 2 minutes. Tip onto a plate to cool. Grind to a fine powder using a mortar and pestle or spice grinder, then combine with 2 tablespoons sweet paprika, 2 teaspoons ground allspice, ½ teaspoon ground cinnamon, 1 tablespoon salt flakes, 5 finely grated garlic cloves and 3 teaspoons Harissa (p. 92). Cut 150 g (5½ oz) lamb fat (shoulder or rump fat works well) into 1 cm (½ in) dice and add to a food processor with the lamb in batches, pulsing until you have a rough hamburger texture. Scoop into a bowl, sprinkle with the spice mix and 3 handfuls chopped wild fennel tops (or ½ bunch finely chopped coriander/cilantro), then combine with your hands, adding 100 ml (3½ fl oz) iced water as you go – you may not need it all, so add a little at a time until the mixture is homogenous and a little sticky. Fry a small patty and taste for seasoning, then adjust the seasoning accordingly. Shape into sausages by hand and place on a lined tray – or transfer the mixture to a piping (icing) bag fitted with a 2.5 cm (1 in) nozzle (or no nozzle, depending on your bag) and pipe onto the lined tray. Chill the sausages for 20 minutes to firm up. (They will keep for up to 3 days in the fridge before cooking, or can be frozen for later use.) To serve, grill the sausages on a hot barbecue for 3 minutes on each side. Serve hot with chips, Harissa (p. 92) and yoghurt, and a salad of chopped tomato and cucumber. Makes about 16.

1 kg (2 lb 3 oz) lamb neck
  pieces
1.5 litres (51 fl oz/6 cups)
  Golden chicken stock
  (p. 54)
2.5 litres (85 fl oz/10 cups)
  water
2 onions, finely diced

6 garlic cloves, finely sliced
3 carrots, finely diced
1 leek, sliced into half-moons
  1 cm (½ in) thick
4 celery stalks, finely diced
2 teaspoons ground cumin
2 teaspoons coriander seeds
60 g (2 oz) pearled barley

60 g (2 oz) black barley
½ bunch of silverbeet
  (Swiss chard), shredded,
  stems and all
juice of 1½ lemons

Staples
EVOO, S&P

Add the lamb, stock and water to a large saucepan and bring to a simmer. Skim off any impurities as they rise, and cook for about 2½ hours, until the meat is tender, topping up the water as needed.

Strain the stock and chill to settle the fat, then skim the fat off and set the stock aside. You should have about 3 litres (101 fl oz/12 cups) of stock – top it up with water if necessary.

Meanwhile, stand the lamb at room temperature until cool enough to handle, then pick and shred the meat.

Heat a good splash of oil in a large saucepan over a medium heat. Add the onion and garlic and sweat for 2 minutes. Add the carrot, leek, celery and spices and cook until softened, about 10 minutes.

Add the pearled and black barley and lamb stock and simmer for 25 minutes, until the barley is tender.

Add the silverbeet and shredded lamb, season with salt and pepper and simmer for 10 minutes. Once the silverbeet is tender, adjust the seasoning as needed, and serve with the lemon juice squeezed over.

Make it different

Braised lamb shank & barley broth. Instead of the lamb neck pieces, use three lamb shanks.

With another grain. If you don't have black barley, use extra pearled barley – or you could replace the barley altogether with farro or brown rice.

Lamb koftas baked with tomato & smoky eggplant, with pine nuts & parsley

Pair with

Cauliflower, barley & parsley salad (p. 477).

Kohlrabi & cucumber salad (p. 549).

Grain salad (pp. 378–80).

This recipe looks more involved than it actually is, with a longish list of staple pantry spices bulking out the ingredients list. It is, in reality, a very simple dish to achieve, and one I commonly make as a midweek meal. **Serves 6**

3 large eggplants
  (aubergines)
100 ml (3½ fl oz) extra-virgin
  olive oil
4 tomatoes, sliced 1 cm
  (½ in) thick
500 ml (17 fl oz/2 cups)
  tomato passata (puréed
  tomatoes)
150 g (5½ oz) firm
  Greek-style feta
30 g (1 oz) pine nuts,
  toasted, to serve

6 flat-leaf (Italian) parsley
  sprigs, leaves roughly
  chopped, to serve

Koftas
400 g (14 oz) finely minced
  (ground) lamb
300 g (10½ oz) finely minced
  (ground) beef
45 g (1½ oz/¾ cup)
  panko breadcrumbs, or
  60 g (2 oz/¾ cup) fresh
  breadcrumbs
1 salad onion, coarsely
  grated

3 garlic cloves, finely grated
50 g (1¾ oz/⅓ cup) pine
  nuts, toasted
1 egg
2½ teaspoons salt flakes
1½ tablespoons Baharat
  (p. 6)
1¼ teaspoons chilli flakes
2 teaspoons dried mint
2 teaspoons tomato paste
  (concentrated purée)

Staples
LMN, S&P

Scorch the eggplants over a gas burner, on a hot barbecue or under a hot grill (broiler) for a few minutes to char the skin, then place on a baking tray and roast for 35 minutes, until collapsing. Set aside to cool.

For the koftas, add the lamb and beef to a large bowl and combine well with your hands. Add the remaining ingredients and combine until evenly mixed. (You can also pulse the mixture in a food processor, if you prefer, but add the pine nuts once combined.) Form into twelve football-shaped koftas or round patties, then chill for 15 minutes to firm up.

Meanwhile, preheat the oven to 200°C (400°F) fan-forced.

Heat half the oil in a large frying pan over a high heat. Fry the koftas for 1½ minutes on each side to seal, then set aside.

Split the eggplants in half and scoop out the flesh into a roasting tin. Arrange the koftas on top, then top with the tomato slices. Squeeze on some lemon juice, spoon the passata over and season with salt and pepper. Crumble the feta over the top and drizzle with the remaining oil.

Cover with baking paper, then foil, and bake for 15 minutes.

Uncover and roast for a further 20 minutes, until bubbling and slightly brown. Scatter with the pine nuts and parsley to serve.

Make it different

Rather than baking them, shape the koftas into torpedoes and grill on a hot barbecue for 8–10 minutes, rotating to cook evenly. Serve with Tahini dip/sauce (p. 71), pitta breads (see p. 854), Zhoug (p. 87), torshi (see p. 639) and a salad of chopped cucumber and tomato.

Crumbed lamb cutlets

Crumbed lamb cutlets are just lovely with Insalata caprese (p. 662) or a green salad, or with Grilled gem lettuce & bagna cauda (p. 556). Allow for 3 cutlets and ½ small lettuce per person. To crumb the cutlets, combine 100 g (3½ oz/1 cup) dried breadcrumbs and 35 g (1¼ oz/⅓ cup) finely grated parmesan in a shallow bowl. Dredge the cutlets in flour, then whisked egg, then coat with the crumb mix. Fry in an even mix of oil and butter over a medium heat for about 2 minutes each side until golden, seasoning as they come out of the pan.

Moussaka

Moussaka has many regional variants – and not just in Greece – but the one most people are familiar with is this relatively modern interpretation. Some maintain that the sauce must be beef, others lamb. It is a recipe that has been modified a lot over the years. The keys for me are making sure the eggplant is well-cooked – so the dish doesn't become wet, which the breadcrumbs also play a vital role in – and not skipping the eggs in the béchamel, as they set the white sauce in a delicious slab, which is a major feature of the dish. This is best served very warm rather than super-hot, as it will hold its shape better. **Serves 8**

Pair with

A simple green salad.

3 large eggplants (aubergines), peeled and sliced 1 cm (½ in) thick
3 large boiling (waxy) or all-purpose potatoes (such as desiree or nicola), peeled and sliced 1 cm (½ in) thick
50 g (1¾ oz) fresh breadcrumbs
1 tablespoon dried Greek oregano (rigani)
150 g (5½ oz) kefalotyri cheese or parmesan, grated

Cheese sauce
3 eggs, whisked

1 × quantity Béchamel (p. 70)
150 g (5½ oz) kefalotyri cheese or parmesan, grated

Meat sauce
80 ml (2½ fl oz/⅓ cup) extra-virgin olive oil
1 onion, finely diced
4 garlic cloves, finely chopped
350 g (12½ oz) minced (ground) lamb
350 g (12½ oz) minced (ground) beef
1 teaspoon ground allspice
1 teaspoon ground cinnamon

1 teaspoon ground black pepper
2 × 400 g (14 oz) tins diced tomatoes
2 tablespoons tomato paste (concentrated purée)
1 litre (34 fl oz/4 cups) White chicken stock (p. 54)
1 tablespoon dried Greek oregano (rigani)
2 teaspoons caster (superfine) sugar
1 egg white, whisked

Staples
EVOO, S&P

For the meat sauce, heat the oil in a saucepan over a medium heat. Cook the onion and garlic until softened, about 5 minutes. Add the lamb, beef and spices, season with salt and cook over a high heat until the meat is well browned, about 10 minutes. Stir in the tomatoes, tomato paste, stock, oregano and sugar and simmer for about 30 minutes, until the sauce has reduced by about one-third. Set aside to cool to room temperature, then stir in the egg white (it helps the sauce to set when baking).

Meanwhile, preheat the oven to 180°C (350°F) fan-forced and line two baking trays with baking paper. Toss the eggplant slices in oil and lay them on the baking trays. Roast for 20 minutes, then set aside to cool.

Add the potato slices to a pot of cold salted water. Bring to the boil and cook until tender, about 15 minutes. Drain well, then drizzle with a tablespoon or so of oil.

For the cheese sauce, whisk the eggs into the béchamel, then stir the cheese through.

To assemble, scatter 2 tablespoons of the breadcrumbs in a deep 20 × 30 cm (8 × 12 in) baking dish. Lay half the eggplant and all the potato slices, alternating them in the dish, so they're overlapping. Spoon half the meat sauce over. Sprinkle with the oregano, then scatter with half the cheese and half the remaining crumbs. Top with the remaining eggplant slices, then spoon the remaining meat sauce over. Top with the remaining crumbs and cheese, flattening with a spatula.

Top with the cheese sauce and bake at 180°C (350°F) fan-forced for about 45 minutes, until the sauce is slightly golden, puffed and bubbling at the edges. Set aside for 20 minutes to set before serving.

Spiced-yoghurt leg of lamb 🄶🄵

This marinade can be employed to roast a bone-in or boned leg, which can be roasted or grilled to a blushing pink, or slowly cooked until very tender. I don't cook lamb leg slowly very often, but marinating overnight in a mixture like this yields excellent results. **Serves 4–6**

Pair with

Serve with Pitta bread (p. 854), torshi (see p. 639) and Tahini dip/sauce (p. 71), chopped tomato and cucumber salad and/or a shaved cabbage salad dressed with oil, vinegar, salt and sugar.

Beetroot tabouleh (p. 419).

Grilled eggplant with tahini, pomegranate & mint (p. 516).

Zaalouk (p. 518).

Cauliflower, barley & parsley salad (p. 477).

Grain salad (pp. 378–80).

2.5–3 kg (5½ lb–6 lb 10 oz) bone-in lamb leg
1 large fennel bulb, sliced 1 cm (½ in) thick, or 4 celery stalks
350 ml (12 fl oz) water

Fennel, sumac & yoghurt marinade
1 tablespoon fennel seeds
1 tablespoon cumin seeds
2 teaspoons black peppercorns
1 teaspoon cardamom seeds
1 star anise
½ cinnamon stick
4 cloves
1½ tablespoons salt flakes
1 tablespoon sweet paprika
1 tablespoon ground sumac

2 teaspoons ground nutmeg
100 g (3½ oz) plain yoghurt
2 tablespoons extra-virgin olive oil
5 garlic cloves, finely grated
4 cm (1½ in) piece of fresh ginger, peeled and finely grated
juice of 1 lemon

For the marinade, toast the whole spices in a dry frying pan over a medium heat until fragrant and slightly darkened, about 1 minute. Grind in a spice grinder or using a mortar and pestle, then combine with the remaining marinade ingredients.

Score the lamb in a crisscross pattern, about 1 cm (½ in) deep. Smother the marinade onto the lamb and refrigerate overnight – 24 hours is even better.

Remove the lamb from the fridge 1 hour before roasting.

Preheat the oven to 180°C (350°F) fan-forced.

Lay the fennel in a roasting tin and place the lamb on top. Pour in the water.

Roast the lamb, basing the timing on 15 minutes for every 500 g (1 lb 2 oz). So, a 2.5 kg (5½ lb) leg would take 1¼ hours, and a 3 kg (6 lb 10 oz) leg would need 1½ hours. If using a thermometer, you're aiming for 45°C (115°F) in the thickest part.

Turn the oven up to 220°C (430°F) fan-forced and baste the lamb with the juices. Roast for a further 10 minutes to brown the crust.

Remove from the oven and rest for 15–20 minutes, loosely covered with foil, before carving.

Make it different

Try slow-roasting the spiced lamb leg. Rather than rosy pink lamb, cooking slowly will yield delightfully tender meat that yields to a little pressure and pulls off the bone with ease. Prepare the lamb as above. Add 600 ml (20½ fl oz) water to the roasting tin, cover with paper, then foil. Roast for 3 hours at 150°C (300°F) fan-forced, then uncover and roast for a further 30 minutes. Increase the oven temperature to 220°C (430°F) and roast for a final 20 minutes, until a deep brown. Squeeze some lemon over to serve.

Barbecue a boned butterflied lamb leg. Cut the leg into the three main muscles (see Barbecued lamb leg, right), then marinate as above. Leave at room temperature for an hour before grilling each piece on a medium–high grill for 8–10 minutes per side. Rest under some foil for 15 minutes before carving. The seasonings here take well to the barbecue, with the smoky char of real coals adding to the intensity – but a gas barbecue will yield a fine result, too.

Easy souvlaki

On a trip to Santorini in the late 1990s, I had the best souvlaki of my life from a tiny shop well off the beaten track. It was a tiny fluffy pitta bread filled with the most tender, smoky meat that had been slowly grilled over coals and scented with lemon, garlic, and dried and fresh oregano, served with a dollop of yoghurt, some shaved onion, iceberg lettuce and a dusting of spice. I'll never know what was in that spice mix, but I have evolved a pleasing replica. **Serves 6**

1 kg (2 lb 3 oz) lamb leg, cut into 3 cm (1¼ in) dice
6 pitta breads (see p. 854)
1 × quantity Yoghurt sauce (p. 312)
2 white onions, 1 very finely sliced, 1 cut into 12 chunks
¼ iceberg lettuce, finely shredded
Greek spice mix (p. 16), to serve

Marinade
3 garlic cloves, smashed
zest and juice of 1 lemon
2 tablespoons extra-virgin olive oil
2 tablespoons red or white-wine vinegar
4 teaspoons dried Greek oregano (rigani)
4 oregano sprigs, leaves chopped
2 fresh bay leaf, crushed

Yoghurt & garlic sauce
250 g (9 oz/1 cup) thick plain yoghurt
juice of ½ lemon
1 tablespoon extra-virgin olive oil
1 large garlic clove, finely grated
1 teaspoon salt flakes

Staples
S&P

Special equipment
6 metal skewers

Combine all the marinade ingredients in a bowl. Add the lamb and toss well to coat. Marinate for as long as you can – 30 minutes at a minimum, but overnight is best.

When ready to cook, preheat a barbecue grill on high.

For the sauce, add all the ingredients to a bowl and combine well.

Season the lamb with salt, then thread onto the skewers, reserving the marinating juices. Thread a chunk of onion onto both ends of each skewer. Cook on the grill for 2 minutes, then rotate, basting with the marinating juices, and repeat again. The lamb will take about 8 minutes to cook and char on all sides.

Rest for 3 minutes before serving; the lamb should have a blush of pink inside.

Meanwhile, warm the pitta breads on the grill, then add some yoghurt sauce, finely sliced onion and lettuce. Slide the meat off the skewers on top, dust with some Greek spice mix and eat immediately.

Barbecued lamb leg with oregano & lemon (GF)

When barbecuing a butterflied lamb leg, I find it better to break the meat down into its major muscles. This ensures you get good colour across the meat without burning (as may happen if you try to truss it); also, it can be hard to handle if opened out. There are three major sections, which will be easy to identify – simply cut along the lines of the muscles. I trim away some of the fat, as it can catch and burn. Score the remaining fat in a crisscross pattern, then season generously with salt and pepper. Squeeze over some lemon, splash over a little red-wine vinegar and drizzle with oil. Throw on a good handful of dried Greek oregano (rigani) and massage everything into the meat. Set aside to marinate for 1 hour at room temperature. Heat a barbecue – or ideally, light a fire and let it die down to even coals. Barbecue the lamb pieces on one side for about 15 minutes (this will naturally depend a bit on the size of the lamb), then flip and cook for 10–15 minutes. When cooking, keep moving the lamb to avoid flare-ups from dripping fat, which can result in an unpleasant flavour. Rest for 10 minutes, loosely covered with foil, then slice across the grain, drizzling the resting juices over to serve.

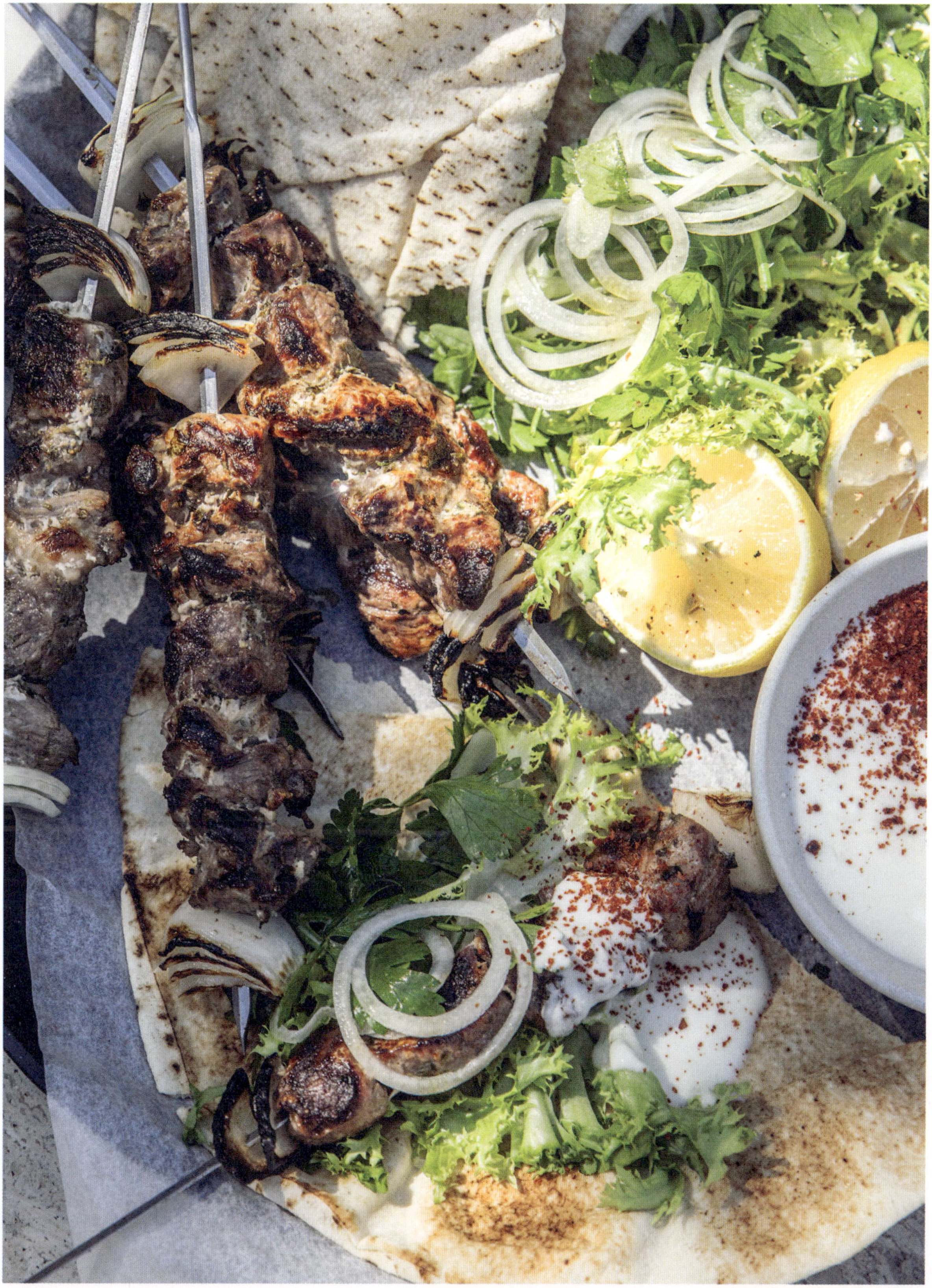

Lamb, spinach, pomegranate & date salad with crisp pitta

This salad is an ideal vehicle for lamb backstrap, with the delicate meat perfectly matched with lemony sumac, cumin and sweetly tart pomegranate molasses, which all work superbly with the fresh celery and spinach, exotic date purée and crunchy pitta. **Serves 8**

100 g (3½ oz/⅔ cup) blanched almonds
4 lamb backstraps
1 tablespoon ground sumac
500 g (1 lb 2 oz) baby English spinach leaves
2 celery hearts, finely sliced on an angle
1 bunch of mint, leaves picked, large leaves torn
2 handfuls of pomegranate seeds

Fried pitta
100 g (3½ oz) butter
100 ml (3½ fl oz) extra-virgin olive oil
5 small pitta breads (see p. 854), each cut into 8 triangles
1 tablespoon ground cumin

Pomegranate dressing
150 ml (5 fl oz) extra-virgin olive oil
150 ml (5 fl oz) pomegranate molasses
juice of 1 lemon
1 garlic clove, finely grated
1½ teaspoons chilli flakes
½ teaspoon salt flakes

Date paste
250 g (9 oz) medjool dates, pitted and finely chopped
300 ml (10 fl oz) boiling water
juice of 1 lemon
2 teaspoons chopped preserved lemon

Staples
EVOO, S&P

For the date paste, bring all the ingredients to a simmer in a small saucepan, then blitz in a blender until smooth. Season with salt and pepper and transfer to a bowl. It should be the consistency of very thick honey; if necessary, add a little hot water to loosen.

For the dressing, combine all the ingredients in a small bowl.

For the pitta, add half the butter and half the oil to a large frying pan over a medium heat. Fry the pitta triangles in batches for about 1½ minutes on each side, adding more oil and butter as needed. Don't rush this and don't crowd the pan, as these need to be crisp. Remove from the pan, sprinkle with some cumin and season with salt and pepper and drain on paper towel. The pitta will crisp up as they cool.

Wipe out the pan, then toast the almonds over a medium heat, tossing regularly until scorched. Tip into a bowl and set aside.

Season and oil the lamb. Cook the backstraps on a very hot griddle plate, barbecue or frying pan for about 5 minutes each side, then cover loosely with foil and rest for 5 minutes. Once rested, slice on an angle. Sprinkle with half the sumac.

Add the spinach, celery and mint to a bowl. Season with salt, dress with a splash of oil and toss.

Spread the date paste around the edges of a large platter, and pile half the salad in the middle. Top with the lamb slices and then the remaining salad. Scatter the almonds and pomegranate seeds around and drizzle the dressing over. Finish with the fried pitta and remaining sumac.

Make it different
If you don't like the idea of frying the pitta, oil the triangles and bake at 170°C (340°F) fan-forced for about 8 minutes, then cool (but remember, the butter tastes so good!).

Pair with

The pomegranate dressing is great for saucing any grilled meat or cheese.

Braised lamb chump chops with potato, jalapeño & oregano (GF)

Preheat the oven to 180°C (350°F) fan-forced. Heat a good splash of extra-virgin olive oil in a heavy-based flameproof casserole dish over a medium heat. Season 6 lamb chump chops with salt and pepper, then cook in batches until brown, about 2 minutes each side. Set aside. Add a splash more oil to the pan, then add 1 large finely diced onion, 4 peeled and sliced garlic cloves, 2 green capsicums (bell peppers), cut into eight pieces, 2 fresh jalapeño chillies, sliced into thick rings, and 2 tablespoons dried Mexican oregano or dried Greek oregano (rigani). Cook until softened, about 6 minutes. Slice 3 creamy yellow-fleshed potatoes into 1 cm (½ in) thick slices and add to the pan with 3 teaspoons ground allspice, then season and cook for about 5 minutes. Stir in 500 ml (17 fl oz/2 cups) Golden chicken stock (p. 54), 80 ml (2½ fl oz/⅓ cup) white-wine vinegar and 2 handfuls plump sultanas (golden raisins), then return the chops, adding a little water if needed to just cover. Bring to a simmer. Cover and transfer to the oven to braise for about 1 hour, until the chops are tender. Once tender, remove the lid and cook for a further 15 minutes or so, for the sauce to thicken and intensify. Adjust the seasoning to taste. Serves 4–6. Great with Baked buttered rice (p. 384), seasonal greens and a tomato and onion salad.

Simply roasted leg of lamb with rosemary & garlic GF

Pair with

I would serve this roasted lamb with a salad. No matter what time of the year it is, I feel the richness of the lamb needs a freshness and an acidic kick to complement.

Vinaigrette lentils (p. 385) finished with tarragon and/ or parsley.

Beetroot tabouleh (p. 419).

Braised romano beans (p. 438).

Borlotti bean braise with cumin (see p. 426).

Borlotti beans with herbs & freekeh (p. 427).

Cauliflower cheese (p. 479).

Roasted cauliflower, barley, feta & almond salad (p. 477).

This is a universal recipe for roasting lamb to achieve a beautifully roasted crust and pink meat. **Serves 4–6**

2.5 kg (5½ lb) bone-in lamb leg
5 garlic cloves, cut in half lengthways
2 rosemary sprigs

2 onions, cut into rings 1.5 cm (½ in) thick
400 ml (13½ fl oz) white wine, or water

Staples
EVOO, S&P

Rest the lamb at room temperature for 1 hour before roasting.

Preheat the oven to 220°C (430°F) fan-forced.

Score the surface of the lamb in a crisscross fashion, then make ten small incisions into the meat using a paring knife. Insert the pieces of garlic and a tuft of rosemary into each incision. Rub the meat with a little oil and season generously with salt and pepper.

Add the onion rings to the base of a roasting tin to make a 'trivet', then put the lamb on top. Pour in the wine.

Roast the lamb for 1¼ hours (15 minutes per 500 g/1 lb 2 oz) for medium-rare, with an internal temperature of 45–48°C (115–118°F).

Remove from the oven and rest, loosely covered with foil, for 15–20 minutes; the internal temperature will rise to 53–54°C (127–129°F). Don't rush the resting, as it will reward you with tender, relaxed meat.

If you want to take it to medium, the rested internal temperature should be around 55°C (130°F), with 65°C (150°F) for medium to well-done – and 75°C (165°F) for well-done, which is not recommended.

Once rested, either carve the whole leg, or cut the three separate lobes of muscle from the bone and then slice. Serve with the pan juices drizzled over.

Make it different
I like thinner pan juices for the lamb – but you can reduce them down further to thicken them, and add a knob of butter for extra gloss, if desired. If you want to thicken the juices even more, combine a few teaspoons of oil with the same quantity of flour until smooth, then whisk into the strained juices with a teaspoon of white-wine vinegar and simmer for 30 seconds or so, until thickened.

Abbacchio al forno

Pair with

A leafy salad.

Polenta (p. 383).

Horta-style greens (p. 552).

Braised romano beans (p. 438).

Borlotti bean braise with cumin (see p. 426).

Borlotti beans with herbs & freekeh (p. 427).

Abbacchio al forno or abbacchio alla romana are quite ancient dishes of wet-roasted suckling lamb. My grandmother made a version with spices and red capsicum (bell pepper), while my chef friend Rita Macali's family made a classic Roman version. It is counterintuitive to a chef to cook the meat without searing it first, but the caramelisation all happens at the end of cooking. This is wonderful baked in a clay vessel, and even better when done in a wood-fired oven. Naturally, the bonito is not traditional, but anchovies often are used for abbacchio, so it's not that wild an inclusion. Plus, you know, the umami and all that. You can also skip the brining step, but it does add that little something extra. **Serves 8–10**

3–3.5 kg (6 lb 10 oz–7 lb 12 oz) lamb forequarter, cut by your butcher into pieces about 4 cm (1½ in) thick, through the bones and ribs
1 large garlic bulb, skin on, cloves bruised
2 tablespoons dried Greek oregano
2 teaspoons salt flakes
2 teaspoons ground black pepper
150 ml (5 fl oz) extra-virgin olive oil
3 onions, sliced
10 slices of guanciale, about 2 mm (⅛ in) thick

10 g (¼ oz) katsuobushi (bonito flakes), or 6 anchovies (optional)
3 Dutch cream or desiree potatoes, peeled and sliced 1.5–2 cm (½–¾ in) thick
2 fresh bay leaves
3 rosemary sprigs, each cut in three
6 thyme springs
6 large tomatoes, cut into 6 slices each – or 2 × 400 g (14 oz) tins diced tomatoes
500 ml (17 fl oz/2 cups) white wine

500 ml (17 fl oz/2 cups) Golden chicken stock (p. 54)
150 g (5½ oz) Grana Padano, finely grated
160 g (5½ oz/2 cups) fresh white breadcrumbs

Brine
5 litres (170 fl oz/20 cups) water
200 g (7 oz) sea salt
150 g (5½ oz/⅔ cup) caster (superfine) sugar
1 tablespoon black peppercorns, crushed

Staples
S&P

Combine the brine ingredients in a large saucepan and heat to dissolve the sugar and salt. Transfer to a container or pot that will fit the lamb and fit in the fridge. Once the brine has cooled, add the lamb and refrigerate overnight.

When ready to cook, drain the meat and dry well.

Preheat the oven to 150°C (300°F) fan-forced.

Toss the lamb with the garlic, oregano, salt flakes, pepper and 2½ tablespoons of the oil.

Spread half the onion in the bottom of two roasting tins, then lay the lamb on top so it fits snugly. Lay the guanciale over the lamb, sprinkle with the katsuobushi or anchovies and scatter the remaining onion over. Poke the potato slices in between the meat, then scatter with the bay leaves, rosemary and thyme, followed by the tomato slices. Pour the wine and stock over, then scatter with the cheese and breadcrumbs. Drizzle with the remaining oil.

Cover with baking paper, then foil, and roast for about 3 hours, until very tender.

Once the meat is falling from the bone, remove the foil and turn the oven temperature up to 200°C (400°F) fan-forced and roast for a further 30 minutes to colour the lamb. Serve with the pan juices spooned over.

Make it faster
Skip the brining step – it's what I do, but it's not traditional.

Make it different
Capretto. The equivalent weight in baby lamb or goat, broken down, can be cooked the same way.

Braised lamb neck with white wine, tomato & oregano ⒼⒻ

This is based on a braise I ate in Santorini many years ago. The depth of tomato and oregano flavour with the succulent lamb was mesmerising, with the potatoes taking up so much flavour. It had a slick of fat and oil on top, stained with tomato, which really helped me understand how important the fat/oil in a dish like this is, and it made sponging up the residual juices in the bowl with bread such a delight. Make sure you get good deep colour on the lamb when browning it; it adds a depth of flavour you can't achieve otherwise. **Serves 8**

Pair with

Plenty of good bread to mop up the juices.

Cooked greens or a leafy salad.

Horta-style greens (p. 552).

Buttered small pasta, such as orzo or stellini.

Boiled greens, such as beans, peas or silverbeet (Swiss chard).

150 ml (5 fl oz) extra-virgin
  olive oil
1.8 kg (4 lb) boned lamb
  neck (about 6 pieces)
3 onions, sliced
6 garlic cloves, sliced
2 fresh bay leaves
½ cup dried Greek oregano
  (rigani)
2 teaspoons ground allspice

30 g (1 oz) brown sugar
1 tablespoon tomato paste
  (concentrated purée)
500 ml (17 fl oz/2 cups)
  white wine
1 litre (34 fl oz/4 cups) White
  chicken stock (p. 54)
200 ml (7 fl oz) tomato
  passata (puréed tomatoes)

4 boiling (waxy) yellow-
  fleshed potatoes (such as
  desiree or Dutch cream),
  peeled and cut in half
1 handful of fresh
  breadcrumbs

Staples
FLR, S&P

Heat half the oil in a large flameproof casserole dish over a medium heat. Toss the lamb in flour, shaking off any excess. Brown all over, about 5 minutes each side, seasoning with salt and pepper as you go. Remove and set aside.

Tip the fat from the dish and wipe clean with paper towel.

Heat the remaining oil in the dish. Add the onion, garlic and bay leaves, season and cook over a medium heat for about 15 minutes, until sticky and caramelised.

Meanwhile, preheat the oven to 160°C (320°F) fan-forced.

Return the lamb to the dish, then stir the oregano, allspice, sugar and tomato paste through. Add the wine and bring to the boil. Stir in the stock and passata, bring to a simmer and add the potato.

Sprinkle the breadcrumbs over the top. Cover with a lid, or baking paper and foil, transfer to the oven and bake for 2 hours.

Uncover and cook for a further 30 minutes, until the sauce has reduced a little and the meat is tender and colouring up at the edges. Serve directly from the pot.

Lamb rogan josh ⒼⒻ

Pair with

Basmati rice, Naan (p. 855)
and Raita (p. 98).

Rogan josh is undoubtedly the most famous Kashmiri dish, an aromatic and often fiery curry of lamb or goat, with a distinct red hue. That colour comes both from Kashmiri chillies, with the powder (and sometimes dried whole peppers) readily available from Indian/Asian grocers, as well as dye liberated from a herb related to borage called ratan jot – it also gives tandoori chicken its ruddy hue. As with many subcontinental curries, the depth, richness and sweetness come from cooking out a lot of onion at the start, which will fully liquefy by the time the curry is ready. Where we might use stock to enrich and fill out the flavour in Western dishes, onions do the same thing in a curry, working in such perfect accord with the spices and chilli. **Serves 8**

80 g (2½ oz) ghee
2 fresh bay leaves
2 brown cardamom pods
8 cm (3¼ in) piece of cassia
  bark
1½ tablespoons fennel seeds
3 red onions, sliced
10 garlic cloves, finely
  chopped
10 cm (4 in) piece of fresh
  ginger, peeled and finely
  julienned

1½ tablespoons salt flakes
2 tablespoons ground
  coriander
3 teaspoons ground
  cardamom
3 teaspoons ground cloves
2 teaspoons ground turmeric
2 teaspoons ground ginger
2 teaspoons Kashmiri chilli
  powder
6 large tomatoes, diced

1 tablespoon tomato paste
  (concentrated purée)
2 long red chillies, finely
  chopped, or 2 dried
  Kashmiri chillies, soaked
  and chopped
1.5 kg (3 lb 5 oz) lamb
  shoulder, cut into 2.5 cm
  (1 in) dice
600 ml (20½ fl oz) water

Melt the ghee in a wide-based saucepan over a high heat. Add the bay leaves, cardamom pods, cassia and fennel seeds and fry for 2 minutes.

Add the onion, garlic and fresh ginger and cook until softened, about 10 minutes. Stir in the salt, ground spices and chilli powder for about 1 minute, until fragrant, then add a splash of water to cool the spices.

Stir in the tomatoes, tomato paste and chopped chilli to combine, then add the lamb and stir to coat well. Add the water and bring to a simmer.

Reduce the heat to low, then cover and cook for about 50 minutes, until the meat is tender. Adjust the seasoning to taste, and reduce the sauce a little if required.

Lamb & eggplant karahi curry GF

The word karahi actually refers to the vessel a curry is often cooked in – a small wok-like pan with two handles. In fact, I'm not entirely sure what makes this a karahi curry, and I do not own the requisite pan. The word karahi is also a potential source of the very non-subcontinental term 'curry'. A western word, 'curry' is a hopeless grouping of a vast array of dishes under the one banner. And if karahi is the etymological source of the word curry, then this is essentially a 'curry curry' … Nonetheless, the base recipe for this came to me as a karahi curry and, though I have modified it substantially, a karahi curry it has remained. After all that, I do love a lamb curry, and it is always a crowd pleaser. The sauce is thickened and enriched with chickpea flour and yoghurt, making for a velvety, soupy sauce, which is what I want in an Indian curry. **Serves 4–6**

Pair with

Basmati rice, Raita (p. 98), Naan (p. 855) and a fresh ginger and tomato chutney with plenty of fresh coriander (cilantro) and/or mint.

- 1½ tablespoons besan (chickpea flour)
- 800 ml (27 fl oz) water
- 350 g (12½ oz) plain yoghurt
- 125 ml (4 fl oz/½ cup) extra-virgin olive oil
- 2 large eggplants (aubergines), partly peeled lengthways in stripes, then cut into 6 wedges each
- 3 heaped teaspoons cumin seeds
- 3 heaped teaspoons fennel seeds
- 3 heaped teaspoons fenugreek seeds
- 2 tablespoons mustard seeds
- 2 onions, sliced lengthways into half-moons
- 6 garlic cloves, sliced
- 10 cm (4 in) piece of fresh ginger, peeled and julienned
- 3 long red chillies, sliced on an angle
- 2 heaped teaspoons ground cumin
- 2 teaspoons ground turmeric
- 3½ teaspoons salt flakes
- 2 teaspoons chilli powder
- 800 g (1 lb 12 oz) lamb shoulder, cut into large dice
- 400 g (14 oz) tin diced tomatoes
- 12 fresh curry leaves (optional)

Whisk the chickpea flour and water in a large bowl until combined. Add the yoghurt and whisk until smooth.

Heat the oil in a large, wide saucepan over a medium heat. Add the eggplant and fry until lightly browned, then remove from the pan.

Fry the whole spices for about 1½ minutes, until fragrant and lightly toasted. Stir in the onion, garlic, ginger and sliced chillies and fry for 2 minutes. Stir in the ground spices, salt and chilli powder and cook for 1 minute, then add the lamb and cook, stirring, for about 4 minutes.

Turn the heat down to low, then cover and cook for 12 minutes. Stir in the yoghurt mixture, eggplant and tomato and bring to a simmer over a medium heat, then mix the curry leaves through.

Turn the heat back down to low. Cover and cook for about 1 hour, until the meat is tender; you may need to add a little water during cooking.

Lamb, pea & mint pancake fritters

Whisk 250 ml (8½ fl oz/1 cup) milk with 2 eggs, then whisk in 150 g (5½ oz/1 cup) self-raising flour. Add 2 teaspoons dijon mustard, 2 teaspoons ground cumin, 1½ teaspoons dried mint or a few handfuls of shredded fresh mint leaves and ½ teaspoon salt flakes. Season with a good grind of pepper and combine, then fold in 300 g (10½ oz) shredded left-over cooked lamb, 120 g (4 oz) frozen peas, thawed and mashed a little with a spoon, and 100 g (3½ oz) chopped baby English spinach. Heat 3 tablespoons extra-virgin olive oil in a large frying pan over a medium heat. Add 2 tablespoons of the mixture for each fritter and fry for 2½ minutes on each side, until lightly golden. Serve with a squeeze of lemon.

Left-over lamb roast shepherd's pie

The genesis of the shepherd's pie is no doubt from repurposing leftovers, which is what always happened in my house growing up, and still does. Problem is, my family just don't leave that many leftovers. If this is the same for you, either opt for a slightly larger roast, or make up the difference with minced (ground) lamb – probably both. I like a strong vegetable presence in my shepherd's pie, and find that using chicken stock and tomatoes helps make an even more delicious filling. **Serves 4–6**

850 g (1 lb 14 oz) left-over lamb – make up the difference with minced (ground) lamb, if necessary
3 tablespoons extra-virgin olive oil
2 onions, finely diced
2 garlic cloves, finely diced
2 carrots, finely diced
2 celery stalks, finely diced
2 rosemary sprigs, leaves finely chopped
1 tablespoon tomato paste (concentrated purée)

300 ml (10 fl oz) red wine, or white wine
1 tablespoon worcestershire sauce
300 ml (10 fl oz) White chicken stock (p. 54), or any meat stock
400 g (14 oz) tin chopped tomatoes
115 g (4 oz/¾ cup) peas
40 g (1½ oz) unsalted butter, diced

Mash
1.5 kg (3 lb 5 oz) boiling (waxy) potatoes (such as desiree or Dutch cream), peeled and cut into 3 cm (1¼ in) chunks
150 g (5½ oz) butter
100 ml (3½ fl oz) milk – or cream for a richer result
5 grates of nutmeg
2 egg yolks

Staples
EVOO, S&P

If using minced lamb, fry it in a little oil in a large saucepan over a high heat until browned, about 10 minutes. Season with salt and pepper, then remove and set aside.

Add the oil to the pan over a medium heat. Cook the onion, garlic, carrot and celery for 15 minutes, until caramelising, adding the rosemary about halfway through. Stir the tomato paste through for 2 minutes, then add the wine and simmer for 2 minutes.

Splash in the worcestershire sauce and stir all the lamb through, then add the stock and tomatoes and simmer for about 20 minutes.

Preheat the oven to 200°C (400°F) fan-forced.

Meanwhile, for the mash, add the potato to a pot of cold salted water, bring to the boil and cook for about 25 minutes, until very tender. Drain well and pass through a ricer, or mash. Stir the butter, milk and nutmeg through, season with salt and pepper, then mix the egg yolks through.

Once the lamb mixture has thickened and the sauce has reduced by about one-third, mix the peas through. Tip into a baking dish measuring about 20 × 30 cm (8 × 12 in). Spoon the mash over and rough up the surface with a fork (these bits will crisp up more readily). Dot with the butter.

Transfer to the oven and bake for about 30 minutes, until the mash is golden with the mixture bubbling beneath.

Make it different
With puff pastry. You can top this with bought or home-made Puff pastry (p. 822). Glaze with a beaten egg and pierce the pastry a couple of times for steam to escape, then bake for the same time until golden.

Lamb & eggplant karahi curry

Also see

Ramen **58–9**

Mussels with chorizo, tomato & white wine **213**

Ragù alla bolognese **283**

Scotch quail eggs **360**

Cassoulet **391**

Mapo-style tofu with beans & pork **436**

Smoked ham hock & borlotti bean soup **425–6**

Jamón, fig, beetroot, goat's curd, watercress & mint salad **702**

Pork

Pork

While pork has never seemed to occupy the spotlight in Australia the way that beef, lamb and chicken have, the market for pork products is a formidable one. Australians now eat a bit more pork than they do beef, and a lot more than they do lamb – which seems a little surprising, until you consider the scale of the processed pork market, which extends well beyond the obvious standard-bearers of ham and bacon, and includes a wealth of salami, charcuterie, partly and fully cured sausages, and a dizzying array of anonymous deli meats.

The annual consumption of pork – fresh and processed – by Australians has increased from under 9 kg (20 lb) per person annually in 1960 to almost 30 kg (66 lb) per person in 2020. That's an awful lot of pork, given that our population has grown during that time from just over 10 million to more than 25 million. Pork is big, big business – and sadly that's how it has been run, with economical efficiencies prioritised over ethical ones.

Pigs, like chickens, have the misfortune of being manipulable enough to be farmed intensively, and are sometimes reared in the most heartbreaking of ways. At worst, intensively farmed pigs are fed a cocktail of growth promotants – including sedatives, antibiotics and anabolic steroids – and are kept indoors, packed in pens, while being pushed to slaughter weight as quickly as possible.

Thankfully, standards in Australia have vastly improved this picture, with antibiotics now only used for welfare reasons (though, as with intensively farmed poultry, those health issues are generally endemic). The stalls the animals occupy are now generally less cramped, and there is a degree of transparency to the industry. However, 'indoor' pigs don't live in remotely natural conditions, still with little room to move, and no opportunity to roam or wallow, and little to no chance of engaging in instinctive, natural behaviours. It's not how I want to see any animals raised. To me, it's still a tragedy.

It's also important to note that although all fresh pork sold here is domestically reared and slaughtered, imported pork makes up something like 75 per cent of the processed pork consumed – with 45 per cent of our *total* pork consumption being imported processed pork. So, any perception of ethical standards for Australian pork are not applicable to almost half the pork products sold here. That's not to say imported pork products are better or worse in terms of welfare issues – but, as always, ask questions and do your research.

At a very base level, there is a wholly selfish reason for eating ethically raised animals: they taste better, far, far better. But hopefully, as a society, we prove to have more noble and humane motivations than that. If we are to eat animals, then we need to do so responsibly. We need to respect the animals, respect natural processes and respect the land. I understand that small-scale, ethical, pasture-raised meat is expensive, and eye-wateringly so at times, but any choices we make to buy better will have a positive impact.

Choose legitimate free-range or organic products, rather than anonymously sourced cheap pork. Eat less, eat better. Demand for ethically raised meat will raise supply, and costs will go down. If low prices are the guide, then cost efficiencies will be the overriding principles for farmers' economic survival. It's important to remember that many of the less-desirable modern farming and animal rearing methods are not necessarily how many farmers want to operate, but rather they are market-driven necessities. Our choices can change that.

Rare breeds of pork, such as Berkshire or Wessex Saddleback, raised with care, and raised slowly, deliver the best flavour. The meat will be rosy and pink with a good amount of fat, often with marbling through the meat, and it will be a pinky brown when cooked. While they eat almost anything, pigs need a richly varied diet, so farming pigs in a near-natural way is somewhat of a

Pair with

Pork takes well to spices, with fennel seeds, coriander seeds, cloves, black and white pepper, nutmeg, star anise, Chinese five-spice and paprika all excellent matches. Rosemary, bay leaves and sage are perfect companions, as are softer herbs such as parsley and coriander (cilantro). Pork likes salt and salty sauces, such as soy and fish sauce, and it loves sweet things, such as maple syrup and honey, just as much as it likes heat, whether it be fiery chilli or relatively mild mustard. Onions, ginger, garlic, cabbage, potatoes, carrots, celery, tomato and bitter leaves are all excellent pairings, as too are oranges, prunes, pickled cherries and apples. Pork also pairs beautifully with pulses, such as lentils and all kinds of dried beans, as well as fresh borlotti (cranberry) beans, and grains such as barley and freekeh.

challenge. But a pig raised on a broad range of grains, vegetables, fruit, legumes, grasses and protein sources will always produce better-tasting pork than ones raised on a narrow diet with supplements to fill in nutritional gaps.

Pigs raised on good natural diets will also produce fat that is simply better for you. Like all animals, pigs fed intensively on diets of corn, soy and the like will end up with more omega-6 fatty acids and fewer omega-3s, while those on a near-natural diet will do the reverse. Acorns are a meaningful part of the diet for some pigs in Europe – famously contributing to the quality of Jamón Ibérico – resulting in flavoursome flesh marbled with fat. That fat is also high in omega-3 fats, with the lard in some cases mimicking the profile of olive oil, consisting of plenty of healthy monounsaturated fat and oleic acid. And that profile is not just true of pigs that gorge on acorns, with properly grazed pigs showing similar benefits. Better for the pigs, better for us. And the flavour is revelatory.

Pigs have been progressively bred to have less subcutaneous and intramuscular fat, while properly reared rare breeds will have more of both, which I believe is healthier, and it is also unarguably – absolutely incontrovertibly – tastier. The twin desire to satisfy a market terrified of fat, and to bring that pork to market quickly, has resulted in animals with less fat, but fat that is less good for you. Very much a lose–lose situation.

Pork is best from a female pig, raising similar ethical quandaries that plague the dairy and egg industries – though male pigs are typically still raised for meat. The issue is 'boar taint', with the meat having a distinctive off-putting aroma. It is something you will recognise quite readily – and you will not forget it. The issue occurs when the pigs reach sexual maturity, so castration can be seen as a solution, with 'immunocastration' the preferred method in Australia (as per the RSPCA guidelines), whereby a 'vaccine' stimulates an antibody response that fights the hormones responsible for sexual development. The other approach is to slaughter the animals before puberty, but the pigs will be at a non-commercial weight for the effort and cost involved. The alternative, which is uncomfortable for many, is to slaughter them as suckling – or, more commonly, weaned – piglets.

The same concerns are raised over veal, although treating male calves as waste, as male chickens are viewed in the egg industry (male chickens are raised for meat production) is hardly a defensible alternative. As it stands, this is a personal choice, but we must all own the realities of where our meat comes from. Opening our eyes and making informed choices is the only way. If this means that buying traceable, ethically raised and slaughtered meat is the right choice for you, then so be it. If this means eschewing meat altogether, then so be it, too – the plant world is a culinary wonderland, after all.

Preparing pork

One of the pervasive myths about pork, in Australia at least, is that it needs to be thoroughly cooked. *Trichinella spiralis* is a parasitic roundworm that can live in pigs (and, according to America's Centers for Disease Control, in bears and cougars, too) – and did so quite prevalently in the early twentieth century, in America and elsewhere, at least. Trichinella has never been identified in Australia, so the recommendations to cook pork thoroughly (even though trichinella is actually killed at lower temperatures) was never applicable here, and it is no longer a problem in America either. That's an incredible amount of overcooked pork! And the tentacles of those fears still cling tenaciously. If you're eating pork on a backpacking adventure in Asia or the like – or indulging in a meal of bear or cougar – then I'd opt for properly cooked meat, but it's not just unnecessary here, it's a disaster.

Cook your pork to the degree you prefer, but please leave at least a blush of pink, especially in leaner cuts such as fillet or loin. Meat from common modern breeds and intensively farmed animals, with their leaner profile, will perform even less well when cooked through. Pork does take well to brining (see p. 333), though, which is a good way to increase the moisture in any cut.

As with beef and lamb, cuts with more connective tissue and fat take well to slow cooking, with shoulder still retaining good moisture if cooked through; it can also be cooked for a long time until meltingly tender and shreddable (see p. 333). I also love to roast the scotch, and butchers will often roll up the cut with some crackling strung tightly to it. Cuts from the leg and loin are less forgiving, as is the fillet, though a loin rack (see p. 343) can be roasted to a blushing pink with a crunchy cap of crackling; it's hard to get a good result on the skin of loin chops, given the much quicker cooking time. Cutting away the rind and cutting the fat in 1 cm (½ in) intervals will produce a great result, with the fat succulent, and no chewy, leathery rind to distract from the texture. Silverside, topside or pork neck are all great for braising, and are fabulous in a ragù or marinated for grilling on skewers (see p. 345). I will buy minced (ground) pork for a ragù, meatballs or dumplings – but I would never buy lean mince. All the flavour and texture come from the fat in the mince, and it is essential to keep a juicy texture. Powdery, dry mince holds no appeal.

Pork belly is perhaps the ideal slow-cooking cut, and probably the most versatile and forgiving cut of all. You can braise, roast, pan-sear, grill and slow-cook pork belly, and it can be rendered succulent in quite a short time, too. A relatively quick braise in shaoxing rice wine, vinegar, soy sauce and spices is on rotation at home (see p. 341), while you can also grill or pan-fry it quickly (see p. 341). It's also marvellous in a Ragù (p. 336). Belly is loved by my family, with the smell of it roasting with fennel seeds on a bed of sliced fennel bulbs bringing the family to the table well before they're called to dinner. A simple apple and fennel slaw (see p. 680) and some roast potatoes and/or carrots completes the picture. Roast pork belly is also perfect for a Bánh mì (p. 332), bao buns, or in a rice noodle salad with Nuoc cham (p. 93).

A smoked ham hock is also a constant at home, with the hock storing well until it's slowly simmered in water with some aromatic vegetables – onion, carrot, celery, garlic, fennel, leek, whatever is on hand – plus a few bay leaves and/or thyme sprigs and some peppercorns. After 1½–2 hours, once the meat is falling from the bone, the meat can be stripped off, with the skin, cartilage and spongy fat discarded. Strain the broth, pressing hard on the vegetables with a spoon or ladle. The simplest course is then to flake the meat into the broth. Serve bowls with a handful of chopped parsley, a poached egg and a good grating of parmesan. Use a hunk of good bread to break open the egg and soak up the broth. The meat can also be stored in some broth, which will gel readily, and be used in risotto (see p. 148) or the like. And any stock you don't use can be frozen for another time – just be aware that it will already be seasoned to a degree. In the warmer months, try moistening some freshly cooked barley or white beans with the stock, add a little dijon mustard, a splash of peppery oil and a dash of your favourite vinegar, then toss the chopped meat through with some chopped tarragon and chives. A handful or two of cooked baby green beans, or a few handfuls of rocket (arugula), would also be wonderful, and crowning with a dollop of Pesto (p. 90) will match it to the season even better. A hock also makes the best Pea & ham soup (p. 334).

People seem to have an obsession with crackling – and a bit of a fear of failure. It is not complicated to achieve, but is fraught if you're ill-prepared or in a rush. The secret is simply reducing the moisture in the skin. Salting the rind for an hour or two, or much longer, will do the job: just wipe off the moisture and season again before roasting. Salting the rind uncovered in the fridge is even more effective, with the dry environment helping things along. I will often scorch the skin with a kettle of boiling water first, which makes the skin supple and easy to score, but it will also help it dry out more effectively in the long run. Towards the end of roasting, check the crackling to see how it's going – a little increase in heat towards the end will help the skin puff. I often do this with the oven grill (broiler) on right at the end, watching it very carefully, as it can burn quickly.

When not slow cooking, or with cuts from the loin and leg (including chops, cutlets, racks and fillet), I find the ideal internal temperature is 66–68°C (150–155°F). The juices will be pink, which is something some older references may advise against, but there is no danger here, with the meat at its succulent best.

I use several cured/fermented pork products to cook with – including good Italian pork and fennel sausages. Although they're essentially a raw product, the seasonings used in the mix dry-marinate and partially cure the sausages, and they're a great shortcut to big flavour. Slit the skins and crumble the meat for a Ragù (p. 335), use to make Polpette (p. 337), or scatter over a pizza (see p. 857). They have such intense flavour and enough fat to moisten and enrich.

Nduja is a paste-like salami from Calabria, which is scented with spices and can be arrestingly hot. In Australia, biosecurity laws prohibit importing genuine nduja (and any uncooked salami), and I find that many local versions lack the traditional – and necessary – chilli punch. If you do find a good one, and they are out there, bring to room temperature and spread on fresh or grilled bread, spoon on roasted scallops, or stir through an oil-based pasta sauce stained with tomato and laden with olives. I also like to warm it through to loosen, then drizzle over grilled calamari with Skordalia (p. 621), say, or a bruschetta smeared with ricotta and topped with sprouting broccoli.

On the more cured side, various types of salami may make it into a pasta dish, be used on a pizza, or find their way into a sandwich, though I usually enjoy them as they are, with a salumi selection and cheeses. I use chorizo – usually the picante version – with mussels (see p. 213) or prawns (shrimp), braised or tray-roasted chicken, in a rabbit braise, to intensify a pot of beans (see p. 390), or to stud a potato croquette. Morcilla, a Spanish cured sausage made from pig's blood, pork, spices, onion and rice, is intense, but when fried it matches superbly with delicate flavours, such as pan-seared scallops. I also use it in my version of frijoles negros (see p. 340).

There are occasions where I will cook with jamón or prosciutto, as for a saltimbocca (pp. 268, 702), though quality jamón or prosciutto is best at room temperature, allowing the fat to gently melt in the warmth of your mouth. I will sometimes use them in a cold dish but will generally enjoy just as they are, as an appetiser with other salumi and Grissini (p. 856). However, there are always hardened stubs that delis will not be able to slice, and these are marvellous diced, then fried in a pasta sauce or side dish where bacon or pancetta might otherwise be used. Waste not.

Pancetta comes in two forms: rolled, or as flat cured belly, much like bacon, though taken to a drier, firmer cure. Either will usually be perfumed with some spices such as juniper, black pepper and fennel seeds. I use rolled pancetta for salumi plates, in a sandwich (perhaps with rocket/arugula and fresh mozzarella) or on a pizza. I prefer flat pancetta or guanciale (cured pork cheek) for starting a ragù and for a pasta such as carbonara, or to throw into a pot of braised beans (see p. 390) or a soup, or to add porky intensity to a Gigantes plaki (p. 380). As with prosciutto, those hard end bits are still full of flavour, so use it all.

Speck can be a little confusing. In northern Italy, in the Südtirol (the part of Alto Adige that merges culturally with southern Austria), speck is cured pork belly, very much like prosciutto. In Germany, speck has come to mean bacon, but what is sold as speck may be smoked belly bacon or smoked back fat. The latter is very similar to Lardo (p. 326), though lardo is not smoked. The term kaiserfleisch seems to be used more broadly still, but to me it is another take on pancetta but with a deeply smoky intensity. I will use it instead of pancetta when I want that more northern European flavour, such as in stews, soups and braises.

Then there's bacon. There are so many types, perfumed with the smoke of various woods, either hot or cold smoked, and cured in all manner of ways. I'm more than happy with the variety, and I cook all types, but always ensure the source of what I'm buying. As with all smallgoods, bacon can be too easily disconnected from the farming source, so ask questions and buy well. However it has been cured, bacon should always feel dry, and while it always requires cooking, it should have an appealing aroma. One oddity to avoid is the somewhat bizarre proliferation of seemingly low-fat bacon, which I would never buy. The fat is an integral part of bacon, whether fat-laced streaky bacon (the belly), or leaner short cut (mainly loin).

A simple way to cook bacon is to lay the rashers or slices flat on a lined baking tray, then roast at 180°C (350°F) fan-forced until done to your liking. They will cook evenly, and there's no danger of sticking. (You can also cook the bacon until quite dark, then cool and crush, if you're ever in need of crisp bacon bits.) This method is particularly useful if you're trying to cook several breakfasts at once and stovetop real estate is at a premium. Set that tray aside for later, too, as it will be coated with the most flavourful fat (especially if you've used a superior smoky bacon) that can be used for roasting potatoes. I will typically roast bacon like this if I have bought a slab, and cut thick slices, which I sometimes glaze with honey or maple syrup for the last minute or so of cooking.

I'm used to having many pans on the go at once, so the bacon will usually hit a heavy cast-iron pan if I'm having a fry-up for breakfast. That pan gets pushed to the back of the stove when the bacon is done. I'll either scrape out the fat to use later instead of oil in a ragù, soup, braise or risotto, or I'll fry off some left-over boiled potatoes in the fat with some rosemary and serve with steak, or add to a salad with green beans, crisp leaves and hot-smoked trout or the like.

Cotechino sausage has a special place in my heart. A traditional semi-cured Italian pork sausage, it has a high fat content and always includes some pork skin in the mix, along with various spices, depending on the region. Poaching whole for 40 minutes or so will cook the sausage, but it is elevated when chilled and then sliced and fried, before serving with condiments such as mustard and Salsa verde (p. 86), which are ideal for cutting through the fat.

I have been cooking a version of cotechino with lentils, a traditional dish of from Emilia-Romagna, in Italy's north, for many years, as well as a take on bollito misto, the classic northern preparation of mixed boiled meats. Both have featured on restaurant menus, with the latter being a celebratory dish or cooked for shared-table Sunday lunches. As well as cotechino, I would typically cook a small chicken, veal shank and pickled veal tongue in a broth with carrot, celery, garlic, rosemary, bay leaves and peppercorns. They'd all be sliced and served with braised cabbage, carrots, celery hearts and small boiled potatoes, with horseradish bread sauce (see p. 70), Salsa verde (p. 86), mustard and chopped mustard fruits on the side, plus plenty of grilled bread to take up the broth. It's quite an event.

Lardo ⓖⒻ

Making lardo is not that difficult, simply requiring a little patience. Well, a lot of patience. Cover an 800 g–1 kg (1 lb 12 oz–2 lb 3 oz) piece of pork back fat completely in rock salt in a non-reactive tray and refrigerate for 2 months until cured. You can also flavour the fat with 1 tablespoon crushed juniper berries, 1 tablespoon black peppercorns, 2 rosemary sprigs and 6 bay leaves. Once cured, brush off the salt and wrap in plastic wrap or baking paper and a tea towel (dish towel). Slice finely and serve with other charcuterie, or drop over a risotto, pasta or cooked pizza, or a side of mushrooms, brussels sprouts or broccoli, and let the residual heat render it deliciously oozing.

Pâté de campagne   GF

Pair with

Serve with mustard, cornichons, confit onions, sherried onions, Quince & apple relish (p. 716) and/or Jerusalem artichoke pickle (p. 545), with a little salad of peppery leaves – mizuna, rocket (arugula), baby kale, mâche (lamb's lettuce/corn salad), nasturtium and tatsoi are all good. And don't forget plenty of charred bread – or enjoy it all in a sandwich the same way.

This recipe is a modified version of a fairly classic country terrine – one that is technically called a pâté en terrine – that I have been making for years in restaurants. Although it's not overtly technical, it is a bit of a labour of love, and it deserves as much attention in the sourcing as it does in the making. The flavour of the pork is so important, the fat content is essential to both the flavour and texture, so have a chat to a trusted butcher and get them to mince (grind) the pork with 12–15 per cent fat included. And don't buy pre-minced pork. If mincing your own meat, ensure everything is well chilled, as it will mince more efficiently and cleanly. Also, make your own quatre épices mix from vibrantly fresh spices – it's not hard, and it makes such a difference. It's also best to plan ahead, as the terrine will improve once made, with the flavours maturing over a couple of days. It also keeps well. Simply seal the top with melted lard or duck fat, then wrap with baking paper, then foil. It will then refrigerate perfectly for up to 2 weeks. **Serves 12**

700 g (1 lb 9 oz) pork shoulder, with at least 12% fat, minced (ground)

350 g (12½ oz) pork back fat, finely minced (ground)

250 g (9 oz) cleaned chicken livers, coarsely minced (ground) or finely chopped

2 large garlic cloves, finely grated

6 thyme sprigs, leaves stripped

6 sage leaves, finely chopped

½ bunch of flat-leaf (Italian) parsley, leaves finely shredded

1½ teaspoons Quatre épices (p. 24)

18 g (¾ oz) fine sea salt

1¼ teaspoons freshly ground black pepper

2½ tablespoons Cognac or decent brandy

2½ tablespoons dry sherry

30 thin slices of flat pancetta, or lardo

1 egg, lightly beaten

60 g (2 oz) pistachio kernels (optional)

Special equipment
terrine mould, about 1.5 litre (51 fl oz/6 cup) in capacity
probe thermometer

Add the pork, pork fat and chicken livers to a large bowl, along with the garlic, herbs, quatre épices, salt, pepper, Cognac and sherry. Thoroughly mix with your hands in a circular motion, slapping the mix against the side of the bowl to form a well-combined, fatty mixture.

Ideally, marinate in the fridge overnight or for at least 2 hours.

Preheat the oven to 160°C (320°F) fan-forced.

Line the terrine mould with 20 slices of the pancetta, overlapping the slices and allowing enough overhang to fold back over the top.

Add the egg and pistachios (if using) to the meat mixture, and combine very well. Press the mixture firmly into the prepared mould, banging it on the bench and pressing to carefully remove any air pockets. Fold the pancetta over the top. Use the extra slices to cover, tucking them in at the edges. Cover with baking paper, then foil, and place in a roasting tin. Pour in enough boiling water to come halfway up the side of the mould.

Transfer to the oven and cook for 15 minutes. Reduce the heat to 140°C (285°F) fan-forced and cook for 45 minutes to 1 hour, until the core temperature reaches 69–71°C (156–159°F).

Once cooked, transfer the terrine mould to a tray and cool for 45 minutes at room temperature, then refrigerate for about an hour. Once the jelly just starts to set on the edges, cut a piece of heavy cardboard to fit inside the mould, place it on the terrine, then weigh down with some tins to compress the terrine, which helps the meat reabsorb the juices. (I have found the initial resting before weighting to be essential. If you compress the terrine too early, the result will be dry because you will push all the juices out of the terrine.) Refrigerate overnight at least, but a couple of days will improve the flavour.

Unmould the terrine and cut into 1.5 cm (½ in) slices to serve. Leftovers will keep for up to a week in the fridge, tightly wrapped in plastic wrap.

Ham hock & leek terrine (GF)

This is based on a simple Burgundian terrine of ham hock and parsley, but I've turned up the dial a little. This is equally good to eat rugged up on a wintery day as it is sitting in the sunshine with a glass of Chablis. You can use smoked ham hocks or, better still, ask your butcher or deli to put aside a couple of hocks left over after slicing that premium rare-breed ham off the bone they sometimes have. **Serves 8–10**

2 large smoked ham hocks
3 litres (101 fl oz/12 cups) Golden chicken stock (p. 54), or water
1 onion, peeled and halved
1 large garlic bulb, cut in half crossways
2 carrots, cut into chunks
2 celery stalks
2 fresh bay leaves
5 thyme sprigs
1 bunch of flat-leaf (Italian) parsley, leaves finely chopped, stems reserved

10 black peppercorns
2 leeks, white part only
1 handful of yellow celery leaves (from the heart)
6 leaves of gold-strength gelatine
2 purple Asian shallots, very finely diced
2 garlic cloves, finely grated
10 small cornichons, finely diced
2 tablespoons well-drained small brined capers

5 small pickled onions, chopped
4 tarragon sprigs, leaves picked
2 tablespoons sherry vinegar
2 teaspoons dijon mustard

Special equipment
26 cm (10¼ in) terrine mould (or use a steel or glass bowl)

Staples
S&P

Pair with

Serve with grilled Sourdough bread (p. 847) or Focaccia (p. 845), pickled mushrooms, cornichons, and/or pickled cocktail onions (see p. 594) and freshly grated horseradish.

Add the hocks and stock to a large saucepan, along with the onion, garlic bulb, carrot, celery, bay leaves, thyme, parsley stems and peppercorns. Top up with water to just cover, if necessary. Bring to a gentle simmer over a medium heat and cook for 2 hours, topping up the liquid as necessary.

Meanwhile, tie the leeks together and simmer in well-salted water for about 20 minutes, until tender. Refresh in cold water, drain well and slice into 1.5 cm (½ in) thick rounds.

Line the terrine mould with plastic wrap, then line the base with half the leek. Scatter over half the celery leaves and some parsley leaves, then chill.

When the meat is coming away from the bones, remove the hocks from the stock and strain the liquid into another saucepan. Bring to the boil and reduce the liquid by almost two-thirds (or to about 1.2 litres/41 fl oz), skimming carefully of all impurities. Once reduced, strain again. Soak the gelatine leaves in cold water for 5 minutes, before squeezing off the moisture and adding to the stock. Stir to dissolve, then strain into a jug.

Remove and discard the skin from the hocks. Cut the meat into large pieces, discarding any cartilage or large pieces of fat. You should have about 500–600 g (1 lb 2 oz–1 lb 5 oz) of meat.

Add the meat to a bowl with the shallot, garlic, cornichon, capers, pickled onion, tarragon, vinegar, mustard and remaining parsley. Grind in plenty of pepper, then combine well. Check for seasoning: the mixture should be highly seasoned, as the intensity will die back when chilled – but just be aware that the stock will be salty from the hocks.

Spoon half the mixture into the mould, then top with the remaining leek and celery leaves, followed by half the hock stock. Tip in the remaining meat mixture, smoothing out gently, then add enough hock stock to just cover.

Refrigerate overnight to set.

Unmould and cut into 1.5 cm (½ in) slices to serve, or into wedges if using a bowl to set the terrine. The terrine will keep covered in the fridge for 3–4 days.

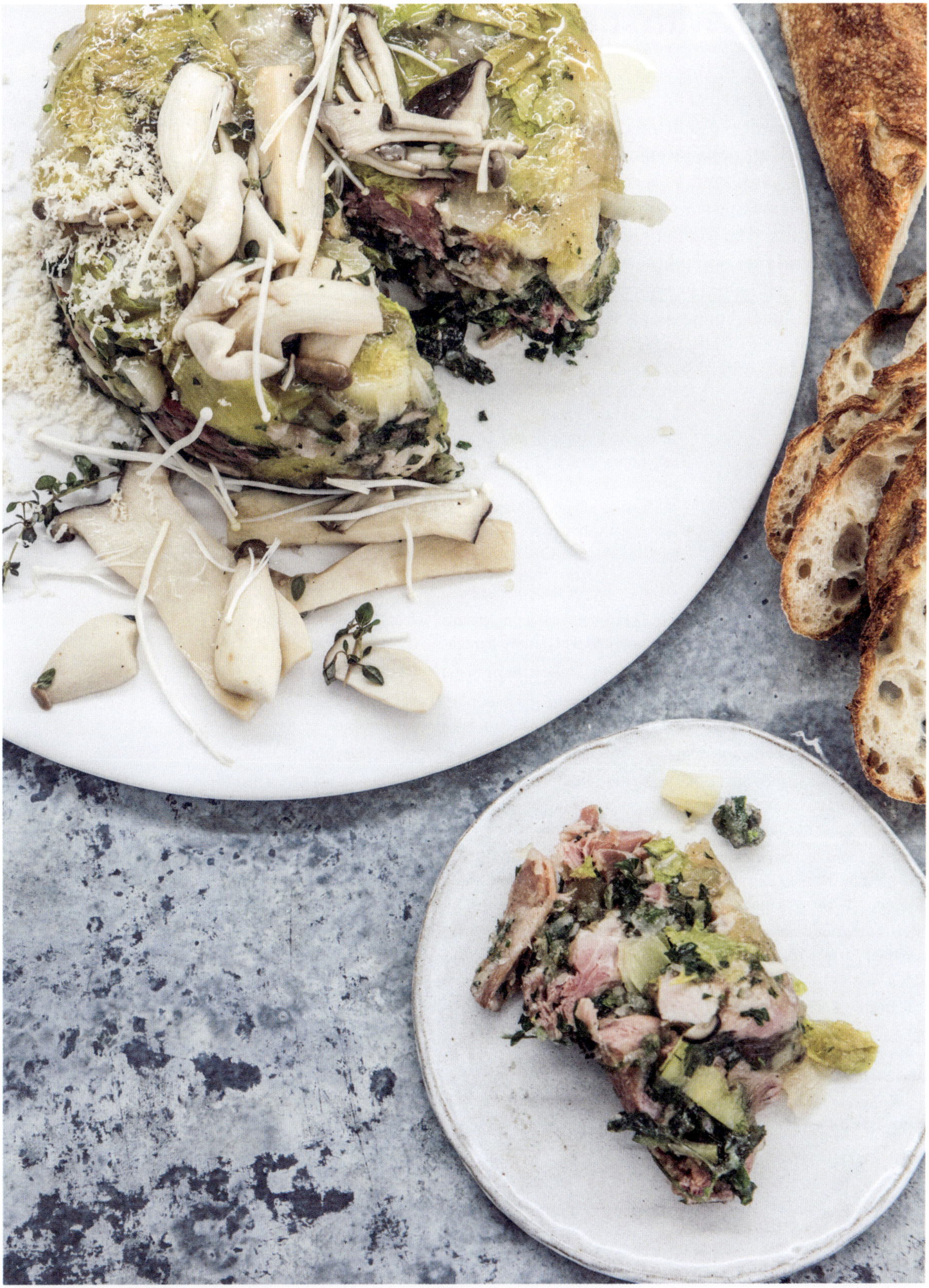

Pork rillettes with sherry ⓖⓕ

If you're interested in making your own charcuterie, mastering rillettes is essential. And that's not just for completing your skill set, but just because it's so satisfying – and they're so delicious. Traditionally, rillettes are made from either pork, rabbit, duck or goose, though I've not employed the latter. Whichever meat you're using, the key is long, slow cooking in pork fat until buttery tenderness is achieved, then making sure you include enough of that delicious fat in the mix before potting. If fat frightens you, or you think you can make a lean version – stop and go and cook something else. However, I have, on occasion, topped up the lard with a little extra-virgin olive oil when I didn't quite have enough. This is not traditional, but neither is the sherry. Both are very successful.

Makes just under 1 kg (2 lb 3 oz)

Pair with

Serve at room temperature with toasts, warm baguette or toasted brioche, or from the fridge with cornichons, pickled onions (see p. 594) and/or Jerusalem artichoke pickle (p. 545).

500 g (1 lb 2 oz) pork shoulder, cut into 5 cm (2 in) dice
500 g (1 lb 2 oz) boneless and rindless pork belly, cut into 5 cm (2 in) dice
150 ml (5 fl oz) dry sherry
4 garlic cloves, peeled and smashed

5 thyme sprigs
30 g (1 oz) salt flakes
1 teaspoon allspice berries
3 teaspoons black peppercorns
2 teaspoons juniper berries
3 teaspoons coriander seeds

300 g (10½ oz) lard, plus extra for sealing
½ teaspoon ground nutmeg

Staples
S&P

Equipment
ramekins or ceramic dishes (any size will do)

Add the pork shoulder and belly to a bowl or container. Pour in 100 ml (3½ fl oz) of the sherry, add the garlic, thyme and salt and toss well. Cover and refrigerate overnight.

The next day, bring the pork to room temperature. Preheat the oven to 130°C (265°F) fan-forced.

Crack the whole spices in a mortar, then tie up in muslin (cheesecloth) or similar. Place in a large flameproof casserole dish with the lard. Melt over a low heat, then add the pork mixture.

Transfer to the oven, partially covered, and cook for about 3 hours, until the meat is meltingly tender.

Cool for 15 minutes, then lift the meat from the lard with a slotted spoon, into a large bowl. Shred the meat with two forks, discarding any gristle. Season with salt and pepper until quite highly seasoned. Add the nutmeg, the remaining sherry and enough fat to bind.

Cool for about 20 minutes, then check the seasoning, as it will dull slightly. Add enough extra fat to make the mixture luscious, then pack the rillettes into ceramic dishes or ramekins (any size will do), flattening and leaving room to seal the tops with lard.

Melt the lard and cool a little before pouring on top of the rillettes. Refrigerate until the lard has set, then top with baking paper, then foil, and refrigerate for a day to mature. Remove the lard and refrigerate for your next batch, or use it to fry or roast potatoes.

The rillettes will keep for about 7–10 days if the fat layer is intact, or 2–3 days otherwise.

Sit the rillettes at room temperature for 20 minutes before serving.

Make it different
With another meat. You can replace the pork shoulder with duck, rabbit or quail meat, and cook them exactly the same way.

Pork spare ribs with maple glaze

If you're intent on diving into the world of American barbecues, then you can ignore this recipe. There's not even a barbecue or smoker in sight – but the result is a very satisfying simulation. These are big flavours, with the sweetness balanced by spice, and the ribs sticky and super moist. **Serves 4**

Pair with

Baked potatoes, charred corn on the cob (see p. 498), Coleslaw (p. 448) and buttered white bread buns.

Sichuan pepper & honey glaze (GF)

This simple glaze takes roast pork in a decidedly Asian direction, ideal to match with rice and greens or to drop into a salad, soup, bao bun (see p. 332) or Bánh mì (p. 332). After cooking the Crispy roasted pork belly (p. 332), strain the juices from the roasting tin into a jug. Set aside at room temperature, then skim off the fat. In a small saucepan, combine 120 g (4 oz/⅓ cup) honey, 2 fresh bay leaves, 2 star anise and 2 teaspoons sichuan peppercorns. Crack 2 tablespoons coriander seeds, and smash 2 garlic cloves with the skin on, and add these too. Simmer for 2 minutes, then stir in the pan juices and simmer for another 3 minutes or so. Dress the sliced pork with the glaze and serve as desired.

125 ml (4 fl oz/½ cup) maple syrup
90 g (3 oz/⅓ cup) dijon mustard
2 kg (4 lb 6 oz) pork spare ribs
150 ml (5 fl oz) white vinegar
150 ml (5 fl oz) water

Sweet smoky spice mix
3 tablespoons fennel seeds, crushed
2 tablespoons salt flakes
1½ tablespoons sweet smoked paprika
1½ tablespoons brown sugar
1 tablespoon garlic powder
1 tablespoon black peppercorns, ground
1 teaspoon chilli powder

Maple glaze
250 ml (8½ fl oz/1 cup) barbecue sauce
100 ml (3½ fl oz) maple syrup
2½ tablespoons extra-virgin olive oil
1½ tablespoons worcestershire sauce

Preheat the oven to 180°C (350°F) fan-forced. Line two roasting tins with foil, then baking paper.

Combine the maple syrup and mustard in a small bowl. In another small bowl, combine the spice mix ingredients.

Smear the mustard mixture all over the ribs in the roasting tins, then dust with the spice mix. Lay the ribs flat. Combine the vinegar and water and pour half into each tin. Cover tightly with baking paper, then foil, and bake for 90 minutes.

Combine the glaze ingredients in a small bowl. Uncover the roasting tin and brush the glaze over the ribs.

Increase the oven temperature to 220°C (430°F) and cook for a further 20–30 minutes, until the ribs are deeply coloured, basting occasionally. Serve hot.

Crispy pork belly salad with sesame spiced dressing, cucumber & coriander (GF)

This is a very simple salad, which I will generally plan for by roasting more pork belly than we can eat for dinner the night before, and reserving what I need – as pork belly has a habit of being eaten, no matter how much I present. **Serves 4–6**

½ bunch of spring onions (scallions), white and most of the green, cut into 5 cm (2 in) batons
2 telegraph (long) cucumbers, peeled and finely sliced
750 g (1 lb 11 oz) Crispy roasted pork belly (p. 332),

at room temperature, finely sliced
½ bunch of coriander (cilantro), leaves and fine stems picked
4 radishes, finely sliced
1½ tablespoons sesame seeds, toasted

1 lime
1 × quantity Spiced sesame & peanut dressing (p. 94)

Staples
S&P

Blanch the spring onion batons in boiling salted water for 10 seconds. Refresh in iced water, then drain.

Cover the base of a serving platter with the cucumber, then lay the pork slices over. Scatter the coriander, radish, sesame seeds and spring onion batons round the edges. Squeeze the lime over and sprinkle with a little salt. Serve with the dressing on the side.

Crispy roasted pork belly (GF)

This is a master recipe for roasting pork belly, with perfectly crackled skin and succulently moist flesh. You can always skew the flavour in a particular direction. For example, roast with sichuan pepper and star anise for a more Asian angle, or for a more Mediterranean feel, rub with cracked fennel seeds and black peppercorns, then roast atop thickly sliced fennel and bay leaves.

Serves 4–6

1.8 kg (4 lb) boneless pork belly, thick end (it can be in two pieces)	2 litres (68 fl oz/8 cups) boiling water 3½ tablespoons salt flakes	1 litre (34 fl oz/4 cups) water **Staples** EVOO, S&P

Lay the pork on a rack in the sink. Pat dry with paper towel, then slowly pour the boiling water over the skin.

Dry the pork, then transfer to a board. The skin will be supple and easy to score. Cut lines or a crisscross pattern into the skin about 1 cm (½ in) apart, and no more than 1 cm (½ in) deep. Rub the skin with 2 tablespoons of the salt flakes.

Place on a rack and refrigerate on a tray, uncovered, for at least 1 hour – preferably overnight. This will dry out the skin and ensure great crackling.

When ready to cook, preheat the oven to 150°C (300°F) fan-forced.

Wipe the salt and any moisture from the pork. Oil the pork and rub the remaining 1½ tablespoons of salt flakes all over. Transfer to a rack in a roasting tin, skin side up. Pour the extra 1 litre of water into the tray.

Transfer to the oven and roast for 1½ hours. Check occasionally to make sure the tray doesn't dry out, as the water keeps the meat moist, stops the dripping fat from burning, and will form a sauce. During the last 20 minutes of roasting, turn the oven up to 220°C (430°F) fan-forced to finish crackling the skin.

Set aside for 5 minutes before slicing. Serve hot or at room temperature, accompanied by the pan juices, skimmed of fat.

Make it different
Serve cold in a salad (see p. 331).

Bánh mì with roast pork belly

Everyone has their favourite way with a bánh mì, so tweak the filling as you will. This is one of those rare dishes that will *not* be improved by sourcing the best bread. Odd, I know. You want an airy roll, with a crust that annoyingly breaks into countless fragments and ends up going everywhere. It needs to be large enough to fill with plenty of stuff, but also insubstantial enough that it can be squashed around those fillings. Unsurprisingly, Vietnamese bakers make the right ones, and they're usually alarmingly economical. Take a seat, artisan sourdough. I don't say that often, so pay heed. **Serves 4**

Pair with

Roast potatoes or roasted pumpkin salad (see p. 630), with Apple, fennel & witlof slaw (p. 680) or a fennel salad (pp. 527–8).

Dress with Sichuan honey glaze (see p. 331) and serve in a bao bun (see opposite) or Bánh mì (p. 332).

Add to rice paper rolls and serve with Coconut hoisin dipping sauce (p. 96).

Add to a rice noodle salad with herbs and shredded vegetables.

Add any left-over pork belly to fried rice (see p. 610).

Drop left-over pork into the shoyu broth (p. 58) with ramen or udon .

Salt & pepper tofu for bánh mì (GF) (V) (VG)

Heat 80 ml (2½ fl oz/⅓ cup) grapeseed oil in a large frying pan over a high heat. Add 4 sliced garlic cloves and fry until golden, about 2 minutes. Add 2 teaspoons cracked coriander seeds, 1 teaspoon ground black pepper and 300 g (10½ oz) firm tofu, sliced into dominos. Toss to colour the tofu slightly, about 3 minutes. Add 1 tablespoon vegan fish sauce and 1 tablespoon light soy sauce and toss for 30 seconds, then take off the heat.

Pair with

Wholesome hoisin sauce (p. 96).

Pork roll

Without going the full bánh mì treatment, a slice of pork in a white roll with a drizzle of Sichuan honey glaze (p. 331), a handful of herbs such as coriander (cilantro), Thai basil and/or Vietnamese mint and a hit of chopped red chilli is quite delicious.

Spicy pork bao

Smother the base of hot steamed bao buns with Gochujang chilli sauce (p. 97), then follow with a slice of roasted pork (opposite), cut to fit. Top with a ribbon of cucumber and a sprig of coriander (cilantro), then dollop with Sesame mayonnaise (p. 75) and serve immediately. You could also smear the bao bun with some Chicken liver parfait (p. 233) or pâté before filling.

Pair with

A simple slaw dressed with vinegar, oil, salt and pepper – or a slaw with a little more complexity (see p. 449). Along with tortillas and a punchy sauce, such as Chimichurri (p. 85), mayonnaise (pp. 74–5) spiked with green chilli, Aïoli (p. 76) spiked with smoked paprika, or a Corn & pineapple salsa (p. 499).

Baked potatoes, charred corn on the cob (see p. 498), Coleslaw (p. 448) and buttered white bread buns.

Roasted root vegetable salads.

4 long crusty white rolls, split lengthways
2 tablespoons Chicken liver parfait (p. 233), or pâté
¼ iceberg lettuce, shredded
1 Lebanese (short) cucumber, finely sliced lengthways
2 carrots, julienned and moistened with fish sauce

8 coriander (cilantro) sprigs, leaves and fine stems picked
3 red bird's eye chillies, sliced
4 long slices of Crispy roasted pork belly (opposite) dressed with Sichuan honey glaze (p. 331)
1 handful of salted peanuts, chopped

Roasted blood plum relish (p. 725), or Spicy malt plum sauce (p. 725), to serve (optional)
8 slices of pickled daikon (see p. 304), to serve (optional)

Staples
BTR, S&WP

Butter the rolls, then smear with the parfait. Top with lettuce, cucumber, carrot, coriander and chilli. Season with salt and white pepper, then top with the pork and peanuts, and the plum sauce and daikon, if using. Serve immediately.

Make it different
Bánh mì with roast chicken. If pork is not your thing, shredded roast chicken will work.

Make it vegetarian/vegan 🅥 🆅🅖
For a tasty alternative vegetarian or vegan filling for bánh mì, substitute pork for Salt & pepper tofu (left), use a vegan fish sauce and skip the parfait (and butter, if vegan) in the roll.

Pulled slow-cooked pork shoulder with cider 🅖🅕

Pork shoulder is the perfect cut to slow roast, retaining so much moisture. Brining it first makes it just that bit more successful. The effort, if not the time, is also quite minimal for what is a very impressive one-pot dish. **Serves 10**

3.5 kg (8 lb 2 oz) square-cut pork shoulder, bone in, skin on
1½ tablespoons Quatre épices (p. 24)
2 teaspoons ground ginger
2 teaspoons sweet smoked paprika
4 fresh bay leaves

1 garlic bulb, cut in half crossways
350 ml (12 fl oz) dry apple cider
300 ml (10 fl oz) White chicken stock (p. 54)

Brine
3 litres (101 fl oz/12 cups) water

500 g (1 lb 2 oz) sea salt
350 g (12½ oz) caster (superfine) sugar
1 garlic bulb
40 g (1½ oz) black peppercorns, cracked
3 fresh bay leaves

Staples
S&P

Add the brine ingredients to a large saucepan over a high heat. Stir until the salt and sugar have completely dissolved, then take off the heat and add 1 litre (34 fl oz/4 cups) cold water – or 1 kg (2 lb 3 oz) ice, which will be quicker – and cool to room temperature. Once cool, add the pork and refrigerate for 10 hours or overnight.

When ready to cook, preheat the oven to 120°C (250°F) fan-forced.

Drain the pork and thoroughly pat dry. Combine the spices in a small bowl, then rub into the flesh side of the pork.

Add the bay leaves and garlic to a large flameproof casserole dish and place the pork on top. Pour in the cider and stock, then lay a piece of baking paper on top of the pork. Cover with the lid and cook for about 7 hours. Once the meat pulls with a fork and is coming away from the bone easily, it's ready. Don't take it too far, as the meat can become powdery if overcooked.

Ladle the cooking juices into another saucepan and reduce by two-thirds, skimming off a little fat as you go. Season with pepper, and salt if necessary.

Peel back the skin from the pork and pour the cooking juices over just before serving.

Pea & ham soup

This is based on my mum's recipe, but I like to use a whole ham hock so that there are large chunks of meat. You could also get the hock sliced through the bone, which will speed up the cooking time a little. **Serves 8**

Pair with

Heavily buttered bread.

1 large ham hock, cut into pieces if possible
100 ml (3½ fl oz) extra-virgin olive oil
3 large onions, cut into 2 cm (¾ in) dice
6 garlic cloves, sliced
4 carrots, cut into 2 cm (¾ in) dice

1 fennel bulb, cut into 2 cm (¾ in) dice
6 celery stalks, finely diced
350 g (12½ oz) green split peas
150 g (5½ oz) pearled or wholegrain barley
400 g (14 oz) tin diced tomatoes

2 fresh bay leaves
1 tablespoon dried Italian oregano
3 litres (101 fl oz/12 cups) cold water, or White chicken stock (p. 54)

Staples
S&P

Add the hock to a large saucepan, cover with water and bring to the boil. Drain immediately and set aside.

Heat the oil in a large saucepan over a medium heat. Cook the onion, garlic, carrot, fennel and celery until the vegetables have softened, about 8 minutes. Season with salt and pepper.

Add the remaining ingredients, bring to the boil, then turn down to a gentle simmer. Cook for 1½–2 hours, stirring occasionally, until the soup has thickened.

Remove the hock from the soup. Discard the skin, then pick the meat, discarding any sinew or large pieces of fat. Flake the meat into the soup. Adjust the seasoning as needed and serve.

Petit salé aux lentilles ⒼⒻ

Puy lentils have been cultivated in Auvergne, in central France, for thousands of years. They even have their own appellation protection and contribute to one of the region's classic dishes, namely this one – a braise of Puy lentils with salted pork. It's something I always crave as the weather cools. **Serves 4–6**

Pair with

Buttered baguette, dijon mustard, a good dollop of garlicky Aïoli (p 76), chopped mustard fruits, and/or a condiment made by stirring 2 tablespoons freshly grated horseradish through Crema fresca (p. 364).

200 g (7 oz) rock salt
1 kg (2 lb 3 oz) boneless pork belly
900 g (2 lb) cotechino
300 g (10½ oz) Puy lentils, or tiny blue-green lentils
2 litres (68 fl oz/8 cups) water
3 parsley stalks, 3 fresh bay leaves and 5 thyme sprigs, tied up as a bouquet garni
1.2 litres (41 fl oz) White chicken stock (p. 54)

4 large French shallots, trimmed and peeled
3 garlic cloves, sliced
4 carrots, cut into large chunks
3 celery stalks, cut into 5 cm (2 in) lengths
2 yellow-fleshed boiling (waxy) potatoes (such as kipfler), peeled and cut into 3 cm (1¼ in) discs

½ celeriac, trimmed, cut in half lengthways and sliced 2 cm (¾ in) thick
1 tomato, cored, cross cut in the base
½ bunch of flat-leaf (Italian) parsley, leaves finely chopped

Staples
S&P

Spread half the salt in a ceramic dish and lay the pork on top. Cover with the remaining salt and refrigerate for at least 6 hours, ideally overnight.

Cook the cotechino in a saucepan of simmering water for 40 minutes. Drain and set aside to cool, then cut into slices 2 cm (¾ in) thick.

Tip the lentils into a saucepan of simmering water. Bring back to a simmer, then drain.

Wipe the salt off the pork with a cloth, then pat the meat dry. Place the pork, skin side down, in a large flameproof casserole dish. Pour in the water, add the bouquet garni and simmer for 1 hour, skimming occasionally. After an hour, the liquid should have reduced by half.

Preheat the oven to 170°C (340°F) fan-forced.

Pour the stock into the casserole dish and bring to a simmer. Turn the pork over, add the lentils and simmer for about 5 minutes. Add the shallots, garlic, carrot, celery, potato, celeriac and tomato. Bring to a simmer and skim, then add the cotechino.

Cover, transfer to the oven and cook for 30 minutes. Remove the lid and cook for a further 20 minutes.

Carefully remove the pork and set aside. Stir in the parsley.

Slice the pork about 1.5 cm (½ in) thick and add back to the pot. Adjust the seasoning with salt and pepper as needed and serve.

Italian sausage ragù

Pair with

Any pasta you like, but pappardelle (see p. 112) and gnocchi (see p. 137) are my favourite pairings.

This recipe can also be the start of a spectacular Lasagne (p. 136).

This is a perfect example of how good the flavour-giving properties of quality Italian sausages are. The seasoning and part-curing of the sausages get this ragù off to a flying start, meaning you'll have a sophisticated and complex sauce after it has simmered for just half or a third of the time you would need if simply using minced (ground) pork. Just add gnocchi (you could make that in the hour it simmers – see p. 137) or pasta. **Serves 8**

150 g (5½ oz) piece of flat pancetta, cut into 2 cm (¾ in) dice
900 g (2 lb) Italian pork and fennel sausages, skins removed
2 onions, cut into 1 cm (½ in) dice
6 garlic cloves, finely chopped
1 carrot, diced

3 celery stalks, finely sliced
2 fresh bay leaves
2 teaspoons fennel seeds, lightly ground
½ teaspoon chilli flakes
2 tablespoons tomato paste (concentrated purée)
400 ml (13½ fl oz) red wine
1 litre (34 fl oz/4 cups) White chicken stock (p. 54)

2 × 400 g (14 oz) tins diced tomatoes
3 rosemary or oregano sprigs
1½ tablespoons dried Greek oregano (rigani)
4 sprigs sage, leaves chopped
100 g (3½ oz) Grana Padano, to serve

Staples
EVOO, S&P

Heat a good splash of oil in a wide saucepan over a medium heat. Add the pancetta and crumble in the sausage meat. Fry until golden brown and catching slightly, about 10 minutes.

Stir in the onion, garlic, carrot, celery, bay leaves, fennel seeds and chilli flakes. Cook for about 15 minutes, until the vegetables are softened and lightly caramelised.

Stir the tomato paste through for a couple of minutes. Add the red wine and reduce by half. Add the stock, tomato, rosemary and dried oregano, and bring to a simmer.

Turn the heat to low and cook for about 1 hour, until the sauce is thick and intensely flavoured. Adjust the seasoning with salt if necessary (the pancetta and sausage meat are salty), and grind in plenty of pepper.

To finish, stir in a few tablespoons of oil, before tossing with pasta or gnocchi and grating the parmesan over the top.

Slow-cooked robust ragù of pork & beef

This is the ultimate bolognese-style ragù. So often a meat of the bolognese style is made from minced (ground) meat, which is perfectly fine – but I also love the more traditional, more robust route, where large pieces are braised, then yield into the sauce or are shredded in at the end. The flavours meld over the three-hour cooking time, with the pork belly enriching the sauce, giving it a silky lusciousness, while the beef adds the meaty depth. Cutting the beef into large chunks results in the ideal size when shredded at the end. Too large and the sauce will clump together; too short and you miss out on the texture that is such a key part of this recipe. **Serves 8–10**

Pair with

Serve with Polenta (p. 383) short pasta, fresh egg pappardelle, Classic potato mash (p. 625) or Gnocchi alla romana (p. 138) and plenty of parmesan.

Pile onto grilled fat slices of rye sourdough rubbed with garlic and grate over plenty of parmesan.

3 tablespoons tomato paste (concentrated purée)

450 ml (15 fl oz) red wine, or white wine

500 g (1 lb 2 oz) boneless pork belly, cut into 5 thick slices, then each cut in thirds across

600 g (1 lb 5 oz) beef topside, chuck or shin, cut into 8 cm (3¼ in) chunks

125 ml (4 fl oz/½ cup) extra-virgin olive oil

2 onions, finely diced

5 garlic cloves, finely sliced

4 celery stalks, very finely diced

1 carrot, finely diced

300 g (10½ oz) Italian pork and fennel sausages, skins removed

1 nutmeg, finely grated

2 teaspoons ground allspice

3 fresh bay leaves

2 rosemary sprigs

4 sage sprigs

1.5 litres (51 fl oz/6 cups) White chicken stock (p. 54), or Brown beef stock (p. 55)

3 × 400 g (14 oz) tins diced tomatoes

1 tablespoon Porcini powder (p. 570)

Staples

S&P

Combine the tomato paste with the wine and set aside.

In a large dry frying pan over a medium heat, sear the pork belly until some fat renders out. Season with salt and pepper and fry until golden, about 3 minutes each side. Remove the pork and fry the beef in the fat, seasoning as you go – you may need to do this in batches so as not to crowd the pan. Cook the beef until golden, about 3 minutes each side. Don't rush this step, as the caramelisation is important to the finished flavour.

Meanwhile, heat the oil in a large wide saucepan over a medium heat. Cook the onion, garlic, celery and carrot for about 15 minutes, until softened and caramelised. Season with pepper. Crumble in the sausage meat and cook until browned, about 6 minutes. Stir in the nutmeg, allspice, bay leaves and rosemary and sage. Add the seared pork and beef, along with half the cooking fat from the pan.

Turn the heat to high, stir in the wine mixture, then reduce by about one-third. Stir in the stock, tomato and porcini powder, then bring to a simmer.

Turn the heat to low, so the ragù is at a lazy simmer. Cook for about 3 hours, until the sauce is thick and silky. You may need to add a little water if it's getting too thick.

Adjust the seasoning as needed, then gently pull the beef and pork apart with a fork.

Pork polpette & potato al forno

This is a comforting meal for me, as my mum made it often when I was growing up – though always with sliced onion. Because the meatballs are rolled in flour, they thicken the sauce a little, as does the starch from the potatoes. Using the meat from quality Italian-style sausages makes the meatballs so fully flavoured, and gives them a soft, succulent texture. **Serves 6**

Pair with

A leafy salad and plenty of bread.

Veal & pork polpette with savoy cabbage, taleggio & truffled pecorino

Cut half of a <u>savoy cabbage</u> into wedges, core, then separate the leaves. Blanch the cabbage in boiling salted water for 2 minutes, then refresh under cold water and drain thoroughly. In a frying pan, cook 100 g (3½ oz) <u>butter</u> and 1 grated <u>garlic clove</u> until fragrant, about 1 minute. Add the cabbage and toss through until changing colour and about halfway cooked, about 3 minutes. Arrange the cabbage and 1 × quantity <u>Pork polpette</u> (right) in a baking dish, then pour over enough <u>Golden chicken stock</u> (p. 54) to come halfway up the contents. Cover with baking paper, then foil, and bake for 30 minutes. Once cooked, carefully pour the juices into a saucepan. Reduce the liquid by half, then pour back into the dish. Push 200 g (7 oz) diced <u>taleggio</u> into the mixture, lay 100 g (3½ oz) truffled or regular <u>pecorino</u> slices on top and push in 150 g (5½ oz) roughly torn <u>Sourdough bread</u> (p. 847) so that the pieces are half submerged. Return to the oven with the grill (broiler) on and cook for about 5–10 minutes, until bubbling and golden. Serves 4–6.

6 large yellow-fleshed boiling (waxy) potatoes (such as desiree, Dutch cream or nicola), peeled and cut into 5 mm (¼ in) thick discs
1 litre (34 fl oz/4 cups) White chicken stock (p. 54)
1 tablespoon tomato paste (concentrated purée)
2 fresh bay leaves
juice of ½ lemon
50 ml (1¾ fl oz) extra-virgin olive oil
1½ tablespoons fresh breadcrumbs

1½ tablespoons finely grated Grana Padano
2 teaspoons dried Greek oregano (rigani)

Polpette
1 onion, finely diced
4 garlic cloves, chopped
400 g (14 oz) finely minced (ground) pork
400 g (14 oz) Italian pork and fennel sausages, skins removed, meat crumbled
150 g (5½ oz/2½ cups) panko or fine breadcrumbs

100 g (3½ oz) Grana Padano, finely grated
1 egg
1½ tablespoons dried Greek oregano
½ nutmeg, finely grated, or 2 teaspoons ground nutmeg
zest of ½ lemon
½ bunch of flat-leaf (Italian) parsley, leaves finely chopped
100 ml (3½ fl oz) extra-virgin olive oil

Staples
EVOO, FLR, S&P

Preheat the oven to 220°C (430°F) fan-forced.

For the polpette, heat a good splash of oil in a frying pan over a medium heat. Add the onion and garlic, season lightly with salt and pepper and cook until softened, about 3 minutes. Tip into a bowl to cool.

Add the pork, sausage meat, breadcrumbs, parmesan, egg, oregano, nutmeg and lemon zest to a food processor and blend into an even paste. Transfer to a bowl and mix in the parsley and cooked onion mixture. Roll the mixture into about twelve large ovals.

Heat 100 ml (3½ fl oz) of the oil in a large frying pan over a medium heat. Working in two batches, roll the meatballs in flour and add to the pan. Cook for about 5 minutes, until brown all over, rolling them around to colour evenly.

Add the meatballs to a baking dish measuring about 25 × 35 cm (10 × 14 in), standing the potato slices up between them.

In a saucepan, bring the stock, tomato paste, bay leaves, half the lemon juice and the oil to a simmer and cook for 3 minutes, then pour it over the meatballs. Combine the breadcrumbs, parmesan and oregano in a small bowl, then scatter over the top.

Cover with baking paper, then foil, and bake for 30 minutes. Uncover and cook for a further 15 minutes, until the meatballs are golden.

Make it different
With pine nuts. Add 80 g (2¾ oz/½ cup) pine nuts to the meatball mixture for a little extra flavour and texture.

Make it a meal
Roll the mixture into about twenty-four large ovals, then simmer in a tomato sugo (see p. 166) with 500 ml (17 fl oz/2 cups) Golden chicken stock (p. 54) for 25 minutes. Serve with pasta.

Porchetta GF

Rome noisily lays claim to porchetta, but it is equally championed by many other regions. The version most of us are familiar with consists of pork belly and loin, seasoned, spiced and rolled, then roasted until the skin crackles. In Italy, that neat roll is just as likely to be a whole pig, boned, spiced and often stuffed with the offal, then rolled and cooked – ideally over coals, and for many hours – until the skin is gloriously blistered. The constants are the inclusion of fennel (either seeds or wild fennel fronds, or both), garlic and rosemary, and for the flesh to be well salted, giving it a cured feel when cooked. Seasoning and leaving overnight is a critical step, so don't be tempted to skip it. The meat is eaten both hot and cold. Hot, it is eaten with sides such as potatoes roasted with garlic and rosemary, and wilted bitter greens such as cime di rape or chicory (witlof/endive) – but more often than not it is hungrily stuffed into a ciabatta or roll with nothing much else, and needing nothing much else, either. Cold, it is sliced more finely and used in a sandwich, much like ham or the like. However you eat it, porchetta is simply marvellous. **Serves 8**

Pair with

Roast potatoes with garlic & rosemary.

Horta (p. 552).

Serve thickly sliced in a crusty hot ciabatta-style role with Simple soused cabbage (p. 340).

An even mix of finely chopped granny smith apple and finely diced mustard fruits.

Mustard or Salsa verde (p. 86).

3 kg (6 lb 10 oz) pork loin, belly attached, or 2.8–3.2 kg (6–7 lb) butterflied boneless pork shoulder
40 g (1½ oz) salt flakes
2½ tablespoons fennel seeds
1 tablespoon black peppercorns

6 garlic cloves, peeled
1 branch of fresh bay leaves (or a good handful if not on the stem), 3 leaves shredded
5 rosemary sprigs, leaves chopped
5 oregano sprigs, leaves chopped

½ bunch of flat-leaf (Italian) parsley, leaves finely chopped
3 onions, cut into 3 fat slices each

Staples
S&P

Place the pork in a colander and pour a whole kettle of boiling water over the skin. Dry with paper towel, then score the skin at 1 cm (½ in) intervals. Place on a tray and rub all over with the salt, getting into all the incisions. Flip the pork over so the skin is facing up, then refrigerate, uncovered, overnight to dry out the skin and lightly cure the meat.

When ready to cook, preheat the oven to 130°C (265°F) fan-forced.

Toast the fennel seeds in a dry frying pan over a medium heat until fragrant, 1 minute. Tip into a mortar, add the peppercorns and a pinch of salt and grind to a rough powder. Add the garlic and crush to a paste. Add the shredded bay leaves, rosemary, oregano and parsley, and grind as finely as you can.

Spread the herb paste on the meat side only of the pork, massaging it into all the pockets. Roll up the pork as tightly as you can, securing tightly at regular intervals with butcher's twine. Place in a roasting tin, using the onion slices and bay leaf branch as a trivet.

Transfer to the oven and roast for 3½ hours, or until the internal temperature is 71°C (159°F).

Remove the pork from the oven and turn the temperature up to 250°C (480°F) fan-forced. Baste the whole roll of pork with the juices in the tray, then and roast for a further 10 minutes or so to finish the crackling. Watch carefully, as it can burn quickly.

Remove from the oven and rest for 20 minutes, then remove the string, slice the pork about 2 cm (¾ in) thick and serve with the pan juices and the onion, if desired.

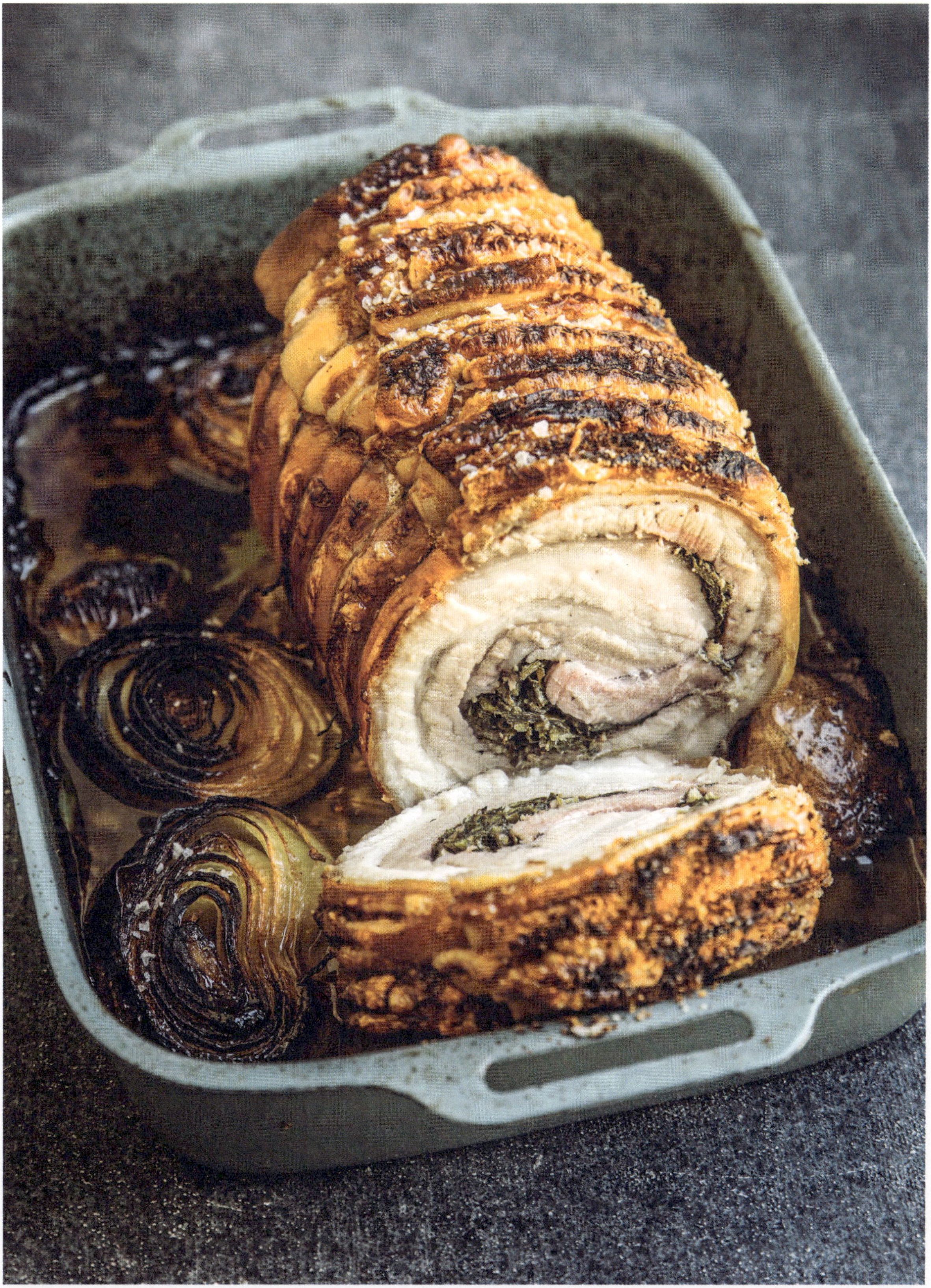

Black turtle bean, pork belly & morcilla braise (Frijoles negros)

Versions of frijoles negros are common in Latin America, though it is perhaps best known as a Cuban dish. It is often made without meat, though ham hocks are not uncommonly employed. For me, pork belly is ideal with this smoky and spicy braise, and the morcilla just adds that little something extra. While cooking in Ibiza, I used a refined version as a base for calamari pan-fried with garlic and parsley. Back home, one of my favourite efforts was in a wood-fired oven, which imbued it with such a fitting smokiness. The borlotti beans are certainly optional, but they add a little burst of creamy texture. **Serves 6–8**

900 g (2 lb) boneless pork belly ribs, each cut into 3 pieces
200 g (7 oz) rock salt
400 g (14 oz) black turtle beans, soaked overnight
150 ml (5 fl oz) extra-virgin olive oil
150 g (5½ oz) morcilla or chorizo, sliced 3 cm (1¼ in) thick
1 large onion, cut into 1 cm (½ in) dice
6 large garlic cloves, skin on, smashed

1 fennel bulb, cut into 2 cm (¾ in) dice
4 celery stalks, sliced
2 fresh bay leaves
2½ teaspoons smoked paprika
1½ tablespoons ground cumin
2 teaspoons cumin seeds
2 star anise
2 teaspoons ground black pepper
2½ tablespoons sherry vinegar

2 tablespoons dark brown sugar
250 ml (8½ fl oz/1 cup) tomato passata (puréed tomatoes)
3 teaspoon pasilla chilli powder (see p. 10)
2 handfuls of freshly podded borlotti (cranberry) beans, if in season; otherwise omit
1.8 litres (61 fl oz) White chicken stock (p. 54)

Staples
S&P

Add the ribs to a dish or container in one layer, then cover with the rock salt. Set aside at room temperature for 2 hours, then shake off the salt and dry with paper towel.

Meanwhile, add the soaked turtle beans to a saucepan and cover with cold water. Bring to the boil for 1 minute, then take off the heat, drain and set aside.

Preheat the oven to 150°C (300°F) fan-forced.

Heat 2½ tablespoons of the oil in a wide-based saucepan over a medium heat. Working in batches, add the ribs and fry until golden all over, about 8 minutes. Remove from the pan, leaving the fat behind.

Fry the morcilla for about 1 minute each side to seal. Remove from the pan, leaving the fat behind.

Add the remaining oil to the pan, then cook the onion, garlic, fennel, celery and bay leaves until the onion is softened and starting to caramelise, about 10 minutes.

Stir the spices through for 1 minute. Deglaze the pan with the vinegar, then stir the sugar and passata through. Add the pasilla powder, black beans and borlotti beans, if using. Stir to coat, then return the ribs and morcilla.

Pour in the stock and bring to a simmer. Partially cover with the lid, transfer to the oven and cook for 2 hours.

When the beans are cooked and the pork is very tender, adjust the seasoning as needed, skim off the fat, then serve.

Pair with

Serve with steamed rice or Baked buttered rice (p. 384), tortillas, some Simple soused cabbage (below) and chipotle mayonnaise, made by combining 300 g (10½ oz) mayonnaise (pp. 74–5), 100 ml (3½ fl oz) chipotle sauce, 1 teaspoon ground cumin and a good squeeze of lemon.

Simple soused cabbage GF V VG

A great side dish to go with Frijoles negros (left) and the like. Take ¼ cabbage and shave it. Toss in a bowl with 2 tablespoons white-wine vinegar, 2 teaspoons caster (superfine) sugar, and salt and pepper to taste. Leave to steep for 10 minutes before serving.

Glazed red pork with cassia, star anise, black vinegar & wood ear fungus

This is based on a specialty of Shanghai, called hong shao rou, or red braised pork. For what is a relatively quick cooking time, the results are quite spectacular, with richly sticky and deeply flavoured pork in a shimmeringly glossy sauce. The wood ear fungus is not a traditional addition, but I love its uniquely rubbery chew against the succulent pork. **Serves 4–6**

Pair with

Steamed rice and greens.

Speedy pork belly with gochujang

Pork belly doesn't have to be cooked slowly. Remove the rind from some boneless pork belly and slice the meat about 4 mm (¼ in) thick. Toss in Gochujang chilli sauce (p. 97) to coat and marinate for 20 minutes, then grill or pan-fry for about 3 minutes each side. Serve with short-grain rice and fresh wombok (Chinese cabbage) tossed in sesame oil and rice-wine vinegar.

Grilled pork fillet, wombok & crispy egg

Preheat a chargrill pan on high until very hot. Heat about 6 cm (2½ in) oil in a saucepan to 180°C (350°F). Coat 3 × 300 g (10½ oz) pork fillets with oil, then grill for about 3 minutes on each of the three sides until, or a little more if you prefer. Remove from the pan, brush with 3 tablespoons kecap manis and rest for 5 minutes before slicing about 2 cm (¾ in) thick. Meanwhile, crack a room-temperature egg into a cup or small bowl and carefully pour into the oil (the egg will splutter, so be careful). Fry for about 2 minutes. Remove the egg with a slotted spoon and drain on paper towel while cooking five more eggs in the same way. Cut ¼ wombok (Chinese cabbage) into wedges and plate, adding some sliced pork and an egg to each plate. Top with 4 shredded makrut lime leaves and 2 handfuls coriander (cilantro) leaves and serve with Satay sauce (p. 104) on the side. Serves 6.

4 boneless pork belly ribs, about 900 g (2 lb), each cut into 6 pieces	250 ml (8½ fl oz/1 cup) shaoxing rice wine	1 litre (34 fl oz/4 cups) White chicken stock (p. 54), or water
12 cm (4¾ in) piece of fresh ginger, peeled and julienned	3 tablespoons dark soy sauce	2½ tablespoons Chinese black vinegar, or brown-rice vinegar
1 bunch of spring onions (scallions), white and green parts, cut into 4 cm (1½ in) batons, plus extra finely sliced spring onion to serve	2 tablespoons light soy sauce	150 g (5½ oz) wood ear fungus, roughly cut, or fresh shiitake mushrooms, sliced 1 cm (½ in) thick
	1 piece of cassia bark	
	3 star anise	
	1½ teaspoons ground white pepper	
	70 g (2½ oz) rock sugar, or demerara sugar	

Heat a wide saucepan over a medium heat. Add the pork to the dry pan and fry until the fat renders out. Cook until golden brown all over, about 10 minutes. Remove from the pan and set aside.

Cook the ginger and spring onion batons for about 4 minutes. Return the pork to the pan and deglaze with the rice wine. Simmer for 1 minute, then add the soy sauces, cassia, star anise and white pepper. Add the sugar and stock, topping up with water to cover, if necessary, then simmer very gently for 40 minutes.

Stir in the vinegar and the shiitake mushrooms, if using. Reduce the sauce down into a syrupy glaze, watching closely, as it can catch. You want it to be thick but still saucy. The liquid and fat residue will come together with the sugar to make a glossy syrup. If reduced too far, the glaze may split, but a little hot water will bring it back.

Add the fungus and wilt slightly, about 1 minute. Serve scattered with extra spring onion slices.

Bo ssäm

It is hard not to be inspired by chef David Chang's interpretation of this Korean classic, famously served at his New York restaurant, Momofuku. This is special occasion stuff – but life's not just about midweek dinners, is it? **Serves 8–10**

100 g (3½ oz) caster (superfine) sugar	1 telegraph (long) cucumber, finely sliced lengthways	steamed short-grain rice, to serve
100 g (3½ oz/¾ cup) sea salt	1 bunch of coriander (cilantro), fine stems and leaves picked	250 g (9 oz) Kimchi (p. 455), to serve
1 × 3 kg (6 lb 10 oz) boned pork shoulder (not rolled), skin on	3 limes, cut into wedges	Pickled radish (p. 639), to serve
150 ml (5 fl oz) rice vinegar	18 oysters, freshly shucked	1 × quantity Gochujang chilli sauce (p. 97), to serve
60 g (2 oz) brown sugar	1 lemon, cut into wedges	1 × quantity Ginger & spring onion sauce (p. 95), to serve
2 heads of butter lettuce, leaves separated	12 steamed bao buns, to serve	

Combine the caster sugar and salt in a large ceramic dish. Add the pork and rub thoroughly with the curing mix. Refrigerate, uncovered, overnight or for at least 4 hours.

When ready to cook, preheat the oven to 160°C (320°F) fan-forced.

Dust any visible cure off the pork with your hands or a damp paper towel. Transfer the pork to a roasting tin, skin side up, discarding any liquid in the dish. Pour the vinegar over, cover with baking paper, then foil.

Roast the pork for 4 hours, then uncover and cook for a further 1½ hours.

Remove the pork skin and set it aside. Rub on the brown sugar and increase the oven temperature to 180°C (350°F). Baste the meat with the juices and roast for about 1 hour, basting every 20 minutes, until the meat is just starting to fall apart. Cover loosely with foil. Set aside.

Increase the oven temperature to 200°C (400°F) fan-forced. Line a baking tray with baking paper.

Scrape any fat or meat from the underside of the skin, then lay the skin on the baking tray, fat side down. Roast for 15 minutes to crisp up, turning on the oven grill (broiler) for the last 5 minutes. The skin won't crackle, but it will become crunchy. Set aside on the tray to crisp further.

Once cooked, transfer the pork, crackling and about half the roasting juices to a serving dish.

Arrange the lettuce, cucumber, coriander and lime wedges on one serving plate, and the oysters and lemon wedges on another. Shred some of the meat with a fork or tongs and turn the meat through the juices. Serve with the bao buns, rice, kimchi, pickles and sauces on the side.

Pork & prawn wontons with chilli & sichuan pepper dipping sauce

These are simple wontons, which can be boiled or steamed and served with the dipping sauce as a snack or appetiser. **Makes 40–50**

40–50 square wonton wrappers
1 egg white, whisked
3 tablespoons cornflour (cornstarch)

Filling
300 g (10½ oz) finely ground pork mince
300 g (10½ oz) green prawn (shrimp) cutlets, tails removed, deveined and finely chopped

2 corn cobs (see p. 498), cooked, kernels removed and finely chopped
5 spring onions (scallions), white parts only, finely sliced
50 g (1¾ oz) ginger, finely grated
1 large garlic clove, finely grated
1 egg
2½ tablespoons soy sauce

2½ tablespoons shaoxing rice wine
1½ teaspoons sesame oil
1 teaspoon ground white pepper

Sauce
3 tablespoons light soy sauce
1 tablespoon hot chilli sauce
2 teaspoons sichuan pepper & mandarin salt (p. 29)

Combine the filling ingredients well with your hands in a bowl.

Lay out a few wonton wrappers on the bench. Brush two edges with egg white, then add 2 teaspoons of filling to the middle. Fold into triangles, pressing the edges together to seal. Place on a plate or tray dusted with the cornflour.

For the sauce, combine the ingredients in a small bowl.

Cook the wontons in batches in boiling water for 3 minutes, then drain and serve immediately with the sauce.

Make it a meal
Drop into bowls of Congee (p. 383), or serve with greens (right).

Pork & prawn wontons with choy sum & kale

Strip the leaves from ¼ bunch of kale and cut into 4 cm (1½ in) widths. Trim ¼ bunch choy sum (Chinese flowering cabbage) and cut into 4 cm (1½ in) widths. Blanch the kale and choy sum in boiling salted water for 1 minute, then drain. In a small bowl, combine 150 ml (5 fl oz) oyster sauce, 80 ml (2½ fl oz/⅓ cup) shaoxing rice wine, 80 ml (2½ fl oz/⅓ cup) light soy sauce, 1 teaspoon sesame oil, 1 teaspoon sugar and ½ teaspoon ground white pepper, stirring to dissolve the sugar. Set aside. Heat a wok over a high heat until very hot. Add 3 tablespoons grapeseed oil and heat until shimmering. Add 100 g (3½ oz) fresh ginger, peeled and julienned, and 4 finely sliced garlic cloves, and fry briefly until golden, then quickly add a 175 g (6 oz) tin water chestnuts, drained and sliced, along with the blanched greens. Stir-fry until the greens start to take on the sauce, about 2 minutes. Add 25 Pork & prawn wontons (left) and the oyster sauce mixture and toss to coat, then simmer for about 3–5 minutes, until the sauce is shiny and has reduced to a glaze. Scatter with 2 handfuls Thai basil leaves. Serve as is, or with steamed rice. Serves 4–6.

Teriyaki pork belly wrapped with shiitake, spring onion & togarashi

Remove the rind from some boneless pork belly and slice the meat finely, allowing three pieces per person. Season with salt and pepper, then lay a couple of thick slices of shiitake mushrooms and spring onion (scallion) batons on each. Roll up tightly, then pan-fry over a medium heat for about 5 minutes, rotating to brown evenly, seasoning with salt and pepper as you cook. The pork will tighten around the filling. Once evenly browned, turn the heat down a little and add some Teriyaki sauce (p. 101), allowing 60 ml (2 fl oz/¼ cup) of glaze for each portion of three. Simmer the glaze for a minute or so, then plate the pork. Reduce the glaze for another 20 seconds or so, then pour over the rolls. Sprinkle with togarashi and serve with short-grain rice.

Roasted rack of pork with fennel (GF)

This is an instance where brining makes a big difference. Being from the loin, the meat in a pork rack is generally leaner, with nothing much in the way of connective tissue – though it will also typically have a generous cap of fat and skin that's ripe for crackling, making it perfect for roasting. The prunes – which are also great with duck – may seem old-fashioned, but the star anise and vinegar take them in a more vibrantly modern direction. **Serves 4–6**

3 kg (6 lb 10 oz) pork rack, skin on	**Brine**	**Spiced prunes**
2 onions, skin on, thickly sliced	5 litres (170 fl oz/20 cups) water	200 ml (7 fl oz) red-wine vinegar
3 fennel bulbs, or carrots or celeriac, sliced lengthways about 3 cm (1¼ in) thick	250 g (9 oz) sea salt	100 ml (3½ fl oz) water
	200 g (7 oz) caster (superfine) sugar	2 star anise
2 small branches of bay leaves	4 fresh bay leaves	500 g (1 lb 2 oz) prunes, pitted
	1 tablespoon white peppercorns	**Staples**
	1 tablespoon allspice berries	EVOO, S&P

In a large saucepan, bring the brine ingredients to a simmer until the salt and sugar dissolve. Remove from the heat and cool. Submerge the pork in the brine in a large container or saucepan, weighing down with a plate. Refrigerate overnight, or for at least 8 hours.

When ready to cook, remove the pork from the brine and rinse. Dry all over, then score the skin at 1 cm (½ in) intervals. Salt just the skin and refrigerate, uncovered, for 2 hours.

Preheat the oven to 220°C (430°F) fan-forced.

Wipe the salt and moisture from the pork, season the skin with salt again and rub all over with oil. Arrange the onion, fennel and bay leaves in a baking tray and put the pork on top, skin side up.

Roast for 30 minutes, until the skin starts to crackle.

Reduce the oven temperature to 170°C (340°F) fan-forced and roast the pork for a further 1½–2 hours, or until the internal temperature is 70°C (160°F). Rest the pork for 20 minutes before carving.

Meanwhile, to spice the prunes, bring the vinegar, water and star anise to a simmer in a saucepan. Add the prunes and simmer for 3 minutes, then turn off the heat and steep for 30 minutes.

Serve the pork with the fennel and onions and a drizzle of pan juices, or purée the vegetables with all the juices. Serve the prunes on the side.

Pork chops with orange & fennel glaze (GF)

The combination of caramelised orange and fennel is a sublime one with pork. This technique of cooking and making a glaze is very versatile, with all manner of cuts working equally well – chops, fillet, neck steaks, scotch steaks. **Serves 2**

Pair with

Braised borlotti beans (p. 426).

Fennel & orange salad (p. 530).

Some simply dressed leaves and boiled potato or Classic potato mash (p. 625).

1½ teaspoons fennel seeds	1 tablespoon extra-virgin olive oil	200 ml (7 fl oz) orange juice (about 2 oranges)
½ teaspoon black peppercorns	2 × 250–300 g (9–10½ oz) rindless pork chops, or 2 × 300 g (10½ oz) pork fillets, or 2 × 250 g (9 oz) pork neck or scotch steaks	50 g (1¾ oz) unsalted butter
2 garlic cloves		2 bronze fennel fronds, or dill sprigs, chopped
1½ teaspoons salt flakes		
2 rosemary sprigs, leaves finely chopped	zest of ½ orange	**Staples** EVOO, S&P

In a mortar, grind the fennel seeds and black peppercorns into a rough powder. Add the garlic and salt and grind to a rough paste. Add the rosemary and oil and grind again. Smear the paste over the pork and refrigerate to marinate for 1 hour.

When ready to cook, bring the pork up to room temperature. Dust the paste off and reserve some of the marinade.

Heat a splash of oil in a frying pan over a medium heat. Add the pork and cook for about 5 minutes on one side (about 4½ minutes for the fillets, or about 4 minutes for the steaks), being careful not to burn the marinade.

Flip the pork over and cook for another 5 minutes, adding the reserved marinade for the last minute of cooking, along with a splash of oil. After another 30 seconds, add the orange zest and juice, leave for 30 seconds, then remove the pork.

Reduce the liquid in the pan by two-thirds, then add the butter and swirl to melt and combine. Add the fennel fronds and swirl to combine. Simmer the sauce until reduced to a thick glaze, about 80 ml (2½ fl oz/⅓ cup).

Spoon the sauce over the chops to serve.

Roasted pork scotch with burnt honey & thyme, scorched grapes & grilled peaches GF

Pork scotch is so lovely to roast. With plenty of connective tissue, it retains moisture exceptionally well. Pairing pork with sweet fruit is pretty classic, but balance is still key. The bitter notes from the scorched honey, the acidity from the vinegar and vincotto, and the char on the peaches provide superb foils. **Serves 6**

1.5 kg (3 lb 5 oz) rolled pork scotch fillet, with skin, at room temperature
2 white onions, peeled
150 ml (5 fl oz) White chicken stock (p. 54)
150 ml (5 fl oz) white wine

2 peaches, halved and pitted
25 grapes

Burnt honey & thyme sauce
100 ml (3½ fl oz) honey
2½ tablespoons white-wine vinegar

2½ tablespoons vincotto, or saba
2½ tablespoons extra-virgin olive oil
6 thyme sprigs

Staples
S&P

Preheat the oven to 160°C (320°F) fan-forced.

Season the pork with salt and pepper and add to a roasting tin with the whole onions, stock and wine. Cover with baking paper, then foil, and roast for 1 hour.

Turn the oven up to 220°C (430°F) fan-forced. Remove the foil and baking paper, then roast the pork for a further 30 minutes, until the skin crackles. Remove the pork and onions from the tray.

Strain and reserve the pan juices. Remove most of the fat, then pour the pan juices into a small saucepan and reduce on the stovetop to about 2½ tablespoons.

Meanwhile, for the sauce, cook the honey in a small saucepan over a high heat until dark brown, 3–4 minutes. Take off the heat and add the vinegar and vincotto, swirling to combine. Add the oil, thyme and a pinch of salt, then set aside.

Grill the peaches, cut side down, on a hot barbecue or in a griddle pan until charred but not cooked through, about 3 minutes. Cut the pieces into quarters and combine with the honey sauce.

Add the grapes to a frying pan over a high heat and cook for about 10 minutes, rolling them around occasionally, until they colour a little and are scorched. Stir into the honey and peach sauce.

Carve the pork and arrange on a platter, then slice the onions into quarters and arrange on top. Spoon the grapes, peaches and honey sauce over, drizzle with the meat juices and serve.

Sage & rosemary pork chops GF

Remove the skin from 4 × 300 g (10½ oz) mid-loin pork chops and score the fat at 1 cm (½ in) intervals. Bring to room temperature, then season with salt and pepper and coat with oil. Heat a large frying pan over a high heat for 2 minutes. Add the chops and cook for 4 minutes. Flip them over and add 60 g (2 oz/¼ cup) butter and a few smashed garlic cloves (skin on). Cook for 4 minutes, then add a few rosemary sprigs and the leaves from ½ bunch sage and cook for 2 minutes. Plate the chops and spoon on the crisp sage leaves and pan juices. Serve with blanched peas, spinach or asparagus, and Classic potato mash (p. 625) or Gnocchi alla romana (p. 138). To dress these up further, spoon some Bagna cauda (p. 83) over the chops and greens.

Pair with

A green salad.

Simply cooked green vegetables.

Left-over pork sandwich

Left-over pork roast of any kind is so great in a sandwich with mustard, fresh slices of apple rubbed with oil and pepper, or a chutney, sriracha, chilli sauce or Fermented cooked chilli sauce (p. 97) or spiced plum sauce (p. 725), along with shaved cabbage, peppery leaves, maybe some cheddar or fresh mozzarella in a high-top sandwich, or all jammed into a fresh baguette or ciabatta roll.

Schnitzel

Butterfly 4 × 180 g (6½ oz) pork loin fillets, or chicken breasts, by placing them on a board and using a sharp knife to cut lengthways down each fillet, but not all the way through, then opening them out. Cover with baking paper and beat with a mallet or rolling pin until just under 5 mm (¼ in) thick. Coat the pork in flour seasoned with a little salt. Dredge in 2 beaten eggs, then coat with 100 g (3½ oz/1⅔ cups) panko breadcrumbs, pressing them in to ensure the fillets are well coated. Preheat the oven grill (broiler) on high. Line a baking tray with baking paper. Heat 125 ml (4 fl oz/½ cup) extra-virgin olive oil in a large frying pan over a medium heat for 3 minutes. Working in batches, add the schnitzels to the pan and cook for about 2 minutes on each side. Drain on paper towel, season and transfer to the baking tray. Serves 6. Great with slaw (see pp. 448, 484), Piperade (p. 465) or a green salad, green beans and Classic potato mash (p. 625), and boiled potatoes tossed in vinegar and oil.

Moorish pork skewers with orange & black olive salsa

These pork skewers, laced with North African spices, are great barbecue fare. The crackle of smokily fragrant spice with the char from the grill are perfectly complemented by the tangy, salty and sweet salsa, cooling yoghurt and fresh mint. The longer these marinate – within reason – the better they get. To further jazz things up, add a pinch of saffron to the marinade; just grind the threads to a powder and soak it in a little hot water first, or use saffron powder and add it to the spice mix. **Serves 8**

1 kg (2 lb 3 oz) pork loin, cut into 3 cm (1¼ in) dice
4 fresh bay leaves
8 medium pitta breads (see p. 854)
200 g (7 oz) plain yoghurt
½ bunch of mint, leaves picked

Moorish spice mix
2 tablespoons coriander seeds
2 tablespoons fennel seeds
1½ tablespoons cumin seeds

5 garlic cloves, peeled
2 teaspoons smoked paprika
1 teaspoon chilli powder
zest of ½ orange
80 ml (2½ fl oz/⅓ cup) extra-virgin olive oil

Orange & black olive salsa
2 oranges, peeled, segmented and chopped
1 roasted red capsicum (bell pepper) (see p. 463), finely diced
1 salad onion, finely diced

2 long red chillies, finely diced
10 black olives, pitted and finely chopped
1 garlic clove, finely grated
½ teaspoon cumin seeds
100 ml (3½ fl oz) extra-virgin olive oil

Staples
EVOO, S&P

Special equipment
Metal skewers (or soaked wooden/bamboo skewers)

For the spice mix, grind the whole spices into a powder in a mortar. Add the garlic, paprika, chilli and orange zest and grind into a smooth paste, then mix the oil through. Transfer to a bowl with the pork and rub in well. Marinate in the fridge for at least 2 hours, ideally overnight.

Near serving time, add the salsa ingredients to a bowl, season with salt and pepper and combine.

Season the marinated pork with salt. Cut each bay leaf into three, then thread the meat onto the skewers with a piece of bay leaf here and there.

Preheat a barbecue or griddle pan on high.

Grill the skewers for about 2 minutes on each side, being careful not to overcook or the pork will dry out. Warm the pitta breads on the grill.

Once off the grill, pull the pork off the skewers, then dress the pork with a little oil and serve in the pitta breads with a dollop of yoghurt, a spoonful of the salsa and a few mint leaves.

Make it different
Moorish chicken skewers with orange & black olive salsa. The skewers can also be made with chicken (make sure it is cooked through).

Also see

Stracciatella soup **55**

Dairy-based sauces **69-73**

Flavoured butters & butter sauces **72-3**

Egg-based emulsions **74-80**

Egg pasta dough **111-3**

Tagliatelle with egg, truffle & Parmigiano Reggiano **119**

Tortilla de patata **623**

Pavlova **784**

Lemon, lime or passionfruit curd **797**

Eggs & Dairy

Eggs & dairy

We had chickens when I was growing up, and I was often tasked with collecting the eggs. I thought them quite the marvel. The whole idea of this firm and perfectly shaped object coming out of a chicken was something that I found utterly fascinating. I also just loved the eggs themselves, and I adore them just as much now.

From the multitude of almost magical uses in baking and pastry applications, yielding such wonders as brioche and souffles, to the simple joy of a well-made omelette or a perfectly poached specimen, eggs are a wondrous ingredient. My life would be the poorer without dishes such as shakshuka, carbonara and a ramen with a perfectly gooey egg. An egg can dress up the simple, like some basic fried rice crowned with a fried egg, some chilli sauce, coriander and a handful of sliced spring onion (scallion). It can add richness to a salad, with a soft yolk saucing and coating. And it is responsible for the emulsifying properties that give us mayonnaise and custard.

My father has always liked eggs a very particular way, cooked in ample olive oil heated to the point where the whites firmed up as soon as they hit the pan, creating a lacy frill of crisp edges. I remember him showing me that a decent pool of oil was important to get the right texture, and he would spoon it over the top to firm up the white, while keeping the yolks runny. It's still how I prefer my fried eggs today, and sometimes I'll have them as Dad did, with the fried egg crowning hot ragù on a slab of well-toasted Sourdough bread (p. 847). Sunday breakfast memories relived, minus the International Roast instant coffee.

Another of Dad's favourite egg dishes was something his mother, my Meme, made. It's a version of the Tunisian dish brik à l'oeuf. She used to seal an egg in a brik pastry parcel with confit tuna and capers, then fry it in very hot oil until crisp, serving it with chilli sauce. It's something Dad still makes when he can find the pastry, and my girls have become big fans, too.

Eggs are extraordinary things. Personally, I find them to be absolutely delicious, and I revel in the silky richness of a good yolk. They are also highly nutritious. But it's the unique properties of eggs that make them so vital for the cook. Naturally, some people eschew all animal products, which I respect, but eggs are tricky to replace for certain applications. Their ability to bind, emulsify and be whipped into fluffy meringue are not easy things to imitate, though recent strides have been made in filling in this gap. Aquafaba (the cooking water from chickpeas) has stepped in for egg white for vegans, holding a foam when whisked.

Like chickens, eggs can be bought at alarmingly low prices, but the cost is huge. A factory farmed egg is a woeful thing, from a culinary, nutritional and moral standpoint. The available economy also downgrades how good an egg can be. Eggs are not mundane, like generic sliced white bread. A good egg is a marvellous thing: nutritious, flavoursome and incredibly versatile. I never, ever skimp on eggs. I value the effort that goes into raising laying birds humanely in a natural environment with a largely foraged diet. I can really taste the difference and, if we are to eat them, it is the only way. As with all animal products, if you are consuming them, source the best you can, with transparent practices placing welfare and environmental goals as priorities. They will cost more, but they will be so much more satisfying. Learn to cherish them.

Pair with

Pair eggs with cream, butter, crème fraîche, sour cream and all manner of cheese, from fresh curds to tangy aged cheeses. Eggs love bacon, and other cured pork, such as pancetta, speck and the like. Scent with soft herbs, such as tarragon, chives, parsley, chervil, watercress, sorrel, coriander (cilantro) and dill, and spice with cumin, pepper, cayenne and chilli. Match with tomatoes, corn, avocado, peas, mushrooms and lettuce, capers, tahini, soy and oyster sauce. Serve with caviar, bottarga, salmon roe, anchovies, smoked fish, prawns (shrimp) and crab.

The colour of an egg yolk will vary with the season and the feed. Indeed, pasture-raised chickens are likely to have more variation than those penned up and fed a consistent ration, but a deep orange hue will generally reflect a more nutritious egg. A marigold-coloured yolk is a lovely thing, but it's not a clear indicator of a good diet and a healthy egg. As with farmed salmon, additives in the feed can be used to manipulate the colour. These additives are generally not sinister in themselves but the deception is. A quality egg will typically have a robust shell, a thick white that holds in a puck when cracked in a pan (also a sign of freshness) with some spreading around it, and a yolk that is similarly robust. An egg that breaks under the slightest tap, gushes out and spreads in the pan, with the yolk oozing like the white is unlikely to have come from a chicken that has seen anything other than a miserable life.

Eggs are generally dated, so freshness is easy enough to determine, however you can test eggs by putting them in bowl of water. Fresh eggs will sink, laying on their side. Older eggs will float and should be discarded. As eggs age, the proteins become less tightly bound, which results in the whites becoming watery. Older egg whites become easier to beat and will produce a greater volume than super-fresh eggs will. Cooks are divided over what makes a better meringue, with some preferring the volume and others the denser structure and greater stability. I prefer using fresher ones. Though it is not always easy to know exactly how old your eggs are and how they will perform, adding a little vinegar will acidify the whites and make them more stable. Working with room temperature eggs is also key to a speedy and successful result.

Eggs that have just been laid are also tricky to peel if boiled. The well-bound proteins mean that the membrane adheres more readily to the shell, where an egg with a little age on it will come away cleanly. Picking shell off an egg can be frustrating and the results are quite the aesthetic turn off, so don't use your freshest eggs for boiling. I also believe that eggs that are promptly and properly cooled, ideally in iced water, are easier to peel, with the shock of the cold water shrinking the membrane away from the shell. Cracking the eggs gently but well all over also makes things easier, and some say that soaking them in cold water for a few minutes after cracking makes it easier still.

Eggs are generally stored and sold at room temperature in Australia, though they are starting to chill them in some places. The recommendation is to refrigerate them. This is due to how they are processed. Commercial eggs are washed as a means of lowering any salmonella contamination risk, but that washing removes a protective barrier, making the eggs more porous so they don't last as long. It's a bit of a win-lose situation. Nonetheless, there is a real salmonella risk from an unwashed eggshell contaminating the egg, especially if grown in an intensive farming operation. So, most eggs are washed. And unless they can be refrigerated through the whole supply chain, including when you take them home, room temperature is a better solution until they land in your fridge. The problem of them going from cold to warm is that the condensation can attract bacteria; given that they're more porous after being sanitised, this can be an issue. Eggs are sold by size, with a 700 g (1 lb 9 oz) and 800 g (1 lb 12 oz) dozens my go-to. These are 'large' and 'extra-large' eggs in Australia, and they're what my recipes are based on – around a 60 g (2 oz) egg, with about 30 g (1 oz) of white and 20 g (¾ oz) of yolk – I don't generally use smaller eggs, excepting quail eggs.

I use a variety of dairy when cooking, from milk to a huge variety of cheeses, but I also like to make my own at times. Admittedly, I haven't dived deeply into the world of cheesemaking, but it's simple and very rewarding to make your own ricotta, or to hang yoghurt to make the simplest preparation of all: Labneh (p. 362). Making your own butter is also a simple and quite cathartic task that yields a high level of satisfaction. Yoghurt takes a little more practice, but successful results return equally big smiles of contentment.

For me, the key with dairy is to always work with full-fat versions. Taking the fat from milk strips it of flavour and texture, rendering it a pallid simulation entirely unsuitable for cooking, in my opinion. Naturally, this applies to any other dairy, whether yoghurt, cheese or cream – the very idea of low-fat cream really has me scratching my head. Unsurprisingly, if making your own dairy basics, the best quality milk will return the best results. I always try to buy organic milk and cream if making ricotta and butter. If you're going to the trouble, then it's worth the extra expense.

Chopped egg tartare GF V

In a medium bowl, thoroughly mix 250 g (9 oz/1 cup) Master olive oil mayonnaise, (p. 74), 2 finely chopped hard-boiled eggs, 2 handfuls chopped dill fronds, 2 tablespoons finely chopped gherkins (pickles) or cornichons, 1 tablespoon finely chopped capers, 2 teaspoons white-wine vinegar, 1 teaspoon caster (superfine) sugar, ½ teaspoon salt flakes, 10 grinds black pepper and 5 shakes hot green jalapeño sauce, such as green Tabasco. The tartare will keep in an airtight container in the fridge for up to 3 days. Makes about 400 g (14 oz).

French-inspired scramble GF V

For two people, add 6 eggs and 3 tablespoons of pouring (single/light) cream to a bowl, season with salt and whisk well, then strain through a fine-mesh sieve (this gives you a finer, creamier mixture that results in a richer flavour and texture). Melt 30 g (1 oz) of butter in a saucepan over a medium heat, then add the egg mix. Stir the mix vigorously with a rubber spatula for about 3 minutes until slightly thickened, then remove from the heat for a moment and continue stirring. Return to the heat, stirring continually. Keep taking on and off the heat to slow down the cooking and judge the texture. When the mix has a creamy consistency and is delicately set, stir in a large tablespoon of Crema fresca (p. 364) or crème fraîche. Season with black pepper and serve immediately.

Boiling eggs

When boiling eggs, it is always better to start with room-temperature eggs, or close to, as they will cook more consistently and there is less chance of the shells cracking. Lowering a fridge-cold egg into boiling water is somewhat of a shock, and the results are unpredictable. Timing is obviously key to getting the eggs cooked the way you like, but there are always variables. The volume of water to the number of eggs will naturally have an impact, with a packed pan dropping the temperature considerably. To cook six eggs, I use 1.2 litres (41 fl oz) water in a saucepan. Bring to the boil, then lower in the room-temperature eggs, adjusting the heat to keep the water at a simmer. For hard-boiled eggs, cook for 10 minutes before refreshing in cold or iced water. Cooking for 6 minutes will yield soft-boiled eggs, where the yolks are still runny and can act as a self-saucing addition to salads, soups or pasta dishes (if you dare to use cold eggs straight from the fridge, 7 minutes will yield a soft-boiled egg). Cooked for 8 minutes, the eggs will have firm whites and jammy yolks, perfect for sandwiches, potato salads and the like. Unless you want the eggs warm, in which case plunge into cold water briefly then quickly peel, cool the eggs very well in iced water, say for 15 minutes, then peel. Boiled eggs can be stored in the fridge in water to stop them drying out. For quail eggs, 5 minutes will yield a runny yolk if cooking in a batch of six, or about 7½ minutes for a hard-boiled result.

Scrambling eggs

Rather than the silky curd-like scrambled eggs, another method is to create pillowy clouds of egg, which almost melt away when eaten. For two people, add six eggs and 3 tablespoons of cream, milk or crème fraîche to a bowl, season with salt and whisk well. Melt 30 g (1 oz) of butter in a saucepan over a low heat, then add the egg mix. Stand without stirring over a low heat for about 2 minutes to start to set, then start to fold the partly cooked egg towards the middle, letting the raw egg flood into the pan, like making an omelette. The idea is to work it minimally, until still a little wet, then serve. You can add grated cheese and herbs about halfway through, or just leave plain, finishing with black pepper.

Poaching eggs

Poaching eggs well takes a little practice, but it's not in itself complicated. You want the water as hot as possible, while not being turbulent. A splash of vinegar helps the outside of the eggs set quickly, making for a cleaner result, but properly fresh eggs, with their tightly bound proteins, will do that anyway. So, vinegar is a good safety measure, but it can impact on the flavour if heavy handed. And room temperature eggs are best, or at least eggs left on the bench for 20 minutes. Bring a saucepan of water to the boil, then reduce to a simmer just under boiling point. If using, add ½ teaspoon of white vinegar. Crack the eggs into a teacup or small glass, then create a vigorous whirlpool in the saucepan with a kitchen spoon, slipping the egg into the middle, then repeat with a second egg while still swirling. Poach the eggs – the water can't boil – for at least 3 minutes, but 4½ minutes is ideal for me, with the white set and the yolk just starting to. Lift the eggs out with a slotted spoon, drain on paper towel and serve. You can also slightly undercook the eggs if you want to serve several at once, then warm in the water for 30 seconds or so before serving.

Cooking a 63°C (145°F) egg

You need an immersion circulator to cook an egg like this, but inexpensive ones are now readily available. The advantage here is that you get eggs that have a similar consistency to poached eggs but with much more intense flavour and an incredibly silky texture the whole way through. The process is simple enough, 60 minutes at 63°C (145°F), which will gently set the egg white and yolk consistently. These can be used as a fancy breakfast, but they're also wonderful slipped out of their shells and dropped on top of some wet polenta with plenty of finely grated Parmigiano Reggiano, shaved truffle and a drizzle of exceptional olive oil.

Omelettes

Making a classic omelette is often seen as a measure of a chef, and it is the fabled test of technique for new cooks trialling in a classical kitchen. An omelette is a simple thing, and not one that requires rarefied skills – but it does take a bit of attention to detail and care, which are signs of any good cook, be they qualified chef or home cook. A traditional omelette should be baveuse, which essentially translates to being moist or runny, where the outside of the omelette is set, but the centre is glossy and a little loose. This is as much about taste as texture, with a fully cooked omelette having a markedly different flavour. That combination of cooked egg and scrambled egg is the aim – well, classically at least, and it is my preference ... but it's your omelette, so do as you will.

The keys to a good omelette are fairly simple. Top-quality fresh eggs are a given, of course, but they're best at room temperature, as they will cook quicker and set better. A well-seasoned or non-stick pan of the right size is also important. Too big and the omelette will be too thin, too small and it will be hard to properly cook the egg without overcooking the outside, and an omelette sticking is probably the main fear for the novice. A non-stick pan solves this, but if you're wary of these, butter is the key; I tend to use a mix of oil and butter, as I like the flavour. It's also important to have the pan up to heat before cooking, as the egg will take up the fat otherwise without actually sealing, and then it will certainly stick. The egg should start to set straight away, with the cooked edges dragged in as they firm to allow uncooked egg to flood the pan, which will ensure you don't overcook the exterior of the omelette. Before the omelette is fully cooked, there is just enough time to drop on any fillings you favour, though a simple, well-seasoned omelette is a lovely thing, too.

Omelettes can be filled with whatever takes your fancy, but it's important to make sure those fillings aren't wet, as this will mar the texture – though a little cheese oozing out is more than acceptable. For any fillings that will seep moisture, blanch or fry them first, then drain.

When I add cheese, I like to do so in chunks or slices, so that I can still see it once served, yielding into the egg, but you can of course grate it, too. Parmigiano Reggiano, gruyère, goat's curd, hard goat's cheese, firm feta, soft marinated feta, brie or washed rind cheese ... anything you like, really.

And while cheese is a wonderful match, so too are prawns (shrimp) with Asian herbs, or smoked salmon ... An omelette is a blank canvas, after all.

Soft polenta with crab, artichoke & poached egg GF

Warm 300 g (10½ oz) cooked crabmeat and 200 ml (7 fl oz) Prawn essence (p. 67) in a small saucepan. In another pan, warm 1 × quantity Braised artichokes with garlic, bay & white wine glaze (p. 534). Divide 1 × quantity Polenta (p. 383) finished with parmesan between six serving bowls. Top each with a poached egg (see p. 351). Spoon the crab and sauce over, then the glazed artichoke pieces, and serve.

Boiled egg on toast with anchovies, onion & paprika

A favourite snack of mine is a sliced boiled egg fanned out on a great piece of toasted and well-buttered Sourdough bread (p. 847), topped with the best anchovies I can get my hands on, along with some finely shaved onion, a sprinkling of tabasco, salt and pepper, and some shredded parsley leaves.

Omelette with pecorino & parsley GF V

A few years back, I stayed in a farmhouse in the Italian countryside, and would often cook omelettes for breakfast – as the eggs, naturally, were local and super fresh, and the pecorino that was typical of the area was young and milky with a soft tang. A little chopped parsley and there's nothing more I could have wished for – though some good hand-cut ham would not have gone astray ... **Serves 1**

3 eggs
1½ tablespoons pouring (single/light) cream
25 g (1 oz) butter

60 g (2 oz) young sheep's milk pecorino, or parmesan, cut into 4 triangular slices

1 handful of flat-leaf (Italian) parsley leaves, very finely chopped

Staples
EVOO, LMN, S&P

Add the eggs and cream to a bowl, season with salt and pepper and beat with a fork to combine.

Heat a splash of oil in a frying pan over a medium–high heat, then melt in the butter. Add the egg mixture and leave undisturbed for about 30 seconds, until it starts to set around the edges. Drag the cooked edges into the centre in ribbons, pushing the runny egg into the pan, then repeat once it starts to set again.

Push the cheese into the egg (or add another filling). Sprinkle with the parsley and season with pepper. Cook to your liking, though traditionally it should still be a little runny in the centre, with a glossy wetness to the egg. If you like it more set, drop the heat a little so the exterior doesn't overcook.

Slide the omelette to one side of the pan and flip it onto itself, to fold closed in a half-moon, or fold the top side over the middle, then roll onto the plate, so that the middle mass folds onto the open edge, resulting in a fat cigar shape. Squeeze on a little lemon and serve immediately.

Make it different

Omelette with blackened roma tomatoes, dill & marinated feta. (GF) (V) You need super-ripe tomatoes for this to work. Heat a splash of oil in a frying pan over a high heat. Cut two ripe roma (plum) tomatoes in half lengthways and add to the pan, cut side down. Cook undisturbed until a little blackened, about 6 minutes. Remove the pan from the stove and slip the skins off. Drizzle 1 tablespoon sherry vinegar over the cut side and season with salt and pepper. Crumble a little marinated feta over the tomatoes and top with a few picked dill sprigs. Add to the omelette when you normally add the filling.

Omelette with smoked salmon, chives & crème fraîche. (GF) To fill, sprinkle the setting omelette with ¼ bunch of finely snipped chives, follow with 100 g (3½ oz) smoked salmon or hot-smoked trout, and spoon over 1 tablespoon crème fraîche.

Omelette with goat's curd & chives. (GF) (V) To fill, sprinkle the setting omelette with ¼ bunch of finely snipped chives, dollop on 2 tablespoons goat's curd and grind on plenty of black pepper.

Omelette with mushroom & taleggio. (GF) (V) Slice a large field or pine mushroom about 1 cm (½ in) thick. Season with salt and pepper and sauté in a knob of butter for about 3 minutes, until a little golden. Remove from the heat, add a handful of finely chopped parsley leaves and a squeeze of lemon and toss through. Dot the setting omelette with 50 g (1¾ oz) finely diced taleggio (or fontina or gruyère), then top with the mushroom before folding. Let the omelette set for a minute or two on the plate to ensure the cheese has melted.

Prawn or crab omelette with oyster sauce. Drizzle the setting omelette with 2 teaspoons oyster sauce, then top with 50 g (1¾ oz) cooked crabmeat or two shelled cooked prawns (shrimp) sliced in half lengthways. Sprinkle over half a sliced long green chilli, a few picked coriander (cilantro) sprigs and a few teaspoons sesame seeds. Once plated, drizzle with a tablespoon of oyster sauce and finish with a little more coriander.

Spinach & cheddar omelette. (GF) (V) Melt a knob of butter in a small frying pan, then add 100 g (3½ oz) baby English spinach leaves and cook until wilted, about 1½ minutes. Season with salt and pepper, then tip onto paper towel to absorb any excess liquid (this may not be necessary, but you don't want water in the filling, so just judge it). Top the setting omelette with the spinach, and sprinkle with 60 g (2 oz) finely grated aged cheddar (or gruyère) before folding.

Silverbeet or zucchini & feta omelette. (GF) (V) Heat a good splash of olive oil in a small saucepan over a high heat. Add four large shredded silverbeet (Swiss chard) leaves (stems removed), or one finely sliced zucchini (courgette). Season with salt and pepper, add 1½ tablespoons water, then cover and cook for 2 minutes. Uncover and cook for another 2 minutes, then set aside, draining if necessary. Sprinkle ¼ teaspoon ground cumin over the setting omelette, top with 60 g (2 oz) crumbled Greek feta, then the silverbeet or zucchini before folding.

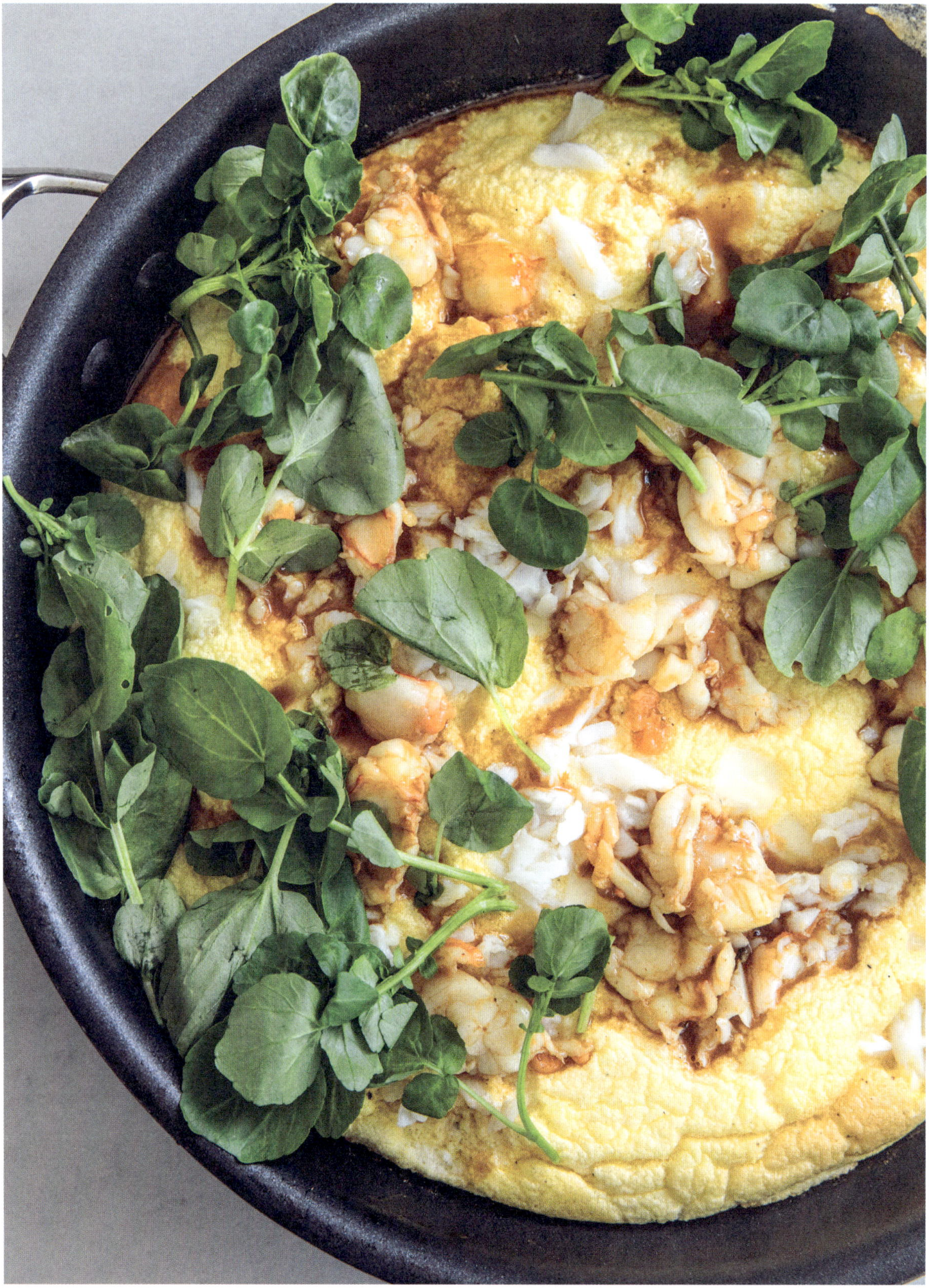

Frittata GF

I often start with a little diced onion and a touch of garlic, cooked in extra-virgin olive oil in a 23 cm (9 in) deep frying pan over a medium heat. Melt in 2 anchovies, then add some greens, such as sprouting broccoli or spinach, and cook covered for a few minutes to soften. Add a handful each of parsley and dill. Whisk 8 eggs together with a large dollop of cream or crème fraîche, season with salt and pepper, then pour over the greens and dot with goat's curd or ricotta. Cook on the stovetop for 10 minutes over a low heat, and then finish in a 170°C (340°F) fan-forced oven for another 10 minutes. Remove and rest, then squeeze over some lemon juice to serve.

Fluffy prawn & crab omelette with prawn essence & watercress GF

This soufflé omelette is a show-off dish, perfect for an elaborate brunch or lunch. It could also be made in two pans and served individually. **Serves 2**

6 eggs, separated
40 g (1½ oz/⅓ cup) grated gruyère, cheddar or stracchino, diced
100 g (3½ oz) crabmeat

3 green prawns (shrimp), peeled, deveined and cut in half lengthways
200 ml (7 fl oz) Prawn essence (p. 67), or

Tangy oyster sauce dressing (see p. 358)
2 handfuls of picked watercress

Staples
BTR, EVOO, S&P

Preheat the oven to 180°C (350°F) fan-forced.

In a large bowl, whisk the egg whites and a pinch of salt to stiff peaks.

In a separate bowl, beat the egg yolks with some salt and pepper to combine, then gently fold into the whites.

Heat a splash of oil and a knob of butter in an ovenproof non-stick or well-seasoned frying pan over a medium–high heat. Pour in the egg mixture, sprinkle with the cheese and crabmeat and cook for 2 minutes.

Transfer to the oven and bake for 5–8 minutes, until the omelette is puffed but still with a little wobble. Slide onto a serving plate.

Heat a splash of oil in a frying pan over a medium–high heat, then add a knob of butter and melt. Add the prawns, season with salt and fry for 1½ minutes, then add the prawn essence and simmer for 30 seconds.

Scatter the watercress over the omelette, then spoon the prawns and sauce over. Serve whole, then cut to serve.

Fluffy goat's cheese & gruyère omelette GF V

Pair with

Buttered toast or a toasted bagel, or a fresh baguette or rye bread.

A soufflé omelette with a more classic cheesy theme. **Serves 2–3**

6 eggs, separated
100 g (3½ oz) soft goat's cheese

100 g (3½ oz) gruyère, or cheddar, grated
6 chives, finely chopped

Staples
EVOO, S&P

Preheat the oven to 180°C (350°F) fan-forced.

In a large bowl, whisk the egg whites and a pinch of salt to stiff peaks.

In a separate bowl, beat the egg yolks with some pepper to combine, then gently fold into the whites.

Heat a splash of oil in an ovenproof non-stick or well-seasoned frying pan over a medium–high heat. Pour in the egg mixture. Crumble the goat's cheese over and sprinkle with the gruyère and chives, then cook for 2 minutes.

Transfer to the oven and bake for 5–8 minutes, until the omelette is puffed but still with a little wobble. Slide onto a serving plate, then cut to serve.

Fluffy prawn & crab omelette
with prawn essence & watercress

Devilled eggs GF V

Devilled eggs have a hallowed place in the history of hors d'oeuvres, right up in the pantheon. And though they may be irredeemably unfashionable to some, I think they're an absolute delight. **Makes 18 halves**

12 eggs
90 g (3 oz/⅓ cup) Master olive oil mayonnaise (p. 74)
2½ tablespoons boiling water
3 teaspoons dijon mustard
1½ teaspoons salt flakes

½ teaspoon smoked paprika
6 drops of hot sauce (such as Tabasco)
3 tablespoons extra-virgin olive oil

snipped chives, picked chervil or picked watercress, to serve (optional)
cayenne pepper, or paprika, to serve (optional)

Carefully lower the eggs into a saucepan of boiling water and cook for 12 minutes. (The time here may seem long, but the mass of eggs will cool the water substantially.) Cool the eggs in cold or iced water and peel carefully. Cut the eggs in half lengthways, then carefully remove the egg yolks. Select the eighteen best-looking halves, reserving the rest for a sandwich or potato salad or the like.

Add the egg yolks to a bowl and mash with a fork. Add the mayonnaise, water, mustard, salt, paprika, hot sauce and oil and blitz with a stick blender until smooth, about 2 minutes, adding a little extra water if needed to make a smooth, pipe-able paste. Transfer to a piping (icing) bag fitted with a star nozzle.

Fill each egg cavity with the mixture, then garnish with the herbs and/or a pinch of cayenne or paprika, if desired. Ideally, serve straight away, but the eggs will keep for a few hours covered in the fridge.

Make it different
With shellfish. Pimp these further by adding half a smoked oyster or mussel for a super-retro feel.

Or top with some caviar, salmon roe, or an anchovy, halved lengthways and rolled in a swirl … have some fun.

Chawanmushi

So finely set that it quivers with the slightest movement, chawanmushi is a beautifully delicate savoury Japanese egg custard. You can change the fillings you add to the custard, but this is a lovely starting point. **Serves 2 as an appetiser**

2 slices of raw chicken breast
2 peeled and cleaned raw prawns (shrimp)
2 fresh shiitake mushrooms, sliced

2 spring onions (scallions), white and green parts, finely sliced
1 teaspoon salt flakes
2 teaspoons sake

Custard
375 ml (12½ fl oz/1½ cups) Dashi (p. 53), or miso soup
3 eggs
2 teaspoons light soy sauce
2 teaspoons mirin

Whisk the custard ingredients in a bowl to combine well, but without aerating too much.

Add the remaining ingredients to a bowl and toss to coat, then divide between two small heatproof serving bowls or teacups – I use Japanese-style handle-less cups.

Strain the custard evenly into the bowls, then skim any bubbles off the surface.

Place in a steamer set to medium–low. Cover and cook for 10 minutes (if you have a steam oven, cook at 80% for 10 minutes).

Once cooked, let stand on the bench for 2 minutes before serving.

Simple Thai-style hard-boiled eggs

I like to serve this simple side with Thai curries, or even with rice and greens for a meal. Cut 6 hard-boiled eggs (see p. 351) in half and arrange on a serving plate. Generously spoon some Nuoc cham (p. 93) over, then sprinkle with 3 very finely shredded makrut lime leaves (ribs removed), and a tablespoon or so of chopped salted peanuts.

Spiced tea eggs

Carefully lower 6 eggs into a saucepan of boiling water and cook for 10 minutes. Plunge into iced water until cool. Crack the shells slightly with a teaspoon all over (this will create the marbled effect in the white), then return to a saucepan and cover with cold water. Add 3 tablespoons dark soy sauce, 3 star anise, 2 cassia bark sticks, 2 jasmine teabags, 2 Russian caravan teabags, 1 teaspoon fine sea salt and 1 teaspoon toasted sesame seeds and simmer very gently for 1 hour. Remove from the heat and set aside to cool for 30 minutes. Refrigerate for 24 hours before peeling and using. The spiced eggs will keep for 5 days in the fridge.

Twice-baked cheese soufflé Ⓥ

Pair with

A green salad, and bread to mop up the sauce.

Truffled eggs ⒼⒻ Ⓥ

The porosity of eggs mean that they will take up flavours, which is a good reason to keep them in their container in the fridge, but it also means you can perfume them with a truffle. It's also a great way to get some mileage out of that most expensive of ingredients. Simply place the eggs in a jar with the truffle, seal and refrigerate for a couple of days. The eggs will be scented marvellously, ready to be made into a simple scramble with some cream. A few shavings of truffle would be an ideal way to finish, with a glass of Champagne making it a wonderfully decadent brunch dish. You can also store truffles in risotto rice (carnaroli, arborio etc.), which will similarly perfume the rice and keep the truffle nice and dry at the same time. Perhaps because of the way the rice is then cooked, I don't find it quite as successful, but it's very good, nonetheless.

Truffled eggs en cocotte ⒼⒻ Ⓥ

For each serve, crack 2 truffled eggs (above) into a small buttered ceramic dish/ramekin that has been rubbed with a garlic clove. Top with a heaped tablespoon of thick (double/heavy cream), season with salt and pepper, then top with 3 slices truffle. Finish with a knob of butter and bake in a bain marie (a dish or roasting tray filled with hot water) at 180°C (350°F) fan-forced for 8–10 minutes, or until done to your liking. Serve with toasted brioche or toast soldiers.

Based on a classic recipe that Stephanie Alexander made famous in Melbourne in the 1980s and 1990s, these soufflés are built around a light-coloured roux to make a thick béchamel. Egg yolks and cheese are then whipped in, which strengthens and stabilises the mixture before the egg white is folded in, then it's baked until risen. It's the second bake that elevates the dish, with the light and airy soufflé so deliciously golden and cheesy. It's also a lot less nerve-racking than making a classic soufflé, where an expertly risen specimen can seem to slump for no apparent reason. **Serves 6**

80 g (2¾ oz) butter
80 g (2¾ oz) plain (all-purpose) flour
380 ml (13 fl oz) milk, warmed
120 g (4½ oz) gruyère cheese, grated

60 g (2 oz) soft or aged goat's cheese
¼ teaspoon freshly ground nutmeg
¼ teaspoon cayenne pepper, or smoked paprika
4 eggs, separated

500 ml (17 fl oz/2 cups) pouring (single/light) cream

Staples
BTR, FLR, S&P

Special equipment
6 × 200 ml (7 fl oz) metal or ceramic moulds

Preheat the oven to 180°C (350°F) fan-forced.

Grease the moulds well. Sprinkle in some flour and rotate the moulds to coat evenly, then tip out any excess.

Melt the butter in a saucepan over a medium heat. Add the flour and stir with a wooden spoon to form a roux. Stir for about 3 minutes to cook out the rawness while still keeping the roux pale, then gradually whisk in the milk. Cook until thickened, about 3 minutes, then remove from the heat. Stir 80 g (2¾ oz) of the gruyère through, and all the goat's cheese, nutmeg and cayenne. Season with salt. Once smooth, stir the egg yolks through until combined, then tip into a large bowl.

In a separate bowl, whisk the egg whites and a pinch of salt to firm peaks, then use a spatula to fold one-third of the egg white into the cheesy egg yolk mixture. Follow with the remaining egg whites, combining completely but keeping the mixture as aerated as possible.

Divide the mixture evenly among the moulds, tapping them a little on the bench to ensure the mixture is touching the bottom of the moulds.

Arrange the moulds in a roasting tin or baking dish, then pour in boiling water to reach halfway up the side of the moulds, to make a bain marie. Transfer to the oven and bake for 28–30 minutes, until puffed and golden.

Remove the moulds from the roasting tin and set the soufflés aside at room temperature to cool.

Once cooled, run a knife around the inside of the moulds, then invert them onto a tray lined with baking paper, with the bottom forming the top of the finished soufflés. Cover and refrigerate until needed; the soufflés will keep for 2 days like this.

To serve, preheat the oven 200°C (400°F) fan-forced. Place the soufflés either in individual ovenproof dishes, or one larger one. Pour the cream over, then sprinkle with the remaining gruyère and grind on some pepper.

Bake for 20 minutes, until puffed and golden. Serve immediately.

Soft-boiled eggs with green mango salad & citrus & chilli relish

This is a delightful way to start a Thai-themed meal – a little morsel to set the tone and prime the appetite. The relish is very punchy and hot, but perfect with the tart mango and soft egg. **Serves 8**

¼ white cabbage, very finely shaved
juice of 1 lime
2 teaspoons fish sauce
8 soft-boiled eggs (see p. 351), peeled
1 large green mango, peeled and finely julienned
2 tablespoons crispy shallots (see p. 600)

2 tablespoons chopped salted peanuts

Citrus & chilli relish
2 teaspoons shrimp paste
4 garlic cloves, sliced
3 tablespoons small dried shrimp
½ teaspoon salt flakes
7 red bird's eye chillies, finely chopped

3 tablespoons finely grated palm sugar (jaggery)
juice of 3 limes
2 tablespoons fish sauce
2 mandarins, tangelos or blood oranges, or 1 grapefruit or pomelo, peeled, segmented and sliced into small triangles

Pair with

A generous stack of prawn or crab crackers, as an appetiser before a feast.

The Citrus & chilli relish is also great with fish, cooked bug tails, barbecued prawn (shrimp), and to top pan-seared, grilled or roasted scallops on the shell.

For the relish, wrap the shrimp paste in a double layer of foil, sealing to make a flat parcel. Heat in a frying pan over a high heat for 5 minutes, then set aside to cool.

Using a mortar and pestle, pound the garlic, dried shrimp and salt into a fine paste. Add the shrimp paste from the foil parcel, and the red chilli. Pound until fairly smooth, then grind in the sugar. Stir the lime juice and fish sauce through to combine, then mix the citrus flesh through. The relish should be thick and a balance of hot, sour, sweet and salty, so adjust as needed.

Dress the cabbage with the lime juice and fish sauce. Cut the eggs in half and arrange on a serving plate. Pile a little cabbage and mango on each. Top with some of the relish, the shallots and peanuts and serve immediately.

Crisp-fried eggs, corn, smoked trout & herb salad with tangy oyster sauce dressing

This dish requires a little swift deftness to fry the eggs and serve them hot, but being organised and understanding the process beforehand makes it very achievable. Frying the eggs in super-hot oil is one of the real keys, achieving puffed whites with a crisp filigreed edge, while retaining a gloriously oozing yolk. Match that with an explosion of herbs, corn, chilli, hot-smoked trout and a tangy oyster sauce dressing, and I'm pretty happy. This is a dish that fits either early or late for me, either for breakfast/brunch or for a late supper. **Serves 6**

4 corn cobs
oil, for deep-frying (see p. 22)
6 eggs
200 g (7 oz) hot-smoked trout fillet, flaked
5 spring onions (scallions), white and green parts, finely sliced
6 Thai basil sprigs, leaves picked

6 coriander (cilantro) sprigs, leaves and fine stems picked
4 makrut lime leaves, finely sliced
2 long green chillies, sliced on an angle
juice of 1 lime, plus extra wedges to serve

Tangy oyster sauce dressing
3½ tablespoons oyster sauce
1½ tablespoons fish sauce
juice of 2 large limes
3 teaspoons caster (superfine) sugar
1½ teaspoons ground white pepper

Pair with

Steamed or fried rice.

Eggs en cocotte, plain or with wilted spinach & parmesan GF V

For each serve, crack 2 eggs into a small, well-buttered ceramic dish/ramekin and top with a heaped tablespoon of thick (double/heavy cream). Season with salt and pepper, then bake in a bain marie (a dish or roasting tray filled with hot water) at 180°C (350°F) fan-forced for 8–10 minutes, or until done to your liking. Fill the base of the dish(es) with some wilted baby spinach, tossed in butter and seasoned – a few grates of nutmeg is nice, too. Finish with a shower of finely grated parmesan before cooking. Serve with toasted brioche or toast soldiers. If you'd prefer this plain, you can omit the spinach, nutmeg and parmesan.

Pair with

Baked buttered rice (p. 384) or steamed basmati.

Naan (p. 855).

Fine parmesan crisps V

Combine 95 g (3¼ oz/1 cup) finely grated parmesan and 20 g (¾ oz) plain (all-purpose) flour in a small bowl. Lightly brush a 20 cm (8 in) frying pan or saucepan with 20 g (¾ oz) melted butter. Evenly sprinkle in a heaped tablespoon of the cheese mixture, in a circle, to cover the pan base. Place over a high heat for 15–20 seconds for the cheese to bubble. Take off the heat and allow to cool a little and firm up. Lift out with a spatula and set aside to cool completely on a rack, or shape over a bottle for curled crisps. Serve on the day of making, once cooled and crisp. Drop the crackers on a little starter salad of peppery leaves such as rocket (arugula) and watercress, sliced radishes and apple or pear, dressed with olive oil, good balsamic vinegar and plenty of black pepper. Dress it up further with a few slices of prosciutto.

Cook the corn in a saucepan of boiling salted water for 6 minutes, then drain. When cool enough to handle, stand the cobs upright and slice off the kernels.

Meanwhile, combine the dressing ingredients in a small bowl. Toss the corn in a small bowl with one-quarter of the dressing.

Heat about 8 cm (3¼ in) of oil in a heavy-based saucepan or deep-fryer until 200°C (400°F).

Place the trout in a bowl with the spring onion, herbs, lime leaves and chilli. Add the lime juice and 2 teaspoons of the dressing and toss gently.

Crack one egg at a time into a small bowl, then carefully slip the egg into the hot oil, from just above the surface. Immediately repeat with another egg; they should puff and crisp immediately. Cook for about 50 seconds. Remove with a slotted spoon, quickly drain on paper towel, then transfer immediately to a plate. Repeat with the remaining eggs.

Divide the corn among serving plates. Top each with an egg and spoon the remaining dressing over. Pile the salad on top and serve with lime wedges.

Make it different

With eel. Use smoked eel instead of trout, or simply garnish with salmon roe.

Egg, tomato & spinach curry with ginger & turmeric GF V

This dish is fabulous as the protein focus of a vegetarian curry spread, or as a standalone meal just with some rice. The yolks will remain runny, saucing and enriching the dish when the whites are poached. **Serves 4**

8 eggs
100 ml (3½ fl oz) extra-virgin olive oil
2 large red onions, sliced into half-moons
5 garlic cloves, sliced
80 g (2¾ oz) fresh ginger, peeled and julienned
8 cm (3¼ in) piece of fresh turmeric, peeled and finely grated, or 2 teaspoons ground turmeric
2 red bird's eye chillies, split lengthways
2 tablespoons yellow mustard seeds

2 teaspoons cumin seeds
2 teaspoons ground coriander
4 large handfuls of baby English spinach leaves
1 tablespoon tomato paste (concentrated purée)
400 g (14 oz) tin diced tomatoes
2 teaspoons salt
300 ml (10 fl oz) Classic white vegetable stock (p. 51), Golden chicken stock (p. 54), or water
200 g (7 oz) plain yoghurt

1 bunch of coriander (cilantro), leaves and fine stems picked and roughly chopped
1 handful of cashew nuts, toasted
cooked rice, to serve

Staples
LMN, S&P

Carefully lower the eggs into a saucepan of simmering water and cook for 5½ minutes. Refresh in cold water for 5 minutes, then peel.

Heat the oil in a wide-based saucepan over a medium heat. Fry the onion, garlic, ginger, turmeric and chilli until softened, about 10 minutes. Add the mustard seeds, cumin seeds and ground coriander and fry for 1 minute, then add the spinach and cook until wilted, about 4 minutes.

Stir in the tomato paste, tomatoes and salt and bring to a simmer. Add the stock and simmer for 5 minutes, then add the eggs and simmer for 5 minutes. Adjust the seasoning as needed.

Serve dolloped with the yoghurt and sprinkled with the coriander, nuts and a squeeze of lemon, accompanied by rice.

Scotch quail eggs

Scotch eggs are often made to be eaten cold, something of a pub snack or picnic staple in the UK, with a hard-boiled egg encased in sausage meat and crumbs, and then cooked – often deep-fried. I like them served hot, with the white of the egg just set when boiled, so that once the crumb is golden and the meat cooked, the egg will be warm and the yolk still runny. Needless to say, timing and temperature are key here, but they'll still be delicious if the egg yolks firm up, so don't stress too much. This version with quail eggs is especially elegant, a lovely pre-dinner snack for a dinner party aimed to impress. **Makes 12**

12 quail eggs
5 French shallots, finely chopped
4 garlic cloves, finely chopped
2 teaspoons fennel seeds
300 g (10½ oz) chicken thigh meat, cut into 5 mm (¼ in) dice

2 Italian pork and fennel sausages, skins removed, meat crumbled
½ nutmeg, grated
2 eggs, 1 separated
100 g (3½ oz/1 cup) finely grated Parmigiano Reggiano

75 g (2¾ oz/½ cup) plain (all-purpose) flour
300 g (10½ oz/3¾ cups) fresh breadcrumbs
oil, for deep-frying (see p. 22)

Staples
EVOO, S&P

Add the quail eggs to a saucepan of boiling water and cook for 5 minutes. Plunge into iced water, stand for at least 5 minutes, then peel.

Heat a good splash of oil in a frying pan over a medium heat. Fry the shallot, garlic and fennels seeds until golden, about 6 minutes. Tip into a bowl and set aside.

In a food processor, blitz the chicken and sausage meat to a smooth paste, about 2 minutes. Add the shallot mixture, nutmeg and egg white. Season with salt and pepper and blitz until smooth, 1–2 minutes. Add the parmesan and blitz to combine.

Transfer the mixture to a bowl and chill for 20 minutes, then divide the mixture into 12 even portions.

In a bowl, whisk the egg and egg yolk to combine. Combine the flour and breadcrumbs in a shallow bowl.

Flatten a portion of the meat in your hand, then add a quail egg to the centre. Form the mince around the egg, pressing to gently create an even layer, then chill on a tray while you coat the remaining eggs.

Once chilled again – which is important to ensure the shape holds well while crumbing – coat in the whisked egg, then roll in the crumbs to coat.

Chill again for at least 5 minutes, then egg and crumb again, to seal the egg in beautifully.

Heat about 8 cm (3¼ in) of oil in a large saucepan until 150°C (300°F); use a thermometer here, as you don't want these to fry too fast – the meat should be cooked, but the egg only warmed.

Starting with the coldest eggs, fry the eggs for 8 minutes, then drain on paper towel and serve.

Pair with
Tartare sauce (see p. 77) or smoked paprika Aïoli (p. 76), and some pickled guindilla peppers or cornichons.

Clarified butter GF V

Clarified butter is fantastic for frying, with the fat having a high smoke point. I use it for shallow frying fritters, battered fish and the like – and it's essential for Pommes anna (p. 624) – but it can be used in the place of oil for any frying application. Simply put, clarified butter is butter where the solids are removed from the fat, yielding a transparent yellow liquid, which will solidify when cold. Removing those solids takes out the elements that will burn, the bits that go brown and nutty when you make a brown butter sauce (see p. 73). You will need about 320 g (11½ oz) of butter to make 200 g (7 oz) clarified butter. Melt the <u>butter</u> gently over a low heat until it splits, leaving the fats at the bottom of the pan. This is a relatively slow process, taking about 10–15 minutes, as you need to keep the heat low to avoid burning the solids and tainting the flavour. Once separated, set aside so all the solids sink, then ladle off the liquid. This will keep refrigerated for a few weeks. Be aware that Indian ghee is usually more intense in flavour. Indian/subcontinental ghee is great for curries and the like (find one you like the flavour of, as brands can be quite different), while clarified butter is better for tasks where a milder flavour is preferred.

Salted butter GF V

Creating a simulation of a quality European cultured butter is very simple, and I do love that sour, fermented flavour, whether using it to butter a slice of Sourdough bread (p. 847), or when I'm baking or making pastry. You can also add a layer of complexity by using a top-notch salt, such as fleur de sel, Celtic sea salt or Murray River salt, or a smoked salt – or you can flavour it with nori powder (see p. 187) or blitzed wakame, or sprinkle with Spring onion ash (p. 602) to finish. **Makes 400–500 g (14 oz–1 lb 2 oz)**

Pair with

Boiled potatoes topped with anchovy crumb (see p. 122).

Spoon over a cooked fish fillet (whiting, garfish, hapuka or blue-eye trevalla work well), then sprinkle with anchovy crumb (see p. 122).

Serve with cured fish (pp. 168, 169, 171) and shaved cucumber.

Dress thinly sliced cucumber and dill as a simple side.

Drizzle over butter lettuce, iceberg or chicory (witlof/ endive), or vegetables for a salad, such as shaved raw asparagus, peas, snow peas (mangetout) or sugar-snap peas.

Spoon over blanched ribbons of zucchini (courgette) and toss with mint, currants and toasted pine nuts.

Drizzle over Basic vinaigrette lentils (p. 385) mixed with finely diced roasted beetroot (beet) and chopped or grated hard-boiled egg.

500 g (1 lb 2 oz) crème fraîche

500 ml (17 fl oz/2 cups) pouring (single/light) cream

500 ml (17 fl oz/2 cups) iced water

2 teaspoons salt flakes

In a food processor or blender, process the crème fraîche and cream for 10 minutes, scraping down the sides every now and then. The mixture will thicken and then split, and the buttermilk will separate.

Drain off the buttermilk and keep in the fridge, to make Buttermilk dressing (below), to marinate chicken in, or to use in scones, pancakes and the like.

Add the iced water to the blender, then blitz for 2 minutes. Transfer the butter to a strainer and drain off any excess liquid.

Tip the butter onto a wooden board, then fold in on itself with a butter paddle, grooved pasta paddle or large spatula. Add the salt, folding in to incorporate. Fold for a couple more minutes.

Shape into a block, wrap in baking paper and refrigerate. It will keep for 2 weeks.

Buttermilk GF V

Buttermilk is what comes from cream when you're churning it to make cultured butter (see p. 361), so it is fermented and somewhat sour. Well, that's what it should be – but what is typically sold in supermarkets is a simulation of buttermilk, with culture added to milk. Make your own by adding the juice of ½ lemon to 250 ml (8½ fl oz/1 cup) full-cream (whole) milk and let it stand for 15 minutes. Use in cakes, pancake mixes and pastries – whenever buttermilk is called for.

Buttermilk dressing GF V

This is a versatile dressing, creamy, tangy and mildly warm from the horseradish and hot sauce. I love it on fish, crunchy leaves and raw and cooked vegetables. **Makes about 300 ml (10 fl oz)**

150 ml (5 fl oz) Buttermilk (above)

100 ml (3½ fl oz) extra-virgin olive oil, or grapeseed oil

1 large French shallot, finely diced

2 tablespoons plain yoghurt, or crème fraîche

1½ tablespoons white-wine vinegar

1 tablespoon freshly grated horseradish (optional)

2 teaspoons dijon mustard

1 teaspoon caster (superfine) sugar

2 drops of hot sauce (such as Tabasco)

Staples
S&P

Add all the ingredients to a bowl, season with salt and pepper and combine. Stand for 5 minutes before using. The dressing will keep in the fridge for about 2 days.

Ricotta GF V

Ricotta is the most accessible and economical type of fresh cheese available, and it's equally useful for sweet and savoury applications. Unfortunately, the freshness can often be lacking. Tubs of supermarket ricotta make me shudder, and the abomination that is smooth ricotta is not worth discussing. You can, of course, buy decent fresh ricotta at most delis, but just make sure it is vibrant-looking with a clean aroma. If there's any hint of it greying or looking dull, it's time to move on. The alternative is to make your own. **Makes about 1 kg (2 lb 3 oz)**

3 litres (101 fl oz/12 cups) full-cream (whole) milk
700 ml (23½ fl oz) pouring (single/light) cream

2 teaspoons salt flakes
125 ml (4 fl oz/½ cup) white-wine vinegar
100 ml (3½ fl oz) water

In a large saucepan over a medium heat, bring the milk and cream to just under the boil, or to 92°C (197°F).

Add the salt. Turn the heat right down to as low as possible. Combine the vinegar and water in a bowl and add to the pan. Stir in thoroughly, then sit over a low heat for 5 minutes – the curds will float to the top. Turn off the heat and stand for 5 minutes.

Line a large strainer with a few layers of muslin (cheesecloth) and set it over a large bowl. Spoon the curds into the strainer and set aside to drain for 30 minutes at room temperature.

You can now use the ricotta, or refrigerate for later use. For a firmer curd, leave the ricotta in the muslin and refrigerate, squeezing out the moisture regularly until the ricotta is the desired consistency.

The ricotta is best enjoyed as fresh as possible, but will keep for several days in the fridge.

Pair with

Serve warm fresh ricotta with new season's olive oil, pepper and salt flakes, with grilled bread on the side.

Tumble on a handful of ripe berries and drizzle with good honey.

Smear on a plate and top with broad beans or freshly podded peas with soft herbs, then drizzle with olive oil and season with black pepper and salt flakes.

One of my favourite breakfasts is freshly made ricotta smothered on top of a charred or toasted piece of bread rubbed with garlic, then dressed with peppery oil and a sprinkling of herbs – chives, basil and/or parsley – and plenty of black pepper and salt flakes.

Or for a sweeter take, ricotta on toast topped with cinnamon, honey and crushed pistachio nuts is also divine, maybe with some sliced fig, too.

Labneh GF V

Labneh is simply yoghurt that has been drained of whey, thickening it into something like a sour cream cheese. Using thick Greek-style yoghurt is best for labneh, as thinner yoghurts will lose much of their mass when you drain them, but any plain yoghurt will work. **Makes about 14 balls**

1 kg (2 lb 3 oz/4 cups) thick plain yoghurt
2 garlic cloves, sliced
180 ml (6 fl oz) neutral-flavoured oil

80 ml (2½ fl oz/⅓ cup) extra-virgin olive oil

Staples
OIL

Line a fine-mesh sieve with a few layers of muslin (cheesecloth). Suspend it over a bowl to catch the whey. Add the yoghurt and refrigerate for 24–36 hours, until firm enough to roll.

Tip the labneh out of the strainer and, with oiled hands, roll into balls. Drop the balls into a jar with the garlic and the combined oils and refrigerate until needed. The labneh can be used immediately and will keep for around 6 weeks under oil.

Make it different
With saffron. Steep six saffron threads in 2 teaspoons boiling water, then stir the mixture through the yoghurt before placing it into the fine-mesh sieve.

Pair with

Roll well-drained Labneh balls in Za'atar (p. 33) or Dukkah (p. 13) and serve with warmed or soft fresh Pitta bread (p. 854) with sliced fresh radishes, pickled green chillies and olives.

Smear on toasted or grilled bread.

It's also lovely on Scones (p. 772), and on Pancakes (p. 768) with jam for breakfast.

Fried haloumi with vine leaves, pistachios, za'atar & pomegranate molasses GF V

Vine leaves crisp up in the pan, encasing delightfully oozing haloumi – with the crunchy pistachios, za'atar and sweet-and-sour caramel tang of the pomegranate molasses perfect foils. As with grilled saganaki, eat this dish as soon as it's made, as the true glory fades a little as the cheese cools and firms again. It makes a wonderful finger food or antipasto. **Serves 8**

4 preserved vine leaves, thoroughly rinsed
500 g (1 lb 2 oz) haloumi
3 tablespoons pomegranate molasses

1 heaped tablespoon Za'atar (p. 33)
1 heaped tablespoon roughly chopped pistachios

1 teaspoon ground aleppo pepper

Staples
EVOO, LMN

Dry any excess moisture from the vine leaves with paper towel. Cut each leaf in half along the stem.

Slice the haloumi into eight fingers. Roll each piece tightly in a vine leaf half.

Heat a good glug of oil in a frying pan over a medium heat. Cook the haloumi on two sides only until golden, about 1½ minutes each side.

Transfer to a plate, drizzle with the pomegranate molasses and squeeze on some lemon. Sprinkle with the za'atar, pistachios and aleppo pepper, if using, and enjoy immediately.

Pair with

Olives, torshi (see p. 639) or other pickles (pp. 470, 520, 531), Yoghurt, cucumber & mint salad (p. 508) and fresh pitta breads (see p. 854).

Using left-over whey

Don't waste the whey left over from making labneh or ricotta, or from hanging yoghurt. The whey can be used in a number of ways. You can use it as the basis for the brine when lacto-fermenting vegetables (see p. 454); it also works well for soaking grains in, as it is acidic and will break down some of the indigestible elements. Whey can also be used as the liquid for making Focaccia (p. 845), or added to Pancakes (p. 768) and the like, or to a falafel mixture instead of plain water. I often set some whey in ice blocks to use in smoothies, or to give to our dog in summer – he loves them! It's also apparently quite good for the garden and pot plants.

Orange-blossom labneh GF V

Spoon 500 g (1 lb 2 oz/2 cups) plain yoghurt into a strainer lined with muslin (cheesecloth). Place over a bowl or tub in the fridge for 24 hours. Once drained, combine the labneh with 2 teaspoons orange-blossom water and a pinch of salt.

Crema fresca 🄶🅅

Crema fresca is a whipped soured cream condiment, which I serve on all sorts of things, from vegetables to fish and meats. Adding a few tablespoons of pure cream makes for a thicker and more luscious mix – but if you don't have any, just use an extra few tablespoons of regular cream. **Makes 300 ml (10 fl oz)**

200 ml (7 fl oz) pouring
  (single/light) cream
2 tablespoons pure cream
  (40–42% fat)

2½ tablespoons plain yoghurt
25 ml (1 fl oz) lemon juice

Staples
S&P

Lightly whip the pouring cream in a bowl, then add the pure cream and yoghurt and whisk to combine. Add the lemon juice, season with salt and pepper, then whisk to combine.

Cover and refrigerate until needed. The crema fresca is best used the same day.

Pair with

Gravlax (pp. 169, 171).

Baked potatoes (see p. 626).

Tacos.

Chicken & corn koftas (p. 249).

Serve on a Blini (pp. 377, 621) with caviar.

Swirl through soups such as tomato, Roasted root vegetable (see p. 472) or Gazpacho (p. 657) just before serving.

Combine with freshly grated horseradish and dollop on a steak.

Stir cooked crabmeat and snipped chives through, then serve on top of a cooked fish fillet with Crustacean essence (p. 52) drizzled over to finish.

Smear on a plate and top with slices of roasted beetroot (beet) tossed in French-style vinaigrette (p. 88) with tarragon and dill, or fermented chilli and sherry vinegar (pictured left).

Break open a roasted smoky eggplant (see p. 519) and spoon on some crema fresca, then serve with barbecued lamb or grilled fish.

Yoghurt GF V

You can buy cultures to make yoghurt, but you can also employ the (rather unfortunately titled) 'backslop' method. This is simply a way of inoculating milk with bacteria by using yoghurt with a live culture in it – a commercially produced yoghurt, in other words. It's much like a sourdough starter or adding yeast, but unlike a sourdough mother, you need to start from scratch every three or four batches. The key is to establish a hospitable environment, which means regulating the ambient temperature, which is an inexact art unless you have a yoghurt maker. If you have an area warm enough, you can make jars of yoghurt on the kitchen bench, as my mother-in-law Lemonia and my meme Grace used to do (much to my father's distaste, as he was force fed room-temperature yoghurt daily as a tonic when he was growing up, and to this day detests it). Mostly, using a jar of warm water or a hot water bottle in a portable drinks cooler, or the oven set on the lowest setting, are the most reliable ways. It's also good to separate your yoghurt-making area from any bread-making or yeasted baking, as these other yeasts can negatively affect the flavour and texture of your yoghurt. **Makes about 1 kg (2 lb 3 oz)**

1 litre (34 fl oz/4 cups) full-cream (whole) milk (sheep's, cow's or goat's milk all work)	30 g (1 oz) full-fat milk powder (optional, for a thicker yoghurt)	125 g (4½ oz/½ cup) plain yoghurt, at room temperature **Special equipment** *Thermometer*

Add the milk to a small saucepan. If using milk powder, stir it into the milk to dissolve.

Over a medium heat, warm the milk to 85–88°C (185–190°F) as best you can, keeping at this temperature for 25 minutes, stirring occasionally.

Take the milk off the heat and leave to cool down to 42–45°C (107–115°F) at room temperature; you can change pans to bring the heat down faster, but don't use a water bath, as the temperature will be hard to regulate.

Once cooled, combine 200 ml (7 fl oz) of the milk with the yoghurt, then stir it back into the rest of the milk to completely disperse. Pour into clean glass jars and seal.

Set the oven to the lowest temperature, ideally close to 40°C (105°F), and put the jars of yoghurt in – or you can turn the oven off when the yoghurt goes in, then bring it back up to temperature every couple of hours.

Or, put the jars in a portable drinks cooler and pop a jar of 38–40°C (100–105°F) water next to the yoghurt, checking every 2 hours and topping it up with hot water to keep the yoghurt warm.

The absolute ideal inoculating temperature is 38°C (105°F) – but people have been making yoghurt since well before they could reliably regulate temperature. If the environment is too hot, the bacteria might be killed off; too cold and it will just take longer.

Leave for 4–8 hours to ferment and thicken, then stand at room temperature for an hour to further develop the flavour.

The yoghurt will keep for about 2 weeks in the fridge. Always set aside a small jar to use as a starter for your next batch. After two more batches, you will need to start again.

Make it different

With spices. Flavour the yoghurt by adding spices to the jar before pouring in the milk. For every 500 ml (17 fl oz/2 cups) milk, add two squashed cardamom pods, half a split vanilla bean, a cinnamon stick, a couple of cloves, or ½ teaspoon rosewater or orange-blossom water.

Also see

Braised lamb neck & barley broth **308–9**

Petit salé aux lentilles **334**

Black turtle bean & pork belly braise (Frijoles negros) **340**

Falafel with broad beans & tahini yoghurt **432**

Harira **461**

Barley 'risotto' with mushrooms & speck **572**

Chickpeas with mushrooms, red-wine vinaigrette & tarragon **574**

Pumpkin, chickpea, cashew & coconut curry **633**

Zucchini flower, wild rice, lentil & yoghurt salad **671**

Rye crackers, Spiced seed crackers **838–9**

Wholemeal & rye sourdough loaves 850–1

Grains, Pulses, Seeds & Nuts

Grains, pulses, seeds & nuts

Today, wholegrains, pulses, nuts and seeds have come to occupy a very significant place in many of our diets. Naturally, they have done so in numerous cultures for thousands of years, but in the West that connection was often broken. Grains ended up meaning wheat, typically stripped of bran and germ and pulverised to flour. Even when I was growing up, muesli bordered on the hippy fringes, and health-food stores, where you needed to go to get such things, were decidedly alternative in feel.

Pearled barley in a lamb soup, the occasional tabouleh, tinned kidney beans in a salad with capsicum (bell pepper) or in a 'con carne' braise were about the extent of things. Seeds were for birds, or the occasional cracker, and nuts were a snack only, while the inclusion of cashew nuts in the stir-fry for our Saturday night visits to the local Oriental Jade restaurant was positively exotic. My pantry now has endless shelves and drawers filled with all sorts of grains, pulses, nuts and seeds, and I use them all regularly, and for all manner of things.

Wholegrains are a delight, both for flavour and texture, with the squeaky chew of barley stunning in a soup, stew or salad, while the pleasingly grainy texture and warming quality of polenta is wonderful topped with a deeply flavoured braise of beef or autumn fungi. I adore the texture and nuttiness of cracked freekeh or bulgur in a herb-heavy salad, and an elaborate presentation of spiced meat and/or vegetables with buttery couscous is a marvel.

I keep bulgur, freekeh, quinoa, amaranth, farro and buckwheat on hand, but barley takes pride of place in my pantry. I am somewhat drawn to the plump, nutty pearls. It ends up in braises, soups and salads, and gets made into a risotto alternative (see p. 572). Freshly cooked barley is tossed with chopped ripe tomatoes, cumin and olive oil to pair with chicken or torn buffalo mozzarella or burrata. Freekeh is also delicious simmered in a braise, or cooked in stock then buttered and served with roast chicken or grilled lamb chops. Both grains are excellent cooked until tender but still chewy, then tossed with lots of chopped soft herbs, oil, vinegar, finely diced onion and some currants plumped in warm vinegar or quick-pickled grapes. Couscous, both the fine version as well as moghrabieh are essential, and I usually have both white and yellow polenta on hand. I opt for the real stuff, but instant polenta is no stranger in my house, either.

I readily keep a few types of rice on hand, with basmati, jasmine, koshihikari, bomba and some type of risotto rice, usually carnaroli (see p. 144), the most used (though glutinous rice, wild rice, brown rice and black rice are usually present, too). Their uses naturally fit with certain cuisine directions – with jasmine essential for Thai dishes, and bomba ideal for croquetas (see p. 190) or paella – but basmati is a handy all-rounder (not for risotto, of course), great for curries but also excellent for Middle Eastern dishes, with the grains deliciously nutty; plus they hold their shape and texture, standing up well in soups. With risotto rice in the pantry, stock in the freezer and butter and parmesan in the fridge, a great risotto is only minutes away, maybe just with soaked dried porcini, or by using the vegetables and herbs on hand, or perhaps a handful of prawns from the freezer.

Walnuts and almonds are on high rotation at my house, with pistachio nuts, pine nuts, macadamia nuts, peanuts and hazelnuts getting their fair share of airtime, too. Red-skinned peanuts end up in Asian dishes, when not on Pesto (p. 90) duty, pine nuts feature in Sicilian-inspired dishes, as well as being used to add texture and a nutty creaminess to salads. Walnuts get roasted and tossed with oil and salt flakes for a snack or to be chopped and dropped on salads. They're made into a paste to smear over baked salmon with tahini, mint and pomegranate molasses, or for a different take on Skordalia (p. 373). Almonds and pistachio nuts get chopped for salads, too, and are constantly in demand as a snack, as are cashew nuts.

Sesame seeds get sprinkled over pies, sausage rolls, hamburger buns and other baked goods, while also getting scattered over noodle salads. I also keep a dedicated sesame grinder (which you can find online and in specialty Japanese supermarkets) on hand to give dressings a nutty flourish. Pepitas are always a lovely addition to a salad, and are marvellous gently toasted, as are sesame seeds. Linseeds end up in crackers (see p. 839) or a loaf (see p. 376) with sunflower seeds and other crunchy delights, the gelling qualities of chia make it ideal to use in puddings, and poppy seeds get sprinkled on bagels and buns.

My stable of pulses extends to several types of lentils (pp. 18–9), including various types for dal (pp. 388–9), elegant Puy lentils and black beluga lentils for warm salads, standard green and brown lentils for soups and braising, and red lentils for soups, purees and patties. I keep split peas for Pea & ham soup (p. 334), and an array of dried beans, from adzuki to kidney, borlotti (cranberry), dried broad (fava) beans, black turtle beans, great northern, kidney, cannellini and haricot (navy), as well as giant Greek white beans for Gigantes plaki (p. 380). Chickpeas are always well stocked, for hummus, and I love them in salads, curries (see p. 633), for Falafel (p. 432), and in Harira (p. 461).

A well-stocked pantry for me is rich with grains, seeds and nuts, but, like with spices, more is not better, as they will all deteriorate over time. Nuts and seeds contain oils that can be very good for you, but they are generally not terribly stable, meaning that they will become rancid under suboptimal conditions or simply over time. Rancid nuts and seeds are woeful things, and they will ruin any dish they end up in. And while dried pulses are somewhat hardier, they do not last forever.

Dried beans, chickpeas and lentils will all deteriorate, with chickpeas in particular becoming almost impenetrably hard, while lentils will become brittle and chalky. Old pulses will cook unevenly, and some may never soften. It's always best to buy from a shop that has a high turnover, and then to ensure that you have a reasonably high turnover, too. They will all last for a long time, and remain in good condition for most of that time, but the quality will dip eventually. Less than a year is a reasonable marker to maintain quality, in my book. I do have the odd tin of chickpeas or beans in the cupboard, for emergencies, but I don't generally use them. I'm not a big fan of the flavour, but if well drained and rinsed, with plenty of spices then braised well to take on flavour, they can work well.

Nuts and seeds need to be used much more swiftly, and should only be bought from busy stores. I have always found Middle Eastern specialty grocers to be very reliable sources of nuts, as they play a big part in the varied cuisines. They're also generally very good sources of spices and dried fruits – currants, plump sultanas (golden raisins) and green raisins are always in my pantry.

No matter what I am storing, I do so in airtight containers or jars in a cool, dark place. Glass jars are an immensely practical way to manage things like pulses and grains, as you can see what's in there and how much is left. It's also a good prompt to remind you to use this or that, factoring it into your meal planning.

If I happen to end up with too many nuts or seeds (I sometimes overestimate my already large appetite for new-season walnuts – a complete joy that is hard to reconcile against the floury and bitter ones that are all too common), I store them in the freezer, which you can do anyway, if you prefer. The freezer is also often a good place for nuts with high oil contents, like macadamia nuts and pine nuts. If there are ever little cobweb-like stringy bits in your nut containers, there is a critter present. It is best to throw them out and wash the container in very hot water, lest they spread through the pantry.

For more on grains, pulses, seeds and nuts, see the Essentials section (p. 6).

Soaking nuts

Soaking grains, nuts, seeds and legumes is quite an ancient process, and while it is naturally speculation to ascribe the exact reasoning to how this practice came about, and persisted, it's not hard to make an educated guess once you understand how seeds operate. I say seeds, as this is what they all are. Grains, nuts, seeds and legumes are all basically plant embryos waiting for the right conditions – soil, water, warmth/light – to deploy their energy stores and grow.

I'm going to leave the hard science to others, but the essence is that a seed is built to survive difficult conditions before it can flourish in optimal ones. It just wouldn't be very good at its job otherwise. In fact, the delivery method for many seeds is essentially hostile, and they often pass through an animal's digestive tract before finding more fertile surroundings. Evolution has ensured that most seeds are quite indigestible, so that they can survive and flourish as plants once their journey is complete.

So, while a seed may have loads of nutritional positives on paper, these are sometimes bound up and not bioavailable. Once that seed finds the right conditions, all of that changes, and the barriers come down, releasing all the inherent goodness to power growth. What soaking does is replicate positive sprouting/growing conditions, and in turn this alters the seeds so that they are more digestible and more nutritious.

Sure, at first, soaking something for 12–24 hours seems like an unimaginable burden, and something that requires too much foresight, but, trust me, it's not. The 10–15 seconds it takes to tip some chickpeas or the like into a bowl with a pinch of salt (with grains, a squirt of acid is best, such as a little lemon juice or vinegar) and then fill with water shouldn't interrupt your day too much, and you don't need to watch them for the 12–24 hours, in fact I would really advise against it – you'd get quite bored. Also, if you soak them for 6 hours, that's better than not at all, and who cares if it's 12 or 24 or even 36 hours. However, buckwheat should only be soaked for up to 6 hours. You can also then cook pulses and leave them in the fridge for a week in their cooking water, ready to add to salads or soups and the like, or to whiz into a dip. Soak first, ask questions later, I say.

Sometimes, I will just soak a few bowls with whatever I have on hand – chickpeas, lima beans, haricot (navy) beans, borlotti (cranberry) beans – and they then form the basis of some meals for the week: buttery soft lima beans tossed with chopped soft herbs and plenty of extra-virgin olive oil, finished with hard-boiled eggs and white anchovies; chickpeas whizzed into hummus, added to a lamb curry, or used to beef up a tabouleh-like salad with tomato and plenty of chopped parsley; haricot (navy) beans mixed through braised chicory (witlof/endive) with a lemon and olive oil dressing; any cooked legume combined with anything you like to eat raw as a salad will be great, just use good oil (always), make sure it's bright with acid (lemon juice, vinegar) and season well, and add some chopped almonds, sliced chilli ... you pick – it's going to be great.

Activating nuts

If you want to soak nuts to 'activate' them (making the nutrients more bioavailable), you will need to dry them once drained. Soaking for 12–24 hours (cashew nuts for 6–8 hours only though, as they can become slimy, with a tainted flavour) with a pinch of salt should do the job, but then they do need to be dehydrated at low temperatures until crunchy again. You can do this in a dedicated dehydrator, if you have one, which may take 12 hours or even 24, but results will vary so just check the nuts occasionally. A very low oven will also work, and, again, the timing will very much depend on the nuts and the temperature of your oven. The key is to do this slowly, though, as the nutrients will be better preserved. You can naturally take them in and out for those times when you need to actually cook something.

Roasting nuts

Always lay nuts and seeds on a lined tray in a single layer and roast, checking regularly. Roast whole almonds, hazelnuts, brazil nuts, cashew nuts, pistachio nuts, walnuts, pecans, macadamia nuts and peanuts at 160°C (320°F) fan-forced for 10–12 minutes; flaked or slithered almonds at 170°C (340°F) fan-forced for 10–15 minutes; and pine nuts, sunflower seeds, pumpkin seeds and sesame seeds at 170°C (340°F) fan-forced for 5 minutes. Then shake and check before roasting for another 5 minutes or so.

Cooking pulses

After soaking, always discard the water and rinse the pulses before cooking. Cook in a large saucepan with ample water. Bring the pulses to the boil for a few minutes, then cook at a rapid simmer. Skim off any impurities as they cook, as these can contain some of the indigestible carbohydrates that can cause digestive issues. To salt the water or not to salt the water? The old wisdom says that salting the water will harden the skins of pulses, but science says the opposite – that it helps to break down any toughness. Both methods will work. Force of habit means I don't salt the water, but it's up to you. If you want to soften the skins, bicarbonate of soda (baking soda) can be your friend, but mainly if you're after a puree. Half a teaspoon in the water while cooking will yield terrifically soft and creamy chickpeas (or any beans), ideal for Hummus (p. 374), but they'll likely be too soft for salads, curries or the like. Without bicarbonate of soda (baking soda), some chickpeas can take from 45 minutes up to 2 hours to cook, especially if they're old. It's hard to generalise about the cooking time of pulses, as they can vary wildly. In general, chickpeas will take the longest, while most other pulses will take between 30 minutes and an hour, if soaked beforehand. Lentils are generally the quickest pulses to cook, usually about 15–20 minutes but up to 30 minutes for some types, and they can become mushy very quickly, so keep an eye on them. If using for salads, I tend to blanch lentils before draining and then cooking, as the flavour can be muddy otherwise. All pulses will take longer if not soaked, and I find they can be brittle and cook unevenly. If I have forgotten, I will soak for as long as possible in hot water. As a rough guide, cooked pulses will yield about double the dried weight.

The warmth of freshly cooked pulses absorbs a vinaigrette or dressing for a salad beautifully, giving them an acid lift and plenty of flavour. Toss freshly cooked chickpeas in a French-style vinaigrette (p. 88) with lots of chopped mint, chives, tarragon, parsley and/or coriander. Or try adding a little crumbled goat's cheese or feta to the mix as well. Cannellini beans, butterbeans also appreciate the same treatment, and you can also experiment by adding a spice as well like some ground cumin or a little fermented chilli or Harissa (p. 92). Freshly cooked puy lentils with vinaigrette, lots of parsley and ham hock meat (see p. 324) is another lovely combination.

Cooking grains

Grains should similarly be drained and washed before cooking in ample water. The cooking time will vary, with quinoa, buckwheat (if these aren't soaked, they need to be rinsed as they have a coating of saponin, which can be very bitter) and cracked freekeh relatively quick, between 15–20 minutes; pearled barley and amaranth are more like 30 minutes. If using wholegrain barley, the cooking time might be closer to an hour, and wholegrain freekeh around 40 minutes. Wild rice, which is not really rice, but seeds from four species of grass, will take about 35 minutes for an al dente result, which I prefer. As with pulses, it's important not to rely on strict timings, but rather to watch and check them. With experience, you will be able to tell to a degree from the appearance of the grains, but tasting is the best indicator. And I always like a little chew left in grains, but that's up to you.

The absorption method

White rice

I don't own a rice cooker. They are economical and effective, but I am a bit stubborn about cooking rice in a saucepan. I think the results are better, and I suppose I have cooked enough of it that I don't find it a burden. Plus, I don't need the extra clutter. Having said that, rice cookers are handy for larger amounts, and they keep the rice hot until needed.

This is the classic absorption method I use. Rinse 400 g (14 oz/2 cups) of jasmine or basmati rice in about three changes of cold water, until the water is mostly clear. Tip the rice into a heavy-based saucepan, then cover with about 600 ml (20½ fl oz) of boiling water, so it comes about 2 cm (¾ in) above the rice (if making a larger batch, never have the rice more than 3 cm (1¼ in) deep, or it won't get the surface heat required). Twist the pan from side to side to even out the level. Add a couple of pinches of salt, then bring the water to the boil. Wrap the saucepan lid with a tea towel (dish towel), knotting it at the handle. Once the water is boiling, turn the heat to as low as it goes, then cover with the lid, ensuring a tight seal. The tea towel will seal in the steam. Cook for 11 minutes, then sit for 5 minutes off the heat, fluffing with a fork before serving.

Japanese rice

Koshihikari is a polished short-grain rice for sushi and Japanese rice dishes. Add 330 g (11½ oz/ 1½) cups of rice and 500 ml (17 fl oz/2 cups) of boiling water to a saucepan. Add a pinch of salt, a pinch of sugar and a strip of kombu (soaked for 5 minutes first, then wiped) on top. Bring to a simmer and then quickly cover, reduce the heat to very low and cook for 12 minutes. Turn off the heat and stir in 1 tablespoon of mirin and 1 tablespoon of rice vinegar. Cover and stand for 5 minutes before using.

Brown rice

Follow the method for white rice, but use 800 ml (27 fl oz) boiling water for 400 g (14 oz/2 cups) rice, and allow the rice to cook for 30 minutes rather than 11 minutes.

Wholegrain black rice

Add 300 g (10½ oz/1½) cups of rice and 500 ml (17 fl oz/2 cups) of boiling water to a saucepan. Bring to a simmer and then quickly cover, reduce the heat to very low and cook for 35 minutes. Turn off the heat and stand for 10 minutes before stirring through.

Food safety concerns

There are some safety issues to be aware of with both rice and dried beans. Dried beans contain lectins that can be toxic, with kidney beans often cited as the most troublesome. Concentrations vary but it is best to play it safe, as improperly cooked beans can cause significant gastrointestinal stress and worse. Soaking then boiling will deactivate lectins, with the advice that 10 minutes at the boil is sufficient to render beans safe. Naturally, beans take a lot longer than this to cook, but starting at a brisk boil is recommended. Never toss beans into a dish that will be cooked very slowly, unless you have boiled them first.

Rice can become hazardous after cooking, with bacteria that is present in the growing conditions sometimes present on the processed grains. Those bacteria are heat tolerant, so cooking will not resolve the issue, with the spores multiplying at warm temperatures. Refrigeration will retard that growth, rendering them innocuous, but if you think you've kept that left-over rice too long, then it's best to start again. The best advice is to refrigerate cooked rice as soon possible, ideally within an hour or two, and to keep leftovers for no more than 4–5 days, and never, ever combine old left-over rice with new left-over rice.

Almond skordalia Ⓥ

Skordalia can be made with nuts, stale bread or potatoes, or a combination. The key to skordalia is actually garlic, though I don't push the flavour too hard here, instead focusing on the almond and sourdough notes. This is lovely with fish or vegetables, or as a dip. **Serves 4–6**

Pair with

Serve as a dip topped with crushed smoked almonds and quick-pickled onions.

Smear onto a platter, top with slices of ripe fig and dressed rocket (arugula) leaves, then drizzle with pomegranate molasses or aged balsamic vinegar.

Dollop on roasted pumpkin (winter squash) or lightly grilled vegetables, such as young asparagus, tender leeks or fennel slices.

Serve under seared fish.

2 large garlic cloves, sliced
100 g (3½ oz/⅔ cup) blanched almonds
180 ml (6 fl oz) full-cream (whole) milk

100 ml (3½ fl oz) water
100 g (3½ oz) Sourdough bread (p. 847), crusts removed, bread torn

Staples
EVOO, LMN

Heat a splash of oil in a deep-sided frying pan over a medium heat. Fry the garlic until fragrant, about 1 minute. Add the almonds, milk and water, season with salt and simmer for 5 minutes. Add the bread and simmer over a low heat for 3 minutes.

Tip the mixture into a blender and blitz, adding a couple of tablespoons of oil to form a thick, smooth paste. Add a little more oil or water to loosen as required.

Squeeze in lemon juice to sharpen, then adjust the seasoning to taste.

Fava ⒼⒻ Ⓥ ⓋⒼ

The name for this classic Greek dip is somewhat confusing, given that fava is another name for broad beans. In Greek, fava (or φάβα) refers to split peas, with the dip made from simmering them with onion and garlic until tender, then blitzing with plenty of oil and lemon juice. It really is a fabulous thing, and best served warm just after making, with freshly baked bread. **Serves 15**

Pair with

Fresh pitta breads (see p. 854).

Horta-style greens (p. 552), roasted vegetables, and feta or fried saganaki cheese.

Top with caramelised onions (see p. 598) with dried Greek oregano (rigani) stirred in at the end of cooking, scattered with capers and finished with a drizzle of oil.

150 ml (5 fl oz) extra-virgin olive oil
1 onion, diced
3 garlic cloves, sliced

400 g (14 oz) yellow split peas, well rinsed
1.75 litres (60 fl oz/7 cups) water

1½ tablespoons sherry vinegar, or any other vinegar

Staples
EVOO, S&P

Heat 50 ml (1¾ fl oz) of the oil in a saucepan over a medium heat. Fry the onion and garlic until lightly golden, about 6 minutes. Stir the split peas through, then add the water. Bring to a simmer, then turn the heat to low and cook for about 45 minutes, until very tender.

Strain off the liquid, reserving 150 ml (5 fl oz).

Add the split peas to a blender with the vinegar and remaining oil. Blitz until smooth, adding a little of the reserved liquid as needed until the dip is the consistency of thick cream.

Season with salt and pepper and serve warm, with a drizzle of oil over the top.

Make it a meal
Serve with skewered meats (see p. 312) or braised eggplant (aubergine), Horta-style greens (p. 552) and warm flatbreads (see p. 852).

Hummus (GF) (V) (VG)

I used to always add olive oil to my hummus – and it's good, very good. But Yotam Ottolenghi's polite but firm correction has seen the practice vanquished to hummuses past. There is no olive oil in hummus. Okay. For a super smooth and fluffy dip, use quality dried chickpeas that are reasonably fresh; left on the shelf too long, they become lethally hard, with uneven results likely, and they are almost impossible to cook. Bicarbonate of soda (baking soda) helps to soften the chickpeas, breaking down the pectins, which can otherwise harden (the minerals in your water can influence this, too); it also reduces the cooking time significantly. The other trick is to drizzle in iced water to finish while adjusting the consistency, to achieve an incredibly fluffy result. **Serves 6–8**

350 g (12½ oz) dried chickpeas, soaked overnight, drained
2 teaspoons bicarbonate of soda (baking soda)

200 g (7 oz) tahini
4 garlic cloves, finely grated
juice of 2 lemons
120 ml (4 fl oz) iced water, approximately

Staples
S&P

Add the chickpeas and bicarbonate of soda to a large saucepan and cover with plenty of cold water. Season lightly with salt and bring to the boil, then simmer for about 40 minutes, until very tender. The timing can vary greatly, but the bicarb will speed things up.

Drain the chickpeas, then tip into a blender and blitz to a stiff paste. Add the tahini, garlic and lemon juice and blitz for a minute or two. Drizzle in some iced water while processing, until the hummus is super smooth, light and fluffy but not too loose.

Adjust the seasoning to taste and serve. The hummus will keep for about a week in the fridge.

Pair with

This is wonderful served still warm with fresh pitta breads (see p. 854) as a standalone dish.

I like to reserve a few tablespoons of the cooked chickpeas to garnish the hummus. Fry a few sliced garlic cloves in oil until a little golden, then add a few teaspoons of roughly ground cumin seeds with the reserved chickpeas, tossing to coat and to toast. Pile the hummus onto a serving plate, drizzle with a little tahini, sprinkle with ground aleppo pepper and drizzle with a little good olive oil. Alternatively, along with the chickpeas, add Fermented cooked chilli sauce (p. 97) stirred through burnt butter (see p. 73).

Sprinkle Za'atar (p. 33) over the top.

Dolmades with rice, pine nuts, currants & lemon GF

These are a labour of love, but I think they are just so wonderful when made from scratch. They are a brilliant addition to a feast of meze, or as a snack to have on hand in the fridge. **Makes 50–60**

Pair with

Tzatziki (p. 507) or Greek yoghurt.

Serve alongside grilled meats and salad.

Pop in a lunchbox as is, or in a wrap with Hummus (opposite) and chilli.

Quick rice & peas GF V

We often have rice as a very quick snack in our house, usually before sport or after school. Add 1 tablespoon of oil, 50 g (1¾ oz) butter and 2 finely grated garlic cloves to a saucepan. Fry for 1 minute over a medium heat. Add 400 g (14 oz/2 cups) long-grain white rice, 600 ml (20½ fl oz) boiling water and 1 tablespoon of chicken or vegetable stock powder. Stir through and bring to a simmer. Cover and cook for 5 minutes over a low heat. Add 115 g (4 oz/¾ cup) frozen peas, cover and cook for 6 minutes. Turn off the heat and stand for 5 minutes, then fluff with a fork and serve with natural yoghurt and a handful of fresh mint, if you have it.

200 ml (7 fl oz) extra-virgin olive oil
1 onion, finely diced
6 garlic cloves, finely chopped
3 tablespoons currants
50 g (1¾ oz/⅓ cup) pine nuts
450 g (1 lb) long-grain white rice
5 anchovies, chopped

1½ teaspoons salt flakes
1 litre (34 fl oz/4 cups) Golden chicken stock (p. 54), or Classic white vegetable stock (p. 51)
1 tablespoon dried mint
juice of 4 lemons
50–60 preserved vine leaves, thoroughly rinsed

1 litre (34 fl oz/4 cups) hot water
1 tablespoon fennel seeds
10 allspice berries, or 3 teaspoons cumin seeds
1 fresh bay leaf

Staples
S&P

Heat 80 ml (2½ fl oz/⅓ cup) of the oil in a saucepan over a medium heat. Fry the onion, garlic, currants and pine nuts until the onion has softened, about 5 minutes. Add the rice, anchovies and salt flakes. Cook, stirring constantly, for 1 minute. Add the stock, mint and half the lemon juice.

Bring to the boil and cook, stirring frequently, until the rice has absorbed the liquid, about 5 minutes. Transfer to a bowl.

Preheat the oven to 180°C (350°F) fan-forced.

Drizzle a little of the oil into an ovenproof casserole dish. Lay a vine leaf flat on the bench and pile on a heaped tablespoon of the stuffing near the stem. Roll the stem end over, folding the edges in, and rolling up like a spring roll. Roll firmly but not too tight, as the rice will expand. Repeat until the mixture runs out. As each vine leaf is rolled, arrange the dolmades in the pan to form two tightly packed layers.

Combine the remaining lemon juice and oil with the remaining ingredients. Add a pinch of salt, then pour into the pan.

Place a circle of baking paper over the vine leaves, then weigh down with a heatproof plate large enough to just fit inside. Cover tightly and bake for 1 hour.

Cool at room temperature before serving or refrigerating. Resting the dolmades first gives the rice a chance to absorb all the liquid. Serve at room temperature.

Make it different
With lamb. Fry 150 g (5½ oz) minced (ground) lamb in the pan before adding the onion.

Make it vegan VG
Omit the anchovies, and add 2 teaspoons white miso paste to the vegetable stock.

Super seed loaf GF V VG

This densely packed gluten-free loaf is quite filling, with deliciously toasty flavours. It's great just with butter or hummus and salt flakes, and makes a lovely building block for your breakfast plate. **Makes 2 loaves**

150 g (5½ oz/¾ cup) white quinoa, rinsed
100 ml (3½ fl oz) maple syrup
650 ml (22 fl oz) water
3 tablespoons coconut oil
2 teaspoons caraway seeds
2 teaspoons fennel seeds
2 teaspoons salt flakes
1½ teaspoons ground black pepper

150 g (5½ oz/1 cup) raw almonds
100 g (3½ oz/⅔ cup) linseeds (flax seeds)
150 g (5½ oz/1¼ cups) sunflower seeds
3 tablespoons chia seeds
80 g (2¾ oz/⅔ cup) pepitas (pumpkin seeds)
35 g (1¼ oz/¼ cup) sesame seeds

40 g (1½ oz) coconut flour
30 g (1 oz) psyllium husk powder
1 tablespoon maca powder

To line the tin
2 tablespoons sesame seeds
2 tablespoons pepitas (pumpkin seeds)
1 tablespoon fennel seeds

Cook the quinoa in a saucepan of boiling water for 8 minutes, then drain well.

Pour the maple syrup and water into a saucepan. Add the coconut oil, spices, salt and pepper and warm through for 2 minutes over a low heat. Set aside.

In a food processor, blitz the almonds, linseeds, sunflower seeds and chia seeds into a fine powder.

Tip into a large bowl, along with the quinoa, pepitas, sesame seeds, coconut flour, psyllium and maca. Mix to combine, then add the maple syrup mixture and mix in well, adding a little more water if needed; the mixture will be stiff.

Line two 23 cm (9 in) loaf (bar) tins with baking paper. Sprinkle the extra seeds evenly in both tins, then divide the dough between them, packing it in firmly. Stand for 2 hours at room temperature, which will soften the seeds and bring the mixture together.

Preheat the oven to 180°C (350°F) fan-forced.

Bake the loaves for 1 hour. Turn the loaves out onto an unlined baking tray and bake for a further 15 minutes to brown the outside of the loaves.

Cool before slicing. The bread will keep in an airtight container or wrapped in the fridge for up to 2 weeks.

Pair with

Simply spread with butter and jam.

Top with Hummus (p. 374) or Almond skordalia (p. 373).

Spread with goat's curd or ricotta and drizzle with extra-virgin olive oil.

Pile scrambled eggs (see p. 351) on top and finish with chopped chives.

Top with avocado with lemon, salt flakes and plenty of pepper, perhaps a curl of gravlax (pp. 169, 171) and a poached egg or two.

Top with Labneh (p. 362) and Sweet Zuni-style pickles (p. 668).

Seasoned pistachio dust GF V VG

This bright green pistachio dust is delicately spiced and is wonderful sprinkled on pâté, Chicken liver parfait (p. 233), pan-fried chicken livers (see p. 234), and pan-seared, grilled or roasted poultry. Simply add 80 g (2¾ oz/⅔ cup) pistachio kernels to a spice grinder, along with 2 juniper berries, ½ teaspoon brown sugar, ½ teaspoon salt flakes, ½ teaspoon ground white pepper and the zest of ½ orange and blitz into a powder. Keep in an airtight container and use within 3 days.

Nutty, salty, sweet & seedy crunch mix ⓥ

Pair with

Yoghurt (p. 365) or Whipped vanilla ricotta (p. 799) with fruit for breakfast.

Use to finish steel-cut oats soaked overnight in yoghurt and water.

Enjoy as is for a snack.

Sprinkle over a green vegetable bowl with rice.

Top a rocket (arugula), pear and parmesan salad.

Scatter over roasted vegetables, such as pumpkin (winter squash) or carrot, and serve with tahini.

Sprinkle over pan-seared haloumi or burrata.

This seed, nut and spice mix is on the savoury side, but the touch of coconut oil, cinnamon and a little maple syrup gives a sweet undertone to the saltiness and makes the seed flavour really prominent. **Makes about 750 g (1 lb 11 oz)**

3 egg whites
3 tablespoons coconut oil
1½ tablespoons extra-virgin olive oil
1 tablespoon light soy sauce
2 tablespoons maple syrup
1½ teaspoons ground cinnamon

1 teaspoon chilli powder, or ground aleppo pepper
1½ teaspoons salt flakes
150 g (5½ oz/1 cup) pepitas (pumpkin seeds)
150 g (5½ oz/1 cup) toasted blanched almonds
150 g (5½ oz/1¼ cups) sunflower seeds

80 g (2¾ oz) buckwheat
80 g (2¾ oz/½ cup) sesame seeds
60 g (2 oz/⅓ cup) pistachio kernels
2 teaspoons fennel seeds
1 tablespoon caraway seeds
1 tablespoon nigella seeds

Preheat the oven to 160°C (320°F) fan-forced. Line two baking trays with baking paper.

In a large bowl, whisk together the egg whites, oils, soy sauce, maple syrup, cinnamon, chilli and salt. And the remaining ingredients and combine well.

Spread the mixture across the baking trays, smoothing it out flat. Bake for about 40 minutes, stirring every 12 minutes to toast evenly, until golden.

Cool, then store in an airtight container in the pantry, where it will keep for about 2 months.

Make it different
Nutty granola. To make granola, add 120 g (4½ oz) shredded or shaved coconut and 150 g (5½ oz/1½ cups) rolled (porridge) oats to the mixture.

Buckwheat blinis ⓥ

Pair with

Top with diced smoked eel, and a little crème fraîche with chives mixed through.

Top with gravlax (pp. 169, 171) or smoked salmon along with salmon roe and crème fraîche or grated hard-boiled egg, crème fraîche and chopped chives.

This is an alternative to potato or straight wheat blinis, with the buckwheat adding a nutty richness. However, you can make them plain by simply omitting the buckwheat flour. **Makes 10–12**

400 ml (13½ fl oz) full-cream (whole) milk, warmed to blood temperature
3 teaspoons dried yeast

2 pinches of caster (superfine) sugar
175 g (6 oz) plain (all-purpose) flour
½ teaspoon fine sea salt

50 g (1¾ oz) buckwheat flour
2 eggs, separated

Staples
BTR, EVOO, S&P

Add the milk, yeast, sugar and a tablespoon of the plain flour to a bowl and whisk well. Set aside for 5–10 minutes, until the yeast activates and foams.

Sift the remaining flours and salt into a large bowl. Add the yeast mixture and combine into a smooth batter. Cover with a damp tea towel (dish towel) and leave in a warm place for 1–1½ hours, until the mixture doubles in size and bubbles.

Whisk the egg whites into stiff peaks. Stir the egg yolks into the batter to combine, then fold in the egg whites. Cover and set aside for 10 minutes.

Heat a large knob of butter and a splash of oil in a large frying pan over a medium–high heat. Add a tablespoon of batter per blini and cook for about 1 minute, until small bubbles appear on top, and the blinis are golden underneath. Flip and cook for 1 minute on the other side. You should be able to cook about four at once.

Repeat for the remaining batter, adding more butter and oil as needed.

Pearled barley, parsley & toasted pepita salad Ⓥ Ⓥ🄶

I love using parsley as a leading flavour in dishes such as tabouleh. Parsley is especially good in the cooler months, deeply green and intense in flavour, whereas summer parsley tends to bolt quickly and become coarse in both flavour and texture. Parsley is fabulous with grains, as tabouleh attests to; smoothly textured and nutty pearled barley is also ideal. Here, pepitas (pumpkin seeds) add even more texture and a toasted accent. **Serves 4–6**

200 g (7 oz) pearled barley
1 garlic clove, finely grated
1 teaspoon salt flakes
1½ teaspoons caster (superfine) sugar
100 ml (3½ fl oz) extra-virgin olive oil

2½ tablespoons white-wine vinegar
juice of 1 lemon
1½ bunches of flat-leaf (Italian) parsley, leaves and fine stalks chopped

1 white salad onion, finely diced
50 g (1¾ oz/⅓ cup) toasted pepitas (pumpkin seeds)

Staples
S&P

Put the barley in a saucepan, cover generously with cold water and bring to the boil. Reduce the heat and simmer for about 20 minutes, until tender but still with a little bite. Drain and set aside to cool.

Add the garlic, salt and sugar to a bowl, then work into a paste with the back of a spoon. Add the oil, vinegar and lemon juice, season with pepper and whisk until emulsified.

Add the barley, parsley and onion to the bowl and toss to combine well. Adjust the seasoning to taste, then pile onto a serving plate. Scatter the pepitas over and serve.

Pair with

Roast lamb or chicken.

Baked or grilled fish.

Dress it up further by adding diced tomato and/or cucumber, with a slab of feta crumbled over.

Wild rice, herb, almond & currant salad 🄶🄵 Ⓥ Ⓥ🄶

Gloriously chewy, nutty and fresh at the same time, this salad is a wonderful side for poultry. **Serves 4–6**

200 g (7 oz) wild rice
80 g (2¾ oz/½ cup) currants
100 ml (3½ fl oz) sherry vinegar
120 g (4½ oz/¾ cup) toasted blanched almonds, crushed

40 g (1½ oz/¼ cup) toasted sesame seeds
6 dill sprigs, fronds roughly chopped
6 coriander (cilantro) sprigs, stalks finely chopped, leaves roughly chopped

150 ml (5 fl oz) extra-virgin olive oil

Staples
S&P

Cook the rice (see p. 371), then drain.

Meanwhile, add the currants and half the vinegar to a small saucepan and simmer for 1 minute, then set aside.

In a large bowl, combine the warm rice, almonds, sesame seeds and herbs.

Add the oil and remaining vinegar to the currants, season with salt and pepper and mix together.

Pour the dressing over the salad and toss, then serve.

Pair with

Grilled or roasted chicken (see p. 229).

Lebanese skewered chicken (p. 247).

Pan-fried haloumi.

Fried tofu.

Braised greens, such as silverbeet (Swiss chard) or spinach.

Byzantine salad Ⓥ ⓋⒼ

The Byzantine diet apparently centred around plenty of grains, legumes, fresh vegetables and fish, which sounds like an extraordinarily good mix, both from a culinary and health perspective. This salad pays homage to the Byzantine passion for grains and pulses, though I can't claim the recipe to be remotely connected with that time or place. It's a textural adventure, with nuts and seeds upping the game even further, with a gentle vinegar tang and sour burst from the barberries, which look brilliant in the salad. I often make versions of this when my family comes together, especially to serve with lamb. It's best at room temperature, tossed through on the day, but it will keep for a few days if there is any left over. Parsley and coriander would also work, but I favour the undertone of dill and the burst of mint freshness on the palate. **Serves 12**

Pair with

Silverbeet & haloumi pies (p. 563).

Slow-roasted lamb shoulder (p. 304).

Slow-roasted pork shoulder (p. 333).

Salt-baked fish (see p. 175) or grilled whole fish.

Roasted vegetables, such as beetroot (beet), carrot or pumpkin (winter squash).

Chicken chops with wild rice salad ⒼⒻ

Slash 6 chicken chops three times each through the skin, then season heavily with salt and pepper and coat with olive oil. Add to a large cold frying pan, skin side down, and place over a medium–high heat. Cook for 10 minutes undisturbed, then flip and cook for 6 minutes; you could add some thyme, sage or rosemary now, too. Remove from the heat, cover loosely with foil and rest for 10 minutes to finish cooking and relax, then serve with the pan juices poured over, or with a sprinkle of sherry, balsamic or white-wine vinegar, and a wild rice salad (see p. 378) on the side.

100 g (3½ oz) barberries and/or currants (barberries are my preference)
80 ml (2½ fl oz/⅓ cup) red-wine vinegar, or sherry vinegar
150 g (5½ oz) green lentils
150 g (5½ oz) pearled barley
150 g (5½ oz) cracked freekeh

70 g (2½ oz/½ cup) sunflower seeds
70 g (2½ oz/½ cup) pepitas (pumpkin seeds)
60 g (2 oz/⅓ cup) blanched almonds, chopped
1 large white salad onion, very finely diced
1 bunch of dill, fronds chopped

1 bunch of mint, leaves picked

Cumin & vinegar dressing
3 teaspoons cumin seeds
3 teaspoons salt flakes
180 ml (6 fl oz) extra-virgin olive oil
120 ml (4 fl oz) red-wine vinegar, or sherry vinegar

Staples
S&P

Put the barberries or currants in a small saucepan with the vinegar. Bring to the boil, then take off the heat and set aside.

Add the lentils, barley and freekeh to separate saucepans of boiling lightly salted water. Cook the lentils for about 18 minutes, the barley for about 35 minutes, and the freekeh for about 20 minutes, until the lentils and grains are tender. Drain and cool to room temperature.

Meanwhile, preheat the oven to 170°C (340°F) fan-forced. Spread the sunflower seeds, pepitas and almonds on a baking tray and toast in the oven until fragrant and lightly coloured, about 8 minutes. Drizzle over a little oil, season with salt and pepper and toss.

Tip the room-temperature lentils and grains into a large bowl, then tip in the seeds and nuts, onion and herbs. Add the barberries and any residual vinegar.

For the dressing, grind the cumin seeds and salt using a mortar and pestle, then add the oil and vinegar and combine. Tip over the salad and toss; the salad should be well dressed and luscious.

Adjust the seasoning to taste, then pile onto a serving plate. It's worth mixing the salad every now and then at the table, as the dressing tends to seep to the bottom.

Black bean, quinoa & cherry tomato salad (GF) (V) (VG)

White quinoa and black beans are striking together, especially with the pops of red from the cherry tomatoes and flecks of green coriander (cilantro). Aside from the visuals, I also find this salad very satisfying to eat, and it's good for you, too, packed with plant protein and micronutrients. **Serves 4**

200 g (7 oz) dried turtle beans, soaked overnight
200 g (7 oz/1 cup) white quinoa, rinsed
500 ml (17 fl oz/2 cups) water
400 g (14 oz) cherry tomatoes, halved

2 French shallots, finely sliced
2 tablespoons extra-virgin olive oil
2 tablespoons white-wine vinegar
¼ teaspoon cayenne pepper

¼ teaspoon freshly ground black pepper
¼ bunch of coriander (cilantro), leaves and fine stems finely chopped
1 teaspoon cumin seeds

Staples
EVOO, S&P

Pair with
Tinned tuna, or a seared piece of fish.

Pitta breads (see p. 854) and Guacamole (pp. 412–3).

Chilli con pollo (p. 232) or beef con carne.

Grilled prawns (shrimp) or a chargrilled steak.

Drain the beans, place in a saucepan and cover generously with cold water. Lightly salt and bring to the boil over a medium heat, then simmer for about 30 minutes, until properly tender. Drain and set aside.

Meanwhile, toast the quinoa in a dry saucepan for 5 minutes until it starts to pop. Add the water and simmer until absorbed, about 15 minutes. Remove from the heat, then cover and allow to steam for 10 minutes.

Heat a good splash of oil in a frying pan over a medium heat. Add about 60 g (2 oz/⅓ cup) of the quinoa and toss frequently for about 10 minutes, until golden. Drain on paper towel; the quinoa will become crunchy once cooled.

In a large bowl, combine the tomatoes, shallot, oil, vinegar, cayenne pepper and pepper. Add most of the coriander.

In a dry pan, toast the cumin seeds until fragrant, about 30 seconds. Tip over the salad, add the quinoa and beans, season with salt and combine.

Finish by scattering the crisp quinoa and remaining coriander over the top.

Make it faster
Instead of turtle beans, mix a drained 400 g (14 oz) tin of black beans through the salad.

Gigantes plaki (GF) (V) (VG)

I have a lot of love for beans cooked like this – such basic ingredients that deliver so much flavour. It's a dish you come across all over Greece, with the beans baked in a tomatoey braise, often weeping a generous amount of good olive oil, and just crying out for bread. As the name suggests, the beans are huge, and become meaty and creamy when cooked. Track down a Greek grocer to get the right ones, and to ensure there's high turnover, as the beans should be quite white and never shrivelled or with a yellow tinge, which would suggest that they're old and won't soften properly or evenly. You can use tinned beans here, if you like – but it's worth going the extra mile. **Serves 4–6**

Pair with
Some hard feta, black olives and good bread.

500 g (1 lb 2 oz) dried
   gigantes beans, or lima
   beans, soaked overnight
   and drained
1 carrot, finely diced
2 fresh bay leaves
100 ml (3½ fl oz) extra-virgin
   olive oil
2 onions, finely diced

2 garlic cloves, finely diced
4 celery stalks, finely diced
400 g (14 oz) tin diced
   tomatoes
1½ tablespoons tomato
   paste (concentrated purée)
2 teaspoons ground
   cinnamon
1 teaspoon chilli flakes

1½ teaspoons caster
   (superfine) sugar
¼ bunch of flat-leaf (Italian)
   parsley, leaves chopped

Staples
LMN, S&P

Put the beans in a large saucepan and cover with about 8 cm (3¼ in) water. Lightly salt, add the carrot and bay leaves and bring to the boil. Simmer for about 35 minutes, until the beans are just tender and the water is mostly absorbed.

Preheat the oven to 180°C (350°F) fan-forced.

Heat the oil in a large saucepan over a medium heat. Fry the onion, garlic and celery until softened and starting to caramelise, about 10 minutes. Stir in the tomato, tomato paste, cinnamon, chilli and sugar, season with salt, then cook over a low heat for 5 minutes.

Stir in the bean mixture; the mixture should be wet but not soupy.

Transfer to a baking dish and bake for 35 minutes.

Serve hot, with the parsley scattered over, and a good squeeze of lemon.

Spiced green soup GF V

Pair with

A dollop of yoghurt and a swirl of sriracha or Fermented cooked chilli sauce (p. 97) is all this needs.

A few handfuls of lentils and a bunch of greens, some curry powder, herbs … nothing fancy, but just so delicious. This soup purées to a richly soothing green, while the brown lentils give it a deep flavour and excellent body. It is best served on the day, while the intense colour is at its most vibrant. **Serves 4**

100 g (3½ oz) butter
1 onion, finely diced
2 garlic cloves, finely
   chopped
150 g (5½ oz) brown lentils,
   or Puy or tiny blue-green
   lentils
2 tablespoons curry powder
2 teaspoons ground cumin
600 ml (20½ fl oz) hot water

1 bunch of silverbeet (Swiss
   chard), or English spinach,
   cut across into 1.5 cm
   (½ in) wide strips
500 ml (17 fl oz/2 cups)
   Golden chicken stock
   (p. 54), White chicken
   stock (p. 54), Vegetable
   stock (p. 51) or water

150 ml (5 fl oz) pouring
   (single/light) cream
½ bunch of coriander
   (cilantro), or flat-leaf (Italian)
   parsley, finely chopped,
   stems and all

Staples
EVOO, S&P

Heat the butter and a splash of oil in a large saucepan over a medium heat. Fry the onion and garlic until softened and starting to colour, about 5 minutes. Add the lentils, curry powder and cumin and stir through for about 2 minutes.

Stir in the water and simmer for 5 minutes. Add the silverbeet and stock, pushing the greens under the liquid as they wilt. Season with salt and pepper and bring to a simmer. Cook for 15 minutes, then stir in the cream and herbs and simmer for 5 minutes.

Transfer to a blender in batches to blitz, or use a stick blender. Adjust the seasoning to taste, and bring back to a simmer before serving.

Japanese mixed rice & grains Ⓥ ⓋⒼ

Here you'll end up with rice that is sticky and glutinous and delightfully chewy. It's an immensely soothing breakfast dish, but can equally step in as a dinner accompaniment. You'll need to start preparing a day ahead. **Serves 6**

2 tablespoons glutinous rice
1 tablespoon black rice
1 tablespoon red rice
2 tablespoons dried adzuki
   beans, or mung beans

1 tablespoon buckwheat
550 g (1 lb 3 oz/2½ cups)
   sushi rice
1 tablespoon toasted
   sesame seeds

1 teaspoon salt flakes
2 tablespoons mirin
2 tablespoons rice vinegar

Staples
S&P

Add the glutinous, black and red rices to a bowl with the beans and the buckwheat. Cover with ample hot water (from a kettle), and leave to soak overnight.

The next day, drain the mixture and add the sushi rice, then tip into a saucepan with the sesame seeds and salt. Cover with boiling water by 2 cm (¾ in), then bring to a simmer. Turn the heat to low, cover and cook for 11 minutes, then turn off the heat and stand covered for 5 minutes.

Fluff the rice with a fork. Mix the mirin and vinegar through.

Serve straight away, or reheat the next day by toasting in a dry frying pan.

Pair with

Serve with finely shaved slices of cooked pork, Kimchi (p. 455), a fried egg and Fermented cooked chilli sauce (p. 97) or sriracha, and top with shaved raw white cabbage – this is breakfast heaven in my book.

I also like this for lunch, topped with pickled cucumber, wakame, pickled ginger and cooked spinach, and maybe a seared fish fillet, sliced White-poached chicken (p. 230) or left-over roast chicken.

Baked polenta with gorgonzola, radicchio, walnuts & balsamic ⒼⒻ Ⓥ

Pour the Polenta (opposite) into individual ovenproof dishes or a larger tray. Set in the fridge for 2–3 hours, then cut into slabs. Top with gorgonzola and stracchino or fontina cheese, and a good grating of parmesan. Bake at 200°C (400°F) for 15 minutes to melt the cheeses and warm the polenta through. Serve topped with crushed walnuts, and radicchio dressed with olive oil, lemon juice and balsamic vinegar.

Baked polenta with stracchino & greens ⒼⒻ Ⓥ

Pour the Polenta (opposite) into a large ovenproof dish. Top with slices of stracchino or taleggio cheese and broccolini. Bake at 180°C (350°F) for 5 minutes to melt the cheese. Serve with boiled greens.

Polenta Ⓥ

Pair with

Abbacchio (p. 315).

Soft-poached eggs with truffles and Parmigiana Reggiano.

Soft-poached eggs with crabmeat, crustacean essence and Braised artichokes with garlic, bay & white wine glaze (p. 534).

A meat Ragù (pp. 259, 283, 335, 336, 535) or Mushroom ragù (p. 576), with plenty of parmesan.

Polenta chips ⒼⒻ Ⓥ

Pour the Polenta (right) into a deep-sided tray, to about 3 cm (1¼ in) deep. Chill for 2–3 hours, until firmly set, then turn out and cut into fat chips. Deep-fry for about 6 minutes at 180°C (350°F). Season with salt and serve with Aïoli (p. 76) or a tomato relish, or grate over parmesan and sprinkle with rosemary salt.

Pair with

Shallow-fry wonton skins for a crunchy textural contrast to the congee.

Roll up toasted nori sheets and snip finely with scissors over the finished dish.

It's not actually traditional, but I like milk in my polenta, as it lends body and flavour. Instead, you can use more stock or water, if you prefer. You can of course also make instant polenta, which I certainly do when time is tight, but the traditional way yields a superior result. **Serves 8–10**

1 litre (34 fl oz/4 cups) full-cream (whole) milk
1.5 litres (51 fl oz/6 cups) Golden chicken stock (p. 54), or water
2 fresh bay leaves
1 teaspoon salt flakes

300 g (10½ oz) traditional polenta
100 ml (3½ fl oz) extra-virgin olive oil
100 g (3½ oz) Grana Padano, finely grated (optional)

Staples
S&P

Add the milk, stock, bay leaves and salt to a large saucepan over a high heat. Just before it simmers, rain in the polenta in a slow and steady stream, stirring continuously with a whisk. Stir for 3 minutes to thicken, then reduce the heat to very low.

Continue to cook for 25 minutes, stirring with a wooden spoon. Once the polenta is coming away from the sides of the pan a little, stir in the oil and parmesan, if using. Season and serve warm.

Congee

I do love congee, and I genuinely crave it when I'm feeling flat. I'm not sure of its genuine benefits, but it does the trick for me. **Serves 4**

4 eggs
80 ml (2½ fl oz/⅓ cup) soy sauce
1 teaspoon sesame oil
100 g (3½ oz) baby English spinach leaves, blanched and drained
150 g (5½ oz) cooked chicken, shredded
4 spring onions (scallions), finely sliced

8 cm (3¼ in) piece of fresh ginger, peeled and julienned
1 long green chilli, finely sliced

To serve
micro cress, or coriander (cilantro) leaves
pickled seaweed
furikake
sriracha sauce
soy sauce

Congee
1.5 litres (51 fl oz/6 cups) hot water
1 litre (34 fl oz/4 cups) White chicken stock (p. 54)
225 g (8 oz/1 cup) sushi rice
2 thick slices of fresh ginger
1 teaspoon salt flakes
1 star anise

Add all the congee ingredients to a large, wide-based saucepan and bring to a simmer. Cook for 45 minutes at a slow simmer, stirring occasionally, until a porridge-like consistency.

Just before serving, fry the eggs sunny side up (see p. 348) in a non-stick frying pan.

Ladle the congee into serving bowls. Drizzle the soy sauce and sesame oil over each, and top with the spinach, chicken, fried eggs, spring onion, ginger and chilli.

Serve with the other ingredients on the side, for people to help themselves.

Make it different

The toppings listed are suggestions only. Left-over roast duck (pp. 258, 264) or pork belly (see p. 332), for example, would be fantastic additions. For a seafood version, pan-fry prawn (shrimp) cutlets and drop on top of the cooked congee.

If you don't have stock, you can make the congee with water and two chicken leg quarters (marylands) in the pot, simmering as instructed.

Coconut & pandan jasmine rice (GF) (V) (VG)

Jasmine rice is delicate and fragrant with a sticky, rich finish, making it ideal for spicy curries and Thai-style salads. This version is perfumed with pandan and coconut, so it's not something that I would serve with coconut-based curries.
Serves 4–6

400 ml (13½ fl oz) coconut milk
500 ml (17 fl oz/2 cups) water
400 g (14 oz) jasmine rice

50 g (1¾ oz/¾ cup) shredded coconut
2 tablespoons finely grated palm sugar (jaggery), or caster (superfine) sugar

1½ teaspoons salt flakes
1 pandan leaf, tied in a knot, or 4 makrut lime leaves

In a saucepan, bring the coconut milk and water to a gentle simmer over a medium heat.

Add the remaining ingredients to a wide saucepan over a high heat and pour in the simmering liquid. Stir through and return to a simmer, then reduce the heat to as low as possible.

Wrap the saucepan lid in a tea towel (dish towel), knotting it at the top. Cover the pan, ensuring it has a snug seal, then cook for 15 minutes.

Turn off the heat and stand for 10 minutes before serving.

Pair with

Hot and spicy Thai salads.

Lighter spicy curries that are not coconut based.

Steamed fish.

Toasted glutinous rice powder (GF) (V) (VG)

Add 100 g (3½ oz/½ cup) glutinous rice to a heavy frying pan and spread out evenly. Toss or stir over medium heat until the rice is a deep golden colour. Remove from the heat to cool a little, then grind to a fine powder in a mortar and pestle. Use this powder to impart a toasty nutty flavour to noodle salads, rice paper rolls, soups or Thai-style braised meats.

Baked buttered rice (GF)

This buttery baked rice, or pilaff, is a constant feature on my table, pairing beautifully with so many things; I just tweak the spicing to match the dish. The rice is golden and slightly crisp on top and stays fluffy underneath, with a rich buttery flavour. This is real comfort food for me. **Serves 4–6**

100 g (3½ oz) unsalted butter
5 garlic cloves, finely sliced
320 g (11½ oz) basmati rice
1 fresh bay leaf, or
  2 teaspoons dried oregano
2 teaspoons salt flakes

800 ml (27 fl oz) Golden chicken stock (p. 54), or water mixed with 1½ tablespoons chicken stock (bouillon) powder

Staples
S&P

Preheat the oven to 200°C (400°F) fan-forced.

Gently melt the butter in a saucepan over a low–medium heat. Add the garlic and cook until softened and lightly coloured, about 3 minutes, being careful not to burn the butter.

Add the rice, bay leaf and salt. Stir through for 2 minutes to coat and warm the rice, then tip into a deep baking dish, about 20 × 30 cm (8 × 1 in).

Return the pan to the heat and add the stock. Bring to a simmer and swirl to deglaze the pan, then pour over the rice. Cover with baking paper, then foil, and bake for 20 minutes.

Uncover and bake for about 20 minutes, until golden.

Make it different
With spices. Add 1 tablespoon cumin seeds and one cinnamon stick when you add the garlic, and add the zest of one lemon when adding the bay leaf.

With coconut & lemon. Preheat the oven to 160°C (320°F) fan-forced. Just before baking in a ceramic baking dish, add 100 g (3½ oz/1⅔ cups) shredded coconut, 1 tablespoon coconut oil and a strip of lemon zest. Place a sheet of baking paper on top. Bake for about 40 minutes, until the rice is cooked and the liquid absorbed.

Pair with

Freshy made Labneh (p. 362) or Tzatziki (p. 507).

Ratatouille (p. 672).

Slow-roasted lamb shoulder (p. 304).

Roast chicken (p. 229).

Curries.

Lebanese skewered chicken (p. 247).

Lamb skewers (see p. 312).

Mejadra GF V

Pair with

Vegetable dishes such as braised silverbeet (Swiss chard) or roasted beetroot (beet).

Roasted chicken and lamb.

Simply cooked fish.

Salad of lentils & smoked trout with dill & horseradish cream dressing GF

Peel and cook 6 new or kipfler (fingerling) potatoes in salted water from cold until tender, then drain well and cut in half. Tip 1 × quantity of Basic vinaigrette lentils (below), made using dill and flat-leaf (Italian) parsley, onto a serving plate. Chop the fronds of 4 dill sprigs and 2 handfuls flat-leaf (Italian) parsley leaves, and add to a bowl with the potatoes. Drizzle with extra-virgin olive oil, season with salt and pepper, then toss to coat. Pile onto the lentils. Flake over the flesh of 300 g (10½ oz) hot-smoked trout fillet. Scatter with 1 punnet snipped mustard cress, and spoon over 1 × quantity Horseradish cream dressing (p. 70). Serves 4–6 people as a starter, or makes for a stunning centrepiece salad to share.

My meme Grace made a version of what I now know to be a classic dish of spiced rice and lentils from the Levant. The modern education is courtesy of Yotam Ottolenghi. Yotam's approach to stir half the fried onions through is a must, adding so much flavour to the rice and earthy, gently spiced lentils. His version doesn't call for fresh herbs, but I can't go without. **Serves 4–6**

250 ml (8½ fl oz/1 cup) extra-virgin olive oil

3 large red or brown onions, sliced 5 mm (¼ in) thick

200 g (7 oz) small green lentils, or large brown lentils

2½ teaspoons cumin seeds

250 g (9 oz/1¼ cups) basmati rice

2 teaspoons ground cinnamon

½ teaspoon ground turmeric

1 teaspoon salt flakes

½ teaspoons ground black pepper

350 ml (12 fl oz) boiling water

1½ teaspoons brown sugar

60 g (2 oz) toasted pine nuts

200 g (7 oz) plain yoghurt

3 dill sprigs, fronds torn

3 mint sprigs, leaves torn

Staples
S&P

Heat 200 ml (7 fl oz) of the oil in a frying pan over a medium heat for 3 minutes. Add half the onion and fry until golden, about 5 minutes. Lift from the oil with a slotted spoon, draining the oil back into the pan. Drain on paper towel, then repeat with the remaining onion.

Put the lentils in a saucepan with plenty of cold water. Bring to the boil over a medium heat, then reduce the heat and simmer for 12 minutes. Drain and set aside.

In a saucepan over a medium heat, fry the cumin in the remaining oil until fragrant, about 1 minute. Add the rice, cinnamon, turmeric, salt and pepper, combining well, then stir the boiling water, sugar and drained lentils through. Simmer for 1 minute, then reduce the heat to low. Cover and simmer for about 15 minutes, until the rice is cooked.

Chop half the cooked onion, then add to the pan with the pine nuts. Mix through with a fork, fluffing the rice at the same time. Cover for 5 minutes off the heat, then adjust the seasoning to taste.

Tip onto a serving plate, and serve topped with the remaining onion, yoghurt and herbs.

Make it a meal

Add 200 g (7 oz) of cooked chickpeas to make this a more substantial dish.

Basic vinaigrette lentils GF V VG

Pair with

Fish, roast poultry or lamb.

Smoked trout, eel or salmon.

Cotechino (see p. 326), fatty pork sausages, confit duck (see p. 260) or Crispy roasted pork belly (p. 332).

Roasted beetroot (beet) (see p. 418) tossed in oil and vinegar.

Crown with ricotta, feta, burrata, goat's curd or buffalo mozzarella.

Serve with the flaked flesh of a cooked ham hock (see p. 324), with Horseradish cream dressing (p 70).

Good heavily buttered bread.

Take this fabulously versatile dish it any direction you like with the herbs. **Serves 6**

200 g (7 oz/1 cup) Puy lentils, or tiny blue-green lentils

1 fresh bay leaf

4 French shallots, sliced

2 garlic cloves, finely chopped

1 celery heart, very finely sliced

80 ml (2½ fl oz/⅓ cup) French-style vinaigrette (p. 88)

6 sprigs of any soft herbs – my favourites are tarragon,

flat-leaf (Italian) parsley, dill or chervil, or half a bunch of chives

Staples
EVOO, S&P

Put the lentils and bay leaf in a saucepan with plenty of cold water. Bring to the boil over a medium heat, then simmer for 12–15 minutes, until tender. Drain well, then tip into a large bowl.

Add a splash of oil to a frying pan over a medium heat. Fry the shallot and garlic until softened, about 5 minutes. Add the celery and stir to warm through for about 5 minutes.

Toss the celery mixture through the lentils. Pour the vinaigrette over, combine well and set aside for 5 minutes for the lentils to take up the dressing.

Just before serving, stir the herbs through and season with salt and pepper.

Tunisian vegetable couscous royale with rosewater labneh (V)

Couscous is traditionally cooked in a couscoussier, a steamer basket that sits atop the pot that holds the stew that is served with the couscous. It's a very sensible way to use the flavourful steam, but it does add a layer of technical complexity – and equipment – to the dish. I am quite happy with quality 'instant' couscous, putting my attention into making the vegetables and/ or meat. I have had many versions of couscous royale, typically with a range of meats, from plump little merguez sausages to quail legs, lamb cutlets and grilled beef skewers; while I adore those versions, I'm just as happy with a tagine of spiced mixed vegetables. You can simply serve with yoghurt if you don't have time to make labneh – but if you're going all out, decorating with rose petals is a nice touch. Whatever you do, you must serve this with plenty of pickled turnip torshi (p. 639). **Serves 8**

Pair with

Fresh Green harissa (p. 92) is wonderful with this. And a garnish of pomegranate seeds wouldn't go astray.

Chickpea, garlic & turmeric salad with witlof (GF) (V) (VG)

Simmer chickpeas with a bulb of garlic sliced in half crossways, a few slices of fresh turmeric and a couple of bay leaves. Once cooked, toss in olive oil with garlic clove slices fried until golden, then squeeze over lemon juice, add some chopped witlof, season with salt and pepper and serve with seared fish, soft-boiled eggs, or toss with some wilted silverbeet (Swiss chard) and serve with slices of ham, corned beef or roast chicken.

400 ml (13½ fl oz) Roasted tomato passata (p. 660), or regular tomato passata (puréed tomatoes)

400 ml (13½ fl oz) water

3 tablespoons vegetable stock (bouillon) powder

¼ kent or jap pumpkin (squash), skin on, seeds removed

2 carrots

2 parsnips

½ celeriac

1 turnip

1 fennel bulb

1 celery heart, cut in four lengthways

2 zucchini (courgettes)

100 ml (3½ fl oz) extra-virgin olive oil

2 onions, diced

8 garlic cloves, sliced

150 g (5½ oz) cooked chickpeas (see p. 371); tinned ones are fine, just drain well

2 × 40 cm (15¾ in) chunks of white cabbage

3 roasted red capsicums (bell peppers) (see p. 463), cut into cheeks

2 long green chillies, split lengthways

1 bunch of coriander (cilantro), leaves and fine stems picked

500 g (1 lb 2 oz) fine instant couscous

juice of 1 lemon

3 tablespoons rosewater

Spice oil

200 ml (7 fl oz) extra-virgin olive oil

2 fresh bay leaves

5 cardamom pods, smashed

2½ tablespoons ground cumin

2 tablespoons ground coriander

1½ tablespoons fennel seeds

1 tablespoon coriander seeds

3 teaspoons ground ginger

3 teaspoons sweet paprika

2 teaspoons ground allspice

2 teaspoons chilli flakes

Rosewater labneh

1 kg (2 lb 3 oz/4 cups) plain yoghurt

2 garlic cloves, crushed with 1 teaspoon salt

2½ tablespoons rosewater

Staples
EVOO, S&P

Combine the labneh ingredients in a bowl. Line a strainer with doubled-over muslin (cheesecloth) and set over a bowl. Add the labneh mixture to the strainer, place in the fridge and leave to drain and thicken for 24–48 hours.

When ready to cook, preheat the oven to 180°C (350°F) fan-forced. Meanwhile, combine the spice oil ingredients in a small bowl. Combine the passata, water and stock powder in a bowl or jug and set aside.

Cut the pumpkin into four wedges, about 4 cm (1½ in) thick. Peel the carrots, parsnips, celeriac and turnip and cut into 3 cm (1¼ in) chunks or wedges, along with the fennel. Cut the celery hearts into quarters, and the zucchini into 4 cm (1½ in) rounds. Set aside.

Heat the olive oil in a large, wide saucepan over a medium heat. Fry the onion and garlic until softened, about 5 minutes. Transfer to a tray and set aside.

In batches, fry the pumpkin, carrot, parsnip, celeriac and turnip for several minutes to colour them, adding the spice oil with each batch and seasoning with salt. Remove and add to the onion.

Add the celery hearts, fennel and zucchini to the pan with any remaining spice oil. Toss through to coat, cook for a minute or two to colour, then add to the onion.

Layer all the sautéed vegetables in a large, wide ovenproof dish. Top with the chickpeas, cabbage, capsicum and chilli, then pour the passata mixture over. Season with salt and pepper and tuck in half the coriander. Top with water to cover, if necessary, and bring to a simmer.

Transfer the dish to the oven and partially cover with the lid. Braise for 30 minutes, until the vegetables are tender and the sauce has reduced a little.

Meanwhile, cook the couscous according to the packet instructions.

Pile the couscous high in the middle of a large serving plate. Stir the lemon juice and rosewater through the vegetables, then arrange decoratively over the couscous. Serve the cooking juices on the side.

Scatter with the remaining coriander and serve with dollops of labneh and a drizzle of oil to finish.

Braised red lentils with turmeric, curry leaves, fried garlic & haloumi ⒼⒻ Ⓥ

Split red lentils on their own can be powdery and a little mushy, but they thicken and flavour a dish wonderfully, so I like to combine them with whole red Persian lentils, which hold their shape well. This is a little lighter than most dal-style dishes that I make, gentle on spice but scented with the explosive fragrance of fresh curry leaves – which I adore – and the earthy scent of turmeric. And yes, the haloumi sticks out here as being culturally misplaced, but it works incredibly well, with its classic squeaky texture quite charming. Use paneer instead, if you prefer. **Serves 4–6 sides**

10 cm (4 in) piece of fresh turmeric, finely grated, or 2½ teaspoons ground turmeric
6 garlic cloves, finely sliced
4 onions, diced
½ celeriac, cut into 1 cm (½ in) dice, or 4 celery stalks, finely diced

125 g (4½ oz/½ cup) Persian red lentils, rinsed
125 g (4½ oz/½ cup) split red lentils, rinsed
½ teaspoon cayenne pepper, or chilli powder
1½ teaspoons salt flakes 800 ml (27 fl oz) water

150 g (5½ oz) haloumi, or paneer, sliced and crumbled
10 fresh curry leaves
1 long green chilli, finely sliced
lime cheeks, to serve

Staples
EVOO, S&P

Heat a splash of oil in a wide-based saucepan over a medium heat. Fry the turmeric and half the garlic until fragrant, about 1 minute. Add the onion and celeriac, and fry until the celeriac starts to colour, about 6 minutes.

Add the lentils, cayenne pepper, salt and water. Stir well, then simmer for about 30 minutes, until the lentils are tender. Adjust the seasoning to taste and tip into a serving bowl.

Meanwhile, heat a splash of oil in a frying pan over a medium heat. Add the haloumi and fry until soft and lightly coloured on both sides, 3–4 minutes, then tip over the lentils.

Add another splash of oil and the remaining garlic to the pan. Fry until fragrant and lightly golden, about 1 minute, then add the curry leaves and cook until fragrant, 20–30 seconds.

Tip the mixture over the lentils. Scatter the chilli over the top, squeeze on some lime and serve.

Tunisian vegetable couscous royale with rosewater labneh

Dal fry GF V VG

This simple dal fry is accidentally vegan and quite delicious. It is largely made with pantry staples and is easy and quick to prepare. It's the sort of thing you eat and just know is good for you. **Serves 4–6**

350 g (12½ oz) red lentils (masoor dal), or pigeon peas (toor dal), rinsed

2 litres (68 fl oz/8 cups) Classic white vegetable stock (p. 51), or water

100 ml (3½ fl oz) extra-virgin olive oil

3 teaspoons cumin seeds

2 teaspoons coriander seeds

1 brown cardamom pod

1 fresh bay leaf

2 onions, finely diced

4 garlic cloves, finely chopped

5 cm (2 in) piece of fresh ginger, peeled and finely diced

2 long green chillies, cut into 2 cm (¾ in) pieces

½ bunch of coriander (cilantro), stalks finely chopped, leaves rough chopped

2 teaspoons tomato paste (concentrated purée)

2 teaspoons garam marsala

1 teaspoon cayenne pepper

2 teaspoons ground turmeric

lime or lemon wedges, to serve

Staples
S&P

Pair with

Naan (p. 855), Raita (p. 98) and steamed rice.

Use to accompany other curries (pp. 317, 318, 359, 581).

Great with carrot, pumpkin (winter squash) and/or cauliflower tossed with Garam masala (p. 15) and oil, and roasted until tender and coloured.

Add a little more liquid, season and serve as a soup topped with crisp fried onions and yoghurt.

Cover the lentils or pigeon peas well with boiling water. Add a pinch of salt and soak for 2–3 hours.

Drain, then add to a medium saucepan with the stock. Bring to the boil over a medium heat, reduce to a simmer and cook for 25 minutes, until tender.

Meanwhile, heat the oil in a medium saucepan over a medium heat. Fry the cumin and coriander seeds, cardamom and bay leaf until fragrant, about 1 minute. Add the onion, garlic, ginger, chilli and coriander stalks, season with salt and cook until the onion is translucent, about 6 minutes.

Stir the spiced onion mixture into the lentils with the tomato paste, garam masala, cayenne and turmeric. Simmer for about 10 minutes, adding more water as needed to keep it a little soupy. Adjust the seasoning to taste.

Serve scattered with the chopped coriander, with a squeeze of lime or lemon.

Black dal GF V

Pair with

Naan (p. 855), Raita (p. 98) and steamed rice.

Use to accompany other curries (pp. 317, 318, 359).

Serve with yoghurt, rice and slow-roasted wedges of pumpkin (winter squash).

This is my version of dal makhani, the Punjabi classic made with black urad dal and red kidney beans. I flavour the dal towards the end by frying aromatics, spices and tomato and stirring these through once the lentils and beans are cooked, which creates layers of deep spice, while retaining a vibrant freshness. The brown butter adds a layer of nutty complexity to the dish, which stands in for the cream that dal makhani normally contains. I often find the cream a little heavy, where the butter adds a toasted flavour and picks up the fat content to make it more luscious. You could also just finish it with knobs of butter dropped onto each bowl when serving. **Serves 6–8**

150 g (5½ oz) dried red kidney beans
150 g (5½ oz) black lentils, or urad dal
2.5 litres (85 fl oz/10 cups) water
1 teaspoon cayenne pepper
1 teaspoon smoked paprika
⅛ teaspoon asafoetida
3 tablespoons extra-virgin olive oil
1 tablespoon cumin seeds

1 thumb-sized piece of cassia bark
1 black cardamom pod
1 large onion, finely diced
6 garlic cloves, finely chopped
10 cm (4 in) piece of fresh ginger, peeled and julienned
6 cm (2½ in) piece of fresh turmeric, julienned
3 long green chillies, finely chopped

4 ripe tomatoes, finely diced
1 tablespoon Garam masala (p. 15)
2 tablespoons dried fenugreek leaves
100 g (3½ oz) butter
4 coriander (cilantro) sprigs, leaves and fine stems picked

Staples
S&P

Soak the kidney beans and black lentils separately in plenty of water overnight.

The next day, drain the beans and lentils. Place the beans and water in a medium saucepan, season lightly with salt and pepper and bring to the boil. Reduce the heat and simmer for 10 minutes, then add the lentils and cook for another 25 minutes.

Stir in the cayenne pepper, paprika and asafoetida. Reduce the heat to low and cook until quite soft, about 10 minutes, adding more water if necessary.

Meanwhile, heat the oil in a medium saucepan over a medium heat. Fry the cumin seeds, cassia and cardamom until fragrant, about 1 minute. Add the onion, garlic, ginger, turmeric and chilli, season with salt and cook until softened, about 5 minutes. Stir in the tomato and cook until softened, about 3 minutes. Add the garam masala and stir through for 1 minute.

Stir the spiced onion mixture through the lentil mixture. Add the fenugreek leaves and more liquid if necessary, then cook for another 20 minutes; the dal should have a pourable consistency when finished. Adjust the seasoning to taste.

To serve, melt the butter in a small saucepan over a medium heat. Cook until nut brown, about 3 minutes, then pour over the dal, finishing with the coriander.

Baked beans with mustard seeds, vinegar & tomato GF V VG

I love baked beans on toast, however they come, but this version is just about my favourite, with a pleasing twist of spice in the background. These improve with a day or two on them, as do so many dishes like this, with the flavour intensifying and melding into a more complete whole. Any white bean will work in this recipe. You can also use tinned beans, but they won't have quite the same robust flavour or texture as ones cooked from scratch. **Serves 6**

250 g (9 oz) dried great northern beans, soaked overnight, drained
140 ml (4½ fl oz) extra-virgin olive oil
2 onions, diced
2 celery stalks, finely diced
6 garlic cloves, finely chopped
1 fresh bay leaf

3½ tablespoons brown sugar
2 tablespoons curry powder
1 tablespoon sweet smoked paprika
1½ tablespoons brown mustard seeds
3 tablespoons apple-cider vinegar
400 g (14 oz) tin diced tomatoes

600 ml (20½ fl oz) tomato passata (puréed tomatoes)
600 ml (20½ fl oz) Golden chicken stock (p. 54), Classic white vegetable stock (p. 51), or water mixed with a stock (bouillon) cube

Staples
S&P

Put the beans in a saucepan and cover generously with cold water. Lightly salt and bring to the boil over a medium heat, then simmer for about 45 minutes, until well cooked. Drain and set aside.

Heat the oil in a heavy-based frying pan over a medium–high heat. Fry the onion, celery, garlic and bay leaf until the onion has softened, about 5 minutes.

Add the beans, sugar, spices and vinegar. Stir in the tomatoes, passata and stock. Bring to a boil, then simmer for 40 minutes, until the beans are tender.

Adjust the seasoning to taste. The beans will keep for about a week in the fridge.

Make it different
With chorizo. Before cooking the onion mixture, fry 250 g (9 oz) finely diced cured chorizo sausage (preferably hot and spicy) in the oil for 4 minutes, until well cooked and deep red. Then add the onion, celery, garlic and bay leaf and continue with the recipe.

Pair with

I think a fried egg or two is essential with these – but opt for poached or scrambled eggs if you prefer.

Spoon the hot beans into a baking dish. Make indentations with a kitchen spoon and crack in some room-temperature eggs. Bake at 220°C (430°F) for about 8 minutes, or until the eggs are cooked to your liking.

Pile onto toasted Turkish bread, then top with avocado. Season well and finish with a fried egg and a toast 'lid'.

Use as a jaffle filling with sharp cheddar.

Serve with a cheese omelette (pp. 352–3, 355).

Cassoulet

Pair with

A green salad, green beans, braised silverbeet (Swiss chard) (see p. 555) or cavolo nero.

This is my version of cassoulet, the famous dish of baked white beans and mixed meats from southern France. People bicker endlessly over what is and isn't the correct composition for cassoulet, with many variants just as traditional as each other. I like to use great northern beans, cotechino sausage, pork belly and duck confit, and have no particular view on whether this is faithful enough to the platonic ideal of cassoulet – just that it makes for a rich, unctuous and utterly delicious meal, perfect for a winter's evening. **Serves 8**

500 g (1 lb 2 oz) dried great northern beans
700 g (1 lb 9 oz) cotechino sausage, or Toulouse sausages
700 g (1 lb 9 oz) thick end of boneless pork belly, cut into 2.5 cm (1 in) dice
160 g (5½ oz/½ cup) rock salt
100 ml (3½ fl oz) duck fat, or confit duck leg cooking oil/fat (see p. 260)
2 onions, diced
6 garlic cloves, chopped
1 celery heart, finely sliced

2 carrots, cut into 3 cm (1¼ in) chunks
8 thyme sprigs
2 fresh bay leaves
6 juniper berries, lightly crushed
3 teaspoons fennel seeds
2½ teaspoons ground allspice
1½ teaspoons ground black pepper
400 g (14 oz) tin diced tomatoes
2 tablespoons tomato paste (concentrated purée)

1.5 litres (51 fl oz/6 cups) Golden chicken stock (p. 54)
1.5 litres (51 fl oz/6 cups) hot water
4 confit duck legs (see p. 260), jointed
125 g (4½ oz/1½ cups) coarse breadcrumbs, made from stale bread
60 g (2 oz) parmesan, grated

Staples
S&P

Soak the beans in plenty of water overnight.

Cook the cotechino in simmering water for 40 minutes. Drain and chill, then slice 1.5 cm (½ in) thick. If you are using Toulouse sausages this step is not necessary.

The next day, toss the pork with the rock salt and refrigerate for 1 hour, then shake off the excess salt. Drain the beans and set aside.

Preheat the oven to 170°C (340°F) fan-forced.

Heat the duck fat in a flameproof casserole dish over a medium heat. Fry the pork belly until quite dark and becoming crispy, about 8 minutes. Remove from the pan, leaving the fat behind. Cook the onion, garlic, celery and carrot in the fat until slightly golden, about 8 minutes. Add the herbs, spices and pepper and stir through for 2 minutes. Stir in the tomatoes, tomato paste and beans, then add the stock and hot water and bring to a boil. Cook at a hard simmer for 20 minutes.

Mix the pork through and if you are using Toulouse sausages add them now. Cover the dish and transfer to the oven. Cook for about 1 hour.

Once the pork is tender, add the confit duck and cotechino slices, pushing them in to submerge. Cover and bake for another 35 minutes.

Skim off about three-quarters of the fat and adjust the seasoning to taste.

Top with the breadcrumbs and cheese, then return to the oven. Set the oven grill (broiler) to high and toast until bubbling and golden; alternatively, you can portion into individual dishes or a ceramic dish before grilling.

No-bake seed bars Ⓥ

This is a simple way to make muesli bars – you don't even need to turn the oven on, and they will set once cool. I always keep them in the freezer, as it prolongs their life substantially, slowing the oxidation of the natural oils. **Makes 25**

Pair with

Enjoy as is for a snack.

Break the bars over some yoghurt and fruit for breakfast.

150 g (5½ oz) honey
150 g (5½ oz) tahini
80 g (2¾ oz) unsalted butter
1½ teaspoons ground
  cinnamon
200 g (7 oz/2 cups) rolled
  (porridge) oats

80 g (2¾ oz/⅔ cup) sunflower
  seeds
80 g (2¾ oz/⅔ cup) linseeds
  (flax seeds)
80 g (2¾ oz/⅔ cup) pepitas
  (pumpkin seeds)
60 g (2 oz/⅓ cup) toasted
  almonds

80 g (2¾ oz/½ cup) sesame
  seeds
60 g (2 oz/⅓ cup) chia seeds
30 g (1 oz/¼ cup) cacao nibs

For topping
1 tablespoon pepitas
  (pumpkin seeds)
1 tablespoon cacao nibs

Line a 30 × 15 cm (12 × 6 in) baking tray with baking paper.

Melt the honey, tahini, butter and cinnamon in a small saucepan over a low heat, stirring until well combined.

In a blender, pulse the oats, sunflower seeds, linseeds, pepitas and almonds until combined but chunky.

Tip into a bowl and add the sesame seeds, chia and cacao nibs. Pour in the warm tahini mixture and massage with your hands until combined.

Press the mixture firmly and evenly into the baking tray – it should be about 2 cm (¾ in) thick. Use the back of a wet spoon to smooth the top, then push the extra pepitas and cacao nibs into the top. Freeze until set, about 2 hours.

Once set, cut into 6 × 3 cm (2½ × 1¼ in) slices, or whatever size suits, and store in an airtight container in the freezer, where they will keep for up to 2 months.

Apricot & sesame oat bars Ⓥ

This is a moist apricot slice, with a gentle sesame flavour – a great snack bar for lunchboxes or as a pick-me-up any time of the day. **Makes about 16**

Pair with

Enjoy as is for a snack.

Break the bars over some yoghurt and fruit for breakfast.

250 g (9 oz) dried apricot
  halves, semi finely diced
300 g (10½ oz/3 cups) rolled
  (porridge) oats
100 g (3½ oz/1 cup) flaked
  almonds
50 g (1¾ oz/⅓ cup) salted
  cashew nuts, roughly chopped

50 g (1¾ oz/½ cup) long
  golden sultanas (golden
  raisins)
40 g (1½ oz/¼ cup) toasted
  sesame seeds
2 tablespoons white chia
  seeds

125 ml (4 fl oz/½ cup)
  extra-virgin olive oil
125 g (4½ oz) honey
125 g (4½ oz) brown sugar
1 tablespoon tahini
1½ teaspoons ground cinnamon

Staples
S&P

Soak the apricots in boiling water for 20 minutes, then drain and quarter.

Meanwhile, preheat the oven to 170°C (340°F) fan-forced. Line a brownie tin with baking paper.

Put half the oats in a blender and blitz for two 15-second pulses to chop lightly. Tip into a large bowl with the whole oats, almonds, cashews, sultanas, sesame seeds and chia seeds.

Bring the oil, honey and sugar to a simmer in a saucepan. Remove from the heat, stir in the tahini and cinnamon, then pour over the oat mixture. Stir until well combined.

Press the mixture into the brownie tin. Lay baking paper on top and press quite firmly with a spatula to flatten. Remove the baking paper and sprinkle with a pinch of salt.

Bake for 45 minutes, until golden all over. Set aside to cool before cutting into bars, or any shape you like. The bars will keep in an airtight container in the pantry for up to 5 days.

Chia pudding GF V VG

Add 350 ml (12 fl oz) almond milk, 250 ml (8½ fl oz/1 cup) coconut water or plain water, 120 g (4½ oz) white chia seeds, 2½ tablespoons smooth peanut butter and 2 tablespoons maple syrup or honey and to a blender and process for 20 seconds. Pour into glasses and set in the fridge for 2 hours. Serve with banana or blackberries. Serves 4.

Coconut bircher V

In a container, combine 500 ml (17 fl oz/2 cups) coconut water, 120 g (4½ oz/½ cup) plain or coconut yoghurt, 250 g (9 oz/2½ cups) rolled oats, 80 g (2¾ oz) desiccated coconut, 2 tablespoons honey, 2 tablespoons sesame seeds and 2 teaspoons ground cinnamon. Leave to soak overnight in the fridge. In the morning, top with fresh grated apple, honey and sesame seeds. Serves 4.

Date, sesame, coconut & macadamia nut balls GF V

These are very handy to have on hand, with plenty of energy, protein and nutrients in each ball. They're also great treats for kids, with all those healthful properties cloaked by their sweet and nutty deliciousness. **Makes about 25**

100 g (3½ oz/⅔ cup) white sesame seeds
350 g (12½ oz) fleshy dates, pitted
100 g (3½ oz/⅔ cup) black sesame seeds
100 g (3½ oz/¾ cup) pepitas (pumpkin seeds)

50 g (1¾ oz/½ cup) ground almonds
50 g (1¾ oz/¾ cup) shredded coconut
3 tablespoons chia seeds
1 tablespoon tahini
2 teaspoons salt flakes
120 g (4½ oz/⅓ cup) honey
100 g (3½ oz) coconut oil

1½ tablespoons dark cocoa powder
3 heaped teaspoons ground ginger
3 heaped teaspoons ground cinnamon
140 g (5 oz/1 cup) crushed macadamia nuts

Lightly toast the white sesame seeds in a dry frying pan over a medium heat until they colour a little and start to crackle, 1–2 minutes. Set aside to cool.

In a small pot, cover the dates in hot water and simmer until the water is gone, about 5 minutes.

Add all the sesame seeds and the pepitas to a food processor and blitz to a coarse powder. Add the dates, ground almonds, coconut, chia seeds, tahini and salt and pulse into a coarse mixture.

Warm the honey, coconut oil, cocoa powder and spices in a small saucepan, stirring until combined, then add to the food processor. Blend with the seed mixture to form a smooth paste, then chill for 20 minutes to firm up.

Roll the mixture into small balls, then roll in the macadamia nuts to coat, pressing them in. The balls will keep in an airtight container in the pantry for up to 7 days.

Left to right: Date, sesame, coconut & macadamia nut balls (above); Apricot & sesame oat bars (opposite); No-bake seed bars (opposite)

Toasted muesli ⓥ ⓥⓖ

I like a muesli full of seeds and nuts, with spice accents – and it's got to be toasted, so that it's extra crunchy and flavourful. This one has a touch of sweetness and some pleasingly sour notes from the barberries. **Serves 16**

400 g (14 oz/4 cups) rolled (porridge) oats
60 g (2 oz/1 cup) shredded coconut
235 g (8½ oz/1½ cups) sesame seeds
125 g (4½ oz/1 cup) sunflower seeds
150 g (5½ oz/1 cup) pepitas (pumpkin seeds)

4 tablespoons chia seeds
150 g (5½ oz/1 cup) whole almonds
50 g (1¾ oz/½ cup) flaked almonds
2 teaspoons ground cinnamon
1 whole nutmeg, freshly grated

125 ml (4 fl oz/½ cup) coconut oil
125 ml (4 fl oz/½ cup) golden syrup, or light treacle
125 ml (4 fl oz/½ cup) maple syrup
60 g (2 oz/½ cup) sultanas (golden raisins)
60 g (2 oz/½ cup) barberries, or goji berries

Preheat the oven to 180°C (350°F) fan-forced. Line two baking trays with baking paper.

In a large bowl, combine the oats, coconut, and all the seeds and almonds. Add the cinnamon and grate the nutmeg over, then toss until well combined.

Add the oil and syrups and rub through the mixture thoroughly with your fingers.

Spread the mixture out in one layer on the baking trays and toast for 20 minutes.

Allow to cool on the trays, then mix the sultanas and barberries through. The muesli will keep in an airtight container in the pantry for up to a month.

Nut yoghurt ⓖⒻ ⓥ ⓥⓖ

While 'vegan yoghurt' is not a combination of words that would normally excite me, this one is really quite delicious, with a creamy texture and a gently sour tang. **Makes about 650 g (1 lb 7 oz)**

250 g (9 oz/1⅔ cups) blanched almonds
250 g (9 oz/1⅔ cups) large raw cashew nuts
1½ teaspoons salt flakes

1 capsule of acidophilus probiotic powder
450 ml (15 fl oz) filtered or purified water

maple syrup, lemon juice, vanilla bean paste or cinnamon, to taste

Pair with

Use as you would regular yoghurt.

Serve as a dip with Dukkah (p. 13) sprinkled on top, with bread or crackers.

Use as a base to serve wilted greens on top of, as a side dish.

Flavour with vanilla and/or maple syrup and use as an icing for cakes.

Put the almonds and cashews in a large heatproof bowl and cover with boiling water. Add 1 teaspoon of the salt, then leave to soak overnight.

The next day, drain the soaked nuts. Place in a blender with the acidophilus powder and remaining salt. Pour in the filtered water, then blitz to a smooth paste.

Transfer to a large jar, making sure the sides are cleaned down, and leave at room temperature for 2 days, until you have a slightly thickened, aerated paste.

Season again and flavour as you like. The nut yoghurt will keep in the fridge in an airtight container for about a week.

Chilled coconut & lime leaf rice pudding (GF)

Pair with

Scoop into bowls and serve as is, or top with some fresh berries, fresh mango, lychees, passionfruit pulp or poached rhubarb (see p. 646).

Drizzle with lemon syrup (see p. 707).

The rice in this is gorgeously coconutty, with a little sharpness from the yoghurt and a burst of freshness from the lime leaves. **Serves 6–8**

200 g (7 oz) arborio rice, or short-grain black rice
650 ml (22 fl oz) full-cream (whole) milk
350 ml (12 fl oz) coconut cream

140 g (5 oz/⅔ cup) caster (superfine) sugar
1 teaspoon salt flakes
1 vanilla bean, split
½ leaf of gold-strength gelatine

2 makrut lime leaves
250 g (9 oz/1 cup) plain yoghurt, or coconut yoghurt

Add the rice to a saucepan and cover with water. Bring to a boil over a high heat, then drain immediately and refresh under cold water.

Return to the pan with the milk, coconut cream, sugar, salt and vanilla bean. Bring to a simmer, then cover and simmer over a low heat for about 15 minutes, until the rice is tender and the liquid has been absorbed.

Meanwhile, soak the gelatine in cold water for about 5 minutes.

Once the rice is cooked, drain the gelatine, squeeze out any excess water and add to the pan with the lime leaves. Stir until the gelatine has dissolved, then transfer to a bowl to cool at room temperature.

Once cooled, remove the lime leaves and vanilla bean, scraping the seeds in. Fold the yoghurt through, then refrigerate until cold before serving.

Rizogalo (GF) (V)

This is my take on the Greek version of rice pudding. I have reduced the sugar a little from the original, as traditionally it's quite sweet. Serve it hot or cold; I even occasionally sneak one in for breakfast. **Serves 4**

250 g (9 oz) short-grain white rice
500 ml (17 fl oz/2 cups) water
1 teaspoon salt flakes
900 ml (30½ fl oz) full-cream (whole) milk

150 g (5½ oz/⅔ cup) caster (superfine) sugar
2 teaspoons vanilla extract or paste
1 cinnamon stick

2 tablespoons cornflour (cornstarch)
3 egg yolks
ground cinnamon, to serve

In a saucepan, bring the rice, water and salt to a simmer, then turn the heat down to as low as possible. Partially cover and cook for about 20 minutes, until all the water is absorbed.

Add 800 ml (27 fl oz) of the milk and 100 g (3½ oz) of the sugar to the pan, along with the vanilla and cinnamon stick. Stir through and bring slowly to a simmer over a low heat. Cook gently, partially covered, for about 15 minutes, until the milk has mostly been absorbed.

Mix the cornflour into the remaining milk and stir into the rice. Cook until thickened, about 3 minutes.

Meanwhile, whisk the egg yolks with the remaining sugar to combine and aerate.

Once the rice mixture has thickened, fold the egg mixture in, then cook for about 3 minutes, until thick and glossy but still pourable.

Serve warm, sprinkled with cinnamon. Or, pour into containers, sprinkle with cinnamon and chill to set, then serve cold.

Vegetables

Asian greens

I must say I baulk a little at the generality of the term, 'Asian greens', as Asia is of course a huge region, and the variety of green things grown there is equally vast. The greens that I am referring to are ones commonly used in Chinese and South-East Asian cooking, and principally the ones that are readily available in the Western markets. An entire book could be written on the topic, but this is not that book.

We grow so many Asian greens in Australia these days, and we have for some time, with various waves of immigration from Vietnam, China and the like ensuring a healthy exposure to different cuisines and unfamiliar fresh produce. I hate to think where we'd be in a culinary and cultural sense without such diversity.

Bok choy (or pak choy) was probably the most ubiquitous green early on, and I think we overdid things a little – I certainly tired of it. Gai lan, or Chinese broccoli as it is still often called, was somewhat more exotic, though it was mainly the province of Chinese restaurants, and typically smothered in oyster sauce – making it even more exotic. Today, gai choy (mustard greens), choy sum (Chinese flowering cabbage), amaranth greens, kang kong (water spinach, Siamese watercress), tatsoi, tung ho (chrysanthemum leaves) and pea and snow pea (mangetout) shoots – which were naturally grown here earlier, but their culinary use had not really been explored – are also readily available in Asian grocers and at more specialised market stalls.

For me, wilted greens accompanying an Asian-inspired dish provide the perfect balance, along with some steamed rice complementing and rounding out a meal, whether hot and spicy or gently fragrant. Stir-frying is the simplest way to cook most greens, though I will typically blanch hardier types such as gai lan first in boiling salted water, then finish the cooking and pick up flavour in the wok; I usually do this with ginger and garlic, and might finish with a good drizzle of oyster sauce or sesame oil and a scattering of sesame seeds. I also add greens to broths at the last minute; greens such as amaranth or kang kong will wilt quickly in a hot wok or stock without any blanching.

When selecting Asian greens, the standard principles apply. Look for bright, vibrant leaves and firm (but not woody) stems. Bok choy and gai lan can vary a bit in size and still be delicious, but avoid overly large specimens, as they will be tough and fibrous. Similarly, the stems of leafy greens will become stringy and tough, so finer ones are best. Leafy cooking greens such as kang kong are best used as soon as possible, as the leaves can wilt and blacken fairly quickly; wrap them in a tea towel (dish towel) and store in the crisper.

Also see

Pork & prawn wontons with choy sum & kale 342

Soba noodles with avocado, sprouts, umeboshi & sesame 410

Sour fish & mussel curry with celery hearts & kang kong 488

Daikon, edamame & avocado salad with sesame, apple & soy dressing 640

Pair with

Asian greens are versatile, taking to chilli, ginger, garlic and spring onion (scallion), as well as sympathetic herbs such as coriander (cilantro), Thai basil and Vietnamese mint. They work beautifully with sesame oil and sesame seeds, XO sauce (p. 98), Fermented cooked chilli sauce (p. 97), hoi sin, fermented black beans and oyster sauce. They are ready foils for pretty much any protein, whether pork, duck, beef, seafood or tofu. Combine them with Asian mushrooms, such as shiitake, or mix with other green vegetables, such as snow peas (mangetout), asparagus or sugar-snap peas.

Preparing Asian greens

Given the broad scope of greens, preparation will naturally differ, but little is typically required. You may need to trim away any mature woody stems or core (from bok choy/pak choy in particular) and discard any blackened leaves. If using things like pea shoots, tough hollow stems are best discarded, as they will not readily soften. Any greens that are wilting a little during storage can be brought back to life by soaking in cold water.

Stir-fried kang kong & wombok with tofu & fermented chilli Ⓥ Ⓥᴳ

The tofu really picks up a lot of personality in this dish, becoming quite soft and really soaking up all the deep and spicy flavours of the sauce. **Serves 4**

Pair with

Serve as a side, or as a midweek meal with rice.

100 ml (3½ fl oz) shaoxing
  rice wine
80 ml (2½ fl oz/⅓ cup)
  light soy sauce
1 teaspoon sesame oil
1 teaspoon sugar
½ teaspoon ground
  white pepper
100 ml (3½ fl oz)
  grapeseed oil

100 g (3½ oz) fresh ginger,
  peeled and julienned
4 garlic cloves, finely sliced
350 g (12½ oz) firm tofu, cut
  into 3 cm (1¼ in) dice
½ inner yellow wombok
  (Chinese cabbage) heart,
  sliced on an angle
200 g (7 oz) kang kong
  (water spinach)

2 teaspoons Fermented
  cooked chilli sauce (p. 97)
2 handfuls of Thai basil
  and/or coriander (cilantro)
  leaves

Combine the rice wine, soy sauce, sesame oil, sugar and pepper in a small bowl, stirring to dissolve the sugar. Set aside.

Heat a wok over a high heat until very hot. Add the grapeseed oil and heat until shimmering. Add the ginger and garlic and fry briefly until just golden, then quickly add the tofu and stir-fry until it takes on a little colour, about 2 minutes. Add the wombok and kang kong and stir-fry until wilted, about 2 minutes.

Stir in the rice wine mixture and cook until dry. Add the chilli paste, tossing through to coat, then serve with the herbs sprinkled on top.

Stir-fried pea shoots with shrimp paste & chilli

Done well, stir-fried pea shoots are one of my favourite greens. This version drifts in a South-East Asian direction with the addition of shrimp paste and plenty of chilli; it should be fresh, vibrant, salty, oily and spicy. **Serves 4**

Pair with

Serve as a side for South-East Asian dishes.

It's also great with steamed fish, noodles, fried rice, stir-fried shellfish (such as pipis, clams and mussels) and grilled calamari.

2 large garlic cloves
1 long red chilli, roughly
  chopped
½ teaspoon salt flakes
80 ml (2½ fl oz/⅓ cup)
  grapeseed oil

1 teaspoon shrimp paste
  (belachan)
400 g (14 oz) pea shoots or
  kang kong (water spinach),
  cut into 3 cm (1¼ in)
  lengths

3 tablespoons Fermented
  cooked chilli sauce (p. 97),
  or 6 crushed fresh bird's
  eye chillies
125 ml (4 fl oz/½ cup)
  White chicken stock (p. 54),
  or water

Stir-fried greens & shiitake with XO sauce

Weigh out 250 g (9 oz) shiitake mushrooms and halve them if they're large – otherwise keep them whole. Split 2 baby bok choy (pak choy) lengthways and trim 2 bunches choy sum (Chinese flowering cabbage), cutting it into 5 cm (2 in) widths. Blanch the mushrooms and greens in boiling salted water for 1 minute, then drain. Heat a wok over a high heat until very hot. Add 2½ tablespoons XO sauce (p. 98) and fry for 2 minutes. Add the mushrooms and greens and toss to coat, then serve. I'm pretty happy simply having this with steamed rice, but it's also great with Crispy roasted pork belly (p. 332) or spicy grilled meats or seafood. Serves 4.

Using a mortar and pestle, pound the garlic, chilli and salt into a paste.

Heat a wok over a high heat until very hot. Add the oil and heat until shimmering, then briefly fry the garlic paste until lightly golden. Add the shrimp paste and fry for 30 seconds.

Stir the pea shoots and chilli paste through, then add the stock. Toss in the wok for a minute or so until the shoots have wilted, then serve.

Make it a meal

A handful of peeled prawns (shrimp) thrown in just after the garlic paste turns golden would be a great way to elevate this dish into more of a meal – simply serve with rice.

Stir-fried choy sum & gai lan with oyster sauce

I never tire of the combination of ginger, garlic and oyster sauce with greens – it's a standing order when I go out, no menu required. **Serves 4–6**

1 bunch of choy sum (Chinese flowering cabbage), trimmed and cut into 5 cm (2 in) widths

1 bunch of gai lan (Chinese broccoli), trimmed
80 ml (2½ fl oz/⅓ cup) grapeseed oil

100 g (3½ oz) fresh ginger, peeled and julienned
4 garlic cloves, finely sliced
150 ml (5 fl oz) oyster sauce
½ teaspoon sesame oil

Blanch the choy sum and gai lan in boiling salted water for 1 minute, then drain.

Heat a wok over a high heat until very hot. Add the grapeseed oil and heat until shimmering, then briefly fry the ginger and garlic until just golden. Add the blanched greens and stir-fry for about 90 seconds. Add the oyster sauce and sesame oil, tossing through to coat, then serve.

Make it different

You could use any Asian greens for this dish, but snow peas (mangetout), sugar-snap peas and/or asparagus would also work well.

Fragrant chicken soup with bok choy 🌀

This is an extremely light and fragrant broth, which is especially good if you are a little under the weather. I always keep galangal, lime leaves, chillies and turmeric in the freezer for when I lack the fresh stuff, which makes pulling a dish like this together so much easier. **Serves 4**

2 litres (68 fl oz/8 cups) White chicken stock (p. 54)
4 cm (1½ in) knob of fresh galangal, or ginger, sliced
1 lemongrass stem, bruised
5 cm (2 in) piece of fresh turmeric
4 makrut lime leaves
2 × 180–200 g (6½–7 oz) chicken breasts

8 shiitake or abalone mushrooms, finely sliced
2 baby bok choy (pak choy), quartered lengthways
2 handfuls of baby English spinach leaves
2 handfuls of bean sprouts
2 handfuls of coriander (cilantro) leaves

2 long red chillies, finely sliced
1 handful of Thai basil (optional) leaves
1 lime, quartered

Staples
S&P

Add the stock to a large saucepan with the galangal, lemongrass, turmeric and lime leaves. Bring to a simmer, then gently simmer over a low heat for 10–15 minutes to allow the aromatics to flavour the stock.

Bring the stock to the boil and lower the chicken in. As soon as it comes back to the boil, turn the heat off and poach for 11 minutes. Remove the chicken, cover with foil and set aside for 5 minutes.

While the chicken is resting, strain the stock into a clean saucepan, discarding the aromatics. Bring to a simmer, adjusting with salt as needed.

Shred the chicken and divide between four bowls, along with the mushrooms, bok choy and spinach, then pour the hot stock over. Finish with the bean sprouts, coriander, chilli, basil (if using) and a squeeze of lime.

Make it faster
Use finely shredded left-over roast chicken.

Make it different
Fragrant seafood soup with bok choy. Replace the chicken with fillets of salmon or blue eye trevalla.

Make it vegetarian **V**
Swap out the chicken stock for Classic white vegetable stock (p. 51), or a broth made from rehydrated dried mushrooms and any aromatics you have on hand. Add some other exotic mushrooms and/or silken tofu in place of the chicken.

Udon noodles with chicken, shiitake, bok choy, miso & kimchi

Heat 2 tablespoons shiro miso paste or 2 sachets of instant miso and 500 ml (17 fl oz/2 cups) water in a saucepan. Add 1 shredded cooked chicken breast (either poached, see p. 230, or left-over roast chicken), 150 g (5½ oz) diced firm tofu, 6 sliced shiitake mushrooms and 1 sliced baby bok choy (pak choy), and simmer for 1 minute. Cook 200 g (7 oz) udon noodles and refresh in cold water, then add to two bowls and ladle the hot broth mixture over. Top with 3 tablespoons chopped Kimchi (p. 455) or shredded toasted nori. Serves 2.

Fried rice with wood ear fungus & cashews

This is fried rice as a sustaining standalone meal. You could use white rice here, but brown rice is heartier and nuttier. Serve with chopped chilli or Fermented cooked chilli sauce (p. 97) on the side. **Serves 6**

1 bunch of choy sum (Chinese flowering cabbage), or gai lan (Chinese broccoli), trimmed
80 ml (2½ fl oz/⅓ cup) light soy sauce
2 tablespoons oyster sauce, or vegetarian oyster sauce
1 teaspoon sesame oil
2 teaspoons sugar
½ teaspoon ground white pepper
2 tablespoons grapeseed oil

1 large onion, finely sliced
5 garlic cloves, sliced
15 cm (6 in) piece of fresh ginger, peeled and finely chopped
200 g (7 oz) salted roasted cashews
2 tablespoons sesame seeds
120 g (4 oz) fresh wood ear fungus, or shiitake or abalone mushrooms, finely shredded

500 g (1 lb 2 oz/2½ cups) long-grain brown rice, or long-grain white rice, cooked and cooled
100 g (3½ oz) bean sprouts
5 spring onions (scallions), white and green parts, finely sliced
1 handful of coriander (cilantro) leaves

Blanch the choy sum in boiling salted water for 1 minute, then drain. Cut into 3 cm (1¼ in) pieces and set aside.

Combine the soy and oyster sauces, sesame oil, sugar and pepper in a small bowl. Stir to dissolve the sugar.

Heat a wok over a high heat until very hot. Add the grapeseed oil and heat until shimmering. Add the onion, garlic, ginger, cashews and sesame seeds and stir-fry until the onion has softened, about 3 minutes.

Add the blanched choy sum and cook for 1 minute, then add the fungus and rice and stir briskly until hot. Add the soy sauce mixture, bean sprouts, spring onion and coriander. Stir to combine, then serve.

Make it vegetarian **V**
Use a vegetarian oyster sauce.

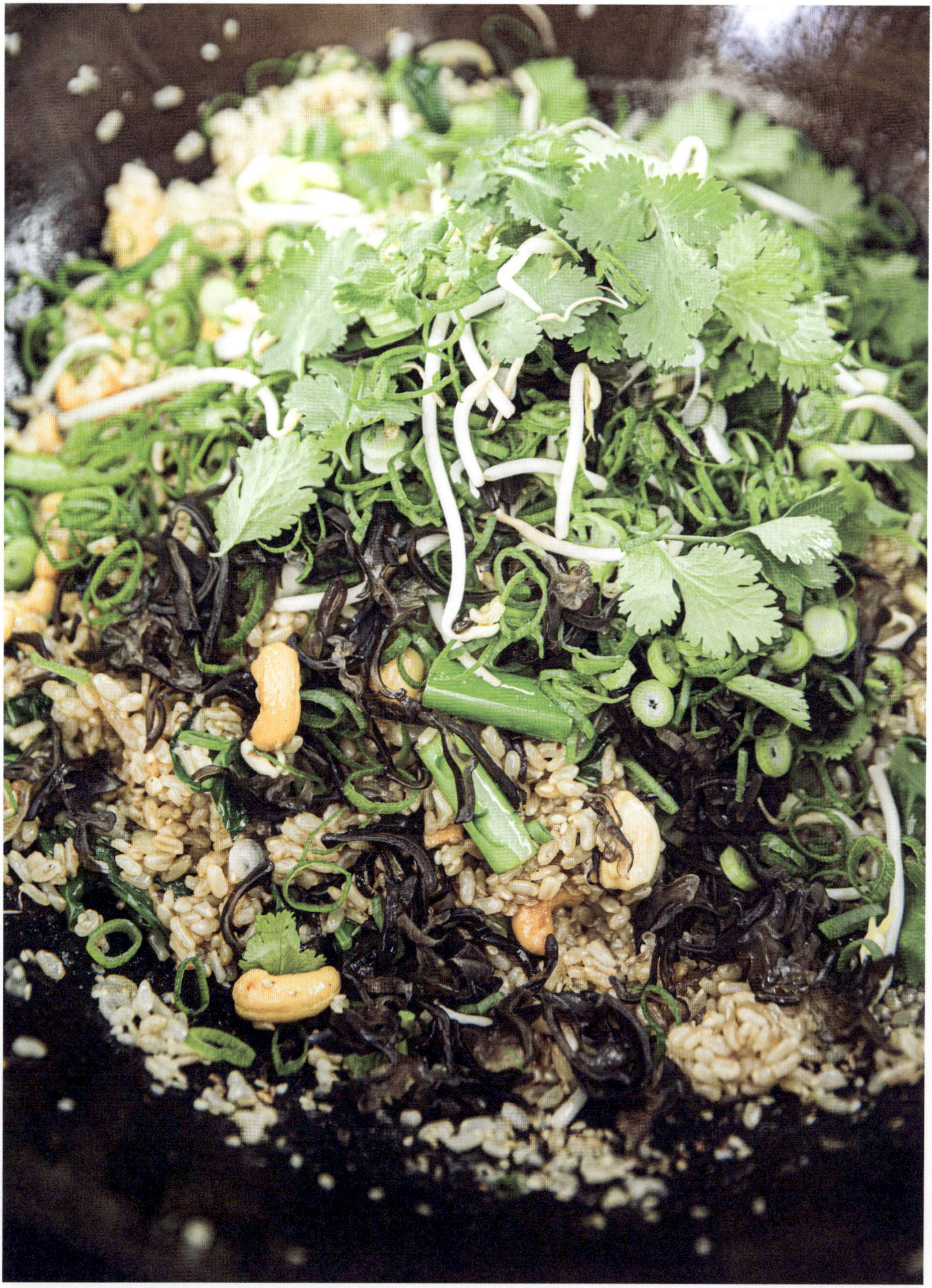

Asparagus

Asparagus has a deliciously brief season, its peak somewhat fleeting and at the mercy of prevailing weather. Rather than this modern obsession with being able to get everything always, I think seasonality is something to celebrate, to look forward to and embrace fully. In Europe, asparagus season is eagerly anticipated – and once you've tasted the flavour of asparagus freshly plucked in the full flush of spring, those spongy-looking hot-house spears will hold no allure.

With asparagus, the early offerings of the season are certainly much better than the last gasps. You can often buy imported asparagus in the depths of winter, but I never would. Besides the environmental problems with shipping a vegetable from one hemisphere to another, the quality will rarely stack up, given the time required to harvest, pack, ship, stock, buy, prepare and eat – so learn to look forward to asparagus at its best, and be patient.

There are different varieties of asparagus. Green and purple hues are due to different cultivars, with the purple being a modern cultivar developed from colour variation in heirloom varieties, while the pallor of white asparagus is simply a result of light deprivation, with soil piled around the spears as they grow, blocking photosynthesis. In Europe, fat spears of white asparagus are the most highly prized, even though more slender specimens are just as enjoyable. White asparagus has a distinctive and slightly nutty flavour, while the green version is earthy and tastes like, well, springtime. The purple varieties generally contain a little more natural sugar, and a greater concentration of antioxidants, vitamins and minerals. Ultimately, you should just buy the freshest asparagus available.

Asparagus does deteriorate reasonably quickly, so only buy what you need. I typically choose finger-thick spears but, in season and in peak condition, spears ranging from the fine to the imposing can be equally delicious. However, mature woody spears will not be. The same can be said of most vegetables, with outsized offerings becoming fibrous and lacking in flavour and sweetness. Asparagus should be vivid in colour, without any soft spots, wrinkles or markings. The tips will tell a story, with dehydration easy enough to spot; they should be closed and tightly packed. Buds that are opening can also indicate over-maturity, as do 'leaves' on the stems. The spears should not look floppy or wilted in any way. And for those inclined to entertain the idea of using tinned asparagus … well, please don't.

Asparagus is most commonly cooked by steaming, boiling or grilling, but it can also be sliced finely and eaten raw in salads.

Also see

*Spring vegetable
risotto* 149

*Porcini & asparagus
risotto* 151

Spring minestrone 531

*White asparagus
with walnut & rye
skordalia* 600

Pair with

*Asparagus loves butter
and extra-virgin olive oil,
lemon, pepper, tarragon and
chervil. It's great with eggs,
whether in an emulsified
sauce, such as hollandaise or
mayonnaise, or any way you
like – fried, poached, scrambled,
hard-boiled (grate the eggs
directly over spears along
with some good parmesan).
Crab, caviar and fish roe
work beautifully, as do fish
and scallops. Pancetta and
bacon, chicken, steak, taleggio,
parmesan, goat's cheese and
cream are natural partners; so
are soy and sesame. And truffles
aren't bad either.*

Preparing asparagus

Trim the base of the asparagus, discarding the woody end, which is usually the bottom 2–3 cm (¾–1¼ in) of the stem. You can simply snap off the woody end, but this is untidy, and not very reliable, as you'll probably also be snapping off some perfectly edible stem. So, just get used to judging the texture; anything remotely woody or fibrous needs to go. You can also use a vegetable peeler to remove the skin from the base, but this is only really necessary for spears thicker than your index finger (depending on the size of your fingers!). White asparagus always needs to be peeled, with the lower two-thirds of the spears typically having tough skin, which can also be quite bitter.

Once trimmed, the spears can be cooked in simmering salted water, for 3½ minutes for finger-thick spears. Dress and eat immediately, or refresh in cold or iced water for a few minutes (but no longer, as they can become waterlogged). They can then be used for salads, or on a pizza with taleggio and mozzarella, or simply rewarmed in butter in a pan; throw in some chopped soft herbs at the end and finish with salt flakes and plenty of black pepper.

Asparagus with poached egg & prosciutto ⒼⒻ

Asparagus, prosciutto, parmesan and eggs are all just so complementary – so much umami right there. Proper pasture-raised eggs are absolutely required here. If I can find it, I'll usually opt for white asparagus, too. **Serves 4**

2 bunches of asparagus, trimmed	¼ bunch of chives, finely chopped	**Staples** *S&P, VNGR*
4 eggs	5 chervil sprigs, leaves picked	
100 g (3½ oz) butter	80 g (2¾ oz) Parmigiano Reggiano	
8 slices of prosciutto, jamón or mojama		

Bring two saucepans of salted water to the boil, one for the asparagus and one for poaching the eggs. Cook the asparagus for 3½ minutes, then drain. At the same time, add a dash of vinegar to the other pan and turn the heat down to a simmer. Gently poach the eggs (see p. 351) for 3–4 minutes, depending on how you like them.

Melt the butter in a frying pan over a medium heat. Once foaming, add the asparagus, season with salt and pepper and toss to coat.

Divide the asparagus among serving plates and top with the eggs. Season with salt and pepper, then add the prosciutto. Scatter with the herbs and shave the parmesan over using a vegetable peeler. Serve immediately.

Grilled asparagus & haloumi salad with fennel, walnuts & pomegranate ⒼⒻ Ⓥ

Chargrilling asparagus takes the flavour in a different direction to steaming or blanching. It retains its signature grassy notes, but the char adds a compelling dimension. It also takes well to different flavours, particularly Middle Eastern ones. This salad makes a great light spring starter. **Serves 6**

Sautéed wild asparagus with tarragon & brown butter ⒼⒻ Ⓥ

If you happen to know where to forage for wild asparagus, then not much needs to be done to bring it to table. Wild asparagus is the same species as cultivated asparagus, but different growing conditions mean that it presents differently. While not so common in Australia, it grows widely in Europe and has somewhat of a foothold in parts of North America. The spears are often finer, wispy even, and the colour can range from green to a burnished coppery brown. Trim any woody ends from the spears and sauté with a generous slab of good butter until just tender. Season with salt flakes and black pepper and finish with chopped tarragon and a healthy squeeze of lemon. Serve simply poached or with baked fish.

Asparagus with bagna cauda ⒼⒻ

Cook a couple of bunches of asparagus, then drain and toss in extra-virgin olive oil with a pinch of salt and a good grind of black pepper. Spread the asparagus on a platter and top with 3 large halved zucchini (courgette) flowers and 2 soft-boiled eggs broken open with your hands. Shave a generous amount of Parmigiano Reggiano on top and spoon over a portion of warmed Bagna cauda (p. 83).

Pair with

Lamb, grilled chicken or fish.

Asparagus soup GF V

To make enough soup for four people, heat 80 g (2¾ oz) butter and a good splash of extra-virgin olive oil in a wide-based saucepan over a low–medium heat. Add 1 finely diced salad onion and 3 finely chopped garlic cloves and cook gently for about 10 minutes to soften, without picking up any colour. Peel and very finely slice 1 all-purpose potato (such as desiree), add to the saucepan and stir to coat well. Cook until tender, about 5 minutes, adding a splash of stock if it is sticking. Add 400 g (14 oz) finely sliced asparagus (too-fat or too-thin spears and offcuts are perfect) and a pinch of sugar, season with salt and pepper and stir to coat. Add 650 ml (22 fl oz) warmed chicken or vegetable stock and 2 tarragon sprigs, if desired, then simmer for 2 minutes. Stir in 150 ml (5 oz) thick (double/heavy) cream and simmer for a further 2 minutes. Remove the tarragon sprigs and blitz the soup using a stick blender, or in batches in a blender. Adjust the seasoning as necessary, then serve with a swirl of cream on top. Take the soup a step further by topping with some cooked asparagus, salmon roe and/or flaked hot-smoked trout, or add a poached egg to each bowl and crumble some crisp pancetta over. A few shavings of black truffle wouldn't hurt, either.

2½ bunches of asparagus, trimmed on an angle
250 g (9 oz) haloumi, cut into 1.5 cm (½ in) slices
3 tablespoons pomegranate molasses
1 tablespoon ground sumac
1 fennel bulb, finely sliced

1 handful of coriander (cilantro) leaves
1 handful of mint leaves, torn
½ pomegranate, seeds reserved
3 tablespoons toasted walnuts, oiled, seasoned and crushed

Lemon garlic dressing
80 ml (2½ fl oz/⅓ cup) extra-virgin olive oil
juice of ½ lemon
1 garlic clove, finely grated

Staples
EVOO, S&P

Preheat a chargrill pan or barbecue grill on high.

Oil the asparagus and season with salt, then grill for 2–3 minutes, rotating the spears regularly, until tender and slightly charred. Lightly oil the haloumi and grill until quite brown, about 1½ minutes on each side.

Add the dressing ingredients to a bowl, season with salt and pepper and combine well.

Drizzle the pomegranate molasses across a serving plate. Lay down the haloumi and asparagus and sprinkle with the sumac. Dress the fennel with half the dressing and pile on top. Scatter with the herbs, pomegranate seeds and walnuts, then drizzle with the remaining dressing and serve.

Crumbed asparagus spears V

This is quite sophisticated party food, or it could be plated up as an appetiser. Leaving the asparagus tips un-crumbed retains some of the natural appeal of the spears, while the crunchy golden sleeve of cheesy panko adds its own charm. Eat these hot while the crumbs are deliciously crunchy. **Serves 4**

250 ml (8½ fl oz/1 cup) oil, for shallow-frying
150 g (5½ oz/2½ cups) panko breadcrumbs

50 g (1¾ oz/½ cup) finely grated Grana Padano
2 bunches of asparagus, trimmed
2 eggs, whisked

Chopped egg tartare (p. 351), to serve

Staples
FLR, S&P

Heat the oil to 170°C (340°F) in a deep frying pan, or use a deep-fryer.

Combine the panko and cheese in a shallow bowl. Dust the asparagus lightly with flour, then dip the spears in the egg, leaving the tips uncoated. Finally, roll the spears in the panko mix to coat.

Fry the asparagus in the hot oil, in batches if necessary, until golden brown, about 3 minutes, turning occasionally to cook evenly. Drain quickly on paper towel, season with salt and serve hot, with chopped egg tartare.

Make it different
Serve with Hollandaise (p. 79) or Rouille (p. 80) instead of the chopped egg tartare.

Avocado

Given their ubiquity today, it is hard to appreciate that avocados were relatively exotic not so long ago – in Australia at least. And while never truffle-expensive, cost often relegated them to the somewhat fancy category. With less varietal diversity, the season was also shorter. Having said all that, my nanna would happily pile an unseemly amount of avocado on toast when I was growing up.

Nanna lived in a big old country house in Benalla, Victoria, with a garden full of fruit trees, particularly citrus. We spent regular holidays there, all the way throughout school. For breakfast, she would often make avocado on wholemeal (whole-wheat) toast with lots of ground white pepper, salt and lemon juice; I remember the toast sagging heavily under the weight. Sometimes a fried egg, from the chooks across the road, would make it onto the plate as well. We'd follow that with half a grapefruit, from the tree in her backyard, sprinkled with a little too much white sugar. And I'd force down a cup of milky tea – her specialty.

A regular breakfast of mine still consists of a ripe avocado smashed on well-toasted Sourdough bread (p. 847) or dark rye with lots of black pepper, salt flakes, a rather large squeeze of lemon or lime, and a drizzle of extra-virgin olive oil. Sometimes it gets a sprinkling of dried chilli flakes, or some fruity, sweet and hot ground aleppo pepper. When time allows, a poached egg or two gets perched on top. Nanna's breakfast with a makeover!

Avocados are a fruit (well, they're actually a berry, which may be fascinating to botanists but somewhat irrelevant to cooks), thought to have originated in what is now Mexico, though they've been cultivated throughout Central and South America and the West Indies for many thousands of years. There are myriad varieties, adapted to growing in climates from the relatively cool to the tropical. Some are classically pear shaped ('avocado pear' is an old-fashioned term) with deep green skin, while others are quite large and almost spherical, with smooth, luridly green skin. Perhaps the most familiar variety is Hass, with its knobbly skin that typically turns a deep green-black when ripe. It has creamy flesh with a rich, nutty flavour, while other varieties are slightly waxier and less rich. Different varieties tend to overlap seasonally, meaning an almost year-round supply in a country as climatically diverse as Australia.

So, the avocado you use will often be dictated by the time of year. Properly ripe, any avocado will do the job, though aficionados may bicker over the detail. The key is ripeness. An unripe avocado is a thing of misery – firm, vegetal, soapy-textured and thoroughly unappetising. And there's no fixing it. It won't really ripen further once cut, and it can ruin a dish if you try to persevere with it. Select specimens that yield to gentle pressure towards the neck. If there are soft spots on the body or noticeably darker and discoloured patches, move on. Hass is the only variety that changes hue when ripe, although some growing conditions retard this change, making colour an unreliable indicator of ripeness.

If buying more than one, remember that a firm avocado will ripen with time, so select the ripeness based on when you intend on using them. To speed up that ripening, pop them in a paper bag; adding a banana, kiwi fruit or apple will make them ripen even faster. If you want to arrest the ripening, just put them in the fridge.

Avocados can also be cold-pressed for their oil, which contains many of the health benefits associated with extra-virgin olive oil, plus a brace of nutrients and antioxidants.

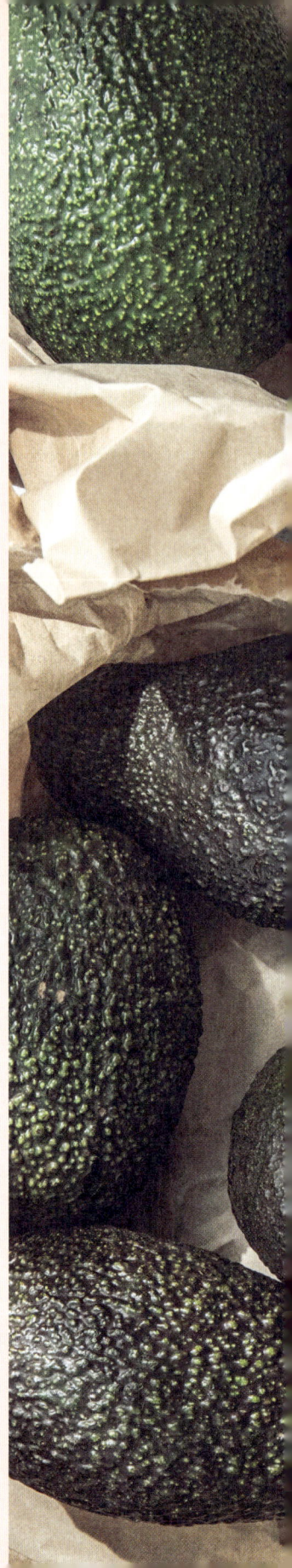

Also see

Chicken & corn koftas with avocado & coriander 249

Broad bean & avocado dip 431

American-style ranch salad 557

Daikon, edamame & avocado salad with sesame, apple & soy dressing 640

Pair with

The rich oiliness of avocado loves a spike of citric acidity from lemon, lime, yuzu and pickled radish, bright fragrant herbs such as mint, coriander (cilantro), chives and parsley, and flavours of smoked paprika, ginger, coriander seeds, cumin, fresh chilli, chilli flakes and ground aleppo pepper. That richness is also great with the earthy nuttiness of pepitas (pumpkin seeds), sesame, sunflower seeds, rye bread, seed crackers and sprouted legumes and seeds. Pair with fennel, corn, zucchini (courgette), tomato, cucumber, cos (romaine) and butter lettuce, peas, pea shoots, spring onion (scallion), charry grilled pineapple and seaweed. Match with chicken, soft-boiled eggs, caviar, smoked fish, raw fish (especially tuna), crab, prawns (shrimp), Moreton bay bugs (flat-head lobsters), scallops and white anchovies.

Preparing avocados

Using a sharp knife, carefully cut along the length of the avocado, right down to the stone, then run the knife all the way around the avocado. Remove the knife. Twist one side free of the stone, then tap the knife blade into the stone and pull it free. Run a large spoon along the inside of the skin and remove the flesh. From there, slice, dice, mash or puree. However you prepare it, avocado flesh will oxidise quickly, so aside from being a great flavour match, lemon juice will also help to keep up appearances. If you're only using half an avocado, leave the stone in the other half, which will help it keep better, and rub some lemon juice on the cut surface. You can also submerge the avocado in a container of water and keep it in the fridge to stop it oxidising.

Soba noodles with avocado, sprouts, umeboshi & sesame GF V VG

I love this combination: the crunchy life-giving sprouts, nutty silken buckwheat noodles and rich avocado, anointed with the salty and sour tang of the umeboshi plum and sesame dressing, is just divine. My children love this salad, too, and have since they were quite little – which makes life easier all round. The quantities here are small, as this is something I generally whip up for lunch when the house is all but empty, or for my girls after school, but you can easily double this recipe. **Serves 2**

125 g (4½ oz) buckwheat soba noodles
1 avocado, flesh diced
4 spring onions (scallions), white part only, finely sliced
1 handful of baby pea shoots
1 handful of mung bean sprouts

1 handful of lentil sprouts
Gomashio (p. 16), to serve, or 3 tablespoons sesame seeds

Umeboshi & sesame dressing
2½ tablespoons extra-virgin olive oil

1 tablespoon rice vinegar
1 tablespoon umeboshi purée
juice of ½ lemon
½ teaspoon sesame oil
¼ garlic clove, finely chopped

Add the dressing ingredients to a small bowl and combine well.

Cook the noodles in boiling salted water for 5 minutes, then drain and refresh under cold water. Drain off any excess water, then coat the noodles with half the dressing.

Pile the noodles into serving bowls, then scatter with the avocado, spring onion, pea shoots, and the mung bean and lentil sprouts. Top with a few shakes of gomashio, spoon the remaining dressing over and serve.

Make it a meal
Add a handful of shredded left-over roast chicken or poached chicken breast. Some fried tofu would be just as good, if you'd like to keep it vegetarian.

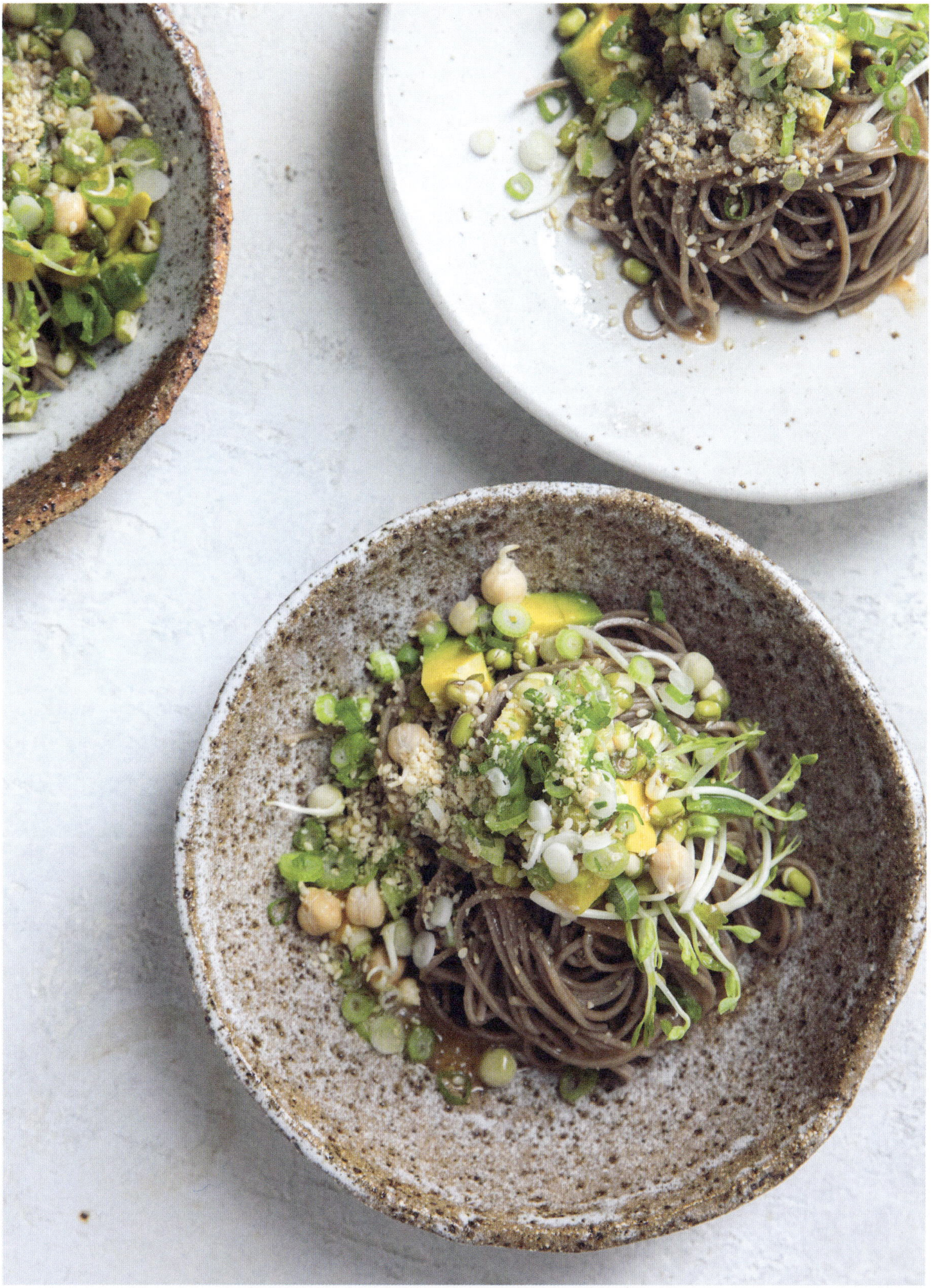

Chocolate & avocado ganache ㊾ Ⓥ ㊰

If the idea of using avocado to ice a cake is a new concept to you, then this ganache will probably seem quite bizarre. But it works incredibly well, with the avocado flavour and colour completely masked by the cocoa, so what you're left with is a luscious, buttery texture. The other upside is that it's healthier than most alternatives. You can, of course, adjust the sugar to taste. **Makes about 600 g (1 lb 5 oz)**

300 g (10½ oz) ripe avocado flesh (about 2 avocados)	125 ml (4 fl oz/½ cup) agave syrup, or brown rice syrup, maple syrup or honey	1 teaspoon vanilla extract
100 g (3½ oz) raw unsweetened cocoa powder	70 g (2½ oz) coconut oil, gently melted if solid	

Blitz all the ingredients in a blender until smooth and glossy. Use straight away.

Pair with

This ganache works beautifully on desserts and cakes where nuts are a feature. It is perfect any time you would like to ice a vegan cake or slice.

Lime leaf & white pepper guacamole ㊾ Ⓥ ㊰

This version of guacamole is particularly good with the Corn & pineapple salsa (p. 499), and its overt limey brightness matches even the most intensely flavoured proteins. Chopping and grinding the lime leaves is a bit of a labour, but the result is stunning. **Serves 10**

5 makrut lime leaves	1½ tablespoons extra-virgin olive oil	1 teaspoon ground white pepper
1 teaspoon salt flakes	2 teaspoons hot green jalapeño sauce (such as green Tabasco)	**Staples**
juice of 2 limes		S&P
3 ripe avocados, roughly diced		

Cut the vein out of the lime leaves, then chop as finely as possible. Add to a mortar with the salt and grind into a very fine powder; it will be incredibly fragrant and bright green. Stir in the lime juice and, washing the powder from the sides of the mortar.

Scrape into a bowl and add the other ingredients. Combine vigorously with a spoon, mashing to a smooth-ish paste. Adjust the salt if needed, and serve straight away.

Pair with

Corn & pineapple salsa (p. 499), with fried fish, white bait or school prawns (shrimp) in a soft tortilla.

Chilli con pollo (p. 232) or other Mexican-inspired dishes.

Floured fried fish, flathead, mirror dory (with skin on), snapper, blue-eye cod or salmon.

Use as a dip for corn chips.

Simple guacamole ㊾ Ⓥ

There are more complicated versions of guacamole, but the simplest are just as delicious. Smash some avocado with salt and pepper and plain yoghurt (one part yoghurt to two parts avocado), then spike with a splash of lemon juice and hot green jalapeño sauce, such as green Tabasco. This version is so simple that my girls regularly made it for a snack from about the age of ten.

Guacamole no. 2 GF V VG

This one's a bit fancier. Using a mortar and pestle, grind ½ small garlic clove with a generous pinch of salt, into a paste. Add the flesh of 2 avocados and mash roughly. Follow with the juice of 1 lime (or lemon, but lime is best here), ½ finely diced red onion, a few handfuls of chopped coriander (cilantro) and a tablespoon of chopped pickled jalapeño chillies. Season with salt and pepper and serve with a drizzle of olive oil on top. You can omit the jalapeños, if you like, or dial up the heat with a few chopped chillies, or a squirt of hot sauce.

Crab with avocado mousse, mint, chilli & sweet pickled cucumber

This is an elegant little starter, with the silky-smooth texture of the avocado mousse a fabulous foil for the delicate and sweet crabmeat. **Serves 6 as a starter**

80 ml (2½ fl oz/⅓ cup) extra-virgin olive oil
juice of 1 lime
1 teaspoon dijon mustard
500 g (1 lb 2 oz) cooked crabmeat (spanner, blue swimmer or mud crab)
4 dill sprigs, fronds chopped
10 small mint leaves, torn
1 long green chilli, finely sliced into rings
1½ tablespoons salmon roe
2 teaspoons ground aleppo pepper

finely sliced crostini or fresh white bread, to serve

Avocado mousse
3 ripe avocados, at room temperature, flesh roughly chopped
juice of 1 lemon
¼ teaspoon cayenne pepper
3 gold-strength gelatine leaves
300 ml (10 fl oz) thickened cream (35% fat), lightly whipped and not very cold

Sweet pickled cucumber
2 Lebanese (short) cucumbers, peeled, seeded and sliced
2 red Asian shallots, very finely sliced
2 teaspoons raw sugar
½ teaspoon salt flakes

Staples
EVOO, S&P

For the mousse, add the avocado flesh to a blender and puree until smooth. Season with salt and pepper, add the lemon juice and cayenne, then blend to combine. Transfer to a bowl and set aside.

Add the gelatine to a little cold water and leave to bloom for 5 minutes. Heat 2 tablespoons of the cream in a small saucepan. Squeeze any excess water from the gelatine leaves, add them to the pan and stir to dissolve, then pour into a bowl and set aside for 5 minutes.

Fold the remaining cream through the avocado puree, then fold in the gelatine cream. Chill for 1–2 hours, until set.

For the pickled cucumber, add all the ingredients to a bowl and toss to combine. Set aside for 5 minutes to soften and slightly pickle.

Combine the oil, lime juice and mustard and use it to dress the crabmeat, tossing gently.

Toss the herbs and chilli through the pickled cucumber, then divide between serving plates, along with the crab. Spoon on some avocado mousse and drizzle with oil. Finish with the caviar and aleppo pepper. Serve with crostini or bread.

Make it different
Prawn cocktail. The mousse could also be used in a prawn cocktail by setting it in the base of glasses. Once set, layer in shredded iceberg lettuce or cos (romaine) heart and cooked prawns (shrimp), with a drizzle of Marie rose sauce (p. 77) to finish.

Present the dish a little more formally by setting the mousse in small dariole moulds, ramekins or the like; you'll need to oil the moulds so the mousse slips out easily. Turn the mousse out onto plates and arrange the other elements around it.

Tuna poké bowl with avocado, shiitake, sesame, wakame & cucumber

The success of poké bowls is not surprising, especially given the recent popularity of 'clean eating' and superfood bowls. I'd be happy to eat this salad, or versions thereof, several times a week. The layering in of goodness, as well as texture and flavour, is deliciously compelling. **Serves 6**

400 g (14 oz) cooked short-grain brown rice, kept warm

kewpie mayonnaise, to serve

12 small cherry tomatoes, rolled in 1 teaspoon sesame oil

250 g (9 oz) daikon, finely julienned and kept crisp in chilled water, then drained

2 ripe avocados, flesh thickly sliced

2 tablespoons furikake seasoning

2 tablespoons pickled white ginger

2 finger limes, split to reveal the pearls, or a splash of lime juice if unavailable

2 long green chillies, sliced into rounds

Lightly cured tuna

450 g (1 lb) sashimi-grade yellowfin tuna, cut into 2 cm (¾ in) dice

1 tablespoon extra-virgin olive oil

½ teaspoon sesame oil

½ teaspoon salt flakes

1 teaspoon caster (superfine) sugar

Cucumber & wakame salad

20 g (¾ oz) dried wakame

2 Lebanese (short) cucumbers, sliced into fine rounds

2 spring onions (scallions), white part only, finely sliced

1 tablespoon rice vinegar

1 tablespoon mirin

Tamari sesame dressing

2 tablespoons mirin

2 tablespoons rice vinegar

1½ tablespoons tamari

½ teaspoon sesame oil

2 tablespoons toasted sesame seeds

Soy shitake mushrooms

2 tablespoons grapeseed oil

1 garlic clove, finely grated

200 g (7 oz) fresh shiitake mushrooms, big ones sliced, small ones quartered

1 tablespoon brown-rice vinegar

1 tablespoon light soy sauce

Staples

S&P, SGR

Combine the tuna ingredients in a bowl and set aside for about 15 minutes.

For the salad, rehydrate the wakame in warm water for about 10 minutes. Drain and roughly chop, then add to a bowl with the cucumber and spring onion. Add the vinegar, mirin and a pinch of salt and sugar. Toss and set aside to pickle for about 5 minutes.

Add the dressing ingredients to a small bowl and combine well.

For the mushrooms, heat the oil in a frying pan over a medium heat. Add the garlic and fry briefly until fragrant. Add the mushrooms and cook for a couple of minutes to soften, before adding the vinegar and soy. Set aside for 5 minutes.

To serve, divide the warm rice among bowls and dot with mayonnaise. Pile on the salad, mushrooms, tomatoes and daikon. Dip the avocado slices in furikake and place a few slices in each bowl. Top with the ginger, finger lime pearls and chilli, then spoon the sesame dressing over and serve.

Make it faster
Poké bowls are very versatile. You can leave elements out or just simplify them, using fresh cucumber rather than the pickled salad, or flaking in some hot smoked trout in place of the tuna. But remember that variety and textural contrasts are what make the dish, so try to layer it up a bit.

Make it different
With chicken. Add White-poached chicken (p. 230).

Beetroot

Beetroot (beet) was a very common vegetable when I was young. Tinned mainly, and usually sitting between two pieces of bread. Either in a burger – a very Australian thing that horrifies many an outsider – or a salad sandwich with shredded iceberg lettuce, or nestled in a cloud of earthy sprouts and grated carrot (usually a plastic-wrapped affair that was always too big to eat in any practical way). A bit fancier were the baby beets sold in a tin, used for salads and the like. Times have changed, and while I have a feeling preserved beetroot was more ubiquitous than popular back then, fresh beetroot has seen an appetising renaissance.

I can't get enough of beetroot now. I love them raw – shaved, julienned, grated – as well as cooked, whether roasted whole, or in wedges, steamed or simmered in salted water until tender. Roasted beets simply dressed with a splash of vinegar and extra-virgin olive oil and a good seasoning of salt flakes and black pepper is about the simplest way to enjoy them cooked. Quite often, I'll also crumble over some firm Greek-style feta, dried wild oregano and shaved salad onion – it's beautiful served alongside grilled fish or slow-roasted lamb shoulder.

You can eat pretty much the whole beetroot, as the leaves and stems are delicious, though they can have a slightly sharp edge. Just treat them a bit like silverbeet (see p. 550), also known as Swiss chard (they are closely related, after all); you can support the beetroot greens with other greens to round that sharpness out. The bulb itself is the taproot of the plant, and the only bits that can be a challenge are the woody probe of the root and the very top, where the stems emerge, as the stems can be quite densely packed and any dirt can be hard to dislodge. Having said that, with a thorough wash baby beets sliced lengthways on a mandoline look quite spectacular with the stems still attached. I just quick-pickle them with a pinch of salt and sugar and a splash of vinegar. They can then be added to a slaw, or used to top a potato salad – or toss them with watercress or herbs, such as mint and parsley, and serve with toasted almonds or walnuts and a fresh curd cheese.

You can buy beetroot in many colours – from deep blood-red to turmeric-yellow to white, with striped varieties, too (known variously as chioggia, target, bullseye and candy stripe). They will all be slightly different in intensity and sweetness, and sizes vary from the petite to almost grapefruit-sized specimens. Whatever the size, the preparation and applications are the same. Sugar beets are also very widely grown, especially in Europe, but their main purpose is for producing refined sugar – second only in volume to cane sugar, globally speaking.

When buying beetroot, I like to select ones with the leaves still attached. Like any vegetable, beets will start to decline after harvest, so vibrantly fresh leaves will be a good signpost for freshness. If you are buying without the leaves, opt for firm and heavy bulbs with no splits or soft spots. If the skin feels baggy or they are a little soft, move on.

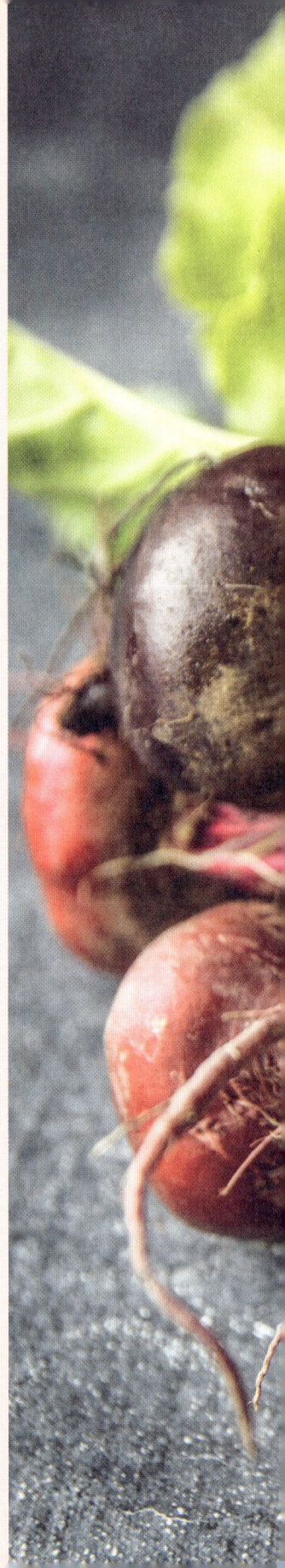

Also see

Kohlrabi, cabbage &
beetroot slaw 548–9

Pickled turnip torshi 639

Jamón, fig, beetroot,
goat's curd, watercress
& mint salad 702

Pair with

*The robust earthiness of
beetroot works beautifully with
slightly sharp dairy, such as
sour cream, yoghurt, ricotta,
cream cheese and goat's cheese.
Accent with almonds, pine
nuts, walnuts, pistachios, rye
bread, garlic, fermented garlic,
olives, anise, ouzo, ginger and
chocolate – and soft herbs
such as thyme, dill, parsley
and chervil, and spices such
as cinnamon, cumin, allspice,
caraway and fenugreek.
Match with bitter greens,
radicchio, silverbeet (Swiss
chard), radish, orange, lemon,
carrot, fennel and onion. Acid
and robust flavours are excellent
foils for their sweetness – try
with vinegar of all types, pickled
onion, pickled fish, smoked
fish and anchovies. Beetroot
stands up to strongly flavoured
proteins such as beef, pork,
lamb and game.*

Preparing beetroot

Beetroot (beets) should be washed before cooking, but can be peeled after roasting, steaming or boiling. So, if cooking them whole, leave the fine end of the taproot and the stem base attached. Both can be removed when you slip the cooked skins off. If using raw, they can simply be peeled with a vegetable peeler before cutting. It's a good idea to leave the stem base on when slicing finely on a mandoline; just be sure to dislodge any dirt trapped in there. If boiling, it's best to keep them whole, with stem and root intact, otherwise they will bleed too much juice. You can also roast them whole, or cut into wedges to speed things along; either way, simply coat the beetroot with oil, season and wrap in foil before roasting at 180°C (350°F). This will take anywhere from 30 minutes to more than an hour for a large whole beet. When they yield easily to a knife, they're done.

Borscht (GF)

This is a soup I really should make more often. It's nurturing and comforting, like a super-big hug in the cooler months. This recipe is based on Ukrainian borscht, which is what most of us would identify as borscht: a beetroot (beet) soup with a meat base. However, beetroot-based borscht (the word is Russian, so that's not even a constant) is easily the most emblematic, and subtle changes in the recipe define national and regional variants, which are no doubt fought over endlessly. Traditionally, this is a sour soup, with the beetroot fermented for several days before cooking. Here, lemon juice at the end fills that gap for me, though I can hear the traditionalists grumbling. This soup keeps well in the fridge for several days and can also be frozen. **Serves 10–12**

Pair with

Serve with buttered toasted rye bread and pickled onions.

3 beef ribs, about 1.5 kg (3 lb 5 oz), or 1 kg (2 lb 3 oz) osso buco
3.5 litres (118 fl oz/14 cups) water
2 carrots, peeled, 1 split lengthways, 1 diced
2 brown onions, 1 skin on and studded with 4 cloves, 1 finely diced
5 parsley stalks
8 allspice berries
2 teaspoons salt flakes

3 large beetroot (beets), trimmed
100 g (3½ oz) butter
6 garlic cloves, finely chopped
1 celeriac, peeled and cut into 2 cm (¾ in) dice
2 turnips, or swedes/ rutabaga, peeled and cut into 2 cm (¾ in) dice
1 parsnip, peeled and cut into 2 cm (¾ in) dice
1 tablespoon tomato paste (concentrated purée)

2 waxy yellow potatoes (such as Dutch cream), peeled and cut into 2 cm (¾ in) dice
500 ml (17 fl oz/2 cups) White chicken stock (p. 54)
2 teaspoons freshly ground black pepper
sour cream, to serve
dill fronds, to serve

Staples
EVOO, LMN, S&P

Preheat the oven to 180°C (350°F) fan-forced.

Add the beef and water to a large saucepan. Bring to a simmer over a medium heat, skimming thoroughly for several minutes. Add the split carrot, whole onion, parsley stalks, allspice and salt. Simmer for about 2½ hours, until the meat is falling from the bone.

Meanwhile, place the beetroot on a double layer of foil. Drizzle over some oil, season with salt and pepper, wrap up and roast on a baking tray for an hour or so, until tender. Once cooked, cool a little before slipping the skins off and cutting the flesh into 2 cm (¾ in) dice.

When the beef is tender, remove from the stock, strip the meat from the bones and cut into small dice. Strain the broth through a fine-mesh sieve, then moisten the meat with a little of the broth to stop it drying out.

Heat the butter in a wide-based saucepan over a medium heat. Add the diced onion and cook until softened but without colour, about 5 minutes. Add the garlic and cook until fragrant. Add the diced carrot, celeriac, turnip and parsnip and cook until starting to caramelise, about 10 minutes.

Stir in the tomato paste and potatoes. Add the meat broth, chicken stock, roasted beetroot and diced beef and bring to a simmer. Reduce the heat to low and simmer gently for 30 minutes. Add the pepper and season with salt as necessary.

Serve in wide, flat bowls, with a dollop of sour cream, a good squeeze of lemon and some dill.

Beetroot tabouleh with currants & sunflower seeds Ⓥ ⓋⒼ

Classic tabouleh has quite a summery feel, while this salad plays down a richer line, presenting just as well in cooler weather as it does in warmer months. The bulgur wheat takes up so much flavour, colour and moisture from the pureed beetroot (beet), making for a wholesome and filling salad. **Serves 4–6**

Pair with

This salad is perfect served with grilled skewered meat, with plenty of yoghurt and warmed flatbread on the side.

Raw quick pickled beetroot ⒼⒻ Ⓥ ⓋⒼ

Trim a couple of baby beetroot, leaving a bit of stalk on. Wash and scrub thoroughly, ensuring you dislodge all the dirt from the stems. Using a mandoline, finely slice lengthways; the idea is to get the full profile of the beetroot, including the stem. Place in a small bowl, splash some wine vinegar or sherry vinegar over and season with a few pinches of salt and sugar. Set aside for about 10 minutes to lightly pickle, then use to garnish the dish.

2 large beetroot (beets), trimmed
250 g (9 oz) fine bulgur wheat, or white quinoa, washed
3 tablespoons currants
60 ml (2 fl oz/ ¼ cup) red-wine vinegar
juice of 1 lemon
1 large garlic clove, finely grated

2 teaspoons ground cumin
1 bunch of flat-leaf parsley, finely shredded, including the top three-quarters of the stalks
½ bunch of mint, leaves picked and torn
2 handfuls of dill fronds
3 tablespoons sunflower seeds

Cumin & garlic dressing
100 ml (3½ fl oz) extra-virgin olive oil
60 ml (2 fl oz/¼ cup) red-wine vinegar
1 large garlic clove, finely grated
2 teaspoons ground cumin

Staples
EVOO, S&P

Preheat the oven to 180°C (350°F) fan-forced.

Place the beetroot on a double layer of foil. Drizzle over some oil, season with salt and pepper, wrap up and roast on a baking tray for an hour or so, until tender.

Meanwhile, add the bulgur wheat to a saucepan of boiling water and cook for 5 minutes (or 10 minutes if using quinoa). Drain, dress with a splash of oil and fluff the grains with a fork.

In a small saucepan, bring the currants and vinegar to the boil, then take straight off the heat.

Cool the cooked beetroot a little, then slip off the skins. Add the flesh to a food processor and blitz to a rough puree. Add the lemon juice, garlic and cumin and blitz again. Tip the puree into a fine-mesh sieve and set aside to drain for 5 minutes.

Add the dressing ingredients to a large bowl, season with salt and pepper and combine. Add the bulgur wheat to the dressing and combine. Mix in the beetroot, then set aside for 5 minutes.

Stir the parsley and mint through, and adjust the seasoning as necessary. Tip into a shallow serving bowl and scatter with the currants, dill and sunflower seeds.

Make it different
With haloumi. Haloumi works particularly well with this salad. Cut a 250 g (9 oz) block into eight slices, then pan-fry with a little oil until golden. Serve alongside the tabouleh with a good squeeze of lemon.

Roasted beetroot, cinnamon & pomegranate dip GF V

Beetroot (beet) and cinnamon are an excellent match, with the deep warmth of the spice playing beautifully with the full earthy flavour and sweetness of the beet. This recipe makes quite a lot of dip, but it can easily be halved. The base dip also keeps well in the fridge, in which case dress the dip with the feta and other elements just before serving. **Makes about 400 g (14 oz)**

Pair with

This dip will complement any meze spread, but also pairs well with grilled lamb, chicken or fish.

500 g (1 lb 2 oz) beetroot (beets), trimmed and cut into sixths
2½ teaspoons ground cinnamon, plus extra to serve
1 teaspoon ground allspice

1 teaspoon chilli powder
150 g (5½ oz) thick plain yoghurt
60 ml (2 fl oz/¼ cup) pomegranate molasses
80 g (2¾ oz) feta

2 handfuls of pomegranate seeds
3 mint sprigs, leaves picked
flatbread, or crostini, to serve
Staples
EVOO, S&P

Preheat the oven to 180°C (350°F) fan-forced.

Add the beetroot to a large baking tray, drizzle with oil, sprinkle with the cinnamon and allspice, season with salt and pepper and toss through to coat evenly. Add a splash of water to the dish, cover with baking paper, then a layer of foil, and roast for about 15 minutes, until the beetroot is just tender. Remove the paper and foil and bake for another 40 minutes, or until the beetroot is tender and starting to caramelise. Set aside to cool.

Once cooled, puree the beetroot with the chilli powder until smooth. Add the yoghurt and pomegranate molasses and process until combined. Adjust the seasoning as necessary.

To serve, spread the beetroot onto a serving plate, crumble some feta over, and sprinkle on some extra cinnamon. Scatter with the pomegranate seeds and mint and serve with flatbread.

Make it different
Spread the dip across a serving plate and pile on a colourful medley of cooked beetroot dressed with a simple French-style vinaigrette (p. 88) and chopped soft herbs.

Beetroot, carrot & pomegranate salad GF V VG

This is part salad and part condiment, so a little goes a long way. Its balance of sweetness and refreshing tartness is a great foil for dishes with spice. **Serves 8**

Pair with

Serve the salad with several dips and flatbread, or pan-fried fish dusted with flour and cumin.

It's also an excellent companion for a Middle Eastern–style stew or tagine.

80 ml (2½ fl oz/⅓ cup) extra-virgin olive oil
2 tablespoons apple-cider vinegar, or white-wine vinegar
2 tablespoons pomegranate molasses

1 pomegranate, seeds reserved from half, the other half juiced
zest of ½ orange
2 teaspoons ground ginger
3 large carrots, coarsely grated

1 large beetroot (beet), coarsely grated
Staples
S&P

Combine the oil, vinegar, molasses, pomegranate juice, orange zest and ginger in a large bowl. Add the carrot and beetroot, season with salt and pepper and combine. Pile into serving bowls and top with the pomegranate seeds. Serve as is, or chilled.

Beetroot jelly ⒼⒻ

This beet and ginger jelly is a beautifully different way to present beetroot, with the jewel-like jelly adding pops of colour, flavour and texture to a dish. Treat it a bit like a condiment, or as an accent in a salad. **Makes about 300 g (10½ oz)**

Pair with

The sweetness and tart vinegary profile, plus the earthy tone of the beetroot, make this an ideal accompaniment for charcuterie and cured fish. Serve with smoked meats, pork terrines (pp. 327–8) or Chicken liver parfait (p. 233) – and also try it with hot-smoked freshwater trout, cured or smoked ocean trout or gravlax (see p. 169), Ocean trout rillettes (see p. 174) or smoked eel pâté or rillettes.

It would also work well with corned or roast beef in a salad or a sandwich, and with goat's and sheep's curd cheeses.

Dice the jelly and use it to dress up a mayonnaise-based potato salad.

4 beetroot (beets), trimmed
150 ml (5 fl oz) white-wine vinegar
2 tablespoons caster (superfine) sugar
1½ tablespoons salt flakes
2 star anise
2 teaspoons sherry vinegar
5 cm (2 in) piece of fresh ginger, peeled and finely grated
12 gold-strength gelatine leaves

Add the beetroot, white-wine vinegar, sugar, salt and star anise to a large saucepan. Cover with water, to about two finger-widths above the beetroot. Simmer for 40–60 minutes, until tender.

Remove the cooked beetroot and strain off the liquid into a bowl. Measure 500 ml (17 fl oz/2 cups) of the cooking liquid and add the sherry vinegar and ginger. Set aside for 15 minutes to infuse, then strain.

Once cool enough to handle, slip the skins off the beetroot and cut the flesh into 1 cm (½ in) dice. Place in a non-reactive bowl or container.

Add the gelatine to a little cold water and leave to bloom for 5 minutes. Warm 100 ml (3½ fl oz) of the infused beetroot liquor in a small saucepan. Squeeze any excess water from the gelatine leaves, add them to the pan and stir to dissolve, then strain again and add back to the remaining infused liquor.

Pour the liquid over the beetroot and refrigerate for at least 2 hours, until set. You can then dice or slice the jelly, or spoon it out to use. The jelly will keep for 7 days in the fridge.

Borlotti beans

In the River Cafe's seminal vegetable book, *Green*, borlotti beans (also known as cranberry beans) are referenced by their Italian synonym, fagioli scritti, or 'written beans', reflecting their pink freckled pods, which are thought to resemble handwriting (about as legible as mine). The beans retain their pretty flecks of colour when dried, but lose their unique markings during simmering. You certainly don't want to eat them raw, though – mature borlotti beans, like many shelling beans, are toxic if not cooked properly, or at too low a temperature (see Pulses, p. 372). Once cooked, borlotti beans are creamy in texture and absorb the flavours of a sauce or vinaigrette, making them incredibly delicious.

Though originally from the Americas, borlotti beans are as embedded in Italian cuisine as tomatoes and potatoes, which are also introduced species. And while I identify borlotti beans very much with Italian cooking (think pasta e fagioli), that association extends around the Mediterranean, with influences from the Middle East, North Africa and Greece yielding just as compelling dishes.

Fresh borlotti beans are typically available from late summer into autumn. Ideally, select pods that are vibrantly coloured and firm. If the pods have dried out, the beans inside may have started to dry also, which may result in uneven cooking and/or a longer cooking time. You can, of course, shell the beans, then dry them completely and use as you would any dried bean. Apparently, they freeze well enough if blanched first, but I'm happier making the most of the harvest and enjoying the dried version in the cooler months. If the pods are looking a bit damp and tired, the beans might still be perfectly good inside, so don't discard without inspecting the beans themselves. A green hue on the beans typically means they are not fully mature, which doesn't impact on their deliciousness, but discoloured or soft specimens are not desirable.

Because they take up flavour so readily, scenting the cooking water with aromatic vegetables such as onion, carrot and fennel, and hard herbs such as rosemary, thyme and bay leaves, imparts them with so much character. The cooked beans can then be added to soups, stews and salads, and don't require much effort to shine. Coat with Salsa verde (p. 86) as a simple accompaniment to steak or fish. Serve tossed in a French-style vinaigrette (p. 88) with lots of parsley or tarragon and a crumbling of soft goat's cheese. Or add ground spices to the vinaigrette and toss with diced lemon or orange flesh and blanched greens. Combine with shaved cabbage, olive oil, wine vinegar and freshly grated Parmigiano Reggiano for an interesting coleslaw-style salad. Or cook them longer with some peeled garlic cloves, then smash to a paste with peppery olive oil and plenty of lemon juice and black pepper for a dip, or to smear on toasted Sourdough bread (p. 847).

Also see

Chilli con pollo with chorizo & beans 232

Black turtle bean, pork belly & morcilla braise (Frijoles negros) 340

Pair with

Borlotti (cranberry) beans love lemons and oranges, tomatoes and red capsicums (bell peppers). They take well to spices such as cumin, allspice and coriander seeds, and sing with peppery extra-virgin olive oil, garlic, and fresh soft herbs such as parsley, mint, coriander (cilantro), dill and chervil. Pair them with fresh or pan-wilted greens – from spinach and rocket (arugula) to bitter leaves such as chicory (witlof/endive), dandelion and cime di rape ('turnip tips'), as well as cooked grains such as barley, farro, freekeh and bulgur wheat. They stand up well against lamb and pork, and full-flavoured and oily fish such as tuna and mackerel.

Preparing borlotti beans

Fresh borlotti (cranberry) beans just need to be removed from their pods, which come away quite easily. Bring them to the boil in a pot of salted water (I like to throw in a bay leaf, garlic clove and a halved onion, too), then simmer until tender, which will take 20–25 minutes. Dried beans are best soaked overnight in water with a pinch of salt, and will take closer to 45 minutes to cook (using fresh lightly salted water). The dried beans will have a heavier flavour and will tend to mash more readily. Note that recipes (including the River Cafe book) will often say *not* to salt fresh or dried borlotti beans during cooking, but in fact they cook more quickly, more evenly and become more tender when salted, as is the case with all dried beans (see p. 371).

Short cut

You can use tinned borlotti beans, but they won't match the flavour and texture of fresh beans. Cannellini beans and kidney beans can be used interchangeably with borlotti beans.

Braised pork shoulder with borlotti beans & taleggio

This is relatively light for a pork braise, with only a hint of tomato, yet it feels substantial thanks to those porky juices penetrating deeply into the fleshy borlotti (cranberry) beans and the melted lusciousness of the taleggio. **Serves 6–8**

Pair with

Serve with braised silverbeet (Swiss chard) or cavolo nero, or buttered cabbage.

1.4 kg (3 lb 1 oz) pork shoulder, cut into 6 cm (2½ in) chunks
125 ml (4 fl oz/½ cup) extra-virgin olive oil
100 g (3½ oz) butter
2 large onions, diced
3 garlic cloves, finely diced
3 celery stalks and some pale inner leaves, finely sliced
2 bay leaves
3 carrots, cut into angled chunks
1 tablespoon tomato paste (concentrated purée)

1 tablespoon ground allspice
350 ml (12 fl oz) white wine
1.5 litres (51 fl oz/6 cups) Golden chicken stock (p. 54)
3 oregano sprigs, leaves picked
500 g (1 lb 2 oz) cooked borlotti (cranberry) beans (see p. 424)
150 g (5½ oz) taleggio, diced
3 handfuls of fresh breadcrumbs
50 g (1¾ oz/½ cup) finely grated Grana Padano

Thyme & oregano rub
1 tablespoon black peppercorns
8 garlic cloves, finely chopped
½ bunch of thyme, leaves stripped
½ bunch of oregano, leaves chopped
5 bay leaves, chopped

Staples
S&P

For the rub, grind the peppercorns using a mortar and pestle. Add the garlic and herbs, then grind to a paste. Rub all over the pork and refrigerate overnight.

When ready to cook, preheat the oven to 160°C (320°F) fan-forced.

Add half the oil and half the butter to a flameproof casserole dish over a medium heat. Brown the pork in batches, seasoning generously with salt as you go. Be careful, as you want colour, but you don't want to burn the marinade. Remove from the pan and set aside.

Add the remaining butter and oil to the pan. Cook the onion, garlic, celery and bay leaves until softened, about 8 minutes. Add the carrot and cook until caramelised, about 10 minutes. Stir in the tomato paste and allspice, then return the pork to the pan. Add the wine and simmer for about 3 minutes. Stir in the stock and oregano, then simmer for 20 minutes.

Add the borlotti beans, cover the pan and transfer to the oven. Braise for about 40 minutes, until the pork is tender.

Remove the dish from the oven, and remove the lid. Turn the oven temperature up to 200°C (400°F) fan-forced. Tuck the taleggio pieces into the braise. Combine the breadcrumbs and parmesan, then sprinkle over the top. Return to the oven and bake, uncovered, until the crumbs are golden, about 10 minutes. Take the dish directly to the table for serving.

Spiced bean & vegetable braise 🅖🅕 🅥 🅥🅖

Pair with

This dish is pretty complete as is, but it's just that bit better served on couscous or brown rice with a spoonful of sheep's milk yoghurt, and diced avocado tossed with lime juice, coriander (cilantro) and salt. You could also use Simple guacamole (p. 412) or Guacamole no. 2 (p. 413).

For this hotpot of goodness, I have used tinned borlotti (cranberry) beans, but you could soak your own. You can buy Egyptian fava beans (ful medames) from Middle Eastern grocers. They have a tart, lemony flavour and are often spiced with cumin, but you could use more kidney beans, or another bean. **Serves 8**

3 red capsicums (bell peppers)
500 g (1 lb 2 oz) podded borlotti (cranberry) beans
100 ml (3½ fl oz) extra-virgin olive oil
2 leeks, white part only, sliced into rounds
2 onions, finely diced
5 garlic cloves, sliced
2 carrots, cut into 1 cm (½ in) dice

4 celery stalks, finely diced
1 tablespoon fenugreek seeds
1 tablespoon fennel seeds
2 teaspoons sweet smoked paprika
2 long red chillies, sliced on an angle
5 thyme sprigs
1 bay leaf
400 g (14 oz) tin red kidney beans, drained

400 g (14 oz) tin Egyptian fava beans, or another tinned bean, drained
400 g (14 oz) tin diced tomatoes
2 tablespoons tomato paste (concentrated purée)
2 tablespoons apple-cider vinegar
5 kale leaves, leaves stripped from stems and torn

Staples
S&WP

Preheat the oven to 200°C (400°F) fan-forced.

Roast the capsicums on a baking tray for 30 minutes, then tip into a bowl and cover with a plate. Set aside to sweat for 10 minutes, then remove the skins and seeds. Cut the flesh into 2 cm (¾ in) squares.

Meanwhile, cook the borlotti beans in simmering salted water for 10 minutes, then drain.

Heat the oil in a large, wide-based saucepan over a medium heat. Add the leek, onion and garlic, season with salt and white pepper and cook until softened, about 10 minutes.

Stir in the carrot and celery, then cook for about 15 minutes, until sticky and caramelised. Add the capsicum, spices, chilli and herbs and cook for a further 5 minutes.

Stir in all the beans, along with the tomatoes, tomato paste and vinegar. Top up with a little water to just cover, then season and bring to a simmer. Stir in the kale and simmer for 45 minutes over a low heat. Adjust the seasoning as needed before serving.

Smoked ham hock & borlotti bean soup

This is based on my mother's recipe for pea and ham soup, using fresh borlotti (cranberry) beans instead of split peas. The ham hock adds so much flavour to the soup as it simmers, underpinning the dish with beautiful smoky tones, and adding a rich viscosity and gloss. The flakes of meat are so tender and unctuous, with the meltingly tender borlotti beans lending a creamy richness. **Serves 6–8**

1 × 1–1.2 kg (2 lb 3 oz– 2 lb 10 oz) smoked pork hock, chopped in half (your butcher can do this)
100 ml (3½ fl oz) extra-virgin olive oil
3 onions, cut into 2 cm (¾ in) dice
6 garlic cloves, chopped

2 carrots, cut into 2 cm (¾ in) dice
4 celery stalks, finely sliced
500 g (1 lb 2 oz) podded borlotti (cranberry) beans
3 large ripe tomatoes, blanched see (p. 655), peeled and cut into 3 cm (1¼ in) dice

120 g (4½ oz/½ cup) pearled barley, or spelt
4 thyme sprigs
3 bay leaves
2.5–3 litres (85–101 fl oz/ 10–12 cups) cold water

Staples
EVOO, S&P

Add the hock pieces to a large saucepan, cover with water and bring to the boil, then drain immediately and set aside.

Heat the oil in a wide-based saucepan over a medium heat. Add the onion and garlic, then sweat until softened, about 8 minutes. Add the carrot and celery and cook for about 10 minutes, until starting to caramelise.

Add the hock pieces and remaining ingredients, season with salt and pepper and cover with the water. Bring to the boil, then turn the heat down to a simmer and cook, stirring occasionally, for 1½–2 hours, or until the meat is coming away from the bone.

Lift out the cooked hock pieces and cool slightly before pulling the meat from the bone. Discard the skin, bone, excess fat, and any hard bits of sinew or tendon. Tear or slice the meat.

You can puree several few cups of the beans and barley to thicken the soup before adding the meat back, or just stir in the meat and leave as is. Adjust the seasoning as needed. Serve with a drizzle of olive oil.

Make it different
Smoked ham hock & pea soup. For a more classic pea and ham soup, use 400 g (14 oz) dried split peas instead of the borlotti beans.

Borlotti bean salad with mustard fruits GF V VG

Dress cooked borlotti (cranberry) beans (either simply boiled, or use the braising recipe, left) with equal parts peppery olive oil and vinegar, then squeeze in the juice from a large lemon. Season generously with salt and pepper and set aside to let the beans take up the vinaigrette. Toss through plenty of chopped parsley and mint, and a few tablespoons of chopped pickled onion and finely diced mustard fruits. Serve as a side for roast chicken or Porchetta (p. 338).

Braised fresh borlotti beans in lemon & cumin stock GF V

Here's a very simple way to cook fresh borlotti (cranberry) beans, layering in plenty of aromatic flavours and spice notes. **Serves 6–8**

3 tablespoons extra-virgin olive oil
60 g (2 oz/¼ cup) butter
1 large onion, finely diced
4 celery stalks, finely sliced
6 garlic cloves, finely chopped

2 bay leaves
100 ml (3½ fl oz) white wine
2 teaspoons ground allspice
2 teaspoons cumin seeds
peel of ½ lemon
500 g (1 lb 2 oz) podded fresh borlotti (cranberry) beans

1 litre (34 fl oz/4 cups) White chicken stock (pp. 54), or Classic white vegetable stock (p. 51)

Staples
S&P

Heat the oil and butter in a wide-based saucepan over a medium heat. Add the onion, celery, garlic and bay leaves and cook until softened, about 6 minutes. Add the wine, allspice, cumin and lemon peel and bring to a simmer.

Add the beans and stock, season with salt and pepper and bring to the boil, then simmer for about 20 minutes, until the beans are tender and the liquid has mostly reduced.

The beans can now be used in other recipes.

Make it different
Make it a side. It doesn't take much to turn this into a delicious side. Dress the beans with French-style vinaigrette (p. 88), or with good olive oil, vinegar, lemon juice, salt, black pepper, and handfuls of chopped parsley. Serve with chargrilled cotechino sausage, braised beef ribs, pan-seared pork chop, Porchetta (p. 338) or quality tinned tuna or sardines in olive oil, or spoon over seared fish fillets.

Borlotti beans with herbs & freekeh Ⓥ

Pair with

Skewered grilled meats.

Fried or grilled haloumi.

Plain yoghurt.

The beans are the hero here, with a tabouleh-like topping adding freshness and texture. You don't need to use both grapes and currants, but it's a nice touch to have the fresh with the dried. If you're using grapes, flame seedless grapes are particularly striking in the finished dish. **Serves 6–8**

120 g (4½ oz) cracked freekeh
2 French shallots, finely sliced
2 handfuls of seedless grapes, and/or 80 g (2¾ oz/½ cup) currants, soaked in red-wine vinegar to cover

½ bunch of flat-leaf (Italian) parsley, leaves finely chopped
2 handfuls of mint leaves, torn
1 × quantity Braised fresh borlotti (cranberry) beans (opposite), warmed

Mint & lemon dressing
80 ml (2½ fl oz/⅓ cup) extra-virgin olive oil
juice of 1 lemon
1 garlic clove, finely grated
2 teaspoons dijon mustard
1 teaspoon dried mint

Staples
S&P

Cook the freekeh in simmering salted water for about 15 minutes until tender. Drain, then place in a large bowl.

Combine the dressing ingredients in a small bowl and season with salt and pepper.

Tip the dressing over the freekeh. Add the shallot, grapes (and/or currants) and herbs, then toss to combine. Set aside for 5 minutes for the flavours to absorb.

Tip the borlotti beans onto a serving platter, then pile the salad on top.

Broad beans

Broad beans are a complete labour of love. One of my earliest memories as an apprentice is of the whole kitchen team standing around towering boxes of broad beans, madly podding into large bowls or empty pots, cracking the pods open, then expelling each bean one pop at a time. Many hands: there is no easier way. Once those boxes were reduced to rubble and the bins were spilling over with broached pods, we'd pick the baby beans out, then mix them back through the larger beans once the larger ones had been double podded. It is always somewhat of a frugal harvest from bulky beginnings, but certainly a delicious one.

The broad beans themselves sit inside a bulky and vibrantly green pod, with a silky cotton-like lining. There is also another layer of skin covering the bean, which is generally best removed, but this is not necessary for the younger beans. While the yield from double-podding broad beans can seem blushingly wasteful, if you grow them yourself, the plants are an amazing source of nitrogen once they've done their job and been slashed and returned to the soil – but that's another matter.

The season for broad beans is quite short, starting in late winter or spring, depending on the climate. As the temperature rises, the beans tend to lose their vibrancy and fresh flavour, at which point drying for extended storage and cooking at a later date becomes the best option. Broad beans grow steadily through winter, ascending upwards with lushly green leaves and rather pretty pale-petalled flowers, with purple to pink to blue to brown accents.

Even before the pods and beans have formed, much of the plant is edible, with the flowers and young leaves lovely raw in salads, and the tips and more mature leaves taking well to an application of heat, too. They also work in stir-fries or as a simple side. You can eat the immature pods whole, either raw or cooked. They can be steamed or pan-fried and served like a flat bean, or presented in a salad with other tender young springtime greens with shaved young goat's cheese and a herb oil such as parsley or basil.

When selecting broad beans, look for smaller pods, as there's a better chance of them being less mature, and therefore sweeter with a crisper texture. The pods should have some tension, rather than being floppy in any way; a limp outer pod will almost always lead to a disappointing result (unlike borlotti/cranberry beans). As they get larger, the beans will swell in the pods, making them quite knobbly, and the colour of the bean skins and the beans themselves will dull from a vibrant green to more of a drab yellow. These mature beans will be starchy and quite mealy, and, I think, thoroughly unappetising when presented as you would tender beans – though they can be cooked longer and mashed with plenty of extra-virgin olive oil and chopped parsley. Dried fully, broad beans are more universally called fava beans (this term is also used for both fresh and dried broad beans, although 'fava' simply means 'bean' in Latin); they can be cooked as you would any dried bean (see p. 371), which then can be used for dips, purees, stews, braises and the like.

Fresh young broad beans are delicious simply tossed in butter with salt and pepper, or with a handful of grated parmesan or pecorino. The cheese will melt, making an instant sauce that just coats them. Toss with herbed peppery extra-virgin olive oil and serve with jamón or prosciutto, or scatter over a carpaccio of beef (see p. 280) with finely shaved Parmigiano Reggiano. Make a simple spring salad by dressing a few handfuls of double-podded broad beans and blanched peas with fruity olive oil, scatter over some crumbled fresh ricotta, then finish with mint leaves and plenty of black pepper. The tender young beans still in their skins tossed with walnut oil and olive oil make a lovely accompaniment to manchego, pecorino or fresh curd cheeses, with rocket (arugula) leaves, baby radishes, chicory (witlof/endive) and olives on the side.

Also see

Spaghetti aglio e olio with mint & broad beans 123

Fennel & buffalo mozzarella salad with broad beans, mint & green sultanas 530

Spring minestrone 531

Braised artichoke, fennel & broad bean salad with orange glaze 536

Pair with

The spring freshness of broad beans can be matched with greens of the season, such as peas, asparagus and sugar-snap peas, as well as tomato, celery and zucchini (courgette). Scent with verdant herbs such as chives, parsley and mint, and spice up with cumin, dried chilli, sumac, garlic, fermented garlic and preserved lemon. Enrich with cream, butter, parmesan, pecorino, goat's curd, feta, sour cream and crème fraîche, and pair with eggs and egg pasta. Excellent protein matches include prawns (shrimp), sardines, tuna, salmon, firm-fleshed white fish (such as blue-eye trevalla), mussels, chicken and lamb.

Preparing broad beans

There are no shortcuts to preparing broad beans. The pods need to be split open, which is just a matter of cracking them roughly in half, then using your thumbnails to tear along the seam, popping the beans out as you go. You can also apply pressure with your thumbs to the beans and they will pop out of the pods. You'll find a technique pretty fast, then try in vain to find a quicker way. Whichever way you do it, just do so directly over a bowl. Those velvet-lined pods are only good for the compost, while the beans just need to be blanched for 2 minutes in boiling salted water. It's best to then refresh them in cold or iced water, stirring the water through to cool them quicker, as they can retain their warmth and continue cooking if they clump together. Naturally, the time here will vary a little depending on the size of the beans, so you can sort them into larger and smaller groups and add the larger ones to the pot first, followed by the smaller ones. Once cooked, the smallest beans can be left in their skins, but the skins of larger ones can tend to be bitter, as well as distract from the texture and flavour of the beans themselves, and so your podding thumbnail, which is now somewhat chlorophyll loaded, can be used to carefully rend the outer skin, with a gentle squeeze expelling the emerald-green beans. The beans will be slippery and often divide into their two halves. Any yellowing, overly firm or crumbling ones will not be that pleasant – do what you will with them. **A kilogram (2 lb 3 oz) of broad bean pods will yield about 250 g (9 oz) of double-podded beans.**

Short cut

Nothing can ever replace fresh broad beans, but frozen ones can be used quite acceptably if smashing them for a paste or a dip.

Cheesy buttered broad beans & peas GF V

This is a rich and luscious side, with one foot in spring and the other still firmly in winter. **Serves 6**

1.5 kg (3 lb 5 oz/3–4 cups) broad beans, podded
3 garlic cloves, finely sliced
100 ml (3½ oz) white wine
150 ml (5 fl oz) cream (35% fat)

250 g (9 oz) peas (fresh or frozen)
80 g (2¾ oz/¾ cup) manchego or Grana Padano, finely grated
50 g (1¾ oz) butter

1 handful of mint leaves

Staples
EVOO, S&P

Blanch the broad beans for 2 minutes in boiling salted water. Lift out and immediately refresh in a bowl of iced water. Drain and double-pod the beans.

Add a splash of oil to a deep-sided frying pan over a medium heat. Add the garlic and cook until fragrant. Add the wine and reduce by a little over half. Add the cream and bring to a simmer, then add the broad beans and peas and cook for a minute or so.

Add the cheese and butter and toss them through. Cook, stirring, until the sauce is bubbling and coating the vegetables evenly. Season with salt and pepper and tip into a serving dish. Top with the mint and serve.

Make it different
With other greens. You could use the same idea here with blanched asparagus, or wilted greens such as silverbeet (Swiss chard).

Pair with

Serve with intensely flavoured meats, such as beef, lamb, venison or even hare, or a golden roasted chicken. Also pairs well with sliced jamón, ham steaks or grilled thick-cut bacon.

Baba ghanoush.

Crumbed fennel.

Crumbed fried fish.

Broad bean & avocado dip GF V VG

A version of this dip was served to me by a good friend cooking from one of Yotam Ottolenghi's recipes – that happens a bit. It was stunning, and a combination that I had never considered instantly made so much sense. This is my version based on eating it. You'll need the flesh from a couple of avocados, with the same weight in chopped cooked broad beans (about 300 g/10½ oz of each). Using a mortar and pestle, smash the beans to a rough paste with a small garlic clove and 1 teaspoon cumin seeds. Work in the avocado, season with salt and pepper and stir through a generous squeeze of lemon juice and a good splash of extra-virgin olive oil. Serve with warmed flatbread.

Broad bean & pea salad with nasturtium leaves, goat's cheese & bagna cauda GF

Nasturtium leaves are very striking, and their distinctive peppery notes really add to this salad, but they can be omitted if you don't have any (or are unsure if they have been sprayed). You can actually buy the leaves, but once planted in the garden nasturtiums tend to proliferate, and the flowers are just as interesting in flavour and are alarmingly pretty. It may seem odd to use both fresh and frozen peas here, but the frozen peas make for a better paste, and are less expensive. Grilled bread may be in order, too. **Serves 4–6**

75 g (2¾ oz/½ cup) currants
50 ml (1¾ fl oz) red-wine vinegar
1 kg (2 lb 3 oz) broad beans, podded
3 handfuls of fresh peas
200 g (7 oz) sugar-snap peas, trimmed

1 large garlic clove, finely sliced
150 g (5½ oz/1 cup) frozen peas, thawed in hot water
½ bunch of mint, leaves roughly chopped
8 small radishes, fine leaves left on

150 g (5½ oz) soft goat's cheese
2 handfuls of nasturtium leaves
1 × quantity Bagna cauda (p. 83)

Staples
EVOO, LMN, S&P

Bring the currants and vinegar to the boil in a small saucepan. Set aside for 15 minutes.

Blanch the broad beans for 2 minutes in boiling salted water. Lift out and immediately refresh in a bowl of iced water. Follow by blanching the fresh peas and sugar-snaps for 1 minute, then refresh in iced water. Drain the greens. Split the sugar-snaps and double-pod the broad beans, leaving the tiny ones un-podded.

Add the garlic, a splash of oil and some salt and pepper to a mortar, then grind to a paste using a pestle. Add the double-podded broad beans, frozen peas and mint and pound to a rough paste. The mixture should be stiff, but add a little oil as necessary. Adjust the seasoning as required.

Add the sugar-snaps, fresh peas, radishes and any remaining broad beans to a bowl, season with salt and pepper, drizzle with oil and toss through.

Spread the paste across a large platter and arrange the pea and broad bean mix on top. Crumble the goat's cheese over, and top with the currants, nasturtium leaves and a squeeze of lemon. Spoon some bagna cauda over and serve with the remaining bagna cauda on the side.

Make it faster
If anchovies aren't your thing, or you'd just like to simplify things, omit the bagna cauda and instead serve the salad with a basic Vinaigrette (p. 88) of well-seasoned extra-virgin olive oil and sherry vinegar.

Make it different
With other spring vegetables. Think of this salad as a celebration of spring, so grilled asparagus spears or baby zucchini (courgettes), with or without zucchini flowers, would also work well, or any tender young vegetables.

With cheese. Burrata or torn fresh mozzarella are lovely alternatives to the goat's cheese.

Make it a meal
A couple of soft-boiled eggs broken over the salad are delicious, and make it more substantial.

Falafel with broad beans & tahini yoghurt (GF) (V)

The broad beans add a fresh lightness to the falafel, making for a mesmerisingly bright-green interior beneath the golden shell. **Makes about 20; serves 6–8**

oil, for deep-frying (see p. 22)
1 handful of mint leaves

Falafel
300 g (10½ oz) dried chickpeas, soaked for 24 hours with 1 teaspoon bicarbonate of soda (baking soda), drained
50 g (1¾ oz) chickpea flour
150 g (5½ oz) fresh or frozen double-podded broad beans (see p. 430), or peas

2 handfuls of flat-leaf (Italian) parsley leaves, finely chopped
½ white salad onion, finely grated
2 large garlic cloves, finely grated
35 g (1¼ oz) sesame seeds
3 teaspoons salt flakes
2 teaspoons baking powder
1 heaped tablespoon ground cumin

1 heaped tablespoon ground coriander
1 teaspoon ground black pepper
½ teaspoon chilli powder, or cayenne pepper

Lemony tahini yoghurt
300 g (10½ oz) natural yoghurt, or crème fraîche
2½ tablespoons tahini
juice of 1 lemon

Staples
EVOO, LMN, S&P

Pair with

All manner of meze, or wrap in pitta bread with some tabouleh (see p. 419) or the like, pickles, cucumber and a good smear of the lemony tahini yoghurt.

Also pairs well with Lebanese talami bread (p. 852) and Moroccan semolina flatbreads (p. 852).

Heat 5 cm (2 in) of oil in a deep frying pan to 175°C (345°F), or use a deep-fryer.

To make the falafel, blitz the chickpeas and chickpea flour in a food processor to a medium crumb. Add the remaining falafel ingredients, except the sesame seeds, and process to a rough paste. Shape the mixture into walnut-sized balls or quenelles, roll in the sesame seeds, then deep-fry until well browned, about 4 minutes. Drain on paper towel.

Combine the lemony tahini yoghurt ingredients, season with salt and pepper, then spread across a serving plate. Dress the remaining broad beans in a little oil, season with salt and pepper and toss the mint leaves through. Arrange the falafel on the plate, scatter with the broad beans and mint and serve with lemon wedges.

Make it different
Plain falafel. (GF) (V) Instead of broad beans or peas, use an extra 100 g (3½ oz) chickpeas.

To dress up the presentation, scatter a handful of the smallest beans over the finished dish. These can be raw in their skins if they are tiny and sweet, or use small double-podded beans if a little larger.

Grilled lamb cutlets with smashed broad beans & hot feta dressing (GF)

I select small racks of lamb for this, as the meat is typically sweeter and juicier – which may mean that cutting double cutlets is preferable. **Serves 6**

2 garlic cloves, smashed
1 tablespoon dried Greek oregano (rigani)
60 ml (2 fl oz/¼ cup) extra-virgin olive oil
16 lamb cutlets
1 handful of Ligurian or wild olives (optional)

Broad bean & pea paste
1.5 kg (3 lb 5 oz/3 cups) broad beans, podded

150 g (5½ oz/1 cup) frozen peas
½ garlic clove, finely grated
1 tablespoon extra-virgin olive oil
6 mint sprigs, leaves roughly chopped

Feta dressing
1½ tablespoons sherry vinegar, or any wine vinegar

60 ml (2 fl oz/¼ cup) extra-virgin olive oil
½ garlic clove, finely chopped
1 tablespoon honey
2 teaspoons dijon mustard
150 g (5½ oz) Greek feta, crumbled

Staples
EVOO, S&P

Preheat a chargrill pan or barbecue grill on high.

Meanwhile, combine the smashed garlic, oregano and oil in a small bowl. Season generously with salt and pepper, then rub into the lamb.

To make the paste, blanch the broad beans for 2 minutes in boiling salted water. Lift them out and immediately refresh in a bowl of iced water. Blanch the peas for 1 minute, then drain and refresh in iced water. Drain both and double-pod the beans.

Chop the beans and peas roughly, then add half to a mortar with the grated garlic and a little salt. Pound while gradually adding the oil, beans and peas until a rough paste forms. Stir the mint through and adjust the seasoning as necessary.

To make the dressing, whisk the vinegar, oil, garlic, honey and mustard in a small saucepan. Season with salt and pepper, then warm gently over a low–medium heat. Just before serving, add the feta and gently warm through.

Meanwhile, grill the cutlets for about 2 minutes on each side, which will keep them quite pink (cook longer if you prefer, or if you're using double cutlets). Rest for a minute or so. Serve with the smashed broad beans to the side, and the olives (if using) and hot feta dressing spooned over the lamb.

Make it different
The broad bean and pea paste is also a delicious topping for bruschetta, perfect with a drizzle of oil and extra ground pepper – and it becomes something quite special with a curl of jamón or prosciutto, cured tuna or kingfish, or some splodges of goat's curd.

Linguine with prawns & broad beans ⒼⒻ

It may seem odd to chop both the broad beans and prawns here, given how beautiful they both are intact – but the intention is to get morsels of both as you eat the pasta, rather than having them sitting apart. You tend to eat the prawns separately otherwise, and the broad beans will just drop to the bottom of the bowl if they're not chopped. **Serves 4**

500 g (1 lb 2 oz) linguine
12 raw prawns (shrimp),
  peeled and deveined, then
  cut into 1 cm (½ in) chunks
3 garlic cloves, finely sliced

2 red bird's eye chillies,
  finely sliced
100 ml (3½ fl oz) white wine
300 g (10½ oz/2 cups)
  double-podded broad
  beans, roughly chopped

½ bunch of flat-leaf (Italian)
  parsley, leaves finely
  chopped
80 g (2¾ oz) butter

Staples
EVOO, S&P

Cook the pasta until al dente in boiling salted water.

Meanwhile, heat a wide-based saucepan over a high heat for 1 minute. Oil the prawn meat and season with salt and pepper, then fry for 2 minutes. Remove from the pan and set aside.

Add a good splash of oil to the pan, along with the garlic and chilli. Cook until fragrant, then add the wine. Reduce for a couple of minutes, then add the prawn meat, broad beans, parsley and butter and cook for a minute or so.

Using tongs, lift the pasta directly out of the water into the pan and toss through, adding a little oil and some of the pasta cooking water to loosen the mix. As the liquid reduces it will start to enrich and thicken the sauce, which will begin to cling to the pasta. Once the pasta is nicely coated, adjust the seasoning and serve.

Linguine with prawns & broad beans

Green beans

Green beans were a welded-on fixture in the meat-and-three-veg era, with khaki-coloured and ruthlessly topped-and-tailed beans ubiquitously nestled next to mashed potato and perhaps equally drab peas and batons of carrot. Those were the days, hey. That period of cooking has been accorded a Dark Ages aura, but the general idea of serving some meat or fish with plenty of vegetables remains a very sound and simple principle. *More* vegetables and less meat, perhaps. Either way, the versatility of green beans means they deserve their ubiquity in these more enlightened culinary times.

Their commonness may be their undoing, however, with their presence in the market seemingly unaffected by the seasons. Perhaps people tire of this, with fleeting appearances by stars such as asparagus and broad beans always stealing the mic. An in-season just-picked green bean is a marvellous thing – so crunchy, tender and packed with distinctive flavour, and requiring little to no cooking. But just because you can buy beans all year round, doesn't mean you should. The green bean season runs through summer and autumn, so try to buy locally grown specimens whenever possible; a farmers' market is generally the easiest way to shop seasonally. No fresh produce is improved by travelling long distances in cold storage, and beans are no exception.

Green beans, French beans, string beans – whatever you call them – are the product of countless different cultivars. The plants grow either as 'bush' beans or 'pole' beans, with the former a self-supporting plant, and the latter requiring something to climb on. 'Runner' beans also grow vine-like, producing typically flatter and slightly coarser pods later in the season, and again there's a dizzying array of types. If you have a vegetable garden, these three types will keep you in beans from spring well into autumn, depending on your local climate. All versions are eaten whole, with the immature beans barely swelling in the pods.

Green may be the dominant colour, but you can also source yellow beans (also called wax beans) and purple types, as well as pods with the distinctive borlotti (cranberry) bean marbling. They can all be eaten cooked or raw, though its maturity will dictate how pleasing a raw runner bean is. I throw raw French beans in my girls' lunchboxes, and also add them to all sorts of soups and braises. They're marvellous with pesto and potatoes, either as a salad or tossed through pasta, which is a Ligurian classic. Just-cooked beans warmed in garlicky extra-virgin olive oil is the most versatile of sides, or toss them with chopped anchovies, butter and parsley. They're also lovely with brown/burnt butter (see p. 73) and toasted hazelnuts or flaked almonds, and can be fried with sambal oelek and minced (ground) pork. While we now favour lightly cooked green beans, retaining some texture, there are plenty of successful dishes where they are braised for longer, though I typically make these dishes with flat beans, such as romano beans (see p. 438).

Finely shredded, most beans can feature in salads or be added to stir-fries at the last moment. French beans are also lovely fried in tempura batter, though anything but an immature runner bean will be too fibrous.

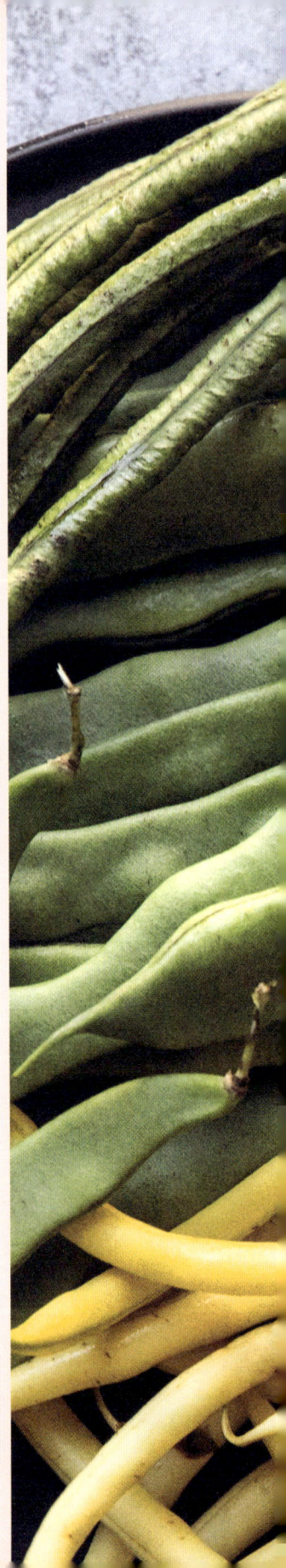

Also see

Seared beef with bean thread noodles, beans, wood ear fungus & gochujang 292

Crunchy lacto-fermented vegetables 508

Genovese salad 624

Spring & Winter minestrone 531, 607

Pair with

Green beans pair beautifully with dairy, such as cream, mascarpone, ricotta, parmesan, fresh mozzarella, feta and yoghurt, as well as cured meats such as bacon, pancetta and nduja. Beans work equally well in western and Asian dishes; match with soy, shrimp paste, sesame, miso, tofu, fermented black beans, fermented chilli and coconut. Scent with herbs such as mint, coriander (cilantro), parsley, chives, oregano, tarragon and basil, and spice with cumin, fenugreek, allspice, sumac, curry leaves, baharat, curry powder and black and white pepper. Pair with onion, spring onion (scallion), garlic, ginger, tomato, rocket, bean sprouts, potatoes, shiitake mushrooms, abalone mushrooms, green papaya and green apple. Beans also love almonds, pistachios, hazelnuts, pine nuts and, as well as olives, anchovies, balsamic and honey. Match with proteins such as chicken, tuna and salmon, as well as beef, pork and lamb.

The other green beans that get a good workout in my kitchen are snake beans, or yard-long beans. Although I associate them heavily with Thai cuisine, they are quite commonly grown in Italy, where they are called fagioli serpenti. It's a little hard to shake that association with fish sauce, volcanically hot chilli and fragrant Thai basil, but they can be braised with tomato to equal effect. I do love the snap and crunch of a raw snake bean, or one in a curry or stir-fry that hasn't yielded much to the heat. The texture and flavour are really quite unique.

When selecting green beans, do exactly that: select individual beans. Feel no shame, and don't be hurried. If you rake them up by the handful, for every fistful of firm and springy beans you'll inevitably pick up some with withered ends or soft spots or the like. One by one. You get quite quick at it after a while. I also favour the smaller, tender beans, so pluck these out as a priority. And the rules for most vegetables apply. Beans should be crunchy and vibrantly coloured, not limp or dull. For classic green beans, the colour should be quite deep and vibrant. Larger beans, unless a function of the variety, tend to be paler and less flavourful. Avoid them. Snake beans should be firm, with a certain rigidity; they will also develop mottled spots when old.

Preparing green beans

'Top and tail' is a preparation method for beans that seems somewhat enduring. In fact, we seem to cut the ends off so many things without questioning whether we need to or not. Do you cut both ends off a clove of garlic? Well, don't. The woody bit isn't great, but where it curls into a point is all garlic, just as the tail of a bean is all bean, and just as tasty as the rest. They look better this way, too. Natural. The double-cropped tubes make me shudder. As a kid, I remember that you'd always cut the stalk off the bean and then peel the attached 'string' off the length of it before cooking. That practice is no longer necessary, as the string has been bred out of most commercial beans. If you're growing or buying old varieties, however, it's worth checking this first, as the strings can get in the way of enjoying a bean. No more needs to be done to a bean before boiling (3–4 minutes in salted water), steaming, pan-frying or eating raw, if that's your thing. Once steamed or boiled, then refreshed, you can split beans along the seam by prying them open with your thumbnails. These will combine well in a salad, taking up the dressing well, and they present nicely. Snake beans similarly need the tough ends cut away, as these will usually have dried out, and then they will need to be cut to manageable lengths – unless you can source baby specimens, which can make a marvellously serpentine tangle of a side dish.

Mapo-style tofu with beans & pork

Mapo tofu is a classic Sichuan dish and a real favourite of mine. I find it quite nurturing and filling, and the sichuan pepper gently mouth-numbing, which I am convinced is what has you coming back for more. My version is really quick to put together and makes a great addition to a feast. You can spice this up a little further – in genuine Sichuan fashion – by adding chopped fresh red chilli or a heaped tablespoon of Fermented cooked chilli sauce (p. 97) with the ginger and garlic. **Serves 4–6**

Pair with

Steamed rice and stir-fried greens make this a complete meal, but it will also star in a spread of Asian-style dishes.

3 tablespoons black beans
2 tablespoons boiling water
½ teaspoon chilli powder, plus extra to serve
2 tablespoons light soy sauce
80 ml (2½ fl oz/⅓ cup) oyster sauce
1½ teaspoons sesame oil
1 teaspoon sugar
75 ml (2½ fl oz) grapeseed oil

10 cm (4 in) piece of fresh ginger, peeled and julienned
5 garlic cloves, finely sliced
350 g (12½ oz) finely minced (ground) pork, or chicken
1 onion, sliced into half-moons from tip to root
350 g (12½ oz) green beans, finely sliced into rounds
2 teaspoons sesame seeds

2 tablespoons spicy fermented broad bean paste
500 g (1 lb 2 oz) silken tofu
½ bunch of coriander (cilantro), leaves and fine stems picked
1½ tablespoons cornflour dissolved in 1 tablespoon cold water (optional)
2 teaspoons sichuan peppercorns, crushed

In a small bowl, soak the black beans in the boiling water for 20 minutes. Add the chilli powder, soy sauce, oyster sauce, sesame oil and sugar, mixing well. Set aside.

Heat a wok or large frying pan over a high heat until very hot. Add half the grapeseed oil and heat until shimmering, then add the ginger and garlic. Cook for about 20 seconds until fragrant, then add the pork and stir-fry vigorously for 3 minutes, until browned. Tip into a bowl and set aside.

Add the remaining oil and the onion, beans and sesame seeds. Stir-fry until softened, about 2 minutes. Return the pork to the wok, add the black bean sauce mixture and the broad bean paste and stir-fry for 2 minutes to coat and combine. Add the tofu, breaking it up with a spatula, then add the coriander and simmer for 30 seconds. If you like a thick sauce, add the cornflour mixture and simmer for an additional 30 seconds.

To serve, tip into a serving dish, sprinkle with the sichuan pepper and dust with a little extra chilli powder.

Tuna, brown rice & green bean salad with sumac (GF)

I just adore this combination of nutty brown rice infused with a lemony sumac vinaigrette. The trick to a rice salad is to dress the rice while it is still warm, so it readily absorbs the flavours. This salad is kept simple with tinned tuna. **Serves 4**

25 green beans, trimmed
280 g (10 oz/1½ cups) cooked brown rice, warm but not hot
125 ml (4 fl oz/½ cup) extra-virgin olive oil
1½ tablespoons sherry vinegar
juice of 1 lemon

2 tablespoons ground sumac
1 × 185 g (6½ oz) tin tuna in olive oil, drained
10 flat-leaf (Italian) parsley leaves, finely sliced
3 mint sprigs, leaves picked and torn
2 spring onions (scallions), finely sliced

3 soft-boiled eggs (see p. 351), peeled and sliced
3 tablespoons pine nuts, toasted

Staples
S&P

Cook the beans in a saucepan of boiling salted water for 3 minutes, then drain and place in a bowl.

Meanwhile, put the rice in another bowl. Whisk together the oil, vinegar and lemon juice, seasoning with salt and pepper. Tip half the dressing over the rice, then stir through with the sumac. Mix the tuna through. Adjust the seasoning to taste, then pile onto a serving plate.

Pour the remaining dressing over the beans. Toss the herbs and spring onion through, then pile on top of the rice. Finish by laying the egg slices on top and scattering with the pine nuts.

Make it vegetarian (V)
Simply omit the tuna. It's all about bringing it to life with the egg, sumac and pine nuts.

Stir-fried green beans with sesame, ginger & oyster sauce

Pair with

Serve over rice or noodles, or as a side for steak, fish or poultry.

This is a very simple and quick side dish to boost the green quotient of any feast. **Serves 4–6**

80 ml (2½ fl oz/⅓ cup) oyster sauce
2 tablespoons light soy sauce
1½ teaspoons sesame oil
1 tablespoon sugar
½ teaspoon chilli powder, plus extra to serve

75 ml (2½ fl oz) grapeseed oil
350 g (12½ oz) green beans, trimmed
10 cm (4 in) piece of fresh ginger, peeled and julienned
3 garlic cloves, finely sliced

4 spring onions (scallions), white part only, sliced on an angle
1 tablespoon sesame seeds, plus extra to serve

Combine the oyster sauce, soy sauce, sesame oil, sugar and chilli powder in a small bowl.

Heat a wok or large frying pan over a high heat until very hot. Add the grapeseed oil and heat until shimmering, then add the beans. Stir-fry for about 4 minutes, then make a little space in the wok and add the ginger and garlic. Cook for about 1 minute until lightly golden, then stir-fry everything vigorously for another minute.

Add the spring onion and sesame seeds and stir-fry for 1 minute. Add the oyster sauce mixture and stir-fry for another minute to coat well, then tip into a serving dish.

Sprinkle with a little extra chilli powder and sesame seeds to serve.

Thai green papaya salad

The first time I had this salad in Thailand, it was served in a plastic bag hanging off one end of a stick that had charred chicken wings threaded onto it, with a bag of sticky rice hanging off the other end – a special food moment. **Serves 4–6**

½ green (unripe) papaya,
  or 2 large green mangoes
4 green Thai chillies, or bird's
  eye chillies, chopped
1 garlic clove, sliced
25 g (1 oz/⅓ cup) tiny dried
  shrimp

120 g (4½ oz/¾ cup) salted
  roasted peanuts
100 g (3½ oz/½ cup) grated
  palm sugar (jaggery)
3½ tablespoons fish sauce
8 snake beans, cut into 4 cm
  (1½ in) lengths

12 cherry tomatoes, halved
juice of 3 limes

Staples
S&P

Peel the papaya and remove the seeds. Finely slice lengthways, about 2 mm (⅛ in) thick, then julienne lengthways to the same thickness; you're after very long matchsticks. (The Thais hold the papaya in their hand and chop lines into it, then slice off the strands. Don't try that at home! You could also use a mandoline.)

Using a mortar and pestle, pound the chilli, garlic and shrimp with a pinch of salt, into a rough paste. Add half the peanuts and pound until combined. Add the papaya, palm sugar and fish sauce and bruise the papaya well. Add the snake beans and tomatoes and keep pounding until the papaya is bruised and has softened enough to absorb the juices.

Add the lime juice and taste for balance. The aim is to achieve a balance between hot, sweet, sour and salty, so adjust according to taste, then serve.

Tuna niçoise ⒼⒻ

This version of the French salad is more composed and substantial than most, and can be served as individual dishes, or plated up to share. It's important that the beans and potatoes are not refrigerated after cooking – they can even have a gentle flush of heat in them – and that the eggs are freshly cooked. **Serves 4**

4 kipfler (fingerling) potatoes,
  skin on, boiled until tender
4 tuna steaks, each 3 cm
  (1¼ in) thick
1 white salad onion, sliced
  into rounds
30 green beans, trimmed
12 ripe cherry tomatoes,
  halved

5 flat-leaf (Italian) parsley
  sprigs, leaves picked and
  sliced, or left whole if small
5 tarragon sprigs, leaves (and
  any flowers) picked
16 black olives, pitted
  and torn
1½ tablespoons tiny capers,
  drained

2 tablespoons extra-virgin
  olive oil
80 g (2¾ oz/⅓ cup)
  mayonnaise (p. 74, p. 75)
4 soft-boiled eggs (see
  p. 351), peeled
½ × quantity Bagna cauda
  (p. 83), warmed

Staples
EVOO, LMN, S&P

Add the potatoes to a saucepan of cold salted water. Bring to the boil and cook until tender, about 20 minutes. Drain and set aside.

Meanwhile, coat the tuna with oil and season with salt and pepper. Set aside at room temperature for at least 10 minutes before cooking. Soak the onion in cold water for 10 minutes, then drain and pat dry.

Cook the beans in simmering salted water for 4 minutes, then drain and split lengthways. Cut the potatoes into slices, or gently crush, then season.

Pair with

Thai meals usually have a multitude of dishes, so you can use this salad to accompany all kinds of salads, curries and grilled or roasted meat, seafood and poultry. Thai fish cakes (p. 192) are a must, too.

This salad is also deliciously refreshing with roasted pork belly, spicy grilled chicken or grilled prawns (shrimp).

Braised romano beans ⒼⒻ Ⓥ ⓋⒼ

Heat 100 ml (3½ fl oz) extra-virgin olive oil in a large, deep-sided frying pan over a medium heat. Add 4 sliced garlic cloves and fry until fragrant and golden, 1–2 minutes. Trim 500 g (1 lb 2 oz) romano or other flat beans and cut any large ones in half on an angle. Add the beans to the pan along with 2 large ripe tomatoes cut into 2 cm (¾ in) dice, season with salt and pepper and cook for about 3 minutes to soften, tossing every 20 seconds or so. Stir in 300 ml (10 fl oz) tomato passata (puréed tomatoes) or Roasted tomato passata (p. 660) and continue to cook until the beans are very tender and the tomato mixture has reduced and starts to cling to the beans, about 10 minutes. These are great with slow-cooked or roasted lamb, or spiced grilled chicken.

Add the beans, tomatoes, herbs, olives, capers and oil to a bowl, season and toss to coat.

Heat a large frying pan over a high heat until very hot (use two pans if it isn't big enough to fit all the tuna). Cook the tuna for 2–3 minutes on one side only, cooking about halfway through.

Dollop the mayonnaise on serving plates. Follow with the potato, then lay the cooked tuna next to the mayonnaise, cooked side down. Top with the bean and tomato mix, then position the eggs next to the tuna. Pierce the eggs with a knife and tear open to expose the yolk. Squeeze some lemon over, then dress everything with the bagna cauda. Top with the onion slices and serve.

Make it faster
You can simplify things by using tinned or jarred tuna, anchovy fillets instead of the bagna cauda, and a dressing of olive oil and vinegar. Toss together with some torn cos (romaine) lettuce for crunch, then break the soft-boiled eggs over the top.

Broccoli, broccolini & cime di rape

The edible head of broccoli is a flower, the bloom of a brassica isolated as a cultivar back in Etruscan times in what is now central Italy. Indeed, the cultivar group covering broccoli is known as the Italica group, and the main broccoli type we would all be familiar with is Calabrian broccoli – though the attribution to the southern Italian region is usually lopped off. Calabrian broccoli has a large head that grows from a central stem, with radiating broad leaves, which are quite edible. The broccoli head can be harvested, and the rest of the plant will regrow, often with smaller stems and heads.

Sprouting broccoli is very similar to Calabrian broccoli, just with more slender stalks and equally compact heads, either green or purple. They are, however, quite different to broccolini, which has more pliable, glossy and deeply green stems, and wispier, less dense heads.

Though broccolini is sometimes called baby broccoli, it isn't. Broccolini is a cross between broccoli and gai lan (Chinese broccoli), and a simple horticultural cross-pollination – nothing sinister about it. Broccolini is also a trademarked name, with broccoletti the work-around for those not paying royalties; confusingly, broccoletti is also a synonym for cime di rape (see below), which is delicious but somewhat different, with small sprouting heads, large soft leaves and a bitter accent. Whatever the name, broccolini is a vegetable that works extremely well in both Western and Asian dishes, standing in for gai lan very effectively, with a slightly deeper flavour profile, making it ideal for stir-fries and the like: just blanch and refresh first. Broccolini is also excellent as a side, blanched then warmed through in oil with garlic and chilli and finished with toasted flaked almonds, or cooked with bacon lardons or speck (see p. 442).

Broccoli, sprouting broccoli and broccolini can all be steamed or cooked in salted water and then dressed with oil or butter, or tossed in a pan, again with garlic and chilli. They all take well to being charred on a grill, which adds another dimension of flavour and texture.

Broccoli was even a little exotic when I was growing up. I actually remember the first time I had it. My mother cooked it in a stir-fry of sorts that included tomato among other incongruous ingredients. It's not a dish that I have chosen to replicate, though broccoli is certainly very successful with Asian flavours. I will typically blanch florets first, then refresh in iced or cold water before adding to stir-fries and the like – you will keep the bright colour this way, and they will cook just enough in the wok, as raw broccoli can be too crunchy in a quick cook like this.

Cime di rape is also known as broccoli rabe and rapini. Rapa (rape is the plural) is the Italian word for turnip, and cime the word for tops, hence they are quite literally translated as 'turnip tops' in the UK, which is immensely confusing. They are not the tops of turnips as we know them, but they do belong to the same brassica subspecies. Cime di rape has some quite wispy broccolini-like florets but, in a culinary sense, it is just as much about the stems and large serrated leaves, and they are sometimes sold with a bloom of tiny yellow flowers. It is a bitter green that takes to richer flavours well. Although it could reside in the chapter with turnips, I find their use more in line with broccoli and broccolini, with either being the best substitute for cime di rape in one of the emblematic dishes of both the vegetable and Puglia: orecchiette con cime di rape.

Also see

Baked polenta with strachino & greens 382

Horta 552–3

Greens & cheese pie 564

Pair with

Broccoli and broccolini soak up flavours incredibly well. They are enhanced by garlic and chilli, and they love Asian flavours – soy, mirin, oyster sauce, fish sauce, sesame. Nuts are good companions – pine nuts, almonds, hazelnuts – especially when the broccoli is charred. Match with hard cheese, such as parmesan and pecorino, or grilled haloumi. Anchovies are exceptionally compatible.

How I love that pasta: anchovies dissolved in plenty of garlicky oil with chilli flakes, tossed with well-cooked greens and the classic 'little ear' pasta of the region, then finished with Pangrattato (p. 123). I have cooked it countless times over the years, both at home and professionally; given that cime di rape has not been reliably available, well-cooked broccoli (including all the stalk) was my go-to. While lacking the bitter twist of cime di rape, it is still delicious, if needing a little extra sharpening with chilli. Cime di rape can be used as a green for a side sautéed with garlic and oil and finished with a good squeeze of lemon at the table – perfect with roast pork, fatty sausages or cotechino with lentils. The young leaves can also be used as salad greens.

Spigariello (also spelt spigarello) or leaf broccoli is starting to appear in more specialised markets, though it is still not easy to come by where I am. It is an ancient plant hailing from southern Italy – potentially via Asia, with the origins apparently given away by its white flowers, rather than yellow. It doesn't have the bitterness of cime di rape, with a sweet broccoli-like flavour to the leaves and stems, and an appearance and texture somewhat like kale. Being ancient, there are many variations, so leaves range from broad to spindly. It can be used like any cooking green.

Broccoli heads are best when the flower nodules are tightly packed, often with a deep green or purplish green hue. Loosely packed broccoli heads will generally indicate faster growing in warmer weather when the plant is bolting, and the flavour and texture will be second rate. Naturally, any floppiness should be avoided. As with all brassicas, if it has been stored too long, broccoli will start to get a little pongy, with a sulphurous character that is quite unpleasant. So, make sure what you buy smells garden fresh and not like a drain.

When buying broccolini, look for vividly coloured examples that aren't wilting, but also check the base of the stem where they have been cut. Produce that has been picked late in the season or when the weather is too hot will tend to have a white circle in the stem, like the ring of a tree trunk, and will almost certainly be fibrous and tough.

Cime di rape will show its age more readily, both if it has been stored too long or if it is overly mature. Being mainly leaf and stem, wilting is pretty apparent, while mature plants will have thick stems, which are sometimes hollow. These stems will not cook down and I regard them as essentially inedible. You can pick off the finer stems and leaves, but your yield will be meagre, so this is probably only useful if you're growing it yourself. So, buy it at its youthful best, or select the most tender parts if growing your own.

Preparing broccoli, broccolini & cime di rape

Broccoli should be a low- to no-waste vegetable, certainly given how it is presented in the market. But if you grow your own, eat those leaves, too. I trim away the woody part of the base where it has been cut, but the stem is perfectly good. (In fact, some even prize the stem more highly than the flower, such as the great Italian cookery writer Marcella Hazan's husband and collaborator Victor: he considers the florets 'an accident of nature, and he refuses to touch them,' she wrote.) I'll trim away any coarse parts where leaves have been snapped off, and sometimes peel if the skin feels tough, but mostly it's not necessary. The same is true of sprouting broccoli, while broccolini may need a bit more of a trim if the stems are woody. But be vigilant with cime di rape, as tough stems can ruin a dish. If you end up with a more mature harvest, just use the fine stems and leaves. Spigariello just needs to be trimmed at the base, with any tough stems discarded. The stalk of broccoli takes a little longer to cook than the flower, so cut them smaller than the floret heads if cooking at the same time.

Broccolini with speck, shallot & garlic (GF)

This is a wintery way to dress up broccolini. You could also add well-cooked cavolo nero leaves or brussels sprouts, as all those dark greens love the rich fattiness of cured pork. Speck adds a robust smoky flavour and richness. **Serves 2**

3 bunches of broccolini, trimmed, or 10 sprouting broccoli stems
150 g (5½ oz) speck, cut into 1 cm (½ in) thick lardons
100 ml (3½ fl oz) extra-virgin olive oil
4 French shallots, thickly sliced
5 garlic cloves, sliced
1 teaspoon chilli flakes
60 g (2 oz) Grana Padano

Staples
S&P

Cook the broccolini in boiling salted water until tender, about 5 minutes.

Meanwhile, fry the speck in a large frying pan over a high heat until the fat renders out and it starts to brown. Add the oil, shallot and garlic and cook until softened and starting to colour, about 3 minutes.

Add the broccolini straight from the boiling water, with the chilli flakes and a splash of cooking water. Toss for another minute or so, reducing the liquid and coating the broccolini well.

Pile onto a serving plate, drizzle with the pan juices and grate the parmesan over.

Charred broccolini with tuna mayonnaise, black barley, egg & anchovy dust (GF)

A meal in itself or a spectacular centrepiece to a feast of smaller dishes. The briny tuna flavour of the mayonnaise will surprise – it's divine. **Serves 3–4**

90 g (3 oz) dried black barley, or regular barley or brown rice
3 bunches of broccolini, trimmed
10 anchovies, drained
juice of ½ lemon
1 tablespoon extra-virgin olive oil
4 soft-boiled eggs, with just-set whites and runny yolks (p. 351)

Tuna mayo
2 × 185 g (6½ oz) tins tuna in spring water, drained
250 g (9 oz/1 cup) mayonnaise (see p. 74)
juice of ½ lemon

Staples
EVOO, LMN, S&P

Smashed broccoli with preserved lemon (GF) (V)

Break a large head of broccoli into florets, cutting the stalk into slices. Cook in boiling salted water until very tender, about 5 minutes, then drain. Smash the broccoli using a mortar and pestle, adding a teaspoon of chopped preserved lemon, a handful of shredded mint leaves, some crumbled feta, salt and pepper, and enough oil to anoint and loosen. Serve with grilled or slow-cooked lamb.

Pair with

Serve with steak, or grilled or roasted chicken.

Well-cooked broccoli with anchovies & pine nuts (GF)

Break down a couple of heads of broccoli into florets, cutting the stems into 1 cm (½ in) thick slices. Cook in boiling salted water until very tender, about 5 minutes, then drain. Heat 100 ml (3½ fl oz) extra-virgin olive oil in a large frying pan over a medium heat. Add 6 or so anchovies and cook until they dissolve in the oil, about 2 minutes. Add a couple of tablespoons of pine nuts and cook until taking on some colour, about 40 seconds. Add the broccoli, a couple of handfuls of chopped parsley leaves, a good grinding of black pepper, and salt if needed. Toss through to warm and coat. Serve as a side for fish or grilled lamb.

Broccoli stems with chilli & garlic (GF) (V) (VG)

Sometimes you just don't want much stalk in a dish, or if you grow your own broccoli, you can end up with more stalk than you might wish to use. Here's a very simple solution. Trim any tough outer skin off about 4 stalks and slice into 2 cm (¾ in) thick pieces. Blanch for 3 minutes in boiling salted water. Meanwhile, gently warm 125 ml (4 fl oz/½ cup) extra-virgin olive oil in large frying pan with 3 sliced garlic cloves and 3 sliced red bird's eye chillies until fragrant, 2–3 minutes. Lift the broccoli out of the water and directly into the pan, then toss through to coat. Add 100 g (3½ oz) blanched almonds that have been cracked in a mortar and cook until lightly browned, 2–3 minutes. Season with salt and lots of black pepper and serve as a side for lamb, poultry, pork or fish.

Cook the barley in lightly salted boiling water for about 35 minutes until tender, then drain and set aside. Blanch the broccolini in boiling salted water for 1½ minutes, then drain.

Meanwhile, preheat the oven to 180°C (350°F) fan-forced. Line a baking tray with baking paper.

Lay the anchovies on the baking tray and bake for 10 minutes, then set aside to cool.

Dress the barley with the lemon juice and oil. Season with salt and pepper and combine.

Blitz all the tuna mayo ingredients in a food processor, seasoning to taste.

Preheat a chargrill pan or barbecue grill on high. Toss the broccolini in oil and season with salt and pepper, then char until the edges blacken, about 3 minutes.

Spoon the tuna mayo across a large serving plate. Scatter the barley over, then pile on the broccolini. Peel the eggs, then break or slice in half, and nestle them against the broccolini. Crumble the baked anchovies over the sauce and broccolini tops. Drizzle with a little oil and serve with lemon on the side.

Orecchiette with broccoli & cime di rape

This is a specialty of the southern Italian region of Puglia. Cime di rape is traditional, but broccoli yields a fine result – just double the amount if you can't find cime di rape. I also enjoy its creamy texture when mashed through the sauce, so this combines the traditional and the available. **Serves 4**

300 g (10½ oz) cime di rape, leaves and finer stems
300 g (10½ oz) broccoli, roughly chopped
500 g (1 lb 2 oz) orecchiette
125 ml (4 fl oz/½ cup) extra-virgin olive oil

3 large garlic cloves, finely sliced
2 bird's eye chillies, finely sliced
10 large anchovies
150 g (5½ oz) pecorino or Parmigiano Reggiano, finely grated

½ bunch of flat-leaf (Italian) parsley, leaves finely chopped
Pangrattato (p. 123), to serve

Staples
EVOO, S&P

Cook the cime di rape in boiling salted water for 5 minutes, then lift from the pan, drain and roughly cut into shorter lengths. Cook the broccoli in the boiling water for 8 minutes. Lift from the pan, drain and set aside, reserving 300 ml (10 fl oz) of the cooking liquid.

Cook the pasta in the boiling salted water until just al dente. (It's quite traditional to cook the pasta and the greens in the same water, but not essential.)

Meanwhile, heat the oil in a wide-based saucepan or large frying pan over a medium heat. Add the garlic, chilli and anchovies and cook for about 3 minutes, until fragrant, without letting the garlic colour. Break up and mash the anchovies as they warm through. Add the broccoli and mash with the back of a spoon. Once heated through, add the cime di rape, parsley and 150 ml (5 fl oz) of the broccoli cooking water. Bring to the boil and season as needed with salt and pepper.

Lift the pasta directly into the sauce, over a high heat. Cook for about 3 minutes, tossing through the sauce, adding a little more of the pasta cooking water as needed; the sauce will start to emulsify and stick to the pasta. Add the cheese and parsley and toss through, loosening with a little more pasta water and oil as required. The sauce should be glossy, but not overly oily.

Serve with a drizzle of oil and a handful of pangrattato, which provides a charming textural crunch.

Make it different
Orecchiette with cauliflower. Replace the broccoli entirely with the same about of cauliflower.

With cavolo nero. Add some cavolo nero leaves (cooked for 8 minutes, then drained well and finely shredded) to supplement the broccoli.

Broccoli with lemon, chilli, fennel seeds & pecorino GF V

Cut 2 heads of broccoli or 2 bunches broccolini into large florets and boil in salted water for 3 minutes, then drain well. Preheat a chargrill pan or barbecue grill on high. Oil the broccoli and grill until charred, 3–5 minutes. Set aside. Warm 100 ml (3½ fl oz) extra-virgin olive oil in a large frying pan over a low heat. Add 5 sliced garlic cloves, 3 long red chillies thickly sliced on an angle, and 2 teaspoons fennel seeds. Cook until fragrant, 3–4 minutes. Add the broccoli, season with salt and pepper and toss through. Add the juice of 1 lemon, toss through again, then tip onto a platter. Serve with 70 g (2½ oz) finely shaved pecorino or Grana Padano on top. Beautiful with Italian-style sausages, Porchetta (p. 338) or pork chops, or grilled fish or baked whole fish. Serves 4.

Charred broccoli, ramen & nori salad GF V VG

I love charring broccoli in a pan or on a grill, as it develops so much nutty character, and is especially good if eating cold in a salad. **Serves 2**

2 heads of broccoli, trimmed
150 g (5½ oz) dried ramen noodles, or soba noodles
1½ teaspoons sesame oil
50 ml (1¾ fl oz) extra-virgin olive oil

2 tablespoons sesame seeds, lightly toasted
100 ml (3½ fl oz) Ponzu (p. 101), or light soy sauce
1½ tablespoons brown-rice vinegar
10 cm (4 in) piece of fresh ginger, peeled, very finely diced

4 spring onions (scallions), white part and most of the green, finely sliced
2 handfuls of coriander (cilantro) leaves, lightly chopped
2 nori sheets, snipped

Staples
EVOO, S&P

Blanch the broccoli in boiling salted water for 1 minute, then refresh in cold water and drain well. Slice lengthways about 2 cm (¾ in) thick, to give you a silhouette of the head and good contact surface for charring.

Cook the noodles in boiling water for 2 minutes, stirring frequently. Drain and refresh briefly under cold water. Drain again and coat lightly with ½ teaspoon of the sesame oil and 2 teaspoons of the olive oil.

Heat a large frying pan over a medium heat, or heat a chargrill pan or barbecue grill on high. Lightly oil the broccoli and cook until lightly blackened, about 2½–3 minutes each side. Break up the broccoli; it will be half-cooked and still a little crunchy.

In a large bowl, combine half the sesame seeds, the remaining sesame oil and olive oil, the ponzu, vinegar and ginger. Add the broccoli, toss and stand for 5 minutes. Finally, add the noodles, spring onion and coriander and toss to combine.

Serve in a large shallow bowl, sprinkled with the nori and remaining sesame seeds.

Make it different
Charred broccoli is perfect with cooked grains, toasted almonds, hazelnuts and the like. Try adding it to a barley or freekeh salad – or serving it with Anchoïade (p. 78), Tuna mayonnaise (p. 74) or Bagna cauda (p. 83).

Make it a meal
Add a few handfuls of shredded poached or left-over roast chicken, or some marinated tofu and a handful of podded edamame.

Cabbage & brussels sprouts

These days, I have an appreciation of cabbage in all forms: raw, fermented, pickled, briefly cooked, and cooked slowly until meltingly tender. Growing up, aside from my meme's long-braised version, I'd only really ever had it in coleslaw. And those coleslaws were always made with sweet commercial mayonnaise, so you never really tasted the cabbage much; it played more of a textural role. And I love the flavour of raw white cabbage. There's a gentle, spicy/peppery note that I find quite addictive, and I'm now also very fond of the sweetly pungent tone of brussels sprouts.

Brussels sprouts are the symbol of childhood distaste, and it's a bias that can persist well into the adult years. My feeling is that the strong flavour of brassicas can be a bit overwhelming for what seems to be a heightened sense of taste in the young. Perhaps familiarity breeds content in some cases, with the flavours eventually finding acceptance with many. And though it would be natural for me to harp on about twentieth century vegetable-overcooking crimes, I'm not going to. Brussels sprouts have a strong flavour, with a classic sulphurous dimension, but in season they're also irresistibly sweet and mildly flavoured, with a creamy texture when just cooked. Feel free not to like them, if you will, but don't judge them by the measure of heavily boiled sprouts with no love other than a little salt.

The simplest way to cook brussels sprouts is in ample boiling salted water for about 4 minutes until tender, then drain and toss in plenty of butter and black pepper. They also roast beautifully, taking on a nutty dimension, which matches beautifully with a drizzle of honey and a sprinkling of Dukkah (p. 13). They like sweet and rich flavours, so saba, vincotto or good balsamic vinegar drizzled over roasted sprouts, with a slick of peppery olive oil and maybe some chopped almonds, would be a delight. A little curd cheese or feta wouldn't hurt, either. They're also lovely raw, with quite a fine cabbage flavour and delicately crunchy texture. They can be used to make a slaw-style salad, and are delicious tossed with roasted mushrooms and parmesan cheese (see p. 453).

A large cabbage can yield a fantastic amount of food, whether shredded for a slaw, sautéed until tender, blanched and stuffed for cabbage rolls (see p. 451), braised slowly or fermented to make plenty of Sauerkraut (p. 454) or Kimchi (p. 455). Cabbages are also very tolerant of cold weather, so it's no wonder they became such a symbol of the common diet in Eastern Europe – though they have been grown widely for a long time, even being known as somewhat of a staple in ancient Greece, Rome and Egypt.

Most readily available cabbage types are green/white, red, savoy and wombok (also known as Chinese cabbage or Napa cabbage). There are in fact many varieties, with many cultivars fitting into the first two colour-coded brackets, but unless you're buying heirloom types, the actual variety is rarely referenced. In a culinary respect, while there may be some variation to hue or sweetness, their uses are the same. Red cabbage, though, is notably sweeter and richer in flavour, especially when braised. Green/white and red cabbages tend to be weighty and dense, and more so for the former than the latter. Savoy cabbage – with its capillary-like ribs and crinkled leaves – and the more cylindrical wombok are leafier, with a looser structure and a finer, less firm texture to the leaves.

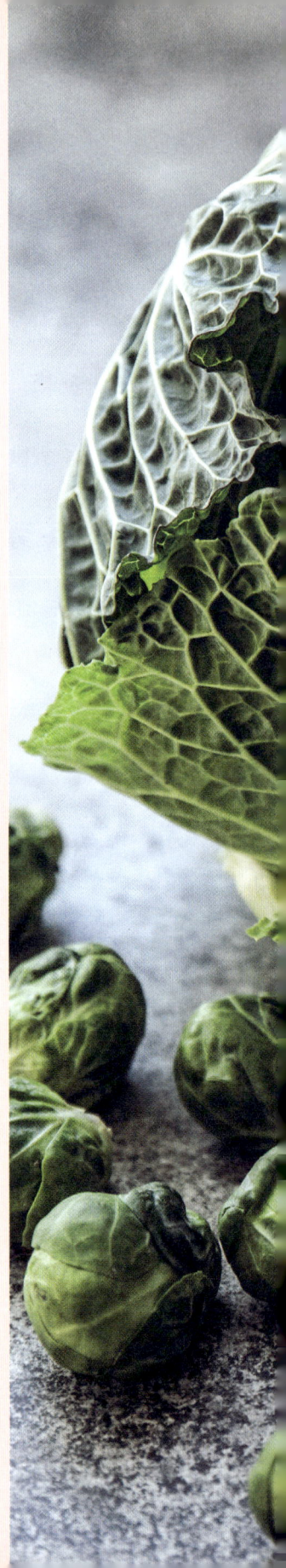

Also see

Simple soused cabbage 340

Grilled pork fillet, wombok & crispy egg 341

Veal & pork polpette with savoy cabbage, taleggio & truffled pecorino 337

Wombok, daikon, shiitake & tofu salad 450

Pork, wombok & ginger dumpling filling 500

Kohlrabi, cabbage & beetroot slaw 548–9

Pair with

Pair cabbage and brussels sprouts with cream, butter, feta, sour cream and parmesan, as well as soy, fermented chilli, miso, sesame, chilli, ginger, vinegar and honey. Spice with black and white pepper, cumin, coriander seeds, caraway, nutmeg and mustard, and match with herbs such as mint, coriander (cilantro), parsley, Thai basil, dill and garlic chives. Pair with onions, spring onions (scallions), carrots, celery, mushrooms, peas, apples, lemon and chestnuts. They love cured and smoked pork, such as bacon, pancetta and lardo, as well as roasted pork and beef.

Savoy cabbage is prized for its colour and texture and is a favourite of classical French cooking. You can use blanched leaves to make a delicate wrapper for stuffing, or shred and sauté with bacon or speck (or just in butter) until tender, finishing with plenty of salt and pepper. Wombok is leafy, with a juicy and crunchy spine to the leaves. It can be stir-fried or served raw in salads.

These days, I like to keep my slaws bright, with plenty of herbs and a vinaigrette rather than mayonnaise, or if I do use mayonnaise it's usually combined with a vinaigrette or lightened with yoghurt, crème fraîche or sour cream. Green/white cabbage and fennel are in peak season at about the same time, so they make happy slaw-fellows, ideally with the fennel fronds chopped and added with some dill, then dressed with oil, vinegar, a tablespoon of mayo and another of whichever of the sour dairy trio you have on hand.

Even simpler, scrunch shredded cabbage in your hands with a pinch of salt and sugar and a splash of white-wine vinegar. This is somewhat like the first step in making sauerkraut, which starts to break down the cellular structure, softening it. Stand for 5–10 minutes, then serve with sausages or roast pork shoulder, or cram into a roll with roasted pork belly and mustard or relish.

When selecting a cabbage, it should be surprisingly heavy in the hand. The leaves of green/white and red cabbages should be tightly packed, and the first few layers of darker outer leaves should clamp around the mass, rather than peeling back. Savoy cabbage or wombok (Chinese cabbage) will naturally be looser, but the leaves should be crisp and vibrant, not floppy or limp. A whole white/green cabbage can last for weeks in the crisper, while savoy cabbage and wombok will be less resilient.

With brussels sprouts, opt for smaller specimens, as they can get starchy when too large. They should be green and vivid; any with yellowing or mottling of the leaves are best avoided. Like cabbage, they should be fairly tightly packed, with off-peak-season specimens lacking the tightly interlaced leaves and being somewhat light on and generally less sweet. Like any brassica, brussels sprouts and cabbages that have been stored for too long will develop a pungent, sulphurous character, so make sure they have a fresh aroma.

Preparing cabbage & brussels sprouts

Brussels sprouts simply need the base of the stem trimmed off where it has dried out, and any tired or loose coarse leaves removed. For cabbages, the darker outer leaves are generally a bit tough and should be peeled away. These can be used to keep sauerkraut submerged, if that's where you're headed, but otherwise it's off to the compost. I will typically remove the core from a cabbage quarter by lying it flat on one side, then angling my knife to remove most of the stem. This may not be necessary on small or young specimens, or if braising. If I'm making a slaw, I'll also cut out some of the thicker ribs or work around them when shredding. The ribs in a savoy cabbage are usually fine and tender enough to begin with, and the crunchy ribs of wombok are a big part of its charm.

Italian-style coleslaw ⓖⒻ Ⓥ

This was a mr. wolf staple, bright, refreshing and quite hearty at the same time. A portion of this accompanies every crumbed schnitzel we send out, along with a big wedge of lemon, and that's something I'd never change. **Serves 4–6**

¼ white cabbage, core trimmed and finely shredded
6 Dutch carrots, peeled and finely sliced lengthways
6 radishes, trimmed and finely sliced
¼ celeriac (optional; increase the cabbage quantity otherwise), julienned

½ white salad onion, finely sliced
5 sprigs of flat-leaf (Italian) parsley, leaves roughly chopped
85 ml (2¾ fl oz) extra-virgin olive oil
35 ml (1¼ fl oz) white-wine vinegar

50 g (1¾ oz/½ cup) finely grated Grana Padano, plus extra to serve

Staples
S&P

Special equipment
Mandoline

Add the cabbage, carrot, radish, celeriac (if using), onion and parsley to a large bowl. Season with salt and pepper and toss together.

Combine the oil and vinegar and pour over the slaw. Add the parmesan and toss to combine. Adjust the seasoning as needed, then grate some extra parmesan over to serve.

White cabbage & pea slaw ⓖⒻ Ⓥ

This is similar to my Italian coleslaw, but the peas and mint make it quite a different affair. **Serves 4–6**

¼ white cabbage, core trimmed and finely shredded
6 radishes, trimmed and finely sliced
½ white salad onion, finely sliced
5 sprigs of mint, leaves torn
1 long green chilli, seeds removed, finely sliced

2 handfuls of fresh or frozen peas, blanched or thawed under hot water
85 ml (2¾ fl oz) extra-virgin olive oil
35 ml (1¼ fl oz) white-wine vinegar

50 g (1¾ oz/½ cup) finely grated Grana Padano, plus extra to serve

Staples
S&P

Special equipment
Mandoline

Pair with

Pizza, grilled or crumbed meat, roasts or pasta.

Classic cabbage slaw
ⓖⒻ Ⓥ

To make the dressing, mix 3 tablespoons white rice vinegar, 3 tablespoons extra-virgin olive oil, 3 tablespoons kewpie mayonnaise, 4 tablespoons plain yoghurt, 3 teaspoons caster (superfine) sugar, 1 teaspoon ground white pepper and 2½ teaspoons salt flakes. Finely shave ½ small white cabbage and thinly slice the white and pale green parts of 6 spring onions (scallions). Toss the dressing through the cabbage mixture and allow to sit for 5 minutes before serving. This slaw is great the next day as well.

Pair with

This is such a great foil for pizza!

It also works particularly well with chilli, as a palate cleanser.

Add the cabbage, radish, onion, mint, chilli and peas to a large bowl, season with salt and pepper and toss together.

Combine the oil and vinegar and pour over the slaw. Add the parmesan and toss to combine. Adjust the seasoning as needed, then grate some extra parmesan over to serve.

Make it a meal

Cut 240 g (8½ oz) haloumi into 1 cm (½ in) thick fingers, then dust the haloumi in flour. Add a splash of extra-virgin olive oil to a frying pan over a medium heat and fry the haloumi in batches until golden, about 2 minutes, turning to colour evenly. Drain on paper towel. Pile the slaw on a serving plate, then top with the fried haloumi. Scatter with the seeds of half a pomegranate.

Savoy cabbage slaw with apple, sour cream, caraway & fennel seed GF V

Pair with

Pork ribs, roast chicken or crumbed veal, or simply grilled steak or fish.

Simple dressed white cabbage GF V VG

In a bowl, combine ¼ finely shaved white cabbage, 1½ teaspoons sugar and 1 teaspoon salt flakes. Set aside for 10 minutes, then dress with 2 tablespoons white-wine vinegar and 2 tablespoons extra-virgin olive oil. Serve with everything from tacos to sausages or grilled barbecue meats, to braised chickpeas or Black turtle bean, pork belly & morcilla braise (frijoles negros) (p. 340).

This is a spritely spring salad and a great alternative to traditional coleslaw. Fresh mint or chopped dill fronds would be a lovely addition. **Serves 4–6**

1 small savoy cabbage, about 1 kg (2 lb 3 oz), core cut out, outer leaves removed, finely shredded
1½ teaspoons salt flakes
1½ teaspoons caster (superfine) sugar
2 granny smith apples, skin on, cut into matchsticks
½ white salad onion, finely diced

3 teaspoons caraway seeds, or fennel seeds, lightly ground

Sour cream dressing
80 ml (2½ fl oz/⅓ cup) extra-virgin olive oil
3 tablespoons sour cream
3 tablespoons mayonnaise (pp. 74–5)
juice of 1 lemon

1½ tablespoons white-wine vinegar
2 teaspoons caster (superfine) sugar
1 teaspoon salt flakes

Staples
S&P

Special equipment
Mandoline

Add the cabbage to a large bowl, sprinkle with the salt and sugar, then scrunch in your hands to soften slightly. Stand for 10 minutes, then drain off any liquid.

Add the cabbage to a large bowl with the apple, onion and half the caraway seeds.

Combine the dressing ingredients in a bowl, then pour over the salad and toss to combine. Pile onto a plate and serve sprinkled with the remaining caraway seeds.

Grace's braised cabbage GF V

This is based on my meme's recipe, which she'd serve with roast pork. While her cooking was largely influenced by Tunisian cuisine, this dish has a distinctly Eastern/Northern European feel. It was the only way that my father would eat cabbage, so my mother had to learn it, too. This interpretation is built from a combination of both of their versions. **Serves 8**

100 g (3½ oz) butter
10 French shallots, sliced
2 garlic cloves, sliced
1.2 kg (2 lb 10 oz) cabbage (savoy/drum/white/red), cored and sliced 4 mm (¼ in) thick

300 ml (10 fl oz) white wine
2 granny smith apples, peeled and sliced
100 ml (3½ fl oz) white-wine vinegar, or apple-cider vinegar

100 g (3½ oz) caster (superfine) sugar (Grace used brown sugar with red cabbage)
1 teaspoon caraway seeds, or 2 bruised juniper berries

Staples
S&P

Pair with

Pork chops, roast pork belly, bratwurst sausages, roast duck or goose – if you're up for the challenge!

Melt the butter in a wide-based saucepan over a medium heat. Add the shallot and garlic, season with salt and pepper and cook until softened, about 5 minutes. Add the cabbage and cook until slightly softened, about 5 minutes. Pour in the wine, then cover and cook for 45 minutes on a very low heat.

Add the apple, vinegar, sugar and caraway seeds. Season again and cook for 30 minutes, with the lid partially open, until the cabbage is meltingly tender. Serve warm.

Wombok, daikon, shiitake & tofu salad V VG

The firm, squeaky tofu, peppery daikon and generous burst of fresh herbs are an amazing combination with the shiitake mushrooms and the crisply crunchy wombok. I very happily eat this salad on its own. **Serves 6**

15 fresh shiitake mushrooms, cut into quarters
1 green chilli, finely sliced
½ wombok (Chinese cabbage), 3 cm (1¼ in) of base trimmed, leaves separated
15 cm (6 in) piece of daikon, finely shaved into ribbons
200 g (7 oz) dry, firm tofu, sliced

1 bunch of Thai basil, leaves picked
½ bunch of dill, fronds picked
½ bunch of mint, leaves picked
2 tablespoons toasted sesame seeds

Ginger & sesame dressing
100 ml (3½ fl oz) extra-virgin olive oil
60 ml (2 fl oz/¼ cup) light soy sauce

10 cm (4 in) piece of ginger, peeled and finely julienned
1 garlic clove, finely grated
juice of ½ lime
½ teaspoon sesame oil
2 teaspoons caster (superfine) sugar
½ teaspoon ground white pepper
a pinch of salt

Pair with

This can be enjoyed as a standalone salad, but it's also a great match with rich and spicy Asian dishes.

Blanch the mushrooms in boiling salted water for 1 minute, then drain.

Combine the dressing ingredients in a large bowl, then add the mushrooms and chilli. Toss to coat, then set aside for 5 minutes.

Shred half the wombok leaves, then add to the mushroom mixture with the daikon, tofu and half the herbs. Toss to coat and combine.

Arrange the remaining wombok leaves on a serving plate and pile the salad on top. Top with the remaining herbs and the sesame seeds. Serve immediately, while fresh and crunchy.

Cabbage rolls with lamb, rice, pine nuts & dill ⒼⒻ

Pair with

Yoghurt and Fermented cooked chilli sauce (p. 97).

Modelled on a dish I enjoyed in Istanbul, these rolls get better after a day or so – the cabbage mellows, the spices soften, and the flavours enrich and meld. Salçasi is a cornerstone of Turkish cuisine, a paste of either tomatoes (domates salçasi) or peppers (biber salçasi). I use the version with peppers here, which adds so much flavour and depth; I wouldn't recommend substituting anything else. Be wary, though, as there are hot and mild versions of the paste. This recipe uses mild biber salçasi; using the same quantity of the hot variety will make these rolls somewhat spicy – some would say explosively so.

Makes 10 rolls

1 white cabbage, core cut out
1.2 litres (41 fl oz) water
250 g (9 oz) mild biber salçasi (see p. 8)
250 g (9 oz/1 cup) passata
juice of 2 lemons
1 tablespoon dried Greek oregano (rigani)
1 tablespoon salt flakes
2 teaspoons long-grain white rice

Filling

2 salad onions, finely diced
4 garlic cloves, finely sliced
60 g (2 oz) pine nuts, lightly toasted
500 g (1 lb 2 oz) minced (ground) lamb, or pork
250 g (9 oz/1¼ cups) long-grain white rice
3 tablespoons mild biber salçasi

2 tablespoons ground cumin
2 long green chillies, finely diced
½ bunch of dill, fronds finely sliced
¼ bunch of flat-leaf (Italian) parsley, leaves finely sliced

Staples
EVOO, S&P

Cook the cabbage in boiling salted water for 10 minutes, then turn it over and cook for another 5 minutes. Drain and cool. Peel the leaves back in one piece. You'll need 10 large leaves – or you can make more rolls if the leaves are smaller. Cut the firm stem out, in a 5 cm (2 in) deep V-shape. Once the leaves are separated, leave to drain well.

(Alternatively, you can separate the cabbage leaves from the raw cabbage, then blanch for 3 minutes and drain. This can be tricky, though, as it is hard to separate the leaves in one piece, unless the leaves aren't very tightly packed.)

Preheat the oven to 170°C (340°F) fan-forced.

To make the filling, heat a splash of oil in a saucepan over a medium heat. Fry the onion and garlic until softened and translucent, about 5 minutes. Tip into a bowl with the pine nuts. Cool for a few minutes, then add the remaining filling ingredients and combine well with your hands.

Divide the mixture amongst the well-drained cabbage leaves, tucking the ends in as you roll them up into parcels. Lay the rolls in a baking dish or casserole dish that fits them snugly.

Add the water, biber salçasi, passata, lemon juice, oregano and salt to a saucepan and bring to a simmer, then pour over the rolls. Sprinkle the rice on top. Weigh the rolls down with a plate, then cover with a lid (or baking paper, then foil).

Transfer to the oven and bake for 1 hour, or until the rice on top is cooked.

Stand for 10 minutes to relax and firm up a little before serving. I also like these cold – and find they're especially good reheated the next day.

Shaved brussels sprouts with roasted king brown mushrooms, manchego & maple dressing GF V

Pair with

Something simple, such as a steak or roast chicken.

Salt-baked celeriac sliced into steaks.

For an interesting starter, serve with soft-boiled or poached eggs.

Tossing the shaved sprouts with cooked mushrooms brings warmth and richness to this salad, which is somewhat heavy on umami – just the way I like it! **Serves 6–8**

300 g (10½ oz) large king brown mushrooms sliced 1 cm (½ in) thick, or shiitake mushrooms
650 g (1 lb 7 oz) small brussels sprouts, trimmed, outer leaves removed, finely sliced
2 handfuls of mint leaves, torn

1 handful of dill fronds
120 g (4½ oz) manchego or Parmigiano Reggiano, half shaved, half finely grated

Maple dressing
80 ml (2½ fl oz/⅓ cup) maple syrup
3 tablespoons sherry vinegar
2 teaspoons dijon mustard

2½ tablespoons lemon juice
1 teaspoon salt flakes
100 ml (3½ fl oz) extra-virgin olive oil

Staples
EVOO, S&P

Special equipment
Mandoline

Preheat the oven to 180°C (350°F) fan-forced. Line a baking tray with baking paper.

Season the mushrooms with salt and pepper and toss with a good splash of oil. Spread them out on the baking tray and roast for 15 minutes, until cooked and slightly golden on the edges. Set aside.

To make the dressing, whisk the maple syrup, vinegar, mustard, lemon juice and salt together, then whisk in the oil until combined.

Add the sprouts and herbs to a large bowl and season with salt. Tip in the mushrooms and pour half the dressing over, then add all the shaved cheese and half the grated cheese and toss gently. Serve with the remaining cheese and dressing over the top.

Roasted brussels sprouts with honey & dukkah GF V

Pair with

Grilled chicken, a seared steak or a roast.

This is a lovely addition to a spread of Middle Eastern dishes.

I never thought about roasting sprouts until I was strongly advised to, and my scepticism was quickly dispelled. It's now my favourite method. They become tender on the inside and crisp and charred on the outside, while taking on a delightfully nutty flavour. They match so well with hummus, dukkah and floral honey. I have conquered many a hater of sprouts with this recipe. **Serves 4–6**

30 brussels sprouts, trimmed
2½ tablespoons extra-virgin olive oil
2 tablespoons fragrant honey

4 tablespoons Dukkah (p. 13)
4 tablespoons Hummus (p. 374)

Staples
EVOO, S&P

Preheat the oven to 180°C (350°F) fan-forced.

Add the sprouts to a baking tray, drizzle with the olive oil and season with salt and pepper. Roast for about 45 minutes, shaking the tray occasionally. When the sprouts are tender and the leaves are curling back, tip into a bowl and drizzle with the honey. Add half the dukkah and toss to coat.

Spread the hummus on a serving plate and pile on the sprouts. Serve sprinkled with the remaining dukkah.

Sauerkraut ⓖⓕ ⓥ ⓥⓖ

When learning to ferment and preserve, sauerkraut is a good place to start, as it's so easy to make and such an ideal way to understand the fermentation process. It's also very safe, which is reassuring when you're starting out.

The basic principle at play is lacto-fermentation, and it is a principle that can be used to ferment and preserve all sorts of vegetables. With sauerkraut, you salt some shredded cabbage, which releases ample water to make a brine, but you can also make a brine at the same or a similar concentration to pickle cucumbers, carrots, olives (see p. 470), fennel ... pretty much anything you like.

Once the vegetables are submerged in brine – which protects them from oxidation and spoilage while they ferment – it's just a matter of tasting occasionally to see if they're fermented enough for your liking, then popping them in the fridge to slow the process down. So simple. The salt kills off any bugs that might develop in a problematic way, then, once fermentation starts, lactic acid is produced from the conversion of fermentable sugars, with the acidic environment (just like the sourness of yoghurt or sourdough bread) hostile to anything ambient trying to grow and spoil the mix.

The key points are that the salt concentration is high enough (2–3 per cent is about right, but you can go a little higher, too), and that the produce stays beneath the liquid. Plus, if you're making a brine, either boil and cool the water first, or use spring water, as chlorinated water can retard fermentation.

Lacto-fermented foods are also very good for you. Fermentation makes their nutrients easier to digest and absorb, while also breaking down so-called anti-nutrients that can block the bioavailability of key vitamins and minerals. Naturally fermented foods are also rich in probiotics, and they can have a very positive effect on your gut biome and overall health. They are also said to reduce inflammation and boost your immune system.

When making sauerkraut, you can you use all sorts of cabbages and flavour the kraut in many different ways. Fennel, caraway and celery seeds are my favourite flavourings, but experiment and find your own. It's key to note, though, that a little spice goes a long way, so don't overload the mix. Different cabbages perform differently, too, with some fermenting faster and some slower, so just taste on the early side and monitor. **Makes a 1.5 litre (51 fl oz/6 cup) jar**

2 drumhead cabbages
(2 kg/4 lb 6 oz after
trimming and shredding)
40 g (1½ oz) fine sea salt
(2.5–3% salt to cabbage
weight is ideal)

1 heaped tablespoon
caraway, dill or fennel
seeds, or any spice you
like (optional)

Special equipment
Mandoline (optional)

Pair with

Corned beef, sausages or hot-smoked fish.

Grilled bratwurst with mustard in a bread roll, or with dill pickles and rye bread.

Add to salads, sandwiches or rice bowls.

I really love sauerkraut for breakfast with scrambled or poached eggs and chilli sauce, or on top of avocado on toast with goat's cheese.

Layer into a toasted sandwich with corned beef, pastrami or ham, with a great cheddar, Comté, fontina or jarlsberg.

Combine two-thirds raw shredded cabbage with one-third sauerkraut, then dress simply with vinegar, oil, pepper and a little salt and sugar; serve with grilled meats, roasted or fried chicken, or a schnitzel (see p. 345).

Remove the loose outer leaves from the cabbages, reserving a couple of leaves to keep the sauerkraut submerged. Cut the cabbage into quarters, then trim away some of the core. Shred into 5 mm (¼ in) slices with a sharp knife or mandoline.

Toss the cabbage and salt well in a large bowl (or two). Stand for 15 minutes; the cabbage will start to weep and soften. Squish with your hands for about 15 minutes to bruise and release more water. (You can also use the end of a rolling pin or similar to soften the cabbage, but be careful not to break it up.) The cabbage will have reduced dramatically in volume (combine the bowls if using two), and there will be a good amount of liquid in the bowl.

Add the spice, if using, and combine. Pack the cabbage firmly into clean jar(s) and top with the brine. Don't pack the jar(s) right to the top, as you need a little space for the cabbage to ferment, and all the cabbage needs to be submerged under the brine, or the exposed parts will go mouldy. If necessary, you can add a little water to supplement the liquid. Use the reserved outer cabbage leaves to keep the kraut submerged by folding them up and pressing them into the jar(s), using the shoulders to hold the cabbage in place. Place the lid on the jar(s) and seal.

Sit the jar(s) on a small tray or in a container, as they will produce more liquid as the cabbage ferments and may overflow when opened. Place out of direct sunlight. While fermenting, it is important to open the jars each day to release gas, then reseal. (Alternatively, you can sit the lids loosely on top, but not seal them – though there is a greater chance of mould developing.)

Test the kraut after a week; it might take another week to be ready. This will depend a bit on temperature and how fermented you like it. The cabbage is perfectly delicious from the start, but the flavour will become more complex as it ferments – and it's better for you, too. Just remember, it is food and not medicine, so ferment it as much or as little as you like – you're eating it, after all.

When tasting, make sure the cabbage is submerged again if you're fermenting it for longer. Once ready, I like it to be a little crunchy and a little shiny, with a lovely sour, moreish flavour. Once you're happy, seal the jars and refrigerate. This will slow down the fermentation process to a very slow tick.

The sauerkraut will last for at least 6 months, but it will get softer and stronger in fermented flavour the longer you keep it.

Kimchi

Pair with

Braised and grilled spiced meats.

Fried rice or steamed rice.

Add to a chicken or prawn (shrimp) stir-fry.

Eat with an omelette.

Make a cheddar cheese and chopped kimchi toasted sandwich.

Add 2 tablespoons finely chopped kimchi and 1 tablespoon toasted sesame seeds to a soy dressing (see p. 94) and serve with White-poached chicken (p. 230).

Serve with dumplings (pp. 231, 342, 500).

Kimchi is essentially a spicy and extra-pungent sauerkraut, with the same process of lacto-fermentation transforming the cabbage into something both delicious and even more healthful. A staple of Korean cuisine, kimchi has countless variations, with radishes sometimes used instead of cabbage. The instantly recognisable wombok (Chinese cabbage) version is made with red kimchi paste, and is fiery in both colour and spicy heat ... but I'm also a fan of the milder type made with white kimchi paste, with plenty of ginger to give a gentler warmth and a fragrant lift. The ingredients list looks long – but you only need one of the kimchi pastes for each new batch, so try one first and give the other a go next time, to see which you prefer. **Makes a 1–1.25 litre (34–42 fl oz/4–5 cup) jar**

1 large wombok
(Chinese cabbage),
weighing 1.5–2 kg
(3 lb 5 oz–4 lb 6 oz)
50 g (1¾ oz) fine sea salt
1 daikon, peeled and cut into
fat matchsticks
6 spring onions (scallions),
white and half the green,
cut into 2 cm (¾ in) lengths
½ bunch of garlic chives
or regular chives, cut into
3 cm (1¼ in) lengths

Red kimchi paste
3½ tablespoons (35 g/1¼ oz)
gochugaru powder (Korean
chilli powder)
2½ tablespoons warm water
1 large apple or nashi pear,
peeled and grated
2 long red chillies, seeded
and finely chopped
5 garlic cloves, finely
chopped
10 cm (4 in) piece of fresh
ginger, peeled and finely
grated
2 tablespoons dried shrimp,
finely chopped
2 tablespoons fish sauce
1 tablespoon raw sugar

White kimchi paste
2 granny smith apples,
peeled, cored and chopped
16 cm (6½ in) fresh young
ginger, peeled and finely
chopped
6 spring onions (scallions),
white part only, finely
chopped
6 garlic cloves, finely
chopped
1 long green chilli, finely
chopped
80 ml (2½ fl oz/⅓ cup) fish
sauce

Cucumber kimchi GF V VG

Semi-peel 5 Lebanese (short) cucumbers and slice into 1 cm (½ in) pieces. In a bowl, combine the cucumbers with 1 finely sliced white salad onion, 2 small finely grated garlic cloves, 130 ml (4½ fl oz/½ cup) white rice vinegar, 2 tablespoons gochugaru powder, 3 teaspoons caster (superfine) sugar, ½ teaspoon sesame oil, 1½ teaspoons salt flakes and 1 tablespoon toasted sesame seeds. Stir to combine and leave in the fridge for at least 30 minutes before serving. Serve chilled with grilled beef, chicken, fish or pork and rice.

Remove and reserve a couple of the loose outer leaves from the wombok, which can be used to keep the kimchi submerged. Quarter the wombok lengthways, then trim off about half the core. Cut into rough 3 cm (1¼ in) squares. Rinse very well, then drain.

Add the wombok and salt to a large bowl and toss well, then massage for about 5 minutes with a moderately firm hand. Stand for 3 hours at room temperature, then rinse well under cold water. Drain, gently squeezing out some of the moisture.

If making the red kimchi paste, add the gochugaru and water to a small bowl and make a paste, then add to a blender with the other ingredients and blitz until smooth.

If making the white kimchi paste, add all the ingredients to a blender and blitz until smooth.

Add the wombok, daikon, spring onion and chives to a large bowl with your chosen kimchi paste. Wearing disposable gloves, thoroughly massage the paste through the cabbage. Pack into a sterilised jar(s) so the ingredients are fully submerged under the liquid, folding up a reserved cabbage leaf to keep the mixture down. Place the lid on the jar(s) and seal.

Sit the jar(s) on a small tray or in a container, as they will produce more liquid as the cabbage ferments and may overflow when opened. Place out of direct sunlight. While fermenting, it is important to open the jars each day to release gas, then reseal. (Alternatively, you can sit the lids loosely on top, but not seal them – though there is a greater chance of mould developing.)

Stand at room temperature for 5–10 days, tasting daily from the five-day mark to check on the progress. The fermentation will take longer at cooler temperatures but, as with Sauerkraut (p. 454), it is a matter of taste when it's ready. You can eat it immediately if you want, but the beneficial bacteria won't be present.

Refrigerate when you're happy with the flavour. The kimchi will continue to ferment slowly in the fridge, becoming more agreeably funky over time. It will keep for up to 12 months in the fridge, but it will continue to ferment and become softer, so consuming within 6 months is advisable.

Kimchi pancakes with a tamari & sesame dipping sauce

Pair with

Serve with seared scotch fillet or porterhouse that has been painted on both sides with a couple of tablespoons of kecap manis while it rests, then slice. To eat, tuck the sliced meat into the lettuce cups with the pancakes.

Grill some fresh shiitake mushrooms, then brush with kecap manis to serve in the lettuce and kimchi cups.

Kimchi pancakes are a popular appetiser or side in Korean cuisine. They are also a good way to use up kimchi that has fermented a little too long and lost some of its crunch. In fact, slightly over-fermented kimchi is ideal for these. The pancakes are quite lovely as they are, but I especially like contrasting the texture and heat with a crisp lettuce leaf and some coriander (cilantro). Adding in a little sliced grilled beef or spiced chicken is even better, but far from necessary. **Makes 12 pancakes**

1 iceberg lettuce
oil, for shallow-frying
½ bunch of coriander (cilantro), fine stems and leaves picked

Kimchi pancakes
150 g (5½ oz/1 cup) plain (all-purpose) flour
150 g (5½ oz) potato starch
2½ teaspoons baking powder

½ teaspoon salt flakes
320 g (11½ oz) kimchi, squeezed of liquid and chopped, 100 ml (3½ fl oz) liquid reserved
200 ml (7 fl oz) water
6 fine spring onions (scallions), white and most of the green, finely sliced
1½ tablespoons toasted sesame seeds

Tamari & sesame dipping sauce
80 ml (2½ fl oz/⅓ cup) tamari
2 tablespoons rice vinegar
¾ teaspoon sesame oil
1 long red chilli, finely sliced

Remove the outer leaves of the lettuce, then cut out the core with a paring knife. Soak the lettuce for 30 minutes in cold water, then carefully pry the leaves away to make lettuce cups, trimming as necessary. Drain upside down on a tea towel (dish towel), then stack for serving.

For the pancakes, add the flour, potato starch, baking powder and salt to a large bowl. Whisk in the reserved kimchi liquid and the water to make a smooth batter. Fold in the kimchi and half the spring onion. The batter should have the consistency of a thick pancake batter; add another 50 ml (1¾ fl oz) water if it is too stiff.

Combine the dipping sauce ingredients in a small bowl.

Heat 2–3 cm (¾–1¼ in) of oil in a large frying pan until it instantly fizzes when a little batter is dropped in.

Using about 2 tablespoons of batter for each pancake, cook three or four at a time over a medium heat for 2½ minutes on one side. Sprinkle a little spring onion and sesame seeds on the uncooked side, then flip and cook for another minute. Drain well on paper towel and repeat, ensuring the oil comes back to temperature before cooking the next batch.

Serve the pancakes with the lettuce cups, dipping sauce and coriander on the side. Dip the pancakes in the sauce, then wrap in the lettuce with some coriander and eat with your hands.

Capsicum

To me, the aroma of roasting sweet capsicum is so familiar, so comforting. My grandmother Grace passed her recipe for the Martini family stuffed capsicums (p. 464) to my mother, who still makes a superb version. It's also a vegetable my father has a strong affection for, so perhaps that's why we ate it so much when I was young. Capsicum (bell pepper) was ubiquitous in the chopped salad (with tomato, cucumber and a lemony vinaigrette) that would accompany wiener schnitzel or crumbed cutlets of pork or veal, or pretty much any other dish. That salad says summer to me, and it's on my table at home more often than not in the warmer months. One of dad's other favourite dishes, again passed from his mother to mine, was her fried capsicum and pumpkin salad, spiked with lemon and cumin (see p. 460). This is the accompaniment for fish, or so I was told. And although I've found many other things that go beautifully with fish, I agree it does have a special affinity.

There's a dizzying array of pepper varieties, from sweet ones to a phalanx of variously hot chilli peppers (p. 492), but for most of my sweet pepper needs, the capsicum (bell pepper) is the workhorse. From crunchily garden fresh to sweet and richly flavoured, capsicums have many dimensions. They can be used as a vegetable raw, or roasted, grilled, stir-fried, braised or stuffed. Charring them over hot coals or a naked flame transforms the flesh into silky sweetness, imbued with a subtly smoky scent. Once peeled, it can be seasoned and dressed with good olive oil, red-wine vinegar or sherry vinegar, and perhaps some torn parsley or basil, then served as a simple antipasto with olives, salumi and the like – or you can add it to a frittata, omelette or Shakshuka (p. 463), serve with fresh cheese such as mozzarella, burrata or ricotta, layer in a sandwich with mozzarella and a smear of pesto, crisscross some plump anchovies over the top and scatter with finely shaved onion, or add to Harira (p. 461).

Besides the more familiar traffic-light trio of red, yellow and green, capsicums also come in other colours, including ivory white and even luridly purple. While there is also a variety that remains green, many green capsicums are simply less-ripe red or yellow capsicums. The flavour follows, too, with green less-ripe peppers having a more grassy, vegetal flavour, compared to the rich, sweet notes of red ones. Capsicums are the only member of their genus to not contain capsaicin. They are the bottom dwellers on the Scoville chilli heat scale, with a reading of zero, as opposed to the 1,500,000–2,200,000 Scoville units allotted to the Carolina reaper pepper, which is classified in the 'dangerous' zone, with the apocalypse scorpion being another diabolically hot pepper with a distinctly demonic appearance.

Bullhorn peppers, named for their shape, have a sweet, pungent flavour and no discernible heat. Thin skinned with quite thin flesh, they're not ideal for roasting (thick-walled capsicums are best for this), but are great for stuffing. They're quite similar to banana peppers and sweet Hungarian peppers (which are used to make sweet paprika) – but be careful, as these mild-mannered versions have a surprisingly hot lookalike. I made this mistake once, using them generously in a salad with my girls! I always taste them now. With their rich flavour, bullhorns and banana peppers are perfect for salads (especially with vinegar, good olive oil, dried Greek oregano (rigani), white onion and hard feta), and are ideal in slow braises and soups. My mother-in-law used to grow a bountiful supply of bullhorns all through the summer months. They'd end up in all kinds of dishes, but one I have a fondness for is when she would split them open, crumble feta inside, scatter oregano over, drizzle with oil and then roast until the capsicums were softened and the feta a little coloured. We'd eat these straight from the oven or at room temperature. Super simple and utterly delicious.

Check capsicums forensically when purchasing, as an otherwise sound specimen may have an isolated soft spot, which is often worse than it first feels, with the flesh melting into a soft mush. The skin should be taut and vibrant, whatever the colour, and not baggy or wrinkled. The stem should also feel firmly attached. If it feels like you could loosen it easily, there's a problem lurking inside.

Also see

Rouille 80

Salsa romesco 84

Harissa 92

Summer vegetable
lasagne 136

Tunisian vegetable
couscous royale with
rosewater labneh 386–7

Melanzane sotto aceto
with banana peppers,
basil & chilli 523

Gazpacho 657

Provençale tomato-stuffed
peppers with olives &
anchovies 662

Ratatouille 672

Pair with

*Capsicums love onion, garlic
and pumpkin (winter squash),
as well as the summer produce
they grow with – such as
eggplant (aubergine), tomatoes
and zucchini (courgette) – and
also herbs such as rosemary,
basil, parsley, dill and coriander
(cilantro). They soak up good
extra-virgin olive oil and vinegar
of almost any kind, particularly
sherry and red-wine vinegars,
as well as genuine balsamic.
Their robustness and sweetness
is complemented by cheese –
especially those with strong,
rich flavours, such as goat's
cheese and feta – as well as
hard-boiled or fried eggs. They
take to other strong flavours
beautifully, such as anchovies,
chillies, capers and olives,
as well as most spices, with
cumin, caraway and coriander
seeds working especially well.
Walnuts, almonds and pine
nuts are natural matches,
as is pomegranate molasses.
Capsicums will complement
most animal proteins, but
I love them with oily fish such
as sardines or tuna.*

Preparing capsicums

Whatever type of capsicum you're using, the seeds, core and stem are not edible and need to be removed, either before or after cooking. The advantage of cooking capsicum whole is that the flesh steams in its own juices, yielding such a rich, velvety and sweet result. If using a pepper raw or adding to a dish in pieces, cut it in half, then cut out the core and remove any seeds; I also cut away most of the white membrane, as there's not much flavour there. You can then just slice or dice as required. The skin is perfectly edible raw, but can become a bit tough when cooked. Fine ones will melt away, but thick skins often remain in a sauce or braise. Like tomato skins, there's no real upside to them, being essentially flavourless and sometimes bitter, and they tend to distract from the texture of a dish. It's easy enough to pick them off with tongs as you cook – I just do so every now and then when I'm stirring or checking the progress of a dish.

Tunisian green capsicum & pumpkin salad (GF)(V)(VG)

This rough paste–style salad was a staple recipe of my grandmother's, and it was always served with fish. Always. No flexibility there. The fish was almost always sand mullet, cut into thick darnes and pan-fried. You don't need to be quite so rigid, as this deliciously tangy and intense salad will sit happily among a spread of dishes. It is great with fish, though ... **Serves 6**

Pair with

Yes, fish... this makes a happy partner to deep-fried crumbed whitebait, pan-fried or grilled fillets of any white-fleshed fish, as well as grilled sardines or a chargrilled piece of tuna.

½ kent pumpkin (winter squash), about 600 g (1 lb 5 oz), peeled and cut into 2 cm (¾ in) thick slices
4 green capsicums (bell peppers), seeded and quartered

oil, for deep-frying (see p. 22)
1 large lemon, segmented and chopped, the juice squeezed out of the membranes and reserved
2 garlic cloves, finely grated
2 teaspoons cumin seeds, ground

2 teaspoons freshly ground black pepper

Staples
EVOO, S&P

Heat about 10 cm (4 in) oil in a deep-fryer or large saucepan to 170°C (340°F).

Working in batches, deep-fry the pumpkin slices for 4 minutes, turning to cook them evenly, until tender and coloured. Drain on paper towel.

Deep-fry the capsicum quarters for 5 minutes, turning to cook evenly, until golden. Drain on paper towel, removing the skins when cool enough. Chop the capsicum and pumpkin finely.

Add the lemon chunks and juice to a bowl with the garlic, cumin, pepper and a little oil. Season with salt and combine. Add the chopped vegetables and stir to combine. Season to taste and serve.

Harira

This is my take on the classic Moroccan soup. Lamb is typical in this, but I like it just as much without the lamb, with the long, slow cooking melding the spices and cooking the legumes until buttery soft. The semolina added towards the end thickens the soup that bit more, giving it a velvety texture, while the lemon sharpens the flavours and enhances the spices. If you can't clearly taste the lemon, add more. **Serves 6**

2 lamb shanks
4 litres (135 fl oz/16 cups) water, plus 150 ml (5 fl oz) water
150 g (5½ oz) chickpeas, or black barley, soaked in lightly salted water overnight
150 g (5½ oz) brown lentils, or other lentils, soaked in lightly salted water overnight
100 ml (3½ fl oz) extra-virgin olive oil
2 large onions, diced
4 garlic cloves, sliced

1 red bird's eye chilli, sliced
½ celeriac, peeled and cut into 5 mm (¼ in) dice
5 celery stalks, cut into 5 mm (¼ in) dice
3 teaspoons ground cumin
1 teaspoon ground black pepper
1½ teaspoons caraway seeds
1½ teaspoons ground turmeric
1 teaspoon ground coriander
400 g (14 oz) tin diced tomatoes
3 red or yellow capsicums (bell peppers), roasted

(see p. 463), cleaned and cut into 2 cm (¾ in) pieces
2 tablespoons fine semolina
juice of 1 lemon
100 g (3½ oz) fine vermicelli, broken
½ bunch of coriander (cilantro), leaves and stems roughly chopped
sheep's milk yoghurt, or plain yoghurt, to serve

Staples
EVOO, LMN, S&P

Heat a large saucepan over a medium heat. Coat the shanks with oil and season with salt, then brown well all over. Add 4 litres (135 fl oz/16 cups) of the water and simmer for 30 minutes, skimming regularly, then turn the heat off.

Meanwhile, drain the chickpeas and lentils, cook in boiling salted water for 15 minutes, then drain.

Heat the oil in a wide-based saucepan over a medium heat. Add the onion, garlic and chilli and cook until softened, about 5 minutes. Add the celeriac and celery, season with salt and pepper and cook for 5 minutes.

Add all the spices and fry for 30 seconds, then stir through the tomatoes, capsicum, chickpeas and lentils. Add the lamb shanks and their liquid and bring to a simmer, then reduce the heat to low. Simmer for about 2 hours, until the lamb is falling off the bone and the lentils have broken down.

Combine the semolina and lemon juice with the 150 ml (5 fl oz) water, mixing to break up any lumps, then add to the soup along with the noodles. Cook until the noodles are tender, about 10 minutes.

Season to taste, adding a little more lemon juice to sharpen, if needed. Just before serving, stir the coriander through.

Serve each bowl with a dollop of yoghurt and an extra squeeze of lemon.

Make it vegetarian Ⓥ
Omit the lamb and add 3.5 litres (118 fl oz/14 cups) water instead. The soup is no less delicious.

Harissa roast capsicum salad with goat's cheese (V)

The sweet tones of roasted capsicum are a natural match to the fiery foil of its siblings – with harissa, the North African chilli paste, being employed here. Harissa also has enough spice (cumin, coriander seeds and so on) to add plenty of flavours, which are all balanced by the addition of fresh herbs, lemon (two ways) and the creamy sharpness of goat's cheese. This salad is layered with complex flavours, but it's super simple to make. **Serves 4–6**

Pair with

Enjoy with grilled meats or fish, or on its own as part of a meze spread.

4 large red capsicums (bell peppers), roasted (see opposite), cleaned and cut into thick slices

2 heaped teaspoons harissa paste (from a tube)

juice of ½ lemon

½ teaspoon very finely diced preserved lemon

1 white salad onion, finely diced

1 garlic clove, finely grated

2 coriander (cilantro) sprigs, leaves finely shredded

3 flat-leaf (Italian) parsley sprigs, leaves torn

100 g (3½ oz) firm goat's cheese

Staples
EVOO, S&P

Add the capsicum slices to a bowl with the harissa, lemon juice, preserved lemon, onion, garlic, coriander and a good glug of oil. Season with salt and pepper and toss. Lay the slices flat on a platter and scatter the parsley over. Crumble the cheese over and drizzle with some oil to finish.

The simplest roasted capsicum salad (GF)(V)(VG)

As the recipe title says, this salad is so simple, with the flavours of the dressing enhancing and never masking the natural flavour of the capsicum. **Serves 10**

Pair with

Seared tuna, schnitzels, crumbed fish or lamb chops.

I often serve this alongside a potato salad or a tabouleh-style salad, or with simply dressed lettuce with boiled eggs and green beans.

6 red capsicums (bell peppers), roasted (see opposite), cleaned and torn into thick strips

Paprika vinegar dressing

80 ml (2½ fl oz/⅓ cup) extra-virgin olive oil

2 tablespoons red-wine vinegar, or sherry vinegar

1 garlic clove, very finely sliced

5 flat-leaf (Italian) parsley sprigs, leaves chopped

2 teaspoons salt flakes

2 teaspoons caster (superfine) sugar

¼ teaspoon smoked paprika

Combine the dressing ingredients in a bowl, then toss the capsicum through. Set aside to marinate at room temperature until ready to serve.

This salad will keep for up to 5 days in an airtight container in the fridge, but bring it back to room temperature for serving.

Shakshuka with capsicum ⓖⓕ ⓥ

Pair with

Toasted flatbread (see p. 852), Lebanese talami bread (p. 852) or Puffed pitta pockets (p. 854).

Dollop with Tahini dip/sauce (p. 71) or fresh Harissa (p. 92), and serve with Moroccan semolina flatbread (p. 852), Simit/koulouri (p. 842).

Roasted charred capsicums ⓖⓕ ⓥ ⓥⓖ

Lightly oil 4 <u>whole capsicums</u> (bell peppers) and place in a roasting tray lined with baking paper. Cook in a preheated 180°C (360°F) fan-forced oven for 30 minutes until blistered. If you want a smokier flavour you can char the capsicums over an open flame for 5 or so minutes, and then roast in the oven for 20 minutes instead of 30. Remove from the oven and allow the capsicums to sit covered for 15 minutes. Drain off any liquid and remove the skins and seeds – you should be able to do this quite easily. Try to leave the capsicums whole if possible.

The origins of shakshuka are not completely clear, and almost certainly never will be. Although many connect it with Israel, its presence across North Africa and the Middle East stretches back into the proverbial mists. The relationship with Israel is one of popularity, with the dish embraced there with uncommon fervour. It's not surprising, really, given that it is so delicious, and also very flexible, being a filling and suitable meal for any time of the day. Although the Western association with eggs will probably always box it into a breakfast and brunch category, this makes for a fine evening meal, too. **Serves 3–6**

1 white salad onion, finely sliced
4 garlic cloves, finely sliced
2 red capsicums (bell peppers), cut into 2 cm (¾ in) pieces
2 yellow capsicums (bell peppers), cut into 2 cm (¾ in) pieces

½ teaspoon chilli powder
2 teaspoons ground cumin
1 teaspoon smoked paprika
400 g (14 oz) tin diced tomatoes
2 tablespoons tomato paste (concentrated purée)
150 ml (5 fl oz) water
2 teaspoons caster (superfine) sugar

6 eggs
3 handfuls of flat-leaf (Italian) parsley, coriander (cilantro) or dill (I'm always alternating, or using a mix!), chopped

Staples
EVOO, S&P

Heat a good splash of oil in a large, deep frying pan over a medium heat. Cook the onion and garlic until softened with a little colour, about 5 minutes. Add all the capsicum and cook until softened, about 10 minutes.

Add the chilli powder, cumin and paprika and stir through quickly, then stir in the tomatoes, tomato paste and water. Season with salt and pepper, add the sugar and bring to a simmer.

Reduce the heat to low and simmer gently for 15 minutes to let the flavours come together and the liquid reduce. Season to taste.

Meanwhile, put the eggs in a heatproof bowl, cover with boiling water and set aside for 10 minutes to warm through. This will help them cook more quickly and more evenly.

Once the sauce is rich and concentrated, make indentations in it, cracking in the eggs as you go. Season the eggs, cover the pan and cook for 5 minutes before checking, then continue cooking to your liking – watch carefully here, as the eggs can go from looking undercooked to being cooked through quite quickly.

Scatter your chosen herbs over and serve.

Make it different
You can serve the shakshuka in individual portions. Simply transfer the cooked sauce to small ovenproof dishes (terracotta dishes are perfect), then crack in the eggs and bake in a 180°C (350°F) fan-forced oven until the eggs are cooked to your liking.

Martini family stuffed capsicums

This is a signature family dish, passed down from my paternal grandmother to my mother. It was always a pleasure to come home and recognise the scent of them cooking. In a way, these were our version of meat and (almost) three veg, just all in the one delicious dish. **Serves 6**

8 red or green capsicums (bell peppers)
2 onions, finely chopped
6 garlic cloves, finely chopped
3½ teaspoons ground cinnamon
2½ teaspoons chilli powder
3½ teaspoons dried mint
1 kg (2 lb 3 oz) minced (ground) beef

2 eggs, lightly beaten
100 g (3½ oz/1¼ cups) fresh breadcrumbs
100 g (3½ oz/½ cup) basmati rice, soaked in boiling water for 15 minutes, then drained
½ bunch of flat-leaf (Italian) parsley, leaves roughly chopped
800 ml (27 fl oz) tomato passata (puréed tomatoes)

600 ml (20½ fl oz) White or Golden chicken stock (p. 54), or water
80 ml (2½ fl oz/⅓ cup) extra-virgin olive oil

Staples
EVOO, S&P

Pair with

Serve with lots of bread to soak up the juices!

For a complete meal, serve with rice, couscous or Classic potato mash (p. 625).

Capsicum & eggplant salad (GF) (V) (VG)

This simple salad is perfect with slow-roasted lamb, or grilled lamb or beef. Slice 1 large eggplant (aubergine), coat with oil and grill on a barbecue until tender, then cut into strips and add to a bowl with the flesh of 2 roasted capsicums (bell peppers), torn into strips. Add some finely grated garlic, a few handfuls of basil leaves, a finely diced ripe tomato, salt flakes and freshly ground pepper. Drizzle in some extra-virgin olive oil and good balsamic vinegar, then toss to combine. Stand for 10 minutes for the flavours to meld before serving.

Preheat the oven to 200°C (400°F) fan-forced.

Cut the stem out of each capsicum with a paring knife, then scoop the seeds out with your fingers and discard them.

Heat a large glug of oil in a large frying pan over a medium heat. Add the onion and garlic and cook until softened, about 6 minutes. Add the cinnamon, chilli and dried mint, then season with salt and pepper and remove from the heat.

Tip the onion mixture into a large bowl. Add the beef, eggs, breadcrumbs, rice and parsley, season generously with salt and pepper and combine well with your hands. Spoon the mixture into the capsicums, packing it in reasonably firmly (but not forcefully), leaving a little space at the top for the rice to expand.

Drizzle a generous amount of oil into an ovenproof dish and nestle the capsicums inside. Bake for 10–15 minutes, or until lightly browned.

Combine the passata, stock and oil, season, then pour the mixture over the capsicums. Scatter the peas over, if using. Cover with baking paper, then foil, and bake for 50 minutes.

Remove the paper and foil and bake for a further 10 minutes before serving.

Make it different

With peas. My grandmother always added peas to this dish just before baking; 155 g (5½ oz/1 cup) frozen peas will do it. They are well and truly cooked after an hour in the oven, but they add real flavour to the sauce. You could simply scatter them over for the last 10 minutes of cooking if you prefer them a bit brighter.

Piperade GF V VG

Pair with

Serve warm with goat's curd, hard feta, black olives and warmed pitta bread or baguette.

Spoon hot piperade over grilled fish.

Serve next to lamb chops, or roasted or chargrilled chicken.

Toss through pasta with olives, chillies and capers, with or without some flaked tuna in oil.

Make a piperade savoury tart with Shortcrust pastry (p. 829).

This recipe was the first step for a red capsicum (bell pepper) terrine I made as an apprentice in my first years at Tansy's restaurant. It was part of a superb autumn plate with a selection of vegetarian delights, pickles, baby herbs and a leaf salad served with olive bread. When I visited Tansy Good's latest restaurant in Kyneton, in rural Victoria, that piperade was on the menu, served with goat's cheese and thyme oil. The memories! And such a delight to eat. The scent of charred capsicum always takes me back to that early dish. This is as much an onion recipe as a capsicum one, with both components contributing so much depth and sweetness. Piperade is originally made with green peppers and includes tomato; this is my version, via Tansy's. This is best enjoyed warm.

Serves 12

6 onions, finely sliced
140 ml (4½ fl oz) extra-virgin olive oil
1½ teaspoons salt flakes
2½ teaspoons smoked sweet paprika

6 large red capsicums (bell peppers), charred and cleaned (see p. 463), cut into 1.5 cm (½ in) thick strips

Staples
S&P

Add the onion, oil and salt to a large bowl and toss to coat. Tip into a wide-based saucepan over a medium heat. Cover for 5 minutes, stir a little, then repeat until the onion has softened. Reduce the heat to low and cook for 40 minutes, stirring occasionally.

Once the onion has caramelised, stir in the paprika, then the capsicum. Cook for about 1 hour, until the mixture has fully reduced and the colour is homogenous.

Season with pepper and adjust the salt to taste. The piperade will keep for 5–7 days in the fridge.

Carrot

I remember getting in trouble with my nanna for eating carrots from her garden before they had grown to their full potential. A quick shake to get rid of the loose dirt, a rinse under the garden tap, and those carrots were just about the sweetest and crunchiest I've ever had. Sure, old memories are like that, but there's something special about the heightened sense of taste as a child, colliding with formative experiences.

Early in my career, I spent hours cleaning countless bunches of carrots, scrubbing the skin off gently with a fine scourer, trimming the tops to leave a little green intact, and soaking to remove any grit. These days, I am more inclined to give them a scrub and roast them with the skin on, as they look great naturally presented and the skin contains plenty of vitamins. In fine dining, carrots used to be peeled and reshaped into uniform sizes. Anyone who has had the pleasure of 'turning' vegetables into unnatural shapes will appreciate the food waste and pointlessness of the task. That was at a time when it was about asserting the cook's hand on the produce. Much has changed.

Carrots have been domesticated and selected for varying qualities for at least 1000 years, with the orange hue that dominates the carrot world appearing and deepening across that timeline, evolving from what were once wild white or purple taproots. This is the story of much of our produce, with simple farming decisions made for flavour, colour, hardiness to climate or other environmental compatibility reshaping vegetables, fruit and livestock into the forms we know today. Indeed, many heirloom varieties are relatively recent steps on this ladder, rather than the original iteration, which would be largely unrecognisable in both appearance and flavour.

The natural shape of a carrot is a beautiful thing and should be celebrated. The rigorously sorted straight carrots we see in supermarkets sadden me. For every straight carrot, there is an equally delicious and far more appealing bent, twisted or otherwise misshapen specimen that ended up as juice, compost or fodder. Celebrate the natural shapes, I say!

And be wary of those that masquerade under the name 'baby carrots' (not to be confused with Dutch carrots, which come in a bunch with stalks and fluffy fronds attached). They're innocent-sounding enough, but baby carrots are machine-peeled-and-sculpted carrots that are bathed in chlorine before being packaged for sale. That level of chlorine is officially deemed safe, akin to levels in tap water; it is something that naturally dissipates over time, but it is essentially unnecessary. The only reason for the chlorine bath is that the carrots are peeled, making them more prone to food-borne pathogens. Originally designed to use misshapen carrots that would be dumped or sold cheap for juice, baby carrots are now often cut from purpose-grown specimens that are processed through energy-heavy machines.

So, buy whole carrots. Celebrate them in all their natural forms. Peel them, if you prefer. Cut them smaller, if you like.

Raw, steamed, boiled, roasted, grilled (broiled), pickled or fermented, carrots are so versatile as to be nearly indispensable. Carrots occupy their own conspicuous space as a flavourful and nutritious vegetable, but they're also an essential anonymous cooking tool. They add depth and sweetness to stocks and sauces – and can be roasted until charred to make that contribution even more robust. They also provide an irreplaceable dimension to sauces, soups and the like when chopped and fried with onion and celery (a mirepoix or soffritto) at the start of cooking, either sweated down until soft and translucent, or caramelised and golden (soffritto dorata).

Roasting carrots is a great way to intensify their flavour, whether whole Dutch carrots, or larger carrots cut on an angle or split down the middle. Toss them in olive oil, season with salt and pepper and throw into a roasting tin along with a splash of water or stock, which just helps them start to steam. Cook in a medium–hot oven until tender and golden at the edges. I'll serve them with all manner of dishes, and not just as a classic roast accompaniment.

Also see

Robust vegetable fumet 51

Beetroot, carrot & pomegranate salad 420

Italian-style coleslaw 448

Crunchy lacto-fermented vegetables 508

Spring & Winter minestrone 531, 607

Vegetable bolognese 576

Carrot cake 742

Pair with

Carrots work well with dairy items, such as cream, butter and soft curd cheeses. They love almonds, walnuts, pistachios, pine nuts, hazelnuts and sesame seeds, and are complemented by cooking with herbs such as thyme, oregano and sage, or dressing with soft herbs such as tarragon, parsley, chervil and coriander (cilantro). Their sweetness is enhanced and complemented by honey, brown sugar, maple syrup, raisins and currants, and they like the foil of mustard, chilli, harissa, garlic and ginger. Cumin, coriander seeds, fennel seeds, caraway, anise seeds and celery seeds are great spice matches, and they are a versatile fit for most proteins, with chicken, rabbit, beef, hare, pork and ham being especially apt.

If you're using larger carrots, steaming is a great way of cooking them, with the denser flesh yielding a very rich, intense flavour. Split lengthways, they will take 10–15 minutes in a steamer basket and can then be tossed in butter with lots of salt and pepper and chopped soft herbs, such as tarragon, parsley or chervil. Carrots can be finely sliced, julienned or grated and added to salads or slaws. Like beetroot (beet), they take well to being salted and sitting for a bit, softening and shedding some water in the process. They can also be lacto-fermented with cabbage to make Sauerkraut (p. 454), used in vinegar-based pickles (see p. 470), or on their own in 3% room-temperature salted water.

When selecting carrots, the general rules of buying vegetables apply. Pick firm specimens without blemishes; they should snap rather than bend. If buying carrots with the tops still attached, bright and lively greens will be the best sign of freshness. You can use those tops for a take on Pesto (p. 90), or add to a green pie (pp. 563–4) or the like. Dutch carrots can go limp somewhat quickly, so are best used soon after purchase, but you can revive them, too. As with greens and herbs, a soak in cold water will bring softening carrots back to life, and splitting them lengthways before soaking will speed things up considerably.

In general, I tend towards small to medium carrots, as they are sweeter with a finer texture, but large carrots can be very flavourful too. Like most vegetables, however, unduly large specimens tend to be fibrous and tough, and you may even need to trim away the core. Today, there are so many types of carrots available to gardeners and an ever-increasing diversity in the markets, from resurgent heirlooms to more modern hybrids. You can now readily buy white, purple, red, yellow and very carrot-coloured orange ones, which all taste more or less similar, though the sweetness and intensity of flavour will vary across cultivars. As for shape, they vary from thick and tapered to cylindrical, to stubby, and spinning-top-like to quite ball-like roots. And if you grow carrots, those flowers are delicious, too, with a delicate carrot flavour and soft herb texture. Use them to dress dishes or add to a green salad.

Preparing carrots

I'll typically peel larger carrots, as the skin can tend to become ragged and a little untidy looking, and not so tasty once cooked (and a tad bitter if raw). With smaller, thin-skinned carrots or Dutch carrots, a scrub to loosen any dirt and roots is a good idea, but peeling just tends to waste too much flesh for no great gain. Thin carrot skins aren't quite the nutritional powerhouses of some other vegetables, but the outer layer of the flesh (and the skin) does carry more of the vitamins, so scrubbing off the tougher bits is the best compromise. When using Dutch carrots, I often leave a few centimetres of the stalk intact for presentation purposes, but just make sure to remove any ingrained dirt from around the top of the carrot, and wash the stalks thoroughly to dislodge any grit.

Roasted carrots with harissa & goat's curd ⓥ

Salty, buttery carrots work so well with a touch of sweetness and a spike of heat. You can skip the goat's curd if you like, but the sharp creaminess is so delicious with the warmth of the fresh harissa. And if you're a harissa fan, like me, some extra harissa dolloped on top doesn't go astray. A mix of coloured heirloom carrots looks great here, too. **Serves 6 as a side dish**

Pair with

Roast or grilled chicken, lamb or beef.

Enjoy with grain salads and simply cooked greens as a starter.

2 tablespoons currants
100 ml (3½ fl oz) red-wine vinegar
2 bunches of Dutch or Chantenay carrots, scrubbed and trimmed
50 g (1¾ oz) butter
2 teaspoons cumin seeds

150 ml (5 fl oz) water
1 heaped tablespoon golden sultanas (golden raisins)
1 white salad onion, finely sliced
4 tablespoons Harissa (p. 92)

4 coriander (cilantro) sprigs, or any mix of soft herbs, fine stems and leaves picked
120 g (4½ oz) goat's curd, or soft goat's cheese

Staples
EVOO, S&P

Preheat the oven to 180°C (350°F) fan-forced.

Bring the currants and vinegar to a simmer in a small saucepan for 2 minutes, then set aside.

Add the carrots to a large ceramic baking dish that fits them loosely. Drizzle with a little oil and season with salt and pepper. Roughly distribute the butter over the carrots and sprinkle with the cumin seeds. Pour the water into the dish, cover with foil and roast for 30 minutes.

Remove the foil and scatter the sultanas and the currants (and any residual vinegar) over, giving the dish a bit of a shake. Roast again until the carrots are tender, about 10 minutes.

Meanwhile, soak the onion in iced water for 5 minutes, then drain and pat dry.

Dollop the harissa onto a platter. Allow the carrots to cool a little before serving, then pile on top of the harissa. Scatter with the onion and coriander, spoon on the goat's curd and serve.

Barbecued Dutch carrot & leek salad ⒼⒻ ⓥ

Dutch carrots are usually sold with a flush of charming green foliage on top – which usually ends up in the bin, or at best the compost. It seems a shame, because you can absolutely eat the tops as well. They have a distinct grassy flavour, which is delicious when made into a pesto-like paste, and they can also be added to a green pie (pp. 563–4), along with greens such as dandelion leaves, which generally grow rampant in my lawn. Just be sure to pick out any wilted or blackened leaves, and don't use thicker stems, as they're far too tough. **Serves 6**

Pair with

Fresh curd cheeses, grilled poultry, pork or steak, Falafel (p. 432) or grilled red capsicum (bell pepper).

Carrots with butter, honey & thyme glaze (GF)(V)

Peel 3 carrots, then slice 2 cm (¾ in) thick, either in rounds or on an angle, or cut into 1.5 × 5 cm (½ × 2 in) batons. Add to a saucepan with 250 ml (8½ fl oz/ 1 cup) water, 2 tablespoons honey and 60 g (2 oz/¼ cup) butter. Season with salt and pepper and simmer over a medium heat until the carrot is tender, and the liquid has reduced to a glaze, then finish with the leaves from a few thyme sprigs. Some fennel, caraway or coriander seeds (any or all) at the start are a good addition, too. Serve as a side dish to pork or chicken, or anything you like. You can elevate the dish to a standalone salad by simmering the carrots with currants, then tossing with heaps of chopped parsley and/or watercress, chopped roasted hazelnuts or almonds, and a splash of vinegar, and then topping with ricotta or goat's curd.

Roasted carrots with Champagne vinegar & maple dressing (GF)(V)

Slice 4 carrots into 1 cm (½ in) discs and toss with olive oil, salt, pepper and 2 teaspoons fennel seeds or anise seeds. Spread out on a lined baking tray and roast at 180°C (350°F) for 30 minutes. Remove from the oven and spoon over a dressing of Champagne vinegar (or white-wine vinegar or sherry vinegar), maple syrup and extra-virgin olive oil – about 1½ tablespoons of each. Leave to sit for a little for the carrots to take on the dressing, then serve with about 30 g (1 oz) parmesan or gruyère grated over the top. Serve as a side dish with fish, steak or chicken, toss through a grain salad or couscous – or serve as a share plate piled on top of a generous spoon of crème fraîche or goat's curd, finishing with a squeeze of lemon and a sprinkling of fresh tarragon, oregano or marjoram.

1 tablespoon currants
2 tablespoons white-wine vinegar
1 leek, white part only
12 Dutch carrots, trimmed, with about 60 g/2 oz soft leafy tops reserved
2 teaspoons ground aleppo pepper

Carrot top dressing
carrot tops, from the salad
½ bunch of flat-leaf (Italian) parsley leaves, chopped
1 garlic clove, peeled
2 tablespoons water
40 g (1½ oz/¼ cup) smoked almonds, chopped
40 g (1½ oz) Grana Padano, finely grated

2 teaspoons ground aleppo pepper
150 ml (5 fl oz) extra-virgin olive oil
1 tablespoon white wine vinegar
1 tablespoon honey

Staples
EVOO, S&P

Preheat the oven to 190°C (375°F) fan-forced. Heat a chargrill pan or barbecue on high.

Bring the currants and vinegar to a simmer in a small saucepan for 2 minutes, then set aside.

Meanwhile, cook the leek in simmering salted water until tender, about 10 minutes. Refresh in cold water, drain well, then place in a tea towel (dish towel) and press out the moisture. Slice into 4 cm (1½ in) rings.

Make a start on the dressing. Coat the reserved leafy carrot tops with a little oil, then grill or barbecue for about a minute on each side, until slightly charred/browned. Set aside to cool, then roughly chop.

Oil the carrots, season with salt and pepper, then grill for about 5 minutes, until charred all over. Spread out on a baking tray and roast in the oven for about 10 minutes, until tender but not soft; the carrots will naturally vary a bit in size, so some may take a little longer than others.

To finish the dressing, add the carrot tops, parsley, garlic and water to a blender and blitz. Add the almonds, Grana Padano, aleppo pepper, oil and a large pinch of salt and blitz again to form a paste. Add the vinegar and honey, then blitz to combine. Adjust the seasoning as needed.

Arrange the leek on a serving plate and dollop on some of the dressing. Toss the carrots with the remaining dressing and pile on top, then sprinkle with the aleppo pepper and vinegary currants.

Pasties

Aside from being delicious, pasties admirably fulfil their original purpose – to provide a complete meal in the one parcel, their crimped pastry seal providing a conveniently disposable handle. Instead of the Olive oil pastry, you could use Pâte brisée (p. 829) or Classic puff pastry (p. 822). **Makes 10**

2 swedes (rutabaga), peeled and cut into wedges
2 carrots, peeled and split in half
2 large potatoes (any variety), peeled and cut into 6 pieces each
2 parsnips, peeled and cut into 4 pieces each
250 g (9 oz) minced (ground) lamb

1 large brown onion, diced
3 garlic cloves, sliced
1 egg, whisked
100 g (3½ oz/⅔ cup) frozen peas
150 g (5½ oz) good cheddar, coarsely grated

Olive oil pastry
500 g (1 lb 2 oz) plain (all-purpose) flour

½ teaspoon salt flakes
60 ml (2 fl oz/¼ cup) extra-virgin olive oil
250 ml (8½ fl oz/1 cup) cold water
1 egg, whisked, for brushing
2 tablespoons sesame seeds

Staples
BTR, EVOO, FLR, S&P

Preheat the oven to 170°C (340°F) fan-forced.

Meanwhile, for the pastry, blitz the flour and salt in a food processor. Drizzle in the oil while processing, followed by the water. Keep processing until the dough comes together in a ball. Tip out onto a lightly floured surface and knead briefly, then wrap in plastic wrap, or cover with a tight-fitting bowl, and rest in the fridge for 2 hours.

Drizzle a generous amount of oil over the swede, carrot, potato and parsnip, season with salt and pepper and toss to coat. Tip into a large roasting tin and roast for about 1 hour, turning occasionally, until tender. Once cooked, the vegetables will have lost quite a lot of their mass, and will have concentrated in flavour. Once cooled, dice roughly.

Turn the oven up to 200°C (400°F) fan-forced. Line two trays with baking paper.

Heat a splash of oil in a frying pan over a medium heat. Add the lamb and fry, breaking up any lumps, until browned and crisping up, about 10 minutes. Season with salt and pepper, drain off any excess oil and tip into a large bowl.

Wipe out the pan and heat another splash of oil and a knob of butter over a medium heat. Add the onion and garlic, season and sweat over a gentle heat until softened, about 10 minutes, then remove from the heat.

Add the onion mixture to the lamb, along with the egg, peas and cheese, and gently mix. Fold the cooled vegetables through until you have an even mix.

Cut the chilled dough into ten pieces, then roll out on a lightly floured surface into circles about 18 cm (7 in) in diameter. Divide the filling into ten portions. Brush the circles with egg, place a portion of filling in the centre of each and bring the edges together, crimping the pasties closed as you go.

Brush the pasties with more egg, sprinkle with the sesame seeds and bake on the prepared trays for 20–25 minutes, until golden. (Alternatively, you can freeze some uncooked pasties for later.) Serve warm, with your favourite relish if you like.

Pickled spring vegetables ⒼⒻ Ⓥ ⓋⒼ

You can use this pickle brine to pickle almost any vegetable, giving a gently sweet and appealing tart vinegary finish. Spring is a wonderful time to make these pickles, as the produce is so tender, brightly flavoured and perfectly formed. **Makes 2 × 1 litre (34 fl oz/4 cup) jars**

10 small French shallots or small pickling onions, peeled
12 Dutch carrots, peeled, cleaned and trimmed
½ cauliflower, cut into florets
¼ small savoy cabbage, outer leaves removed, cut into 4 wedges
1 celery heart, quartered lengthways, leaves intact
2 small fennel bulbs, cut into 8 wedges each
10 mini cucumbers, halved lengthways
2 long red chillies, sliced on an angle
20 g (¾ oz) fine sea salt

Pickling medium
400 ml (13½ fl oz) white-wine vinegar, rice vinegar or apple-cider vinegar
200 ml (7 fl oz) water
200 g (7 oz) caster (superfine) sugar
20 g (¾ oz) fine sea salt
4 garlic cloves, peeled and bruised
2 dill sprigs
2 fresh bay leaves
2 tablespoons white mustard seeds
1 teaspoon black peppercorns

Pair with

Finely chop to add a zing to a tabouleh (see p. 419) or chopped lettuce salad.

Serve alongside a terrine (pp. 327–8) and/or salumi.

Serve with rolled Labneh (p. 362) and pitta bread (see p. 854).

Add the shallots to a bowl. Combine all the other vegetables in a large bowl. Divide the salt between the shallots and vegetables and rub through with your hands. Weigh each down with a plate for 1–2 hours.

Drain off the shallots and set aside. Drain the liquid off the other vegetables, gently squeezing out the excess moisture, then pack into sterilised jars (see p. 40).

In a saucepan, bring the pickling medium ingredients to a simmer for 5 minutes. Take off the heat, add the shallots and cool at room temperature.

Add the shallots and pickling medium to the jars, distributing the aromatics evenly. Ensure all the ingredients are submerged, then seal and refrigerate.

These pickles need to stand for another day before eating, but a little longer is best. They will keep in the fridge for about a month before losing their crunch.

Moroccan carrot, date & green chilli salad (GF) (V) (VG)

Simmering carrots with spices infuses the flavours right through their flesh – then dressing them hot means that all the lemon and seasoning penetrates deeply as well. All this makes for some very flavourful carrots, with the dates adding deep bass notes of sweetness cut with fresh chilli and fragrant coriander (cilantro).

Serves 6

Pair with

This is perfect with lamb – grilled, roasted or pan-seared.

I also serve it with rich, oily fish (such as tuna, mackerel or sardines) that has been rubbed with chermoula or masala paste and grilled.

It's also delicious served with Falafel (p. 432).

It makes a fine accompaniment to a firm and salty cheese such as feta, ricotta salata or grilled haloumi, as well as fresh curd cheeses, such as ricotta, goat's curd and mozzarella di bufala.

7 medium–large carrots, peeled and sliced on an angle about 2.5 cm (1 in) thick
2 teaspoons caraway seeds
2 teaspoons coriander seeds

80 ml (2½ fl oz/⅓ cup) extra-virgin olive oil
3 lemons, 1 juiced and 2 segmented
6 dates, pitted and sliced

2 green chillies, finely chopped
1 bunch of coriander (cilantro), leaves picked

Staples
S&P

Add the carrot, caraway seeds and coriander seeds to a saucepan of simmering salted water. Cook until tender, about 25 minutes, then drain well.

Add the oil and lemon juice to a large bowl, season with salt and pepper and mix to combine. Toss the carrot through, then stand for about 15 minutes to cool and take up the dressing.

Toss the date, chilli and coriander through, then serve.

Roast carrot & root vegetable soup with cinnamon & ginger (GF)

This is a warming and generous-feeling soup, with robust root vegetable flavours accented by a vibrant dose of ginger and some gentle spices. **Serves 8–10**

½ dense-fleshed pumpkin (winter squash; such as kent or jap), peeled and cut into large chunks
6 carrots, scrubbed and cut into large chunks
2 parsnips, peeled, cored and cut into large chunks
1 large sweet potato, randomly pricked with a knife

3 onions, sliced
6 garlic cloves, peeled and sliced
15 cm (6 in) piece of fresh ginger, peeled and diced
1 cinnamon stick
2 teaspoons anise seeds
1.5 litres (51 fl oz/6 cups) White or Golden chicken stock (p. 54), or use stock bouillon cubes

Greek-style yoghurt, to serve
coriander (cilantro) leaves, to serve
1 handful of pepitas (pumpkin seeds)
freshly grated horseradish, to serve (optional)

Staples
LMN, OIL, S&P

Preheat the oven to 170°C (340°F) fan-forced. Line two baking trays with baking paper.

Coat the pumpkin, carrot and parsnip with oil, season with salt and pepper and arrange on the baking trays with the sweet potato. Roast for 1 hour, until tender.

Meanwhile, add a good glug of oil to a wide-based saucepan over a medium heat. Add the onion, garlic and ginger and cook until starting to caramelise, 8–10 minutes. Add the cinnamon stick and anise seeds and stir to combine.

Once the vegetables have finished roasting, halve the sweet potato and scoop out the flesh. Add to the onion mixture with the pumpkin, carrot and parsnip. Stir in the stock and simmer for 30 minutes.

Remove the cinnamon stick, then puree the soup using a stick blender. Adjust the seasoning as needed.

Serve topped with a dollop of yoghurt, a sprinkling of coriander leaves and pepitas, some horseradish if desired, and a squeeze of lemon.

Carrot, chervil & gruyère loaf (GF)(V)

This recipe takes me right back to some of my earliest days of classical cooking. We made this at Tansy's Restaurant as a vegetable accompaniment for roast pork and roast chicken dishes. The sweetness of the carrots is really intensified, which is nicely coiled up in the umami-rich intensity of the gruyère, the flavours melding together seamlessly. This loaf is recommended for both the carrot lover and the carrot averse. **Serves 12**

100 g (3½ oz) butter
6 French shallots, very finely sliced
800 g (1 lb 12 oz) carrots, finely grated

60 g (2 oz) caster (superfine) sugar
100 ml (3½ fl oz) dry sherry
150 g (5½ oz) gruyère, grated

3 eggs, lightly whisked
1 bunch of chervil, lightly chopped

Staples
S&WP

Quick-pickled carrots (GF)(V)(VG)

Slice 3 carrots about 2 mm (⅛ in) thick lengthways, using a mandoline. Leave them in long strips, or finely julienne, then season with salt and caster (superfine) sugar and set aside for 10 minutes to soften. Drain off the liquid and sprinkle with white-wine vinegar or rice vinegar, depending on how you're using them. Either eat as is to accompany other dishes, or combine with dressed shaved fennel and/or celery.
Go a step further by making a paste out of 2 roasted garlic cloves (see p. 66) combined with chopped oregano leaves, black pepper and olive oil to loosen. This makes a perfect side for pan-fried chicken breast or roast chicken, along with some dressed rocket (arugula) leaves. Or combine the pickled carrot with sliced radish and a simple sesame dressing (see p. 94) and serve on short-grain rice with wilted spinach and miso-grilled fish (see p. 184). They're also great stuffed into a Bánh mì (p. 332) with roasted Crispy pork belly (p. 332) or turmeric chicken (see p. 246).

Carrot paste salad with lemon, caraway & nigella seeds (GF) (V) (VG)

Peel 6 large carrots and cut into rounds 1.5 cm (½ in) thick. Peel 2 large creamy yellow-fleshed potatoes (such as Dutch cream) and cut into similar-sized pieces to the carrot. Add the carrot and potato to a saucepan of simmering salted water along with 3 teaspoons caraway seeds. Cook until the vegetables are tender, about 25 minutes, then drain well. Reserve some of the carrot rounds for garnishing, then mash the remaining carrot and potato in a large bowl with a fork. Add the juice of 1 large lemon and 60 ml (2 fl oz/¼ cup) extra-virgin olive oil and mash to a coarse paste. Adjust the seasoning as needed, then pile into a serving bowl. Toss the reserved carrot in a little bit of extra-virgin olive oil and coat with 2 teaspoons nigella seeds, then drop on top of the paste. Garnish with a handful of coriander (cilantro) leaves. Serves 6–8, and is excellent with grilled sardines, fried fish, grilled or oil-preserved tuna, chargrilled calamari, roast chicken and grilled lamb chops with sumac. You could also try it in a sandwich with some confit tuna, boiled egg and fresh herbs.

Preheat the oven to 180°C (350°F) fan-forced. Line a 20–22 cm (8–8¾ in) loaf (bar) tin or brownie tin with baking paper.

Melt the butter in a small saucepan over a low heat. Add the shallot and sweat for 10 minutes, to soften but not colour. Add the carrot and sugar and sweat until the carrot is tender and most of the moisture has evaporated, about 15 minutes. Add the sherry and reduce until evaporated, about 5 minutes, then remove from the heat.

Transfer the mixture to a bowl, then cool for about 5 minutes. Stir in the gruyère, eggs and chervil. Season well with salt and white pepper and mix to combine.

Pour the batter into the loaf tin. Cover the tin with baking paper, then foil. Place the tin in a roasting dish and three-quarters fill with hot water to make a bain marie. Bake for about 30 minutes, until the cake is firm to the touch.

Remove from the oven and cool in the tin for 20 minutes, then unmould, slice and serve warm.

Make it different

With mushroom. With the gruyère, stir in 300 g (10½ oz) diced mushroom, such as pine mushroom or slippery jack, that have been cooked in 60 g (2 oz/¼ cup) butter. A superb autumn addition.

Cauliflower

Buried in memories of mistreatment, cauliflower took some time to re-emerge as a vegetable of significant merit. But re-emerge it has. In times past, where ensuring vegetables were thoroughly boiled seemed to be something of a priority, or at least a hard-to-shake habit, the worst side of cauliflower was expressed, with it becoming rather pungently odorous.

Cauliflower is a member of the brassica family, as are broccoli, cabbage, turnip and radish – all of which contain a form of sulphur in their makeup, which is very good for you, but does contribute to their distinctive aroma. That sulphurous character is particularly noticeable when brassicas are overcooked, and perhaps more apparent when the vegetables are less fresh or harvested late in their natural season (though this is just anecdotal).

Cauliflower is such a versatile and rewarding vegetable, with a hearty profile that stands up to myriad intense flavours and textures, although it can also highlight some very delicate ones, too. Just be careful not to overcook it when steaming or boiling, for reasons already mentioned – plus the texture will end up about as unappealing as the aroma. You can even eat cauliflower raw, when it is super fresh and crunchy. My favourite cooking method is roasting, whether in fat slices, florets or even whole, in a medium-hot oven. Naturally, the flavour intensifies in the oven as the moisture is drawn out, but there's also something about the toasty, nutty flavour and gentle crunch that's quite special, with a little char adding even more complexity. Grilling is a compelling method, too.

You can buy cauliflower in various forms, from petite single-serve versions to significantly weighty specimens, though the flavour is not significantly different. Colours vary from white to green to orange to purple, with the variations largely due to selective breeding. The colour of the orange version is due to the presence of carotenoids – yes, they make carrots orange, too – so it has another nutritional dimension, while the purple version is rich in anthocyanins, which are antioxidants and also healthful. The green types are sometimes called broccoflower (broccoli and cauliflower are variants of the same species, but green cauliflower is not a cross of the two), with the Roman favourite romanesco also part of the family, with its mesmerising cosmic array of seemingly endless spirals upon spirals. While the flavour is essentially the same across the cauliflower colours, romanesco trips more into broccoli territory in flavour, and is generally a little firmer in texture than cauliflower, but it can be used in recipes for either.

There's also something called 'caulini' or 'caulilini' (the latter being a registered trademark, I believe), which announces itself both in name and in its miniature tree-like appearance as a cross between cauliflower and broccolini – yet it isn't. It is in fact a type of cauliflower, but can be used just like you might broccolini. It cooks rather quickly, so 60–90 seconds in boiling salted water is typically enough, and it can then be tossed in butter or oil and served as a side dish (some garlic and/or crisp pancetta wouldn't hurt, either). Caulini can be used in stir-fries, and it loves Bagna cauda (p. 83). I've also draped it over a beef carpaccio with Parmigiano Reggiano and parsley, with a scant drizzle of cream on top.

A fresh cauliflower announces itself rather proudly, with crisply attentive leaves and a radiant glow across the off-white 'flower'. Over time, those leaves will droop, and the 'flower' will take on a yellow-ish hue, with clusters of small dark spots an indication of some oxidation, which will lead to mould. No prizes for guessing the cauliflower you're best buying. Having said that, a few spots on a cauliflower shouldn't mean it needs to be discarded. These can be sliced off if you've left it a little too long in the crisper, but be wary of a cauliflower that has gone flaccid, with the florets falling away from each other. A pungent vegetable anyway, an old cauliflower will be unappealingly sulphurous, and cooking will only make it even more malodorous.

Also see

Orecchiette with cauliflower 444

Pickled spring vegetables 470–1

Crunchy lacto-fermented vegetables 508

Kohlrabi, cauliflower & fenugreek soup 548

Pair with

Cauliflower loves cream, butter, yoghurt and cheese of any type, as well as pine nuts, hazelnuts, almonds, walnuts, sesame and tahini. Natural vegetable partners include eggplant (aubergine), carrot, onion, spinach, silverbeet (Swiss chard), pomegranate, tomato and chilli. Spices such as cumin, curry powder, coriander seeds, garlic, ginger, turmeric, chilli, black pepper, allspice and fennel seeds, and herbs such as parsley, coriander (cilantro), chives, oregano, sage and dill all pair well. Salmon, scallops and white fish are perfect protein partners.

Preparing cauliflower

You can eat the whole cauliflower, with only the woodiest bit of the stem best sent to the compost. So, don't discard those leaves, either. Most of the coarse leaves will have been removed by the time of purchase, so those fine leaves, depending on freshness, are very edible. They can be cooked along with the rest, with the charred leaves of a whole roasted cauliflower presenting quite dramatically on the plate. The smallest curled leaves also look great in pickles, while the larger ones can simply be sliced first. You can then slice off the florets with a paring knife and slice the remaining stem. Or cut the head in half, then divide into florets. You can also stand it on its base and cut into thick slices for roasting or grilling, or leave whole.

Roasted cauliflower & turmeric soup with yoghurt & poached egg GF V

Cauliflower works so well with spices. Stained with golden, earthy turmeric, it is one of my favourite vegetables in Indian curries. Perhaps this is why this soup makes so much sense to me. The pungent top note of fenugreek makes it so aromatic, with the curry powder (make sure it's a good one) filling in the spice gaps with minimal effort. This soup is deeply nourishing as is, a fine salve for winter, but adding in poached eggs, yoghurt and chilli sauce transform it into quite the elegant one-bowl meal. **Serves 6–8**

1 kg (2 lb 3 oz) cauliflower, sliced 3 cm (1¼ in) thick
6 cm (2½ in) piece of fresh turmeric, peeled and finely grated
3 teaspoons fenugreek seeds
3 teaspoons cumin seeds
1 large (180 g/6½ oz) creamy yellow-fleshed potato (such as Dutch cream), peeled, finely sliced on a mandoline

1.5 litres (51 fl oz/6 cups) Golden chicken stock (p. 54), or Classic white vegetable stock (p. 51)
600 ml (20½ fl oz) cream (35% fat)
120 g (4½ oz) butter
1 tablespoon extra-virgin olive oil
1 small onion, finely sliced
1 leek, white part only, finely sliced

3 teaspoons curry powder
poached eggs (see p. 351), to serve
plain yoghurt, to serve
Fermented cooked chilli sauce (p. 97), or sriracha, to serve

Staples
EVOO, S&P

Preheat the oven to 180°C (350°F) fan-forced. Line a baking tray with baking paper.

Lay the cauliflower on the baking tray, in one layer. Drizzle generously with oil, sprinkle with the turmeric, fenugreek and cumin seeds, then season with salt and pepper. Roast for about 45 minutes, until the cauliflower is tender and lightly charred. Set aside.

Meanwhile, add the potato to a saucepan with the stock and cream. Bring to a simmer, then cook for about 10 minutes, until the potato is quite soft, topping up the water as needed to keep it just covered.

Heat the butter and oil in a large saucepan over a medium heat. Add the onion and leek, and sweat until translucent but without any colour, about 8 minutes. Add the roasted cauliflower and curry powder and stir through for a minute or so, then add the stock and potato mixture. Simmer for 5 minutes, adjusting the seasoning to taste, then blitz until smooth.

Serve the soup with a poached egg in each bowl, topped with a dollop of yoghurt, some chilli sauce and a drizzle of oil.

Roasted whole cauliflower GF V VG

Roasting a whole cauliflower makes for a very dramatic dish indeed, and a valid candidate for the centrepiece of a meal. Roasting from scratch can take a very long time, and you run the risk of burning the outside before the stem is properly cooked – so instead, bring the whole head to a simmer from cold in a large saucepan of water (ensure the whole head is submerged), then simmer for about 5 minutes. Drain well and pat dry, then place on a lined baking tray. Drizzle with oil, rubbing it all over, then season with salt and pepper, and scatter with cumin and/or fennel seeds, if you like. Roast at 170°C (340°F) fan-forced for 1½ hours, or until golden. Dress with your favourite dressing and serve. This is great drizzled with some Greek-style yoghurt, then topped with currants, capers, pine nuts and chopped parsley, then a last drizzle of good oil. Or try it with Tahini dip/sauce (p. 71), with pomegranate molasses or Fermented cooked chilli sauce (p. 97) and a good scattering of pomegranate seeds, or Green harissa (p. 92).

Cauliflower puree GF V

Add equal amounts of cauliflower and potato to a saucepan with a peeled garlic clove. Add just enough milk and water (in equal measure) to cover, then simmer until tender. Drain and blitz in a blender, adding extra-virgin olive oil until smooth. You're looking for a consistency like thick honey – add a little milk to loosen, if required. Season well with salt and pepper (white pepper if you're a food-colour purist) and use as a base for seared scallops, roasted pork belly, crumbed oysters, or smoked or pan-fried fish fillets.

Roasted cauliflower, barley & parsley salad with scorched almonds & feta Ⓥ

I will probably never make this salad exactly like this again. And not because I don't like this version. I do, very much. It's just that I cook it in subtly different ways each and every time, and it's always a huge hit. Who knew cauliflower could be so loved! The combination of roasted nutty florets and slippery barley is such a pleasing texture and flavour base to work from; adding some spices and herbs, acid in various forms, and salty sharp feta takes it somewhere else altogether. **Serves 6–8**

Pair with

This salad is at home with anything off the barbecue, as smoky flavours play well with the roasted cauliflower.

It's also great with a rice and lentil salad with caramelised onions and/or a Turkish-style pumpkin dip (p. 632).

Cauliflower steaks ⒼⒻ Ⓥ

Cut a cauliflower into 'steaks' 3–4 cm (1¼–1½ in) thick, across the head. Line a baking dish with baking paper and lay the steaks flat. Pour in water or stock to come halfway up the cauliflower, then drizzle with oil. Season with salt and pepper and scatter cumin and/or fennel seeds over; a few knobs of butter wouldn't hurt either. Roast at 170°C (340°F) fan-forced for about 45 minutes, until the steaks are tender and golden and the liquid has evaporated. Top with ricotta and chopped almonds or a spicy mayo (see p. 620), or try them with Zaalouk (p. 518) and Labneh (p. 362), or Tahini dip/sauce (p. 71) – or bake with a Béchamel (p. 70) spiked with taleggio or gorgonzola, or with curry powder, for another angle on cauliflower cheese.

½ cauliflower, cut into small florets, the stalk sliced 1 cm (½ in) thick
1 teaspoon cumin seeds
60 g (2 oz) blanched almonds
100 g (3½ oz) cooked pearled barley (see p. 371), or freekeh, black barley or farro, at room temperature

1 bunch of flat-leaf (Italian) parsley, leaves and fine stems finely chopped
2 spring onions (scallions), white part and most of the green, finely sliced
1 handful of pomegranate seeds
100 g (3½ oz) sheep's or goat's milk feta

Spiced lemon dressing
80 ml (2½ fl oz/⅓ cup) extra-virgin olive oil
juice of 1 lemon
2 garlic cloves, finely grated
1 teaspoon coriander seeds, toasted and crushed
½ teaspoon ground allspice

Staples
EVOO, S&P

Preheat the oven to 180°C (350°F) fan-forced. Line a baking tray with baking paper.

Toss the cauliflower with the cumin seeds and a good splash of oil. Season with salt and pepper and spread on the baking tray. Roast for about 30 minutes, until tender and slightly charred, then cool on the tray.

Meanwhile, scorch the almonds (see p. 566), then roughly crush or chop.

Combine the dressing ingredients, seasoning with salt and pepper as needed.

Add the barley, parsley and spring onion to a large bowl. Drizzle with the dressing and combine. Add the cauliflower and gently combine, then tip onto a serving platter.

Scatter with the almonds and pomegranate seeds, crumble the feta over and serve.

Make it different
With dressings. This is also delicious with a tahini dressing dolloped on top. Combine 250 g (9 oz/1 cup) Greek-style yoghurt with 2 tablespoons tahini, a glug of extra-virgin olive oil, one finely grated garlic clove and some salt. You won't need it all, but the leftovers are also delicious on a grain salad, and with grilled meat or chicken. Or, try serving the salad with Tahini dip/sauce (p. 71).

Gado gado with roasted cauliflower, cucumber & eggs

This is one of those dishes where any recipe you write will probably make traditionalists wince. The reality is, this national dish of Indonesia has countless variants in its homeland, though I concede this is almost certainly not one of them. Which I'm okay with, as the combination of vegetables, eggs and spicy peanut sauce is magical. **Serves 6**

1 small cauliflower, sliced 3 cm (1¼ in) thick
2 Lebanese (short) cucumbers, sliced 5 mm (¼ in) thick on an angle
3 pale inner celery stalks, leaves picked, stalks finely sliced
1 lime, segmented

2 makrut lime leaves, finely shredded
4 coriander (cilantro) sprigs, leaves and fine stems picked
4 boiled eggs with just-set yolks (see p. 351), or 6 soft-boiled quail eggs, cut in half

1 × quantity Satay sauce (p. 104)
1 handful of salted roasted peanuts

Staples
EVOO, S&P

Preheat the oven to 180°C (350°F) fan-forced. Line a baking tray with baking paper.

Lay the cauliflower slices on the baking tray. Drizzle with oil and season with salt and pepper. Roast for about 45 minutes, until tender and lightly charred.

Combine the cucumber, celery, lime segments, lime leaves and coriander in a small bowl. Dress with a little oil and season.

Arrange the roasted cauliflower on a serving plate. Top with the cucumber mixture, then the eggs. Finish by dolloping on about half the satay sauce and scattering the celery leaves and peanuts over. Serve with the remaining satay sauce on the side.

Make it different

With other vegetables. You can swap in any vegetables you like here, such as boiled potatoes or blanched green beans; raw vegies are great, too, such as wedges of cabbage or snake beans.

With tofu. Fried tofu is a classic inclusion – use 200 g (7 oz).

With kimchi. Add 150 g (5½ oz) finely chopped Kimchi (p. 455) on top of the eggs.

Pair with

This is a meal in itself, but it also accompanies grilled chicken or beef particularly well.

Cauliflower rice (GF) (V) (VG)

Use this it instead of rice, or add to patties, fritters and savoury muffins, but my favourite use is in salads. It stands in nicely for barley, freekeh or the like in a grain salad, holding its shape and providing its own nutty character. To make cauliflower rice, break a cauliflower into manageable pieces and, working in batches, pulse in a food processor with a little salt. A dozen or so pulses for a second each should yield fairly uniform pieces, perhaps resembling large couscous more than rice. Tip onto a cloth, then tie into a firm ball to slightly bruise and soften the cauliflower. It's then ready to use in salads. If you like, it can be fried quickly in a little oil in a hot pan to scorch slightly and warm through – but don't be tempted to steam it, unless you want mush.

Cauliflower salad (roasted & raw) (GF) (V)

I often like to make salads with both raw and cooked (and pickled) elements of the same vegetable. Cauliflower has a distinctly appealing texture and flavour when raw or 'undercooked', adding a layer of detail and depth to the charred character of the roasted florets. The nutty elements are enhanced by the tahini and almonds, and accented by the sweet sultanas. **Serves 12**

50 g (1¾ oz) golden sultanas (golden raisins)
80 ml (2½ fl oz/⅓ cup) apple-cider vinegar
1 large red onion, skin on, cut into 6 wedges
1 cauliflower, cut into uneven florets (including the stalk)

¼ bunch of dill, fronds picked and chopped
3 tablespoons flaked almonds, toasted

Tahini & yoghurt dressing
150 g (5½ oz) plain yoghurt
juice of ½ lemon

125 ml (4 fl oz/½ cup) extra-virgin olive oil
2 tablespoons apple-cider vinegar
1½ teaspoons tahini

Staples
EVOO, S&P

Pair with

This is perfect in a vegetarian feast with other salads and vegetable dishes, or to serve with roast chicken or fish.

Cauliflower cheese (V)

Preheat the oven to 180°C (350°F) fan-forced. Cook 1 large whole cauliflower in a large saucepan of boiling salted water for 20 minutes. Drain well, then cut into 3 cm (1¼ in) thick slices, or break into large florets. Melt 90 g (3 oz/⅓ cup) butter in a saucepan over a medium heat, then add 3 teaspoons yellow mustard seeds and 90 g (3 oz) plain (all-purpose) flour. Bring together into a paste and stir constantly until you have a medium-brown roux, 1–2 minutes. Pour in 750 ml (25½ fl oz/3 cups) warmed full-cream (whole) milk, while whisking constantly, until incorporated. Turn the heat to low and cook for about 3 minutes, until the béchamel sauce thickens slightly. Now whisk in 150 g (5½ oz) grated cheddar or gruyère until melted, and season with salt and pepper. Arrange the cauliflower in an ovenproof dish, then season. Pour the sauce over, sprinkle with 2 teaspoons poppy seeds and bake for about 25 minutes, until golden. Serve hot. Serves 6 as a side dish.

Preheat the oven 180°C (350°F) fan-forced. Line a baking tray with baking paper.

Bring the sultanas and vinegar to a simmer in a small saucepan, then set aside.

Coat the onion with oil, season with salt and pepper, then add to one end of the baking tray. Coat half the cauliflower with oil, season and spread on the tray. Roast for about 45 minutes, until both vegetables are tender and slightly charred, then set aside to cool.

Meanwhile make 'rice' out of the remaining cauliflower (left).

Combine all the dressing ingredients, seasoning to taste.

Add the cauliflower rice to a large bowl, then toss with half the dressing. Add the roasted cauliflower and half the sultanas, season and combine. Tip onto a serving plate and scatter with the roasted onion and dill. Spoon over the remaining dressing and finish with the almonds and remaining sultanas.

Celeriac

Celeriac has long been called 'celery root', and still sometimes is, which is a little misleading: celeriac and celery are related both botanically and in flavour, but they are different plants. The main edible part of celeriac is the bulbous, tuber-like storage organ. That bulb starts its life as the bridge between the first roots and the stalks and leaves, then swells to store nutrients, water and carbohydrates to keep the plant viable.

Harvested celeriac consists of the knobbly, ball-like bulb with celery-like stalks, which grow individually rather than interlaced in a bunch, and a manic web of roots protruding from the base. Aside from the rugged skin and roots, everything is edible – though you'll need to use the stalks and leaves when they're very young. The flavour of celeriac is very much akin to celery, but the flesh has a dense and very distinct texture and spicy richness, and a mildly earthy, sweet character. Celeriac is also often said to echo the flavour of parsley – which isn't so surprising, given they're from the same family.

Celeriac is a very handy and delicious vegetable, and a distinctly underappreciated one. Once peeled, the wild appearance of the exterior gives way to a creamy white interior. The flesh can be cooked down until silky and smooth, or left raw and distinctly crunchy; I like it as a mash, just as much as I like it raw. Add diced celeriac to soups and stews, puree into soups, poach in milk and whiz into a silky mash, or add to a potato mash for a spicy, savoury note. Roast thickly sliced celeriac and serve as you might wedges of pumpkin (winter squash) as a side, or dice and sauté with butter, oil and smashed garlic. Add julienned raw celeriac to a slaw or shredded salad, or finely grate and add to a mayonnaise dressing for a take on potato salad. Match its crunch with shredded apple and shaved fennel, with plenty of fennel fronds and lemon juice, for a side to accompany pork chops or roasted pork belly.

Select small to medium celeriac that feel dense and heavy in the hand, with firm skin. Although it can keep for months in the right conditions, it will eventually dry out in the centre, becoming hollow and woody. If the green stalks are still attached, it's best to remove these if storing celeriac for a longer period. Those stalks can be eaten like celery, though only from very youthful specimens, as they will be tough and fibrous otherwise. The leaves, too, can be used as a herb, but they won't have the delicacy of flavour or texture of the pale yellow leaves from a celery heart. Typically, the leafy applications are really only considerations if you're growing celeriac yourself, with the stalks usually shorn off before they make it to market.

Also see

Celeriac & parsnip
purée 285–6

Duck, celeriac & verjuice
ragù 259

Tunisian vegetable
couscous royale with
rosewater labneh 386–7

Italian-style coleslaw 448

Pair with

*Celeriac loves dairy, including
butter, cream, yoghurt and
mayonnaise, and cheeses
such as pecorino, gruyère
and parmesan. Pair it with
parsley, mint, thyme, sage, cress,
mustard, curry, cumin, pepper,
turmeric, fennel seeds, allspice
and chilli. It's also great with
nuts (pistachios, pine nuts,
hazelnuts, walnuts, almonds),
fruits (apples, pears), vegetables
(celery, endive, cauliflower,
potato, onion, witlof, leek,
spinach, mushroom), meats
(crumbed meats, roast beef or
chicken, cured meats, oxtail, beef
cheeks), white fish, smoked fish
and scallops.*

Preparing celeriac

Use a sharp knife to trim both ends of the celeriac and peel away the skin. There is a bit of waste in the process, as you need to remove all of the knobbly skin. The exposed flesh will oxidise and discolour reasonably rapidly, so it's advisable to rub the surface with a cut lemon, or to drop the cut celeriac pieces into a bowl of water acidulated with a splash of lemon juice or vinegar until needed. If using the celeriac raw, tossing it into your intended dressing as you cut each piece achieves the same effect. If roasting diced or sliced celeriac, lemon shouldn't be necessary; simply oil and roast the pieces immediately after cutting.

Warm celeriac salad with yoghurt, aleppo pepper, pine nuts & sultanas GF V

There is something quite engaging about the pairing of yoghurt and roasted celeriac in this salad. And those clean, bright flavours love a spot of fruity heat from aleppo pepper and the nutty, woody, piquant notes of roasted cumin. The raw celeriac adds texture, as well as a vibrantly fresh, spicy note, in beautiful contrast to the caramelised tones. I've used green sultanas here, which for me have a real Middle Eastern feel, but currants would work well, too. **Serves 4–6**

Pair with

Baked or fried fish fillets, spiced lamb or roasted chicken.

Enjoy as part of a shared table of Middle Eastern dishes.

Serve with Baked buttered rice (p. 384).

50 g (1¾ oz) green sultanas
2 tablespoons white-wine vinegar
1½ celeriac bulbs
2 teaspoons cumin seeds, lightly ground
½ lemon

250 g (9 oz/1 cup) plain yoghurt
2 handfuls of mustard cress, or watercress or shredded curly kale leaves
50 g (1¾ oz/⅓ cup) toasted pine nuts

1 tablespoon ground aleppo pepper

Staples
EVOO, S&P

Preheat the oven to 180°C (350°F) fan-forced. Line a baking tray with baking paper.

Add the sultanas and vinegar to a small saucepan. Simmer for 1 minute, then set aside for about 15 minutes.

Peel the whole celeriac, cut into 4 cm (1½ in) dice, and immediately toss the pieces in some oil and the cumin. Season with salt and pepper, spread out on the baking tray and roast for 40 minutes, until tender and golden at the edges. Squeeze the lemon over the cooked celeriac as it comes out of the oven, then cool for 5 minutes.

Add the cooked celeriac to a large bowl with the yoghurt. Peel and finely grate the remaining celeriac half and fold through, along with the sultanas and any vinegar remaining in the saucepan. Adjust the seasoning as necessary.

Spread the mixture on a serving plate. Scatter the cress and pine nuts over, then the aleppo pepper. Drizzle with a little oil to finish.

Make it different
With potato & parmesan. Boil enough diced potato to match the roasted celeriac, drain well, then toss in 1½ tablespoons vinegar. Combine with the other ingredients as per the recipe, but also add 80 g (2¾ oz) finely grated parmesan and a handful or two of chopped flat-leaf (Italian) parsley.

Roasted whole celeriac – several ways (GF) (V) (VG)

Roast a whole celeriac bulb a bed of rock salt at 170°C (340°F) fan-forced for about 1¼ hours for a medium-sized specimen, until easily skewered. Once cooked, slice off the skin and cut the flesh as desired; it will be pearly with a rich, almost meaty flavour. You can simply drizzle with good olive oil and season generously with salt flakes and freshly ground black pepper, or drizzle with a few tablespoons of tahini mixed with 250 g (9 oz/1 cup) yoghurt, some olive oil, grated garlic, salt and pepper, a good squeeze of lemon juice and some mint and/or dill to finish – perhaps with a sprinkling of Dukkah (p. 13) and aleppo pepper. Or, try drizzling with Tahini dip/ sauce (p. 71). Down a similar road, top with Labneh (p. 362), drizzle with tahini, and finish with chopped toasted walnuts and smoked paprika. The intensity of flavour will also marry well with a Mushroom ragù (p. 576), or a Béchamel (p. 70) laced with taleggio or gruyère. Or for a side dish, mash the flesh and pour over some Burnt butter sauce with lemon, capers & parsley (p. 73), then finish with toasted pine nuts and parsley.

Celeriac, fennel & rice brodo with ricotta bruschetta (V)

I cook many versions of this soup, sometimes finished like the Greek classic avgolemono, and sometimes just like this, with an imposing slab of bruschetta sinking into the broth. I love it either way, with the well-cooked rice thickening the gently spicy, anise-tinged chicken soup to make it just about the most soothing and comforting dish I know. **Serves 6**

1½ celeriac bulbs
1 fennel bulb, diced, fronds reserved and roughly chopped
2 large onions, finely sliced
6 garlic cloves, finely sliced, plus 1–2 whole cloves to rub on the bruschetta
2 fresh bay leaves

2½ teaspoons fennel seeds, ground
150 g (5½ oz) risotto rice
2 litres (68 fl oz/8 cups) Golden chicken stock (p. 54), or Classic white vegetable stock (p. 51)
1 litre (34 fl oz/4 cups) water

¼ bunch of flat-leaf (Italian) parsley, leaves finely sliced
6 thick slices of Sourdough bread (p. 847)
200 g (7 oz) ricotta

Staples
EVOO, LMN, S&P

Preheat the oven to 180°C (350°F) fan-forced. Line a baking tray with baking paper.

Peel the celeriac bulbs and cut into 3 cm (1¼ in) dice, tossing the pieces in oil as you go. Season with salt and pepper and spread out on the baking tray. Roast for about 30 minutes, until tender and turning golden.

Heat a generous glug of oil in a wide-based saucepan over a medium heat. Add the diced fennel, onion, garlic, bay leaves and fennel seeds, season and cook until golden, about 15 minutes. Add the roasted celeriac and cook until golden and caramelised, about 5 minutes.

Add the rice, stock and water, then bring to a simmer. Cook for about 40 minutes, until the rice is well cooked and the soup has thickened. Stir in the parsley, bring back to the boil and turn off the heat. Stand for 15 minutes before serving.

Just before serving, grill or toast the bread well, then rub with a cut garlic clove and drizzle with oil. Smother with ricotta, season and finish with the fennel fronds.

Serve the bruschetta resting on the lip of each bowl. Finish with a squeeze of lemon and an extra drizzle of oil.

Make it different
With pancetta. Sprinkle some crispy pancetta or bacon on top of the bruschetta.

With anchovies. Warm up some anchovies and extra-virgin olive oil in a small saucepan. Once the anchovies have started to dissolve, sprinkle in some chilli flakes, then spoon over the top of the soup and bruschetta.

With egg & lemon. Omit the celeriac, and instead use two fennel bulbs. Whisk three eggs in a small bowl with the juice of one lemon and 100 g (3½ oz) finely grated Grana Padano. Just before serving, stir the mixture through until it sets in strands and thickens the soup.

Make it a meal
Cook some chicken meatballs in the soup. Add 250 g (9 oz) minced (ground) chicken, one egg, a couple of handfuls of fresh breadcrumbs, a handful each of grated parmesan and chopped parsley to a food processor and season with salt and pepper. Blitz until combined, then roll into small balls and drop into the soup 10–15 minutes before it has finished cooking.

Celeriac remoulade GF V

If celeriac has an emblematic dish, this is it. Part salad, part condiment, remoulade is a penetrating foil for fatty, salty and rich foods, while being somewhat rich itself. Have it with a little salami, sit it next to a charred steak, stuff it into a roll with roast pork ... If this one dish was the only use celeriac had, it would be enough. **Serves 6**

1 celeriac bulb
4 flat-leaf (Italian) parsley sprigs, leaves very finely shredded
1 handful of yellow or light green celery leaves, very finely shredded

Creamy mustard dressing
120 g (4½ oz) Master olive oil mayonnaise (p. 74)
2 tablespoons wholegrain mustard
1 tablespoon crème fraîche, or sour cream or yoghurt
1 tablespoon extra-virgin olive oil

3 teaspoons apple-cider vinegar, or sherry vinegar
2 teaspoons raw sugar
1 small garlic clove, very finely grated using a microplane

Staples
EVOO, S&P

Pair with

Try this with a grilled or roasted mid-loin pork chop, your favourite cut of steak, or a paillard of chicken (butterflied chicken breast, pounded flat).

It also eats very well with crumbed meats.

Serve with smoked trout, or a baked side of ocean trout or salmon.

Match with cured meats and charcuterie.

Add to a sandwich with thickly cut ham and pickles.

Serve with a pile of flaked hot-smoked trout, fat green olives and some rye sourdough.

Add all the dressing ingredients to a bowl and whisk until smooth.

Peel the celeriac and cut it into julienne strips, tossing them immediately through the dressing as you go. Fold in the parsley and celery leaves, then stand for 10 minutes before serving.

Make it different
With nuts. Add 50 g (1¾ oz) toasted roughly chopped hazelnuts or walnuts, with a dash of their nut oil, if available; this remoulade will then go particularly well with pork and chicken.

With shallots & pickles. For a more tangy remoulade, add finely chopped French shallots and dill pickles.

With apple or pear. Add a sliced granny smith apple or nashi pear to serve with pan-fried pork chops or pork loin.

Celeriac, apple & kale slaw with anchovy GF

This salad is decidedly delicious with pork, but it's also a very convincing meal on its own, deeply flavoured, salty and bound up with layers of umami. A handful of chopped smoked almonds would push it even further into standalone territory. **Serves 6**

12 anchovies
1 bunch of kale, stalks removed, leaves shredded
4 mint sprigs, leaves torn
1 small celeriac bulb, peeled and julienned
2 granny smith apples, skin on

Sour cream roast garlic dressing
1 large garlic bulb, roasted (see p. 66)
150 g (5½ oz) sour cream
80 ml (2½ fl oz/⅓ cup) extra-virgin olive oil
juice of 1 lemon

2 tablespoons white-wine vinegar
2 teaspoons caster (superfine) sugar

Staples
EVOO, S&P

Pair with

Try the slaw with a crumbed pork cutlet (cotoletta) or chicken schnitzel, or some slow-cooked pulled lamb shoulder or pork shoulder.

Preheat the oven to 180°C (350°F) fan-forced. Line a baking tray with baking paper.

Lay the anchovies on the baking tray and bake for about 5 minutes, until brown and powdery looking. Set aside to cool and dry out.

For the dressing, squeeze the roasted garlic cloves out of their skins into a bowl, and mash with a fork. Mix in the remaining dressing ingredients, adding a splash of water to loosen. Season with salt and pepper.

Put the kale and mint in a large bowl. Peel the celeriac, cut into julienne strips and add to the kale, then pour the dressing over and toss to coat. Finely slice the apples and cut in half, then mix them through the salad.

Tip onto a platter and crumble the dried anchovies over.

Roasted celeriac, parsnip, potato & fennel with ras el hanout ⓖⓕ ⓥ

This recipe takes standard roasted vegetables up a notch, with a dusting of the heady Moroccan spice blend ras el hanout, and a drizzle of cream that bubbles and caramelises in the oven. **Serves 6**

4 parsnips, peeled, quartered lengthways, woody core removed

5 kipfler (fingerling) potatoes, washed well, sliced 4 mm (¼ in) thick on an angle

1 small fennel bulb, cut into 2 cm (¾ in) slices

1 celeriac bullb

10 garlic cloves, skin on, smashed

6 thyme sprigs

3 teaspoons Ras el hanout (p. 25)

150 ml (5 fl oz) water

150 ml (5 fl oz) cream (35% fat)

Staples
OIL, S&P

Preheat the oven to 180°C (350°F) fan-forced.

Arrange the parsnip, potato and fennel in a baking dish. Peel the celeriac and cut into 1 × 6 cm (½ × 2½ in) batons, then add to the baking dish. Scatter with the garlic, thyme and ras el hanout, season with salt and pepper and drizzle generously with oil. Add the water to the dish, cover with foil and roast for 25 minutes.

Remove the dish from the oven and take off the foil. Pour the cream over, stir gently, then roast for a further 20 minutes, until golden and bubbling.

Pair with

Serve as you would any roasted vegetables alongside a roast or the like, with some braised silverbeet (Swiss chard) or a simply dressed salad of bitter greens.

Celeriac & mustard condiment for steak ⓖⓕ ⓥ ⓥⓖ

Celeriac has a natural affinity with beef. This condiment was an essential companion to bistecca alla fiorentina (a charred Florentine-style steak, see p. 278) that was a staple at the Melbourne Wine Room for 15 years or so. Finely grate celeriac and horseradish in a ratio of three to one, then combine with extra-virgin olive oil, dijon mustard and lemon juice in equal measure to bind. Season with salt and pepper – and that's it. This condiment is my ideal companion for charred beef, along with a thick lemon wedge and more dijon mustard.

Warm celeriac salad with yoghurt, aleppo pepper, pine nuts & sultanas (p.482)

Celery

I fear that the best part of celery – a much-maligned workhorse vegetable that I have a deep affection for – is often either never consumed, or consumed past its best. It makes some sense that you eat a head of celery from the outside in, breaking off the stalks as needed, but I suspect the last inner portion too often sinks into oblivion at the base of the crisper. But that last bit, just like the heart of a lettuce, is the best. It has the most delicate yet still intense flavour, and the leaves make a beautiful herb, with a sublime savoury sweetness.

While perhaps ignored by many, the heart is certainly prized by chefs, though waiters will shoot them more than the occasional hateful look when their staff meals absorb the glut of outer celery stalks; you can never make enough stock to use them all. I'd certainly encourage you to prize the heart, and use it at its best, but the rest of the celery is of course just as useful in the kitchen.

Celery is an essential aromatic vegetable, adding a vital herbaceousness to so many dishes. It's a foundation flavour for most stocks, and with onion and carrot is one of the three elements of an Italian soffritto and French mirepoix, which form the basis of most European sauces, soups and braises. Celery can also be used as a vegetable in stews, soups and the like, and the beloved heart braised as a standalone side. A finely sliced celery heart, with all the leaves, is stunning in a Panzanella (p. 658). I love the pale stalks and leaves, and they also pickle successfully. Use the pale leaves to garnish leaf salads or sprinkle over cooked fried fish or toss into Shoyu ramen broth (p. 58).

Celery is also a perfect snacking vegetable as is, or with the hollow of the stalks filled with peanut butter or cream cheese and sultanas. That's a nostalgic snack for me, and although my girls were sceptical at first, they came around quickly enough. Celery is also an essential garnish for a bloody Mary, with celery salt being an equally essential seasoning.

You can make your own Celery salt (p. 9) using either dehydrated leaves blitzed with salt flakes (see p. 9), or celery seeds (p. 9), which I love, or both. Celery seeds don't come from the same celery plant, but rather from a spindly family ancestor, also known as smallage or leaf celery. Then there's wild celery, which looks quite similar to their shared cousin, parsley. The leaves can be used as a herb, and have a pungent celery flavour, as do the seeds, though they lean into anise more heavily.

There's no great secret to selecting celery, though I tend towards those with broader stalks, with the compact dark-green stems tending to be fibrous and just a bit too coarse and vegetal in flavour. That said, this doesn't necessarily account for potential heirloom cultivars, which may perform differently. Mostly, however, the celery you'll buy will be of the regular type, if varying somewhat in size. There is a purple variety, too, with its flavour somewhat prized, though I have not come across it often enough to comment on.

Also see

Celery salt 9

Deep-fried red mullet with celery & olive salad 188

Spiced bean & vegetable braise 425

Spring & Winter minestrone 531, 607

Sour fish curry with okra & celery heart 581

Pear, fennel, celery heart, Roquefort & poppy seed salad 710

Pair with

Celery is great with lemon, lime and orange, as well as with vinegar and extra-virgin olive oil. Enjoy it with butter, cream, sour cream and cream cheese; with tarragon, ginger, mint, parsley, spring onion (scallion), green capsicum (bell pepper), eggplant (aubergine), cauliflower, olives, grapes, onion, tomato, apple, pineapple, green mango, walnuts, crumbed meat, chicken and sardines.

Preparing celery

I use most of a head of celery, with the outer stalks heading for stock, along with some of the leaves. The slightly paler inner stalks get used for snacks, soffritto and in soups and the like, while those paler still and the prized heart, along with all the yellow leaves, are used in salads and as a sophisticated touch in other recipes. The only part I don't use is the more mature leaves. Adding too many to a stock tends to overwhelm the flavour and, as with mature parsley leaves, I don't enjoy them in salads or as a finishing herb, as their texture and flavour are just too coarse.

To prepare celery, simply peel the stalks back until they snap off at the base, which is where most of the dirt will reside, so give them a careful wash, then trim. The stalks can then be used as required. Celery that has gone a little soft, though not completely limp, responds to a bath in ice-cold water like few other vegetables, springing back to all its crunchy glory in no more than 15 minutes.

Sour fish & mussel curry with celery hearts & kang kong

My affection for sour fish curries runs deep, with this one pushing in a Thai direction. And although the ingredients list looks long, I have included a couple of tricks to make a genuinely impressive curry that's quick and easy to make. The hot-smoked trout adds a depth of flavour that means you don't need stock, as do the mussels when they contribute their liquor. The frying of the fish skin at the start also releases the fat and plenty of flavour from under the skin, which adds even more intensity. And I've also used tamarind paste, which is a lot easier than soaking and straining tamarind from a block (see p. 30), though you can. **Serves 6**

Pair with

All you need is steamed jasmine rice, but the fish curry will happily sit alongside other Thai-inspired curries or salads.

2 tablespoons coconut oil
1 × 1.2 kg (2 lb 10 oz) fillet of thick white-fleshed fish (such as blue-eye trevalla or hapuka), skin on, cut in half lengthways, then into 6 pieces
150 g (5½ oz) hot-smoked trout, flaked
2 tomatoes, diced
1 teaspoon chilli powder
3 tablespoons tamarind paste, mixed with 800 ml (27 fl oz) water
2 tablespoons fish sauce

2 celery hearts, sliced 4 cm (1½ in) thick on an angle (reserve the leaves)
6 makrut lime leaves
500 g (1 lb 2 oz) black mussels, scrubbed, hairy beards removed
2 handfuls of kang kong (Siamese watercress), or spinach
2 handfuls of pale celery leaves
2 handfuls of Thai basil leaves
2 limes, plus extra to serve

Curry paste
4 red Asian shallots, sliced
3 garlic cloves, sliced
8 cm (3¼ in) piece of fresh turmeric, peeled and sliced
5 cm (2 in) piece of fresh ginger, peeled and sliced
3–4 red bird's eye chillies, sliced
2 tablespoons coconut oil
1 tablespoon small dried shrimp
1 tablespoon caster (superfine) sugar
3 teaspoons shrimp paste
2 teaspoons ground white pepper

Blitz the curry paste ingredients with a splash of water in a blender, until you have a rough paste. Set aside.

Heat a wide-based saucepan or deep frying pan over a high heat until quite hot. Add the oil and seal the fish for 1 minute, skin side down, then remove from the pan.

Add the curry paste and fry over a medium heat until fragrant, about 2 minutes. Add the trout, tomato and chilli powder and fry until the tomato has softened, about 2 minutes. Add the tamarind water and fish sauce and bring to a simmer, then add the celery hearts and lime leaves and simmer for a further 2 minutes.

Add the mussels and cook until starting to open, about 5 minutes, then nestle the fish fillets into the sauce, followed by the watercress and celery leaves. Cover and gently simmer over a low heat for 4–5 minutes.

Turn off the heat and stand for a minute to finish cooking the fish. Scatter the basil over, squeeze in the limes and serve with extra lime wedges.

Caponata bianco with toasted walnuts (GF) (V) (VG)

Pair with

Serve as part of an antipasto selection, with fresh ricotta or a wedge of sharp pecorino.

Grilled haloumi.

Fried fish, skewered or roasted lamb, or grilled chicken with a smoky spiced crust.

Grilled Italian pork and fennel sausages.

Porchetta (p. 338).

Caponata is a warm roasted salad, and a Sicilian classic with so many variations. Most are richer and darker in colour than this one, but I'm very fond of my bianco version. Many dishes are born out of necessity, either due to scarcity or glut; this one is the latter. Anyone who grows vegetables at home in meaningful amounts will struggle at one time or another to find enough recipes for zucchini (courgettes) or pumpkins (winter squash) or the like, with the charm of home-grown produce being outpaced by the dread of eating your way through a sea of squash. One year, my in-laws had an especially good year for banana chillies (peppers), so their glut became ours (happily, I might add). This was one of the memorable dishes from that season. It's a pale and delicate result, a fresh and juicy caponata salad that can be enjoyed warm or cold. **Serves 8–10**

2 large eggplants (aubergines), peeled and cut into 8 cm (3¼ in) batons
5 large yellow banana chillies (peppers)
3 pale inner celery stalks
2 white salad onions, sliced into 1 cm (½ in) rings
8 garlic cloves, finely sliced
½ bunch of oregano, leaves picked

5 ripe tomatoes (I like to use green or black Russians), diced
80 ml (2½ fl oz/⅓ cup) white-wine vinegar
1 tablespoon caster (superfine) sugar
2 handfuls of dried black olives, pitted
2 tablespoons tiny capers, drained

1 bunch of flat-leaf (Italian) parsley, leaves very finely shredded
150 g (5½ oz/1½ cups) toasted walnuts, roughly chopped

Staples
EVOO, LMN, S&P

Preheat the oven to 180°C (350°F) fan-forced. Line two baking trays with baking paper.

Toss the eggplant batons in a generous amount of oil, season with salt and pepper and spread out evenly on one of the baking trays. Roast for 20–25 minutes, until golden. Add the banana chillies to the other tray, toss in a little oil and roast for about 25 minutes, until soft and blistered. Tip into a bowl and cover with a plate to sweat for 20 minutes, then peel the banana chillies, deseed and roughly dice the flesh, and drain off the excess liquid.

Add the celery, onion, garlic and oregano to a baking dish and drizzle generously with oil. Season and toss well, then cover tightly with foil. Bake for 20 minutes, then remove the foil. Mix the eggplant and tomato through and bake for a further 20 minutes uncovered.

Remove the dish from the oven and stir in the banana chillies, vinegar, sugar, olives, capers, parsley and half the walnuts. Squeeze in some lemon juice, then combine well.

Adjust the seasoning and serve with the remaining walnuts scattered over the top. Serve warm, or at room temperature; you may need to drain off the juices a little once the salad relaxes.

Caponata bianco with toasted walnuts

Waldorf salad with roast chicken wrapped in iceberg ⓖⓕ

The original Waldorf salad (from 1893, credited to one Oscar Tschirky, or 'Oscar of the Waldorf', as he was known) was just celery, apple and mayonnaise served on a bed of lettuce. The lettuce doesn't appear to be an ingredient as such – just a bed for the salad – but the crackle of iceberg lettuce certainly makes a valid contribution, as do walnuts, which populate most versions. Whatever the history, the essential combination is great, and a perfect match to chicken. Make sure, though, that you don't use fridge-cold meat, and ideally, make it a still-warm roasted bird. **Serves 6**

1 firm iceberg lettuce
½ warm roast chicken, meat picked and shredded finely by hand
2 granny smith apples, skin on, julienned
6 radishes, julienned
4 celery stalks, sliced lengthways into thirds, then finely sliced
1 chicory (witlof/endive), finely sliced on an angle

3 spring onions (scallions), white and pale green parts, finely sliced
5 flat-leaf (Italian) parsley sprigs, leaves finely chopped
5 dill sprigs, fine fronds whole, coarse ones chopped
1 large handful of toasted walnuts, or pine nuts, roughly chopped

Lemon mustard dressing
125 g (4½ oz/½ cup) Master olive oil mayonnaise (p. 74)
juice of ½ lemon
2 tablespoons plain yoghurt
2 tablespoons extra-virgin olive oil
3 teaspoons white-wine vinegar
2 teaspoons dijon mustard

Staples
EVOO, S&P

Cut 4 cm (1½ in) off the base of the lettuce to remove the core, then add the lettuce to a large bowl of iced water, cut side down; this helps the lettuce leaves separate easily. After 15 minutes or so, carefully pry the leaves apart intact, and stand the cups upside down on a tea towel (dish towel) to drain.

Combine the dressing ingredients thoroughly in a large bowl, seasoning with salt and pepper. Add the remaining salad ingredients, reserving some walnuts to garnish, then season and combine.

Fill the lettuce cups with the salad and arrange on a platter; you can either roll up the lettuce cups, or simply leave them open. Scatter with the reserved walnuts and serve.

Make it faster
The most basic version is to dice one apple and two celery stalks, then combine with a handful of chopped toasted walnuts, some picked roasted chicken meat, a little mayo and a dash of yoghurt or sour cream to bind. Drizzle in a little oil and a splash of vinegar, season with salt and pepper and wrap in flatbread.

Make it different
Waldorf salad & roast chicken wraps. Wrap in flatbread as an alternative to lettuce.

With more vegetables. Add finely diced celeriac, fennel and/or raw beetroot (beet).

Make it vegetarian ⓥ
Omit the chicken and add four chopped hard-boiled eggs.

Celery, lemon & parsley salad with a fried garlic & fennel seed dressing (GF) (V) (VG)

Pair with

Try the salad with thick pork sausages, cotechino sausages with lentils, a rich braise of lamb, grilled lamb cutlets or roast chicken.

The salad is superb with fish, whether grilled, baked or pan-fried.

This kind of salad is something that I refer to as a 'condiment salad', sitting somewhere between the two. A condiment salad is something that you probably wouldn't sit down to a bowl of by itself, but rather it's an intense salad that both complements and accents a dish, while also providing a bit of relief. A condiment and a salad – I rest my case. This one is zippy and bright, with a big herbal punch from the celery leaves and parsley, accented by the nutty tones of fried garlic and the anise spike of fennel seeds. It's great with fatty proteins and seafood. **Serves 4–6**

2 small Lebanese (short) cucumbers, halved lengthways, seeds removed, flesh cut into 5 mm (¼ in) slices

2 celery hearts, leaves picked and reserved, hearts cut into 5 mm (¼ in) slices

2 teaspoons caster (superfine) sugar

2 teaspoons salt

3 lemons, segmented (see p. 694) and cut into 3–4 pieces each, membranes reserved

80 ml (2½ fl oz/⅓ cup) extra-virgin olive oil

5 large garlic cloves, sliced

2 teaspoons fennel seeds

½ bunch of flat-leaf (Italian) parsley, or dill or mint, leaves picked

Staples
S&P

Add the cucumber and celery slices to a colander and sprinkle with the sugar and salt. Lightly toss with your hands and set aside.

Add the lemon segments to a bowl, picking out any errant seeds. Squeeze the juice from the reserved membranes into the bowl.

Heat the oil in a small frying pan over a medium heat. Add the garlic and fry until just golden and fragrant. Add the fennel seeds, then take off the heat and allow to cool for a minute or so, before pouring over the lemon. Season with salt and pepper and combine.

Squeeze the celery and cucumber lightly to remove any excess moisture, then add to the bowl along with the parsley and reserved celery leaves. Toss through, then stand for 10 minutes before serving.

Make it faster
Simplify this salad by sprinkling sliced celery hearts with salt and sugar, standing for 5 minutes, then mixing with lemon segments, pale celery leaves and any soft herbs you have on hand. Some good olive oil is all that's then needed to bring it together.

Make it different
With fennel, capers & dill. Add some shaved fennel and small capers and dill.

Celery, lemon, orange & parsley salad. (GF) (V) (VG) Omit the cucumber and combine the remaining ingredients with a few sliced, peeled oranges and a shaved fennel bulb, perhaps with some shredded radicchio and a handful of black olives.

Chilli

The world of chillies is a vast and well documented one, with aficionados not just obsessing over the wildly explosive heat of those at the top of the register, but also at the variety of flavours offered, from grassy and sharp to fruity and mellow. However, that fruity mellowness can often come with explosive heat, so the untempered palate is unlikely to detect the detail. I will leave the subtleties of the chilli canon to others, and instead focus on those that I use habitually.

My two standard chillies are bird's eye chillies, for intense heat, and long red and green chillies for milder heat, and where I want more of the pepper's flavour and textural contribution. The chilli lover will recoil at the generic term 'long chilli', which simply reflects how they are typically sold here; in our markets, those chillies are quite likely to be a type of cayenne pepper. The type we see here tend to be a bit fatter and milder than the thin cayenne chilli, which can be challengingly hot – for me at least. A pepper like the anaheim would serve a similar purpose, though they're milder again.

There is more than one type of bird's eye chilli, with the most common having a small bullet-like shape – hence the synonym 'bullet chilli'. They are common in Thai cuisine and are also called scuds. They are variably spicy, but always on the hot end of things, so should be sliced or chopped finely. I occasionally find Thai chillies that are similarly small but quite spindly, and these are typically hotter again. They are great for genuinely fiery Thai dishes.

I also use jalapeño chillies from time to time, and pickle them when I can. They have a reputation for fierce heat, and though they are certainly hot, they are not abrasively so. They're great raw or pickled to add pops of genuine heat without overwhelming dishes, with a very distinctive grassy and herbaceous flavour.

It seems that the more sinister a chilli looks, the hotter it is, with size another moderately reliable indicator. Smaller chillies are typically hotter than large ones, but if they're unfamiliar, always test a sliver on your tongue before jumping in. It's also always worth checking chillies before using, as the season can dictate how hot they are. The staple long chillies I use can be fiercely hot when the weather is right, while they can be devoid of heat when not. It's therefore important to always treat chilli quantities in recipes as guides only, both for personal preference and for seasonal variation.

Dried chillies (see p. 10) are another category entirely, with Mexican chillies, for example, taking on an array of complex flavours, sometimes with plenty of heat, and sometimes little to none. Some can be quite chocolatey, with overtones of raisin, dried fig and even date, a little like Pedro Ximénez sherry – it's no wonder that a Mexican mole often contains cacao, as the flavours are very complementary. These chillies are often toasted in a dry pan to intensify the smoky caramelised notes even further; I will typically then soak them in boiling water, then discard the seeds as they can be bitter. They can then be added to braises, stews or a mole.

Also see

<u>Herb & chilli oil</u> 86

Harissa 92

Thai-style chilli jam 96

Chilli crab 199–200

<u>Oysters with fire ice</u> 208

Red curry paste 266–7

Citrus & chilli relish 358

Thai green papaya salad 438

Kimchi 455–6

Spiced corn & manchego loaf 858

Pair with

Chillies are great with oils of any type, citrus juices and vinegars, as well as soy sauce, ginger, garlic, fish sauce and mustard; they also spice up noodles, rice, breads and pasta. Chillies work well with eggs, cheeses (including fresh curd and pulled-milk cheeses), pumpkin (winter squash), green beans, cucumber, avocado, tomatoes, capsicum (bell pepper) and zucchini (courgette), and pair with proteins such as fish, seafood, beef, pork and chicken.

Preparing chillies

The stem of a chilli is the only part that needs to be trimmed away. Both the seeds and the membrane are the source of much of the heat, so they can be discarded if a milder result is desired. Chillies naturally vary in intensity, but when handling them, even small amounts of relatively mild chillies can cause discomfit – and hot chillies can be very painful. Once a chilli has been sliced, the oils will transfer readily to another surface or to your hands – and if you then happen to rub your eyes, mouth or even nose, the outcome can be quite unpleasant. If preparing a small amount, simply wash your hands, the knife and the board immediately afterwards. If preparing a large amount, always wear gloves, as it will invariably start to irritate your skin. If you're working with a chilli that is patently hazardous, such as a scotch bonnet or carolina reaper – though I'm not sure why you would be! – then both gloves and eye protection are essential, no matter the quantity. Also, heat will make lots of those hot oils ambient, so frying in any quantity can be the source of much coughing and spluttering.

Fermented red cooked chilli paste GF V VG

Finely slice 1 kg (2 lb 3 oz) red chillies, then blitz in a blender with 50 g (1¾ oz) salt. Set aside in a container for 3 days, then blitz again. Add 50 g (1¾ oz) sugar and 225 ml (7½ fl oz) white vinegar, then tip into a saucepan and cook for 20 minutes until thick.

Sliced pickled jalapeños GF V VG

This is one of those items that I always used to buy from the sliver of shelf space allocated to alarmingly inauthentic Mexican food in the supermarket. These are somewhat better. **Makes 3 × 500 ml (17 fl oz/2 cup) jars**

800 g (1 lb 12 oz) jalapeño chillies, rounds sliced finely, seeds and all

Pickling medium
700 ml (23½ fl oz) rice vinegar
100 ml (3½ fl oz) filtered water
100 g (3½ oz) raw sugar
80 g (2¾ oz) sea salt
15 g (½ oz) coriander seeds
3 garlic cloves, sliced

Pack the chilli slices into jars.

Add the pickling medium ingredients to a saucepan and simmer over a medium heat for 1 minute. Cool the hot liquid, then pour over the chillies to cover. Seal the jars.

Cool to room temperature, then refrigerate for a day to pickle. These will keep for up to 6 months in the fridge. Use after 1 day.

Pair with

Serve with Mexican-themed fare, such as tacos, tortillas, quesadillas, guacamole, mole and the like, or add to a salsa.

Chop finely and sprinkle over soft curd cheeses as part of a spread of appetisers or to spread on a toasted sandwich.

Spike a simple green salad with some of these, finely chopped.

Slice and use whenever a bit of pickled heat is welcome, in a burger, a roast chicken roll or Bánh mì with roast pork belly (p. 332).

Blitz with some mayonnaise (see pp. 74–5) for a spicy dipping sauce.

Drop on top of scrambled eggs and wrap in pitta bread (see p. 854).

Whole pickled chillies & a simple fermented chilli sauce GF V VG

This is a very basic lacto-fermentation method to make both whole pickled chillies and the simplest of fermented chilli sauces, which happens to also be one of my favourite chilli sauces. **Makes 1 × 3 litre (101 fl oz/12 cup) jar**

30 long red or green chillies, each pricked once with a knife

2 litres (68 fl oz/8 cups) filtered water
50 g (1¾ oz) salt

4 garlic cloves, peeled
1 teaspoon fennel seeds

Pair with

Serve the pickled chillies whole, sliced or chopped with a meze spread, or use to spike other dishes with heat and a pickled note.

Keep the sauce on hand to eat with cured or grilled meats or fish, or add to braises, soups or pastas. It's a real all-rounder, not bound to any particular cuisine.

Dried chilli flakes, chilli powder & chilli salt GF V VG

Chillies are very easy to grow, even in a small pot. And if you grow a few varieties, you'll invariably have too many on hand at one time or another – in which case you can either pickle them (see opposite) or dry them. Spread them out on a baking tray and dehydrate in the bottom of a very low oven set at about 70°C (160°F) for 12 hours or longer, until brittle. Break into flakes and keep in an airtight jar, or blitz finely to make chilli powder. Using a mix of chillies can make for very interesting notes – smoky, sweet, pungent and even chocolatey. The colour will be dictated by the mix of chillies you have, so don't despair if it's a little darker than what you find on the supermarket shelf. I leave the seeds in for a delightfully pungent and punchy heat, but you can omit if preferred. To make chilli salt, grind 2 teaspoons of your chilli powder with 2 tablespoons salt flakes until you have a lightly pink salt.

Roasted chillies GF V VG

Roast long red chillies in a hot oven or under a grill (broiler) until blistering, then slip off the skins, scrape away the seeds and cut the flesh into fine strips. Pop into a jar, cover with extra-virgin olive oil and refrigerate. Use on pizzas, or to dress a bruschetta with tomato, sardines, cured fish or smashed boiled egg – or drape over a tuna crudo or Vitello tonnato (p. 297) for a non-traditional burst of heat.

Pair with

Subcontinental-style curries, especially hot ones.

Fish, lightly dusted in rice flour and flash-fried.

Split grilled prawns (shrimp), or chicken or pork skewers with rice.

Fried spring rolls.

Pack the chillies into jars.

Pour 1 litre (34 fl oz/4 cups) of the water into a small saucepan. Stir in the salt, garlic and fennel seeds and bring to the boil. Pour into a bowl, add the remaining water and cool to room temperature.

Pour the brine over the chillies and stand at room temperature out of direct sunlight, with the lid sitting on top but not sealed. Set aside somewhere warm to ferment, making sure the chillies are submerged.

The time it takes varies depending on the ambient temperature and the chillies, but they will change from vibrantly coloured to somewhat duller as they ferment, and they will soften in texture. Taste after 3 days, then periodically until you're happy with the pickled flavour and the texture; I like my chillies still a bit crunchy.

Once ready, seal the jars and refrigerate. The chillies will keep for many months like this, but they will keep fermenting slowly and become soft over time - you can always blitz these for sauce.

To make a smooth chilli sauce with a good spike of pickle flavour, I like to ferment the chillies on the bench for a few days longer than my ideal crunchy chilli. Again, this is personal preference, but once you're happy with the flavour and texture, strain off the liquid and reserve. Remove and discard the chilli stems, then blitz the chillies in a blender, adding a little of the brine to get the desired consistency. Once bottled, the sauce will easily keep for up to 6 months in the fridge.

Make it different

You can slice the chillies first (just wear gloves!) and pickle them like that. They will ferment a little more quickly and are great to have on hand to pep up a burger, taco or the like, or to mix through a salad.

Mango, ginger & chilli relish GF V VG

I really enjoy a relish like this with a hot curry. And though this has a chilli component, it is more to balance the sauce than make it overly warm.

Makes 1.25 litres (42 fl oz/5 cups)

400 g (14 oz) brown sugar
300 ml (10 fl oz) rice vinegar
1 brown onion, finely diced
15 cm (6 in) piece of fresh ginger, peeled and diced
3 long red chillies, sliced finely into rounds

2 teaspoons yellow mustard seeds
1 star anise
1 kg (2 lb 3 oz) mango flesh, cut into 2 cm (¾ in) dice
80 g (1¾ oz/⅔ cup) sultanas (golden raisins)

2 teaspoons ground ginger
2 teaspoons salt flakes
1 stem of fresh curry leaves

Put the sugar in a wide saucepan with the vinegar, onion, fresh ginger, chilli, mustard seeds and star anise. Bring to a simmer over a medium heat, then cook for 3 minutes, until the sugar has dissolved and the onion is translucent.

Stir in the mango, sultanas, ground ginger and salt. Bring to a simmer, then reduce the heat to low and cook for 1½ hours, placing the curry leaves on top for 1 hour, then removing. The relish will darken slightly, but you will still have visible mango pieces.

Spoon the hot relish into hot sterilised jars (see p. 40) and seal, then turn upside to help form a vacuum seal. The relish will keep jarred in the pantry for 6 months. Once opened, refrigerate and use within 1 month.

Make it different

With fish sauce & lime. Sharpen the flavour by adding a splash of fish sauce, the juice of a few limes and some chopped coriander (cilantro) when serving. You could also add some finely sliced shallots and chilli to elevate it even further.

Corn

I have a very fond memory of a sun-splashed day eating boiled sweet corn slathered in butter. I was about eight, and we kids were exiled to the big old wooden verandah, lest we drip butter all throughout the house. It was one of those indelible food memories, where one chases the raw simplicity of that moment endlessly, and it is still one of my favourite ways to eat corn. I also love charring it on the barbecue, with the smoky notes complementing the sweetness beautifully.

Maize, or field corn as it is also known, is thought to have been first cultivated in Mesoamerica some 10,000 years ago, in what is now Mexico. Sweet corn is a naturally occurring mutation of maize, resulting in greater sugar production in the kernels – a variation that ancient civilisations such as Native North Americans, Incas, Aztecs and Mayans recognised, isolated and grew domestically. Since then, many hybrids have emerged, as well as many genetically modified (GM) cultivars. If you're keen to avoid GM foods, corn is one to be particular about, as it has been tinkered with like few others. The simplest way to avoid GM foods is to buy certified organic.

Maize and sweet corn are a cereal grain: a grass, essentially. In fact, in terms of volume, maize is the number one grain in the world, even if much of it never ends up on the dinner table. Besides being ground into flour (masa) and meal products (such as polenta, cornmeal and grits), it is used for all manner of things, from animal feed to ethanol production. Unlike sweet corn, maize is dried on the plant before harvest.

If you are keen to grow sweet corn, there are many heirloom varieties available, some with quite distinctive colouration, from the standard sunny yellow to white, blue and a range of ruddy hues. The kernels can even be a variety of colours on the one cob, including some that are so varied and colourful as to look almost surreal. Colour is not a great indicator of flavour or sweetness, as these are determined by the cultivar; corn has been bred to be sweet to different degrees, with some almost cloyingly so. Climate and the time of season will also determine sweetness and intensity of flavour. In terms of nutrition, the oldest varieties are the best, with selective breeding favouring yield, durability, sweetness, pest resistance, colour and the like at the expense of both nutritional value and flavour.

Baby sweet corn is just that, immature sweet corn cobs, picked when they're around finger-length in size. They're ideal to throw into stir-fries or serve with Asian greens; try them stir-fried with black fungus, shiitake mushrooms and Black bean & ginger sauce (p. 100). Popping corn is different, though, with specific varieties suited to making the cinema staple.

The maturation process of corn is one where sugars are eventually turned to starches, which occurs naturally on the plant. Ideally, however, we want to catch the corn before those sugars get converted. Harvesting triggers the process, which is partly outside your control unless you are growing it yourself – so it is important to eat corn as quickly as practicable after purchase if you want the best results. All vegetables are seasonal, but corn is one that really suffers if grown in less than optimal conditions, or when held up in the supply chain. A just-picked ear of sun-kissed corn is a thing of beauty; imported husked cobs wrapped in plastic on a supermarket tray are not. Enjoy corn at its best in the full flush of summer.

Select ears of corn that have bright, tightly fitting husks that are not dry and papery. You can pull down the top of the husk a little way to check the kernels, but keep the husk on to maintain freshness. The kernels should be plump and firm, not shrivelled or dull. Avoid corn that has been trimmed in its husk, as this is usually done to cut away a husk and corn silks that are showing signs of age. If storing corn for a day or two, leave the husks on and keep it in the crisper to help preserve the nutrients and slow down that sugar conversion. The main area of the fridge is too dry an environment for keeping corn fresh, so if the crisper is full, store it in a bag or container in the fridge.

Also see

Chicken & corn koftas with avocado & coriander 249

Spiced corn & manchego loaf 858

Pair with

Corn loves butter and oil, parmesan, and citrus such as lemon and lime. It sings with soft herbs such as coriander (cilantro), parsley, chives and chervil. Its sweetness is an ideal foil for chilli, whether fresh or preserved, and it loves the tang of onion, shallots and garlic. It pairs with fresh and vibrant flavours such as avocado and tomato, but equally it knits into rich and creamy dishes, marrying well with dairy and eggs. Chicken is an excellent match, as is crabmeat, and its vibrant flavour and sweetness marries well with Asian flavours, playing well against spice, salt and heat.

Fried corn cakes with chilli jam & smashed avocado ⓥ

There's no need to relegate corn cakes to breakfast and brunch. This version, with Thai-style chilli jam and a nod to Mexican ingredients, may seem like a cultural mash-up, but the flavours just work so well with corn, and so well together. The fritters themselves are quite soft and sweet – a perfect foil for the punchy accents here, although you can, of course, dial down the chilli. Blitzing the coriander roots into the batter adds a fresh burst to the base flavour. **Serves 4**

¼ bunch of coriander (cilantro), with roots attached
4 corn cobs, kernels stripped (about 450 g/1 lb)
2 red Asian shallots, roughly chopped
2 garlic cloves, roughly chopped

2 long green chillies, seeds removed, chopped
3 eggs, lightly beaten
2 tablespoons brown sugar
2 teaspoons salt flakes
150 g (5½ oz/1 cup) plain (all-purpose) flour
2 teaspoons baking powder
1 heaped teaspoon ground white pepper

500 ml (17 fl oz/2 cups) oil, for frying
2 avocados
2 limes, plus extra wedges to serve
150 g (5½ oz) sour cream
Thai-style chilli jam (p. 96), to serve

Staples
FLR, S&P

Pick the leaves off the coriander and set aside. Cut off the coriander roots and wash them thoroughly. Finely chop the roots and stems, keeping them separate.

Add three-quarters of the corn kernels to a blender, along with the coriander roots, shallot, garlic, chilli, eggs, sugar and salt. Blitz on high for about 3 minutes, until smooth. Tip into a bowl with the remaining corn kernels, flour, baking powder, pepper and coriander stems, combining well; the mixture should be wet but spoon-able, so add a little more flour if necessary.

Heat the oil in a deep frying pan to 180°C (350°F).

Working in batches, spoon 1 heaped tablespoon of mixture per fritter into the hot oil. Don't crowd the pan, or the oil temperature will drop. Fry until golden and crisp, 3–4 minutes, then drain on paper towel.

In a small bowl, smash or dice the avocado flesh roughly, season with salt and pepper, squeeze in the juice from the limes and combine.

Serve the corn cakes warm, topped with the avocado, sour cream, coriander leaves and a drizzle of chilli sauce, with extra lime wedges on the side.

Make it gluten-free ⒢
Instead of plain flour, use 200 g (7 oz) rice flour or besan (chickpea flour).

Make it a meal
Serve with eggs fried in hot oil until lacy and crispy at the edges, and some deep-fried pork belly pieces or pulled pork or chicken.

Charred corn & cheddar fritters ⓥ

These are more traditional, rustic corn cakes or fritters, like a corn and cheese flavoured hotcake or pancake. Turn them into a tasty hors d'oeuvre or finger food by making tiny fritters and topping with crème fraîche and Thai-style chilli jam (p. 498). **Makes 10 large or 18 small fritters**

Pair with
These fritters will take all your favourite corn cake toppings, from bacon and crisp pancetta to hot-smoked trout or poached eggs … it's up to you.

Barbecued whole corn ⒢ ⓥ ⓋⒼ

Peel back the husks from a few ears of corn and remove the silks, then tie the husks in a knot, just above the stem. Char them evenly over low coals for 8–10 minutes, using the knotted husks as handles to turn the cobs; those same handles are just as useful when eating them. Dress the cooked corn however you like; a knob of citrus-flavoured butter works well. You can also barbecue the whole cobs, husk and all, then peel the husks back to reveal the cooked kernels that have steamed in their jackets. First, simply peel back the husks, remove the silks and cover the cobs with the husks again, then soak them in water for about an hour to stop them burning too easily. Cook them slowly on a cool part of the grill, turning occasionally, for 15–20 minutes, until tender. You can also char peeled cobs of corn on a hot gas barbecue or chargrill pan on the stove over a high heat for 6–8 minutes, rotating regularly.

Pair with
Bacon or grilled ham steaks.

Top with a fried egg and a dollop of Roasted tomato passata (p. 660).

Poached or fried eggs, with some sliced avocado, roasted tomato and/or wilted spinach.

Pure corn purée ⒢ ⓥ

Using the coarse side of a box grater, grate 8 corn cobs onto a tray to catch all the juice. (Do this carefully, as it is very easy to grate more than just corn!). Add the kernels and any juice to a small saucepan, along with 80 g (2¾ oz) unsalted butter. Stir over a medium heat with a spatula to lift everything off the base and out of the corners. The corn will let down and start to thicken after about 3 minutes. Once it has turned into a chunky puree, season with salt and serve immediately. Serves 4–6 as a side dish. Great with Fried buttermilk chicken (p. 230), Fried artichokes (see p. 539) or spooned over crème fraîche, then garnished with fried capers or sage leaves and served with crumbed meats or roast chicken.

Pair with

Battered or crumbed fish in a soft tortilla.

Pork taco, such as al pastor.

Barbecued prawns (shrimp) (see p. 202) and rice.

Fish cakes with parsley (p. 190).

Chilli con pollo (p. 232) with all the trimmings: guacamole (pp. 412–3), sour cream or Crema fresca (p. 364), tortillas, shaved cabbage.

Add a tin of drained pinto beans to the salsa and serve with grilled or fried whole fish.

Spoon over a grilled hand-cut ham steak and serve with Smoked paprika aïoli (p. 76).

Pulled slow-cooked pork shoulder with cider (p. 333).

6 corn cobs, husks and silks removed
150 g (5½ oz/1 cup) plain (all-purpose) flour
100 g (3½ oz) cornflour (cornstarch)
1½ teaspoons baking powder
¼ teaspoon salt flakes

2 teaspoons caster (superfine) sugar
1 teaspoon ground coriander
1 teaspoon ground cumin
2 eggs
125 ml (4 fl oz/½ cup) full-cream (whole) milk
100 g (3½ oz) cheddar, coarsely grated

2 spring onions (scallions), white only part only, finely sliced
½ bunch of flat-leaf (Italian) parsley, finely chopped, stalks and all

Staples
OIL, S&P

Heat a chargrill pan or barbecue grill on high.

Grill the corn cobs for 6–8 minutes, rotating them to cook evenly. When cool enough to handle, slice off the kernels and place in a large bowl.

Sift the flour, cornflour and baking powder into a large bowl. Stir in the salt, sugar and ground spices and make a well in the centre.

In a separate bowl, whisk together the eggs and milk. Gradually whisk the egg mixture into the dry ingredients until you have a stiff but smooth batter.

Add the cheddar, spring onion and parsley to the bowl of corn kernels, season with salt and pepper and toss together. Pour in the batter and combine well.

Heat a few tablespoons of oil in a non-stick frying pan over a medium heat. Add 2 heaped tablespoons of batter per fritter and cook, in batches of three or four fritters, for about 2 minutes on each side, until golden, then drain on paper towel. Repeat, adding more oil to the pan as needed.

Serve warm, or at room temperature.

Corn & pineapple salsa

This addictive salsa is bright and fresh, suffused with a gentle smokiness, and a present but not overpowering heat, and freshened by an abundance of coriander (cilantro). Choose a pineapple that is slightly under-ripe, as the salsa can be too sweet if very ripe, even with the chilli and salt – the balance is important.
Serves 10

2 corn cobs
½ slightly under-ripe pineapple, peeled and cut into long wedges, most of the core removed
1 white onion, sliced 2 mm (⅛ in) thick
1 bunch of coriander (cilantro), leaves and stems finely chopped

2 long green chillies, finely diced

Chilli, lime & brown sugar dressing
2 tablespoons extra-virgin olive oil
1½ tablespoons white-wine vinegar
1 tablespoon brown sugar
2 teaspoons fish sauce

1 teaspoon salt flakes
½ teaspoon ground white pepper
½ teaspoon ground cumin
juice of 1 lime
½ teaspoon hot green jalapeño sauce (such as green Tabasco)

Staples
EVOO, S&P

Preheat the barbecue on high; alternatively, you can use a metal rack set over a stovetop gas burner.

Grill the corn for 5 minutes or so, until scorched and blackened – the time will vary a bit depending on your barbecue. Lightly oil the pineapple, season with salt and grill until scorched.

Meanwhile, combine the dressing ingredients in a small bowl.

Slice the corn kernels from the cobs. Cut the pineapple into 1 cm (½ in) pieces. Add both to a bowl, then add the onion, coriander and chilli, tossing to combine. Pour the dressing over and toss to coat.

Leave to stand for about 5 minutes before using. The salsa is best enjoyed same day.

Prawn, corn & shiitake pot-sticker dumplings

This technique yields a combination of soft and silky steamed dumplings with a crisply fried base sporting a lacy, crunchy crust – a shimmeringly beautiful combination in my mind. Prawn (shrimp) is the predominant flavour here, with the finely minced chicken giving it a mousse-like texture. The addition of flour and water creates a crust across the pan, which will form as the last of the water evaporates and the residue caramelises. This is a good recipe to make in bulk, as the dumplings freeze very well. **Makes 25**

25 round white gow gee wrappers
3 tablespoons neutral-flavoured oil
2 heaped teaspoons plain (all-purpose) flour
500 ml (17 fl oz/2 cups) water
hot chilli oil, to serve (optional)
Filling
8 raw prawn (shrimp) cutlets, peeled and deveined, then finely sliced

200 g (7 oz) minced (ground) chicken thighs
1 large cooked corn cob, kernels stripped
4 fresh shiitake mushrooms, very finely sliced
8 cm (3¼ in) piece of fresh ginger, peeled and finely diced
3 spring onions (scallions), white part only, finely sliced
1 tablespoon oyster sauce
1 tablespoon light soy sauce
½ teaspoon sesame oil

Soy, sesame & ginger dipping sauce
3 tablespoons light soy sauce
1 long red chilli, finely sliced
1 tablespoon julienned fresh ginger
1 teaspoon caster (superfine) sugar
½ teaspoon sesame oil

Pork, wombok & ginger dumpling filling

To make a classically flavoured filling for pot-sticker dumplings (left), add 400 g (14 oz) fatty minced (ground) pork to a bowl, season lightly with salt and combine. Add ¼ finely shredded small wombok (Chinese cabbage), an 8 cm (3¼ in) piece of fresh ginger, peeled and finely diced, 5 finely sliced spring onions (scallions; white and light green parts), ½ teaspoon ground white pepper, 2 tablespoons light soy sauce, 1 tablespoon oyster sauce and ½ teaspoon sesame oil and combine very well. Proceed with the instructions for making and cooking dumplings (left). These are perfect paired with Crispy garlic & soy vinegar dressing (p. 94).

To make the filling, mix the prawn and chicken together in a bowl, then add all the other filling ingredients and combine well.

Lay several gow gee wrappers on a clean, dry surface. Using your finger or a brush, wet the edge of one half with a little water. Place 1 tablespoon of filling in the centre of each wrapper, then fold the edges together, pressing in little pleats to seal. Repeat until all the filling is used, refrigerating each batch of dumplings on a tray until you are ready to cook, so they don't become soggy.

At this point, the dumplings can also be frozen. Place them on a tray in a single layer without touching each other, then seal in a bag or in airtight containers. Use them within a month or two, slowly thawing them in the fridge overnight before cooking.

When ready to serve, combine all the dipping sauce ingredients in a bowl.

Heat a large non-stick frying pan over a high heat. Add the oil and heat, then add half the dumplings, pleated side up (alternatively, you could cook them all in two large frying pans at the same time). Cook until deep golden on the bottom, about 3 minutes. For each batch of dumplings, whisk half the flour into the half the water and add to the pan. Place a tight-fighting lid on the pan, or cover with another frying pan. Cook until the water has evaporated, about 8 minutes – but take a peek after 5 minutes. Once the liquid has gone, remove the lid and keep cooking briefly until you can see a lacy golden crust across the pan; it's important to watch closely at this point.

Turn off the heat and sit for 30 seconds, then use a spatula to carefully unstick the crust and slide the whole thing onto a plate. If you're not using two pans, cook the remaining dumplings in the same way. Serve immediately, with the dipping sauce on the side; a splash of hot chilli oil is delicious, too.

Make it different
Pork, wombok & ginger dumplings. Make these by following the filling recipe (right).

With other proteins. Change the protein mix in this to your liking: use just prawn (shrimp) or just chicken, or use crabmeat or minced (ground) pork.

Corn chowder with potato & dill (GF)(V)

Corn chowder is often dressed up with chicken or seafood, but here it is in its simplest form. Well, you could make it even simpler, but this version is so luscious and soothing, with an underlying savoury richness from the cheese. **Serves 4**

120 g (4½ oz) butter
1 large onion, finely chopped
1 leek, white part only,
    finely sliced
2 garlic cloves, finely grated
1 teaspoon cumin seeds
3 boiling (waxy) potatoes
    (such as desiree or Dutch
    cream) peeled, finely sliced

4 corn cobs, kernels stripped
    (about 450 g/1 lb)
1 litre (34 fl oz/4 cups)
    Classic white vegetable
    stock (p. 51), or White
    or Golden chicken stock
    (p. 54)
4 dill sprigs, fronds chopped,
    plus extra to garnish

125 g (4½ oz/1 cup) grated
    cheddar, or gruyère
1 teaspoon smoked paprika
sour cream, to serve

Staples
S&P

Melt half the butter in a wide-based saucepan over a medium heat. Add the onion and leek and sweat until softened and lightly golden, about 8 minutes. Add the garlic and cumin seeds and cook until fragrant, about 1 minute.

Add the potato slices and remaining butter, stirring to coat. Cook until translucent, about 3 minutes, then season with salt and pepper and stir in the corn.

Pour in the stock and bring to the boil, then reduce the heat and simmer for 15 minutes.

Blitz the soup with a stick blender, but don't take it too far, as you still want a little texture. Add the dill and simmer for 1 minute. Stir in the cheddar and paprika. Adjust the seasoning to taste and serve with a little sour cream and extra dill on top.

Make it different
With a protein. Add some cooked crabmeat, flaked hot-smoked fish or shredded poached chicken at the end to warm through.

With parsley. Instead of dill, use parsley.

Corn with chilli & lime glaze (GF)(V)

In a large saucepan, place 4 halved corn cobs, 3 sliced garlic cloves, 2 teaspoons smoked paprika, 1 tablespoon salt flakes and 1 tablespoon caster (superfine) sugar. Add water to just cover. Simmer for 8 minutes, then remove the corn and return the pan to the heat to reduce by half over a high heat. Add 100 g (3½ oz) unsalted butter, and 2 sliced green chillies and cook to thicken. Return the corn to the pan, toss to coat, then squeeze over the juice of 1 lime. Great at any barbecue, with salads or with Mexican-style dishes.

Chicken, corn & noodle soup

This soup is a hybrid of a silky Asian chicken and corn soup, and a more European chicken noodle soup. And it is about the simplest version that I make. Building the broth from the chicken leg quarters means you don't need stock on hand, and it yields a full-flavoured result because of the ratio of meat (using bones would require a lot more time to extract any depth of flavour). **Serves 6**

50 g (1¾ oz) butter
2½ tablespoons extra-virgin
    olive oil
½ onion, finely diced
3 large garlic cloves, finely
    sliced
6 cm (2½ in) piece of fresh
    ginger, finely diced
1 celery stalk, cut lengthways
    in thirds, then finely sliced
2 corn cobs, kernels stripped

120 g (4½ oz) spaghettini
2 tablespoons cornflour
    (cornstarch), dissolved in
    2 tablespoons water
3 eggs, lightly whisked
1 teaspoon sesame oil
1 tablespoon soy sauce

Chicken broth
2 chicken leg quarters
½ onion, skin on
3 garlic cloves

1 vegetable stock (bouillon)
    cube
1 teaspoon white
    peppercorns, or
    black peppercorns

Staples
S&P

Add all the broth ingredients to a large saucepan and cover with water – about 2 litres (68 fl oz/ 8 cups). Bring to a simmer and cook for 40 minutes, then strain off the broth. Set the chicken quarters aside until cool enough to handle, then pick off and roughly shred the meat.

Heat the butter and oil in a saucepan over a medium heat. Add the onion, garlic and ginger and sweat for a couple of minutes, until softening. Add the celery and sauté for about 5 minutes. Add the corn, season with salt and pepper and cook, stirring, for about 2 minutes.

Pour in the broth and snap the pasta into the pan. Bring to a simmer and cook for 5 minutes. Add the chicken meat and simmer for 2 minutes.

Stir the cornflour slurry through, then pour in the beaten eggs, stirring constantly. As soon as the soup thickens and the egg has set in ribbons, ladle into bowls, drizzle each one with the sesame oil and soy sauce and serve.

Make it a meal
Add chicken meatballs, such as the Japanese-style chicken meatballs (p. 251), and allow to heat through before serving.

Corn, black bean & pomegranate salad (GF) (V) (VG)

I'm torn between calling this a salad or a salsa. It is almost one of those salads that I like to call condiment salads, which are more substantial than a sauce, but a bit too intensely flavoured to serve as a standalone lunch. This one, though, you could enjoy either way. The pomegranate seeds add a surprise texture and sour–sweet zing, which is just stupendously good with the sweetness of corn. **Serves 4–6**

Pair with

Serve in a tortilla with avocado, sour cream and slow-cooked pork, beef or chicken, or grilled or fried fish fillets dusted with ground cumin.

Spoon over cooked cracked freekeh or Baked buttered rice (p. 384) with yoghurt.

Serve as a side for flour-dusted and fried fish fillets, such as flathead, with a wedge of iceberg lettuce heart.

3 corn cobs, husks and silks removed
400 g (14 oz) cooked black turtle beans, either from a tin, drained and well rinsed, or cooked from 250 g (9 oz) dried beans (see p. 371)
1 red capsicum (bell pepper), finely diced
1 poblano chilli, or jalapeño or long green chilli, very finely diced
1 ripe, fleshy tomato, finely diced

1 salad onion, very finely diced
½ pomegranate, seeds reserved
10 mint leaves, very finely sliced
5 coriander (cilantro) sprigs, chopped, stems and all

Lime & pomegranate dressing
80 ml (2½ fl oz/⅓ cup) extra-virgin olive oil
juice of ½ pomegranate
juice of 1 lime

1 large garlic clove, finely grated
1 tablespoon white-wine vinegar, or sherry vinegar
1 tablespoon dried Mexican oregano, or dried oregano
1 teaspoon ground coriander
1 teaspoon ground cumin
½ teaspoon smoked paprika

Staples
S&P

Heat a barbecue grill or chargrill pan on high.

Grill the corn cobs for 6–8 minutes, rotating them to cook evenly. When cool enough to handle, slice off the kernels and set aside.

Combine the dressing ingredients well.

Add all the remaining salad ingredients to a bowl with the cooled corn. Season with salt and pepper, pour the dressing over and toss together. Serve within an hour or so, to keep the flavours fresh.

Cucumber

My daughter Amber is addicted to cucumbers. 'I *have* eaten, Mum. I had two cucumbers!' Two to three cucumbers a day, every day, that's up to twenty-one cucumbers a week, over 1000 a year. And that's just her. We all love cucumbers in my house. Amber loves the refreshment of them, as do I, plus that addictive slippery crunch. They are such a common vegetable, but far from mundane.

If cucumbers were just good for snacking and salads I'd still be in their thrall, but they also make extraordinary pickles (see opposite), can be marinated and even cooked. I particularly love them with something sour, so sousing in vinegar or citrus juices – and always plenty of salt and pepper – is a favourite, with the cool refreshment of the cucumber working so well with the acidity.

You can add chunks of cucumber to a prawn (shrimp) stir-fry for the last 30 seconds, so they still retain crunch, and they're delicious dropped into a soup such as Tom yum (p. 201) or a fish curry at the last minute; you want the cucumber to warm through but still be crunchy. It might take a bit of mental retraining to accept cooked cucumber, but trust me.

Mostly, it is the cooling crunchy quality of cucumber that is its strength; it speaks to warm weather and hot food, laced through yoghurt for Tzatziki (p. 507) or Raita (p. 98) for chilli relief, piled into a Greek or Thai salad, stuffed into a spicy bánh mì, or even slipped into a cool glass of Pimm's or a gin and tonic. And cucumbers preserve so well, too, making them staples through the cooler months, lending tang to a plate of charcuterie, a roast beef sandwich or pulled pork roll. So many uses! Why persist with floury tasteless tomatoes in winter – up the cucumber quotient instead.

I've been known to make a Greek-style salad laden with cucumbers on the road while filming. I'm usually armed with a bottle of locally sourced extra-virgin olive oil and olives (I'll always buy them when travelling), so a salad isn't too hard to muster, and it's miles better than eating yet another burger. In fact, salads like this sustained me through my apprenticeship as a poor trainee, watching *Rage* after a long service and soaking up the dressing with a chunk of stale – but excellent – bread pocketed from the restaurant. And they sustain me to this day.

Cucumbers come in many shapes and sizes, with the most common perhaps being the long, thin telegraph cucumber (also called a continental cucumber or English cucumber), which is typically sold sheathed in plastic. The shorter and thicker-skinned Lebanese cucumber, as I know it (and as others know as a Persian cucumber), has taken more real estate at my local markets, and it's my go-to cucumber. The larger and deep-green version with firm bumps and large seeds is more common in other countries and is loosely known as a slicing cucumber, though it is the product of different varieties. There are also many types of pickling cucumbers, with their distinctive shape and knobbly skin, which can be harvested in an array of sizes.

Apple cucumbers are round to oval with yellowish-green skin that is quite tough; the flesh is crisp, and the seeds are large. Armenian cucumbers are long, pale green and thin-skinned, with corrugated stripes running their entire length that look quite decorative when sliced. They have a gentle cucumber flavour, though they are not actually a cucumber at all, but rather a species of muskmelon. For the cook, however, they are firmly cucumbers.

I can sometimes buy 'wild cucumbers', although I'm pretty certain they're not foraged from the wild. (There is actually a member of the cucumber family that is commonly referred to as 'wild cucumber', but it is quite a tenacious weed with inedible fruit.) They are typically dark-skinned and quite curly. I suspect only the straight ones are selected to be plastic wrapped and sold at supermarkets; these are telegraph (long) cucumber rejects, in other words, and therefore quite perfect in my book.

Pair with

Cucumbers love tomatoes, fennel, onion, mint, coriander (cilantro), dill, watercress and oregano, as well as sour cream, yoghurt, crème fraîche and salty cheese such as feta and haloumi. Extra-virgin olive oil, sesame oil, salt, and both white and black pepper enhance cucumber so much; they're also complemented by miso paste, seaweed, sichuan pepper, peanuts and fish sauce. Match with pork, duck and seafood.

Crunchy lacto-fermented dill pickles GF V VG

This is a European-style pickle with a distinctly satisfying crunch. Fermenting guru Sharon Flynn, from The Fermentary, taught me that tannin is the secret to crispness in a pickled cucumber, and it works wonderfully well. Tannin can be added to the brine by adding fresh vine leaves or oak leaves, or a few loose black or green tea leaves, to the jar(s). Boil water with a ratio of 2½ tablespoons fine sea salt to 1 litre (34 fl oz/4 cups) water, then cool completely; this will help to shed any chlorine from tap water. If using filtered water, simply heat enough to dissolve the salt. Pack sterilised 1 litre (34 fl oz/4 cup) jars with firm, crunchy cucumbers; to each, add a few split garlic cloves, 3 teaspoons black and/or white peppercorns, 1 teaspoon white mustard seeds, a few dill fronds and ½ teaspoon black or green tea leaves (or a vine or oak leaf). Top with the brine, making sure the cucumbers are submerged, then seal. Stand at room temperature – ideally at 15–22°C (59–72°F) – out of sunlight for 5–10 days; fermenting will happen more quickly when the ambient temperature is warm. Each day, release the gas by opening the lids, then seal again. Check after 5 days, to see if the cucumbers taste pickled enough. Once ready, refrigerate to slow the process down.

Wrapping telegraph (long) cucumbers in plastic extends their shelf life by about a week. I'm not sure this directly translates to a reduction in food waste, but I don't really want my food wrapped in plastic. Buy fresh, use fresh. The need to extend the life of a product by that much also just suggests to me that it has probably travelled a bit to get to my table. Plant-based wrappers are a significantly better solution, though it's still another layer of manufacturing that to me seems largely unnecessary.

When selecting cucumbers, look for firm-feeling specimens. Take the time to check them all over, as soft spots can be hidden on otherwise taut-skinned cucumbers. The skin should look vibrant and not dull, with larger specimens best avoided, as the seeds can become tough. If your cucumber is wrapped in plastic, be especially diligent about checking for softness – the plastic can conceal issues, especially at the tips.

Also see

Cucumber, celery heart & herb salad 240

Sweet pickled cucumber 413

Cucumber & wakame salad 415

Kohlrabi & cucumber salad with lemon yoghurt dressing 549

Pickled arame salad 622

Preparing cucumbers

A cucumber doesn't need much done to it aside from what is required for a recipe. Trim both ends only as much as you have to, and that's about it. Some varieties have tough skin and may be better peeled, but for most it's unnecessary, and simply a cook's choice. There are times when I prefer to peel a cucumber, then halve and deseed. It's a choice of texture and also how much liquid you might want, or not want, in a dish. Again, cook's choice. There are cucumber varieties with larger seeds, and more mature ones will typically have larger and sometimes quite tough seeds, so it may be best to discard these; the simplest method is to halve lengthways, then run a spoon down the length.

Pickled Lebanese cucumbers GF V VG

This quick and simple pickle is ready in a couple of hours. It's all about gentle flavour and texture, rather than preservation, so it needs to be eaten on the day of making. The cucumbers can be sliced, cut into chunks or left whole. You can also pickle baby cucumbers whole. **Serves 6**

6 Lebanese (short) cucumbers, or 12 mini Lebanese cucumbers	200 ml (7 fl oz) white-wine vinegar	130 g (4½ oz) caster (superfine) sugar
2 teaspoons salt flakes	3 tablespoons lemon juice	500 ml (17 fl oz/2 cups) water
	2 tablespoons lime juice	

Peel the cucumbers lightly. If you sink your peeler in to its full extent, you'll dig too deep into the flesh and waste a lot, so be gentle. Split them lengthways and coat with the salt. Set aside for 1 hour.

In a bowl, combine the vinegar, lemon juice and lime juice. Add the sugar and stir until dissolved – do not heat. Stir in the water until combined. Add the liquid to a vacuum bag or sealed bag.

Briefly rinse the salt off the cucumbers under running water, then dry well. Add to the bag and press as much air out as possible before sealing – this will pickle the cucumbers more evenly.

Refrigerate for 1 hour, then remove from the liquid to serve.

Pair with

Serve with prawns (shrimp) or crabmeat in a prawn cocktail-style starter.

Slice and coat with chopped herbs or gomasio as an accompaniment to pan-seared fish or grilled seafood.

Coat in some dill or mint and eat with charcuterie or smoked fish.

Slip into a sandwich or bagel with smoked salmon or gravlax (pp. 169–71).

Remove the seeds and fill with cream cheese or avocado mousse (see p. 413) and top with smoked salmon or the like.

The pickles also make excellent crudités for dips.

Japanese quick-pickled cucumber & wakame salad V VG

A quick-pickled salad like this is all about those briny, sweet and acidic pickle flavours, with the cucumber just starting to give in to the pickling medium, but holding on to its freshness as well. It makes a lovely little palate-cleanser on the side, or can be added to salads or cooked dishes. **Serves 8–10**

10 g (¼ oz) dried wakame, soaked in warm water to rehydrate, then drained	2 spring onions (scallions), white part only, finely sliced	1 teaspoon caster (superfine) sugar
3 Lebanese (short) cucumbers, sliced into 5 mm (¼ in) rounds	1½ tablespoons rice vinegar	**Staples**
	1 tablespoon mirin	S&P, SGR
	½ teaspoon salt flakes	

Chop the wakame reasonably finely and add to a bowl with the remaining ingredients. Season with salt, black pepper and a pinch of sugar. Toss, then set aside for 5 minutes before serving.

Pair with

Add to all sorts of Japanese-inspired salads.

Serve over freshly cooked rice with a piece of grilled salmon, kingfish or other fish.

Stir into freshly cooked ramen or soba noodles with Sesame dressing (p. 94).

Chilled cucumber & sesame salad with shiso & garlic chives ⓖⓥⓥⓖ

Pair with

Red glazed pork.

Steamed fish with ginger (see p. 177).

Rendang curry (p. 292).

Fish marinated with white miso (p. 184).

Mapo tofu with chicken (see p. 436).

Bashing half-frozen cucumbers with a rolling pin may not seem the most elegant manner of preparation, but the result is amazing. The extra chill makes the cucumbers shatter more readily, yielding appealing shards, and makes them even more refreshingly crisp, and strangely crunchier. This salad is also laced with garlicky sesame flavour, with a limey spike of acid. It is stunning with intense, spicy dishes. **Serves 6–8**

6 Lebanese (short) cucumbers, semi-peeled in stripes
1 handful of coriander (cilantro) leaves
10 garlic chives, or regular chives, cut into batons

5 shiso leaves, torn
2 tablespoons toasted sesame seeds

Sesame & lime dressing
2 tablespoons extra-virgin olive oil

2 tablespoons iced water
2 teaspoons sesame oil
juice of 2 limes
2 teaspoons salt flakes
½ teaspoon ground white pepper

Wrap the cucumbers in a tea towel (dish towel) and chill for 30 minutes in the freezer. Chill a large bowl and serving plate.

Add the dressing ingredients to a small bowl and combine well.

Bash the cucumbers with a rolling pin in the tea towel to smash them into shards – you want them to split and break apart, but don't pulverise them. Unwrap them and tip into the chilled bowl. Pour the dressing over and toss through well, then tip onto the chilled serving plate.

Sprinkle with the herbs and sesame seeds and serve immediately.

Tzatziki ⓖ Ⓥ

Pair with

Serve as a dip with flatbread, crudités, olives, pickled vegetables and other mezes.

Serve alongside Slow-roasted lamb shoulder (p. 304). The next day, dollop some left-over lamb with tzatziki and roll up in a flatbread with tabouleh (see p. 419) or another salad.

Smear onto a plate and top with Falafel with broad beans (p. 432).

Zucchini & haloumi fritters with burnt honey sauce (p. 673).

Not that I haven't done it, but buying ready-made tzatziki is so unnecessary. Trust me: you simply cannot buy a commercial tzatziki as good as you can make yourself. It tastes so good that people must think there's an art to it. Sure, there are some tricks, but it's devilishly simple. It will also keep well for a week, and is so cost effective. **Makes about 600 g (1 lb 5 oz)**

500 g (1 lb 2 oz/ 2 cups) Greek-style yoghurt
4 Lebanese (short) cucumbers
1 small garlic clove, finely grated

5 mint sprigs, leaves finely chopped
1 heaped teaspoon dried mint
100 ml (3½ fl oz) extra-virgin olive oil

Staples
EVOO, S&P

Hang the yoghurt in a very fine-mesh sieve or muslin (cheesecloth) for 1 hour, to drain off the excess liquid.

Grate the cucumbers coarsely, season lightly with salt and pepper, and stand in a colander or sieve for 10 minutes. Gently squeeze out the excess liquid with your hands, then add the cucumber to a bowl.

Add the garlic, fresh mint, dried mint and three-quarters of the oil. Season with salt and pepper and mix together. Fold the yoghurt through, then refrigerate for a couple of hours to let the flavours develop.

To serve, pile into a bowl and drizzle with the remaining oil.

Yoghurt, cucumber & mint salad/dip (GF)(V)

This is a chunky tzatziki, more or less – a salad and a dip, or a condiment salad, as I like to call things like this. It can be eaten as is with plenty of pitta bread, but this is my go-to with lamb, especially a slow-roasted shoulder served with pitta. **Serves 4–6**

3 large Lebanese (short) cucumbers, peeled, seeded and cut into 1 cm (½ in) dice
500 g (1 lb 2 oz/2 cups) Greek-style yoghurt

2 garlic cloves, finely grated
½ bunch of mint, leaves finely chopped
juice of ½ lemon
1½ tablespoons extra-virgin olive oil

2 teaspoons sweet paprika or ground sumac

Staples
S&P, SGR

Add the cucumber to a colander and lightly sprinkle with salt and sugar. Set aside for 10 minutes to drain off the excess water.

Combine the yoghurt, garlic, mint and lemon juice in a bowl. Season with salt and pepper and stir the oil through. Add the cucumber and combine, then serve.

Serve dusted with the paprika or sumac.

Pair with

Slow-roasted lamb shoulder (p. 304).

Byzantine salad (p. 379).

Falafel (see p. 432).

Barbecued lamb chops (see p. 303).

Koftas (pp. 249, 309) and kebabs.

Grilled fish.

Cucumber, grape & herb salad with shallot dressing (GF)(V)(VG)

This is truly one of my favourite ways of serving cucumber. The pleasure is all in the simplicity – it even works without the grapes. The secret is the way in which the cucumbers are scored and then cut thickly, so the dressing coats and the herbs stick. Whenever you need a bright refreshing salad, this will do the trick. **Serves 4–6**

3 Lebanese (short) cucumbers
3 mint sprigs, leaves torn
3 dill sprigs, fronds picked and roughly chopped
3 French tarragon, or chervil, sprigs (optional), leaves torn

20 seedless green grapes, cut into thirds

Shallot dressing
1 garlic clove, cut in half
3 French shallots, very finely sliced
1½ teaspoons salt flakes

½ teaspoon caster (superfine) sugar
3 tablespoons extra-virgin olive oil
1½ tablespoons sherry vinegar, or white wine vinegar

Semi-peel the cucumbers in stripes lengthways, then run the tines of a fork down the length all the way around to make grooves – these will catch and take up the dressing. Cut into 2.5 cm (1 in) chunks and set aside.

For the dressing, rub the garlic halves around the inside of a large bowl several times, then reserve for another use. Add the shallot, salt and sugar and pinch together with your hands, then set aside for a couple of minutes to soften. Add the oil and vinegar, mixing well.

Toss the herbs through. Add the cucumber, then the grapes, crushing some to add to the dressing. Toss together and serve.

Pair with

Roast chicken or lamb shoulder, baked fish or grilled prawns (shrimp).

Serve simply with burrata or sliced fresh mozzarella.

Lamb souvlaki (p. 312).

Horta or wild weed pie.

Crunchy lacto-fermented vegetables (GF)(V)(VG)

The dill pickles recipe (see p. 505) can be used on all kinds of vegetables, from green beans to carrots, fennel and cauliflower. You could also add bay leaves, horseradish slices, caraway, fennel or celery seeds, star anise and split bird's eye chillies … whatever pleases you. I also tend to use 2 tablespoons salt per litre (34 fl oz/4 cups) of brine for softer vegetables, such as green beans, and 3 tablespoons salt for carrots and the like.

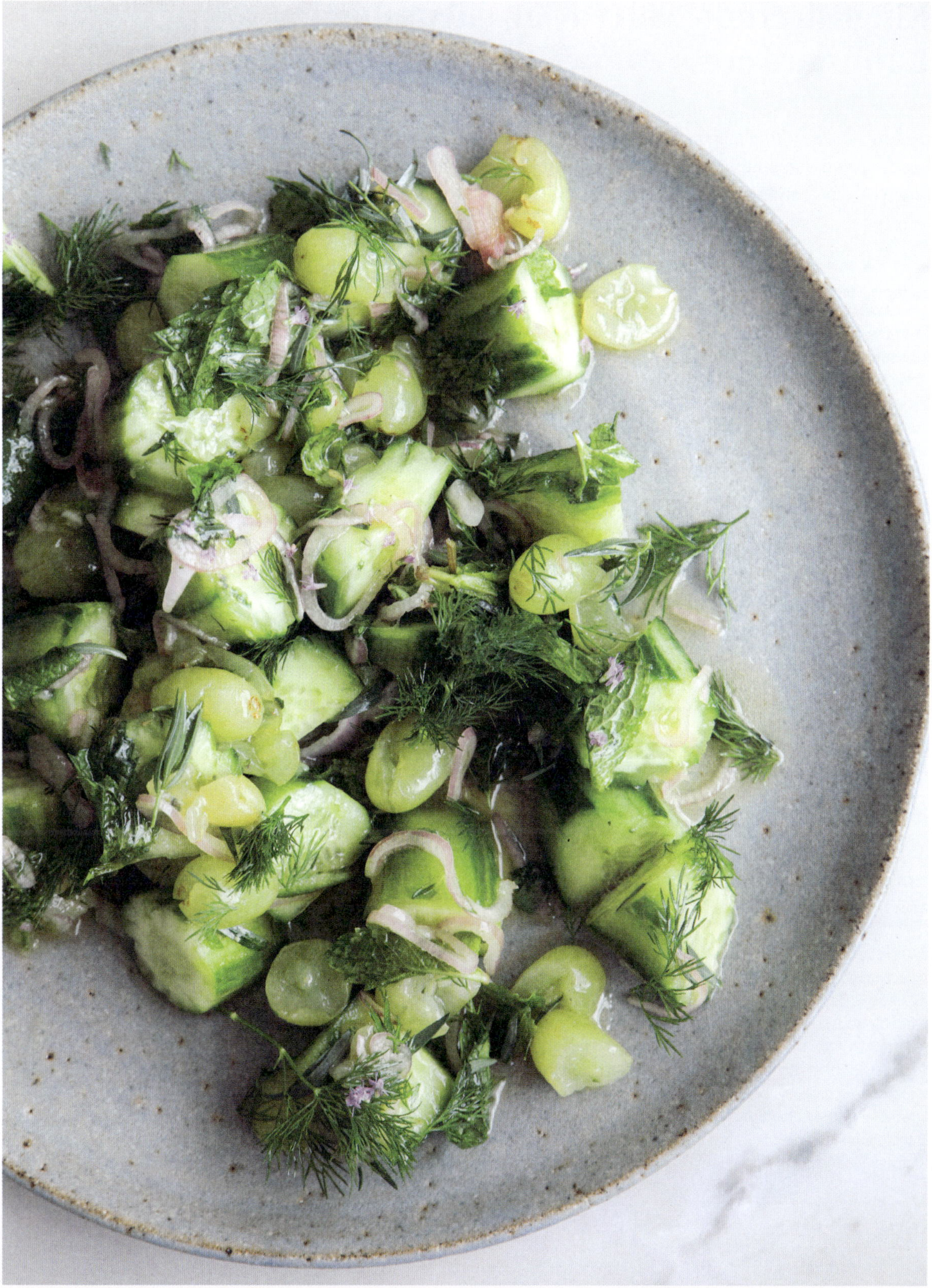

Kingfish crudo with caviar, cucumber & mustard cress ⒼⒻ

This dish is an elegant, composed ceviche. The acid in the lime juice cures the fish quickly, resulting in a textured flesh. This is a delicate, detailed and very pretty starter that relies on the flavour of exquisite extra-virgin olive oil and some careful plating to make it really sing. **Serves 4–6 as a starter**

500 g (1 lb 2 oz) mid-loin piece of sashimi-grade kingfish, salmon or ocean trout, skin and bones removed

1 Lebanese (short) cucumber, peeled, seeded and julienned

5 spring onions (scallions), white part only, finely sliced

2 handfuls of mustard cress sprouts

20 g (¾ oz) salmon roe

2 finger limes, or 1 large lime peeled and chopped into segments

Ginger, lime & olive oil dressing

125 ml (4 fl oz/½ cup) extra-virgin olive oil (use something a bit special), plus extra

10 cm (4 in) piece of fresh ginger, peeled, finely grated

and squeezed for the juice (about 1 tablespoon juice)

juice of 1 lime

1 teaspoon caster (superfine) sugar

½ teaspoon ground white pepper

Staples
S&P

Add the dressing ingredients to a bowl, season with salt, then whisk until emulsified.

Slice the kingfish like sashimi, just under 1 cm (½ in) thick. Lay flat in a dish and drizzle with half the dressing, which will marinate and cook the fish slightly. Stand for 5 minutes.

Lay the fish out on a serving plate, top with the cucumber and spring onion, then spoon the rest of the dressing over. Scatter with the cress, salmon roe and the 'caviar' from the finger limes. Drizzle with a little more oil and serve immediately.

Oyster shooters with cucumber, ginger vinegar & white pepper jelly

This sultry combination is sure to get lunch or dinner off to a good start. It's so simple to put together, and will deliver a wow factor right from the beginning. You'll need tall good-looking shot glasses to have the right impact. **Serves 6–12**

2 large Lebanese (short) cucumbers, peeled

12 large Pacific oysters, freshly shucked and detached from the shell (see p. 208)

2 long green chillies, seeds removed, finely diced

2 tablespoons Japanese ginger vinegar, or 100 ml

(3½ fl oz) brown-rice vinegar infused with pickled ginger for 3 days

12 slices pickled white ginger

12 teaspoons wasabi tobiko (flying fish roe with wasabi)

1 lime

White pepper jelly

400 ml (13½ fl oz) clear apple juice

1 teaspoon white pepper

7 leaves of gold-strength gelatine, soaked in cold water for 5 minutes

Staples
S&P

Special equipment
12 elegant shot glasses, chilled Small Parisian baller

Stir-fried cucumber with wood ear fungus & snow peas Ⓥ ⓋⒼ

Mix together ½ teaspoon sesame oil, 1 tablespoon light soy sauce, 2 teaspoons black vinegar or brown-rice vinegar and a pinch or two of sugar; set aside. Peel and deseed a telegraph (long) cucumber, then cut into 3 cm (1¼ in) chunks. Roughly chop a handful of fresh wood ear fungus, trim a handful of snow peas (mangetout), cut some garlic chives into batons and/or roughly chop some coriander (cilantro). Get a wok blisteringly hot, then pour in a splash of neutral-flavoured oil, which will shimmer. Add a smashed garlic clove and some julienned fresh ginger and stir-fry until fragrant. Add the cucumber and cook for 30 seconds, then add the other ingredients and stir-fry quickly. Serve with steamed fish, roast pork or duck.

Sesame saganaki with quick-pickled cucumber Ⓥ

In a bowl combine 3 Lebanese (short) cucumbers, peeled and finely sliced, 1 long green chilli (seeds removed and finely sliced), 3 finely sliced spring onions (scallions, white part only), 2 teaspoons sherry vinegar, 1 teaspoon caster (superfine) sugar and 1 teaspoon salt flakes. Stand for 5 minutes, then mix through 2 teaspoons nigella seeds and the chopped fronds of 3 dill sprigs. Heat a large frying pan over a medium heat, then add 100 ml (3½ fl oz) extra-virgin olive oil. Spread 2 tablespoons white sesame seeds on a plate. Slice kefalograviera cheese into 4 slices 1.5–2 cm (½– ¾ in) thick. In batches, dip the cheese slices in water, shake off the excess, then coat both sides in the sesame seeds. Once the oil is hot, fry the slices until golden on both sides, about 2 minutes each side. Serve hot, with lemon cheeks, and the cucumber pickle on the side. Serves 4.

Cucumber sandwiches (V)

An old-fashioned favourite of mine, which my mother sometimes made when I was young. I loved them. I have sent them to school in my girls' lunchboxes, but they don't quite get the same reaction: rather a firm thumbs down. You need brown bread – soft and delicious – spread generously on both sides with quality butter that's been smashed up with snipped chives. Peel the cucumber (choose your favourite variety) and slice finely, then layer up on top of the butter, season with a little salt and lots of white or black pepper, then close firmly with the other slice. To be faithful to my memory, you'll also need to trim off the crusts and cut into triangles. To make these a little bit fancier, top the cucumber with some picked watercress and serve with freshly shucked oysters or cooked prawns (shrimp) – heaven!

To make the jelly, heat the apple juice in a small non-reactive saucepan to just below boiling. Add the white pepper and a pinch of salt. Take off the heat and add the gelatine, squeezed of water, stirring to dissolve. Pour into a flat-sided rectangular dish, so the jelly is about 1 cm (½ in) deep. Refrigerate for 1 hour.

Using a small Parisian baller, make tiny pearls of cucumber flesh, avoiding the seeds. (If you don't have a Parisian baller, you could peel and deseed the cucumber, then finely dice.)

Pile the cucumber pearls into the shot glasses. Follow with an oyster and a little of its salty juices, then drop on some green chilli.

Remove the jelly from the fridge. Slice the jelly lengthways, and then across into dice. Carefully place the jelly cubes on top of the oysters. Drizzle with the ginger vinegar. Top with the ginger slices and roe, then squeeze the lime over. Chill for 5 minutes before serving.

Cucumber & lime granita with gin jelly, yoghurt sorbet & minted cucumber (GF)

This is the lightest and most refreshing of summery desserts, leaning heavily on those most refreshing of things – cucumber, mint, lime and gin. There's a much simpler drink in that combination, but the icy sophistication here is somewhat compelling, and it's actually pretty easy to make. This doesn't need to be dessert, of course; serve it as a little pick-me-up at the start of an event, or as a refresher somewhere in the middle. **Serves 8**

	Granita	Gin jelly
150 g (5½ oz) caster (superfine) sugar	3 telegraph (long) cucumbers	8 leaves of gold-strength gelatine
100 ml (3½ fl oz) water	100 g (3½ oz) caster (superfine) sugar, plus an extra 1½ tablespoons	200 ml (7 fl oz) filtered water
1 telegraph (long) cucumber		300 ml (10 fl oz) aromatic gin
1 handful of mint leaves, finely shredded	zest of 2 limes	**Special equipment**
500 ml (17 fl oz/2 cups) yoghurt sorbet	100 ml (3½ fl oz) lime juice	*Small Parisian baller*

For the granita, grate the cucumbers into a large bowl. Sprinkle the extra 1½ tablespoons sugar over and set aside for 10 minutes. Strain the liquid through a fine-mesh sieve, into a bowl, squeezing out the juice with your hands. Discard the solids.

In a small saucepan, gently warm the lime zest, lime juice, and remaining 100 g (3½ oz) sugar over a low heat, stirring until the sugar has dissolved – don't let this get too warm or the flavour will dull. Tip into the bowl of cucumber juice and stir to combine. Pour into a shallow dish, then cover the granita and freeze for 5–6 hours or overnight.

For the gin jelly, add the gelatine leaves to a small jug or bowl of cold water and set aside for 5 minutes. Gently warm the water in a small saucepan and take off the heat. Add the gelatine, squeezed of excess water, then stir to dissolve. Add the gin and stir to combine. Pour into eight serving glasses and refrigerate for about 3 hours, until set.

Meanwhile, add the sugar and water to a small saucepan and bring to the boil. Stir until the sugar has dissolved, then refrigerate until cold and syrupy.

When ready to serve, use a small Parisian baller to scoop out balls of cucumber, into a bowl. Add the mint and enough of the chilled sugar syrup to coat. Toss gently and add to the serving glasses, along with small scoops of sorbet. Scratch the surface of the granita with a fork until fluffy, then spoon on the top of each glass. Serve immediately.

Greek salad GF V

A lot of Greek-style salads are made in our house; the girls automatically start looking for tomatoes and cucumbers if a salad is required. There are few rules with a Greek salad (the Greeks have more than one salad, but you know what I'm referring to). The starting point is tomato, lots of cucumber, feta, onion, kalamata olives (or whatever we have), dried Greek oregano (rigani) and onion. The onion might be red onion, even spring onion (scallion), but mostly I use white salad onions, soaked in water to reduce the astringency, then thoroughly dried. I'll use radish if we have any, too, and in winter, wedges of fennel sometimes get tucked in on the side. I like to peel the cucumbers in strips and then cut into chunks, and the tomato into chunks, too ... but do what pleases you. Good extra-virgin olive oil makes a big difference, which I combine with half the amount of wine vinegar, a smashed garlic clove to add perfume (don't eat that), plenty of salt and pepper – and a splash of ouzo or pastis if I'm feeling fancy. I'll always dress the salad and let it sit for a little just to let the flavours meld. Sometimes I drop slabs of feta on top, and sometimes crumble them through ... again, it's up to you.

A quick pantry snack

Tinned sardines can take on a new life in seconds. Tip them from the tin, draining off the never-very-good oil, and into a small bowl. Dose them up with extra-virgin olive oil and sherry vinegar. Throw in some finely sliced chilli and peeled, finely shaved cucumber, grind in plenty of pepper, then pile up on your favourite cracker. An icy cold beer is advised.

An inspiration from ajo blanco

Smoked salmon & cucumber canapés GF

Run the tines of a fork down the length of 4 Lebanese (short) cucumbers, all the way around to make grooves, then cut into 2.5 cm (1 in) thick rounds. Using a teaspoon or melon baller, scoop out some of the soft, seedy core, to create little cucumber bowls. Discard (or consume) the scrapings. In a separate bowl, mix 2½ tablespoons room-temperature cream cheese with the juice of ½ lemon using a fork. Dice 4 slices smoked salmon, and cut another 2 slices into 1 cm (½ in) wide strips. To the cream cheese mixture, add the diced salmon, 1 tablespoon grated fresh horseradish (or unsweetened horseradish from a jar), 10 finely chopped chives and ½ teaspoon cayenne pepper and mix well. Use a teaspoon or small piping (icing) bag to fill the cucumber bowls with the cream cheese mixture. Top each with a salmon strip rolled into a scroll. Finish with a dill frond (you'll need 2 sprigs), a squeeze of lemon, an extra sprinkle of cayenne pepper, some salmon roe and another fine dill frond. Makes 14–16 pieces.

An inspiration from ajo blanco

From Andalusia in Spain, gazpacho is the world's most famous cold soup. But Andalusia's other significant cold soup – yes, they have more than one – is ajo blanco, which is arguably the precursor for gazpacho. In its simplest form, it is made from bread, almonds, garlic (ajo), oil and vinegar. Sometimes cucumber makes its way in, and sometimes grapes; I like generous amounts of both. This is my take on the soup, but used as a sauce for an elegant dinner party dish. Preparing the ajo blanco the day before is preferable for the flavours to cohere, making it even easier for entertaining. **Serves 12**

170 g (6 oz) blanched almonds
1 garlic clove, peeled
550 ml (18½ fl oz) water
2 Lebanese (short) cucumbers, peeled and roughly chopped
40 small seedless green grapes
1 long green chilli, roughly chopped
3 slices soft white bread, crusts removed, roughly torn

100 ml (3½ fl oz) extra-virgin olive oil
2 tablespoons sherry vinegar
12 cooked king prawn (shrimp) tails, thickly sliced

To serve
torn Sourdough bread (p. 847) chunks, toasted in the oven until crisp on the outside but soft inside, crushed
sliced green grapes

spring onions (scallions), white part only, very finely sliced
a few sprigs of watercress
roughly smashed toasted almonds
green hot sauce (such as green Tabasco; optional)

Staples
EVOO, LMN, S&P

In a small saucepan, bring the blanched almonds, garlic and 200 ml (7 fl oz) of the water to the boil over a medium heat. Cook until the water has mostly evaporated, about 4 minutes. Set aside to cool.

Add the mixture to a blender with the cucumber, grapes, chilli, bread, oil, vinegar and remaining 350 ml (12 fl oz) water. Pulse to start, then blitz until smooth. Season to taste with salt and pepper, then chill for 2 hours, or preferably overnight, for the flavours to infuse.

Squeeze a little lemon over the prawns and drizzle with oil, then arrange in shallow bowls or plates with some toasted bread, sliced grapes, spring onion and watercress. Spoon some of the chilled ajo blanco on the side, then sprinkle with smashed almonds. Finish with a drizzle of oil and a splash of hot sauce, if using, and serve.

Make it different
With other seafood. The ajo blanco pairs happily with lots of different seafood. Seared scallops, lobster or crabmeat would also be excellent companions.

Make it vegan VG
Skip the seafood altogether and serve this as a soup with the same garnishes.

Eggplant

Mention the word eggplant, or aubergine, and for many of us, a large, deeply shiny, round-bottomed purplish-black ovoid vegetable immediately springs to mind – but in fact, eggplants come in a range of shapes and hues, from pea-sized pods to ribbed tomato-like fruits, to the dark, slender fingers of the Lebanese version, to striped heirloom varieties and long, skinny gourds, with colours ranging from black through to white, green, red, orange, purple ... and their uses are just as diverse. Originating in India, they occupy an important place in many cuisines across Asia, the Middle East and the Mediterranean. And while they're not particularly forgiving – an undercooked eggplant has about as much charm as a raw potato – handled with just a little care, they are incredibly versatile and one of my absolute favourite vegetables. You can steam, boil, fry, grill, roast, braise, stuff, pickle and puree them, and they take to European and North African flavours just as well as they do to those from China, Japan and South-East Asia.

My kitchen bench is often adorned with a large bowl of glossy eggplants, as I find them quite beautiful. When selecting eggplants, look for bright, unblemished specimens with smooth, glossy and taut skin. They should feel heavy in the hand, and not hollow or soft. Bought in good condition, they will keep quite well in the crisper, but are best used reasonably promptly – like most vegetables.

The recipes in this book are all based around the large, egg-shaped, deeply purple eggplant most of us are familiar with, though that doesn't mean they are limited to it. Just be aware that some varieties are best suited to specific dishes or methods that have evolved over time. I remember first having the tiny pea eggplants in a curry by chef David Thompson, one of Australia's foremost proponents of Thai cuisine. Their bitterness made revelatory sense with the fierce heat and underlying sweetness, but good luck making baba ghanoush from them! Usually, someone who sells more exotic specimens will be able to help out here. So, as always, ask questions.

Also see

Orecchiette with eggplant, oregano, balsamic & ricotta 132–3

Summer vegetable lasagne 136

Lamb koftas baked with tomato & smoky eggplant, with pine nuts & parsley 309–10

Moussaka 310–1

Lamb & eggplant karahi curry 318

Caponata bianco with toasted walnuts 489

Capsicum & eggplant salad 464

Ratatouille 672

Pair with

Eggplant (aubergine) loves good olive oil and the acidity of lemon, plain yoghurt, vinegar, balsamic glaze or vinegar, and the sweetly tart tang of pomegranate molasses. It shines in tomato sauces, and takes to spices very well – cumin, allspice, white and black pepper, cinnamon, fresh or dried chilli, curry flavours and shrimp paste. Sesame and tahini are natural companions, as are many fresh herbs such as parsley, oregano, coriander (cilantro), mint, basil and Thai basil; so too is dried oregano, especially the wild Greek variety. Garlic, onion, shallots, spring onions (scallions) and capsicum (bell pepper) hum in pretty much any form. Walnuts, pine nuts and almonds pair well, and peanuts sing if working a spicy Asian angle. I love the richness of lamb with eggplant. Fish also works beautifully, especially varieties with large flaky textures and big flavours – think tuna, swordfish, mackerel, blue-eye trevalla or hapuka, for example.

Preparing eggplant

The old wisdom used to be that eggplants needed to be salted before cooking, either by submerging in brine for 30–45 minutes and then draining and drying, or by liberally covering the cut flesh with salt and leaving for 30–45 minutes, then washing and drying. Neither is typically necessary. Salting removes bitterness, but bitterness is not generally a problem with the eggplants that are sold today (apart from the pea-shaped Thai varieties whose bitterness is a prized foil in curries and soups). However, if the seeds are dark, it means the eggplant is mature, and salting is recommended. Some heirloom or less familiar cultivars may also need salting, so cook a small slice first if you're unsure. Salting reduces moisture, which means that the flesh won't soak up oil quite as readily, and the eggplant will cook a little more quickly. So, this becomes a time-based and personal decision.

The only inedible parts of the eggplant are the stem and green collar, so they just need to be trimmed if slicing or dicing, though they can be left on if roasting or grilling whole. Whether you're frying or grilling or steaming, just make sure that you cook the eggplant fully, as it can be unpleasant and somewhat of an irritant to the palate and tongue. (Some Thai varieties are traditionally served raw in salads, so, again, just be aware of the cultivar that you are using.) Eggplant is generally at its best immediately after cooking, with its fluffy, pearly texture changing as it cools.

Raw eggplant really acts like a sponge, and you can go through a lot of oil in the process of frying. A hot pan and hot oil will help with this, sealing the flesh quickly and keeping some oil in the pan to help with the cooking. If you're grilling eggplant, brush slices with oil just before they hit the (hot) grill, or they will soak up the oil before the cooking starts.

Grilled eggplant with tahini & yoghurt dressing, pomegranate, chilli & mint GF V

Eggplant is beautiful cooked on the grill, the char accentuating its meatiness, which takes to spice and acidity extremely well. This is a simple and pretty salad of bold flavours. **Serves 6–8**

4 large eggplants
  (aubergines), cut
  lengthways into slices
  2 cm (¾ in) thick
2 teaspoons cumin seeds
300 g (10½ oz) plain yoghurt

2 tablespoons tahini
2 garlic cloves, finely grated
juice of 1 lemon
¼ bunch of mint, leaves
  picked
1 long green chilli, sliced

1 long red chilli, sliced
  (optional)
½ pomegranate, seeds
  reserved
pomegranate molasses,
  to serve

Staples
EVOO, S&P

Preheat a grill pan or barbecue grill on high.

Brush the eggplant slices with oil and season with salt and pepper. Grill for a few minutes on each side, until scorched and tender but still holding their shape. Lay them out separately to cool.

Using a mortar and pestle, roughly grind the cumin seeds with two good pinches of salt. Add the yoghurt, tahini, garlic and lemon juice and mix well.

Lay the eggplant on a serving plate and spoon the dressing over. Scatter with the mint, chillies and pomegranate seeds, then drizzle with a little pomegranate molasses and some more oil. This salad is best made near serving time.

Make it different
Roasted pumpkin with tahini & yoghurt dressing, pomegranate, chilli & mint. GF V
Instead of eggplant (aubergine), use roasted pumpkin (winter squash) wedges.

Eggplant puree with chilli oil & walnuts GF V VG

Preheat the oven to 200°C (400°F) fan-forced. Cut 2 large eggplants (aubergines) in half lengthways and score the flesh deeply, in slashes about 2.5 cm (1 in) apart. Coat the cut surfaces of the eggplant with extra-virgin olive oil and season with salt. Place on a baking tray, cut side up, and roast for about 30 minutes, until soft and collapsing. Set aside to cool. Scoop out the eggplant flesh and puree in a food processor. Add the juice of 1 lemon, 2 handfuls torn mint leaves, and season to taste with salt and pepper. Gradually add enough oil to create a smooth and silky paste. Drizzle the puree with some Chilli oil (see p. 86), scatter over 80 g (2¾ oz/¾ cup) roughly chopped toasted walnuts, and serve with lemon on the side. Delicious served as a bed for tuna, swordfish, snapper and blue-eye trevalla, as well as lamb chops and grilled haloumi.

Pair with

Spiced barbecued meat or poultry.

Serve as part of any Middle Eastern-style spread.

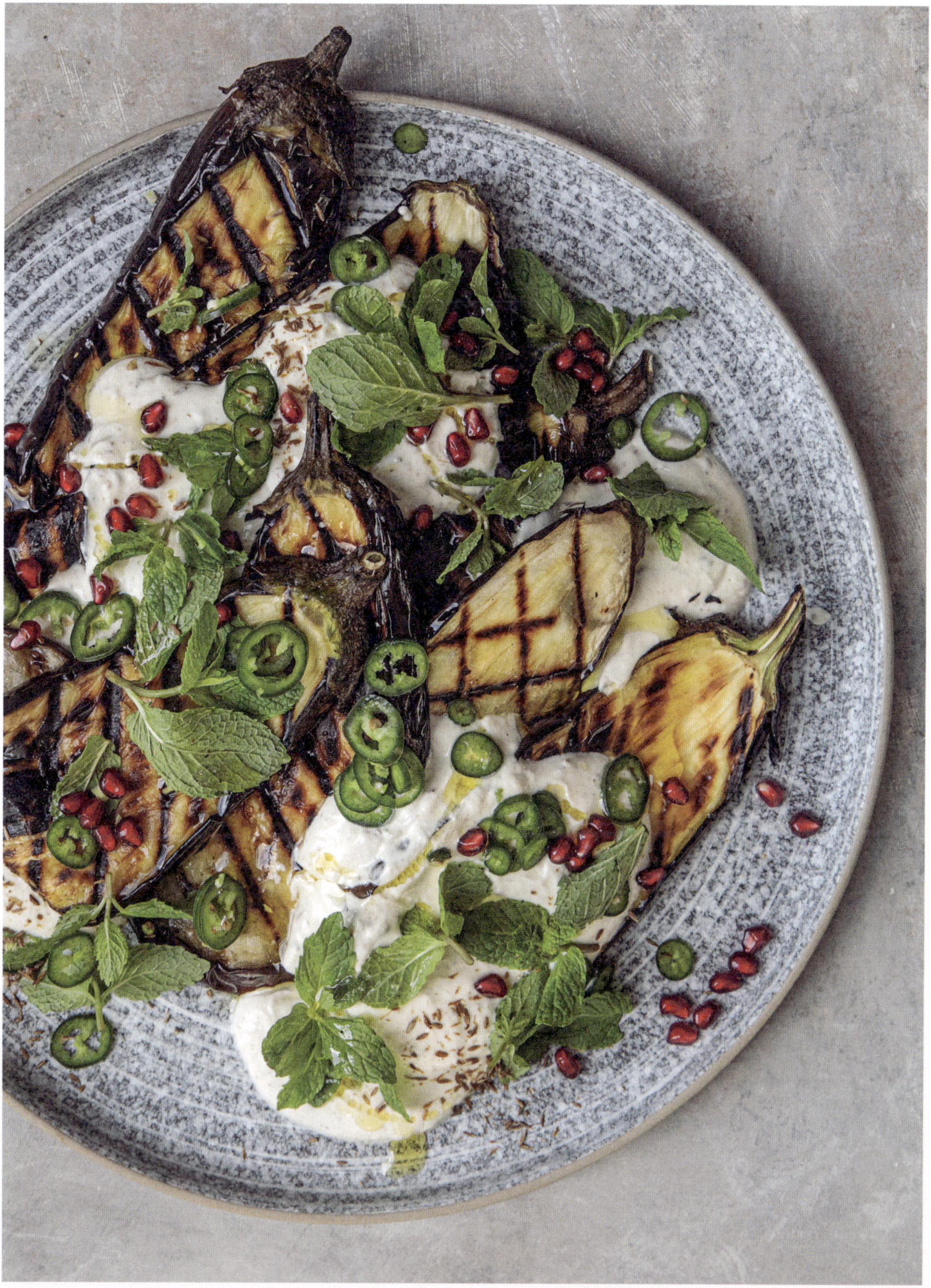

Eggplant, sesame, egg, olive & radish salad (GF)(V)

This salad echoes the flavours in one of the world's best sandwiches – the Israeli pitta called sabich, which is stuffed with fried eggplant (aubergine), hard-boiled eggs, chopped salad and a tahini dressing. It presents beautifully, especially if you go the extra step and deep-fry the eggplant skin to create a wispy black halo across the plate. **Serves 4–6**

4 eggs, at room temperature
1 large eggplant (aubergine), peeled and cut into 2 cm (¾ in) dice
juice of ½ lemon
100 g (3½ oz/⅔ cup) toasted pine nuts
1 tablespoon toasted sesame seeds
60 g (2 oz/⅓ cup) black olives, pitted and roughly chopped

2 teaspoons ground sumac, plus extra to serve
1 teaspoon chilli powder
1 long green chilli, seeded and finely sliced
6 radishes, tops well washed, larger ones halved
6 mint sprigs, leaves picked
½ bunch of watercress, picked
½ white salad onion, finely sliced in rings, then soaked in iced water for 10 minutes

Dukkah (p. 13), to serve (optional)

Tahini dressing
2½ tablespoons tahini
½ garlic clove, finely grated
juice of ½ lemon
1 tablespoon water

Staples
EVOO, S&P

Add the dressing ingredients to a screw-top jar, season with salt and pepper and shake vigorously.

Lower the eggs into a small saucepan of boiling water and simmer for 6 minutes. Plunge the eggs into iced water for 5 minutes, then peel and dice as neatly as possible.

Add the eggplant and lemon juice to a saucepan of simmering salted water and cook for 10 minutes, or until tender. Drain very well, absorbing any excess liquid on paper towel.

Add the diced egg to a large bowl with the eggplant, pine nuts, sesame seeds, olives, sumac, dried and fresh chilli, a tablespoon of the dressing and a couple of tablespoons of oil. Season and combine, then tip into a bowl about 20 cm (8 in) wide and gently press.

Gently invert the bowl onto a serving plate to form a rough mound. Spoon the remaining dressing over and garnish with the radishes, mint and watercress. Pat the onion dry and scatter over the salad, followed with some extra sumac, and dukkah if using.

Make it different
Julienne the eggplant skin and fry in 2 cm (¾ in) of oil over a high heat for 1 minute, then drain; it will crisp as it cools. Use to garnish the salad.

Zaalouk (V)(VG)

A classic Moroccan dish, zaalouk is something of a cross between a cooked salad and a dip. The oil is important to protect the tomatoes while they cook, but you won't need it all in the finished dish, so keep any left-over oil for roasting vegetables, or flavour cooked pasta with it. **Serves 8**

3 eggplants (aubergines)
10 ripe roma (plum) tomatoes, cores removed
4 garlic cloves, peeled
150 ml (5 fl oz) extra-virgin olive oil

3 teaspoons ground cumin
3 teaspoons ground caraway
1 tablespoon harissa (ready-made, from a jar)
½ bunch of mint, leaves finely chopped

½ bunch of coriander (cilantro), stalks and all, finely chopped
juice of 1 lemon

Staples
S&P

Pair with

This eats so well on its own with soft Turkish-style bread or crisp pitta bread!

It is also lovely with grilled meats, chicken or fish.

Eggplant chips (V)

I've always avoided serving potato chips/fries in my restaurants. They can become a default snack, and there are enough people around frying chips. At the Melbourne Wine Room, it was polenta chips instead. At mr. wolf, it was fried eggplant (aubergine) chips with cumin and sesame, served with lemony yoghurt; and at the time of writing, it still is, as they've been immensely popular. Cut some eggplant (aubergine) into thick fingers, then dust with flour, dredge through beaten egg whites and coat with breadcrumbs and sesame seeds. Deep-fry at 170°C (340°F) for 3–4 minutes until deeply golden, then sprinkle with a mix of salt and cumin. Stack the fingers alternately, so they don't go soggy, and serve with Mayonnaise (p. 74) and plain yoghurt (mixed in equal amounts) spiked with chopped lemon segments. These are best eaten quickly, while the eggplant flesh is fluffy and glorious.

Pair with

Enjoy as a dip with flatbread, or as an accompaniment to grilled meat, poultry or fish.

Cauliflower steaks (p. 477).

A pie filled with horta or wild weeds.

Baba ghanoush GF V

Versions of this dip are found all through the Middle East and much of the Mediterranean, but the core principle is the same: well-charred eggplant (aubergine). If you don't have a fire nicely settled into ashes, the next best option is to pop a few eggplants (prick them with a fork first) directly onto the gas burners of a stove. Turn them with tongs as they blister, and once they are blackened, pop them in a moderate oven for about 20 minutes, until they collapse. Alternatively, you can grill the whole eggplant over a barbecue grill for 30 minutes, rotating constantly. Cool for 15 minutes, then cut them in half lengthways and scoop out the flesh. Stand in a colander to drain for a few minutes to wick away excess moisture, then chop roughly, or finely if you prefer. Combine the flesh with a grated garlic clove, a few good dollops of plain yoghurt, a spoonful of tahini, a glug of extra-virgin olive oil and enough lemon juice to sharpen. Season with salt and pepper and serve with flatbread, koftas (pp. 249, 309), Falafel (p. 432), or grilled or roasted lamb, fish or chicken. Or serve topped with a sprinkle of aleppo pepper, a handful of pomegranate seeds and a handful of chopped mint as part of a meze spread. You could also drizzle with black tahini at the last minute.

Preheat the oven to 200°C (400°F) fan-forced.

Scorch the eggplants directly over gas burners (or on a hot barbecue) until blackened all over, about 10 minutes. Place in a roasting tin and bake until soft, about 20 minutes. Set aside to cool, before scooping the flesh from the skin and chopping it roughly. Discard the skin.

Reduce the oven temperature to 150°C (300°F) fan-forced.

Add the tomatoes, garlic and eggplant flesh to a shallow baking dish, season with salt and pepper and drizzle the oil over. Roast for 1 hour, then stand for 20 minutes, before pulling off and discarding the tomato skins.

Heat some of the roasting oil in a saucepan over a medium heat. Add the spices and harissa and cook for about 20 seconds, until fragrant. Stir in the eggplant and tomatoes, reserving the roasting oil. Cook for 2–3 minutes, until the mixture comes together as a thick paste, then set aside to cool.

Tip the mixture into a bowl, adding a little more of the roasting oil to loosen it. Stir in the herbs and lemon juice, season to taste and serve.

Smoked eggplant soup with kefalograviera GF

This is a soup of robust flavours, rich and very satisfying. Cooking the potato for 10 minutes while stirring may seem a little laborious, but it's what gives this soup a super-silky texture and mouthfeel, which works beautifully with all that cream, butter and umami-rich chicken stock. **Serves 6–8**

4 eggplants (aubergines)
80 ml (2½ fl oz/⅓ cup) extra-virgin olive oil
5 French shallots, finely sliced
3 garlic cloves, finely sliced
50 g (1¾ oz) butter

2 yellow-fleshed potatoes (such as Dutch cream), peeled and very finely sliced
500 ml (17 fl oz/2 cups) White chicken stock (p. 54)
500 ml (17 fl oz/2 cups) water
200 ml (7 fl oz) pouring (single/light) cream

100 ml (3½ fl oz) oil, for frying
2 triangles of kefalograviera cheese (about 150 g/5½ oz), each cut into 6 pieces
toasted sesame seeds, to serve

Staples
LMN, S&P

Preheat the oven to 180°C (350°F) fan-forced.

Scorch the eggplants directly over gas burners (or on a hot barbecue) until blackened all over, about 10 minutes. Place in a roasting tin and bake until collapsing, about 20 minutes. Set aside to cool, before scooping the flesh out of the skin and chopping it roughly. Discard the skin.

Heat the olive oil in a saucepan over a medium heat. Add the shallot and garlic and cook until lightly golden, about 5 minutes. Add the butter and potato, season with salt and pepper and stir constantly until tender and falling apart, about 10 minutes. Add the eggplant and stir for 2 minutes.

Stir in the stock and water. Bring to the boil, then reduce the heat and simmer for 10 minutes. Add the cream and simmer for 5 minutes. Leave to cool a little, then blitz in a blender until very smooth. Adjust the seasoning to taste.

Just before serving, heat the frying oil for 3 minutes in a heavy frying pan over a medium heat. Fry the cheese triangles for 30 seconds or so until golden, then flip and repeat. Drain briefly on paper towel.

Serve the soup topped with the warm cheese, a scattering of sesame seeds and a squeeze of lemon.

Make it different
With goat's cheese. Instead of fried kefalograviera, crumble some soft goat's cheese over the soup, dollop on some crème fraîche, and finish with chopped dill or mint.

With tahini & feta. Drizzle in some tahini and top with crumbled firm feta.

Eggplant & tomato kasundi GF V VG

Kasundi is a rich and unctuous pickled sauce, originating in India. This version has a gentle curry undertone with just a smidgeon of heat, as opposed to the fieriness kasundi can often have. The salting of the tomatoes and the roasting of the eggplant (aubergine) beforehand are the secrets to the depth of flavour and texture. **Makes 1.25 litres (42 fl oz/5 cups)**

1.5 kg (3 lb 5 oz) eggplants (aubergines)
150 ml (5½ fl oz) extra-virgin olive oil
100 ml (3½ fl oz) water
1.5 kg (3 lb 5 oz) tomatoes, peeled (see p. 655) and cut into 2 cm (¾ in) dice

2 tablespoons salt flakes
2 teaspoons black peppercorns
2½ tablespoons coriander seeds
2 tablespoons cumin seeds
2 teaspoons fenugreek seeds

350 g (12½ oz) onions, finely chopped
450 ml (15 fl oz) white-wine vinegar
180 g (6½ oz) caster (superfine) sugar
2 teaspoons chilli powder

Preheat the oven to 200°C (400°F) fan-forced.

Put the whole eggplants on a baking tray and rub with 3 tablespoons of the oil. Pierce each eggplant a few times, then add the water to the tray. Roast for 1 hour, until soft and a little wrinkly, then cool in the tray.

Meanwhile, add the tomato to a colander and sprinkle with 1 tablespoon of the salt. Leave to drain for 1 hour.

Using a spice grinder or mortar and pestle, grind the peppercorns with the coriander, cumin and fenugreek seeds. Set aside.

Remove the eggplant from the tray and trim off the tops, then cut into rough 4 cm (1½ in) dice.

Add the remaining oil to a wide saucepan over a medium heat. Fry the onion to soften but not colour, about 4 minutes. Stir the ground spices through for a minute, then add the drained tomato and remaining salt flakes. Cook for 5 minutes to soften, then add the vinegar, sugar and chilli and bring to a simmer.

Gently stir the eggplant through, so as not to break it up. Cook over a low heat for 2½–3 hours, stirring regularly to stop the mixture catching, until you have a chutney consistency.

Spoon the hot kasundi into hot sterilised jars (see p. 40) and seal, then turn upside down to help form a vacuum seal. The kasundi will keep for 6 months in the pantry. Once opened, refrigerate and use within 1 month.

Pair with

Grilled lamb chops or roast chicken (see p. 229).

Barbecued poultry, pork or fish.

It's great on steamed rice with yoghurt and a handful of herbs when no-one wants to cook.

Spoon over stir-fried okra or beans.

Serve with a good sharp cheddar and crackers, or in a toasted cheddar sandwich.

Spoon over fried eggs, or a goat's feta omelette (see p. 353).

It's also lovely on steamed fish or roasted scallops in the shell.

Baked lamb-stuffed eggplant

I have fond memories of stuffed eggplants from my first trip to Greece. It was the kind of food I could afford in the tavernas in my twenties, and I was taken by the simplicity and incredible depth of flavour. This is real comfort food for me now. **Serves 4**

½ onion, finely diced
4 garlic cloves, finely sliced
500 g (1 lb 2 oz) minced (ground) lamb, or beef or pork
60 g (2 oz/¾ cup) fresh breadcrumbs

1 egg
½ bunch of flat-leaf (Italian) parsley leaves, roughly chopped
1 teaspoon ground allspice
2 teaspoons ground cinnamon

1 teaspoon chilli flakes
150 g (5½ oz/1½ cups) finely grated Grana Padano, or hard Greek cheese such as kefalograviera or an aged mizithra

Pair with

Serve with Baked buttered rice (p. 384) or tiny pasta (such as pastina or orzo), and a green salad.

Pasta alla Norma GF V

Tomato and eggplant (aubergine) have a natural affinity, nowhere better expressed than in pasta alla Norma, a classic Sicilian dish named after the Bellini opera of the same name. Cut 2 eggplants in half lengthways, score the cut surface in a crisscross fashion, drizzle with olive oil and season with salt and pepper, then roast for about 30 minutes in a 180°C (350°F) oven until tender. Scoop out the flesh and chop roughly. Fry a few sliced garlic cloves in plenty of olive oil with a big pinch of chilli flakes until fragrant, then add the eggplant and fry for a minute or so. Tip in 350 ml (12 fl oz) tomato passata (puréed tomatoes) and simmer for about 5 minutes. Adjust the seasoning to taste, tear in plenty of basil leaves, then toss with hot al dente pasta (a 'short' variety, such as penne, ziti, macaroni). Top with crumbled fresh ricotta and grated parmesan, or just coarsely shredded ricotta salata (or other firm, salted sheep's milk cheese). Finish with a little more basil and a generous anointing of good olive oil.

Pair with

Japanese short-grain rice and greens, such as stir-fried snow peas (mangetout) or spinach with sesame and soy.

Simply grilled fish, including salmon, ocean trout and mackerel.

---

1 tablespoon dried Greek oregano (rigani)
4 eggplants (aubergines), cut in half lengthways
2½ tablespoons extra-virgin olive oil

500 ml (17 fl oz/2 cups) White chicken stock (p. 54)
400 g (14 oz) tin diced tomatoes
3 tablespoons tomato paste (concentrated purée)

2 bay leaves
Staples
EVOO, S&P

Preheat the oven to 200°C (400°F) fan-forced.

Heat a good splash of oil in a heavy-based saucepan over a medium heat. Add the onion and garlic and cook until lightly golden, about 5 minutes. Remove from the pan.

Add the onion and garlic to a food processor with the lamb, breadcrumbs, egg, parsley, spices, chilli, half the cheese and half the oregano. Season well with salt and pepper and blend to a smooth paste.

Scoop out half the eggplant flesh (a melon baller or teaspoon works well here), trying to leave an even layer on the skin, then season the shells. Stuff the shells with the lamb mixture and top with the remaining cheese. Place in a baking dish and bake for 10 minutes.

Meanwhile, add the oil, stock, tomatoes, tomato paste and bay leaves to a saucepan. Add the eggplant flesh and remaining oregano, season and bring to the boil. Pour into the baking dish and cover with baking paper, then foil. Reduce the oven temperature to 170°C (340°F) fan-forced and bake for 35 minutes.

Uncover the dish and increase the oven temperature to 200°C (400°F) fan-forced. Bake for another 5 minutes or so to brown the top a little, then serve.

Make it vegetarian V

Combine the cooked onion and garlic with 120 g (4½ oz/1½ cups) breadcrumbs, 150 g (5½ oz) diced haloumi and 250 g (9 oz) cooked spelt (or pearled barley or green lentils). Add the spices and chilli, bind the mixture with 2 beaten eggs, then stuff into the eggplant shells. Use Classic white vegetable stock (p. 51) instead of chicken stock and continue the recipe as written.

Eggplant with miso glaze & spring onions

Ever versatile, eggplant (aubergine) is marvellous with Japanese flavours. Roasting thick slices means the flesh steams as it roasts, yielding a pillowy texture, which really soaks up the flavours of the glaze. **Serves 6–8**

3 eggplants (aubergines), cut into discs 4 cm (1½ in) thick, scored in a crisscross pattern on both sides
2 tablespoons grapeseed oil
1 tablespoon sesame seeds
3 spring onions (scallions), white part only, finely sliced

katsuobushi (bonito flakes), to serve
Miso glaze
3 tablespoons white miso paste
3 tablespoons mirin
2 tablespoons grapeseed oil

2 tablespoons water
1 tablespoon caster (superfine) sugar
1½ teaspoons sesame oil
1 teaspoon dashi powder

Preheat the oven to 200°C (400°F) fan-forced.

Coat the eggplant discs with the oil and lay them on a baking tray. Roast for about 30 minutes until quite soft, then transfer to a baking dish.

Turn the grill (broiler) on high.

For the glaze, blitz all the ingredients in a jug using a stick blender.

Pour the glaze over the eggplant, sprinkle with the sesame seeds and grill until the glaze is bubbling, 5–8 minutes. Sprinkle with the spring onion and katsuobushi to serve.

Deluxe eggplant parmigiana with anchovies

Likely a dish borne of necessity or narrow abundance, eggplant parmigiana is a southern Italian classic said to originate in Naples, where it is still quite beloved, with eggplant (aubergine) and cheese standing in for pasta and meat, making for a very rich and fulfilling lasagne-style dish. I've upped the ante here, with a creamy wealth of dairy and a salty punch of anchovy taking it firmly outside the cucina povera category – but the inspiration is very much the same. **Serves 4–6**

Pair with

A fresh green salad.

Horta-style greens (p. 552).

400 ml (13½ fl oz) oil, for frying
3 large eggplants (aubergines), peeled in alternating stripes, then cut lengthways into slices about 1.5 cm (½ in) thick (about 12 slices)
150 g (5½ oz/1 cup) plain (all-purpose) flour
3 eggs, beaten

400 g (14 oz) fresh breadcrumbs
1 litre (34 fl oz/4 cups) tomato passata (puréed tomatoes)
150 g (5½ oz) Grana Padano, finely grated
150 g (5½ oz) finely sliced fontina or smoked scamorza
3 large balls of fresh mozzarella (about 120 g/ 4½ oz each), sliced

250 g (9 oz) mascarpone
250 ml (8½ fl oz/1 cup) thick (double/heavy) cream
10 anchovies
2 tablespoons dried Greek oregano (rigani)
6 basil sprigs, leaves picked

Staples
EVOO, S&P

Preheat the oven to 170°C (340°F) fan-forced.

Heat one-third of the frying oil in a frying pan over a medium heat.

Working in batches, coat the eggplant in the flour, then dredge in the egg and finally coat with breadcrumbs. Fry on the first side until golden, about 3 minutes, then flip and cook on the other side until golden and tender – reduce the heat if colouring too quickly, as the slices need to be cooked through. Season them with salt and pepper as they cook, and drain on paper towel. You will have to wipe out the pan and change the oil several times, as any excess crumbs will burn.

Spoon a little passata into a 55 × 40 cm (22 × 16 in) baking dish and sprinkle with some Grana Padano. Layer on some eggplant slices, then some fontina and mozzarella. Dollop on some mascarpone and cream and lay a few anchovies over. Sprinkle with some oregano and basil, then season and drizzle with a little oil. Repeat until all the ingredients are used, finishing with the passata and a little cheese.

Cover with baking paper, then foil, and bake for 20 minutes. Uncover and bake for about 15 minutes, until golden. Serve hot.

Make it gluten free (GF)
Skip the crumbing, oil the eggplant slices and roast them on lined baking trays at 170°C (340°F) fan-forced for 35 minutes.

Make it vegetarian (V)
Simply omit the anchovies.

Crispy eggplant with spiced caramel & fried Thai basil

The crisp eggplant yields to reveal a fluffy interior that is swamped by salty, sweet and tangy caramel. This is also a very pretty dish, making it great for entertaining. **Serves 4–6**

Pair with

Serve with steamed fish, rice and stir-fried greens.

Melanzane sotto aceto with banana peppers, basil & chilli (GF) (V) (VG)

Peel 8 medium eggplants (aubergines), then slice lengthways into 1 cm (½ in) thick batons. Add to a large bowl with 200 g (7 oz) fine sea salt and toss well. Place in a colander, cover with a plate and weigh down overnight to drain. The next day, rinse the eggplant to get rid of the excess salt, then squeeze well to extract the moisture. Add to a large bowl with 600–800 ml (20½–27 fl oz) white-wine vinegar, weigh down with a plate and stand again overnight. The following day, drain the eggplant and squeeze the vinegar out firmly until compressed. Add to a bowl with 4 seeded and finely sliced banana peppers, 4 finely sliced garlic cloves, the leaves from 5 basil sprigs, 20 grinds pepper and 1½ teaspoons ground cloves, then toss well. Stuff the mixture into three 300 ml (10 fl oz) sterilised jars (see p. 40) with a red bird's eye chilli, split lengthways, in each. Combine 500 ml (17 fl oz/2 cups) extra-virgin olive oil with 500 ml (17 fl oz/2 cups) neutral-flavoured oil, then pour evenly into the jars and seal; you may need a little more or less oil. Store in a cool, dark place for 2 weeks before using. The jars will keep for 6–12 months in the pantry. Once opened, refrigerate and use within 1 month.

oil, for deep-frying (see p. 22)
4 egg whites
½ teaspoon salt flakes
2 eggplants (aubergines), semi-peeled in stripes, then cut into wedges about 2.5 cm (1 in) thick (or use a selection of small eggplants, split in half or cut on an angle)
500 g (1 lb 2 oz) rice flour
3 handfuls of Thai basil leaves
1 × quantity Thai caramel (p. 105)
1 handful of salted beer nuts
3 tablespoons dried shrimp, blitzed to a floss in a blender
lime cheeks or wedges, to serve

Heat 4 cm (1½ in) of frying oil in a deep heavy-based frying pan or deep-fryer until 170°C (340°F).

Whisk the egg whites with the salt until light and fluffy.

Working in batches, dust the eggplant wedges in the rice flour, dredge in the egg white, then coat in the rice flour again. Fry for 4 minutes in total, flipping to cook evenly, then drain on paper towel while frying the remaining eggplant. Toss and season.

Fry the basil leaves for 30 seconds and drain. They will crisp up as they cool.

Arrange the eggplant on a serving plate and spoon the Thai caramel over. Finish by scattering with the nuts, basil and shrimp floss. Serve immediately, with lime on the side.

Fennel

I have significant affection for fennel. As a chef, I love its versatility, both raw and cooked, and I love it as a vegetable and a herb – but my feelings run deeper than that. Its anise flavour and crisp crunch are hardwired to some very strong childhood recollections, and its fragrance stirs up more recent memories of gathering sheaves of wild fennel to adorn a restaurant that we ran for one sunny season in Ibiza.

Mum used to slice fennel and drop it into iced water for a snack, or to settle the stomach after a meal. Us kids would dive into that bowl, depleting it well before dinner hit the table and then fight over who got to drink the liquorice-scented icy water. I've passed that tradition on to my girls, too – not the fighting so much – and I put chunky fennel wedges in their winter lunchboxes.

Nestled into a secluded cove was our little open-air restaurant, only accessible by a too-long trip down a pitted dirt track, or by gliding through the cobalt waters of the Balearic Sea by boat. The rocky hills around the restaurant were thick with wild fennel, and I used to gather the flowering stems both to detail the dining area, and to harvest the pollen to scatter over a crudo of fish (similar to kingfish), dressed with wild lemon juice and shimmering-green local olive oil.

The stems were also used to perfume sea bass on the grill. The fish was soaked in a slurry of seawater and sea salt for 30 minutes, before being roasted on the asador grill under a bed of wild fennel. I'd leave the scales on, which the server would peel back at the table, like the lid on an old-fashioned tin of sardines, revealing the slightly smoky and ever-so delicate flesh. A charred lemon and a pot of Sauce vierge (p. 82) on the side would complete the picture, with the diner digging their feet a bit deeper into the sand in satisfaction (or so I imagine). Memories, hey!

You're likely to encounter fennel in two ways – most noticeably as the swollen, ribbed white bulb at the market, ideally with its beautiful plume of feathery fronds intact. But you probably come across the wild version more often than you realise. Common or wild fennel broadcasts its seeds on the wind readily, and it happily grows almost anywhere they settle. You'll often see it growing by railway lines, on riverbanks, or in any piece of land left vacant for long enough for it to grow – which isn't very long. The wild version is characterised by quite tall and spindly stalks, with a blurred fuzz of fronds and a spray of vibrant yellow flowers at the top.

Both types are essentially the same species, within the carrot family. Bulb or Florence fennel is a cultivar developed several hundred years ago, while the wild version doesn't have an enlarged edible bulb, instead being valued as a herb. The wild version is stronger in anise flavour, but the fronds, fine supple stalks, flowers and seeds of both have the same culinary applications. Young wild fennel stalks can be used in stock, or to stuff things such as whole fish to add flavour, and the fronds can be used as an anise-tinged herb. The vibrant flowers and pollen are quite pungent, adding sophisticated flavour and colour when finishing dishes. The seeds (actually fruits, but let's not go there) can be used as a spice (see p. 13), and are quite different in flavour and texture when fresh and 'wet', compared to dried. There is a third decorative variety called bronze fennel, which is similar to wild fennel, but with a slightly burnished hue.

Bulb (Florence) fennel is what most of us are familiar with. It is at its best in winter and early spring, with small baby bulbs entering the market in summer. These are harvested earlier, as the hotter season makes them woody and coarse if left to mature to full size, but the flavour and sweetness hasn't developed properly for me and I find them bland and stringy. I'm happy to wait.

The fennel bulb can be eaten raw or cooked in all manner of ways. It adds a flavoursome and crunchy dimension to salads, and can star in a gratin, or as a chunky vegetable in a stew or soup. Or use it more subtly as an aromatic vegetable finely diced in a soffritto. Bulb offcuts (or the stalks and fronds) can strongly perfume a fish or crustacean stock, or add subtle spice notes to a chicken stock. You can pickle it in chunks, or lacto-ferment with cabbage for a riff on Sauerkraut (p. 454).

Also see

Cured kingfish with fennel, paprika & pepper 171

Roasted flounder with charred fennel 176

Shaved fennel, artichoke & almond salad 535–6

Braised artichoke, fennel & broad bean salad with orange glaze 536

Apple, fennel & witlof slaw with buttermilk dressing 680

Pair with

Fennel loves acid, whether citrus juices, sherry vinegar or wine vinegar. It's enhanced simply with some good extra-virgin olive oil, and even more so with a sprinkling of salt flakes and fresh black pepper. Its strong anise profile marries well with strong and salty ingredients such as olives, salumi, bottarga, anchovies and good parmesan or pecorino cheese. It also knits into the rich and luscious – so cream, mayonnaise, butter, fresh mozzarella and eggs all make it sing, as do dill, thyme, saffron and chilli. Match it with cannellini beans, lima beans, lentils, chickpeas and fresh borlotti (cranberry) and broad beans, and it accompanies most proteins, from fish and calamari to pork and beef.

Simply shaved fennel (a mandoline is best here) – and some shaved raw artichoke, if you like – works beautifully dressed in an emulsion of extra-virgin olive oil and lemon juice seasoned with plenty of salt flakes and freshly ground black pepper. Serve with fish, or top finely sliced raw beef fillet with shaved curls of Parmigiano Reggiano and crisp fried shallot rings. Fennel is stunning with oranges, also peaking in winter, and a salad of the two simply dressed or with olives, mint and/or hard feta is a staple on my table in the coolest season. As you can see, fennel is a very versatile ingredient!

When selecting fennel, as a starting point I always insist on some of the fronds being attached. It's a sure way to judge freshness, and I always want them to use as a herb – plus I love their decorative value. From there, I choose fat rounded bulbs, ideally with no bruising – this can be hard to avoid, but if there are dark or soft spots, move on. The rounder the bulbs, the denser and more layered they are, and they also present better on the plate. You will sometimes see fennel bulbs in a flatter form, almost rectangular. Some say this is just natural variation, others that it is the difference between male and female plants, or that the flatter bulbs are due to the plants bolting in warmer weather … I'm not sure which, if any, of these notions are true, but I find the flatter specimens quite inferior, and never buy them.

Caramelised fennel

Fennel cooked this way takes on a much deeper flavour profile, sweet and rich. Slice 2 fennel bulbs 1 cm (½ in) thick. Heat 80 g (2¾ oz) butter and 50 ml (1¾ fl oz) extra-virgin olive oil in a wide-based saucepan or large frying pan over a medium heat. Lay the fennel slices in the pan, season with salt and pepper and sprinkle with a tablespoon of caster (superfine) sugar. Cook for a few minutes before stirring, then reduce the heat and cook for about 40 minutes, until you have a very tender, golden rough mash, stirring frequently. In the last few minutes, add any fennel tops you have, and season as needed. Serve with a seared salmon fillet or pork chop, stir into a plain risotto with chopped prawns (shrimp), or toss through spaghetti with some smashed tinned sardines, a handful of toasted pine nuts, a pinch of chilli flakes and a splash of sherry vinegar.

Preparing fennel

Depending on how long your fennel took to get to market, or if it had a rough time on the way, the very outer cuff of the bulb can be bruised and should be removed for most uses, though it will work fine in stock or can be braised. If it's in good condition, or only slightly scuffed, it doesn't need to be discarded. Trim off the green stalks and the woody base. Pick the fennel fronds from the stalks, discarding any tough stems, and chop or tear into smaller pieces to add to your dish or use as a garnish once finished. The green – and often hollow – stalks can be used in a stock, so pop these into the crisper if not using immediately. The bulb can then be diced, sliced, shaved finely or cut into wedges, depending on the application. The core, at the base, only needs to be trimmed away if tough, and depending on the use. Soaking sliced fennel in cold or iced water will make it crunchier; just drain and pat dry before using in salads.

Malloreddus with prawns & fennel

This is a risotto-style pasta dish, using slippery malloreddus pasta instead of rice. It's important to extract all the juices from the prawn (shrimp) heads at the start, as that's where the depth of flavour comes from, though you could also use those heads to make a Prawn essence (p. 67) and use that with stock, which will really up the intensity. **Serves 4**

140 ml (4½ fl oz) extra-virgin olive oil

8 large raw prawns (shrimp), peeled and deveined, then split in half lengthways, heads reserved

1 litre (34 fl oz/4 cups) Golden chicken stock (p. 54), or Fish stock (p. 52)

6 ripe tomatoes, quartered, or a 400 g (14 oz) tin diced tomato, drained

1 teaspoon ground fennel

½ fennel bulb, fronds picked, bulb finely diced

4 garlic cloves, sliced

400 g (14 oz) malloreddus

100 ml (3½ fl oz) dry white wine

300 ml (10 fl oz) water

1 large knob of butter

Staples
LMN, S&P

Heat 2 tablespoons of the oil in a saucepan over a medium heat. Fry the prawn heads, squashing them with your spoon to extract all the juice, until they have changed colour, about 3 minutes. Add the stock and simmer for 3 minutes.

Heat the remaining oil in a large heavy-based saucepan over a high heat. Cook the tomatoes until softened but still holding their shape, 2–3 minutes. Lift them out and set aside.

Add the prawn meat and ground fennel to the pan, season with salt and pepper and fry for about 2 minutes to just colour but not cook through. Remove from the pan, leaving the oil behind, and set aside with the tomatoes.

Add the diced fennel and garlic to the pan, season and cook over a medium heat until lightly coloured and softened, 6–8 minutes. Stir in the malloreddus and wine, then reduce the liquid for 3 minutes. Strain in the stock and add the water, then bring to a simmer and cook for 15 minutes, stirring frequently to prevent sticking.

Return the prawn meat and tomato to the pan and cook for another 3 minutes. Turn the heat off, stir the butter through, cover and stand for 2 minutes.

To serve, scatter with the fennel fronds and squeeze over some lemon juice.

Make it different

With broad beans. When in season, stir through a few handfuls of double-podded broad beans at the last minute. You could use peas, too.

With short pasta. Substitute the malloreddus for gnocchi sardi (see p. 131) or pennette.

Roasted & raw fennel salad with mint & egg yolk ⓥ

Fennel is so versatile, and highlighting that adaptability in a salad adds so much depth and detail. Whether crisply fried, raw or pickled, a combination of techniques elevates the complexity of any dish. In this simple salad, roasted fennel contrasts with crunchy slivers of raw fennel, with sourdough crumbs adding another textural dimension. Select a bulb with lots of feathery fronds for this. **Serves 4**

Pair with

Serve as a standalone starter, or with simply grilled or pan-seared fish.

1 large fennel bulb, fronds roughly chopped
¼ bunch of mint, leaves picked and torn
2 slices of Sourdough bread (p. 847), well toasted or charred and dressed with oil

2 hard-boiled egg yolks

Chilli garlic dressing
100 ml (3½ fl oz) extra-virgin virgin olive oil
juice of ½ lemon
½ garlic clove, finely grated
½ teaspoon chilli flakes

Staples
EVOO, S&P

Special equipment
Japanese mandoline

Preheat the oven to 180°C (350°F) fan-forced.

Cut half the fennel bulb into wedges, coat the wedges with oil, season with salt and pepper and spread on a baking tray. Roast for about 30 minutes, until tender and golden at the edges. Cool a little, then lay out on a serving plate.

Add the dressing ingredients to a large bowl, season and combine. Using a mandoline, finely slice the remaining fennel bulb, then add to the dressing, along with the fennel fronds and mint. Toss to coat, then pile on top of the cooked fennel.

Smash the toasts into a rough crumb, season with salt and pepper and sprinkle over the salad. Finely grate the egg yolks over the top and serve immediately.

Make it different
With preserved fish. This salad is delicious with a punch of briny preserved fish. Try adding tuna, a few chopped plump pink anchovies to the salad, or shaving some bottarga or tuna over to serve.

Malloreddus with prawns & fennel

Charred fennel salad with tarragon GF V VG

The anise flavour marriage of tarragon and fennel is such a winter thing for me, especially when you add in orange – all at their peak, and just so harmonious together. The key with this salad is to get a good char on the fennel. **Serves 4–6**

1 large fennel bulb, cut 8 mm (⅓ in) thick lengthways, fronds roughly chopped

Orange & tarragon dressing
zest and juice of ½ orange
2 tablespoons Champagne vinegar, or white-wine vinegar

1 tablespoon extra-virgin olive oil
2 spring onions (scallions), white part only, finely sliced
1 garlic clove, finely grated
5 winter tarragon sprigs, or oregano, parsley or marjoram, leaves finely chopped

1 teaspoon brown sugar
1 teaspoon salt flakes

Staples
EVOO, S&P

Preheat a barbecue grill or chargrill pan on high.

Coat the fennel with oil, season with salt and pepper and set aside for a few minutes.

Combine the dressing ingredients in a large bowl.

Grill the fennel pieces for about 3 minutes on each side, until tender and charred. As the fennel pieces come off the grill, add them to the dressing, tossing them through.

Tip onto a serving plate, finish with the fronds and serve.

Make it different

With fried haloumi. Simply crumble some haloumi into hot oil and shallow-fry until golden, then drain and scatter over the fennel. Or for a simpler version, dollop on some goat's curd.

With other vegetables. You can add different grilled vegetables to this, such as spring onions (scallions) or halved Dutch carrots.

With orange. Add sliced or segmented orange to the salad after charring the fennel.

Pair with

This salad works beautifully alongside roasted or grilled meat or chicken.

It is also a perfect partner for a baked whole fish, or pork or Lamb koftas (p. 309).

Serve with a rich braise or stew.

It can even take the spotlight with a bit of support from a grain salad or buttery couscous.

Fennel gratin GF V

Lay thickly cut fennel wedges or slices on lined baking trays. Season with salt and pepper, then drizzle with oil. Keep it as simple as this, or add some butter, fennel seeds, fennel fronds and/or thyme sprigs. Now add a splash of water or wine and roast in a 180°C (350°F) fan-forced oven for about 40 minutes. Serve as is, or drizzle with cream and sprinkle with grated parmesan before returning to the oven until golden. Either way, this is great alongside fish, a pork chop, slow-roasted pork shoulder, steak or roast chicken.

Baked fennel & leek with provolone sauce V

This riff on cauliflower cheese has a bit more zip and intensity than its original inspiration, with the sweetly anise-tinged fennel a perfect partner to the sharply salty provolone. **Serves 4–6**

2 large fennel bulbs, trimmed
4 thin leeks (no more than two fingers wide), trimmed
75 g (2¾ oz) provolone, grated

Provolone sauce
750 ml (25½ fl oz/3 cups) full-cream (whole) milk
1 fresh bay leaf
60 g (2 oz/¼ cup) butter
60 g (2 oz) plain (all-purpose flour)

75 g (2¾ oz) provolone, grated
¼ whole nutmeg, freshly grated, or 1 teaspoon ground nutmeg

Staples
BTR, EVOO, S&P

Pair with

Roast pork, brined roast chicken (see p. 245) or pan-seared fish fillets.

Preheat the oven to 170°C (340°F) fan-forced.

Cook the fennel bulbs in a large saucepan of boiling salted water for 20 minutes, adding the leeks for the last 5 minutes. Drain well, pressing the moisture out of the leeks using a tea towel (dish towel). Cut the leeks into 4 cm (1½ in) lengths, and slice the fennel lengthways, about 2–3 cm (¾–1¼ in) thick. Set aside.

Cevapcici with wild fennel

This is a simple skinless sausage that I enjoyed as a child. Chopped fennel fronds from common wild fennel or bronze fennel were used quite generously in the mix, like you might use parsley. My mother learnt the recipe from my grandmother Grace, and my version is not too far removed. Combine 500 g (1 lb 2 oz) slightly fatty minced (ground) pork (or a mix of beef and lamb mince, if you prefer) with a few handfuls of dried breadcrumbs. Season with salt and pepper, scatter in some fennel seeds, a generous pinch of ground cinnamon, and chilli flakes to your liking. Add a few handfuls of chopped wild or bronze fennel fronds and combine well with your hands. Form into sausages the size of your index finger, then pan-fry in olive oil until golden and cooked through. Serve hot or cold with bread, pickles and roasted capsicum (bell pepper).

Pair with

This dish would work with any fish, or simply grilled or roasted chicken or pork.

This is also great with cooked greens, such as silverbeet (Swiss chard), and/or a grain salad for a vegetarian winter spread.

To make the sauce, bring the milk to a simmer with the bay leaf, then remove from the heat.

Melt the butter in a saucepan over a medium heat. Once foaming, add the flour and stir together into a paste, stirring until the raw aroma of the flour has been cooked out, about 1 minute. Over a low heat, gradually whisk in the milk until thickened, about 3 minutes. Remove from the heat, then stir in the provolone and nutmeg. Season with salt and pepper.

Rub a shallow baking dish with butter, then lay the fennel out. Scatter the leek over and season. Pour the sauce over the top, sprinkle with the remaining provolone, then bake for about 25 minutes, until lightly golden. Serve hot.

Braised fennel with tomato & olives 🟢Ⓥ🟢

When fennel is braised, it develops a lovely softness that absorbs flavours beautifully, so cooking it in an intensely aromatic sauce such as this one is ideal. The potato will have mostly broken down when this is ready, thickening and adding a silkiness to the sauce. **Serves 4–6**

2 fennel bulbs, trimmed
100 ml (3½ fl oz) extra-virgin olive oil
1 small onion, finely sliced
2 garlic cloves, finely sliced
2 thyme sprigs
1 pinch of saffron threads
1 teaspoon fennel seeds

2 creamy yellow-fleshed potatoes (such as Dutch cream), peeled and cut into 2 cm (¾ in) dice
150 ml (5 fl oz) white wine
1 tablespoon small capers
1 tablespoon raw sugar, or demerara sugar

1 tablespoon tomato paste (concentrated purée)
1 fresh bay leaf
2 tomatoes, roughly diced
400 ml (13½ fl oz) water
15 manzanilla olives, or your choice

Staples
EVOO, S&P

Cook the fennel bulbs in a saucepan of boiling salted water for 10 minutes, then lift out and drain well. Slice the fennel 2–3 cm (¾–1¼ in) thick lengthways.

Heat the oil in a wide-based saucepan over a medium heat. Add the onion, garlic, thyme, saffron and fennel seeds and cook to soften slightly, about 3 minutes. Stir in the potato and cook for about 3 minutes to coat well and warm through. Add the wine, capers, sugar, tomato paste and bay leaf and bring to a simmer.

Stir in the diced tomato and water and simmer for about 4 minutes.

Add the fennel and simmer for 20–25 minutes, until the fennel is tender but still holding its shape, and the sauce has thickened a little.

Add the olives, season with salt and pepper and drizzle with a little oil. To serve, lift the fennel slices onto a plate (or plates) and spoon the sauce over.

Fennel, black pepper & garlic paste 🟢Ⓥ🟢

There's something about the flavours in this very simple little paste that naturally enhances the flavours of all manner of meals – from boosting stir-fries to adding complexity to Western dishes. **Makes about 125 g (4½ oz/½ cup)**

Pair with

Use as a base to pan-fry or stir-fry prawns (shrimp), strips of scotch fillet, diced chicken, clams (vongole), mussels, tofu or diced pumpkin (winter squash). There is enough paste to cook 2 kg (4 lb 6 oz) mussels.

2 tablespoons black peppercorns
2 tablespoons fennel seeds
2 teaspoons salt flakes
6 garlic cloves, peeled

Using a mortar and pestle, roughly grind the peppercorns and fennel seeds. Add the salt and garlic and grind to a wet paste. Use immediately.

Fennel & buffalo mozzarella salad with broad beans, mint & green sultanas ㉾ Ⓥ

You could absolutely use fresh cow's milk mozzarella here, but the flavour of buffalo milk mozzarella is simply divine. Its milky, sharp and slightly sour flavour works so well with the mint, chilli and broad beans, as well as the sweetness from the sultanas. You can serve this salad with any bread you like, but properly charred Sourdough bread (p. 847) is a must for me. **Serves 4**

50 g (1¾ oz) green sultanas
3 tablespoons sherry vinegar
2 large buffalo mozzarella balls
350–400 g (12½–14 oz/ 2 cups), podded broad beans (see p. 430), blanched for 1 minute,

refreshed and podded again
4 spring onions (scallions), white part only, finely sliced
1 long red chilli, finely sliced into rings, or ½ teaspoon chilli flakes
4 mint sprigs, leaves torn

1 fennel bulb, shaved using a mandoline, fronds roughly chopped
2½ tablespoons extra-virgin olive oil

Staples
S&P

Special equipment
Japanese mandoline

Bring the sultanas and 2 tablespoons of the vinegar to a simmer in a small saucepan. Set aside for 15 minutes, then chop the sultanas.

Tear the mozzarella balls into pieces and arrange on a serving plate. Season with salt and pepper.

Add the remaining vinegar to a bowl, along with the sultanas, broad beans, spring onion, chilli, mint, fennel fronds and oil. Season, then gently toss to combine.

Arrange the shaved fennel next to the mozzarella. Spoon the dressed salad over and serve.

Make it different

With balsamic vinegar. Drizzle with some quality balsamic vinegar or saba (grape-must reduction) to finish. Their complex sweetness is a perfect foil for the mozzarella's milky richness.

With pickled fennel. Mix some Pickled fennel (p. 531) with the fresh fennel.

With cured meat. Add some jamón, prosciutto, bresaola or salami.

Pair with

This salad works particularly well with a grilled steak or fish – but it's delicious as is with some charred bread.

Fennel, potato & sausage tray bake

Cut a fennel bulb into thin wedges, and 2 potatoes into 5 mm (¼ in) slices. Toss everything with extra-virgin olive oil and season with salt and pepper. Spread evenly in a roasting tin, scatter with some dried oregano (I love wild Greek oregano/rigani), then tip in a splash of water or white wine. Take 4 Italian pork and fennel sausages, split the skins and crumble the meat over the vegetables. Roast at 180°C (350°F) fan-forced for about 30 minutes, until the vegetables are tender and golden.

Fennel & orange salad with olives, currants & chilli ㉾ Ⓥ ㉦

Fennel and navel oranges are both at their best in winter, and their flavours just marry so well together. This is based on a classic southern Italian salad, and can be tweaked and simplified as required. The two main ingredients at their prime, simply seasoned and dressed with good olive oil, is about all that is required for success. **Serves 6–8**

80 g (2¾ oz) currants
80 ml (2½ fl oz/⅓ cup) red-wine vinegar
a pinch of chilli flakes
½ large red onion, finely diced
60 g (2 oz) black kalamata olives, pitted

80 ml (2½ fl oz/⅓ cup) extra-virgin olive oil
3 navel oranges, or blood oranges, peeled and sliced, pips removed
1 large fennel bulb, cut into 1 cm (½ in) wedges, fronds roughly chopped

4 mint sprigs or dill or parsley, leaves torn

Staples
S&P

Pair with

Pasta or risotto with lamb ragù, or a rich braise.

Sweet pickled fennel (GF) (V) (VG)

Cut 2 trimmed fennel bulbs (fronds reserved) into twelve wedges, or slice into pieces 4 mm (¼ in) thick lengthways. Pack the fennel, ½ long red chilli, split lengthways, and 1 peeled and squashed garlic clove into a clean 1 litre (34 fl oz/4 cup) jar, along with any fennel fronds. For the pickling medium, to a small saucepan add 200 ml (7 fl oz) water, 150 ml (5 fl oz), white-wine vinegar or brown-rice vinegar, 80 g (2¾ oz/⅓ cup) caster (superfine) sugar, 40 g (1½ oz/⅓ cup) salt flakes and ½ tablespoon white mustard seeds. If you like, you could also add 1 teaspoon black peppercorns, a fresh bay leaf and/or a thyme sprig. Bring to just under a simmer, to dissolve the sugar and salt. Set aside to cool, then add 2 tablespoons lemon juice. Pour the cooled pickling medium into a 750 ml (25½ fl oz/3 cup) jar, making sure the fennel is submerged. Seal and refrigerate for 2 hours or overnight before eating. These pickles will change over their brief life, and I enjoy them lightly and more heavily pickled – but after 2 weeks they will soften dramatically. You could also try this pickle with Dutch carrots, celery or daikon.

Fennel chips

Slice a fennel bulb 2–3 mm (⅛–⅙ in) thick using a mandoline (you can slice into long or round chips, and there's no need to remove the core). Lightly dust the slices with flour and fry in 165°C (330°F) oil for about 4 minutes, turning to cook evenly. Once golden, drain on paper towel, season with salt and set aside to cool. These can be used as a contrast on top of a freshly shaved fennel salad served with a seared fillet of fish, for example.

In a small saucepan, bring the currants, vinegar and chilli to a simmer over a medium heat. Remove from the heat and stir in the onion, olives and oil. Set aside to soften the onion and cool the mixture.

Add the orange, fennel, fennel fronds and mint to a large bowl, season with salt and pepper and toss. Tip into a serving bowl and dress with the currant and olive mixture.

Make it different

Fennel & mandarin salad with olives, currants & chilli. Use mandarins in place of the orange.

With pine nuts. A few tablespoons of toasted pine nuts adds another dimension to this salad.

With radicchio. Serve on shredded radicchio to add a welcome winter bitterness.

Spring minestrone (GF)

Minestrone conjures up thoughts of wintery days with a steaming bowl of vegetable, legume and pasta-filled soup with thick-cut bread for dunking. And while this image tells a wonderful story, minestrone can echo other seasons just as effectively. Making a light springtime minestrone is all about highlighting the green bounty – slow cooking is out, and quick blanching is in. Tomatoes also get the boot, as we're after those delicate verdant tones. To top off the seasonal message, springtime minestrone is crowned with a big dollop of pesto, which can be stirred through at the table. The French make a similar soup called pistou, from Provence, which can be in the mould of a hearty minestrone, but I have also seen refined versions like this, which are all about delicate greens.

Serves 4–6

50 g (1¾ oz) butter
1 onion, finely diced
4 garlic cloves, finely sliced
5 Dutch carrots, finely sliced
1 celery heart, finely sliced
1 fennel bulb, finely diced
2 zucchini (courgettes), sliced
1 bunch of asparagus, sliced
12 green beans, cut into
    short lengths

1 litre (34 fl oz/4 cups)
    Golden chicken stock
    (p. 54)
500 ml (17 fl oz/2 cups) water
400 g (14 oz) tin cannellini
    beans, drained and rinsed
115 g (4 oz/¾ cup) fresh peas
140 g (5 oz/¾ cup)
    double-podded broad
    beans (see p. 430)

½ bunch of flat-leaf
    (Italian) parsley, leaves
    finely chopped
Pesto (p. 90), to serve

Staples
EVOO, LMN, S&P

Melt the butter with a good glug of oil in a large wide-based saucepan over a medium heat. Add the onion, garlic, carrot and celery, season with salt and pepper and cook for about 5 minutes, until softened. Turn the heat down to medium–low and cook until sticky but not quite caramelised, about 10–12 minutes.

Add the fennel, zucchini, asparagus and green beans, turn up the heat and cook for a few minutes, until softening. Pour in the stock and water, stir in the cannellini beans and bring to the boil. Add the peas, broad beans and parsley and cook for another minute or so – the vegetables should be bright and just cooked. Remove from the heat and season to taste.

To serve, top with a dollop of pesto and a drizzle of oil.

Make it different

Rocket & basil pesto. (GF) (V) Making the pesto with a mix of half rocket (arugula) and half basil adds a peppery kick that works particularly well here.

Globe artichoke

When I was growing up, fresh artichokes were an uncommon sight. You certainly didn't see them in supermarkets like you do now. I have a treasured memory of my grandmother Grace preparing artichokes; I was quite little, and it was the first time I had ever seen them. She would seek them out from Melbourne's Queen Victoria Market, mainly from Greek and Italian stalls. Grace would simply trim the stems, then wedge them into her largest pot with salt, a slice or two of lemon, and water to cover, then simmer with the lid on until they could be easily pierced with a skewer. She would make the simplest vinaigrette, and you'd peel the leaves off and dip them into it, then pull a leaf over your bottom teeth to scrape the morsel of flesh off the base. Labour intensive, but delicious! Once you got to the pale-yellow heart, that was the reward for persevering with the fiddly leaves and their tantalisingly small offerings.

Globe artichokes are quite beautiful, though somewhat confronting, vegetables. They are thistles essentially, and the main edible part is the base from which the leaves and flowers emerge (one head gives rise to a spray of vibrant blue-purple flowers). Once bloomed, they are unmistakably thistle-like – striking but essentially inedible.

From a cook's perspective, we're after the head in an armoured state, with most of the thorny petals clamping inwards. Once the petals of a harvested artichoke start to relax and peel backwards, and the stem starts to soften, the artichoke is in a state of decline and far from its best. So, select firm artichokes that are heavy in the hand, and ideally with thick stems, as these are delicious when peeled, too.

Although overly mature artichokes are not desirable, the size of an artichoke is not always a great indicator of quality, given the diversity of cultivars. Some are classically globe-shaped, while others are more elongated. Some are quite compact and others more substantial. And the colour can vary from vibrant green to deep purple. A younger artichoke, of any type, will have a less developed spiky choke (these are the nascent flowers) that doesn't need to be removed, while in a more mature specimen that choke can be fibrous (typically with purple tips) and unpleasant to eat. The heart of either should be equally delicious. Artichokes are classically a spring crop but, depending on growing conditions and variety, the harvest now spills into other seasons.

Jerusalem artichokes and globe artichokes are unrelated, with the former being the tuber of a species of sunflower. The shared nomenclature is due to a supposed similarity in flavour. The link to the Holy Land is a bit more tenuous.

For those unfamiliar with preparing them, there can be a lot of anxiety associated with artichokes. Much like making mayonnaise, peeling an artichoke (see p. 534) seems to terrify new cooks but, once accomplished, it will become transparently simple. Trust me.

Once prepared, artichokes can be cooked until tender simply in salted water, or with wine and aromatics; they can be battered and fried; stuffed then baked or poached; or shaved finely and eaten raw. Then there's the very Italian method of stuffing them with breadcrumbs, parsley, garlic, lemon zest and oil, then trussing and simmering them in salted water until tender (you can steam or bake them, too).

Also see

Soft polenta with crab, artichoke & poached egg 352

Mezzanotte paste 588

Green olive, artichoke & kale tapenade 590

Pair with

Artichokes are quite versatile and work equally well with lamb, chicken, fish and even crabmeat. They're also great with pork sausages, bacon or chorizo. Soft cheeses such as ricotta or goat's curd, hard cheeses such as Parmigiano Reggiano, and washed-rind cheeses such as taleggio also provide lovely combinations – as do soft herbs (parsley, mint, dill), lentils, olives, fresh porcini mushrooms, and orange and lemon.

Preparing globe artichokes

This is step one in each of the following artichoke recipes.

Firstly, gloves aren't a bad idea. The outer leaves can be very bitter, and they will leave a residue on your hands, which can transfer to other foods. (Otherwise, wash up well after the artichokes have been prepared.) Peel off most of the outer leaves until you see the light yellow flesh at the base, then cut off the top 5 cm (2 in) from the remaining leaves. Trim the stalk to about 5 cm (2 in) in length, then use a paring knife to pare away the outer skin to reveal the light green inner flesh. You should end up with a thick disc attached to a slender stem. Remove any remaining tough outer leaves until they are an even yellow. Scoop out the hairy choke from the centre with a spoon (baby artichokes may not have a developed choke), and immediately rub the entire surface of the artichoke with cut lemon to stop discolouration. (You can do this as you go if you're not quite on top of the method yet.) While you see to any remaining artichokes, keep the prepared ones in a bowl of water with a good squeeze of lemon juice.

Short cut

Quality jarred artichokes will work perfectly well in most recipes, too.

Braised artichokes with garlic, bay & white wine glaze (GF) (V) (VG)

Prepare (see left) and quarter 5 large artichokes (or use 12 baby artichokes). Heat 200 ml (7 fl oz) extra-virgin olive oil in a wide-based saucepan over a high heat. Add the artichokes, season with salt and pepper and turn until evenly golden, about 5 minutes. Add 3 sliced or smashed garlic cloves, 1 tablespoon whole coriander seeds, 3 thyme sprigs and 1 bay leaf to the pan; stir and briefly cook the garlic until lightly golden. Add the juice of ½ lemon, 200 ml (7 fl oz) white wine and a splash of water. Turn the heat to low, then simmer gently with a cartouche over the top until just tender, 10–15 minutes. Turn the heat off and cool the artichokes for 15 minutes in the liquor. If you're using the artichokes immediately or don't require the glaze, you can skip this next step. Otherwise, remove the artichokes, leaving the garlic and herbs in, and simmer the liquid over a medium heat until reduced by half, to create a glaze. Dress the artichokes with the glaze and serve, or store the artichokes in the glaze in a jar in the fridge for up to 7 days. Makes 20 pieces.

Lamb, artichoke & mint ragù (GF)

I first made this ragù for my Italian-inspired menu at the Melbourne Wine Room, all those years ago, and have been cooking it ever since. The flavours are just a natural fit in my cook's brain. **Serves 6**

400 g (14 oz) jar or tin of artichoke hearts, drained and quartered
1 kg (2 lb 3 oz) lamb shoulder, cut into 4 cm (1½ in) dice
2 brown onions, finely diced
4 garlic cloves, finely chopped
3 celery stalks, finely sliced

4 oregano sprigs, leaves picked
2 bay leaves
350 ml (12 fl oz) white wine
1 litre (34 fl oz/4 cups) White chicken stock (p. 54), or lamb or light beef stock
2 handfuls of finely grated parmesan or pecorino, plus extra to serve

120 g (4½ oz) butter
2 handfuls of mint leaves, torn
short pasta of your choice, or Gnocchi (p. 136), mash or Polenta (p. 383), to serve

Staples
EVOO, S&P

Preheat the oven to 200°C (400°F) fan-forced. Coat the artichoke hearts with oil and spread out on a baking tray. Roast for about 20 minutes, until brown and a little blistered.

Meanwhile, heat a generous splash of oil in a wide-based saucepan over a medium heat. Season the lamb with salt and pepper and brown very well on all sides; remove from the pan, leaving the oil and rendered fat behind. Add the onion and garlic, season with a little salt and cook for a few minutes until softened. Add the celery, oregano and bay leaves and caramelise gently, then return the lamb to the pan. Stir in the wine and simmer until reduced by half, about 5 minutes. Stir in the stock and simmer for 30 minutes.

Add the roasted artichokes and simmer for 30 minutes or so. The lamb should be meltingly tender, but be careful not to overcook it or stir too much, as the meat will break up and become stringy. The sauce should be looser if serving with pasta, but you will need to reduce it more if serving with mash or polenta.

Adjust the seasoning and finish by stirring in the cheese, butter and mint. If using pasta or gnocchi, stir it through until the sauce is glossy and clings to it. Otherwise, spoon the ragù over mash or polenta.

Make it different

Veal, artichoke & mint ragù. (GF) The lamb can also be swapped for diced veal.

With braised artichokes. Simple braised artichokes (see opposite) would elevate the flavour even more; just add them during the cooking.

With dried mint. If you're particularly partial to the lamb and mint combination, dried mint can be used instead of the fresh oregano, but 1½ teaspoons are sufficient.

Shaved fennel, artichoke & almond salad (GF)(V)

Pair with

Serve as part of a varied shared table, or pair it with roast chicken or steak.

Eating raw artichokes may seem a bit unusual, but they are in fact quite delicious. It's critical, though, that you dress the slices as quickly as possible before their colour dulls to an unappetising grey. **Serves 6 as a side**

100 ml (3½ fl oz) extra-virgin olive oil
juice of 1 lemon
3 large artichokes, prepared (see opposite)
½ large fennel bulb, fronds picked and reserved

150 g (5½ oz) fresh ricotta
50 g (1¾ oz) Parmigiano Reggiano
2 handfuls of toasted blanched almonds, crushed

Staples
S&P

Special equipment
Mandoline

Add the oil and lemon juice to a bowl, season with salt and pepper and combine well.

Using a mandoline, slice the artichokes very finely lengthways and immediately toss them through the dressing. Slice the fennel bulb a little thicker, but still finely, then toss with the fronds in another bowl.

Break the ricotta into chunks and arrange on a platter. Top with the fennel, then the artichokes, pouring all the residual dressing over the top. Finish by finely grating or shaving the Parmigiano over and scattering with the walnuts.

Make it faster
Shaved artichokes dressed simply with lemon juice and extra-virgin olive oil, and seasoned with salt and pepper, make a delicious accompaniment to roast chicken or Risotto bianco (p. 148).

Make it different
With cured fish or meat. Finish the salad with grated bottarga, or shaved mojama, jamón or prosciutto.

With goat's cheese. Goat's cheese would marry beautifully in place of the ricotta.

With more vegetables. Add some blanched asparagus or some double-podded broad beans.

With fried artichoke. Or for some drama and crunch, dust some artichoke slices in rice flour or cornflour (cornstarch) and shallow- or deep-fry at 170°C (340°F) until golden, then drain on paper towel and use to garnish.

Braised artichoke, fennel & broad bean salad with orange glaze GF V

This salad came together one day at a good friend's vineyard. 'Just bring a salad,' they said. Anyway, with some ingredients in hand and some plucked from their garden, this is what we ended up with, more or less. **Serves 6–8**

Pair with

Works beautifully with barbecued meats, and would accompany roasted or grilled chicken or a lamb braise equally well.

1 quantity Braised artichokes (p. 534) – minus the garlic, bay & white wine glaze
3 oranges
80 ml (2½ fl oz/⅓ cup) extra-virgin olive oil
50 ml (1¾ fl oz) sherry vinegar
1 kg (2 lb 3 oz) broad beans, double podded (see p. 430)

2 handfuls of mint leaves, torn
1 handful of dill fronds
120 g (4½ oz/1¼ cups) finely grated Parmigiano Reggiano
1 large fennel bulb, finely shaved using a mandoline

Orange glaze
juice of 3 oranges
1 teaspoon fennel seeds, crushed
1½ tablespoons extra-virgin olive oil

Staples
S&P

Special equipment
Mandoline

For the orange glaze, add the orange juice and fennel seeds to a small saucepan and gently reduce by two-thirds, then combine in a large bowl with the oil. Season with salt and pepper. Toss the artichokes through and set aside.

Slice the peel and any pith off two of the oranges, then cut into five or six slices each.

Combine the oil and vinegar in a bowl, seasoning with salt and pepper. Add the broad beans, herbs and parmesan and toss to coat.

Arrange the shaved fennel and orange slices on a platter, then spoon the broad bean mixture over. Arrange the artichokes on the salad and spoon their dressing over. Grate half the zest of the remaining orange directly over the salad and serve.

Make it a meal
You could dress this up further with fresh ricotta, kalamata olives and finely sliced salad onion.

Artichoke, anchovy & gruyère gratin

Preheat the oven to 200°C (400°F) fan-forced. In a bowl, combine 120 g (4½ oz) room-temperature cream cheese, 100 g (3½ oz) mayonnaise, 2 teaspoons dijon mustard, ½ teaspoon cayenne pepper, ½ teaspoon smoked paprika, the leaves from 6 thyme sprigs and a pinch of salt in a bowl until you have a paste. Drain, dry and finely chop 600 g (1 lb 5 oz) jarred or tinned artichoke hearts, then add to the cream cheese mixture along with 150 g (5½ oz) diced gruyère or fontina and 50 g (1¾ oz/½ cup) grated Grana Padano. Press the mixture into a baking dish and cover with 100 g (3½ oz/1¼ cups) fresh white breadcrumbs. Arrange 8 anchovies in a crisscross pattern on top, then bake for 20 minutes, until bubbling. Squeeze the juice of ½ lemon over and serve immediately, with focaccia (see p. 845), flatbread or crackers.

Braised lamb, artichokes, lemon & cinnamon with couscous

While it's not a classic recipe, this draws on the flavours of my Tunisian heritage. The combination of lemon, cinnamon, cumin and garlic works so well with lamb shoulder – simple, yet with an exotic feel, too. But the artichokes elevate it even further, working so well with the aromatic and lusciously textured braise. Using lamb shoulder is key here, as it's a full-flavoured cut that yields a richly sticky stew, rather than the stringy and lean result that is more likely if using lamb leg. You can use Braised artichokes (p. 534) here, but a quality jar will do just fine. **Serves 6**

1 kg (2 lb 3 oz) lamb shoulder, cut into 4–5 cm (1½–2 in) dice
2 large brown onions, cut into thick rounds
6 garlic cloves, smashed
2 bird's eye chillies, split lengthways
6 thyme sprigs
2 bay leaves
2 teaspoons cumin seeds
1 cinnamon stick
1 teaspoon black peppercorns, ground

2 tablespoons tomato paste (concentrated purée)
1 large lemon, peeled in strips, then halved for squeezing
350 ml (12 fl oz) dry white wine
1 litre (34 fl oz/4 cups) White chicken stock (p. 54)
6 silverbeet (Swiss chard) leaves, cut across the stem into 4 cm (1½ in) widths
400 g (14 oz) jar of artichoke hearts, drained and halved

plain yoghurt, to serve

Couscous
2 tablespoons extra-virgin olive oil
370 g (13 oz/2 cups) instant couscous
500 ml (17 fl oz/2 cups) boiling water

Staples
EVOO, S&P

Preheat the oven to 160°C (320°F) fan-forced.

Add a generous splash of oil to a flameproof casserole dish over a high heat. Add the lamb and season generously with salt, then cook all over until evenly browned. Add the onion, garlic, chilli, thyme, bay leaves, cumin, cinnamon and pepper and cook for about 5 minutes to soften and meld the flavours. Add the tomato paste and lemon peel and stir to coat. Stir in the wine and simmer until reduced by half, about 2 minutes.

Add the stock and bring to a simmer. Pile the silverbeet and artichokes on top, but don't stir them through. Cover with the lid, place in the oven and cook for 1½ hours.

Once the lamb is tender, remove the dish from the oven, remove the lid and reduce the liquid over a medium heat until it has a sauce consistency, adjusting the seasoning as necessary.

For the couscous, rub the oil through the grains in a heatproof bowl until well coated. Pour the water over and cover with plastic wrap. Uncover after 5 minutes, then fluff the grains with a fork.

Squeeze the peeled lemon into the braise. Serve with the couscous and a large dollop of yoghurt.

Make it different
Braised chicken, artichokes, lemon & cinnamon with couscous. This recipe also works beautifully with an equal weight of boned chicken thighs in place of the lamb.

With olives & harissa. Throw in a few handfuls of cracked green olives and serve dolloped with green or red harissa (see p. 92).

Make it vegetarian Ⓥ
Cut a peeled head of celeriac into large dice and brown off as you would the lamb, with an extra splash of oil. Swap out the chicken stock for 600 ml (20½ fl oz) vegetable stock and reducing the cooking time to 1 hour.

Braised artichoke, egg, olive & watercress salad ⓥ

This starter salad is super simple in its presentation, but it certainly delivers complex flavours. I'd have this on its own as a light lunch with some great bread, or it could be part of a larger affair. **Serves 4–6**

1 quantity Braised artichokes with glaze (p. 534), warmed
2 handfuls of flat-leaf (Italian) parsley leaves, torn
1 handful of mint leaves

3 handfuls of picked watercress
4 soft-boiled eggs, halved
100 g (3½ oz) fromage frais
12 black olives

80 g (2¾ oz/ ½ cup) toasted blanched almonds, lightly crushed
grilled bread, to serve

Staples
EVOO, S&P

Toss the artichokes and glaze with the parsley and mint. Scatter half the watercress over a platter. Spoon on the artichokes and glaze, then arrange the eggs on top. Dollop the fromage frais around, then scatter with the olives, the remaining watercress and the almonds. Season with salt and pepper, then drizzle with some oil to finish. Serve with grilled bread.

Roman-style fried artichokes Ⓥ ⓋⒼ

Short cut

Use jarred or tinned artichoke hearts. Press all the liquid out of them and dry thoroughly, then rub in a 50-50 mix of semolina and flour, pushing the petals open. Deep-fry for 5–8 minutes until crisp.

Carciofi alla giudia ('artichokes in the Jewish style') is one of Rome's classic dishes – one of necessity perhaps, typically associated with the Jewish ghetto, which was established there in the mid 1500s. That's not to say a version of the dish didn't exist before, but frying was a key method of cooking, and this dish became very popular. Well, in the ghetto at least: wider acceptance took a little while. The Romanesco artichoke variety, which is generally less spiny with a less prickly choke, is typically used, but any baby artichokes will work. My version employs a batter, which is not traditional, but delicious nonetheless. Enjoy as a starter or as part of an antipasto selection, either on their own, with lemon, or with mayonnaise spiked with lemon and/or capers. Or for something different, sprinkle the cooked artichokes with aleppo pepper and salt. **Serves 6**

juice of 1 lemon
60 ml (2 fl oz/¼ cup)
  extra-virgin olive oil
1 teaspoon salt flakes
10 baby artichokes, trimmed
  and quartered, in acidulated
  water (p. 534)
oil, for deep-frying (olive oil is
  best; see p. 22)

Batter
150 g (5½ oz/1 cup) plain
  (all-purpose) flour
1 teaspoon salt flakes
50 ml (1¾ fl oz) extra-virgin
  olive oil
150 ml (5½ fl oz) lukewarm
  water, plus extra

Staples
EVOO, S&P

Special equipment
Mandoline

To make the batter, combine the flour and salt in a large bowl, making a well in the centre. Combine the oil and water, then pour into the well while whisking vigorously. The batter should be quite liquid, similar to thick (double/heavy) cream; adjust with a little more water if it's too thick. Set aside for 30–60 minutes at room temperature.

Meanwhile, combine the lemon juice, oil and salt in a large bowl. Drain the artichokes, shaking them in a colander to get rid of any excess water. Add them to the bowl, mixing well with your hands. Set aside for at least 30 minutes.

Add the cooking oil to a deep frying pan or shallow saucepan, to a depth of at least 6 cm (2½ in), then heat to 165°C (330°F).

Drain the artichokes and shake off any excess liquid, then add to the batter and mix well to coat. Working in batches so that they are well spaced, add the artichokes, one by one, to the hot oil; it should bubble up around each piece as it hits the oil. Regulate the heat so that the artichokes don't fry too fiercely, as they need to cook for 3–4 minutes – if the oil is too hot, the batter will cook before the artichokes are tender. During cooking, turn the artichoke pieces in the oil so they brown evenly on both sides. Drain well on paper towel, then season with salt and pepper and serve.

Make it different

You could also try frying whole artichokes, if you come across very small and tender specimens. After marinating, force open the leaves a little before dipping them in the batter, and double the frying time.

Make it a meal

At mr. wolf we served these with a quality tin of sardines or anchovies and plenty of crostini. They'd also be great on a niçoise-style salad, crumbled over a simple potato salad with boiled egg, or with Petit salé aux lentilles (p. 334).

Slice the fried artichokes and toss with parsley, dill and/or mint, tiny capers and very finely sliced lemon, and serve with any seared fish fillet or roasted whole fish.

Jerusalem artichoke

Jerusalem artichokes are perhaps the most confusingly named vegetable of all, having no relationship with either of their two identifying words. The synonym 'sunchoke' is a little more revealing, as they are, in fact, a variety of sunflower, native to North America. With equally bright – though significantly smaller – flowers than those the word 'sunflower' evokes, Jerusalem artichokes were cultivated by Native Americans and adopted by settlers who exported them to Europe, where they flourished. Indeed, they thrive in most conditions, to the point that they were regarded as an invasive weed for some time in the United States. This period coincided with a lack of appreciation of them as a foodstuff, though they are very nutritious, and really quite delicious.

Jerusalem artichokes have an additional stain on their reputation outside of their vigour, which is due to their high concentration of inulin – an indigestible fibre that can't be broken down by our digestive enzymes, passing through to the colon, where it becomes prime food for our gut flora, which will devour it and flourish. In other words, it is a prebiotic, which is great – but this process also does produce an extraordinary amount of carbon dioxide and methane. Slow roasting, cooking in acidulated water and pickling will all moderate some of these gaseous effects, though the most health benefits are gained by eating the raw chokes. You'll have to decide your path on this one. Moderation is not a bad angle.

The edible end of a Jerusalem artichoke is found below ground, where small knobbly tubers – looking like something between ginger and a potato – flourish. The skin is typically an ivory or parchment colour, but it can be a quite bright red or magenta as well. The flavour is said to resemble that of a globe artichoke, accounting for part of the nomenclature, though I'm not so sure about the connection. To me they have a distinctive earth-scented but sophisticated vegetal profile that is thoroughly individual.

You can simply cook the tubers in salted water until tender (10–20 minutes, depending on size), but I much prefer them either raw or roasted, which enhances their sweetness and deeply nutty, caramelised character. Simply oil and season with salt and pepper, then roast in a moderate oven until tender and golden, which will take 40 minutes to 1 hour. They can be eaten as is, or left to cool a little and tossed with plenty of chopped soft herbs and mayonnaise, crème fraîche or a vinaigrette. The raw tubers are delicious sliced and roasted in a gratin with potato (p. 627) – or sliced thin and layered with potato in pommes anna (p. 624). They can also be sliced and pan-fried in butter and oil, then salted generously and served like chips – or dice them and sauté with bacon lardons for a side to accompany steak or chicken.

Choose artichokes that are firm, unblemished and free from any harvesting cuts. Selecting the less eccentrically shaped specimens will make your life significantly easier if you intend to peel or slice them finely, but is not so relevant if roasting or boiling. They will store reasonably well in the fridge, but they need to be kept in a relatively high-humidity environment, so make sure they are in a bag or sealed container. You can also freeze them.

Also see

*Beef carpaccio with
Jerusalem artichokes* 280

Pair with

Jerusalem artichokes adore
soft herbs such as mint, chives,
tarragon and parsley. Their
nuttiness is enhanced by tree-nut
oils such as hazelnut and
walnut, and with the actual
nuts themselves. The richness
of the tubers pairs well with
cheeses, but is delicate enough
to marry with seafood, too. Try
them with beef, either roasted
or grilled, or raw as a carpaccio.
They also work very well with
pork and mustard fruits.

Preparing Jerusalem artichokes

I sometimes freeze Jerusalem artichokes before using, as it seems to reduce their gassy effects. You'll still get enough beneficial fibre, but won't need to quarantine yourself after dinner. Some tubers are quite regular and more potato-like, while others will have multiple bulbous protrusions – so the choice here is whether to peel or not, with an inevitable loss of yield with the more irregular specimens, not to mention a rabbit hole of lost time. The benefit of peeling is the colour in the finished dish, so for a bright and pale soup or puree, peeling is essential. But if this doesn't concern you, then a good scrub will suffice – dirt hides in all those protrusions, so do this thoroughly. Just note that retaining the skin can steer the result towards grey in hue. Your choice. If you do peel or slice, just pop them in some acidulated water, as they discolour just like their namesake.

Roasted Jerusalem artichoke salad with horseradish & salmon roe (GF)

I love the nutty complexity Jerusalem artichokes take on when roasted, partnering so well with robust flavours, such as the pungent kick of fresh horseradish. This is a simple warm salad, with a luxuriously salty pop of salmon roe. **Serves 4**

800 g (1 lb 12 oz) Jerusalem artichokes, scrubbed, large ones halved
100 g (3½ oz) crème fraîche

4 cm (1½ in) piece of fresh horseradish
30 g (1 oz) salmon roe, or trout roe

2–3 dill sprigs, fronds picked and chopped
Staples
EVOO, S&P

Preheat the oven to 180°C (350°F) fan-forced.

Toss the artichokes in oil in a roasting tin, season with salt and roast for 40–50 minutes, until golden and tender. Remove from the oven and leave until cooled but still with some residual warmth.

Toss the still-warm artichokes with the crème fraîche and pile onto a serving plate. Finely grate the horseradish over, season with salt and pepper and dot with the salmon roe. Scatter with the dill and serve.

Make it vegetarian (V)
Skip the salmon roe, and instead grate 100 g (3½ oz) manchego or Parmigiano Reggiano over the top. A mix of Jerusalem artichokes and roast potatoes works well, too.

Slow-roasted Jerusalem artichokes with roe & pan-fried scallops (GF)

A rich sweetness and umami dimension develop with slow-roasting. Pile whole Jerusalem artichoke tubers on rock salt on a baking tray and roast at about 160°C (320°F) for an hour or so. Once tender, split lengthways and stuff with Horseradish cream (p. 70), salmon or trout roe, or caviar if your budget stretches there. Top with some pan-fried scallops (or warmed crabmeat) and sprinkle with some chopped herbs such as dill or chives.

Pair with

Serve as part of a shared table feast.

Serve as a side for fish.

With cheese rather than roe, this is particularly good with roast beef or a grilled steak.

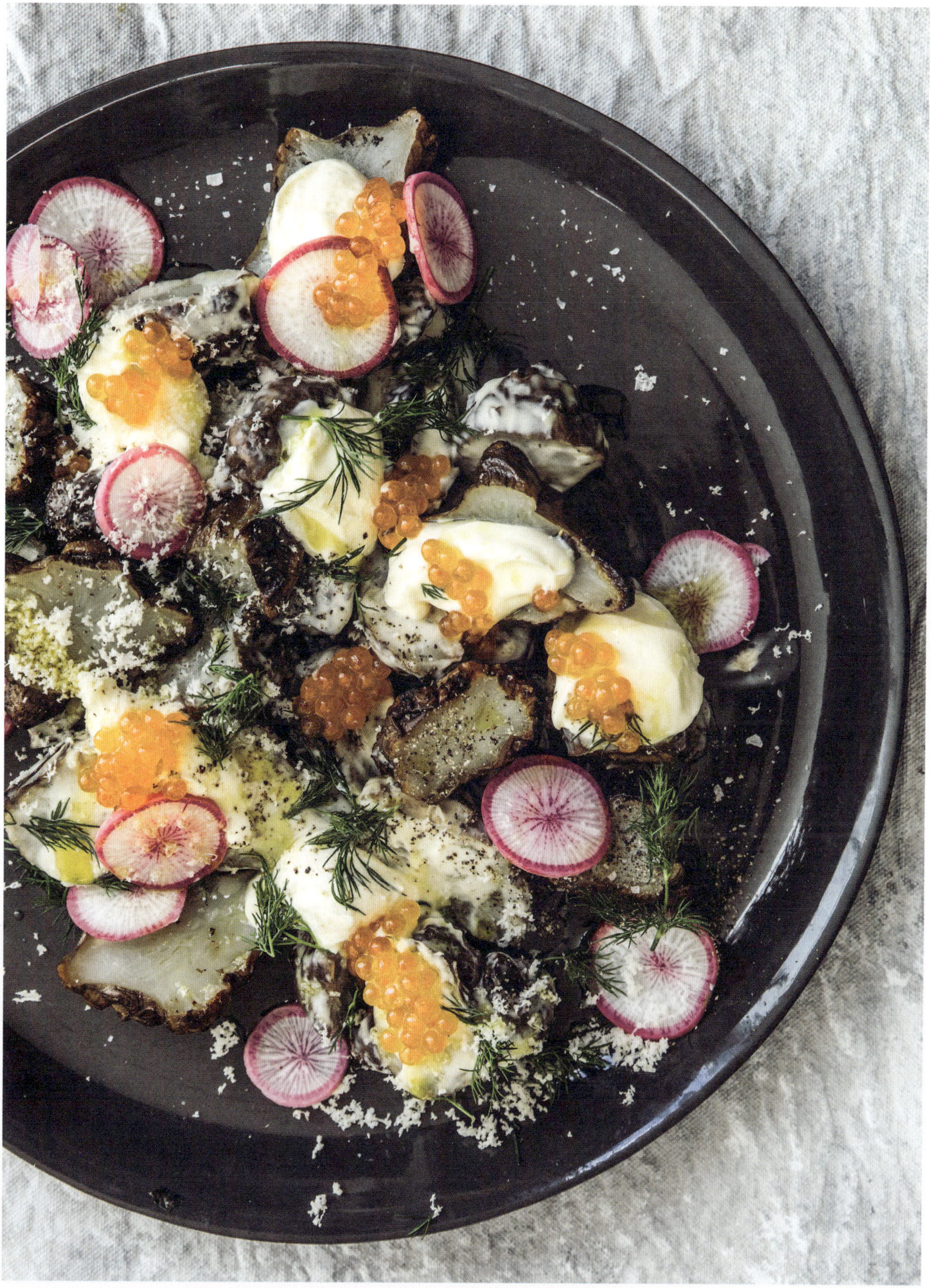

Jerusalem artichoke soup (GF)

This is such a velvety, rich and luscious soup, with deeply earthy, sweet and nutty flavours. It is by no means complicated to prepare, but it makes for a sophisticated and elegant starter, especially if you're inclined to dress it up a little with some sliced truffle or seared scallops. Although it is a little more work, using roasted artichokes gives so much depth of flavour, with layers of caramelisation lending resoundingly rich bass notes. **Serves 8–10**

750 g (1 lb 11 oz) Jerusalem artichokes, scrubbed
200 g (7 oz) yellow-fleshed potatoes (such as Dutch cream)
1.2 litres (41 fl oz) Golden chicken stock (p. 54)

500 ml (17 fl oz/2 cups) cream (35% fat)
80 g (2¾ oz) butter
1 small onion, finely sliced
1 leek, white part only, finely sliced
2 garlic cloves, sliced
1 whole nutmeg

snipped chives or picked watercress, to serve

Staples
EVOO, S&WP

Special equipment
Mandoline

Preheat the oven to 180°C (350°F) fan-forced.

Toss 500 g (1 lb 2 oz) of the artichokes in oil in a roasting tin, season with salt and roast for 40–50 minutes, until golden and tender. Remove from the oven, leave until cool enough to handle, then dice roughly.

Meanwhile, peel the remaining raw artichokes and potatoes, then finely slice using a mandoline.

Add the roasted artichokes and raw artichoke and potato slices to a saucepan. Pour in the stock and cream and bring to the boil. Turn the heat down to a slow simmer and cook until very tender. It's important to cook slowly, as you don't want to reduce the stock level much.

Meanwhile, melt the butter in a large wide-based saucepan over a low–medium heat. Add the onion, leek and garlic and sweat until softened and translucent but not coloured, about 10 minutes.

When the potato and artichokes are cooked, add the whole mixture to the onion pan. Season with salt and white pepper and bring to a simmer, then turn off the heat.

Blitz the soup with a stick blender, or in batches in a blender. Pass through a fine-mesh sieve into a clean saucepan, then season as needed and grate in nutmeg to taste.

Reheat the soup and serve with a garnish of chives or watercress. The soup will keep in an airtight container in the fridge for up to a week.

Make it different

With cheese toast. Just before serving, drop a grilled cheese toast (featuring gruyère, raclette or fontina) on the soup. Or serve with well-buttered toast with a crumbling of soft goat's cheese.

With seafood. Take it a step further by placing some diced smoked eel, oysters or pan-fried scallops in each bowl before pouring the soup in.

With egg, crème fraîche & caviar. Finish the soup with a poached egg, a crostini with crème fraîche, and an overly generous dollop of caviar or salmon roe.

With truffle. A few shavings of fresh truffle would also be divine on this soup.

Roasted & raw Jerusalem artichoke salad (GF) (V)

Make a dressing of equal parts grapeseed oil and walnut or hazelnut oil, a splash of chardonnay vinegar and about one-third of the volume again of crème fraîche. Dress some shaved raw Jerusalem artichoke tubers, then pile on top of some roasted ones, tipping all the dressing over. Top with peppery lettuce, baby kale, mustard cress, sliced chicory (witlof/endive) or the like (a mix would be great), then crumble over some Roquefort or grated Parmigiano Reggiano or gruyère. Finish with chopped toasted hazelnuts and snipped chives, drizzle with a little olive oil and serve.

Raw Jerusalem artichoke salad with broad beans & cheese (GF) (V)

Take the time to meticulously peel some Jerusalem artichoke tubers, then slice very finely using a mandoline. Dress with lemon juice and extra-virgin olive oil (a dash of walnut oil would be nice, too), then toss with some double-podded broad beans and soft herbs. Season well, being especially generous with the pepper, and over the top scatter some ricotta, goat's curd, stracciatella di bufala or other fresh mozzarella. A few white anchovies are not essential, but a nice touch, and there you have a simple and superb little starter or share plate.

Jerusalem artichoke pickle (GF)(V)(VG)

Pair with

Use anywhere you would use a pickle.

Slice and eat with cheese, charcuterie or with terrines.

Use in sandwiches, or enjoy as a snack.

Slice or julienne and serve with sliced raw fish.

Slice finely and serve on a Beef carpaccio (p. 280) or with Vitello tonnato (p. 297).

Add to a salad with chicken or quail.

Dice or julienne and add to a grain salad.

A long-lost version of this pickle is buried deep in my early memories of cooking professionally, as it was used in salads at Tansy's restaurant, where I was an apprentice. I have never forgotten staring at jars and jars of the pickled barrel-shaped tubers while endlessly prepping. And even though I had the written recipe, I never actually made it at the restaurant, and have since searched widely for that recipe but to no avail! So, I have based this version on a Stephanie Alexander recipe, which has American origins, and tweaked it to more closely resemble the less-sweet pickle that I remember from way back when. It takes some time to fully cure but is worth the patience, as it is both delicious and somewhat less gas-inducing than other forms of preparation.

Makes 25

25 Jerusalem artichokes, scrubbed and peeled

Pickling medium
1.5 litres (51 fl oz/6 cups) white-wine vinegar
1½ tablespoons salt flakes

700 g (1 lb 9 oz/3 cups) caster (superfine) sugar
4–5 cm (1½–2 in) piece of fresh turmeric, peeled and sliced on an angle, or 1 tablespoon ground

1 tablespoon white or yellow mustard seeds
2 teaspoons celery seeds
2 cinnamon sticks
2 teaspoons ground ginger

Add the pickling medium ingredients to a saucepan and simmer for 15 minutes. Set aside to cool.

Pack the artichokes into a sterilised jar (or jars; see p. 40) and pour the cooled syrup over. Seal the jar tightly, then refrigerate and leave for about 3 months to pickle.

Kohlrabi

To be honest, I came to kohlrabi quite late. Although it has been generally available in markets for some time, it took a while for my curiosity to take control. And I wish I hadn't been so sluggish. Kohlrabi is a wonderful vegetable, somewhere between a turnip and a radish in flavour, with a cucumber freshness thrown in. It has the best textural crunch of pretty much any vegetable, and it's juicy as well: a good combination, in my mind. This vibrant flavour, texture and attendant juiciness means it is something I rarely think about cooking, although you can. In fact, it is widely cooked in Europe, especially in the north-east.

Kohlrabi is sometimes called 'German turnip', with the name translating as 'cabbage turnip' (kohl means cabbage, and though rübe is the word for turnip, rabi is a dialect variant), rightly placing it in the brassica family. Kohlrabi comes in green and purple hues, but if there is a flavour difference, I'm not receptive to it. Green and purple kohlrabi can be used interchangeably in dishes and, once peeled, will be indistinguishable from each other. Cooked kohlrabi is somewhat like braised daikon or turnip, and can be added to soups, curries and stews, or used as a side.

Taking up spices beautifully during braising, kohlrabi features in northern Indian cooking, and is also well appreciated in Vietnam, where it is called su hao. There it is used both cooked and raw, featuring in soups, stir-fries and salads. It's not hard to see it used in Thai-inspired dishes, too: julienned kohlrabi would make an interesting alternative in a Green papaya salad (see p. 438), or add it to an Asian slaw with prawns (shrimp), sliced roast pork or fried tofu. In my house, kohlrabi is shaved finely, julienned or diced and ends up in super-bright salads, or is pickled.

Select bulbs with bright, unblemished skin and firm texture. If possible, buy kohlrabi with the leaves still attached. Firstly, you can eat them. And, secondly, as with many vegetables, vibrant foliage is a good sign of recent harvest. The bulbs can certainly store for some time in your crisper, but I'd always prefer the freshest specimen, and those leaves are delicious. Avoid overly large bulbs, as they can become woody and fibrous.

Pair with

Kohlrabi loves lemon and lime juice, wine and rice vinegar, soy, sesame, pickled ginger, garlic, spring onion (scallion), salad onions, and the tart richness of crème fraîche, yoghurt, parmesan, sour cream and mayonnaise. Accent with parsley, mint, curry leaves, makrut lime leaves and coriander (cilantro), as well as spices such as cumin, celery seeds, black pepper, aleppo pepper, chilli, fenugreek and curry powder. Delicious with olives, cucumber, celeriac, radish, apple and firm persimmon, and with proteins such as boiled egg, pork (try a crumbed schnitzel!) and grilled fish.

Preparing kohlrabi

Remove the leaves and stems from the kohlrabi bulb, chop them as you like, depending on their size, then sauté, steam or blanch them as your first priority. Don't relegate them to the crisper as a secondary product; they are lovely but will deteriorate quickly. (If the leaves are young and small and the stems quite fine, they can be used in salads. For example, slice them finely and add to a slaw with the julienned bulb.) Trim off the woody taproot and peel the bulb using a vegetable peeler or paring knife. The core of the root can be fibrous inside the bulb, so trim this or just avoid when slicing. (One bulb of kohlrabi can go a long way, so only peel as needed, as the left-over portion will keep longer this way.) The texture of raw kohlrabi is quite firm and crisp, which makes it great for salads, but it will need to be sliced finely or julienned; a mandoline is made for jobs like this. You could, I suppose, grate it – but I don't, preferring the texture from a clean cut. If cooking, the bulb can be sliced or diced, and then steamed, sautéed or boiled until tender.

Kohlrabi, cauliflower & fenugreek soup (GF) (V) (VG)

I find the flavour of cooked kohlrabi quite mild with a subtle sweetness, which works well with the gentle spices in this coconut-based soup. The cauliflower and pungent fenugreek add depth. **Serves 4–6**

½ cauliflower, cut into florets
1 onion, sliced
2 garlic cloves, sliced
2 kohlrabi, peeled and cut
    into rough 3 cm (1¼ in) dice
1½ tablespoons ground
    fenugreek

2 teaspoons curry powder
500 ml (17 fl oz/2 cups)
    coconut milk, plus extra
    to serve
400 ml (13½ fl oz) Classic
    white vegetable stock
    (p. 51), or water

4 dill sprigs, chopped,
    stalks and all

Staples
EVOO, S&P

Preheat the oven to 180°C (350°F) fan-forced.

Spread the cauliflower on a baking tray, drizzle with oil and season with salt and pepper. Roast for about 40 minutes, until tender and golden.

Add a good splash of oil to a large saucepan over a medium heat. Add the onion and garlic and cook until softened, about 5 minutes. Add the roasted cauliflower, kohlrabi, fenugreek and curry powder and season with salt and pepper, then stir through for a minute or so. Add the coconut milk and stock, then simmer for about 25 minutes, until the vegetables are very tender.

Stir in the dill, then blitz with a stick blender until smooth. Serve with a swirl of extra coconut milk.

Kohlrabi, cabbage & beetroot slaw (GF) (V) (VG)

This salad is crisp and vibrant, but also quite rich and fulfilling, with the peanut-laced 'mayonnaise' giving it ample body and depth. **Serves 8**

4 small beetroot (beets), trimmed
¼ white cabbage
2 carrots, peeled
1 kohlrabi, peeled
½ celeriac, peeled
½ bunch of Thai basil,
    or mint, leaves picked

5 spring onions (scallions),
    white part only, finely sliced
2 long red chillies, finely sliced
1 tablespoon julienned pickled
    white ginger
1 × quantity Tofu 'mayonnaise'
    (p. 75)

2 tablespoons chopped
    peanuts
1 tablespoon poppy seeds

Staples
S&WP, SGR

Special equipment
Mandoline

Quick kohlrabi pickle (V) (VG)

In a small saucepan, combine 200 ml (7 fl oz) rice vinegar, 100 ml (3½ fl oz) mirin, 1 smashed garlic clove, 2 tablespoons caster (superfine) sugar, 2 teaspoons salt, 10 black peppercorns, 5 cloves and 2 star anise and boil for 1 minute. Pour the mixture into a heatproof bowl and leave to cool down until warm. Peel 1 kohlrabi and cut it into wedges 1 cm (½ in) thick. Pack the kohlrabi into a sterilised jar (see p. 40) large enough to submerge the kohlrabi and pour in the pickling liquid and aromatics to cover. Seal tightly and leave to stand for at least 30 minutes before using; it will be more flavourful if left overnight. The pickle will keep for about 1 month in the fridge. This pickle has an Asian feel, but you can use white-wine vinegar in place of the rice vinegar and mirin to suit other uses. Great in a salad, a slaw, Bánh mì (p. 332), bao (see p. 333), or a fried rice or noodle dish, and with rich meat dishes, such as lamb, Confit duck (p. 260) and Crispy roasted pork belly (p. 332).

Pair with

Crumbed and fried eggplant (aubergine) or field mushrooms.

Crispy roasted pork belly (p. 332).

Stuff in a roll with grilled skewered meat or vegetables, or a crumbed chicken schnitzel.

Using a mandoline, shave the beetroot finely, then toss with a pinch of sugar and set aside.

Shave the cabbage finely. Shave the carrots on an angle. Shave the kohlrabi and celeriac, then stack the two together and slice with a knife into strips. Add them all to a bowl with the basil, spring onion, chilli and ginger. Season lightly with salt and white pepper and toss.

Tip the mayonnaise over the salad, toss to combine, then pile onto a serving plate.

Blot the shaved beetroot with paper towel, then scatter over the salad, along with the peanuts and poppy seeds. Serve immediately.

Kohlrabi & cucumber salad with lemon yoghurt dressing GF V

This is a crunchy and refreshing little number, perfect for contrasting a rich and full-flavoured dish. It's also a very pretty addition to the table. **Serves 6**

Pair with

I like the contrast of this refreshing salad with intense flavours such as charred or spiced barbecued meats or roasts.

It's also great with slow-braised lamb shoulder.

It will also knit into a spread of dishes, especially with a Middle Eastern bent, such as Falafel (p. 432), koftas (pp. 249, 309) or grilled skewered meat or vegetables. Bring in some Hummus (p. 374), Baba ghanoush (p. 519), tabouleh (see p. 419), freshly cooked pitta breads (see p. 854) and … you get the picture.

1 kohlrabi, peeled and cut into 3 cm (1¼ in) dice
1 telegraph (long) cucumber, peeled and seeded, cut into 2 cm (¾ in) chunks
1 teaspoon caster (superfine) sugar
1 teaspoon salt flakes

1½ teaspoons cumin seeds, roughly ground
1 handful of soft herbs (such as dill, mint and/or tarragon leaves), torn
1½ pomegranates, seeds reserved

Lemon yoghurt dressing
200 g (7 oz) plain yoghurt
60 ml (2 fl oz/¼ cup) extra-virgin olive oil
juice of ½ lemon
1 garlic clove, finely grated

Staples
S&P

Combine the dressing ingredients in a bowl, season with salt and pepper and chill.

Toss the kohlrabi and cucumber in the sugar and salt and set aside at room temperature for 20 minutes. Drain the liquid from the vegetables, then toss the vegetables with the dressing.

Pile the salad onto a serving plate. Sprinkle with the cumin, herbs and pomegranate seeds. Serve.

Make it different

With pomegranate molasses. Drizzle with a little pomegranate molasses to add a tart sweetness.

With aleppo pepper. Sprinkle with aleppo pepper to add some gentle, fruity heat.

With apple. Add a diced granny smith apple with the dressing for a little more sweetness.

Leafy vegetables & salad leaves

Leafy vegetables, from buttery soft lettuce to sharply bitter chicory (witlof/ endive), are some of my very favourite things. A perfectly dressed mixed salad, with each leaf chosen carefully to balance flavour, texture and bitterness is a true delight. From the peppery lift of rocket (arugula) to darkly bitter radicchio to the gently earthy tones of crunchy cos (romaine) and a wiry burr of curly endive (frisée), there can be so much going on in the humblest of salads. And a meal without one – of one sort or another – just seems a little incomplete to me.

My love for a proper mixed salad started early in my restaurant career, where my first prep job was to meticulously pick, wash, dry, sort and carefully combine lettuces for the well-loved salads at Tansy's. There were also herbs in the blend, chervil and parsley mostly. Making the salad dressing was quite a ritual as well, with perfectly pitched balance essential. A dressed salad, always tossed with open fingers so as not to crush the lettuces, was scrutinised daily to make sure it was perfect. Besides pristine leaves that have been well washed, then perfectly dried – wet leaves are a no-no – I always use well-chilled leaves and room-temperature vinaigrette, dressing the salad just before serving so it stays bright and crisp.

But leafy vegetables naturally go beyond salads, with a brace of iron-rich greens, such as kale, silverbeet (Swiss chard), cavolo nero and spinach, and then there are those that can be plucked from an unkempt garden, such as dandelion greens, mallow, fat hen or nettles. They're all wonderfully nutritious and can make for a healthful side dish, be used to green up a soup (see p. 558) or braise, be packed into a pie with cheese (pp. 563–4) or used to fill an omelette (see p. 353) or frittata. One of my favourite sides is the simple Greek preparation horta, which are boiled wild greens.

Traditionally, horta would have been made up of a large variety of 'weeds' with various health-giving properties. It's a staple food of necessity, a pauper's meal, if you like, foraged rather than cultivated, and it's as marvellous as most food that was once consigned to the diets of the poor. It is also often linked to the notable longevity of some communities in the 'blue zones'.

Silverbeet and Swiss chard are the same thing, the difference merely nomenclature. However, where I'm from the white-stalked and green-leafed version is usually called silverbeet, while the red and golden cultivars are typically called chard, and a bunch of varying hues from yellow through golden to pink to purple and on to a deep beetroot red are composed of the stems from different plants. All those types taste a little different, though they are essentially in the same vein, just a little earthier or sweeter here and there.

English spinach is the ubiquitous leafy green, and it can be employed as a simple wilted or pureed side with butter and a squeeze of lemon at the last minute, or be used to fill a pie (see p. 564) or pastry (see p. 828). It can contribute to a curry (see p. 359) or be the hero of one, such as with saag paneer. Baby spinach also makes a tasty and quite robust salad leaf (see p. 267), or it can be wilted at the last minute for a pasta (see p. 124) or to add to an omelette (see p. 353). Native warrigal greens can be used in place of spinach, but it's recommended not to eat them raw, as they are rich in oxalates, which can lead to kidney stones. Another spinach-like green is amaranth, which often has a reddish hue and is sometimes called Chinese spinach – it's great in stir-fries or dropped into soups.

Also see

Green goddess dressing 89

Green harissa 92

Ricotta & spinach ravioli 116

Green aglio e olio 122

Chicken livers with witlof & radicchio fatoush salad, currants & sumac 234

Lamb, spinach, pomegranate & date salad with crisp pitta 314

Pork & prawn wontons with choy sum & kale 342

Spiced green soup 381

Celeriac, apple & kale slaw with anchovy 484–5

Waldorf salad with roast chicken wrapped in iceberg 490

Apple, fennel & witlof slaw with buttermilk dressing 680

Cheese, silverbeet & hazelnut filling for sambouseks 833

A note on foraging

Dandelion, mallow, fat hen, chickweed, wood sorrel (oxalis) and nettles are all readily identified, but some caution is advised. Naturally, nettles require gloves, as they can be quite painful if handled improperly (blanching in boiling water will neutralise the stings), but it's important that you know something about the places you are foraging. Councils will spray for weeds, and many urban environments have dubious soil profiles, with high-traffic areas often carrying the legacy of lead from car exhausts.

Kale comes in a few variants, from fine Russian red kale that works in salads, to the more robust curly kale and cavolo nero, which are more suited to braised side dishes and soups, stews and the like. The latter two need a bit of cooking to tenderise, with cavolo nero particularly robust, holding its shape and deepening in colour over a long, slow braise.

That said, I often use cooking greens raw. Spinach, of course, but also finely shredded silverbeet (Swiss chard), and even kale, with a rest in the dressing breaking down any overt toughness.

Collard greens aren't commonly found in Australian markets, which is a shame. They have some bitterness, but I also find them to have a sweetness, with a flavour a little reminiscent of brussels sprouts. They are a brassica, so this is not surprising, with large fan-shaped leaves with thick ribs. Although they are often cooked for a long time, I have found that they are quite delicious quickly sautéed with garlic until tender.

Rocket is one of the easiest salad leaves to grow, with it reaping a good harvest over many weeks, even months. It grows rapidly, and the flavour changes as it matures, becoming more intensely peppery as the plant gets bigger. It's quite lovely harvested when youthful and wispy, and can be dropped on a fish crudo or the like, while the more mature leaves are ideal for a Carpaccio (p. 280) or to fill a roll with fresh mozzarella and salami. I like it with oil, lemon juice and salt for the simplest salad, or with shaved Parmigiano Reggiano, my best olive oil and some serious balsamic. And however you make that salad, it will be delicious tucked into a folded slice of Pizza margherita (p. 857). Quite mature leaves can also be sautéed with olive oil as a side, or made into a Pesto (p. 90) just as you would with basil (I quite like to use walnuts instead of pine nuts when doing this, but both work equally well).

To keep rocket producing, harvest the leaves regularly and snip off any flowers. Left to their own devices, especially in warm weather, rocket will bolt, going to flower and seed quickly, with the leaves quite small and sparse. That's not a tragedy, mind you, with the flowers very pretty and beloved by bees. They are also as tasty as the leaves and can be dropped on a dish for both culinary and aesthetic reasons. Try them scattered over fior di latte or burrata, perhaps with some prosciutto, bresaola or capocollo – some ripe figs split open would also be welcome. Left to die out and dry, one rocket plant will provide you with ample seeds for later crops. It really is a must for even the most casual of gardeners – and you can grow it in pots, too.

Watercress is another flavourful leaf with an intense pepperiness to it. The picked leaves and fine stems (fatter ones are typically woody) are wonderful in a salad, or dressed and served solo alongside chicken, fish or grilled steak. Watercress also makes wonderful soup (see p. 558). It's something that needs to be used quickly, usually on the day of purchase. Mustard cress also has a pungent peppery flavour, which can be added to salads or scattered over a dish to finish. Nasturtiums can also play this role, with the flowers and leaves both pretty and tasty, with the peppery heat coming late on the palate. If you're foraging for nasturtium, then also look for dandelion leaves, chickweed and wood sorrel, which all add an interesting angle to a salad.

Sorrel is also very easy to grow, and it is a perennial, so it just keeps on giving. It is also very hardy, so another good option for the keen cook but not always attentive gardener. Sorrel may not be commonly used these days, but it should feature more. It's not the hardiest once picked, so it's no surprise that it's not available in supermarkets, hence dropping out of view for most. It has the most delightful lemony flavour and tang to it, and I love it in leaf salads, or shredded in a slaw or potato salad.

Sorrel keeps its vibrant zing when cooked, but it breaks down into essentially a puree when heated, which with butter can be used to sauce fish, but I generally toss it in with other wilted greens, such as spinach, at the last minute to serve on the side of some pan-seared dory or snapper. I also add it to stir-fried noodles or a fish curry, or finely shred it and mix through fried rice or a Vietnamese-style rice paper roll.

Chicory is a broad family that includes radicchio and witlof but, when I use the term, I am referring to catalogna chicory, whose leaves look like elongated dandelion leaves in an upright and fairly tightly packed bunch. The leaves and stems are bitter, which I find appealing, especially in a mix for

Kale chips

Preheat the oven to 120°C (250°F) fan-forced. Line two baking trays with baking paper. Strip the leaves from the stems of 1 bunch of curly kale. Compost the stems and tear the leaves into large pieces. Drizzle a little oil over the leaves, toss to just coat, and massage a little with 1 teaspoon salt flakes. Spread out on the baking trays without crowding or layering. Season with salt and dehydrate in the oven for 15–20 minutes, until crisp. Leave to cool, then store in an airtight container and use within 3 days. You could also spray the chips with sherry vinegar using an atomiser, then eat straight away, toss in vinegar powder (which you can buy from specialty stores and some supermarkets) or dust with togarashi for a Japanese angle.

Horta

You can include any greens in a horta mix, but I always like to include plenty of bitter greens, such as chicory (witlof/endive) or dandelion leaves – and cime di rape (see p. 440) is a favourite inclusion. You can wilt in the pan with garlic and oil, or remove any tough stems and cook in plenty of boiling salted water until tender. The greens will naturally take different times to cook, and this will vary greatly depending on how mature they are. Drain well, then press out any excess liquid and chop finely. Sauté with plenty of olive oil, a smashed garlic clove or two and a teaspoon or so of ground fennel, season with salt and pepper and mix through a few sprigs of picked parsley or dill before squeezing in some lemon and serving. This can be served as a side for lamb, chicken, pork sausages or cotechino with lentils and fish, but it can be used for so many other things, too. Pile the greens onto some white beans dressed with oil and lemon juice, then top with feta or pecorino. Spoon the horta over fried eggs, or pile onto well-buttered toast with goat's cheese, taleggio or gruyère. The bitterness works wonderfully with dishes containing guanciale, pancetta, Lardo (see p. 326), bacon and pancetta. Spoon over Risotto bianco (p. 148) finished with Parmigiano Reggiano and a squeeze of lemon. Add to a plate of seared sardine fillets with segmented oranges and capers, or serve with simply seared swordfish, mackerel or blue-eye trevalla. Mix through a couple of tablespoons of chopped mustard fruits and serve with slow-roasted pork belly. Serve over sliced fresh mozzarella or burrata – some very finely sliced lemon, rind and all, cut into small triangles and tossed through the greens first is a lovely addition. Add the chopped greens to a braise of lamb or pork in the last 10 minutes of cooking. Stir through pan-fried pine or field mushrooms and pile onto bruschetta with melted fontina, taleggio, gruyère or fresh mozzarella.

horta, which is marvellous paired with roasted pork (see p. 338) or baccalà with grated hard-boiled eggs and grilled Sourdough bread (p. 847). I find it's best to boil the chicory in salted water for an extended amount of time, until softened, then to squeeze out the excess water, chop and dress with oil and lemon and a whisper of garlic. It's great stirred through cooked mussels and served with chargrilled bread.

Bitter leaves are essential. They make a salad sing, and they're an ideal foil for sweet or fatty foods, especially with a sharp vinaigrette. It's rare that I wouldn't include radicchio and witlof when making a proper mixed salad. Radicchio can also be used to finish gnocchi with blue cheese, chopped walnuts and balsamic (see p. 602) or a Duck ragù (p. 259), and it's marvellous with pickled cherries and burrata (see p. 566), or tossed in a pasta with tuna (see p. 125). Radicchio is also excellent paired with things such as charred calamari and potatoes in a warm salad topped with Pangrattato (p. 124) and chilli, or torn and tossed into an orange and fennel salad with olives. Radicchio is generally available in two cultivars, chioggia, which is spherical, and treviso, which is elongated, a little like witlof.

Witlof's firm crispness is a textural delight. The leaves also make great little 'spoons', ready to be filled with delicate morsels for canapés or to be used to scoop up salmon rillettes or a beef tartare (see p. 279). They are also excellent with Bagna cauda (p. 83), along with an assortment of young vegetables. The denser structure also means that witlof can be cooked like a vegetable, by braising in stock and butter (see p. 554). You can generally buy witlof in two colours, white or red.

Although the proliferation of more glamorous leaves has rendered iceberg lettuce somewhat unfashionable, you can't beat its crunch and watery refreshment value. It's naturally unmatched for making lettuce cups for spring rolls (see p. 575) or san choy bao (see p. 555), but it is also lovely torn and dropped into a mixed salad or to make a shredded salad with finely sliced salad onion and a vinegar-heavy dressing. I don't mind oak leaf and coral lettuces in a mix, and I really enjoy the texture and flavour of butter lettuce, which comes in a variety of cultivars, including green and red mignonette. Tatsoi, mizuna and mibuna (the latter pair being mustard greens) are all greens that I will use in a mix, and lamb's lettuce (mâche) is a bit of a favourite, with its petite soft leaves and buttery, nutty flavour. I also use youthful Russian red kale and baby rainbow chard to some salads, which are more deeply earthy and texturally interesting, as is curly endive (frisée), though I find the outer dark-green leaves can be a little too wiry at times.

Cos (romaine) is another crisp lettuce that holds its structure well, meaning it works so well in a salad with more robust ingredients, such as in that most famous of salads, the caesar. You can also grill, then braise it (see p. 561). Cos gives maximum crunch in a sandwich or roll, perhaps with some shredded roast chicken and a good dollop of mayo. The cos hearts are my favourite for salads, as they're delicately flavoured and extra crunchy. Buying small heads guarantees more crunch. These are generally sold as baby cos, but they are simply a cultivar that produce a small head. I find the large heads of mature cos a little wasteful, as I don't find a lot of value in the outer leaves. The cosberg – a hybrid of fairly obvious parentage – is also an excellent crunchy option.

Preparing leafy vegetables & salad leaves

When preparing salad leaves and greens, it is important to wash them well, as many harbour plenty of sandy grit, which will ruin a dish. A good soak in ample water with a degree of agitation to dislodge any grains is required. If doing this in a bowl, always list the greens out into a colander to drain; upending the bowl in a colander will only tip that dirt back over the greens. Salad greens need to be thoroughly dried, which can be achieved most effectively with a salad spinner. Cooking greens, on the other hand, benefit from a little water, helping to steam a little if wilting in a pan.

I will discard any discoloured or soft outer leaves from lettuces, while the woodiest parts of cooking greens will also end up in the compost, but aside from that there should be no waste. For things like silverbeet (Swiss chard), rainbow chard, kale, cavolo nero and English spinach, I trim the end couple of centimetres (about an inch) from the stalks, then finely slice the remaining stalks and roughly slice the leaves (depending on their use, of course).

If you are boiling or blanching greens, it is always best to do so in a large amount of water at a rolling boil. This will ensure that they stay brightly green. As they cook, the cell walls are broken down to reveal chlorophyll, which makes them appear more vividly coloured, and this is further enhanced by stopping that cooking by refreshing in cold or iced water, then reheating very quickly in boiling water as needed. If you drop the water temperature too much, chlorophyll will leach out over a longer cooking time, resulting in duller leaves. The other thing that will dull their appearance is acidity. But I do love a spike of lemon juice with cooked greens. In fact, I demand it. Simply ensure you squeeze lemon over just before serving.

Braised witlof with ginger GF V

The texture and flavour of cooked witlof is glorious, with the bitterness subsiding and giving over to a luxuriously gentle quality. This is a substantial vegetable side that is perfect with rich and/or charred meats, such as steak, duck and pork.
Serves 4

- 100 g (3½ oz) unsalted butter
- 4 large chicory (witlof/endive), cut in half lengthways
- 6 cm (2½ in) piece of fresh ginger, peeled and finely grated
- 2 tablespoons brown sugar
- 300 ml (10 fl oz) Golden chicken stock (p. 54), or Classic white vegetable stock (p. 51)

Staples
S&P

Melt the butter in a deep frying pan over a medium heat. Add the witlof, cut side down, and cook for about 3 minutes, until browned.

Turn the witlof over and add the ginger and sugar. Season with salt and pepper and cook for 2 minutes. Turn the witlof over again and add the stock, then simmer until tender, 15–20 minutes. Reduce the sauce a little longer if needed.

Transfer the witlof to a serving plate, then spoon the sauce over and serve.

Make it different

With cream. Once the witlof is cooked, remove and keep warm. Add 100 ml (3½ fl oz) cream and reduce until you have a sauce consistency, then drizzle over the witlof on a serving plate.

With ham & cheese. To take it further, you could also wrap each piece of witlof in a slice of ham, then a slice of Jarlsberg or gruyère cheese, while the sauce thickens. Arrange in a baking dish, then pour over the sauce. Top with breadcrumbs and grated parmesan and bake at 180°C (350°F) fan-forced for about 20 minutes until golden and bubbling.

Witlof, rocket & macadamia salad with pork & fennel sausage, mustard & honey

Preheat a chargrill pan or barbecue on high. Slice 2 red onions, skin on, into sixths lengthways. Oil the onion lightly, then grill until charred and soft on both sides, about 10 minutes. Grill 8 Italian pork and fennel sausages until cooked, then split lengthways. Make a mustard and honey dressing by combining the following in a bowl: 2 finely sliced French shallots, 2 finely grated garlic cloves, the juice of ½ lemon, 125 ml (4 fl oz/½ cup) extra-virgin olive oil, 3 tablespoons red-wine vinegar, 2 tablespoons wholegrain mustard, 1 tablespoon dijon mustard, 2 tablespoons honey and 1 tablespoon water. Season with salt and pepper. Put 3 trimmed chicory (witlof/endive), leaves separated, 2 handfuls wild rocket (arugula), 1 punnet baby red sorrel leaves or mâche (lamb's lettuce/corn salad) and 2 handfuls flat-leaf (Italian) parsley leaves in a large bowl with 100 g (3½ oz) toasted and roughly chopped macadamia nuts. Dress with half the dressing and toss to coat. Arrange the sausage and onion pieces on a serving plate, then top with the salad. Scatter another 100 g (3½ oz) nuts over, drizzle with the remaining dressing and serve. Serves 4–6.

Shiitake, tofu & cashew san choy bau Ⓥ ⓋⒼ

A crisp lettuce cup filled with a freshly cooked, punchy filling is always a fabulous way to start a meal. I often opt for a seafood san choy bau when I'm out, but I am rather partial to this meat-free version. **Serves 6 as a starter**

Pair with

Wholesome hoisin sauce (p. 96).

Braised silverbeet with garlic & lemon ⒼⒻ Ⓥ ⓋⒼ

Trim the end couple of centimetres off the stalks from a bunch of silverbeet (Swiss chard) or rainbow chard, then finely slice the remaining stalks and roughly slice the leaves. Sauté the stalks first in plenty of olive oil and garlic over a high heat for a few minutes, then add the leaves. Keep stirring until they wilt down, then add about 200 ml (7 fl oz) water, turn the heat to low and cover the pan. Cook for about 15 minutes until well braised and dark green, letting most of the liquid evaporate towards the end of cooking. Season with salt and pepper, then squeeze over plenty of lemon juice, dress with some oil and serve. These are also delicious cold, but it's best to add the lemon juice when serving, as the greens will discolour. This can be made with spinach, which will take about half the time, or cavolo nero or kale, which will take more like 25–30 minutes. Serve with Slow-roasted lamb (p. 304), yoghurt, a slab of feta and some pitta bread (see p. 854). These are also lovely with a simple grain salad (pp. 378, 379) or with Baked buttered rice (p. 384), fried egg and Fermented cooked chilli sauce (p. 97). Drained of liquid, the greens are also good in a frittata or omelette, or add to some ricotta, feta and an egg and fold into a few layers of filo pastry brushed with butter to make a quick filo triangle mix.

1 iceberg lettuce
80 g (2¾ oz/½ cup) raw cashew nuts
1 bunch of coriander (cilantro)
2 tablespoons grapeseed oil, or peanut oil
½ red onion, finely sliced
2 garlic cloves, finely diced
10 cm (4 in) piece of fresh ginger, peeled and finely diced
½ teaspoon Chinese five-spice

10 fresh shiitake mushrooms, sliced
10 green beans, finely sliced
2 celery stalks, finely diced
2 tablespoons shaoxing rice wine
250 g (9 oz) firm tofu, diced
80 g (2¾ oz) bean sprouts
1 large carrot, finely julienned
¼ wombok (Chinese cabbage), finely sliced
2 long red chillies, finely sliced
Wholesome hoisin sauce (p. 96), to serve

Cooking sauce
2 tablespoons light soy sauce
1 tablespoon brown rice vinegar
1 teaspoon brown sugar
½ teaspoon sesame oil
½ teaspoon ground white pepper

Remove the core from the lettuce. Soak the lettuce in iced water for 20 minutes, then drain and ease the leaves away intact. Trim away any untidy edges, if you like, then drain again and stack on a plate.

Combine the cooking sauce ingredients in a small bowl. Set aside.

Heat a wok or large frying pan over a high heat, then add the cashews and toast until scorched, about 3 minutes. Tip out of the pan and set aside.

Thoroughly wash three of the coriander roots and chop them. Pick the leaves from all the coriander, and chop half of them, keeping them all separate.

Add half the oil to the wok, then the onion, garlic, ginger, coriander root and five-spice. Fry for 1 minute, then add the mushrooms, beans, celery and remaining oil and stir-fry for 2 minutes.

Add the rice wine, then the tofu, and stir just long enough to heat through. Stir the cooking sauce through.

Add the cashews, bean sprouts, carrot, wombok, chilli and chopped coriander and toss through.

Drain off the excess liquid, then serve the mixture in a bowl, garnished with the coriander leaves, with the lettuce leaves stacked next to it, and the hoisin sauce on the side.

Make it different
Shiitake, duck & cashew san choy bau. Swap the tofu for shredded roast duck (see p. 258)

Shiitake, chicken & cashew san choy bau. Swap the tofu for roasted or White-poached chicken (p. 230).

Rainbow chard & chickpea salad GF V VG

Iron-rich chard loves a good braise. The leaves take on gentle notes of cumin and cinnamon, while becoming soft and yielding, with lemon juice and vinegar giving a brightening lift at the end. **Serves 6 as a side**

250 g (9 oz) dried chickpeas, soaked overnight and drained
2 cinnamon sticks
150 ml (5 fl oz) extra-virgin olive oil
3 large garlic cloves, finely grated
1 small onion, sliced

2 teaspoons cumin seeds
1 bunch of rainbow chard, cut on an angle into strips 5 cm (2 in) wide
500 ml (17 fl oz/2 cups) Golden chicken stock (p. 54), Vegetable stock (p. 51), or water

2 handfuls of flat-leaf (Italian) parsley leaves
1 tablespoon white-wine vinegar
juice of ½ lemon
2 handfuls of dill fronds

Staples
S&P

Add the chickpeas and a cinnamon stick to a large saucepan and cover generously with water. Simmer for about 1 hour until tender, then drain. Remove any loose skins and set aside at room temperature.

Heat half the oil in a large saucepan over a medium heat. Fry the garlic and onion until fragrant and softened, about 5 minutes. Add the other cinnamon stick, along with the cumin seeds, chard and half the stock. Stir until the chard has wilted, about 5 minutes.

Season with salt and pepper, then cover and cook over a low heat until tender, about 10 minutes.

Add the chickpeas and remaining stock, then cook for 10 minutes over a medium heat.

Stir in the parsley and adjust the seasoning to taste. The chickpeas will have absorbed some of the liquid by now.

To serve, dress with the vinegar, lemon juice, remaining oil and dill.

Make it a meal
Add a handful of pepitas (pumpkin seeds) and sunflower seeds and a big dollop of yoghurt.

Instead of rainbow chard, you could use kale, silverbeet (Swiss chard) or spinach.

Pair with
Serve as a side with roasted chicken, lamb or baked fish.

Grilled gem lettuce & bagna cauda GF

Barbecue (or sear in a griddle or chargrill pan) halved gem or baby cos (romaine) lettuces for 5 minutes on the cut side. Dress with Bagna cauda (p. 83) with 1½ tablespoons cream stirred through (one quantity will dress six to eight lettuce halves), then scatter over some thinly sliced spring onion (scallion), blanched peas and torn mint leaves, or grate parmesan over to serve.

Baby chard & curly endive salad with soft-boiled egg dressing & honey bacon GF

This salad is based around a classic French bistro salad of curly endive (frisée), egg and bacon. It makes a lovely starter or light meal. **Serves 4**

4 kipfler (fingerling) potatoes, scrubbed
4 thick slices of double-smoked bacon
1 tablespoon honey
30 g (1 oz) gruyère, grated
2 handfuls of baby chard

2 handfuls of rocket (arugula)
2 handfuls of curly endive (frisée)
1 handful of chervil
4 cornichons, sliced

Soft-boiled egg dressing
2 eggs

70 ml (2¼ fl oz) extra-virgin olive oil
1 tablespoon sherry vinegar
½ teaspoon dijon mustard

Staples
S&P

Cook the potatoes from cold in salted water until tender, then drain and slice.

Meanwhile, for the dressing, cook the eggs in boiling water for 4 minutes, then drain and run under cold water to cool slightly. Crack into a tall container or jug, then add the oil, vinegar and mustard. Season with salt and pepper and mix with a stick blender to make a frothy dressing.

Fry the bacon until crisp, then take off the heat and brush with the honey.

Arrange the warm potato on a serving plate, then season. Scatter the gruyère over, then some of the leaves. Lay the bacon on top. Scatter the rest of the leaves over, then spoon on the dressing.

Scatter with the cornichons and serve.

American-style ranch salad GF V VG

Pair with

Steak, lamb chops or grilled or roasted chicken.

Braised spiced beans or lentils.

A chickpea salad.

This is a side with plenty of punch, with the soft lettuce and rich avocado nicely offset by the chilli and pickled onions. **Serves 4**

2 large heads of butter lettuce, trimmed
1 large ripe oxheart tomato, peeled (see p. 655) and diced
1 ripe avocado, flesh diced

1 small garlic clove, finely grated
juice of 1 lemon
2 pickled green chillies (jalapeños work well), finely sliced

3 small pickled onions, sliced into rounds

Staples
EVOO, S&P

Separate the lettuce leaves and arrange on a serving plate.

Put the tomato, avocado, garlic and lemon juice in a large bowl. Add a good splash of oil and season with salt and pepper. Toss gently, then tip over the lettuce.

Scatter the chilli and pickled onion over, drizzle with more oil and serve.

Make it different

With cheese & croutons. Add torn fresh mozzarella or finely grated gruyère or tangy cheddar, then drop on some garlicky toasted croutons for added texture. Some charred sweetcorn sliced off the cob would also be nice.

With a dressing. Dress with Buttermilk dressing (p. 361).

Spinach, lentil & yoghurt salad with brown butter GF V

The first wilted green I remember enjoying was English spinach with butter, salt and pepper. I still love its sheer simplicity, but my tastes have developed somewhat. There's an earthiness to spinach, especially as it wilts slightly when you add hot lentils. I love the addition of brown butter at the end, adding toasty tones to the tang of the yoghurt. **Serves 4**

100 g (3½ oz) Puy lentils, or tiny blue-green lentils
1 fresh bay leaf
500 g (1 lb 2 oz) baby English spinach, half shredded
100 ml (3½ fl oz) extra-virgin olive oil

1 garlic clove, finely chopped
4 spring onions (scallions), white part only, finely sliced
12 sprigs of parsley, mint, tarragon and/or dill (at least 2), chopped
200 g (7 oz) plain yoghurt

60 g (2 oz/¼ cup) butter

Staples
EVOO, S&P

Add the lentils and bay leaf to a saucepan, cover with cold water, season lightly with salt and bring to a simmer. Cook until tender, 10–15 minutes, then drain.

Add the hot lentils and spinach to a large bowl and combine. Add the oil, garlic, spring onion and herbs, season with salt and pepper and combine. Stir the yoghurt through and pile onto a serving plate.

Melt the butter in a small saucepan. When it's a nut-brown colour, pour over the salad. Serve immediately.

Pair with
Steak, koftas (pp. 249, 309), fish, chicken, or with a spread of salads.

Watercress & potato soup GF V

These flavours are so good together, with the brightness of the greens given weight by the cream and potato, which makes this soup ever so silky. This soup is lovely by itself, but it is quite stunning and sophisticated served with a little garnish of fresh oysters or crabmeat. **Serves 10**

120 g (4½ oz) unsalted butter
1 small onion, finely sliced
1 leek, finely sliced
500 g (1 lb 2 oz) watercress, chopped
500 g (1 lb 2 oz) butter, gem or cos (romaine) lettuce, chopped

200 g (7 oz) creamy yellow-fleshed potatoes (such as Dutch cream), peeled and sliced very finely
1 litre (34 fl oz/4 cups) White chicken stock (p. 54), or Classic white vegetable stock (p. 51)

1 litre (34 fl oz/4 cups) pouring (single/light) cream
20 g (¾ oz) fresh horseradish, peeled and finely grated

Staples
S&P

Melt the butter in a large saucepan over a medium heat. Add the onion and leek, season with salt and pepper and cook until soft but not coloured, about 8 minutes. Add the watercress and lettuce and sweat to soften and wilt, about 3 minutes.

Meanwhile, in a saucepan, bring the potato, stock and cream to the boil over a medium heat. Cook until the potato is very tender, about 8 minutes.

Add the potato mixture to the other pan and puree with a stick blender – or transfer in batches to a blender.

Stir in the horseradish and season to taste, then pass through a fine strainer into a bowl over an ice bath, which will help fix the vibrant colour.

Serve cold, or gently reheat for serving.

Pair with
Garnish with crème fraîche and caviar or salmon roe.

Serve topped with fried crumbed oysters, or fresh oysters gently warmed in butter, with sliced black fermented garlic and the briny juices, and toasted rye bread.

Serve with diced avocado and cooked prawns (shrimp) or crabmeat.

Watercress & potato soup

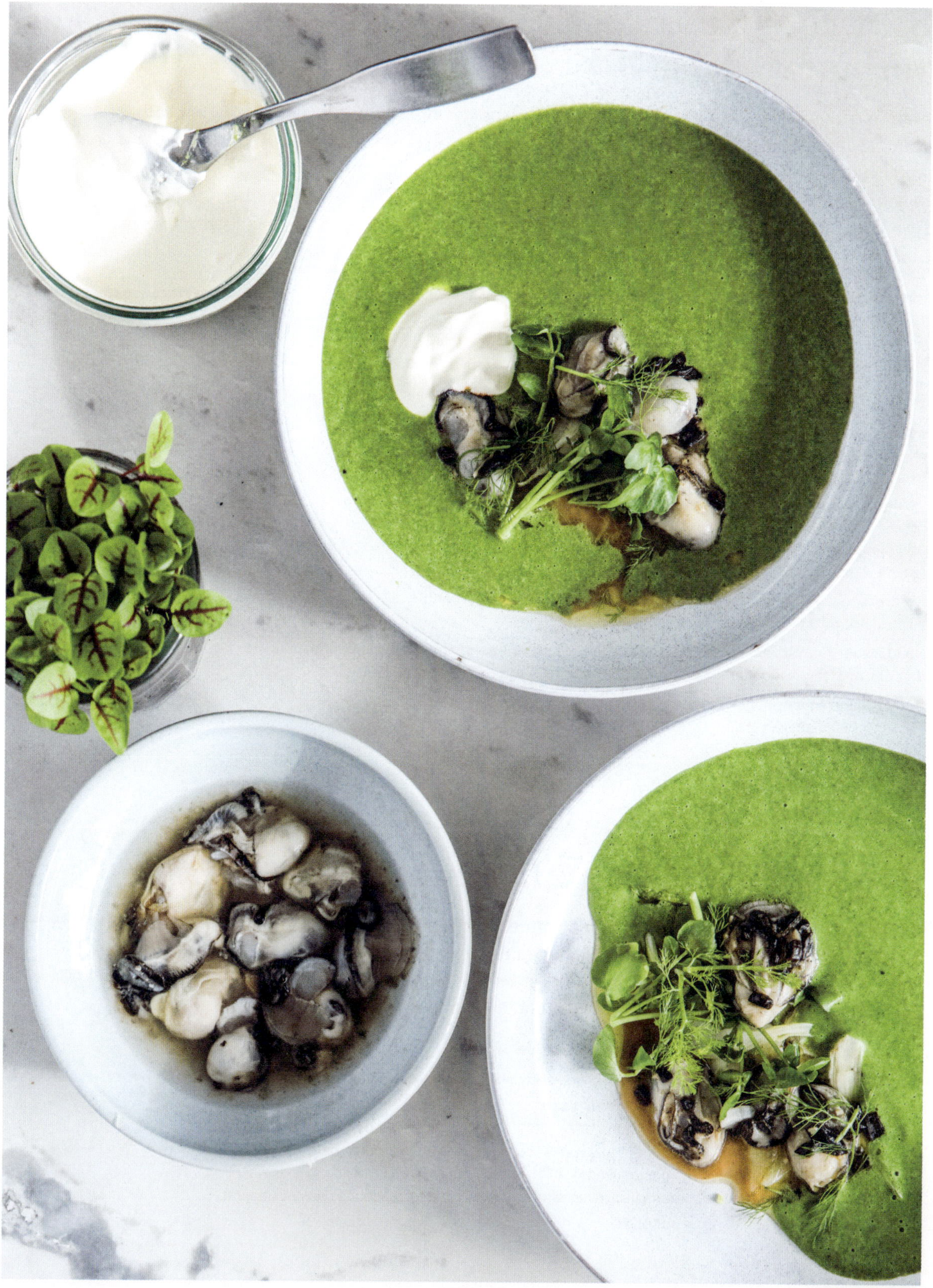

Spinach, mint & rice salad with yoghurt dressing ⒼⒻ Ⓥ

Many a culinary crime has been committed in the name of rice or pasta salad, with mayonnaise-laced ones a bit of a barbecue staple when I was growing up. And while this one has the expected creaminess, it is achieved via the sour tang of good yoghurt, rather than the often rancid-smelling vegetable oil and elevated sweetness of many commercial mayos. **Serves 4–6**

Pair with

I do love this salad with spicy dishes – think spiced and grilled chicken or lamb, with the coolness of the yoghurt and greens a refreshing salve.

- 5 handfuls of baby English spinach leaves
- 10 sorrel leaves, finely shredded
- 2 handfuls of mint leaves
- 2 dill sprigs, fronds picked
- 3 spring onions (scallions), white part only, sliced
- 65 g (2¼ oz/½ cup) small fresh or frozen peas, blanched or thawed
- 400 g (14 oz/2 cups) basmati rice, cooked by the absorption method (see p. 372)
- ½ pomegranate, seeds reserved
- 50 g (1¾ oz/½ cup) toasted flaked almonds

Yoghurt dressing
- juice of ½ lemon
- ½ garlic clove, very finely grated
- 2 teaspoons tahini
- 200 g (7 oz) thick plain yoghurt
- 80 ml (2½ fl oz/⅓ cup) extra-virgin olive oil

Staples
EVOO, S&P

Add the spinach, sorrel, mint, dill, spring onion and peas to a large bowl. Drizzle with oil, season with salt and pepper and toss.

For the dressing, combine the lemon juice, garlic, tahini and a pinch of salt in a bowl. Add the yoghurt and oil and combine.

Combine the rice with half the dressing and pile onto a serving plate. Spoon the remaining dressing over, then top with the spinach mixture.

Scatter with the pomegranate seeds and almonds and serve.

Make it different

With chicken. Serve with shredded poached or roasted chicken on top.

With trout. Add some flaked hot-smoked trout.

Raw silverbeet, sorrel & hazelnut salad ⒼⒻ Ⓥ

While I love silverbeet well braised, it's also quite delicious raw, with the hazelnut dressing softening it just enough, and the sorrel adding a welcome lemony tang. It's best to use smaller, youthful silverbeet (Swiss chard) leaves here and to shred them finely, or the texture and flavour can be too coarse. **Serves 4**

Pair with

Fried or grilled haloumi.

Grilled chicken or lamb.

Cooked asparagus.

- 1 bunch of silverbeet (Swiss chard), stems removed, leaves finely shredded
- 1 handful of sorrel leaves, finely shredded
- 2 handfuls of chickpea sprouts or other sprouts
- 50 g (1¾ oz/½ cup) finely grated Parmigiano Reggiano
- 100 g (3½ oz) hazelnuts, roasted (see p. 371), skins removed, roughly chopped

Hazelnut vinegar dressing
- 80 ml (2½ fl oz/⅓ cup) hazelnut oil
- 2 tablespoons extra-virgin olive oil
- 1½ tablespoons sherry vinegar

Staples
S&P

In a large bowl, toss together the silverbeet, sorrel, sprouts and parmesan.

Combine all the dressing ingredients in a small bowl, season with salt and pepper and whisk to emulsify. Add half the hazelnuts, pour the dressing over the greens and toss to evenly coat.

Tip into a serving bowl, sprinkle the remaining hazelnuts over the top and serve immediately.

Make it different
Raw silverbeet, mint & pistachio salad. (GF) (V) Use pistachio nuts and mint, instead of sorrel and hazelnuts.

Pressed spinach with sesame (Horenso gomaae)

Pair with

Some shaved raw vegetables, such as cauliflower, daikon or charred spring onions (scallions) that have been seasoned with salt flakes and sesame oil.

Grilled, fried, steamed or pan-fried fish.

Simply cooked shredded chicken.

The sesame dressing also works well over freshly cooked snow peas (mangetout) or sugar-snap peas.

The chilled spinach really soaks up the nutty sesame dressing in this simple Japanese dish. It's flavour rich and full of key umami notes, yet there is a freshness that I find quite cleansing and revitalising. It's a dish I like as a solo course at the start of a meal, but it makes a lovely side, too. **Serves 2–4**

600 g (1 lb 5 oz) English spinach, trimmed

Black sesame dressing
1½ tablespoons black sesame seeds

1½ tablespoons white sesame seeds, toasted
1 tablespoon caster (superfine) sugar
2 tablespoons light soy sauce

1½ tablespoons mirin
2 teaspoons tahini
2 teaspoons fish sauce
1 teaspoon bonito powder

Blanch the spinach in boiling salted water for 1½ minutes. Drain and plunge in iced water, then drain again once cool.

Press the liquid out of the spinach, then compress in a sushi mat (or plastic wrap) to form a log about 4 cm (1½ in) thick. Chill for 15 minutes to firm up.

For the dressing, grind all the sesame seeds to a powder using a mortar and pestle. Add the sugar and grind to combine. Stir the remaining ingredients through. The consistency should be like honey, so add a little water to loosen, if needed.

Unwrap the spinach and cut into four pucks. Arrange on a serving plate, cut side up. Drizzle the dressing over and serve.

Seared ocean trout with grilled lettuce, peas & pea tendrils (GF)

This is an elegant little dish, with the peas, the grilled and braised lettuce doused in butter, and the reduced stock making a lovely accompaniment for the seared fish draped in lardo, which gently melts in the residual heat. **Serves 4**

2 baby cos (romaine) lettuces, cut in half lengthways
3 garlic cloves, finely sliced
120 g (4½ oz) unsalted butter
100 ml (3½ fl oz) Golden chicken stock (p. 54), or water

150 g (5½ oz/1 cup) fresh or frozen peas
4 large French shallots, roasted (see p. 595)
4 × 150 g (5½ oz) ocean trout fillets
4 slices of lardo (see p. 326)

2 large handfuls of pea tendrils or sprouts

Staples
EVOO, LMN, S&P

Preheat a chargrill pan or barbecue on high.

Oil the lettuce, then grill, cut side down, until charred and starting to wilt, 2–3 minutes.

Heat a splash of oil in a frying pan over a medium heat. Fry the garlic until fragrant, 1–2 minutes. Add a knob of the butter and the lettuce. Season with salt, then add the stock and reduce by two-thirds, about 2 minutes. Add the peas, shallots, and the rest of the butter little by little, taking off the heat when the sauce is thick and glossy.

Meanwhile, heat a large frying pan over a high heat for a couple of minutes. Coat the fish with oil and season with salt and pepper. Cook the fish, skin side down, for 1½ minutes, then flip over and cook for another 1½ minutes.

Lay the lardo slices on the fillets and take off the heat, resting for 30 seconds in the pan before plating.

Serve the fish with the lettuce to the side, with the peas and sauce spooned over. Finish by scattering the pea tendrils over and squeezing on some lemon.

Silverbeet & haloumi pies Ⓥ

Pair with

Tzatziki (p. 507) or plain yoghurt.

Grilled chicken or sausage.

Byzantine salad (p. 379).

Rainbow chard & chickpea salad (p. 556).

I find the savoury pastries of the Middle East really most engaging, and I adore the combination of haloumi and greens, especially silverbeet (Swiss chard) – with the big earthy flavour of the greens matched by the salty intensity of the cheese. The citric acid is optional, but it's a handy trick in pastries such as this, adding a lemony lift that brightens the filling, whereas lemon juice can make the mixture too wet. **Makes 28**

80 ml (2½ fl oz/⅓ cup) extra-virgin olive oil
1 onion, diced
5 garlic cloves, finely diced
1 bunch of silverbeet (Swiss chard), half the stem trimmed off, the rest of the stem finely shredded
1½ tablespoons ground coriander
3 teaspoons Ras el hanout (p. 25)

3 eggs
250 g (9 oz) haloumi, coarsely grated
50 g (1¾ oz) Grana Padano, finely grated
6 dill sprigs, fronds chopped
2 handfuls of flat-leaf (Italian) parsley leaves, chopped
50 g (1¾ oz/⅓ cup) sesame seeds
1 teaspoon citric acid powder (optional)

7 shortcrust pastry sheets, or 500 g (1 lb 2 oz) Classic puff pastry (p. 823), or Cream cheese shortcrust pastry (p. 830)
nigella seeds, or sesame seeds, to garnish (optional)

Staples
S&P

Preheat the oven to 200°C (400°F) fan-forced. Line two baking trays with baking paper.

Add half the oil to a large frying pan over a medium heat. Fry the onion and garlic until softened, about 5 minutes. Add the silverbeet and cook until wilted, about 5 minutes, then cover and cook until very tender, about 15 minutes, sprinkling in the coriander and ras el hanout in the last minute or so. Tip into a colander to drain off any excess liquid.

Transfer the silverbeet to a large bowl. Add two of the eggs, the cheeses, herbs, sesame seeds and citric acid, if using. Season with salt and pepper and combine well. Beat the other egg with a pinch of salt for glazing.

Cut each sheet of pastry into four, or roll out the pastry to 3–5 mm (⅛–¼ in) thick and cut into 15 cm (6 in) squares. Brush the edges of one of the pastry squares with the beaten egg. Dollop about a heaped tablespoon of the mixture in the middle, then bring each point of the square up to meet in the middle. Seal by pinching the edges together, then brush with egg. Sprinkle with the nigella seeds, if using, then repeat with the remaining pastry and filling. (The pies can now be frozen, if you like.)

Bake the pies on the lined baking trays for about 25 minutes, until lightly golden; they will take a little longer if baking from frozen.

Enjoy warm or cold.

Make it different
With meat. Try these pies with 250 g (9 oz) minced (ground) chicken, or Italian pork and fennel sausages, skins removed. Heat a splash of oil in a frying pan over a medium–high heat and crumble in the meat. Fry until lightly golden, then tip into a bowl to cool. Add the cooked silverbeet, reduce the haloumi to 100 g (3½ oz) and proceed with the recipe.

Greens & cheese pie ⓥ

I can't imagine how many versions of spanakopita I have made in my life, though they have rarely just been spinach pies, with me favouring silverbeet (Swiss chard) for the bulk of the greens, and often accenting it with some other bitter greens. Spanakopita has become my fallback term – though in truth my versions should be called hortopita, or 'greens pie'. Mostly I use commercial filo pastry, but it is a lovely thing to go the extra yard and make it yourself. Now, I'm not talking about learning some arcane skill where you stretch out transparent pastry that drapes over your entire kitchen table; rather, this version achieves a lovely layered effect, with the baked pastry fabulously crispy and a little chewy, and it won't take a lifetime to perfect. It presents stunningly, too, making a wonderful centrepiece. **Serves 6–8**

Filling

1 white salad onion, finely diced
4 garlic cloves, finely chopped
1 bunch of silverbeet (Swiss chard), sliced 2 cm (¾ in) wide, including most of the stalk (about 350 g/12½ oz)
200 g (7 oz) English spinach and/or cime di rape
200 g (7 oz) rocket (arugula), sorrel, chicory (witlof/endive) and/or dandelion leaves

4 spring onions (scallions), white and most of the green, finely sliced
¼ bunch of flat-leaf (Italian) parsley, stems and leaves roughly chopped
2 eggs
350 g (12½ oz) ricotta
100 g (3½ oz) firm Greek-style feta, crumbled
¼ bunch of dill, fronds finely chopped
½ nutmeg, finely grated

Filo pastry

500 g (1 lb 2 oz) plain (all-purpose) flour
1 teaspoon fine sea salt
225 ml (7½ fl oz) water
1 egg
sesame seeds, chopped pistachios or pepitas (pumpkin seeds), for sprinkling

Staples

BTR, EVOO, FLR, S&P

For the filling, melt a small knob of butter in a large saucepan over a medium heat. Fry the onion and garlic until softened, about 5 minutes. Stir the silverbeet and spinach through, then cover and cook for 15 minutes over a low heat.

Mix the rocket through and cook for about 5 minutes, until wilted. Season with salt and pepper and add the spring onion and parsley. Tip into a sieve, draining off all the excess liquid by pressing lightly. Cool for 5 minutes, then chop.

Add the eggs, ricotta, feta, dill and nutmeg to a large bowl. Season and combine, then add the greens mixture and combine.

For the pastry, combine the flour and salt in a large bowl, making a well in the centre. Beat the water and egg in another bowl, then add to the flour. Stir to combine, then bring together into a ball. The dough should be smooth and elastic. Cover the bowl and rest for 1 hour.

Preheat the oven to 200°C (400°F) fan-forced. Line a baking tray with baking paper; a heavy cast-iron one is best to brown the base of the pie.

Cut the dough in half, then set one half aside, covered with a tea towel (dish towel). For the pie base, roll the other piece of dough out to about 60 cm (24 in). Cut a 26 cm (10 in) round in the middle, then cut the rest of the dough around the circle into six to eight irregularly shaped but roughly equal pieces, keeping them as flat pastry strips. Brush the round and the offcuts with oil and sprinkle with a little flour. Lay the pieces on top of the round to cover it. This will be messy, with pastry laying on top of other pieces and hanging over the edges, but try to get a roughly even distribution. Dust again with flour, then roll out to an even thickness, into about a 40 cm (15¾ in) round.

Transfer the pie base to the baking tray. Spread the filling over the base, to about a 26 cm (10 in) diameter, then fold the edges over the filling, pleating them to enclose.

Repeat the rolling instructions for the other piece of dough, to form another layered 40 cm (15¾ in) circle. Take the round and drop it on top of the pie as a lid, pulling it into folds so that it sits over the base more or less exactly, with a ruffled texture across the top.

Brush generously with olive oil, sprinkle with the sesame seeds and bake for about 30 minutes, until golden. If you don't have a heavy baking tray, check the base to make sure it is cooked, as it may need a little longer.

Make it faster

You can, of course, use this filling and commercial filo. Using a 40 cm (15¾ in) pie dish, butter each filo sheet and layer half the packet into the dish, leaving an overhang all around. Fill the pie, then fold in the edges. Butter the remaining sheets and layer on top, again ruffling layers to go on top to create a crisp and crunchy finish.

Seared radicchio with burrata, balsamic-pickled cherries & scorched almonds (GF)(V)

This may seem an unusual dish, but the combination of strong flavours, with charry bitter notes, sweet and sour balsamic cherries, milky fresh cheese and scorched almonds is quite magical. Serve as an antipasti or starter. **Serves 4**

Pair with

Freshly baked focaccia (see p. 845) or chargrilled Sourdough bread (p. 847).

25 large red cherries, pitted
2 French shallots, finely sliced
2 tablespoons caster (superfine) sugar
¼ teaspoon ground white pepper

80 ml (2½ fl oz/⅓ cup) balsamic vinegar
1 tablespoon red-wine vinegar
½ head of tightly packed radicchio, cut into 6 thick slices, core attached

80 g (2¾ oz/½ cup) blanched almonds
1 large burrata, or 2 balls of mozzarella
3 tablespoons peppery extra-virgin olive oil

Staples
EVOO, S&P

Add the cherries to a saucepan that fits them snugly in one layer, then place over a high heat. Sprinkle the shallot over the top, then add the sugar and season with the white pepper and some salt. Once everything is hot, add the vinegars. Toss the cherries in the sizzling liquid to coat, cook for 2 minutes, then take off the heat. Set aside to gently pickle.

Heat a large frying pan over a high heat for 2 minutes. Coat the radicchio in a little oil, then lay flat in the hot pan. Cook for 4–5 minutes to char on one side, then take off the heat and leave to wilt further in the residual heat.

In a dry frying pan over a high heat, toast the almonds for about 8 minutes, jiggling and tossing the pan every now and then to blacken and scorch. Set aside to cool. Tossing in a little oil, season and crush roughly using a mortar and pestle.

Lift the cherries out of the syrup and reduce the liquid by one-third, then return the cherries and cool.

Lay the radicchio on a serving plate, piling the cherries and liquid on top. Position the cheese on the plate, then drizzle with the peppery oil and season. Sprinkle with the almonds and serve.

Make it different
With cured meat. Adding some finely sliced mortadella, bresaola or capocollo would work nicely.

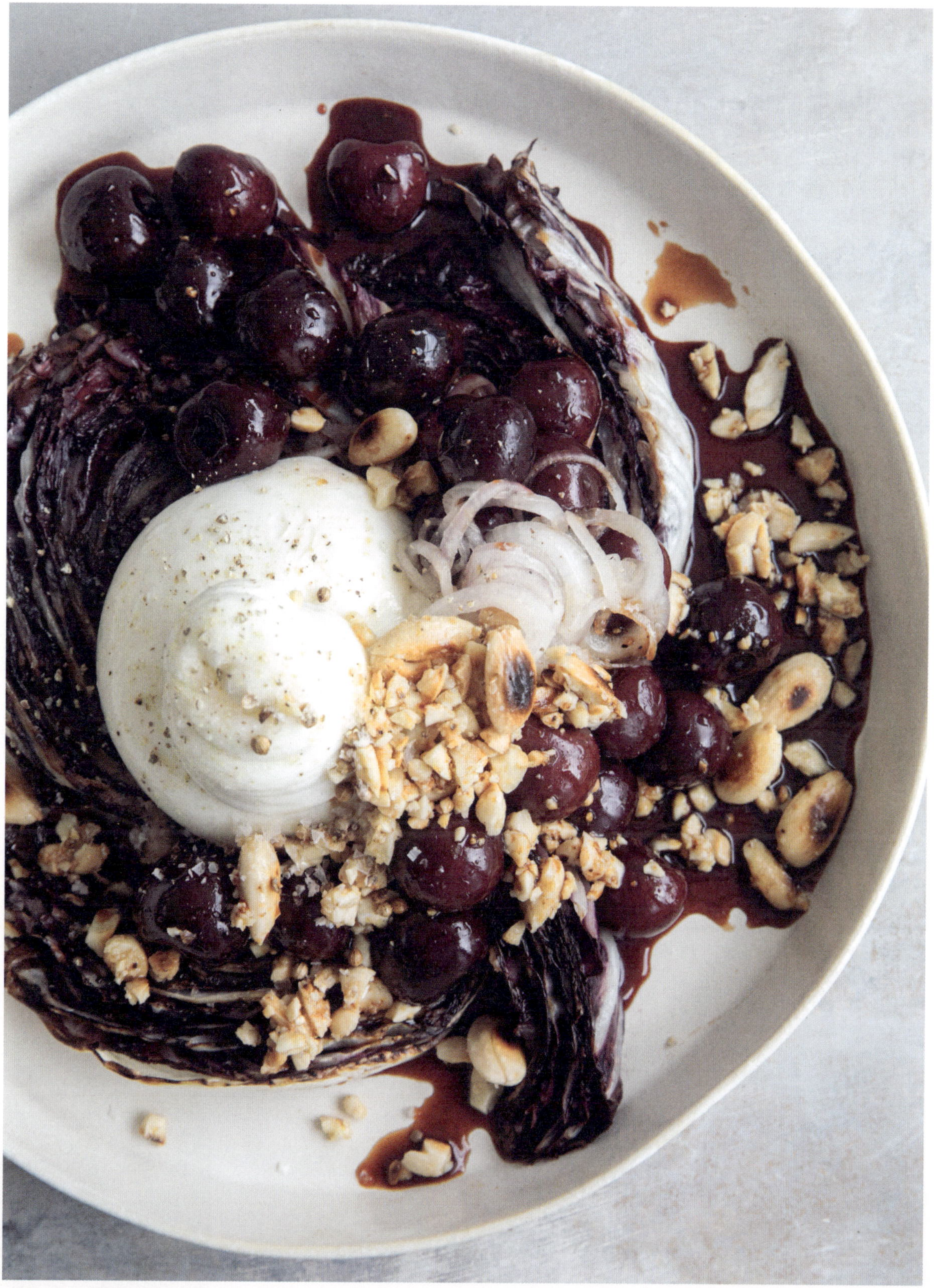

Mushroom

These days, when hunting for wild mushrooms, it is increasingly common to bump into fellow foragers with arms hooked into baskets and eyes trained on the ground. However, not long ago your venture would have been a solitary one, and any fellow mushroom hunters would likely have picked up the habit from their (or their parents') homeland in Europe.

Many of the imported species that grow wild in Australia would be instantly recognisable to someone who has foraged in Europe, as the main species hitched a ride when trees were imported for timber and colonial 'beautification'. As kids, we used to forage with our neighbours, though our bounty mainly consisted of large field mushrooms – what we called 'horse mushrooms' – with stern warnings given about the species not to touch. Those field mushrooms would end up sliced and fried in ample butter, parsley, plenty of salt and pepper and served with toast and sometimes fried eggs.

Foraging for mushrooms is a true delight. Wild mushrooms are a real delicacy, their flavour and texture unmatched by cultivated species. And the fact that they can be picked for free is quite the bonus – especially when you consider how cruelly expensive they are at the market and on restaurant menus.

I am now confident picking slippery jacks and pine mushrooms, and have done so many times with the girls and our dog, Rudi. It's such a relaxing, calm and beautiful thing to do. If the yield is good, I drop some off at the restaurant on the way back, and then take the rest home to make a ragù with Gnocchi (p. 136) or the like. Some mushrooms might get pickled, and I always leave a few in the fridge for a quick fry-up over the next day or so.

While wild mushrooms are the source of much excitement, most of the time cultivated mushrooms are what's available, and there is a large range to choose from. There are numerous Asian fungi grown, and an assortment is readily available from Asian grocers. And while their sheer variety and exoticism may make it tempting to employ them in Western wild mushroom dishes (such as risotto), the flavours often don't work in those applications – for me at least. Having said that, king brown mushrooms are prevalent in both Europe and Asia, and can cross over better than, say, wood ear fungus, and shiitakes can pair well with field or swiss brown mushrooms.

In Western dishes, the main cultivated mushrooms I use are the progeny of the *Agaricus bisporus* species, or common or white mushroom. I'm not one to lean heavily on scientific names, but the reason here is that we have a slew of names attached to what is essentially the same mushroom, albeit in different stages of maturity: champignon, button, chestnut, cup, cremini, portobello, 'field' (real field mushrooms are a different species, but the term is often used), flats and various other names are indeed all *Agaricus bisporus* at different stages of development. When young, they are delicately flavoured with a firm-ish, squeaky texture, and they become meatier when mature. In fact, Swiss browns are *Agaricus bisporus*, too, but they have a superior flavour in my book. Their name remains constant and they are sold by size, with the cost somewhat higher than their sibling.

Most of the variety in cultivated fungi species is actually found in Asian mushrooms, from the fine mop of delicate enoki mushrooms that need only the briefest application of heat, to the texturally robust kelp-like chew of wood ear fungus – with king browns having a foot in both camps. That idea of texture is an important and highly valued one – especially so in regional Chinese cuisine, for example – and that contrast in mouthfeel and bite between different types of fungi can add significant complexity and interest to a dish.

Also see

Simple porcini risotto 150

Tagliatelle with egg,
truffle & Parmigiano
Reggiano 119

Chicken noodle broth with
porcini polpette 253

Truffled eggs 357

Fried rice with wood ear
fungus & cashews 402

Shiitake, tofu & cashew
san choy bau 555

Pair with

*Mushrooms love butter, cream,
eggs and fresh curd cheeses
such as ricotta and goat's
cheese. Pair with ham, lardo,
guanciale, bacon and pancetta.
Mushrooms work with most
herbs; thyme, parsley, rosemary,
sage, oregano, marjoram,
chives, chervil and tarragon
are all excellent companions.
Spike with the acidity of
vinegar – sherry, red or white
wine, balsamic, rice wine – or
lemon juice. Garlic, ginger
and chilli all work beautifully,
as do all onions, whether
spring (scallion), shallot or
red or brown dry onion, and
also cabbage, peas, eggplant
(aubergine), potatoes, leeks
and asparagus. Pair with soy
sauce, nori, wakame, sesame,
white pepper, black pepper
and sichuan pepper.*

*Pair truffles with eggs, cream,
butter, buffalo mozzarella,
Parmigiano Reggiano, potatoes,
leek, cabbage, pork, poultry
and shellfish.*

Of the Asian mushrooms, shiitake are probably king, with their intensely distinctive flavour profile and a pleasing rubbery bite. They also have naturally high levels of glutamate, making them umami-loaded, while drying increases their level of guanylate, a natural salt that enhances flavour. Shiitakes are actually not that hard to cultivate, though they are a tree fungus that feed off carbohydrates in wood, so a decent number of un-dried logs are required to harvest any volume. I am mad for shiitakes cooked with soy, rice vinegar and sesame (see p. 415). Keep them on hand in the fridge, or use straightaway in noodle, rice dishes and salads.

Autumn and wild mushrooms are generally synonymous, though some species, such as morels, will appear in spring. What is needed, however, is humidity, with rain typically preceding a bountiful harvest. A dry season can lead to no meaningful season at all, while a year in which the ideal conditions remain constant can result in a long window of opportunity.

It's important to stress – *overstress* even – the importance of experience when foraging for mushrooms. Some poisonous (not always deadly, but certainly unpleasant) mushrooms look very much like edible ones. If you ever find ones you're totally unfamiliar with, it's worth remembering that the charmingly named death cap is quite a common and unassuming-looking fungus. If consumed, the death cap will make you very sick in a day or so, then you'll seemingly recover – before likely succumbing to liver failure a few weeks later. Then there's the eerily named destroying angel … It's serious stuff, so take care.

Native to Europe, pine mushrooms – also known as saffron milk caps – are wonderful mushrooms, with their distinctive coppery orange colour and delicate gills instantly recognisable. Meaty and intensely flavoured, they retain their marvellous colour during cooking, standing up to extended cooking, as well as being good candidates for a quick sauté. The cap is the prize, with the stems woody and not palatable. They are an easy mushroom for an amateur to identify, based on their striking appearance, and the fact they grow in pine forests. However, the advice still stands to only forage with an experienced guide. Always.

Slippery jacks are similarly common in pine forests, though not exclusively so. They have a spongy texture, a sticky cap, and the underside has an aerated texture, rather than serried gills. For the inexperienced, however, they are a less reliable pick, as there are lookalikes – so best avoided. Once cooked, slippery jacks are a little like a porcini mushroom in texture (being from the same genus), though not with quite the same depth of flavour and intrigue. While it is certainly not a gateway mushroom for the mushroom averse – their texture is more for the fungi aficionado – they are a lovely mushroom. Unlike pine mushrooms, the stem provides most of the flesh.

Porcini mushrooms, or ceps, are just about the most prized of mushrooms, both fresh and dried. They are similar to slippery jacks but have a deeper, more umami-laced character. They similarly grow near conifers, and were once thought not to be adaptable to Australian conditions. However, pockets of porcini have been quietly cherished in the Adelaide Hills, and elsewhere, for decades – and no doubt we'll be seeing more of them. Until relatively recently, most of my experience has been cooking with dried porcini (see p. 25), which have an extraordinary amount of flavour, and can fill the void most of the year when wild mushrooms aren't in season.

Like pine mushrooms and slippery jacks, morels grow both here and around the world. Australian morels are mostly not imported but native species of the same genus, producing similar distinctive caps that look something like a cross between honeycomb and a sea sponge. Internationally, the number of morel species is a matter of some conjecture, and though they are all recognisably similar, the shape of the cap can vary from a quite slender and elongated cone, to the wavy flicker of a cartoon candle, to ball-like; the hue has similar variance, from almost black to reddish brown to light tan. The one to be wary of is the 'false morel' – or false morels, as there are several species – some are apparently edible, but others can be fatal. True morels are quite the delicacy, though their intensity of flavour varies from species to species, age and the season, with a tendency to become woody and a bit dull at their worst. Morels need to be cooked before consumption.

Porcini powder

Add 20 g (¾ oz) porcini to a high-speed blender or spice grinder and blitz to a powder. For a more general mushroom powder, add 100 g (3½ oz) shiitake mushrooms along with the porcini and blitz as above. This is great for adding a umami kick to meat or vegetable braises, soups, eggs, sauces and dumpling mixes. I also use mushroom powder if I'm short on chicken or vegetable stock. It will keep in an airtight container at room temperature for up to 3 months.

Chanterelles, or girolles, are one of the most prized mushrooms in Europe and North America. They have an intense flavour for their compact size, resembling an unkempt calla lily in shape. They are not readily available in Australia, though there is a native species that is somewhat similar in appearance, and apparently flavour, but I have not had any experience with them.

Another cultivated mushroom I love is lion's mane. White and bulbous, they look quite unusual but have a pleasing scallop-like texture. I simply pan-fry with butter and serve with lemon and parsley or with a little balsamic vinegar drizzled over them.

True field mushrooms grow, as you may expect, in fields. The wealth of manure in grazing paddocks is a particular encouragement for them. They are possibly the most prosaic of the edible wild mushroom family, but they are very meaty in flavour, and marvellous cooked simply in butter with garlic and parsley. Most mushrooms labelled as field mushrooms are also called flats, which are just common mushrooms grown to full maturity.

Truffles are expensive, brutally so. Though prices are improving in Australia, where production is excellent, and booming; through July and August you will find black truffles with perfect punch for reasonable prices. Invest and indulge. I say it's a must. After all, truffles are one of nature's great gifts. The aroma of a truffle – and this is essentially what a truffle is prized for – is haunting, complex and utterly unique. It's not universally loved, with some rather ardent opponents, though to be truly decisive, one must have had a proper truffle served simply. Truffle oil does not count.

Truffles are subterranean fungi that grow within the web of roots of certain deciduous trees, mainly oak and hazelnut. They are unassuming tuber-like lumps, ranging from white to deeply black, with enough fragrance leeching above ground to attract the keen olfactory capacity of trained truffle hogs or dogs. Once sliced into, that fragrance is released further, and a pretty brain-like web of marbling is revealed. Heat will enhance the aroma more, though the delicacy of the aroma will suffer when cooked too much, and it is the clarity of that flavour that should be the focus. Hence, a beautiful bowl of hand-made egg pasta tossed in a buttery sauce with a wilfully large amount of fresh truffle shaved over it at the table is just about the best way to consume them. Also magnificent is a very simple risotto with Parmigiano Reggiano and with truffle shaved over at the last minute.

When selecting mushrooms, look for bright and vibrant specimens, with darker brown hues on white mushrooms a sign of age. They will also soften and become a little woody and shrivelled as they dry out. As the paper mushroom bags at markets suggest, these mushrooms shouldn't be stored in plastic, as they will sweat and become slimy. Pine mushrooms are particularly fragile, so both rough treatment and having been picked some time ago will be very evident. The gills will show this somewhat clearly, with the delicate filaments easily bruised. As with all wild mushrooms, they really should be eaten within a day or so of being picked. They are best stored upside down in a single layer and covered with a tea towel (dish towel) to stop them drying out.

Truffles should smell like truffles. Sounds obvious, but there are old specimens sold sometimes, and less scrupulous chefs have been known to boost dishes with truffle oil as a result. Use your nose when buying truffles – that's what you're paying for.

All mushrooms can be refrigerated, as can truffles – but they need to be in the crisper, as it's the warmer part of the fridge. Storing a truffle in dried rice for risotto will perfume it, as will storing them with eggs, with the porous shells taking up the flavours. Otherwise, store wrapped in paper towel. Just remember that the aroma of a truffle will diminish over a week or so, which means they should be used fairly promptly. Truffles are now reliably cultivated, with Australian examples now of world standard.

Preparing mushrooms

Most wild mushrooms need to be cooked before eating. The preparation for mushrooms varies a little depending on type, but most will soak up water, so washing is ill advised. In general, mushrooms can be either wiped with a slightly damp cloth to get rid of dirt and debris, or brushed with a pastry brush or the like. Pine mushrooms and slippery jacks in particular pick up a lot of material, and pine needles are not terribly tasty, so be thorough. The stems of white mushrooms are generally edible, but more mature specimens are less palatable than younger ones; if using, trim off any woody or discoloured ends. The stems on pine mushrooms are woody in the extreme. Shiitake stems are equally unfriendly, but they are a brilliant addition to a stock if working with complementary flavours. Enoki mushrooms simply need the base trimmed, which will separate the individual stems, which can just be added to hot broth or thrown into noodle or rice dishes at the last minute. White mushrooms and wild European mushrooms will soak up butter or oil very readily, so it is generally best to sweat them down in some fat, then add more towards the end of cooking to sauce to the desired degree.

Barley 'risotto' with mushrooms & speck

This take on risotto pairs the nutty quality of barley with meaty, earthy mushrooms and smoky speck – a very good match in my book. **Serves 4**

250 g (9 oz) pearled barley

1 litre (34 fl oz/4 cups) Golden chicken stock (p. 54)

120 g (4½ oz) speck, or pancetta, diced

3 large French shallots, finely diced

5 garlic cloves, finely chopped

90 g (3 oz) butter

350 g (12½ oz) mixed slippery jack, pine and field mushrooms (Swiss, king brown or lion's mane would also work well), thickly sliced

3 thyme sprigs

150 ml (5 fl oz) white wine

60 g (2 oz) Grana Padano, finely grated

Staples
S&P

Pair with

Braised silverbeet (Swiss chard) or cavolo nero with garlic and oil, or simply dressed peppery greens such as rocket (arugula), mustard cress or young curly red kale.

Simmer the barley in lightly salted water for 15 minutes, then drain well. Set aside.

Bring the stock to a gentle simmer in a small saucepan.

Meanwhile, fry the speck in a heavy-based saucepan over a medium heat until it renders out fat and crisps up, about 5 minutes. Add the shallot and garlic and cook in the fat until softened, about 3 minutes.

Add 40 g (1½ oz) of the butter, the mushrooms and thyme. Season with salt and pepper and cook to soften, about 5 minutes. Add the barley and wine and reduce by half.

Add about one-third of the stock, stirring until absorbed. Repeat the process, just like making risotto, until the barley is cooked; the grains should have a chewy resistance. If you run out of stock, use a little hot water.

Once the barley is cooked, stir in the parmesan and remaining butter and serve.

Make it different

With parsnip chips. Garnish with parsnip chips (p. 606) for crunch and a sophisticated presentation.

With crispy sage. In a small frying pan, fry the leaves from four sage sprigs in about 30 g (1 oz) butter until they crisp up, drain on paper towel, season and sprinkle over the 'risotto' just before serving.

Make it vegetarian Ⓥ

Drop the speck. Instead of chicken stock, use vegetable stock, enhanced by dissolving a few teaspoons of Porcini powder (p. 570), and a few teaspoons of shiro miso or brown rice miso paste, in a little of the stock. Add it after the wine, then continue with the recipe.

Chickpeas with mushrooms, red wine vinaigrette & tarragon (GF) (V) (VG)

I stumbled across this delightfully unusual little salad at the legendary La Boqueria market in Barcelona, Spain. It was about 8 am, and workers had finished their shifts and were pulling up seats at a tapas bar in the market. They were pointing at fresh produce they wanted grilled – prawns (shrimp), clams (vongole) or little sausages, which were served with a darkly hued chickpea side. Intrigued, I pulled up a seat beside them and copied their orders, just to be served this salad. This is based on what I tasted. **Serves 4–6 as a side**

250 g (9 oz) dried chickpeas, soaked overnight, then drained
1 fresh bay leaf
½ teaspoon bicarbonate of soda (baking soda)
6 large Swiss brown or field mushrooms, stalks removed

¼ bunch of tarragon, leaves picked

Red-wine vinaigrette
350 ml (12 fl oz) red wine
100 ml (3½ fl oz) extra-virgin olive oil
1 large garlic clove, finely grated

50 ml (1¾ fl oz) sherry vinegar
3 teaspoons dijon mustard
¼ bunch of tarragon, leaves chopped

Staples
EVOO, S&P

Preheat the oven to 180°C (350°F) fan-forced.

Add the chickpeas to a large saucepan of lightly salted water with the bay leaf and bicarbonate of soda. Cook until tender, which will take 30–50 minutes, depending on the chickpeas. Drain very well.

While the chickpeas cook, place the mushrooms, gill side up, on a baking tray. Drizzle with some oil, season with salt and pepper and roast for about 25 minutes, until dark and well cooked. Blitz the mushrooms in a food processor, along with any juices in the tray.

Meanwhile, for the dressing, reduce the wine in a small saucepan to about 3 tablespoons. Tip into a large bowl, along with the remaining ingredients. Season and beat until emulsified.

Add the mushroom puree to the dressing, mixing well. Add the warm chickpeas and combine. Adjust the seasoning as needed.

Tip into a serving bowl and finish with the tarragon leaves and a drizzle of oil.

Pair with

Serve with grilled meat, fatty sausages, roast chicken or grilled prawns (shrimp).

Make a more generous serve to add a robust note to a vegetarian feast, alongside some Zucchini & haloumi fritters (p. 673) or grilled haloumi.

Cream of mushroom soup (GF)

I'm hesitant about this recipe title, as it conjures up images of tinned soup. But the name is worth reclaiming, as this soup is creamy and velvety. So, what else would you call it? As with many silky pureed soups, I cook potato in butter at the start until tender, which lends a texture that you just can't replicate. **Serves 6–8**

20 g (¾ oz) dried porcini mushrooms, rehydrated in 100 ml (3½ fl oz) boiling water
180 g (6½ oz) butter
1 onion, finely diced
6 garlic cloves, finely sliced

3 large boiling (waxy) potatoes (such as desiree or Dutch cream), finely sliced
800 g (1 lb 12 oz) portobello or field mushrooms (the darker and meatier the better), sliced
250 ml (8½ fl oz/1 cup) white wine

1 litre (34 fl oz/4 cups) Golden chicken stock (p. 54)
300 ml (10 fl oz) pouring (single/light) cream
3 thyme sprigs, leaves stripped
1 tablespoon dijon mustard

Staples
S&P

Pair with

Top with a dollop of crème fraîche or goat's curd.

Fry small chunks of bread in a little olive oil until golden with some smashed garlic cloves to make rustic croutons to drop on the soup.

Top with crispy pancetta or bacon, and serve with grilled bread smeared with ricotta.

Champignons with garlic, wine & cream (GF) (V)

Add about 15 small trimmed champignons to a dry frying pan over a high heat, stem side up. Cook until the cap is browned, about 5 minutes, then drizzle in some olive oil and add a sliced garlic clove. The garlic will cook quickly, so when it is just changing colour, add a splash of white wine or dry sherry. Season with salt and pepper and reduce for about 30 seconds, then add 100 ml (3½ fl oz) pouring (single/light) cream. Toss the mushrooms through the sauce until it clings to them, then cool at room temperature. Toss the cooled mushrooms with chopped parsley, tarragon or thyme and plenty of freshly ground black pepper, and salt to taste. Serve as an antipasto or side, or with steak or chicken.

Grilled mushrooms (V) (VG)

Add 2 tablespoons balsamic or sherry vinegar, 2 tablespoons extra-virgin olive oil and 1 tablespoon light soy sauce to a bowl. Add a few rosemary sprigs, leaves stripped and finely chopped (or use thyme, or fresh or dried oregano). Season with salt and pepper and combine, then marinate trimmed portobello or field mushrooms in the dressing for an hour. Grill, gill side down first, for 2 minutes, then flip and continue to cook for about 5 minutes until tender, then serve as a side, or with eggs for breakfast or brunch. You can also melt some cheddar, gruyère or blue cheese over the mushrooms, or serve hot from the grill on toast with crème fraîche or mascarpone spooned over, and some caramelised onions (see p. 598); popping the whole lot in a toasted brioche or ciabatta bun is also delicious. Or instead of the cooked onions, try adding some garlic and parsley butter (see p. 73), a sprinkle of cayenne or smoked paprika, and some finely shaved raw onion.

Strain the rehydrated porcini, reserving the liquid, then finely chop the flesh.

Melt the butter in a large, heavy-based saucepan. Sauté the onion and garlic until softened, about 5 minutes. Add the potato slices, season with salt and pepper and stir to coat. Cook, stirring continuously, until the potato is translucent and starts to break up, about 6 minutes.

Add the sliced mushrooms and porcini, season and cook for about 5 minutes. Splash in the wine and reduce by half. Pour in the stock, reserved porcini liquid and cream, stir in the thyme and mustard, then bring to a simmer. Cook until the potato is tender and breaking down, 8–10 minutes.

Once cooked, ladle out and reserve about one-quarter of the soup. Use a stick blender to blitz the soup in the pan. Stir the unblended soup back in, then adjust the seasoning as needed. You could, of course, puree the whole soup, if preferred. Serve warm.

Vietnamese spring roll with crab, prawn & shiitake

These are on the deluxe side – but I think if you're going to the trouble of making spring rolls at home, it's worth dialling them up a bit. To eat, drop a spring roll in a lettuce cup, add some herbs and roll up, then dip in the sauce. **Makes 24**

1 iceberg lettuce
250 g (9 oz) raw prawn (shrimp) cutlets, peeled and deveined, tails removed, meat chopped
1 garlic clove, finely grated
1 tablespoon fish sauce
1 teaspoon sesame oil
1 teaspoon caster (superfine) sugar

½ teaspoon ground white pepper
150 g (5½ oz) cooked crabmeat
5 shiitake mushrooms, stems removed, diced
6 spring onions (scallions), white part only, finely sliced
60 g (2 oz) Pickled daikon (see p. 304), or water

chestnuts, chopped (optional)
1 egg white, lightly beaten
24 medium (20 cm/8 in) spring roll wrappers
oil, for deep-frying (see p. 22)
½ bunch of Vietnamese mint
½ bunch of Thai basil
Nuoc cham (p. 93), to serve

Cut the core out of the lettuce. Stand the lettuce in a bowl of cold or iced water for 10 minutes or so, then invert in a colander to drain well. Carefully separate the leaves and pat dry, then refrigerate until needed.

Add the prawn meat, garlic, fish sauce, sesame oil, sugar and white pepper to a food processor and blitz until smooth, about 30 seconds. Scrape into a large bowl. Add the crabmeat, shiitake, spring onion, and daikon if using, and combine well.

Brush the egg white on three edges of a wrapper. Line 1 tablespoon of prawn filling along the unbrushed edge, leaving space at each end, then fold the sides over and roll tightly into a cigar shape. Repeat until all the wrappers and filling are used up. (The spring rolls will hold for a couple of hours kept covered in the fridge, so you can get organised beforehand – or, once rolled they can be frozen; defrost for 25 minutes on the bench before frying.)

Heat about 8 cm (3¼ in) of oil in a deep frying pan until 180°C (350°F).

Fry the spring rolls in batches for 2–3 minutes, flipping them halfway through, until golden brown. Drain on paper towel.

Serve hot, with a stack of lettuce cups, the herb sprigs and the nuoc cham on the side.

Vegetable bolognese GF V VG

This sauce was my way of upping the vegetable content for my daughters when green was their least favourite colour. It's sneaky, but sometimes you need to be. Oh, and it's also quite delicious, which is good for all concerned. **Serves 6–8**

8 large field mushrooms

125 ml (4 fl oz/½ cup) extra-virgin olive oil

1 large onion, finely diced

4 garlic cloves, finely diced

2 teaspoons dried Greek oregano (rigani)

4 celery stalks, finely diced

3 carrots, finely diced

4 zucchini (courgettes), cut into 1 cm (½ in) dice

3 tablespoons tomato paste (concentrated purée)

800 g (1 lb 12 oz) tomato passata (puréed tomatoes)

400 g (14 oz) tin diced tomatoes

1 tablespoon caster (superfine) sugar

200 ml (7 fl oz) Vegetable stock (p. 51), or water

Staples
EVOO, S&P

Preheat the oven to 200°C (400°F) fan-forced.

Season the field mushrooms with salt and pepper and dress with oil. Roast them for 20 minutes, then dice.

Heat half the oil in a large wide-based saucepan over a medium heat. Add the mushroom and fry until browned, about 8 minutes. Remove from the pan and set aside.

Add the remaining oil to the pan with the onion, garlic and oregano. Cook for 3 minutes, then add the celery, carrot and zucchini and cook for 15–20 minutes, until soft and golden.

Return the mushroom to the pan and stir the tomato paste through. Stir in the passata, tomato, sugar and stock. Lightly season with salt and pepper, bring to a simmer, then cook over a low–medium heat for about 40 minutes, until the sauce is reduced and intensely flavoured. Adjust the seasoning as needed.

The sauce will keep for up to 5 days in the fridge, and 3 months in the freezer.

Make it different

Pork bolognese. Make it meat-based by frying 400 g (14 oz) Italian pork sausages (skins removed) or minced (ground) pork instead of the mushrooms. Use Golden chicken stock (p. 54) instead of vegetable stock.

With porcini mushroom. Enhance by adding 15 g (½ oz) soaked and chopped porcini mushroom. You could also dissolve a few teaspoons each of Porcini powder (p. 570) and shiro miso or brown-rice miso paste in a little of the stock.

Pair with

Your choice of pasta and plenty of grated parmesan.

Simple fried mushrooms GF V

The simplest way to cook a trimmed whole medium-sized mushroom or a thickly sliced larger one is to sauté it in a heavy-based frying pan over a high heat with enough olive oil to coat the bottom of the pan. Throw in the mushrooms, but don't crowd the pan, or they will stew rather than sauté; if the mushrooms let out too much water, tip this out of the pan and continue to brown. Season with salt and, once coloured and becoming tender, add a good knob or two of butter and some finely chopped garlic. Cook for about 3 minutes, tossing frequently until the mushrooms are tender, but still with a little bite. Squeeze in some lemon and toss with herbs, such as parsley, chervil, thyme or chives. Serve on toast, over eggs, in an omelette, or add a dash of cream or crème fraîche to sauce them up a little further and toss through pasta, or serve on top of a steak or with chicken.

Mushroom ragù GF

When wild mushrooms are abundant, this is on high rotation for me – though you can make it with field mushrooms and small king browns as well. I particularly like it with pine mushrooms, as they stand up to the relatively long cooking, have a rich flavour profile, and the colour is stunning. **Serves 6–8**

600 g (1 lb 5 oz) pine and field mushrooms

25 g (1 oz) dried porcini mushrooms, rehydrated in 100 ml (3½ fl oz) boiling water

100 g (3½ oz) butter

2 tablespoons extra-virgin olive oil

6 French shallots, finely diced

4 garlic cloves, very finely chopped

3 thyme sprigs, leaves stripped

1 fresh bay leaf

150 ml (5 fl oz) white wine

500 ml (17 fl oz/2 cups) Golden chicken stock (p. 54)

Staples
EVOO, S&P

Pair with

Gnocchi (pp. 131, 136). Finely grate about 120 g (4½ oz) Parmigiano Reggiano. Stir through most of the cheese, along with a couple of knobs of butter, when you add the gnocchi to the ragù. Serve the remaining cheese on the side.

Pasta or on Polenta (p. 383).

Try on bruschetta, with stracciatella cheese or burrata.

Pan-fried chicken.

A good shaving of good truffle on top.

Preheat the oven to 180°C (350°F) fan-forced.

Scrape the gills from the field mushrooms and reserve, then cut the flesh into 5 mm (¼ in) dice. Trim the pine mushrooms, then slice, halve or leave whole, depending on how large they are. Add the pine and field mushrooms to a baking tray, season with salt and pepper, drizzle with oil and roast for 25 minutes.

Strain the rehydrated porcini, reserving the liquid, then finely chop the flesh.

Heat the butter and oil in a heavy-based saucepan over a medium heat. Add the shallot, garlic, thyme and bay leaf and cook for 15 minutes over a low heat until golden. Stir in the chopped porcini and roasted mushrooms with any juices, then add the wine and reduce by half over a medium heat.

Add the stock and reserved porcini liquid. Bring to a simmer, then cook for 30–40 minutes over a low heat to develop the flavours.

To finish, add the reserved field mushroom gills to the ragù, then adjust the seasoning as needed.

Okra

As a child, I ate okra much more often than I realised. My Meme used to cook them slowly in a spiced lamb braise with cumin, garlic and preserved lemon until the pods yielded their shape and thickened the braising juices into a rich sauce. The spritely finger-like, rocket-shaped green pods you see in the markets were a mystery to me until much later. In fact, although they're popular throughout the Middle East, Asia, Africa, the Caribbean, the United States and the Mediterranean fringe, in Australia for a long time you'd generally only find okra in specialist grocers, sometimes fresh but often frozen, and usually in suburbs with a concentration of migrants, be they Greek, African or Indian.

Today, okra even features on some supermarket shelves in summer, although I suspect they still remain somewhat mysterious to many. I liken the flavour to just-cooked eggplant (aubergine), with a green bean flavour in the background. Perhaps okra's most famous use, in the Western world at least, is in gumbo – the famous stew of Louisiana, in America's Deep South. The word 'gumbo' is said to have its etymological roots in west African languages, where it was fashioned by time from the word for okra. There are countless gumbo variants, with regional location and ingredients dictating the rules, and okra acting as a thickening agent, either on its own or in conjunction with a roux, with the seeds lending a unique texture.

The texture of the liquid that oozes from the seeds of okra when cooked is more often than not described as 'slimy' – or that delightfully evocative but somewhat creepy word, 'mucilaginous'. Its thickening quality and gelatinous, satiny texture is either prized or reviled, with few people being indifferent to the mouthfeel. Having said that, cooking okra whole or frying slices quickly won't produce this result, instead transforming okra into an engagingly crisp and distinctively flavoured vegetable. If you're on the other side of the fence, simply split okra in half or cut into slices and cook in a stew, soup, curry or the like until it yields up its textural glory.

I find one of the simplest ways with okra is to fry small pods in olive oil for 2–3 minutes, until they turn bright green. They'll still be crunchy, and will 'pop' when you bite into them. I season them with salt flakes and dust with a little ground cumin and/or sumac and serve on yoghurt as a side dish or meze. They're also delicious cooked this way and finished with a drizzle of light soy sauce and Chilli oil (p. 86). You can pop them into a braise for the last 15 minutes or so of cooking, and they'll be yieldingly tender but still holding their shape. I enjoy okra as a standalone vegetable, and like it crunchy and cooked out until quite soft. It's a great addition to a sour curry, particularly with seafood, and you can also slice them and use in fritters or pakoras.

When selecting okra, the smaller specimens are typically recommended, but I have had just as much success with larger ones, too. Like any vegetable, they will become fibrous if particularly large, but you'd rarely see such examples in a market. The common wisdom is that smaller okra is less slimy, which may be true, but not overcooking them has the same result. Occasionally, you'll see super-fresh okra that are a fuzz of brilliant blemish-free green, but a little browning of the stem cap is common and acceptable. Just be wary when the pods start to discolour and dull, with soft spots a good reason to cook something else instead. The pods should always be firm, with a crunchy snap to them – avoid any that feel hard and dried out.

Although I've commonly seen them in markets in Morocco and Spain, tiny fingertip-sized pods are hard to come by where I live, unless buying them frozen. And while most frozen vegetables are off my shopping list, with some notable exceptions (peas … and broad beans, sometimes), these can be quite a successful addition to a braise or any well-stewed okra recipe.

Pair with

Okra loves extra-virgin olive oil, tomato, onion, garlic and ginger, and spices such as coriander seeds, cumin, cinnamon, curry leaves, mustard seeds, pepper and dried chilli. Match it with soft herbs such as parsley, mint and coriander (cilantro), or dried herbs such as oregano. Quality sharp and creamy goat's and sheep's milk yoghurt are great fits, as are sour foils such as wine vinegar, tamarind, lemon and lime juice – and it will work with most proteins, from lamb, chicken and beef braises to fish, prawns (shrimp) and shellfish.

Preparing okra

Aside from washing and drying, okra require minimal preparation. All I do is trim off the very tip of the stem, where it will have browned and become woody. Occasionally, you may need to peel the stem cap with a paring knife if the pods are more mature, but I never really find it necessary – I'll leave that up to you. They're then ready to cook whole, or they can be sliced, depending on the use. Just remember, if you cut them and add to a liquid, they will thicken and alter the texture, so leave them whole if this is not desired.

Greek-style braised okra (bamies) 🟢 🅥 🅥🅖

This is based on a classic Greek braise with sweet and sour accents. Cooking okra this way enhances and intensifies the flavour, with the pods addictively tender and deeply perfumed. Serve these hot or cold. **Serves 6 as a side dish**

100 ml (3½ fl oz) extra-virgin olive oil
4 garlic cloves, sliced
500 g (1 lb 2 oz) okra
3 large ripe tomatoes, cut into 2 cm (¾ in) dice

200 ml (7 fl oz) tomato passata (puréed tomatoes)
30 ml (1 fl oz) red- or white-wine vinegar
1 tablespoon brown sugar

2 teaspoons dried Greek oregano (rigani)
½ teaspoon ground allspice

Staples
S&P

Heat the oil in a large, deep frying pan over a medium heat. Add the garlic and fry until fragrant and golden, about 2 minutes.

Add the okra and tomato, season with salt and pepper, then toss every 20 seconds or so until softened, about 3 minutes.

Stir in the remaining ingredients and cook on a low heat for about 20 minutes, until the okra is tender, and the passata has reduced and starts to cling to the pods.

Make it different
With extra red-wine vinegar. Sharpen the flavour further with a good glug of red-wine vinegar just before serving.

Pair with

Serve with grilled meats, fish or braised lamb with Baked buttered rice (p. 384).

Match with a soft fresh cheese such as ricotta, or one that is salty and flavourful, such as feta, and serve with plenty of bread.

Tempura okra 🅥 🅥🅖

Okra look and taste wonderful with a crisp veil of Tempura beer batter (p. 187). Dust finger-length okra pods lightly in flour, dredge in batter and fry for about 3 minutes, until crisp and a very pale golden hue, then drain on a wire rack to keep them crisp. Serve with soy sauce mixed with finely grated fresh ginger, a few drops of sesame oil and a squeeze of lemon as a dipping sauce, or simply dust with Sichuan pepper salt (p. 29). Fried okra can be served with a mix of vegetables and seafood with Tempura dipping sauce (p. 98).

Sour fish curry with okra & celery heart ⓖⓕ

Pair with

Serve with simply steamed rice, coconut rice, stir-fried greens (see p. 401) and/or Naan (p. 855) or paratha.

This is another one of those dishes that I cook many tweaked versions of, such as employing Thai accents rather than Indian spicing, and using all manner of sea creatures. Curries soured with tamarind are amazing with seafood, and this method gently poaches the fish, resulting in such a delicate and perfectly cooked texture. Blitzing the sauce and simmering it is a handy shortcut, too – it couldn't be simpler. Make sure you use properly ripe tomatoes here, as the depth of the sauce depends on it. **Serves 4–6**

5 garlic cloves, sliced

6 cm (2½ in) piece of fresh ginger, peeled and chopped

6 dense-fleshed tomatoes (such as roma/plum), roughly diced

1½ teaspoons ground black pepper

1 tablespoon brown mustard seeds

2 teaspoons coriander seeds

2 teaspoons cumin seeds

2½ tablespoons coconut oil

20 okra

2 celery hearts, quartered, pale leaves picked and reserved

1½ white onions, finely sliced into half-moons

2 tablespoons dried fenugreek leaves

4 red bird's eye chillies, sliced

1 tablespoon salt flakes

20 fresh curry leaves, on the stem

2½ tablespoons tamarind paste

500 ml (17 fl oz/2 cups) Fish stock (p. 52), or White chicken stock (p. 54), or water

6 × 200 g (7 oz) fillets of firm white-fleshed fish (such as blue-eye trevalla or rockling)

1 lime, cut in half

1 bunch of coriander (cilantro), leaves picked and fine stems chopped

Staples

S&P

Add the garlic, ginger, tomato and pepper to a blender, along with 2 teaspoons of the mustard seeds, 1 teaspoon of the coriander seeds and 1 teaspoon of the cumin seeds. Puree until smooth.

Heat the oil in a wide-based saucepan or deep frying pan over a medium heat. Stir-fry the okra and celery to soften slightly, about 3 minutes, then remove from the pan and set aside.

Add the remaining mustard seeds, coriander seeds and cumin seeds and briefly fry until the mustard seeds pop. Add the onion and cook until softened and picking up some colour, about 5 minutes. Stir in the spiced pureed tomato mixture, fenugreek, chilli and salt flakes. Add the curry leaves, then simmer for 2 minutes.

Add the tamarind and stock and bring to a simmer. Turn down the heat to a very slow simmer and cook for 10 minutes.

Nestle the fish into the sauce, then scatter with the stir-fried okra and celery, and the reserved celery leaves. Cover and cook for 5 minutes, then turn off the heat and stand, covered, for 2 minutes, to finish gently poaching the fish.

Remove the curry leaves. Adjust the seasoning as needed, squeeze in the lime, scatter with the coriander and serve.

Make it different

With fried curry leaves. Fried curry leaves make a striking and very fragrant garnish. Simply flash-fry a few stems of curry leaves in hot oil for about 30 seconds until crisp, then drop on top of the finished curry.

With more seafood. You could also add mussels, clams (vongole) or seared prawn (shrimp) cutlets with the fish – or use other fish varieties such as snapper, mackerel or rockling, cut into darnes or cutlets.

Okra with shiso, soy & toasted sesame seeds (V) (VG)

This started out as a totally experimental recipe. I'd always eaten okra stewed in a heavier oil-based style, deep-fried or in a curry. Here, simply cooked in a pan with oil, the okra stays bright and fresh, while being tender enough to take up all the flavour of the Japanese-themed dressing. This is a great way to introduce okra to those who haven't tried it before. **Serves 4–6**

400 g (14 oz) okra
½ teaspoon ground
   white pepper
20 tiny shiso leaves or
   6 shredded large leaves,
1½ tablespoons toasted
   sesame seeds, lightly
   ground

Sesame & mirin dressing
80 g (2¾ oz) fresh ginger,
   finely grated and
   squeezed for juice
   (20–30 ml/¾–1 fl oz)
1½ tablespoons extra-virgin
   olive oil
1 tablespoon light soy sauce

1 tablespoon mirin
½ teaspoon sesame oil
3 ripe tomatoes, cut into
   5 mm (¼ in) dice

Staples
EVOO, S&P

For the dressing, combine the liquid ingredients in a bowl, then stir the tomato through. Set aside to infuse for 15 minutes.

Heat a good splash of oil in a large frying pan over a high heat. Add the okra, season with salt and pepper and cook until it turns bright green, about 4 minutes.

Tip the okra into the dressing, then stand for 5 minutes to let it take on the flavours.

Plate the okra, drizzling any residual dressing over the top. Scatter the shiso leaves over, sprinkle with the ground sesame seeds and serve.

Make it different
With a heavier dressing. Try it with Sesame dressing (p. 94).

Pair with

Enjoy the okra with simply cooked fish.

Spoon over Japanese-style rice, and snip some toasted nori over.

Serve alongside freshly sliced raw tuna or kingfish.

Spiced okra with curry leaves (GF) (V)

This was loosely based on an Indian dry masala recipe, but I took it in another direction by adding liquid and finishing with butter, which softens the flavours and gives a saucy sheen. **Serves 6 as a side dish**

2 teaspoons yellow
   mustard seeds
15–20 fresh curry leaves
1 onion, finely sliced
2 garlic cloves, sliced

2 teaspoons curry powder
2 teaspoons ground cumin
1 teaspoon chilli flakes
500 g (1 lb 2 oz) okra
100 ml (3½ fl oz) water

80 g (2¾ oz) butter
lime wedges, to serve

Staples
EVOO, S&P

Heat a good splash of oil in a frying pan over a medium heat. Add the mustard seeds and cook until they pop, about 1 minute. Add the curry leaves and fry until they change colour, about 20–30 seconds.

Add the onion and garlic and cook until softened and taking on some colour, about 3 minutes.

Quickly stir the curry powder, cumin and chilli through, then add the okra. Coat with the spices, then turn the heat to low and cook until fragrant, about 3 minutes, tossing frequently.

Add the water, then cover and cook until the okra is just tender and the pan is drying out, about 3 minutes.

Season with salt and pepper, then add the butter, tossing well to coat. Finish with a squeeze of lime.

Pair with

Enjoy with fish, or in a spread of other vegetable dishes and curries.

Serve with spiced rice, or a fresh, lively herb-based salad and flatbread.

Spiced okra with curry leaves

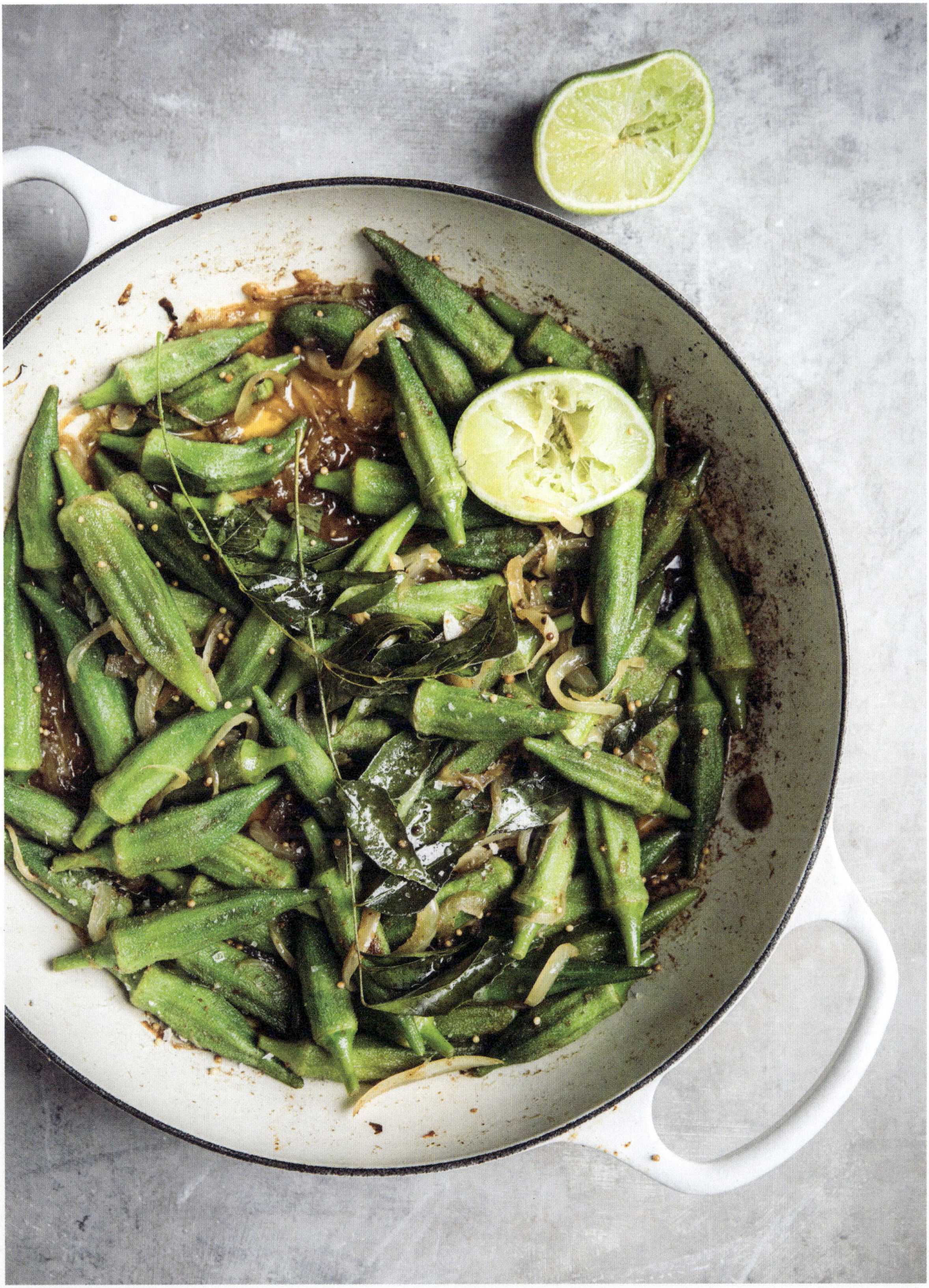

Olives

Olives have been celebrated throughout history for their fruit and oil, with the latter used for anything from culinary purposes, to providing a protective barrier to stop wine oxidising, to oiling up wrestlers for tournaments in ancient Greece, to keeping the Olympic flame lit – literally. Olives and extra-virgin olive oil are two of my favourite things. But it *has* to be extra-virgin olive oil. Anything labelled otherwise – olive oil, light olive oil, blended olive oil – has gone through some chemical process to get to bottle.

Olives have been cultivated for millennia. There are still a handful of extant trees that are thousands of years old – and they're still producing olives. The most famous is the Olive Tree of Vouves, in Crete. Like most truly ancient olive trees, it is hollow, making radiocarbon dating impossible, but it is conservatively estimated to be 2000 years old – with some estimates as high as 4000 years, making it a substantially old tree, even by the end of the Bronze Age.

Green olives were the thing in my childhood – large green 'queen' olives. My father loved them. And those same unpitted fat green olives were often in my lunchbox at school, along with hand-cut bread filled with salami, and wedges of fennel and capsicum (bell pepper). As you can imagine, the aroma of my lunchbox was very different to those packed with white bread and jam sandwiches and a bag of chips. I now see mum was doing me a favour, even though I felt a little differently back then. I really did love those fleshy green olives, though. The woeful black Spanish olives that were ubiquitous at the time, contributing their flavourless black rings to pizzas across the land, were not allowed past the threshold at home.

There's always a jar or two of olives in my fridge, and usually some that I've marinated, along with brined black and green ones. If I'm travelling, I'll quite often buy a jar of local olives in brine and a bottle of extra-virgin olive oil, because there is so much individuality, so much variety to olives and olive oil – somewhat like buying wine from different regions. Many a makeshift meal starts with a bowl of olives to get things moving, or sometimes after a long day of cooking and tasting, all I feel like is a glass of wine and a bowl of olives. That will tend to get my appetite going, and I'll be cooking again in no time.

In my house, olives go in pasta, they get smashed to a paste with anchovies, capers and parsley, then loosened with good oil to make tapenade – which I use for all manner of things, from spreading on bruschetta or crostini, to tossing through pasta, or spooning onto grilled tuna or lamb chops. Olives get thrown into braises towards the end, they are a defining part of a proper Greek salad (p. 512) and the Provençal classic, Pissaladière (p. 599), and are an essential pizza topping. Toss them with roasted red capsicums (see p. 463), scatter over a block of feta with dried oregano and a drizzle of extra-virgin olive oil for an antipasto, push into a focaccia (p. 845) before baking, or just serve as is, simply brined. And a martini isn't a martini without an olive.

There's a seemingly endless variety of olives, with more than 1500 distinct types recognised. Some are more favourable for oil production, and some better as table olives (see p. 586). And while olive trees are hardy and seem to grow in the most unlikely of places, often seemingly bereft of soil, growing an olive tree from seed is no easy undertaking. The sheer volume of fruit means that plenty of seeds germinate in the wild, but there are many more that don't, making it a frustrating prospect for a gardener. And, if you do manage to grow one, you may not quite get what you expect, with the vast number of varieties being hybrids and grown from cuttings, which revert to their original form when grown from an olive pit. You'll typically get what is referred to as a wild olive, which usually has small fruit with a scant amount of flesh; they're still delicious, mind you.

Also see

Spaghetti puttanesca 117

Celery & olive salad 188

**Orange & black olive
salsa 345**

Greek salad 512

**Braised fennel with
tomato & olives 529**

Pissaladière 599

Pair with

*Olives are at home with so
much classic Mediterranean
and Middle Eastern produce:
tomato, eggplant (aubergine),
capsicum (bell pepper), chilli,
cucumber, garlic, onion,
fennel, lemon, orange, dried
beans, chickpeas, and nuts
such as almonds and walnuts.
Rosemary, oregano and thyme
match their robustness, but
olives are equally good with
soft herbs such as basil, parsley
and coriander (cilantro). They
take to fennel seeds, coriander
seeds, cinnamon, cumin,
black pepper and saffron
especially well, and marry with
the tartness of good yoghurt
and the tang of sourdough
bread. Fresh curd-style cheeses,
feta and haloumi are sublime
matches, as are strongly
flavoured cooked-curd cheeses,
such as Parmigiano Reggiano,
mizithra and pecorino. Olives
work with rich meats, especially
lamb and beef, and braised
rabbit and poultry, but also
accompany fish very well.*

Olives are inedible before being cured. Their rich antioxidant properties are due to the polyphenol oleuropein, which is found in other plants, too. That back-palate burn you get from super-fresh olive oil is because of this polyphenol, which has purported cancer-fighting properties, amongst other benefits. And while in the oil it may provide some heat, oleuropein is acridly bitter in the fruit until cured.

Cured olives can be green through to a mild purply brown to an almost obsidian black. Green olives are simply picked earlier, before they have changed colour (just as wine grapes go through veraison as they ripen), so colour is not a function of variety – though the different hues can be quite marked between cultivars. Even picked with a gentle shift away from green, the olives will deepen significantly in colour once cured. Left to go quite black on the tree, olives can become soft and will not be easy to cure without becoming mushy. Ripe black olives, however, can be sun-dried naturally in arid climes, or artificially dried in an oven or dehydrator. They are typically dry-salt cured and have a prune-like appearance and deeply concentrated and distinctive flavour – they're well worth seeking out.

Curing your own olives is not technically difficult, and engenders a similarly rewarding feeling to sourdough baking, using only two primal additives, salt and water – so the process seems somewhat miraculous. It's worth having a go (see p. 586), but it can take an awfully long time to see the results, depending on the type and ripeness of the olives. Marinating your own olives is somewhat quicker, and the results are stunning. Just buy some brined olives, flavour them with your chosen aromatics and spices (see p. 591) and marinate in oil. It couldn't be simpler.

Simple cured olives

Curing olives by brining them is a very simple process, but one that can take a meaningful amount of time. Essentially it involves lacto-fermentation, much like Sauerkraut (p. 454) and, while there are ways of speeding things up, it is still the province of the patient. The first batch is the hardest, as it feels like the results will never come – but once you're in the swing, and with last year's crop still seeing you through, you will soon relax into the rhythm of things. It's also worth brining a good quantity of olives, as there is not much more work involved and, if you've waited months for a result, it can be disheartening to see your slowly brined olives disappear in a day or two.

You can buy olives at the market, but do ensure they are freshly picked, as they will deteriorate very quickly, and you will end up with a poor result. Depending on where you live, you might encounter olive trees growing in neighbourhood yards and gardens. The influx of European immigrants to Australia has certainly been largely responsible for the wealth of olive trees in the suburbs of Melbourne and, as with so many other fruits, that resource is often not used. Often a tree that looks to be neglected is just that – but please ensure you knock on the door before helping yourself to any overhanging fruit. You will also find a lovely array of varieties, all tasting quite different and yielding diverse results in terms of texture and acidity. Picking your own really is a lot of fun, and the connection to where they have grown is infinitely more satisfying than having bought them. The other key factor is that you can pick them as they ripen to your liking, then ferment in smaller jars, ensuring you make the most of the harvest. You want firm, freshly picked specimens, free of blemishes and insect holes.

I find it best to select olives that are still green but have lightened in tone, often with white speckles on them. When pressed between thumb and index finger, they will be firm, but once the flesh yields the juice will be a little milky. If they have just started to turn darker in hue, they are also ready, but I find ones that are more black than green less successful for brining, with the texture becoming quite soft once cured – though these can still be blitzed for Tapenade (opposite). Even when picked green, if ripe enough, the olives will darken to a reddish brown to black colour.

As soon as they are picked, cover the olives with cold water and stand for a day, then drain and repeat each day for a week. This will leach out some of the bitterness before you brine them. You can do this in a large tub, weighing them down with a plate – or a simple method is to use large jars, then curl a small piece of olive twig with leaves attached inside the shoulder of the jar to keep the fruit submerged. I will keep these on the kitchen bench and then upend them each day and refill. It's very easy, and less cumbersome, but do what suits you.

After a week, combine ¼ cup of good granular salt in a saucepan with 1 litre (34 fl oz/4 cups) water and 60 ml (2 fl oz/¼ cup) apple-cider vinegar or red-wine vinegar; you can also add garlic cloves, chillies, bay leaves and the like, but I tend to prefer adding flavours when I marinate, as the base olives are then more versatile. How much brine you need will naturally depend on how much you need to cure, but you can measure this by filling your jars with water, then pouring it off into a measuring jug. I boil the brine for a few minutes, which will kill off anything undesirable, as well as reducing the chlorine, then leave to cool before covering the olives, ensuring they are submerged. Seal the jars and set them somewhere out of direct sunlight to cure, opening the jars every now and then to release some of the gas.

And then, you wait. A month, two months, six months, a year … all are possible. It's simply a matter of tasting occasionally (always using a scrupulously clean spoon) for the right balance of flavour and bitterness.

If you want to speed matters up, before you begin the process use a paring knife to make an incision lengthways in each olive, which will allow the brine to penetrate more quickly. Alternatively, some people bash the olives to crack them open, but I like my olives un-bashed.

A mould can sometimes develop on top of the brine, typically a white film, which is quite normal and can be scooped off. But any mould that develops on the olives themselves is an issue. This will usually only occur on olives that have floated to the top, and they can be discarded. But if for some

A note on lye-cured olives

Traditionally, olives are cured simply in water, brine or dry salt, whereas modern commercial olives are first treated with lye before they are brined briefly. Lye is sodium hydroxide – the active ingredient in drain cleaner. Yes, not terribly appealing, but lye-cured olives go back to ancient times, using lye pulled from wood ash.

Lye takes the bitterness out of olives and softens the flesh more quickly than brining, so it can turn a crop into a saleable product very quickly. However, if done purely for expediency, once the lye is rinsed out and the olives are packaged, the flesh lacks that briny distinctiveness that I so love.

The Spanish are particularly fond of lye-curing olives, and while a good Spanish olive is a thing of wonder – and many of these are cured, in part, with lye – you need to know what you're buying, as many of the Spanish olives can be tasteless and soapy.

reason the salt concentration is too low and the olives don't ferment properly to raise the acidity and drop the pH, then they will spoil and will need to be discarded.

Once the olives are cured to your satisfaction – and some jars may be ready earlier than others – drain them off, make up a fresh batch of brine, then bottle in sterilised jars (see p. 40) and seal. They will continue to soften if kept on the bench, or can be refrigerated to slow the process down.

Once opened, I always refrigerate the olives, as frequently accessing the jar will always introduce ambient microbes which will often lead to surface mould. Kept in the fridge, the olives will last well for a year or longer.

Olives ascolana

The laborious task of pitting, stuffing, crumbing and frying an olive may not be something that fits your schedule that often, but these are just so delightful. We served them at the Melbourne Wine Room for many years, and they're one of my favourite snacks to have with drinks, whether a glass of white wine, sherry or an icy and crisply dry martini. Be a little wary, as the filling can become volcanically hot – but don't let them sit for too long, as they're at their best piping hot. The name 'ascolana' is derived from the province of Ascoli Piceno, in the Marche region, where they are a specialty. **Makes 40**

Pair with

These are aperitivo snacks without rival and don't need any adornment, though a lemon wedge is a nice touch, and some Aïoli (p. 76) would also be welcome.

Quick olive tapenade GF

For a super-quick tapenade, throw a few handfuls of pitted fleshy black olives in a food processor with 3 anchovies, 1 garlic clove and a small handful of flat-leaf (Italian) parsley leaves, then blitz for a couple of minutes. Add heaps of ground black pepper and about 100 ml (3½ fl oz) extra-virgin olive oil, then blitz until smooth. This is a simple version, but it is so punchy and perfect to be spread on crostini or in sandwiches, perhaps with fresh mozzarella, salami, tomato and basil leaves, or tossed into pasta at the last minute. It will keep for a week comfortably, but a slick of oil on top will preserve it for longer.

Quick olive dip GF

This is an extension of the quick tapenade (above), and is similarly no frills. Soften a 250 g (9 oz) block of cream cheese on the bench for an hour or two, then blitz with the tapenade until smooth. Serve as you would any dip, with crackers, bread or crudités. This will also keep for at least a week.

	Stuffing	
40 large green olives, preferably unpitted	100 g (3½ oz) mild salami, roughly chopped	1 rosemary sprig, leaves very finely chopped
250 g (9 oz/1⅔ cups) plain (all-purpose) flour	150 g (5½ oz) minced (ground) veal, or beef	2 teaspoons fennel seeds, toasted and ground
4 eggs, lightly beaten	150 g (5½ oz) minced (ground) pork	¼ nutmeg, finely grated
300 g (10½ oz/3¾ cups) fine fresh breadcrumbs	finely grated zest of ¼ lemon	1 teaspoon salt flakes
oil, for deep-frying (see p. 22)		

You can work with pitted olives, but using a small paring knife to cut the flesh from the pit in one piece will give you the best result – it just takes a little practice. Cut crossways across the top of an olive against the pit, but not all the way through, then make a cut along the length of the pit in one action and shave off the flesh in a barrel, and finish by taking off the other tip, so you're left with a continuous strip of olive.

For the stuffing, blitz the salami in a food processor until you have a paste. Add the remaining ingredients and pulse until just combined. Divide into 40 portions and roll into balls in the palm of your hand. Wrap each ball with an olive and close to re-form the olive shape.

Put the flour, egg and breadcrumbs in separate bowls. Roll each olive in flour, then dredge through the egg and finally coat with breadcrumbs, gently shaking off any excess. Refrigerate the olives for at least 1 hour to firm up before frying. The olives can also be frozen now on a tray, spaced well apart, then combined in a bag or container once solid.

Heat 5 cm (2 in) of oil in a deep heavy-based frying pan or deep-fryer until 170°C (340°F).

In batches, without crowding the pan, fry the olives, turning to cook evenly, until golden, about 5 minutes (fry for an extra 30 seconds if cooking from frozen). (Crowding the pan will mean the oil temperature will drop, and the olives will soak up oil and not become golden.) Drain briefly and serve.

Baked olives, grapes & ricotta Ⓥ

This combination of olives and grapes is fabulous. The briny intensity of the olives and sweetness of the grapes concentrate in the oven, and both are stunning with the oven-burnished ricotta, which firms and takes up the herby chilli-flecked oil. This is pretty special straight from the oven, and always has people asking for the recipe. **Serves 6–8**

450 g (1 lb) ricotta, well
   drained and cut into 3 cm
   (1¼ in) thick slices
125 ml (4 fl oz/½ cup)
   extra-virgin olive oil
150 g (5½ oz) seedless
   grapes, stems removed

50 g (1¾ oz) pitted manzanilla
   or kalamata olives
¼ bunch of oregano,
   leaves picked
4 thyme sprigs
1 tablespoon red-wine vinegar
½ teaspoon chilli flakes

bread, to serve

Staples
S&P

Preheat the oven to 210°C (410°F) fan-forced.

Lay the ricotta slices in a ovenproof dish. Season with salt and pepper and drizzle with half the oil.

Using your hands, gently break open the grapes and olives in a bowl. Add the herbs, vinegar and remaining oil, season and toss to coat. Scatter over the ricotta, then sprinkle with the chilli.

Bake for about 25 minutes, until the ricotta is firm and golden at the edges. Serve with bread.

Pair with

This is a delicious appetiser with plenty of bread, or serve as part of a spread of small dishes.

This approaches light meal territory when combined with Braised silverbeet with garlic & lemon (p. 555).

Mezzanotte paste ⒼⒻ

Mezzanotte means 'midnight' in Italian, and it lends its name to various versions of 'midnight pasta' – cooked in a flash after a night out – which are sometimes as simple as aglio e olio (garlic and oil), and sometimes with more ingredients harvested from the pantry cupboard, such as anchovies, capers, olives and chilli flakes. This paste riffs on that idea. It's certainly not something you'd whip up for a round of spaghetti mezzanotte, but you'll be very appreciative of your foresight when the craving strikes. In reality, I developed this recipe many years ago, and it wasn't done with late-night pasta cravings in mind, so it has countless other applications. **Makes about 650 g (1 lb 7 oz)**

250 g (9 oz) purple
   manzanilla olives or
   black mammoth olives,
   pitted and chopped
150 g (5½ oz) artichoke
   hearts, drained and
   roughly chopped
1 tablespoon capers
   in brine, drained and
   roughly chopped

6 anchovies
150 ml (5½ fl oz) extra-virgin
   olive oil
1 tablespoon red-wine
   vinegar
100 g (3½ oz) ground
   almonds
1 roasted garlic bulb (p. 66)
1 small garlic clove

3 red bird's eye chillies,
   finely chopped
1 teaspoon dried
   Greek oregano
½ teaspoon chilli powder

Staples
EVOO, S&P

Add all the ingredients to a blender, grind in about 20 turns of a black pepper mill and blitz until smooth. Pack into a clean jar and top with a little oil to seal. The paste will keep in the fridge for up to 2 months.

Pair with

Dollop on pizza (see p. 856) or focaccia (see p. 845) before baking.

Serve with seared tuna or roasted lamb rump with roasted capsicum (see p. 315).

Toss through any pasta and serve with grated parmesan or pecorino.

Stir into a braise of chicken or rabbit at the last minute for a pop of flavour.

Use as you would tapenade.

Flip into a dip by whizzing with softened cream cheese or ricotta.

Smear on crostini and top with a slice of hard-boiled egg or fig.

For a stunningly simple starter, dollop over a plate of bresaola, then drop on some fig slices, lightly dressed rocket (arugula) and some Grissini (p. 856).

Loosen the paste with a little vinegar and olive oil, then drizzle over Vitello tonnato (p. 297) – perhaps with some sliced egg.

Baked olives, grapes & ricotta

Queen green tapenade GF

Queen green olives are the same fat and fleshy olives I loved as a kid, and they're still up the top of the rankings for me. Green olives give tapenade a lighter and fresher flavour. **Makes about 450 g (1 lb)**

180 ml (6 fl oz) extra-virgin olive oil
250 g (9 oz) pitted green olives (preferably queen green olives), roughly chopped

2 heaped tablespoon capers, drained and roughly chopped
4 anchovies, roughly chopped
2 garlic cloves, roughly chopped

2 green chillies, roughly chopped
¼ bunch of flat-leaf (Italian) parsley, leaves roughly chopped

Add all the ingredients to a high-speed blender and puree to a smooth paste, about 3 minutes. The tapenade will keep covered in the fridge for about a week.

Make it different

Garlicky green olive tapenade. Add a few tablespoons of roasted garlic paste (see p. 66) for a richer tapenade, which is perfect to smear over a pizza base and top with fresh mozzarella, and possibly a few quality anchovies as well, with lightly dressed rocket (arugula) dropped on top.

Green olive, artichoke & kale tapenade. Add 300 g (10½ oz) drained and squeezed artichoke hearts, two extra anchovies, an additional 50 ml (1¾ oz) extra-virgin olive oil and 100 g (3½ oz) blanched kale or cavolo nero (squeezed of excess liquid).

Pair with

Dollop the tapenade on crostini.

Stir it through ricotta with diced haloumi to make a filling for simple filo triangles.

Whisk through a vinaigrette and spoon over pan-seared or grilled chicken or fish.

Toss boiled new potatoes in a mix of mayonnaise and yoghurt or sour cream, then top with Pangrattato (p. 123) and some of the tapenade.

Dollop on seared mackerel, tuna, swordfish or red mullet.

Serve on top of pasta or gnocchi tossed with tomato sauce or mascarpone.

Serve with Lebanese skewered chicken (p. 247).

Oven-baked poussins with tomato, sherry, fennel & olives GF

This recipe has Iberian roots, and is especially successful in a wood-fired oven, with the smoky scents and depth of colour adding something special. It is pretty amazing in a regular oven, too, with the juices of the birds mingling with the reducing sauce, scented with sherry, bay leaves and fennel, to come together beautifully in its short cooking time. You could easily make this a midweek meal with bone-in chicken thighs, or impress weekend guests with the poussin or even quail. **Serves 4**

4 × 600 g (1 lb 5 oz) poussins, spatchcocked (see p. 229), or jumbo quail
2 white salad onions, sliced 3 mm (⅛ in) thick
5 garlic cloves, finely sliced
1 fennel bulb, cut into wedges
1½ tablespoons fennel seeds

5 ripe tomatoes, cut into large dice
150 ml (5 fl oz) dry sherry, or white wine
2 fresh bay leaves
250 ml (8½ fl oz/1 cup) Golden chicken stock (p. 54)

150 g (5½ oz) black mammoth olives, or kalamata or large green olives, pitted

Staples
EVOO, S&P

Preheat the oven to 180°C (350°F) fan-forced.

Coat each poussin with oil and season with salt and pepper.

Heat a large deep frying pan over a medium heat. Sear the poussin for about 5 minutes, skin side down, until golden, then flip and cook for 2 minutes on the other side. Transfer to a baking dish, skin side up.

Pair with

A green salad and Baked buttered rice (p. 384).

Classic potato mash (see p. 625), pan-fried Gnocchi (p. 137) or baked semolina gnocchi (see p. 138).

Marinated olives GF V VG

I love to marinate a mix of olives to have on hand for a snack, or to pull together some antipasti on the fly. Fill a jar with any cured olives. Gently warm a mixture of two-thirds extra-virgin olive oil and one-third neutral-flavoured oil (to stop the olive oil solidifying in the fridge) with a few smashed garlic cloves, some black peppercorns, crushed coriander seeds, a split red chilli, a strip of orange or lemon rind, a sprig of rosemary or thyme and a bay leaf or two. Pour the mixture over the olives, then refrigerate and use as needed. The olives will become more flavourful over time, and the oil fragrant and flavourful, so it can be used in pasta dishes and the like as the jar empties. Adding the oil to a pasta with some of the olives, a splash of tomato passata (puréed tomatoes) and torn basil is a super-quick way to make a delicious meal; for a quick pasta puttanesca, add in some anchovies and capers. The marinated olives are best at room temperature, so either sit what you need on the bench until ready, or warm gently in a pan. To get the oil quantity right, measure it first by filling the jar of olives with water, then draining the water into a measuring jug to establish the quantity. If doing this, it's advisable to drain the olives well before tipping the warmed oil in.

Add a good glug of oil to the same frying pan over a medium heat. Add the onion and garlic, season and cook until softened, about 5 minutes. Add the fennel and fennel seeds and cook to slightly soften, about 5 minutes. Stir in the tomato and cook until it lets down, about 3 minutes. Add the sherry and bay leaves and simmer for about 2 minutes, then add the stock and bring to a simmer.

Pour the sauce mixture over the poussin, scatter the olives over and bake uncovered for 30 minutes. (If using quail, reduce the cooking time to 20 minutes). Serve straight from the baking dish.

Make it different

For a nice golden crust, scatter a handful of breadcrumbs over the dish just before it goes in the oven.

Onion & leek

Where would we be without onions? So many dishes start with the humble onion. It is the foundation ingredient that enhances the flavour of countless recipes, while being anonymous in most. But onions can star, too: they can be sharp and pungent, or rendered into sweetly caramel tones with great umami richness. And while you could remove onion from so many recipes, it is almost always at the expense of depth, sweetness and complexity.

Onions are instrumental in most cuisines the world over, though they and other alliums (garlic, leeks, chives) are shunned in Ayurvedic cooking, in the belief that they promote passion and ignorance, while also centering the consciousness in the physical world, thus being a barrier to enlightenment. Personally, I'm taking that risk. I adore onions.

My everyday onion is the humble brown onion, which ends up in stocks – always with the skin, as it adds flavour – and is diced to form a flavour base of almost any braise or stew, with the pungency converting to sweetness over time. In the absence of stock, a base of well-cooked onions adds so much intensity to a dish. You'll often see this in curry recipes, where a few onions are cooked down over a reasonably intense heat – not to stew and caramelise, but rather to let them catch a little without burning, yielding a bit more light and shade to the finished flavours; they will then be smashed in a mortar or blitzed, to thicken and intensify the gravy.

Red onions (sometimes called Spanish onions) are richer in flavour and sweeter than brown onions, and so are often used raw in salads and the like; in Indian cuisine they are more readily used than brown onions to form the base for curries. Red onions become quite luscious when roasted or slowly cooked (see p. 598).

I tend to increasingly use white onions raw these days, but they can also replace a brown onion as a cooking workhorse. If using raw, I'll soak them in water or quickly pickle to remove some harsh astringency, but I adore their crunch and gentle heat. On a purely aesthetic level, I love their brilliant whiteness as a contrast against other ingredients.

Whether, brown, white or red, all onions will sweeten when cooked slowly, and all can be stuffed and roasted (see p. 598).

Cipollini onions are small (from the Italian cipolla meaning 'onion', and the suffix ini meaning 'small'), with a squat disc shape, like a squashed ball, and delicate loose skin. They are mild and sweet fleshed and can be roasted (see p. 598) to intensify that sweetness, making them a candidate as a standalone vegetable – an unusual position for an onion to occupy.

An array of onion varieties grow in tight formation to produce a small, tightly packed bulb that is ideal for pickling; these are often generically labelled as 'pickling onions' at the market. Then there are the similarly small pearl onions, which are actually closely related to leeks and elephant garlic, and are also ideal for pickling.

Salad onions come in a range of shapes, sizes and colours – from spring onions (scallions) taken to swollen maturity, to large green or purplish discs. They are all milder, sweeter and much less astringent than other onions. Like spring onions, salad onions are harvested and sold 'green', rather than being dried, and are good in salads and sandwiches.

What I call spring onions are also (erroneously) called shallots in some parts of Australia; elsewhere, they are also (far more defensibly) known as green onions, scallions or bunching onions. Spring onions are the immature shoots of a type of onion that doesn't produce a pronounced bulb. Shallots (or eschalots), on the other hand, are small bulb-like onions, often elongated, that separate into cloves when the outer papery skin is peeled. The skin can be golden in the case of French shallots, or quite purplish red in the case of red Asian shallots, and the flesh white with magenta highlights.

Also see

A quick Bordelaise sauce with bone marrow & roasted shallots 68

Black onion spice 281

Ham hock & leek terrine 328

Barbecued Dutch carrot & leek salad 468–9

Shallot dressing 508

Baked fennel & leek with provolone sauce 528–9

Pair with

Leeks and onion love dairy, such as butter, cream and eggs, and cheeses, such as goat's curd, gruyère, feta, young pecorino and parmesan. Pair with garlic, chilli, tomato, capsicum (bell pepper) and peppers, chillies, daikon, potatoes, corn, olives, pineapple and grapes. Spice with cumin, coriander seeds, fennel seeds, coconut, curry leaves, white and black pepper, and fenugreek, and match with herbs such as thyme, sage, rosemary, parsley, bay leaves, oregano and tarragon. Pair with lentils, chickpeas, white beans, walnuts, sesame and almonds. Leeks and onions work well with cured and smoked pork, beef, chicken, salmon, sardines, mackerel and swordfish.

You can use nearly the whole length of a spring onion. The greener parts are ideal as a garnish, being milder in flavour, while the white and pale green parts can take some heat – they're great raw, too, making fine contributions to potato salad and the like (though I'll often rub them with salt and sugar first to soften the sharpness). Sometimes I also leave the roots on when grilling, as they present beautifully all charred and wiry. Charring a spring onion only takes a few minutes on a hot grill with a little oil, and the complexity it adds is exceptional. You can present them whole, as a side, or chop into a salad. Soaking sliced spring onion in water for 10–15 minutes will make them curl up in a visually appealing way, which makes for a great garnish for Asian dishes.

Shallots have an intense flavour, but lack the brash sharpness of, say, a brown onion. They can be used raw, and are particularly good in Thai salads such as larb gai, and finely diced to make a mignonette (see p. 207) for oysters. They also cook extremely well, their intensity and delicacy making them essential for French sauces such as Beurre blanc (p. 69), and are superb roasted (see opposite) and served as a companion for beef. Finely sliced shallots, deep-fried until golden and crisp (see p. 600), are also a fundamental garnish for many Asian dishes.

Leeks are in the same genus as onions, but descended from the same wild or broad-leafed leek that spawned pearl onions and elephant garlic. The leek plant is basically a sheaf of leaves, arrayed like the rings in a tree trunk. As with growing white asparagus, leeks are 'blanched', with earth mounded up to stop them turning green and fibrous in the light – hence the need for careful washing. Leeks can be used in lieu of onions, though their flavour is very distinctive. They are great in stocks, and their gentle oniony richness is a welcome addition to soups (see p. 252), pie fillings (see p. 603), and sautéed to use in an omelette with goat's curd and chopped soft herbs, for example. They're perfect with cream and cheese – think quiches, tarts and the like.

There are many tricks to stopping tears when chopping onions, and some of them actually work. Poking your tongue out is said to attract the gases that make you teary before they reach your eyes, but I tend to just soldier on, unless I have a commercial load to work through. Halving and peeling an onion, then soaking in cold water for 15 minutes or so, will help the slicing and dicing proceed more or less dry-eyed.

Onions can be quite astringent when raw, depending on both the type and ripeness. Simply soaking wedges or rings in cold/iced water for 10–15 minutes will take the edge off them considerably, and enhance their crispness – simply drain, pat dry and add to a salad, sandwich, or scatter over a dish as a finishing touch. Coating them generously with sumac adds a lemony zing and ups the presentation substantially.

To soften the flavour even further, quickly pickle sliced onion. Dissolve a pinch of salt and sugar in a splash of vinegar, massage into the onion and set aside for 5 minutes or so, then throw into a dressing or salad, or mix with a few soft herbs and crown a piece of meat or fish. I use these a lot to complement rich, big-flavoured dishes or charcuterie, or to give a sharp lift to a grain salad or roasted vegetables. With this method you'll convert quite a few of those who are otherwise ardent in their distaste for raw onion.

The anonymous ubiquity of onions can be a problem for those who have a food intolerance to them (FODMAP, fructose malabsorption). While it won't make dining out any easier, onions can be omitted in almost all recipes that they're not the hero of, and celery or fennel can be used to build flavour instead – though these may also inflame some with more extreme sensitivities.

Red, white and brown onions are dried before sale, so the skin should be dry and the onion firm, with no soft spots. I always press my thumb at the shoot end to check there is no rotting within. Squeeze shallots fairly firmly all over, as they can look perfectly fine, but still be soft inside – I often reject quite a few before buying what I need. Spring onions (scallions) should look vibrant and crisp, without too many layers peeling off.

A leek should feel firm and tightly packed – with a longer white/pale green trunk giving you more yield. If the layers are loose and slipping, it's not as fresh as it could be. I always opt for medium to small specimens, and love the super-fine youthful ones. Too large, and the core can be quite inedible, and the layers don't really soften when cooked.

Quick-pickled onions

Peel 4 white salad onions or red onions, or 12 red shallots, and evenly slice 4–5 mm (¼ in) thick. (A mandoline is useful for this, but not essential.) Soak in cold water for 10 minutes, then drain and add to a large bowl. Warm 250 ml (8½ fl oz/1 cup) white-wine vinegar, 100 ml (3½ fl oz) water, 100 g (3½ oz) caster (superfine) sugar and 1½ tablespoons salt flakes in a small saucepan to dissolve the sugar and salt, then cool at room temperature. Pour the liquid over the onions, toss through and stand for 10 minutes. This makes enough for 10–12 serves. The pickles are then ready to serve (in sandwiches or salads, with charcuterie and cheeses, or scattered over barbecued steak or chicken), or can be refrigerated in the liquid for up to a week.

Fried onion rings

Not just great to garnish fish or steak! Scatter them over a caesar salad or chicken salad, or serve with fried squid or whitebait. Serve stacked up as a starter with some spicy mayonnaise (see p. 620), Black aïoli (p. 76) or Anchoïade (p. 78), or dust with paprika and simply serve with sour cream. Cut a few brown onions into 3 cm (1¼ in) thick rings and soak in milk with a squeeze of lemon for at least 15 minutes, and up to 1 hour. Drain well. Liberally dust with an even mix of flour and fine semolina, then deep-fry in oil in batches until golden, about 4 minutes. Drain on paper towel, season with salt and keep warm in a low oven while cooking the remaining onion rings.

Preparing onions & leeks

A brown, white or red onion needs to be peeled. Cut the shoot end off, leaving the root end intact (which is said to contain more sulphur-rich, tear-inducing compounds; some discard it entirely, but this is wasteful). Rest it on the cut end, halve lengthways (unless cutting rings, where a mandoline is handy) and peel. Lay it on the large cut side to slice or dice. Shallots are best peeled with a paring knife, after separating into individual cloves. Spring onions just need the roots trimmed and any loose skin removed. When the green tops get too coarse and large, I will lop them off, but otherwise I try to use as much of the spring onion as possible.

With leeks, trim off and discard the root, then cut off the dark green top, which you can use for stock (just the less coarse bits, though). Slice the pale part lengthways, discarding any less-tender outer layers. Wash well, as dirt will intrude between the layers, and you can't rid of grit once it's in your dish. If slicing into rings, submerge them in water for a little, then change the water a few times to purge any grit. The useable part of the leek is the white and the tender green.

Salt-roasted shallots ⓖⒻ Ⓥ ⓋⒼ

Pair with

Season with salt and pepper and toss in good vinegar, some chopped parsley or tarragon and/or grated horseradish, and serve with steak or roast chicken.

Serve with roast beef or a steak, spooned atop Beurre rouge (p. 69).

Toss through cooked lentils, freekeh or barley with mint, and serve as a salad with some crumbled hard feta or a curd cheese.

Serve in Dashi (see p. 53) with ramen noodles, sliced shiitake mushrooms, greens, sliced seasoned tofu or shredded cooked chicken.

Toss in quality balsamic vinegar and serve on a simple risotto (see p. 148), with steak or grilled fish, or on bruschetta with fresh ricotta, goat's cheese or taleggio.

Blitz the shallots with some oil, sharpening the flavour with a dash of vinegar, mustard or horseradish. Serve as an onion sauce with chicken, steak, fish or even roasted cauliflower (see p. 476).

The magic happens in the parcel and in the skins, roasting and steaming in their juices until tender and lusciously sweet. They can be warmed up and added to sauces and salads, or used as a side for rich meat dishes. **Makes 16**

200 g (7 oz) rock salt
16 French shallots, or white onions, skin on

6 thyme sprigs
Staples
EVOO

Preheat the oven to 170°C (340°F) fan-forced.

Stack three lengths of foil together, then pile on the rock salt, followed by the shallots. Drizzle with oil and top with the thyme. Seal the foil into a parcel and roast for 40 minutes.

Once cooked, open the parcel slightly for the steam to escape, then set aside for 5 minutes to cool a little. Slip the skins off the shallots before using. Any leftovers will keep for up to 3 days in the fridge.

French onion soup

This dish is about as classic as it gets, and one that celebrates the caramelised sweetness of onions cooked low and slow – in this case, for about 5 hours. But don't let that put you off, as most of that time is spent in the oven. Recipes for French onion soup will vary by small calibrations, and ardent loyalists will decry minor deviations. For me, it should be rich and intense, with acidity and a vaguely boozy touch from the wine and sherry, and the depth of a good stock – ideally beef (see p. 55), though a Golden chicken stock (p. 54) also yields an exceptional result. The other essential is crowning with a cheesy raft of toasted baguette. **Serves 6**

80 ml (2½ fl oz/⅓ cup) extra-virgin olive oil	70 g (2½ oz) butter	**To serve**
4 large red onions, sliced 1 cm (½ in) thick	7 thyme sprigs	1 sourdough baguette, sliced
4 large brown onions, sliced 1 cm (½ in) thick	80 ml (2½ fl oz/⅓ cup) water	dijon mustard, for spreading
6 garlic cloves, finely sliced	200 ml (7 fl oz) white wine	3 spring onions (scallions), finely sliced, or Spring onion ash (p. 602)
1 celery heart, finely sliced	1.5 litres (51 fl oz/6 cups) Brown beef stock (p. 55)	250 g (9 oz) gruyère, grated
2 star anise	2½ tablespoons dry sherry, or madeira	**Staples** S&P

Preheat the oven to 130°C (265°F) fan-forced.

Heat the oil in a large flameproof casserole dish over a medium–high heat. Add the onions, garlic, celery and star anise and cook until lightly caramelised, about 10 minutes. Season lightly with salt and pepper, then add the butter, thyme and water. Stir through.

Cover tightly, place in the oven and bake for 4½ hours.

Place the casserole dish on the stovetop over a medium heat. Remove the star anise and allow the liquid to reduce, stirring constantly until almost dry. Deglaze with the wine and reduce until almost dry. Stir in the stock and simmer for 10 minutes. Add the sherry and season with salt and plenty of pepper. Simmer for a couple of minutes, then take off the heat.

To serve, toast the bread slices, then smear with mustard. Sprinkle with the spring onion and gruyère and grill (broil) until the cheese is melted. Drop on top of the soup in bowls and serve immediately.

You can also make up the toasts, ladle the soup into the bowls – usually squat goblet-like ones that keep the soup ultra-hot and fit a disc of baguette neatly in their opening – under the grill (broiler) to melt the cheese, which is how it's classically done in restaurants.

Make it different

With an indulgent French finish. Mix together 3½ tablespoons crème fraîche and two egg yolks. Before serving the soup, divide the egg mixture between the serving bowls before proceeding to serve as above.

Sherry vinegar–glazed shallots & taleggio on toast ⓥ

This is cheese on toast taken to a new level, and fancy enough as a standalone starter or supper dish. Brown about a dozen peeled whole shallots in oil and butter, season well, then roast with some thyme and 150 ml (5 fl oz) water in a 180°C (350°F) fan-forced oven for about 25 minutes. Once tender, and the water has cooked out, dress with 3 teaspoons each of sherry vinegar and balsamic vinegar and place over a medium heat. Add 30 g (1 oz) butter and toss through to melt and gloss. Toast some Sourdough (p. 847), then top with 1 cm (½ in) slices of taleggio and melt under a grill (broiler). Spoon the shallots and sauce over and serve immediately. Some picked bitter greens or rocket (arugula) is a nice touch, too.

Pickled shallots & currants with parsley & cornichons ⒼⒻ ⓥ ⓋⒼ

Add 300 ml (10 fl oz) white-wine vinegar, 5 cloves, 1 fresh bay leaf, 2½ tablespoons caster (superfine) sugar and 1 tablespoon salt flakes to a small saucepan and bring to a simmer over a medium heat. Add 8 large peeled French shallots and 80 g (2¾ oz/½ cup) currants, bring back to a simmer and cook for 1 minute. Remove from the heat and stir 100 ml (3½ fl oz) sherry vinegar through. Stand at room temperature for 3 hours, then separate the layers of the shallots. The shallots will keep under the vinegar for a month or two. To serve, drain off some shallots, toss with some cornichons, parsley, pepper and a splash of extra-virgin olive oil. Serves 8, and adds a tangy zing of acidity and flush of sweetness as an accompaniment to charcuterie or strong cheeses.

Sweet pickled onions GF V VG

Pair with

*Charcuterie, terrines (pp. 327–8)
or rillettes (see p. 330).*

*Slice and serve with a sharp
cheddar and Oatcake crackers
(p. 840).*

*Add to a ploughman's
lunch plate.*

*Slice for a sandwich with
sliced roast beef, dijon mustard
and cheddar.*

*Serve with Beer-battered
flathead & twice-cooked
potato cakes (p. 187).*

These sweet and sharp pickled onions make a wonderful foil for sharp cheeses and cured or roast meats, especially beef, but they're also delicious as a snack on their own, or with a beer or two. **Makes a 1 litre (34 fl oz/4 cup) jar**

600 g (1 lb 5 oz) pickling
  onions or French shallots,
  peeled
20 g (¾ oz) fine sea salt

Pickling medium
400 ml (13½ fl oz) white-wine
  vinegar, or malt vinegar

200 ml (7 fl oz) water
200 g (7 oz) caster (superfine)
  sugar
50 g (1¾ oz) salt flakes
1 tablespoon white mustard
  seeds

1½ teaspoons black
  peppercorns
2 fresh bay leaves

Add the onions and salt to a large bowl, then toss and rub the salt in with your hands. Weigh down with a plate and stand for at least 6 hours or overnight.

Drain off any liquid, dry with a clean tea towel (dish towel) and pack into a hot, sterilised jar (see p. 40).

Bring the pickling medium ingredients to a simmer in a saucepan for 2 minutes. Pour the hot liquid over the onions, making sure they are submerged. Seal the jar, then invert on the bench until cool.

Pickle at room temperature in the pantry for at least 3 weeks; after 6 weeks they will taste even better. Once opened, refrigerate and use within 6 months.

Pearl onions à la grecque GF V VG

Pair with

*Slice and toss with chopped
soft herbs to crown cooked fish
or a simple steak.*

*Serve with charcuterie, terrines
and the like.*

*Plate with roasted capsicums
(bell peppers), olives and
boiled eggs.*

*Slice and drop on top of
a potato salad.*

*Pair with oily smoked fish,
such as mackerel.*

Vegetables à la grecque, or in the Greek style, are a French classic. In fact, it's hard to imagine a preparation like this appearing in Greek cuisine. The Greek reference is apparently an epithet that was applied to recipes originally inspired by immigrants who moved to France in the Middle Ages, with many of them evidently Greek. The classic preparation is basically one of vegetables (try a mix of any varieties you fancy) that are just-cooked in a spiced, acidic liquid, somewhat resembling pickling liquor. This version is somewhat simplified and employs pearl onions alone – though if serving as a starter, I would offer up a more traditional version using a range of vegetables. Serve at room temperature. **Makes 35**

35 small pearl onions,
  or round green onions,
  trimmed and peeled
250 ml (8½ fl oz/1 cup)
  white wine
100 ml (3½ fl oz) tomato
  passata (puréed tomatoes)

3 thyme sprigs, or
  2 rosemary sprigs
3 garlic cloves, peeled
juice of 1 lemon
3 teaspoons coriander
  seeds
2 teaspoons salt flakes

1 teaspoon ground black
  or white pepper
125 ml (4 fl oz/½ cup)
  extra-virgin olive oil

Bring all the ingredients except the oil to a simmer in a saucepan. Cook over a low heat for 20 minutes, then add the oil and cool to room temperature before serving.

These onions will keep for a week refrigerated; just bring back to room temperature before serving.

Simple caramelised onions (GF) (V) (VG)

This simple staple recipe can be used as a topping for pizza or tarts, or as a sweet condiment for strong cheese or charcuterie. The type of onion will determine the finished sweetness, with red onions cooking a little faster and becoming the sweetest – but I don't necessarily prefer one over the other. **Makes 250–300 g (9–10½ oz/about 1½ cups)**

6 brown or red onions, sliced 5 mm (¼ in) thick
1 tablespoon water
125 ml (4 fl oz/½ cup) extra-virgin olive oil

1½ tablespoons sherry vinegar, wine vinegar or vincotto
5 thyme sprigs, leaves stripped

Staples
S&P

Toss the onion with the oil in a bowl to coat, then season with salt and toss again. (Coating the onions first helps them to cook down more quickly.)

Add to a large saucepan over a medium heat. Season with salt and stir until softening down, about 5 minutes. Add the water and stew the onion for about 1 hour, until caramelised. You will need to stir every 5 minutes to begin with, then once softened, turn down the heat and stir about every 10 minutes.

Once the onion has changed colour to a light brown, you're done. Stir in the vinegar and thyme, then either use or store.

The caramelised onion will keep in an airtight container in the fridge for a week, as long as you keep it well covered in the oil, which also has a great onion flavour. You can use the oniony oil to start a rich braise, sauce or soup to add extra flavour; just be sure to keep it in the fridge, as it may go sour otherwise.

Slow-roasted red onions (GF) (V) (VG)

Once cooked, the herb-scented red onion flesh is just so rich and sweet, making it a perfect foil for beef or strong, sharp cheeses. You can also take this simple dish a step further by crumbing (see right) and serving as a side or antipasto. **Makes 6**

6 red onions, or cipollini onions, skin on, cut in half
2 fresh bay leaves

4 thyme sprigs
1 rosemary sprig

Staples
EVOO, S&P

Preheat the oven to 150°C (300°F) fan-forced.

Tightly pack the onions, cut side up, and herbs into a baking tray or dish. Season generously with salt and pepper and drizzle with oil. Roast for about 1½ hours, until soft and just starting to brown.

To colour them more if already tender, turn the oven up to 200°C (400°F) fan-forced and roast for another 15–20 minutes. Any leftovers will keep for up to 3 days in the fridge.

Make it a meal

Slow-roasted red onion quiche. (GF) Bake these onions into a quiche (see p. 829) with ham and/or mushrooms.

Slow-roasted red onion frittata. (GF) (V) Add the onions to a Frittata (p. 355) with feta and peas.

Potato & slow-roasted red onion salad. (GF) (V) (VG) Toss through boiled new potatoes and dress as you would a potato salad.

Pair with

Use for Pissaladière (opposite) in place of oven-roasted shallots.

Spread the onion over 400 g (14 oz) rolled-out pizza dough (see p. 856). Top with 4 figs, each sliced into 3–4 pieces, plus 50 g (1¾ oz) sliced or crumbled gorgonzola cheese and the leaves from 6 thyme sprigs. Bake at 200°C (400°F) for 30 minutes, until golden.

Serve with terrines (pp. 327–8), pâté (see p. 233) or strong cheeses.

Add to a frittata with goat's cheese, or to a quiche.

Use atop a grilled steak.

Add to freshly cooked grains or pulses to make a salad with soft herbs, Vinaigrette (p. 88) and crumbled goat's cheese.

Thyme-crumbed onions (V)

Preheat the oven to 180°C (350°F) fan-forced. To make the crumb, add 3 large torn slices of Sourdough bread (p. 847), the leaves of 6 thyme sprigs, 4 roughly chopped flat-leaf (Italian) parsley sprigs, 2 tablespoons finely grated Grana Padano, 40 g (1½ oz) butter and 1 chopped garlic clove to a food processor. Season heavily with salt and pepper and blitz. Tip the crumbs over 1 × quantity warm Slow-roasted red onions (left) and roast for about 15 minutes to toast. Sprinkle with a little extra-virgin olive oil and red- or white- wine vinegar before serving warm, or at room temperature. Dollop with fresh goat's curd or ricotta, and sprinkle with chopped black olives, vinegar-soaked currants and chilli powder. Serves 6.

Pissaladière

While pissaladière is a classic dish of Nice, in the south of France, it is reasonable to link its origins with an Italian staple from Liguria, which many also credit as being the first modern pizza. Either way, there's something very special about the interplay of sweetly caramelised onions and the briny pop of olives and anchovies. You can make this tart with bread/pizza dough – as they do in Genoa, and quite commonly in Nice, too – but I do love it with the savoury, short, buttery crumb of this sour cream shortcrust. **Serves 8**

Pair with

Serve warm with something peppery – such as radish and rocket (arugula) or mustard cress.

Onion sauce

This onion sauce is perfect for steak, rissoles and meatballs. You can make this sauce while your protein finishes in the oven and then rests. After a steak, rissoles or meatballs have been seared, wipe out the pan and then, in a little oil, sauté a few finely sliced brown onions or half a dozen or so shallots and a sliced garlic clove. Cook slowly until sweet and caramelised, about 15 minutes. Add a knob of butter, some thyme leaves and a tablespoon of flour and stir through for a minute or so. Add a good splash of red or white wine, or dry sherry vinegar, and reduce for a minute, then add 250 ml (8½ fl oz/1 cup) of reduced Beef stock (p. 55). Add a teaspoon of mustard and simmer until thickened. Season with salt and pepper and serve with the protein.

Sour sherry onions (GF) (V) (VG)

Add 2 finely sliced red onions, 50 ml (1¾ fl oz) sherry vinegar, 2 tablespoons caster (superfine) sugar and ½ teaspoon salt flakes to a saucepan over a medium heat. Cover and cook for 15 minutes, stirring occasionally, until the onion has softened and turned bright pink.

1½ tablespoons extra-virgin olive oil
600 g (1 lb 5 oz) French shallots, peeled and sliced in thirds
5 garlic cloves, peeled
30 g (1 oz) butter
150 ml (5 fl oz) water
1½ tablespoons sherry vinegar, or red-wine vinegar
4 thyme sprigs, leaves stripped

16 anchovies
20 black olives, pitted
2 teaspoons baby capers
Sour cream shortcrust pastry
400 g (14 oz/2⅔ cups) plain (all-purpose) flour
230 g (8 oz) unsalted butter, chilled and cut into 2 cm (¾ in) dice
85 g (3 oz) sour cream
2 egg yolks

Staples
S&P

Preheat the oven to 160°C (320°F) fan-forced.

For the pastry, pulse the flour and butter in a food processor until the mixture resembles fine breadcrumbs, about 1 minute. Add the sour cream and egg yolks and pulse for a few seconds, until the dough comes together. Turn out onto a bench and bring together by hand, into a smooth dough. Wrap in plastic wrap and chill until needed.

Heat the oil in a large ovenproof frying pan over a medium heat. Add the shallot and garlic, season with salt and pepper and cook until golden at the edges, about 10 minutes.

Add the butter and water. Transfer to the oven and roast for 25 minutes, until the shallot is soft and golden, stirring halfway through. Once cooked, stir the vinegar and thyme through, adjust the seasoning as needed and cool to room temperature.

Turn the oven up to 180°C (350°F) fan-forced. Take a baking tray (ideally a heavy one, to conduct heat better) and line with baking paper.

Roll the dough out until just over 1 cm (½ in) thick, then cut out a rectangle about 36 × 25 cm (14½ × 10 in). You will have about 200 g (7 oz) dough left over, which can be frozen.

Lay the pastry on the baking tray. Spread the shallot mixture over, leaving a border of pastry all around. Crisscross with the anchovies and dot with the olives and capers.

Grind some pepper over and bake for 35 minutes, until the pastry is golden. Cut into tiles and serve warm.

Make it different
With another pastry. Instead of the pastry, you could use 375–400 g (13–14 oz) butter Puff pastry (p. 822, or buy a good commercial block) or 400 g (14 oz) Pizza base (p. 856) rolled out to 1–1.5 cm (½ in) thick. Increase the oven temperature to 200°C (400°F).

With green olive paste. Instead of the black olives, dollop with Queen green tapenade (p. 590) when the pissaladière comes out of the oven.

Leek with walnut & rye skordalia ⓥ

When leeks are in full swing, tender and small to medium in size, they become meltingly delicious when cooked. Their delicate, creamy flavour is nicely offset by walnuts and the mealy, earthy flavour of rye. This dish can be made with slender juvenile leeks, and also larger – though not oversized – ones. Adjust the cooking time accordingly. **Serves 6**

150 ml (5 fl oz) sherry vinegar
1 teaspoon brown sugar
1 teaspoon salt flakes
100 g (3½ oz) golden or
    green sultanas, or currants
50 g (1¾ oz/½ cup) walnuts
6–8 small leeks, about 3 cm
    (1¼ in) thick, trimmed

3 tarragon, chervil or flat-leaf
    (Italian) parsley sprigs,
    fronds picked and chopped
Spring onion ash (p. 602),
    to serve

Walnut & rye skordalia
3 tablespoons extra-virgin
    olive oil

2 large garlic cloves, sliced
100 g (3½ oz/1 cup) walnuts
150 ml (5 fl oz) milk
100 ml (3½ fl oz) water
100 g (3½ oz) rye bread,
    crusts removed, bread torn

Staples
EVOO, LMN, S&P

Preheat the oven to 160°C (320°F) fan-forced.

Bring the vinegar, sugar and salt to a simmer. Add the sultanas and simmer for 2 minutes over a low heat, then set aside for 30 minutes. Strain the vinegar, reserving the sultanas, and combine with an equal amount of oil to make the dressing.

For the skordalia, heat a splash of the oil in a saucepan over a medium heat. Add the garlic and cook until fragrant, about 1 minute. Add the walnuts, milk and water, season with salt and pepper and cook to soften and reduce, about 5 minutes. Add the bread and simmer over a low heat for 3 minutes. Tip into a blender and blitz on high, adding the remaining oil as you go to emulsify. If it's not smoothing out, add a little more oil and/or a tablespoon or so of hot water. Sharpen with lemon juice and adjust the seasoning to taste.

Meanwhile, roast the walnuts on a baking tray until toasted, about 10 minutes. Toss in a little oil and salt, then roughly chop and set aside.

Tie the leeks in two bunches, secured at both ends, then cook in salted simmering water for about 8 minutes, until tender. Drain well, gently pressing the water out. Wrap in a tea towel (dish towel) and press out any excess moisture, then cut into 4 cm (1½ in) lengths.

Toss the leeks with the sultanas, herbs and dressing in a bowl.

To serve, spread the skordalia on a serving plate and top with the leek mixture. Dust with the spring onion ash and scatter with the walnuts.

Make it different
White asparagus with walnut & rye skordalia. ⓥ Replace the leeks with poached fat spears of white asparagus (see p. 404), which occupy a similar space in terms of flavour.

Roasted pumpkin with walnut & rye skordalia. ⓥ Instead of braised leeks, serve the walnut and rye skordalia under a pile of warm roasted pumpkin (winter squash). You could do the same with cauliflower.

Pair with
This is so delicious as a vegetable starter, or serve it with a cheese tart or pie (pp. 564, 828).

Crisp fried shallots ⒼⒻ ⓥ ⓋⒼ
Fried shallots are wonderful to have on hand, adding crunch and a hit of golden onion flavour to Asian soups, salads, meat, fish and noodle dishes. Add 5 cm (2 cm) of frying oil to a saucepan. Add 12 shallots, peeled and sliced 3 mm (⅛ in) thick, to the cold oil and place over a medium heat. Bring the oil up in temperature while stirring frequently and watching closely. The shallot slices will fry and slowly change colour to a light golden brown, about 8 minutes. As soon as they turn lightly golden, strain them off, then transfer to paper towel to drain, spreading out in one layer. The shallot slices will crisp up as they cool, and darken slightly. Don't be tempted to let them darken too much in the oil, as by the time they cool down they will be a little bitter and burnt. Season with salt as soon as they come out of the oil and store in an airtight container.

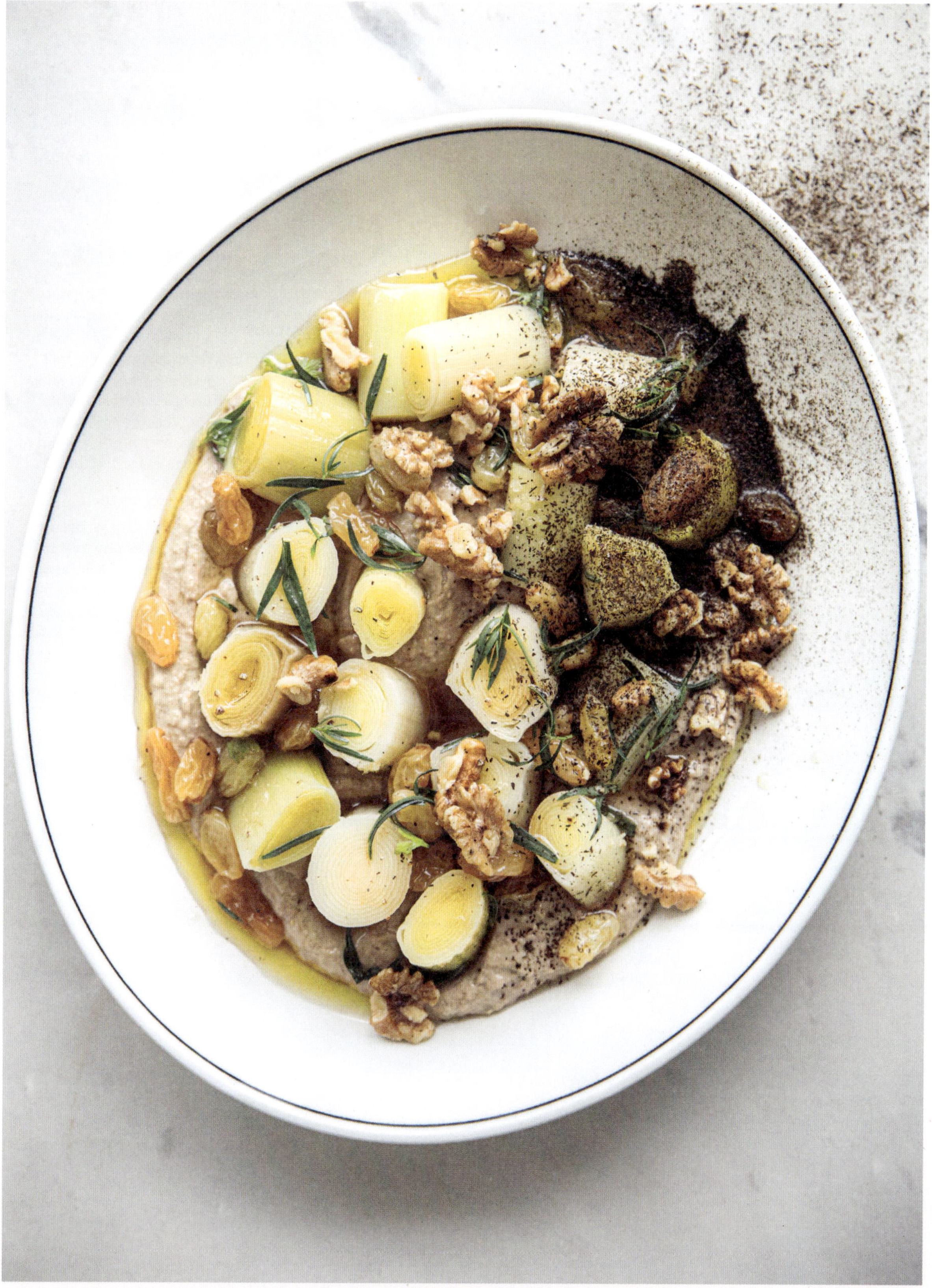

Gnocchi with leek & gorgonzola (GF)

This was the first way I ever served gnocchi in a restaurant. The pure flavour of potato against the rich and piquant gorgonzola sauce with buttery soft leeks and toasted breadcrumbs is a wonderful combination. While simple to pull together, the flavours are complex, while still letting the flavour and texture of the gnocchi shine. **Serves 4**

120 g (4½ oz/1½ cups) fresh breadcrumbs
4 leeks, trimmed
50 g (1¾ oz) butter
300 ml (10 fl oz) pouring (single/light) cream

160 g (5½ oz) gorgonzola, or your favourite blue cheese
500 g (1 lb 2 oz) freshly cooked Gnocchi (p. 136), coated lightly with oil or butter and kept warm in a low oven

100 g (3½ oz) Grana Padano, finely grated

Staples
EVOO, S&P

Add the breadcrumbs to a large frying pan with a drizzle of oil over a medium heat and toss until golden, about 5 minutes. Season with salt and pepper and drain on paper towel.

Poach the leeks in simmering salted water until tender, about 10 minutes. Drain well, gently pressing the water out. Wrap in a tea towel (dish towel) and press out any excess moisture, then slice into fine rounds.

Melt the butter in a large frying pan over a medium heat. Add the leek and toss through to coat. Stir in the cream and bring to a simmer. Turn the heat to low and crumble in the gorgonzola, letting it melt in gently.

Add the gnocchi and parmesan. Grind in plenty of black pepper, and salt if needed (check first). Toss through, or gently mix with a metal spoon – a wooden spoon will mash the gnocchi, especially if home-made.

Serve immediately.

Make it different

With nuts. This is also delicious topped with toasted walnuts, pine nuts or hazelnuts.

With spring onion 'ash'. Garnish with Spring onion ash (right).

Pair with

A salad of mixed greens is all that's needed – but include something like radicchio or chicory (witlof/endive) for a bitter accent.

Spring onion 'ash' (GF) (V) (VG)

This adds a very restauranty touch to a dish. The flavour is a gentle charry onion note, and it has quite a dramatic visual effect. Sprinkle over eggs, fish crudo, pasta, risotto, roasted vegetables, salads, curd cheeses, piperade tart … so many things. It also features in the leeks with Walnut & rye skordalia recipe (p. 600). Spread a bunch of spring onions (scallions) out on a baking tray and roast at 160°C (320°F) fan-forced for about 2 hours, until deep brown-black and totally dried. Set aside to cool, then pulverise in a food processor or blender.

Spring onion 'ash'

Chicken, leek & mushroom pie

Pair with

A lightly dressed green salad is all this pie needs.

The velouté (a stock-based sauce thickened with a roux) is key to the success of this sauce, so make sure you use an intensely flavoured chicken stock, preferably home-made (see p. 54). If you must buy stock, use the best you can find, not the stuff in tetra packs in the supermarket. The pastry is also critical, so genuine all-butter puff is essential, whether store-bought or home-made (see p. 822). Regular puff pastry sheets are handy for some things, such as sausage rolls and the like, but for this marvellous pie they're not really thick enough to give the lid enough rise and sufficient flaky foil for the silky filling. **Serves 4**

8 chicken thighs, skin on, bone in
1.2 litres (41 fl oz) Golden chicken stock (p. 54), hot
4 leeks, finely sliced
½ onion, finely diced
3 garlic cloves, finely chopped
65 g (2¼ oz) butter

200 g (7 oz) Swiss brown mushrooms, finely diced or sliced
3 thyme sprigs, leaves stripped
40 g (1½ oz) plain (all-purpose) flour
2 tablespoons thick (double/heavy) cream
1 tablespoon dijon mustard

1 handful of flat-leaf (Italian) parsley leaves, or dill or tarragon, chopped
375 g (13 oz) Classic puff pastry (p. 822), Rough puff pastry (p. 823), Pâte brisée (p. 829), or use a quality store-bought puff pastry
1 egg, whisked

Staples
EVOO, S&P

Heat a splash of oil in a wide-based saucepan over a medium heat. Season the chicken with salt and cook, skin side down, until golden brown, about 10 minutes. Flip the thighs over, cook for a couple of minutes, then pour the stock over. Simmer, uncovered, for about 25 minutes, until the chicken is cooked.

Strain the stock into a saucepan and skim off most of the fat. Reduce on the stove over a medium heat until reduced to about 400 ml (13½ fl oz), then set aside. Set the chicken aside to cool, then strip the meat and skin off the bones. Tear or chop the flesh and skin.

Heat another good splash of oil in a large frying pan over a medium heat. Add the leek, onion and garlic and sweat until soft but barely coloured, about 15 minutes. Add 25 g (1 oz) of the butter, the mushrooms and thyme, season with salt and pepper and cook until the mushrooms are tender, about 5 minutes.

Preheat the oven to 190°C (375°F) fan-forced.

Melt the remaining butter in a saucepan over a medium heat. Once foaming, add the flour and stir to make a roux. Stir for about 1 minute to cook the rawness out of the flour, then add the reduced chicken stock. Cook, whisking constantly, until smooth and thick, 2–3 minutes. Cool for 15 minutes, then whisk in the cream and mustard.

Combine the creamy sauce with the chicken, mushroom mixture and parsley. Season as needed.

Roll out the pastry so you can cut out a lid 3 cm (1¼ in) larger than a 25–28 cm (10–11 in) pie dish. Brush the edge of the dish with the egg, then tip the filling in and drop the pastry on top. Crimp to seal the pastry onto the dish, and decorate the top with any pastry scraps. Make an incision or two in the top and brush with more egg.

Bake for about 40 minutes, until golden and puffed. Stand for 5 minutes before serving.

Parsnip

When my grandmother Monica (my mother's mother) used to roast duck or chicken, she would also roast a separate tray of parsnip, which no-one else ate. Parsnips are a bit like that, adored by some and loathed by others (well, my father hated them), and generally treated with a little suspicion. They don't even get a hard time, really; they just don't get much airtime at all. My mother certainly never cooked them.

Parsnips are an intriguing vegetable, with such a distinctive flavour that I liken to white sweet potato spiked with cinnamon. They are sweet, but not cloyingly so, and they have earthy and nutty notes that are enhanced when roasted. I always use healthy amounts of parsnip in my winter minestrone (see p. 607) and pasties (see p. 469), and they also mash extremely well, with a more richly flavoured and earthy result than using potato alone (see p. 606). For me, parsnips are also an essential companion to a traditional winter roast.

Parsnips are from the same botanical family as parsley and carrots, with references to them dating back to the earliest times. Carrots are thought to have been first domesticated in Afghanistan, while parsnips are indigenous to Eurasia (Kazakhstan), and both of them found their way into the diets of the ancient Greeks and Romans. Early records of tapered white root vegetables exist, though given that carrots at the time were often white, coupled with a vagueness of nomenclature, means it's sometimes hard to discern which is being referenced. The Romans certainly grew parsnips, however, and valued their sweet flesh highly, reputedly even accepting them as tribute payments.

That sweetness is a key feature of parsnips, and indeed they were used as a source of sugar prior to the introduction of cane sugar. Parsnips are primarily winter vegetables – though they spill into autumn and spring – and that sweetness develops when starch is converted to sugar after a frost. Bought outside of season, parsnips will either be imported from elsewhere or have been stored for an extended period, neither of which is ideal.

As with all vegetables, large specimens are best avoided, but parsnips can become particularly fibrous and woody when mature. Larger than average parsnips can still be delicious, but are best peeled and cored. Modestly sized roots can be sweet and delicate and won't need peeling, and they will cook rather quickly, somewhat like Dutch carrots - too long in the oven and you won't be left with much of anything. Select examples that are firm and ivory coloured with no blemishes. An old parsnip will lose its vividness of colour and start to go a little spongy, so is best avoided. I also look for parsnips that taper into the root tip more gradually, as you get more usable flesh from these; a long tapering root is essentially the same as the core – all fibrous strands and little joy.

Also see

Celeriac & parsnip
purée 286

Tunisian vegetable
couscous royale with
rosewater labneh 386–7

Borscht 418

Pasties 469–70

Roast carrot & root
vegetable soup with
cinnamon & ginger 472

Roasted celeriac, parsnip,
potato & fennel with
ras el hanout 485

Pair with

*Parsnips work well with cream,
butter and yoghurt, as well as
flavourful hard cheese such
as Parmigiano Reggiano and
gruyère. The natural sweetness
of maple syrup knits in well
with their earthy sweetness,
while wine and sherry vinegars
are excellent foils. Parsnips
love spice (pepper, cinnamon,
nutmeg, turmeric, allspice,
clove, cumin, fennel seed, anise
seed, curry powder), herbs
(parsley, tarragon, chives)
and nuts (pecans, walnuts,
pine nuts, almonds). Pair with
potatoes, onions, carrots, fennel
and apple, and with proteins
such as smoked fish, lamb,
duck and beef.*

Preparing parsnips

I tend to always peel parsnips, unless they are very young, and core them depending on how dense that core is, which is largely influenced by maturity. Even medium-sized parsnips are usually best cored. The cap, where the greenery once sprouted, can just be sliced off, but smaller specimens need nothing done. If roasting, the spindly end of the tap root will tend to burn before the thicker section is tender, so these can be cut away. It's not always easy to get even chunks for roasting, but leaving the tapered section whole and cutting the main barrel of the root into rounds or chunks gets close enough. If roasting whole, choose small to medium evenly sized parsnips and oil well. Leave the tender ends intact and they will caramelise and darken – I think it adds to the charm, and they are a thing of beauty done like this.

Parsnip & potato purée GF V

This versatile puree is a little like skordalia (see p. 373) in feel, but is just that bit sweeter, earthier and more deeply flavoured. **Serves 4**

250 g (9 oz) peeled and cored parsnips, cut into evenly sized pieces
200 g (7 oz) peeled all-purpose potatoes (such as desiree), cut into evenly sized pieces
2 garlic cloves, peeled
125 ml (4 fl oz/½ cup) extra-virgin olive oil
125 ml (4 fl oz/½ cup) cold milk

Staples
S&P

Add the parsnip, potato and garlic to a saucepan of boiling salted water. Simmer until very tender, about 10–15 minutes, then drain well.

Blend in a food processor while still hot, gradually adding the oil, then the milk, through the feeder. Season as needed with salt and pepper and keep warm in an airtight container or piping (icing) bag until needed. Use within 3 hours of making.

Make it vegan VG
You can make this dairy-free by using oat milk.

Roasted parsnip & purple sweet potato with cinnamon, nutmeg & garlic GF V VG

There are many varieties of sweet potatoes, but I'm a big fan of the white-fleshed sweet potato with bright purple skin. It has a delicious nutty flavour of cooked chestnuts when roasted – but you could, of course, use any sweet potato for this. Parsnip and sweet potato both have a rich sweetness that loves spice, especially warm spices such as cinnamon and nutmeg. **Serves 4–6**

4 parsnips, peeled and cored, cut in half
1 purple or white sweet potato, cut into 3 cm (1¼ in) rounds
10 garlic cloves, peeled
6 thyme sprigs
1 cinnamon stick
½ whole nutmeg, finely grated
80 ml (2½ fl oz/⅓ cup) extra-virgin olive oil
100 ml (3½ fl oz) water

Staples
S&P

Roasted parsnip with anise, maple syrup & gruyère GF V

Preheat the oven to 180°C (350°F) fan-forced. Line a baking tray with baking paper. Trim and peel 5 parsnips. Cut 2.5 cm (1 in) rings from the thick ends of the parsnips, then once halfway down, cut in half lengthways. Toss in extra-virgin olive oil and 3 teaspoons ground anise seeds, season with salt and pepper and spread out on the baking tray. Roast for about 30 minutes, until golden and tender. Once cooked, sprinkle over 50 ml (1¾ fl oz) sherry vinegar, then pile onto a serving plate. Drizzle with 100 ml (3½ fl oz) maple syrup and grate over the 80 g (2¾ oz) gruyère over before serving. Serves 4–6.

Pair with

Serve with rabbit, quail, chicken, pork or steak.

Use as a base for roasted parsnips.

Parsnip chips GF V VG

Peel 3 large parsnips, then slice into fine rounds using a mandoline or sharp knife. Heat 2 cm (¾ in) of frying oil in a large frying pan over a high heat. Once hot enough to sizzle, add a handful of the parsnip discs and cook briefly until light brown. Drain on paper towel, seasoning with salt while hot. They will crisp up as they cool, but don't pile them up or they will go soggy. Repeat until all the parsnip is cooked.

Pair with

Serve as a side instead of potatoes with roast chicken, beef or steak.

Add to a freekeh or other grain salad (pp. 378–80) on a bed of yoghurt with a burnt honey dressing (see p. 673) with a handful of mint.

Confit parsnip salad (GF) (V)

Parsnips cooked in olive oil take on a buttery flavour, rich and simply delicious. Peel 2 large parsnips, then cut in half lengthways and remove the core. Leave like this, or cut into large chunks. Add to a saucepan with a couple of garlic cloves and half a dozen thyme sprigs, season with salt and pepper and just cover with olive oil. Bring to a slow simmer over a low heat, then cook for 10 minutes until tender. Lift from the oil while still warm, but not hot, and toss in a little lemon juice with some soft peppery leaves, tarragon or parsley, and a few shavings of parmesan. Top with Parsnip chips (opposite), if you like. This salad pairs well with a grilled steak or roast chicken. You can also simply serve the warm parsnip with roast beef and some horseradish cream on the side.

Raw parsnip salad (GF) (V) (VG)

When at their peak, you can eat parsnips raw. Peel away the skin, then use a vegetable peeler to remove the flesh in long shavings until you reach the core. Work around the parsnip to remove all the flesh. Dress the shavings lightly with extra-virgin olive oil and a splash of wine vinegar, season with salt and pepper and toss with rocket leaves or baby red kale and some picked flat-leaf (Italian) parsley. Enjoy as is, or toss through some shaved parmesan, chopped hazelnuts and a pinch of ground cumin. Eat as a salad, or pile onto grilled Sourdough bread (p. 847) rubbed with garlic and smothered with ricotta.

Preheat the oven to 180°C (350°F) fan-forced.

Add the vegetables, garlic, thyme and spices to a roasting tin. Drizzle with the oil, season with salt and pepper and toss to combine. Pour in the water, cover with foil and roast for 15 minutes.

Remove the foil and roast for about 20 minutes, until tender and golden. Serve warm.

Winter minestrone with roasted root vegetables

Minestrone is a seasonal thing. And I don't mean that it's something one only huddles over in winter, inhaling the steam scented with vegetables, stock and herbs … though it is, and it is good! What I mean is that minestrone can be tuned to the seasons, celebrating produce from spring as much as winter. This version fits in the more classic camp, full of hearty vegetables, beans and pasta. Yes, it's one to huddle over. For another layer of flavour, crumble some roasted chestnuts into the soup just before serving. Textural, buttery and rich, they really fill the dish out further for an even more robust meal – making for even more concerted huddling. **Serves 6–8**

125 g (4½ oz) small dried haricot (navy) beans, or cannellini beans, soaked overnight
3 carrots, peeled and cut into rough 3 cm (1¼ in) dice
3 parsnips, peeled and cut into rough 3 cm (1¼ in) dice
3 white sweet potatoes, peeled and cut into rough 3 cm (1¼ in) dice
2 teaspoons fennel seeds
2 large brown onions, finely diced

6 garlic cloves, sliced
4 celery stalks, diced
1 fennel bulb, diced
3 cm (1¼ in) thick piece of pancetta, diced
1 fresh bay leaf
3 thyme sprigs
3½ tablespoons tomato paste (concentrated purée)
10 cm (4 in) piece of parmesan rind (optional)
1.5 litres (51 fl oz/6 cups) Golden chicken stock (p. 54)

1 litre (34 fl oz/4 cups) water
200 g (7 oz) green beans, cut into 4 cm (1½ in) lengths
½ bunch of rainbow chard or silverbeet (Swiss chard), cut into 2 cm (¾ in) widths, including most of the stem
80 g (2¾ oz) short pasta
finely grated Grana Padano, to serve

Staples
EVOO, S&P

Preheat the oven to 180°C (350°F) fan-forced. Line a baking tray with baking paper.

Cook the soaked beans in simmering salted water for 20 minutes, until just tender but not fully cooked. Drain and set aside.

Meanwhile, tip the carrot, parsnip and sweet potato onto the baking tray. Scatter with the fennel seeds, drizzle the oil over, season with salt and pepper and toss to coat. Roast for 30 minutes.

Heat a splash of oil in a large heavy-based saucepan over a medium heat. Add the onion, garlic, celery, fennel and pancetta and sweat for 15 minutes. Add the bay leaf, thyme and tomato paste and cook, stirring, for 2 minutes. Stir in the cooked beans and parmesan rind, if using.

Pour in the stock and water and bring to a simmer. Add the green beans and chard and cook for 15 minutes, adding the pasta for the last 8 minutes of cooking. Keep an eye on the liquid level; it should be a thick soup, but you may have to stir in a little more water.

Adjust the seasoning; you can remove the parmesan rind if you like, but it will keep imparting flavour if you're not serving all the soup at once. Serve hot, with a drizzle of oil and some grated Grana Padano.

Peas

As kids, we were never made to whistle while we shelled peas – it's supposed to stop you eating them, or at least alert the cook that you are. Perhaps we should have been, as the yield was typically meagre when I was on the job. I've always loved peas like that. Fresh, sweet and crunchy. I still find them irresistible.

There are many different types of garden peas – for the gardener, that is. It's highly unlikely that you'll see them sold as anything other than just humble peas. Cooking enhances their sweetness and makes the nutrients a bit easier to absorb, but a just-picked pea is a marvellous thing raw. Like corn, peas will quickly start converting sugars to starch once harvested, which is what they eventually do on the plant before drying out and releasing their seeds. Picking them flicks that switch early, which means peas should be eaten as quickly as possible to get the most pleasure out of them. Left too long they will become floury and, well, starchy. The same can be said of overly mature peas, which are on their way to being more useful dried fully, then used as split peas for soup, dal and the like. (The other source of split peas is the closely related field pea, which is treated as a grain and only used once dried.)

A just-picked peak-season pea needs next to no cooking. Blanching for 30 seconds will do the trick, or just pour boiling water over and sit for 30 seconds before draining and refreshing in cold water. Either method will take the rawness off, without really cooking the peas, which is unnecessary when they're in their prime. Toss with some good oil, salt flakes and plenty of pepper and use them in other dishes, or throw in a handful of chopped herbs (mint, dill, chervil, parsley) and pile onto a bruschetta smothered with ricotta, goat's cheese, soft feta or bocconcini. Or tear open a large burrata on a plate and pile the peas on top, drizzle a little more oil over and serve as a starter or antipasto. They can also be combined with double-podded broad beans for any of those applications, or cook them a bit further and mash together with mint, garlic and oil, then smear on grilled Sourdough bread (p. 847) with some prosciutto draped over the top, or on fried Pitta bread (p. 854) with a drizzle of tahini.

Peas love fresh herbs and work beautifully with fish, squid and shellfish, but they can go into almost anything, and knit happily into countless cuisines as a stunning last-minute addition to so many dishes, be it a hearty stew, sauce, ragù, curry, soup or pasta. They're great in fritters, and are mandatory in fried rice (see p. 610). They're also handy to boost a side dish of greens, such as broccoli and green beans, or to fill out some wilted baby spinach (you always end up with less than you think!). Then there is the Italian classic Risi e bisi (p. 613), where you use the pods to flavour a stock for a soupy risotto. Of late, I have taken to making an omelette filled with goat's cheese, warmed peas and a handful of chopped parsley or basil; I tend to be quite heavy-handed with the peas, so they burst out the side in an ooze of cheese.

A fresh pea is just heavenly, but what their frozen counterpart may lack in springtime romance, they more than make up with their versatility. There is no vegetable that freezes as well as a pea, and they take mere seconds to prepare. They don't need cooking (they're actually cooked before they're frozen), just warming through, so they can go straight in the pot or just be refreshed under a hot tap. My girls don't even bother with that. They've been eating them frozen by the spoonful since they were little.

Sugar-snap peas and snow peas (mangetout) are from the same family as peas – although with these two varieties, it is the squeaky, waxy pods that are eaten whole (including the small immature peas within), as these pods don't have the tough, indigestible fibres found in garden peas. They are both delicious as a just-cooked vegetable, and are marvellous in or stir-fries.

Also see

Lamb, pea & mint pancake fritters 319

Pea & ham soup 334

Quick rice & peas 375

Cheesy buttered broad beans & peas 430

Broad bean & pea salad with nasturtium leaves, goat's cheese & bagna cauda 431

Broad bean & pea paste 432–3

White cabbage & pea slaw 448–9

Stir-fried cucumber with wood ear fungus & snow peas 510

Seared ocean trout with grilled lettuce, peas & pea tendrils 561–2

Zucchini, ham & pea slice with feta 672–3

Pair with

Peas are ideal with all their green springtime companions, as well as potatoes, leek, avocado, tomato and cucumber. They pair with pretty much any soft herb, such as parsley, mint, chives, chervil, coriander (cilantro), basil and watercress, as well as harder herbs such as thyme and sage. Butter, cream and most cheeses are natural pairings, and they are particularly good with goat's cheese, from soft curds to firmer, more mature specimens. They are also a fine match for smoky cured meats, such as pancetta, ham, chorizo and bacon, as well as hot-smoked fish, and squid and shellfish. And they are synonymous with lamb, for very good reasons, too.

The shoots from all types of peas are edible, too, with a gentle pea flavour and a grassy springtime freshness. The fine shoots can be picked and used in salads, while the larger stems can be stir-fried, if they're not too mature; when they get larger, they become fibrous and quite tough, which cooking further won't resolve. You can also buy pea and snow pea (mangetout) shoots as sprouts, which are deliciously fresh microgreens for salads and the like.

It's worth stating again that garden peas need to be super fresh to maximise their flavour and texture, given their rapid conversion of sugar to starch once picked. And while it's not often possible to know exactly when they were harvested, it's important to only pick pods that are vibrantly fresh. Waxy, crunchy and vivid pods make for a good pea experience. Also, avoid overly large pods, or ones that have pronounced pea bulges, as these are likely to be too mature, lacking in flavour and somewhat floury. Snow peas and sugar-snap peas should be similarly vibrant, with dull pods best avoided.

Preparing peas

Fresh garden peas simply need to be removed from their pods by rending open the pods with your thumbnails, then the peas can be easily flicked into a bowl – some hide at the ends, so be thorough. With sugar-snaps and snow peas (mangetout), simply trim the stalk, then use whole or sliced. In general, cooking of any type of pea should be minimal, to preserve their fresh texture and flavour. A quick dip in a big saucepan of boiling salted water for 30 seconds or so will have them ready to be added to salads and other dishes at the last minute. If super-fresh and petite, err on the side of less cooking (although older ones may require a little more cooking). To retain their colour and stop the peas overcooking, plunge in iced or cold water, then drain once cold.

Fried rice with peas, prawns & egg

Fried rice is a great way to use up left-over rice and any other small morsels. This is a good base recipe, but don't be shy about adding to it. For example, that small piece of roast pork you're not sure what to do with is a prime candidate. Just please make this with cold cooked rice. If it's warm, it ends up being too wet and a bit mushy. You want the rice to dry out and firm up a bit, so if you're making rice specifically for this dish, refrigerate it until properly cold. The best approach, though, is to just buy a few extra prawns (shrimp) for that Asian feast and cook too much rice. You'll be thankful the next day. **Serves 4**

20 g (¾ oz/½ cup) dried shrimp
2 tablespoons soy sauce
1 teaspoon caster (superfine) sugar
½ teaspoon ground white pepper
2 tablespoons grapeseed oil
6 raw prawns (shrimp), peeled and deveined, then cut into chunks

350 g (12½ oz/about 2 cups) cold cooked long-grain rice
90 g (3 oz/½ heaped cup) fresh or frozen peas, blanched or thawed under hot water
2 eggs, whisked

Chilli paste

4 red Asian shallots, or ½ onion, roughly chopped
3 garlic cloves, roughly chopped
2 long red chillies, roughly chopped
4 cm (1½ in) piece of fresh ginger, peeled and roughly chopped
2 tablespoons grapeseed oil

Cover the dried shrimp with boiling water and stand for 5 minutes, then drain. Blitz to a rough paste in a blender, or using a mortar and pestle. Set aside.

Blitz or pound the chilli paste ingredients into a coarse paste.

In a small bowl, combine the soy sauce, sugar and pepper.

Heat a large frying pan or wok over a high heat until very hot. Add the oil, then the chilli paste. Fry until fragrant, about 2 minutes. Add the shrimp paste and fry until it turns a deep pinkish brown, about 1 minute. Add the sliced prawns and fry until opaque, 1–2 minutes.

Now add the rice, peas and soy sauce mixture and stir-fry to combine. Once the rice separates and everything is warm and combined, clear the middle of the wok and tip the whisked eggs in. Fry until the egg starts to set, then use your spatula to chop it up. Once set, mix the rice back through and serve.

Make it different

There are few rules here, so add in whatever you please. Chopped left-over pork belly or diced ham would be great, left-over Asian greens, chopped and added towards the end … whatever you have on hand, really, and whatever makes sense to you. A big handful of coriander (cilantro) or Thai basil would be lovely stirred through at the finish; add a glug of oyster sauce or a dollop of XO sauce (p. 98), if you like.

Buttery minted peas GF V

Tip a few handfuls of fresh or frozen peas into a saucepan and add about 1 cm (½ in) water. Drop in a large knob of butter, ½ teaspoon sugar and a few pinches of salt, and bring to a fast simmer. Cook for 2 minutes, then stir a handful of mint leaves through. The butter and water should start to thicken and gloss over the peas. Adjust the seasoning to taste and serve as a side dish to fish, lamb or roast chicken. To make it different, add the sliced heart of a cos (romaine) lettuce to the finished peas. You could also spoon the cooked peas over grilled cos (romaine) lettuce (see p. 562), then crisscross with anchovies and grate over Parmigiano Reggiano.

Crab, pea & potato samosas

Making your own samosas, pastry and all, is hardly something you'd squeeze in for a midweek dinner after work. It's something that requires a little effort – so I think that effort deserves the luxury of some silky crabmeat included in the classic potato and pea-dominated filling. Even without the crab, these are so rewarding to make, and well worth the effort. **Makes 12**

Pair with

These are delicious with the Raita (p. 98) but they are even better with a dollop of spiced tamarind chutney (see below).

Sweet & sour tamarind sauce (GF) (V) (VG)

To a small saucepan, add 4 tablespoons tamarind paste, 260 ml (9 fl oz) water, 200 g (7 oz) palm sugar (jaggery), 2 teaspoons salt flakes, ½ teaspoon cayenne pepper, 1 teaspoon ground cumin and 1½ teaspoons ground ginger. Simmer for 5 minutes, then strain and chill. Serve with Crab, pea & potato samosas (right), along with a couple of tablespoons of cooked peas.

Pea & mozzarella salad (GF) (V)

Preheat a barbecue on high, or a chargrill pan for 5 minutes over a high heat, until very hot. Very finely slice ½ white salad onion, then season with salt, pepper and sugar and set aside to soften. Combine 2 tablespoons plain yoghurt and 2 tablespoons extra-virgin olive oil in a bowl, season, then tear 3 large balls mozzarella or fior di latte and mix through. Tip into a flat serving bowl. Toss 180 g (6½ oz/1½ cups) fresh baby peas, 250 g (9 oz) cherry tomatoes (larger ones halved), 20 torn basil leaves, 2 tarragon sprigs, leaves stripped, ¼ bunch of snipped chives and the softened onion with 1 tablespoon white-wine vinegar and 1 tablespoon extra-virgin olive oil. Season, then tip over the mozzarella. Serve with lemon wedges and dijon mustard on the side. side. Great served with scotch fillet steaks or roast chicken. Serves 4.

1 teaspoon white mustard seeds
80 g (2¾ oz/½ cup) frozen peas, thawed under hot water
2 long green chillies, finely chopped
3 teaspoons Garam masala (p. 15)
½ teaspoon ground turmeric
2 large potatoes (any variety), boiled, peeled and roughly diced

150 g (5½ oz) cooked crabmeat
½ bunch of coriander (cilantro), leaves roughly chopped, stems finely chopped
4 cm (1½ in) piece of fresh ginger, peeled and finely grated
2 teaspoons amchur (mango powder; see p. 6)
oil, for deep-frying (see p. 22)
1 × quantity Raita (p. 98), to serve

Sweet & sour tamarind sauce (left), to serve

Samosa dough
300 g (10½ oz/2 cups) plain (all-purpose) flour, plus extra for dusting
2 tablespoons fine semolina
1 teaspoon salt
2½ tablespoons extra-virgin olive oil
140 ml (4½ fl oz) warm water

Staples
EVOO, S&P

For the dough, combine the flour, semolina and salt in a bowl. Add the oil and mix through with your hands, to a crumb texture. Make a well in the centre, then add the water and work until all the ingredients are incorporated and the bowl is clean of flour.

Tip the dough onto a lightly floured surface and knead for a few minutes, until smooth and silky, dusting lightly with flour if it's too sticky. Wrap in plastic wrap and rest on the bench for 20 minutes.

For the filling, heat a good glug of oil in a large frying pan over a medium heat. Add the mustard seeds and peas and cook for 2 minutes. Add the chilli, garam masala and turmeric, and cook until fragrant, about 1 minute.

Remove the pan from the heat and add the potato, crab, coriander, ginger and amchur. Season with salt and pepper and combine.

Heat about 10 cm (4 in) of oil in a deep-fryer or large saucepan to 170°C (340°F). Preheat the oven to 100°C (210°F) fan-forced.

Divide the rested dough into six even balls. Roll out one ball on a floured bench, into a circle about 2 mm (⅛ in) thick. Cut in half and rub a little water along the straight edge of one of the halves. Form into a cone by sealing one half of the straight edge with the other half. Support the open end of the cone over your thumb and index finger (the pastry is quite delicate) – much like you might hold a piping bag to fill it. Spoon in some filling, leaving about 2 cm (¾ in) free at the top, then wet the open edges and stretch to seal shut; this end becomes the bottom of the samosa.

Fry the samosas as you make them, turning to cook evenly, until golden brown, about 5 minutes. Keep them warm in the oven while you cook all the samosas. Serve warm, with the raita and the tamarind sauce.

Make it different

Pea & potato samosas. (GF) The crabmeat is a complete indulgence. If omitting the crab, increase the peas to 115 g (4 oz/¾ cup).

Seared squid & pea salad with tomato & chilli (GF)

This salad is based around a starter that was very popular early in my career, and I still love the combination of flavours today. I've reworked this since, adding peppery nasturtium and the textural component of puffed wild rice, though the salad is also delicious without them. **Serves 4–6**

400 g (14 oz) cleaned squid, with tentacles

200 g (7 oz/1⅓ cups) frozen baby peas

250 g (9 oz) small cherry tomatoes, quartered or sliced into rounds

5 garlic cloves, sliced

3 red bird's eye chillies, finely sliced

2 tablespoons coriander seeds, ground

10 basil leaves, torn

3 teaspoons sherry vinegar

Staples
EVOO, LMN, S&P

Divide the squid tentacles into sets of two at the base, then cut the tentacles into manageable lengths. Cut the hoods open and slice into 3 mm (⅛ in) wide strips, or angle your knife and slice into thin ribbons on a 45-degree angle.

Pour boiling water over the peas to thaw and refresh, then drain. Mash the peas with the back of a spoon or potato masher; you're after an uneven texture, with chunky pea pieces in a mash. Season with salt and pepper.

To a large frying pan over a high heat, add a splash of oil and the cherry tomatoes. Season with salt and pepper and cook for 3 minutes to sear. Add a little more oil, then the garlic and chill. Cook without stirring until the garlic is lightly coloured. Add the ground coriander and toss through for 30 seconds or so. Oil the squid and add to the pan, cooking briefly until it changes colour.

Spoon the remaining mashed peas onto a serving plate and top with the squid mix. Squeeze over some lemon.

Frugal pea supper (V)

The hours of a chef are long, and as an apprentice you are poorly remunerated. Tired and hungry, my go-to late-night meal was rice cooked by the absorption method (about 11 minutes), with frozen peas rained in, sometimes with a big knob of butter, then left to warm through for a few minutes. I'd dollop on some Greek-style yoghurt and drizzle with chilli sauce, or instead add 1 tablespoon of light soy sauce, and that was that. And although this supper was born out of frugality, I am still fond of it. When pressed for time, I'll serve it to my girls as well, minus the chilli sauce.

Risi e bisi ⒼⒻ

This is a classic Venetian dish, made only when peas are at their tender best. The pods are traditionally simmered in water to create a pea stock, though many classic Italian writers reference chicken stock, which is what I use. It sits somewhere between a risotto and a soup, with the rice just submerged in a silky, starchy broth. I have deviated a bit here by using sugar-snap peas, which have such a beautifully sweet and pure flavour. **Serves 4**

1.5 litres (51 fl oz/6 cups) White or Golden chicken stock (p. 54), or Vegetable stock (p. 51), or water
1 teaspoon sugar
1 teaspoon salt
900 g (2 lb) sugar-snap peas, trimmed and podded, pods reserved
2 cm (¾ in) thick slice of flat pancetta, or guanciale
1 small onion, finely diced

1 teaspoon fennel seeds
1 fresh bay leaf
225 g (8 oz/1 cup) risotto rice (use vialone nano or carnaroli for the creamiest result)
200 g (7 oz) fresh peas, podded
50 g (1¾ oz) Grana Padano, finely grated, plus extra to serve
30 g (1 oz) butter

1 handful of mint leaves, finely chopped

Staples
EVOO, S&P

Heat the stock, sugar and salt in a large saucepan. When boiling, add the pods of the sugar-snap peas and cook for 6 minutes. Turn the heat off and lift the pods from the stock using a slotted spoon.

Working in batches, blitz the pods in a blender with some of the stock to loosen, then pass through a medium-mesh strainer back into the stock.

Add a good glug of oil to a large saucepan over a medium heat. Add the pancetta and cook to render out some of the fat and take on some colour, about 5 minutes. Add the onion, fennel seeds and bay leaf and cook until softened and fragrant, about 5 minutes.

Stir the rice through until coated and hot to touch, about 2 minutes. Pour in about one-third of the stock and cook, stirring, for 5 minutes. Pour in the remaining stock and cook for 12 minutes, or until the rice is cooked but still has a slight bite.

Add the podded sugar-snaps and the other peas. Season with salt and pepper and cook for 2 minutes. Turn the heat off and remove the pancetta. Stir the parmesan and butter through until creamy.

Adjust the seasoning as needed, then serve with the mint sprinkled on top, and some extra parmesan on the side.

Lebanese peas with lamb ⓖⓕ

This dish is decidedly peas with lamb, not the other way around, and goes a long way with a relatively small amount of meat. The peas add a lovely lingering sweetness, which works perfectly with the chilli and spices, and balances the richness of the lamb. This is one of those dishes that improves as it stands, so leftovers are even more of a treat. **Serves 4**

Pair with

Delicious with a big dollop of plain yoghurt, or mashed or boiled potatoes, or buttered short pasta.

- 100 ml (3½ fl oz) extra-virgin olive oil
- 400 g (14 oz) minced (ground) lamb
- 1 large onion, finely diced
- 2 garlic cloves, chopped
- 2 teaspoons ground allspice

- 1 teaspoon ground black pepper
- 1 teaspoon chilli flakes
- 2 teaspoons dried mint
- 3 large ripe tomatoes, diced
- 2 heaped tablespoons tomato paste (concentrated purée)

- 750 g (1 lb 11 oz) frozen peas
- 700 ml (23½ fl oz) water
- ¼ bunch of mint, leaves chopped, to serve

Staples
LMN, S&P

Heat the oil in a large saucepan over a medium heat. Add the lamb and cook until browned, about 8 minutes. Push the lamb to the side of the pan and add the onion and garlic. Fry until softened, about 5 minutes.

Stir in the allspice, pepper, chilli and dried mint, season with salt and pepper and cook for 3 minutes. Add the diced tomatoes and cook until softened, about 5 minutes.

Stir in the tomato paste, peas and water, then bring to a simmer and cook for about 20 minutes. Season to taste.

To serve, scatter with the fresh mint and squeeze some lemon juice over.

Make it different

Layer this with cooked potato and some haloumi, then finish with a layer of cheesy Béchamel (p. 70) and bake in a 180°C (350°F) fan-forced oven for about 25–30 minutes, until golden.

Omit all of the spices (but not the mint) and instead use 1½ tablespoons Baharat (p. 6).

Pea salad with a golden garlic, sichuan pepper & ginger dressing ⓥⓥⓖ

It's a joy to make a salad of tender young green vegetables, highlighting the sweet seasonal harvest with little or no cooking. This salad features all three common pea varieties, pitching their verdant freshness against a spike of chilli, with nutty garlic, briny soy and the spicy citrus of sichuan pepper supporting. **Serves 4–6**

Pair with

This is a perfect accompaniment to richer dishes served with rice, or serve it with simply steamed fish, chicken or silken tofu.

- 150 g (5½ oz) snow peas (mangetout)
- 150 g (5½ oz) sugar-snap peas, split lengthways
- 150 g (5½ oz/1 cup) fresh peas
- 2 handfuls of snow pea (mangetout) sprouts
- 2 handfuls of micro coriander (cilantro), or mint, shiso or chives

- 1½ tablespoons toasted sesame seeds

Golden garlic, sichuan pepper & ginger dressing
- 5 garlic cloves, finely sliced
- 100 ml (3½ fl oz) extra-virgin olive oil
- 4 long red chillies, sliced on an angle

- 2 teaspoons sichuan peppercorns, lightly toasted, then ground
- 1 teaspoon sesame oil
- 2½ tablespoons soy sauce
- 2½ tablespoons black vinegar
- 5 cm (2 in) piece of fresh ginger, peeled and finely grated

For the dressing, add the garlic and olive oil to a small saucepan and slowly bring to a gentle simmer over the lowest heat. Once the garlic is lightly golden, stir the chilli through, then lift the garlic and chilli from the oil with a slotted spoon, drain on paper towel and set aside. Add the sichuan pepper and sesame oil to the warm oil, then cool for 2 minutes before stirring in the soy sauce, vinegar and ginger.

Blanch the snow peas and sugar-snaps in boiling salted water for 30 seconds. Add the peas, cook for 10 seconds, then drain all the greens. Immediately refresh in cold or iced water, then drain again.

Pile the greens onto a serving plate and top with the snow pea sprouts. Sprinkle with the crisp garlic and chilli and spoon the dressing over. Scatter with the coriander and sesame seeds to finish.

Potato & sweet potato

Potatoes originated in South America, and they have been domesticated and farmed across the Americas for thousands of years. Potatoes, along with corn, became critical exports after the Spanish occupation, with both – although slowly taken up – becoming staples in Europe, North Africa and further east, which fuelled population growth and fed the masses. However, there's a cautionary tale with both. And they're lessons that resonate today.

Maize is a nutrient-dense food, but only if prepared properly, with many of those nutrients not bioavailable. The Mesoamerican process of nixtamalization unlocks that potential by boiling the grain in an alkaline solution (employing wood ash, mineral lime or limestone rocks). It took epidemics of pellagra (niacin deficiency) on different continents to recognise the value of this ancient method.

In the instance of potatoes – which are also an excellent nutrient source – a narrow range of varieties were cultivated, making the crop susceptible to large-scale failure if disease struck, which it most famously did to fuel Ireland's Great Famine of the nineteenth century. While South America had thousands of potato cultivars, all performing differently, this dependence on a couple was the root of devastating tragedy.

The lessons? Ancient methods, developed over many hundreds or thousands of years are not to be ignored because we believe that as an 'developed' society we know better. We have evolved with foods that have seen humanity flourish, and while we don't need to be slaves to the past, we ignore it at our own peril.

Secondly, biodiversity is key. A richly diverse world of plants, animal and insect species that have evolved to thrive is a wonderous thing. Our efforts to reduce this diversity can have devastating effects. On a personal level, having one or two varieties of potatoes – rather than say 100 (that's a lot, you say, but it's about 2 per cent of known cultivars) – is a miserable palette for a cook to work with. And it's not long ago that this was mostly the case.

I recall standing around an old fan-forced oven in the tiny restaurant kitchen, waiting for a couple of arthritic finger-like potatoes to cook. We could barely wait for them to cool down to try what was then a very strange tuber. I can't tell you how good they tasted: crispy, firm and waxy in texture with a lovely distinct and fresh flavour, scented with olive oil. They went straight on the menu. I know this might sound a little odd now, but it was a truly memorable moment, savouring the flavour of that unfamiliar potato – the kipfler (fingerling).

That was in 1989, or thereabouts, when I was an apprentice. It's not that long ago, but it says a lot about how far we have come. The range of produce back then was narrow across the board. Supermarkets had the supply chain by the neck, and uniformity and durability were their demands, not flavour, not character. Back then, potatoes came as brushed and washed, and that was about it.

In Melbourne, it's fair to say that the tide was turned largely by Dobson's potatoes, who started growing a range of 'exotic' potatoes in the 1980s. That started with some patrones as a trial, but the yellow flesh was roundly rejected by wholesale markets. That saw Geoff Dobson go direct to retail and restaurants, where people like me stood around staring at an oven like they were watching the moon landing.

Also see

Classic potato
gnocchi 137–8

Twice-cooked potato
cakes 187

Brined roast chicken
with magic smashed
potatoes 245

Moussaka 310–1

Left-over lamb roast
shepherd's pie 319

Roasted celeriac, parsnip,
potato & fennel with ras el
hanout 485

Corn chowder with potato
& dill 502

Crab, pea & potato
samosas 611

Roasted parsnip &
purple sweet potato with
cinnamon, nutmeg &
garlic 606–7

Greens, potato & cheese pie
with olive oil pastry 828

Potato bread 844

Pair with

Potatoes love dairy – butter, cream, sour cream, crème fraîche, yoghurt and all manner of cheeses – and cured pork, such as bacon, pancetta, chorizo and ham hock. Pair with leaves such as watercress, radicchio, chicory (witlof/endive) and curly endive (frisée), as well as herbs – chives, basil, parsley, chervil, tarragon, marjoram, oregano, rosemary, sage, thyme, bay leaves. Partner with fennel, capsicum (bell pepper), tomatoes, beetroot (beet), mushrooms, peas, broccoli, celeriac, garlic, onion, spring onion (scallion), olives, lentils and barley. Scent with curry spices, turmeric, saffron and garlic, and spike with vinegar, mustard or chilli. Pair with beef, rabbit, lamb, chicken, prawns (shrimp), squid, fish and smoked fish, such as salmon, trout and eel, as well as fish roe.

Today, there are many other growers that have joined the ranks alongside Dobson's, and a decent array of potatoes is readily available – though a lot less than the 5,000 purported cultivars – with farmers' markets inevitably turning up the greatest bounty. Even supermarkets offer more choice these days, though the range is still quite limited and uninspiring. Supermarkets often sell potatoes by generic brand name, rather than variety, with similar types used at varying times of the year to achieve year-round consistency. How effective this is I don't know, as I avoid them.

The boom in potato varieties has come with a little confusion, with varieties more suited to certain applications than others. But the overarching rule is easy enough to understand.

Potatoes range from starchy to waxy, with quite a few in the middle that can be used for pretty much anything. A very starchy/floury potato won't hold together when boiled, but they go wonderfully fluffy when roasted or fried as chips, and they make excellent mash. A waxy/starchy potato retains its shape well, so they are good for salads or to use in a soup or braise or the like, but they also make silky smooth mash. There are also boiling (waxy) potatoes that make great chips, just different to the classic fish and chip shop chip. The key is to avoid disasters, like making a potato salad out of a very floury potato.

The coliban is a potato that I have little time for. It is *the* standard Australian potato, at the floury end of the spectrum. A disaster boiled, it technically bakes and mashes well, but it doesn't ever have much flavour no matter how hard you try. I just avoid them. Pink-skinned desiree potatoes, on the other hand, are readily available and an excellent allrounder, being somewhere in the middle of the waxy to floury scale. They hold their shape well but also make superb silky mash. They are also excellent for Gnocchi (see p. 136), as are Dutch cream, nicola and royal blue – three of my absolute favourites, which have creamy yellow flesh and wonderfully rich flavour and are readily available in Australia.

I use Dutch cream and nicola (also a Dutch variety) for almost anything, except if I'm after a classic fluffy deep-fried chip – which is not something I make at home often – but they do make marvellous potato cakes (see p. 187) – I serve potato cakes with fish, but they are also stunning with Taramasalata (p. 182) spread over the top with sour cream and caviar or salmon roe. Another Dutch variety, the bintje potato is similarly yellow-fleshed and creamy and can also be used broadly.

Sebago and pontiac, and the less commonly found Otway red and wilwash, are also good allrounders (excepting pontiac for frying), while rarer still is the Andean sunrise, a yellow-fleshed potato from Peru, with a lineage that stretches back thousands of years – it is creamy, full flavoured and versatile. These varieties all make terrific mash, along with spunta, which also holds well in a salad. Allrounders and boiling (waxy) potatoes work well with the Italian approach of frying diced potatoes in plenty of olive oil until golden, tossing almost constantly to cook evenly. Some chopped rosemary at the end adds a wonderful perfume. The Spanish do this in a similar way, but in slices and often with capsicum (bell pepper), too, which can be served as a side or made into a tortilla (see p. 623).

Kennebec, russet Burbank, spunta and sebago are perfect for making chips or cooking in duck fat, crisping up while maintaining a fluffy interior. But I also adore waxy kipflers fried. King Edward is an old variety at the floury end, which makes excellent mash or roast potatoes. Maris piper and Yukon gold are also both fine roasting potatoes.

Kipflers are excellent in salads, holding their shape and having a buttery texture, as are the similarly shaped and textured pink fir apple. I adore small ones of either variety boiled, then peeled quickly and tossed in butter and chopped parsley and chives. Patrone are also at the waxy end and an ideal salad potato, retaining a pleasingly firm texture when cooked. Tasmanian pink eye potatoes are another potato that I favour for salads, but they mash very well, too. Any of these, boiled, then roughly mashed with a fork, seasoned with salt and pepper and dosed with good olive oil makes for a deliciously quick side.

Purple potatoes can be a rich purple to almost black, with the Toolangi delight having white flesh, while the blue moon (also called royal blue) is yellow fleshed; both are good allrounders. Toolangi delight is often presented as an ideal gnocchi potato, but this has not been my experience. This may be due to not using egg in my recipe, but nevertheless, I'll stick with desiree, nicola or Dutch cream.

Purple congo is a vibrant purple all the way through, as is the almost black-skinned midnight pearl. Both retain this colour once cooked. Midnight pearl is densely fleshed and floury, while purple congo is waxier and on the drier side. Purple-fleshed potatoes are especially nutrient dense, with the purple hue due to lots of anthocyanins, which are antioxidants, while they are also high in vitamin C.

There are naturally many more varieties, but those selling specialist potatoes will invariably be armed with their best applications, so a few questions should raise the veil. The other common terms used are new potatoes and chats. The former just refers to potatoes dug earlier in the season, with the skins thin and the flesh sweet, while chats are simply small potatoes – either can be of any variety.

I must confess, sweet potatoes are not really my thing. I do appreciate purple sweet potato, as the roasted flesh has a great waxy and fluffy texture, which is not as wet as the normal sweet potato. The flavour is delicate, reminding me of roasted chestnuts. Orange-fleshed sweet potatoes, of various types, are the most commonly sold in markets near me, and I find the sweetness overwhelming at times. When balanced in a dish, that sweetness can be moderated. Or, pricked with a fork and roasted in the flesh, the decadence of that flesh can be lovely with lots of butter or oil and plenty of salt and pepper when served against something spicy or fatty, such as roast pork or smoked meats. Sweet potatoes are also excellent for tempura, and, in this case, I favour the purple varieties.

Select firm potatoes that are free of soft spots, dark blemishes or cuts from harvesting. It's also advisable to handle them with a little care, as they can bruise. Potatoes should be stored in the dark, so a sturdy paper bag is ideal. Cooler temperatures are also best, as this will hinder the tubers sprouting, but refrigeration is not recommended. When stored too cold for an extended period, starches can convert to sugars, which also sees the production of acrylamide, which is thought to be a carcinogen.

If potatoes sprout, the sprouts can be knocked off with the flesh unaffected. However, green potatoes are best avoided. The green hue that you sometimes see is from extended light exposure, with chlorophyll being produced. But it's the presence of glycoalkaloids that can cause problems. Those compounds are toxic and, while generally not a lethal threat, they can cause some digestive discomfort. In the interests of not being wasteful, the parts that are not green are unaffected, so they can be trimmed with a paring knife to remove the offending areas.

Preparing potatoes

Potatoes should be scrubbed or just washed, and can be peeled or not before cooking, depending on their use. Peeled potatoes may take up a little more water, so are not always ideal for mash or gnocchi, but any excess liquid can be steamed off in a dry pan if needed. I certainly don't always want to wait for whole potatoes to cook, plus you can control the size if you peel and cut into chunks first, meaning they will cook more evenly. If peeling after cooking, then cradle the potatoes in a tea towel (dish towel) and scrape off the skin with a paring knife. I do like the skin of a potato, as it has an earthier flavour, but there are times when it just doesn't suit a dish. I was certainly brought up thinking that most of a potato's goodness was held in the skin, but that is not so. The skin does hold a lot of the fibre and iron and some vitamins, but the flesh still has plenty of nutritional value. When boiling, I always start potatoes in well-salted cold water. The reason, which Harold McGee can scientifically explain much better than I, is to do with an enzyme that is released between 50–70°C. That enzyme helps the potato to retain its shape, meaning that they are less likely to break down when fully cooked, effectively firming up the outside while the water comes up to temperature. It is also said to cook them more evenly; if you are cooking from boiling, the interior has a chance of being undercooked when the outside is tender. And there are few things that I like less than an undercooked potato.

Crisp sweet potato chips with paprika mayo ⓥ

The crispy coating on these really delivers a crunch, contrasting wonderfully with the tender flesh inside. You can eat these without the mayo, but it does work particularly well. **Serves 4**

4 sweet potatoes, scrubbed and cut into 2 cm (¾ in) thick chips
oil, for deep-frying (see p. 22)
2 egg whites
1 tablespoon water
150 g (5½ oz/1 cup) tapioca flour

100 g (3½ oz/⅔ cup) plain (all-purpose) flour
50 g (1¾ oz) cornflour (cornstarch)
1 tablespoon Celery salt made using white pepper (p. 9), plus extra to serve

1 × quantity Mayonnaise (p. 74) seasoned with smoked paprika, to serve

Staples
EVOO, S&P

Pair with
Salads.
Grills.
Serve in place of potato chips.

Preheat the oven to 180°C (350°F) fan-forced. Line a baking tray with baking paper.

Tip the potato chips onto the baking tray and drizzle generously with oil. Season with salt and toss to coat, then spread out evenly, leaving space between each. Roast for 15 minutes, then set aside to cool on the tray.

Heat about 8 cm (3¼ in) of frying oil in a deep heavy-based frying pan or deep-fryer until 180°C (350°F).

In a bowl, whisk the egg whites with the water.

In another bowl, whisk the flours, cornflour and celery salt to combine.

Coat the cooled chips in the flour mix, dusting off any excess, then dredge through the egg-white mixture and lower into the oil. Fry for about 2 minutes, until crisp.

Drain on paper towel, seasoning with a little more of the celery salt. Serve immediately, with the spicy aïoli.

Make it different
With sauces. Instead of the paprika mayo, serve the wedges with Spicy aïoli (p. 76), or mix sweet chilli sauce or Fermented cooked chilli sauce (p. 97) through the mayo to taste.

Potato skordalia GF V

Pair with

Steak or braised beef.

Grilled or seared fish, scallops, prawns (shrimp) or crayfish.

Steamed asparagus or artichokes, or grilled vegetables such as fennel or carrots, with a smashed herb and olive oil dressing and a garnish of crisp fried onions or toasted and crushed nuts.

The key to skordalia is garlic – with skórdo being the Greek word for garlic. This is a silky-smooth version, with potato taking the lead, though soaked left-over bread or nuts are also often used in skordalia. This version dials down the garlic a bit, making it a more versatile purée, with the olive oil enriching and taking it away from being a classic mashed potato. This makes a great bed for crumbed meat, seafood or vegetables. **Serves 4–6**

450 g (1 lb) boiling (waxy) all-purpose potatoes (such as desiree)	125 ml (4 fl oz/½ cup) extra-virgin olive oil	**Staples** S&P
2 garlic cloves, peeled	125 ml (4 fl oz/½ cup) cold milk	

Peel the potatoes and cut each one into six even pieces. Cook with the whole garlic cloves in boiling salted water for about 20 minutes until the potatoes and garlic are very tender.

Drain well, then, while still hot, blitz in a food processor while adding the oil (through the feeder tube), then the milk. Season with salt to taste, then transfer to a bowl.

Keep warm until needed, but use within 3 hours of making.

Make it vegan VG
Oat milk is a good substitute for cow's milk.

Potato blinis V

Pair with

Top with diced smoked eel, and a little crème fraîche with chives mixed through.

Top with Gravlax (pp. 169, 171).

Top with smoked salmon and crème fraîche along with salmon roe, or grated hard-boiled egg and snipped chives.

This recipe is from the early mists of my professional time in the kitchen, possibly from Tansy's, but it's hard to say exactly. It's a fragment, thankfully not entirely lost to time. Back then we used to serve these as little snacks or canapés with smoked eel, crème fraîche with chives and a fine sprig of ferny chervil – and to me that doesn't sound dated at all. **Makes about 25**

250 g (9 oz) peeled desiree potatoes, cut into 4 cm (1½ in) dice	1 egg 2 egg whites 2 tablespoons thickened (whipping) cream	100 g (3½ oz) Clarified butter (p. 360)
2 tablespoons full-cream (whole) milk	¼ bunch of chives, finely chopped (optional)	**Staples** S&P
2 tablespoons plain (all-purpose) flour		

Cook the diced potato in boiling salted water until tender, about 12 minutes, then drain well. Pass through a ricer or food mill into a bowl.

Beat the milk into the hot potato with a spoon until well incorporated and smooth. Stand for about 3 minutes. Sift the flour over and stir in well, then incorporate the egg, following with the unbeaten whites. Use a whisk to combine until smooth, then stir in the cream and chives, if using.

Heat the clarified butter in a large frying pan over a medium heat. Add a tablespoon of batter for each blini, which will spread out to about 6 cm (2½ in). Cook for 1–2 minutes, until the tops start to bubble and blister, then flip and cook for about 1 minute on the other side until golden.

Dress with your chosen toppings and serve, or keep warm in a low oven while you cook all the batter, then serve warm. You can always make the batter earlier, but these are best served freshly cooked.

Tuna & sweet potato sesame patties with pickled arame salad

Ginger and sweet potato really sing with tuna, with their inherent sweetness working well with tuna's intense flavour. I like to accent these patties with a sharp little salad of arame, cucumber and radish. The key here is to roast the sweet potatoes for a long time, as the mixture will be too wet otherwise. **Serves 4**

2 large golden sweet
  potatoes
300 g (10½ oz) tinned tuna,
  drained well
2 eggs, lightly beaten
2 spring onions (scallions),
  white part only, finely sliced
5 cm (2 in) piece of fresh
  ginger, peeled and finely
  grated
300 g (10½ oz/3¾ cups) fresh
  breadcrumbs, made from
  stale bread
1½ tablespoons sesame
  seeds, lightly toasted

oil, for shallow-frying
a handful of coriander
  (cilantro) leaves

Pickled arame salad
10 g (¼ oz) arame,
  rehydrated in warm water
  for 5–10 minutes, then
  drained
3 Lebanese (short)
  cucumbers, finely sliced
  into rounds
8 radishes, finely sliced

Pickling medium
200 ml (7 fl oz) brown-rice
  vinegar
50 g (1¾ oz) caster
  (superfine) sugar
2 teaspoons salt flakes
½ teaspoon mustard seeds
1 star anise

Staples
LMN, S&P

Preheat the oven to 180°C (350°F) fan-forced.

Add the pickling medium ingredients to a small saucepan and simmer over a medium heat for 2–3 minutes, stirring to dissolve the sugar and salt. Put the arame in a bowl, pour the pickling medium over and cool to room temperature.

Prick the sweet potatoes all over with a fork, then roast on a baking tray for about 50 minutes, until tender.

Split the sweet potatoes lengthways and scoop the flesh into a large bowl. Roughly mash, then add the tuna, egg, spring onion and ginger, half the breadcrumbs and half the sesame seeds. Season with salt and pepper and combine.

Combine the remaining sesame seeds and breadcrumbs in a shallow bowl.

Divide the sweet potato mixture into eight portions (or any size you like), then roll into balls and flatten a little. Coat the patties in the crumb mixture on both sides, pressing in to coat well all over.

Heat about 3 cm (1¼ in) of oil in a large frying pan over a medium heat. Once hot, cook the patties in two batches for about 3 minutes on each side, being careful when you flip them. Drain briefly on paper towel, then serve or keep warm in a low oven while you cook the second batch.

To serve, add the cucumber and radish to the pickling mixture, tossing through to coat. Drain off the pickling liquid and serve the salad piled on top of the patties. Scatter some coriander over the top and serve with a squeeze of lemon.

Pair with

Eat these hot or cold, with any leftovers ideal for the lunchbox.

Stack a few up for a light dinner with the salad and a flavoured Mayonnaise (pp. 74–5) of your choice.

Creamed mustard kipfler potatoes GF V

In a bowl, toss together 1 sliced white salad onion, 1 teaspoon salt, 1 teaspoon caster (superfine) sugar, then set aside to soften. Meanwhile, peel, slice and boil 8 large kipfler (fingerling) or yellow-fleshed creamy potatoes in salted water for 15–20 minutes, until quite tender (just before they fall apart), then drain. Transfer the warm potato to a bowl. Add the onion, 200 ml (7 fl oz) pouring (single/light) cream, 2½ tablespoons dijon mustard and 2 tablespoons wholegrain mustard. Season with salt and pepper, then gently toss through and serve. Serves 4.

Tortilla de patata GF V

This recipe comes courtesy of my friend Emma Warren, who is one of my go-to references for the traditional dishes of Spain. Rather than the oven, the Spanish use the stovetop a lot more than the rest of Europe, and this requires a little care in the technique to make sure it doesn't catch, which is where a properly seasoned cast-iron pan comes in handy – although a non-stick one will work just as well. Avoid cutting the potatoes and storing them in water, as you'll lose the creaminess from the starch; instead, you could pre-cook them and then reheat when you're ready to make the tortilla. Choose a quality potato on the waxy side, such as Dutch cream or desiree, which will hold its shape and have that buttery, rich taste. Slow and low is the go to let everything really marry. **Serves 8–10**

250 ml (8½ fl oz/1 cup) extra-virgin olive oil
1 kg (2 lb 3 oz) boiling (waxy) potatoes (such as desiree or Dutch cream), peeled, cut in half and sliced 2 mm (⅛ in) thick

1 large onion, finely sliced and cut across twice
6 eggs
Staples
S&P

Heat the oil in a 24 cm (9½ in) non-stick or well-seasoned heavy-based frying pan over a medium heat. Add the potato and mix through to coat. Add the onion, stir through to coat, then reduce the heat to low.

Cook until the potatoes are soft but not browning or breaking apart, and the onion is translucent, 8–10 minutes. Carefully turn the mixture at regular intervals with a flat spatula for even cooking.

Tip into a colander over a bowl to catch the oil.

In a large bowl, beat the eggs with a pinch of salt, then add the potato mixture. Stand for 10–15 minutes to allow the potato to absorb some of the egg.

Add 2½ tablespoons of the reserved oil back to the frying pan over a medium heat. Add the egg mixture and cook until the edges start to firm up, about 1 minute.

Reduce the heat to low, then stir for 1 minute to move the heat through the mixture and break up the cooked egg from the base. Once stirred evenly, flatten out the mixture. As it cooks, loosen the edges with a spatula, to allow some airflow and stop it sticking. Cook for 6–8 minutes, until the edges are well-sealed and golden. The top will still be a bit runny.

Invert a dinner plate over the top, then place your hand on top and flip the whole thing over so the tortilla is on the plate. Add a splash more of the reserved oil to the pan and slide the tortilla back in, tucking in the edges with a spatula. Cook for 6–8 minutes, then shake the pan to make sure it is not stuck.

Flip again onto a dinner plate, then set aside for 15–20 minutes to finish cooking in the residual heat.

If you prefer your eggs really well done, or aren't up for the flipping component, once the mixture is flattened out in the pan, bake it in a preheated 170°C (340°F) fan-forced oven for 30–40 minutes.

Serve sliced, with a sprinkling of salt flakes. This tortilla is delicious at room temperature or still warm, but for best results eat on the day and don't refrigerate.

Pair with

This makes a lovely pre-dinner or late afternoon snack with some fat green olives and a glass of dry sherry – or include it in a feast of tapas.

Chermoula (p. 90).

Potato rösti with ocean trout

Peel 1 kg (2 lb 3 oz) chipping potatoes (such as kennebec) and add to a saucepan of cold salted water and bring to the boil. Turn down the heat and simmer for 5 minutes. Drain, then set aside until just cool enough to handle. Coarsely grate the potatoes onto a tray and divide into four even portions. Add 1 tablespoon of plain/all-purpose flour and 1 tablespoon of extra-virgin olive oil to one of the portions (you will need a total of 50 g/1¾ oz/⅓ cup flour and 80 ml/2½ fl oz/⅓ cup oil), then season with salt and pepper. Depending on your waffle maker, make one or two at a time, but only flour each portion just before cooking. Combine gently by mixing with open fingers, then shape into a loosely formed patty. Add to the waffle maker and cook until golden, about 4 minutes; you can keep the cooked waffles warm in a low oven if necessary. (If you don't have a waffle maker, make two rösti from each pile and shallow-fry in batches for 2½ minutes on each side until golden, then drain.) Top each waffle with some Sour sherry onions (p. 599), Raw quick pickled beetroot (p. 419), a dollop of Horseradish cream dressing (p. 70), chunks of hot-smoked rainbow trout (you'll need 250 g/9 oz) and chopped chives (you'll need 3 tablespoons). Drizzle with a little oil and serve with lemon wedges on the side. Serves 4.

Pommes anna GF V

Although so simple in terms of its ingredients, this classic French preparation yields a devastatingly impressive result. A potato cake, in a way, it is sliced or cut into wedges to reveal all the layers, with a beautifully burnished and crisp exterior. You can slice the potatoes using a sharp knife and a steady hand, but it's easy and quick with a mandoline, and the result will be consistent. **Serves 4–6**

1.2 kg (2 lb 10 oz) potatoes (I use Dutch cream, desiree, king edward or nicola), peeled and finely sliced

220 g (8 oz) Clarified butter (p. 360), warmed to liquify

Staples
S&WP

Special equipment
Mandoline

Preheat the oven to 150°C (300°F) fan-forced. Line a 20 × 35 cm (8 × 13¾ in) or a 30 cm (12 in) round cake tin or ceramic baking dish with baking paper.

Add the potato slices to a large bowl, pour the butter over and toss to coat. Make layers of potato either in a circle, lines or as a spiral, filling in the middle to make it even, and seasoning with salt and white pepper as you go. Continue until all the potato is used, gently pressing flat as you go, then drizzle any residual butter over.

Cover with baking paper, then foil. Bake for 2 hours, then uncover and cook for 45 minutes to colour and crisp the outside.

Stand for 5 minutes to settle, before unmoulding and cutting into wedges or slices.

To reheat, warm the cut slices in a pan on the stove or in a moderate oven, serving the crisp side down to show off the layered effect.

Make it different
With oregano. Sprinkle a little dried Greek oregano (rigani) between every second layer.

With another vegetable. Add another vegetable cut in the same way, such as parsnip or celeriac, or even sweet potato or Jerusalem artichoke, and alternate with the potato and oregano, finishing with a squeeze of lemon once cooked.

Vinaigrette potatoes with cornichons, dill, caperberries, crème fraîche & fried egg GF

This is a personal favourite, a dish I would happily have for breakfast or brunch; it works equally well for lunch, or even supper if that's something you do. It's also a wonderful way to use up left-over corned beef, bacon or ham off the bone at Christmas, with those salty and vinegary/pickled tones, a bright burst of herbs and chilli heat, and the eggs and potatoes such ideal companions. **Serves 4**

10 new potatoes
2 tablespoons white-wine vinegar
2 tablespoons extra-virgin olive oil
4 eggs
2 handfuls of flat-leaf (Italian) parsley leaves, torn

1 handful of dill fronds, torn
10 tiny cornichons, cut in half lengthways
2 spring onions (scallions), white part only, finely sliced
2 long green chillies, finely sliced

12 thin slices of cooked Corned beef (p. 289)
8 caperberries, cut in half lengthways
4 tablespoons crème fraîche

Staples
EVOO, S&P

Pair with
This is so good with roast beef or steak, roast chicken (see p. 229), pan-seared scallops, or even a delicate fish dish.

Genovese salad V

Add 400 g (14 oz) potato cut into 2 cm (¾ in) chunks to a large saucepan (you will cook the pasta in this, too) of cold salted water. Cover and bring to the boil, then cook until tender, about 15 minutes. Add 500 g (1 lb 2 oz) dried linguine or pennette and cook for 6 minutes. Add 200 g (7 oz) green beans cut into 4 cm (1½ in) lengths and cook for 3 minutes, then add 50 g (1¾ oz) fresh or frozen peas (this is not traditional, but I like the addition) and cook for another minute before draining, reserving 125 ml (4 fl oz/½ cup) of the cooking water. Tip the pasta mix into a large bowl. Combine the pasta water and 350 g (12½ oz) Pesto (p. 90) in a bowl to make a loose sauce, then add to the pasta and toss before serving with plenty of parmesan. This is just as good at room temperature as it is hot, but only use short pasta if serving as a salad. You may need to adjust the cooking time of the pasta depending on the type you are using (refer to the packet).

Sweet potato fritters (GF) (V)

Coarsely grate 1 large sweet potato, add 2 teaspoons salt, let sit for 10 minutes, then squeeze out the excess water. In a bowl, combine the potato with 150 g (5½ oz/1 cup) cornflour (cornstartch), 1 grated onion, a whisked egg, 1 microplaned garlic clove, 1½ teaspoons ground cumin, 1½ teaspoons salt flakes, 1 teaspoon chilli flakes and ½ teaspoon turmeric. Divide into four patties and heat a little extra-virgin olive oil in a frying pan. Cook for 3 minutes each side, then drain of excess oil and serve with avocado salsa, fried egg, sour cream and salmon, or Corn & pineapple salsa (p. 499) and bacon.

Pair with

Roasted or grilled meats.

Roast chicken (p. 229) or duck (pp. 258, 264).

Classic potato mash (GF) (V)

Boil 1 kg (2 lb 3 oz) peeled yellow-fleshed potatoes (such as Dutch cream or nicola), or all-purpose potatoes (such as desiree) in salted water for 20 minutes. Drain well in a colander, then pass through a food mill or ricer into a large bowl. Meanwhile, warm 100 ml (3½ fl oz) each of pouring (single/light) cream and full-cream (whole) milk, then beat into the hot potato along with 200 g (7 oz) diced cold unsalted butter until smooth and fluffy. (The hotter the potato the better, as it is easier for the potato to absorb the milk, cream and butter – this results in a fluffy mash). Season with salt and black pepper.

Mustard mash (GF) (V)

Follow the Classic potato mash recipe (above) and, when adding the butter, add 2 teaspoons each of English mustard and dijon mustard.

Cook the potatoes in boiling salted water until tender, then drain well. Slice in half and add to a large bowl with the vinegar and oil. Season with salt and pepper and toss through gently. Set aside for 5–10 minutes to absorb the vinaigrette.

Heat a splash of oil in a frying pan over a medium heat. Add the eggs, season with salt and pepper and fry until the whites are just set.

Meanwhile, add the parsley, dill, cornichons, spring onion and chilli to the potato and toss gently to combine.

Divide the salad among serving plates, then tuck in the corned beef. Top with the eggs and caperberries, dollop on the crème fraîche and serve immediately.

Make it different

With other meat or seafood. Instead of corned beef, this dish is equally delicious with hot-smoked trout, pastrami, crispy bacon, gravlax (pp. 169, 171) or smoked eel.

Make it vegetarian (V)

Simply omit the corned beef.

Taleggio mash (V)

Here is an indulgent way with mash – a richly cheesy, pungently scented and silkily textured affair, perfect as a side to impress at a dinner party. For even more indulgence, grate a few slivers of fresh truffle over the mash at the table. If making the mash ahead and refrigerating it, give it a good 20–30 minutes in a hot oven to properly heat through and colour, depending on the size of your serving dish or dishes. **Serves 4–6**

1 kg (2 lb 3 oz) yellow-fleshed potatoes (such as Dutch cream or nicola), or all-purpose potatoes (such as desiree), peeled	50 ml (1¾ fl oz) pouring (single/light) cream 20 g (¾ oz) unsalted butter 180 g (6½ oz) taleggio, diced	50 g (1¾ oz) fresh breadcrumbs 50 g (1¾ oz/½ cup) grated parmesan

Preheat the oven to 200°C (400°F) fan-forced.

Boil the potatoes in salted water until very soft. Drain well in a colander, then pass through a food mill or ricer into a large bowl.

Meanwhile, warm the cream and butter in a small saucepan to melt and combine.

Fold 150 g (5½ oz) of the taleggio through the hot potato, then whisk in the cream and butter, whisking hard to achieve a smooth consistency.

Transfer to individual dishes or a large baking dish. Top with the remaining taleggio, poked just below the surface, then top with the breadcrumbs and parmesan.

Bake for 10 minutes to crust the top.

Roasted potatoes with thyme Ⓥ ⓋⒼ

A properly roasted potato is a beautiful thing, especially if cooked perfumed with thyme (or any sturdy herb) right at the end of cooking. Even though harder herbs can be roasted, if left too long they will burn. Adding them at the end to release their flavours in the residual heat ensures a sublimely fresh flavour but also softens them so they meld into the cooked potatoes beautifully. **Serves 4**

1.2 kg (2 lb 10 oz) Dutch cream potatoes, peeled and quartered, or kipfler (fingerling) potatoes, peeled
100 g (3½ oz) duck fat, or extra-virgin olive oil

1½ tablespoons plain (all-purpose) flour or fine semolina
6 thyme sprigs, leaves stripped; rosemary or

oregano would also work well
Staples
S&P

Preheat the oven to 200°C (400°F) fan-forced. Heat a heavy deep-sided baking tray in the oven.

Add the potatoes to a saucepan of salted cold water. Bring to the boil over a medium heat, then reduce the heat and simmer for 10 minutes.

Drain the potatoes and place in a large bowl. Add a generous tablespoon of the duck fat or oil and toss to coat. Add the flour and toss through.

Remove the preheated tray from the oven and add 2 tablespoons of the duck fat. When the fat has melted, add the potatoes and gently toss to coat, seasoning with plenty of salt.

Quickly return the tray to the oven. Bake for 20 minutes, then remove from the oven and turn the potatoes with tongs. They should be starting to develop a golden crust. If the tray seems dry, add the remaining duck fat.

Return to the oven and bake for about 20 minutes, until golden.

Once cooked, sprinkle the potato with the thyme, then rest in the tray for 5 minutes, moving occasionally to allow them to absorb the aroma of the herb. Transfer to a platter and serve.

Greek-style lemon & oregano potatoes Ⓥ ⓋⒼ

I first had potatoes like these while backpacking in 1991, from the canteen on a ferry in Greece, somewhere between islands. Not only did they help with sea sickness, they were stunningly, memorably delicious. **Serves 4–6**

7 large waxy yellow-fleshed potatoes (such as Dutch cream or nicola), peeled and cut into wedges

150 ml (5 fl oz) extra-virgin olive oil
150 ml (5 fl oz) water
juice of 2 lemons
3 garlic cloves, finely grated

1½ tablespoons dried Greek oregano (rigani)
1 tablespoon fine semolina
Staples
S&P

Preheat the oven to 200°C (400°F) fan-forced.

Spread the potato wedges out in a large roasting tin, leaving a little space between each.

Combine the oil, water, lemon juice, garlic and half the oregano in a bowl, then pour the mixture over the potatoes. Season well with salt and pepper.

Bake for about 40 minutes, until a golden crust has formed. Remove the tray from the oven and toss the potatoes, then sprinkle with the remaining oregano and the semolina.

Roast for 30–40 minutes, stirring occasionally to colour evenly, until deeply golden.

Pair with

Roast beef, lamb or poultry.

Whole baked fish, or pan-fried snapper (see p. 158).

Hasselback potatoes with paprika & bay leaves ⒼⒻ

Preheat the oven to 180°C (350°F) fan-forced. Using a sharp knife, make incisions down the whole length of 8 boiling (waxy) potatoes (such as desiree), about 2 mm (⅛ in) apart and two-thirds of the way through. Slide a piece of bay leaf into an incision in each potato (you'll need 4 large leaves split in half lengthways). Add ½ finely sliced brown onion to a baking dish and season with salt. Arrange the potatoes on top, cut side up, and season with salt and pepper. Sprinkle 2 tablespoons sweet paprika over, then pour in 250 ml (8½ fl oz/1 cup) heated Golden chicken stock (p. 54) and distribute 30 g (1 oz) butter in knobs over the potatoes. Cover with foil and bake for 50 minutes, then uncover and bake for about another 20 minutes to brown. Serves 4.

Pair with

Braised lamb (see p. 316), Slow-roasted lamb shoulder (p. 305), or lamb on the spit.

Grilled fish.

Chargrilled octopus (p. 218) with Greek salad.

Dauphinoise potatoes GF V

Pair with

Braised beef or roasted poultry or meat.

Dauphinoise with camembert GF V

Dauphinoise is a delight as is, but is truly indulgently magnificent finished with camembert – and if you're into Baroque levels of excess, finished with a flurry of shaved truffle … that's up to you, and your resources, of course. Once the foil has been removed, slice a ripe wheel of Camembert crossways and arrange over the potatoes, cut side up. Bake uncovered for 15–20 minutes, until the cheese is bubbling and with a crust forming, turning on the oven grill (broiler) if necessary. It is perfect with a beef rib roast or grilled rib-eye steaks, and some blanched or wilted seasonal greens.

This is arguably *the* essential gratin. While many gratins feature cheese to create a golden crust, this version achieves a cheesy result by cooking down and concentrating the cream and butter. It's a magnificent thing, rich and intense, but charmingly earthy, too – a wonderful wintery side. **Serves 4–6**

500 ml (17 fl oz/2 cups) pouring (single/light) cream
100 g (3½ oz) unsalted butter
1 large garlic clove, finely sliced

6 thyme sprigs
1.5 kg (3 lb 5 oz) Dutch cream or nicola potatoes, peeled

Staples
S&P

Special equipment
Mandoline

Preheat the oven to 180°C (350°F) fan-forced.

Add the cream, butter, garlic and thyme sprigs to a medium saucepan. Warm through over a medium heat to melt the butter, then season with salt and pepper.

Meanwhile, slice the potatoes about 2 mm (⅛ in) thick using the mandoline (or slice by hand, but they need to be evenly cut). Add to a large bowl. Tip the cream mixture over and gently toss through to coat.

Ladle a little of the liquid into a ceramic baking dish or heavy copper pan, about 26 cm (10 in) in diameter and 8–10 cm (3¼–4 in) deep. Spread a layer of potatoes in the bottom, overlapping a little; season lightly. Build up layers, seasoning lightly and spooning the cream over, gently flattening a little as you go. Finish by pouring the residual cream over.

Cover with baking paper, then foil. Bake for 40 minutes, then uncover and bake for another 15 minutes, until golden.

Stand for 5 minutes before serving.

Pumpkin

All pumpkins are winter squash – but not all winter squash are pumpkins. Well, that depends on where you come from. In fact, squash are not really named according to seasons; rather, some varieties are harvested earlier and some later, with summer squash eaten as juvenile fruits, and winter ones taken to full maturity (although usually picked in autumn). Mature summer squash are largely unpleasant and sometimes bitter, while winter squash generally improve in flavour and sweetness. Winter squash will have thicker (and sometimes quite hard) skin, and large seeds that are not digestible unless dried.

In Australia, winter squash are generally all called pumpkins – mind you, we don't have the huge array of squash that are available in the Americas, where they are native. Botanically, pumpkins aren't classified separately but rather by custom, hence the nomenclature disparity between countries.

The main pumpkins in my local markets are kent, jarrahdale, Queensland blue, butternut and golden nugget (minikin squash), with the musquee de provence variety cropping up more frequently at farmers' markets. There is, of course, a huge range of heirloom and hybrid pumpkins and squash, with many being cultivated in small quantities by specialised growers.

The butternut pumpkin (or butternut squash – with its pumpkin credentials questioned by some) is very versatile and easy to handle, with thin edible skin that is easily peeled, or can be left on, as it is not particularly tough. The flesh is sweet and quite firm and retains its shape when cooked, while also making a compelling soup or purée. Kent (a variety of Japanese kabocha squash) is my go-to pumpkin, with excellent flavour and sweet flesh that is rarely stringy. It will hold some texture, but purées well also, and is far more visually appealing on a plate than, say, a butternut. Jarrahdale is an heirloom Australian crossbreed that can grow quite large. It has grey skin and bright orange flesh that is reasonably sweet; it's a good all-rounder. The Queensland blue is another heirloom variety, and one of the most widely grown pumpkins in Australia. It is also cultivated around the world, with seeds first exported to the US back in the 1930s. It has a reasonably dry texture, so holds its shape well, with deeply coloured sweet flesh. Another heirloom variety, golden nuggets are compact, as the name suggests, typically fitting amply into the palm of your hand. They have sweet, finely textured flesh and are ideal for roasting whole or stuffing and roasting. The musquee de provence has a richly golden, dense and full-flavoured flesh with superb flavour. They are a very attractive pumpkin, too – they look good on the bench, that's for sure – with exaggerated bulging segments, like a caricature of a pumpkin.

Spaghetti squash, of which there are many cultivars, are also a type of winter squash, which are characterised by flesh that separates into spaghetti-like strands when cooked. They can be eaten as a side, or some people, though not me, use them as a pasta substitute. To cook them, cut them in half lengthways, remove the seeds, rub the flesh with oil, then season and roast in a 180°C (350°F) fan-forced oven for about 45 minutes, until tender.

There are also some quite compact heirloom varieties, as well as a dizzying array of other possibilities, with many seeds gathered from all over the world now available from specialist suppliers. The main pumpkin varieties are more or less interchangeable in terms of use, though you might well develop a preference for one or the other for different applications. When using less-familiar varieties, however, you will find many that are great for some purposes and not so good for others. Some will become very 'wet' when cooked, some will be noticeably stringy, while others will be significantly less sweet than what you might be used to. As always, talk to the seller – who in these cases is often the grower – and they can guide you.

Also see

Tortelloni with pumpkin, sage & mustard fruits, with burnt butter sauce 114

Tunisian green capsicum & pumpkin salad 460

Spiced pumpkin & olive oil loaf cake 742–3

Pumpkin, anchovy & ricotta pizza 857

Pair with

Pair pumpkin with eggs and dairy – yoghurt, butter, sour cream, crème fraîche, parmesan, feta, goat's curd, haloumi and taleggio. Its sweetness takes to an acid spike from lemon juice, vinegar, caperberries, pickled onions and pomegranate molasses or the sharpness of raw onion, its richness being enhanced by roasted garlic, fermented chilli, soy, coconut cream, honey and maple syrup. Warming spices work well – cloves, ginger, cinnamon, chilli, smoked paprika, allspice, cumin, cardamom, nutmeg, pepper – and so many herbs, including coriander (cilantro), sage, rosemary, parsley, thyme, bay leaves, dill, sorrel, chives and tarragon. Pumpkin marries so well with nuts and seeds – walnuts, pine nuts, almonds, hazelnuts, peanuts, cashews, sesame seeds – as well as raisins, currants and sultanas. Pair with pulses, couscous and potatoes, or pork, lamb, chicken, and fried or baked fish.

The less water involved when cooking pumpkin, the better, as the flesh can tend to become mushy or watery. I never boil pumpkin, unless it is cooking in a curry or the like. Steaming is the best wet method for a purée, while roasting is by far my preferred method in general, though grilling on the barbecue can produce spectacular results. The great advantage with roasting is that it dehydrates the flesh, concentrating the flavour and texture. When adding pumpkin to a soup, I will often roast it first, for added flavour and caramelised complexity. You can also roast pumpkin whole (pierce it at the top first, or slice the top, so it doesn't burst in the wrong places) or as halves, but you will get a wetter result, which makes for a wonderfully flavourful purée; it just depends on the texture you're after.

When stored properly, pumpkins keep incredibly well. Whole pumpkins, that is. If you come across a farmers' market with a range of interesting varieties, don't be shy about buying up, as they can keep for many months. Pumpkins should be heavy for their size and blemish-free. Any soft spots will mean a pumpkin should be used as quickly as possible, so break it down, discarding any soft flesh, and use or refrigerate. Check the stem to make sure it is firmly attached, as sometimes moisture pooling in the depression around the stalk can cause it to rot, which will spell doom for your storage plans. Pumpkins will keep best in a well-aired, cool place, although whole pumpkins have occupied my benchtop for many, many weeks without harm – and just happen to be strikingly decorative.

Preparing pumpkin

A pumpkin can be a dangerous thing. Not proactively so, but cutting into a whole pumpkin does require a bit of pressure with a large sharp knife, so any slip can be catastrophic. Take it slowly and don't force things, and you'll be okay. With the pumpkin sitting on its base on a stable chopping board, start by inserting the tip of a large, sharp knife into the flesh just below the stalk; a tap on the pommel of your knife will make this easier. Now gently rock the knife, bringing the handle down to split the flesh. Work down, rocking the knife to cut and split open, then repeat on the other side. Once halved, things should get easier, but the flesh can still grip the blade tightly, and the skin of some varieties is quite tough and can deflect a not-so-sharp blade – so proceed with reasonable caution. Remove the seeds and any stringy membranes. Once halved, you can peel with a knife by slicing the skin off, or cut into wedges or slices and then slice off the skin – which can be easier to manage. I usually leave the skin on if roasting. I quite like the way it presents on the plate, but it can also be easily peeled away once cooked. The skin on many pumpkins is perfectly edible, especially when roasted, though plenty of people seem to find the idea off-putting. As said, the skin peels away easily, so you can leave that up to your diners.

Grilled pumpkin salad with pumpkin oil dressing, pickled grapes & goat's cheese GF V

The depth of flavour in the pumpkin works so well with the tart sweetness of grapes, and grilling the pumpkin adds a smokiness that I think is a welcome addition to the sweet pumpkin flesh. Patience is needed when grilling, though, as there isn't really that much moisture in the flesh – so be watchful and turn as needed, as it does take a while to cook. **Serves 6**

Pair with

This is an intense salad that makes a beautiful vegetarian centrepiece, perhaps with some dolmades and yoghurt.

Pair with a roast chicken, grilled lamb cutlets or Salt-baked fish (p. 175).

½ kent or jap pumpkin, skin on, cut into 3 cm (1¼ in) slices
2 teaspoons ground allspice
3 tablespoons pumpkin seeds (pepitas), lightly toasted
1 garlic clove
3 tablespoons pumpkin oil
1½ tablespoons extra-virgin olive oil

1½ tablespoons red-wine vinegar
2 teaspoons very finely diced preserved lemon
200 g (7 oz) Greek-style yoghurt, or Labneh (p. 362)
80 g (2¾ oz) soft marinated goat's feta, or shanklish
¼ bunch of mint, leaves picked and torn

Pickled grapes
80 ml (2½ fl oz/⅓ cup) red-wine vinegar
1 tablespoon caster (superfine) sugar
1 tablespoon salt flakes
25 red grapes, sliced into rounds (use seedless grapes, or remove the seeds)

Staples
EVOO, S&P

Preheat the barbecue on medium.

Coat the pumpkin with olive oil, season with salt and pepper, dust with the allspice and coat evenly. Grill the pumpkin for about 15–20 minutes on each side, until charred and tender. You may need to flip the slices over several times so they don't burn, so keep checking on them.

Using a mortar and pestle, grind half the pumpkin seeds with the garlic, into a paste. Add the pumpkin oil, olive oil and vinegar. Season with salt and pepper, then combine.

For the pickle, combine the vinegar, sugar and salt in a small bowl, stirring until dissolved. Toss the grapes through, then set aside for 15 minutes.

Stir the preserved lemon through the yoghurt, then spread over a large serving plate. Lay the pumpkin on top, then dot with the feta. Stir the pickled grapes and half the pickling liquid into the pumpkin seed dressing, then spoon over the top. Finish by scattering over the remaining pumpkin seeds and mint.

Lemonia's pumpkin & feta pie with olive oil pastry (V)

This is a deeply golden and beautifully rustic-looking pie, and it always presents well in a spread. The pastry has a firm crunch once cooked, which is a perfect foil for the sweet and lusciously textured pumpkin. It's also a tribute to the beautiful Lemonia, my mother-in-law, who loved it so very much. **Serves 6–8**

1.5 kg (3 lb 5 oz) kent or jap pumpkin, peeled and cut into 2 cm (¾ in) dice
2 leeks, white part only, finely sliced
5 eggs
200 g (7 oz) feta

120 g (4½ oz) Grana Padano, finely grated
1 teaspoon ground cinnamon
4 rasps of whole nutmeg
a handful of walnuts, toasted and roughly broken

1 × quantity Short olive oil pastry (p. 828), or Filo pastry (see p. 564)

Staples
BTR, EVOO, S&P

Preheat the oven to 165°C (330°F) fan-forced. Line a baking tray with baking paper.

Toss the pumpkin in oil, season with salt and pepper and spread out on the baking tray. Roast for 30–40 minutes, until the flesh is well cooked and has dried out, but not coloured much. Set aside to cool.

Meanwhile, melt a knob of butter in a saucepan. Add the leek and cook over a medium heat for about 10 minutes, until softened but not coloured, adjusting the heat as needed. Season and set aside.

In a food processor, purée half the pumpkin, four of the eggs, half the feta, and all the parmesan, cinnamon and nutmeg to a smooth paste, then season as needed.

Turn the oven temperature up to 170°C (340°F) fan-forced. Grease a 30 cm (12 in) pie dish and line the base.

Roll out the pastry into a large even circle, about 5–8 mm (¼–⅓ in) thick, allowing enough overhang so that when it is in the pie dish, the edges can be folded over to form a lid. (It doesn't need to cover all the filling, but it needs to come up the sides with enough to fold over some of the top.) Ease the pastry into the pie dish.

Pour the pumpkin purée onto the pastry, smoothing it out evenly. Press the remaining pumpkin pieces into the purée. Spoon the leek over, crumble the remaining feta over, and scatter with the walnuts. Pull the edges of the pastry in to form a lid, pleating to make a petal-like pattern with a hole in the centre. Beat the remaining egg and brush it over the pastry.

Bake for about 45 minutes, until golden brown. Serve warm or cold.

Pair with

Serve with a bitter leaf salad, braised greens or a grain salad (pp. 378–80) as a complete meal.

Lovely as a side to chicken or lamb dishes.

Roasted pumpkin with cinnamon, chilli, pickled onion, yoghurt & feta (GF)(V)

Slice a kent or jap pumpkin into 6 cm (2½ in) thick wedges and toss with a generous amount of olive oil. Season with salt and pepper and dust with ground cinnamon (or allspice or ginger), then spread on a lined baking tray with the wedges standing up or lying flat. Roast at 180°C (350°F) fan-forced for about 30 minutes, until tender. Cool a little and pile onto a serving plate, spoon on some Greek-style yoghurt or Labneh (p. 362) and scatter some soft herbs over, such as parsley, coriander (cilantro) or mint. Squeeze on some lemon, sprinkle with chopped chilli and sliced pickled onion or vinegar-plumped currants, then crumble over some feta, ricotta or goat's curd. Serve with roasted beef, pork, chicken or lamb.

Pumpkin, rosemary & taleggio risotto `GF`

The pumpkin melts into the rice as you cook this risotto, delivering a richly golden result. A small drizzle of properly expensive balsamic vinegar would be a good move as a flourish at the table. **Serves 6 as a main**

1 kg (2 lb 3 oz) pumpkin (winter squash), peeled and cut into 3 cm (1¼ in) dice
1 tablespoon ground allspice
2 litres (68 fl oz/8 cups) Golden chicken stock (p. 54)

6 rosemary sprigs
1 onion, finely diced
4 garlic cloves, finely sliced
2 fresh bay leaves
500 g (1 lb 2 oz) arborio rice
200 ml (7 fl oz) white wine

60 g (2 oz/¼ cup) unsalted butter, diced
50 g (1¾ oz/½ cup) finely grated Grana Padano
120 g (4½ oz) taleggio, diced

Staples
EVOO, LMN, S&P

Preheat the oven to 160°C (320°F) fan-forced. Line a baking tray with baking paper.

Coat the pumpkin in oil, season with salt and pepper, sprinkle with the allspice and toss to coat. Spread out on the baking tray and roast for 1 hour, until well caramelised.

Meanwhile, add the stock and rosemary to a saucepan and keep just off the simmer.

Heat a good splash of oil in a heavy-based saucepan over a medium heat. Add the onion, garlic and bay leaves, season lightly with salt and pepper. Sweat until softened but not caramelised, about 5 minutes.

Add the rice to the pan. Stir constantly until the grains are hot to the touch, about 2 minutes, then add the wine. Stir until the wine has reduced to almost nothing, then start adding enough hot stock to cover the rice. Stir until almost dry again, then add a couple more ladles of stock and keep stirring.

Continue the process of stirring and ladling in stock, adding the pumpkin after 5 minutes. Cook for 15–20 minutes from the first stock application, until the rice is just cooked, with a slightly nutty centre. It should be fairly wet at this stage; add more stock if needed.

Once just al dente, add the butter, then gradually stir in the parmesan. Squeeze in a little lemon juice, adjust the seasoning as needed, then stand for 2 minutes.

Fold in the taleggio and stand for 1 minute, so the cheese is just starting to melt, but is still visible in chunks. Serve on warm plates.

Make it different

With cured meat. Sprinkle with fried pancetta, bacon or guanciale lardons.

With crispy sage. Spoon over some sage leaves fried in nut-brown butter.

Turkish-style pumpkin & walnut dip `GF` `V` `VG`

This is not necessarily authentic, but it is delicious. Black or regular tahini will work to finish the dish, but black yields a more dramatic presentation. **Serves 4–6**

1 kg (2 lb 3 oz) kent or jap pumpkin, skin on, cut into 6 cm (2½ in) wedges
1 teaspoon ground cinnamon
1 teaspoon ground allspice
100 g (3½ oz/1 cup) walnuts, toasted
2 tablespoons water
2½ tablespoons extra-virgin olive oil

3 tablespoons tahini
3 tablespoons pomegranate molasses
3 teaspoons salt flakes
finely grated zest of ½ lemon
juice of 1 lemon

To finish
1 small white onion, sliced into rings and soaked in cold water

1½ tablespoons black tahini, or regular tahini
50 g (1¾ oz/½ cup) walnuts, toasted and tossed in oil and salt, then roughly broken
1 handful of coriander (cilantro) leaves

Staples
EVOO, LMN, S&P

Quick pumpkin & cashew dip `GF` `V` `VG`

Soak 150 g (5½ oz/1 cup) raw cashews in water overnight, then drain. Preheat the oven to 180°C (350°F) fan-forced. Line a baking tray with baking paper. Peel 500 g (1 lb 2 oz) pumpkin (winter squash), then dice into 3 cm (1¼ in) pieces. Toss the pumpkin with a splash of extra-virgin olive oil, 2 teaspoons ground cumin or cinnamon (or a mix) and 1 teaspoon salt flakes, then spread out on the baking tray. Roast for about 35 minutes, until tender and dehydrated. Add the pumpkin and cashews to a food processor and blitz to a smooth paste. You can adjust the texture by adding some oil or warm water to loosen. If you like, squeeze in some lemon juice to sharpen the flavour; add 100 g (3½ oz) ricotta, feta or goat's curd to make the flavours more complex; or add a little Fermented cooked chilli sauce (p. 97) or chilli powder to give it some kick. You can serve on toast with eggs, as a dip with crackers, flatbread (see p. 852) or with crudités, such as fennel, radish or celery heart on toast with eggs, or you can spoon the dip onto a plate and top with poached eggs, cooked greens, something pickled for sharpness and a sprinkling of your favourite seeds. Makes about 500 g (1 lb 2 oz).

Pair with

Serve with Simit/koulouri (p. 842) or Puffed pitta pockets (p. 854).

Preheat the oven to 180°C (350°F) fan-forced. Line a baking tray with baking paper.

Toss the pumpkin with the cinnamon and allspice, then spread out on the baking tray. Dry roast for about 1 hour, until coloured and tender. Set aside to cool.

Process the walnuts in a blender until quite finely crumbed, then add the water in a thin stream, followed by the oil, to form a paste. Scoop the pumpkin flesh from the skin and add to the blender, along with the tahini, pomegranate molasses, salt, lemon zest and lemon juice. Blend until smooth.

Drain the onion and pat dry. Add to a small bowl and toss with a little oil and pepper.

Spoon the pumpkin dip onto a serving plate. Drizzle with the black tahini, scatter over the onion, walnuts and coriander. Finish with another squeeze of lemon juice.

Pumpkin, chickpea, cashew & coconut curry (GF)(V)(VG)

This is a rich and super-fragrant vegan curry that becomes almost dry once cooked. The zesty tang of the lime leaves and juice beautifully complements the sweetness of the pumpkin, which becomes quite intensely rich when cooked like this. **Serves 4–6**

Pair with

Wilted greens and steamed jasmine rice.

Roast pumpkin slices for pizza, frittata or a simple tart (GF)(V)(VG)

Preheat the oven to 180°C (350°F) fan-forced. Slice pumpkin (winter squash) about 4 mm (¼ in) thick, rub with olive oil, and season with salt and pepper. Roast on a lined baking tray in the oven for about 10 minutes, then cool. Use to top a pizza with mozzarella, fresh oregano and anchovies, then finish with ricotta and a drizzle of good olive oil when cooked. Or, use the slices on a square of quality puff pastry with some strongly flavoured cheese, such as feta or taleggio, then bake in a hot oven for a simple tart. Finish with dressed peppery leaves as a simple starter or light lunch. Or, add the slices to a frittata with goat's cheese and poached leeks (see p. 355).

30 g (1 oz) coriander seeds (4½ tablespoons)
50 g (1¾ oz/⅓ cup) cashews
1 onion, finely diced
5 garlic cloves, sliced
10 cm (4 in) piece of fresh ginger, peeled and sliced
1 lemongrass stem, white part only, finely sliced
20 curry leaves
3 red bird's eye chillies, chopped
1 bunch of coriander (cilantro), leaves picked,

stems and roots washed well and finely sliced
80 ml (2½ fl oz/⅓ cup) melted ghee, coconut oil or olive oil
1½ tablespoons curry powder
2 teaspoons ground cardamom
1 heaped tablespoon salt flakes
800 g (1 lb 12 oz) pumpkin (winter squash), peeled and cut into rough 6 cm (2½ in) chunks

400 g (14 oz) cooked chickpeas (a drained tin, or see p. 371)
850 ml (28½ fl oz) water
400 ml (13½ fl oz) coconut cream
30 g (1 oz) palm sugar (jaggery)
7 makrut lime leaves, 3 very finely shredded, to serve
1 lime, to serve

Toast the coriander in a dry frying pan over a medium heat until toasted and fragrant, about 1½ minutes. Grind lightly using a mortar and pestle.

Toast the cashews in the same pan over a high heat until golden and scorched, about 6 minutes.

Add the onion, garlic, ginger, lemongrass, curry leaves, chilli and coriander stems and roots to a blender with a tablespoon of the ghee or oil and blitz to a rough paste.

Add the remaining ghee to a large saucepan over a medium heat and fry the paste until fragrant, about 4 minutes. Add the ground coriander, curry powder, cardamom and salt, then stir through for 30 seconds. Stir in the pumpkin to coat.

Add the chickpeas, water, coconut cream, palm sugar and whole lime leaves. Bring to a simmer and cook over a low heat for about 45 minutes, stirring in the cashews during the last 10 minutes.

Serve topped with the shredded lime leaves and coriander leaves and a good squeeze of lime.

Make it different
With chicken. You could add chicken thighs to this, with or instead of the chickpeas. Dice 400 g (14 oz) chicken thigh fillets into 3 cm (1¼ in) pieces and add to the pan with the dry spices.

Roast pumpkin soup with Thai flavours

This is far from traditional, but the sweetness of pumpkin works so well with the punchy Thai flavours. This soup freezes well, but freshen it with some lime juice once reheated; you may also need a little salt or a splash of fish sauce. **Serves 10**

2.5 kg (5½ lb) kent or jap pumpkin, cut in half, seeds removed
3 red onions, peeled and cut into quarters
2½ tablespoons coconut oil
4 garlic cloves, finely sliced
3 red bird's eye chillies, finely sliced
3 tablespoons tom yum paste
2 tablespoons fish sauce, plus extra to serve

1½ tablespoons grated palm sugar (jaggery)
1 litre (34 fl oz/4 cups) coconut water
600 ml (20½ fl oz) water
juice of 1 lime
150 ml (5 fl oz) coconut cream
½ bunch of coriander (cilantro), leaves and fine stems picked
1 young coconut, flesh sliced (optional)

Shrimp floss (see p. 523), Toasted glutinous rice powder (see p. 384) or fried shallots (see p. 600), to serve (optional)
Fermented cooked chilli sauce (p. 97), to serve (optional)

Staples
EVOO, S&P

Preheat the oven to 160°C (320°F) fan-forced. Line a baking tray with baking paper.

Coat the pumpkin and onion with olive oil, season with salt and spread out on the baking tray. Roast for about 1 hour, until tender. Once cool enough to handle, scoop out the pumpkin flesh and set aside.

Heat the coconut oil in a wide-based saucepan over a medium heat. Add the roasted onion, garlic and chilli and cook for about 3 minutes. Add the tom yum paste and fry until fragrant, about 1 minute. Stir in the pumpkin flesh, fish sauce, sugar, coconut water and water. Bring to a simmer and cook for 20 minutes.

Add the lime juice and purée with a stick blender. Adjust the seasoning as needed with a little more fish sauce.

Serve with a swirl of coconut cream and some coriander leaves. If you want to dress it up further, finish with some young coconut slices, prawn floss and a dollop of chilli paste.

Make it different
With shellfish. Take this soup to another level by crowning it with a mound of cooked crabmeat or pan-fried prawns (shrimp) before serving.

Make it vegan 🅥🅖
Use vegan tom yum and fish sauces.

Slow-roasted pumpkin with red onion, garlic & crème fraîche 🅖🅕 🅥

Cut a golden nugget (minikin squash) or small kent or jap pumpkin in half. Scoop out the seeds, then rub with olive oil, season with salt and pepper and dust with ground cumin. Fill the cavities with wedges of red or white onion, or peeled shallots, a few thyme sprigs and a couple of smashed garlic cloves. Drizzle the onion with oil and season, then cover with foil and roast on a baking tray for 30 minutes at 160°C (320°F) fan-forced. Remove the foil, turn the heat up to 180°C (350°F) fan-forced and roast for another 30 minutes, until tender and golden. To serve, scatter over a handful or two of currants that have been soaked in warm red-wine vinegar for 10 minutes, then dollop on some crème fraîche, sour cream or goat's curd. Serve with Fermented cooked chilli sauce (p. 97), charred flatbread (see p. 852), a grain salad (pp. 378–80) – black barley is especially good with this – and grilled meat, chicken or fish.

Spiced pumpkin, date, almond & moghrabieh salad ⓥ

Here, the caramel notes of the dates enhance the sweetness of the pumpkin. I find the slippery texture of moghrabieh a real pleasure, but it's the dressing with toasted flaked almonds and chilli that makes this salad really sing. **Serves 4**

Pair with

This works as a standalone salad, but is also excellent served with spiced roast chicken.

800 g (1 lb 12 oz) kent or jap pumpkin, cut into 1.5 cm (½ in) thick slices
3 teaspoons ground cinnamon
3 teaspoons ground cumin
1 lemon, cut in half
80 g (2¾ oz) flaked almonds
150 g (5½ oz) butter
3 long red chillies, sliced on an angle

3 tablespoons extra-virgin olive oil
juice of 1 lemon
1 litre (34 fl oz/4 cups) Classic white vegetable stock (p. 51)
250 g (9 oz) moghrabieh (pearl couscous), washed well

6 medjool dates, pitted and cut lengthways into 6 batons
2 mint or coriander (cilantro) sprigs, leaves picked

Staples
EVOO, S&P

Preheat the oven to 180°C (350°F) fan-forced. Line a baking tray with baking paper.

Coat the pumpkin generously with oil. Rub on half the spices, season with salt and lay out on the baking tray. Roast for about 30 minutes, until tender. Set aside at room temperature.

Meanwhile, oil the cut side of the lemon halves and char in a pan over a high heat until blackened, about 3 minutes. Set aside for serving.

Toast the almonds in a dry frying pan over a high heat, tossing until golden and a little scorched, about 5 minutes. Add the butter, chilli, oil and the remaining spices. Warm through and combine, then add half the lemon juice and take off the heat.

Bring the stock to a simmer in a saucepan. Add the moghrabieh and cook for about 12 minutes, until tender. The liquid will have mostly reduced or been absorbed, but drain off any excess. Cool for 5 minutes or so. Add the remaining lemon juice, the dates and a splash of oil to coat, then toss.

Arrange the pumpkin slices on a serving plate. Top with the moghrabieh mixture. Spoon over the spiced butter and almond mixture, finish with the mint and serve with the charred lemon.

Radish, daikon & turnip

Radishes and turnips are from the same family and share similar attributes. Both consist of an edible taproot, with equally edible green stalks and leaves. Radishes tend to be quite peppery and can be very hot, while turnips have a milder heat. Both can be eaten raw or cooked, though most would associate radishes with salad-like applications and turnips with more hearty foods, which mirrors their growing seasons – mostly.

I love to dip radishes straight into salt flakes, and then straight into the mouth, with the hit of salt evened out by their natural sweet pepperiness. Dipping the radishes into whipped cultured butter after the salt is even better – and with some freshly baked wholemeal bread, is better still. That combination of butter and salt on radishes is a very French one, thought to have originated in produce markets. It has that feel of improvisation to it, a snack on the fly. Radishes were certainly a go-to snack when I was a young cook working in cold larder.

Radish leaves are perfectly edible, though I imagine they're rarely eaten. I'll always keep a few of the smaller leaves on whole, halved or quartered radishes, whatever I'm using them for. The larger leaves can be a bit raspy, with a cat's tongue texture, but cooking will change that, and any of the fine leaves can be used in salads. There are also radish varieties that have a nominal taproot, with the leaves being the prize. They are probably most famously used to make summer kimchi in Korea, called yeolmu kimchi. Regular radish leaves can simply be wilted like spinach for a side or added to a stir-fry, curry or soup.

Radishes come in many guises, but they can be separated into spring/summer radishes and winter radishes. Those grown in the warmer months are the common salad radishes we're all accustomed to. They come in many shapes, colours and sizes, whether classically round and red, the white-tipped cylinders of breakfast radishes, or candy-striped like Chioggia beetroot (beets). They're generally very fast growing, maturing in a few weeks from seed to harvest, unlike winter radishes that take several months to reach maturity.

Black radishes and daikon are the most common winter radishes, though the former are hardly common at all. Black radishes, or Spanish radishes, are very old cultivars, and were largely forgotten when the fast-growing, warm-season radishes became popular throughout Europe in the last few centuries. They are well worth seeking out, however, with their strikingly black exterior and equally starkly white interior. Black radishes are dense, very crisp and can pack a bit of heat. They are lovely in salads, or finely sliced and eaten with butter and rye bread. They can also be added to soups and stews.

Daikon is the most common winter radish and is popular throughout Asia. They are also known as icicle radishes in the West, which goes some way to explaining both their shape and hue. Resembling a large white carrot, daikon has a milder peppery heat to, say, a black radish. Like all radishes, they have a brightly crisp texture, making them perfect for salads when finely sliced, julienned or grated, yet daikon is often cooked, too.

The first time I ever saw whole turnips was as bunches of baby turnips piled high on a bench, as an apprentice at Tansy's. I was handed a metal scourer and directed to a sink full of cold water to clean the delicate skins off (along with plenty of my own skin). I had encountered them before, without realising it: my grandmother Grace pickled them with beetroot (beets) to make pink-hued pickles, or torshi (see p. 639). Back then, baby turnips were quite prominent in classical cooking, often featuring with turned baby carrots and the like, while mature turnips were seen as a somewhat old-fashioned bulking vegetable of peasant food from Eastern Europe and the United Kingdom. Turnips were also commonly grown as feed for livestock, no doubt contributing to their lowly reputation.

Also see

Pickled daikon & mint salad 304

White cabbage & pea slaw 448–9

Wombok, daikon, shiitake & tofu salad 450

Kimchi 455–6

Pair with

Radish and daikon are lovely with lemon and orange, sesame, soy sauce and ginger, olive oil, sugar, honey and maple syrup, fish roe, and smoked goods such as smoked fish, bacon, pancetta, ham and Chinese sausage. They love a dose of dairy such as butter, cream and crème fraîche, herbs such as mint, dill, parsley and shiso, and vegetables such as cucumber, carrot and potato.

I often have radishes in the fridge, whether to eat whole (the salt's always close by) or to add pep and crunch to a curried egg sandwich or the like. And I always include radishes in a crudité selection, keeping a small plume of vibrant leaves on each. Radishes sliced paper-thin with a mandoline are a lovely addition to a simple leaf salad, or scattered over Vitello tonnato (p. 297), Beef carpaccio (p. 280), or over a crudo of tuna, snapper or kingfish – their pepperiness and crisp texture a delightful foil.

Pair turnips with cream, butter and mayonnaise. Spice with cumin, caraway and white and black pepper, and scent with thyme, sage, rosemary and bay. Pair with carrots, potatoes, beetroot (beet) and lemon, as well as walnuts and prunes. Turnips can also match up to intense proteins such as lamb, hare, rabbit, ham, pork, braised beef, pigeon and quail.

Turnips still don't get a lot of attention, and although I don't cook them a lot, I enjoy them when I do – which is often well-cooked and simply dressed with butter and lots of pepper. They can, however, be used like any root vegetable, in soups, stews and the like, or be mashed alone or with celeriac and/or potato for a hearty winter mash for braises or roasted meats. Young turnips can also be eaten raw, much like you would a radish. And those young turnip tops make for a fine vegetable side dish, or can be added to soups, stews and braises.

I must admit, I also rarely cook with swedes (rutabagas), which are related to turnips, but I do have strong memories of them. So named because they are thought to be a Swedish discovery, swedes are not a horticultural creation, but rather a natural cross-pollination between a turnip and cabbage or kale, found in the wild in the seventeenth century. They don't appear to have been exclusive to Sweden, but the name has stuck. They are easy to grow and, like parsnips, their flavour and sweetness is improved after a frost. My nanna used to boil them, then mash with plenty of butter and seasoning to serve with roasted meat in winter. The aroma of a boiling swede can be quite confronting, even more so if the root is overly mature or has been stored for an extended time. It's not an aroma you'll easily forget. Swedes can also be cooked in soups and stews. I sometimes add them to pasties, roasting a mix of vegetables before making the filling (see p. 469).

The rules for selecting radishes, turnips and swedes are the same as for so many vegetables. You're after firm and bright-looking specimens, with vibrant foliage – wilted leaves are not a great sign and, after all, you want to eat them. Turnips and swedes should be heavy in the hand for their size; lighter ones will likely be fibrous and woody. While softening radishes can be halved and crisped up with a bath in cold water, I would never buy them like this. Radishes, turnips and swedes are all brassicas, so they will become pungent if stored for too long, whether revived or not.

Pair with

Quickly pickle sliced radish in white-wine vinegar, salt and sugar, then toss with shredded mint or parsley and serve in a roast pork or beef sandwich, or in a bánh mì with pork or seasoned firm tofu. You could also bind the lightly pickled radish with yoghurt and serve with Cevapcici (p. 529) or Slow-roasted lamb shoulder (p. 304), or wrap in a Pitta bread (see p. 854) with Falafel (p. 432) and salad.

Daikon, cut into chunks, is delicious braised with dashi and finished with butter.

Grated daikon is essential to Tempura dipping sauce (p. 98).

For a super-refreshing salad, toss julienned or shaved daikon with sugar-snap peas or snow peas (mangetout), cherry tomatoes, some rice vinegar, soy sauce, grated ginger, sesame oil and sesame seeds.

Preparing radishes, daikon & turnips

Radishes can go soft in the crisper quite quickly, and will fare better in an airtight container with a bit of moisture from washing keeping the flesh crisp. Use the trimmed leaves promptly, as they will wilt quickly. A soak in cold water will revive a softening radish and further crisp an already crunchy one. Finely sliced radish soaked for 10 minutes or so, then dried, will add extra textural sparkle to salads and the like. The spindly end of the taproot doesn't offer much, so I trim it away – but not all the way back, as a radish looks best with its natural shape intact; I also leave a few fine leaves and stalks on, after giving the stem a good wash to dislodge any dirt. That's if I'm serving them whole or halved – otherwise the stem and leaves are a useful handle if slicing finely on a mandoline. For presentation, I like to leave the (well-washed) stem on baby turnips, like you might with Dutch carrots, and rather than peeling, I usually scrub the delicate skin off with a scourer, which wastes less flesh.

Mature turnips and swedes need to be peeled, with the stalk and any woody part of the taproot removed before cooking.

Pickled radishes (GF) (V) (VG)

Pair with

Serve with smoked or cured meats, terrines (pp. 327–8), smoked fish or rillettes (see p. 174).

Chop and slice and add to an egg and/or potato salad.

These are a must with Tunisian vegetable couscous royale (p. 386).

Pickled turnip torshi (GF) (V) (VG)

Ubiquitous at mealtimes, and even breakfast, torshi are Middle Eastern pickles, with countless variants of spicing and vegetables employed. Peel 1 kg (2 lb 3 oz) turnips and 1 small beetroot (beet), then cut into batons 1.5 cm (½ in) × 6–8 cm (2½–3¼ in) long. Pack the beetroot and turnip tightly into two sterilised 600 ml (20½ fl oz) jars (see p. 40). To a saucepan, add the pickling medium ingredients: 750 ml (25½ fl oz/3 cups) water, 250 ml (8½ fl oz/1 cup) white-wine vinegar, 35 g (1¼ oz/¼ cup) salt flakes, 2 smashed garlic cloves and 1 fresh bay leaf. Bring to the boil and turn off the heat. Set aside to cool completely, then pour into the jars. Seal the jar lids and stand at room temperature for 3 days to pickle, then refrigerate – or refrigerate straight away and leave for twice as long to pickle. Either way, these pickles will keep for about 1 month before they lose their crunch.

This is a fairly traditional vinegar pickle, perfect for whenever you need a good sour, peppery kick to balance out rich and fatty foods, or to snack on straight from the jar. **Makes 1.2 kg (2 lb 10 oz)**

600 g (1 lb 5 oz) radishes, trimmed, roots attached

Pickling medium
250 ml (8½ fl oz/1 cup) water

500 ml (17 fl oz/2 cups) white-wine vinegar, or apple-cider vinegar
150 g (5½ oz/⅔ cup) caster (superfine) sugar

3 teaspoons salt flakes
6 black peppercorns
1 fresh bay leaf

Add the pickling medium ingredients to a saucepan and bring to simmer, then set aside to cool to room temperature.

Pack the radishes into two sterilised 600 ml (20½ fl oz) jars (see p. 40), then pour in the pickling medium, seal with the lids and refrigerate.

The radishes are ready after 24 hours, and will keep for up to 10 days. They will still be perfectly edible, but they will start to soften; I like them crunchy.

Spiced Chinese pickles ⒼⒻ Ⓥ ⓋⒼ

This recipe is based on pickles Kylie Kwong used to make, which I had many years ago in the original cheek-to-jowl Billy Kwong in Crown Street, Sydney. I was obsessed with them, and with much of Kylie's food at the time. Truly wonderful and indelible memories. This is my version of those pickles.

Makes 3 × 1 litre (34 fl oz/4 cup) jars

1 daikon, peeled and sliced 5 mm (¼ in) thick

1 bunch of radishes, trimmed and quartered

½ wombok (Chinese cabbage), shredded 2 cm (¾ in) wide on an angle

4 Lebanese (short) cucumbers, cut lengthways, then sliced 1 cm (½ in) thick

1 celery heart, yellow leaves attached, cut into 1.5 cm (½ in) slices on an angle

1 fennel bulb, finely sliced lengthways

60 g (2 oz) fine sea salt

2.5 litres (85 fl oz/10 cups) white vinegar

800 g (1 lb 12 oz) caster (superfine) sugar

6 garlic cloves, smashed

12 slices of fresh ginger, about 4 mm (¼ in) thick

6 small dried chillies

2 teaspoons sichuan peppercorns

4 star anise

Add the daikon and radish to a bowl or container, the wombok and cucumber to another, and the celery and fennel to a third. Sprinkle the salt over evenly, then toss each mixture to coat. Cover and refrigerate overnight.

In a medium saucepan, bring the vinegar and sugar to the boil. Stir to dissolve the sugar, turn the heat down and simmer for 30 minutes. Refrigerate until chilled.

Drain the vegetables, gently squeezing out any excess liquid with your hands. Add each pair of vegetables to a separate jar, then pour the pickling liquid over to cover.

Divide the garlic, ginger, chillies and peppercorns between all the jars. Divide the star anise between the fennel jar and the cucumber jar.

Refrigerate for 2 days before using. These pickles will keep in the fridge for up to 2 weeks.

Pair with

Dumplings (pp. 231, 342, 500).

Grilled or roasted spiced meats.

Bao with roast pork (see p. 333) or duck (see p. 263).

Serve as a pre-dinner snack.

Quick-pickled turnips with soy & rice vinegar ⒼⒻ Ⓥ

Peel or scrub some baby turnips, then halve or cut into fat wedges. Toss with a few generous pinches of salt and stand in a colander for 30 minutes to drain off any excess liquid. Rinse off the salt and shake off the water. Pack into a sterilised jar (or jars; see p. 40) and cover with even parts brown-rice vinegar and light soy sauce, with a teaspoon or so of sugar per jar. Stand on the bench for a couple of hours before using. Serve with fish or tempura, or slice and add to salads. It will keep refrigerated for 3 days.

Daikon, edamame & avocado salad with sesame, apple & soy dressing ⒼⒻ Ⓥ

This is a refreshingly zingy salad that is crunchy, sweet, sharp and refreshing. The grated apple is the trick to the dressing, with the sweetness and acidity combining perfectly with the sesame and soy. Some tiny red or yellow vine tomatoes would also add a sweet tang. **Serves 4**

1 butter lettuce, core trimmed, leaves separated

2 handfuls of mizuna, or tatsoi

1 small daikon, peeled and finely julienned

60 g (2 oz/⅓ cup) edamame (frozen is fine, just thaw first)

1 avocado, cut into 8 wedges or chunks

3 spring onions (scallions), white and pale green parts, sliced very finely on an angle

Gomashio (p. 16), for sprinkling

Sesame, apple & soy dressing

1 tablespoon finely grated fresh ginger

3 tablespoons brown-rice vinegar

1 tablespoon caster (superfine) sugar

1 granny smith apple, peeled and finely grated

3 tablespoons extra-virgin olive oil

3 tablespoons light soy sauce

1½ teaspoons sesame oil

Pair with

Serve with meat, seafood or poultry off the grill, or braised in a Japanese/Korean style.

For the dressing, combine the ginger, vinegar and sugar in a small bowl. Add the remaining ingredients and combine.

Build the salad in a large shallow bowl, starting with the lettuce, then the mizuna, daikon, edamame, avocado and spring onion. Spoon the dressing over, sprinkle with gomashio and serve immediately.

Daikon & shiitake braised in soy dashi & brown butter sauce

Even after long cooking, the texture of daikon will still have some integrity and bite – and in this dish it will have taken up the rich umami flavour from the dashi and shiitake mushrooms, which is further enhanced by the nut-brown butter. **Serves 4**

5 g (¼ oz) wakame (optional)
500 ml (17 fl oz/2 cups) Dashi (p. 53)
1 daikon, about 500 g (1 lb 2 oz), peeled and trimmed, cut into 4 cm (1½ in) thick discs

8 fresh shiitake mushrooms, or 4 dried shiitake that have been soaked in boiling water for 30 minutes, sliced
100 ml (3½ fl oz) mirin
80 ml (2½ fl oz/⅓ cup) light soy sauce

1 thumb-sized knob of fresh ginger, cut into 2 mm (⅛ in) slices
120 g (4½ oz) butter

Reconstitute the wakame by covering with boiling water and standing for 20 minutes, then drain and chop.

In a saucepan, simmer the dashi, daikon, mushrooms, mirin, soy sauce and ginger over a low heat for about 45 minutes, until the daikon is very tender.

Once cooked, remove the daikon and mushrooms and reduce the liquid by half.

Brown the butter in another saucepan over a medium heat, about 2½ minutes. Once nut brown, whisk in the reduced liquid until emulsified.

Pour the buttery sauce over the daikon and mushrooms, then sprinkle with the wakame.

Make it different
Turnip & shiitake braised in soy dashi & brown butter sauce. You could also braise some baby turnips or larger trimmed turnip slices in the same way. They will cook in about the same time.

Pair with
Simply serve with rice.

Match with grilled or slow-braised beef or pork.

Miso-grilled fish (see p. 184).

Eggplant with miso glaze (p. 521).

Raw turnip with walnut oil, celery leaves & parsley
GF **V** **VG**

When turnips are in full season, they are almost sweet and can be eaten raw. Coarsely grate a peeled turnip or two and season with salt and pepper. Combine a tablespoon each of honey, walnut oil, extra-virgin olive oil and apple-cider vinegar and pour over the grated turnip. Add a handful of chopped parsley, mint and pale yellow celery leaves and combine. Serve with some coarsely chopped walnuts scattered over the top. I have also made a similar salad with raw celeriac. Either version could be served with melted cheese on toast, pork sausages or cotechino with braised lentils, or with Duck leg confit (p. 260) or rabbit.

Lamb navarin

This is a classic braise from the Normandy region of northern France. Navet is the French word for turnip, though some contend that the dish celebrates a nineteenth century battle in the Bay of Navarino, where the Ottoman Empire allied with Egypt were defeated by France in league with Russia and Britain. Larousse points to the dish existing before the battle, so we'll defer to the humble turnip taking naming rights. The dish originally featured mutton, with the vegetables changing depending on whether it was made in winter or spring. The key is to use lamb with plenty of connective tissue, as this is what yields a rich braise. Shoulder is perfect, and you could also use a two-point forequarter rack cut between the bones. You can simplify, too, by not straining out the diced vegetables; however, straining them does produce a more polished result, and would be done in a restaurant kitchen – if that's important to you. **Serves 4–6**

1.6 kg (3½ lb) lamb shoulder, cut into 5 cm (2 in) dice
150 g (5½ oz) butter
1 onion, finely diced
4 garlic cloves
2 celery stalks, finely diced
1 carrot, finely diced
1 turnip, peeled and cut into 2 cm (¾ in) dice
1½ tablespoons plain (all-purpose) flour
250 ml (8½ fl oz/1 cup) white wine

5 tomatoes, blanched, peeled (see p.655), seeded and diced
2 rosemary sprigs
4 thyme sprigs
1 fresh bay leaf
1 litre (34 fl oz/4 cups) Golden chicken stock (p. 54)
10 small–medium kipfler (fingerling) potatoes

10 Dutch carrots, peeled and trimmed, with some stem left on
12 baby turnips, peeled and trimmed, with some stem left on
10 roasted shallots (see p. 595), flesh pushed from the skins

Staples
EVOO, S&P

Preheat the oven to 175°C (345°F) fan-forced.

Season the lamb well with salt and pepper. Drizzle on some oil and massage into the meat. Sear the meat in batches in a flameproof casserole dish over a medium heat, adding half the butter with the first batch. Cook until golden brown all over, about 6 minutes per batch, then set aside.

Add the remaining butter to the pan. Add the onion, garlic, celery and carrot and cook until softened, about 5 minutes. Add the diced turnip and cook for 2 minutes. Add the flour and stir for 1 minute to coat the vegetables. Return the meat and add the wine. Reduce the wine by half, then add the tomato and herbs. Season with salt and plenty of pepper, then add the stock. If it doesn't cover the mixture, top up with water to just submerge the meat and vegetables. Bring to a simmer.

Cover the dish, place in the oven and cook for about 1 hour, until the meat is tender.

Meanwhile, peel the potatoes and cook for 6 minutes in boiling salted water, then remove with a slotted spoon. Peel and trim the Dutch carrots, leaving some stem on, and blanch in the boiling water for 1 minute. Drain and set aside.

When the lamb is tender, return the dish to the stovetop. Carefully remove the lamb pieces. Strain the sauce, then add back to the rinsed pan. Return the meat to the pan, along with the potatoes, Dutch carrots, baby turnips and shallot. Gently simmer over a low heat for 20 minutes. Adjust the seasoning as needed and serve.

Pair with

You could serve this as is, but I find it hard to resist serving it with Classic potato mash (p. 625), or a combination of mashed celeriac and potato, which would be very wintery indeed.

Roasted radishes with thyme (GF) (V)

Pack a few bunches of radishes, with some of the leaves still attached, into a ceramic baking dish. Season with salt and pepper, dot with butter and drizzle with extra-virgin olive oil. Add 200 ml (7 fl oz) water or a light chicken stock and about 10 thyme sprigs. Roast for about 30 minutes at 180°C (350°F) fan-forced, until tender and pink. These are great served with braised beef ribs, roast beef, roast chicken or a pork chop, or drop them on top of a dish of roasted potatoes or a Baked buttered rice (p. 384). You can also serve them tossed with fried bacon and onion to go with a red wine braise, or with steak and Beurre rouge (p. 69).

Baby turnips with butter glaze (GF) (V)

Scrub the skin off 10 baby turnips and trim the stems, leaving 1 cm (½ in) or so of stubble. Simmer in 400 ml (13½ fl oz) light vegetable or chicken stock or water with 50 g (1¾ oz) butter, 1 teaspoon caster (superfine) sugar and a little salt and pepper until tender. Once cooked, remove the turnips to a warm serving dish and reduce the liquid to a glaze, seasoning as needed, then pour back over the turnips. You could also add some tender turnip leaves right at the end to wilt before serving. This is ideal with braised lamb, or the gamey flavours of hare and venison.

Rhubarb

Like many, I met rhubarb courtesy of a crumble. My mother's apple and rhubarb crumble, no less, served with thick, cold custard – although mum probably bucked the trend a little, showcasing rhubarb's tart side, with the sugar a minor player. I still enjoy rhubarb done simply, usually poached in orange juice with a little sugar and served with rich, thick yoghurt, clotted cream or the like; it also makes its way into jams, chutneys, mixed compotes and pickles, and even features in savoury dishes.

Most authors like to point out that rhubarb is a vegetable, and not a fruit. I'm very much of the opinion that as cooks we refer to fruits or vegetables based on their use – but rhubarb is a leafy stalk that resembles rainbow chard, and is very hard to mistake for a fruit. Rhubarb is a vegetable, and it can be used as such, but you do need to balance the sourness, as you do in sweet applications. I use it in a lamb braise (see p. 647), where the sourness cuts through the rich and fatty lamb; it can be used as a tart accent in a Green papaya salad (p. 438); and it works shaved into fine curls and tossed with fennel, extra-virgin olive oil, a little lemon and a healthy crowning of shaved parmesan as a side salad.

Rhubarb has such a distinctly appealing rosy pink-red hue – except when it doesn't. In reality, rhubarb can be red or green, and though there is said to be some flavour variation, the general consensus appears to be that they are very similar. You'll often read that red rhubarb is sweeter than green, though I can't ever recall having sweet red rhubarb, either. Rhubarb is tart, and alarmingly so. As with quinces, sugar is typically used to bring rhubarb into balance, sitting on the other side of the scale to acidity. When there's some harmony, you can start to appreciate the flavour.

Rhubarb is a perennial, so technically it doesn't have a season, but the stalks tend to be more compact and intensely flavoured in cooler weather, due to the slower growth, and many rhubarb dishes are similarly suited to cooler weather. Rhubarb is also grown under 'forced' conditions, which sounds horrible, but simply means they're grown in dark sheds. The practice started in the nineteenth century, with rhubarb first grown outside for two years to become frost hardy, then grown in darkness but with heat, so the plant strives to find light. The lack of photosynthesis results in less-tart stalks and an absence of bitterness. It is a very effective and creative piece of adaptive thinking, where rhubarb can be grown outside of the prime season, harvesting the warmth of the sun but not the sunlight. The stalks grow 2–3 cm (¾–1¼ in) per day, so those sheds are said to be full of the creaking, groaning and popping of rhubarb growing. Eerie stuff.

While rhubarb leaves may look vaguely edible to those keen on avoiding food waste, please don't eat them. Ever. The leaves contain toxic levels of oxalic acid, which is present at lower concentrations in many fruits and vegetables, as well as in rhubarb stalks. The levels in the leaves, however, can cause serious stomach upset and vomiting, and an elevated level of oxalic acid in the diet can result in kidney stones.

When selecting rhubarb, I look for stalks a little bigger than my index finger that are brightly coloured, firm and crisp. If the leaves are useful for anything, it is as an indication of freshness – steer away from any sad and wilted-looking ones. I am always drawn to brightly coloured specimens, but that's not to say that green rhubarb isn't just as tasty. I suppose it's just an association that's hard to shake. You eat with your eyes, as they say – so, it's red rhubarb for me.

Also see

Rhubarb muffins 732

Pair with

Rhubarb loves ginger, cloves, star anise, pepper, thyme, vanilla, rosewater, rose geranium and gin aromatics. It is enriched by butter, yoghurt, cream, crème fraîche, ice cream, custard and meringue. Pair it with raspberries, strawberries, plums, lemons and limes, as well as hazelnuts, pistachios and almonds. Use it as a foil for rich meats such as lamb, duck and quail.

Preparing rhubarb

Rhubarb simply needs to be trimmed of the pale, woody base, with the toxic leaves sent to the compost. There was a time when rhubarb was routinely peeled or 'stringed', where the tougher fibres were removed from the corrugations on the stalks. I remember celery was often treated the same way when I was little. Beans also required stringing. Now, not so much for any of them. This is no doubt largely due to selective breeding, though I imagine overly mature or out-of-season rhubarb may require the same intervention – not that I would buy either of these. Rhubarb can then be sliced or left as whole stalks before poaching or roasting. Just be wary, as rhubarb cooks quite quickly, so you'll need to keep an eye on it unless you don't mind a purée – and don't stir or agitate, or it will start to break down.

Roasted rhubarb, blood plum & ginger chutney GF V VG

This sweet, tart and savoury relish pairs well with rich meats. You could use any plums, but the colour from blood plums is particularly dramatic set against the blush of the rhubarb. **Serves 20**

Pair with

Pork, duck or quail, baked Christmas ham, terrines (pp. 327–8), sharp aged cheddar.

6 rhubarb stalks, trimmed and cut into 3 cm (1¼ in) pieces on an angle
4 blood plums, quartered
5 cm (2 in) piece of fresh ginger, peeled and cut into matchsticks
120 g (4 oz) brown sugar
2 teaspoons black peppercorns
1½ tablespoons sherry vinegar, or red-wine vinegar
4 thyme sprigs
2 teaspoons salt flakes

Preheat the oven to 200°C (400°F) fan-forced.

Add all the ingredients to a ceramic baking dish and combine well, then smooth out in an even layer. Set aside for 15 minutes.

Roast for 10 minutes, then remove from the oven and stir through gently. Roast for a further 15 minutes, or until the rhubarb is tender. Set aside to cool completely without stirring.

Serve as needed, or refrigerate in a clean airtight container for up to 2 weeks.

Spiced lamb shanks with rhubarb, honey & fried vine leaves GF

Cooking meat and fruit together is a very old practice, and one we don't really dabble with much in the West, whereas in the Middle East it is a lot more common. When you think of the rich fattiness of slow-cooked lamb, especially when cooked with spices, using dried fruit, dates, pears or quince starts to make a lot of sense. Adding rhubarb isn't going to add the sweetness of, say, dates, but the sourness lifts the flavours and cuts through the fat, while the honey adds richness, and the flavours of both are just so stunningly complementary in this.
Serves 6

500 g (1 lb 2 oz) rhubarb stalks, trimmed and cut into 6 cm (2¾ in) lengths on an angle
2 teaspoons salt flakes
6 Frenched lamb shanks
12 French shallots, peeled and left whole
8 garlic cloves, peeled and crushed

2 red bird's eye chillies, split lengthways
1 tablespoon cumin seeds
1 cinnamon stick
1 tablespoon red-wine vinegar
1 tablespoon tomato paste (concentrated purée)
115 g (4 oz/⅓ cup) honey
1.5 litres (51 fl oz/6 cups) Golden chicken stock (p. 54)

250 ml (8½ fl oz/1 cup) water
oil, for shallow-frying
4 large vine leaves in brine, rinsed and dried
50 ml (1¾ fl oz) extra-virgin olive oil
rice or couscous, to serve

Staples
EVOO, S&P

Preheat the oven to 170°C (340°F) fan-forced.

Season the rhubarb with the salt flakes and a generous grind of black pepper. Set aside.

In a large flameproof casserole dish (with a lid), heat a few tablespoons of oil over a medium heat and brown the lamb shanks all over, turning now and then; this will take about 10 minutes to do properly. Season well with salt and pepper, remove from the pan and set aside.

Wipe the pan out with paper towel, then heat another splash of oil over a medium heat. Add the whole shallots, garlic cloves, chillies, cumin and cinnamon. Cook for 15 minutes, stirring often.

Return the shanks to the pan, along with the vinegar, tomato paste and honey. Stir, then pour in the stock and water. Bring to a simmer and cook for 10 minutes, then cover, transfer to the oven and cook for 2 hours.

Meanwhile, heat 2–3 cm (¾–1¼ in) of oil in a deep frying pan until it sizzles when you drop in the vine leaves. Cook for 20 seconds on both sides, then drain on paper towel. They will crisp up as they cool.

Add the rhubarb to the casserole dish and cook for 20 minutes. When the meat is just starting to fall from the bone, remove the casserole dish from the oven.

Remove the shanks, rhubarb and shallots, allowing the liquid to drain back into the casserole dish. Arrange the shanks, rhubarb and shallots in a baking dish, leaving a little space between each shank.

Turn the oven up to 200°C (400°F) fan-forced.

Reduce the sauce in the casserole dish over a medium–high heat by one-third, then whisk in the olive oil. Pour the sauce into the baking dish, ensuring that the shanks are not submerged.

Bake for 10 minutes to darken and crisp the exposed lamb.

Serve with the vine leaves piled on top, and rice or couscous on the side.

Emma's pickled rhubarb GF V VG

This pickling method was borrowed from my good friend and brilliant cook Emma Warren. Emma and I have worked on countless shoots and events together, and she was my right hand when we ran a restaurant for a season in Ibiza. She also cooked in Spain for a decade prior, and has written two books (so far) on regional Spanish cooking. This recipe hails from Menorca. These pickles are crunchy and sharp with a touch of sweetness; use as you would cornichons or small pickled onions. **Makes 800 g (1 lb 12 oz)**

400 g (14 oz) rhubarb stalks, trimmed

Pickling medium
300 ml (10 fl oz) apple-cider vinegar

300 ml (10 fl oz) water
300 g (10½ oz) caster (superfine) sugar
1 tablespoon fennel seeds

2 teaspoons black peppercorns
1 teaspoon salt flakes

Cut the rhubarb into lengths the size of the jar(s) you have on hand, then pack reasonably tightly.

Add the pickling medium to a small saucepan and bring to a rolling boil over a high heat. Stand off the heat for 5 minutes, then pour into the clean jar(s). If not quite full, add a little more vinegar.

Seal the lids and cool to room temperature, then refrigerate for a week before using. These pickles should keep for at least 6 months in the fridge.

Pair with

Serve with a terrine (pp. 327–8), Pork rillettes (p. 330) and other charcuterie.

These pickles work particularly well with the nutty sharp flavour of cheese made from sheep's milk, such as manchego, or mixed-milk cheeses.

Slice finely and add to a salad for a tartly sweet accent.

For someone who has everything, a jar of this also makes a lovely and unusual gift.

Roasted rhubarb & strawberries with rose geranium GF V VG

You can use this recipe as a base for lots of different desserts, or just serve with some cream, custard or ice cream. You can get your grocer to order in rose geranium, but heading to a nursery is a better option, then you'll have it on hand for this dish, plus it is lovely infused into custard, ice cream or jelly. You'll also get a beautifully fragrant plant with pretty pink flowers – a win–win situation. **Makes about 800 g (1 lb 12 oz)**

1 bunch of rhubarb, trimmed and cut into about 12 cm (4¾ in) lengths
400 g (14 oz) strawberries, hulled

400 g (14 oz/1¾ cups) caster (superfine) sugar
½ lemon, zest peeled
4 rose geranium sprigs

150 ml (5 fl oz) Prosecco, or other sparkling or white wine

Preheat the oven to 220°C (430°F) fan-forced.

Add the rhubarb, strawberries, sugar and lemon zest to a roasting tin and toss through. Set aside for 1 hour.

Add the geranium sprigs to the dish and pour in the Prosecco. Roast for 20 minutes, or until the liquid is bubbling around the edges.

Remove from the oven and gently shake the dish. Set aside on the bench for 5 minutes before serving.

Pair with

Ice cream, frozen yoghurt, custard, cream or Italian meringue (p. 807).

Chilled vanilla custard, honey and shards of crisp, layered filo pastry (see p. 564).

This is great with chocolate cake.

Serve with Greek-style yoghurt for an indulgent weekend breakfast.

Rhubarb tartlets ⓥ

I had been indulging in little tartlets like these ones at a local farmers' market some years back, but that market was a monthly affair, and sometimes I just couldn't wait that long. This is my interpretation, with the delicate, buttery pastry the perfect match for the sharp and sweet rhubarb compote. These are one-or-two-bite morsels, but you could make larger single-serve tarts. This compote could also be spooned over yoghurt, stirred through a cream fool or served with custard. **Makes about 18**

8 × 30 cm (12 in) rhubarb stalks, cut into 2 cm (¾ in) pieces
250 g (9 oz) raw sugar
150 ml (5 fl oz) orange juice
125 g (4½ oz/1 cup) raspberries

200 ml (7 fl oz) thick (double/heavy) cream
icing (confectioners') sugar, for dusting

Sweet pastry
180 g (6½ oz) unsalted butter
75 g (2¾ oz) icing (confectioners') sugar

2 egg yolks
25 ml (1 fl oz) water
250 g (9 oz/1⅔ cups) plain (all-purpose) flour

Special equipment
Fluted mini-tart tins (about 5 cm/2 in) or muffin tray

Preheat the oven to 170°C (340°F) fan-forced.

For the pastry, cream the butter and sugar in a food processor. Add the egg yolks and water and blitz, then add the flour and blitz until combined. Tip out onto a benchtop and form a ball, then wrap in plastic wrap and chill for 30 minutes.

Meanwhile, add the rhubarb and sugar to a saucepan and mix well. Add the orange juice and stand for 15 minutes, then cook over a medium heat for 10 minutes, until the rhubarb is cooked and just tender. Add the raspberries, turn off the heat and cool to room temperature.

Once the pastry has rested, roll it out between two sheets of baking paper until 4 mm (¼ in) thick. Cut circles about 1 cm (½ in) larger than the tart tins, re-rolling the scraps to use up all the pastry. Line the tart tins with the pastry and chill for 15 minutes, then fill the pastry shells with foil and dried beans and bake for 6–10 minutes, until the edges are golden. Set aside to cool.

To serve, spoon the rhubarb mixture into the tart shells, dollop with cream and dust with icing sugar. Serve immediately.

Make it faster
If you're short on time, buy ready-made tart cases to simplify things. But I would highly recommend trying the full recipe when time allows, as the pastry is stunning with the compote.

Rhubarb galette ⓥ

This is sublime, and it's always a showstopper. If you have guests over, have it prepped in the fridge until ready to bake. The aroma alone towards the end of an evening will be enough to impress, but when the burnished golden pastry lands on the table with its chevrons of rosy rhubarb ... well, I can hear the gasps already! **Serves 4–6**

Pair with

Custard, cream, ice cream or crème fraîche.

250 g (9 oz) caster (superfine) sugar
juice of ½ lemon
1 vanilla bean, split in half (optional)
300 ml (10 fl oz) water
800 g (1 lb 12 oz) rhubarb stalks, trimmed and cut into 8 cm (3¼ in) lengths

2 tablespoons demerara sugar
1 egg white, beaten

Sweet galette pastry
250 g (9 oz/1⅔ cups) plain (all-purpose) flour, plus extra for dusting
60 g (2 oz/½ cup) icing (confectioners') sugar

100 g (3½ oz) chilled butter, diced
2 yolks, beaten
2 tablespoons iced water
a pinch of salt flakes

Hazelnut base
100 g (3½ oz) toasted hazelnuts
50 g (1¾ oz) caster (superfine) sugar

Add the caster sugar, lemon juice, vanilla bean and seeds and water to a large saucepan over a high heat until the liquid is simmering and the sugar is dissolved. Add the rhubarb and reduce the heat to very low. Poach, turning gently, until the rhubarb is glossy and deepens in colour, about 5 minutes. (The rhubarb will not be totally cooked, as it will cook again in the galette.) Refrigerate the rhubarb in the syrup until thoroughly chilled. Once cool, thoroughly drain off the syrup, reserving the syrup.

For the pastry, tip the flour onto a benchtop and add the sugar and butter. Work in your fingers to form a coarse crumb, then incorporate the egg yolks, iced water and salt. Lightly knead with the heel of your hand until the pastry comes together into a soft dough. Flatten into a thick disc between two sheets of baking paper and rest in the fridge for 1 hour.

Roll the rested pastry out on a lightly floured surface, or between two sheets of baking paper, to a rough 40 cm (16 in) round, then trim to a neat 36 cm (14 in) circle. Transfer to a baking tray lined with baking paper and refrigerate until firm, about 30 minutes.

Preheat the oven to 200°C (400°F) fan-forced.

For the base, pulse the hazelnuts and sugar in a food processor until coarsely chopped. Scatter over the rested pastry, leaving a 3 cm (1¼ in) border all round. Arrange the rhubarb on top, in any pattern you like. You can cut on an angle and make chevrons, or be more organic – in this instance, I like a pattern. Once the surface is covered with rhubarb, fold the pastry edges in, crimping to seal. Brush the pastry edges with egg white, then scatter the demerara sugar over the exposed pastry and rhubarb.

Bake until the pastry is golden and the rhubarb is cooked, about 25 minutes. Serve hot, with the reserved rhubarb syrup.

Tomato

My Mediterranean heritage saw me fall heavily for tomatoes. We had a second kitchen in our house at one point, and my meme, Grace, used to buy produce at the market and cook it in large batches for the weeks ahead, or preserve for later. In summer, big pots of tomatoes simmered slowly downstairs and ended up tossed with short pasta, peas, oregano and ricotta, or used to sauce baked ricotta cannelloni, to add to a ragù, for stuffed sweet capsicums (bell peppers), or poured over cooked tuna that was first preserved under oil.

Tomato still occupies my home as steadfastly as it did then. In summer, the tomato is king, tumbling from bowls laden with all manner of varieties – some destined for salad, some for sauce, some for preserves. Greek salad (p. 512) with tomato, feta, olives and dried oregano is a welded-on fixture at home. The deliciousness of a fresh heirloom tomato sauce seems to be continuously revelatory, no matter how often I make it, and tomatoes tossed with milky buffalo mozzarella, burrata, basil and quality balsamic vinegar just need salt, pepper and good oil to sing. Tomatoes have an amazing affinity with extra-virgin olive oil that is beyond compare. The unique peppery green fruitiness of cold-pressed extra-virgin olive oil matched with the sweetly tart, vibrant but rounded acidity of a peak-season tomato is just sublime. Though not just any old tomato, mind you.

Oh, the horrible injustices we have subjected this magnificent fruit to are hard to reconcile. For decades, despite being blessed with a panoply of wondrous cultivars we – as a society – sought to banish them all in favour of a durable red orb of nothingness. The tomato is the most emblematic symbol of the disastrous horticultural quest to make 'perfect' fruit and vegetables for supermarkets: uniform in colour and size, hardy for long storage, and hard to blemish. Also, hard to eat, as well as being a nutritional vacuum.

Tomatoes were bred to perform commercially, but sadly taste was never a factor. The process of selective breeding that created the supermarket abomination we all know so well unwittingly selected out many genes responsible for flavour. As a consequence, over 90 per cent of commercial tomatoes lack a critical flavour gene that is present in wild and heirloom varieties.

When tomatoes are available all the time, we lose perspective on how a ripe and luscious in-season tomato should taste, and slowly start to accept what modern agriculture can generate all year round. As far as I'm concerned, that floury, fuzzy, powdery and bland fruit that occupied space in white bread sandwiches while I was growing up, and still proliferates, is not a tomato – it's a deception. I'm not sure why anyone would like them.

The other issue with tomatoes – well, with how we treat them – is that they don't like being refrigerated. Cold temperatures shut down the genes that produce flavour, so while the tomatoes might ripen further, they will still be tasteless. I think that's a fairly well-known effect these days, but I guarantee that those supermarket tomatoes have slumbered in cold storage long enough to void their essentially flavourlessness further – so, storing them at room temperature after purchasing is largely useless, despite at least appearing to ripen over a day or so.

That's a bit of a rant, I know, but it simply reflects how besotted I am with real tomatoes. And, thankfully, there is a widening appreciation for the real deal, and they are becoming more readily available. Outside of farmers' markets, where heirloom varieties are eagerly cleared from trestles by enthusiasts, there is a growing culture of growing your own, with backyard plants proliferating. It's a wonderful sight.

Also see

Smoky tomato dressing 84

Tabouleh 87

Simple tomato sugo 116

Bucatini amatriciana 121

Iraqi chicken with tomato & cardamom rice 242–3

Ragù alla bolognese 283

Egg, tomato & spinach curry with ginger & turmeric 359

Greek salad 512

Eggplant & tomato kasundi 520

Pasta alla Norma 521

Vegetable bolognese 576

Pizza margherita 857

Pair with

Tomatoes love, love, love extra-virgin olive oil, as well as vinegar, whether sherry, wine, cider or balsamic. Basil springs to mind for herbs immediately, then perhaps oregano, but tarragon, coriander (cilantro), chives, mint, parsley, sorrel and bay leaves are wonderful, too. And saffron, cinnamon, allspice, chilli, cumin, fennel seeds, coriander seeds and black pepper are great spices with tomato. So many cheeses match beautifully – haloumi, parmesan, pecorino, goat's curd, fresh mozzarella, burrata, feta – as do crème fraîche, butter, labneh, cream and eggs. Garlic and onions of all types are perfect, as are peas, okra, spinach, fennel, cucumber and potatoes. Also pair with grains and pulses, poultry, lamb, beef, pork, fish and shellfish.

Tomatoes grow either on a bush or a sprawling vine. The former grow to their full height, flower, fruit and produce essentially one crop, then die off. The latter will keep growing without ever supporting its own weight, so the vines need to be tied, and will continue to produce fruit until frost ends the struggle as autumn fades to winter. Naturally, each has its merits for the home gardener, with bush tomatoes ripening in more or less the same window of time, which is ideal for making passata or the like, while vine tomatoes will provide a crop over an extended period. And it is not uncommon for gardeners to uproot late-season plants and hang them inside somewhere warm to ripen the last of the fruit. Or if still luridly green, a pickle is the way to go, or layering them in oil with salt, vinegar and oregano (see p. 656).

There are too many varieties of tomatoes to expand on here, with a huge diversity in size, colour, shape and flavour. There are tomatoes that are green when fully ripe, some that are almost black, and others that have distinctly smoky flavours. There are tomatoes not much bigger than a redcurrant, and those that need to be carried with two hands. There are some that cook down to a dense pulp, and those that break down into mostly liquid. It's a wonderful, wonderful non-uniform world.

There are some very good modern hybrid tomatoes, as well as superb heirlooms. Generally, more densely fleshed tomatoes are considered best for sauce, as they yield a thicker result more readily, but any impeccably ripe and tasty tomato will make a beautiful quick sauce. If you're preserving passata for later use, then opt for something with a bit more dense matter.

Plum tomatoes, which include roma and the legendary San Marzano (the only tomato used for authentic pizza margherita), are ideal for sauce, being thick-walled and densely fleshed. Beefsteak tomatoes – such as oxheart – have a higher water content and will cook down in volume more, but the sauce will taste great if kept on the fresher side rather than stewing down, emphasising the sun-flushed flavour. Similarly, any heirloom will make a stunning quick pan sauce.

Beefsteak varieties are large, multi-chambered tomatoes that are ideal for salads such as Insalata caprese (p. 662) – though again, any properly ripe heirloom will work wonderfully. I often use a mix in tomato-dominant salads, including sweet cherry or pear tomatoes, often red and yellow, contrasting with fat slices of beefsteak tomatoes and sometimes green zebras, tigerellas or black Russians, among others. Cherry tomatoes are usually always available, but they are generally miserably tart when out of season, whereas they should be a pop of juicy sweetness.

While I have pressed the point of seasonality here rather strongly, there are times when a tomato is required, even though the wind is lashing in icy tendrils, with windows chattering in their sashes. Yes, no-one's perfect. In those moments of desperation, the Kumato variety can be somewhat of a salvation – though it's not infallible. Kumato is a tightly controlled commercial cultivar resembling a black Russian, though its actual parentage is a well-guarded secret. They are unusual in that they can be eaten at all stages of ripeness, becoming very sweet and flavourful when fully ripe. Mostly, though, stick to tinned and preserved tomatoes in the coolest months, though if you have tomatoes that are good, but not great, Tomato confit (p. 656) is the way to go.

When selecting tomatoes, look for ones that are heavy in the hand for their size. Some heirloom varieties are prone to splitting, which is not necessarily a problem. One of the most important considerations with tomatoes is what you're going to use them for. Oozingly ripe tomatoes may not make a great salad, but they will make an extraordinary sauce. Black spots, leaking juices and mould are more concerning, as those tomatoes can carry 'off' flavours. Mind you, black spots can be cut away and the rest used for sauce. Use your nose. The one thing you shouldn't do is use the model of a red spherical tomato as some sort of Platonic ideal, as 'real' tomatoes come in all shapes, colours and sizes. You may need to become familiar with the varieties to see which you prefer, but that's a very enjoyable journey. And remember, never refrigerate your tomatoes – unless you've cooked or pickled them first.

Preparing tomatoes

The only inedible parts of a tomato are the stem, and the small core where it attaches, which simply needs to be cut away – although you can eat the core if you like. Usually, a tomato just then needs be sliced or diced as required; however, tomato skins aren't that awesome once cooked. You can peel them (see below), but that's a fussy process only required for certain applications. Mostly, if I'm roasting or braising with whole tomatoes or large pieces of tomato, I will just pull the skins off as they peel away, or pick them out of the sauce with tongs. You don't have to get them all, but if the skins are thick, they can be quite tough and don't have any real flavour. Some contest that tomato seeds can be bitter, but there's a lot of flavour in the gel-like pulp between the membranes, and I've never had any problem with bitterness. In classical French cooking, the pulp and seeds are often removed before the flesh is diced, which does make sense in some vinaigrette sauces, but it's usually done for some sense of aesthetic order, which I have little interest in.

Peeling tomatoes

You need to blanch tomatoes to peel them. Blanching just scalds the skin enough to be able to remove the skin easily (without cooking the tomato), so the flesh can be used in salads, or in a vinaigrette sauce such as Sauce vierge (p. 82). Remove the core/stem with a paring knife, then score a cross in the base to just cut through the skin. Drop the tomatoes into a saucepan of boiling water for 2 minutes, then lift out and plunge into cold or iced water. Once cooled, peel off the skins from the cross in the base.

Bruschetta Ⓥ Ⓥ🄶

This is one of those combinations that simply can't be improved on. Naturally, the success is all about the quality of the ingredients, and when tomatoes are at their best, you don't even need the vinegar, or not much, with the tangy and sweet juice and seeds so perfectly balanced. One real key here is to make sure the bread is well toasted and crunchy but with a little give in the middle – so, cut it thickly and toast it well. **Serves 4**

70 ml (2¼ fl oz) extra-virgin olive oil

1 tablespoon vinegar (balsamic, sherry or wine vinegar)

2 garlic cloves, 1 finely grated, 1 peeled

4 ripe tomatoes, finely diced

10 basil leaves

4 slices Sourdough bread (p. 847), about 2 cm (¾ in) thick

Staples
S&P

Add the oil, vinegar and grated garlic to a bowl, season with salt and pepper and combine. Add the tomato and roughly tear in the basil. Toss to combine, then set aside for 10 minutes.

Toast or grill the bread well so that it's firm and scorched on the outside. Rub the toast with the whole garlic clove – it will grate into the toast a little and perfume it. Spoon on the tomato mixture and serve.

Make it different
With cheese. Dress this up further by topping the toast with a good smear of goat's cheese or ricotta before piling on the tomato.

With heirloom tomatoes. If you have some large ripe heirloom tomatoes at the peak of the season, simply slice thickly and drop on the oiled garlicky toast, season, then scatter over a little basil. This is a common breakfast for me in the summer months.

Pan con tomate with soft-boiled eggs & celery salt Ⓥ

Pan con tomate is a somewhat messier Spanish version of Italian bruschetta. Rather than piling on tomato, the tomato is rubbed into the toast, pushing in the flesh and juices. It's gloriously inelegant and absolutely delicious. This version dresses that process up a little more with soft-boiled eggs and a flurry of pale-yellow celery leaves. **Serves 4**

Pair with

Serve as is, or with anchovies, smashed sardines, stuffed olives and shaved jamón or other salumi as an aperitivo snack.

4 eggs, at room temperature
4 slices Sourdough bread (p. 847), about 2 cm (¾ in) thick
1 large garlic clove, peeled

4 very ripe tomatoes, cut in half crossways
2 teaspoons Celery salt (p. 9)
1 handful of pale-yellow celery leaves

Staples
EVOO, S&P

Bring a small saucepan of water to the boil over a high heat. Carefully lower the eggs into the water with a spoon, then cook for 5½ minutes. Refresh in cold water for 40 seconds, then place in egg cups.

Meanwhile, toast or grill the bread well so that it's firm and scorched on the outside. Rub the toast with the garlic. Rub the cut edge of the tomatoes on the toast, pushing the flesh into the toast. Drizzle heavily with oil, season with pepper and some celery salt, then leave whole or cut into fingers.

Scatter the celery leaves over the toast and serve with the hot soft-boiled eggs, with the remaining celery salt on the side.

Tomato confit ⒼⒻ Ⓥ ⓋⒼ

These tomato gems need a little preparation but once done, they are so convenient to have on hand to bring that touch of spiced tomato flavour to all sorts of dishes. The flavour intensifies when they are cooked slowly, making them a little similar to a semi-dried tomato in flavour concentration, but they have been peeled and are not chewy. They are a complete delight, and you can use them as you would a semi-dried tomato. **Makes 30**

Pair with

Serve at room temperature with a splash of sherry vinegar, some manchego or Comté, a few black olives and some good bread.

Layer into a deluxe roll, maybe stuffed with slow-cooked lamb, rocket (arugula) and feta.

Add to salads, or chop and add to dressings and vinaigrettes.

Use to enhance sauces, or toss through spaghetti with prawns (shrimp) or crabmeat and plenty of good oil.

Top toast or a seed cracker with confit tomato and some goat's cheese, parmesan or fermented almond ricotta.

Serve as a salad dressed with pomegranate seeds and molasses topped with goat's curd or mozzarella.

2 kg (4 lb 6 oz) tomatoes ripe, peeled (see p. 655) and cut in half
200 ml (7 fl oz) extra-virgin olive oil
5 garlic cloves, very finely sliced

½ bunch of oregano, leaves picked
½ bunch of thyme, leaves picked
2 teaspoons ground cumin
3 teaspoons smoked paprika

3½ teaspoons caster (superfine) sugar
3 teaspoons salt flakes

Staples
OIL, S&P

Preheat the oven to 120°C (250°F) fan-forced. Line two baking trays with baking paper.

Add all the ingredients to a large bowl with about 20 grinds of pepper. Toss to combine, then arrange the tomatoes, cut side down, on the baking trays and bake for 4 hours. Allow to cool completely on the trays, which will help to preserve their shape.

Preserve these tomatoes for up to a month by layering them in a sterilised wide-mouthed jar (see p. 40). Pour in extra-virgin olive oil blended evenly with a neutral-flavoured oil (this will stop the olive oil solidifying) to cover, then seal and refrigerate.

Gazpacho GF V

Pair with

Serve with diced ripe avocado, soft herbs, pickled onion and a dollop of crème fraîche.

Use this soup as a base to serve seafood with, such as chopped prawns (shrimp), fried school prawns, crabmeat, fried bug (flat-head lobster) tails or crayfish.

Serve the gazpacho mix as a party-style drink in shot glasses, adding a touch of dry sherry or vodka if desired.

This is a recipe that has evolved a little in my hands, but it was originally passed to me by my friend and fellow chef Emma Warren. Emma worked in Spain for a decade and has a great passion for this classic cold soup. **Serves 6–8**

2 kg (4 lb 6 oz) ripe tomatoes, cut into 3 cm (1¼ in) chunks
2 red capsicums (bell peppers), cut into 3 cm (1¼ in) chunks
4 Lebanese (short) cucumbers, cut into 3 cm (1¼ in) chunks
1 white onion, cut into 3 cm (1¼ in) chunks
3 flat-leaf (Italian) parsley sprigs, leaves picked, stalks chopped

2 teaspoons salt flakes
1 loaf of ciabatta or Sourdough bread (p. 847)
3 garlic cloves, germ removed if green
3 tablespoons sherry vinegar, plus extra to serve
150 ml (5 fl oz) water
150 ml (5 fl oz) extra-virgin olive oil

Optional garnishes, to serve
small tomatoes, sliced
Lebanese (short) cucumber, finely sliced
white onion, finely sliced
red capsicum (bell pepper), finely sliced

Staples
EVOO, S&P

Preheat the oven to 150°C (300°F) fan-forced.

Add the tomato, capsicum, cucumber, onion and parsley stalks to a large bowl. Add the salt and combine. Set aside for 1 hour.

Meanwhile, cut the bread into thick slices, removing and discarding any hard crusts. Place on a baking tray and bake for 30 minutes, turning the slices over every now and then to dry out evenly. The aim is to dry the bread without actually toasting it. When the bread is crunchy, remove from the oven and turn the temperature up to 180°C (350°F) fan-forced.

Firmly rub the bread all over with the garlic and place in a large bowl, setting one slice aside for garnishing. Mix the vinegar, water and 75 ml (2½ fl oz) of the oil in a small bowl and pour over the bread. Set aside until the bread has softened, 5–10 minutes.

Rip up the reserved garlic bread and coat well in oil. Return to the oven and toast until golden.

Blitz the soaked bread and the tomato mixture in a food processor, pouring in the remaining 75 ml (2½ fl oz) oil while processing – you will need to do this in batches. Pass the purée through a sieve, then adjust the seasoning as needed. You may need a splash more vinegar, too.

Serve the gazpacho with the toasted croutons, parsley leaves, an extra splash of sherry vinegar and a drizzle of oil. Serve the garnishes on the side to add to the gazpacho, with extra croutons if desired.

Make it different

Tomato & cherry gazpacho. GF V For a deluxe blush colour and a touch of tart sweetness, when cherries are at their peak, substitute the tomato for 400 g (14 oz/2 cups) pitted fresh ripe cherries.

An inspiration from ajo blanco. To make what is arguably the precursor to gazpacho, see p. 513.

Panzanella with buffalo mozzarella ⓥ

This is a merging of two of my favourite tomato salads – panzanella and caprese. Well, two of my all-time favourite salads, tomato or not. Panzanella is a triumph of invention, utilising stale bread and seasonal vegetables, so sneaking in Parmigiano Reggiano and milky buffalo mozzarella is certainly a little outside its cucina povera origins, but the combination is a stunning one. The basil seeds are absolutely optional – they swell a little like chia seeds do, and add a prettily dramatic touch to the presentation. **Serves 4**

Pair with

I'd happily sit down to this for a meal, but it will go beautifully with so many things, too. Try it with grilled steak or lamb chops, fried or barbecued fish, or grilled chicken.

1 tablespoon basil seeds (optional), plus 1 tablespoon white-wine vinegar and 2 tablespoons water
3 thick slices of Sourdough bread (p. 847) (can be a few days old)
1 garlic clove
3 very ripe oxheart tomatoes, or another large, densely fleshed tomato
140 ml (4½ fl oz) extra-virgin olive oil

2½ tablespoons sherry vinegar
1 teaspoon caster (superfine) sugar
1 celery heart, finely sliced, leaves picked
100 g (3½ oz) Parmigiano Reggiano, some shaved, most finely grated
250 g (9 oz) mixed cherry tomatoes, cut in half
20 basil leaves

½ white onion, very finely sliced into rounds and soaked in cold water for 10–15 minutes
2 large balls of buffalo mozzarella, torn into chunks if desired

Staples
S&P

If using the basil seeds, place them in a small bowl with the white-wine vinegar and water. Set aside for the seeds to swell and reconstitute.

Meanwhile, toast or grill the bread well so that it's firm and scorched on the outside. Rub the toast with the whole garlic clove on both sides. Tear the toast into chunks and drop into a large bowl. Coarsely grate in one of the oxheart tomatoes.

Add 100 ml (3½ fl oz) of the oil, the sherry vinegar and sugar to a small bowl. Season with salt and pepper, then combine. Pour half the dressing over the toast chunks and toss to coat. Add the celery heart and leaves, and grated parmesan, then toss to combine.

Slice the remaining oxheart tomatoes into rounds about 1.5 cm (½ in) thick and lay on a plate. Pile on the dressed toast chunks and scatter the cherry tomatoes over, then spoon over the remaining dressing. Tear the basil leaves and scatter with the shaved parmesan. Drain and pat dry the onion and scatter over the top, then crown with the mozzarella.

Spoon the basil seeds over, if using. Season and dress with the remaining oil.

Pasta with fresh tomato sauce ⓥ

This will forever be a much-loved and oft-cooked pasta at our home. It's so simple, but also a clear contender for my all-time favourite pasta, perfect for when the cupboard is bare and the tomatoes are beyond ripe. Cook a good dried pasta in plenty of boiling salted water. Choose a couple of big handfuls of over-ripe tomatoes, preferably heirloom and fleshy, and roughly dice. Slice a clove or two of garlic and add to a frying pan over a medium heat with what seems like too much extra-virgin olive oil. Fry until the garlic is fragrant and just coloured, then add the tomato with any juices on the board. Season with salt and pepper and cook until the tomato melts into the oil and reduces a little, about 5 minutes. Add a fistful of basil or oregano, then lift the al dente pasta from the water and into the pan, taking some pasta water with it. Toss the pasta until the sauce glosses and sticks to it. Throw in a few handfuls of finely grated parmesan or pecorino and toss through to melt. Drizzle over a little more oil, grind in some more pepper and serve immediately. A scoop of fresh ricotta will usually make an appearance at home, as will a sprinkle of chilli flakes, but neither is essential. Don't make this with standard supermarket tomatoes no matter how ripe – the magic just won't be there.

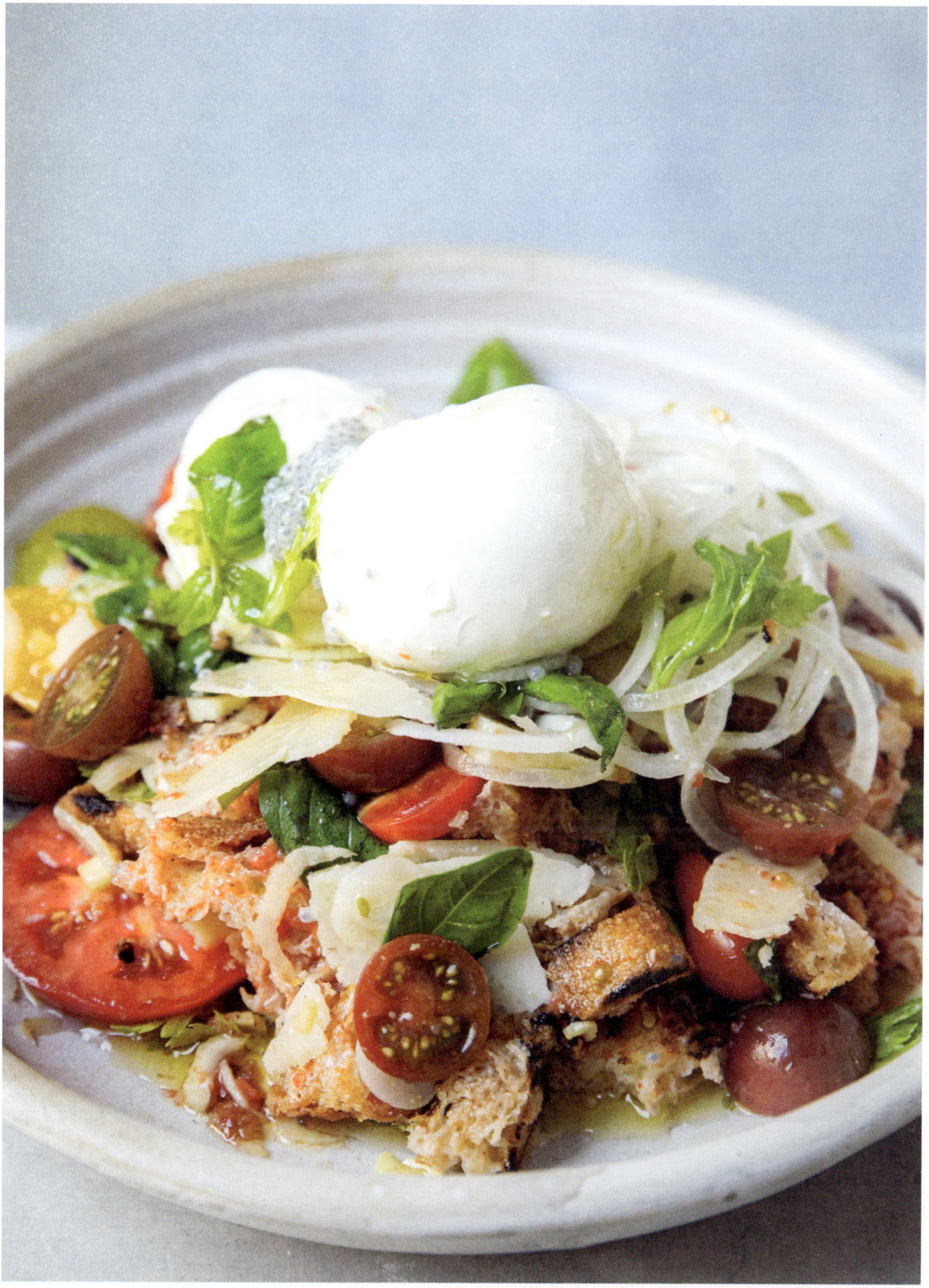

Tomato tarte tatin with manchego, thyme & dried olives Ⓥ

This take on tarte tatin is a celebration of tomatoes, so they need to be at their very best – no hydroponic ones here, please. So often we talk about peak-season tomatoes eaten raw – which is an undeniable delight – but when done right, a ripe sun-flushed heirloom tomato cooks so beautifully, retaining the fresh flavours while also concentrating and intensifying them. Quality all-butter puff pastry is essential. **Serves 4–6**

Pair with

This makes for a lovely light meal with some simply dressed leaves.

375 g (13 oz) Classic puff pastry (p. 822), rolled into a 6 mm (¼ in) thick square and rested in the fridge for 1 hour
50 g (1¾ oz) butter
400 g (14 oz) oxheart tomatoes, or any ripe, densely fleshed tomatoes, sliced 1 cm (½ in) thick

100 g (3½ oz) caster (superfine) sugar
5 French shallots, finely sliced into rings
4 garlic cloves, finely sliced
2½ tablespoons sherry vinegar
5 thyme sprigs, or tarragon

50 g (1¾ oz) manchego, cut into 2 cm (¾ in) dice and chilled in the freezer
12 dried black olives, pitted
120 g (4½ oz) goat's curd, to serve

Staples
S&P

Cut the pastry about 3 cm (1¼ in) larger than a 30–35 cm (12–13½ in) ovenproof frying pan or similar, then chill until needed. Generously grease the pan with the butter and line with a piece of baking paper.

Season the tomatoes with salt, then set aside for about 10 minutes to draw out some moisture.

Meanwhile, preheat the oven to 220°C (430°F) fan-forced.

Add the sugar to a frying pan over a high heat and shake to melt. Once it turns to a caramel, add the shallot, garlic and vinegar and swirl to combine.

Pour the caramel into the lined pan, distributing it evenly. Scatter the thyme around and season with salt and pepper.

Lift the tomato slices out of their juices and shake a little to get rid of any residual liquid. Arrange the slices in the pan; the base will be the top of the tart, so take some care with this. Dot the tomato with the manchego and olives, then lay the pastry on top. Bake for 25–35 minutes, until golden.

Once cooked, reshape the overhanging pastry, which will have shrunk, down the sides of the pan with a spatula, then rest for 5 minutes.

Place a plate on top of the pastry, then flip the whole tart over and unmould. Dollop on the goat's curd to serve.

Roasted tomato passata ⒼⒻ Ⓥ Ⓥ Ⓖ

This is one of the most delicious basics to have on hand. It can be used in all applications that call for tomato passata (puréed tomatoes), but it has a good deal more flavour than a regular purée. Overripe tomatoes, especially densely fleshed heirlooms, are perfect for this. **Makes 1.5 litres (51 fl oz/6 cups)**

25 ripe roma (plum) tomatoes, core removed
20 smaller yellow and red tomatoes, core removed
12 French shallots, sliced into 3 mm (⅛ in) thick rounds

12 garlic cloves, sliced or smashed
5 thyme sprigs, leaves picked
1 tablespoon dried Greek oregano (rigani)

400 ml (13½ fl oz) extra-virgin olive oil

Staples
S&P

This can be used wherever passata is called for, but given how intense and flavourful it is, you can use it sparingly for a big impact.

Toss hot pasta in the passata with some torn black olives and a handful of basil, then serve with a big dollop of fresh ricotta.

Add to a pot of mussels while they steam open.

Stain an aglio e olio sauce and serve with linguine or spaghetti and prawns (shrimp) or a mix of seafood.

Toss with home-made Gnocchi (p. 136) and serve with parmesan or pecorino.

Boost a sauce with a good spoonful of this at the end of cooking to keep those roasted flavours nice and present.

Preheat the oven to 120°C (250°F) fan-forced.

Arrange the tomatoes in a deep baking dish that fits them snugly. Scatter the shallot, garlic and herbs over, season generously with salt and pepper, then pour the oil over.

Roast for about 1½ hours, until the tomatoes have softened and the skins are papery.

Once cool, pull off the skins. Mash the tomatoes into the oil infusion with your hands, squeezing the pulp between your fingers.

Store in a jar or airtight container in the fridge, and use within a week.

Insalata caprese ⓖⓕ ⓥ

This salad relies on beautifully sun-kissed tomatoes. So, please make this only when tomatoes are genuinely in season – sweet, intensely flavoured and irresistible. Brightly coloured hot-house tomatoes in the depth of winter may look appealing, but they will be tart and flavourless. Wait, look forward to it, and enjoy it even more. **Serves 4**

3 tablespoons plain yoghurt
2½ tablespoons extra-virgin olive oil
2 large fior di latte, or buffalo mozzarella, balls
4 very ripe tomatoes, sliced 1 cm (½ in) thick

250 g (9 oz) yellow pear or cherry tomatoes, cut in half
½ white salad onion, finely sliced
5 basil leaves
2 tablespoons aged balsamic vinegar

Basil oil
12 basil leaves
½ garlic clove
100 ml (3½ fl oz) extra-virgin olive oil

Staples
S&P

Pair with
Bread! Yes, bread can – and should – be served with so many things, but here it is beyond essential. It would be a crime to waste the juices of this classic salad. And please match them with equally good Sourdough bread (p. 847) (fresh or chargrilled are both perfect).

For the basil oil, grind the basil, garlic and a pinch of salt in a mortar until you have a paste, then mix the oil through.

Add the yoghurt and oil to a bowl, season with salt and pepper and combine. Tear the mozzarella into pieces and drop into the bowl, then toss to coat.

Arrange the tomatoes on a serving plate, season, then top with the cheese mixture. Scatter the onion and basil over, then drizzle with the basil oil and balsamic and serve.

Provençale tomato-stuffed peppers with olives & anchovies

Capsicums (bell peppers) are great candidates for stuffing – in this case, tomato with garlicky bread, olives and herbs, finished with anchovies. You could also go a step further and crown these with a slice of fresh mozzarella or a dollop of crème fraîche or mascarpone as soon as they come out of the oven. These can be served hot or cold. **Serves 4**

2 thick slices Sourdough bread (p. 847)
3 garlic cloves, 2 finely chopped, 1 peeled
500 g (1 lb 2 oz) cherry tomatoes, cut in half
16 black olives, pitted and finely chopped

4 oregano sprigs, leaves torn
4 flat-leaf (Italian) parsley sprigs, leaves chopped
125 ml (4 fl oz/½ cup) extra-virgin olive oil
4 red capsicums (bell peppers), cut in half lengthways, seeds removed

16 anchovies, split lengthways
2 tablespoons red-wine vinegar

Staples
EVOO, S&P

Pair with
Great with Salt-baked fish (p. 175) or simply cooked fish fillets.

Serve with a schnitzel or minute steak.

Make these the centrepiece of a vegetable feast with a selection of roasted vegetables, grain salads and the like.

Preheat the oven to 150°C (300°F) fan-forced.

Toast or grill the bread well so that it's firm and scorched on the outside. Rub the toast with the whole garlic clove on both sides. Smash the toast into rough crumbs.

Toss the toast crumbs into a bowl. Add the tomatoes, olives and herbs, season with salt and pepper, drizzle in half the oil and combine.

Lay the capsicum halves in a baking dish so they fit snugly, then fill with the tomato mixture. Crisscross with the anchovies, then drizzle with the vinegar and remaining oil.

Bake for 1 hour, until the capsicum shells are coloured and collapsing.

Fried green tomatoes ⓖⓕ ⓥ

Tomatoes that don't ripen can still be used for preserving or pickling, or they can be fried. Dust <u>tomato</u> slices in <u>semolina or cornmeal</u> – or dip in <u>egg white</u> and <u>milk</u> first to make a heavier coating – then pan-fry to crisp the outside and soften the tomato. Serve with Spicy aïoli (p. 76) or hot sauce by themselves, or with bacon and eggs or fresh mozzarella and soft herbs.

Baked tomatoes stuffed with rice, feta & pine nuts GF

Filled with gently spiced rice, laced with cheese and pine nuts, these roasted tomatoes are a true delight. You can serve them hot or cold to equally impressive effect, whether as a side to lamb or fish, or as a light meal with a dollop of yoghurt and a salad. **Serves 4–6**

Pair with

These benefit from a dollop of Yoghurt (p. 365) or Tzatziki (p. 507).

Serve with grilled fish or Slow-roasted lamb shoulder (p. 304).

Pan-seared tomatoes on toast with feta & dill V

Dice a few very ripe tomatoes and slice a clove of garlic. Add the garlic and 100 ml (3½ fl oz) extra-virgin olive oil to a frying pan and bring up to a warm temperature over a medium heat. When the garlic is fragrant and starting to colour, add the tomato and season with salt and pepper. Cook for a minute or so to soften, then spike with a couple of teaspoons of sherry vinegar and cook for 5 minutes. Toast some thick Sourdough bread (p. 847), then butter generously. Throw a handful of chopped dill into the pan, toss, then pile onto the toast. Crumble over some feta or drop on some fried haloumi and serve. This is also great with some thickly cut grilled or pan-fried bacon.

12 vine-ripened tomatoes
1 white onion, finely diced
4 garlic cloves, finely chopped
2 teaspoons dried Greek oregano (rigani)
1½ teaspoons ground cinnamon
1 teaspoon ground allspice

450 g (1 lb oz) short-grain white rice
800 ml (27 fl oz) White chicken stock (p. 54)
100 g (3½ oz) feta, crumbled
80 g (2¾ oz) parmesan, or a Greek hard cheese (such as Mizithra)
80 g (2¾ oz/½ cup) pine nuts, toasted

1½ teaspoons dried mint
juice of 1 lemon
80 ml (2½ fl oz/⅓ cup) white wine
150 ml (5 fl oz) water

Staples
EVOO, S&P

Cut the tops off the tomatoes and scoop out the flesh. Reserve the tops and pulp separately. Season the inside of the tomatoes with salt and turn upside down to drain a little.

Heat a few tablespoons of oil in a saucepan over a high heat. Add the onion and garlic and fry until golden, about 4 minutes. Add the tomato flesh, oregano and spices, season with salt and pepper and stir to combine. Add the rice and stir for a minute, then stir the stock through.

Bring to a simmer, then reduce the heat to low. Cover and cook for about 12 minutes, until the rice is just under-cooked. Cool to room temperature.

Meanwhile, preheat the oven to 165°C (330°F) fan-forced.

Add the feta, parmesan, pine nuts, dried mint and lemon juice to the rice and combine well, seasoning as needed. Stuff the mixture firmly into the tomatoes and arrange in an oiled ceramic baking dish. They should fit in neatly without being too snug. Top with the reserved tomato tops. Pour the wine and water into the dish and drizzle over a few tablespoons of oil.

Cover with baking paper, then foil. Bake for 40 minutes, then uncover and cook for a further 20 minutes.

Stand for 5 minutes before serving.

Make it different
Baked zucchini stuffed with rice, feta & pine nuts. Stuff hollowed-out zucchini (courgette) halves in the same way, chopping up the scooped-out flesh along with a tomato, and proceeding as per the recipe.

Make it vegetarian/vegan V VG
Simply use Classic white vegetable stock (p. 51) instead of chicken stock.

Use vegetable stock, omit the cheese and increase the pine nuts by half, with the same weight in currants (added with the stock). Double the parsley.

Domatokeftedes ⓥ

These are a classic Greek appetiser originating in Santorini, where they are often served during Lent. Orthodox Lent is pretty strict on the food front, with all animal products prohibited. So, these are vegan, on religious grounds. And though they may have developed through a process of exclusion, they want for nothing, being intensely flavoured and quite delicious. **Makes about 20**

80 g (2¾ oz) semi-dried tomatoes, or Tomato confit (p. 656)
500 g (1 lb 2 oz/2 cups) peeled (see p. 655), seeded and diced ripe tomatoes
½ large white onion, finely diced
3 garlic cloves, finely chopped

½ bunch of spring onions (scallions), white part only, finely sliced
175 g (6 oz) plain (all-purpose) flour
1 tablespoon baking powder
¼ bunch of flat-leaf (Italian) parsley, leaves very finely chopped

¼ bunch of mint, leaves very finely chopped
1 tablespoon dried Greek oregano (rigani)
oil, for deep-frying (see p. 22)
Greek yoghurt, to serve

Staples
EVOO, LMN, S&P

Pair with

Tahini dip/sauce (p. 71).

Smashed peas.

Use whole to garnish a potato salad.

Serve with tuna or sardines, green beans, olives and soft-boiled eggs, with a dressing of lemon, olive oil and oregano.

Add to a Greek or niçoise salad.

Soak the semi-dried tomatoes in hot water for 20 minutes, then drain well and chop finely.

Season the fresh tomato lightly with salt, then drain off any juices in a colander for about 15 minutes.

Heat a splash of oil in a small frying pan over a medium heat. Add the onion and garlic and fry until just golden, about 4 minutes. Tip into a large bowl.

Add the fresh and dried tomato, spring onion, flour and baking powder, season with salt and pepper, and combine. Stand for 15 minutes before mixing the herbs through.

Heat about 8 cm (3¼ in) of oil in a deep frying pan over a medium heat until about 170°C (340°F).

Working in batches, use a tablespoon to take some of the mixture, flatten it with another spoon, then slip into the oil. Fry for about 3 minutes, turning to cook evenly, then drain on paper towel. The tomato will tend to make the fritters go dark and they won't turn golden, so it's worth breaking one open to check they're cooked.

Serve on a bed of yoghurt with a squeeze of lemon and a sprinkle of salt. The domatokeftedes are best enjoyed hot, but can also be eaten cold.

Green tomato salsa with dill & mint

This is not a recipe for unripe tomatoes, but rather for ripe green-hued varieties, although it works with any good heirloom tomato. When I can get them, green zebra tomatoes are my choice. **Makes about 600 g (1 lb 5 oz/1½ cups)**

3 ripe green or yellow tomatoes (such as zebra), finely diced
1 lemon, peeled, segmented and chopped
2 long green chillies, finely sliced

1 small garlic clove, finely grated
2 handfuls of mint leaves, finely chopped
2 handfuls of dill fronds, finely chopped

80 ml (2½ fl oz/⅓ cup) extra-virgin olive oil
1 tablespoon sherry vinegar
1 tablespoon fish sauce
2 teaspoons ground cumin

Staples
S&P

Pair with

Grilled prawns (see p. 202) or calamari (see p. 223).

Soft tortillas and fried fish.

Slow-baked pulled pork shoulder.

Twice-cooked pork belly with chipotle.

Lay some anchovies on charred bruschetta and spoon the salsa over.

Smear charred bruschetta with ricotta and spoon the salsa over.

Steam open some mussels (see p. 205) and toss with the salsa, or pull off the top shells, arrange the mussels on a platter and spoon the salsa over.

Add all the ingredients to a bowl, season with salt and pepper and combine. Set aside for 15 minutes for the flavours to infuse and mesh before using. The salsa is best enjoyed on the same day.

Spiced creamed tomato soup with bacon (GF)

Pair with

Toast dripping with butter.

Toasted double cheddar and provolone sandwiches.

The secret to this soup is the roasting, which intensifies the flavour of the tomato while taking on the spices. **Serves 10–12**

3 red onions, finely sliced into half-moons

10 garlic cloves, sliced

6 thyme sprigs, leaves picked

2 tablespoons ground cumin

1 tablespoon ground fennel

200 ml (7 fl oz) extra-virgin olive oil

4 × 400 g (14 oz) tins whole tomatoes, or 1.2 kg (2 lb 10 oz) fresh tomatoes, peeled and chopped, juice reserved

2 tablespoons tomato paste (concentrated purée)

1 tablespoon sweet smoked paprika

3 litres (101 fl oz/12 cups) Golden chicken stock (p. 54)

450 ml (15 fl oz) pouring (single/light) cream

8 smoked bacon rashers, guanciale or spec, cut into batons

6 flat-leaf (Italian) parsley sprigs, leaves finely chopped

sour cream, to serve (optional)

Staples
EVOO, S&P

Preheat the oven to 180°C (350°F) fan-forced.

Add the onion, garlic, thyme, cumin, fennel and oil to a roasting tin, season with salt and pepper, then toss to combine. Roast for 15 minutes, then stir and bake for another 5 minutes.

Add the drained tomatoes, tomato paste and paprika to the roasting tin. Season with salt and pepper, toss through and bake for 45 minutes.

Tip the roasted tomato mixture into a large saucepan. Stir in the reserved tomato juice and stock and simmer over a medium heat for 25 minutes.

Blitz the soup with a stick blender. Mix the cream through, bring back up to the boil and turn off the heat. Adjust the seasoning if needed.

Fry the bacon in a frying pan over a medium heat until golden and crisp (you may need some oil, depending on how much fat renders from the bacon). Toss the bacon with the parsley.

Serve the soup with a dollop of sour cream and the bacon mixture sprinkled on top.

Zucchini

Mild in flavour, the zucchini (courgette) is somewhat of a workman-like vegetable that doesn't immediately wow. But I have become quite fond of it over the years. A versatile vegetable, its gentle taste takes on intense flavours very effectively, whether chilli, anchovies, bottarga or punchy cheeses such as parmesan and pecorino. Zucchini can be pickled, stuffed, grilled, braised, roasted, added to soups and stews, eaten raw, baked into fritters or a slice, and even made into a stunning cake (see p. 674). Plus, the flowers are quite a delicacy.

The zucchini is essentially a group of summer squash cultivars, developed some centuries after squash were introduced to Italy from Mesoamerica in the 1500s. We are all familiar with the dark-green version, though there are also pale green, striped and vividly yellow ones. All summer squash belong to the same family, *Cucurbita pepo*, which also includes marrows (simply some varieties of squash that are grown to maturity). Like pumpkins, marrows store well, but they have more limited culinary interest (for me, at least) – though young marrows can be prepared and eaten like zucchini.

Zucchini are the dominant type of summer squash where I live. At farmers' markets you'll sometimes see spaghetti squash (which forms spaghetti-like strands when cooked – but is actually a winter squash), a range of heirloom varieties, as well as scallop or pattypan squash – those small yellow flying saucer–shaped ones, which I find almost universally wanting for both flavour and textural interest. In more specialised stalls and Middle Eastern markets, you will also often find Lebanese zucchini (kusa squash or white zucchini). They are compact and sightly bulbous, typically with a thin, pale-green skin flecked with white, and sweet flesh; they are quite similar to Mexican squash. Lebanese zucchini are ideal for stuffing, then roasting or braising, standing in for stuffed tomato and pepper recipes.

The golden trumpet-like flowers of zucchini are delightful in salads, tossed through pasta at the last minute, or draped over a pizza with buffalo mozzarella and anchovies. Or stuff them with cheese, dip in batter and fry until golden (see p. 668). Zucchini flowers can be both male and female, and are interchangeable in a culinary sense, though the female flower blossoms directly from the fruit (yes, zucchini are fruit – berries, actually – and in fact, each is the ovary of its flower). The female flowers are usually sold with an immature zucchini attached, while the males bloom from a stem. Often, cooks remove the stamen from the male flowers and pistil from the female flowers, and indeed I always used to – but this is not necessary, as they simply taste somewhat like the rest of the flower. I will, however, sometimes remove them when stuffing to make a little more room.

There are many vegetables that seem to always get cooked and are rarely enjoyed raw. I think this is often due to entrenched practices passed down from one generation to the next. But so many vegetables that we normally cook are spectacular raw, such as beetroot (beets), corn, celeriac, brussels sprouts and, of course, zucchini. They have a gentle resistance to the bite, a very pleasing texture and a delicately verdant and creamy flavour. Julienne, grate, finely slice or shave them with a peeler or mandoline into ribbons and add to salads, or quickly pickle in a little vinegar and salt first.

Select zucchini with smooth, unblemished skin; any trace of sliminess or sponginess are warning signs of old produce. Avoid overly large zucchini or ones with thick skins, as their optimal harvest day was missed some time ago. Zucchini in its prime will have quite delicate skin and should be handled with care. Small and medium specimens are best, as they will have the sweetest and most delicate flesh. That's not to say you should discard larger ones if you have them, but they will grow to quite a substantial size if left to their own devices. What we eat are essentially juvenile fruits. Once mature, the seeds develop, the flavour drops away and they can become bitter. Apparently, thorough cooking can render them edible, but I have avoided this necessity so far.

Also see

Summer vegetable lasagne 136

Asparagus with bagna cauda 406

Vegetable bolognese 576

Baked zucchini stuffed with rice, feta & pine nuts 663

Zucchini, coconut & macadamia muffins with lime cream cheese icing 734

Pair with

Zucchini pair well with other typically Mediterranean vegetables such as tomatoes, eggplant (aubergine) and capsicum (bell pepper), as well as peas, garlic and chilli, and herbs such as basil, oregano, marjoram, dill, mint and parsley. Spike them with acid, whether citrus juice or vinegar. Match with cheeses such as mozzarella, burrata, ricotta, Parmigiano Reggiano, pecorino or a sharp goat's curd. They are also a great foil for anchovies and bottarga.

Zucchini 'chips'

At mr. wolf, we served crumbed and fried eggplant (aubergine) and zucchini (courgette) with sesame, cumin and lemon yoghurt. Designed as alternatives to potato chips, they have taken on a life of their own and are extremely popular. Cut zucchini into 2 × 2 cm (¾ × ¾ in) thick fingers, then dust with plain (all-purpose) flour, dredge through beaten egg white and coat with breadcrumbs and sesame seeds. Deep-fry until golden, then sprinkle with a mix of salt and cumin. Stack alternately, so they don't go soggy, and serve with Mayonnaise (see p. 74) and Greek-style yoghurt combined in equal amounts, spiked with chopped lemon segments. These are best eaten quickly – huddle over the plate and devour them, with no polite lingering over the last chip.

Preparing zucchinis

The rough tip of the base should be sliced away, as well as the prickly cuff that attaches to the plant, but nothing else needs to be done. If you need to peel your zucchini (courgettes) and they have large seeds, then you've bought some mature specimens (or probably grown them yourself – it's hard to eat them all in time!), and I have no advice on cooking them. Sorry. In general larger zucchini are better for braising (see p. 671) or slower cooking, while petite ones are best for raw preparations.

Sweet Zuni-style pickles ⓖ ⓥ ⓥⓖ

These pickles are inspired by the version made famous by San Francisco's legendary Zuni Café. They're a modern classic popular for their mustardy sweetness and vibrant crunch. I try to keep them in the fridge for snacking year-round. **Makes 2 × 500 ml (17 fl oz/2 cup) jars**

600 g (1 lb 5 oz) zucchini (courgettes) cut into 1 mm (1/16 in) thick ribbons or 2 mm (1/8 in) thick rounds
1 French shallot, finely sliced
1 garlic clove, finely sliced
1 jalapeño, finely sliced in rounds

3 tablespoons salt flakes
600 ml (20½ fl oz) water

Pickling medium
500 ml (17 fl oz/2 cups) white-wine vinegar, or apple-cider vinegar
230 g (8 oz) raw sugar or white sugar

5 cm (2 in) piece of turmeric, peeled and finely sliced or 1 teaspoon ground turmeric
2 tablespoons yellow mustard seeds
2 teaspoons celery seeds

Add the zucchini, shallot, garlic, jalapeño and salt to a bowl and toss through to coat, then add the water and let stand for 45 minutes.

Meanwhile, bring all the pickling medium ingredients to a simmer over a medium heat. Simmer for 1 minute, then cool completely at room temperature.

Tip the zucchini mix into a colander and drain for 10 minutes to remove all excess water, then pack the mix into the sterilised jars (see p. 40). Pour over the pickling medium to cover completely, then seal with the lids and refrigerate. The pickles can be used once chilled for at least 45 minutes, but they will improve over the next few days. These will keep refrigerated for up to 3 weeks – after that they're still fine to eat but tend to soften.

Stuffed zucchini flowers ⓥ

There's a bit of wow to these stuffed zucchini (courgette) flowers, both visually and when the crisp veil of batter yields to the bite, releasing molten cheese spiked with chilli, lemon and mint. You can play with other cheeses, or dial down or omit the chilli. Plate as a starter, or serve as aperitivo snacks. **Makes 10**

10 zucchini (courgette) flowers, with baby zucchini attached
600 ml (20½ fl oz) Tempura beer batter (p. 187)
oil, for shallow-frying

Ricotta stuffing
250 g (9 oz/1 cup) ricotta, well drained
80 g (2¾ oz) melting cheese (such as manchego or gruyère), finely grated
50 g (1¾ oz) Grana Padano, finely grated

¼ teaspoon chilli powder
1 jalapeño (fresh or pickled), finely diced
15 mint leaves, finely sliced
zest of ½ lemon

Staples
FLR, LMN, S&P

Pair with

Add to steak sandwiches (or a vegetarian version with a grilled garlicky field mushroom), hamburgers, or a rye sourdough sandwich with cheddar and corned or roast beef.

Chicken & corn koftas (p. 249).

Also great to top grilled vegetables, to drop on a grain salad or to accompany a fleet of meze.

Grilled zucchini salad ⓖ ⓥ

Cut a few zucchini (courgettes) into 5 mm (¼ in) slices. Grill on a hot barbecue until tender and charred, then toss gently in good olive oil with a squeeze of lemon or splash of vinegar. Season with salt and pepper, then add some chopped herbs, such as marjoram, basil or mint. Serve with feta, goat's cheese, ricotta or mozzarella. A few currants soaked in vinegar and some toasted pine nuts tossed through would work well, too – or simply squeeze over lots of lemon juice.

Zucchini baba ghanoush (GF)(V)(VG)

I've had the pleasure of cooking with Yotam Ottolenghi on a few occasions, and I never fail to pick up something deliciously new. One time in London, he made a zucchini (courgette) version of baba ghanoush, which was simply delicious. Grill whole zucchini on a hot grill (preferably coals) until charred, then cook on a cool or elevated part of the grill or transfer to a baking tray and oven-roast at 175°C (345°F) fan-forced for 20–30 minutes until soft. Split the zucchini lengthways and scoop out the flesh, discarding the skin. Roughly, for each 200 g (7 oz) of flesh, add a small clove of crushed garlic, a teaspoon of tahini, the juice of ½ lemon and a couple of tablespoons of extra-virgin olive oil, then season with salt and pepper and combine well. Serve as a dip with flatbread or crudités, or with poached eggs or grilled fish. Or, shave raw zucchini into thin ribbons, season with salt and pepper and toss with mint, parsley, virgin oil and a splash of lemon juice or vinegar and pile on top a bed of the purée for a salad for fish, chicken or lamb, or as a contribution to a feast of small dishes.

Add the stuffing ingredients to a bowl, season with salt and combine well. Transfer to a piping (icing) bag fitted with a large nozzle and refrigerate until needed.

Carefully pull back the petals of the zucchini flowers and remove the pistils. Cut the zucchini stalks in half lengthways, about three-quarters of the way up towards the flower end; this will ensure the zucchini cooks evenly. Pipe the mixture into the flowers, dividing evenly, then twist the end of the petals together to seal.

Heat 6 cm (2½ in) of oil in a wide heavy-based saucepan or deep frying pan over a medium heat until 180°C (350°F).

Working in batches, dredge the zucchini in flour, shaking off any excess, then dip in the tempura batter, letting the excess run off. Fry until golden, 3–4 minutes, turning to colour evenly. Season with salt as soon as they come out of the fryer and serve immediately, with lemon wedges.

Crumbed zucchini flowers with crab mayonnaise & peas

This very pretty and delicious starter tends to create a bit of a buzz at the table. It's really not very technical, though, avoiding the fuss that comes with stuffing the flowers. I love the heavy textural crumb on these, and they can be coated ahead of time. If you prefer a lighter coating, you could always use Tempura beer batter (p. 187). **Serves 4**

80 g (2¾ oz/½ cup) peas, fresh or frozen, blanched
160 g (5½ oz/2 cups) fresh white breadcrumbs
zest of 2 lemons
2 eggs
½ teaspoon salt
1 tablespoon water
8 zucchini (courgette) flowers, with baby zucchini attached

oil, for shallow-frying
1 garlic clove, finely chopped
250 g (9 oz) cooked crabmeat
200 g (7 oz) Mayonnaise (p. 74)
125 ml (4 fl oz/½ cup) pouring (single/light) cream, lightly whipped
3 heaped tablespoons plain yoghurt

1 spring onion (scallion), white part only, finely sliced
½ teaspoon cayenne pepper
½ bunch of chives, finely snipped
½ bunch of chervil, leaves picked, to serve
Staples
EVOO, FLR, S&P

Add the peas to a small bowl, season with salt and pepper, drizzle with oil and toss to coat.

Add the breadcrumbs to a shallow bowl and mix in the lemon zest. Beat the eggs with the salt, water and about 10 grinds of pepper.

Cut the baby zucchini in half lengthways, about three-quarters of the way up towards the flower end; this will ensure it cooks evenly. Dredge the zucchini in flour and shake lightly to remove any excess. Dip in the egg and drain off the excess. Coat with the breadcrumb mixture and set aside, uncovered, for 10 minutes.

Heat about 6 cm (2½ in) of oil in a large heavy-based saucepan or deep frying pan over a medium heat until 180°C (350°F).

Meanwhile, add a splash of oil to a small saucepan over a low heat. Add the garlic and fry gently until fragrant, about 30 seconds. Take off the heat and stir the crabmeat through.

Add the mayonnaise, cream, yoghurt, spring onion and cayenne pepper to a bowl, squeeze in half a lemon and combine. Add the crabmeat, season with salt and pepper and combine gently.

Fry the zucchini until golden, 3–4 minutes, turning to colour evenly. Drain on paper towel.

To serve, spoon the crab mixture onto each plate, then top with the zucchini flowers. Scatter the peas and herbs over the top and serve with a lemon wedge.

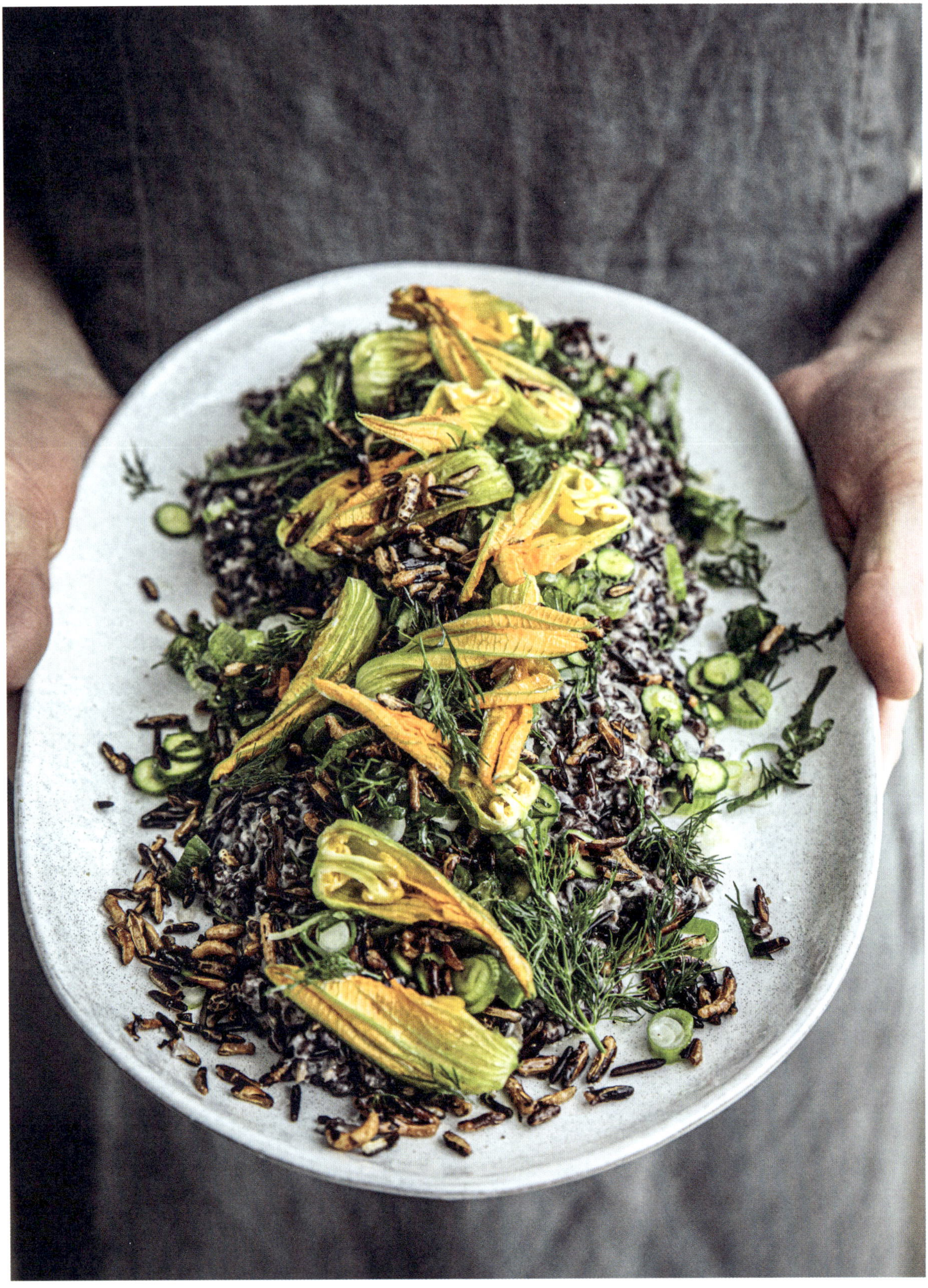

Zucchini flower, wild rice, lentil & yoghurt salad (GF) (V)

This filling salad is both fresh and earthy, with a wealth of textural contrasts. It makes for a delicious light meal, and is also great the next day. **Serves 4**

Pair with

Serve with grilled koftas (pp. 249, 309), Falafel (p. 432), baked fish (pp. 175–6) or a simple roast chicken (see p. 229).

Southern Italian fried zucchini (GF) (V) (VG)

This very simple preparation captures the flavours and rustic simplicity of southern Italian cooking. Thickly slice some zucchini (courgettes) and deep-fry in quality olive oil (the flavour is important here) for a few minutes until golden. Drain and cool a little, then toss with plenty of torn mint leaves, some chilli flakes and a generous squeeze of lemon, seasoning to taste. Serve as a warm side to grilled fish, minute steak, lamb chops or the like, or as an antipasto.

Braised zucchini with fresh tomato & herbs (GF) (V)

A slightly more mature zucchini (courgette), say 20 cm (8 in) long, works well braised. Cut 3 zucchini into 4 cm (1½ in) thick rounds and add to a casserole dish with 3 smashed garlic cloves, a bay leaf, 100 ml (3½ fl oz) extra-virgin olive oil and 200 ml (7 fl oz) water. Season well with salt and pepper, cover tightly with a lid and braise for about 40 minutes at 160°C (320°F) fan-forced. Finely dice 2 large ripe tomatoes and combine with a good squeeze of lemon juice and a few handfuls of mint, parsley and/or coriander (cilantro). Pile the tomato mix on top of the zucchini and serve with a big dollop of thick yoghurt. Great with lamb, grilled chicken, baked whole fish or couscous.

---

150 g (5½ oz/¾ cup) black wild rice
2 teaspoons cumin seeds
120 g (4½ oz/⅔ cup) green lentils
oil, for shallow-frying
6 zucchini (courgette) flowers, with baby zucchini attached

1 garlic clove, finely grated
juice ½ lemon
150 g (5½ oz) Greek-style yoghurt
2 spring onions (scallions), white part only, finely sliced
1 handful of mint leaves
1 handful of dill fronds

Staples
EVOO, S&P

Special equipment
Mandoline

Add 100 g (3½ oz) of the wild rice and the cumin seeds to a saucepan of lightly salted simmering water and cook until just tender, about 20 minutes, then drain. Meanwhile, add the lentils to another saucepan of lightly salted cold water, bring to a simmer and cook until tender, about 12 minutes, then drain.

Meanwhile, heat 3 cm (1¼ in) of oil in a small saucepan until about 200°C (400°F). Fry the remaining wild rice in batches until it puffs up, which will only take a few seconds – if it doesn't puff quickly, the oil is too cool. Drain on paper towel.

Detach the flowers from the zucchini. Split the flowers in half, or quarters if large. Finely slice the zucchini in rounds using a mandoline.

Add the sliced zucchini, garlic and a splash of oil to a large bowl, season with salt and pepper and toss. Add the boiled wild rice and combine. Add the zucchini flowers and lemon juice and toss gently.

To another bowl, add the lentils, yoghurt, spring onion, mint, most of the dill and a splash of oil, season and combine.

Spread the lentil mixture on a serving plate. Top with the wild rice mixture. Scatter the puffed wild rice and remaining dill over and serve.

Make it faster
You can skip the step of frying the wild rice, and simply use puffed rice or pepitas (pumpkin seeds).

Make it different
With zucchini. If zucchini flowers are not available, you could use two small white or green zucchini, and either finely shave them raw, or blanch very quickly in boiling water and refresh in cold. Garnish with nasturtium or marigold flowers.

Make it a meal
Make the salad more substantial by adding grilled asparagus, and topping with a few halved soft-boiled eggs.

Ratatouille GF V VG

A classic Provençal preparation, ratatouille is one of those dishes that inspires great loyalty for particular renditions, from the rustic to the decidedly fancy, with separately cooked and carefully assembled components. I prefer the former, and for me a slick of good oil is absolutely key. This can be served warm or at room temperature – and like almost any braise, stew or ragù of this nature, it is always better the next day. **Serves 8–10**

3 large eggplants (aubergines), pricked with a fork
4 red capsicums (bell peppers)
150 ml (5 fl oz) extra-virgin olive oil
2 onions, sliced
6 garlic cloves, finely chopped
2 fresh bay leaves
2 tablespoons dried oregano
6 zucchini (courgettes), cut into 2 cm (¾ in) rounds
400 g (14 oz) tin diced tomatoes
1 tablespoon tomato paste (concentrated purée)
2 teaspoons brown sugar
zest of ½ orange
juice of 1 orange

Staples
EVOO, LMN, S&P

Preheat the oven to 180°C (350°F) fan-forced.

Add the eggplants to a roasting tin and bake for 1 hour, until tender. Once cooled, cut them in half, then scoop out and roughly chop the flesh.

Scorch the capsicums directly on stovetop burners until charred and tender; you can also grill or barbecue them on high heat. Add to a bowl, cover with a plate and set aside to sweat for 15 minutes. Remove the skins and discard the seeds, then dice the flesh into rough 3 cm (1¼ in) squares.

Heat the oil in a large saucepan over a medium heat. Add the onion and garlic and cook until softened, about 5 minutes. Add the herbs and cook for 5 minutes, then add the capsicum and cook for about 10 minutes.

Stir in the eggplant flesh, zucchini, tomato, tomato paste, sugar, orange zest and juice. Season with salt and pepper and simmer slowly for about 45 minutes, until the zucchini is tender but still just holding its shape. The mixture will be quite stiff to start with, but the zucchini will let out quite a bit of water as it cooks. It's important to stir regularly so it doesn't catch.

Squeeze in some lemon juice before serving warm or cold.

Make it different
Warm some ratatouille in a baking dish. Make hollows in the mixture with a kitchen spoon and crack an egg in each. Bake in a moderate oven until the whites are set. This is a delicious breakfast dish – but some white anchovies or quality pinked-fleshed anchovies in oil criss-crossed over the top at the end make it a more serious brunch, lunch or even supper offering.

Pair with
Eat on its own with toasted Sourdough bread (p. 847), or top the bread with ricotta or melted mozzarella and spoon some ratatouille over.

Serve as a side with baked whole fish, grilled lamb or chicken, or as an addition to a vegetarian feast.

Sear sardine fillets, skin side down, until cooked and golden, then serve with ratatouille spooned over the top.

Roasted zucchini with anchovy, oregano & chilli GF

Cut a few zucchini (courgettes) into 3 cm (1¼ in) pieces. Toss with a few chopped anchovies, dried oregano, chilli flakes, salt and pepper and lots of extra-virgin olive oil. Roast in a baking dish for 25 minutes at 180°C (350°F) fan-forced until colouring at the edges. Squeeze lemon juice over just before serving. Serve with lamb chops, couscous, braised beans or fish.

Zucchini, ham & pea slice with feta

This slice is a lunchbox favourite in my house, and a handy option in the fridge for those hungry afternoon moments – for people of all ages. And it's loaded with vegetables and protein. You could use gluten-free flour in this, if preferred. **Serves 10**

Pair with
Serve with Tzatziki (p. 507) or Hummus (p. 374) and cherry tomatoes as an after-school snack.

Zucchini & cream soup with cumin ⒼⒻ Ⓥ

In a saucepan, bring 1 litre (34 fl oz/4 cups) Golden chicken stock (p. 54) or Classic white vegetable stock (p. 51) and 2 finely sliced boiling (waxy) potatoes (such as desiree or Dutch cream) to the boil. Cook until tender, about 10 minutes. Stir in 300 ml (10 fl oz) pouring (single/light) cream and 2 teaspoons dijon mustard, then turn off the heat. Melt 150 g (5½ oz) butter in a large saucepan over a medium heat. Add 1 finely diced onion and 5 finely sliced garlic cloves and cook until softened, about 5 minutes. Add 500 g (1 lb 2 oz) diced zucchini (courgette) and 3 teaspoons ground cumin, and season with salt and pepper. Cook, stirring frequently, for about 10 minutes, then add another 500 g (1 lb 2 oz) zucchini and cook until just tender, about 5 minutes. Add the stock mixture and bring to a simmer. Use a stick blender to blitz the soup until smooth, or remove one-quarter of the soup, blitz what's in the pan and then return the rest, which gives a mix of silky soup and chunky texture. Serve with a drizzle of oil. For a greener, more herbaceous result, omit the cumin and add a few handfuls of basil, coriander (cilantro) and/or mint before blitzing. Serves 6–8.

Pair with

These fritters are great served with Tzatziki (p. 507) or just some minted yoghurt.

They also go well with chicken, grilled lamb or fish.

- 500 g (1 lb 2 oz) zucchini (courgettes), coarsely grated
- 4 spring onions (scallions), white and most of the green parts, finely sliced
- 2 garlic cloves, finely grated
- 150 g (5½ oz) smoked ham, finely diced
- 2½ teaspoons ground cumin
- 6 eggs, lightly beaten

- 180 g (6½ oz) self-raising flour
- 1 teaspoon baking powder
- 200 g (7 oz) feta, crumbled, or grated cheddar
- 100 g (3½ oz) Grana Padano, finely grated
- 100 g (3½ oz/⅔ cup) frozen peas, thawed
- ½ bunch of flat-leaf (Italian) parsley, leaves finely chopped

Toppings
- 1 small zucchini (courgette), finely sliced
- 2 tablespoons pepitas (pumpkin seeds)
- 2 tablespoons sunflower seeds
- 1½ teaspoons cumin seeds

Staples
EVOO, S&P

Preheat the oven to 175°C (345°F) fan-forced. Line a 25 cm (10 in) springform tin with baking paper.

Sprinkle the grated zucchini with salt and set aside in a colander to drain. After 15 minutes, squeeze out the excess liquid, then add to a large bowl and set aside.

Heat a good splash of oil in a frying pan over a medium heat. Add the spring onion and garlic and cook until softened, about 2 minutes. Add the ham and cumin and cook for 2–3 minutes.

Tip the ham mixture in with the zucchini. Add the remaining slice ingredients and combine well.

Pour the mixture into the springform tin, scatter the toppings over and bake for 40–45 minutes, until cooked through. Serve hot or cold.

Make it different

Grease a muffin tin, then roughly line each hole with half a slice of ham. Continue as per the recipe, but adjust the cooking time to 20–25 minutes, baking until puffed and golden.

Make it a meal

Because it's already full of vegetables and protein, it only takes a simple dressed salad to turn this into a meal.

Zucchini & haloumi fritters with burnt honey sauce Ⓥ

The burnt honey sauce adds sweetness, naturally, which is a great foil for the salty haloumi, but it also layers in a caramelised intrigue to these verdant fritters. These can be served as a starter or finger food at a party. **Serves 4–6**

- 6–8 zucchini (courgettes)
- 100 g (3½ oz/⅔ cup) plain (all-purpose) flour
- 100 g (3½ oz) cornflour (cornstarch)
- 2 teaspoons baking powder
- 2 teaspoons ground cumin
- ½ teaspoon salt flakes
- 2 large eggs
- 150 g (5½ oz) baby peas, fresh or frozen, blanched

and processed to a roughly smooth paste
- 2 spring onions (scallions), white part only, sliced
- 1 garlic clove, finely grated
- ¼ bunch of mint, leaves chopped
- 200 g (7 oz) haloumi, cut into 5 mm (¼ in) dice
- 300 ml (10 fl oz) oil, for shallow-frying

Burnt honey sauce
- 250 g (9 oz) honey
- 100 ml (3½ fl oz) sherry vinegar
- 2 tablespoons extra-virgin olive oil
- ½ teaspoon ground white pepper
- ¼ teaspoon salt flakes

Staples
LMN, S&P

For the honey sauce, heat the honey in a small saucepan over a high heat until it turns a medium to dark colour, 5–6 minutes. Stir the vinegar through. Bring to a simmer, then take off the heat. Stir in the oil, pepper and salt. Cool to room temperature before using.

Coarsely grate the zucchini (you should have 500–600 g/1 lb 2 oz–1 lb 5 oz), season with salt and stand for 5 minutes, then squeeze out the excess moisture. Once salted and squeezed you should have about 350–400 g (12½–14 oz)

Sift the flour, cornflour, baking powder and cumin into a large bowl. Add the salt and combine. Make a well in the centre.

In a separate bowl, whisk the eggs, then mix in the zucchini and peas. Gradually add the zucchini mixture to the dry ingredients until you have a smooth, stiff batter. Fold in the spring onion, garlic, mint and haloumi.

Heat the oil in a frying pan over a medium heat, until the oil is hot enough that it sizzles when a small amount of batter is dropped in. Working in batches to keep the oil temperature up, spoon in 2 tablespoons of batter per fritter and cook until the underside of each fritter is golden, about 2 minutes. Flip and cook until golden on the other side. Drain on paper towel, then serve warm, with the honey sauce.

Make it different

Skip the honey sauce and serve the fritters with bacon and poached eggs for breakfast.

For a main course, serve with Tzatziki (p. 507), lemon wedges and a salad.

The honey sauce can also be served with grilled skewers of fish, lamb or pork, with fresh pulled curd cheeses such as burrata and fior di latte, or drizzled over charred vegetables.

Spiced zucchini & walnut cake ⓥ

Given the amount of zucchini (courgette) in this cake, I think I'm entitled to call it healthy. Plus, there's the antioxidant-rich extra-virgin olive oil, walnuts and protein-rich eggs. There is admittedly a little sugar, too, but I'm turning a blind eye to that. The texture of this cake is so luscious and moist. You can actually dial the sugar down a bit – even by half – and the cake is still very successful, if a little less moist and caramelised. Many cakes like this call for a neutral-flavoured oil, such as vegetable, but extra-virgin olive oil is so much better for you, and I love the richness of flavour it adds. **Serves 8–10**

3 eggs
250 ml (8½ fl oz/1 cup) extra-virgin olive oil
300 g (10½ oz) light brown sugar
2 teaspoons vanilla extract
300 g (10½ oz/2 cups) plain (all-purpose) flour

2 teaspoons ground cinnamon
1½ teaspoons ground cloves
2 teaspoons ground ginger
1½ teaspoons bicarbonate of soda (baking soda)
1 teaspoon baking powder
1 teaspoon salt

270 g (9½ oz /2 cups) grated zucchini (courgette), squeezed gently of excess moisture
160 g (5½ oz/1⅔ cups) toasted walnuts, chopped

Preheat the oven to 175°C (345°F) conventional. Grease and flour a 21 cm (8¼ in) ring (bundt) tin or a standard loaf (bar) tin of 22–25 cm (8¾–10 in).

Beat the eggs with the oil, using a hand whisk or electric beaters. Add the sugar and vanilla and beat until creamy.

Sift or whisk the dry ingredients, then fold into the egg mixture with the zucchini and nuts, combining well.

Pour into the cake tin and bake for 55–60 minutes, until springy to touch and deeply golden.

Zucchini & pesto pasta ⓥ

Shredded zucchini (courgette) tossed through pasta with a generous amount of pesto is delicious. I only discovered this when experimenting with using zucchini as a replacement for the pasta itself. I can appreciate the nutritional benefits of doing so, and the motivation if one has a gluten intolerance – but for me, nothing can replace good pasta. Happily, a 50–50 compromise didn't taste like a compromise at all, rather a verdantly delightful and quite nutritious meal. Cut zucchini into ribbons a similar thickness to your pasta; a tagliatelle shape works well. To feed four to six people, use 500 g (1 lb 2 oz) pasta to 500 g (1 lb 2 oz) zucchini, adding the zucchini to the pasta pot for the last 30 seconds of cooking, then toss with plenty of Pesto (p. 90). I like to use hazelnuts instead of pine nuts in the pesto for this, which just adds a bit more depth of flavour, though the creamy texture and flavour of pine nuts are a great match for zucchini, too – you choose.

Pair with

Top with a basic Cream cheese icing (p. 803) or simple lemon icing (see p. 802).

Zucchini & haloumi fritters with burnt honey sauce (p. 673)

Fruit

Apple

I used to work on a signature apple dessert at Tansy's when I was an apprentice. It was one of those dishes with a 20-minute-wait caveat on the menu. You don't see that very often anymore. We would hollow out golden delicious apples and par-bake them, before stuffing them with spiced granny smith flesh studded with fruit and nuts and bound with egg yolks and cream. They were then roasted and served on a puff pastry base, and finished with a Calvados, apple cider and apple butter sauce. Served with heavenly cinnamon ice cream, the dish embraced apples from many angles, with different textures and real complexity of flavour. A lot of work, for sure, from the apples to the house-made ice cream and puff pastry – but so worth it.

Apples are the most common of fruit, ubiquitous in the markets year-round, and perhaps taken for granted because of it. But a tree-ripened apple in the flush of its season is a thing of immense beauty, and well worth celebrating. Apples are ready-made snacks, with any intervention entirely unnecessary – but they are also marvellous cooked, and I love their sweetness buttressed with crunchy texture and bracing acidity in savoury dishes, too.

The apples readily available to us are limited to a handful of varieties, mainly crossbred to be pleasingly sweet, with fresh but not jarring acid, a low presence of phenolic tannins (the grippy stuff in wine grapes and wine) and good storage properties. Some of these apples are unquestionably delicious, but when you consider there are more than 7000 apple cultivars, we must be missing out just a little.

In terms of eating apples, that balance of sweetness, freshness, flavour and lack of astringency makes a lot of sense. If, however, you want to cook with them, more acidity and even a bit of grip can work extremely well. Making cider? Well, some of the harshly tannic apples lend structure and flavour nuance to the brew – though you certainly wouldn't want to eat them raw.

For the home, some eating and cooking apples are all that's really required, but it's worth expanding your horizons during autumn at farmers' markets, as a host of intriguing varieties are sold only in season, being not great candidates for long-term cold storage. Aside from a couple of varieties such as royal gala, which are also picked in late summer, the majority of apples are harvested in autumn.

Apples can be kept in cold storage for a few months, and heightened measures such as reducing the oxygen level in their storage facility and introducing a molecule that shuts down an apple's ethylene receptors, will inhibit further ripening and keep them for as long as 12 months. I am guilty of buying apples all year round, so I'm not going to stand in judgement of these methods – but please do engage with apples when they are abundant and in the shimmering peak of their season.

Granny smiths have long been a real workhorse apple in Australia, since first being discovered as a chance mutation in the garden of a Mrs Smith in New South Wales in the 1860s. They are great as a cooking apple, becoming fluffy and luscious, and make for a great purée, but for those who enjoy tartly crunchy eating apples, they also fit the bill well. They also hold their shape when raw, so when julienned for a salad, they remain reliably crisp. What the granny smith is to Australia, the bramley is to Britain, being a fabled cooking apple. Both have excellent flavour and similarly tart acidity, meaning that the sweetness of the cooked apple is balanced and intense but not cloying.

Golden delicious apples are a bit of a favourite, and ones I love to cook with, their sugars caramelising readily and picking up real depth of flavour. They are probably one of the lightest and crispest of apples – except when they're not. Golden delicious are marvellous when ripe, but picked green and kept too long in storage, or just past their peak, and their texture becomes soft and floury,

Also see

Soy, sesame & apple vinaigrette 102

Celeriac, apple & kale slaw with anchovy 484–5

Waldorf salad with roast chicken wrapped in iceberg 490

Quick quince & apple relish 716

Caramelised spiced cider apples 769

Apple, blueberry & blackberry galette 818

Pair with

Apples love sugar, maple syrup, honey, vanilla, butter, cream, brandy, sherry, and warm spices such as cinnamon, cloves and allspice. Nuts such as pecans, walnuts and almonds are fine matches, as is sesame/tahini and dried fruit. Spike with lemon juice and sherry vinegar and pair with cheese (gruyère, cheddar, aged goat's cheese, and sheep's feta are great), pork, bacon and chicken.

and they lose much of their charm as an eating apple. Ideally, they should be ripened fully on the tree. Red delicious share little with golden delicious other than their name, being from different parentage, but they do also have a tendency to be disappointing if not at their peak – and they are not terribly inspiring even at their best.

Pink Lady is one of the most prominent apples in our markets. It's about my favourite readily available eating apple, along with the red fuji, a Japanese cultivar developed in the 1930s from two American apples.

They're both good everyday apples, a little sweet, aromatic, with a full apple flavour, a lovely refreshing tartness and good crisp crunch. Pink Lady is actually a trademark, with the growing and distribution of the apples tightly controlled. It's not that you can't grow the same variety, which is called cripps pink – an Australian cross of lady williams and golden delicious; it's just that the Pink Lady mark is reserved for apples that meet a colour and quality level. Which, mind you, is not to say that a cripps pink grower doesn't sell apples of the same standard.

Less easy to find, but marvellous as a flavourful, crisp eating apple, is the early-season akane apple, another 1930s Japanese cultivar.

Jonathan apples were once the emblematic American apple, and they were the quintessential lunchbox apple when I was growing up. They're generally a good size for children, with a fine apple flavour, snappy bite and a lovely balance of sweetness and acidity. They are somewhat less prevalent these days, but they're a lovely eating apple. They also happen to help pollinate most other apple cultivars, so their presence in orchards is unlikely to ever disappear, even if their market share has dropped drastically.

Cox's orange pippin is an English heirloom variety that is hard to find in Australia. It has a short season and is not often commercially available, but is worth seeking out at farmers' markets. It's red–orange in colour and very aromatic, bright and crisp, with rich, sweet flavours and a fresh tartness. It's the apple variety that seems to be the standard bearer for reintroducing heritage varieties, and it's a worthy choice. If you're considering the long haul of planting your own apple tree, put this one right at the top of your list.

Unlike pears, apples are typically sold ready to eat. They should be firm in the hand, with vibrant skin. That doesn't mean they need to be glossy – wax can fool you here – but apples shouldn't look dull or tired. Naturally, avoid those with any soft spots or dents. Apples that have been held in cold storage for an extended period will have a short shelf life, so they will need to be eaten reasonably soon after purchase. The time of year should be a guide here, with apples perhaps best avoided in early to mid summer – and with all that stone fruit around, who's buying apples anyway?

Preparing apples

Apples require no special preparation. Sometimes I'll leave the stem and core in place when cooking, to keep the natural form. I'll only ever remove the skin when it gets in the way, intruding on the texture of cooked apple at times. If slicing, take the cheeks off from two sides, and then between the remaining two, avoiding the core, then lay flat and slice. Cut apple will oxidise reasonably quickly, though not as aggressively as, say, an artichoke. As with artichokes, lemon juice will halt the browning process. In general, though, slice apple when needed, rather than prepping too early.

Apple, fennel & witlof slaw with buttermilk dressing GF V

This a somewhat fancy slaw. The marriage of these ingredients is just so complementary, with sweet and tangy apple, fresh aniseedy fennel and the gently bitter witlof being brought together with the rich, sour buttermilk dressing. **Serves 6**

2 granny smith or Pink Lady apples, julienned
1 fennel bulb, sliced into 2 mm (⅛ in) rounds
2 chicory (witlof/endive), one with leaves separated, the other sliced on an angle 2 cm (¾ in) thick
½ white salad onion, finely sliced into half-moons
5 flat-leaf (Italian) parsley stalks, leaves picked, large ones torn
1 × quantity Buttermilk dressing (p. 361)
50 g (1¾ oz) toasted almonds or pecans, tossed in oil, seasoned and chopped

Add the apple, fennel, sliced witlof, onion and parsley to a large bowl and combine.

Arrange the witlof leaves on a plate, with the cup side facing up, and pile in the slaw mixture. Drizzle the dressing over and stand for 2 minutes, then scatter with the nuts and serve.

Make it different
With cheese. To enrich this further to serve with grilled steaks or roasted meats, finish the salad with a veil of finely grated parmesan, or crumble over some gorgonzola and finish with plenty of freshly ground black pepper.

Pear, fennel & witlof slaw with buttermilk dressing. GF V Replace the apple with pear.

Pair with

Schnitzel-style crumbed meats or pork chops.

Seared fish fillets, or smoked trout, salmon or eel.

Vegetable salads featuring roasted beetroot (beet) or celeriac.

Quick apple & witlof salad GF V VG

Finely julienne an apple, any variety you like, as long as it's crisp and tasty. Toss with finely sliced chicory (witlof/endive), or drum head or savoy cabbage, and dress with lemon juice and an exceptional oil – extra-virgin olive, or cold-pressed walnut or hazelnut oil – and season well with salt and pepper. Serve with roast chicken, or a chunk of premium cooked curd cheese. A handful of new-season walnuts would also be lovely.

Simply cooked apples GF V

This is an easy way to cook apples for a pie filling, turnover or cake, to to serve with crepes or to partner custard or ice cream. **Makes about 350 g (12½ oz)**

60 g (2 oz/¼ cup) unsalted butter

2½ tablespoons caster (superfine) sugar, or brown sugar

6 golden delicious or granny smith apples, peeled and cut into 2 cm (¾ in) dice
juice of ½ lemon

Add the butter and sugar to a large frying pan over a medium heat. Once melted, add the diced apple and toss once. Cover, reduce the heat to low and cook for 10 minutes.

Uncover the pan. Squeeze in the lemon juice and toss through once. Cook for a further 3 minutes, until the apple is golden, translucent and caramelised.

Make it different

With spices. Add ½ vanilla bean, ½ teaspoon vanilla extract, 1 clove or ½ teaspoon ground cinnamon.

Without sugar. Cut a plain cooked apple into 1 cm (½ in) dice, then spread out in a large frying pan over a high heat. Cook for 8–10 minutes, until tender, stirring gently three times with a spatula to keep the dice intact; the apple will steam lightly in its own juices.

Apple & cherry turnovers V

Pair with

Cream or ice cream.

Mum often served us turnovers as kids, and they were always so satisfying, especially with a generous drizzle of cream or a scoop of ice cream. The dried cherries in these provide an appealing flavour and texture contrast to the cooked apple. **Makes 12–14**

150 g (5½ oz) dried cherries, roughly chopped
100 ml (3½ fl oz) cherry liqueur, or brandy
6 Pink Lady apples, peeled and cut into 2 cm (¾ in) dice

70 g (2½ oz) unsalted butter
70 g (2½ oz) caster (superfine) sugar
2 tablespoons honey
3–4 Puff pastry (p. 822) sheets, each cut into 4 squares

1 egg, whisked
2 tablespoons flaked almonds
icing (confectioners') sugar, for dusting

Add the cherries to a small bowl with the liqueur and set aside to rehydrate for 30 minutes.

Add the diced apple, butter, caster sugar and honey to a large frying pan over a medium heat and cook for 5 minutes. Stir in the cherries and liqueur and cook for about 15 minutes, until the fruit is soft and the liquid is reduced and sticky. Set aside to cool completely.

Preheat the oven to 200°C (400°F) fan-forced. Line two baking trays with baking paper.

Brush the edges of a pastry square with egg. Place a heaped tablespoon of the filling in the centre, then fold one corner of the pastry over to the opposite corner, making a triangular parcel. Press the edges together and twist the corners to seal, then place on a baking tray. Repeat until the filling is used.

Brush the parcels with more egg and scatter with the almonds.

Bake for 20–25 minutes, until golden. Dust with icing sugar and serve.

Make it different

Fruit-spiked apple & peach turnovers. V The cherries can be replaced with dried peaches soaked in fruit brandy. You could also use apricots.

Tarte tatin ⓥ

This is a classic tarte tatin, bursting with buttery, caramelised apple flavour. It's such a simple presentation, yet it takes my breath away every time I flip it over. And the scent of apples cooking in the house almost sets me in a trance – I find the aroma so soothing. This dish may seem a little intimidating at first, but it's really not hard to get a great result. A copper tarte tatin pan is perfect, or you can use any appropriately sized ovenproof pan with curved sides (and preferably with a removable handle). This recipe is rather special, as it's from my sister Odette, who is a fabulous pastry chef. **Serves 6–8**

Pair with

Whipped cream, ice cream or Vanilla crème anglaise (p. 800).

400 g (14 oz) Classic puff pastry (p. 822), Rough puff pastry (p. 823), or a 400 g (14 oz) block of quality puff pastry

200 g (7 oz) chilled unsalted butter, finely sliced
200 g (7 oz) caster (superfine) sugar

1 vanilla bean, sliced on an angle (optional)
12 large granny smith apples

Roll out the pastry to about 1.5 cm (½ in) thick, then cut out a 30 cm (12 in) circle. Rest on baking paper in the fridge until required. (Always rest the pastry after rolling, and keep it chilled, otherwise it will shrink too much.)

Line a 28 cm (11 in) ovenproof pan or copper tatin pan with the butter, smearing it in to cover evenly. Evenly sprinkle over one-third of the sugar. Scatter with the vanilla, if using.

Peel the apples, then cut the flesh away from the cores in cheeks. Slice about 5 mm (¼ in) thick, fanning the apples into the pan as you slice, working in a spiral from the middle out, continuing until the base is covered and you have used half the apple.

Sprinkle another third of the sugar evenly over the top, then fan the remaining apple slices around in the same fashion, finishing with the remaining sugar.

Cover the apples with a circle of baking paper, then seal with foil. Place the pan over a low heat and cook for 45 minutes. The apples will cook and the sugar will caramelise very slowly.

Near the end of cooking, preheat the oven to 210°C (410°F) fan-forced.

Take the pan off the heat and remove the foil and paper. There will be quite a bit of liquid, which may seem odd, but don't worry. Cover the pan with the pastry, quickly tucking the overhang down the sides of the pan.

Bake for about 30 minutes, until the pastry is golden. There will be syrup bubbling at the edges of the pan; it's important to let this set and be absorbed before trying to invert.

Remove from the oven and stand for about 20 minutes, until the syrup has started to thicken.

Cover the pastry with a serving plate larger than the pan, then gently flip the tart over. Serve warm or cold.

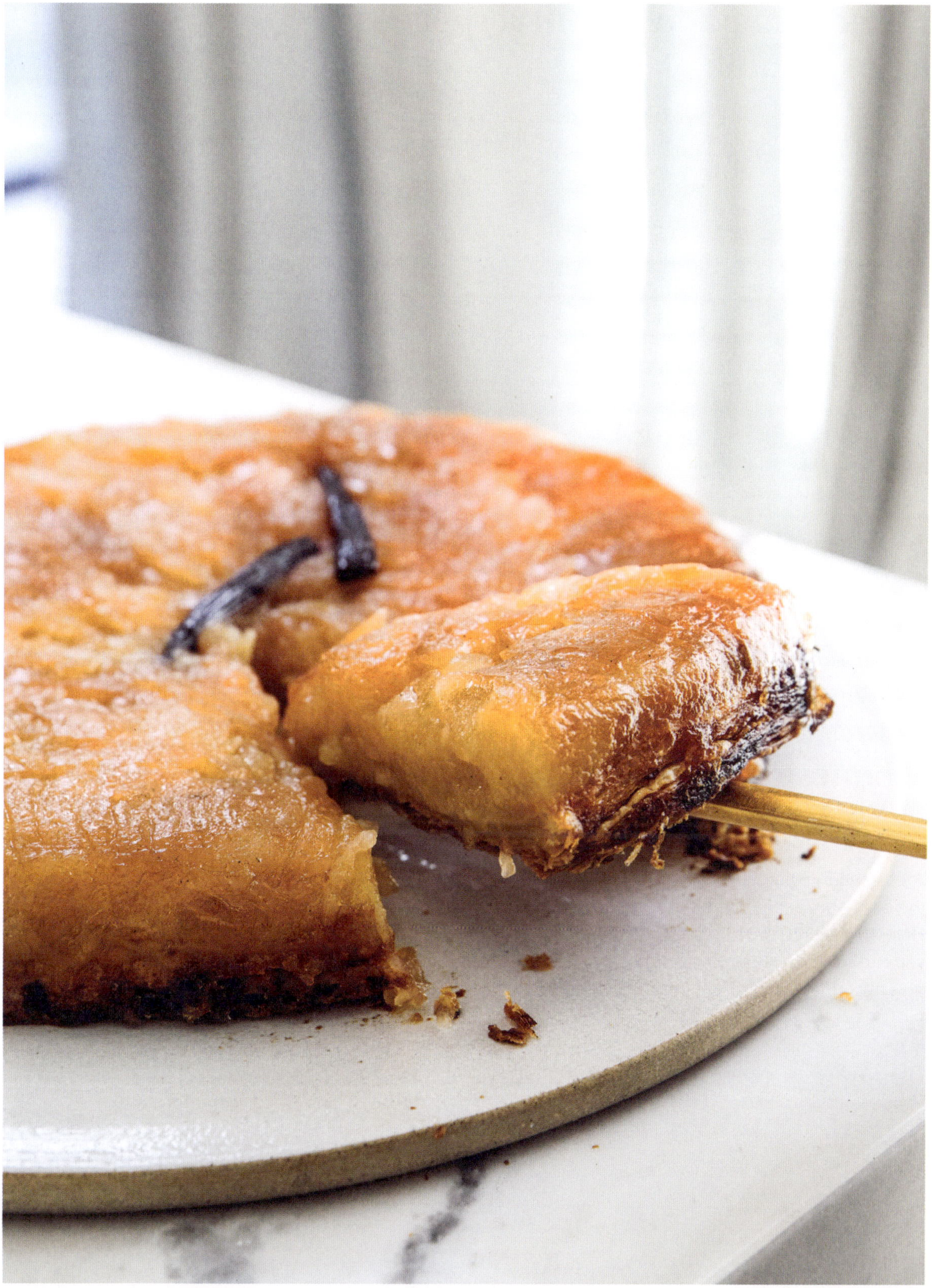

Baked whole apples with verjuice & a clove crumb (V)

This is quite a dramatic-looking apple crumble, like a wild apple pie with stems poking out of deconstructed pastry. It's super simple and absolutely delicious – just be sure to use small, tasty apples. **Serves 6**

40 g (1½ oz) butter
10 small apples, peeled, leaving the stems attached
100 ml (3½ fl oz) verjuice
120 g (4½ oz) caster (superfine) sugar

peel of ½ lemon, pith removed
clotted cream, to serve

Clove crumb
150 g (5½ oz/1 cup) plain (all-purpose) flour

120 g (4½ oz) brown sugar
60 g (2 oz/¼ cup) butter
2½ tablespoons extra-virgin olive oil
2½ teaspoons ground cloves

Preheat the oven to 180°C (350°F) fan-forced. Line a baking tray with baking paper.

Add all the crumb ingredients to a large bowl and rub together with your fingers until combined. Spread over the baking tray and bake for 12–15 minutes, until golden. Set aside to cool.

Grease a baking dish with the butter and add the apples.

In a small saucepan, simmer the verjuice, sugar and lemon peel over a medium heat until the sugar has dissolved. Pour the syrup over the apples.

Bake, uncovered, for about 30 minutes, until the apples are tender and slightly coloured.

Crumble the clove crumb over the apples and serve with clotted cream.

Make it different
Savoury baked whole apples. (V) Add a splash of vinegar and a bay leaf to the baking dish, skip the crumb and season with salt and pepper. Great as a side for roast pork.

Baked whole pears with verjuice & a clove crumb. (V) Simply replace the apples with small pears.

Viennese strudel (V)

Strudel always reminds me of afternoon tea with my aunt, who has Austrian heritage. When I was a bit older, she arranged a visit for me and a cousin to a relative in Vienna, who made simply the best strudel I have ever tasted, the pastry brittle, light and crisp. I don't have that recipe, but this comes very close. The secrets are the vinegar in the dough, which relaxes the gluten so you can stretch it super fine, and the toasted toffee crumbs, which swell as they absorb the juices from the apple, preserving the flakiness of the ultra-thin pastry. **Serves 10**

Quick apple sauce for roast duck or pork (GF) (V)

Pink Lady and granny smith apples are great for a quick sauté. For four serves, peel and slice 3 large apples, about 2 cm (¾ in) thick. Add 25 g (1 oz) butter to a large frying pan over a high heat, then add the slices flat, in one layer (cook in batches if necessary). Sprinkle over 1 tablespoon sugar, ½ teaspoon salt flakes and a little ground white pepper. After 2 minutes, flip the slices and cook for 2 minutes on the other side. Tip into a bowl, sprinkle in a teaspoon of vinegar and toss with a few thyme leaves. Serve with roast pork or duck, or a pork chop.

Pair with
Serve with cream, ice cream or clotted cream.

60 g (2 oz/¼ cup) unsalted
  butter
120 g (4½ oz) fine dry
  breadcrumbs
80 g (2¾ oz/⅓ cup) caster
  (superfine) sugar
2 teaspoons ground
  cinnamon
70 g (2½ oz) sultanas (golden
  raisins), or currants
3 tablespoons rum
  or brandy

850 g (1 lb 14 oz) peeled
  and sliced granny smith or
  golden delicious apples,
  tossed in lemon juice
50 ml (1¾ fl oz) melted
  unsalted butter

Strudel/pastry
300 g (10½ oz/2 cups) plain
  (all-purpose) flour
120 ml (4 fl oz) lukewarm
  water

45 ml (1½ fl oz) grapeseed oil
1 tablespoons white vinegar
1 teaspoon fine sea salt

Cinnamon sugar
90 g (3 oz/¾ cup) icing
  (confectioners') sugar
3 teaspoons ground
  cinnamon

Staples
FLR, OIL

For the pastry, add half the flour and all the other ingredients to a bowl and combine into a slurry with a fork. Add the remaining flour and bring together to form a dough. Tip onto a lightly floured bench and knead for about 15 minutes, until smooth. If the dough is sticky, add a small amount of extra flour and knead again until smooth. Drop the pastry into an oiled bowl and rotate to coat the dough. Cover with a plate and stand for 1 hour on the bench to relax and loosen.

Melt the butter in a frying pan over a medium heat. Add the breadcrumbs and cook, tossing constantly, to toast evenly. Once golden, about 5 minutes, remove from the heat and toss the sugar and cinnamon through. The sugar will caramelise quickly and coat the crumbs. Tip into a bowl and set aside to cool.

Add the sultanas and rum to a small saucepan and bring to a simmer. Set aside for about 10 minutes to soften, then drain. Add to the apple with a handful of the sugared breadcrumbs and combine.

Preheat the oven to 200°C (400°F) fan-forced. Line a baking tray with baking paper.

Roll the pastry out on a lightly floured bench. You may need to flour the rolling pin, but do so frugally. When the pastry is about the size of an A4 sheet of paper, pick it up and drape it over the back of your hands. Use your fingers and knuckles to stretch the dough very gently. Keep working, straightening out any wrinkles to get a uniformly thin rectangle that is translucent. The dough is very soft and will stretch easily, but don't take it too far. It should be about 30 × 40 cm (12 × 16 in) and be of an even thickness (the edges will be thicker).

Lay the pastry down on the bench (you can lay it on a large cloth to make rolling easier). Brush half the pastry along the short edge with the melted butter. Spread the crumbs over the other half, leaving a 5 cm (2 in) border. Top the breadcrumbs with the apple mixture, then fold the three overhanging sides over the apple, but leave the other end unfolded.

Carefully support the pastry (or use the cloth to help roll, if using) as you roll up the strudel, finishing at the open buttered end.

Transfer to the baking tray, seam side down. Brush with the remaining butter and bake for about 35 minutes, until the pastry is golden.

Remove the strudel from the oven and leave to cool for 10 minutes.

Combine the cinnamon sugar ingredients in a sifter or fine-mesh sieve, then dust heavily over the warm strudel. Cut into slices about 5 cm (2 in) wide and serve warm.

The strudel will keep for around 4 days refrigerated, and I enjoy it just by itself at room temperature.

Berries

At home, we gorge on seasonal fruit when it's at its best. We devour cherries around Christmas, plunder apricots, peaches, nectarines and plums when they peak in summer, let the sticky juices run down our arms for weeks on end when watermelon is bursting with flavour and the sun beats down hard. In autumn, the bench is laden with new-season pears and apples, and furry golden quinces, while winter sees citrus star. When most stone fruit is hogging the limelight – reasonably, mind you – berries are also at their best. And there is nothing more compelling than a freshly plucked berry.

There has been many a holiday in summer when blackberries were rambling, and my partner Michael and I have literally driven around for hours to pick enough blackberries to make a crostata, often with thumbs pricked and shirts torn for that one tart with its sweet crusted buttery pastry smothered in jam and fresh berries … and it's worth it, every time. Berry picking with kids can also be a very enjoyable experience.

Like so many fruits, berries are often available outside of their season, though they are never at their best and will always be expensive. Not usually worth it, in my opinion. Also, berries are wonderful when served generously – a lone raspberry or fanned strawberry on a dish is more annoying than enjoyable. Frozen berries are very useful, and I will always freeze any excess fresh ones that I have. They can't replace the beauty of a fresh berry, but they are wonderful for smoothies, cakes, muffins, jellies, a quick jam and the like – and they're also significantly cheaper than fresh berries.

Strawberries are the most common of berries, which is not surprising given they can be grown successfully in different climates. They are grown in many regions all around Australia, extending the season to be the longest of any of the berries, and essentially stretching across most of the year. Having said that, you need the right conditions for good flavour development, as they sometimes achieve maturity without actually acquiring much sweetness and only the faintest whisper of flavour. The more intensely a berry smells, the better it will taste, but this is especially true for strawberries. They are impossible to resist when perfectly ripe and fragrant, with a juicy sweetness and texture quite unlike any other berry.

Raspberries are the most delicate of berries, and also one of the most distinctive. The flavour of raspberries has been immortalised – and to some degree bastardised – by so many types of confectionery. With such a radiantly individual flavour, it is no surprise to see it both widely employed and mimicked. There is nothing like true raspberry flavour, whether fresh, or cooked-out in jam or the like. The fragile nodules of the berries also make for a pleasingly juicy eating experience, though that fragility is somewhat of an issue for harvesting and packing, no doubt contributing to their generally high costs. Raspberries are both sweet and acidic, making them perfect for providing balance in desserts. The darker the raspberries, the better the flavour.

Blueberries are relatively new to our shores, and they certainly weren't common when I was growing up. That's all changed, with their popularity now at fever pitch. That fascination is as much about the flavour as it is about their purported health benefits, wearing that most excitable of epithets: superfood. Blueberries don't have the overtly distinctive scent and flavour of, say, strawberries or raspberries, but their tart sweetness and the way they pop in the mouth is more than a little pleasing. Plus, the colour is dramatic when presented against something like a meringue, as is the internal star pattern when halved.

Mulberries are one of my favourite berries, though their season is extremely short and they are rarely available at the markets. Most harvests are likely from backyard trees. Yes, they grow on trees, which make them somewhat of a commitment for the home gardener, as those trees can grow to significant heights. A blueberry bush or two – always in full sun – is likely a better option.

Also see

Roasted rhubarb & strawberries with rose geranium 648

Friands 734–5

Coconut & raspberry cake with chocolate ganache 746

Coconut, cherry & pistachio slice 761

Strawberry sorbet 785

Chianti & raspberry granita with ice cream 784–5

Apple, blueberry & blackberry galette 818

Pair with

Cream and yoghurt, chocolate, vanilla, spices such as cloves and pepper, mint, basil, rhubarb, pastry, sugar, nuts, liqueurs and spirits such as grappa, Grand Marnier, gin and vodka, balsamic vinegar, lemon vincotto, watermelon, rockmelon, lemon, and stone fruits such as peaches and cherries.

Super-simple roasted raspberry jam GF V VG

Preheat the oven to 170°C (340°F) fan-forced. Add 1.2 kg (2 lb 10 oz) fresh or frozen raspberries to a large ceramic baking dish. Add 900 g (2 lb) caster (superfine) sugar to another dish and roast both for 45 minutes. Remove both dishes from the oven and tip the berries into the sugar tray. Stir through the juice of 1 large lemon. Return to the oven for 10 minutes, then remove and stir through again, making sure all the sugar has dissolved and is fully incorporated. You could add a split vanilla bean or a sprig of rose geranium at this stage, too. Transfer to jars and seal, then store in the fridge once cooled. Makes 945 g–1.26 kg (2 lb 1 oz–2 lb 12 oz/ 3–4 cups). Use as you would any jam – on crumpets, toast, muffins, Scones (p. 772) or to fill a sponge cake (see p. 689).

Blackberries also have a short season, in the flush of summer. They have long been a noxious weed in Australia, dominating creek banks and farmland like so many coils of barbed wire abandoned in no man's land. They were a well-meaning import, but a real scourge when I was growing up, and the pleasure of picking them was always tempered by concerns about them being sprayed with herbicide. Like prickly pears, that invasion is now under control. Boysenberries are related to blackberries, but also to raspberries and loganberries (a raspberry and blackberry hybrid), with a red fruit and milder flavour to the inky wild depth of a blackberry. Blackberries make compelling jam, but can also accompany game meats, such as venison, hare, duck or pigeon.

We're more likely to see blackcurrants here than redcurrants, and certainly more than white currants. Blackcurrants or cassis (cassis is 'blackcurrant' in French) is a flavour that is often associated with cabernet sauvignon among wine tasters, and would be instantly recognisable to generations of Australians (and those in the UK) as a flavour of cordial purportedly high in vitamin C. Redcurrants are wonderfully decorative (like tiny edible Christmas baubles) and have a pleasingly tart character, while white currants are somewhat sweeter with less acid. Currants have a very short season, so are usually only available fresh for a month or so in summer.

Most berries are very fragile, and will typically be sold in sealed punnets. Unfortunately, this involves quite a bit of plastic, so a better solution is needed. Compostable punnets are being made, but they are not convenient enough for the industry yet, and it's important to remember that compostable items actually do need to be composted – not tossed into landfill, where they will rot slowly and anaerobically like other rubbish.

Flipping the plastic punnets over is the best way to gauge the health of the fruit, as blemished and squashed berries are often more apparent there. You should also look for vibrant colours. Strawberries with a blush of red fading to white and green will taste exactly as they look, and will never fully ripen. Mulberries, blackberries, blackcurrants, blueberries and the like should be deeply coloured. Berries are best eaten within a day or so.

Smashed berry sauce GF V VG

I love to bruise raspberries or blackberries to make a sauce. If they're sweet, then liberating the juice and spooning over a slice of tart, panna cotta or ice cream is all that's needed. If they're a little tart, add a pinch of icing (confectioners') sugar or a drizzle of vincotto or quality balsamic vinegar. A little lemon juice can really make the flavour shine too.

Preparing berries

Aside from hulling strawberries (removing the stalk with a paring knife), berries require no preparation beyond washing. I tend not to muck around with them too much, but I often add a squeeze of lemon juice as it really sharpens and enhances the flavour of all berries.

Berry crumble ⓥ

This is a snap to pull together. It also reheats well, and is just as delicious cold. If you have fresh berries, reduce the cooking time by 5 minutes or so. You can also assemble the crumble in individual dishes. **Serves 6**

600 g (1 lb 5 oz) frozen mixed berries
3 tablespoons brown sugar
2 tablespoons plain (all-purpose) flour
zest and juice of 1 lemon

½ teaspoon salt flakes
Cinnamon crumble
120 g (4½ oz) plain (all-purpose) flour
1 teaspoon ground cinnamon

1 teaspoon baking powder
100 g (3½ oz) unsalted butter
100 g (3½ oz) brown sugar
100 g (3½ oz/1 cup) rolled (porridge) oats or raw granola

Preheat the oven to 220°C (430°F) fan-forced.

For the crumble, add the flour, cinnamon and baking powder to a bowl, then crumble in the butter. Pinch together to combine until you still see some flecks of butter here and there. Mix the sugar and oats together, then add to the bowl and combine gently with your hands. Set aside.

Reserve a handful of berries for the topping. Add the rest to a bowl with the remaining ingredients and combine, then spoon into a 25 cm (10 in) baking dish. Top with the crumble mixture and finish with the reserved berries.

Bake for about 25 minutes, until the berries are molten and bubbling. Serve hot or cold.

Pair with

Vanilla ice cream or clotted cream.

Berry turnovers ⓥ

Using a soup bowl as a guide, cut some Sweet galette pastry (p. 813) into rounds. Pile a little hazelnut base (see p. 650) on the pastry rounds, then top with as many raspberries as you can fit and still fold the pastry over. Pinch or roll the edges to seal, glaze with beaten egg and sprinkle with a little demerara sugar. Bake on a lined tray at 180°C (350°F) fan-forced for about 20 minutes, until the pastry is golden. Serve warm or at room temperature, with cream. These turnovers are also great with other berries, such as blackberries or boysenberries.

Strawberries romanoff ⓥ

Temperature is the key to this dessert, hence the chilled serving bowls. **Serves 4**

500 g (1 lb 2 oz) strawberries, hulled and sliced 5 mm (¼ in) thick
3 tablespoons orange liqueur (such as Grand Marnier)
juice of 1 lemon

3½ tablespoons caster (superfine) sugar
200 ml (7 fl oz) thickened (whipping) cream
2½ tablespoons pouring (single/light) cream
½ teaspoon vanilla extract

vanilla ice cream, to serve
4 mille-feuille pastry shards, dusted with icing (confectioners') sugar (see p. 824)

Special equipment
4 chilled coupes or small bowls

Combine the strawberries, liqueur, lemon juice and 2½ tablespoons of the sugar in a medium bowl. Chill for 1 hour.

Whip the creams, vanilla and remaining 1 tablespoon sugar until stiff. Fold 2 tablespoons of the strawberry macerating liquor into the cream.

Add a quenelle or small scoop of vanilla ice cream to the bottom of each serving glass. Spoon the macerated strawberries over the top, then pile the whipped cream up high.

Serve the mille-feuille in the side of the bowls, with a few extra strawberries, if you have them.

Pair with

Instead of mille-feuille, you could serve this with fried Churros (p. 775), cat's tongue biscuits or the like, a tuile (see p. 788), a warm Madeleine (p. 788), or diced fresh Classic sponge cake (p. 748).

Berry, coconut & mint smoothie ⓖⓕ ⓥ

Use 2 heaped tablespoons frozen mixed berries, 2 heaped tablespoons yoghurt, 100 ml (3½ fl oz) coconut water or any type of milk, a squeeze of lemon or lime juice, 4 mint leaves and 3 ice cubes per person and whiz until smooth. You can sweeten with honey or maple syrup if you like, too.

Summer berry & chia pudding loaf (V) (VG)

The addition of chia seeds to this British classic is a neat trick here, ringing a few health bells and masking the liqueur, but also taking up moisture and thickening the juices in a jelly-like way. This is best made when fresh berries abound, with the fresh berry salad at the end an important serving element. You can use frozen berries in the pudding, then use whatever you can find fresh to finish. **Serves 6–8**

500 g (1 lb 2 oz) blueberries
300 g (10½ oz) blackberries
400 g (14 oz/1¾ cups) caster
  (superfine) sugar
125 ml (4 fl oz/½ cup) crème
  de cassis (blackcurrant
  liqueur)

80 g (2¾ oz/½ cup) white
  chia seeds
juice of 1 lemon
500 g (1 lb 2 oz) raspberries
  (fresh or frozen)

500 g (1 lb 2 oz) strawberries,
  hulled and sliced in
  4 lengthways
1 large unsliced loaf of white
  high-top bread (preferably
  slightly stale)

Line a 20–22 cm (8–8¾ in) loaf (bar) tin or terrine mould with plastic wrap so that it overhangs enough to be able to fold over the completed pudding.

Add half the blueberries, half the blackberries, 350 g (12½ oz) of the sugar and 100 ml (3½ fl oz) of the liqueur to a saucepan over a high heat. Boil for 5 minutes, stirring to dissolve the sugar. Take the pan off the heat and stir in the chia seeds and half the lemon juice. Now stir the raspberries, half the strawberries and the remaining blueberries through. Set aside. Reserve the remaining blackberries, strawberries, sugar, liqueur and lemon juice for serving.

Slice the crusts from the bread, then cut the loaf into four even slices lengthways. Cut the best-looking slice (this will be the top) to fit the bottom of the tin. Cut another slice in half lengthways and use to line the sides of the tin, then cut another to fit in both ends, leaving one slice for the top of the tin.

Spoon the berry mixture into the middle, pressing the berries into the bread with your spoon. Leave some liquid in the bowl. If the berries don't quite fill the cavity, you can always use some of the reserved ones. Top the pudding with the last slice of bread, cut to fit, then tip the remaining juices on top to stain the bread. The juice pattern will look a little patchy, but will even out as it sits overnight.

Pull the plastic wrap over to seal tightly, the weigh the pudding down with a couple of food tins laying on their sides. Place on a tray in the fridge overnight.

Just before serving, combine the remaining berries, sugar, liqueur and lemon juice in a bowl.

Unwrap the plastic and turn the pudding out onto a platter, then spoon over the berry mixture and juices. Cut into 3 cm (1¼ in) slices and serve.

Pair with

Whipped cream, frozen yoghurt or ice cream.

Heavenly sponge filled with cream & strawberries (V)

Split a cooled Classic sponge cake (p. 748) and fill with whipped cream sweetened with a little caster (superfine) sugar and vanilla extract. Pile on sliced strawberries that have been tossed in caster (superfine) sugar, lemon juice and a dash of vincotto or balsamic vinegar and left to steep for 5 minutes. A little strawberry jam on the sponge before piling on the cream would also be nice.

Balsamic pepper strawberry & chicken sandwiches

Slice strawberries 3 mm (⅛ in) thick and toss with ground black or white pepper, torn basil leaves and a dash or two of the best balsamic vinegar you can get your hands on. Combine with shredded roast chicken tossed in a little mayonnaise mixed with sour cream or yoghurt. Use as a filling for white ribbon sandwiches.

Raspberry toffee coulis (GF) (V) (VG)

Before you make the toffee, add 600 g (1 lb 5 oz) frozen raspberries to a food processor, leaving them whole. Heat 400 g (14 oz/1¾ cups) caster (superfine) sugar and 100 ml (3½ fl oz) water in a saucepan over a high heat. Cook to a medium coloured toffee, about 8 minutes. Now blitz the berries and pour in the toffee in a steady but fast stream, which will melt the berries. Keep the motor running until you have a smooth purée, then add the juice of ½ lemon. Strain the coulis through a fine-mesh sieve. Makes 1 litre (34 fl oz/1 cup).

Citrus

Citrus has its origins in Asia, but the fruits that are familiar to us today are largely due to mutations and hybrids that occurred both spontaneously and by design all around the world, with citron, pomelo, mandarin and papeda the main ancestors. In its varying forms, citrus accounts for vital components of the culinary identity of so many regions, whether preserved lemon and orange-blossom water in the Middle East, lime and lime leaves in South-East Asia and the subcontinent, the bitter Seville oranges of Spain, cedro in Southern Italy, the dried limes of Iran, the British – via the Iberian Peninsula – staple of marmalade, as well as the stunning finger limes of Australia that are finally getting their due after years of Indigenous ingredients being trivialised.

And citrus in all its forms has just as large a part in my cooking, appearing as often in savoury dishes as it does in sweets and desserts. Even when it's not playing the lead role, it is quite apparent that it is making everything else look its best, whether through a squirt of juice or the pungently aromatic quality of the oils in the peel.

A squeeze of lemon over almost anything before serving will improve it beyond what seems reasonable for such a humble gesture. Lemon juice adds freshness with its vibrant flavour and high acidity, but it also enhances, sharpens and heightens flavours, essentially seasoning – it is almost a magical ingredient.

The scent of lemon zest in a butter-rich pastry case or in a custard, or the subtle hint of orange zest in a sponge or biscuit elevates immeasurably. Citrus adds flavour and it balances. The addition of lemon zest and juice to an almond paste, for example, enhances the almond flavour and cuts through the sweetness, and it balances the richness of a cheesecake or lemon meringue pie, both of which would be ponderous without a spike of citrus.

Lemons are rarely the hero of a dish, excepting the simple glory of a lemon tart or the like, but there are few ingredients I find as essential. For me, a kitchen is barren without a big bowl of lemons on the bench, no matter how well it might otherwise be stocked.

The 101 advice from me for less-experienced cooks is to taste your food, then season properly with salt and pepper, and brighten with a squeeze of lemon – perhaps not always, but often enough. It's a simple mantra that makes the ordinary good and the good sublime. Lemon juice is also a useful way to drop the apparent saltiness of an over-seasoned dish – it happens to the best of us. Lemon juice, oil, salt and pepper also makes the simplest of dressings, marvellously fresh and vibrant, ideal for salad leaves, raw vegetables or sliced raw fish.

I often use the finely grated zest or a strip of peel for an even punchier kick of flavour, but restraint is important here, with lemon a tricky flavour to mask later. Grated zest will make it into dressings or marinades, or to finish a pasta, while a strip of peel often gets dropped into a stew or braise. Sliced lemons or lemon leaves get tucked into whole fish with fennel fronds and herbs. If a lemon is thin skinned, I'll cut slices into little triangles to add to a mayonnaise, dressing or salad, or I'll whip thicker skins off and do the same just with the flesh.

Lemons come in a few notable varieties, with Lisbon and eureka lemons being the most commonly found at the market. The former is generally larger with a thicker skin, while the latter is more compact, thinner skinned and with less seeds. They are interchangeable in terms of application, both with a brightly acidic profile. Meyer lemons are originally from China – an old hybrid, with mandarin part of their make-up, which reveals itself in a softer acid profile, rounder flavour and elevated sweetness. They still have good acidity, though, and are really quite a beautiful fruit –

Also see

Fresh ponzu 101

Tagliatelle with lemon cream 123–4

Citrus-cured gravlax 169

Spiced lemon dressing 477

Scorched lemon syrup 707

Lime & coconut cheesecake 738

Italian blood orange breakfast cake 740

Orange & almond cake with glacé orange 744

Crepes suzette 771

Candied orange & lemon peel 790

Lemon, lime or passionfruit curd 797

Lemon tart 814–5

Pair with

Cream, meringue, butter, brown butter, yoghurt, eggs, coconut, spring onion (scallion), onions, chilli, broad beans, spinach, rocket (arugula), kale, avocado, fennel, mint, coriander (cilantro), olives, cannellini beans, butter beans, lentils, borlotti beans, chickpeas, freekeh, tamari, soy, tahini, honey, fish sauce, palm sugar, cumin, cinnamon, black pepper, turmeric, ginger, shellfish, oysters, fish, beef, veal, lamb, chicken, duck, quail.

a favourite of mine that make wonderful preserves (p. 696), are ideal in a Lemon tart (p. 814) and roast beautifully with chicken (see p. 229).

Less common is the lemonade, a naturally occurring hybrid that was discovered in the 1980s in New Zealand. These are sweeter again than Meyer lemons, which they are speculated to be related to, perhaps crossed with a mandarin, dropping the lemon genes down even further in favour of mandarin. They are great eaten as is, juiced or added to salads, but not so much to use as an acidity spike. Ancestor to them all is the citron, which is more pith than flesh, with the fragrant pith and peel used in Asian cuisines. The Italians call the fruit cedro, candying the fleshless halves to use in cakes, biscuits and desserts. It is also used to perfume drinks.

The most common orange varieties at my local markets are Valencia and navel, with the former a summer orange and the latter ripening in winter, ensuring oranges are in season for most of the year. Another orange that appears more frequently is the cara cara navel, which is a seedless, red-fleshed mutation of the Washington navel (the most common cultivar), which in turn is also a mutation. Seville oranges are a rare sight where I live, but they are perfect for marmalade, with an appealing bitterness to both flesh and zest. They are a cooking orange, being too bitter as an eating or juicing orange, but the flavour is sublime when balanced with sweetness. The blossoms of Seville orange trees are also incredibly fragrant. They are used to make orange-blossom water.

Blood oranges have a relatively short season, from winter tripping into early spring, and they're something I really look forward to. There are actually a few varieties – though they're not typically labelled as such – some with deeply coloured red flesh, and others with mostly orange flesh flecked with red. The flavour profile is quite distinct, and often said to be berry-like, pairing with some more familiar citrus notes. They are also often said to be lower in acidity, which I don't think is universally true. Some varieties are certainly more sweet than sour, but others will be noticeably tart, while still flavour ripe.

We used to churn through countless boxes of blood oranges at the Melbourne Wine Room, squeezed to order with a generous slug of Campari. It's a great combination, and we made a somewhat compelling sorbet from that marriage, which also works exceptionally well for jam or marmalade (see p. 699). Blood orange juice also works well in jellies, puddings and cakes. The segmented flesh is sublime in a salad with sliced fennel, olives and onion.

Grapefruit are a cross between sweet orange and pomelo, with a characteristic combination of very sour acidity and a pleasing bitterness, with red grapefruits notably sweeter and lower in acidity than yellow ones. Either type is marvellous juiced – Campari is also an ideal way to spike it, if that's your thing – and

I sometimes use them instead of orange for a salad with fennel, or the juice can be used to flavour sorbets or jellies. Pomelo has a similar flavour to grapefruit without the bitterness. Unlike so much citrus, pomelo is not a hybrid, with its genes contributing to so many other citrus fruits, regular sweet orange included, which is a cross between mandarin and pomelo.

There are several types of mandarins, including tangerines, grown in Australia, with the seasons of each meaning supply stretches across the cooler months, from autumn, through winter and spilling into the first flush of spring. The most recognisable variety is the imperial mandarin, with its characteristically ill-fitting skin. It's an understandable lunchbox favourite, being easy to peel for little hands, and having few seeds, good flavour and relatively low acidity. The skin is also full of flavourful oils, making the zest ideal for cakes, tarts and biscuits, or it can be dehydrated and used to make a spice dust or added to a marinade. The other common variety is the Ellendale, which has tighter fitting skin.

Tangors are a cross between a tangerine and an orange, with honey murcott and clementines the most commonly available. They are characterised by being easier to peel than an orange, with individual segments that are somewhat more tightly connected to each other than a true mandarin. I consider them more a mandarin in terms of use than an orange, and I use them for juice, in salads, desserts, sorbets, ice creams and jellies.

Small smooth-skinned cumquats can be eaten as is, peel and all. In fact, the sweetness is in the peel, along with a lot of the distinct aromatic flavour, with the flesh very sour. For me, though, cumquats are for preserving, making wonderfully tart marmalade.

In Australia, you're unlikely to come across a lime that is not a Tahitian lime, with the Mexican or key lime rarely seen in markets. The two are related, with the Tahitian lime, also known as Persian lime, a hybrid of lemon and Mexican lime. Tahitian limes are a little sweeter and less acidic, but the two are interchangeable in a culinary sense.

Limes are critical for Thai cooking – one of my favourite cuisines – and lemon juice is not a suitable substitute. Lime juice is particularly dulled by cooking, so it should be added to curries and the like at the last minute, with any leftovers needing a fresh squeeze to brighten again. The other important lime for the Thais is the makrut lime (also known as the kaffir lime), with its knobbly, brain-like skin and hyper-fragrant leaves. It is indeed the glossy leaves that are mostly used in curries, stir-fries, salads and desserts, with the grated zest employed to provide a similar punch of flavour. The flesh and juice, though, are incredibly tart and not often used in cooking.

Desert limes are another species of native citrus, growing in arid zones in eastern Australia. Long a bush food for first nations people, colonists took to using the flavourful and tart fruit, employing it to make European-style jams, jellies, cordials, chutneys and the like. While that general use has not persisted, the fruit is now commercially grown, and is worth seeking out for its distinctive flavour. Although they are quite small, only a few centimetres across, the fruit has a thin edible skin, so peeling is unnecessary. They are mostly sold frozen, or as a puree.

The other lime of note is more about process than variety, with brined and dried limes used in the Middle East to add a citric freshness to soups, curries and braises. They can be added whole to a braising liquid or the like, where they will rehydrate to a degree and impart the zesty notes of the skin, or they can be crushed to a powder and used as a zesty dusting spice to finish a dish.

In Australia, we are also blessed with native limes, or finger limes. There is a fantastic array of types, with the shape of the fruit unsurprisingly finger-like (though some are more spherical). These limes have a tough outer sheath that is split to reveal the 'caviar' inside, which ranges from luminous yellow to shockingly vibrant red. The flavour and level of acidity differs between these varieties, but all add sweetness and acidity to a dish, while also contributing pops of texture. I particularly love using them on raw fish, scattered over a crudo at the end (see p. 510). They are incredibly pretty, too, making them an added visual treat on any dish, but I do especially love them on a canapé (see p. 168).

Now available locally, if not commonly, yuzu rounds out my citrus use. It's a fruit that is used in Japan, Korea and China, with an appearance a little like a spherical lemon with knobbly skin. The flavour hovers somewhere between lemon, lime, grapefruit and mandarin, with a very aromatic and tart profile. It can be used in dressings and marinades, and it has also taken off as a cocktail ingredient, with a small dose adding a lot of flavour and acid.

When selecting any citrus, the fruit should feel heavy in the hand, laden with juice. Citrus should have a strong aroma, with the oils in the skin vibrantly present. Colour is not always a reliable indication of flavour and quantity of juice. I'm sure we've all sliced into a handsome-looking orange to find a web of dry membrane and not much else, while a juicy and flavoursome organic lemon will not always have the glossy sheen and bright yellow hue that has become the platonic ideal. But, needless to say, fruit that is dull or looking old is best avoided, and soft spots in any citrus are undesirable.

Green oranges, lemons and the like will not advance to ripeness on the bench. The exception to this is Valencia oranges, with the green tinge a product of summer ripening. Green lemons are usable, though somewhat sour. Imperial mandarins will have baggy skin when ripe, but other varieties should all have a more tailored appearance. Limes are often picked green and, as they ripen, they will yellow a little (Tahitian limes) or a lot (Mexican limes).

If you have the good fortune to have a citrus tree, it is generally the best way to store the fruit, with lemons and grapefruits keeping especially well on the tree, so pick as needed. Most citrus will keep for at least a couple of weeks on the bench if in good condition and the temperatures are mild, but refrigeration will extend their life meaningfully.

Limes will yellow markedly as they age, and both lemons and limes will lose the oil in their peel, which will see them shrink and eventually harden. Although you would avoid either in this condition – unless desperate – they are not necessarily a write-off. Older lemons and limes can still have quite viable juice, if the flavour has mellowed and the acidity dropped a little. Too old, and they will pick up fermented flavours and be of little use. As always, trust your nose.

Lemon seeds are also a handy tool for jam-making, especially when dealing with fruits that are naturally low in pectin, like apricots, peaches and strawberries. Lemons are high in pectin, which you can extract readily from the seeds without skewing the flavour of the jam. Simply save the seeds whenever you squeeze lemons – they will keep indefinitely in the freezer – and tie up in muslin (cheesecloth) to add to jams. The amount you need will depend on the fruit and the pectin in the seeds, but twenty to thirty seeds for 1 kg (2 lb 3 oz) of fruit is a good guide.

Preparing citrus

I try to buy organic lemons where possible, as they are generally more flavoursome, but also because they will not be waxed. The wax on a lemon is not particularly easy to spot, and naturally it is regarded as non-toxic, but I personally prefer to not eat wax. And given that I use the zest frequently, unwaxed lemons it is. You can apparently remove the wax by covering the lemons with boiling water and then scrubbing, but it's hard to tell how effective this is. Mandarins and oranges are also waxed, though I use their zest less frequently. Again, the wax is not toxic, so whether this is a concern or not is entirely personal.

When juicing limes, a good trick is to roll them firmly on the bench before cutting, which will soften them and make the juice easier to extract. I typically then just squeeze by hand, rather than breaking the membrane too much with a juicer. The membrane and pith contain limonin, which can be bitter if treated too roughly, and juicers are intentionally brutal. The other method, which is more classically Thai, is to slice off the cheeks (which also look great as garnish, and they're much easier to use – a lime wedge is an awkward and frugal-looking thing), which will then squeeze easily, while the central disc can be twisted to extract all the juice. For any citrus, juice as needed, and please never use bottled lime or lemon juice, as the flavour and acidity is always compromised.

I use the zest of citrus in two ways, either by slicing off some peel with a paring knife to infuse a braise or syrup, or I'll use a microplane and use immediately if adding to a marinade, gremolata or dressing, or to a cake batter or the like. It may sound obvious, but it's easier to zest fruit before you squeeze it. Citrus that has had the zest removed will not last as long, so use as a priority.

Supreming (segmenting) citrus

For citrus that doesn't break into ready segments, you can remove the flesh from the membrane by slicing off the top and bottom of the fruit, then standing on one end to slice off the peel and white pith (the pith on citrus is often bitter) with a sharp knife. Taking the peeled fruit in your palm, cut along the membrane on both sides of a segment to remove the flesh, repeating until all segments have been removed – the seeds can then easily be picked out. Do this over a bowl to catch any juices, then squeeze the juice from the membrane. You can then use the flesh in salads or desserts, with the juice added to a dressing or sauce – or use for another purpose, or drink.

Easy preserved lemons (GF) (V) (VG)

I had to search high and low for this recipe, which had been misplaced. It was a favourite at the Melbourne Wine Room, and I'm pretty sure the method was born from being impatient and wanting to make my own preserved lemons – quickly! The flavour is softer and a little mellower than with the traditional method, and the subsequent paste you can make is extremely versatile.

Makes a 1 litre (34 fl oz/4 cup) jar

6 large lemons
125 ml (4 fl oz/½ cup)
  grapeseed oil
90 ml (3 fl oz) extra-virgin
  olive oil
35 g (1¼ oz) salt flakes

Pair with

Chop and use as you would regular preserved lemon to add flavour to tagines, stews and braises.

Mix through grain salads with plenty of chopped herbs.

Pour the juice from one of the lemons into a 1 litre (34 fl oz/4 cup) sterilised jar (see p. 40). Seal the jar and shake to coat the inner surface of the jar well with the juice, then tip out and reserve the juice.

Whisk the oils in a jug or bowl to combine.

Slice the remaining lemons crossways to 5 mm (¼ in) thick. Lay some in the bottom of the jar, sprinkle in some salt, then repeat until the jar is about one-third full. Add some of the reserved lemon juice and combined oils to cover, then continue to layer, adding more juice and oil after another one-third of the lemon slices, then topping to cover after the final third.

Seal the jar and set aside in a cool, dark place. These preserved lemons will be ready after 4 days, but will mellow and cure further with time. When testing them, it's important to remove the lemons with a very clean spoon, or they can become contaminated and spoil.

Once you're happy with the texture and flavour, these will keep in the fridge for about a month.

Make it different
With spices. Add a little more flavour by layering in some dried oregano, smoked paprika, black pepper or dried chilli.

Preserved lemons with bay & cinnamon GF V VG

This is the more classic way to make preserved lemons, and it takes a little longer, but the results are stunning. It's best to match the jar to the size of your lemons, so that you can stuff them in snuggly. **Makes 1 large jar or 2 smaller jars**

10 thick-skinned lemons, scrubbed
250 g (9 oz) coarse salt or rock salt

4 fresh bay leaves, roughly torn
10 cloves

2 cinnamon sticks, split into shards lengthways
juice of 4 lemons

Cut the lemons lengthways from the tip down, but not through the base, then at a right angle to make a cross, leaving the base attached.

Squeeze a lemon in your hand over a small bowl, then push some salt down into the cuts. Add a bay leaf and a sprinkling of salt to the jar(s), then push in the lemons, interspersing with the cloves, cinnamon shards and remaining bay leaves.

Scatter salt over the top, about a heaped tablespoon, then top up with the extra lemon juice and any juice left in the bowl. Push the lemons down to compact and submerge them, then seal the jar(s).

Stand at room temperature out of direct sunlight for 2 weeks, then refrigerate for 2 months before using. These will keep for up to 1 year in the fridge.

To use, remove a lemon, rinse off the salt and chop finely before adding to dishes.

Make it different
Preserved lemons with bay & star anise. GF V VG Omit the cinnamon and instead add four star anise.

Pair with

Chop finely and use to add flavour to tagines, stews and braises.

Mix through grain salads with plenty of chopped herbs.

Preserved lemon paste GF V VG

This recipe uses Easy preserved lemons (left). After setting the preserved lemons aside for 4 days, drain off and reserve the oil. Add the preserved lemon slices to a blender and blitz into a paste with 1 teaspoon ground cumin and ½ teaspoon ground chilli seeds. Gradually work in about half the reserved oil mixture to make a smooth, pourable paste. Use the paste in marinades and dressings, stir into mayonnaise and eat with grilled fish or shellfish, or add to dips, braises and stews.

Lemon cream & cherry possets GF V

This is a lovely dessert to have at Christmas, when cherries are abundant – at least in my part of the world. The freshness is perfect after an exhaustive meal, but it's equally suited to finishing a meal on a summer evening. **Serves 10**

600 g (1 lb 5 oz) cherries, some with stalks
80 g (2¾ oz) demerara sugar
50 g (1¾ oz) raspberry jam
½ teaspoon vanilla paste
juice of ½ lemon

Lemon cream
zest and juice of 2 lemons (about 125 ml/4 fl oz/½ cup juice)
150 g (5½ oz) demerara sugar

500 ml (17 fl oz/2 cups) thick (double/heavy) cream
200 ml (7 fl oz) pouring (single/light) cream

Set aside ten of the most perfect cherries with stalks to garnish each serve. Pit the remaining cherries and cut in half. Add to a large bowl with the sugar and toss to combine. Set half the cherries aside to macerate for 1 hour.

Meanwhile, add the remaining cherries to a saucepan, with the jam, vanilla paste and lemon juice. Cook over a medium heat for 5 minutes, until softened.

Blitz the cooked cherry mixture in a blender until smooth, then pass through a fine-mesh sieve. Divide the purée among ten serving glasses.

Once the remaining cherries have finished macerating, spoon them into the glasses and refrigerate.

For the lemon cream, blitz the lemon zest and sugar in a food processor until well combined. Transfer to a saucepan with both of the creams and bring to a gentle simmer over a low–medium heat until the sugar dissolves.

Remove from the heat and stir in the lemon juice. Strain immediately and divide between the glasses. Chill for 3–4 hours, until set.

Serve each posset garnished with a reserved cherry.

Preserved Meyer lemons with ginger & star anise GF V VG

I have been obsessed with Meyer lemons since I was a young cook. I love the sweet and tart flavour they deliver. When preserved, they lend the same character, being a little sweeter and less potent than classic preserved lemons. **Makes a 1–1.5 litre (34–51 fl oz/4–6 cup) jar**

500 ml (17 fl oz/2 cups) filtered water (or boiled and cooled)
100 g (3½ oz) fine sea salt

1 kg (2 lb 3 oz) Meyer lemons, washed
juice of 2 limes
100 g (3½ oz) peeled fresh ginger, finely grated and

squeezed to give 40 ml (1¼ fl oz) juice
3 star anise

Pair with

Use these as you would preserved lemons.

Try them chopped up in stuffings, in grain salads, and in marinades for fish (such as Chermoula, p. 90).

Boil half the water and add the salt, stirring to dissolve, then add the remaining water. Cool completely at room temperature.

Cut the lemons in half lengthways. Working over a bowl to catch any juices, cut out any central membranes and remove any visible seeds. Add the juice to the cooled brine with the lime and ginger juices.

Add one of the star anise to a large sterilised jar (see p. 40) that will fit all the lemons. Fill halfway with the lemons, cut side down. Add another star anise and pour in the brine to cover. Pack in the remaining lemons, top with the last star anise and fill with the remaining brine, leaving a 2–3 cm (¾–1¼ in) space below the rim of the jar.

Seal and store in a cool, dark place for 12–14 weeks to mature (but the longer the better), then taste to see if you're happy with the result, and use or leave for longer.

The preserved lemons will keep unrefrigerated for up to 12 months, but can be stored in the fridge for even longer. Finely chop both the flesh and the soft rind to use.

Lemon cheesecake ⓥ

This classic cheesecake has a lemony flavour that is splendidly vibrant.
The mix of cheeses in the cake is the secret to its light, velvety texture. **Serves 8**

500 g (1 lb 2 oz/2 cups) ricotta
150 g (5½ oz) cream cheese
150 g (5½ oz) mascarpone
50 g (1¾ oz) fromage frais or
    goat's curd, or extra cream
    cheese
220 g (8 oz) caster (superfine)
    sugar
4 eggs
zest of ½ large lemon, plus
    70 ml (2¼ fl oz) lemon juice

2 pinches of salt flakes
1 teaspoon vanilla extract or
    paste
1½ tablespoons cornflour
    (cornstarch)

Base
150 g (5½ oz/1 cup) plain
    (all-purpose) flour
90 g (3 oz) unsalted butter,
    diced and chilled

50 g (1¾ oz/½ cup) ground
    almonds
50 g (1¾ oz) caster
    (superfine) sugar
2 grates of lemon zest
1 teaspoon vanilla extract
    or paste

Staples
BTR

Preheat the oven to 160°C (320°F) fan-forced. Grease a 23 cm (9 in) springform cake tin.

In a bowl, combine the ingredients for the base, working in the butter until crumbs form. Press into the cake tin, then bake for 30 minutes, until lightly golden and smelling cooked.

Remove from the oven and set aside to cool. Reduce the oven temperature to 150°C (300°F).

Blitz all the cheeses and the sugar in a food processor until smooth, 1–2 minutes. Add the remaining ingredients and process until smooth, 1–2 minutes. Pour the mixture into the cake tin, smoothing out evenly.

Bake for 1 hour, then turn the oven off. Set the door ajar and leave the cheesecake in the oven for another hour to finish setting. Cool to room temperature, or refrigerate before serving.

The cheesecake will keep in an airtight container in the fridge for up to 5 days.

Make it different
With spiked sultanas. Warm 55 g (2 oz) pale-coloured sultanas (golden raisins) in a little dark rum or brandy. Set aside for 15–20 minutes to plump up, then arrange on top of the cooked crumb base before pouring in the filling.

With lemon sherbet. Dust the cooled cheesecake heavily with 80 g (2¾ oz) icing (confectioners') mixed with 1 tablespoon citric acid powder.

Pair with

Sliced strawberries or a compote of blueberries.

Dust with icing (confectioners') sugar and sprinkle with grated lemon zest.

To add a sherbetty zing, dust with a mixture of icing (confectioners') sugar and citric acid powder.

Warm equal parts honey and lemon juice in a small saucepan, then smooth over to glaze, finishing with grated lemon zest.

Dollop with Lemon or lime curd (p. 797).

Serve with Cherry compote (p. 723).

Citrus delicious pudding ⓥ

My mother often made a version of this for dessert when I was young. The original uses just lemons, but a mix of lemon and lime works extremely well. **Serves 6**

2 limes
2 lemons
360 g (12½ oz) caster
    (superfine) sugar

100 g (3½ oz) unsalted
    butter, softened
3 eggs, separated
70 g (2½ oz) self-raising flour

380 ml (13 fl oz) full-cream
    (whole) milk

Staples
ISGR

Preheat the oven to 170°C (340°F) fan-forced.

Finely grate the zest of one lime and one lemon, then juice all the citrus. You will need 150 ml (5 fl oz) of combined juice.

Pair with

Cream, Clotted cream (p. 800), crème fraîche, thick (double/heavy) cream or ice cream.

Cream the sugar, butter and citrus zest in a food processor until pale. Add the egg yolks and blitz to just combine, then follow with the flour and milk and blitz until smooth. Add the citrus juice and blitz again until smooth; the mixture will be quite runny. Pour into a bowl.

Whisk the egg whites in another bowl until soft and fluffy, then fold through the egg yolk mixture.

Pour the batter into a 1 litre (34 fl oz/4 cup) ceramic baking dish. Place in a small roasting tin and pour in hot water to come halfway up the side of the baking dish, to make a bain marie.

Carefully transfer to the oven and bake for 55 minutes.

Allow to cool slightly, then dust with icing sugar before serving.

Make it different

With mandarin. Use imperial mandarins instead of limes.

With makrut lime leaf. To lift the limey fragrance, add a finely shredded makrut lime leaf with the zest.

Blood orange & Campari marmalade GF V VG

This marmalade is ruby in colour with brilliant clarity and intense flavour. The Campari notes don't dominate; rather, they accent and enhance the flavour of blood orange, adding tartly sweet and spiced notes – just what I want in a marmalade. Needless to say, make this when oranges are at their juicy best.
Makes about 3 litres (101 fl oz/12 cups), or 6 × 500 ml (17 fl oz/2 cup) jars

2 kg (4 lb 6 oz) blood oranges, or a mix with navel oranges	2 kg (4 lb 6 oz) caster (superfine) sugar 1 litre (34 fl oz/4 cups) fresh orange juice	juice of 2 lemons 250 ml (8½ fl oz/1 cup) Campari

Cut the oranges in half from stem to base. Slice them 5 mm (¼ in) thick, discarding the bits at the very tip and base, then cut in half lengthways, so you have 5 mm (¼ in) thick quadrants.

Add the orange slices to a large non-reactive saucepan, then top with water. Bring to a gentle simmer over a medium heat, then strain and repeat.

Return the oranges to the pan, cover with water and simmer gently for about 20 minutes, until the rind is tender.

Add the sugar and bring back to a simmer over a medium heat. Simmer for 30 minutes, skimming off any impurities now and then.

Stir in the orange and lemon juices and continue to simmer for about 30 minutes, until the mixture reaches setting point – which is usually 104°C (219°F) or just above on a thermometer; to check, you can simply spoon a little onto a frozen plate, then place in the fridge for a couple of minutes and it should have thickened.

Once ready, turn off the heat and stir the Campari through. Pour into hot sterilised jars (see p. 40) and seal. Cool to room temperature and use, or store in a cool, dark place for up to 1 year. Refrigerate after opening; with its high sugar and acid content, this marmalade will keep very well for 1 year.

Make it different

Without Campari. For a straight blood orange marmalade, simply omit the Campari.

With whisky. Replace the Campari with 100 ml (3½ fl oz) peaty whisky.

With cardamom. Add 2 teaspoons freshly ground cardamom seeds instead of the Campari.

With rosemary. Omit the Campari and infuse four rosemary sprigs into the hot jam as soon as it comes off the stove, then remove the sprigs before jarring. this will keep for 1–2 years.

Pair with

Fresh buttered toast.

Crepes suzette (p. 771).

Classic sponge cake (p. 748).

Crumpets (p. 769).

Lemon, date & orange-blossom marmalade
GF V VG

Slice 3 lemons (preferably Meyer lemons) into 3 mm (⅛ in) slices and remove the seeds. Cover the lemon slices with boiling water and steep overnight on the bench. Drain the steeped lemon and add to a wide heavy-based saucepan with 200 ml (7 fl oz) lemon juice, 400 g (14 oz) caster (superfine) sugar, 1 cinnamon stick and 500 ml (17 fl oz/2 cups) water. Gently cook over a low heat, so that the liquid is just ticking over, for about 1 hour, until the pith is translucent. Remove the pan from the heat, then lift out the lemon slices. Cool a little before cutting into small pieces and returning to the pan, along with 12 fleshy dates that have been pitted and quartered. Bring back to a simmer, then remove from the heat and stir in 2 teaspoons orange-blossom water. Cool before serving; the syrup will keep for 3 months in a sealed jar in the fridge.

Fig

It's one of my fondest memories: lost on a winding road on a hot summer's afternoon in southern Italy, far from where we were supposed to be. But it really didn't matter, as there was tree after tree laden with figs, drooping towards the stony, sandy earth, fruit falling to the ground. We climbed the fence and feasted. I'd never tasted better, with the perfume of the leaves filling my nostrils as I reached for the ripest fruit. We picked enough to fill our T-shirts, stretched into hammocks. And then had to find our way home before they were all squashed. We eventually turned up grinning, covered in sticky, itchy sap, several days' worth of figs our trophies.

We ate those figs with thick yoghurt and fragrant local honey. We tore them into salads with ripe tomatoes and peppery oil to eat with grilled fish. We ate them with sheep's curd cheeses and fresh mozzarella, salty sweet prosciutto and basil and oregano oil. Such delicious memories!

Native to the Middle East and Asia, figs are thought to be one of the first food plants to be domesticated, predating grains and pulses by a good thousand years. It's not surprising, then, that the symbology of the fig is prominent in many ancient cultures, often representing fertility. And figs just feel exotically ancient, much like pomegranates, quinces and dates, which have similarly been cultivated for millennia.

There are several hundred varieties of common fig (and also, in Australia, many native species, as well as those with inedible or no fruit). They range in colour from pale yellowy green to vibrant green (with some species developing a purple hue when ripe), to deeply brown-red, to purple, to almost black. Whatever the exterior colour, the inside of a ripe fig will have crimson filaments and be oozingly juicy – if the interior looks dry, chances are it won't be very tasty. Fig trees fruit in late summer, with the fruit ripening over autumn, although some varieties will provide a ripe crop in summer, too.

Figs are essentially inward-facing 'flowers', which makes a lot of sense when you consider their internal structure. While this presents a clear problem for pollination, the many fig varieties have attendant wasp species that have evolved alongside them. These wasps are tiny, with the female entering a fig through a hole in the base, losing her antennae and wings in the process. She then lays eggs and dies, with enzymes in the fig consuming her body. Once hatched, the males fertilise the females, then dig out escape routes – but die before making it out; the females then exit the fig, carrying pollen to new figs, and so it begins again. It's fascinating, if a little gruesome. Commercially, figs can be pollinated without the intervention of wasps.

My go-to fig is green-skinned with bright white flesh and a jammy, cherry-red centre. Black figs can be just as beautiful and perhaps a bit more textural, with a typically more rounded shape and a higher ratio of seedy inner 'flower' to flesh. Whatever the type, the scent of a ripe fig is truly magnificent. The leaves carry the same aroma, which can be liberated by steeping them in a syrup or custard; they make a stunning panna cotta (see p. 707).

Figs are one of those rare fruits that work beautifully in sweet and savoury applications, and perhaps in equal measure. Their natural sweetness can be enhanced, or it can be used as a counterpoint, with the flavour complementing salty cured meat and blue cheese just as well as it does ice cream or meringue.

Ripe figs are perfect simply sliced and served with any goat's cheese, gorgonzola or Roquefort, or with jamón, prosciutto and/or bresaola and fresh mozzarella. Smear some Mezzanotte paste (p. 588) on crostini, then top with goat's curd or aged goat's cheese and slices of fresh fig. Sliced figs with super-fresh ricotta and a drizzle of floral honey make for a delicious breakfast treat. Drizzle figs with good balsamic vinegar, vincotto or saba for a sweetly savoury accompaniment to salumi and

Also see

Chocolate panforte with almonds, figs & sour cherries 760–1

A simple frangipane fruit tart 796

Gorgonzola, fig & walnut pizza 857

Pair with

Figs love cured meats (ham, jamón, prosciutto, bresaola, pancetta) and cheese (fresh mozzarella, burrata, Parmigiano Reggiano and Grana Padano, blue cheeses, manchego, goat's cheese, mascarpone). Match with tomatoes, fennel, onion, raspberries, blackberries, citrus and fresh ginger. Figs are enhanced by spices such as fennel seeds, white and black pepper, anise, cardamom and cinnamon, herbs such as thyme, basil, sage, rosemary, bay leaves and oregano, as well as pine nuts, walnuts, hazelnuts and almonds. Drizzle with honey, maple syrup or a good thick balsamic vinegar, vincotto or saba. Figs work beautifully with cream and butter, as well as buttery and flaky pastry, meringue and honeycomb. Pair with proteins such as quail, chicken, duck or veal.

cheese. Stuff figs with blue cheese, wrap in prosciutto and grill. Serve them fresh, toffeed (see p. 705) or brûléed (see p. 707), with Crème caramel (p. 781), Rice pudding (p. 395) or Clotted cream (p. 800) and meringue. Figs dehydrate well, too, and can be kept on hand as a snack or accompaniment for cheese plates and the like. When really ripe, they also work superbly on pizza (see p. 856) or Focaccia (p. 845) with caramelised onions and gorgonzola, and maybe a sprinkling of toasted walnuts, hazelnuts or pine nuts. Some shaved prosciutto or jamón wouldn't be amiss.

When figs are good, they are very, very good – but when they are bad, they are horrid. Don't bother with figs that are light in weight or dry; they will never ripen and will always be tasteless. Sometimes the season doesn't result in sweet figs – too much or too little water, for example. Sometimes you can just get a tree that turns out duds, while other trees are reliably magnificent. Unless making large amounts of jam, or dehydrating them, it would be very hard for a standard household to consume the entire crop from a mature fig tree. If you don't have your own tree, establish a relationship with someone who does. Fig trees proliferate in my local suburbs, and much of the fruit goes to waste. Because of their fragility, figs are often expensive at the market, but there's probably a tree nearby groaning under the weight of a crop.

Figs are quite perishable, so look for specimens that are heavy in the hand, soft but not squishy. A split or weeping fig is not necessarily a problem, rather a sign of ripeness, but if those juices have started to ferment or develop mould, move on. If you have a tree, all those ripe figs will make wonderful jam (see p. 706). Just note that figs are not a high-pectin fruit, and pectin naturally degrades when fruits become overripe – so oozingly ripe figs may not gel as well, though they'll still be delicious. Most green figs will start to blush purple and soften when ripe, and rather than protruding directly on their stem, they will start to droop. An easy way to test if a fig is ready is to twist gently: if there's resistance in the stalk, leave for a little longer; a ripe fig will come away without much pressure. An unripe fig will never ripen off the tree, but a mostly ripe fig will soften further on the bench, though it won't necessarily build more flavour. The flavour develops on the tree, but there are many creatures – birds, possums, bats – that are well acquainted with the pleasures of a ripe fig, so daily attention is required. If you have a fig tree, a net is a worthwhile investment.

Preparing figs

Whether you need to peel a fig will depend a little on the variety and the season. Sometimes the skins can be tough and will need to be peeled, but more often than not I will use the whole fig. Just taste and make a judgement based on the produce, as well as your preference. If peeling, you will just be able to do so from the stem down with your hands, or use a paring knife for less waste. Try not to waste any of the harvest – imperfect figs can be poached or made into jam.

Jamón, fig, beetroot, goat's curd, watercress & mint salad (GF)

The success of this simple salad rests heavily on the quality of the ingredients. Well, it solely does, as there's nothing remotely technical about it, but with a little flair in the presentation, it is quite a showstopper. **Serves 4–6**

Pair with

Some good bread of any kind works here, but grilled Sourdough bread (p. 847) drizzled with fragrant oil is best.

2 beetroot (beets), peeled and cut into wedges
125 ml (4 fl oz/½ cup) extra-virgin olive oil
3 tablespoons sherry vinegar

12 slices of jamón
3 handfuls of picked watercress sprigs
6 mint sprigs, picked, large leaves torn

6 ripe figs, thickly sliced
150 g (5½ oz) goat's curd

Staples
EVOO, S&P

Preheat the oven to 200°C (400°F) fan-forced. Line a baking tray with baking paper.

Toss the beetroot in a little oil and season with salt and pepper. Spread out on the baking tray and roast for about 30 minutes, until tender. Set aside to cool.

Combine the 125 ml (4 fl oz/½ cup) oil and vinegar, season and beat to emulsify.

Arrange half the jamón slices on a serving plate, then scatter with half the watercress and mint. Arrange the figs, beetroot and remaining jamón on top. Dollop on the goat's curd, season with salt and plenty of pepper, then finish with the remaining mint and watercress. Drizzle with the dressing and serve immediately.

Veal saltimbocca with fresh figs (GF)

Saltimbocca is a classic dish often associated with Rome, though many attribute its origins further north in Lombardy. Marsala isn't always included in the sauce, though it's worth noting that Marsala is from Sicily, while prosciutto is a northern speciality – so it's likely that saltimbocca is more pan-Italian, rather than a regional dish. It has also taken on something of its own life in the New World, being a staple in old-school 'Italian' restaurants (remember, Italy does not in truth have a national cuisine; it has intensely regional ones). In the past, most restaurant kitchens in Australia seemed to have a bottle of the same type of generic imitation marsala, whether they used it in the dish or not; however, it (and products like it) are nothing like the real thing – though, for some, the nostalgia of the dish may not be replicable without it. Genuine Marsala is not hard to come by, nor is it expensive, but oloroso sherry would also work – or just use more white wine. The addition of fresh fig slices adds a lovely touch of sweetness to complement the saltiness of the prosciutto. **Serves 4**

Pair with

A mixed salad with some bitter leaves such as radicchio and chicory (witlof), dressed with French-style vinaigrette (p. 88), and rosemary and garlic potatoes (see p. 626).

Buttered peas.

Classic potato mash (p. 625).

Figs poached in syrup GF V

Make a simple sugar syrup by adding equal parts caster (superfine) sugar and water to a saucepan, then heat until the sugar dissolves. Spike with fragrant honey and a shot or two of grappa, enough that you can taste it, or try cassis liqueur and lemon juice. Gently poach whole or halved figs until tender – this will only take a few minutes. Cool completely in the syrup, then serve with cold custard or ice cream, or drain off the syrup and top some Puff pastry (p. 822) rounds with Frangipane (p. 796) and then the figs, and bake to make simple tarts. Serve with a drizzle of the poaching syrup and ice cream or Chocolate & honey sauce (p. 793).

---

800 g (1 lb 12 oz) veal backstrap or tenderloin, sliced on an angle into 8 even pieces
8 slices of prosciutto
8 large sage leaves
100 g (3½ oz) butter

100 ml (3½ fl oz) white wine, or dry sherry
100 ml (3½ fl oz) Marsala
100 ml (3½ fl oz) Golden chicken stock (p. 54)
6 ripe figs, sliced into thick rings

Staples
EVOO, FLR, LMN, S&P

Special equipment
Strong, sharp toothpicks

Evenly beat out the veal with a mallet or the flat side of a large knife. Wrap each piece in prosciutto. Pin a sage leaf to the top of each with a toothpick and thread the toothpick through the meat, then back through again to secure the prosciutto in place. Coat the pieces in flour.

Heat two large frying pans over a high heat. Add a splash of oil to each. Divide the saltimbocca between the pans, with the sage facing down. Add one-quarter of the butter to each pan and cook for about 1½ minutes, until well coloured. Season with salt and pepper, then turn and brown for about 1½ minutes on the other side.

Add the wine and marsala and reduce by half, then add the stock, the remaining butter and figs to just warm through.

Plate the saltimbocca and figs, then reduce the sauce to a silky consistency. Squeeze in some lemon and pour the sauce over the saltimbocca to serve.

Fig & filo honey stack

This airy, honey-flavoured cream is a delight with the crisp filo and lusciously textured figs. You can play this any way you like – make a stack or deconstruct, plate individually or make a platter … it's just as delicious whichever way. **Serves 6**

6 ripe figs, thickly sliced
2 tablespoons honey
60 g (2 oz/⅔ cup) toasted flaked almonds (optional)

Honey sabayon cream
300 ml (10 fl oz) pouring (single/light) cream

60 g (2 oz) caster (superfine) sugar
1 egg and 2 egg yolks
1½ leaves of gold-strength gelatine, soaked in cold water
2 teaspoons honey, or 1 teaspoon orange-blossom water

Honey filo crisps
12 filo pastry sheets
120 g (4 oz) unsalted butter, melted
80 g (2¾ oz/⅓ cup) caster (superfine) sugar
3 tablespoons honey

For the sabayon, whip the cream into soft peaks, then set aside at room temperature. Whisk the sugar, egg and egg yolks in a large bowl. Suspend the bowl over a saucepan with a few inches of simmering water in it, then whisk for about 10 minutes until thick and fluffy. Squeeze the gelatine leaves of excess water and add them to the bowl with the honey, then whisk until well incorporated. Fold the cream through and refrigerate until set, about 1 hour.

Preheat the oven to 180°C (350°F) fan-forced. Line two baking trays with baking paper.

For the filo crisps, lay a pastry sheet on a board and brush with some of the butter. Sprinkle with sugar, then lay another filo sheet on top, sprinkle with more sugar and top with a third sheet. Repeat with the remaining filo sheets, to make four stacks. Cut into strips or triangles, then transfer to the baking trays and drizzle with the honey. Bake for about 10 minutes until golden, then cool.

Dollop some sabayon on a plate, top with a piece of filo, more sabayon and a slice of fig, then repeat, making it as orderly or chaotic as you like. Finish by drizzling the honey over, then sprinkling with almonds if desired.

Toffeed figs (GF) (V) (VG)

Cut 4 ripe figs into 2 cm (¾ in) slices. Fill a large bowl with cold water. Add 400 g (14 oz/1¾ cups) caster (superfine) sugar and 80 ml (2½ fl oz/⅓ cup) water to a small saucepan over a high heat. Stir to combine, then cook for 6–8 minutes, until you have a light to medium caramel. Dip the base of the saucepan into the cold water for a minute or so to stop the caramel cooking further, then remove. Using a fork, dip the fig slices into the caramel to coat, then lay on baking paper to set. Eat within the hour, as they will start to weep otherwise. Serve with ice cream or crème fraîche with crushed biscotti over the top, or go even more deluxe and set the figs on a base of Chocolate crème pâtissière (p. 798).

Fried sardines with tomato & fig

Late-season tomatoes are so delicious, and figs are at their prime then as well, and will kick on through late autumn. While not everything in season goes with everything else peaking at the same time, there are still plenty of seasonal synergies – and though this combination may seem unusual at first, it is a very successful one. **Serves 4–6 as a starter**

6 black Russian tomatoes, or another ripe tomato, thickly sliced
5 figs, thickly sliced
1 tablespoon fish sauce
1 tablespoon sherry vinegar
oil, for deep-frying (see p. 22)
100 g (3½ oz) fine semolina

100 g (3½ oz/⅔ cup) plain (all-purpose) flour
16 whole sardines, cleaned, backbone removed (see p. 168)
1 white salad onion, finely sliced on a mandoline, then soaked in cold water and drained

2 handfuls of fresh fenugreek leaves, dill or flat-leaf (Italian) parsley
1 tablespoon ground sumac

Staples
EVOO, LMN, S&P

Special equipment
Mandoline

Lay the tomato and fig slices on a platter, season with salt and pepper, sprinkle with the fish sauce and vinegar, then drizzle with oil.

Heat 4 cm (1½ in) of oil in a deep heavy-based frying pan or deep-fryer until about 180°C (350°F). Combine the semolina and flour in a flat bowl.

Dust the sardines in the semolina mixture, then fry in two batches for 3–4 minutes until lightly golden, turning to cook evenly. Lay directly on top of the figs and tomato, then finish with the onion and fenugreek. Squeeze over some lemon and dust with the sumac. Serve immediately.

Make it different
With whiting or flathead. Use small sand whiting, whole or filleted, or fried pieces of flathead fillets.

Fig & ginger jam GF V VG

If you have a fig tree, you'll need to know how to make fig jam, which is devilishly simple. Fig and ginger are so complementary, with the ginger sharpening the flavours and pegging back the sweetness. **Makes about 1 litre (34 fl oz/4 cups)**

Pair with

This jam has all the normal uses, of course, but I do particularly like it with Saffron scones (p. 772) or spooned over a tart with mascarpone.

1.2 kg (2 lb 10 oz) ripe figs, sliced 1.5 cm (½ in) thick
800 g (1 lb 12 oz/3½ cups) caster (superfine) sugar

100 g (3½ oz) fresh ginger, peeled and very finely sliced
1 vanilla bean, splintered into 4 pieces on an angle

100 ml (3½ fl oz) water
juice of 2 lemons

Add the figs, sugar, ginger, vanilla beans and water to a wide, heavy-based saucepan. Mix with your hands to roughly combine. Put the pan over a medium heat and bring to a simmer, skimming off any foam or impurities as they appear. Cook for 20 minutes, very gently stirring now and then, taking care not to break up the figs.

Add the lemon juice and cook for about 10 minutes, until a teaspoon of jam gels on a chilled plate. If you have a sugar thermometer, the jam is ready when the temperature reaches 105–106°C (221–223°F).

Once at gelling stage, pour the hot jam into sterilised jars, right to the top – the jam will shrink as it cools. Seal the jars and store in a cool, dark place for up to 6 months. Refrigerate after opening.

Vanilla & fig leaf panna cotta with scorched lemon syrup

Fig leaves carry the same distinctive smoky scents as the fruit, and you can extract that flavour quite easily to perfume a custard, panna cotta or the like. You could also serve this with some slices of fig. **Serves 10**

370 ml (12½ fl oz) full-cream (whole) milk
750 ml (25 fl oz/3 cups) pouring (single/light) cream
120 g (4 oz) caster (superfine) sugar
½ vanilla bean, seeds scraped
8 freshly picked fig leaves

5 leaves of gold-strength gelatine, soaked in cold water
amaretti or pistachio biscotti, to serve

Scorched lemon syrup
250 g (9 oz) caster (superfine) sugar

zest and juice of 5 lemons (about 350 ml/12 fl oz juice)

Special equipment
10 × 125 ml (4 fl oz/½ cup) dariole moulds

Warm the milk, cream, sugar and vanilla bean pod and seeds in a saucepan over a medium heat. Roll up the fig leaves to break the fibres and release flavour, then add to the pan. Bring to a simmer and take straight off the heat.

Squeeze the gelatine leaves of excess water and add them to the pan, stirring to dissolve. Stand for 15 minutes to infuse.

Strain the panna cotta mixture through a fine-mesh sieve. Pour into ten 125 ml (4 fl oz/½ cup) dariole moulds to the top (or ramekins or small dishes that you can serve in). Refrigerate overnight, or for at least 6 hours.

For the syrup, add the sugar to a medium saucepan over a high heat until the sugar liquefies, shaking the pan to colour evenly, but without stirring. Continue to cook for about 8 minutes. You're aiming for a dark caramel, but don't let it burn or it will be bitter. Remove from the heat and add the lemon zest and juice. Be careful, as it's extremely hot and will spit! Stir and return to the heat. Bring to a simmer, stirring until the caramel is fully amalgamated with the juice. Take off the heat and refrigerate until cold and syrupy.

To serve, with the tip of your finger, gently pull the top edge of the panna cotta away from the side of the moulds – this will break the seal. Rotate the moulds gently and then turn out onto plates. (If using dishes, you can simply serve the panna cotta in them.) Spoon some syrup over and serve with biscotti, either whole or crumbled over the top.

Pair with

The scorched lemon syrup could also be spooned over Classic sponge cake (p. 748), Blintzes (p. 771) or Crepes (p. 771).

Brûléed figs ⒼⒻ Ⓥ ⓋⒼ

This is a super simple and very attractive way to serve figs for dessert. Heavily dust fig halves or thick slices with caster (superfine) sugar, then place under a very hot grill (broiler) for the sugar to melt and scorch, or use a kitchen blowtorch, if you have one. Cool, then serve with custard, ice cream or Honey sabayon cream (see p. 703).

Pear

I didn't really appreciate that there was more than one variety of pear until I worked in a proper kitchen. Pears – probably mainly packham at the time – were the less durable partner to apples in the uneaten school fruit department, ones that could turn a schoolbag into a miserable mess when ripe, while apples happily endured for days. Pears were also not so widely cooked, again ceding to the apple – though they were often bought cooked, in tins of syrup. Poaching a pear was only the province of the ambitious home cook, and red-wine poached pears certainly never graced our dinner table for a midweek dessert.

There is something classical and elegant about a poached pear, perfectly peeled with its natural shape intact and a spike of stem in place. I have now peeled and poached many a pear, and while we grow only a handful of the estimated 3000 cultivars available to us, they are not all the same.

Bartlett pears are also known as williams pears, which is the original (though not necessarily most common) name. They were first widely propagated and named by a Mr Williams in England, then subsequently 'rediscovered' – though it was just the name and not the variety that was unknown – in America, where a Mr Bartlett lent the cultivar his surname. They are a good all-round pear, which begin their life green and turn yellowish when ripe. They are a fine eating pear, but also hold their shape well when cooked, so can be successfully roasted or poached. The red sensation is essentially a red-skinned bartlett pear, the product of a natural mutation in an Australian orchard in the 1930s.

Beurre bosc and josephine pears both have a deeply golden nectar-like flavour, especially when slowly cooked. Both are good for roasting for sweet and savoury applications, and eat well fresh, matching especially well with hard umami-rich cheeses such as Parmigiano Reggiano and gruyère. Beurre bosc pears are elongated, with a rough skin that has a tarnished coppery hue. They're very elegant looking, evoking an Old Master still life. They have a slightly grainy flesh when raw, but excel when cooked, developing rich caramel tones. Josephines, or Joséphine de Malines to be precise, are a Belgian pear. They are rounded with swollen fat bottoms, with lovely soft and juicy flesh and ample flavour when ripe. They poach beautifully, with the flesh becoming almost translucent.

The packham pear is an Australian cultivar developed in the 1890s in Molong, New South Wales. It looks very similar to a bartlett/williams pear in shape and hue, though with noticeably bumpy skin. One of the packham's parents is indeed a bartlett, with the original aim of Mr Packham to create a late-season pear. It is that, and it has a longer season, making it a significant commercial variety, accounting for about 60 per cent of Australia's production. It is also an excellent eating pear, with sweet, juicy flesh and vibrantly clear and intense flavour. Packhams also poach and roast extremely well.

Corella pears are often regarded as an Australian pear, named after a colourful native parrot, and thought to have been developed by the German settlers of the Barossa Valley in South Australia sometime in the 1800s. However, the essentially identical forelle pear is actually a very old German pear, with forelle meaning 'trout'. Both terms describe how the green to yellow skin blushes red with ripeness. Whether there is an actual genetic difference is irrelevant to the cook, as they are culinarily identical. They are a very pretty and compact fruit with sweet flesh and some tartness. While they cook well, I tend to like them raw, especially paired with hard cheeses such as parmesan, gruyère and pecorino. They can be eaten both quite firm as well as soft.

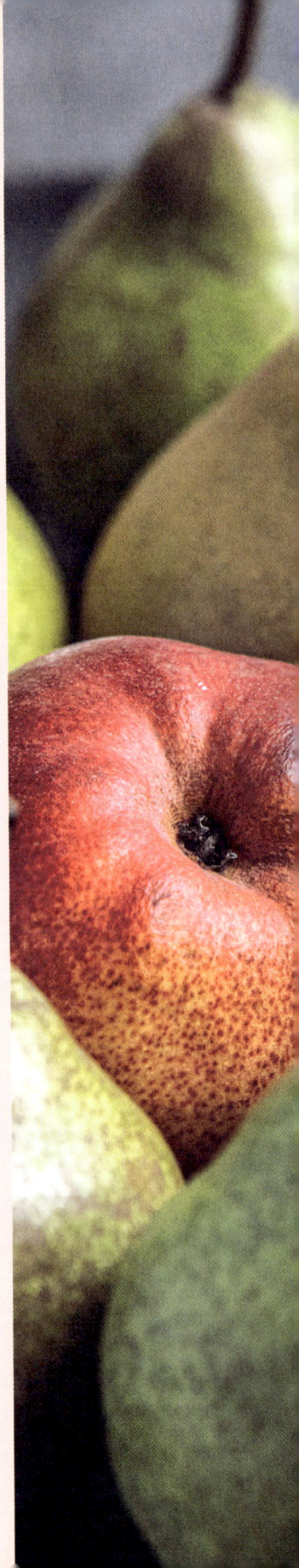

Also see

Quail saltimbocca with caramelised pears 268–9

Celeriac remoulade with pear 484

Pear, fennel & witlof slaw with buttermilk dressing 680

Baked whole pears with verjuice & a clove crumb 684

Saffron-poached pears 724

Pair with

Pears love cream, butter, buttery pastry and umami-rich cheeses, such as Parmigiano Reggiano and gruyère, and they have a special affinity with blue cheeses. Spice them with cinnamon, cloves, black pepper, allspice and ginger, and match with vanilla, maple syrup, dark chocolate, balsamic, vincotto, saba, brown sugar and toffee – and they're amazing poached in red wine. Pears adore walnuts, almonds, hazelnuts and pecans, and are a perfect foil in savoury dishes for bitter or peppery leaves such as rocket (arugula), radicchio and chicory (witlof/ endive).

The nashi is a pear that looks very much like an apple. Sometimes called a nashi pear or Japanese pear, 'nashi' is the Japanese word for pear – so call it 'pear pear', if you will. It also grows throughout China and Korea, and the word 'pear' is often qualified with those countries, too. Nashis can be eerily perfect in their symmetry, and range from being quite pale green yellow to brown with a spray of yellow speckles. They have a high water content and are easily bruised, but the flesh has a light and ultra-crisp texture, delicate flavour, light sweetness and a real sense of refreshment. They're great for cutting into matchsticks to toss with salads.

Like apples, pears are candidates for long-term storage. Pears aren't ripened on the tree and can be kept in stasis for some time, if not quite as long as some apples. At home, a refrigerated pear will store for weeks, and will come to eating maturity after a couple of days on the bench.

When selecting pears, unripe-ness is the curious goal. Pears are very delicate when ripe, so buying ripe pears has some hazards, as you're unlikely to get pristine examples. Any pears with soft spots, cuts or dents should be rejected. Given that pears ripen off the tree, there is no harm in a hard pear, so long as it has been brought to maturity on the tree. How ripe you like your pear is a matter of taste, with some preferring them a little crunchy, while others like them juicy and ultra-sweet. The best way to test a pear is to apply gentle pressure towards the stem, with a little give indicating sufficient ripeness.

Sliced pears roasted with maple syrup, thyme & white pepper (GF) (V) (VG)

Preheat the oven to 180°C (350°F) fan-forced. Cut 3 firm unripe pears (beurre bosc, corella or red sensation) lengthways into 1.5 cm (½ in) slices, including core and stem. On a baking tray, toss the pears, 1½ tablespoons extra-virgin olive oil, 2 tablespoons maple syrup, ½ teaspoon ground white pepper, ¼ teaspoon salt flakes and the leaves of 5 thyme sprigs. Spread out in one layer. Roast for about 25 minutes, until the pear slices are a little shrunken and brown at the edges. Cool to room temperature before using. Serves 6, with cheese. You could also add it to a salad with peppery leaves and chicory (witlof/endive) tossed with a sharp dressing of sherry vinegar and extra-virgin olive oil, with toasted walnuts or hazelnuts and crumbled blue cheese over the top. Alternatively, arrange on top of Puff pastry (p. 822) and bake for 20 minutes at 200°C (400°F) fan-forced. Once cooked, crumble goat's cheese over the top, then drizzle with saba or vincotto.

Preparing pears

After washing, nothing needs to be done to a raw pear, besides removing or avoiding the core. The skin is nutritious, digestible and appealing, though it should be peeled away for poaching. If poaching whole pears, you can either leave the core in, or remove the hard core and seeds from the base with a melon baller or small spoon, leaving the shape of the pear intact; the stem looks elegant when left on. Pears will oxidise and brown once cut, so it's best to cut them just before use. Acid will retard this oxidation, so lemon juice (or a vinaigrette, if using in a savoury application) will keep them pristine.

Pear, fennel, celery heart, Roquefort & poppy seed salad GF V

As autumn leans towards winter, with pears at their peak and fennel slipping into season, this is a lovely light but intensely flavoured salad. Tangy, salty blue cheese with pear is a timelessly beautiful combination. **Serves 4**

2 ripe but firm packham pears, sliced 3 mm (⅛ in) thick
3 teaspoons poppy seeds
½ large fennel bulb, finely sliced lengthways on a mandoline
1 celery heart, finely sliced, pale yellow leaves picked

2 spring onions (scallions), white part only, finely sliced
2 dill sprigs, fronds picked
100 g (3½ oz) Roquefort, or other blue cheese, crumbled

Sherry vinegar dressing
100 ml (3½ fl oz) extra-virgin olive oil
2½ tablespoons sherry vinegar

2 tablespoons pouring (single/light) cream
1 teaspoon caster (superfine) sugar

Staples
EVOO, S&P

Special equipment
Mandoline

Pair with

This works as a standalone salad, or you could serve it with roasted or grilled beef, or crumbed veal or chicken.

Serve alongside Braised witlof (p. 554).

Add the dressing ingredients to a small bowl, season with salt and pepper, then beat to combine.

Add the pear to a bowl and drizzle a little oil over. Season with salt and pepper, add the poppy seeds and toss to coat, then tip onto a serving plate.

Combine the fennel, celery heart and leaves, spring onion and dill in a bowl, then pile on top of the pear. Crumble the cheese around, then spoon the dressing over.

Make it different
With radicchio & walnut. Add some torn radicchio leaves and top with a handful of toasted walnuts, broken with your hands.

Spiced red wine pears GF V VG

This is a very classic way of cooking pears. If you used wine alone, you'd never get the rich infusion of colour that make these so keen on the eye. That comes from the berries, which also add layers of flavour and depth. **Serves 6**

6 pears
1 cinnamon stick
Red-wine poaching liquid
750 ml (25½ fl oz/3 cups) red wine
500 g (1 lb 2 oz) caster (superfine) sugar

300 g (10½ oz) frozen blackberries or blackcurrants
juice of 1 lemon, and zest of ½ lemon
juice of 1 orange, and zest of ½ orange

1 thumb-sized piece of fresh ginger, sliced
4 cloves
2 fresh bay leaves
10 fennel seeds
1 rosemary sprig

Pair with

Whipped cream.

Cold Thick vanilla custard (p. 801).

Panna cotta, Chocolate mousse (p. 782) or meringue and cream.

Serve with cinnamon or chocolate ice cream, or frozen yoghurt parfait.

Rice pudding (p. 395) or a Chocolate pudding (p. 782).

Roasted pears with earl grey tea, marsala, cinnamon & orange GF V

Preheat the oven to 170°C (340°F) fan-forced. For a spiced tea syrup, add 400 ml (13½ fl oz) water, 350 ml (12 fl oz) Marsala, 250 g (9 oz) caster (superfine) sugar or honey, 4 earl grey teabags or bergamot tea, the peel of 1 orange, 1 cinnamon stick, 6 black peppercorns and 4 cloves to a small saucepan over a medium heat. Bring to the boil, simmer for about 8 minutes, then remove the teabags. Peel and cut 5 beurre bosc pears in half and arrange in a baking dish that fits them very snugly, then pour the syrup over. Roast for about 45 minutes, until coloured and tender. Spoon the syrup over to serve. Serves 5. Delicious with Spiced honey cake (p. 740), Rice pudding (p. 395) or Crème brûlée (p. 780), or simply with double cream, ice cream or Clotted cream (p. 800).

Pair with

Thick vanilla custard (p. 801) or a sabayon (see p. 703).

Ricotta, goat's curd, fromage frais or Clotted cream (p. 800), and crushed amaretti biscuits or crushed cantuccini.

Serve the pears and syrup with a crepe filled with a mixture of cream cheese, goat's cheese and ricotta.

Serve with a hard cheese such as parmesan, pecorino or gruyère.

Toss in a salad with rocket (arugula) or watercress and shavings of parmesan.

Slow-roasted lamb shoulder (p. 304).

Roasted pears with earl grey tea, marsala, cinnamon & orange

Add the poaching liquid ingredients to a saucepan and simmer for 10 minutes, then strain into a large saucepan.

Peel the pears, then core them from the bottom using a melon baller or small spoon, keeping the stems intact.

Add the pears and cinnamon stick to the pan. Cover with a plate to keep the pears submerged. Bring to a simmer, then turn the heat down to as low as possible and poach for about 45 minutes, until tender.

Once cooled a little, very carefully lift the pears from the liquid and chill.

Reduce the liquid on the stovetop by two-thirds. Strain the syrup and serve over the cold pears.

Roasted pears with honey, verjuice, rosemary & bay leaves GF V

Hard herbs give these part-roasted, part-poached pears a savoury touch and sophisticated flavour. **Serves 8**

6 firm beurre bosc pears

Verjuice poaching liquid
400 ml (13½ fl oz) verjuice, or white wine

250 ml (8½ fl oz/1 cup) honey
1 vanilla bean, split and sliced on an angle
4 fresh bay leaves

2 rosemary sprigs
1 teaspoon white peppercorns (optional)
1½ teaspoons salt flakes

Preheat the oven to 180°C (350°F) fan-forced.

Bring all the poaching ingredients to the boil in a saucepan, then take off the heat.

Peel the pears and cut in half lengthways. Remove the cores, leaving the stems intact.

Lay the pears in a ceramic dish that will fit them snugly. Pour the poaching liquid over the top. Cover with baking paper, then foil. Bake for 40 minutes.

Remove the foil and baking paper. Turn the pears a couple of times in the hot syrup.

Bake for a further 30 minutes or so, until tender, turning the oven grill (broiler) on for the last 10 minutes to colour the pears.

Once cooked, the sauce should be quite reduced, but if it's a little runny, remove the pears and reduce the liquid for a minute or so on the stovetop.

Quince

The Owl and the Pussy-Cat **was one of my favourite poems as a child, and I read it to my girls even before they were born. Later, they quizzed me – as did I my parents – on why 'they danced in the light of the moon', and what the 'mince' and 'slices of quince' were that they dined on. What was this exotic fruit!**

My first encounter with a quince, however, was somewhat less fanciful. I have an early memory of discovering a quince tree on a neighbouring property at my grandmother's, with low-slung fruit that I took for apples. I promptly cut up the very hard 'apples' to share and got quite a shock. With their astringent and sandy texture, they were utterly unpleasant. And although both my grandmothers cooked them, it wasn't until my early days of professional training that I began to really appreciate the transformative cooking process. Whenever I smell quinces poaching, it takes me back to those early training days, preparing box after box to make the most of the short autumn season.

Quinces undergo an amazing makeover when cooked, from entirely inedible to jelly-like and hauntingly scented with the most appealing reddish amber hue. It is the necessity of this process that perhaps stops quinces being as popular as they should be. It's a labour that seems beyond most, but it's not difficult and it's one worth trying. While I find quinces quite beautiful to look at when raw, somewhat like a painting of themselves – a fruit evolved to be still-life subject matter – the colour once properly cooked is fair reward for sacrificing them to the pot.

Unlike the loss of the reddish flecks on borlotti (cranberry) beans, or the fading of the vibrant blue of a swimmer crab, cooking enhances the colour of quince in the most wonderful way. This has to do with the colour compounds (anthocyanins) in the quince flesh and skin being bound up by tannin, which is what makes them so astringently unpalatable when raw, with much the culinary charm of an uncured olive. Once cooked, those bonds are broken, with the colour unfurling and the tannins dissolving, too. As I said, quite the transformation.

I often store quinces on the bench for aesthetic purposes – and always with some of the beautiful leaves attached – as they last for months, slowly turning from a greenish yellow to deeply golden, like the fading late autumn light, with their rosy scent quite transfixing. As the fruit ripens, the pectin levels drop, making them less suitable for jellies, pastes and the like – but they are still marvellous roasted or poached for a purée.

Quinces grow in similar conditions to apples and pears – to which they are related – with the generally short season extended by varieties that favour slightly warmer and cooler zones, stretching out the harvest at both ends. Those varieties are grafted onto rootstock, rather than grown from seed, with the cultivars producing differently shaped fruit, from apple-like to the larger irregularly bulbous pear-like specimens that are the more familiar mental image of the fruit.

Varieties of quince will differ a little in how well they set for jellies, and the colour once cooked will also vary, from pale pink to deep amber to crimson, though long cooking will always bring out the deepest colour. However, it is uncommon to have quinces sold by cultivar, excepting the pineapple quince, which has a distinctive – you guessed it – pineapple flavour. As always, a conversation with the seller will likely reveal the characteristics and the best uses, but, in general, all varieties can be used for the recipes here.

And while quinces are typically used for sweet applications, or to pair with pungent cheeses, they also have savoury applications. Roasted quinces with chestnuts (p. 716) are lovely with fatty meats such as duck, pork and lamb, or try adding quarters or cheeks of quince to the tray with a lamb shoulder spiced with a little cumin, then slow-roast until meltingly tender. I find the combination quite stunning, with a distinctly ancient feel to the pairing of lamb and exotic fruit.

Also see

Persian roast chicken on buttered rice with quince paste & bay leaves 250

Roasted stone fruit & ginger clafoutis 721

Even simpler frangipane tarts 797

Frangipane crostata 826

Pair with

Quinces take to spices such as cinnamon, cloves, star anise, mustard seeds and ginger, and are lovely perfumed with vanilla or bay leaves. Cook slowly in honey, sugar, verjuice or wine. Partner with duck, quail, pork, lamb and chicken, as well as rhubarb, apple, lemon, almonds and hazelnuts. Quince also loves chocolate and cheese (especially sheep's milk, goat's milk and blue cheese), yoghurt, cream and buttery pastry.

The best source of quinces, in my opinion, is from the vast and largely unused orchard that exists in suburban streets. Along with apple, pear, olive, lemon, orange, mandarin, fig, loquats and the like, I see so many quince trees while walking or driving, with the fruits so often left to fall and rot. This is sad. I'm not advocating jumping fences, but a little conversation with a neighbour will generally liberate the fruit and save them from having to clean up the rotting mess later; some quince paste or jelly as a thank you is always a nice touch. Wherever you obtain your quinces from, select ones that are fragrant and heavy in the hand.

Preparing quinces

All quinces will come with a layer of fuzz, which is best left on until just before cooking, protecting them while they are objects of admiration on your kitchen bench or table. If not peeling, this fuzz is best brushed off before cooking. I often leave the peel on and the cores in, as this tends to enhance the colour, but this is not critical. I also like to leave the fruit as intact as possible if roasting, as I favour the way they present at table. It's important to be very careful when cutting into a quince, as they can be difficult to handle; they tend to grab the knife as you cut, making accidents more likely. A stable surface, a sharp knife and patience are key. If peeling, a regular vegetable peeler will do the job. Then, once cut in half or quarters, the core and any of the sandy flesh can be removed with a paring knife or melon baller. It's best to drop the fruit into acidulated water (a lemon squeezed in, with the halves dropped in, too) to stop discolouration until ready to cook.

Slow-roasted quince with honey, cinnamon & cloves (GF)(V)

This is a wonderful way to cook quince, with the halved fruit in its natural form – core and all – beautifully burnished in the oven. The baking dish is also sauced with the most lusciously intense juices, full of rosy perfume and warm spice notes. **Serves 10**

5 quinces, brushed	zest and juice of 1 lemon	2 fresh bay leaves
400 g (14 oz/1¾ cups) caster (superfine) sugar	zest and juice of 1 orange	350 ml (12 fl oz) verjuice
100 g (3½ oz) honey	6 cloves	1 tablespoon sherry vinegar
	2 cinnamon sticks	

Preheat the oven to 140°C (285°F) fan-forced.

Carefully cut the quinces in half lengthways and place in a ceramic baking dish, cut side up. (You can core the quinces, but I like to leave the cores in.) Sprinkle with the sugar and drizzle with the honey. Scatter the zest, cloves, cinnamon sticks and bay leaves around the dish, then pour the verjuice and citrus juices over. Cover with baking paper, then foil, and bake for 2 hours.

Uncover and cook for a further 2 hours, until the quince is tender and the colour has transformed. The actual hue will vary depending on type and ripeness (see p. 712).

As soon as you remove the cooked quinces from the oven, splash the vinegar over. There will be a thick syrup in the baking dish, which is as precious as the jewel-like quince flesh.

Serve warm or at room temperature; the syrup will set into a jelly, so gently reheat the syrup to loosen it.

Poached quince (GF)(V)(VG)

Have a bowl of acidulated water (see p. 6) at the ready. Peel a quince and cut it into quarters, then cut out the core and the sandy part around it, reserving the peel and trimmings. Drop the quince quarters into the water to stop discolouration. Repeat with 7–9 more quinces. Add the quince peels and core trimmings to a medium saucepan. Pour in 2 litres (68 fl oz/8 cups) water and bring to a simmer over a medium heat, then cook for 20 minutes. Meanwhile, preheat the oven to 140°C (285°F) fan-forced. Strain and reserve the water from the pan. Measure the water and combine in a saucepan with an equal weight of caster (superfine) sugar (about 2 kg (4 lb 6 oz). Bring to a simmer over a medium heat, stirring to dissolve the sugar. Drain the quince pieces and arrange in a glass or ceramic baking dish. Add 1 cinnamon stick or star anise and 1 split vanilla bean, then pour the syrup over to cover. Press a piece of baking paper over the top to keep the quince submerged, then cover the dish tightly with foil. Bake for 3½ hours before checking. It's important to be patient to achieve a deep colour, so after that time, keep checking in 30-minute intervals until ready. Cool the quince in the syrup, then refrigerate in the syrup to store. It makes 20 serves and will keep for up to 1 month.

Pair with

Cream or ice cream.

Creamed rice.

Chocolate mousse (p. 782) and pouring (single/light) cream.

I especially like these served warm with plenty of Thick vanilla custard (p. 801).

If the syrup sets well, use on cheese platters, or to fill a sponge.

Roasted quince & chestnuts GF V

This is a wonderful side for roasted meats, especially rich and fatty ones such as roast duck or pork. The quinces need only be cooked until just tender, and the chestnuts hot and softened. While often I will cook quinces until deeply coloured and very tender, I find the texture and flavour en pointe for pairing with savoury dishes. The key to this recipe is finding a baking dish that fits them snugly. **Serves 4–6**

3 large quinces, peeled, halved and cored
150 g (5½ oz) roasted chestnuts (you can buy these, or roast them yourself)

2½ tablespoons brown sugar
4 tablespoons fragrant honey
2 fresh bay leaves
4 thyme sprigs
50 g (1¾ oz) unsalted butter
200 ml (7 fl oz) verjuice

2 tablespoons red-wine vinegar

Staples
S&P

Pair with
Twice-cooked duck (p. 264).
Roast pork (p. 338).
Roast chicken (see p. 229).
Slow-roasted lamb shoulder (p. 304).

Preheat the oven to 200°C (400°F) fan-forced.

Peel the quinces, cut in half and remove the cores. Place, cut side up, in a baking dish that holds them snugly. Add the chestnuts, season with salt and pepper, then sprinkle with the sugar and drizzle with the honey. Add the bay leaves and thyme, then drop on the butter in knobs. Pour the verjuice and vinegar over.

Seal with paper, then foil. Bake on the bottom shelf of the oven for 1 hour.

Carefully pour the juices from the dish into a small saucepan. Reduce by half over a medium–high heat until slightly thickened.

Serve the quinces and chestnuts with the juices spooned over the top.

Quick quince & apple relish GF V VG

Bursting with spice and floral notes, this sweet relish is perfect with charcuterie and pork. It's very quick to cook, but seems to improve the longer it sits, lasting an incredibly long time in the fridge. **Makes about 1 litre (34 fl oz/4 cups)**

1.2 kg (2 lb 10 oz) quinces
1.2 litres (41 fl oz) water
500 g (1 lb 2 oz) apples, peeled and cut into 2 cm (¾ in) dice
1 kg (2 lb 3 oz) caster (superfine) sugar

350 ml (12 fl oz) apple-cider vinegar
100 ml (3½ fl oz) red wine
4 cm (1½ in) piece of fresh ginger, peeled and finely grated
peeled zest of ½ lemon

3 fresh bay leaves
2 star anise
2 cinnamon sticks
1 vanilla bean, split
2½ tablespoons mustard seeds
2 teaspoons salt flakes

Pair with
Charcuterie.
Sharp cheddar.
Roast pork (see p. 338).
Terrine, pickles and a salad.
Dollop on a grilled pork chop.

Quarter the quinces, remove and discard the cores, then cut into 2 cm (¾ in) dice. Add to a saucepan with the water and simmer for 1 hour, until the quince is tender.

Strain the liquid into a saucepan, reserving the quince pieces.

Add the remaining ingredients to the pan with the liquid and cook over a medium heat until the apple is very tender, and the liquid has reduced by about half.

Return the quince pieces to the pan and simmer until a jam-like consistency, 10–15 minutes.

Spoon the relish into hot sterilised jars (see p. 40) and seal, then invert on the bench until cool.

The relish will keep for 6 months in the pantry. Once opened, refrigerate and use within 1 year.

Quince paste (GF) (V) (VG)

Pair with

Firm sheep's milk cheeses, such as manchego or Ossau-Iraty, as well as hard cooked goat's cheese or soft blue cheeses.

Smear on toast, with or without cheese on top.

Use to make a Crostata filled with ricotta & quince (see p. 826).

Dice and add to a Friand (p. 734) mixture.

When making quince paste, I always look for fruits that are greenish rather than a deeper golden, as younger specimens have higher pectin levels, meaning that the paste will set well. **Makes about 1.5 kg (3 lb 5 oz)**

2.5 kg (5½ lb) quinces	1 kg (2 lb 3 oz) caster
2 litres (68 fl oz/8 cups) water	(superfine) sugar
peeled zest and juice of	1 vanilla bean, split
1 lemon	1 teaspoon salt flakes

Have a bowl of acidulated water (see p. 6) at the ready. Peel a quince and cut it into quarters, then cut out the core and the sandy part around it, reserving the peel and trimmings. Drop the quince quarters into the water to stop discolouration. Repeat with all the quinces.

Add the quince peels and core trimmings to a saucepan. Pour in the water and bring to a simmer over a medium heat, then cook for 20 minutes.

Strain the cooking water and add to a large saucepan with the lemon zest and quince quarters. Bring to a simmer over a medium heat, then cook for about 30 minutes, until the quince is tender.

Strain off and reserve the liquid. Purée the quince in a blender, then add back to the pan with the cooking liquid, sugar and vanilla. Cook over a low heat, stirring to dissolve the sugar, then add the lemon juice. Cook over a very low heat for 1½–2 hours, stirring regularly to stop the mixture catching, until it thickens and becomes very deeply coloured. Be careful here, as it is volcanically hot. Once ready, stir in the salt and, if you like, remove the vanilla bean.

Line a 24 cm (9½ in) cake tin, or two 1 litre (34 fl oz/4 cup) loaf (bar) tins – or any other mould or container – with plastic wrap, then pour or scoop the quince paste in.

Set in the fridge overnight. Unmould the paste and wrap in baking paper, then plastic wrap. The paste will keep in the fridge for about 3 months.

Quince jelly (GF) (V) (VG)

Pair with

Blue cheese, goat's curd and/ or aged goat's cheese with rye bread.

Dollop on warm Scones (p. 772), followed by whipped rosewater-scented cream.

Fill a pavlova with whipped cream and raspberries, then dollop the quince jelly on top.

Use in a trifle.

Warm the jelly and use it to glaze a Christmas ham.

Quince jelly is one of those old-fashioned things my nanna said should be in the back of the cupboard, she said, as you never know when you might need it. It's a view I now heartily endorse. **Makes about 1 litre (34 fl oz/4 cups)**

7 quinces	1.25 kg (2 lb 12 oz)	125 ml (4 fl oz/½ cup) lemon
4 litres (135 fl oz/16 cups)	caster (superfine) sugar,	juice
water	approximately	

Chop the quinces into even chunks, but don't peel or core them. Place in a large saucepan, pour in the water and bring to the boil, then reduce the heat and simmer until very soft, up to 30–40 minutes. Line a strainer with doubled-over muslin (cheesecloth) and set it over a bowl. Strain the liquid through the strainer, but don't press the quince flesh or force it in any way, or the liquid will become cloudy – just allow to slowly strain.

Measure the liquid, then combine in a saucepan with an equal weight of sugar. Stir over a low heat to dissolve the sugar. Add the lemon juice, then bring to the boil. Skim off any foam as it boils, continuing until the jelly reaches setting point, 20–30 minutes. You can test the jelly by placing a teaspoonful on a saucer that has been in the freezer, then returning the saucer to the freezer for 2 minutes to see if the jelly sets.

Once ready, pour the jelly into hot sterilised jars (see p. 40) and seal. Invert on the bench until cool.

The jelly will keep for 6 months in the pantry. Once opened, refrigerate and use within 3 months.

Stone fruit

There are few of my childhood memories of true seasonality that are as insistent as those associated with stone fruit. So many other fruits and vegetables were available out of season, even if they were woefully sad iterations. In fact, available tomatoes, for example, were generally terrible no matter the season, unless you grew them yourself or knew someone who did. But stone fruit was in season, or it wasn't, and the deep flavour, intense sweetness and dripping juiciness of a supremely ripe peach, nectarine or the like was something that even the most unevolved palate was an expert on.

Stone fruit said summer, and it was a true pleasure, an indulgence, but an accessible one, and one that was celebrated as being healthy. Summers were happy times. And that idea of seasonality went even deeper, with the cherry harvest heralding in the warmer weather leading up to Christmas, then exploding in a festive gorging on the fruit, a pair joined by a wishbone of stem draped across an ear or two.

And then cherries vanished not long after, banished until next season. But even as apricots faded and plums started to occupy more space in the fruit bowl, heralding in autumn, those peaches and nectarines kept the hope alive that summer would roll on forever. Of course, it never did.

In fact, when I grew up, we had the benefit of fruit trees in the yard, so that connection was even stronger. I was roped into climbing the apricot, plum and nectarine trees in a race against the birds to pick all the fruit – though I ate a lot in the process – for mum to then make jams, or she would poach the nectarines to eat with custard or make a crumble out of – but never jam from the nectarines.

Today, the windows of availability have expanded a little, due to a raft of varieties that ripen at different times, but I rarely find much difference now than I did then, with early and late season fruit generally lacking, and fruit not adequately ripened on the tree always disappointing.

Nectarines and peaches are essentially the same fruit, or rather nectarines are a smooth-skinned peach variety. The flavour is suitably different, though. Peaches originated in China but were cultivated in ancient Persia (their botanical name is *Prunus persica*) and across the Mediterranean, resulting in many different cultivars, the catalogue of which has expanded dramatically in modern times in the search for new varieties that fulfill various goals, from flavour to frost and disease resistance to filling a certain ripening window.

That wealth of varieties is not something that is a feature at the market, though, with peaches and nectarines generally sold as white or yellow and either clingstone or freestone, which is self-explanatory. There are also those referred to as semi-clingstone or semi-freestone varieties, which is the same thing said in different ways. I generally opt for freestone fruit when cooking, as they are much easier to prepare, with clingstone varieties not suitable for poaching and the like. Clingstones are best for devouring ripe, with the juices invariably racing down your arm. Whichever type you choose, the fruit should have no soft spots and smell extravagantly when ripe. While they will ripen on the bench, it is best to pick fruit that has spent most time ripening on the tree. Green fruit should be rejected.

I have particular affection for white peaches and nectarines, with the flavour and fragrance so pure and elegant, and generally sweeter than yellow varieties. That's not to say that yellow stone fruit is not delicious. It is, and the general firmness of the flesh, while still being ripe, also makes it suitable for grilling. A thickly sliced yellow peach brushed with oil and grilled until a little charry and softened, but still firm in the middle, served with some bresaola and bitter leaves is a wonderous thing. Or serve with fresh mozzarella and a sauce of smashed green olives, capers and extra-virgin olive oil spooned over the top.

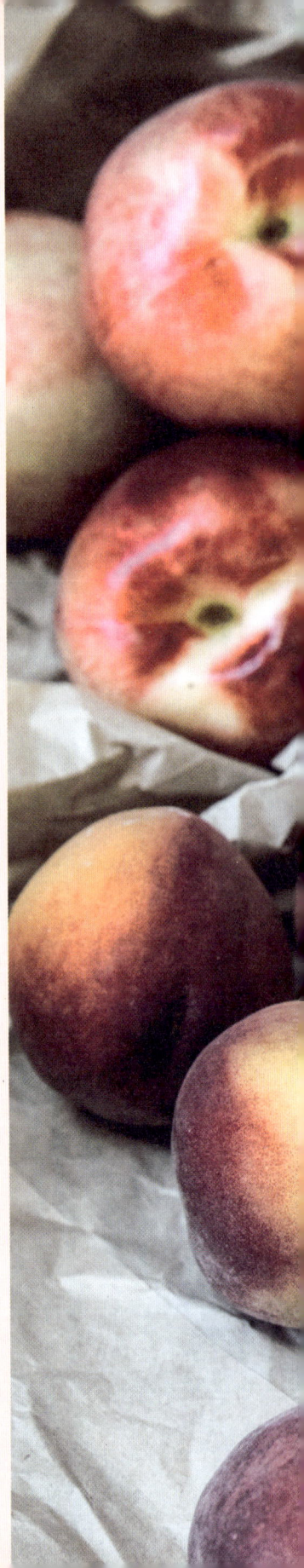

Also see

Seared duck breast with roasted plum & hoisin sauce for pancakes or bao 263

Asian brisket with vinegared blood plums 291

Seared radicchio with burrata, balsamic-pickled cherries & scorched almonds 566

Roasted rhubarb, blood plum & ginger chutney 646

Apple & cherry turnovers 681

Apricot, semolina, almond & yoghurt cake 753

Free-form stone fruit tart 814

Cherry puff pastry tart 824–5

Pair with

Stone fruit loves dairy, cream, milk, ice cream, crème fraîche and mascarpone, and works well with burrata, fresh mozzarella and fresh curd cheeses in savoury dishes. Pair with liqueur, sparkling wine, honey, brown sugar, verjuice, balsamic and caramel. Scent with vanilla, cinnamon, star anise, white pepper, thyme, bay leaves, lemon verbena, mint. Pair with almonds, orange and lemon and spice up with chilli and vinegar.

Cherries similarly come in numerous varieties, with more than eighty in commercial production in Australia across their brief season. Like peaches, cherries are rarely sold by variety but that diversity is apparent by the variations in size and hue, from, well, cherry red, to black. Mostly, cherries are sold by premium, with prices varying widely based on the grade. However, I find the only reliable indicator of a quality cherry is by eating one, which most sellers will encourage – always ask, though. Cherries with their stems will last longer, so buying them sans stem is not a great idea. Although uncommon in Australia, sour cherries will appear at the market at times. These will typically be morello cherries, and they can be used in baking or to make preserves.

Apricots have a similarly short season, though they're typically present through the summer months. There are various cultivars grown for commercial production, but the moorpark variety is the most celebrated. It's an old cultivar, developed in England in the seventeenth century, and it is said to produce the most flavoursome fruit. Moorpark apricots can be reasonably large, though I typically choose smaller specimens, whatever the variety, as they generally seem to be tastier and juicier. I also look for a patch of rosy blush, which was what we looked for on the tree at home. To me, that always meant they were properly sun-ripened, though no doubt some varieties present differently.

Plums have the longest season, stretching from late spring through summer and deep into autumn. That span is due to the diversity of varieties, with the fruit quite varied in colour, size, flavour and acidity. Unlike other stone fruit, plums are usually sold by variety. For me, blood plums are the finest eating plums, and they're wonderfully dramatic to cook with, having such intensely coloured flesh. There are many varieties of blood plum, all originally hailing from Japan, with a raft of other Japanese cultivars – santa rosa being perhaps the best known – combining to make up a lot of the commercial market in Australia.

The balance is made up of 'European' plums, which are generally less firm, with a softer acid profile and more sweetness. While not easy to source, it's worth seeking out greengage plums, which are a European variety that remain green when ripe while having very sweet and richly flavoured flesh. Davidson plums are also becoming more readily available. They're a native Australian plum with a sour profile, making them ideal to cook with. They also pack an extraordinary amount of vitamin C.

Peaches, nectarines, apricots, plums and cherries are all from the *Prunus* genus and are related to almonds, with the kernels of peaches and apricots tasting like the nut. Both are used to make almond substitute products, while apricot kernels are used for snacks or to add a bitter almond note to desserts in Asia. A word of caution, though, as apricots kernels also contain cyanide. This can be deactivated by processing, but it's best not to try this yourself. It's safer to just discard them. Cherry pits, however, contain pectin, and they can be cracked and used to gel Cherry jam (p. 723), as the flesh is naturally low in pectin.

Preparing stone fruit

Choosing freestone stone fruit makes preparation simple, with the stone readily dropping out of the halved fruit. For cherries, a cherry pitter is a good investment if you're making jam or the like. Aside from that, the only preparation required would be if a recipe calls for the fruit to be peeled. Peaches and nectarines can be peeled by blanching the fruit as you would a tomato (see p. 655).

Roasted stone fruit GF V VG

Classically, I was trained to poach stone fruit, as it's a delicate way of cooking what are quite delicate fruits. These days, I prefer a more robust flavour and method. And it's a lot easier to roast the fruit and control the temperature and cooking time. You still get some liquid in the tray to make a sauce.
Makes about 500 g (1 lb 2 oz)

Pair with
Ice cream and a drizzle of the roasting juices.

Cold Thick vanilla custard (p. 801).

Use in fruit tarts.

Pair with Vanilla crème pâtissière (p. 798) in a tart (pp. 812–3).

Use for topping a Pavlova (p. 784).

1 kg (2 lb 3 oz) peaches, nectarines, apricots or plums

100 g (3½ oz) caster (superfine) sugar

200 ml (7 fl oz) orange juice, verjuice or white wine

Preheat the oven to 170°C (340°F) fan-forced.

Cut the stone fruit down the natural seam with a small knife, then split open and remove the stones, using a paring knife if needed to carefully dig the stones out.

Arrange the fruit halves, cut side up, in a ceramic, glass or enamel baking dish that fits them quite snugly. Evenly scatter with the sugar, then pour the orange juice over. Cover with baking paper, pressing down to connect with the fruit, then wrap the dish tightly with foil.

Bake for 30 minutes for peaches and nectarines, 20 minutes for apricots, and 20 minutes for plums.

Set the dish aside on the bench to finish cooking the fruit in the residual heat for 30 minutes, before slipping off the skins.

Serve, or refrigerate the fruit in the roasting juices, which will keep for 5–7 days.

Make it different
To add some colour and a more roasted flavour, you can also roast the fruit uncovered for an extra 15 minutes after the suggested cooking time.

Roasted peaches stuffed with ricotta & chocolate, with crushed biscotti V

While a roasted peach served with a little cream or ice cream is a marvellous thing, stuffing them and roasting further certainly ups the stakes. These are just as good at room temperature as they are hot. **Serves 4**

200 g (7 oz) ricotta
100 g (3½ oz) dark chocolate, chopped
2 tablespoons caster (superfine) sugar
zest of 1 lemon

1 × quantity freshly roasted peaches (above), still in the baking dish
4 amaretti biscotti, roughly crushed

Red wine, orange & coffee sauce
150 ml (5 fl oz) rich red wine (such as shiraz)
100 g (3½ oz) brown sugar
60 ml (2 fl oz/¼ cup) freshly brewed espresso coffee
4 strips of orange zest

Heat the oven to 200°C (400°F) fan-forced.

In a bowl, combine the ricotta, chocolate, sugar and lemon zest, mixing well. Divide the mixture among the peach halves, then spoon some of the roasting juices over the top.

Bake for 15 minutes, or until the topping is slightly puffed and the chocolate has melted.

Meanwhile, add all the sauce ingredients to a small saucepan and bring to the boil over a medium heat. Simmer for 4 minutes, then strain and cool.

To serve, spoon the sauce over the peaches, then scatter with the crushed biscotti.

Roasted apricot & ginger clafoutis (V)

Clafoutis is a traditional French dessert of cherries baked in batter – but the batter works just as well with apricots or other stone fruit, and indeed with poached pears, rhubarb or quince. **Serves 6**

9 apricots, halved and pitted
4 cm (1½ in) piece of fresh young ginger, peeled and julienned
80 g (2¾ oz) caster (superfine) sugar, plus extra to dust the moulds

Batter
100 g (3½ oz) caster (superfine) sugar

60 g (2 oz/½ cup) ground almonds
10 g (¼ oz) plain (all-purpose) flour
a pinch of fine sea salt
250 ml (8½ fl oz/1 cup) pouring (single/light) cream
2 eggs
3 egg yolks

Staples
BTR, ISGR

Special equipment
6 × 13 cm (5 in) ceramic ramekins or a 22 × 32 cm (8¾ × 12½ in) ceramic baking dish

Add the apricot halves, ginger and sugar to the ramekins or baking dish and toss through, then set aside for 20 minutes.

Meanwhile, preheat the oven to 180°C (350°F) fan-forced.

Turn all the apricots cut side up in the dish. Transfer to the oven and bake for 10 minutes, then rest for 10 minutes.

For the batter, add the sugar, ground almonds, flour and salt to a food processor and blend for 1 minute. Add the cream, eggs and egg yolks and process until smooth, about 2 minutes.

Grease the ramekins or baking dish with butter and line with caster sugar, tapping them lightly to shake off any excess. Divide the apricots, cut side up, among the dishes, then pour the batter over.

Bake for 15–20 minutes, until the batter is puffed, golden and has set in the middle.

Dust with icing (confectioners') sugar and serve immediately.

Make it different
Cherry & ginger clafoutis. (V) Instead of apricots, use eighteen fresh cherries, pitted but left whole and unroasted.

Berry & ginger clafoutis. (V) Replace the apricots with a punnet of fresh berries – no need to roast these first.

Roasted apricot & orange blossom clafoutis. (V) Replace the ginger with a splash of orange-blossom water.

Roasted apricot & almond clafoutis. (V) Replace the ginger with natural almond extract.

With other stone fruits. Try this with Poached quince (p. 714), roasted or poached rhubarb (see p. 646), poached stone fruit (see p. 724) or Roasted stone fruit (opposite).

Pair with

Ice cream, pouring (single/light) cream or crème fraîche.

Peach caramel sauce (GF)(V)(VG)

Cut 2 firm but ripe peaches into 3 cm (1¼ in) wedges, then roast for 20 minutes at 180°C (350°F) fan-forced. Caramelise 250 g (9 oz) caster (superfine) sugar in a saucepan over a high heat until a dark caramel. Carefully mix the roasted peach wedges through; the caramel will be molten hot. Add the juice of 1 lemon and simmer for 5 minutes, then cool for 15 minutes. Purée, then strain. Use as a sauce for drizzling over ice cream, waffles, sponge cake or roasted fruit.

A simple peach dessert (GF)(V)

A perfectly ripe peach is a wondrous thing, requiring no embellishment, but you can enhance its beauty in simple ways, too. Slice peaches finely and fan in coups or martini glasses, drizzle with a little sugar syrup (see p. 703) or poaching syrup (see p. 724), and top with a scoop of proper vanilla ice cream. Serve at the table by pouring over some sparkling wine – Champagne if decadence is your thing, but Prosecco will do just fine.

Cherry & almond burnt butter torte ⓥ

Employing that magical match of almonds, vanilla and cherries, this is such a simple tart, with no pastry to worry about. And although it is simple, it presents quite beautifully, especially when heavily dusted with icing (confectioners') sugar and adorned with glossy fresh cherries. **Serves 8–10**

1½ vanilla beans
180 g (6½ oz) cold
 unsalted butter
5 egg whites
340 g (12 oz/2¾ cups) icing
 (confectioners') sugar

110 g (4 oz/¾ cup) plain
 (all-purpose) flour
100 g (3½ oz/1 cup) ground
 almonds
½ teaspoon natural almond
 extract

300 g (10½ oz) pitted
 cherries, halved
2 tablespoons flaked
 almonds

Staples
ISGR, S&P

Preheat the oven to 160°C (320°F) fan-forced. Spray a 24 cm (9½ in) loose-based fluted flan (tart) tin with oil, and line the base with baking paper.

Cut the vanilla beans in half lengthways and scrape the seeds into a small saucepan. Cut the vanilla pods into splinters and add to the pan with the butter. Cook over a medium heat until the butter is brown with a nutty aroma, 4–5 minutes. Tip into a bowl and cool to room temperature.

Using an electric stand mixer, whisk the egg whites with a pinch of salt until forming peaks, then slowly rain in half the icing sugar until combined and glossy. Fold in the flour, ground almonds and remaining icing sugar with a spatula, then fold in the almond extract and the melted butter mixture, being careful to keep the mix aerated.

Pour into the flan tin, flattening gently with a spatula. Drop the cherries all over, keeping a few aside to garnish the cooked torte, then sprinkle the almonds over.

Bake for 30–40 minutes, until the torte is puffed and very lightly golden – don't bake until darker. Cool to room temperature before unmoulding.

Serve heavily dusted with icing sugar, with the reserved cherries tumbled on top.

Make it different
Berry & almond burnt butter torte. Adjust the torte to the season by using the same quantity of raspberries, blueberries or blackberries instead of the cherries.

Pair with
Crème fraîche, Clotted cream (p. 800) or cold Thick vanilla custard (p. 801).

Grilled peaches or nectarines ⒼⓋⓋⒼ

Thickly slice firm but ripe peaches or nectarines. Coat with oil, season with salt and pepper and chargrill for 1–2 minutes on each side to give char marks and soften the flesh a little. Serve with burrata, shaved jamón or prosciutto and a scattering of basil or rocket (arugula), or serve as a starter with well-charred Sourdough bread (p. 847) slices drizzled with peppery olive oil.

Cherry, vanilla & balsamic compote ⒼⓋⓋⒼ

Cherries cooked quickly like this hold their shape and fresh intensity, with their colour remaining deeply vibrant and ever so inviting. **Serves 4**

400 g (14 oz) cherries, pitted
100 g (3½ oz) caster
 (superfine) sugar

1 teaspoon natural vanilla
 extract
100 ml (3½ fl oz) balsamic
 vinegar

1 knifepoint of bitter almond
 extract

Place the cherries, sugar and vanilla in a medium saucepan. Cook over a high heat for 3 minutes, shaking the pan frequently to caramelise the sugar evenly. Add the vinegar and bring to a simmer, then stir the almond extract through and cook for 2 minutes.

Lift out the cherries with a slotted spoon, then reduce the syrup for 1 minute.

Set aside to cool for about 10 minutes, then pour the syrup back over the cherries to serve.

Pair with
Serve warm or chilled, with Classic panna cotta or Yoghurt panna cotta (p. 781).

Spoon over vanilla ice cream with some cherry liqueur and top with a wafer.

Serve with a dark Chocolate tart (p. 817) or torte (see p. 751).

Cherry, raspberry & vanilla jam (GF) (V) (VG)

Pair with

Scones (p. 772), Crumpets (p. 769), Pancakes (p. 768) and toast.

Stir a little grappa through the jam and serve with Classic panna cotta (p. 781).

Cherry compote with brioche & crème fraîche (V)

Serve this quick and simple compote for dessert, or a somewhat decadent brunch. Place 100 g (3½ oz) caster (superfine) sugar in a dry frying pan over a high heat. After about 2 minutes, when the sugar melts and lightly caramelises, lay 2 thick slices of brioche in the caramel. Leave for 20 seconds or so, then carefully flip to coat and lightly toast both sides; this is a quick process, as the caramel is extremely hot. Transfer to two serving plates. Repeat with another 2 thick slices of brioche, placing them on another two serving plates. If the caramel becomes too dark during cooking, clean out the pan and start again. To serve, smear 250 g (9 oz) crème fraîche over the brioche slices, then pile on 1 × quantity Cherry, vanilla & balsamic compote (opposite), along with the balsamic syrup. You could also try this with roasted peaches, plums or nectarines (see p. 720), sauced with their roasting juices.

I adore cherry jam – and cherries most ways – with the late-season cherries in my local markets tending to be of a darker variety, which are ideal for jam. They also tend to be a little cheaper, which is also ideal for jam, given you'll need a couple of kilos; please don't halve this recipe. The addition of the cherry pits adds a bitter almond undertone, which is lovely with the cherry flavour, while the raspberries ensure a brilliant colour. **Makes 4 × 500 g (1 lb 2 oz) jars**

1.8 kg (4 lb) pitted cherries (select darker-coloured ones)	1.3 kg (2 lb 14 oz) caster (superfine) sugar peeled zest of ½ lemon, and the juice of 1 lemon	2 vanilla beans 500 g (1 lb 2 oz) frozen raspberries

Stone the cherries. Wrap fifty cherry pits in an old clean tea towel (dish towel), then use a rolling pin or meat mallet to crack them open. Wrap tightly in muslin (cheesecloth), tie into a parcel with kitchen twine and set aside.

Put the cherries, sugar and lemon zest in a large bowl. Cut the vanilla beans in half lengthways and scrape the seeds into the bowl. Finely slice the vanilla pod on an angle and add to the bowl. Mix until thoroughly combined and stand for 30 minutes.

Transfer the mixture to a large, wide saucepan and add the cherry pits. Slowly bring to a simmer over a low heat, then cook for 45 minutes.

Stir in the lemon juice and raspberries, then simmer for another 15 minutes. Check the setting point by placing a small blob on a saucer that has been in the freezer, then returning the saucer to the freezer for 2 minutes to see if the jam sets.

Once ready, remove the parcel of cherry pits. Pour the jam into hot sterilised jars (see p. 40) and seal, then invert on the bench until cool. The lids will suck down once cooled, indicating a good seal.

The jam will keep for 1–2 years in the pantry. Once opened, refrigerate and use within 6–8 months.

Honey & white wine poaching syrup for stone fruit (GF) (V)

Honey and vanilla lend a deep and mellow sweetness to the stone fruit once poached, allowing the natural flavour to shine through. Select fruit that is firm but ripe. Overripe fruit is not ideal for poaching, as it tends to turn mushy instead of cooking evenly, but it can still be stirred into a Butter cake (p. 736) or used in a crumble-style dessert (see p. 688). The spices listed below are optional, but pears and apricots in particular benefit from the exotic combination of cinnamon, cardamom, saffron and pepper. **Serves 6**

6 peaches or nectarines, or 10–12 apricots, halved and pitted	450 g (1 lb) caster (superfine) sugar	8 cardamom pods 10 black or white peppercorns
1.5 litres (51 fl oz/6 cups) water	150 ml (5 fl oz) honey juice of 1 lemon, plus 3 strips of lemon zest	3 pinches of saffron threads (optional)
500 ml (17 fl oz/2 cups) white wine	1 vanilla bean, split 1 cinnamon stick	

Place the fruit in a wide saucepan so it fits in one layer. Add the remaining ingredients and bring to a simmer over a medium heat. Cover with baking paper cut to fit the inside of the pan, then use two saucers to keep the fruit submerged. Turn the heat down as low as possible.

Poach cherries for about 5 minutes, apricots or plums for about 15 minutes, nectarines for about 20 minutes, and peaches for about 30 minutes – or up to an hour if the peaches are peeled and left whole.

Carefully lift the fruit out with a slotted spoon into a container or dish. Cool a little before slipping the skins off.

Covered with the poaching syrup, the fruit will keep in the fridge for up to 7 days. The syrup can also be reused for another batch, or to dress a finished dessert.

Make it different

Saffron-poached pears. **GF** **V** Peel 6 pears and cut out the core from the base with a melon baller or teaspoon, then poach for about 20 minutes or until tender. You can also use this syrup for rhubarb, 10–15 minutes, or figs, 8 minutes. Serve with Chocolate pudding (p. 782), Crème caramel (p. 781) or Chocolate mousse (p. 782), or with a simple Chocolate tart (p. 817).

Pair with

Enjoy the fruit for breakfast in the syrup, with Greek-style yoghurt. You could reduce the syrup by half and have with granola, if you like.

Use the fruit in a clafoutis (see p. 721).

Use to top a Frangipane tart (pp. 796, 797).

White peach & rosewater jelly **GF**

The honey and white wine syrup from poaching peaches (see p. 723) can be easily transformed into an elegant and refined dessert jelly. Soak six gold-strength gelatine leaves in cold water for 5 minutes. Strain 300 ml (10 fl oz) of the poaching syrup (left) into a small saucepan, then warm through over a medium heat. Squeeze the excess water from the gelatine, add the leaves to the syrup and stir to dissolve. Take off the heat and stir in 250 ml (8½ fl oz/1 cup) water and 1 tablespoon rosewater. Pour into six dariole moulds or ramekins, then refrigerate for about 3 hours, until set. Serve the jelly with the poached peaches and a scoop of vanilla ice cream or yoghurt sorbet.

A simple poaching liquid for stone fruit **GF** **V** **VG**

For a very simple poaching liquid, bring 500 ml (17 fl oz/ 2 cups) white wine, 600 g (1 lb 5 oz) caster (superfine) sugar, the juice of 1 lemon and 1.5 litres (51 fl oz/6 cups) water to a simmer, then proceed with the poaching instructions.

Spicy malt plum sauce

Pair with

Roasted or grilled poultry or pork.

Fried wontons (see p. 342).

Stir into noodle dishes.

Roasted blood plum relish GF V VG

To a ceramic baking dish large enough to fit the plums in one snug layer, add 12 stoned and quartered blood plums, a very finely sliced red onion, a 10 cm (4 in) piece of fresh ginger, peeled and finely chopped, 2 red bird's eye chillies, split lengthways, 120 g (4 oz/½ cup) brown sugar, 2½ tablespoons red-wine vinegar, 1½ tablespoons tomato paste (concentrated purée), 1 star anise, and 2 teaspoons each of ground white pepper, salt flakes and sichuan peppercorns. Toss to combine well, then spread out evenly and stand for 15 minutes. Preheat the oven to 180°C (350°F) fan-forced. Roast the plums for 10 minutes, stir, then roast for a further 15–20 minutes, until the plums are tender. Set aside to cool undisturbed for a chunky sauce or, for a smoother consistency, stir vigorously to break down the plums. Spoon the relish into hot sterilised jars (see p. 40) and seal, then invert on the bench until cool. This makes about 1 litre (34 fl oz/4 cups) and will keep in the fridge for up to 6 months. Adds a punch of flavour to fatty meats and spiced dishes, such as roasted spiced pork belly (see p. 333), Twice-roasted duck (p. 264) or fried quail. You could also serve as a condiment with pâté/parfait (pp. 233, 327) or a terrine (p. 327).

I have a lot of affection for this sauce, and for plum sauces in general. My mother and her mother used to make a version that my father especially loved, full of anise notes with lots of five-spice and sugar, which was very exotic indeed back then. This dials up the exoticism even more. It's a dark and malty sauce that has incredible depth of flavour and a gentle spike of heat. This recipe makes a lot of sauce but can be halved, if you like. If you prefer a smoother sauce, remove the star anise once the sauce is cooked, then blitz until smooth with a stick blender before bottling. **Makes about 3 litres (101 fl oz/12 cups)**

2.5 kg (5½ lb) plums, pitted and roughly chopped
300 g (10½ oz) red onions, finely diced
6 large garlic cloves, finely grated
15 cm (6 in) piece of fresh ginger, peeled and finely grated

3 long red chillies, finely sliced
700 g (1 lb 9 oz) brown sugar
300 g (10½ oz/1⅓) cups caster (superfine) sugar
500 ml (17 fl oz/2 cups) malt vinegar
200 ml (7 fl oz) Chinese black vinegar
200 ml (7 fl oz) red wine

2 tablespoons fish sauce
1 tablespoon salt flakes
1 tablespoon mustard seeds
3 teaspoons ground ginger
1½ teaspoons chilli flakes
½ teaspoon Chinese five-spice
3 star anise
2 fresh bay leaves

Add all the ingredients to a large, wide saucepan. Stir over a medium heat to combine, then bring to a simmer. Reduce the heat to low and cook for 1½ hours, stirring regularly to stop the mixture catching on the pan.

Once thick and syrupy, spoon into hot sterilised jars (see p. 40) and seal, then invert on the bench until cool. The lids will suck down once cooled, indicating a good seal.

Stand for at least 24 hours before using; the sauce will keep in the pantry for up to 6 months. Once opened, keep in the fridge and use within 2 months.

Make it different
With a sour note. Stir in 15 g (½ oz) Davidson plum powder once the sauce has reduced.

Also see

Rhubarb galette **650**

Apple & cherry turnovers **681**

Tarte tatin **682**

Roasted apricot & ginger clafoutis **721**

Lemon tart **814–5**

Chocolate tart **817**

French strawberry shortcake with crème pâtissière **819**

Jam crostata **826**

Sweet baking & desserts

Sweet baking & desserts

I have more of a savoury tooth than sweet, but that doesn't mean I don't appreciate great yeasted buns, sugary doughnuts and buttery delicate biscuits, just-set cheesecakes, deeply rich chocolatey mousses, perfectly poached peaches, poached cherries or macerated strawberries with a crisp tuile and chantilly cream, or tender roasted rhubarb topped with a buttery crumble, creamed simmered rice and shimmering jellies, almost collapsing panna cottas and delicate creams with lashings of caramel.

The truth is, I learned and understood sweet baking a little later in my career. Even though there was great structure in my early training, it's not until you start creating your own, and getting into the nitty-gritty of it, that you really get a feel for it. When making savoury dishes, I very much have a free-form and intuitive approach. It's based on honed techniques, sure, but it's worlds away from baking and making sweets and desserts.

With most savoury cooking, I rarely ever weigh anything. Spices? Sometimes. If I'm making a brine? Yes, as the percentages are important. Or if I'm making terrines, where I can't adjust the salt or spicing later. With savoury cooking, you generally do have the chance to adjust as you go, and there are lots of variables that require responsive action. I'm always tasting and tweaking, narrowing down on the perfect result.

Baking and desserts are mostly different. Good luck adding that bit more sugar to a cooked sponge cake, or resetting that not-quite-set jelly. Or trying to judge the perfect panna cotta ratio by eye.

No, the sweet end of the meal is a much more precise affair, more disciplined and structured, where recipes need to be followed closely. With sweets and baking, it's about reducing those variables to gossamer margins. A light dusting of flour here, a splash more milk there, a little more or less spice to account for potency – or usually a lack of it. It's all about preparation, patience and precision.

But don't forget, it's also supposed to be relaxing!

It all sounds very rigid, but that doesn't mean there is a lack of freedom. It's simply that many of the processes in making sweet things, and baking in general, rely on very specific reactions to be successful. And some are more forgiving than others. Often you can dial down the sugar on a cake and get a good – if slightly different – result. However, fiddle with something like pastry or an anglaise recipe at your own peril!

The art of sweet cooking can bring such joy and a real sense of pride. It's rewarding, but it can certainly be challenging, too. All those chemical reactions turn decidedly simple things into marvellous, transformative creations, so it's also a bit of a buzz. With savoury cooking, you often start with beautifully vibrant ingredients, many of which are lovely just as they are, but with sweet cooking so many wondrous creations are magicked out of raw ingredients that are somewhat more prosaic: flour, sugar, milk … we'll leave chocolate out of this.

Baking and cooking sweets is about understanding techniques that can open many doors. Just remember you don't need to open them all at once. Patience is important. I'm not a natural baker, but I am a natural cook, so I have learned from my mistakes, and now know when to rein in that cavalier spirit.

In learning all the skills and techniques, there have been times when my cakes have collapsed or been raw in the middle, a pie has slumped or a custard curdled. It's all part of the process. Cracks and splits can be covered by bountiful berries and cream, icing, dustings of icing (confectioners') sugar or cocoa powder, Nutty praline (p. 786) or Chocolate gravel (p. 783) or a tuft of Persian fairy floss – and all of these distractions look and taste good. Don't be disheartened – improvise!

What is most important is to work out what went wrong so you don't repeat the issue next time. Sometimes, it can be an ingredient that is too processed, like most so-called ricotta. Its texture has been manipulated and will not set the same or behave as it should in cakes or icings. Sometimes, a temperature or weight was off, or the fan in the oven hadn't been switched on. Sometimes, your kitchen is just too hot as you rush to cook multiple courses at once – as with pastry, heat and humidity will affect some things where temperature and moisture content are important, altering the consistency of a dough or filling, or turning a lustrous meringue soft and tacky. Sometimes, a different flour takes up more water, or the proteins in your eggs are more resilient than other times.

Sometimes, things just don't go your way. But it happens to the best of us. Dust yourself off and work out what might have been the problem to adjust next time. I even write notes in pencil on the pages of cookbooks! Over time, you will start to absorb the lessons, and it will all come more naturally.

You will begin to feel the tension on the spoon as an anglaise thickens to the right point, shimmering into a glossy sheen. You will learn to instantly recognise the moment a shortbread fully transforms from dough to friable delight, while remaining ever so blond. Your ears will prick up with the faint crackle of a cake or a sponge finishing its cooking on the bench just before you turn it out of the tin. And if all this sounds lofty, unattainable – well, it's not. All this detail comes from doing. It will become part of your process.

Once you know the rules, you'll be armed with all sorts of components that can be borrowed or adapted from this recipe or that, then flavoured, baked, set, spun and frozen and constructed however you like. In other words, there are parameters, but there is so much freedom and potential creativity within those boundaries. And then there's the joy of seasonality, making the most of an abundance of fruits – poaching, roasting, macerating, or framing in their pristine natural state.

A recipe is the starting point. Read it through once. And then again. Make sure it makes sense to you, then follow it. Don't deviate. Make sure you have the necessary equipment. Weigh and measure the correct ingredients out, be clean and be organised. Take a breath, be calm. It's relaxing, remember.

Equipment (see p. 34) is important with baking and making sweets. Various stainless steel bowls, a reliable digital probe thermometer, a sturdy whisk, an electric stand mixer (ideally, but not essentially), various tins and trays, and pastry cutters are all part of the armoury, but the thing I would really recommend investing in straight-up is a good set of digital scales.

Many recipes are okay with measuring in cups, and some measurements I may give in spoons or cups are due to a little variance not being critical – but weighing most things is so important. It is often the difference between a good and a great result, and occasionally between failure and success. I weigh pretty much everything, including water.

The other key piece of equipment is your oven, and it is generally a less reliable tool. I test everything in my oven at home, and, as you may imagine, it's not a component of our home renovation that I skimped on. It's the centre of everything I do, both for work and pleasure, and luckily those things overlap significantly. I know that if I cook any of these recipes again, they will work in my oven more or less right on the given timing – but that may not be your experience.

All this banging on about precision generates a good deal of panic – sorry! – but while temperatures are exact, your conditions are different, and sometimes appreciably so. You really need to watch and start to understand how your oven responds to cooking times, then adjust your thinking accordingly. Don't pull that cake out after 50 minutes just because the recipe says so. You need to look at temperatures and times as a guide. A good guide, but not an infallible one.

In this chapter, I have tried to curate many of the recipes I might feel like all year round. It's a pretty hard job, really, and easily a hefty book in itself. I've also tried to cover a range of processes and techniques in the recipes, but there are a couple of general notes on ingredients and methods that are worth covering before you begin, with many more notes in the Essentials section (see p. 6).

Flour

Naturally, you can use cake flour in the cake recipes, but I've listed plain (all-purpose) flour, as it is both readily available and yields successful results.

Chocolate

When it comes to chocolate, use a brand you like, one you enjoy eating as is. Baking, melting or setting doesn't make bad chocolate good – so don't skimp. When a recipe calls for proper dark chocolate, you can't just substitute a lower-cocoa milk chocolate, as it won't perform the same or taste the same. Milk chocolate and white chocolate are generally interchangeable, though.

When melting chocolate, make sure there is no water on any of the utensils, as this can ruin the texture, making it grainy. I always melt over a double boiler; it's simple enough to rest a heatproof bowl over a saucepan about one-quarter full of water, but important that the bowl doesn't touch the water and that the heat is turned down to low once the water has reached a simmer. Add either chocolate melts (buttons) or evenly chopped chocolate to the bowl and stand for 3 minutes before stirring. Leave the bowl on the pan if the chocolate hasn't melted quite enough, or you can rest it on the bench to finish melting, stirring through again to help it finish. Stirring too much will compromise the texture, so intrude on the process as little as possible.

You can also melt chocolate in a microwave for 1 minute on high, then in 10–20 second bursts, again stirring only as much as necessary. It's a very efficient way to do it, but I don't own a microwave, so a double boiler it is.

If adding cream or milk to melt chocolate, heat the liquid first, then pour over the chopped chocolate in a large heatproof bowl and whisk gently from the centre to melt smoothly and not cause air bubbles. Always melt chocolate just before you need to use it, as it will set again if it gets too cold.

Eggs

When whisking egg yolks, never leave unwhisked sugar on the yolks, as it will 'cook' or burn the yolks, causing a graininess and lumps that are difficult to strain out.

When whisking egg whites, any yolk or water can ruin the result, so make sure the whites are just whites, and your equipment is scrupulously clean and dry. Older eggs will yield a less successful result, too, with the structure having nowhere near as much integrity. Additionally, work with room-temperature eggs, as cold egg whites can take twice as long to beat. It's also necessary to whisk egg whites as you need them, as they will 'weep' and break down if left too long.

Cream, butter & dairy products

As with whisked egg whites, whipped cream loses its pep if it sits around for too long, so it's best to whip cream as it's needed. A little pure cream (40–42% fat) in the mix (see p. 12) will help stabilise things, for those times when a cake or the like needs to sit for a bit and be admired before it's cut. I whisk cream by hand and by machine – and while the latter is quick and easy, do be wary, as that convenience can easily result in butter if you're not watching closely. You're aiming for a doubling of volume that holds rounded peaks when you drag the whisk out of the cream.

If you can, opt for cultured butter for baking, as the flavour it adds is stunning. The better the butter, the better the flavour.

One last note: do not, under any circumstances, swap any full-fat dairy for 'light' lower-fat options, as this will severely compromise the result. And, margarine is not butter!

Cakes, cupcakes & muffins

Vanilla cupcakes Ⓥ

These classic vanilla cupcakes couldn't be simpler – five minutes in the food processor and you're away. **Makes 18**

Pair with

Basic sugar icing (p. 802).

Vanilla frosting (p. 803).

Lemon icing (p. 802).

Berry icing (p. 802).

Smashed blueberry glaze (p. 774).

Coffee icing (p. 804).

Chocolate fudge icing (p. 805).

Italian meringue butter cream (p. 807).

Mascarpone citrus curd icing (p. 803).

250 g (9 oz/1 cup) unsalted butter, softened at room temperature

250 g (9 oz/1⅔ cups) self-raising flour, sifted

200 g (7 oz) caster (superfine) sugar

2 teaspoons baking powder

4 eggs

2½ teaspoons natural vanilla extract or paste

120 ml (4 fl oz) full-cream (whole) milk

Preheat the oven to 175°C (345°F) fan-forced. Line two cupcake trays with 18 paper cases.

Add all the ingredients, except the milk, to a food processor and blend until smooth, then add the milk gradually until smooth.

Divide the mixture among the cupcake moulds, about two-thirds full.

Bake for 15–20 minutes, until springy to the touch. Lift the paper cases out from the tin and cool on a wire rack.

The cupcakes will keep in an airtight container at room temperature for up to 5 days.

Make it different
Coffee cupcakes. Dissolve 2 teaspoons instant espresso-style coffee granules in the milk.

Red velvet cupcakes with Italian meringue icing Ⓥ

Fluffy moist and buttery, with a bang of colour and a hint of chocolate. **Makes 18**

Pair with

Sprinkle some freeze-dried raspberry powder or shaved chocolate over the icing.

Instead of Italian meringue, you could also use Italian meringue butter cream (p. 807) or Vanilla frosting (p. 803).

250 g (9 oz/1 cup) unsalted butter, softened at room temperature

200 g (7 oz) caster (superfine) sugar

4 eggs

240 g (8½ oz) self-raising flour

35 g (1¼ oz) dark Dutch (unsweetened) cocoa powder

2 teaspoons baking powder

2½ teaspoons natural vanilla extract or paste

120 ml (4 fl oz) full-cream (whole) milk

2 tablespoons red food colouring

1 × quantity Italian meringue (p. 807)

Preheat the oven to 175°C (345°F) fan-forced. Line two cupcake trays with 18 paper cases.

In a food processor, blitz the butter, sugar, eggs, flour, cocoa powder, baking powder and vanilla until well combined, about 3 minutes. Gradually add the milk and food colouring, processing until smooth.

Spoon the batter into the cupcake moulds, about two-thirds full.

Bake for 15–20 minutes, until springy to the touch. Cool for 5 minutes, then transfer to a wire rack to cool completely.

Pipe or spoon the Italian meringue onto the cupcakes. The cupcakes will keep in an airtight container at room temperature for up to 5 days.

Classic muffins ⓥ

These plain vanilla muffins are perfectly delicious, with a beautifully tender crumb, but they can also be accessorised in all manner of ways, by adding fruit, chocolate, spices, coconut flakes ... whatever takes your fancy.

Makes 12–14 large muffins

380 g (13½ oz) self-raising
  flour
220 g (8 oz) caster (superfine)
  sugar
1¼ teaspoons baking
  powder

½ teaspoon fine sea salt
200 ml (7 fl oz) extra-virgin
  olive oil, or any neutral-
  flavoured oil
150 ml (5 fl oz) full-cream
  (whole) milk

1 egg
2 teaspoons natural vanilla
  paste

Preheat the oven to 180°C (350°F) fan-forced. Line a large muffin tray with paper cases.

Whisk the dry ingredients in a large bowl, then make a well in the centre.

Whisk the remaining ingredients in another bowl, then pour into the well and mix to combine. At this point, leave as is for plain muffins, or stir through fruit or flavourings.

Divide the mixture among the muffin moulds and bake for 25–30 minutes, until a skewer comes out clean.

Lift the paper cases from the tray and cool the muffins on a wire rack. Once cooled, store in an airtight container. The muffins are best enjoyed the same day, but will keep in an airtight container at room temperature for 2–3 days.

Make it different

Berry, toasted almond & chocolate muffins. ⓥ Stir 80 g (2¾ oz) toasted flaked almonds through the batter, along with 100 g (3½ oz) milk chocolate melts (buttons) and 250 g (9 oz/2 cups) frozen or fresh raspberries, blueberries, blackberries (or a mix).

Berry & chocolate muffins. ⓥ Add 80 g (2¾ oz) dark or white chocolate melts (buttons) and 400 g (14 oz) frozen or fresh raspberries, blueberries, blackberries (or a mix) to the batter.

Blackberry & coconut cheesecake muffins. ⓥ Dice 250 g (9 oz/1 cup) cream cheese and bring to room temperature. Mix through the batter with 250 g (9 oz/2 cups) frozen or fresh blackberries and 80 g (2¾ oz) flaked coconut.

Carrot, cinnamon, pecan & cream cheese muffins. ⓥ Dice 250 g (9 oz/1 cup) cream cheese and bring to room temperature. Stir through the batter with 300 g (10½ oz) finely grated carrot, 80 g (2¾ oz) chopped pecans or walnuts and 2 teaspoons ground cinnamon.

Rhubarb or apple muffins. ⓥ Stir 250–300 g (9–10½ oz) poached rhubarb (see p. 646) or apple through the batter.

Mashed banana & coconut muffins. ⓥ Mash 250–300 g (9–10½ oz) bananas and stir through the batter along with 30 g (1 oz/½ cup) coconut flakes.

Spiced muffins. ⓥ Add 2 teaspoons ground ginger, mixed spice or cardamom to the batter.

Hazelnut streusel muffins. ⓥ Before baking, top the plain muffins with the crumb from the Hazelnut plum streusel cake (p. 741).

Mazaresi cakes Ⓖⓥ

To make these little Sicilian fairy cakes, preheat the oven to 160°C (320°F) fan-forced. Line a standard muffin tray with twelve paper cases. Blanch 200 g (7 oz/1⅓ cups) pistachio kernels in simmering water for 1 minute, then drain and dry thoroughly in a tea towel (dish towel), rubbing off their skins. Blitz the nuts to a fine paste in a food processor with a pinch of salt. Whisk 2 egg whites with a pinch of salt until soft peaks form. In another bowl, whisk 4 egg yolks and 150 g (5½ oz/⅔ cup) caster (superfine) sugar to combine, then add 50 g (1¾ oz) potato starch, the zest of 1 orange and the pistachio paste and whisk again until combined. Fold in the egg whites to combine. Divide the mixture among the muffin moulds and bake for about 18 minutes, until lightly puffed. Cool the cakes completely in the tray. When ready to serve, remove from the paper cases and slice off the tops. Dollop with 250 g (9 oz) crème fraîche or whipped ricotta, top with 2 cherries each, sprinkle with 3 tablespoons roughly chopped pistachio kernels, and sit in fresh paper cases. Top with the lids and dust with icing (confectioners') sugar to serve. The cakes will keep in an airtight container at room temperature for up to 3 days. Makes 12.

Blackberry & coconut
cheesecake muffins

Zucchini, coconut & macadamia muffins with lime cream cheese icing (GF) (V)

These are moist and delicious, with a delightful crunch from the macadamias. The zucchini adds a bright green hue and a natural sweetness. **Makes 8–10**

100 g (3½ oz) sultanas (golden raisins)
300 g (10½ oz) grated zucchini (courgette)
1 teaspoon salt flakes
150 g (5½ oz/⅔ cup) caster (superfine) sugar
2 eggs
125 ml (4 fl oz/½ cup) extra-virgin olive oil

100 g (3½ oz) rice flour
100 g (3½ oz/⅔ cup) gluten-free self-raising flour
½ teaspoon bicarbonate of soda (baking soda)
½ teaspoon baking powder
100 g (3½ oz) desiccated coconut
½ teaspoon xanthan gum

100 g (3½ oz) toasted macadamia nuts, roughly chopped
1 × quantity Vanilla frosting (p. 803)
zest of 1 lime
30 g (1 oz) toasted shaved coconut

Preheat the oven to 180°C (350°F) fan-forced. Line a large muffin tin with paper cases.

Add the sultanas to a small saucepan and just cover with water. Bring to a simmer for 1 minute, then set aside.

Toss the zucchini with the salt and a tablespoon of the sugar and set aside in a colander to drain.

Using an electric stand mixer, whisk the eggs, oil and remaining sugar on medium–high speed until pale and creamy, about 4 minutes. Add the flours, bicarbonate of soda, baking powder, coconut and xanthan gum, then beat until well combined. Squeeze the zucchini lightly to extract moisture, then add with the macadamias and sultanas, taking a teaspoon or so of the sultana liquid with them, and fold through.

Divide the mixture among the muffin moulds. Bake for about 20 minutes, until golden.

Cool for 5 minutes in the tray, then transfer the muffins to a rack to finish cooling.

Ice the cooled muffins with the cream cheese icing, then sprinkle with the lime zest and coconut. The muffins will keep in an airtight container at room temperature for up to 3 days.

Make it different
Zucchini, coconut & macadamia loaf with lime cream cheese icing. Use a standard loaf (bar) tin of 22–25 cm (8¾–10 in) and increase the baking time to 45–50 minutes.

Friands (V)

These delightful buttery cakes are an absolute favourite of mine. There are very few trips to a bakery without buying one – or maybe two. **Makes 16**

180 g (6½ oz) unsalted butter
200 g (7 oz) icing (confectioners') sugar
120 g (4½ oz) ground almonds

60 g (2 oz) plain (all-purpose) flour
1½ teaspoons ground cloves
½ teaspoon salt flakes
150 g (5½ oz) egg whites
zest of 1 lemon or orange

50 g (1¾ oz) raspberries or blueberries
Staples
BTR
Special equipment
16 friand moulds

Pair with

Smashed blueberry glaze (p. 774).

Berry icing (p. 802).

Lemon icing (p. 802) and Candied lemon peel (p. 790).

Preheat the oven to 200°C (400°F) fan-forced.

Melt some extra butter, then use to lightly brush your friand moulds. Refrigerate the moulds until needed.

In a small saucepan, cook the butter over a medium heat until nut brown, about 7 minutes, swirling to colour evenly. Set aside to cool for 15 minutes.

In a large bowl, whisk the icing sugar, ground almonds, flour, cloves and salt, to remove any lumps.

Beat the egg whites with a fork until gently frothy, then pour into the almond mixture, along with the brown butter and citrus zest. Mix with a spoon until smooth. Fill the friand moulds about two-thirds full, then add a berry to each one.

Bake for 10 minutes, then reduce the oven temperature to 190°C (375°F) fan-forced and cook for 8 minutes.

Set aside to cool completely, before removing from the moulds. The friands are best enjoyed same day.

Madeleines ⓥ

Light and buttery, these are an absolute delight, and they really do almost melt in the mouth. You really need to buy or borrow a good mould for these, as the shell-like appearance is an absolute must if you're going to call them madeleines. And while these are something you need to eat on the day, you can prepare the mixture a day prior. The other keys are to grease the moulds well, chill before filling, and to use a piping (icing) bag to fill the moulds evenly. **Makes 24**

Pair with

Lemon, lime or passionfruit curd (p. 797).

Mascarpone citrus curd icing (p. 803).

140 g (5 oz) plain (all-purpose) flour
25 g (1 oz) baking powder
½ teaspoon fine sea salt
165 g (6 oz) eggs

110 g (4 oz/½ cup) caster (superfine) sugar
120 g (4½ oz) butter
10 g (¼ oz) soft brown sugar
10 g (¼ oz) honey

Staples
BTR

Special equipment
24 madeleine tins or moulds

Sift the flour, baking powder and salt into a bowl. Set aside.

Warm the bowl of an electric stand mixer using hot water, then dry thoroughly. In the warm bowl, whisk the eggs and caster sugar on medium–high speed for 1 minute to combine. Increase the speed to high and whisk until pale, foamy and doubled in size, about 4 minutes.

Meanwhile, add the butter, brown sugar and honey to a small saucepan over a low heat, stirring for about 2 minutes to dissolve and combine. Remove from the heat.

Using the whisk from the stand mixer, fold half the flour mixture into the egg mixture by hand until combined, then fold in the rest until just combined. Use a spatula to ensure that everything from the bottom of the bowl and the side has been incorporated. Drizzle in the warm honey mixture, folding in until smooth.

Transfer to an airtight container and refrigerate for a minimum of 4 hours; overnight or even up to 2 days is fine, too.

When ready to bake, grease the madeleine tins with butter and chill for an hour or so before using. Preheat the oven to 180°C (350°F) fan-forced.

Transfer the madeleine mixture to a piping (icing) bag fitted with a plain nozzle. Pipe generous tablespoons of the mixture – about 20 g (¾ oz) – into the tin indentations, then tap the tins on the bench to even the mixture out. They should be about two-thirds full.

Bake for 8 minutes, until lightly browned; you can also test with a skewer. Tip the madeleines onto a cooling rack and serve warm, or leave to cool and top with an icing. Enjoy the same day.

Simple butter cake ⓥ

Serve this cake as a simple treat for afternoon tea, or easily cut into layers or shapes to then ice into a decorative birthday cake. It's also the ideal recipe if you want to divide the batter and dye with food colourings for a rainbow cake. Plus, it has such a classic flavour that you can dress it with any icing you fancy. **Serves 6–8**

Pair with

Lemon, lime or passionfruit curd (p. 797).

6 eggs
100 ml (3½ fl oz) full-cream (whole) milk
2 teaspoons natural vanilla extract or paste
200 g (7 oz/1⅓ cups) self-raising flour, sifted

100 g (3½ oz/⅔ cup) plain (all-purpose) flour, sifted
1 teaspoon salt flakes
300 g (10½ oz) caster (superfine) sugar

300 g (10½ oz) unsalted butter, diced, well softened at room temperature

Staples
BTR

Preheat the oven to 170°C (340°F) fan-forced. Grease a 22–24 cm (8¾–9½ in) loose-based cake tin and line with baking paper, or grease a ring (bundt) tin.

Hand-whisk the eggs, milk and vanilla in a bowl until combined.

Using an electric stand mixer with the paddle attachment, mix the flours and salt on low, then pour in the sugar while mixing. Gradually add the butter to combine. Add half the egg mixture and beat on medium–high for 1 minute. Scrape down the bowl with a spatula, then add the rest of the egg mixture in two batches, beating until incorporated.

Pour into the cake tin and bake for about 45 minutes, until a skewer comes out clean.

Set aside for 15 minutes before turning out. Once completely cool, ice the cake, or cut into layers or shapes.

The cake will keep in an airtight container at room temperature for up to 5 days.

Make it different

Marble cake. Ⓥ Dissolve 2½ tablespoons Dutch (unsweetened) cocoa powder in 2 tablespoons boiling water and combine with half the cake batter until incorporated. Pour the remaining batter into the tin, then top with the chocolate mixture. Drag a skewer quickly through the cake batter in four intervals, then bake as normal; it will marble as it cooks.

Lime & coconut cheesecake Ⓥ

Bright, zesty and rich, this citrus-laced coconut cheesecake really delivers. It's a step up from a basic blitzed biscuit base with a cream cheese filling, but it's a relative breeze compared to making a classic curd tart with a blind-baked pastry – though you should do that, too. **Serves 10**

1 × quantity No-bake nutty biscuit base (right)
50 g (1¾ oz) shaved coconut
400 ml (13½ fl oz) Basic whipped cream (p. 799)
1 lime

Lime & coconut filling
395 g (14 oz) tin condensed milk
2 eggs
2 egg yolks
zest and juice of 3 limes
zest and juice of 1 lemon (200 ml/7 fl oz lime and lemon juice combined)

250 g (9 oz/1 cup) cream cheese, diced and softened at room temperature
150 ml (5 fl oz) thick coconut cream

Staples
BTR

Preheat the oven to 170°C (340°F) fan-forced. Grease a 23 cm (9 in) loose-based cake tin, and line only the base with baking paper.

Firmly press the nutty base into the cake tin with the base of a glass or a spoon, then chill.

Meanwhile, spread the coconut on a baking tray and toast until golden, checking at about the 6 minute mark. Set aside to cool.

For the filling, add the condensed milk, eggs, egg yolks and citrus zest and juices to a food processor and process until smooth, about 3 minutes. Add the cream cheese and coconut cream and blitz until smooth.

Pour over the chilled biscuit base and bake for 40 minutes, or until the filling is set, with a slight wobble in the middle. Set aside at room temperature to cool completely.

Once cooled, unmould and pipe on the cream. Sprinkle with the toasted coconut and finely grate the zest of the lime over just before serving.

The cheesecake will keep in the fridge for up to 2 days.

Make it different
With meringue. Pipe on a half quantity of Italian meringue (p. 807), then toast with a kitchen blowtorch or place under an oven grill (broiler) for 2–3 minutes. Finish with the coconut and zest.

Make this in small flan (tart) tins, large lined muffin moulds, or small flan rings on a lined baking tray.

No-bake nutty biscuit base Ⓥ

This recipe was developed for the Lime & coconut cheesecake (left) but it would also work with any cheesecake or slice, or as the base of a small sweet tart. You can omit the coconut, and compensate with more biscuits or nuts. In a food processor, blitz 150 g (5½ oz/1 cup) toasted and cooled <u>Brazil nuts</u> in 30-second bursts, until finely crumbed. Add 200 g (7 oz) roughly crushed <u>unsweetened oat biscuits</u> and blitz into fine crumbs. Tip into a bowl and combine with 140 g (5 oz) <u>unsalted butter</u>, melted, 80 g (2¾ oz) <u>brown sugar</u>, 50 g (1¾ oz) <u>desiccated coconut</u> and ½ teaspoon <u>salt flakes</u>. Press into a flan (tart) tin firmly with the base of a glass or a spoon, then chill for 15 minutes before topping with your chosen filling.

Basque cheesecake Ⓥ

This is based on the classic Basque cheesecake, which is baked super-hot to burnish the exterior to a deeply caramelised hue, while the interior is cooked to a smooth, silky texture. I have added goat's cheese and salt for a savoury edge. Don't be concerned when it lifts loftily in the oven and then promptly sinks. **Serves 6–8**

600 g (1 lb 5 oz) cream cheese, diced, softened at room temperature
300 g (10½ oz) firm but spreadable goat's cheese

300 g (10½ oz) caster (superfine) sugar
6 eggs, at room temperature
1 teaspoon salt flakes
zest of ¼ lemon

400 ml (13½ fl oz) pouring (single/light) cream
30 g (1 oz) plain (all-purpose) flour

Staples
BTR

Preheat the oven to 180°C (350°F) fan-forced. Grease a 23 cm (9 in) springform tin and line with baking paper, making sure the paper is double the height of the tin, as this cake will rise a lot.

Using an electric stand mixer, whisk the cream cheese, goat's cheese and sugar on medium–high speed until smooth, about 3 minutes. Add the eggs one at a time, beating until just incorporated, then add the salt and lemon zest. Add the cream, then the flour, and mix for 2 minutes.

Pour into the cake tin and bake for 35 minutes. Increase the oven temperature to 240°C (465°F) fan-forced and bake for 10 minutes to colour deeply. The tart should have risen quite a lot, with a wobble in the middle.

Cool completely before unmoulding and serving as is. The cake will keep in an airtight container in the fridge for up to 5 days and at room temperature for up to 2 days.

Italian blood orange breakfast cake ⓥ

This is a little like a madeira cake, though the blood orange gives it a slightly different hue, and the flavour is a little sweeter and more fragrant. Naturally, it isn't just restricted to breakfast, but for me it always brings back memories of a fabulous breakfast spread at a little Italian hotel, on our first visit to Italy that we could afford a hotel instead of hostels; I was totally besotted with the fact you could be offered this just-baked warm cake for breakfast. Don't be put off by blood orange's short season, either, as this works perfectly well with regular oranges. **Serves 6–8**

3 blood oranges
3 eggs
300 g (10½ oz) caster
  (superfine) sugar
250 ml (8½ fl oz/1 cup)
  extra-virgin olive oil

250 g (9 oz/1⅔ cups)
  self-raising flour, sifted
1 teaspoon fennel seeds
  or anise seeds, finely
  ground

Orange syrup
140 ml (4½ fl oz) orange juice
40 g (1½ oz) caster
  (superfine) sugar

Staples
BTR

Preheat the oven to 180°C (350°F) fan-forced. Grease a 20 cm (8 in) loose-based cake tin and line with baking paper.

Cook the whole oranges in simmering water for 45 minutes. Drain, then cut into quarters and remove any seeds and core membrane. Dice the orange quarters, including the skin, and add to a colander set over a bowl. Weigh down lightly with a plate and drain for 1 hour at room temperature, then blitz in a food processor until smooth, about 4 minutes. Weigh out 300 g (10½ oz) of the purée for the cake.

Using an electric stand mixer, whisk the eggs and sugar on medium–high speed until pale and creamy, about 4 minutes. Add the oil and beat until thick and frothy, about 2 minutes. Detach the whisk and use it to fold in the orange purée, flour and ground fennel to make a smooth, airy batter.

Pour into the cake tin and bake for about 50 minutes, until a skewer comes out clean.

Meanwhile, for the syrup, add the orange juice and sugar to a small saucepan over a medium heat and reduce to about 80 ml (2½ fl oz/⅓ cup). Set aside.

When the cake comes out of the oven, cool in the tin for 2 minutes, then spike with a skewer five times around, and once in the middle. Pour the syrup over and cool for about 25 minutes, then unmould and serve warm.

This cake is best warm or at room temperature, but will keep overnight on the bench in an airtight container.

Spiced earl grey tea & honey cake ⓥ

Soft, aromatic and moreish, this cake is lovely as is for afternoon tea, or with a good dollop of thick cream. Preheat the oven to 180°C (350°F) fan-forced. Grease a 900 g (2 lb) loaf (bar) tin or 20–22 cm (8–8¾ in) cake tin with butter and line with baking paper. Infuse 2 earl grey tea bags in 125 ml (4 fl oz/½ cup) boiling water for 10 minutes, then discard the tea bags. In a large bowl, whisk 2 eggs, 125 ml (4 fl oz/½ cup) extra-virgin olive oil, 130 g (4½ oz) honey, 70 g (2½ oz) demerara or soft brown sugar and the zest of 1 orange to combine. In a bowl, dry whisk 175 g (6 oz) plain (all-purpose) flour, 1 teaspoon baking powder, 2½ teaspoons ground cinnamon, 2 teaspoons ground ginger and ½ teaspoon bicarbonate of soda (baking soda), then fold into the egg mixture with the tea. Pour the batter into the cake tin and bake for about 45 minutes, until a skewer comes out clean. Stand for 5 minutes, then unmould and serve. The cake will keep in an airtight container at room temperature for 3–5 days. Serve with clotted cream or cold custard and poached/roasted pears or quinces.

Hazelnut plum streusel cake ⓥ

Pair with

*Whipped or Clotted cream
(p. 800).*

*Hot or cold Thick vanilla custard
(p. 801).*

This cake might seem slightly complicated, but it is well worth the few extra steps, as the end result is a masterpiece of buttery, nutty spiced crumb and roasted plums. It's a cake to impress with. **Serves 10**

200 g (7 oz/1⅓ cups) plain
  (all-purpose) flour
2 teaspoons baking powder
1 teaspoon salt flakes
150 g (5½ oz) unsalted butter
150 g (5½ oz/⅔ cup) caster
  (superfine) sugar
1 tablespoon hazelnut liqueur
  or brandy
2 teaspoons natural vanilla
  extract or paste
zest of 1 lemon
2 eggs
200 g (7 oz) sour cream

Plum base
100 g (3½ oz) soft brown
  sugar
10 angelina plums, or
  8 blood plums, halved and
  pitted, quartered if larger
30 g (1 oz) unsalted butter

Streusel mix
80 g (2¾ oz/½ cup) hazelnuts
  or blanched almonds,
  lightly toasted, skins
  removed, chopped
55 g (2 oz) plain (all-purpose)
  flour

55 g (2 oz/¼ cup) soft brown
  sugar
55 g (2 oz) unsalted
  butter, softened at room
  temperature
2 teaspoons ground
  cinnamon
1 teaspoon ground cloves

Staples
BTR

Preheat the oven to 180°C (350°F) fan-forced. Line a baking tray with baking paper. Grease a 23 cm (9 in) loose-based cake tin and line with baking paper.

For the plum base, sprinkle half the sugar over the base of the cake tin, then layer in the plums, skin side down, jamming them in firmly. Sprinkle with the remaining sugar and dot with the butter in knobs. Bake for 20 minutes.

Meanwhile, add the streusel mix ingredients to a bowl and rub together with your fingers into crumbs. Spread out on the baking tray and bake until golden and lightly crunchy, 10–15 minutes. Cool, then crumble in your hands to rough crumbs. Sprinkle half the streusel mix over the cooked plums.

For the cake, whisk the flour, baking powder and salt in a bowl.

In a food processor, cream the butter, sugar, liqueur, vanilla and lemon zest until pale, about 4 minutes. Add the eggs one at a time, followed by the sour cream and flour mixture, blitzing into a thick smooth batter.

Tip into a large bowl and fold the remaining streusel mix through.

Transfer to the cake tin, set on a baking tray and bake for 50–60 minutes, until a skewer comes out clean.

Stand for 30 minutes, then turn out and serve warm. The cake will keep in an airtight container in the fridge for up to 5 days, and up to 2 days at room temperature.

Carrot cake ⓥ

A classically moist carrot cake, with so much flavour and richness from the extra-virgin olive oil. So many cakes like this call for industrial horrors like canola oil, but don't do it. And for those who perpetually insist that you need a neutral oil here ... well, you don't. **Serves 8–10, or makes 12 cupcakes**

220 g (8 oz) plain (all-purpose) flour, sifted
175 g (6 oz) soft brown sugar
1 teaspoon baking powder
1 teaspoon bicarbonate of soda (baking soda)
1 teaspoon ground cinnamon
1 teaspoon ground ginger
1 teaspoon ground turmeric
1 teaspoon salt flakes

400 g (14 oz) peeled and grated carrot, gently pressed to remove a little liquid
100 ml (3½ fl oz) extra-virgin olive oil
2 eggs, lightly beaten
zest and juice of 1 orange
100 g (3½ oz) sultanas (golden raisins)

80 g (2¾ oz) walnuts, chopped
1 × quantity Cream cheese icing (p. 803), or Maple syrup, brown sugar & cinnamon icing (p. 804)

Staples
BTR

Preheat the oven to 175°C (345°F) fan-forced. Grease a 23 cm (9 in) cake tin and line with baking paper, or line a 12-hole cupcake tray with 12 paper inserts.

Combine the flour, sugar, baking powder, bicarbonate of soda, spices and salt in a bowl.

In another bowl, combine the carrot, oil, eggs, and orange zest and juice. Fold the sultanas and walnuts through, then add to the dry ingredients and mix until combined, but don't over-mix.

Spoon into the cake tin, or divide between the cupcake moulds. Bake the cake for 45–50 minutes, or 15–20 minutes for cupcakes, until a skewer comes out clean.

Cool completely before unmoulding and icing. A little orange zest finely grated over the top is a nice touch, too. The cake will keep in the fridge for about 6 days.

Make it different
Spiced pineapple & walnut cake. Replace the carrot with 400 g (14 oz) chopped fresh pineapple or drained tinned pineapple.

Spiced pumpkin & olive oil loaf cake ⓥ

This loaf cake is soft and yielding, with gentle spice notes. I find it very hard to eat just one slice of this, especially just after its been baked, as it's so good warm, but it keeps well, too. **Serves 8–10**

Pair with
Serve with crème fraîche, mascarpone, whipped ricotta or double cream, or warm through and serve with salted butter.

900 g (1 lb 11 oz/about ½) kent or jap pumpkin/winter squash
250 g (9 oz/1⅔ cups) plain (all-purpose) flour
1½ teaspoons baking powder
½ teaspoon bicarbonate of soda (baking soda)
1 tablespoon ground cinnamon

1 tablespoon ground ginger
1 whole nutmeg, finely grated, or 3 teaspoons ground nutmeg
2 teaspoons ground cardamom
250 ml (8½ fl oz/1 cup) extra-virgin olive oil
175 g (6 oz/¾ cup) caster (superfine) sugar

100 g (3½ oz) dark brown sugar
3 tablespoons chopped glacé ginger, plus extra to garnish if desired
1½ teaspoons salt flakes
3 eggs

Staples
EVOO, BTR, S&P

Preheat the oven to 175°C (345°F) fan-forced. Line a baking tray with baking paper. Grease a standard loaf (bar) tin of 24–26 cm (9½–10¼ in) and line with baking paper.

Roast the pumpkin in one piece for 1½ hours. Cut the pumpkin into six wedges and season with salt. Roast on the baking tray for a further 1½ hours to dry bake. Set aside to cool, then remove the skin and roughly chop the flesh into a paste. Weigh out 500 g (1 lb 2 oz) and discard the rest (or save to use elsewhere).

Sift the flour, baking powder, bicarbonate of soda and spices into a bowl.

Put the pumpkin in the bowl of an electric stand mixer. Add the oil, sugars, chopped ginger and salt and whisk on medium speed until smooth, about 2 minutes. Add the eggs one at a time, beating after each addition to combine. Add the flour mixture and whisk on low speed until smooth, about 2 minutes.

Pour the mixture into the loaf tin and bake for 60–70 minutes, until it springs back to the touch or a skewer comes out clean.

Cool in the tin for 30 minutes before unmoulding, then cool for 30 minutes before slicing. The loaf will keep in an airtight container at room temperature for up to a week.

Orange & almond cake with glacé orange ⓥ

I have baked this wonderful cake so many times. It was a staple in my repertoire in the 1990s, and it's something I never tire of eating, typically with a big dollop of clotted cream. There is only a tiny amount of flour in this recipe, which helps to stabilise the crumb, but there's no problem omitting it for a gluten-free version. **Serves 8–10**

3 oranges
6 eggs
350 g (12½ oz/2½ cups) ground almonds
220 g (8 oz) caster (superfine) sugar

1 tablespoon plain (all-purpose) flour
1½ teaspoons baking powder
1 × quantity Glacé orange (p. 790)

Staples
BTR

Cook the whole oranges in simmering water for 45 minutes. Drain, then cut into quarters and remove any seeds and core membrane. Dice the orange quarters, including the skin, and add to a colander set over a bowl. Drain for 1 hour at room temperature, lightly weighed down with a plate.

When ready to cook, preheat the oven to 170°C (340°F) fan-forced. Grease a 22 cm (8¾ in) springform tin and line with baking paper.

Add the drained orange to a food processor and blitz until smooth, about 4 minutes. Add the eggs, ground almonds, sugar, flour and baking powder and blitz to a smooth batter, about 1 minute.

Pour the batter into the cake tin and bake for about 45 minutes, until firm and lightly golden.

Cool completely in the tin before unmoulding, then arrange the slices of glacé orange on top.

The cake will keep in the fridge for about 5 days.

Pair with

Clotted cream (p. 800) or thick (double/heavy) cream.

Coconut butter pandan cake ⓥ

After eating traditional green chiffon cakes in Thailand on multiple holidays, pandan has become a real favourite of mine. I find it has a gentle vanilla flavour with hints of almond and rose, and it's wonderful with coconut. This cake is a little like a pound cake, with a moist buttery crumb, but the flavour is worlds away from that classically Western invention. You can buy pandan extract – or can easily make your own using fresh pandan leaves (see right). **Serves 10**

250 ml (8½ fl oz/1 cup) coconut cream
70 ml (2¼ fl oz) pandan extract (right)
30 g (1 oz/⅓ cup) desiccated coconut

340 g (12 oz) unsalted butter, softened at room temperature
400 g (14 oz/1¾ cups) caster (superfine) sugar
½ teaspoon salt flakes

4 eggs
360 g (12¾ oz) plain (all-purpose) flour
3½ teaspoons baking powder

Staples
BTR

Pair with

Smother with Berry icing (p. 802) or Lime icing (p. 802) and top with lime zest or shredded makrut lime leaves; serve with slices of red papaya, mango, rambutans and/or lychees.

Pandan extract ⒼⒻ ⓥ ⓋⒼ

Finely slice 12 fresh green pandan leaves. Grind or blitz them with 100 ml (3½ fl oz) water and then strain; this will yield 70 ml (2¼ fl oz) of strained extract to use in the Coconut butter pandan cake (left). If you can't get hold of the fresh pandan leaves, look for frozen ones – but don't use dried pandan.

Preheat the oven to 180°C (350°F) fan-forced. Grease a standard loaf (bar) tin of 22–25 cm (8¾–10 in) or a 23 cm (9 in) springform tin and line with baking paper.

Heat the coconut cream in a saucepan to just below a simmer, then remove from the heat. Add the pandan extract and desiccated coconut, then stand for 5 minutes to infuse.

Using an electric stand mixer, whisk the butter, sugar and salt on medium–high speed until pale and fluffy, about 5 minutes. Add the eggs one at a time, mixing until well incorporated, then add the pandan infusion and mix on low to combine.

Sift the flour and baking powder into a large bowl. Add the wet mixture in two batches, quickly folding in with a spatula.

Tip into the tin(s) and bake for 45–50 minutes, until a skewer comes out clean. Cool for 10 minutes, then unmould onto a rack to cool completely.

The cake will keep in an airtight container at room temperature for up to 5 days.

Make it different

Lime coconut butter pandan cake. Stir 100 ml (3½ fl oz) Lemon or lime curd (see p. 797) through Basic whipped cream (p. 799), then spread over the cake, or use to sandwich two halves of a layered cake. Garnish with two very finely chopped makrut lime leaves.

Plain coconut cake. **V** Omit the pandan extract and increase the desiccated coconut to 50 g (1¾ oz).

Sticky chocolate ginger cake **V**

I love the flavours of ginger and chocolate together. Even as a kid, I was obsessed with this quite adult combination. Needless to say, I love this recipe, with the joys of gingerbread and chocolate cake combined. **Serves 8**

180 g (6 oz) unsalted butter
150 g (5½ oz) soft brown
  sugar
150 g (5½ oz) black treacle
150 g (5½ oz) golden syrup,
  or light treacle
2 tablespoons finely grated
  fresh ginger
1 teaspoon ground ginger

1 teaspoon ground cloves
1 teaspoon ground cinnamon
1¼ teaspoons bicarbonate of
  soda (baking soda)
250 ml (8½ fl oz/1 cup)
  full-cream (whole) milk
2 eggs
280 g (10 oz) plain
  (all-purpose) flour, sifted

30 g (1 oz/¼ cup) dark
  Dutch (unsweetened)
  cocoa powder
150 g (5½ oz) dark or milk
  chocolate chips
1 × quantity Chocolate
  ginger icing (p. 805)

Staples
BTR

Preheat the oven to 160°C (320°F) fan-forced. Grease a 20 cm (8 in) square cake tin and line with baking paper, or line a 30 × 20 cm (12 × 8 in) brownie tin.

Melt the butter in a large saucepan over a medium heat. Add the sugar, treacle, golden syrup, fresh ginger and spices and warm to melt and combine.

Dissolve the bicarbonate of soda in the milk.

Lightly whisk the eggs in a large bowl, then whisk in the butter mixture. Add the milk mixture, flour and cocoa powder and combine until smooth, then fold the chocolate chips through.

Pour into the cake tin and bake for 40 minutes, or until springy to the touch. Cool completely before icing.

Ice the cake and stand for about 30 minutes to set. The cake will keep in an airtight container at room temperature for up to 5 days.

Coconut & raspberry cake with chocolate ganache (GF) (V)

A stand-and-stir cake, this is as technically uncomplicated as it gets. The combination of coconut and almond deliver such a moist and buttery crumb, while the raspberries provide a tangy counterpoint. **Serves 8**

170 g (6 oz/1⅔ cups) ground almonds
220 g (8 oz) caster (superfine) sugar
90 g (3 oz/1 cup) desiccated coconut
4 eggs
2 teaspoons natural vanilla extract or paste

200 g (7 oz) vegan margarine, melted and cooled to room temperature
150 g (5½ oz) fresh or frozen raspberries
1 × quantity Chocolate & avocado ganache (p. 412), or Berry icing (p. 802)

To decorate
125 g (4½ oz/1 cup) raspberries
1½ tablespoons cacao nibs
2 handfuls of shaved coconut

Staples
BTR

Preheat the oven to 180°C (350°F) fan-forced. Grease a 22 cm (8¾ in) springform or loose-based cake tin and line with baking paper.

Combine the ground almonds, sugar and coconut in a large bowl.

Whisk the eggs and vanilla in a large bowl to combine. Gradually whisk in the melted butter, then stir into the almond mixture until combined.

Pour into the cake tin, then dot with the raspberries.

Bake for 45–50 minutes, until the cake is golden and the top springs back when pressed lightly. Cool completely in the tin before unmoulding.

Ice the cake with the ganache, then decorate with the raspberries, cacao nibs and coconut.

The cake will keep in an airtight container at room temperature for up to 5 days.

Deluxe chocolate galette cake (V)

This is a sophisticated brownie-style cake that leans heavily on decadence. It's a perfect birthday cake, with a two-finger sliver more than enough for most – though not all. I first cooked this in my very early days in professional kitchens, and it has featured on countless menus over the years. **Serves 6–8**

180 g (6½ oz) dark chocolate melts (buttons) – 70% cocoa
180 g (6½ oz) unsalted butter, diced
3 eggs

200 g (7 oz) caster (superfine) sugar
1 teaspoon natural vanilla extract or paste
110 g (4 oz/¾ cup) plain (all-purpose) flour, sifted
1 teaspoon salt flakes

180 g (6½ oz) toasted macadamias or walnuts, chopped
1 × quantity Chocolate ganache (p. 806)

Staples
BTR

Pair with

Serve as is, or with a dollop of crème fraîche.

Raspberries are a pleasing addition to the top, or try this with vanilla or chocolate ice cream.

Preheat the oven to 180°C (350°F) fan-forced. Grease a 26 cm (10¼ in) springform cake tin and line with baking paper.

Add the chocolate and butter to a heatproof bowl and place over a saucepan of simmering water for about 5 minutes, ensuring the bowl doesn't touch the water. When two-thirds of the chocolate has melted, stir through twice. Remove the bowl to finish melting the chocolate in the residual heat.

Using an electric stand mixer, whisk the eggs, sugar and vanilla on medium–high speed until light and fluffy, about 5 minutes. Add the flour and salt and beat to combine. Fold the chocolate through, then the nuts.

Pour into the cake tin and bake for 20–25 minutes, until firm to the touch. Cool completely in the tin before unmoulding.

Spread a layer of ganache on the cake. Sit for 5 minutes to set a little, then coat again and leave to set before serving. The cake will keep in an airtight container at room temperature for up to 5 days.

Brown sugar dark chocolate loaf cake ⓥ

Pair with

Sprinkle with cacao nibs, chopped nuts or praline (see p. 786).

For me, this is the quintessential chocolate cake, the image that snaps into my consciousness when the words 'chocolate' and 'cake' are mentioned in tandem. There's always a glass of milk, too, with chocolate cake always making me incredibly thirsty as a kid, and very cold milk being the only cure. **Serves 8–10**

100 g (3½ oz) dark chocolate (68% cocoa minimum), chopped
30 g (1 oz/¼ cup) dark Dutch (unsweetened) cocoa powder
80 ml (2½ fl oz/⅓ cup) cold water
120 ml (4 fl oz) boiling water

½ teaspoon bicarbonate of soda (baking soda)
175 g (6 oz) soft brown sugar
100 g (3½ oz) unsalted butter, softened at room temperature
125 g (4½ oz) condensed milk
2 eggs

3 teaspoons corn syrup or trimoline
200 g (7 oz/1⅓ cups) plain (all-purpose) flour, sifted
2 teaspoons baking powder
1 × quantity Chocolate fudge icing (p. 805)

Staples
BTR

Preheat the oven to 160°C (320°F) fan-forced. Grease a 20 cm (8 in) round cake tin or 19 cm (7½ in) loaf (bar) tin and line with baking paper, or use cupcake moulds.

Add the chocolate to a bowl.

Combine the cocoa powder and cold water in a bowl to make a paste, then whisk in the boiling water. Tip over the chocolate and stir to melt. Add the bicarbonate of soda and stir through.

Using an electric stand mixer, whisk the sugar, butter and condensed milk on medium–high speed until very smooth, about 5 minutes. Add the eggs and corn syrup and mix for about 1 minute to combine. Add half the flour and all the baking powder and beat to incorporate. Add the chocolate mixture and remaining flour and beat until smooth.

Tip the mixture into the cake tin and bake for 50 minutes. Cool completely in the tin, then unmould and smother with the icing.

The cake will keep in an airtight container at room temperature for up to 5 days.

Classic sponge cake ⓥ

Cooking a simple sponge cake is something that seems to inspire a decent amount of fear for many cooks. The best sponges are marked by a fine crumb and airy lightness, an effortlessness. Every dedicated sponge cook has their own failsafe recipe – and they differ somewhat – but there are some simple rules to getting a fine result, rather than a heavy and ponderous one. As with all baking, be precise and weigh everything carefully. Always use a glass or stainless steel bowl for mixing, and always use very fresh eggs at room temperature. It's also important to not work the batter too much, just enough to incorporate. A tip from my sister Odette (the pastry chef) is to use the whisk attachment from the stand mixer to fold in the flour, which is gentle and effective. If you overmix, the gluten can toughen, meaning you won't get that fine crumb. In this recipe, I also heat the egg and sugar first, which stabilises the egg, and helps to achieve a good, even rise. Also, always bake on the middle shelf, which is true for all cakes, and *never* skewer a sponge cake to test if it's cooked – a light touch with your fingers to feel for a little springiness is enough. That sounds like a lot of rules, but they're relatively simple, and you'll get a feel for it soon enough. **Serves 8**

250 g (9 oz) eggs
125 g (4½ oz) caster (superfine) sugar
a pinch of salt flakes
110 g (4 oz/¾ cup) plain (all-purpose) flour

30 g (1 oz/¼ cup) cornflour (cornstarch)
1 teaspoon baking powder
40 g (1½ oz) butter, melted, cooled to room temperature

Staples
BTR

Special equipment
Sugar thermometer

Preheat the oven to 170°C (340°F) fan-forced. Grease and line a 24 cm (9½ in) round cake tin, or 2 × 20 cm (8 in) cake tins, or a 20 × 30 cm (8 × 12 in) lamington tray if making Lamingtons (opposite).

Bring a saucepan of water to just under a simmer. Add the eggs, sugar and salt to a large heatproof bowl and place over the pan, ensuring the bowl doesn't touch the water. Whisk constantly until 40°C (105°F), about 5 minutes.

Transfer the mixture to the bowl of an electric stand mixer. Whisk on medium speed, gradually increasing to high and beat for 5 minutes.

Meanwhile, sift the flour, cornflour and baking powder into a bowl.

When the egg mixture is a pale and fluffy foam, take the bowl off the machine. Use the whisk attachment from the machine to fold in the flour mixture in a circular motion, to scrape down the sides and incorporate. It may take five mixes with your whisk, but don't overwork it.

Pour in the melted butter and mix a couple of times with the whisk, then use a spatula to scrape around the bowl and incorporate.

Transfer the mixture to the cake tin(s) and bake for 20 minutes, until springy to the touch.

Remove from the oven and cool for 5 minutes, then unmould the cake onto a tea towel (dish towel; to stop you marking the top) on a wire cake rack.

Invert the cake and cool for 45 minutes before dressing. The sponge will keep in an airtight container in the pantry for up to 3 days.

Pair with

Use in a Tiramisu (p. 776).

Layer in a trifle.

Use to make Lamingtons (opposite).

Berries & cream sponge cake filling Ⓖ🅕

Bake a Classic sponge cake (left) and leave to cool. Whip 300 ml (10 fl oz) pouring (single/light) cream to stiff peaks. Use a sharp serrated knife to evenly cut the cooled cake into two layers, through the middle. Spread the cut side of the bottom half of the sponge with 150 g (5½ oz) raspberry or strawberry jam, or Lemon or lime curd (see p. 797). Top with half the whipped cream, then 250 g (9 oz) fresh whole berries or sliced strawberries, then the remaining cream. Top with the top half of the sponge, cut side down, then dust with icing (confectioners') sugar. You could also decorate with more fruit, if you like. Serve on the day of making, but leftovers will keep for up to 2 days in an airtight container in the fridge.

Lamingtons Ⓥ

Short cut

Use store-bought sponge.

I never liked lamingtons – until I made my own. That's not me blowing my own trumpet; there's just a little magic in a home-made lamington, and little to none in most commercial ones. It's a bit of a sticky and messy job, but really well worth the trouble. Naturally, you'll be making your own sponge cake (which is better a little on the stale side) … and using your own jam propels them into very special territory indeed. **Makes 20**

1 × quantity two-day-old Classic sponge cake (opposite), baked in a 20 × 30 cm (8 × 12 in) lamington tray
150 g (5½ oz) Super-simple roasted raspberry jam (p. 687)

100 g (3½ oz) shaved coconut
250 g (9 oz) shredded coconut

Chocolate glaze
500 g (1 lb 2 oz/4 cups) icing (confectioners') sugar

60 g (2 oz/½ cup) dark Dutch (unsweetened) cocoa powder
140 ml (4 fl oz) full-cream (whole) milk
50 g (1¾ oz) unsalted butter
100 ml (3½ fl oz) boiling water

For the glaze, whisk the icing sugar and cocoa powder in a large bowl.

Warm the milk and butter in a saucepan over a medium heat until the butter melts, then tip into the bowl, along with the boiling water. Whisk until smooth, and the consistency of thin cream. Set aside.

Using a sharp serrated knife, cut the sponge cake horizontally. Spread the bottom half with the jam, then sandwich back together and chill for 15 minutes.

Cut the slab in half lengthways, then cut each half in half again lengthways. Cut each length into five pieces, yielding 20 lamingtons. Chill for 15 minutes to firm up a little.

Toss the shaved and shredded coconut in a shallow container. Carefully add a chilled cake cube to the glaze, then rotate using two forks to completely coat. Lift out, letting the excess icing drain back into the bowl, then drop into the coconut and rotate to coat well. Lift the lamington onto a wire rack, then repeat.

Stand for 20 minutes to dry before serving. The slab cake will keep in an airtight container at room temperature for up for 5 days.

Torta caprese all'arancia e cioccolato (Dark chocolate & almond torte) (GF)(V)

This is based on a very old recipe I found in Capri many moons ago. This flourless cake is quite complex and sophisticated, both in flavour and texture, and it's something I make for special occasions, often popping up at Christmas. I love the texture you get from grinding your own almonds, giving a delightful chewiness that you just won't get with commercial ground almonds – not to mention the freshness. **Serves 8–10**

Pair with

Crème fraîche.

Candied orange peel (p. 790).

Chocolate ganache (p. 806).

Torta caprese bianco cioccolato (GF)(V)

This white chocolate and almond torte is very similar to the <u>Torta caprese</u> (right), but the flavours are pitched differently, with white chocolate and lemon taking the lead. Proceed with the recipe, but replace the dark chocolate with 200 g (7 oz) <u>white chocolate</u>. Add the zest of 1 <u>lemon</u> and 60 ml (2 fl oz/¼ cup) lemon juice when folding the ground almond mixture through the whisked <u>egg</u> yolks. Then, when stirring in the melted chocolate mixture, add 30 ml (1 fl oz) <u>Strega or limoncello</u>. Carefully fold the whisked egg whites through the batter, then pour into the cake tin. Sprinkle with 40 g (1½ oz) <u>flaked almonds</u> and bake for 20 minutes. Top with 50 g (1¾ oz) chopped white chocolate and bake for another 25 minutes, until a skewer comes out clean. Cool completely before unmoulding. Dust with <u>icing (confectioners') sugar</u> to serve.

200 g (7 oz) dark chocolate (70% cocoa), chopped
200 g (7 oz) unsalted butter, diced
250 g (9 oz/1⅔ cups) blanched almonds

200 g (7 oz) caster (superfine) sugar
½ teaspoon salt flakes
5 eggs, separated
¼ teaspoon orange essential oil

Dutch (unsweetened) cocoa powder, for dusting

Staples
BTR

Preheat the oven to 160°C (320°F) fan-forced. Grease a 24 cm (9½ in) loose-based cake tin and line with baking paper.

Add the chocolate and butter to a heatproof bowl and place over a saucepan of simmering water for about 5 minutes, ensuring the bowl doesn't touch the water. When two-thirds of the chocolate has melted, stir through twice. Remove the bowl to finish melting the chocolate in the residual heat.

Blitz the almonds in a food processor until finely ground, then add the sugar and salt and pulse about five times until you have a medium–fine meal.

Whisk the egg yolks by hand in a large bowl until foaming, then stir the almond mixture through. Add the melted chocolate and orange oil and stir to combine.

Whisk the egg whites until firm peaks form, then carefully fold them through the almond mixture to retain as much air as possible. Transfer the mixture to the cake tin.

Bake for about 45 minutes, until the cake is puffed and golden and a skewer comes out clean. Cool completely before unmoulding. Dust with cocoa powder to serve.

The torte will keep in an airtight container at room temperature for up to 5 days.

Sicilian cassata-style ricotta cake ⓥ

I reserve this cake for the most special of occasions. It's a true labour of love, but a lot can be done ahead of time. In fact, the cake can be stored in the freezer, and the icing is virtually indestructible – so you can prepare much of the cake in advance so that you're well rested for the task of decorating. **Serves 8–10**

100 ml (3½ fl oz) Basic sugar syrup (p. 793) – or the syrup from the amarena cherries, below

100 ml (3½ fl oz) almond or cherry liqueur, or brandy

1 × 24 cm (9½ in) Classic sponge cake (p. 748); quality bought sponge is also fine

20 amarena cherries, in syrup

1 × quantity Chocolate crème pâtissière (p. 798), in a piping (icing) bag fitted with a 1 cm (½ in) nozzle

Chocolate ricotta filling

250 g (9 oz/2 cups) icing (confectioners') sugar

750 g (1 lb 11 oz/3 cups) fresh ricotta, drained

1 tablespoon natural vanilla extract

zest of ½ lemon

150 g (5½ oz) dark chocolate (56–80% cocoa), roughly chopped

2 tablespoons finely chopped mixed candied peel

60 g (2 oz/⅔ cup) toasted flaked almonds

Pistachio & almond marzipan icing

100 g (3½ oz/⅔ cup) pistachio kernels

100 g (3½ oz/⅔ cup) blanched almonds

150 g (5½ oz) icing (confectioners') sugar mixture

50 g (1¾ oz) icing (confectioners') sugar

½ egg white (20 ml/¾ fl oz)

50 ml (1¾ fl oz) Basic sugar syrup (p. 793)

½ knife tip of bitter almond essence

3 drops of green food colouring

To decorate

350 ml (12 fl oz) pouring (single/light) cream

50 ml (1¾ fl oz) thick (double/heavy) cream (40–42% fat)

150 g (5½ oz/1⅓ cups) toasted flaked almonds

12 amarena cherries, in syrup

Staples
BTR

Grease a 24 cm (9½ in) springform tin and line with baking paper.

For the ricotta filling, blitz the icing sugar in a food processor to remove any lumps. Add the ricotta, vanilla and lemon zest, then blitz for 2 minutes. Tip into a bowl and fold in the chocolate, peel and almonds, then refrigerate for at least 30 minutes.

Combine the sugar syrup and liqueur in a small bowl.

Cut the sponge cake in half horizontally with a sharp serrated knife. Fit the top of the sponge into the cake tin, cut side up, pressing it in. Drizzle with half the liqueur mixture, then spread half the ricotta mixture over, smoothing flat with a spatula. Stud the mixture with the cherries. Pipe in the crème pâtissière in a spiral, starting from the centre and radiating out to the edge. Top with the remaining ricotta mixture, smoothing over with a spatula. Drizzle the remaining liqueur mixture over the cut side of the remaining sponge, then invert onto the top of the cake, pressing down evenly. Wrap tightly with plastic wrap, then freeze for at least 6 hours or overnight. (The cake can also be frozen for about a month if needed.)

For the icing, blitz the pistachios and almonds until finely ground. Add the icing sugar mixture and icing sugar and blitz. Add the egg white, sugar syrup, almond essence and food colouring and blitz to form a crumb. Tip onto a clean bench and bring together, kneading about six times with the heel of your hand to form a smooth paste; add about 2 teaspoons sugar syrup or water if the mixture won't come together. Wrap in plastic wrap, then refrigerate for 2 hours before using. (The icing will keep for about a month in the fridge.)

When ready to decorate the cake, thaw in the fridge for 30 minutes, then unmould. Smooth the edges over, but don't worry too much about the sides, as these will be covered with cream.

Using an electric mixer, whip the cream and thick cream until stiff.

Cut the icing in half. Form one portion into a ball, then flatten and roll out to about 3 mm (⅛ in) thick, to fit the top of the cake. Cut out a 28 cm (11 in) round and lay it on top of the sponge.

Classic poppy seed loaf ⓥ

Preheat the oven to 165°C (330°F) fan-forced. Grease a standard loaf (bar) tin of 22–25 cm (8¾–10 in). Cream 180 g (6½ oz) softened butter and 240 g (8½ oz) caster (superfine) sugar until pale. Add the zest of 1 lemon, 3 tablespoons poppy seeds, 2 teaspoons vanilla extract, 80 g (2¾ oz) yoghurt and 2 eggs and combine. Fold in 310 g (11 oz) self-raising flour and the juice of the lemon (about 100 ml/3½ fl oz) to make a thick batter. Pour into the loaf tin and bake for 1 hour. Cool, then ice with Lemon icing (p. 802).

Press the overhang around the edge of the cake. Use a cake spatula to apply the whipped cream smoothly around the side of the cake, about 1.5 cm (½ in) thick. Press the almonds into the cream to fully coat the cream border. Roll the left-over icing into cherry-sized balls (or any shape you like) and use them to decorate the top edge, alternating with the cherries. The cake will keep in the fridge for 3 days.

Make it simple
Skip the pistachio and almond marzipan icing, and instead increase the cream by 200 ml (7 fl oz) and entirely cover the cake in whipped cream.

Apricot, semolina, almond & yoghurt cake Ⓥ

This cake has a large, moist crumb and a high fruit-to-cake ratio – just the way I like it. **Serves 8**

Pair with

Serve warm with cream, Clotted cream (p. 800), crème fraîche or Thick vanilla custard (p. 801).

10 ripe apricots, cut in half and pitted
zest of ½ orange, and juice of 1 orange
80 g (2¾ oz) soft brown sugar
1½ teaspoons anise seeds
170 g (6 oz) unsalted butter, softened at room temperature

175 g (6 oz/¾ cup) caster (superfine) sugar
3 eggs, lightly beaten
100 g (3½ oz) plain yoghurt
zest of ½ lemon
60 ml (2 fl oz/¼ cup) lemon juice
135 g (5 oz) fine semolina
135 g (5 oz/1⅓ cups) ground almonds

70 g (2½ oz) plain (all-purpose) flour, sifted
2½ teaspoons baking powder
50 g (1¾ oz) flaked almonds

Staples
BTR

Preheat the oven to 160°C (320°F) fan-forced. Grease a 23 cm (9 in) round cake tin and line with baking paper.

In a bowl, gently toss together the apricots, orange zest and juice, brown sugar and anise seeds. Set aside for 15 minutes or more, gently tossing the apricots through the liquid every now and then.

Whisk the butter and caster sugar using an electric stand mixer on medium–high speed until pale and fluffy, about 5 minutes. Add the egg in two additions, mixing after each addition until just incorporated. Add the yoghurt, lemon zest and juice, then beat until combined.

In a bowl, combine the semolina, ground almonds, flour and baking powder, then fold into the mixture until smooth and well mixed.

Pour the batter into the cake tin and poke the apricots in the top, reserving the macerating juices in the bowl. Sprinkle the flaked almonds over the top and bake for about 50 minutes, until a skewer comes out clean.

Meanwhile, add the liquid from the apricots to a small saucepan and reduce on the stovetop until the consistency of honey.

When the cake comes out of the oven, brush or drizzle the top with the syrup. Cool for 15 minutes before unmoulding and serving.

The cake will keep in an airtight container at room temperature for up to 5 days.

Make it different
Cherry, semolina, almond & yoghurt cake. Ⓥ Instead of apricots, use thirty pitted cherries soaked for 1 hour in boiling water, then drained. Depending what is in season, you could also use fresh peaches, blood plums, nectarines or blackberries.

With spices. Play with the spice profile by adding ground ginger or saffron, or both.

Biscuits, slices & sweet buns

Dark chocolate & hazelnut biscuits Ⓥ

You can roll these biscuits in any type of nut you like, but hazelnuts with dark chocolate is the winning combination for me – with crushed pistachios being a fairly close second. These make lovely gifts, and will keep for weeks sealed in cellophane bags. **Makes 12–14 large biscuits, or about 25 smaller biscuits**

250 g (9 oz) dark chocolate (70% cocoa), chopped
50 g (1¾ oz) unsalted butter, diced
2 eggs

100 g (3½ oz) soft brown sugar
75 g (2½ oz/⅓ cup) caster (superfine) sugar
80 g (2¾ oz) plain (all-purpose) flour

½ teaspoon baking powder
½ teaspoon salt flakes
250 g (9 oz/1¾ cups) hazelnuts, lightly toasted, skins removed, roughly chopped

Add the chocolate and butter to a heatproof bowl and place over a saucepan of simmering water for about 5 minutes, ensuring the bowl doesn't touch the water. When two-thirds of the chocolate has melted, stir through twice. Remove the bowl to finish melting the chocolate in the residual heat.

Using an electric stand mixer, whisk the eggs and sugars on medium speed until thick and fluffy, about 5 minutes. Fold in the chocolate mixture, then the flour, baking powder and salt until combined. Refrigerate for 20 minutes.

Preheat the oven to 180°C (350°F) fan-forced. Line two baking trays with baking paper.

Form the mixture into twelve to fourteen balls, or about twenty-five balls for petite biscuits, then roll in the hazelnuts, pressing them into the mixture. (You could freeze them now for up to a month, and thaw in the fridge for 4 hours before baking.)

Arrange on the baking trays about 5 cm (2 in) apart. Bake large biscuits for 12 minutes, or 8 minutes for smaller biscuits. Cool to room temperature before serving.

The biscuits will keep for up to a month in an airtight container.

Chocolate biscuit sandwiches with sesame cream Ⓖ Ⓕ Ⓥ

These softly chewy chocolate biscuits are easy to master, and make for a very rich and satisfying treat – marvellous party fare. **Makes 16**

600 g (1 lb 5 oz) dark chocolate (70% cocoa), chopped
80 g (2¾ oz) unsalted butter, diced
4 eggs
300 g (10½ oz) light brown sugar

40 g (1½ oz/⅓ cup) dark Dutch (unsweetened) cocoa powder

Sesame cream cheese filling
75 g (2½ oz) cream cheese
60 g (2 oz) tahini

40 g (1½ oz/⅓ cup) icing (confectioners') sugar
750 ml (25½ fl oz/3 cups) thick (double/heavy) cream
1½ tablespoons toasted sesame seeds

Vanilla butter biscuits Ⓥ

Soften 175 g (6 oz) unsalted butter at room temperature. Cream the butter and 200 g (7 oz) caster (superfine) sugar in a food processor until pale, about 3 minutes. Add 2 eggs and 2 teaspoons natural vanilla extract or paste and process for 1 minute. Add 450 g (1 lb/3 cups) plain (all-purpose) flour, 1 teaspoon baking powder and 1 teaspoon salt flakes, then process briefly until the mixture just comes together. Tip onto a clean bench and form into a flattened disc, then cut in half to make it easier to roll later. Refrigerate between sheets of baking paper for 45 minutes. Preheat the oven to 170°C (340°F) fan-forced. Line two baking trays with baking paper. Roll the rested dough out until about 5 mm (¼ in) thick, then cut out your desired shapes. Re-roll the scraps to use all the dough; you can chill it again for 10 minutes if it isn't cold to the touch. Transfer to the baking trays, leaving 3–4 cm (1¼–1½ in) between each. Bake for 7–10 minutes; the biscuits will spread a little once cooked. Cool completely on the trays. If desired, spoon or pipe Basic sugar icing (p. 802) or Lemon icing (p. 802) onto the cooled biscuits, then set aside to dry on a rack. The biscuits will keep in an airtight container for up to a week. Makes 16–20.

Cat's tongue biscuits (Lengua de gato) Ⓥ

Preheat the oven to 210°C (410°F) fan-forced. Line two baking trays with baking paper. Dice 120 g (4½ oz) unsalted butter and warm to room temperature. Cream the butter, 120 g (4½ oz) caster (superfine) sugar and 1 teaspoon natural vanilla extract or paste in a food processor until pale, about 3 minutes. Gradually add 80 g (2¾ oz) room-temperature egg whites until incorporated. Add 100 g (3½ oz/⅔ cup) plain (all-purpose) flour and process until combined. Transfer to a piping (icing) bag fitted with a 1 cm (½ in) nozzle. (You can portion the mixture with a spoon, but this is the best way to get a consistent result.) Pipe into 10 cm (4 in) lengths on the baking trays, leaving 5 cm (2 in) between each. Sprinkle with 50 g (1¾ oz/½ cup) flaked almonds. Bake for 7–8 minutes, until golden at the edges. Cool completely on the trays. Melt 200 g (7 oz) dark chocolate (56–70% cocoa) and transfer to a piping bag. Pipe the chocolate over the cooled biscuits in a crisscross fashion, then put aside on a rack to set. The biscuits will keep for about 3 days in an airtight container. Makes 24 biscuits.

Preheat the oven to 180°C (350°F) fan-forced. Line two baking trays with baking paper.

Add 250 g (9 oz) of the chocolate to a heatproof bowl, with the butter. Place over a saucepan of simmering water for about 5 minutes, ensuring the bowl doesn't touch the water. When two-thirds of the chocolate has melted, stir through twice. Remove the bowl to finish melting the chocolate in the residual heat.

Using an electric stand mixer, whisk the eggs and sugar on medium speed until thick and fluffy, about 5 minutes. Fold in the chocolate mixture, then the cocoa powder and remaining chopped chocolate. Transfer to a piping (icing) bag fitted with a 1.5 cm (½ in) nozzle.

Pipe 32 even rounds (in batches, if needed) onto the baking trays, leaving about 5 cm (2 in) between each.

Bake for about 9 minutes, until they form a crust. Cool on the trays before filling – they will be very soft when they come out of the oven.

For the filling, whisk the cream cheese, tahini and icing sugar on slow speed using an electric stand mixer to combine. Add the cream and sesame seeds, then combine on slow speed – be cautious not to over-whisk, or the mixture will split.

Use about 2 teaspoons of the filling to sandwich the biscuits together. Serve straight away.

Make it different
With fillings. Sandwich the biscuits with 2 teaspoons of salted Dulce de leche (p. 795), Chocolate ganache (p. 806) or Cream cheese icing (p. 803).

Salted nut & choc chip biscuits Ⓥ

This is the staple chocolate chip cookie in my house. It's a classic that I don't tinker with. The only change I will ever make is to vary the nuts. And, in truth, I almost always use hazelnuts – but walnuts, pecans, macadamias or peanuts would all work beautifully. **Makes about 26**

250 g (9 oz/1 cup) unsalted butter, well softened at room temperature	450 g (1 lb/3 cups) self-raising flour	150 g (5½ oz) dark chocolate melts (buttons)
200 g (7 oz) caster (superfine) sugar	100 g (3½ oz/1 cup) ground almonds	100 g (3½ oz) milk chocolate melts (buttons)
200 g (7 oz) light brown sugar	½ teaspoon natural vanilla extract or paste	150 g (5½ oz) toasted nuts of your choice, roughly chopped
2 eggs	1 teaspoon salt flakes, plus extra for sprinkling	

Line two baking trays with baking paper.

Using an electric stand mixer, cream the butter and sugars on medium–high speed with the paddle attachment until thick and creamy, about 5 minutes. Add the eggs one at a time, beating on low–medium speed until each egg is incorporated. Add the flour, ground almonds, vanilla and salt and beat until combined, then fold in the chocolate and nuts. Refrigerate for 10 minutes to firm up.

Scoop the mixture with a spoon and roll into balls of about 60 g (2 oz) each. Place on the baking trays 8 cm (3¼ in) apart, then refrigerate for 45 minutes. (You can freeze these, too; just thaw for 4 hours in the fridge before baking.) Before baking, press down slightly to flatten and sprinkle with salt flakes.

Preheat the oven to 180°C (350°F) fan-forced.

Bake the biscuits for about 13 minutes, swapping the trays on the shelves halfway through to cook evenly. Once cooked, they will spread and be slightly golden at the edges.

Cool on the trays for 10 minutes, then transfer to a wire rack to cool completely. The biscuits will keep in an airtight container for up to a month.

Anzac biscuits (v)

Anzac biscuits are a triumph of simplicity, and one of my favourite biscuits – all oaty, caramelised and buttery, with a gentle soft give in the centre. Their durability is also legendary, gaining their association with the diggers of World War I due to their capacity to remain edible – enjoyable, even – after a long sea voyage. The inclusion of coconut is controversial for some, but there are very old recipes that list it ... and I like the subtle flavour it lends, so in it goes. **Makes 12**

170 g (6 oz) rolled (porridge) oats
220 g (8 oz) plain (all-purpose) flour
200 g (7 oz) soft brown sugar

100 g (3½ oz) shredded or flaked coconut
185 g (6½ oz) unsalted butter
80 g (2¾ oz) golden syrup, or light treacle

100 ml (3½ fl oz) water
1½ teaspoons bicarbonate of soda (baking soda)
½ teaspoon salt flakes

Preheat the oven to 175°C (345°F) fan-forced. Line two baking trays with baking paper.

Combine the oats, flour, sugar and coconut in a bowl.

Gently melt the butter and golden syrup in a saucepan over a medium heat. Combine the water, bicarbonate of soda and salt in a bowl, then add to the pan and stir. Tip onto the dry ingredients while still foaming, then mix through with a spoon until incorporated. Chill for 20 minutes.

Divide the mixture into twelve portions and roll into balls. Place on the baking trays with about 5 cm (2 in) between each. Flatten the balls slightly with a spatula.

Bake for about 18–20 minutes, until the biscuits spread and are bubbling at the edges. The biscuits will keep in an airtight container for at least a week.

Make it different
With macadamia nuts. Add 100 g (3½ oz/¾ cup) crushed macadamia nuts and reduce the oats to 120 g (4½ oz).

Gingerbread Christmas cookies (v)

For many years now, I have collected biscuit cutters for making gingerbread cookies, so there is quite an array of shapes on offer on my Christmas table. Making a little hole in the top before baking can also turn these into edible decorations for the Christmas tree – just thread with ribbon and hang. **Makes about 30–40 (depending on shape/size)**

160 g (5½ oz) unsalted butter
140 g (5 oz/⅔ cup) caster (superfine) sugar
180 g (6½ oz) brown sugar
3 eggs
2½ tablespoons molasses

600 g (1 lb 5 oz/4 cups) plain (all-purpose) flour, plus extra for dusting
1½ teaspoons baking powder
2 tablespoons ground ginger
3 teaspoons mixed spice

2½ teaspoons ground cinnamon
1 × quantity Lemon icing (p. 802)

Using a food processor, cream the butter and sugars until pale, about 3 minutes. Add the eggs and molasses and process until combined. Add the remaining ingredients and process until you have a smooth but quite sticky dough. (If your food processor is small, you may need to do this in batches, but I don't use an electric stand mixer as it can aerate the mixture.)

Tip out onto baking paper, then fold over to cover. Refrigerate for 2 hours.

Top to bottom: Sugared butter custard biscuits (p. 759), Anzac biscuits (above), Salted nut & choc chip biscuits (p. 755)

Preheat the oven to 170°C (340°F) fan-forced. Line two baking trays with baking paper.

Lightly flour a 70 cm (28 in) long sheet of baking paper. Place the dough on top and cover with another sheet of baking paper. Use a rolling pin to roll out the dough to about 1 cm (½ in) thick.

Lift off the top sheet, flour lightly, then turn out onto a clean bench. Flour the other side, then work quickly to cut out the shapes, transferring them with a palette knife to the baking trays, leaving 3 cm (1¼ in) between each. Work swiftly, as the dough will heat and soften quite readily; return to the fridge if needed. Re-roll any of the scraps between paper and cut out as many shapes as possible.

Bake for 10–12 minutes, until lightly golden. Cool on the tray for 10 minutes, then transfer to a wire rack to cool completely.

Dip the cooled biscuits in the icing, or decorate using a squeeze bottle or piping (icing) bag, then stand at room temperature to set. The biscuits will keep in an airtight container for up to a month.

Almond & pistachio biscotti GF V

These biscotti are so nutty and delightfully chewy – and look dazzlingly bejewelled when studded with a glacé cherry. **Makes about 50**

120 g (4½ oz/¾ cup) blanched almonds
570 g (1 lb 4 oz) caster (superfine) sugar
4 egg whites, one kept separate
100 g (3½ oz) hazelnuts, toasted, skins removed

300 g (10½ oz/3 cups) ground almonds
80 g (2¾ oz) unsalted butter
1 tablespoon honey
200 g (7 oz/1⅓ cups) pistachio kernels, roughly chopped

150 g (5½ oz/1 cup) pine nuts, roughly chopped
50 g (1¾ oz) glacé cherries or blanched almonds, or a mix (optional)

In a food processor, blitz the almonds, 270 g (9½ oz) of the sugar and 3 egg whites until smooth. Tip the mixture into a large bowl.

Put the remaining sugar and egg white in the food processor. Add the hazelnuts, ground almonds, butter and honey and blitz until well combined.

Tip into the bowl with the almond mixture and combine. Cover and refrigerate for 1 hour.

Preheat the oven to 140°C (285°F) fan-forced. Line two baking trays with baking paper.

Combine the pistachios and pine nuts. Roll the chilled biscotti mixture into walnut-sized balls, then roll in the nuts and stud with a cherry or almond (if using). Place on the baking trays, leaving 4 cm (1½ in) between each. Flatten out slightly.

Bake for 20 minutes, until pale golden. Set aside to cool. The biscotti will keep in an airtight container for about 4 days.

Amaretti biscotti GF V

You see these classic almond biscotti stacked in bakeries all over Italy. They are perfect with an espresso coffee as an afternoon pick-me-up, or after dinner with a glass of grappa or vin santo. Don't be tempted to buy ground almonds for these, as the less-perfect texture you get from blitzing almonds yourself adds a chewy texture that I love. **Makes about 50**

Almond bread V

This is a simple recipe that yields two loaves. Preheat the oven to 180°C (350°F) fan-forced. Grease two standard loaf (bar) tins of 22–25 cm (8¾–10 in) and line with baking paper. Using an electric stand mixer on medium–high speed, whisk 95 g (3¼ oz) egg whites with a pinch of salt for 1 minute. Rain in 180 g (6½ oz) caster (superfine) sugar, then whisk until thick, about 5 minutes. Fold in 180 g (6 oz) plain (all-purpose) flour, 180 g (6½ oz) whole almonds and 1 teaspoon ground cinnamon until combined. Divide the mixture evenly between the tins, smoothing the tops flat. Bake for about 25 minutes, until slightly risen and golden. Set aside to cool in the tins. At this stage you can freeze the loaves until ready to use them, or just chill well in the fridge overnight. When ready to finish baking the loaves, preheat the oven to 150°C (300°F) fan-forced. Line two baking trays with baking paper. Slice the loaves 2–3 mm (⅛–¼ in) thick with a sharp serrated knife, then lay on the baking trays. Bake for 5–8 minutes, until lightly coloured. Set aside to cool on the trays and crisp up. These are best eaten fresh, but can be stored in an airtight container for about 3 days. The loaves will freeze for up to 6 months. If freezing, thaw for 20 minutes on the bench, then slice and bake – they are easy to slice thinly when semi-frozen, and you can refreeze the unused portion.

420 g (15 oz/1⅔ cups) whole blanched almonds
90 g (3 oz) egg whites
280 g (10 oz/1¼ cups) caster (superfine) sugar

30 ml (1 fl oz) amaretto liqueur, or 1 drop of bitter almond extract
1 teaspoon natural vanilla extract or paste

For rolling
150 g (5½ oz/⅔ cup) caster (superfine) sugar
150 g (5½ oz/1¼ cups) icing (confectioners') sugar

Preheat the oven to 170°C (340°F) fan-forced. Line two baking trays with baking paper.

Blitz the almonds in a food processor, until finely ground.

Using an electric stand mixer, whisk the egg whites and 150 g (5½ oz) of the sugar on medium–high speed until stiff peaks form, about 5 minutes. Fold in the ground almonds, liqueur, vanilla and remaining sugar.

For rolling, spread the caster sugar and icing sugar in separate shallow bowls. Using two teaspoons, shape the biscotti mixture into balls the size of heaped teaspoons. The mixture will be a little wet, so carefully roll in the caster sugar, then the icing sugar to coat.

Place on the baking trays, leaving 5 cm (2 in) between each. Press down on each ball slightly to split the edges a little.

Bake for 15 minutes; the biscotti will have spread and look a little cracked. Set aside undisturbed on the trays until completely cool. The biscotti will keep in an airtight container for up to a month.

Sugared butter custard biscuits Ⓥ

These are delicate, crisp and buttery, with a hint of spice – an understated, melt-in-the-mouth sugar-coated biscuit. **Makes about 26**

190 g (6½ oz) unsalted butter, well softened at room temperature
140 g (5 oz/⅔ cup) caster (superfine) sugar
½ teaspoon natural vanilla extract or paste

200 g (7 oz/1⅓ cups) plain (all-purpose) flour, sifted, plus extra for dusting
30 g (1 oz) custard powder
½ teaspoon bicarbonate of soda (baking soda)
1½ teaspoons ground cloves

1 teaspoon salt flakes
50 g (1¾ oz) demerara sugar

Special equipment
6 cm (2½ in) pastry cutter

Cream the butter, caster sugar and vanilla using an electric stand mixer on medium–high speed with the paddle attachment until thick and creamy, about 5 minutes. In two batches, fold in the flour, custard powder, bicarbonate of soda, cloves and salt.

Once a dough forms, tip out and press into a disc. Refrigerate for 30 minutes.

Preheat the oven to 160°C (320°F) fan-forced. Line two baking trays with baking paper.

Roll the dough out between two lightly floured pieces of baking paper until about 6 mm (¼ in) thick – I generally re-flour on both sides about halfway through rolling to prevent sticking. Use a 6 cm (2½ in) pastry cutter to cut out as many circles as you can, then re-roll the scraps. If the dough is soft, chill to firm up, then cut out more circles, using as much of the dough as possible.

Transfer to the baking trays, then sprinkle with the demerara sugar. Bake for 15 minutes, until slightly puffed, swapping the trays on the shelves halfway through to cook evenly.

Set aside undisturbed on the trays until completely cool. The biscuits will keep in an airtight container for up to 5 days.

Odette's best banana bread (V)

Courtesy of my sister, Odette, this is the best banana bread recipe that I have yet come across – and boy are there a few out there! As with any banana bread, use bananas that are almost stomach-churningly overripe. It's a mystery why, but the intensity and purity of flavour is only improved once blackened and arrestingly decrepit. **Serves 8–10**

340 g (12 oz) plain
(all-purpose) flour
2 teaspoons baking powder
2 teaspoons bicarbonate of
soda (baking soda)
200 ml (7 fl oz) extra-virgin
olive oil

100 g (3½ oz) plain yoghurt
2 eggs
½ teaspoon salt flakes
400 g (14 oz) mashed very
ripe banana
220 g (8 oz) caster (superfine)
sugar

To decorate
1 banana, sliced 1 cm (½ in)
thick

Staples
BTR

Preheat the oven to 170°C (340°F) fan-forced. Grease a 25 cm (10 in) loaf (bar) tin and line with baking paper.

Whisk the flour, baking powder and bicarbonate of soda in a bowl.

Combine the oil, yoghurt, eggs and salt in another bowl.

Using an electric stand mixer, beat the mashed banana and sugar on medium speed with the paddle attachment for 2 minutes. Reduce the speed, then gradually add the egg mixture until incorporated. Add the flour mixture and beat for 3 minutes to incorporate.

Pour the mixture into the loaf tin and top with the sliced banana.

Bake for 30 minutes, then set aside to cool in the tin completely before unmoulding and slicing.

The banana bread will keep in an airtight container in the fridge for 5–7 days, or for 2–3 days at room temperature.

Chocolate panforte with almonds, figs & sour cherries (V)

I usually make this version of the Sienese classic at Christmas time, serving thin slices after lunch with plenty of filter coffee to buoy the spirits while I marshal my strength for dinner. It keeps so well, lasting for a couple of months – but only if you make enough of it! **Serves 50**

150 g (5½ oz/1 cup) blanched
almonds
100 g (3½ oz) hazelnuts
50 g (1¾ oz/⅓ cup) pistachio
kernels
200 g (7 oz/1⅓ cups) plain
(all-purpose) flour
100 g (3½ oz) Dutch
(unsweetened) cocoa
powder
2½ teaspoons ground ginger
2 teaspoons ground
cinnamon

1 teaspoon ground cloves
2 teaspoons ground black
pepper
150 g (5½ oz) candied orange
or cedro, cut into 1 cm
(½ in) dice
100 g (3½ oz) dried figs,
stems removed, cut into
1 cm (½ in) dice
50 g (1¾ oz) dried sour
cherries
zest of ½ orange
zest of ½ lemon

1 teaspoon salt flakes
150 g (5½ oz) dark chocolate
(70% cocoa), chopped
250 g (9 oz) honey
175 g (6 oz/¾ cup) caster
(superfine) sugar

Staples
ISGR

Special equipment
Rice paper (the type used for
nougat), for lining the tin
Sugar thermometer

Banana & blueberry slab cake (V)

Preheat the oven to 165°C (330°F) fan-forced. Line a deep 26 × 40 cm (10 × 15¾ in) baking tray with baking paper. In a bowl, combine 400 g (14 oz) mashed very ripe banana, 2 eggs, 50 ml (5 fl oz) extra-virgin olive oil, 100 ml (3½ fl oz) coconut oil, 150 ml (5 fl oz) maple syrup, 80 ml (2½ fl oz/⅓ cup) full-cream (whole) milk, 100 g (3½ oz) oat bran, 2 teaspoons ground cinnamon and 1½ teaspoons natural vanilla extract or paste. Set aside for 15 minutes. Once the mixture has rested, sift in 230 g (8 oz) spelt flour or plain (all-purpose) flour and 3 teaspoons baking powder and combine. Transfer to the baking tray, then scatter 300 g (10½ oz) fresh or frozen blueberries, or other berries over. Bake for 35 minutes, until a skewer comes out clean. Dust with icing (confectioners') sugar to serve. The slab cake will keep in an airtight container on the bench for 2–3 days. Take it up a notch with Maple cream cheese icing (p. 804).

Coconut, cherry & pistachio slice GF V

Preheat the oven to 170°C (340°F) fan-forced. Grease a 23 cm (9 in) cake tin and line with baking paper. Add 100 g (3½ oz) dark chocolate (68% cocoa) to a heatproof bowl and place over a saucepan of simmering water for about 5 minutes, ensuring the bowl doesn't touch the water. When two-thirds of the chocolate has melted, stir through twice, then remove the bowl to finish melting the chocolate in the residual heat. Pour the melted chocolate into the cake tin, tipping to spread the chocolate evenly over the base. Refrigerate for 25 minutes to set. To a large bowl, add 150 g (5½ oz/⅔ cup) caster (superfine) sugar, 100 g (3½ oz/1⅓ cups) shredded coconut, 100 g (3½ oz) desiccated coconut, 50 g (1¾ oz/⅓ cup) pistachio kernels, 50 g (1¾ oz) flaked almonds, 50 g (1¾ oz) dried cherries, 30 g (1 oz) dried barberries or cranberries and 20 g (¾ oz) cacao nibs. Pour in 100 g (3½ oz) melted unsalted butter, stirring to coat well. Whisk 2 eggs well, then stir them through until well combined. Pile the mixture on top of the set chocolate, flattening it out a little, but not too perfectly. Bake for about 20 minutes, until slightly puffed and a little golden, turning the tin around halfway through. Cool for 20 minutes at room temperature, then refrigerate for 2 hours. Once cooled, unmould the slice, remove the baking paper and cut into bars. These will keep for about a week in a sealed container in the fridge. Makes 20 pieces.

Preheat the oven to 160°C (320°F) fan-forced.

Roast the almonds and hazelnuts on a baking tray for 10 minutes, then turn the oven temperature down to 100°C (210°F) fan-forced. Rub the skins off the hazelnuts. Roughly chop the hazelnuts and almonds and return to the tray, along with the pistachios. Keep warm in the oven.

Sift the flour and cocoa powder into a bowl. Add the spices, candied and dried fruit, citrus zests and salt, combining well.

Add the chocolate to a heatproof bowl and place over a saucepan of simmering water for about 5 minutes, ensuring the bowl doesn't touch the water. Stir once, then turn off the heat.

Heat the honey and sugar in a saucepan over a medium–high heat, stirring only to dissolve. Then heat without stirring until 114°C (237°F) – it won't take long. Once at temperature, pour it over the flour mixture and combine quickly. Add the warm nuts and chocolate and combine well. The mixture will be stiff, but just work at it.

Turn the oven up to 160°C (320°F) fan-forced. Line a 20 cm (8 in) square tin with rice paper. Tip the mixture into the tin, flattening it out evenly.

Bake for 15 minutes, until the panforte swells slightly; it won't really colour. Leave to cool at room temperature, then remove from the tin.

The panforte will keep for up to 2 months in an airtight container – it actually gets better with age. Slice finely with a sharp serrated knife to serve.

Odette's chewy triple chocolate brownies Ⓥ

This recipe is just sensational, chewy and chocolatey, but still with a little cake-like texture. My sister Odette is a genius. Always use the best chocolate you can for this. The chocolate is the star, and is highlighted through the different textures, not disguised by them. The other key is not to get excited and cut into this brownie too early, as it needs to set fully as it cools down. **Serves 6–8**

190 g (6¾½ oz) dark chocolate (at least 60% cocoa), chopped
190 g (6½ oz) unsalted butter, chopped
3 eggs

250 g (9 oz) soft brown sugar or caster (superfine) sugar
115 g (4 oz) self-raising flour
1 teaspoon fine sea salt
150 g (5½ oz) walnuts, pecans or hazelnuts, chopped

60 g (2 oz) white chocolate melts (buttons)
60 g (2 oz) milk chocolate melts (buttons)

Preheat the oven to 160°C (320°F) fan-forced. Line a 30 × 20 cm (12 × 8 in) brownie tin with baking paper.

Add the chopped chocolate and butter to a heatproof bowl and place over a saucepan of simmering water for about 5 minutes, ensuring the bowl doesn't touch the water. When two-thirds of the chocolate has melted, stir through twice. Remove the bowl to finish melting the chocolate in the residual heat, then whisk to fully combine.

Using an electric stand mixer, whisk the eggs and sugar on high speed until pale and foamy, and ribbons can be formed, about 3 minutes. On low speed, add the warm chocolate mixture, combining for 30 seconds only.

Sift the flour and salt into a bowl, then fold into the chocolate mixture. Add the nuts and chocolate melts, then fold in until evenly combined. Tip into the brownie tin, spreading flat evenly.

Bake for about 40 minutes, until a crust has formed. Set aside to cool for at least an hour before slicing, as the chocolate chips need to set and add texture. The brownies will keep in an airtight container for up to a week.

Make it different
Mocha brownies. Ⓥ For a slight coffee edge, add 2 tablespoons freshly ground coffee to the eggs and sugar.

Rum & chocolate brownies. Ⓥ Make this all dark chocolate by swapping out the milk and white chocolate, and add 30 ml (1 fl oz) rum to the eggs and sugar.

Chocolate babka with hazelnuts Ⓥ

If I can find a bright moment in the pandemic of 2020, it's having the unbroken attention to perfect this chocolate babka. That, and spending more time with my immediate family … but that babka! It was my sourdough, my triumph of isolation baking. I had tasted many in the past, and never attempted making it myself. But here we have it, and boy does it deliver. Somewhat like sourdough, there's a good deal of satisfaction in nailing this. When you slice into it and reveal those layers of egg-enriched yeasted crumb swirled with dark-brown chocolate, studded with hazelnuts and scented ever-so gently with spice … it's all the about the babka! Don't be scared, just do it. **Makes 2 loaves**

Use for

The Yeasted dough is also a great base dough for other scrolls and buns, such as the Poppy seed, sour cherry & vanilla scrolls (p. 764) and the Cinnamon & cardamom buns (p. 766) – for the cinnamon buns, you will yield 20 buns.

Yeasted dough

160 ml (5½ fl oz) full-cream (whole) milk

12 g (½ oz/4 teaspoons) dried yeast

3 eggs

550 g (1 lb 3 oz/3⅔ cups) plain (all-purpose) flour, plus extra for dusting

100 g (3½ oz) caster (superfine) sugar

½ teaspoon salt flakes

140 g (5 oz) unsalted butter, diced, at room temperature

1 egg, beaten with a pinch of salt

1 × quantity Basic sugar syrup (p. 793)

Chocolate hazelnut filling

120 g (4½ oz) unsalted butter

80 g (2¾ oz/⅓ cup) caster (superfine) sugar

80 g (2¾ oz) dark brown sugar

140 g (5 oz) dark chocolate (at least 60% cocoa), chopped

50 g (1¾ oz) dark unsweetened (Dutch) cocoa powder

4 teaspoons ground cinnamon

1½ teaspoons ground cardamom

120 g (4½ oz) roasted and peeled hazelnuts

For the dough, combine the milk and yeast in a small bowl, then add the eggs and whisk to combine.

Add the flour, sugar and lemon zest to the bowl of an electric stand mixer. Mix on low speed with the dough hook. Add the milk mixture and mix for 1 minute, then increase the speed to medium and mix for 3 minutes.

Add the salt, then the butter in thirds, combining before each addition. Once combined, mix on medium speed for 10 minutes, scraping down the sides as needed – the dough should come together in one soft mass. Transfer to a large container and seal; the dough will increase in size by at least half, so make sure the container is large enough. Refrigerate overnight, or for at least 6 hours.

When ready to bake, grease two 23 × 10 cm (9 × 4 in) loaf (bar) tins and line with baking paper.

To make the filling, melt the butter in a small saucepan over a medium heat. Add the sugars and stir through to dissolve, then remove from the heat and add the chocolate, cocoa powder and spices. Stand for about 3 minutes before stirring through gently. Set aside to cool, so it is still pliable but not hot.

Cut the dough in half. Roll out one piece of dough on a lightly floured bench until about 20 cm × 30 (8 × 12 in). Turn so the long side is closest to you. Spread half the filling over the dough, leaving a 1.5 cm (½ in) border, then sprinkle with half the hazelnuts. Using the long edge, roll the dough up to form a 30 cm (12 in) log, gently pressing the ends together to seal. Roll onto the seam. Use a sharp knife to cut in half lengthways, so that the two halves are lying side by side with the filling exposed. Lift one end on top of the other, with the cut side up, then lift the bottom piece over the top, then alternate to braid together. Press the ends together a little to compact lengthways, then lift into one of the loaf tins, putting the ends in first, then gently pressing the middle in. Cover with a damp tea towel (dish towel), then repeat for the other piece of dough.

Set aside to rise at room temperature for 1½–2 hours, until the dough puffs to fill the tins.

Preheat the oven to 200°C (400°F) fan-forced.

Glaze the loaves with the egg wash, then bake for 20 minutes, rotating the tins after 10 minutes. Reduce the oven temperature to 165°C (330°F) fan-forced and bake for a further 10 minutes, until richly golden.

Transfer the tins to a cooling rack, then brush the loaves with the syrup, using all of it. Cool the babka until lukewarm, then use the paper to lift them from the tins. If you get impatient and try to remove them too early, they will break up, so be patient and enjoy the mesmerising aroma.

The babka will keep in a sealed container for about 3 days. You can also freeze the whole loaves, thaw them completely in the fridge, then reheat in a 150°C (300°F) oven for 20 minutes.

Bottom to top: Chocolate babka with hazelnuts (opposite); Poppy seed, sour cherry & vanilla scrolls (p. 764)

Poppy seed, sour cherry & vanilla scrolls ⓥ

I'm obsessed with these scrolls (pictured on the previous page). I think perhaps it's the poppy seed filling that really captures my attention, as well as the soft, tender and buttery nature of the buns. These are best eaten 20 minutes after baking, or at least on the day, but of course they can be eaten the next day as is, or reheated. They are particularly good with coffee for breakfast, which makes reheating them the likely scenario at that time of day – unless you're in the habit of rising in the middle of the night to ensure the family has oven-fresh poppy seeds scrolls for breakfast. Be sure to make the filling well before rolling, as it needs to be at room temperature; if it's too warm, it will make the dough very hard to handle. You can also halve this recipe. **Makes 16**

1 × quantity Yeasted dough (p. 763)
1 × quantity Basic sugar syrup (p. 793)
1 egg, beaten with a pinch of salt

Poppy seed & sour cherry filling
300 g (10½ oz/2 cups) poppy seeds

200 ml (7 fl oz) full-cream (whole) milk
150 g (5½ oz/⅔ cup) caster (superfine) sugar
150 g (5½ oz) light brown sugar
50 g (1¾ oz) honey
100 g (3½ oz/⅔ cup) dried sour cherries, chopped
zest of 1 lemon

4 teaspoons ground cinnamon
1 tablespoon vanilla paste or extract
¼ teaspoon bitter almond extract
80 g (2¾ oz) unsalted butter
2 eggs, whisked

Staples
BTR

For the filling, grind the poppy seeds in a spice grinder or blender for 3 minutes.

Add the milk and sugars to a saucepan over a medium heat, stirring to dissolve. Add the poppy seeds and stir to combine. Stir in the honey, cherries, lemon zest, cinnamon, vanilla and almond extract and simmer for 1 minute, then remove from the heat and stir in the butter until melted and combined. Pour into a heatproof bowl and cool for 20 minutes, then whisk in the eggs until you have a shiny paste. Set aside at room temperature to cool completely.

Cut the dough in half. Roll out one piece into a 40 × 30 cm (15¾ × 12 in) rectangle. Turn so the long side is closest to you. Spread half the filling over the dough, leaving a 1.5 cm (½ in) border. Using the long edge, roll the dough up into a 40 cm (15¾ in) log. Lift onto a tray, then repeat with the other piece of dough. Chill for 20 minutes.

Meanwhile, grease and line two 23 cm (9 in) round cake tins.

Cut each dough log into seven pieces. Place one in the middle of each tin, lying flat, with the pastry spiral exposed. Arrange six more around the central one, leaving space between each, as the dough will rise during proving. Set aside to rise for 1½–2 hours, until the dough puffs and doubles in size. Make sure the buns have risen properly before baking – don't rush it.

Preheat the oven to 190°C (375°F) fan-forced.

Brush the tops with the beaten egg. Bake for 10 minutes, then rotate the tins and bake for another 15–20 minutes, until golden. When cooked, the internal temperature will be 90°C (195°F).

Transfer the tins to a cooling rack, then brush the buns with the syrup, using all of it. Cool for 15–20 minutes before serving.

The buns are best enjoyed just baked, or on the day, but can be reheated the following day.

Chocolate hot cross buns Ⓥ

It's quite handy having a sister who is an excellent pastry chef, and doubly so when that pastry chef is married to one of Australia's best bakers. Adapted from Tony Dench's award-winning recipe, these buns are moist, spicy and chocolatey, with a lovely chewiness to them. The chocolate is a great alternative to the traditional version – not necessarily better, just different – but you can easily turn this recipe in a more classic direction, too. **Makes 12**

1 large orange
40 g (1½ oz) peeled fresh ginger, chopped
2 teaspoons (7 g/¼ oz) dried yeast
230 ml (8 fl oz) warm water
400 g (14 oz/2⅔ cups) plain (all-purpose) flour
100 g (3½ oz/⅔ cup) wholemeal (whole-wheat) flour
50 g (1¾ oz) unsalted butter, diced, at room temperature

35 g (1¼ oz) caster (superfine) sugar
15 g (½ oz) Sweet spice mix for baked goods (p. 792)
12 g (½ oz) Dutch (unsweetened) cocoa powder
10 g (¼ oz) fine sea salt
2 drops of orange essence oil
60 g (2 oz) dark chocolate melts (buttons)
50 g (1¾ oz) milk chocolate melts (buttons)

Basic sugar syrup (p. 793), for glazing

Chocolate crosses
30 g (1 oz) plain (all-purpose) flour
60 ml (2 fl oz/¼ cup) cold water
2 teaspoons grapeseed oil
20 g (¾ oz) Dutch (unsweetened) cocoa powder

Boil the whole orange for 45 minutes. Cut into quarters and remove the seeds and any central membrane, but leave the peel on. Blitz with the ginger in a blender until smooth. You will need about 220 g (8 oz) of the orange purée.

Dissolve the yeast in the water and set aside for 5 minutes for the yeast to activate and foam. Line a baking tray with baking paper.

Add the flours, butter, sugar, mixed spice, cocoa, salt and orange oil to the bowl of an electric stand mixer. Add the orange purée and mix on medium speed with the dough hook. Pour in the yeasted water and mix for about 10 minutes, until you have a soft dough. Add all the chocolate melts and mix for 3 minutes to combine. Tip the dough onto a clean bench and rest for 20 minutes.

Portion the dough into 95 g (3¼ oz) pieces and roll into balls. Place on the baking tray, 2–3 cm (¾–1¼ in) apart. Set aside for 2–3 hours, until doubled in size.

When ready to bake, preheat the oven to 220°C (430°F) fan-forced.

To make the crosses, combine the ingredients in a bowl, then transfer to a piping (icing) bag fitted with a 4 mm (¼ in) nozzle. Pipe crosses onto the buns, then bake for 25 minutes, until risen and coloured.

Brush the buns with sugar syrup as soon as they come out of the oven. Set the buns aside to cool a little before eating warm, or toast them if reheating. Eat warm, or toast and enjoy over the next few days.

Cinnamon & cardamom buns ⓥ

These knotted macramé-like buns are an immensely popular sweet treat in Sweden, where they are called kardemummabullar when flavoured with cardamom, while kanelbullar, which are perfumed with cinnamon, are perhaps the most emblematic Swedish pastry. Here, I'm running with a best-of-both-worlds approach, with the exotic flavours of that most fragrant of spices, cardamom, coupled with the warming and comforting tones of cinnamon. When enmeshed with the scent of baking dough, the result is rather intoxicating, perfuming your house all day. It's essential to source fresh spices or grind your own for these buns, as cardamom loses its intensity very quickly once ground.

Makes 16

Cardamom dough
330 ml (11 fl oz) full-cream (whole) milk
2 teaspoons (7 g/¼ oz) dried yeast
600 g (1 lb 5 oz/4 cups) plain (all-purpose) flour, plus extra for dusting
60 g (2 oz/¼ cup) caster (superfine) sugar
55 g (2 oz/¼ cup) demerara sugar
85 g (3 oz) unsalted butter, softened at room temperature

1 tablespoon ground cardamom
1 teaspoon fine sea salt

Cardamom butter filling
250 g (9 oz/1 cup) unsalted butter
100 g (3½ oz) caster (superfine) sugar
100 g (3½ oz) demerara sugar
2 tablespoons ground cardamom
3 teaspoons ground cinnamon
1 teaspoon salt flakes

For topping
1 egg, beaten with a pinch of salt
60 g (2 oz/¼ cup) caster (superfine) sugar
60 g (2 oz/¼ cup) demerara sugar
3 teaspoons ground cardamom
2 teaspoons ground cinnamon

For the dough, warm the milk to body temperature in a small saucepan, then add the yeast and set aside for 5 minutes for the yeast to activate and foam.

Add the milk mixture to the bowl of an electric stand mixer, along with the remaining dough ingredients. Mix with the dough hook on slow speed for 2 minutes. Increase the speed to medium and mix for 3 minutes, then beat a little faster for 5 minutes, until you have a very smooth dough.

Tip the dough onto a clean bench and press out into a rough 20 × 30 cm (8 × 12 in) rectangle. Place on a tray, cover with a tea towel (dish towel) and chill for 2 hours.

Add all the filling ingredients to a large bowl and mix with a spoon, into a smooth, non-aerated paste. Set aside at room temperature.

Line two baking trays with baking paper.

Tip the dough onto a lightly floured bench, then roll out into a rectangle, measuring about 38 × 48 cm (15¼ × 19¼ in). As you roll, pause, as the dough will contract, then roll again until the right size. Dollop the filling over the dough, then spread out evenly using an offset spatula. From the short side, fold one-third of the dough over to cover the middle third, then the other side over that in a letter fold. Press flat gently with your hands and scrape off any filling that oozes out. With a folded edge facing you, cut into sixteen pieces.

Take one length, which will be about 30 cm (12 in) long. Stretch it out to about 45 cm (18 in), then wrap it around your fingers into a coil and then, when you are nearing the end, use the last part to wrap around the coil over the top of your fingers, slipping it off at the same time and tucking the end into the middle. Place on one of the baking trays and repeat for the other lengths. These may look a little messy, but they will fill out when they rise a little more and during baking. Cover with a tea towel and set aside for 1 hour to prove.

Preheat the oven to 230°C (445°F) fan-forced.

Brush the buns with the egg wash, then combine the other topping ingredients and sprinkle on top of each. Bake for 11 minutes, then reduce the oven temperature to 180°C (350°F) and bake for a further 6 minutes, until the buns are golden brown, and the sugar and butter surrounding each bun is lacy in appearance.

Cool completely on the tray. As the buns cool, each will have its own little sugar bottom to enjoy. The buns are best enjoyed just baked, or on the day, but can be reheated the following day.

Make it different

Cinnamon buns. ⓥ Omit the cardamom from the dough, the butter filling and the topping.

Pancakes, doughnuts, scones & crumpets

American-style pancakes Ⓥ

These are classically fluffy and fat pancakes, perfect for crowning with butter and dousing in maple syrup. You could make these with plain flour, but I find the texture more appealing and interesting with wholemeal (whole-wheat) flour. **Makes 16**

200 g (7 oz/1⅓ cups) wholemeal (whole-wheat) flour
150 g (5½ oz/1 cup) plain (all-purpose) flour

30 g (1 oz) baking powder
1 pinch of cream of tartar
230 ml (8 fl oz) full-cream (whole) milk
2 eggs

50 g (1¾ oz/¼ cup) caster (superfine) sugar
¼ teaspoon fine sea salt
350 g (12½ oz) plain yoghurt

Pair with

Maple syrup and butter or plain yoghurt, with fresh banana or berries, or a blueberry compote.

Bacon and maple syrup.

Caramelised spiced cider apples (opposite), yoghurt and maple syrup.

Sift the flours, baking powder and cream of tartar into a large bowl, then add back half the bran from the sieve.

In a bowl, whisk together the milk, eggs, sugar and salt, then add the yoghurt and whisk to combine. Make a well in the flour and add the milk mixture. Whisk just to bring together, then rest for 15 minutes. The batter will be thick, but still pourable.

Heat a large non-stick or cast-iron pan over a medium–high heat. (I don't use any oil, but you can wipe or spray with a little oil if you like.) Add a heaped tablespoon of the batter and let it form a natural round, spreading out a little with a spoon if necessary; you may be able to cook three pancakes at once, depending on your pan. Cook for 2½ minutes, until bubbly on top, then flip and cook for about 30 seconds, until a little springy to touch.

Repeat with all the batter, serving the pancakes as you cook, or you can keep them warm in a low oven.

Ricotta & blueberry hotcakes Ⓥ

While not exactly a kale smoothie or green bowl, these are somewhat more healthful than your standard stack of pancakes. Whether that's important to you is another matter, but these are quite delicious regardless, with the ricotta enriching but also keeping them light and delicate. You can, of course, skip the blueberries if fruit gets in the way of your sense of indulgence. **Makes about 14**

350 g (12½ oz) fresh ricotta
180 ml (6 fl oz) full-cream (whole) milk
4 eggs, separated
150 g (5½ oz) plain (all-purpose) flour

1 teaspoon baking powder
½ teaspoon fine sea salt
1 teaspoon ground cinnamon
125 g (4½ oz) blueberries

Staples
BTR

Pair with

Whip softened butter with maple syrup to taste, and serve with the pancakes along with plain yoghurt and sliced banana. Top with Honeycomb (p. 789) to be really decadent.

Combine the ricotta, milk and egg yolks in a large bowl.

Sift the flour, baking powder, salt and cinnamon into a bowl, then add to the ricotta mixture and just combine.

Using an electric mixer, whisk the egg whites to soft peaks, about 3 minutes. Fold them through the batter in two batches.

Heat a large frying pan over a medium–low heat and lightly grease with butter. Drop 2 tablespoons of batter per hotcake into the pan and top with some blueberries. Don't crowd the pan; three hotcakes is the most you should cook at once. Cook for about 2 minutes, until golden underneath, then flip and cook until golden on the other side. Repeat with the remaining batter.

Serve immediately, or keep warm in a low oven and serve once all are cooked.

Make it different
With another fruit. Instead of blueberries, use blackberries or apple compote.

Crumpets Ⓥ

Crumpets are surprisingly simple to make – another one of those things that seems like the sole preserve of commercial kitchens that is actually very achievable at home. **Makes about 12**

Pair with

Simply spread with butter and jam.

For something a little more fancy, top with Whipped vanilla ricotta filling (p. 799) and drizzle with fragrant honey.

Caramelised spiced cider apples ᴳᶠ Ⓥ

Peel and core 4 granny smith apples, then slice into 1 cm (½ in) thick rings. Melt 100 g (3½ oz) unsalted butter in a large frying pan over a medium heat. Add the apple rings and cook to caramelise and colour, about 3 minutes each side. Sprinkle with 1 teaspoon salt flakes, 1 teaspoon ground cinnamon, ½ teaspoon ground ginger and ½ teaspoon ground nutmeg, then scatter 80 g (2¾ oz/⅓ cup) caster (superfine) sugar and 80 g (2¾ oz) soft brown sugar over and toss well. Stir in 150 ml (5 fl oz) dry apple cider (alcoholic or not) and 1 tablespoon white-wine vinegar, then simmer slowly over a medium–low heat to reduce and soften the apple. Keep cooking for about 10 minutes, until the sauce is glossy and glazes the apples, with some excess sauce in the pan.

340 ml (11½ fl oz) warm water	440 g (15½ oz) plain (all-purpose) flour	**Staples** *BTR*
240 ml (8 fl oz) full-cream (whole) milk, warmed	3 teaspoons baking powder	
50 g (1¾ oz) unsalted butter, melted	2 teaspoons caster (superfine) sugar	**Special equipment** *12 egg rings, or 10 larger rings*
14 g (½ oz/4 teaspoons) dried yeast	2 teaspoons fine sea salt	

Combine the water, milk, butter and yeast in a bowl. Set aside for 5 minutes for the yeast to activate and foam.

Combine the dry ingredients in a large bowl. Make a well and add the yeast mixture. Combine until smooth, then cover and set aside at room temperature for 1½ hours, until bubbly and aerated.

Melt a knob of butter in a small frying pan over a medium–low heat. Spray or grease egg rings, or larger rings, and place in the pan. Ladle in enough batter so the rings are about three-quarters full. Cook for about 10 minutes, until the top is fully covered in holes, then flip and cook for about 3 minutes, until golden. Repeat with the remaining batter.

Enjoy warm, or store in an airtight container (or wrapped in baking paper in the fridge) for up to 2–3 days, until ready to toast.

Crepes V

Crepes are wonderful served simply with lemon and sugar, then rolled and devoured, or dipped into thick yoghurt as you go. They're also quite lovely in the boozy retro classic, Crepes suzette (left), and when made savoury (below). I'm a more recent – and somewhat more ardent – convert to cheese-filled Blintzes (below) dressed with a lemony butter sauce. **Makes 12 × 22 cm (8¾ in) crepes**

Pair with

Dust with icing (confectioners') sugar and serve with sliced fruit and Basic whipped cream (p. 799).

Drizzle with Brown butter & lemon sauce (below).

Crepes suzette V

Fold 12 Crepes (right) into quarters. Finely julienne the zest from 2 oranges, then juice the oranges and set aside. In a large frying pan over a medium heat, cook 100 g (3½ oz) unsalted butter until nut brown, 5–6 minutes, swirling to colour evenly. Add 100 g (3½ oz) caster (superfine) sugar and swirl until dissolved, about 2 minutes. Stir in the orange juice and simmer for 2 minutes, then add the orange zest, 3 tablespoons Cointreau and 2 tablespoons brandy and simmer for 1 minute. Add the crepes to the sauce and swirl around for 2 minutes to warm through. For a bit of old-fashioned theatre, you can ignite the sauce at the table as you serve. Serve with Basic whipped cream (p. 799).

Brown butter & lemon sauce for crepes & blintzes GF V

Use this to sauce plain or filled sweet crepes or blintzes (right). Heat 100 g (3½ oz) unsalted butter in a small saucepan over a medium heat, cooking until nut brown and swirling to colour evenly, about 6 minutes. Remove from the heat and stir in 50 ml (1¾ fl oz) lemon juice and ½ teaspoon salt flakes. Immediately spoon over hot plain crepes that have been heavily dusted in icing (confectioners') sugar, or spoon over unfilled crepes and serve with whipped cream or yoghurt.

250 g (9 oz/1⅔ cups) plain (all-purpose) flour	40 g (1½ oz) unsalted butter, melted	**Special equipment**
¾ teaspoon fine sea salt	100 g (3½ oz) unsalted butter, softened	*An 18 cm (7 in) iron or non-stick crepe pan is best, but a flat frying pan or skillet will also work*
4 eggs		
450–500 ml (15–17 fl oz) full-cream (whole) milk		

Sift the flour and salt into a medium bowl. Make a well in the middle and crack the eggs in, then pour in the milk. Gradually incorporate the flour, whisking until you have a smooth, thinnish batter, then whisk in the melted butter. Strain through a fine-mesh sieve, then refrigerate for at least 1 hour, but ideally overnight.

When ready to cook your crepes, heat the pan for 3 minutes over a medium heat. Brush the pan with butter, then add 3 tablespoons of the batter. Swirl the pan to spread the mixture out finely and evenly. Cook for 1½ minutes, then flip with a palette knife and cook for another 30 seconds or so. They say the first crepe is always a dud, so enjoy it as a snack and move on.

Make it different

Savoury crepes. Fill with some Béchamel (p. 70) and stracchino or gruyère cheese, along with some sautéed mushrooms, leg ham or spinach, and whatever fine soft herbs you have on hand, such as chives or chervil.

Blintzes V

These are a delight. Blintzes are traditionally rolled in a cigar shape, but I'm quite fond of the folded option here. **Serves 4–6**

80 g (2¾ oz/½ cup) currants	1 × quantity Cream cheese & ricotta filling (p. 799)	icing (confectioners') sugar, for dusting
80 ml (2½ fl oz/⅓ cup) brandy	12 Crepes (above)	
40 g (1½ oz) unsalted butter, melted	1 × quantity Brown butter & lemon sauce (left)	

In a small saucepan, bring the currants and brandy to a simmer over a medium heat, then set aside for the currants to plump up.

Preheat the oven to 180°C (350°F) fan-forced. Take a baking dish, measuring about 30 × 25 cm (12 × 10 in), and brush well with the butter.

Lay the crepes flat, on a clean work surface. Add about 2 tablespoons of the filling in one-quarter of a crepe, then sprinkle with ½ teaspoon of the currants. Fold the crepe over into a half-circle, then fold again into a quarter. Repeat for all the crepes.

Place the filled crepes in sets of two or three, depending on how many to want to serve, overlapping in the baking dish. Bake for about 25 minutes, until slightly coloured and plump. (The crepes can also be refrigerated in the dish for a day before baking, if needed.)

Serve dusted with icing (confectioners') sugar, with the sauce spooned over.

Blintzes

Classic scones ⓥ

Scones can go horribly wrong. It's not that they're necessarily complicated, but a heavy hand will result in damper-like bricks that no amount of jam and cream will remedy. The dough is a shaggy one, and this is what gives the scones their light and crumbly texture. It's essential to bring the dough together gently, or the scones won't rise; using a butter knife to do this helps to avoid activating the gluten in the flour, which makes for tough scones – so apart from two quick kneads to finish combining, don't work it any more than this. Remember, you're not making bread here. Preheating the tray and arranging the scones close together also helps them rise properly and evenly. As with all baking, you'll become familiar with the feel and texture after a few attempts. As soon as they're done, split them open and slather on some whipped cream or butter and your favourite jam. **Makes 9**

300 ml (10 fl oz) milk, plus extra for brushing
150 ml (5 fl oz) pouring (single/light) cream

450 g (1 lb/3 cups) plain (all purpose) flour, plus extra for dusting
2½ teaspoons baking powder

½ teaspoon fine sea salt
50 g (1¾ oz) unsalted butter, diced and chilled

Preheat the oven to 200°C (400°F) fan-forced.

Combine the milk and cream in a bowl or jug.

Sift the flour, baking powder and salt into a large bowl. Rub in the butter with your fingertips until combined into a crumb. Make a well and pour in the milk, then mix together using a butter knife to form a rough, shaggy dough.

Turn out onto a floured bench. Gently pat into a flat square about 5 cm (2 in) thick. Cut out scones with a 20 cm (8 in) square cutter.

Preheat a baking tray in the oven for 5 minutes. Lightly flour the tray, then arrange the scones on it, close together but not touching. Brush the tops with a little milk.

Bake for about 12–15 minutes, until risen and lightly golden. Transfer to a wire rack, covering with a tea towel (dish towel) to keep warm until ready to serve.

Make it different

Saffron scones with lemon, date & orange-blossom marmalade & labneh. ⓥ Flavour with saffron (right), and serve with the Orange-blossom labneh (p. 363) and Lemon, date & orange-blossom marmalade (p. 699).

Savoury scones. ⓥ Make the Cheddar & feta scones with mixed seeds (p. 859).

Pair with

Your favourite jam, and Basic whipped cream (p. 799) or Clotted cream (p. 800).

This dough also works beautifully as a cobbler-style scone rolled into rough balls and dropped on Beef bourguignon (see p. 284) to cover. Bake until the scones are golden on top and the stew is bubbling beneath.

Saffron scones ⓥ

It's easy to add an exotic touch to the Classic scones (left). Pour half the milk into a small saucepan, add 2 pinches saffron threads and gently warm through. Set aside to infuse for 5 minutes, then combine with the remaining milk and cream and proceed as per the recipe.

Mini cinnamon-bomb doughnuts ⓥ

I have a few burnt-in doughnut memories. The first was as a kid lining at up at Melbourne's Queen Victoria Market for a fried cinnamon-sugared doughnut with scorching hot jam inside – bribery went a long way back then on shopping trips. The second was visiting Rome for the first time and drinking espresso and eating a bombolone filled with lemony vanilla custard, rolled in sugar, and presented in a very pretty piece of printed paper. The other key doughnut memory – let's face it, there are more – is from my morning ritual in Santa Gertrudis, Ibiza. At the local bakery in mid-morning – no-one rises early on that island – we'd get a bag of hot anise-scented gems straight from the fryer with a couple of cortado coffees to go, before a very, very long day at work. These dainty little doughnuts are delightfully puffy and golden. Serve as is, or dress up with a sauce. **Makes about 40**

Pair with

Chocolate & honey sauce (p. 793).

Honey & orange-blossom syrup (p. 792).

Cream- or jam-filled doughnuts ⓥ

Pipe larger Cinnamon-bomb doughnuts (right), making them about two and a half times bigger. Fry for 4 minutes a side, then drain. Cool for 20 minutes, before piping Vanilla crème pâtissière (p. 798) or jam into them.

Orange & anise doughnuts ⓥ

Combine 150 g (5½ oz/⅔ cup) caster (superfine) sugar, 1 teaspoon anise seeds and the grated zest of ½ lemon and ½ orange, then toss the hot, just-fried Mini cinnamon-bomb doughnuts (right) through the mixture.

Doughnuts in honey & orange-blossom syrup with ricotta & pistachios ⓥ

Soak the Mini cinnamon-bomb doughnuts (right) in warm Honey & orange-blossom syrup (p. 792) for 10 minutes, then serve in the syrup. For a more structured dessert, spoon on some fresh plain ricotta and sprinkle with 40 g (1½ oz/⅓ cup) crushed pistachios.

---

80 g (2¾ oz) unsalted butter
480 ml (16 fl oz) full-cream (whole) milk
14 g (½ oz/4 teaspoons) dried yeast
60 g (2 oz/¼ cup) caster (superfine) sugar

4 eggs
650 g (1 lb 7 oz/4⅓ cups) plain (all-purpose) flour, sifted
2 pinches of fine sea salt
oil, for deep-frying (see p. 22)

Cinnamon sugar
150 g (5½ oz/⅔ cup) caster (superfine) sugar
2½ teaspoons ground cinnamon

Warm the butter in a saucepan over a low heat until just melted, then add the milk and warm until about body temperature. Whisk in the yeast and half the sugar until smooth, then set aside for 5 minutes for the yeast to activate and froth.

Whisk the eggs until light and frothy, then whisk into the yeast mixture.

Add the flour, remaining sugar and salt to the bowl of an electric stand mixer, then mix on low speed with the dough hook. Add the milk mixture and mix until the dough comes together, 2–3 minutes.

Once combined, increase the speed to medium–high and mix until the dough is smooth, shiny and elastic, about 5 minutes.

Either place the dough in a bowl and cover, or divide the dough between three disposable piping (icing) bags, securing the ends with rubber bands, and leaving plenty of space to prove; this method will yield the best shape. Set aside to rest for 1 hour at room temperature.

Combine the cinnamon sugar ingredients in a shallow bowl.

When ready to cook, heat at least 15 cm (6 in) of oil in a wide heavy-based saucepan or deep-fryer until 170°C (340°F).

If not piping the dough, use two spoons to drop heaped teaspoons of the dough into the oil. Alternatively, pipe out the dough and snip off portions with scissors dipped in the hot oil to stop them sticking. Fry the doughnuts, spinning them in the oil to cook evenly, until puffed and golden, 2–3 minutes.

Once cooked, drain briefly on paper towel, toss in the cinnamon sugar and serve hot.

Classic doughnuts ⓥ

These more readily align with a North American interpretation of a doughnut. They're more substantial, they take a glaze well, and they have a hole in them. I like to make a few glazes (see right) and offer a little variety. If you're going to the effort of frying your own doughnuts, then whipping up two or three glazes isn't that much of a stretch. **Makes 12**

230 ml (8 fl oz) full-cream (whole) milk
14 g (½ oz/4 teaspoons) dried yeast
40 g (1½ oz) caster (superfine) sugar
200 g (7 oz) unsalted butter
4 eggs

500 g (1 lb 2 oz/3⅓ cups) plain (all-purpose) flour, plus extra for dusting
2 pinches of salt flakes
oil, for deep-frying (see p. 22)

Special equipment
2 cm (¾ in) and 8 cm (3¼ in) pastry cutters

Warm the milk in a small saucepan until about body temperature. Remove from the heat and whisk in the yeast and half the sugar until smooth. Set aside for 5 minutes for the yeast to activate and froth.

Using an electric stand mixer, whisk the butter and remaining sugar on medium–high speed until smooth and pale, about 3 minutes. Whisk in the eggs, one at a time, then follow with the milk mixture.

Change the whisk for the paddle attachment. Add the flour and salt and mix on slow speed until smooth, about 5 minutes.

Scrape the dough into a large bowl, then cover. Ideally, refrigerate the dough overnight until it doubles in size. Alternatively, set it aside somewhere warm for 1 hour to prove and double in size, then refrigerate for 30 minutes to make it easier to handle.

Tip the chilled dough onto a lightly floured bench, then roll into a round, about 30 cm (12 in) in diameter and 2.5 cm (1 in) thick. Use an 8 cm (3¼ in) pastry cutter to cut out as many rounds as you can, then use a 2 cm (¾ in) cutter to cut out the centres. Re-roll any dough scraps, to cut out as many more doughnuts as you can. Transfer the doughnuts to a lined tray and stand for 20 minutes to puff slightly.

When ready to cook, heat 15 cm (6 in) of oil in a wide heavy-based saucepan or deep-fryer until 170°C (340°F).

Working in batches, so as not to crowd the pan, fry the doughnuts for about 2 minutes each side, until golden. Drain on paper towel before tossing in Cinnamon sugar (p. 773).

The doughnuts are best eaten promptly, or at least on the same day. Doughnuts are for eating! Time improves no doughnut.

Pair with

Crème fraîche glaze (p. 804).

Nutella icing (p. 805).

Coffee icing (p. 804).

Chocolate fudge icing (p. 805).

Vanilla frosting (p. 803).

Miso doughnut glaze with sesame ⓖⓕ ⓥ

This glaze is nutty and slightly tart, with an intriguing umami note from the miso, and makes enough to glaze six Classic doughnuts (left). In a bowl, combine 2 teaspoons white miso paste, 1 tablespoon sour cream and the juice of 1 lemon. Sift in 150 g (5½ oz/1¼ cups) icing (confectioners') sugar and stir until smooth. Once the doughnuts come out of the hot oil, drain on paper towel and sit on a wire rack to cool for 5 minutes, then drizzle the glaze over the doughnuts. Sprinkle with 2 tablespoons toasted sesame seeds and ½ teaspoon salt flakes, then leave to set for 30 minutes before serving.

Smashed blueberry glaze ⓖⓕ ⓥ

This makes enough to glaze six Classic doughnuts (left). In a small saucepan, combine 60 g (2 oz) blueberries and 1 tablespoon orange juice over a low heat. Mash the berries with a spoon, then simmer for 20 seconds. Remove from the heat and add another 1 tablespoon orange juice. Sift in 150 g (5½ oz/1¼ cups) icing (confectioners') sugar and stir until smooth. Once the doughnuts come out of the hot oil, drain on paper towel and sit on a wire rack to cool for 5 minutes, then drizzle the glaze over the doughnuts. Leave to set for 30 minutes before serving.

Thick real hot chocolate GF V

Wonderful with Churros (right), this hot chocolate has some real body to it, as well as great balanced flavour – it will warm you right to your toes, and makes enough to serve two. In a small bowl, combine 2 tablespoons dark Dutch (unsweetened) cocoa powder, 2 teaspoons pure icing (confectioners') sugar, 1½ teaspoons cornflour (cornstarch), 2 pinches ground cinnamon and 2 pinches salt flakes; set aside. In a heatproof bowl, place 100 g (3½ oz) chopped dark chocolate and 1 teaspoon natural vanilla extract or paste. Bring 400 ml (13½ fl oz) full-cream (whole) milk to a simmer in a saucepan, then pour over the chocolate. Whisk until the chocolate is melted and incorporated, then whisk in the cocoa mixture. Pour the mixture back into the pan. Bring to a simmer over a low heat, whisking until thickened. Serve immediately, with churros or skewered Mini cinnamon-bomb doughnuts (p. 773) – or enjoy on its own, perhaps with a few marshmallows dropped in.

Churros V

Churros are like an Iberian answer to a doughnut, or the other way around – depending on who you talk to. Churros dough is more like choux pastry, so they're naturally quite different in texture to doughnuts, but with the whole fried dough and cinnamon sugar thing going on, there certainly are similarities. Churros are more robust, and they take to being dipped in proper hot chocolate, which is how they are traditionally served. Spanish hot chocolate for churros is more like melted chocolate thinned with a little milk than it is chocolate-flavoured milk, so it coats the churros luxuriously. **Makes about 16**

100 ml (3½ fl oz) full-cream (whole) milk
100 ml (3½ fl oz) water
80 g (2¾ oz) unsalted butter
1½ tablespoons caster (superfine) sugar
½ teaspoon fine sea salt

120 g (4½ oz) plain (all-purpose) flour
3 eggs, lightly beaten
oil, for deep-frying (see p. 22)
Thick real hot chocolate (left), to serve

Cinnamon sugar
120 g (4½ oz/1 cup) pure icing (confectioners') sugar
½ teaspoon ground cinnamon

In a small saucepan, bring the milk, water, butter, sugar and salt to a simmer over a medium heat. Add the flour and stir in quickly. Cook for 5 minutes, constantly stirring until smooth.

Tip the mixture into a food processor and add the eggs. Process until smooth, about 2 minutes. Scoop into a piping (icing) bag fitted with a 1 cm (½ in) star nozzle.

Heat 15 cm (6 in) of oil in a wide heavy-based saucepan or deep-fryer until 175°C (345°F).

Combine the cinnamon sugar ingredients in a shallow bowl.

Pipe lines of the dough directly into the hot oil, snipping them off with scissors dunked in the oil so they don't stick; be sure not to overcrowd the pan. Fry the churros for about 2 minutes on each side, until golden. You can also dip a wide spatula in the oil, then pipe a figure-eight shape about 7 cm (2¾ in) long onto the blade – it's a little trickier, but they look marvellous. Otherwise, a circle is a little simpler and also looks great.

Drain on paper towel, then toss in the cinnamon sugar and serve straight away, with the thick hot chocolate.

Puddings & other desserts

Tiramisu ⓥ

This recipe is based on a tiramisu from my travels in Rome when I was younger. True, some would say a tiramisu is not a tiramisu without savoiardi biscuits, and you *can* use a quality store-bought sponge cake – but your own is always going to be better. Try it. You won't go back. I also think it's important that a tiramisu is not overly sweet, with the bitter notes of the coffee still present; for me, good dark chocolate is also essential. I also prefer tiramisu somewhat boozy and on the wetter side, rather than like a cake; it should hold its form and be scoopable at the same time. In the coffee syrup, I like to include some Strega – an Italian liqueur coloured with saffron. It has a distinctive herbal character, which I just love in tiramisu against the richer coffee and cocoa notes, and the rounded tones of Marsala and amaretto. If making the tiramisu a day ahead, finish with the chocolate and cocoa just before serving. **Serves 10–12**

Short cut

Use store-bought sponge cake.

1 × 26–30cm (10¼–12 in) Sponge cake (p. 748) – or 24 savoiardi (lady finger) biscuits (not as good, but still good)
250 g (9 oz) dark chocolate (minimum 56% cocoa), roughly chopped
30 g (1 oz) unsweetened (Dutch) cocoa powder
750 g (1 lb 11 oz) mascarpone

10 Amaretti biscotti (p. 758, or store bought is fine)
1 × quantity Basic whipped cream (p. 799), chilled

Coffee syrup
200 ml (7 fl oz) very strong black coffee, hot
80 g (2¾ oz/⅓ cup) caster (superfine) sugar
100 ml (3½ fl oz) Marsala (not too sweet)

80 ml (2½ fl oz/⅓ cup) amaretto
60 ml (2 fl oz/¼ cup) Strega

Zabaglione
2 eggs
4 egg yolks
150 g (5½ oz) caster (superfine) sugar
150 ml (5 fl oz) Marsala (not too sweet)

Special equipment
Sugar thermometer

For the coffee syrup, add the coffee and sugar to a bowl and stir to dissolve, then add the remaining ingredients. Set aside to cool.

Using a sharp serrated knife, cut the sponge cake in half crossways, as evenly as possible.

Pulse the chocolate in a food processor in three-second bursts to make an unevenly chopped rubble. Tip into a bowl, then toss in 2 teaspoons of the cocoa powder. Add the rest of the cocoa powder to a fine-mesh sieve and set aside.

Put the zabaglione ingredients in a large stainless steel bowl (over 30 cm/12 in), whisking by hand to combine. Set the bowl over a saucepan with a little simmering water in it, ensuring the bowl doesn't touch the water. Whisk constantly in a figure-eight motion until you have a light, airy, thickened mixture, about 8 minutes. You should be able to form thick ribbons over the mixture when you hold the whisk up. The temperature should be 60°C (140°F), and the last 10°C (50°F) moves quite quickly, so monitor with a digital sugar thermometer after 4 minutes.

Using an electric stand mixer, whisk the zabaglione on high speed for 8 minutes, until cooled. On low speed, add the mascarpone in three additions. You should have a light and airy mixture, like thick whipped cream. Do not over-whisk, or the cheese will curdle and go grainy. Chill for 30 minutes in the bowl.

Before assembling, it's important that all the ingredients are cold. Add half the mascarpone mixture to a 30 cm (12 in) round dish, 6–8 cm (2½–3¼ in) deep, then lightly sieve some of the cocoa powder on top.

Pour one-third of the coffee syrup onto the cut side of one of the sponge halves, then lift into the dish and dust liberally with more cocoa powder. Sprinkle over one-third of the chocolate, then crumble in the biscotti. Top with the remaining mascarpone mixture and dust with a little more cocoa.

Pour another one-third of the syrup over the cut side of the remaining sponge, then lift into the dish. Dust liberally with more cocoa, scatter another one-third of the chocolate over, then drizzle with the remaining syrup.

Spoon the whipped cream over the top, leaving a little border so you can see what's beneath. Scatter the remaining chocolate around the edge, then dust with cocoa; I like to leave some of the cream plain in the middle, as it's a nice visual contrast.

Chill for 3 hours, the serve in scoops, or cut into rough wedges and lift from the dish. The tiramisu can be made the day before, and leftovers will last for 5 days in the fridge.

Sticky date pudding (v)

My mother made the best sticky date pudding around, with lots of dates and lots of caramel sauce. This is her recipe, though I do always tinker … **Serves 8**

280 g (10 oz) pitted dates, cut in half
450 ml (15 fl oz) water
1½ teaspoons bicarbonate of soda (baking soda)
90 g (3 oz/⅓ cup) unsalted butter, softened at room temperature

225 g (8 oz/1 cup) caster (superfine) sugar
1 teaspoon natural vanilla extract or paste
3 eggs
250 g (9 oz/1⅔ cups) self-raising flour

1½ teaspoons ground cinnamon
1 teaspoon ground ginger
1 × quantity Golden syrup butter caramel sauce (p. 793)

Staples
BTR

Preheat the oven to 180°C (350°F) fan-forced. Grease a 30 × 25 cm (12 × 10 in) roasting tin and line with baking paper, or use a greased ceramic dish to serve directly at the table.

In a saucepan, boil the dates and water for 2 minutes. Add the bicarbonate of soda and stir to break up the dates a little, then set aside.

Using an electric stand mixer, whisk the butter and sugar on medium speed until pale and fluffy, about 5 minutes. Add the vanilla, then the eggs one at a time, until combined.

Sift the flour, cinnamon and ginger into a large bowl, then fold into the butter mixture. Next, fold in the date mixture to just combine.

Pour the batter into the roasting tin and bake for about 30 minutes, until a skewer comes out clean.

Stand the pudding for 2 minutes, then pour half the caramel sauce over. Scoop out portions and serve with ice cream or cream, with the remaining sauce on the side.

Pair with
Vanilla ice cream or cream.

Christmas pudding (v)

My preferred Christmas pudding recipe is my Nana's with the addition of Pedro Ximénez sherry; brandy is a perfectly good fall-back option. I have added glacé ginger, too, as I adore the flavour among the usual suspects, and though some may turn their nose up at the thought, the prunes are an absolute must. This pudding can be made well ahead of time, with many believing that a good pudding should sit to develop flavour and texture. Nana Hughes often made it much closer to the day, and it was always stunning. **Serves 8–10**

200 g (7 oz) mix of sultanas (golden raisins) and raisins
150 g (5½ oz/1 cup) currants
150 g (5½ oz) prunes, pitted and chopped
30 g (1 oz) dried sour cherries
30 g (1 oz) glacé ginger, finely chopped
250 ml (8½ fl oz/1 cup) Pedro Ximénez sherry or brandy
100 g (3½ oz/⅔ cup) plain (all-purpose) flour
35 g (1¼ oz) cornflour (cornstarch)

1 teaspoon baking powder
80 g (2¾ oz) unsalted butter, diced and chilled
200 g (7 oz/2½ cups) breadcrumbs, made from fresh white bread
200 g (7 oz) soft brown sugar
1½ teaspoons salt flakes
2 teaspoons Sweet spice mix for baked goods (p. 792)
2 teaspoons ground ginger
2 teaspoons ground cloves
1 whole nutmeg, finely grated

1 large apple, peeled and grated (130 g/4½ oz)
zest and juice of 1 orange
200 g (7 oz) eggs
80 ml (2½ fl oz/⅓ cup) full-cream (whole) milk

Special equipment
2 litre (68 fl oz/8 cup) pudding basin (mould)

Staples
BTR

Deluxe bread & butter pudding (v)

Preheat the oven to 180°C (350°F) fan-forced. To make vanilla custard, in a large bowl whisk 4 eggs, 100 g (3½ oz) caster (superfine) sugar, 500 ml (17 fl oz/2 cups) full-cream (whole) milk, 200 ml (7 fl oz) pouring (single/light) cream and 1 tablespoon natural vanilla extract until well combined. Slice 500 g (1 lb 2 oz) almond or plain croissants (about 6) on an angle (you could also use Sourdough bread (p. 847) or pannettone). Lay the croissant pieces in a large ovenproof baking dish measuring about 30 × 25 cm (12 × 10 in), alternating with 300 g (10½ oz) ricotta cheese sliced 2 cm (¾ in) thick. Scatter with 100 g (3½ oz) dark chocolate melts (buttons), then pour the custard over. Set aside for 15 minutes for the custard to soak into the croissants. Sprinkle over 50 g (1¾ oz) demerara sugar and 2 tablespoons flaked almonds. Bake for about 25 minutes, until golden and slightly puffed. Serves 6–8.

Pair with
Thick vanilla custard (p. 801), whipped cream or ice cream.

Christmas pudding semifreddo (V)

This is a great way to use up left-over Christmas pudding or Christmas cake. Tip 1.5 litres (51 fl oz/6 cups) vanilla ice cream into a large bowl and soften at room temperature for about 25 minutes. Line a 26 cm (10 in) stainless steel bowl or 2 litre (68 fl oz/8 cup) loaf (bar) tin with two layers of plastic wrap. Stir the ice cream with a spatula, then crumble in 350 g (12½ oz) Christmas pudding (opposite) or Christmas cake and mix to combine. Tip into the bowl or tin and flatten down. Top with a piece of baking paper and freeze overnight. To serve, turn the semifreddo out onto a frozen plate, then slice or cut into wedges. Pour over 1 × quantity Golden syrup butter caramel sauce (p. 793) and scatter over 50 g (1¾ oz) toasted flaked almonds.

Combine the dried fruit, glacé ginger and sherry in a medium saucepan and warm over a low heat for 5 minutes. Set aside to infuse for 1 hour.

Add the flour, cornflour and baking powder to a large bowl. Rub in the butter between your fingertips, into a fine crumb. Add the soaked fruit and sherry, along with the breadcrumbs, sugar, salt, spices, apple and orange zest and juice, then gently combine. Lightly beat the eggs and milk and add to the mixture, then combine.

Grease the pudding basin and pour the mixture in. Smooth the top and cover with a piece of baking paper. Tie a double layer of foil under the pudding basin's lip with twine.

Place the pudding basin in a large saucepan, then pour in hot water to reach three-quarters of the way up the side of the basin. Bring to a simmer with the lid partly on and cook for 3 hours. The water will need topping up a few times, so keep checking on it.

Cool the pudding at room temperature, then refrigerate for up to 2 weeks, before reheating in a saucepan of simmering water for 1 hour prior to serving.

You can also unmould the pudding once cooled, then wrap in plastic wrap, seal in a sealed bag and freeze for up to 3 months. To thaw, sit the pudding in the fridge for 3 days, then reheat in the pudding basin in a saucepan of simmering water for about 1 hour.

Crème brûlée 🄶🅅

I somehow always have room for this French bistro classic. The aroma is enticing enough, but I'll never tire of the crack of the burnt caramel when you bust through into the smooth vanilla custard. It's best to buy a kitchen blowtorch for this; they are not expensive, and can also be used for torching Italian meringue (p. 807). With an oven grill, you generally don't get a good crust, if at all, and end up with a curdled, scrambled texture. **Serves 8**

100 g (3½ oz) caster (superfine) sugar
1 vanilla bean, split, or 2 teaspoons natural vanilla extract or paste

800 ml (27 fl oz) pouring (single/light) cream
10 egg yolks

To serve
120 g (4½ oz) caster (superfine) sugar

Special equipment
Kitchen blowtorch
8 × 150 ml (5 fl oz) ramekins or moulds

Preheat the oven to 100°C (210°F) fan-forced.

Put the sugar in a large bowl, then scrape in the vanilla seeds and set aside.

Add the vanilla pod to a small saucepan with the cream. Bring to a simmer over a medium heat, then remove from the heat and set aside.

Add the egg yolks to the sugar, then whisk in by hand for about 3 minutes, until the sugar has dissolved, but the mixture is not aerated and pale – the yolks should be runny.

Whisking continuously, gradually add the hot cream until incorporated. Set aside for 5 minutes, then strain through a fine-mesh sieve to remove any set egg.

Place a tea towel (dish towel) in the base of a deep baking tray or roasting tin, then arrange the ramekins on top. Divide the mixture between the moulds, then fill the tray with hot water to the same level as the top of the custards. Bake for 45 minutes. The custard edges should be firm, with the middle only having a little wiggle.

Set aside until cooled, then refrigerate for 4 hours. At this stage, they will keep for 5–7 days.

When ready to serve, evenly sprinkle a 5 mm (¼ in) layer of the caster sugar over the top of each custard. Wipe any sugar off the sides, then scorch with a kitchen blowtorch until the sugar bubbles and turns dark caramel. Cool for a moment so the caramel sets, then serve.

Pair with
Cat's tongue biscuits (p. 755).

Coffee granita 🄶🅅🆅🄶

These icy coffee shards are a lovely contrast to richly creamy Tiramisu (p. 776), or a silky Chocolate mousse (p. 782) with a sprinkling of Chocolate gravel (p. 783) and a dollop of crème fraîche. In a saucepan, combine 400 ml (13½ fl oz) strong coffee, 100 g (3½ oz) caster (superfine) sugar and 2 tablespoons trimoline or liquid glucose. Stir over a medium heat for 3 minutes to dissolve. Pour into a tray or ceramic dish so that the liquid is about 2 cm (¾ in) deep. Freeze for 4 hours, before scraping the granita with a fork to serve. The granita will keep in the freezer for a couple of weeks, and makes about 500 ml (17 fl oz/2 cups).

Tapioca pearls in coconut with tropical salad & caramel sauce 🄶🅅

Use any tropical fruit you like for this refreshing summer dessert option, with the slippery little tapioca balls a textural delight. You can also omit the caramel sauce, and simply top the tapioca with a little extra palm sugar. **Serves 8**

1.8 litres (61 fl oz) water
150 g (5½ oz) tapioca pearls
150 ml (5 fl oz) coconut cream
1½ teaspoons salt flakes
1 × quantity Salted coconut caramel (p. 794), or Dulce de leche (p. 795)

Salted caramel & almond popcorn (p. 788), to serve (optional)

Mango & pineapple salad
2 mangoes, peeled and cut into 2 cm (¾ in) dice
½ pineapple, peeled and cut into 2 cm (¾ in) dice

juice of 1 lime
4 makrut lime leaves, very finely shredded
2 tablespoons finely grated palm sugar (jaggery)

Easy vanilla crème caramel (GF)

For the caramel, add 250 g (9 oz) caster (superfine) sugar and 150 ml (5 fl oz) water to a small saucepan, swirling to wet the sugar. Brush any sugar from the side of the pan with a pastry brush so it doesn't burn. Place the pan over a high heat and boil for about 8 minutes, until a dark caramel, then remove from the heat and add 40 ml (1½ fl oz) water to stop it burning. Carefully pour the caramel into ten 120 ml (4 fl oz) metal or plastic moulds, dividing it as equally as possible. Allow to set at room temperature for about 20 minutes. Add 700 ml (23½ fl oz) pouring (single/light) cream, 300 ml (10 fl oz) full-cream (whole) milk, 160 g (5 oz) caster (superfine) sugar and 1 split vanilla bean or 2 teaspoons natural vanilla extract or paste to a small saucepan and bring to a simmer. Remove from the heat and set aside to infuse for 20 minutes, then scrape the vanilla bean seeds (if using a vanilla bean) into the milk. Soak 4 leaves gold-strength gelatine in cold water for 5 minutes. Add the gelatine leaves, squeezed of excess water, to the pan, gently stirring to dissolve. Strain through a fine-mesh sieve, into a jug. Holding a spoon over the spout to slow the flow and avoid air bubbles, gently pour the cream mixture on top of the caramels, filling the moulds three-quarters full. For best results, refrigerate on a tray overnight, or at least for 8 hours, as the cream mixture softens the caramel, making the sauce when tipped out. To serve, lay one of the moulds on its side in your palm, then use a finger to gently pull one edge of the set cream away from the side of the mould. This will break the surface tension and make it easy to remove. Invert onto serving plates and serve immediately.

Bring the water to the boil in a large saucepan, then add the tapioca. Boil for about 5 minutes, until the tapioca is almost transparent, then remove from the heat. Cover and set aside for 10 minutes to finish cooking in the residual heat, then drain and refresh under cold water.

Tip the tapioca into a bowl. Combine with the coconut cream and salt, then spoon into individual serving dishes or large glasses, or a large container to scoop the mixture out of when set.

Refrigerate for at least 30 minutes before serving.

To serve, toss all the salad ingredients in a bowl to combine. Drizzle the tapioca with caramel sauce or spoon on some dulce de leche, then pile on the fruit. Finish with some caramel popcorn, if using.

Yoghurt panna cotta (GF)

The slightly sour note of yoghurt blends beautifully with milk and cream, making this panna cotta a great example of a balanced and not overly sweet dessert. This is also lovely with fromage frais, if you can find it. **Makes 10**

4 leaves of gold-strength gelatine

300 ml (10 fl oz) pouring (single/light) cream

300 ml (10½ fl oz) full-cream (whole) milk

160 g (5½ oz) caster (superfine) sugar

1 vanilla bean, split, seeds scraped, or 2 teaspoons natural vanilla extract or paste

400 g (14 oz) yoghurt or fromage frais

250 g (9 oz/2 cups) ripe raspberries, to serve

Honeycomb (p.789), to serve

Special equipment
10 × 120 ml (4 fl oz) metal or plastic moulds

Soak the gelatine leaves in cold water for 5 minutes.

In a saucepan, heat the cream, milk, sugar and vanilla (including the vanilla pod, if using) over a medium heat, stirring to combine, until up to a boil – but do not allow to boil, as this will mar the flavour. Add the gelatine leaves, squeezed of excess water, then stir to dissolve.

Set aside for 10 minutes for the vanilla to infuse, then strain into a jug. Stir through the yoghurt to combine well. Divide the mixture evenly among the moulds, then set in the fridge for 6 hours or overnight. At this point, the panna cotta will keep covered in the fridge for up to a week.

To serve, turn a mould on its side, then separate the wall of the panna cotta from the mould by pulling an edge away with your fingertip to break the surface tension. Turn out onto serving plates Bruise the ripe raspberries in a bowl with the back of a spoon, then spoon over the plated panna cottas. Finish with shards of honeycomb.

Make it different
Classic panna cotta. (GF) Increase the cream by 400 ml (13½ fl oz), to 700 ml (23½ fl oz), and omit the yoghurt or fromage frais.

Cinnamon panna cotta. (GF) Omit the vanilla and add 1 teaspoon ground cinnamon and 1 cinnamon stick at the start.

Honey panna cotta. (GF) Replace 80 g (2¾ oz) of the sugar with 80 g (2¾ oz) honey.

Chocolate mousse GF V

Chocolate mousse has been somewhat bastardised and commercialised over the years, with junket-like versions set with all manner of things and tasting chocolate-like, rather than intensely chocolatey. For me, a good chocolate mousse is enriched with egg yolks and cream, lightened with whipped egg whites, and always flavoured with the very best dark chocolate. Set the mousse in serving coupes or glasses, or in a large container to scoop into quenelles.

Makes 850 ml (28½ fl oz); Serves 6

230 g (8 oz) dark chocolate, chopped and blitzed in a food processor
100 g (3½ oz) unsalted butter, diced, at room temperature

3 tablespoons white rum, brandy or Frangelico
4 eggs, separated
60 g (2 oz/¼ cup) caster (superfine) sugar

350 ml (12 fl oz) pouring (single/light) cream

Add the chocolate, butter and rum to a heatproof bowl and place over a saucepan of simmering water for about 5 minutes, ensuring the bowl doesn't touch the water. When two-thirds of the chocolate has melted, stir through twice. Remove the bowl to finish melting the chocolate in the residual heat.

In another large heatproof bowl set over the saucepan, whisk the egg yolks and half the sugar until pale and foaming, about 3 minutes. Remove from the heat and fold the chocolate through.

Whip the cream to soft peaks, then set aside at room temperature (don't chill).

Whisk the egg whites and the remaining sugar to soft peaks, then fold half into the chocolate mixture. Follow by folding in half the whipped cream, then the remaining egg white, then the remaining cream.

Transfer the mixture to a bowl, or portion into individual moulds or glasses. Chill for about 2 hours, until set, then scoop or quenelle to serve, unless serving in individual moulds.

The mousse will keep in the fridge for about a week.

Pair with

Cream or crème fraîche.

Honeycomb (p. 789).

Salted caramel sauce (p. 794) and Salted caramel & almond popcorn (p. 788).

Coffee granita (p. 780) and Chocolate gravel (p. 783).

Spoon into a Pavlova (p. 784).

Pile some Chocolate gravel (p. 783) on a plate, top with a quenelle of mousse and some Sesame brittle (p. 786).

Self-saucing chocolate pudding V

My mother often cooked this dessert in the colder months, though the credit for this version goes to my sister, Odette. I have added the salt flakes, as I love a bit of a savoury touch. **Serves 6**

160 g (5½ oz) self-raising flour
120 g (4½ oz) caster (superfine) sugar
2 teaspoons unsweetened (Dutch) cocoa powder
½ teaspoon fine sea salt

150 ml (5 fl oz) full-cream (whole) milk
1 egg
1 egg yolk
200 g (7 oz) dark chocolate (56% cocoa or higher)
20 g (¾ oz) unsalted butter

For topping
250 g (9 oz) soft brown sugar
1½ tablespoons unsweetened (Dutch) cocoa powder
350 ml (12 fl oz) boiling water
1½ teaspoons salt flakes

Chocolate mousse

Chocolate gravel (GF) (V)

Use this quick and simple chocolate rubble to decorate Chocolate mousse (opposite), Chocolate tart (p. 817), Tiramisu (p. 776), Pavlova (p. 784), and other cakes and desserts. Chop 250 g (9 oz) extra dark or milk chocolate and place in a food processor. Pulse into a gravel-like consistency, then tip into a bowl. Sift 40 g (1½ oz) dark unsweetened (Dutch) cocoa powder over the top and toss to coat.

Preheat the oven to 180°C (350°F) fan-forced

Whisk the flour, sugar, cocoa powder and salt in a bowl.

In another bowl, beat the milk, egg and egg yolk with a fork until combined.

Add the chocolate and butter to a heatproof bowl and place over a saucepan of simmering water for about 5 minutes, ensuring the bowl doesn't touch the water. When two-thirds of the chocolate has melted, stir through twice. Remove the bowl to finish melting the chocolate in the residual heat.

Once the chocolate has fully melted, fold in the egg mixture to combine, then follow with the flour mixture to make a pourable batter.

Tip the mixture into an ovenproof ceramic dish, measuring about 20 × 28 cm (8 × 11 in), with sides at least 5 cm (2 in) high. Smooth flat with a spatula.

For the topping, combine the sugar and cocoa powder, then sprinkle evenly over the batter. Pour the boiling water over in a zig-zag pattern, then sprinkle with the salt.

Bake for about 35 minutes, until the pudding resembles a chocolate brownie, with a slight bubbling of sauce at the side. Serve warm, straight from the dish at the table.

Coconut panna cotta with coconut jelly, black sesame tuiles, mango & lime leaf (GF)

The contrast of the silky coconut panna cotta with the firm brightness of the coconut jelly on top is refreshing and enticing, especially when paired with fresh tropical fruit or lychees. This is the kind of dessert I serve at the end of a feast featuring spicy South-East Asian flavours. **Serves 6**

6 black Sesame tuiles (p. 788)
3 ripe mangoes, peeled and cut into 2 cm (¾ in) dice
4 makrut lime leaves, very finely shredded

Coconut jelly
6 leaves of gold-strength gelatine
100 ml (3½ fl oz) lychee juice

100 ml (3½ fl oz) coconut water
40 g (1½ oz) palm sugar (jaggery), finely grated or chopped
30 ml (1 fl oz) lime juice

Panna cotta
4 leaves of gold-strength gelatine
300 ml (10 fl oz) coconut cream

150 ml (5 fl oz) full-cream (whole) milk
35 g (1¼ oz) palm sugar (jaggery)
2 pinches of salt flakes

Special equipment
6 × 120 ml (4 fl oz) metal or plastic moulds

For the jelly, soak the gelatine leaves in cold water for 5 minutes.

Whisk all the other jelly ingredients in a small saucepan over a medium heat and bring to the boil. Remove from the heat and add the gelatine leaves, squeezed of excess water, stirring to dissolve. Strain into a jug, then divide evenly among the moulds. Set in the fridge for 1 hour.

For the panna cotta, soak the gelatine leaves in cold water for 5 minutes.

Put the remaining panna cotta ingredients in a saucepan, stirring to combine over a medium heat until hot – do not allow to boil. Add the gelatine leaves, squeezed of excess water, then stir to dissolve. Set aside to cool to room temperature, then pour onto the set jelly and refrigerate for about 6 hours, until set. The panna cottas will keep for about 5 days like this.

To serve, turn a mould on its side, then separate the wall of the panna cotta from the mould by pulling an edge away with your fingertip to break the surface tension. Turn out onto serving plates. Serve with a tuile set against each panna cotta, and the mango sprinkled with the shredded lime leaves to the side.

Pavlova (GF)

Making meringue is not too tricky, unless you're feeling a bit slapdash. You need to be particular about everything. If you're making a pavlova, I recommend using a citrus curd (see p. 797), as the contrast of tang is awesome with the whipped cream, sweet meringue and fruit – whether passionfruit pulp, raspberries, strawberries, roasted apricots or peaches, grilled peppered pineapple (p. 784) … whatever takes your fancy. **Serves 8**

240 g (8½ oz) egg whites, at room temperature
420 g (15 oz) icing (confectioners') sugar, well sifted, or blitzed in a food processor
4½ tablespoons cornflour (cornstarch)

1½ teaspoons cream of tartar
1 tablespoon white vinegar
450 ml (15 fl oz) Basic whipped cream (p. 799), or plain whipped cream

600–700 g (1 lb 5 oz–1 lb 9 oz) fruit
Lemon, lime or passionfruit curd (p. 797)
lemon or lime zest, to serve

Preheat the oven to 110°C (230°F) fan-forced. Line a baking tray with baking paper.

Using an electric stand mixer, whisk the egg whites on high speed until soft peaks form, about 3 minutes. Add the icing sugar in three additions and keep beating until glossy and stiff, about 5 minutes. Test by spooning some meringue back onto the mass: if it holds its form, it's ready. Gently fold in the cornflour, cream of tartar and vinegar until incorporated.

Tip the meringue onto the baking tray, in a 28 cm (11 in) round, then gently smooth into a dome, but don't flatten the top. Bake for 1½ hours, then turn the oven off, leave the door ajar and cool completely in the oven. To assemble, gently crack the top of the meringue to make a crater, spoon in the cream, slot in your chosen fruit, then pipe with the curd. Grate on some lemon or lime zest to finish, then serve. Unfilled pavlova will keep in an airtight container in the pantry for up to a week.

Make it different

Giant meringues. (GF) (V) You can leave the meringue mixture plain, or stir in a few drops of pink food colouring. Spoon large kitchen spoonfuls onto the baking tray, leaving 2 cm (¾ in) between each. Bake for 1 hour 20 minutes, then turn the oven off, leave the door ajar and cool completely in the oven. The meringues can be dusted with freeze-dried raspberry powder and enjoyed as is. Or you can bake the meringues as discs, and make mini pavlovas by sandwiching two discs with whipped cream, topping with more cream and finishing with fresh fruit – or use in an Eton mess–type dessert with Basic whipped cream (p. 799) and fresh berries.

Grilled pineapple with pink peppercorns for pavlova (GF) (V) (VG)

Using a mortar and pestle, roughly grind 3 tablespoons pink peppercorns with 200 g (7 oz) soft brown sugar. Tip into a large bowl. Add the juice of 3 limes. Peel and core a ripe pineapple, cut into sixteen wedges, then toss through the sugar mixture. Grill on a baking tray lined with baking paper for 8–10 minutes, until the pineapple is starting to caramelise. Set aside to cool on the tray, before slotting into the cream in the pavlova.

Chianti & raspberry granita with ice cream (GF)

This is a great way to finish a relaxed Italian-themed lunch, when you have eaten too much and need something to finish that's not too filling. It's not overly sweet, the colour is amazing, and perhaps most importantly, it's extremely refreshing. **Serves 6**

400 ml (13½ fl oz) decent Chianti
120 ml (4 fl oz) water
80 g (2¾ oz/⅓ cup) caster (superfine) sugar

20 g (¾ oz) glucose powder
2 strips of lemon zest
2 leaves of gold-strength gelatine, soaked in cold water

250 g (9 oz/2 cups) fresh raspberries
6 scoops of vanilla ice cream

Pair with

Fresh berries.

Strawberry or watermelon sorbet GF V VG

The key to this very simple recipe – aside from great fruit – is the glucose powder, which yields a perfect texture every time. Hull and chop 1 kg (2 lb 3 oz) strawberries or trim and chop the same amount of watermelon. Blitz in a blender with 240 g (8½ oz) caster (superfine) sugar, 70 g (2½ oz) glucose powder and 30 ml (1 fl oz) lemon juice until smooth, then strain through a fine-mesh sieve. Churn in an ice-cream churner according to the manufacturer's instructions, then freeze for 1 hour before serving. The sorbet can be frozen for up to 2 weeks. Makes about 1.2 litres (41 fl oz). Serve strawberry sorbet with sliced strawberries tossed in rosewater and icing (confectioners') sugar. Serve watermelon sorbet with diced watermelon splashed with vodka and chilled for 20 minutes.

Pair with

Serve with smashed fresh blackberries, boysenberries, raspberries or fresh passionfruit pulp spooned over.

Drizzle with Chocolate & honey sauce (p. 793) or Salted caramel sauce (p. 794), and scatter with Nutty praline (p. 786) or Salted caramel & almond popcorn (p. 788).

Serve with Nutty praline (p. 786) dropped on top, and seasonal roasted or fresh fruit – peaches, nectarines or apricots all work so well with the burnt honey.

Add the wine, water, sugar, glucose and lemon zest to a small saucepan over a medium–high heat, then simmer for 4 minutes. Pour into a heatproof bowl, then add the gelatine leaves, squeezed of excess water, stirring to dissolve.

Strain into a shallow 30 × 15 cm (12 × 6 in) dish. Scatter the raspberries over the top and freeze for about 4–6 hours, until set.

Meanwhile, freeze six serving glasses.

Add a scoop of vanilla ice cream to the glasses. Use a fork to scrape the granita onto the ice cream, then serve immediately.

Make it different

For a family-friendly version, omit the wine. Simmer the water, sugar, glucose and lemon zest as usual, then cool for 10 minutes. Add the gelatine leaves, then add 400 g (14 oz) finely strained strawberry purée.

Scorched honey & yoghurt parfait GF V

I find the scorched honey flavour in this creamy parfait so captivating, with the sweetness offset with a lightly tart tang from the yoghurt and lemon juice. This is a lovely way to make an ice cream–like dessert when you don't have a churn.
Serves 10

100 g (3½ oz/½ cup) honey
3 egg whites
180 g (6½ oz) caster (superfine) sugar
30 ml (1 fl oz) water

250 ml (8½ fl oz/1 cup) pouring (single/light) cream, softly whipped
300 g (10½ oz) plain yoghurt
30 ml (1 fl oz) strained lemon juice

Staples
BTR

Special equipment
Sugar thermometer

Grease a 25 cm (10 in) loaf (bar) tin and line with baking paper.

Heat the honey in a small saucepan over a medium heat until a medium-dark caramel, about 5 minutes.

Meanwhile, add the egg whites to the bowl of an electric stand mixer with the whisk attached, but don't start beating yet.

Add the sugar and water to a saucepan over a high heat. When the sugar starts to boil, begin to whisk the whites on medium–high speed.

When the sugar reaches the soft-ball stage (117°C/242°F), increase the mixer speed to high and slowly pour the sugar into the whites in a thin, steady stream while whipping. Once all the sugar has been added, turn the speed down to medium–high and beat for about 3 minutes, until cooled.

Add the burnt honey (warm it through again if it has become too stiff), then continue beating for about 2 minutes, until completely cool.

Fold the cream into the meringue until combined, then fold in the yoghurt and lemon juice. Spoon into the loaf tin and freeze overnight, or until firm.

To serve, unmould the parfait and slice. Serve immediately on frozen plates. The parfait will keep in the freezer for up to 2 weeks.

Sweet essentials & snacks

Sesame brittle GF V

Use these glassy shards as accompaniments or decorations for cakes and desserts. **Makes about 20 pieces**

200 g (7 oz/1⅓ cups) white
   sesame seeds

150 g (5½ oz/⅔ cup) caster
   (superfine) sugar
150 g (5½ oz) liquid glucose

75 g (2½ oz) unsalted butter
1 teaspoon salt flakes

Pair with

Ice cream.

Chocolate mousse (p. 782).

Classic panna cotta (p. 781).

Preheat the oven to 170°C (340°F) fan-forced. Line a baking tray with baking paper, and have a second tray at the ready. Lay out two sheets of baking paper about 40 cm (15¾ in) long on a clean bench that can tolerate heat, with two other sheets at the ready.

Spread the sesame seeds out on the baking tray and toast for 12 minutes, stirring halfway through, until deeply golden.

Add the sugar, glucose and butter to a small saucepan over a medium heat. Stir to combine, then bring to the boil. Stir in the warm sesame seeds.

Pour half the mixture onto a sheet of baking paper, and the rest onto a second sheet, then top with the extra sheets. Roll with a rolling pin to about 2 mm (⅛ in) thick, then slide onto the baking trays.

Remove the top pieces of paper and bake for 20 minutes. Set aside to cool and harden on the trays, then break into shards.

The sesame brittle will store in an airtight container in the freezer for several weeks.

Nutty praline GF V VG

Use whichever nuts suit you in this master praline recipe. Macadamias, almonds, walnuts, pecans, peanuts are good … but hazelnuts are always my favourite. **Makes 500 g (1 lb 2 oz)**

250 g (9 oz) raw nuts
250 g (9 oz) caster (superfine)
   sugar

50 g (1¾ oz) liquid glucose
50 ml (1¾ fl oz) water

Pair with

Use the crushed praline to decorate any cake.

Sprinkle over a Panna cotta (pp. 707, 781).

Mix half the smashed praline with one quantity of Basic whipped cream (p. 799) or Whipped vanilla ricotta filling (p. 799). Use the mixture to fill cannoli; fill a sponge cake, then ice with Chocolate ganache (p. 806); layer between Compressed puff pastry (p. 822) or Honey filo crisps (see p. 703); or serve with roasted peaches (see p. 720) and fresh raspberries.

Preheat the oven to 160°C (320°F) fan-forced.

Spread the nuts on a baking tray and roast for 10 minutes. Remove the tray from the oven and reduce the oven temperature to 90°C (195°F) fan-forced.

Rub off any skins in a tea towel (dish towel), then chop the nuts roughly. Tip onto a baking tray lined with baking paper and keep warm in the oven.

Meanwhile, in a saucepan, bring the sugar, glucose and water to a simmer over a high heat. Cook, without stirring, to a light golden caramel, about 7 minutes. Add the warm nuts and stir with a wooden spoon to coat.

Tip the mixture back onto the tray, tilting the tray to spread it out. Cool completely until hardened, before smashing or blitzing.

Store the toffee in an airtight container in the freezer to stop it getting tacky. It will keep for up to 3 months.

Clockwise from top left: Sesame brittle (above), Honeycomb (p. 789), Nutty praline (left)

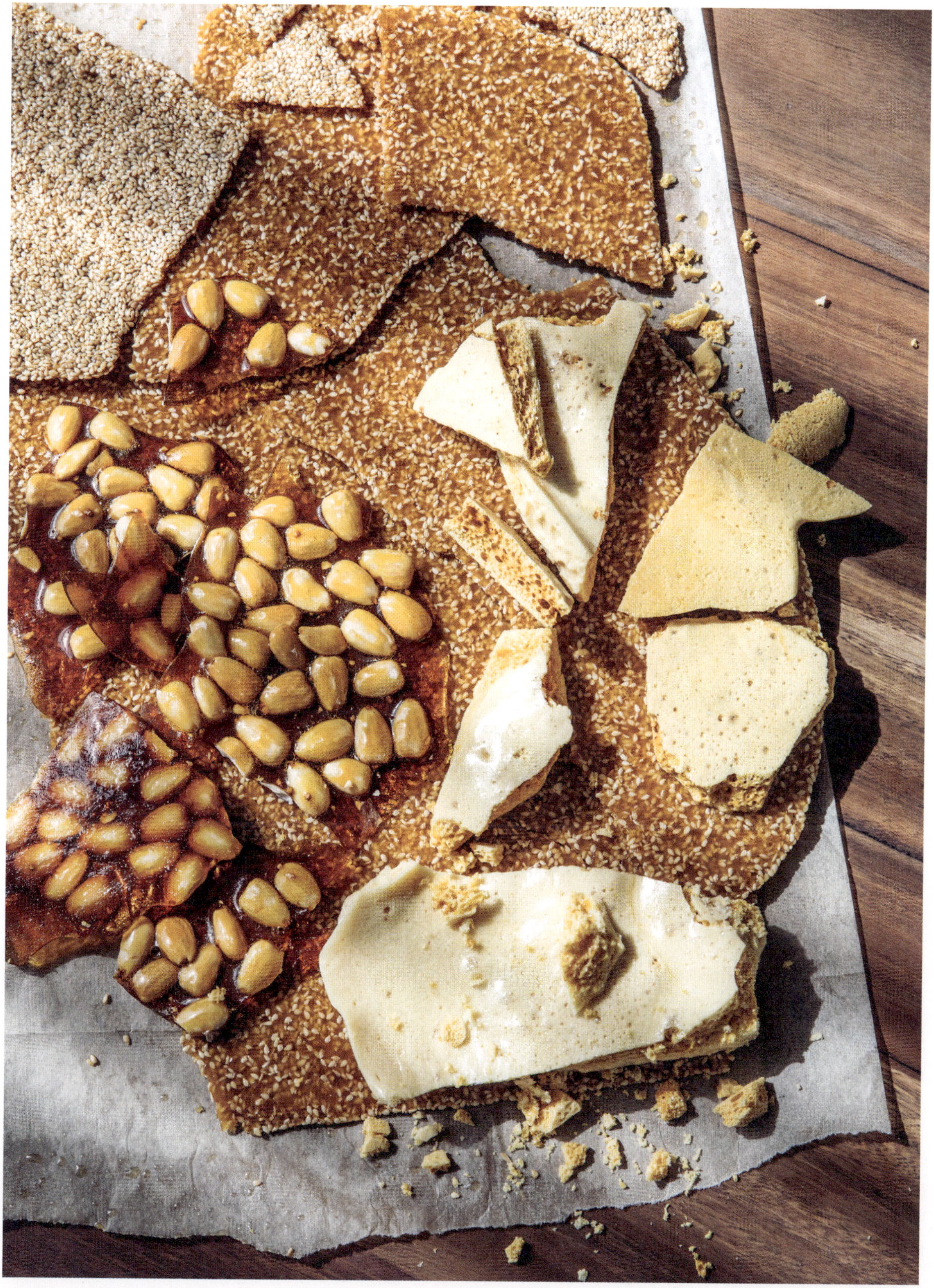

Sesame tuiles ⓥ

These thin and lacy snaps are ideal for gracing desserts, especially ones with tropical fruit and an Asian or Middle Eastern accent. **Makes 20**

50 g (1¾ oz/⅓ cup) black or white sesame seeds
165 g (6 oz/¾ cup) caster (superfine) sugar
35 g (1¼ oz/¼ cup) plain (all-purpose) flour

60 ml (2 fl oz/¼ cup) orange juice
1 teaspoon lemon juice
40 g (1½ oz) unsalted butter, softened at room temperature

1 heaped teaspoon black or white tahini
¼ teaspoon fine sea salt

Preheat the oven to 150°C (300°F) fan-forced. Line two baking trays with baking paper.

Blitz the sesame seeds to a powder in a food processor, 1–2 minutes. Add the sugar and flour, then blitz to combine. Add the orange and lemon juice and blitz to combine.

In a bowl, mix the butter, tahini and salt until incorporated, then add the sesame mixture and combine well.

Dollop about 1½ tablespoons of the mixture per tuile onto the baking trays, leaving ample space between each, as they will spread a lot. Smooth out to about 4 mm (¼ in) thick in whatever shapes you like.

Bake for about 10 minutes, until they start to bubble, then set aside to cool. While still warm and flexible, you can shape them around a rolling pin or cup to make curved tuiles.

The tuiles are best used on the day, but will hold for 2–3 days in an airtight container.

Pair with

Coconut panna cotta (p. 783).

Sliced mango and Salted caramel sauce (p. 794).

Any fresh tropical fruit and vanilla ice cream.

Semifreddo (p. 779).

Salted caramel & almond popcorn ⒼⒻ ⓥ

A perfectly tasty salty sweet treat by itself, this popcorn also makes a fabulous garnish when paired with some Salted caramel sauce (p. 794). **Makes 4 cups**

200 g (7 oz/1 cup) popcorn kernels
20 ml (¾ fl oz) extra-virgin olive oil
200 g (7 oz) unsalted butter
230 g (8 oz/1 cup) caster (superfine) sugar

180 g (6½ oz) soft brown sugar
180 g (6½ oz) honey
80 g (2¾ oz) toasted flaked almonds
3 teaspoons natural vanilla extract or paste

2½ teaspoons salt flakes
2 teaspoons bicarbonate of soda (baking soda)

Add the popcorn and oil to a large heavy-based saucepan over a high heat, stirring to coat the kernels. Cover and wait for a few minutes, until they start to pop, then shake the pan every now and then until the popping subsides. Tip into a large bowl and cool.

Clean out the pan and put it back over a high heat. Add the butter. Once melted, add the sugars and honey. Simmer for about 4 minutes, then add the almonds, vanilla, salt and bicarbonate of soda. Remove from the heat and stir the popcorn through to coat well.

Tip onto a lined tray and spread out to cool totally, before breaking into pieces and storing in an airtight container. The popcorn will keep in the freezer for about 1 month.

Make it different
With nuts. Instead of flaked almonds, use chopped roasted salted peanuts.

Pair with

Serve over ice cream smothered with Salted caramel sauce (p. 794).

Use to garnish Chocolate mousse (p. 782), Scorched honey & yoghurt parfait (p. 785) or Banana custard (p. 801).

Honeycomb GF V VG

To make 450 g (1 lb), line a 20 × 30 cm (8 × 12 in) brownie tin with baking paper. Add 320 g (11¼ oz) caster (superfine) sugar, 125 g (4½ oz) liquid glucose, 50 g (1¾ oz) golden syrup or light treacle and 60 ml (2 fl oz/¼ cup) water to a large heavy-based saucepan over a medium–high heat. Stir only at the start to combine, then cook for 10–12 minutes, until the temperature reaches 154°C (309°F). Remove from the heat and whisk in 15 g (½ oz) bicarbonate of soda (baking soda) well. The toffee will swell like molten lava. Pour into the brownie tin and leave to set for 30 minutes at room temperature. Once cooled, crack the honeycomb into shards. Use straight away, or store in an airtight container in the pantry. It will become tacky if kept in a humid environment, so keep it tightly sealed. It will keep in the freezer for up to 2 weeks. It's especially addictive if dipped in melted chocolate soon after making (cool at room temperature on baking paper to set).

Salted caramel & almond popcorn

Salted macadamia & almond caramels GF V

Wrap these in cellophane as gifts, or serve as after-dinner delights with coffee. These tender chewy caramels have just the right amount of salt to pair with the rich caramel, buttery macadamia and flaked almonds. **Makes about 60**

240 g (8½ oz/1½ cups) macadamias, toasted
100 g (3½ oz) flaked almonds, toasted
1 tablespoon salt flakes, plus 3½ teaspoons for topping

150 g (5½ oz) unsalted butter
375 ml (12½ fl oz/1½ cups) pure cream (40–42% fat)
240 g (8½ oz) soft brown sugar
150 g (5½ oz) honey

150 g (5½ oz) liquid glucose

Special equipment
Sugar thermometer

Preheat the oven to 150°C (300°F) fan-forced.

Toast the macadamias and almonds on separate baking trays for 10–15 minutes, until lightly toasted, checking from time to time. Remove from the oven and set aside.

Line a 20 cm (8 in) square tin with baking paper and sprinkle some of the extra topping salt over the base.

Add the nuts to a bowl.

Melt the butter in a saucepan over a low heat. Add the cream, sugar, honey, glucose and 1 tablespoon of the salt, then stir until combined and starting to bubble. Increase the heat to medium and bring to the boil, without stirring. Cook until the mixture reaches 126°C (257°F), which might take 20 minutes.

Once at temperature, immediately remove from the heat and pour over the nuts, then stir through.

Tip into the lined baking tin, then flatten out with a heatproof spatula. Sprinkle with the remaining salt, then leave to set for 1 hour.

Once cooled, remove from the tin and cut into 5 × 2 cm (2 × ¾ in) pieces. The caramels will keep in an airtight container for up to a week.

Glacé orange GF V VG

Slice 2 large unpeeled oranges 1 cm (½ in) thick, add to a container and cover generously with boiling water. Stand at room temperature overnight. The next day, add the orange slices and 700 ml (23½ fl oz) water to a saucepan. Bring to a simmer, then drain and set the orange slices aside. Place the pan back over a medium heat and add 300 g (10½ oz) caster (superfine) sugar, 1 split vanilla bean or 2 teaspoons natural vanilla extract or paste and 600 ml (20½ fl oz) water. Heat until the sugar dissolves, then add the orange slices. Turn the heat as low as possible and cook for 1 hour, then set aside to cool. Store the orange slices in the syrup until using; they will keep for up to 6 months. Serves 8–10.

Candied orange & lemon peel GF V VG

Peel 2 oranges and 2 lemons with a paring knife. Press the skin flat, pith side up, then scrape off and discard the white pith. Julienne the peel as finely as you can, then place in a saucepan and cover with water. Bring to the boil, then strain off the water. Repeat three more times. Add 300 g (10½ oz) caster (superfine) sugar and 400 ml (13½ fl oz) water to a saucepan over a medium heat and stir to dissolve the sugar. Add the blanched peel and cook over a low heat for 2–3 hours, with the water barely moving, until the peel is translucent. Cool, then store in the syrup in the fridge. Use the peel as is, or chop. When using as a finishing garnish, a little of the syrup can also be drizzled over.

Raspberry sherbet marshmallows GF

Reserve these mainly as an indulgent treat, rather than something you'd toast over a campfire or drop into a hot chocolate. **Makes about 30**

300 g (10½ oz) frozen raspberries, thawed, or passionfruit pulp
9 leaves of gold-strength gelatine, soaked in cold water
550 g (1 lb 3 oz) caster (superfine) sugar

150 ml (5 fl oz) water
80 g (2¾ oz) egg whites, at room temperature
a pinch of salt

Dusting sugar
60 g (2 oz/½ cup) icing (confectioners') sugar

30 g (1 oz/¼ cup) cornflour (cornstarch)
2 tablespoons citric acid

Special equipment
Sugar thermometer

Lightly grease a 23 cm (9 in) square tin and line with baking paper.

Blitz or mash the raspberries, then strain through a fine-mesh sieve into a bowl. Drain the gelatine leaves, squeezing out any excess water, then stir through the raspberries.

Combine the dusting sugar ingredients in a small bowl, then use some of it to heavily dust the base of the tin, reserving some for dusting over the marshmallows.

Add the sugar and water to a large saucepan, stirring over a low heat until the sugar dissolves. Increase the heat to medium and cook for 8–10 minutes, until 125°C (257°F). Remove from the heat and stir in the raspberry mixture.

Using an electric stand mixer, whisk the egg whites and salt on medium–high speed until soft peaks form, about 3 minutes. While beating on medium, gradually add the hot raspberry mixture in a steady stream. The mixture will double in size and become thick and glossy.

Pour into the lined tin, flattening with a spatula. Leave at room temperature for 3–4 hours, until firm.

Once cooled, turn out onto a board and cut into cubes. Roll in the remaining dusting sugar and store in an airtight container in the pantry for up to a week.

Pair with

Enjoy this for the confectionery treat that it is, or use to decorate a Pavlova (p. 784) or cake.

Dark chocolate truffles with nutty praline GF V

Preheat the oven to 150°C (300°F) fan-forced. Line a 20 × 10 cm (8 × 4 in) container with plastic wrap. Make Nutty praline (p. 786) with half almonds and half pistachio kernels and soften 40 g (1½ oz) unsalted butter at room temperature. Line a baking tray with baking paper. Blitz 400 g (14 oz) 70% cocoa dark chocolate in a food processor until it has a gravelly texture. In a small saucepan, bring 180 ml (6 fl oz) pouring (single/light) cream and 55 g (2 oz) liquid glucose to the boil. Pour into the food processor with the chocolate and blitz until melted. Add the butter and blitz until smooth. Transfer to a heatproof bowl and cool for 10 minutes. Fold half the crushed praline through, reserving the rest. Pour into the lined container and leave to set overnight at room temperature. Once set, use a spoon or large melon baller dipped in hot water to scoop out walnut-sized balls of the truffle mixture. (You can also slice rectangles off, and gently roll into egg or barrel shapes.) Dip one side of each truffle into 50 g (1¾ oz) roughly ground cacao nibs, and the other half into the crushed praline. The truffles will keep in an airtight container for up to 10 days. Makes about 40.

Icings, fillings, syrups, sauces & glazes

Sweet spice mix for baked goods GF V VG

So much more interesting than off-the-shelf mixed spice, this is the perfect little sweet spice mix for all sorts of things. The mahleb seeds are optional, but they add lovely bitter almond and cherry flavours. **Makes about 80 g (2¾ oz/½ cup)**

20 green cardamom pods
1 tablespoon fennel seeds
14 whole cloves
1½ whole nutmegs

3 teaspoons mahleb seeds (optional)
2 tablespoons ground ginger

2 tablespoons ground cinnamon
2 teaspoons ground white pepper

Using a mortar and pestle, squash the whole cardamom pods to pop the pods open, then shake through a coarse colander to gather the seeds.

Add the cardamom seeds to a small frying pan, along with the fennel seeds, cloves and nutmeg, and the mahleb seeds, if using. Toast over a medium heat for 3 minutes, tossing constantly, until the seeds are quite warm. Tip into a bowl to cool, then finely grate in the nutmeg.

Using a spice grinder (or mortar and pestle), finely grind the toasted spices, then add the ginger, cinnamon and pepper, and blitz or grind again to combine.

Store in an airtight container or jar. The spice mix will be at its best for up to 2 months, and last for about 6 months.

Use for

Hot cross buns (p. 765).

Cinnamon & cardamom buns (p. 766).

Christmas pudding (p. 778).

Böreks (p. 831).

Combine with sugar to toss freshly cooked Doughnuts (pp. 773, 734) in.

Honey & orange-blossom syrup GF V

This gently fragrant citrus and honey syrup is lovely drizzled over all sorts of sweets, from crepes to little fried doughnuts, to fruit and ice cream. **Makes about 500 ml (17 fl oz/2 cups)**

200 g (7 oz) honey
200 g (7 oz) caster (superfine) sugar
100 ml (3½ fl oz) water

1 cinnamon stick
zest and juice of 1 lemon
1 tablespoon orange-blossom water

Combine all the ingredients in a medium saucepan and stir over a low heat until the sugar dissolves, about 5 minutes. Bring to the boil, then simmer for 3 minutes.

Turn off the heat and serve warm. The syrup will keep in a sealed jar for up to a month.

Pair with

Crepes (p. 771) with cream.

Classic or Yoghurt panna cotta (p. 781), with sliced fruit or berries.

Drizzle over stone fruit after roasting, or on a Free-form stone fruit tart (pp. 814).

Soak mini fried Doughnuts (p. 773) in the syrup and serve as is, or finish with ricotta and pistachios (see p. 773).

Serve drizzled over sliced peaches, nectarines or apricots with vanilla ice cream.

Slice a Classic sponge cake (p. 748) in half and soak in the syrup, then fill with Mascarpone citrus curd icing (p. 803) or Whipped vanilla ricotta filling (p. 799).

Chocolate & honey sauce (GF)(V)

I keep this lovely sauce in a squeeze bottle in the fridge, and simply pop the bottle in a jug of hot water and stand for 5 minutes before using. You could, of course, also use a small pan or the microwave to loosen and gently warm the sauce. **Makes 400 ml (13½ fl oz)**

Pair with

Drizzle over Crepes (p. 771) or Pancakes (p. 768).

Pour over profiteroles filled with Crème pâtissière (p. 798).

Drizzle over ice cream.

Use to dip Mini cinnamon-bomb doughnuts (p. 773) or Churros (p. 775) in.

Drizzle over an individual Frangipane tart (pp. 796, 797) with poached pear (see p. 710) or Poached quince (p. 714).

200 g (7 oz) dark chocolate (60% cocoa minimum), chopped
100 ml (3½ fl oz) pouring (single/light) cream

60 g (2 oz) honey
25 g (1 oz) Dutch (unsweetened) cocoa powder
75 ml (2½ fl oz) water

1 teaspoon natural vanilla extract or paste
25 g (1 oz) unsalted butter, diced

In a small saucepan, melt the chocolate, cream and honey together over a low heat.

Whisk the cocoa powder, water and vanilla in a bowl to combine, then add to the chocolate mixture and stir constantly until combined and almost boiling.

Remove from the heat and stir in the butter, which will gloss the sauce.

The sauce will keep in the fridge for up to 2 months. Warm gently to use.

Golden syrup butter caramel sauce (GF)(V)

This caramel sauce is deep, rich and creamy, decadent even. Serve hot. **Makes 700 ml (23½ fl oz)**

Pair with

Sticky date pudding (p. 778).

Christmas pudding semifreddo (p. 779).

Basic sugar syrup (GF)(V)(VG)

This is the sugar syrup I use for glazing all manner of buns and sweet yeasted loaves, and while you can make it just with sugar, adding liquid glucose stops the syrup crystallising, so you can have the syrup on hand, rather than having to make it fresh each time. Add 200 g (7 oz) caster (superfine) sugar, 2 tablespoons liquid glucose and 160 ml (5½ fl oz) water to a small saucepan. Bring to a simmer to dissolve the sugar, then cool. This will make about 500 ml (17 fl oz/2 cups) and keep in the fridge almost indefinitely.

150 g (5½ oz/⅔ cup) caster (superfine) sugar
30 ml (1 fl oz) water
75 g (2½ oz) unsalted butter

120 g (4½ oz) soft brown sugar
100 ml (3½ fl oz) golden syrup, or light treacle

350 ml (12 fl oz) pouring (single/light) cream
1 teaspoon salt flakes

Special equipment
Sugar thermometer

Heat the caster sugar and water in a saucepan over a low heat until the sugar dissolves. Increase the heat to high and cook to a medium caramel, about 8 minutes

Remove from the heat and stir the butter through. Stir in the brown sugar to combine, then the golden syrup, cream and salt, stirring after each addition.

Return to the heat and bring to the boil, then reduce the heat to medium–low and simmer until the caramel reaches 113°C (235°F).

Pour into a jug and cool a little before using. If the sauce is too thick, loosen with a little hot water.

The sauce can be made ahead of time, and reheated when required. It will keep in a sealed jar in the fridge for up to a week.

Salted caramel sauce GF V

Once cooled to room temperature, this sauce is thick and deluxe. Warm it a little and its viscosity is perfect for an indulgent drizzle over cakes, chocolate mousse, ice cream, cheesecake or a banana split. Salted caramel & almond popcorn (p. 788) is an ideal garnish with this sauce. **Makes about 600 ml (20 fl oz)**

300 g (10½ oz) caster
  (superfine) sugar
1 tablespoon liquid glucose
80 ml (2½ fl oz/⅓ cup) water

160 g (5½ oz) unsalted butter,
  diced, at room temperature
250 ml (8½ fl oz/1 cup)
  pouring (single/light) cream
2 teaspoons salt flakes

Add the sugar, glucose and water to a large heavy-based saucepan over a low heat and stir to dissolve the sugar. Turn the heat up to high and cook until a medium-dark caramel, 8–10 minutes.

Remove from the heat and add the butter and cream, being careful as the mixture is molten and can spit.

Pour the caramel into a clean glass or metal container and cool to room temperature, then refrigerate. It will keep in the fridge for up to 2 months. Serve cold or at room temperature.

Make it different
Salted coconut caramel. GF V Use coconut cream instead of cream.

Pair with

Serve warmed with tarts and cakes.

Cheesecake (pp. 698, 738).

Chocolate mousse (p. 782).

Apple pie (p. 818).

Apple & cherry turnovers (p. 681) or fritters.

Drizzle over Tapioca pearls with tropical salad (p. 780).

Drizzle over ice cream or a banana split.

Mango with salted caramel, ginger & lime V

Here's a quick dessert idea when you have some Salted caramel sauce (left) on hand. Slice the cheeks off 3 large firm but ripe mangoes. Cut a lattice pattern into the flesh without cutting the skin, then push on the skin to expose the flesh, leaving the skin on. Cut 100 g (3½ oz) glacé ginger into small tiles about 2 mm (⅛ in) thick and scatter over the mango flesh. Squeeze on the juice of 2 limes or bush limes, then drizzle with salted caramel sauce. Sprinkle with 2 tablespoons toasted shredded coconut and serve with 6 gingernut biscuits (cookies), wafers or Sesame tuiles (p. 788), either whole or crushed.

Dulce de leche GF V

Dulce de leche is traditionally made from milk slowly cooked until the sugars caramelise, turning it into a luscious syrup to be drizzled over desserts. This version employs condensed milk, so you get the sugar and milk sugars caramelising, making for a sweeter and somewhat more decadent result. This method seems somewhat cavalier, but it works wonderfully well, yielding a super-rich milk caramel. Be a little careful, though: if the pot boils dry, you're liable to have that caramel redecorate your kitchen – and it's molten hot, so there is a genuine safety issue. Don't be afraid of it, though. Just keep the water topped up, and set a timer to remind you. Also, if you're thinking of skipping or reducing the salt, I'd advise against it. I love the salty contrast with the intense toffee sweetness. Without salt, it's way too sweet, and salt also sharpens and enhances the flavours, so there's a lot to be gained by using the salt here.

Makes 2 × 395 g (14 oz) tins

2 × 395 g (14 oz) tins condensed milk, labels removed

3 teaspoons salt flakes

Put the tins in a large saucepan and pour in enough water to cover them by about 5 cm (2 in). Bring to a simmer, then turn the heat to medium–low. Partially cover with a lid and cook at a gentle simmer for 5½ hours. Top the water up as needed to always keep the tins fully covered, as the tins may explode if exposed.

Remove from the heat and leave to cool for 1 hour in the water.

Remove the tins from the water and leave to cool at room temperature before opening, as the contents can be volcanically hot. The dulce de leche will then be ready to use, or will keep sealed in the tin in the pantry for 3 months. Once opened, store any leftovers in a sealed container in the fridge, where they will keep pretty much indefinitely.

Before using, stir 1½ teaspoons of the salt into each tin.

Pair with

Serve at room temperature, or while still a little warm, with ice cream, tarts and cakes.

Add to Crepes (p. 771) filled with cream cheese.

Use to sandwich chocolate biscuits together (see p. 754).

Drizzle over Tapioca pearls with tropical salad (p. 780).

No-churn dulce de leche ice cream GF V

Line a standard loaf (bar) tin of 22–25 cm (8¾–10 in) with plastic wrap and chill in the freezer. Using an electric stand mixer, whisk 390 g (14 oz) Dulce de leche (right) with 600 ml (20½ fl oz) pouring (single/light) cream and 50 ml (1¾ fl oz) pure cream (40–42% fat) on medium speed, until you have a thick voluminous cream, about 5 minutes. Spoon half the mixture into the loaf tin, then dollop in 40 g (1½ oz) dulce de leche. Sprinkle with 1 teaspoon salt, then top with the remaining cream mixture, another 40 g (1½ oz) dulce de leche and another teaspoon salt. Freeze for 1 hour before using. It is best used on the day, as the consistency will change if left to sit too long. Makes about 1 litre (34 fl oz/4 cups).

Frangipane ⓥ

Frangipane is a traditional sugared almond filling used in sweet tarts as a base layer for fruit, nuts, chocolate and the like to sit in, or to fill almond croissants. Its nutty, sweet richness marries the flavours and texture of the filling and pastry. You could also introduce some ground hazelnuts or pistachios to the frangipane mixture (replacing about one-quarter of the almonds), to match your dish. **Makes about 500 g (1 lb 2 oz)**

150 g (5½ oz/1½ cups) ground almonds
130 g (4½ oz/1 cup) icing (confectioners') sugar
2 eggs

1 egg yolk
125 g (4½ oz) unsalted butter, softened at room temperature

30 g (1 oz) plain (all-purpose) flour
3 teaspoons brandy (optional)

Preheat the oven to 180°C (350°F) fan-forced.

Sift the ground almonds and icing sugar through a coarse-mesh sieve into a bowl.

Whisk the eggs with the egg yolk, then set aside.

Cream the butter in a food processor until very soft and smooth. Add the almond mixture and blitz to combine well. Gradually add the whisked eggs, blending to combine. Add the flour and brandy, then blitz again to combine.

Spoon into a piping (icing) bag fitted with a plain nozzle and refrigerate until needed. It will keep for up to a week.

Pair with

Use as a base layer in a simple tart with Classic puff pastry (p. 822) or Crostata (see p. 826).

Combine with Vanilla crème pâtissière (p. 798) to make a custardy fruit tart (see p. 826).

A simple frangipane fruit tart ⓥ

To skip all the blind baking business, take 500 g (1 lb 2 oz) Classic puff pastry (p. 822) or Sweet galette pastry (p. 813) and roll out about to 5–8 mm (¼–⅓ in) thick. Cut a 26 cm (10¼ in) circle out of one end and place on a lined baking tray. Beat an egg with a pinch of salt and brush over the pastry. Brush the remaining pastry with more beaten egg, then cut into 2 cm (¾ in) wide strips. Create a border around the circle by pleating the strips to make a decorative edge, with half overhanging the edge of the circle. Once the outside border is done, use the remaining strips to create a border inside the first, overlapping it slightly. Warm a few tablespoons of jam (to match the fruit you're using) and brush the central disc of pastry. Pipe in a double quantity of Frangipane (left), working in a spiral to completely cover the base. Top with 500 g (1 lb 2 oz) of your chosen sliced fruit – strawberries, figs, apple, apricots, nectarines, blood plums. Dust heavily with icing (confectioners') sugar. Bake in a preheated 220°C (430°F) fan-forced oven for about 35 minutes, until the pastry is golden and the frangipane puffed. Brush with more warmed jam and serve with cream or crème fraîche and poached stone fruit (p. 724).

Lemon, lime or passionfruit curd (GF)

Emphasising bright freshness over sweetness, this light and zingy curd holds its shape at room temperature and is easy to pipe. **Makes about 800 ml (27 fl oz)**

220 g (8 oz) eggs
220 g (8 oz) caster (superfine) sugar
220 g (8 oz) lemon juice, lime juice or strained passionfruit juice

2 leaves of gold-strength gelatine
zest of 1 lemon or lime
280 g (10 oz) unsalted butter

In a large bowl, whisk the eggs and sugar until combined. Add the juice and whisk until combined.

Add the gelatine leaves to a jug of cold water and set aside.

Tip the egg mixture into a saucepan and whisk constantly over a medium heat for a few minutes, until it thickens. Whisk over a low heat for a further 3 minutes, then remove from the heat and whisk for another 3 minutes to cool.

Squeeze any excess water from the gelatine leaves and add them to the pan. Whisk to combine.

Tip the mixture into a blender, along with the zest and half the butter, and blend. Add the remaining butter and blend until smooth.

Scoop into a piping (icing) bag fitted with a small plain nozzle and chill for at least 30 minutes. The curd will keep in the fridge for up to a week.

Pair with

Pipe onto a Pavlova (p. 784) with Basic whipped cream (p. 799).

Layer into a trifle.

Pipe onto Madeleines (p. 736).

Serve with Friands (p. 734).

Use to fill a Classic sponge cake (p. 748) along with Basic whipped cream (p. 799), and ice with Passionfruit icing (p. 802).

Fill small cooked tart shells (pp. 812–3) with the curd, top with Italian meringue (p. 807) and scorch with a kitchen blowtorch or under a very hot grill (broiler).

Even simpler frangipane tarts (V)

Cut out a 12 cm (4¾ in) round of your chosen pastry, brush with egg wash (see p. 13), then smear 1½ tablespoons of Frangipane (opposite) in the centre. Top with some sliced fresh fig, ½ poached pear (see p. 710) or slices of Poached quince (p. 714) or Roasted quince (pp. 714, 716). Bake on a lined baking tray for about 14 minutes at 220°C (430°F) fan-forced until golden. Serve with vanilla ice cream and Chocolate & honey sauce (p. 793). You can also bake the pastry just with the frangipane, then top with fresh raspberries or roasted peaches or nectarines (see p. 720), and serve with Raspberry toffee coulis (p. 689) and ice cream.

Clockwise from left: Vanilla crème pâtissière (p. 798), Chocolate crème pâtissière (p. 798), Lemon curd (above)

Vanilla crème pâtissière ⒼⒻ Ⓥ

This delicious, pipe-able vanilla custard is a true workhorse of the classical pastry kitchen, holding its form well and not weeping into pastry. It can be used as is to fill tarts or choux pastry, or can be combined with Frangipane (p. 796) or lightened with whipped cream. **Makes about 650 ml (22 fl oz)**

380 ml (13 fl oz) full-cream (whole) milk
280 ml (9½ fl oz) pouring (single/light) cream
1 vanilla bean, split, seeds scraped, or 2 teaspoons natural vanilla extract or paste

90 g (3 oz) caster (superfine) sugar
60 g (2 oz) egg yolks
40 g (1½ oz/⅓ cup) cornflour (cornstarch)
40 g (1½ oz) unsalted butter

Pair with

French strawberry shortcake (p. 819).

Mille-feuille (p. 824).

Use to fill Cannoli (p. 820).

Spoon or pipe into small cooked tart shells (see pp. 812–3) and top with berries.

Pipe into Éclairs or Profiteroles (p. 821).

Add the milk, cream, vanilla bean and seeds to a medium saucepan with half the sugar. Bring to a simmer, then remove from the heat.

In a heatproof bowl, whisk the egg yolks, cornflour and remaining sugar by hand until thick and pale, about 4 minutes. Gradually add the milk mixture in a steady stream, whisking until incorporated.

Tip the mixture back into the pan. Cook over a medium–low heat, whisking constantly for a few minutes until thickened. Whisk constantly for a further 3–4 minutes, until thick and shiny, then remove from the heat.

Add the butter and whisk for a few minutes, until cooled a little.

Pour into a container lined with plastic wrap, making sure to cover the top of the mixture directly with the wrap to stop a skin forming, or spoon into a disposable piping (icing) bag and refrigerate until completely cold before using.

The crème pâtissière will keep for up to a week in the fridge.

Make it different

For dishes with Spanish or Italian flavours, add the zest of half a lemon and/or two drops of natural almond extract to the milk.

Chocolate crème pâtissière ⒼⒻ Ⓥ

A deeply chocolatey version of the classic. **Makes about 600 ml (20 fl oz)**

450 ml (15 fl oz) milk
60 g (2 oz) egg yolks
60 g (2 oz/¼ cup) caster (superfine) sugar

20 g (¾ oz) custard powder
10 g (¼ oz) Dutch (unsweetened) cocoa powder

100 g (3½ oz) dark chocolate (70% cocoa or higher), chopped
30 g (1 oz) unsalted butter

Pair with

Cassata cake (p. 752).

Mille-feuille (p. 824).

Use to fill Cannoli (p. 820).

Spoon or pipe into small cooked tart shells (pp. 812–3) and top with berries.

Pipe into éclairs or profiteroles (p. 821).

Warm the milk in a medium saucepan until about body temperature.

Whisk the egg yolks in a large bowl, then slowly rain in the sugar while whisking for a few minutes, until pale. Add the custard powder and cocoa and whisk until incorporated. Gradually whisk in the milk in a steady stream until incorporated.

Tip the mixture back into the pan. Cook over a medium–low heat, whisking constantly for a few minutes until thickened. Whisk constantly for a further 3–4 minutes, until thick and shiny, then remove from the heat.

Add the chocolate in two additions, whisking until melted before adding the next, then add the butter and gently whisk until incorporated.

Pour into a container lined with plastic wrap, making sure to cover the top of the mixture directly with the wrap to stop a skin forming, or spoon into a disposable piping (icing) bag and refrigerate until completely cold before using.

The crème pâtissière will keep for up to a week in the fridge.

Cream cheese & ricotta filling GF V

Pair with

Crostata filled with ricotta & quince (p. 826).

Use to fill Crepes (p. 771).

Pipe into small cooked tart shells, then top with poached rhubarb (see p. 646), fresh strawberries or balsamic cherries (see p. 566).

This is a richer and creamier version of the Whipped vanilla ricotta filling (below), spiked with hazelnut liqueur – but you could use any liqueur you like, or brandy. **Makes about 700 g (1 lb 9 oz)**

375 g (13 oz) drained fresh ricotta

250 g (9 oz/1 cup) cream cheese, diced, at room temperature

80 g (2¾ oz/⅓ cup) caster (superfine) sugar

1½ teaspoons natural vanilla extract or paste

zest of ½ large lemon

40 ml (1½ fl oz) hazelnut liqueur or brandy

Add all the ingredients to a food processor and blitz for 4 minutes, until very silky and smooth.

The filling will keep in the fridge for up to 2 days.

Whipped vanilla ricotta filling GF V

Pair with

Use to fill Cannoli (p. 820).

French strawberry shortcake (p. 819).

Strawberries romanoff (p. 688).

Raspberry toffee coulis (p. 689).

Pasta frolla tarts (pp. 825–6).

Pipe onto layers of cooked Compressed puff pastry (see p. 822), dust with icing (confectioners') sugar, and serve with Chocolate & honey sauce (p. 793).

Use this filling as a lighter alternative to crème pâtissière for cannoli, tarts and things like mille-feuille. **Makes about 450 g (1 lb)**

375 g (13 oz) drained fresh ricotta

80 g (2¾ oz/⅓ cup) caster (superfine) sugar

1½ teaspoons natural vanilla paste

zest of ½ large lemon

Add all the ingredients to a food processor and blitz for 4 minutes, until very silky and smooth.

The filling will keep in the fridge for up to 2 days.

Basic whipped cream GF V

Pair with

Tiramisu (p. 776).

Éclairs and Profiteroles (p. 821).

Lime & coconut cheesecake (p. 738).

Mille-feuille (p. 824).

Coconut butter pandan cake (p. 744).

Layer in a trifle.

This is my version of chantilly cream (a classically French and somewhat more luxurious filling than whipped cream for cakes, cannoli, tiramisu, éclairs, tarts and the like). If you're after a more classic chantilly, you can sweeten it further to taste. **Makes about 700 ml (23½ fl oz)**

350 ml (12 fl oz) thickened (whipping) cream, chilled

3 tablespoons pure cream (40–42% fat)

2 tablespoons icing (confectioners') sugar, sifted

1½ teaspoons natural vanilla extract or paste

Ideally, chill the bowl of an electric stand mixer, before whisking all the ingredients on medium-high speed until soft peaks form, 2–3 minutes – watch carefully, as you're not trying to make butter. Chill until needed, but whip again just before using.

Coffee mascarpone cream GF V

A more adult filling for sponge cakes or sandwiching biscuits. **Makes about 400 g (14 oz)**

3 teaspoons instant espresso
  coffee granules
1½ tablespoons boiling water
250 ml (8½ fl oz/1 cup)
  pouring (single/light) cream

80 g (2¾ oz/⅓ cup) caster
  (superfine) sugar
1 teaspoon natural vanilla
  extract or paste

150 g (5½ oz) mascarpone,
  softened at room
  temperature

In a bowl, dissolve the coffee in the boiling water. With a hand whisk or electric beaters, whisk in the cream, sugar and vanilla until firm peaks form. Whisk in the mascarpone for about 15 seconds to just combine.

The filling will keep in the fridge for up to 2 days.

Pair with

*Use to fill a Classic sponge cake
(p. 748), then ice with ganache
(see p. 806).*

*Serve with Chocolate mousse
(p. 782), topped with Nutty
praline (p. 786) and flaked
almonds.*

*Use to sandwich shortbread
biscuits (see p. 813) together and
serve with ice cream.*

Clotted cream GF V

This classic preparation yields very thick and gently vanilla-scented cream, with a delightful crust of caramelised milk sugars. **Serves 12**

500 ml (17 fl oz/2 cups) pure
  cream (40–42% fat)

½ vanilla bean, split
  lengthways, or 2 teaspoons
  natural vanilla extract
  or paste

10 g (¼ oz) caster (superfine)
  sugar

Preheat the oven to 100°C (210°F) fan-forced.

Add the cream to a saucepan. Scrape in the vanilla bean seeds and add the pod as well, along with the sugar. Warm through until just about to simmer, then remove from the heat.

Pour into a 22–23 cm (8¾–9 in) ceramic baking dish and bake for 4–5 hours, until a light golden crust forms.

Leave to cool slightly, then carefully transfer to the fridge without disturbing the cream. Chill for about 3 hours, until solid. The clotted cream will keep covered in the fridge for up to 10 days.

Scoop straight from the dish to serve, so that there are spoonfuls of cream with a layer of caramelised crust on top.

Pair with

*Anything you would normally
serve with cream or thick
(heavy/double) cream – cakes,
scones, tarts, chocolate pots …*

Vanilla crème anglaise GF V

Crème anglaise is a custard, but an incredibly light and velvety one, used as cold saucing custard for desserts or as the base for ice cream. I distinctly remember when I first understood how to make the perfect anglaise, as it was a pure revelation to tease the reactions out of egg yolks, sugar, milk and cream with gentle heat and dedicated focus to create the silkiest of vanilla custards. As with emulsifying a sauce or making sourdough bread, understanding those transformations by doing is such a key to becoming a confident and capable cook. **Makes about 600 ml (20½ fl oz)**

Pair with

Apple pie (p. 818).

*Roasted fruit (pp. 711, 714, 716,
720) or fresh berries.*

Poached peaches (see p. 724).

*Strawberries romanoff (p. 688)
with Puff pastry shards
(pp. 822, 823).*

*Self-saucing chocolate pudding
(p. 782).*

Berry crumble (p. 688).

*Hazelnut plum streusel cake
(p. 741).*

Doughnuts (p. 774).

*To make vanilla ice cream,
churn in an ice cream churner
following the manufacturer's
instructions.*

Banana custard GF V

Slice 4 ripe bananas and squeeze ½ lemon over. Layer the banana and some of the slightly cooled Thick vanilla custard (below) in a serving dish, finishing with a layer of custard and 45 g (1½ oz/½ cup) shredded coconut. Grate ½ whole nutmeg over the top. Refrigerate until set, then serve as is, or topped with whipped cream, Salted caramel sauce (p. 794) or Chocolate & honey sauce (p. 793). Go a step further by scattering on some Salted caramel & almond popcorn (p. 788) or Honeycomb (p. 789).

250 ml (8½ fl oz/1 cup) full-cream (whole) milk
250 ml (8½ fl oz/1 cup) pouring (single/light) cream

1 vanilla bean, split, or 2 teaspoons natural vanilla extract or paste
5 egg yolks

100 g (3½ oz) caster (superfine) sugar

Special equipment
Sugar thermometer

Set a heatproof bowl over a bowl of iced water.

Add the milk and cream to a saucepan. Scrape in the vanilla seeds and drop in the pod. Bring to a simmer, then remove from the heat.

Whisk the egg yolks and sugar in a large bowl until pale and frothy, about 1 minute. Pour in one-third of the hot milk mixture and whisk constantly for 1 minute, then whisk in the remainder.

Tip the mixture back into the pan, over a medium heat. Stir with a wooden spoon, in a figure-eight movement, until the anglaise reaches no more than 82°C (179°F), about 8–10 minutes; it's generally safer to stop at 80°C (175°F) and remove from the heat. The anglaise will coat the back of the spoon, and you should be able to draw a distinct line in it with your finger.

Pour the anglaise into the bowl on top of the iced water bath to cool and arrest the cooking process. There will be a little amount of scrambling in the corner of the pan, which is fine, being an indication the anglaise is properly cooked.

Once cooled, strain through a fine-mesh sieve, into a glass container or jar (plastic can hold other pungent food flavours, which can mar the custard).

The crème anglaise will keep for 7 days in the fridge. Serve cold.

Pair with

Apple pie (p. 818).

Roasted fruit (pp. 711, 714, 720) or fresh berries.

Poached peaches (see p. 723).

Strawberries romanoff (p. 688) with Puff pastry shards (pp. 822, 823).

Self-saucing chocolate pudding (p. 782).

Berry crumble (p. 688).

Hazelnut plum streusel cake (p. 741).

Thick vanilla custard GF V

Delicious hot or cold, this is a classic, full-bodied custard for pies and desserts. While an anglaise requires a bit more technical focus, this is much more foolproof, with the cornflour making it more robust. If you like your custard a little sweeter, replace the cornflour with custard powder.
Makes about 1.2 litres (41 fl oz)

150 g (5½ oz/⅔ cup) caster (superfine) sugar
50 g (1¾ oz) cornflour (cornstarch)

1 vanilla bean, split, seeds scraped, or 2 teaspoons natural vanilla extract or paste
6 egg yolks

650 ml (22 fl oz) full-cream (whole) milk
450 ml (15 fl oz) pouring (single/light) cream

Combine the sugar, cornflour and vanilla seeds in a large heatproof bowl, then whisk in the egg yolks until combined.

Add the milk, cream and vanilla pod to a medium saucepan. Bring to a simmer over a medium heat and cook for 2 minutes, then remove the vanilla pod. Pour over the egg mixture, whisking until amalgamated.

Pour the custard back into the pan and cook over a medium heat until thickened, about 5 minutes, stirring or whisking constantly. Once the custard is the desired consistency and free of lumps, pour into a jug and serve.

You can also refrigerate and serve cold, or reheat. The custard will keep for about a week in the fridge.

Basic sugar icing (GF) (V) (VG)

This is as simple as it gets, a thin icing for cakes, biscuits and cupcakes.
Makes enough for 10–12 cupcakes or 1 cake

300 g (10½ oz/2½ cups)
  icing (confectioners')
  sugar mixture

juice of ½ lemon
40 ml (1½ fl oz) hot water
food colouring (optional)

Add the sugar and lemon juice to a small bowl. Add just enough hot water to make a thick paste, adjusting until the desired consistency. Add some food colouring, or not, then spoon or pipe onto cooled biscuits or a cake and set aside to dry on a wire cooling rack.

Pair with

Gingerbread Christmas cookies (p. 757).

Simple butter cake (p. 736).

Vanilla butter biscuits (p. 754).

Blackberry or raspberry icing (GF) (V) (VG)

This bright candy-pink drizzle icing is lovely finished with some fresh berries.
Makes enough for 12–14 cupcakes or 1 cake

80 g (2¾ oz) blackberries or
  raspberries, plus extra to
  garnish

2 teaspoons lemon juice
250 g (9 oz/2 cups) icing
  (confectioners') sugar

In a bowl, mash the berries with the lemon juice, then push through a fine-mesh sieve to extract the juice. You should have about 45 ml (1½ fl oz) of juice.

Sift the icing sugar into a bowl, then stir in the berry juice. You can add a little more berry juice or lemon juice to loosen the icing further, if you like. Spoon over your cake(s) and garnish with whole berries.

Pair with

Simple butter cake (p. 736).

Classic sponge cake (p. 748).

Friands (p. 734).

Cupcakes (p. 730).

Lemon, lime or passionfruit icing (GF) (V) (VG)

This is a pourable icing that can be used on cakes or cupcakes, and garnished with passionfruit pulp or finely grated citrus zest. **Makes enough for 12–14 cupcakes or 1 cake**

350 g (12½ oz) icing
  (confectioners') sugar

50 ml (1¾ fl oz) passionfruit
  pulp, or lemon or lime juice

Sift the icing sugar into a bowl, then add the citrus juice or passionfruit pulp and stir to combine. Spoon over your cake(s) and garnish as desired.

Pair with

Simple butter cake (p. 736).

Classic sponge cake (p. 748).

Cupcakes (p. 730).

Mascarpone citrus curd icing GF

This rich lemon curd cream is a gorgeous icing for Madeleines (p. 736), or to fill or top cakes, cupcakes, muffins or a pavlova, or to fill a sponge cake. **Makes enough for 12–14 cupcakes or 1 cake**

300 g (10½ oz) Lemon curd (p. 797)

300 g (10½ oz) mascarpone, softened at room temperature

Using an electric stand mixer, whisk the lemon curd on slow speed for 1 minute, then add the mascarpone and mix for 1 minute to combine. Don't over-whisk, or the fat will become lumpy.

Any left-over icing will keep in the fridge for up to a week.

Pair with

Coconut butter pandan cake (p. 744).

Simple butter cake (p. 736).

Cupcakes (p. 730).

French strawberry shortcake (p. 819).

Use to sandwich meringues (see p. 784) together with some fresh passionfruit pulp.

Top a Pavlova (p. 784) with the curd, then finish with fresh fruit.

Use to fill a Classic sponge cake (p. 748), or a sponge cake soaked in Honey & orange-blossom syrup (p. 792).

Cream cheese icing GF V

This whipped icing has a good citrus kick. **Makes enough for 12–14 cupcakes or 1 cake**

150 g (5½ oz/1¼ cups) icing (confectioners') sugar
100 g (3½ oz) unsalted butter, softened at room temperature

zest of 1 lemon, or 2 limes
100 ml (3½ fl oz) lemon or lime juice
500 g (1 lb 2 oz/4 cups) cream cheese, diced,

softened at room temperature
125 ml (4 fl oz/½ cup) pure cream (40–42% fat)

Using an electric stand mixer with a paddle attachment, beat the icing sugar, butter and citrus zest on medium speed until smooth, about 3 minutes.

Add the cream cheese in three batches, beating until incorporated. Add the cream and mix until light and fluffy, about 3 minutes. Beat in the juice until combined and aerated.

Any left-over icing will keep in the fridge for a week.

Make it different

With ginger. Add 1 tablespoon ginger juice – squeezed from a 6 cm (2½ in) piece of grated fresh ginger – for a Carrot cake (p. 742) or Sticky chocolate ginger cake (p. 745).

With orange. Replace the lemon with strained orange juice, plus the zest from one orange. Add ½ teaspoon ground anise or fennel seed. Use with any chocolate and/or almond cake or citrus-flavoured cake.

Pair with

Zucchini muffins (p. 734).

Use to sandwich chocolate biscuits together (see p. 754).

Vanilla frosting GF V

A thick, pipeable frosting to be used generously. **Makes enough for 20 cupcakes**

500 g (1 lb 2 oz/4 cups) icing sugar
200 g (7 oz) butter, softened

350 g (12½ oz) cream cheese, room temperature

3 teaspoons natural vanilla extract or paste
1 teaspoon salt flakes

Sift the icing sugar into the bowl of an electric stand mixer with a paddle attachment, then beat with the butter on medium speed until smooth, about 3 minutes.

Add the cream cheese in three batches, beating until incorporated. Beat in the vanilla and salt flakes until combined and aerated.

Any left-over icing will keep in the fridge for a week.

Pair with

This icing can be coloured and used on cupcakes (p. 730), Simple butter cake (p. 736) or Classic sponge cake (p. 748).

Crème fraîche glaze GF V

A pourable and dippable glaze for all sorts of things, from pastries, to doughnuts, to sponge cakes, to fruit turnovers. **Makes enough for 6–8 doughnuts**

80 g (2¾ oz) crème fraîche or sour cream

200 g (7 oz) icing (confectioners') sugar, sifted

juice of ½ lemon

Slowly whisk the ingredients by hand in a bowl, then faster once combined. The mixture will seem to seize, but will then relax into a pourable consistency. Use immediately.

Make it different

With cinnamon & lemon. Add 2 teaspoons ground cinnamon and the zest of 1 lemon.

With cardamom & orange. Add 1 teaspoon ground cardamom and the zest of 1 orange.

With salted dulce de leche. Add 2 tablespoons Dulce de leche (p. 795) and 1 teaspoon salt flakes.

Pair with

Doughnuts (p. 774).

Simple butter cake (p. 736).

Classic sponge cake (p. 748).

Vanilla cupcakes (p. 730).

Apple & cherry turnovers (p. 681).

Coffee icing GF V

You can finish this icing with a few instant coffee granules, chocolate-dipped coffee beans, or some chopped walnuts, which all work beautifully with the coffee flavour. **Makes enough for 12–14 cupcakes or 1 cake**

45 ml (1½ fl oz) hot milk
1 tablespoon liquid glucose

3½ teaspoons instant coffee granules

250 g (9 oz/2 cups) icing (confectioners') sugar

In a bowl, mix together the milk, glucose and coffee, stirring until well combined. Sift in the icing sugar and stir to combine. Spoon over your cake(s) and garnish as desired.

Pair with

Simple butter cake (p. 736).

Brown sugar dark chocolate loaf cake (p. 747).

Vanilla cupcakes (p. 730).

Chocolate brownies (p. 762).

Maple syrup, brown sugar & cinnamon icing GF V

Laced with cinnamon and maple syrup, this cream cheese icing is good on any spiced cake or simple vanilla cake, and is marvellous for dressing up a carrot cake. **Makes enough for 12–14 cupcakes or 1 cake**

100 g (3½ oz) unsalted butter, softened at room temperature
90 g (3 oz) soft brown sugar
90 ml (3 fl oz) maple syrup

1 teaspoon ground cinnamon
250 g (9 oz/1 cup) cream cheese, diced, softened at room temperature

Using an electric stand mixer with the paddle attachment, beat the butter, sugar, maple syrup and cinnamon on medium–high speed until light and airy, about 4 minutes. Add the cream cheese in three lots, then continue to beat for about 3 minutes, until smooth. Spoon over your cake(s) and garnish as desired.

Pair with

Simple butter cake (p. 736).

Banana bread (p. 760).

Spiced pumpkin & olive oil loaf cake (p. 742).

Vanilla cupcakes (p. 730).

Carrot cake (p. 742).

Spiced zucchini & walnut cake (p. 674).

Nutella icing ⓖⒻ Ⓥ

Pair with

Chocolate brownies (p. 762).

Doughnuts (p. 774).

Hazelnuts and chocolate are one of my favourite combinations of the sweet world, so this icing makes so much sense to me. This is a drippy, runny sort of icing, rather than a thick ganache. **Makes enough for 12–14 cupcakes or 1 cake**

100 g (3½ oz) Nutella or finely chopped gianduja chocolate

100 g (3½ oz) milk chocolate (56% cocoa), finely chopped

140 ml (4½ fl oz) pouring (single/light) cream

Add the Nutella and milk chocolate to a heatproof bowl.

Heat the cream in a small saucepan until it starts to simmer around the edges, then pour over the chocolate. Stand for 3 minutes, then stir to combine.

Use the icing straight away; it will be pourable.

Chocolate fudge icing ⓖⒻ Ⓥ

Pair with

Brown sugar dark chocolate loaf cake (p. 747).

Simple butter cake (p. 736).

Cover cooled cakes, cupcakes or slices with the icing and sprinkle with cacao nibs, chopped nuts or Nutty praline (p. 786).

Use to sandwich Shortbreads (p. 813) together, or Dark chocolate & hazelnut biscuits (p. 754) or Cat's tongue biscuits (p. 755).

This is a thick, fudgy frosting that was originally made for a Brown sugar dark chocolate loaf cake (p. 747), but it's also quite delicious on other chocolate or vanilla treats. **Makes enough for 12 cupcakes or 1 cake**

150 ml (5 fl oz) full-cream (whole) milk
80 g (2¾ oz) soft brown sugar
1 tablespoon treacle

2 tablespoons Dutch (unsweetened) cocoa powder
2 tablespoons cornflour (cornstarch)

225 g (8 oz) dark chocolate (minimum 54% cocoa), chopped
1 teaspoon natural vanilla extract
35 g (1¼ oz) butter

In a saucepan, off the heat, combine the milk, sugar, treacle, cocoa and cornflour until smooth. Place over a low heat and slowly bring to a simmer, which will take about 5 minutes.

Remove from the heat and stir in the chocolate until smooth and glossy.

Stir the vanilla and butter and through to combine. Use at room temperature.

Chocolate ginger icing ⓖⒻ Ⓥ

Pair with

Sticky chocolate ginger cake (p. 745).

Chocolate brownies (p. 762).

For when you want a gentle lift and zing in your chocolate icing. **Makes enough for 1 cake**

80 g (2¾ oz) unsalted butter
40 g (1½ oz/⅓ cup) dark Dutch (unsweetened) cocoa powder

8 cm (3¼ in) piece of fresh ginger, finely grated, juice squeezed out and reserved
25 ml (¾ fl oz) lemon juice

180 g (6½ oz/1½ cups) icing (confectioners') sugar

Heat the butter and cocoa powder in a heatproof bowl over simmering water until melted. Whisk in the ginger and lemon juices, then whisk in the icing sugar until dissolved and smooth.

Whipped white chocolate ganache GF V

This luscious white chocolate ganache icing works well with berries and sponge cakes – and, surprisingly, with dark chocolate, too. **Makes enough to fill and ice 1 cake**

200 g (7 oz) white chocolate, chopped
200 ml (7 fl oz) pure cream (40–42% fat)

300 ml (10 fl oz) pouring (single/light) cream

Add the chocolate to a heatproof bowl.

Pour the pure cream into a saucepan and bring to just under a simmer. Pour the cream over the chocolate and stand for 3 minutes, then stir through to combine. Cover and refrigerate for 6 hours.

Add the chilled mixture to the bowl of an electric stand mixer with the pouring cream. Whisk on medium speed until spreadable, but not quite as thick as whipped cream, or the ganache will go grainy.

The ganache is best used on the day of making.

Pair with

Coconut butter pandan cake (p. 744).

Chocolate brownies (p. 762).

Deluxe chocolate galette cake (p. 746).

Torta caprese bianco cioccolato (p. 751).

Use to fill a Classic sponge cake (p. 748), along with sliced strawberries, then ice the cake with the ganache.

Chocolate ganache GF V

This was another revelation in my early years of training – mixing just the right amount of cream and butter into melted chocolate results in such a smooth pourable icing that sets with a glossy sheen, and then melts on contact with your palate. The temperature balance is important when making this ganache. If the cream is straight from the fridge, it will set the chocolate. You can place the bowl back over the pan of simmering water for a minute, then let the chocolate sit before stirring it through, but it's best to avoid having to fix it. **Makes enough for 1 large cake**

300 g (10½ oz) dark chocolate (68–70% cocoa), chopped
40 g (1½ oz) unsalted butter, chopped

120 ml (4 fl oz) pouring (single/light) cream, at room temperature

Add the chocolate and butter to a heatproof bowl. Set the bowl over a saucepan with a little simmering water in it, ensuring the bowl doesn't touch the water. Leave to stand for about 5 minutes.

Remove the bowl and set aside for 3 minutes, before stirring the mixture a couple of times. Once the chocolate has fully melted, mix the cream through until evenly incorporated. Use immediately.

When icing, stand for 5 minutes to set the first layer, then add another layer.

Pair with

Cakes (pp. 736, 746, 751).

Vanilla cupcakes (p. 730).

Spread the ganache over a cake, then decorate with nuts, morello cherries, Nutty praline (p. 786), cacao nibs, gold leaf or flowers, or just dust the edges with cocoa powder.

Use to sandwich chocolate biscuits together (see p. 754).

Lemon meringue pie

Fill a blind-baked 22 cm (8¾ in) tart shell (pp. 812–3) with Lemon, lime or passionfruit curd (p. 797), top with the Italian meringue (opposite), piped on or spread on with a spatula, leaving peaks or wavy edges to caramelise, then scorch with a kitchen blowtorch or under a hot grill (broiler) for a couple of minutes before serving.

Italian meringue & Italian meringue butter cream ⓖⓕ ⓥ

Italian meringue is beaten egg white that is cooked with sugar syrup as you whisk, resulting in a soft, spreadable but glossy and stable meringue that can be used to ice or decorate cakes. You can leave as is, or burnish with a kitchen blowtorch to singe the peaks of piped dollops, or curls made with a spatula. Taking it one step further, it also makes for the best butter cream icing. To be honest, I'm not generally a fan of butter creams, but this one is delicious, vibrantly white, soft, slick and silky, and it's also easy to apply, with a smooth finish easy to achieve. Either option will work on cakes and cupcakes, but the Italian meringue is also wonderful on curd tart. Just don't torch the butter cream option! **Makes enough for 12 cupcakes or 1 cake**

Pair with

Classic sponge cake (p. 748).

Red velvet cupcakes (p. 730).

Brown sugar dark chocolate loaf cake (p. 747).

Pipe the Italian meringue over a scoop vanilla of ice cream and Lime curd (p. 797), splash on some Angostura bitters and serve with Cat's tongue biscuits (p.755).

Pipe the Italian meringue on top of a Lime & coconut cheesecake (p. 738) and caramelise with a kitchen blowtorch.

Bombe Alaska ⓥ

Line a 20 cm (8 in) bowl with a double layer of plastic wrap and chill. Fill with 500 ml (17 fl oz/2 cups) of slightly softened vanilla ice cream, followed by 500 ml (17 fl oz/2 cups) of softened strawberry or raspberry ice cream, then 500 ml (17 fl oz/2 cups) chocolate ice cream, making distinct layers. Fold the plastic wrap over the top, then freeze for about 4 hours, until the ice cream is firm. Cut a piece of Classic sponge cake (p. 748) to fit the base of the bowl. Unwrap the top of the plastic wrap and place the sponge on top of the ice cream. Cover the bowl with a plate and invert to remove from the bowl. Freeze again for a few hours, until very firm. To serve, smear or pipe Italian meringue (right) all over the dome, then scorch with a kitchen blowtorch. Pour on some warmed brandy or liqueur and light with a kitchen blowtorch, then take to the table, soaking in the theatre of it all.

Italian meringue
120 g (4½ oz) egg whites
¼ teaspoon cream of tartar
200 g (7 oz) caster (superfine) sugar
100 ml (3½ fl oz) water

For the butter cream
270 g (9½ oz) unsalted butter, softened at room temperature, until like a thick mayonnaise

1½ teaspoons natural vanilla extract or paste
40 ml (1½ fl oz) warm water

Special equipment
Sugar thermometer

For the Italian meringue. Add the egg whites and cream of tartar to the bowl of an electric stand mixer with the whisk attached, but don't beat yet.

Add the sugar and water to a saucepan over a high heat, without stirring. As soon as the syrup reaches 115°C (240°F), turn the mixer on high speed.

When the temperature reaches 121°C (250°F), pour the syrup in a slow stream into the whisking whites. This will cook the egg whites and increase the volume threefold. Keep whisking for about 5 minutes, until cool.

The Italian meringue can now be used to ice cupcakes, or be piped onto a citrus curd tart or the like and be torched.

To make the meringue butter cream. Keep whisking the meringue just below high speed and add the butter 2 tablespoons at a time until combined, stopping and scraping down the sides of the bowl about halfway through. Once all the butter is incorporated, add the vanilla, then the water. Beat for 3 minutes, then use or store at room temperature in a sealed container for up to 2 days.

You can flavour the meringue butter cream with Lemon, lime or passionfruit curd (see p. 797), a shot of your favourite liqueur, or whip in 100 g (3½ oz) cooled melted chocolate and a few drops of orange-blossom water or rosewater to taste.

Also see

Olive oil pastry **469**

Filo pastry **564**

Sour cream shortcrust pastry **599**

Sweet pastry for tartlets **649**

Sweet galette pastry **650**

Strudel pastry **685**

Pastry

Pastry

Pastry can seem like a terrifying art, a complex highwire act where simple ingredients are spun and woven into the most magical of creations. And it is quite the specialty. That's if you judge your success by turning out perfectly burnished croissants, for example, with countless vanishingly thin layers of crisp pastry loaded with enough butter to make you blush with shame.

That's a measure of success for sure, but let's not allow such perfect ambitions be the enemy of less-technical – yet equally delicious – creations that you can achieve with basic techniques. Besides, for me, a rustic free-form tart is just as beautiful as a perfectly glazed one with neatly patterned fruit and an immaculately fluted crust. Both are more than achievable for the home cook, but the latter may take a little more practice and be just a little less forgiving.

Even making your own puff pastry is well and truly within reach, or choux pastry to make profiteroles (arraying them into a towering croquembouche is entirely up to you, though somewhat unnecessary in my book – but don't let that deter you!). The results may not be perfect first time but will still be great, and they'll get better each and every time.

This chapter has the basic pastry recipes that I use all the time, with accompanying tarts and other applications, both sweet (from p. 812) and savoury (from p. 828). There are also many other uses dotted throughout the book.

Pastry essentials

Using quality unsalted butter is important. Pastry and sweet baking are about control and precision, which includes adding salt in perfect measure or excluding it entirely. Salt enhances many sweet dishes, but it is not always called for. Additionally, the quality of the butter has a great influence on the flavour, so please, please don't skimp. The same is true of flour, with a freshly milled quality plain (all-purpose) flour ideal. Flour with a high protein content will become tough, even when lightly handled.

When working with pastry, temperature is a critical factor, so a hot kitchen can be your enemy. Your fridge or freezer can come to the rescue, with a short sojourn in a cold environment saving a pastry whose butter is surrendering to the heat. But left too late this will be irredeemable, so pay attention!

Some commercial kitchens with dedicated pastry sections will have chilled rooms to work in and sometimes chilled marble benches, too. This is not easy to replicate, of course, but planning and timing when you make pastry can solve this problem – remembering that most pastry can rest in the fridge for a day or so before being rolled. So, make that pastry first thing, before you get the stocks and sauces on the stove and things roasting in the oven, or take over the dining room table for a spell. Some people chill all their bowls and utensils, which helps to keep things cool.

The other important factor is to handle the pastry as little as possible when bringing the dough together and rolling it out. This is vital for two reasons: clearly the first is so the warmth of your hands doesn't overheat the butter; and the second is to not overwork the dough, which can activate the gluten in the flour – heavily handled pastry will be leaden and bready.

In preparations such as Classic puff pastry (p. 822) and Rough puff pastry (p. 823), those layers of cold butter are what make the pastry rise and crisp; if they melt into the dough, you simply won't get the same result – it will be pastry sans puff. So, when an instruction says chilled butter, this is vital to achieving the best outcome.

When rolling out, I now typically do so between two large pieces of baking paper (which I always reuse). I very lightly flour them, as you would the bench, then I find it very easy to roll without sticking, plus you can move and flip the pastry without really having to handle it. Depending on use, I will either fill the tart or pie dish, then rest it in the fridge for around 30 minutes, or rest between the paper if making a free-form tart or cutting a lid for a pie or the like. The key, though, is that I always rest the pastry, which stops if from shrinking too much when baked.

Also, while it may be tempting to skip the blind-baking step (see below) when making tarts, please don't. Baking the shell first will mean you can cook it to perfection, regardless of how long the filling takes to cook, and it will also develop the crust, meaning your pastry won't be doughy and soggy – the texture of pastry, whether flaky and light or dense and crumbly, is as critical as the flavour.

Blind-baking pastry shells

For a 20–26 cm (8–10¼ in) pastry shell, roll out 500–600 g (1 lb 2 oz–1 lb 5 oz) of your chosen pastry to about 5 mm (¼ in) thick. (I almost always roll pastry between two large sheets of lightly floured baking paper, to make it easy to shift the pastry without it sticking.) Roll it onto the rolling pin to support the weight without tearing the pastry. Unroll gently over your lightly greased or sprayed flan (tart) tin, then work the pastry into the tin by pulling the pastry edge back towards the centre of the tart and gently pushing into the corner to fit snugly. Do this gently all around the tin, until the pastry fits neatly. Once fitted, push the pastry firmly into position all over the tin, leaving the excess to hang over the side (this can be sliced off with a sharp serrated knife once cooked, as it will shrink a little as it bakes), gently pulling it outwards to help it stay flush with the tin in the oven.

Before baking, chill the pastry shell for about 30 minutes in the fridge, or 15 minutes in the freezer, which will help minimise shrinkage during baking.

Preheat the oven to 180°C (350°F) fan-forced. Line the chilled tart shell with foil, making sure it sits smoothly against the pastry. Fill with dried rice or beans. Fold the top of the foil over the edge of the pastry. Bake for 20 minutes, then flick the foil up to release some steam; bake for about another 10 minutes, until the edges are golden brown.

Turn the oven down to 130°C (265°F) fan-forced. Remove the foil and beans and bake for a further 5–10 minutes, until the pastry is golden all over, then set aside to cool completely.

If baking smaller tarts, simply reduce the cooking time, looking for colour as a guide.

Sweet

Pâte sucrée (Sweet shortcrust) Ⓥ

This is the classic workhorse sweet pastry for all sorts of tarts. It's easy to work and rolls well, as it's not super short; the more butter to flour there is, the 'shorter' a pastry is, meaning it binds less well and is more affected by heat. This is a pastry that is best made in a decent-sized batch like this, as the pastry is just more successful – plus, it keeps well in the freezer. **Makes about 1 kg (2 lb 3 oz)**

360 g (12 oz) unsalted butter, diced, at room temperature
150 g (5½ oz/1¼ cups) icing (confectioners') sugar
4 egg yolks

50 ml (1¾ fl oz) water
500 g (1 lb 2 oz/3⅓ cups) plain (all-purpose) four
½ teaspoon fine sea salt

Add the butter to the bowl of an electric stand mixer. Using the paddle attachment, cream on low speed until smooth, about 5 minutes. Add the icing sugar and mix to combine, keeping the speed low to avoid aeration.

Lightly beat the egg yolks and water in a bowl, then add to the mixer and combine well – the mixture may look split, but that's fine. Turn off the mixer and add the flour and salt. Mix on low speed to combine, then mix for 1 minute.

Tip the dough onto a clean bench. Knead firmly with the heel of your hand, to work in any unincorporated flour and butter. Bring the dough into a ball and flatten into a disc. Wrap in plastic wrap and refrigerate for 1 hour before rolling.

Once rested, the pastry is now ready to use. Alternatively, you can double wrap tightly in plastic wrap and refrigerate for up to 3 days, or freeze for 10–12 months. Thaw frozen pastry in the fridge for about 4 hours before using.

Rolling out the pastry for a 20–24 cm (8–9½ in) flan (tart) tin. Cut 500–600 g (1 lb 2 oz–1 lb 5 oz) of the pastry into six even pieces. On a lightly floured bench, press out a piece with the heel of your hand, bringing it back over itself. Do this three times, then repeat with all the pieces. Bring the pieces back into one ball again; this process makes the dough evenly malleable while still being cool. Press the ball into a flat disc, then roll twice with a rolling pin. Turn and roll twice again. Repeat this process – working quickly so the dough doesn't heat up too much – until you have a circle about 5 mm (¼ in) thick. It should be still cold but supple. Ease the pastry into the greased flan (tart) tin. Proceed with the blind-baking instructions (see p. 811), keeping a little pastry aside to repair any cracks by smearing the pastry into any breaks in the warm shell, and brushing with beaten egg to seal.

Make it different
Chocolate sweet shortcrust. Ⓥ Reduce the icing sugar to 130 g (4½ oz), and add 25 g (1 oz) dark Dutch (unsweetened) cocoa powder.

Use for
Lemon tart (p. 814).

Simple custard tarts (p. 815).

Piperade tart (p. 829).

Gluten-free shortcrust pastry for a tart base ⒼⒻ Ⓥ

In a blender, grind 50 g (1¾ oz) white chia seeds to a flour. Dice 120 g (4½ oz) unsalted butter and set aside until room temperature. In a food processor, blitz the chia seeds, butter, 120 g (4½ oz) rice flour, 100 g (3½ oz) besan (chickpea flour), 1 tablespoon gluten-free cornflour (cornstarch), 120 g (4½ oz) ground almonds, 2 tablespoons soft brown sugar (optional) and 1 teaspoon salt flakes until the mixture resembles breadcrumbs. Add 2 eggs and 2 tablespoons water and blitz until the dough forms clumps. Tip onto a clean bench and knead five times to bring the dough together. Shape into a disc and wrap tightly in baking paper or plastic wrap. Chill for 30 minutes, then your pastry is ready to roll. It will keep in the fridge, wrapped tightly in plastic wrap, for up to 5 days, or up to 3 months in the freezer; thaw the frozen pastry in the fridge for about 4 hours before using. This recipe makes about 600 g (1 lb 5 oz) of pastry, and you can sub this in wherever regular sweet shortcrust pastry is required. Omit the sugar for savoury uses.

Pâte sablée (French shortbread) Ⓥ

This classic French pastry is often used for tarts and biscuits. This version is too short for tart shells, but it makes delightfully crumbly shortbread. This is one of those recipes that is super handy to have in the freezer, as you can slice off and bake what you need and pop the rest back in for next time. **Makes about 20**

180 g (6½ oz) unsalted butter
100 g (3½ oz) caster (superfine) sugar

3 teaspoons pouring (single/ light) cream
1 egg yolk

250 g (9 oz/1⅔ cups) plain (all-purpose) flour

Cream the butter and sugar in a food processor until pale, about 3 minutes. Add the cream and egg yolk and blitz until smooth, 1–2 minutes.

Sift the flour onto a clean bench. Tip the butter mixture on top, and rub into the flour between the tips of your fingers, working until it resembles coarse breadcrumbs. Smear the mixture with the heel of your hand to make sure all the butter is well incorporated, then bring it together into a log.

Cover with plastic wrap and chill for 2 hours before using. The pastry can also be frozen now for up to 3 months; thaw for 20 minutes on the bench before slicing, then return the unused portion to the freezer.

Preheat the oven to 160°C (320°F) fan-forced. Line two baking trays with baking paper.

Unwrap the log and slice 1.5 cm (½ in) thick. Roll with a rolling pin to 5–6 mm (¼ in) thick, then use a cutter to cut the desired shapes, or leave them a bit free-form.

Transfer to the baking trays and bake for about 8 minutes, until lightly golden. Cool completely on the trays. The shortbreads will keep in an airtight container for 3 days.

Pair with

Dairy-based desserts such as Panna cotta (pp. 707, 781, 783) or Crème caramel (p. 781).

Serve with a scoop of Chocolate mousse (p. 782).

French shortbread sandwiches with mascarpone cream, almonds & praline Ⓥ

Make a dessert by sandwiching Pâte sablée (right) together with Coffee mascarpone cream (p. 800) or ice cream, with some toasted flaked almonds or Nutty praline (p. 786) sprinkled around the edges.

Sweet galette pastry Ⓥ

This pastry is ideal for making rustic, free-form fruit tarts – no tart tin or blind-baking required! **Makes about 950 g (2 lb 2 oz)**

500 g (1 lb 2 oz/3⅓ cups) plain (all-purpose) flour
120 g (4½ oz/1 cup) icing (confectioners') sugar

200 g (7 oz) unsalted butter, diced and chilled
4 egg yolks, beaten

80 ml (2½ fl oz/⅓ cup) iced water
½ teaspoon fine sea salt

Tip the flour onto a clean bench and add the icing sugar and butter. Work with your fingers to form a coarse crumb, then incorporate the egg yolks, iced water and salt. Lightly knead with the heel of your hand until the pastry comes together into a soft dough.

Flatten into a thick disc between two sheets of baking paper, then rest in the fridge for 30 minutes before using; it will keep in the fridge for up to 2 days.

Wrap any left-over pastry tightly with plastic wrap and freeze for up to 3 months; thaw in the fridge for about 4 hours before using.

Use for

Rhubarb galette (p. 650).

Free-form stone fruit tart (p. 814).

Fill with Frangipane (p. 796) and top with fresh berries, or add whipped ricotta and chunks of chocolate or quince paste in with the frangipane.

The possibilities are endless – this is a pastry without restraint.

Free-form stone fruit tart (v)

This generous and organically shaped tart is a great way to feed a few, though you can also halve the quantities. The pastry is very forgiving, with no blind-baking required. Fill it with whatever fruit the season is giving you. **Serves 8–10**

Pair with

Custard (p. 801), cream, ice cream or crème fraîche.

1 × quantity Sweet galette pastry (p. 813), rested but not blind-baked

150 g (5½ oz) nuts (such as hazelnuts or almonds)

100 g (3½ oz) caster (superfine) sugar

2 teaspoons ground cinnamon or cloves

800 g (1 lb 12 oz) fresh pitted stone fruit, sliced 3 cm (1¼ in) thick, tossed with 150 g (5½ oz/⅔ cup) caster (superfine) sugar

and 1 tablespoon cornflour (cornstarch)

1 egg, beaten with a pinch of salt

75 g (2½ oz/⅓ cup) demerara sugar

Roll the rested pastry out between two sheets of baking paper, to about a 50 cm (20 in) rough oval. Trim any ragged edges, if you like. Transfer to a baking tray lined with baking paper and refrigerate until firm, about 30 minutes.

Preheat the oven to 200°C (400°F) fan-forced.

In a food processor, pulse the nuts, caster sugar and cinnamon until coarsely chopped, then scatter over the rested pastry.

Leaving a 4 cm (1½ in) border, arrange the stone fruit over the pastry. Fold the pastry border over the filling, pleating and crimping as you go. Brush the pastry edges with the egg wash, then sprinkle the demerara sugar over the pastry.

Bake for 45 minutes, until the pastry is golden. Rest for 5 minutes before serving. The tart will keep at room temperature for up to 2 days before the pastry goes soft, and the tart loses its integrity.

Make it different

Replace the fresh stone fruit with apple compote and a few handfuls of berries. Instead of hazelnuts or almonds, use walnuts or pecans.

Lemon tart (v)

There's nothing so sublime as a perfectly balanced, just-set lemon tart, with that tangy sweet curd yielding effortlessly to the spoon, before a little more pressure is needed to part the buttery pastry ... I do love a lemon tart. This version is based on Philippa Sibley's recipe, which she shared with me during a brief stint at the Melbourne Wine Room. Philippa is a world-class pastry chef, just about the best I've worked with – so, lucky me ... and you. **Serves 8**

Pair with

Serve as is, or with Clotted cream (p. 800).

300 g (10½ oz) caster (superfine) sugar

zest of 3 large lemons (for a softer and sweeter result, use Meyer lemons)

9 eggs

250 ml (8½ fl oz/1 cup) lemon juice

280 ml (9½ fl oz) pouring (single/light) cream

1 × 22–24 cm (8¾–9½ in) Pâte sucrée tart shell

(p. 812), blind-baked see (p. 811) and still in the tin

icing (confectioners') sugar, for dusting

Add the sugar and lemon zest to a food processor and blitz to release the oils in the zest. Tip into a bowl with the eggs and whisk until foamy. Stir in the lemon juice, then stir the cream through, being careful not to aerate. Set aside at room temperature for 1 hour.

Preheat the oven to 130°C (265°F) fan-forced.

Whisk the filling mixture gently, then skim off any bubbles with a spoon. Place the blind-baked tart shell on a baking tray and half-fill with the curd mixture. Position the tray in the oven so you can still reach the tart, then pour in the remaining filling. Slide the tart into the middle of the oven.

Bake for 50 minutes, then check. The curd should be set around the edges, but still have a wobble in the middle. If it's still loose, give it another 5–10 minute before checking again.

Cool in the tin for 45 minutes, then trim the pastry edge with a sharp serrated knife. Slice into wedges and dust with icing sugar to serve.

This tart will keep for 3 days in the fridge, but the pastry will soften a little after a day or so.

Simple custard tarts ⓥ

Short cut

Use pre-baked tart shells.

These are my homage to the little custard tarts you used to find in every local bakery, alongside neenish tarts and vanilla slice. Aside from the pastry shells – and you can buy those if you want – there's no baking here, with the custard setting at room temperature. **Makes 8 small tarts**

½ × quantity Pâte brisée (p. 829), or Pâte sucrée pastry (p. 812)

Eggless custard
250 ml (8½ fl oz/1 cup) full-cream (whole) milk

120 g (4½ oz) custard powder
1 teaspoon natural vanilla extract or paste
500 ml (17 fl oz/2 cups) pouring (single/light) cream

80 g (2¾ oz/⅓ cup) caster (superfine) sugar
1 whole nutmeg

Special equipment
8 × 10–12 cm (4–4¾ in) foil tart tins

Preheat the oven to 180°C (350°F) fan-forced.

Roll out the pastry until about 2 mm (⅛ in) thick. Cut out circles 2 cm (¾ in) bigger than the tins, then line them with the pastry. Line each shell with foil, fill with dried rice or beans.

Bake for 15–20 minutes, until golden. Remove the beans and foil and set aside to cool.

For the custard, whisk 150 ml (5 fl oz) of the milk in a large heatproof bowl with the custard powder and vanilla to combine.

Heat the cream, sugar and remaining milk in a saucepan over a medium heat to just under a simmer, then pour over the custard mixture. Whisk very well, then tip back into the pan and whisk over a medium heat for 5 minutes. Once thickened, pour into a jug.

Divide the custard between the tart shells. Grate the nutmeg over and leave to set at room temperature for 20 minutes.

The tarts will keep at room temperature for up to 2 days.

Chocolate tart ⓥ

Aside from the blind-baking, this tart barely sees any oven time, just enough to set the filling to a silky, mousse-like consistency, which is sublime with the brooding sophistication of the dark chocolate. It's one for serious chocolate aficionados. **Serves 6–8**

Pair with

Cream and fresh raspberries, slices of perfectly ripe fig or roasted rhubarb (see p. 648).

Serve as is – or dust with cocoa powder and serve with Clotted cream (p. 800) or crème fraîche.

Dust with cocoa powder and garnish with Chocolate gravel (p. 783).

300 g (10½ oz) dark chocolate (70% cocoa), chopped
210 g (7½ oz) unsalted butter, diced, at room temperature

2 eggs
2 egg yolks
40 g (1½ oz) caster (superfine) sugar
1 teaspoon salt flakes

1 × 22–24 cm (8¾–9½ in) Chocolate sweet shortcrust tart shell (p. 812), blind-baked (see p. 811) and still in the tin

Preheat the oven to 150°C (300°F) fan-forced.

Add the chocolate and butter to a heatproof bowl and place over a saucepan of simmering water for about 5 minutes, ensuring the bowl doesn't touch the water. When two-thirds of the chocolate has melted, stir through twice. Remove the bowl to finish melting the chocolate in the residual heat.

Using an electric stand mixer, whisk the eggs, egg yolks, sugar and salt until a ribbon consistency, about 5 minutes. Fold in one-third of the melted chocolate mixture to combine, then fold in the remainder until combined, but don't mix any more than necessary.

Pour into the blind-baked tart shell and bake for about 10 minutes, until the filling puffs slightly at the edges.

Once completely cool, trim the pastry edge with a sharp serrated knife. To serve, dip a knife in a jug of hot water, wipe dry, then slice. It will keep at room temperature in an airtight container for about 3 days.

Baked custard tart ⓥ

I have an obsession with custard tarts. My maternal grandmother made a wonderful version with a particularly deep layer of rich baked custard. Happily, there was always a warm tart on arrival for school holidays in Benalla, in country Victoria. **Serves 4–6**

Pair with

Serve as is, or with Clotted cream (p. 800).

1 × 24 cm (9½ in) Pâte sucrée pastry shell (p. 812), blind-baked see (p. 811) and still in the tin

Vanilla custard
650 ml (22 fl oz) pouring (single/light) cream
150 g (5½ oz/⅔ cup) caster (superfine) sugar
3 eggs

4 egg yolks
1 tablespoon cornflour (cornstarch)
2 teaspoons natural vanilla extract or paste
1 whole nutmeg

Preheat the oven to 130°C (265°F) fan-forced. Set the tart tin (with the pastry shell) on a baking tray.

For the custard, add the cream and half the sugar to a saucepan. Bring to a simmer over a medium heat, then take straight off the heat.

In a large heatproof bowl, whisk the eggs, egg yolks, cornflour, vanilla and remaining sugar to combine. Whisk in a little of the cream mixture, then gradually whisk in the rest until incorporated.

Strain the custard into the pastry shell, then grate the nutmeg over. Transfer the tray to the oven.

Bake for about 50 minutes, until the custard is set around the edges, but with a slight wobble in the middle.

Set aside to cool, then serve warm or cold. The tart will keep at room temperature for up to 2 days before the pastry goes soft and the tart loses its integrity.

Top to bottom: Baked custard tart; Chocolate tart

Apple, blueberry & blackberry galette ⓥ

This impressive-yet flat-looking pie sits in a proud golden mound, bejewelled with caramelised demerara sugar – not to mention the scent of clove-spiced apples and the pleasing pop of berries throughout. **Serves 6–8**

1 × quantity Pâté brisée
  (p. 829)
50 g (1¾ oz) tahini
700 g (1 lb 9 oz) peeled
  and cored cooking apples

(such as golden delicious
  or granny smith)
zest of ½ lemon
100 g (3½ oz) caster
  (superfine) sugar
1½ teaspoons ground cloves

200 g (7 oz) mixed
  blueberries and
  blackberries
1 egg, beaten with a pinch
  of salt
50 g (1¾ oz) demerara sugar

Cut the pastry in half and form into two flat discs. Roll each piece out between two pieces of floured baking paper to 3–5 mm (⅛–¼ in) thick, then cut out two 38–40 cm (15–15¾ in) rounds. In one of the rounds, which will be the top, make about nine 1.5 cm (½ in) long slits, then rest that portion on a tray in the fridge for 15 minutes, to help stop the pastry shrinking.

Meanwhile, preheat the oven to 200°C (400°F) fan-forced.

Lay the pastry base on a lined baking tray. Smear the pastry with the tahini.

Cut each apple into 6 mm (¼ in) dice and toss in a bowl with the lemon zest, caster sugar and cloves. Pile on top of the pastry, then sprinkle with the berries. Brush the pastry edges with the egg wash.

Carefully roll the chilled pastry lid onto a rolling pin, then unroll over the top of the pie. (Don't try to lift it on, as it may tear.) Press the edges together and roll or crimp, making the finish as neat and decorative as you can. Don't be too fussy, though, as the pastry is forgiving and becomes golden once cooked. Brush the whole top with more egg wash, then completely coat with the demerara sugar. Cut 2cm (¾ in) holes in the lid.

Bake for 30 minutes, then reduce the oven temperature to 180°C (350°F) fan-forced and bake for a further 20 minutes, until deeply golden. Stand for 5 minutes before serving.

The pie will keep in an airtight container at room temperature for up to 3 days.

Make it different

Sugar-crusted apple pie. ⓥ For a more classic apple pie, omit the berries.

With cherries. Add dried sour cherries.

Pair with

Serve hot with ice cream, Thick vanilla custard (p. 801), cream or crème fraîche. This pie is also very good cold.

Deep-dish apple pie ⓥ

After rolling out the Pâté brisée for the Apple, blueberry & blackberry pie (left), cut out two 28 cm (11 in) circles. Line a 24 cm (9½ in) pie dish with one of the pastry circles and brush the edges with the egg wash (see p. 13). Pile the apple mixture (with or without the barberries) in the middle, then top with the other pastry round. Press the edges together, then trim to neaten, leaving about 4 cm (1½ in) overhang. Roll the edges in, pinching to crimp, and lifting off the dish edge as you go to stop the pastry sticking. Decorate the top with pastry scraps, if you like. Glaze the exposed pastry with more egg wash, then sprinkle the demerara over. Make about five slashes on top to release steam. Bake on a baking tray at 190°C (375°F) fan-forced for 30 minutes, then turn the oven down to 160°C (320°F) fan-forced and bake for about 25 minutes, until deeply golden. Rest for 5 minutes or so before serving.

French strawberry shortcake with crème pâtissière (V)

Sablé breton is a classic French short pastry, a little like Italy's Pasta frolla (p. 825), but it has more lift and is somewhat crumbly when cooked. It's also simple to make and use, much like pasta frolla, and is perfect for making a strawberry shortcake. It can also be cooked off into light and crumbly biscuits, somewhat less dense and short than those made with Pâte sablée (p. 813). As the name suggests, this pastry originates in Brittany, where butter is somewhat revered. **Serves 6–8**

1 × quantity Vanilla crème pâtissière (p. 798)
300 g (10½ oz) strawberries, sliced
icing (confectioners') sugar, for dusting

Sablé breton
220 g (8 oz) plain (all-purpose) flour
10 g (¼ oz) baking powder

4 egg yolks
½ teaspoon natural vanilla extract or paste
3 teaspoons dark rum or brandy (optional)
160 g (5½ oz) caster (superfine) sugar
160 g (5½ oz) unsalted butter, well softened at room temperature

1 egg, beaten with a pinch of salt
2 tablespoons demerara sugar
40 g (1½ oz) flaked almonds

Staples
BTR

Preheat the oven to 160°C (320°F) fan-forced. Grease a 23–26 cm (9–10¼ in) fluted loose-based flan (tart) tin or springform cake tin.

To make the pastry, sift the flour and baking powder into a bowl.

Using an electric stand mixer, whisk the egg yolks, vanilla and rum (if using) on medium–high speed. Add the caster sugar and beat until pale, about 4 minutes.

Beat the butter with a fork to soften it further. On slow speed, add the butter in two additions, whisking well after each to keep the mixture aerated. Fold in the flour mixture until combined.

Tip onto a lightly floured bench. Bring the dough together and form into an oval, then wrap with plastic wrap and chill for 15 minutes.

Once chilled, cut off pieces of pastry and press into the base of the flan tin, about 2 cm (¾ in) thick, with a slightly higher border at the edge. Brush the base and edges with the egg wash, then sprinkle the raw sugar and almonds over. Any left-over dough can be re-rolled and cut to make biscuits (see left).

Bake for 20–25 minutes, until the pastry is lightly golden and quite swollen, but it should stay rather blonde to maintain the buttery texture. Set aside to cool to room temperature.

Top the cooled tart with the crème pâtissière, then the strawberries, finishing with a good dusting of icing (confectioners') sugar.

The tart will keep at room temperature for up to 2 days before the pastry goes soft, and the tart loses its integrity.

Make it different
With whipped ricotta. Replace the crème pâtissière with Whipped vanilla ricotta (p. 795).

With raspberries or cherries. Instead of strawberries, use fresh raspberries or pitted cherries.

Galani dough for crostoli & cannoli ⓥ

This galani dough makes two quite delightful things: crunchy, sugar-dusted crostoli, a simple and satisfying treat that is associated with Venice and in particular Carnevale, and the Sicilian classic cannoli, filled with sweetened ricotta. If you're making cannoli, you will need something to wrap them in that can go in the fryer. A quick trip to the hardware store for dowel (see below) will solve that, but you can also buy dedicated stainless steel cannoli moulds.

Makes about 24 cannoli or seadas, or 30–40 crostoli

oil, for deep-frying (see p. 22)

Galani dough
460 g (1 lb) plain (all-purpose) flour
10 g (½ oz) caster (superfine) sugar
5 g (¼ oz) fine sea salt
60 g (2 oz/¼ cup) unsalted butter, diced
1 egg, lightly beaten
25 ml (¾ fl oz) white vinegar
100 ml (3½ fl oz) dry white wine, or water

For crostoli
honey, for drizzling
icing (confectioners') sugar and/or ground cinnamon, for dusting

For cannoli
1 egg white, beaten
100 g (3½ oz) chopped chocolate (any kind)
zest of ½ lemon
1 × quantity Whipped vanilla ricotta (p. 795)

Vanilla crème pâtissière, (p. 798), Chocolate crème pâtissière (p. 798), or ½ quantity smashed Nutty praline (p 786), mixed with 1 quantity Basic whipped cream (p. 799)

Special equipment
Pasta machine, 4–6 pieces of dowel or bamboo, each 3 cm (1¼ in) in diameter, and 12 cm (4¾ in) long

To make the galani dough, blitz the flour, sugar and salt in a food processor for 30 seconds to combine. Add the butter and process until well combined, 2–3 minutes. Add the egg and vinegar and process to combine, then add half the wine and process again. You may need to reposition the dough as it can get stuck on the blade. Add a splash more wine and process again until absorbed. Pinch a small amount of dough with your fingers – if it sticks together, it is the right consistency; it should just form a ball when you push it together. If not, add a splash more wine. Wrap in plastic wrap and refrigerate for 20 minutes.

Roll out the chilled dough on the bench and divide in three. Ensure any dough you're not working with is kept covered, as it will dry out easily. Flatten out one piece until thin enough to pass through the pasta machine rollers, then pass through the machine, dropping the settings until the dough is about 3 mm (⅛ in) thick. Repeat with the other pieces.

Heat 15 cm (6 in) of oil in a large heavy-based saucepan or deep-fryer until 170°C (340°F).

To make crostoli. Use a fluted pastry/pasta cutter or knife to cut the galani dough into 15 × 3 cm (6 × 1¼ in) ribbons, then cut a 5 cm (2 in) slit in the middle of each with a knife. Fold one end through each slit, or tie in a loose knot. Fry in batches for 3–4 minutes, until the dough is golden and bubbling. Drain thoroughly on paper towel, then drizzle with honey and dust with icing (confectioners') sugar, or sprinkle with 1 teaspoon ground cinnamon combined with 3 tablespoons icing sugar. These are best enjoyed on the day.

To make cannoli. Cut 10 cm (4 in) rounds out of the galani dough, then brush one-third of each round with beaten egg white. Working in batches, wrap a piece around each dowel, with the brushed edge facing out, then lift the unbrushed edge over and press to seal. Fry for 3–4 minutes, until the dough is golden and bubbling. Drain on paper towel, slipping the shells off the dowel and repeating. The cannoli will keep in an airtight container for up to 3 days before filling.

To fill the cannoli, fold the chopped chocolate and lemon zest through the whipped ricotta, then pipe into each end of the shells. Pipe in the crème pâtissière or the praline whipped cream. You can dress these up further by topping the exposed filling with more chopped chocolate, chopped pistachios, glacé fruit or preserved cherries.

Pâte à choux for éclairs & profiteroles Ⓥ

Choux pastry is one of those classic staples that is worth mastering, even if your ambitions aren't set on making a towering sugar-webbed croquembouche for the next special occasion. I'll leave such things to pastry cooks with deeper architectural ambitions, but for me a beautifully made profiterole or éclair filled with whipped cream or crème pâtissière and dipped in good chocolate is a thing of wonder. **Makes 10–12**

Choux dough
240 g (8½ oz) water
120 g (4½ oz) unsalted butter
2 g (⅛ oz) fine sea salt
175 g (6 oz) plain (all-purpose) flour
35 g (1¼ oz) caster (superfine) sugar

250 g (9 oz) eggs, whisked
For éclairs
1 × quantity Chocolate crème pâtissière (p. 798), or Basic whipped cream (p. 799)
200 g (7 oz) dark chocolate (70% cocoa), melted
smashed Sesame brittle

(p. 786), or Nutty praline (p. 786), for sprinkling

For profiteroles
1 × quantity Vanilla crème pâtissière (p. 798), or Basic whipped cream (p. 799)
200 g (7 oz) dark chocolate (70% cocoa), melted

Set up an electric stand mixer with the whisk attachment.

For the choux dough, bring the water, butter and salt to a simmer in a small saucepan over a medium heat. Once simmering, remove from the heat and add the flour and sugar. Stir with a wooden spoon to a paste, then return to the heat for 1–2 minutes while stirring.

Once the dough starts to pull away from the side of the pan and is glossy and smooth, immediately tip into the bowl of the stand mixer and whisk on slow speed for 30 seconds. Add one-third of the egg and mix until incorporated, then add half the remaining egg and beat until incorporated. Add the remaining egg and turn the speed to medium. Beat for 20 seconds, then check the dough. It should hold a peak, then slowly droop down over itself.

Spoon the dough into a piping (icing) bag fitted with a 1 cm (½ in) plain or star nozzle. Chill for 30 minutes.

Preheat the oven to 200°C (400°F) fan-forced. Line two baking trays with baking paper.

To make éclairs. Pipe the dough onto the baking trays in lines about 7 cm (2¾ in) long and 5 cm (2 in) apart. Use an atomiser to spray the dough with a mist of water, or flick on some water with your fingers (practise first); the steam this creates will aid rising. Slide the trays into the oven and immediately turn the temperature down to 180°C (350°F) fan-forced. Bake for 12 minutes, until puffed and lightly golden, then rotate the trays from front to back. Reduce the temperature to 160°C (320°F) fan-forced and bake for another 10 minutes. Set aside to cool for at least 45 minutes before filling and serving.

To fill the éclairs, slice the cooled choux shells open and fill with the chocolate crème pâtissière or whipped cream, then dip the tops in melted chocolate. Sprinkle the sesame brittle or praline over the top, then serve. The éclairs are best enjoyed fresh.

To make profiteroles. Pipe tablespoon-sized rounds on the baking trays, about 5 cm (2 in) apart. Atomise or flick with water, then bake and cool as for the éclairs.

To fill the profiteroles, pipe the crème pâtissière or whipped cream into the cooled choux shells; alternatively, slice the shells open and fill. Dip in melted chocolate, then serve. Best enjoyed fresh.

Classic puff pastry ⓥ

Puff pastry is the king of pastries, and so satisfying to make. Master Rough puff pastry (opposite) first, then make this. Both are buttery and flaky, but this method yields beautifully defined and consistent layers, and the more you fold and roll, the more you will get – up to a point! As with the rough puff, keeping everything cool is vital, so don't try to make this in your kitchen when the oven is on full tilt and pots are simmering. Usually I make twice this amount, but I have reduced the recipe here to make it easier to master. By all means double the recipe if you're experienced, or just confident, with any left-over pastry lasting much longer in the freezer than you will ever need it to. **Makes about 600 g (1 lb 5 oz)**

250 g (9 oz/1 cup) unsalted
   butter, softened at room
   temperature

Détrempe
250 g (9 oz/1⅔ cups)
   plain (all-purpose) flour

25 g (1 oz) unsalted butter,
   finely diced and chilled
¼ teaspoon fine sea salt
60 ml (2 fl oz/¼ cup)
   pouring (single/light)
   cream

60 ml (2 fl oz/¼ cup) water
25 ml (¾ fl oz) lemon juice

Staples
FLR

Use for

Fish pie (p. 188).

Chicken, leek & mushroom pie (p. 603).

Pissaladière (p. 599).

Apple & cherry turnovers (p. 681).

Frangipane fruit tarts (p. 796).

Pies (pp. 188, 284, 503, 603).

Pasties (see p. 469).

Compressed puff pastry

Preheat the oven to 200°C (400°F) fan-forced. Divide ½ × quantity Classic puff pastry (left) in half. Roll out into two sheets, each about 20 × 30 cm (8 × 12 in). Chill the pastry in the freezer for 15 minutes before baking, to stop it shrinking. Line a baking tray with baking paper, and have a second one at the ready. Place the chilled pastry on the baking tray and bake for 8 minutes, then put another tray on top and bake for 5 minutes to compress and finish cooking. Use for Mille-feuille (p. 824), Classic panna cotta (p. 781), Crème caramel (p. 781) or Strawberries romanoff coulis (p. 688). You could also pair the compressed pastry with Basic whipped cream (p. 799) or crème fraîche with Raspberry toffee coulis (p. 689), fresh raspberries and roasted peaches (see p. 720). For something simple, use a sharp serrated knife to cut the pastry into desired shapes. Dust heavily with icing sugar, leave to cool a little and serve with ice cream.

To make the détrempe, which is the basic dough, pulse the flour, butter and salt in a food processor until a sandy texture. Add the cream, water and lemon juice and pulse in 10-second intervals until it all comes together. Press the dough into a ball. Wrap in plastic wrap, or place in a clean freezer bag, and rest for 45 minutes at room temperature.

Meanwhile, place the block of butter between two pieces of baking paper, then use a rolling pin to flatten into an even rectangle about 2 cm (¾ in) thick. Refrigerate for 15 minutes, until firmed up but still malleable.

Once the détrempe has rested, cut a deep cross into the dough. Working from the centre, use your palm to press out the four sections of dough, to form four flaps in a cross shape. Use a rolling pin to flatten the dough flaps, pushing outwards from the main body of the dough. The aim is to form a cross, with the centre about 3 cm (1¼ in) thick, and the arms about 1 cm (½ in) thick. You're trying to make the centre large enough to take the slab of butter. Roll the centre towards and away from you, into a rectangle about 2.5 cm (1 in) thick.

Add the butter to the centre of the dough. Fold over the flaps from the top, then the bottom, followed by each side, ensuring the butter is completely encased with dough. Press down a little on the corners with the heel of your hand to ensure they are sealed, then lightly dust the dough with flour. You may need to dust the dough or rolling pin as you proceed, but do so with as little flour as possible.

If the butter breaks out of the dough at any time, sprinkle flour generously over the tear, and the butter will absorb the flour and repair the hole once turned and rolled. If the butter is bursting out in hard lumps, it's too firm to roll, so rest at room temperature for 5–10 minutes, then continue, sprinkling with extra flour as you go.

Roll the dough out to a rectangle about 20 × 45 cm (8 × 18 in). Then, with the short edge facing you, fold in three, like a letter. Turn so that an open edge faces you, then roll out into a 45 cm (18 in) long strip and fold in three again. Wrap in plastic wrap and refrigerate for 25 minutes. This process is called the first turn.

Once rested, repeat the process of rolling with the open edge facing you, folding, then turning, rolling, folding and resting again for the second turn.

Repeat again for the third turn, but rest for 1 hour before using. At home, three turns are enough, but in a professional kitchen we'd typically do six turns – that's up to you.

After the final resting, the pastry will be ready to use. Alternatively, you can double wrap tightly in plastic wrap and refrigerate for up to 3 days, or freeze for 10–12 months. Thaw frozen pastry in the fridge for about 4 hours before using.

Rough puff pastry ⓥ

Use for

Fish pie (p. 188).

Chicken, leek & mushroom pie (p. 603).

Pissaladière (p. 599).

Apple & cherry turnovers (p. 681).

Cherry puff pastry tart (p. 824).

Pies (pp. 188, 284).

Rough puff and classic puff pastry work on a similar principle, with similar results, as both doughs are loaded with butter. As the pastry cooks, the water expands and tries to escape, while the fat in the butter stops the flour forming bonds and creating structure – so the pastry puffs, and you get these flaky layers enriched with butter. It's a gorgeous little reaction. The more layers you have, the flakier the pastry. With Classic puff pastry (opposite), the butter is pressed into distinct layers between the dough, while rough puff simply incorporates everything together. With rough puff, you won't get defined layers, but you still get a flaky and buttery result, with less effort. It's a great place to start your puff pastry journey, and it's really not hard at all. However, it is very important to work quickly and with well-chilled butter. A hot kitchen or warm butter will mean you'll need to add too much extra flour, which will make the pastry heavy. Streaks of butter through the dough are exactly what you're looking for, so don't panic if it's not uniform. Remember, it's *rough* puff. **Makes about 1 kg (2 lb 3 oz)**

500 g (1 lb 2 oz/3⅓ cups) plain (all-purpose) flour
1 teaspoon fine sea salt

400 g (14 oz) unsalted butter, diced and well-chilled
2 teaspoons lemon juice

225 ml (7½ fl oz) water

Tip the flour and salt onto a clean bench, then top with the chilled butter. Chop through with a pastry scraper or large spatula until roughly incorporated. Make a well, then pour in the lemon juice and water. Combine quickly into a rough dough. If the dough is sticky, add a little more flour – but you shouldn't need to if working while the butter is still cold. Wrap in plastic wrap or place in a clean reused freezer bag and rest for 30 minutes in the fridge.

With your hands, shape the rested dough into a rough rectangle, then roll out to about 30 × 40 cm (12 × 15¾ in). Fold in three as you would a letter, ensuring that the pastry meets neatly at the corners. Wrap and rest for another 20 minutes in the fridge.

Place the rested dough on the bench, with an open edge facing you. Roll out to 30 × 40 cm (12 × 15¾ in), fold in three again, then chill again for 20 minutes.

Repeat the process, refrigerating for another 20 minutes.

The pastry is now ready to use. Alternatively, you can double wrap tightly in plastic wrap and refrigerate for up to 3 days, or freeze for 10–12 months. Thaw frozen pastry in the fridge for about 4 hours before using.

Mille-feuille ⓥ

Mille-feuille calls for a compressed puff pastry – the method creates a golden piece of pastry that is just as buttery and flaky as regular puff pastry, but with a robust quality that makes it ideal to layer for mille-feuille, or serve as biscuit-like shards with other desserts. **Serves 10**

½ × quantity Compressed puff pastry (p. 822)

2 × quantities Vanilla crème pâtissière (p. 798), or Chocolate crème pâtissière (p. 798)

icing (confectioners') sugar, for dusting, or Basic sugar icing (p. 802)

Sandwich the compressed puff pastry together in big slabs with a double quantity of the crème pâtissière, then dust heavily with the sugar or sugar icing before serving.

Make it different
Chocolate mille-feuille. ⓥ You could also ice with Chocolate ganache (p. 806) or Chocolate fudge icing (p. 805).
White chocolate & strawberry mille-feuille. ⓥ Sandwich the pastry together with Basic whipped cream (p. 799) and 250 g (9 oz) sliced strawberries or whole raspberries, then ice with White chocolate ganache (p. 806).

Cherry puff pastry tart ⓥ

This is somewhat more elaborate than a simple fruit tart, with the creamy and nutty filling buoying the roasted cherries on a rich, custard-like bed. It's very much a dessert tart, rather than an afternoon treat. Serve this in large, decadent pieces. **Serves 6–8**

650 g (1 lb 7 oz) pitted cherries
2 tablespoons caster (superfine) sugar
juice of ½ lemon

300 g (10½ oz) Frangipane (p. 796)
300 g (10½ oz) Vanilla crème pâtissière (p. 798)
1 × 25 cm (10 in) Rough puff pastry tart shell (p. 823),

blind-baked (see p. 811) and still in the tin
icing (confectioners') sugar, for dusting

Preheat the oven to 200°C (400°F) fan-forced.

Toss the cherries, caster sugar and lemon juice in a bowl. Set aside for about 30 minutes to macerate the cherries.

Combine the frangipane and crème pâtissière in a bowl, then smooth into the blind-baked tart shell, spreading it out evenly. Arrange the cherries on top, then spoon the juices over. Dust heavily with icing (confectioners') sugar.

Bake for 20 minutes, then reduce the oven temperature to 190°C (375°F) and bake for a further 25–30 minutes, until the pastry is puffed and deeply golden on the edges, with the frangipane centre slightly puffed.

Cheesecake-flavoured biscuit turnovers (V)

Preheat the oven to 165°C (330°F) fan-forced. Line a baking tray with baking paper. Cut 1 × quantity Pasta frolla dough (right) in half. Roll out into two 60 × 12 cm (24 × 4¾ in) rectangles, about 5 mm (¼ in) thick. Roll between baking paper to stop it sticking. With a short edge facing you, brush the long left-hand side of one strip with an egg wash (see p. 13). On the other long side, using a piping (icing) bag, pipe eight evenly spaced 1 tablespoon portions of your chosen filling – either 1½ quantities Whipped vanilla ricotta (p. 795), or 1 × quantity Cream cheese & ricotta filling (p. 799) – just like making ravioli. Fold the egg-washed side over, pressing gently to seal at the edges, and between the filling. Cut between each mound with a knife or fluted pastry/pasta cutter. Repeat with the other piece of pastry, yielding eight portions from each strip, and sixteen portions in total. Transfer to the baking tray and bake for about 15 minutes, until slightly golden at the edges. Dust with icing (confectioners') sugar as they come out of the oven. These are best served warm on the day of making.

Set aside at room temperature, and serve warm or cooled. The tart is best enjoyed same day, and should not be refrigerated.

Make it different

With other fruits. Other stone fruit will work in this – try sliced nectarines, blood plums or apricots. Strawberries work well, too!

With crème fraîche. While the tart is perfect as is, a dollop of crème fraîche is a marvellous addition.

Pasta frolla (Italian sweet pastry) (V)

Pasta frolla is the classic Italian sweet pastry. It's ideal for a Jam crostata (p. 826), which is the simplest of tarts – and also the first tart I ever baked – as well as Crostata filled with ricotta & quince (p. 826). I now add fine polenta to the dough, which adds textural complexity and gives the pastry a very golden hue once baked. The pastry is easy to make and very forgiving, with a lovely buttery crumb. It's a great pastry to keep on hand in the freezer, so you can whip up a treat in no time at all. **Makes 650 g (1 lb 7 oz)**

260 g (9 oz) plain
  (all-purpose) flour
150 g (5½ oz/⅔ cup) caster
  (superfine) sugar
80 g (2¾ oz) fine polenta

1 teaspoon salt flakes
½ teaspoon baking powder
180 g (6½ oz) unsalted butter,
  diced and chilled
3 egg yolks

1 teaspoon natural vanilla
  extract or paste
zest of 1½ lemons

Combine the flour, sugar, polenta, salt and baking powder in a bowl, then tip onto a clean bench. Top with the butter, then rub in the butter between your fingertips until a sandy crumb – a small lump of butter here and there is okay.

Make a well and add the egg yolks, vanilla and lemon zest. Break the yolks with your fingers and stir into the vanilla. Start pinching in the dough mixture to combine, bringing it together with your fingers, until you have a cohesive dough. This will take a few minutes.

Bring into a ball, then gently knead a couple of times and press into a disc. Wrap in baking paper and refrigerate for 30 minutes before using; it will keep in the fridge for up to 2 days.

When rolling out, use as little flour as possible. This pastry will keep tightly wrapped in the freezer for up to 6 months; thaw the frozen pastry in the fridge for about 4 hours before using.

Jam crostata (v)

While not exactly my first memory, jam crostata features in some foggy food reminiscences. It was made at every family gathering on my father's side, and was the quintessential slice of something nice after a long lunch. Just when you thought you couldn't possibly eat another thing, your aunty would offer you a slice, and it would be hard to say no … As a child, I really didn't appreciate the pastry to jam ratio, but the key with this tart is the buttery pastry with a golden crumb that is dominant over the jam. Delicious dusted liberally with icing sugar and served with a good dollop of cream. **Serves 6–8**

1 × quantity Pasta frolla (p. 825)

400 g (14 oz) jam (such as blackberry, apricot, or

Blood orange & Campari marmalade, (p. 699), chilled

1 egg, beaten with a pinch of salt

80 g (2¾ oz) raw flaked almonds

Staples
FLR, ISGR

Preheat the oven to 180°C (350°F) fan-forced.

Cut one-third of the pastry off and chill. Press the larger piece of pastry into a disc, then gently roll between two pieces of baking paper into an even circle. The aim is to roll out to a 35 cm (13¾ in) circle about 5 mm (¼ in) thick – but to stop it sticking, about halfway through rolling, peel off one piece of paper, dust lightly with flour, then replace the paper. Flip and repeat on the other side, then continue to roll.

Once the dough is the right size, remove the paper and roll up the pastry on the rolling pin to support the weight without tearing the pastry. Unroll gently over a 24 cm (9½ in) loose-based flan (tart) tin, then work the pastry into the tin by pulling the pastry edge back towards the centre of the tart, and gently pushing into the corner to fit snugly. Do this gently all around the tin until the pastry fits neatly. Push the pastry firmly into position all over the tin, leaving the excess to hang over the side. Roll the rolling pin over the top to cut off the excess dough, then chill the pastry case in the fridge for about 15 minutes.

Once chilled, fill the pastry shell with the jam.

Roll the remaining dough out between baking paper, into a circle about 4 mm (¼ in) thick. Cut ribbons of dough about 2 cm (¾ in) wide, then use a palette knife to lay them on an angle across the tart, then repeat on the opposite diagonal to form a lattice. Trim any overhanging dough by pushing down on the edges of the tart to sever, then brush with the egg wash and drop the flaked almonds around the edge.

Bake for about 40 minutes, until the pastry is puffed and golden. Dust heavily with icing (confectioners') sugar and serve. The crostata is great hot, but can also be served cooled. It will keep in an airtight container for 2–3 days at room temperature; do not refrigerate.

Make it different

Jam tarts. (v) The crostata can also be made into 8 cm (3¼ in) tarts; just bake for 20 minutes or so until golden.

Frangipane crostata. (v) Instead of jam, fill the tart with a double quantity of Frangipane (p. 796), studded with chopped chocolate.

Crostata filled with ricotta & quince (v)

Rita Macali and I made a version of this back in the 1990s when we ran a restaurant together as co-head chefs – both occupying a lead role for the first time. We found it hard to keep up with demand for this tart. The jewel-like quince floats in the creamed ricotta, and the buttery sweet pastry is just heavenly with it. We poached the quinces back then, but quince paste is an easy and quite wonderful substitute. Make the Cream cheese & ricotta filling (p. 799), but include 3 eggs in the mixture. Blind-bake a Pasta frolla pastry shell (p. 825) as per the Jam crostata (left) recipe. Fill with the ricotta filling, then top with 300 g (10½ oz) diced quince paste. Lattice the top with the extra pastry as per the crostata recipe, glaze with a beaten egg and sprinkle with 1 tablespoon demerara sugar. Bake in a preheated 150°C (300°F) fan-forced oven for 50 minutes, until golden. Instead of the quince paste, you could use 300 g (10½ oz) poached quinces (see p. 714) or roasted rhubarb (see p. 648), or 250 g (9 oz) blackberries, or 4 sliced figs.

Savoury

Short olive oil pastry Ⓥ Ⓥⓖ

This is one of the simplest pastries you will ever make. It's forgiving, soft, supple and very easy to use once rested. It cooks to a crisp finish with a short bite and golden hue. **Makes enough for 2 × 20 cm (8 in) tarts**

500 g (1 lb 2 oz/3⅓ cups) plain (all-purpose) flour
½ teaspoon salt

80 ml (2½ fl oz/⅓ cup) extra-virgin olive oil
240 ml (8 fl oz) warm water

Blitz the flour and salt in a food processor. Drizzle in the oil while processing, then follow with the warm water. Once a ball forms, tip onto a floured surface and knead briefly into a smooth dough, about 2 minutes. Roll into a ball and wrap in plastic wrap, then rest in the fridge for 1 hour before using.

Gruyère & confit garlic tarts Ⓥ

This tart is so good straight from the oven. Cut it up on a shared serving board, then stand around and eat it there and then – though it's also pretty good cold. Experiment with the cheeses, as a mix is good. A hard sheep's cheese would work, or a little goat's cheese, but the majority should be gruyère or cheddar. **Makes 2 × 20 cm (8 in) tarts**

100 ml (3½ fl oz) extra-virgin olive oil
12 garlic cloves
350 g (12½ oz) gruyère or cheddar, half diced, half grated

¼ teaspoon cayenne pepper, or chilli powder
1 × quantity Short olive oil pastry (above)

Staples
FLR, S&P

Preheat the oven to 200°C (400°F) fan-forced.

In a small saucepan, simmer the oil, garlic and a big pinch of salt over a low heat for 15–20 minutes, until the garlic is soft and caramelised, being careful that it doesn't burn. Cool completely, then strain and reserve the oil.

Divide the rested pastry into four balls. Roll out two of the balls on a lightly floured bench until about 4 mm (¼ in) thick. Evenly divide the diced and grated cheese between the discs, leaving a pastry border to seal with the lids. Top with the garlic, squashed slightly with your fingers, then sprinkle with the cayenne and season with pepper. Roll out the other balls and place on top, pinching the edges together to seal.

Brush the pastry with the garlic oil, season with salt flakes and pierce the top of each with a knife. Bake for 15–20 minutes, until golden.

Use for
Pumpkin & feta pie (p. 631).

Greens, potato & cheese pie with olive oil pastry Ⓥ

Roll the rested Short olive oil pastry (left) out into a large round about 4 mm (¼ in) thick and place on a heavy baking tray. Wilt a bunch of silverbeet or spinach in a little oil for about 10 minutes until tender, then drain off the liquid and chop the greens. Combine with 160 g (5½ oz/1 cup) of diced cooked potato, a beaten egg and a couple of handfuls of grated cheddar along with a handful or two of grated or diced melting cheese, such as mozzarella, fontina or stracchino. Season with salt and pepper to taste, then pile onto the pastry offset from the middle. Fold the pastry over the top, then roll and pinch the edges together to seal into a large half-moon, like a calzone. Cut four 1 cm (½ in) incisions in the top to release steam, then brush all over with egg wash (p. 13). Bake for about 25 minutes at 200°C (400°F) fan-forced until lightly golden.

Pair with
Serve the tarts straight from the oven on a chopping board, with some dressed greens on the side – rocket (arugula), watercress and nasturtium would work well.

Some cornichons or dill pickles (see p. 505) and pickled onions (p. 594) or Pearl onions à la grecque (p. 597) on the side would be a nice touch.

Pile some Salt-roasted onions (see p. 595) tossed in vinegar and chopped soft herbs on top.

Delicious with Leek with walnut & rye skordalia (p. 600).

Pâte brisée (shortcrust pastry) Ⓥ

I use this workhorse shortcrust pastry for pies and tarts, both savoury and sweet – especially when I don't want to introduce more sweetness. The cooked pastry has a textural crunch and is divinely flaky. **Makes 700 g (1 lb 9 oz)**

380 g (13½ oz) plain (all-purpose) flour
1¼ teaspoons fine sea salt
1 teaspoon caster (superfine) sugar

¼ teaspoon baking powder
280 g (10 oz) unsalted butter, diced, at room temperature
50 ml (1¾ fl oz) water

20 ml (¾ fl oz) lemon juice or apple-cider vinegar

Whisk the flour, salt, sugar and baking powder in a large bowl. Rub in the butter and between your fingertips, working until it resembles coarse breadcrumbs. Combine the water and lemon juice and add to the bowl, then bring the mixture together with your hands.

Tip onto a lightly floured bench and knead a couple of times with the heel of your hand, until a smooth dough – don't overwork. Shape into a disc about 3 cm (1¼ in) thick, then wrap in plastic wrap and chill for 1 hour. You can also freeze the pastry for up to 6 months, wrapped tightly in a double layer of plastic wrap.

Once rested, the pastry can be rolled out about 5 mm (¼ in) thick and cut into two 40 cm (15¾ in) rounds to make a galette tart (see p. 650); or rolled out to line a 24 cm (9½ in) pie dish, with enough pastry for a lid. Or, roll about 3 mm (⅛ in) thick to line and blind-bake (see p. 811) two 24 cm (9½ in) tart tins. Or, roll about 2 mm (⅛ in) thick to line and blind-bake mini tart shells or a muffin tray.

Piperade tart Ⓥ

The intensely rustic braise of caramelised capsicum (bell pepper) and onions, laced with paprika, is stunning in a savoury custard tart studded with goat's cheese and enriched with gruyère, with the flaky shortcrust pastry an ideal base.
Serves 6

4 eggs
200 ml (7 fl oz) pouring (single/light) cream
½ × quantity Piperade (p. 465)

23–24 cm (9–9½ in) Pâte brisée tart shell (see above), blind-baked (see p. 811) and still in the tin
80 g (2¾ oz) gruyère, grated

80 g (2¾ oz) marinated goat's feta
Staples
S&P

Preheat the oven to 180°C (350°F) fan-forced.

Crack the eggs into a medium bowl. Season with salt and pepper and beat with a fork. Stir the cream through with the fork to combine but not aerate. Strain into a jug.

Drain off the excess cooking oil from the piperade (use it to dip bread in for a snack, or save for frying eggs in). Spread the piperade over the base of the tart shell. Scatter the gruyère over and crumble the feta on top, in large chunks.

Put the tart on a baking tray and place in the oven, towards the front. Pour the egg mixture into the tart (there should be cheese poking out of the custard), then slide into the middle of the oven. Bake for 20 minutes.

Reduce the oven temperature to 160°C (320°F). Bake for about 15 minutes, until the custard is a little golden on top, with a slight wobble.

Remove from the oven and leave for 5 minutes to set further, then serve hot, warm or cold. The tart will keep covered in the fridge for about 3 days.

Use for

Blind-bake for quiches and savoury tarts, such as a Piperade (below), and savoury pies, such as Chicken, leek & mushroom pie (p. 603).

Blind-bake for sweet Tarts (p. 815) or Apple pie (p. 818).

Fill small tart shells with cream cheese and chives, or horseradish combined with Crema fresca (p. 364). Top with cured or smoked trout or salmon (p. 168).

Fill small tart shells with kingfish or Ocean trout rillettes (p. 174). Top with salmon roe, or chopped egg bound with Mayonnaise (pp. 74–5) and finished with caviar.

Fill small tart shells with Lemon, lime or passionfruit curd (p. 797), top with Italian meringue (p. 807) and scorch with a kitchen blowtorch, or under a very hot oven grill (broiler).

Fill small tart shells with Whipped vanilla ricotta (p. 799) or Crème pâtissière (p. 798) and top with raspberries or strawberries.

Fill small tart shells with Chocolate mousse (p. 782). Top with Sesame brittle (p. 786), or Basic whipped cream (p. 799) and chopped Chocolate gravel (p. 783).

Pair with

Serve with a crisp green salad with French-style vinaigrette (p. 88).

Cream cheese shortcrust pastry ⓥ

This recipe was originally based on a buttery Turkish pastry, but it has developed over time, and I can't recall exactly how far removed it is from those origins. Either way, it's so soft and yielding, rich with a delicate crumb, and a soft rather than crisp finish – perfect for pasties, or to make sublime Böreks (opposite). **Makes about 850 g (1 lb 14 oz)**

500 g (1 lb 2 oz/3⅓ cups) plain (all-purpose) flour

200 g (7 oz) unsalted butter, diced and chilled

125 ml (4 fl oz/½ cup) pure cream (40–42% fat)

100 g (3½ oz) cream cheese

1 egg

1½ tablespoons fine sea salt

1 teaspoon white vinegar

1 teaspoon caster (superfine) sugar

1 teaspoon baking powder

Add all the ingredients to the bowl of an electric stand mixer. Using the paddle attachment, mix on low speed until just forming a dough, about 3 minutes. There will be streaks of butter, but this is what makes the pastry flaky.

(If making by hand, combine the dry ingredients in a bowl, then rub in the butter between your fingertips until a crumb. Add the remaining ingredients and bring together to form a dough.)

Press the pastry into a ball, wrap in plastic wrap and chill for 30 minutes before using. The pastry will keep for 3 days in the fridge, or 1 month in the freezer; thaw in the fridge before using.

Use for

Sausage rolls and pasties, or for savoury tarts when you want a soft, buttery pastry.

Silverbeet & haloumi pies (p. 563).

Böreks with cheese ⓥ

Böreks have become very popular of late, where I live at least, but I must say they do vary somewhat in style. That they are savoury morsels filled with cheese (and sometimes greens) or spiced meat is a constant, but the pastry they are wrapped in varies – from different types of filo, to a softer buttery pastry, to being encased in a bread-like exterior. I lean to the middle option, with a pastry rich with butter, cream and cream cheese my absolute favourite. These are lovely for a snack or for breakfast, and will happily do me for lunch with a leafy salad.
Makes 16

1 × quantity Cream cheese shortcrust pastry (opposite)
1 egg, beaten with a pinch of salt
2 tablespoons nigella seeds
2 tablespoons sesame seeds

Mixed cheese filling
2 garlic cloves, finely sliced
375 g (13 oz) fresh ricotta
200 g (7 oz) firm feta, crumbled
200 g (7 oz) haloumi, grated

1 egg
1½ tablespoons Baharat (p. 6)

Staples
EVOO, FLR

Preheat the oven to 180°C (350°F) fan-forced.

For the filling, fry the garlic in a good splash of oil over a medium heat until just golden, then tip into a bowl. Add the cheeses and egg and combine well. Set aside.

Cut the rested dough in half on a very lightly floured bench. Roll out into rectangles about 20 × 60 cm (8 × 24 in). Cut each in half lengthways. Now cut each strip crossways, into four portions. This should yield a total of sixteen pieces, each about 15 × 10 cm (6 × 4 in).

Brush the short edge of one piece of pastry with the egg wash. Add about 1½ tablespoons of the filling to the middle of the pastry, allowing a 2 cm (¾ in) border from the edges. Sprinkle a pinch of baharat on top. Fold the un-brushed edge over the mixture towards the middle, then fold the other edge over the top of it, to overlap slightly, gently sealing together. Then press the open ends down gently to seal.

Brush the pastry with more egg wash, then sprinkle some nigella and sesame seeds on top. Repeat with all the pastry.

Bake for about 12 minutes, until golden. The pastries can also be frozen at this point, and baked for 20–25 minutes from frozen.

Make it different
With fried sausage. Remove the skins from about four spicy pork and fennel or merguez sausages. Crumble the meat, then fry in a little oil until brown and crisp. Sprinkle over the cheese filling before continuing as per the recipe. You can also use this filling with Lebanese talami bread dough (p. 852).

With greens. Squeeze 300 g (10½ oz) of cooked greens, such as spinach and/or silverbeet (Swiss chard) leaves (seasoned lightly and cooked in oil for 6–8 minutes). Finely chop the cooked greens and combine with the cheese filling along with four sprigs of chopped dill, then proceed as per the recipe. You can also use this filling with Lebanese talami bread dough (p. 852).

Böreks with cheese

Sambouseks Ⓥ

An extremely popular snack right across the Middle East, sambouseks are typically savoury pastries shaped in a half-moon, though not always. They are often filled with cheese, or cheese and greens, or onion and spiced meat (typically lamb, with pine nuts and baharat), though fillings vary from country to country and region to region. The similarity with empanadas and samosas is unmistakable, and their kinship fairly well established, with the Persian version being the elder of the trio. They can be either baked or fried, but I do prefer the latter, with the pastry blistering and bubbling marvellously. I use a little self-raising flour in my pastry, to give it some rise, though it is not a traditional feature. These are lovely hot or cold. **Makes 20**

150 g (5½ oz/1 cup) self-raising flour
150 g (5½ oz/1 cup) plain (all-purpose) flour
1 teaspoon fine sea salt

1 teaspoon caster (superfine) sugar
125 ml (4 fl oz/½ cup) warm water

50 ml (1¾ fl oz) extra-virgin olive oil
1 egg, beaten with a pinch of salt, if baking

Combine the flours, salt and sugar in a bowl. Add the water and oil, and bring together into a dough with your hands. Tip onto a lightly floured bench and knead for about 5 minutes, until soft and smooth. Cover with a tea towel (dish towel) and rest at room temperature for about 1 hour, until pliable.

Set a deep fryer to 170°C (340°F) or preheat the oven to 180°C (350°F) fan-forced. Line a baking tray with baking paper.

Divide the rested dough into 20 pieces, then roll each one out to 10–12 cm (4–4¾ in) diameter circles, about 3 mm (⅛ in) thick.

Add 1 heaped tablespoon of your chosen cooled filling (see opposite) to the middle of the discs. Press the two halves of each circle together, pressing with a fork or your fingers to firmly close. For a more decorative edge, sit the sealed pastry on the straight edge, then starting at one tip, pull the pastry edge up and over your index finger, rolling it over and pressing firmly to seal, creating a rope effect in about 5 mm (¼ in) increments.

Transfer the pastries to the baking tray and chill for 10 minutes.

Deep-fry the pastries in batches for 5 minutes, until golden, then drain. Alternatively, brush with the egg wash and bake for about 10 minutes, until puffed and golden.

The sambouseks are delicious warm from the oven, but will keep in an airtight container at room temperature or 2–3 days.

Lamb & pine nut filling for sambouseks (GF)

My take on a traditional sambousek filling with baharat-spiced lamb, pine nuts, and the sweet tang of pomegranate molasses. **Fills 20 sambouseks**

Pair with

Serve hot or warm, with a minted Labneh (p. 362).

40 g (1½ oz/¼ cup) pine nuts
300 g (10½ oz) minced (ground) lamb or beef

1 onion, diced
2 teaspoons Baharat (p. 6)
1½ tablespoons pomegranate molasses

Staples
EVOO, S&P

Toast the pine nuts in a frying pan over a medium heat to colour slightly, about 5 minutes, then tip into a bowl.

Heat a good splash of oil in the pan and fry the meat for about 5 minutes, until starting to colour slightly. Add a splash more oil and the onion and cook for about 5 minutes to soften. Stir the baharat through. Season with salt, stir in the pine nuts and take off the heat.

Stir in the pomegranate molasses and chill before using.

Cheese, silverbeet & hazelnut filling for sambouseks (V)

Hazelnuts and currants add a charming twist to a classic pairing of wilted greens and feta, with plenty of acidic zip coming from the molasses and lemon juice.
Fills 20 sambouseks

Pair with

Serve with minted Labneh (p. 362) or pomegranate molasses drizzled over at the last minute.

400 g (14 oz) silverbeet (Swiss chard) leaves, no stem, finely shredded
1 onion, very finely diced
1 garlic clove, finely chopped
150 g (5½ oz) firm feta, crumbled

80 g (2¾ oz) toasted hazelnuts, chopped
40 g (1½ oz) currants, covered with boiling water for 10 minutes, then drained
1 tablespoon pomegranate molasses

2 teaspoons Baharat (p. 6)
juice of ½ lemon

Staples
EVOO, S&P

Heat a good splash of oil in a large frying pan over a high heat. Add the silverbeet, season with salt and pepper and fry for about 10–15 minutes, until well cooked. Tip into a colander and squeeze to drain well, then chop reasonably finely. You should have about 300 g (10½ oz) silverbeet.

In a frying pan, heat a few more tablespoons of oil over a medium heat. Cook the onion and garlic until softened, about 4 minutes. Stir the silverbeet through to combine, then tip into a large bowl.

Crumble the feta into the bowl, then add the remaining ingredients. Combine well and chill before using.

Also see

Super seed loaf **376**

Pasties **469–70**

Carrot, chervil & gruyère loaf **472–3**

Silverbeet & haloumi pies **563**

Lemonia's pumpkin & feta pie with olive oil pastry **631**

Böreks with cheese **831**

Sambouseks **832**

Savoury baking & breads

Savoury baking & breads

A meal is not a meal without bread, my father always said. He still does. Hand-sliced bread was on the table for every meal, and in my lunchbox, too, bookending slices of salami and some young pecorino or the like, with a few olives and some slices of fennel accompanying.

That was seen as exotic when I was growing up, with jam sandwiches or ones sprinkled with hundreds-and-thousands the popular choice in the playground. It's quite frightening when you think about it: a white bread sandwich filled with margarine and confectionery for a school lunch. Vegemite was popular, too, but I didn't try that until much later, with my father having an unusually passionate hatred for it – though Vegemite does have that effect on people. When I got to it, I loved it.

I wouldn't say the bread in my house growing up was overly sophisticated, mind you – a Vienna loaf or pasta dura, or similar. Sometimes my grandmother Grace would make what she called a fricassee. The original from Provence is somewhat different, flat and often cut to look like an ear of wheat – but her fougasse was dough fried in a hotdog bun shape that would get stuffed with marinated tuna with boiled egg and a Carrot paste salad (p. 473). Grace would also use the same dough to bake Pissaladière (p. 599).

Those were the basic breads of my childhood, along with pitta bread, grissini, a hard Italian biscuit known as Taralli (p. 842), and stale bread toasted to make crostini to eat with pecorino, or be smeared with tuna paste and topped with roasted peppers – usually alongside small bowls of olives, chunks of fennel, sliced ripe tomatoes, boiled eggs, chilli salami, cold crumbed schnitzel, sliced cucumbers, braised broad beans … we ate well, most of the time.

We certainly didn't have access to the extraordinary wealth of sourdough options that are available today, along with the equally extraordinary wealth of faux sourdough on the market. Yes, sourdough has sadly become a marketing term and can be misused at no legal peril. A little sourdough culture added to a loaf essentially baked with commercial yeast can be called sourdough, but it's not. Real sourdough is fermented with wild yeast and bacteria, with very positive implications for your digestion and gut health, along with the joyous flavour, crust and crumb structure that is not replicable with commercial yeasts.

Supermarkets are full of this faux sourdough, but don't be sucked in. Real sourdough will just contain flour, water and salt, along with any seeds or flavourings that may be included. No yeast, no enzymes, no lecithin, no xanthan gum, no vegetable or soy oil … The sourdough starter may have employed things like fruit or yoghurt to get the culture moving, but once active, it'll just be flour, water and salt for the loaf. That's it. Buy the real stuff, or even better, make it yourself (see p. 847) – it's hard to express how much of a satisfying process it is, and you'll have the best-tasting bread that will only cost you a few coins.

Although I had a fairly decent start, my repertoire of bread has grown somewhat since I started cooking professionally, with all sorts of yeasted loaves and buns, along with sourdough options, being added to the catalogue – not to mention pretzels, savoury scones, oatcakes, crispbreads, crackers, savoury pastries … and pizza! We can't forget pizza, with my former pizzeria, mr. wolf, edging towards its second decade.

As with sweet baking, some recipes require a bit of accuracy, with the ratios for doughs needing to be fairly exact to produce reliable results, and ambient temperature and humidity sometimes skewing the process. But once you have cooked these recipes a couple of times, you'll get a feel for them, and know if you need a little dusting of flour to get the right smooth texture in a dough, or a little more liquid to loosen; you'll know to come back to a proving dough a bit earlier in a warm kitchen, and to relax a little longer when it's cold.

This chapter is devoted to many of my favourite breads, crackers and other savoury recipes, and you'll find plenty of other ideas recipes dotted throughout the book, from tarts to pies and savoury pastries. During a normal year, it would be typical for all of these to be made in my house at one point or another, with some built for special feasts, and others very much everyday staples.

Rye crackers **ⓥ**

These extremely crisp and crunchy crackers are made with a high proportion of rye flour, which is stunning with the earthy anise tones of caraway seeds. These are the crackers I always like to have on hand for entertaining, for snacking, or for grazing lunches. You may need to adjust the cooking time depending on the rye flour you use, as they can vary quite meaningfully in respect to how much liquid they absorb. You can also make this without a pasta machine, just by using a rolling pin, but the results will be much less consistent.

Makes 20–40, depending on size

14 g (½ oz/4 teaspoons) dried yeast

250 ml (8½ fl oz/1 cup) warm full-cream (whole) milk (37–40°C/98–105°F)

2 tablespoons golden syrup, or light treacle

150 g (5½ oz/1½ cups) rye flour

170 g (6 oz) plain (all-purpose) flour

1 teaspoon caraway seeds

1 teaspoon fine sea salt

Staples
FLR

Special equipment
Pasta machine

Pair with

Top with chopped egg or sliced ham.

Serve with cheese and dips.

Great as an antipasto with cured meats.

Chicken liver parfait (p. 233) and Beetroot jelly (p. 421).

Ocean trout rillettes (p. 174) and salmon caviar.

Gravlax (p. 169) with cream cheese and chives.

Pork rillettes (p. 330) with plum relish (see p. 725).

Ham hock & leek terrine (p. 328).

Whisk the yeast and milk in a small bowl to combine. Set aside for 5 minutes for the yeast to activate and foam, then whisk in the golden syrup to combine.

Sift the flours into the bowl of an electric stand mixer. Add the caraway seeds, salt and yeast mixture. Using the dough hook, mix on medium speed until a sticky, wet dough forms, about 5 minutes. Cover and set aside somewhere warm for 2 hours, until almost doubled in size.

Line four trays with baking paper (if you don't have four trays, then use what you have and rotate the trays in the oven).

Tip the dough onto a well-floured bench and shape into a rectangle. Cut into three, then roll out with a rolling pin.

Set the pasta machine to its widest setting. Dust the dough with flour, then roll each piece through twice.

Turn down the dial and roll through twice again, dusting with flour as needed. Repeat until about 3 mm (⅛ in) thick.

Cut the dough into 5 × 8 cm (2 × 3¼ in) pieces, or any shape or size you like, and transfer to the baking trays. Cover with a tea towel (dish towel) and rest for 15 minutes.

Preheat the oven to 165°C (330°F) fan-forced.

Brush with a little water and bake for about 15 minutes, until the crackers have shrunk slightly and are gently golden at the edges. Once cooked, cool on the trays to firm up.

If you want them extra crisp, turn the oven off and leave the door open for 5 minutes before returning the trays to cool completely in the closed oven.

The crackers will keep in an airtight container for up to 1 month.

Top to bottom: Spiced seed crackers and Rye crackers

Spiced seed crackers ⓖⓕ ⓥ

Pair with

Perfect with fresh goat's curd.

Smear with avocado, season with salt flakes and plenty of black pepper, and squeeze on some lemon.

Serve with Steak tartare (p. 279).

Serve alongside tuna tartare or Ocean trout rillettes (p. 174).

Almond skordalia (p. 373).

Top with Tomato confit (p. 656).

Crumble over a salad.

Crumble over poached eggs with avocado.

Cured kingfish with Crema fresca & lime (p. 168).

These crackers are wonderful to have on hand. Delicious as is, or with some butter and a sprinkling of salt, they are also marvellous with a beef (see p. 279) or kingfish tartare (see p. 166), cured fish, egg and avocado. **Makes about 60**

500 g (1 lb 2 oz) linseeds (flax seeds)

100 ml (3½ fl oz) tamari or Enhanced soy sauce (p. 101)

100 g (3½ oz/⅔ cup) sesame seeds

100 g (3½ oz/¾ cup) pepitas (pumpkin seeds)

1½ tablespoons fennel seeds, roughly ground

2 teaspoons salt flakes

1½ teaspoons ground black pepper

2 teaspoons curry powder

2 teaspoons chilli powder

1 teaspoon celery seeds

Add the linseeds and tamari to a large bowl. Cover with water by about 4 cm (1½ in), then stand overnight.

The next day, preheat the oven to 110°C (230°F). Line three baking trays with baking paper.

The linseeds will have swollen and be a little gel-like. Add the remaining ingredients and combine well.

Spread the mixture onto the baking trays and dehydrate in the oven for 2–3 hours, until crisp and firm, flipping the crackers over about halfway through. Remove from the oven and cool on the trays.

Once cooled, break into shards. The crackers will keep in an airtight container for 2–3 weeks.

Lavoche-style olive oil crackers Ⓥ

The savoury glaze of egg yolk, soy sauce and salt, with or without seeds, ups the umami content of these crisp crackers. Roll them out thinly for elegantly fine crackers, or leave them on the chunky side. **Makes 30**

400 g (14 oz/2⅔ cups) plain (all-purpose) flour
1 teaspoon fine sea salt
200 ml (7 fl oz) warm water
100 ml (3½ fl oz) extra-virgin olive oil

Rich soy glaze
2 egg yolks

3½ tablespoons water
1 teaspoon light soy sauce
½ teaspoon salt flakes

Optional toppings
2 tablespoons sesame seeds
2 tablespoons nigella seeds
1 tablespoon fennel seeds

Staples
FLR, S&P

Special equipment
Pasta machine

Pair with
Serve with a selection of cheeses.

Labneh (p. 362).

Taramasalata (p. 182).

Chicken liver parfait (p. 233).

Kingfish kibbeh nayyeh (p. 166).

Steak tartare (p. 279).

Ocean trout rillettes (p. 174).

Gravlax (p. 169) with cream cheese and chives.

Pork rillettes (p. 330) with plum relish (see p. 725).

Ham hock & leek terrine (p. 328).

Combine the flour and salt in a bowl. Add the water and oil, then bring together into a dough with your hands. Tip onto a clean bench and knead for about 5 minutes, until soft and smooth. Cover with a tea towel (dish towel) and rest at room temperature for 30 minutes, until pliable.

Preheat the oven to 165°C (330°F) fan-forced. Line four baking trays with baking paper. If you don't have four baking trays, leave half the dough in the fridge and roll out as needed after each batch is baked.

Divide the rested dough into 30 pieces, then roll out with a little flour into rectangles. Set the pasta machine to its widest setting. Dust the dough lightly, then roll each piece through twice.

Turn down the dial and roll through twice again, dusting with flour as needed. If you want a thicker and more robust cracker, pass through the machine until 3–4 mm (⅛–¼ in) thick. For a fine and crisp cracker, repeat until you reach the second-thinnest setting.

Cut the pieces into whatever size you like, making sure you can fit them on the baking trays efficiently – there will be a lot, and space will be at a premium. Once the pieces are laid on the trays, don't try to move them, as the dough will be sticky and will stretch.

In a small bowl, beat the glaze ingredients with a fork, then carefully brush over the dough. Top with fennel seeds or sesame seeds, try a mix of sesame and nigella seeds, or simply leave as is.

Bake for 8–10 minutes for thinner crackers, adding 5–6 minutes for thicker crackers, until golden and crisp.

Cool on the trays, before storing in an airtight container; they will keep fresh for up to a week.

Oatcake crackers Ⓥ

Blue cheese or sharp, earthy cheddars are just made for oatcakes. Their rich mealy quality, gentle hum of sweetness and friable, buttery crumb are built to tackle the most assertive of cheeses, harmonising effortlessly without ever being swamped. **Makes 16**

340 g (12 oz) plain (all-purpose) flour
60 g (2 oz) rolled oats, plus 2 tablespoons for topping
60 g (2 oz) raw sugar

2 teaspoons baking powder
1 teaspoon fine sea salt
150 g (5½ oz) unsalted butter, softened at room temperature

20 ml (¾ fl oz) full-cream (whole) milk

Staples
FLR, S&P

Pair with
Fruit or quince paste or Roasted pears (p. 711) with strongly flavoured cheeses, such as blue cheese and sharp cheddar.

In a food processor, blitz the dry ingredients for 5 seconds. Add the butter and blitz for about 20 seconds, until a crumb consistency. Add the milk and blitz again for about 30 seconds to bring together into a soft dough. Transfer to a bowl, cover and rest for 20 minutes.

Preheat the oven to 160°C (320°F) fan-forced. Line a baking tray with baking paper.

Roll out the dough on a lightly floured bench until about 5 mm (¼ in) thick. Cut out circles with an 8 cm (3¼ in) cutter and transfer to the baking tray. Sprinkle with the remaining oats and some salt flakes.

Bake for about 15 minutes, until slightly golden. Set aside to cool completely on the trays.

The oatcakes will keep in an airtight container for up to 2 weeks.

Pretzels ⓥ

I'm sure this recipe may not satisfy all traditionalists, but in my mind these are very close to the real thing. The classic shape is ideal, but if it doesn't work out, don't stress too much, as they'll taste just as good. **Makes 12–14**

Pair with

Serve as is, or with butter, whipped cream cheese and chives, or Taramasalata (p. 182).

A chopped egg and mayonnaise salad.

Beer.

Gorgonzola with port-steeped muscatels & oatcakes ⓥ

The combination of sharp cheese, crumbly oatcakes and muscatels plumped in port is just sublime. If blue cheese is not for you, a sharp cheddar or aged goat's cheese works well, too. To serve 4, add 2 bunches dried muscatels to a saucepan. Add 125 ml (4 fl oz/½ cup) port or Madeira and 55 g (2 oz/¼ cup) caster (superfine) sugar. Boil over a medium heat for 2 minutes, then set aside to cool. Serve the muscatels in syrup with Oatcake crackers (opposite) and 200 g (7 oz) gorgonzola picante, at room temperature.

250 ml (8½ fl oz/1 cup) full cream (whole) milk, warmed
250 ml (8½ fl oz/1 cup) warm water
75 g (2½ oz) soft brown sugar
10 g (¼ oz) dried yeast
675 g (1½ lb) baker's flour

2 teaspoons fine sea salt
60 g (2 oz/¼ cup) unsalted butter, diced, at room temperature
3 tablespoons coarse sea salt or salt flakes, or fennel, poppy or sesame seeds

Poaching bath
150 g (5½ oz) bicarbonate of soda (baking soda)
1.2 litres (41 fl oz) water

Staples
EVOO, FLR

Add the milk, water, sugar and yeast to the bowl of an electric stand mixer, stir through and stand for 5 minutes for the yeast to activate and foam. Add the flour and salt and start mixing on low speed with the dough hook. After about 3 minutes, the dough will start coming together. Add the butter and mix on medium speed until smooth and elastic, about 6 minutes.

Tip out and shape into a ball, then cover in a lightly oiled bowl and set aside to prove for 1½–2 hours, until doubled in size.

Tip the dough onto a very lightly floured surface and knock the air out gently. With a dough cutter or knife, divide into 12 portions. Roll one portion into a finger-thick snake about 70 cm (28 in) long, then curve into a U-shape, with the opening away from you. Take the ends and bring them back towards you, crossing over each other in the middle, then twisting once and laying each end over the base of the U, to form a rough love heart, tucking the ends under a little to tidy up.

Arrange on two lined baking trays and chill, uncovered, for 30 minutes, to set the skin before poaching.

Preheat the oven to 220°C (430°F) fan-forced.

For the bath, add the water and bicarbonate of soda to a wide saucepan over a medium heat until just under a simmer. In batches of three, poach the pretzels for 20 seconds on each side, then carefully remove and place back on the trays.

Score the top of each pretzel twice with a sharp knife, then sprinkle with the salt or seeds. Bake for 10–12 minutes, until deep brown.

The pretzels are best consumed on the day of baking, but can be stored in an airtight container for up to 3 days; warm through or toast if desired.

Taralli ⓥ ⓥⓖ

I find the fennel seed, pepper and salt combination in these Italian crackers particularly engaging, and they're salty enough to make you a little thirsty, making them a great aperitivo snack, without being too filling to ruin your appetite for the meal ahead. **Makes 50–60**

80 ml (2½ fl oz/⅓ cup) warm water
7 g (¼ oz/ 2 teaspoons) dried yeast
60 ml (2 fl oz/¼ cup) extra-virgin olive oil
60 ml (2 fl oz/¼ cup) white wine

200 g (7 oz/1⅓ cups) plain (all-purpose) flour
100 g (3½ oz) fine semolina
1 tablespoon fennel seeds, plus 3 teaspoons for topping
1½ teaspoons fine sea salt

1 teaspoon ground black pepper
½ teaspoon garlic powder
1 tablespoon bicarbonate of soda (baking soda)

Staples
FLR, S&P

Whisk the water and yeast in a small bowl. Set aside for 5 minutes for the yeast to activate and foam, then whisk in the oil and wine.

Combine the flour, semolina, fennel seeds, salt, pepper and garlic powder in a large bowl, then add the yeast mixture. Mix with your hands until it comes together into a rough dough, then tip onto a lightly floured bench and knead for a few minutes, until a smooth and supple dough.

Cover and set aside for about 1 hour, until doubled in size.

Once proved, divide the dough into ten pieces on a lightly floured bench. Roll each into a 1 cm (½ in) thick sausage, then cut each into four. Coil each piece into a ring, pressing the ends together. Place on lined baking trays, cover with a slightly damp tea towel and set aside for 30 minutes.

Preheat the oven to 160°C (320°F) fan-forced.

Add the bicarbonate of soda to a large wide saucepan of simmering water. In batches, poach the taralli for 2 minutes, until swollen. Lift out with a skimmer or large slotted spoon, allowing the water to drain off before laying on the baking trays.

Sprinkle the taralli with the remaining fennel seeds and season with salt flakes and pepper.

Bake for 30 minutes, then turn off the heat and leave in the oven to fully cool and crisp up.

The taralli will keep in an airtight container for up to 2 weeks.

Simit/koulouri ⓥ

This simple bread is a favourite breakfast street food of Turkey and Greece. Whether in Turkey (simit) or Greece (koulouri), the bread is very similar, though I have seen the twisted version more commonly in Greece. There is an intense sesame flavour, with a good chewiness, and a hint of sweetness from being dunked in grape molasses or, more commonly in Greece, a sugar syrup. **Makes 10**

375 ml (12½ fl oz/1½ cups) warm water
2 teaspoons caster (superfine) sugar
7 g (¼ oz/ 2 teaspoons) dried yeast
3 teaspoons pouring (single/light) cream

1 tablespoon extra-virgin olive oil
475 g (1 lb 1 oz) baker's flour
2 teaspoons sea salt
For coating
100 ml (3½ fl oz) grape molasses, or 1½ tablespoons soft brown sugar

100 ml (3½ fl oz) warm water
150 g (5½ oz/1 cup) sesame seeds

Staples
FLR

Pair with

At Hero we call these Greek bagels and serve them with Taramasalata (p. 182), but they pair perfectly with any dip (pp. 374, 420, 519, 632).

Marinated olives (p. 591) and/ or other meze.

Eat for breakfast with Labneh (p. 362).

Add the water, sugar and yeast to the bowl of an electric stand mixer, stir to combine, then stand for 5 minutes for the yeast to activate and foam. Add the cream and oil and stir to combine. Add the flour and salt, then mix on medium speed with the dough hook to form a smooth dough, about 5 minutes.

Tip out and shape into a ball. Cover in the stand mixer bowl and set aside to prove for 1½–2 hours, until doubled in size.

Preheat the oven to 230°C (445°F) fan-forced. Line two baking trays with baking paper.

For the coating, combine the grape molasses and water in a shallow bowl.

Tip the dough onto a lightly floured bench and divide into ten pieces. Roll each into a rough ball and allow to rest, uncovered, for 5 minutes.

Take the first ball you rolled and cut it in half. Roll each piece into two strips about 30 cm (12 in) long, then twist the strips together to intertwine. Press the ends together to join them into a twisted circle of dough – or, for a more classic Greek version, roll the balls into 30 cm (12 in) snakes (they can be fatter along one edge, as pictured) and overlap and press the ends together to make rings.

Dip the shaped dough into the molasses bath, then shake off the excess liquid and coat with the sesame seeds.

Place on the baking trays and bake for 15–20 minutes, until golden, rotating the trays halfway through. These are best enjoyed as fresh as possible, though a reheat the next day may be attempted.

Top to bottom: Potato bread (p. 844) and Simit/koulouri

Potato bread

This is a modern interpretation of focaccia Pugliese, and is based on a tried and true recipe I've been baking for decades. It's very dear to my heart, as my grandmother Grace was quite taken with it when I first made it – endorsements like that matter, with her being a wonderful cook and food lover, and, well, being my grandmother. This focaccia is extremely light and fluffy due to the double rise, so for the best results be patient and don't rush it. The potato makes this a very sticky dough, but this is what results in a crispy, golden crust with a fluffy but strong honeycomb texture throughout. Persevere, and keep your hands oiled when handling the dough, as the temptation to add flour will be strong. Resist it! The other key, as with making gnocchi, is to ensure the potato mash is hot when the dough is made. **Serves 8–10**

300 g (10½ oz) waxy or all-purpose potatoes (such as desiree or jersey royal), peeled and cut into 4 cm (1½ in) chunks
500 g (1 lb 2 oz/3⅓ cups) plain (all-purpose) flour
2 teaspoons fine sea salt
375 ml (12½ fl oz/1½ cups) warm water

7 g (¼ oz/ 2 teaspoons) dried yeast
Topping
250 g (9 oz) yellow or red cherry tomatoes, as small as possible, halved
80 g (2¾ oz/⅔ cup) pitted black olives, torn

1 tablespoon dried Greek oregano (rigani)
1 tablespoon red-wine vinegar
1 teaspoon caster (superfine) sugar
5 quality anchovies, split lengthways

Staples
EVOO, S&P

Cook the potatoes from cold in salted water for about 20 minutes, until they fall apart when tested with a fork. Drain well, then pass through a ricer or food mill. Weigh out exactly 250 g (9 oz) of mash for the focaccia and immediately start making the dough, as the mash can't cool down too much.

Add the hot mash, flour and salt to a large bowl and combine loosely with your hands, then tip into the bowl of an electric stand mixer.

Combine the water and yeast, then add to the stand mixer. Mix with the dough hook on low speed for 2 minutes, then increase the speed to medium–high and mix for about 6 minutes, until the dough is sticky and shiny.

Scrape the dough off the hook into the bowl. Cover with plastic wrap to seal, then set aside to prove for about 1 hour, until doubled in size.

Preheat the oven to 190°C (375°F) fan-forced. Take a 40 × 60 cm (15¾ × 24 in) baking tray, about 5 cm (2 in) deep, and line with baking paper.

Tip the dough into the baking tray. Coat your hands in oil, as the dough is very sticky, and stretch the dough to fit the tray as evenly as possible, then coat well with oil to cover. Cover with plastic wrap to seal, then set aside for about 45 minutes, until the dough almost fills the height of the tray.

Once the dough has risen, make indentations with your fingers randomly across the top, then lay on the anchovies and pour the tomato mixture over.

Bake for about 40 minutes, until well puffed and golden. Set aside to cool, before slicing while warm. If you want the crust extra crispy, leave for about 15 minutes, remove the cooked focaccia from the tray and bake on a rack in the oven for 6 minutes, then cool again before slicing.

The focaccia is best enjoyed fresh, but will keep for a few days in an airtight container on the bench, and comes up well when toasted or grilled, or flashed in a hot oven.

Basil & tomato topping for focaccia 🟢 Ⓥ 🟢

This is a wonderful topping when you have a glut of ripe tomatoes. Chop 3 large tomatoes into 5 mm (¼ in) dice and dress with 3 tablespoons extra-virgin olive oil. Season with salt and pepper and a teaspoon of sugar, then sit for 10 minutes. Stir through 12 finely shredded large basil leaves just before pouring over the focaccia (right), then baking.

Anchovy, tomato & basil topping for focaccia 🟢

Take 250 g (9 oz) yellow or red cherry tomatoes, as small as possible, and halve them. Add to a bowl with 80 g (2¾ oz/⅔ cup) torn pitted black olives, 1 tablespoon dried Greek oregano (rigani), 1½ tablespoon red-wine vinegar, 3 tablespoons extra-virgin olive oil and 1 teaspoon caster (superfine) sugar. Season with salt and pepper and toss to combine. Set aside for at least 30 minutes before using. Lay on 5 quality anchovies, split lengthways, then pour over the tomato mixture and bake.

This is a traditional Tuscan way of making focaccia with wine grapes from the yearly harvest. I like to use a mix of dried and fresh grapes, making the flavours a little more layered and intense. Soak 200 g (7 oz) dried muscatel grapes or sultanas (golden raisins) in hot water for 1 hour. Cut 200 g (7 oz) fresh small red or green grapes in half. Toss in a medium bowl with the drained muscatels, 1 tablespoon crushed fennel seeds or anise seeds, 1 tablespoon chopped rosemary leaves and 1 teaspoon salt flakes. On the second rise of the focaccia (right), push your fingers deep into the dough, then sprinkle with the grape mixture and 2 tablespoons caster (superfine) sugar. After 20 minutes of baking, tip up the tray and pour off and save any excess juice to brush on the finished focaccia. Serve with gorgonzola, Parmigiano Reggiano, aged pecorino or a Sardinian-style aged sheep's milk cheese, and dessert wine.

Slow-rise focaccia Ⓥ

You can turn this focaccia around quite promptly if needed – but it's *so* much better if you slow the ferment down in the fridge. The flavour improves and the texture is much better, with larger pockets of air, and longer and stronger structural fibres, rather than the cake-like, friable quality you get after a quick rise. Anointing the dough with cream before baking creates a richly flavoured and stunningly golden crust. It is not essential – but please try it at some point. Keep this plain, top with rosemary, or add olives or onions for a little more flavour. **Makes 1 tray of deep focaccia**

800 g (1 lb 12 oz) unbleached baker's flour
15 g (½ oz) fine sea salt
7 g (¼ oz/ 2 teaspoons) dried yeast
680 ml (23 fl oz) water
100 ml (3½ fl oz) extra-virgin olive oil

1 tablespoon honey
150 ml (5 fl oz) pouring (single/light) cream (optional)

Optional flavourings
200 g (7 oz) soft-fleshed black olives, pitted and chopped

2 rosemary sprigs, leaves stripped
1 red onion, finely sliced

Staples
EVOO, S&P

Add the flour, salt and yeast to the bowl of an electric stand mixer. Using the dough hook, mix on low speed to combine, then add the water, oil and honey. Once it starts to come together, add the olives (if using) and turn the speed to medium. Mix for about 10 minutes to a smooth, wet dough. Rest at room temperature for 30 minutes, then chill.

Transfer to a large oiled bowl or container, then cover and refrigerate overnight. (For baking on the same day, use warm water and prove in a warm spot for about 1 hour, until doubled.)

Take a deep baking tray, measuring about 30 cm × 45 cm (12 in × 18 in), and line with baking paper, then coat the paper with oil. Tip the dough in and flatten out gently to fill the tray, being careful not to push all the air out. Set aside to prove for about 1 hour, until the dough is puffed and springs back when touched.

Preheat the oven to 240°C (430°F) fan-forced.

Gently make indentations all over the dough with your fingers. For the simplest focaccia, drizzle oil over to coat and sprinkle with salt flakes – or scatter on some rosemary or onion slices as well, then oil and season. For a more deluxe version, finish by pouring the cream over before drizzling with oil and seasoning with salt.

Bake for 15 minutes, then reduce the oven temperature to 200°C (465°F) and bake for about 15 minutes, until golden.

Remove from the tray and cool on a rack for 10 minutes before slicing.

The focaccia is best enjoyed fresh, but will keep for a few days in an airtight container on the bench, and comes up well when toasted or grilled.

Make it different
Flatbread-style focaccia. Ⓥ Line two baking trays instead of one, and divide the dough between the two trays. Bake for 12 minutes, then reduce the oven temperature to 200°C (400°F) and bake for about 5 minutes, until golden.

Slow-rise focaccia

Classic dinner knot rolls Ⓥ Ⓥ🄶

I recently found this recipe lurking in the back of a Gustav Klimt notebook from my days at Tansy's some decades ago, early in my career. We made these rolls daily, along with a wholemeal (whole-wheat) loaf. If we were lucky, there were rolls left at the end of the night, and supper would be one of them split open and doused in French vinaigrette, then jammed full of mixed leaves – and not much else. But I was pretty happy with that. This recipe calls for bread improver, though it's not strictly necessary; it's a vestige from the original recipe, which I'm trying to be faithful to the memory of. Bread improver is basically a mix of yeast and enzymes that aid the dough's rising, and yields an extra soft and fluffy crumb, which is one of the joys of these dinner rolls. **Makes 20**

14 g (½ oz/4 teaspoons) dried yeast
1½ teaspoons bread improver
½ teaspoon ground ginger
½ teaspoon caster (superfine) sugar

625 ml (21 fl oz/2½ cups) warm water
1 kg (2 lb 3 oz) unbleached baker's flour
50 ml (1¾ fl oz) extra-virgin olive oil
20 g (¾ oz) fine sea salt

1 egg, beaten with a pinch of salt
2 tablespoons poppy seeds
2 tablespoons sesame seeds

Staples
S&P

Add the yeast, bread improver, ginger and sugar to a bowl. Whisk in 125 ml (4 fl oz/½ cup) of the water, then set aside for 5 minutes for the yeast to activate and foam.

Tip the yeast mixture into the bowl of an electric stand mixer with the remaining water, half the flour and all the oil. Using the dough hook, mix on low speed for 3 minutes, into a wet dough. Set aside for 15 minutes.

Once rested, add the remaining flour and the salt, then mix on low speed for about 6 minutes, until a smooth soft dough. Tip out of the bowl and knead twice, then return to the bowl and cover with a damp tea towel (dish towel). Set aside in a warm place to prove for about 45 minutes, until the dough doubles in size.

Halve the dough. Cut each half into ten pieces and cover with a damp tea towel. Take one piece and roll with your palms into a 28–30 cm (11–12 in) long snake. Tie the dough into a simple knot by passing one end over the other side of the dough, then thread it back through the loop. Fold both ends under the knot, pinching them together to fasten on the underside, then place on a lined baking tray. Repeat for all pieces.

Cover with slightly damp tea towels and set aside to prove for about 30 minutes, until the dough puffs up, with any gaps in the knots filled in.

Preheat the oven to 230°C (445°F) fan-forced.

Gently brush the risen rolls with the egg wash, then sprinkle with the poppy and sesame seeds and some salt flakes. Bake for about 18 minutes, until puffed and deeply golden. Cool a little, before serving warm.

These rolls are best the same day. Store leftovers in a sealed bag for a filled roll the next day; they can also be warmed in a moderate oven. You can also par-bake the rolls for 10 minutes, then cool and freeze. They will bake from frozen in about 10 minutes.

Sourdough bread Ⓥ

I have the pleasure of having some extremely good bakers in my life. My close friend Daniel Chirico and Tony Dench, my brother-in-law, are two of this country's finest sourdough bakers, world-class artisans. So, I have always been surrounded by exceptional bread, and baking it myself always seemed like less of an imperative – so many other things to cook! But I cannot tell you how unusually good it felt to make my first sourdough loaf from a starter that I had nurtured myself.

It's quite a relationship you build with that starter, and the magic that happens in the oven with just flour, water and salt is positively alchemical. Tucking into that first loaf – and each one subsequently, to be honest – with the appreciation of crust, crumb and flavour is a wondrous thing. But perhaps because of those humble beginnings, and the extraordinary transformation, sourdough baking seems shrouded in mystery, like some unfathomable skill. It's not. Sure, perfecting the craft is something else, but being able to bake beautiful, flavoursome loaves is within everybody's reach – absolutely everyone's.

The other positive about sourdough bread is that it is easier to digest, with gluten being broken down during the natural fermentation. The culture also acts as a prebiotic, feeding good bacteria in your gut. Naturally, if you have a gluten intolerance, it will be entirely individual whether or not you can stomach sourdough bread, although those loaves made with longer ferments are the most likely to be agreeable.

Aptly named, the starter (or 'mother') is where it all begins. The starter culture is the centre of the process for each and every loaf, and it needs to be maintained in good health. Essentially a colony of ambient yeast and active lactic bacteria, it needs to be fed with flour and water and carefully nurtured to begin with. But once established, it is not difficult to manage, and can be kept refrigerated to slow down the fermentation, meaning it doesn't need to be fed as frequently.

Much is said about starters, with their flavours varying from place to place, depending on local populations of microbes, and also those from the flour used. I have made more or less identical starters at the same time, yet they fermented differently, smelt different, and baked different loaves. The differences were subtle, but they were real. I can only put this down to slightly varied colonies of yeast and bacteria, whose populations multiplied in different ways. It's part of the charm, and both loaves were delicious.

It's important to note that you need to use or discard half or more of the starter each time you feed it. This can be hard to do when beginning, as it does feel wasteful – but if you feed it with less than what is in the jar, there won't be enough food for all the microbes, and the ferment will become stressed and can start producing off-putting aromas and become excessively sour. An established and healthy culture will have a sour but fruity aroma, often with a stone fruit character. If the starter (or levain, see p. 849) has any unpleasant or overly acetic characters, discard most of it and feed what's left to get it back on track.

Once the starter is active – meaning that it has fed on and fermented the flour you added to it (converting simple sugars into lactic acid, acetic acid and carbon dioxide, amongst other things) – you are ready to make your loaf. First, a portion of starter is used to make the levain, which is the basis of the dough, providing an active colony of microbes to ferment the flour and weave its magic. The biggest mistake made when starting to bake sourdough is not having a properly active starter and/or levain, which results in flatter loaves with less flavour. So, take your time, and get that right.

The dough doesn't actually require kneading. Rather, it just undergoes a process of folding and resting over 3 hours or so, which takes a few seconds of labour every 30 minutes. In fact, this is very much the theme with making sourdough, where there is not that much work required, but it needs your attention, and you need to plan ahead.

Sourdough bread

Once stretched and folded, then shaped and rested, you can bake the dough on the same day – but resting in the fridge overnight or longer will build more flavour and a better structure. Again, it's about planning. Sourdough is not for the impatient.

Once ready to bake, you need to crank your oven to its full capacity, 250°C (480°F), with a heavy cast-iron pot in it. A camping stove does the trick, though it's best not to use your favourite Le Creuset, as it will suffer a little over time; a second-hand or older one is ideal. You can also bake in a preheated cast-iron skillet, though the sealed environment within a lidded cooking pot provides the best rise and crust, with the steam generated building the glassiness of the crust. (If using a skillet or the like, a tray of boiling water on the bottom shelf will help improve the crust.)

Scoring the top of the loaf will help it split open evenly as it rises, releasing steam, rather than exploding at the weakest points without rising properly. Once dropped in the pot, the blast of heat in the first 20 minutes or so of baking will expand the gas produced by the fermentation and give the bread its final shape. Another 20–30 minutes is then needed to finish cooking and create a crisp, caramelised crust.

The type and quality of flour will naturally have a large impact on the flavour, and though any flour will work, a generic one will produce a generic result. I buy the best flour I can find, with it ideally freshly milled. Baker's flour is the starting point, with a high protein content, but unbleached flour is vastly better, and organic is always my preference. I find that unbleached organic flour ferments more effectively – presumably as those useful microbes haven't been stripped away through chemical farming methods and/or processing. Its taste and texture is also vastly better, and the nutritional value markedly higher. I also always include some rye flour in my loaves, even white loaves. It contributes a soft plushness to the texture, boosts flavour, and tends to help the bread keep for longer. Just note that if you decide to play with the amount of rye, it does absorb more water, so you may need to add a little more of it to the recipe.

It's important to use filtered water, as chlorine can kill or retard the fermentation, offing the good bacteria along with the bad. You can boil tap water in a saucepan, then leave to cool, which should remove most of the chlorine, but chloramines (formed when chlorine and ammonia are present) are often used to disinfect mains water, and these are a lot more stubborn to remove. How much of an issue this is depends on where you live, and the way your mains water is treated. I have found a quality domestic water filter does the job, or genuine spring water (not the tap water branded as spring water). However, you don't want purified/distilled water, as the minerals in water also affect the finished loaf. Without the minerals, you won't achieve the quality of crust or textural tension that is so delightful in sourdough.

It is also best to weigh everything – including water – to achieve consistent results. Flours will vary in volume, so cups are not a good measure. If you're going the extra yard to mill your own flour, or buying from someone who does, the flour will be light and fluffy, whereas a bag of commercial flour that has settled will be quite compacted, throwing volume measures wildly off.

The final ingredient is salt, and it's important to use a quality one. Truth be told, you can use basic table salt, and it will be, well, salty. But unprocessed salt from a good source has plenty of essential trace elements and minerals, which only enhance the nutritional content of the bread.

It's just flour, water and salt, after all, and there's no reason to skimp.

Making the mother/starter

150 g (5½ oz) filtered water (tap water is chlorinated and can kill the ferment), plus extra to feed the starter

40 g (1½ oz) organic unbleached baker's flour, plus extra to feed the starter

40 g (1½ oz) rye flour, plus extra to feed the starter
20 g (¾ oz) plain yoghurt
10 raisins

I generally begin with the water at about 20°C (68°F), but it's not necessary to be precise – a warm, though not hot, environment will encourage fermentation.

Combine the starter ingredients in a large jar and set aside at room temperature out of direct sunlight. Some advocate leaving the lid sitting loosely on top, while others leave it off to pick up ambient microbes. Either way, there will be enough microbes on the flour, and in the air when you mix it, not to mention the raisins and yoghurt, to kick off the ferment. I tend to leave the lid off during the day and put it on overnight. There's no science to that; it's just what I do – tuck it in for the night, I guess. (You can also make a starter with equal amounts of water and flour only, but the above is what I have had the most success with.)

After 48 hours, the mixture should start bubbling and smell slightly sour, or like ripe fruit, and have tiny little bubbles around the sides or across the top. If not, just leave it another day – at a cooler room temperature it will simply take longer.

On day three or four, the mixture will have separated and look grey, especially around the raisins, but this is fine. Fish the raisins out and feed the culture with 40 g (1½ oz) baker's flour, 40 g (1½ oz) rye flour and 80 g (2¾ oz) warm filtered water. I have found using a chopstick is a good way to fully incorporate the flour. Set aside at room temperature for another 24 hours.

By day four or five, the mixture should be frothing a little, with some surface bubbles, and a slightly sweet and sour aroma. Discard three-quarters of the mixture, then feed with 100 g (3½ oz) baker's flour and 100 g (3½ oz) warm filtered water, mixing in to fully incorporate. Set aside at room temperature for another 24 hours.

On day five or six, repeat the discarding and feeding, then set aside again at room temperature for 24 hours. The starter should now be active, with bubbles forming, a sweet and sour smell, and a little creamy in colour.

On day six or seven, remove about 50 g (1¾ oz) of the starter to make the levain. The levain is the basis for baking, while the residual in the jar is the starter, which you can maintain indefinitely.

Maintaining the starter

Once enough starter (50 g/1¾ oz) has been removed to make the levain, discard half of what's left in the jar and feed with 80 g (2¾ oz) baker's flour and 80 g (2¾ oz) lukewarm filtered water, put the lid on and keep in the fridge. If baking regularly, you can feed the starter as you use it; otherwise discard half and feed again every few days. Because of the lower temperature in the fridge, the starter will ferment slowly and can be fed less rigorously, even weekly. If you are a very regular baker, you can leave the starter at room temperature and it will be very active and ready to go all the time.

If the starter is well-established and refrigerated, only real neglect (or heavily chlorinated water) will kill it. Even if it looks a little sad, with water separating out and an acetic (vinegary) aroma, if you empty the jar, then feed it, there are usually enough active microbes left behind in the jar to get the starter going again. If it doesn't restart, you'll need to begin again.

A back-up option is to freeze a small portion of the starter, then simply thaw and feed to restart.

Preparing to bake – feeding the levain

Feed the levain with 100 g (3½ oz) baker's flour and 100 g (3½ oz) warm water, then put the lid on and set aside at room temperature for 12 hours. This levain is enough to make one loaf, based on the recipes that follow – but adjust the quantity based on your needs.

The aim is for the levain to double in size within this time, which will depend on the strength of the starter, the flour used and the ambient temperature. (To judge this, you can pop a mark or rubber band on the jar once you've fed the levain.)

Don't rush this stage, as you need the starter nice and active to bake properly. If it doesn't double, discard half and feed again. You can also now feed in six-hour intervals to accelerate this process. A young starter can take a few days to become properly active, but once established, your levain should be active after the first feed.

Once the levain doubles and is laced with bubbles, you're ready to bake. You can also test whether it is ready by dropping a tablespoon into a bowl of water – if it's ready, it will immediately float. If it sinks, it is not ready and you will need to feed it again.

Weigh out 200 g (7 oz) of the levain to be precise.

Baking

There are myriad recipes for sourdough baking, using all manner of flours, methods and shaping, to make everything from buns, to loaves, to pancakes ... and with your starter active, you're ready to attempt any and all of them. That's a rabbit hole for another book, but my aim is to get you moving and to equip you with the basic skills. The recipes below are for two loaves that are excellent all-rounders: a basic white loaf, with a little rye; and a wholemeal (whole-wheat) and rye loaf. I include some rye in the white loaf as it softens the texture and adds to the flavour; a white loaf can be a little brittle in texture and lacking in flavour otherwise. The method for both loaves is the same.

White country loaf Ⓥ
200 g (7 oz) active levain
320 g (11½ oz) filtered water, ideally at
   25°C (77°F)
400 g (14 oz) unbleached baker's flour
100 g (3½ oz) rye flour
18 g (¾ oz) fine sea salt

Wholemeal & rye loaf Ⓥ
200 g (7 oz) active levain
420 g (15 oz) filtered water, ideally at
   25°C (77°F)
360 g (12½ oz) unbleached baker's flour
140 g (5 oz) wholemeal (whole-wheat) flour
100 g (3½ oz) rye flour
18 g (¾ oz) fine sea salt

Combine the levain and water in a large bowl. Disperse well with a spatula or your hands; it won't completely combine, so don't be too fussy. Add the flours and combine with a spoon or spatula until the flour has been absorbed. The dough will be quite rough and shaggy. Cover the bowl with a tea towel (dish towel) and set aside for 20–30 minutes. This process is called autolysis, and it allows the flour to hydrate more effectively. Autolysis also activates enzymes that help to provide sugars for the ferment, as well as make the dough more elastic. Not every baker does this, but I'd recommend not skipping this resting step, as I believe it delivers a welcome chewiness to the loaf.

Once rested, scatter the salt over the top of the dough, then mix in by pinching and squeezing until absorbed. The dough will start to come together into a more even mass. Finish by taking one edge of the dough and pulling it up and outwards, folding it back over the mass. Repeat this to stretch and fold from the four compass points. Cover with a tea towel and set aside at room temperature and rest for 30 minutes.

Now repeat the stretching and folding, then rest again. Do this every 30 minutes, over a total time of 3½ hours. The dough will become smoother and it will start to feel puffy. If the dough isn't smoothing out as much as you'd like, just add a few more stretch and folds. The ambient room temperature will affect this process, so if the conditions are cold, you may need to let the dough sit at room temperature for another hour or so without folding until it becomes more active, or find a warmer place for it.

Pair with

It's bread, so naturally use it as you normally would – but I do love sourdough warm from the oven with plenty of good butter and flakes of salt, or dunked into peppery olive oil.

Or serve with oil, chunks of Parmigiano Reggiano and young raw broad beans.

It also grills beautifully, for then rubbing with a garlic clove and drizzling with oil to serve with soup or a fish stew, or top with good anchovies and a sprinkling of fresh thyme.

Top grilled slices with Taramasalata (p. 182) and salmon roe.

Spread with fresh ricotta and dust with chilli powder.

Top with smashed broad beans and peas (see p. 432) and drape with shaved jamón.

Top with roasted capsicums (see p. 463) and dot with soft goat's cheese. Cut into fingers and grill, then wrap while hot with finely sliced Lardo (p. 326), guanciale or prosciutto, then drizzle with oil, grind over some pepper and eat immediately.

Serve with Piperade (p. 465).

Liberally dust a baker's banneton – or a 25 cm (10 in) mixing bowl lined with a tea towel – with flour, to stop the loaf sticking. A mix of rice flour or rye flour and wholemeal (whole-wheat) flour works especially well here, but you can use whatever you have on hand.

Tip the dough out of the bowl, lightly flour the top, then flip onto the floured side. Pull one edge out and fold it towards the centre of the mass, then repeat for the other side to just overlap. Rotate and repeat on the open edges, then roll the ball towards you to flip it over, with the smooth side facing up. Use a dough scraper to turn the dough by running the scraper along the bench until it makes contact with the loaf, then dragging the dough away from you and to the left. Repeat this process so that the base catches slightly on the bench. As you turn, it will create surface tension across the dough. Do this a few times to tighten the dough into a smooth, even round. You will get used to this process as you get a feel for it, and you can use a little flour to dust if it's a little sticky – but do so sparingly.

Sit for 20 minutes on the bench, then repeat this process, finishing by picking up the shaped dough from underneath with both hands, and gently flipping into the bowl or banneton, with the seam side facing up. Fold the tea towel over the exposed dough, gently tucking it in to fully cover but not restrict its expansion.

The loaf can now be proved at room temperature for 2½–3 hours before baking – but for a more developed and complex flavour, which I much prefer, prove the dough in the refrigerator for 12–24 hours. As the fridge is a very dry environment, ensure the dough is well covered, or it can dry out (a reused light plastic bag, with the tea towel over the top, works well for this). If making two loaves, you can bake one on the day, and one the day after.

When ready to bake, preheat the oven to 250°C (480°F) fan-forced. Preheat a cast-iron pot with the lid on for at least 20 minutes. If the dough has been refrigerated, remove from the fridge for 20 minutes before baking.

Once properly heated, remove the pot from the oven. Spread some flour or rice flour over the · exposed dough so that it doesn't stick, then place a small chopping board over the top of the bowl and invert the loaf onto the board, lifting off the tea towel and bowl.

Using a very sharp knife, razor blade or scoring lame, quickly score four lines in the top to make a large square. You can experiment with other patterns, such as a cross, or slash in stripes – you just need to make room for the dough to expand, or the loaf will split.

Lift the lid off the pot, then slide in the loaf, guiding it in with a hand on top. If you need to centre the loaf better, just shake the pot slightly (wearing oven mitts!) to move around. (You can skip the chopping board and just drop the loaf in directly, then score, but the pot is super-hot, the loaf not terribly easy to score once in, and you can knock the air out if you're too rough.)

Immediately cover with the lid, pop in the oven and bake for 20 minutes.

Remove the lid and bake for about 30 minutes (adding 5–10 minutes for the larger wholemeal loaf), until the crust is deeply coloured. You can take the colour quite far, until deeply caramelised, which just adds more flavour and texture.

Once cooked, remove from the oven and lift the loaf out of the pot with a large spatula or kitchen spoon. Cool on a rack for 45 minutes before slicing.

The loaf will feel relatively light for its size, and the base will sound hollow when tapped. Don't be tempted to cut into it too early, as the crumb will come out a little wet. Still, there is nothing like a fresh loaf of sourdough with a gentle warmth to it – enough to ease some butter out of its solid state. This is a heavenly moment, trust me.

Lebanese talami bread with spiced tomato topping ⓥ

Rich with olive oil, this yeasted bread is so beautifully soft. It has a tantalising tang that goes with pretty much everything as part of a meze feast – or with the tomato topping, it is a snack unto itself. Or, you can simply brush the dough with oil and sprinkle with sesame or nigella seeds before baking, making it a lovely mop for dips and the like. The dough can also be filled before baking, encasing cooked greens and cheese, and eaten piping hot. **Makes 15–20**

21 g (¾ oz/6 teaspoons)
   dried yeast
1 tablespoon caster
   (superfine) sugar
620 ml (21 fl oz) warm water
250 ml (8½ fl oz/1 cup)
   extra-virgin olive oil
930 g (2 lb 2½ oz) plain
   (all-purpose) flour
50 g (1¾ oz) milk powder
1½ tablespoons fine sea salt

Turkish tomato & sesame topping
1 white onion, finely diced
5 large tomatoes, coarsely
   grated
juice of ½ lemon
100 ml (3½ fl oz) extra-virgin
   olive oil
50 g (1¾ oz/⅓ cup) sesame
   seeds

2 heaped tablespoons biber
   salçasi, or chilli paste,
   to taste (optional)
1½ teaspoons citric acid
2 teaspoons ground cumin
2 teaspoons cumin seeds
2 teaspoons ground black
   pepper

Staples
S&P

Whisk the yeast, sugar and 125 ml (4 fl oz/½ cup) of the water in a bowl. Set aside for 5 minutes for the yeast to activate and foam, then whisk in the remaining water and the oil.

Add the flour, milk powder and salt to the bowl of an electric stand mixer, then add the yeast mixture. Using the dough hook, mix on medium–high speed for 5–8 minutes, until smooth and elastic.

Transfer to a clean bowl, then cover with a damp tea towel (dish towel) and set aside to prove for about 30 minutes, until doubled in size.

Meanwhile, for the topping, season the onion with salt and drain in a sieve for 10 minutes, then squeeze out any excess moisture. Add to a bowl with the other ingredients and combine well.

Divide the rested dough into 15–20 even pieces. Roll into balls and place on lined baking trays, smooth side up. Prove for 15–20 minutes, until slightly puffed.

Preheat the oven to 240°C (465°F) fan-forced.

Roll the balls into rounds about 1 cm (½ in) thick. Rest for 2 minutes on the trays, then dent a little with your fingers and top with the tomato mixture.

Bake for 5–7 minutes, until the bottom and the edges are golden, being careful not to overbake, as they will dry out quickly. These are best the same day, but can be refrigerated for up to 2 days and reheated or toasted.

Make it different
Lebanese talami bread topped with za'atar. ⓥ Rather than the tomato topping, drizzle with oil and top with Za'atar (p. 33), or sprinkle with sesame seeds, nigella seeds and salt flakes. Serve warm.

Cheese-filled Lebanese talami bread. ⓥ Add 2 tablespoons of Mixed cheese filling (p. 831) to each rolled round, then fold over into half-moons and press to seal. Bake for 8–10 minutes, until golden and puffed.

Lebanese talami bread with cheese & greens. ⓥ Roll each piece of dough into a rough square, then add 1½ tablespoons of the Mixed cheese filling with greens (p. 831). Bring the corners in towards the middle, then press together along the edges to form a parcel, with the centre a little open so you can see the filling. Bake for 8–10 minutes, until golden and puffed.

Pair with
Pair with dips (pp. 182, 374, 420, 519, 632), marinated olives and/or other meze, or eat for breakfast with Labneh (p. 362).

Moroccan semolina flatbreads ⓥ ⓋⒼ

Dissolve 25 g (1 oz) dried yeast in 650 ml (22 fl oz) warm water and set aside for 5 minutes for the yeast to activate and foam. In a large bowl, combine 500 g (1 lb 2 oz/3⅓ cups) plain (all-purpose) flour, 400 g (14 oz) fine semolina and 1 tablespoon salt flakes. Make a well, then gradually incorporate the yeasted water with your fingers, into a rough, sticky dough. Tip onto a lightly floured bench and knead for about 10 minutes, until smooth and elastic. If the dough is too sticky, flour your hands lightly and keep kneading until you get the right consistency. Divide the dough into ten pieces. Take one piece and fold the rough edges into the middle to make a ball, then roll on the bench with your palm into a smooth, even ball. Repeat for all the dough, lining up in the order they were shaped. Dust the bench with a little semolina, then pat the first ball you rolled into a round, about 15 cm (6 in) in diameter. Lift onto a tea towel (dish towel), then dust with more semolina. Repeat with all the dough. Set aside, uncovered, for about 30 minutes, until doubled in thickness. Once rested, heat two dry frying pans over a medium heat. Carefully transfer a pitta to each and cook for 4–5 minutes on one side, then flip and cook for another 4–5 minutes, until coloured on both sides and a little hollow-sounding when tapped. Stack on top of each other to cool before using. Best eaten fresh with dips, Lamb koftas (p. 309), Falafel (p. 432) or the like. Makes 8.

Soft pitta bread for wraps, souvlaki or dips ⓥ

These are a fluffy style of pitta, and my favourite for serving freshly cooked with Slow-roasted lamb shoulder (p. 304). Their beauty is that they're light and soft, but not too thick, making them perfect to wrap around souvlaki, while yielding easily to the bite, rather than having the papery tug of some commercial pitta breads. They're also great for dips. **Makes 12–18**

10 g (¼ oz) dried yeast
2 teaspoons caster
 (superfine) sugar
300 ml (10 fl oz) warm water
100 g (3½ oz) plain yoghurt

40 ml (1¼ fl oz) extra-virgin
 olive oil
600 g (1 lb 5 oz/4 cups) plain
 (all-purpose) flour, plus
 extra for dusting

2 teaspoons fine sea salt
3 tablespoons fine semolina

Staples
EVOO

Whisk the yeast, sugar and 50 ml (1¾ fl oz) of the water in a large bowl. Set aside for 5 minutes for the yeast to activate and foam.

Whisk the yoghurt, remaining water and oil into the yeast mixture, then mix in the flour and salt. Bring the dough together into a ball, then tip onto a lightly floured bench and knead for about 10 minutes, until smooth and elastic. (You can also use an electric stand mixer fitted with the dough hook, mixing on medium speed for 5 minutes.)

Cover the dough with a tea towel (dish towel) and set aside to prove for about 1½ hours, until doubled in size.

Tip the dough onto a lightly floured bench. Divide into twelve pieces for large pitta breads, or eighteen pieces for smaller ones. Shape into balls, then roll out to 5 mm (¼ in) thick. Dust with the semolina and transfer to lined baking trays to rest for 10 minutes.

When ready to cook, heat a dry frying pan over a medium–high heat, or heat the barbecue on high. Prick the dough rounds all over and cook for about 2 minutes on each side, until puffed and charred. Stack the cooked pittas, keeping them warm by wrapping in paper and foil or tea towels.

Store any leftovers in an airtight container or tightly wrapped. They can be reheated in the oven, or flashed on both sides in a pan or on a barbecue grill. Once cooked, these can also be frozen. To reheat, wrap in foil and place in a hot oven for 10 minutes, before flashing over a barbecue grill or in a hot pan.

Pair with

These are my favourite with a Slow-roasted lamb shoulder (p. 304) served with Tzatziki (p. 507) and a chopped salad or tabouleh (see p. 419).

Serve with dips (pp. 182, 374, 420, 519, 632) and/or other meze.

Easy souvlaki (p. 312).

Falafel (p. 432).

A fried or grilled fish wrap, with chilli salsa and salad.

Puffed pitta pockets ⓥ Ⓥⓖ

These balloon in a super-hot oven in no time, making classic double-sided pitta breads, perfect for splitting and filling with falafel or lamb and salad, or anything else that takes your fancy. They're also great for dipping, whether freshly baked, or cut into triangles and toasted in the oven until crisp. **Makes 12**

14 g (½ oz/4 teaspoons)
 dried yeast
1 tablespoon caster
 (superfine) sugar
500 ml (17 fl oz/2 cups)
 warm water
40 ml (1¼ fl oz) extra-virgin
 olive oil

600 g (1 lb 5 oz/4 cups) plain
 (all-purpose) flour
120 g (4½ oz) wholemeal
 (whole-wheat) flour
1½ teaspoons fine sea salt

Staples
EVOO

Pair with

Split and fill with Falafel (p. 432) and Tabouleh (p. 419).

Split and fill with Slow-roasted lamb (p. 304) and salad.

Use as a wrap for lunches.

Serve with dips (pp. 182, 374, 420, 519, 632) and/or other meze.

Saganaki (p. 510) and olives.

Chargrilled octopus (p. 218).

Lamb & date salad (p. 314) with fried pitta bread (see p. 854).

Whisk the yeast, sugar and water in a bowl. Set aside for 5 minutes for the yeast to activate and foam, then whisk in the oil.

Add the flours and salt to the bowl of an electric stand mixer. Using the dough hook, mix on low speed while pouring in the yeast mixture. Once starting to form a rough dough, increase the speed to medium–high and mix for 7 minutes, until smooth and elastic but still a little tacky.

Turn out and form into a ball. Transfer to an oiled bowl, cover with a tea towel (dish towel) and set aside to prove for about 2 hours, until doubled in size. (Alternatively, prove overnight in the fridge, which will develop more flavour and a better structure.)

Preheat the oven to 250°C (480°F) fan-forced, with a heavy baking tray on the middle shelf.

Divide the dough into 12 pieces and roll into balls. Working with four at a time, roll the balls out on squares of baking paper to about 12 cm (4¾ in) in diameter – the dough is sticky, and will be hard to transfer otherwise.

Slide the rounds, still on the paper, onto the tray. Bake for about 5 minutes, until puffed and lightly golden. Stack the cooked pittas, keeping them warm by wrapping in paper and foil or tea towels.

Store any leftovers in an airtight container, or tightly wrapped. They can be reheated in the oven, or flashed on both sides on a barbecue grill.

Naan Ⓥ

Pair with

Any subcontinental curry.

Lamb rogan josh (p. 317).

Lamb & eggplant karahi curry (p. 318).

Butter chicken (p. 248).

Egg, tomato & spinach curry (p. 359).

With some exceptions, subcontinental curries are incomplete without bread. Tearing off a piece of freshly cooked naan and using it to pincer up some curry and rice, dripping in raita, is a mighty, mighty thing. Making your own naan is not such a stretch. A special-occasion thing, perhaps – but if you've gone to the trouble of making a few curries with sides ... well, it would be remiss not to make your own naan as well. **Makes 12**

14 g (½ oz/4 teaspoons) dried yeast	200 ml (7 fl oz) warm water	80 g (2¾ oz) unsalted butter, melted
2 teaspoons caster (superfine) sugar	200 ml (7 fl oz) full-cream (whole) milk, warmed	600 g (1 lb 5 oz/4 cups) plain (all-purpose) flour
	200 g (7 oz) plain yoghurt	2 teaspoons fine sea salt

Whisk the yeast, sugar, water and milk in a bowl. Set aside for 5 minutes for the yeast to activate and foam, then whisk in the yoghurt and butter.

Add the flour to a large bowl and gradually stir in the liquid, until you have a rough dough. Tip onto a lightly floured bench and knead for about 5 minutes, until soft and pliable, then put back in the bowl, cover with a tea towel (dish towel) and set aside for about 1 hour, to prove and double in size.

Once proved, tip the dough out and divide into six pieces. Roll and stretch each into a rough teardrop shape.

Heat a cast-iron pan over a high heat for about 6 minutes, until extremely hot, or preheat the barbecue on high. Add a piece of dough to the pan or barbecue. It should puff pretty much immediately. Cook for 2 minutes, then flip (it should be a little scorched) and cook for 2–3 minutes on the other side.

Stack in a tea towel as they're cooked to keep warm, and serve as soon as possible.

Make it different
These are also delicious brushed with oil or warmed ghee loaded with finely chopped garlic, then sprinkled with salt flakes.

Pizza base Ⓥ ⓋⒼ

This pizza base is chewy and light with good flex, supports toppings well, and I've found it works very well even in a standard domestic oven. It's important to let the dough ferment slowly, which creates excellent structure with large pockets of air and a pleasing chew. The flavour will also be markedly better. You can make it more quickly, but please try not to. Also, using a high-quality unbleached baker's flour adds even more to the flavour of the base, which is such a critical part of a good pizza, and not simply a support for cheese and toppings. The other key element is heat. You need your oven as hot as it can go, and it needs to preheat for a long time. Also, be aware that the heat drops when you open the oven, so once one pizza is baked, bring the oven back up to temperature. Ideally, using a pizza stone is best, as it will conduct more heat directly through the pizza base. Just remember they need to preheat with the oven. You can also preheat a baking tray, then slide the pizza on top. It will need to be a heavy-duty tray, though, as most domestic trays will buckle. This quantity will feed a crowd, but you can halve the recipe if cooking for fewer, or if you just want to make some grissini. **Makes 8 × 28 cm (11 in) round pizzas, or two 30 × 40 cm (12 × 15¾ in) pizza trays along with 10 grissini**

800 g (1 lb 12 oz) unbleached
  baker's flour
140 g (5 oz) fine semolina
14 g (½ oz/4 teaspoons)
  dried yeast

585 ml (20 fl oz) water
12 g (⅙ oz) fine sea salt
60 ml (2 fl oz/¼ cup)
  extra-virgin olive oil

Staples
FLR

Whisk the flour, semolina and yeast in a bowl.

Add the water to the bowl of an electric stand mixer, then the flour mixture. Using the dough hook, combine on low speed for 5 minutes to form a dough. Add the salt and mix thoroughly, about 3 minutes. Pour in the oil and mix for 3 minutes, then turn the speed up to medium and mix for 10 minutes, until a smooth, elastic dough.

Transfer the dough to a large container with a lid (the dough will double, so make sure there's enough space). Rest for 2 hours, then refrigerate for 12 hours for the best result, but you will get a good return after 12 hours, too. (If really pressed for time, you could make the dough with the water at around 22°C/75°F, then prove on the bench for 2 hours – but please try to plan ahead, as the result is vastly better. The latter method can be used if making grissini, but halve the dough.)

Once proved, portion the dough into 190 g (6½ oz) pieces for 28 cm (11 in) pizzas, or cut off 200 g (7 oz) to make grissini, then halve the remainder if baking in two 30 × 40 cm (12 × 15¾ in) trays (you can, of course, use larger trays and use all the dough).

Cover the dough and set aside to puff and relax at room temperature for 30 minutes before pushing and stretching. If you rush this step, you can lose the integrity of the dough structure.

Set up a small bowl of flour on the bench. Dip one of the portions in the flour to coat, then coax it into the desired shape on the bench by pressing with your fingers to stretch it out, leaving the edges a little thicker. Don't use a rolling pin, as you don't want to press all the air from the dough or to flatten the edges. Just gently stretch into a 28 cm (11 in) round in a round pizza tray or on a paddle/board, or stretch into shape on the larger trays as evenly as possible.

The pizzas are now ready to top and bake. Ideally, have a pizza stone preheated in a 250°C (480°F) fan-forced oven, then slide the pizza onto the stone and bake for 8–10 minutes, until the crust is coloured. Because the dough has a high hydration level, it can be hard to slide off a tray, so you can bake the round pizzas on the pizza trays for 4–5 minutes, then slide onto the stone to finish, or cook entirely on the tray, which will take 10–12 minutes. The larger trays will take about 25 minutes.

Grissini Ⓥ ⓋⒼ

Cut the pizza dough (left) into 20 g (¾ oz) pieces. With the middle of both palms lying flat, fingers curled up slightly, roll them with a little flour or semolina to form long even snakes about 40 cm (15¾ in) long, and less than 5 mm (¼ in) thick. Lay crossways on a semolina-dusted baking tray, about 1.5 cm (½ in) apart, with the ends overhanging both sides of the tray. Trim the ends so that they fit the tray. (You can reroll the scraps if you like, or you can roll them shorter and not trim, but I prefer the aesthetics of them being more even, with enough natural variation in their shaping.) Bake at 170°C (340°F) fan-forced for about 12 minutes, until lightly coloured. Drizzle with oil, season with salt and pepper, then bake for another 5 minutes, until crisp. Set aside to cool. These are best fresh, but can be reheated the next day to crisp again for 3 minutes at 170°C (340°F).

Pizza 'number 1'

This was the first pizza listed at mr. wolf, rather grandly replacing the ubiquitous garlic pizza/bread in a way I find particularly engaging. Spread 3 tablespoons Green tapenade (p. 590), or Mezzanotte paste (p. 588) over the pizza base, then scatter with 40 g (1½ oz) shredded mozzarella. Arrange 60 g (2 oz) torn fresh mozzarella on top, followed by 20 g (¾ oz) finely grated parmesan. Season with salt and pepper and bake. Once cooked, dollop on 2 tablespoons ricotta. Dress 2 handfuls rocket (arugula) with the juice of ½ lemon and 1 tablespoon extra-virgin olive oil, season, then crown the pizza and serve immediately.

Coeliac pizza base (GF) (V) (VG)

It's a challenge to create a similarly crusted pizza base with no gluten, and you can't simulate the gloriously puffed structure of a yeasted dough, but this dough has a lovely strong chewiness and holds its toppings well. To make about twelve 28 cm (11 in) bases, preheat the oven to 180°C (350°F) fan-forced. Heat a pizza stone or several baking trays in the oven. Add 1 kg (2 lb 3 oz) gluten-free self-raising flour, 1.5 litres (51 fl oz/6 cups) water, 100 ml (3½ fl oz) extra-virgin olive oil, 2 tablespoons caster (superfine) sugar, 1 tablespoon fine sea salt and 2 teaspoons xanthan gum to the bowl of an electric stand mixer. Using a K-beater or paddle, mix on medium speed for 5 minutes, until well combined; it will be more of a batter than a dough. Spoon about 210 g (7½ oz) of batter onto a piece of baking paper at least 30 cm (12 in) square, then push out with your fingers to almost 28 cm (11 in). Top with another piece of paper. Press down gently to even out and spread a little, to a 28 cm (11 in) diameter. In batches, transfer the pizza bases to the pizza stone or baking trays and bake for 10 minutes, then cool before using; stack the bases in their papers until all are cooked. The pizza bases are now ready to top and bake again for serving. You can wrap and freeze the pizza bases for up to 3 months, or keep them in the fridge for up to 2 weeks. When ready to top and bake, ideally have a pizza stone preheated in a 250°C (480°F) fan-forced oven, then slide the pizza onto the hot stone and bake for 10–12 minutes, until the topping is cooked; the base won't colour like a traditional pizza base.

Pizza margherita (V)

Pizza margherita is the starting point – and, for some, the end point: the peak of pizza perfection. **Tops 1 × 28 cm (11 in) pizza**

1 × quantity Pizza base (opposite)
2 tablespoons Simple tomato sugo (p. 116)
¼ teaspoon dried oregano

40 g (1½ oz) mozzarella, shredded
60 g (2 oz) buffalo or cow's milk mozzarella
4 basil leaves

Staples
EVOO, S&P

Spread the pizza base with a little oil, then the sugo. Scatter on the oregano and shredded mozzarella. Tear the fresh mozzarella and arrange on top, then drizzle with a little more oil and season with salt and pepper. Bake as per the pizza base instructions (see opposite). Tear the basil over before serving.

Make it different

Salami pizza. Add twelve slices of spicy sopressa or calabrese-style salami after the mozzarella.

Napolitana. Add a handful of pitted black olives and a few anchovies.

Pizza diavolo. Omit the shredded mozzarella, and scatter on four anchovies. Tear the fresh mozzarella in three and drop it on, then scatter with ten black pitted and torn olives, 2 teaspoons small capers, a finely sliced red bird's eye chilli (or two pinches of chilli flakes), four roasted garlic cloves (see p. 66), skins removed, and 20 g (¾ oz) finely grated parmesan. Finish with the oil, salt and pepper. Omit the basil.

Pizza bianco with prosciutto & rocket. Skip the sugo and oregano. Sprinkle 20 g (¾ oz) finely grated parmesan on top of the fresh mozzarella. Once cooked, top with four slices of prosciutto. Dress two handfuls of rocket (arugula) with the juice of half a lemon and a tablespoon of oil. Season. Omit the basil.

Pizza bianco with sausage, roasted cauliflower, chilli & cherry tomatoes. Skip the sugo and oregano, and scatter five roasted cauliflower florets (see p. 476) and chunks of a pork and fennel sausage (skin removed) over the top of the shredded mozzarella. After the fresh mozzarella, add 20 g (¾ oz) finely grated parmesan, slices of half a red bird's eye chilli and three halved cherry tomatoes. Season with the salt and pepper, but omit the drizzle of oil and the basil at the end.

Gorgonzola, fig & walnut pizza. (V) After the mozzarella, sprinkle over 20 g (¾ oz) finely grated parmesan. Cut one and a half ripe figs into 5 mm (¼ in) slices and arrange over the top. Break 20 g (¾ oz) walnuts in your hands and drop on top, followed by 60 g (2 oz) gorgonzola and the leaves from two thyme sprigs. Season with the salt and pepper, but omit the drizzle of oil at the end.

Pumpkin, anchovy & ricotta pizza

The sweet roasted pumpkin here works particularly well with the dried oregano, rich cheese and salty foil of the anchovies. **Tops 1 × 28 cm (11 in) pizza**

4 × 5 mm (¼ in) thick kent or jap pumpkin (winter squash) slices, skin on
1 × quantity Pizza base (opposite)
40 g (1½ oz) mozzarella, shredded

60 g (2 oz) buffalo or cow's milk mozzarella
20 g (¾ oz) parmesan, finely grated
3 anchovies

2 tablespoons ricotta cheese
1 teaspoon dried oregano

Staples
EVOO, S&P

Preheat the oven to 220°C (430°F) fan-forced. Line a baking tray with baking paper.

Lay the pumpkin on the baking tray, drizzle with oil and season with salt and pepper. Bake for about 8 minutes, until tender but not really coloured.

Spread a little oil over the pizza base, then scatter with the shredded mozzarella. Lay the pumpkin on top, then tear the fresh mozzarella and arrange on top, followed by the parmesan. Lay on the anchovies, scatter the ricotta and oregano over, season with salt and pepper and bake.

Spiced corn & manchego loaf Ⓥ

This corn-studded cheese loaf has an extra-golden crumb from the polenta, with the goat's curd keeping it moist. If you can't find manchego cheese, cheddar or gruyère will work just as well. The muffins can be served warm from the oven or cold, but I like them best oven-warm with cold salted butter or goat's curd.

Serves 6–8

160 g (5½ oz) manchego, grated
1 tablespoon dried oregano
3 cooked corn cobs, kernels stripped
150 g (5½ oz) goat's curd
320 ml (11 fl oz) full-cream (whole) milk
2 eggs

125 ml (4 fl oz/½ cup) extra-virgin olive oil
400 g (14 oz/2⅔ cups) self-raising flour
½ teaspoon baking powder
100 g (3½ oz) instant polenta
3 teaspoons ground cumin
1 heaped teaspoon salt flakes

6 fresh jalapeño chillies, or long green chillies, sliced
3 teaspoons smoked paprika

Staples
S&P

Special equipment
Muffin tray, paper cases

Preheat the oven to 180°C (350°F) fan-forced. Line a 26 cm (10¼ in) springform cake tin, or a loaf (bar) tin.

In a bowl, combine the manchego and oregano with most of the corn kernels, reserving some kernels for garnishing.

Add the goat's curd, milk, egg and oil to another bowl and combine well.

In a large bowl, combine the flour, baking powder, polenta, cumin and salt, making a well in the centre. Pour in the milk mixture and bring together with a spoon. Stir the corn mixture through until combined.

Spoon into the tin and top with some of the chilli and reserved corn kernels, pressing them in lightly. Sprinkle with the paprika and bake for 30–35 minutes, until the loaf is golden and a skewer inserted in the middle comes out clean.

Cool slightly before serving, or cool completely before storing in an airtight container. This loaf is best kept unrefrigerated, but will keep for up to 5 days in the fridge. A quick warm-through in the oven or microwave will bring it back to life.

Make it different
Cheesy lunchbox muffins. Ⓥ Line a muffin tray with paper cases. Omit the jalapeños and paprika. Substitute the manchego for cheddar, and the goat's curd for ricotta. Reduce the baking time to 20 minutes. Instead of the corn, you could also use about 100 g (3½ oz/1 cup) cooked cauliflower or broccoli, and/or ham.

With capsicum & red onion loaf. Ⓥ Top with roasted red capsicum (bell pepper) or fine red onion rings before baking.

Cheddar & feta scones with mixed seeds Ⓥ

Pair with

Serve for morning or afternoon tea, or as a light supper, with some quality butter.

Top with sour cream and chopped chives and serve with soup.

The key to scones is to barely bring the mixture together, which is why you use a butter knife to drag and fold into a fairly rustic-looking dough. It may feel a little odd, but it's key to the texture. This savoury version is buttery and cheesy, with the seeds adding a charming textural touch, and the hint of mustard powder a savoury undertone, without dominating. **Makes 12**

200 ml (7 fl oz) full-cream (whole) milk
200 ml (7 fl oz) pouring (single/light) cream
juice of ½ lemon
500 g (1 lb 2 oz/3⅓ cups) self-raising flour
2 teaspoons baking powder

2 teaspoons mustard powder
a pinch of salt flakes
100 g (3½ oz) unsalted butter, diced and chilled
75 g (2½ oz) cheddar, finely grated
75 g (2½ oz) feta, crumbled

4 tablespoons mixed seeds (such as sunflower, chia, pepitas/pumpkin seeds) and linseeds/flaxseeds), or 3 tablespoons finely grated parmesan

Staples
FLR

Preheat the oven to 220°C (430°F) fan-forced. Place a heavy baking tray in the oven to heat.

Combine the milk, cream and lemon juice in a bowl.

In a large bowl, combine the flour, baking powder, mustard powder and salt. Rub in the butter between your fingertips to a crumb consistency. You will still be able to see lumps of butter, but that's okay. Add the cheese and mix through with open fingers. Reserve 1 teaspoon of the milk mixture, then add the remainder to the bowl. Mix through with a butter knife to drag and bring together into a soft, shaggy dough.

Turn the dough out onto a lightly floured bench. Bring together gently with your hands, but don't knead – you don't want to activate and strengthen the gluten, or the scones will be heavy. Shape into a 30 × 20 cm (8 × 12 in) rectangle, a little more than 4 cm (1½ in) thick. Cut in half lengthways, then across to yield twelve pieces.

Remove the tray from the oven and lightly flour. Turn the oven down to 200°C (400°F) fan-forced.

Sprinkle half of the seeds on the base of the tray (leave as is if not using seeds) and arrange the scones on top in two lines close together but not touching. Brush with the reserved milk mix, sprinkle over the remaining seeds (or parmesan) and bake for about 12 minutes until puffed and golden. These are best eaten within 2 hours but can be kept in an airtight container for 2 days and reheated to serve.

Index

NOTE: The italicised entries refer to
Make it different recipes and underlined
entries refer to sidebar recipes.

A

abalone mushrooms
  Fragrant chicken soup with bok choy
    401–2
  Fried rice with wood ear fungus & cashews
    402
acidulated water 6

adzuki beans 7
  Japanese mixed rice & grains 382

agnolotti 113
  Agnolotti del plin 115

aïoli
  Aïoli 76
  Black aïoli 76
  Black aïoli with cured meat 76
  Spicy aïoli 76
ajo blanco, An inspiration from 513
ajwain seeds 6

aleppo pepper 6
  Aleppo chilli salt 6
  Barbecued Dutch carrot & leek salad
    468–9
  carrot top dressing 469
  Chargrilled poussins with a lemon, chilli,
    herb & golden sultana salad 236
  Crab with avocado mousse, mint, chilli
    & sweet pickled cucumber 413
  Crispy lamb's brains, pancetta & feta, with
    curly endive & mint 308
  Fried haloumi with vine leaves, pistachios,
    za'atar & pomegranate molasses 363
  *Kohlrabi & cucumber salad with
    aleppo pepper* 549
  Left-over corned beef, egg & cabbage salad
    with smoked salt 289
  Warm celeriac salad with yoghurt, aleppo
    chilli, pine nuts & sultanas 482

almonds 368–71
  activating 370–1
  Almond & pistachio biscotti 758
  Almond bread 758
  Almond skordalia 373
  Amaretti biscotti 758–9
  An inspiration from ajo blanco 513
  Apricot & sesame oat bars 392
  Apricot, semolina, almond & yoghurt cake
    753
  Berry, toasted almond & chocolate muffins
    732
  Braised artichoke, egg, olive & watercress
    salad 538

Breton shortbreads with almonds
  & demerara 819
Broccoli stems with chilli & garlic 443
Butter chicken 248–9
Byzantine salad 379
carrot top dressing 469
Cat's tongue biscuits (Lengua de gato) 755
Cauliflower salad (roasted & raw) 478–9
Cherry & almond burnt butter torte 722
Cherry, semolina, almond & yoghurt cake
  753
Chia pudding 393
Chocolate panforte with almonds,
  figs & sour cherries 760–1
Coconut & raspberry cake with chocolate
  ganache 746
Coconut, cherry & pistachio slice 761
Dark chocolate truffles with nutty praline
  791
Date, sesame, coconut & macadamia
  nut balls 393
Even simpler frangipane tarts 797
Frangipane 796
French shortbread sandwiches
  with mascarpone cream, almonds
  & praline 813
French strawberry shortcake with crème
  pâtissière 819
Friands 734–5
Gluten-free shortcrust pastry for a tart base
  812
Lamb, spinach, pomegranate & date salad
  with crisp pitta 314
Lemon cheesecake 698
Mezzanotte paste 588
No-bake seed bars 392
nut meal 21
Nut yoghurt 394
Nutty, salty, sweet & seedy crunch mix 377
Orange & almond cake with glacé orange
  744
pistachio & almond marzipan icing 752
Quick herb salad 267
Roasted apricot & ginger clafoutis 721
Roasted cauliflower, barley & parsley salad
  with scorched almonds & feta 477
sablé breton 819
Salsa romesco 84
Salted caramel & almond popcorn 788
Salted macadamia & almond caramels 790
Salted nut & choc chip biscuits 755
Seared radicchio with burrata,
  balsamic-pickled cherries & scorched
  almonds 566
Shaved fennel, artichoke & almond
  salad 535–6
Sicilian cassata-style ricotta cake 752–3
Spinach, mint & rice salad with yoghurt
  dressing 560

Super seed loaf 376
Toasted muesli 394
Torta caprese all'arancia e cioccolato
  (Dark chocolate & almond torte) 751
Torta caprese bianco cioccolato 751
Tunisian dukkah 13
Wild rice, herb, almond & currant salad
  378
Za'atar 33

amaranth 6, 368, 550
  cooking 371
amchur 6

anchovies 6
  Abbacchio al forno 315–6
  Anchoïade 78
  Anchovy, tomato & basil topping for
    focaccia 844
  Bagna cauda 83
  Boiled egg on toast with anchovies, onion
    & paprika 352
  Cafe de Paris butter 72
  Celeriac, apple & kale slaw with anchovy
    484–5
  Celeriac, fennel & rice brodo with anchovies
    483
  Charred broccolini with tuna mayonnaise,
    black barley, egg & anchovy dust 442–3
  Deluxe eggplant parmigiana with
    anchovies 522
  Dolmades with rice, pine nuts, currants &
    lemon 375
  Frittata 355
  Linguine vongole 127
  Mezzanotte paste 588
  Orecchiette with broccoli & cime di rape
    444
  Orecchiette with eggplant, oregano,
    balsamic & ricotta 132–3
  Orecchiette with tomato, mint & anchovy
    sauce 132
  Pissaladière 599
  Pizza diavolo 857
  Pizza napolitana 857
  Potato bread 844
  Provençale tomato-stuffed peppers with
    olives & anchovies 662
  Pumpkin, anchovy & ricotta pizza 857
  puttanesca sauce 117
  Queen green tapenade 590
  Quick olive tapenade 587
  *Roasted & raw fennel salad with preserved
    fish* 527
  Roasted zucchini with anchovy, oregano &
    chilli 672
  Rustic salsa verde with potato 86
  Spaghetti aglio e olio 123
  Spaghetti puttanesca 117
  Toasted anchovy crumbs 122
  tomato, mint & anchovy sauce 132

Well-cooked broccoli with anchovies
& pine nuts 442
white anchovies 33
Anchoïade 78
anise seeds 6
Anzac biscuits 757
apples 678–9
  Apple muffins 732
  A simple frangipane fruit tart 796
  Apple & cherry turnovers 681
  Apple, blueberry & blackberry galette 818
  Apple, fennel & witlof slaw with buttermilk
    dressing 680
  Baked whole apples with verjuice & a clove
    crumb 684
  Caramelised spiced cider apples 769
  Celeriac, apple & kale slaw with anchovy
    484–5
  Celeriac remoulade with apple 484
  Christmas pudding 778–9
  Deep-dish apple pie 818
  Grace's braised cabbage 450
  Kimchi 455–6
  Kohlrabi & cucumber salad with apple 549
  Left-over pork sandwich 344
  Quick apple & witlof salad 680
  Quick apple sauce for roast duck or pork
    684
  Quick quince & apple relish 716
  red kimchi paste 456
  Ricotta & apple compote hotcakes 768–9
  Savoury baked whole apples 684
  Savoy cabbage slaw with apple, sour
    cream, caraway & fennel seed 449
  Seared scallops with chorizo & apple
    210–1
  sesame, apple & soy dressing 640
  Simply cooked apples 681
  Soy, sesame & apple vinaigrette 102
  Sugar-crusted apple pie 818
  Tarte tatin 682
  Viennese strudel 684–5
  Waldorf salad with roast chicken wrapped
    in iceberg 490
  white kimchi paste 456
  white pepper jelly 510
apricots 718–9
  A simple frangipane fruit tart 796
  Apricot & sesame oat bars 392
  Apricot, semolina, almond & yoghurt cake
    753
  Fruit-spiked apple & peach turnovers 681
  Honey & white wine poaching syrup for
    stone fruit 723–4
  Jam crostata 826
  Puff pastry tart with fruit 824–5
  Roasted apricot & ginger clafoutis 721
  Roasted stone fruit 720
arame 6
  Tuna & sweet potato sesame patties with
    pickled arame salad 622
Arancini 148

artichokes, globe 6, 532–4
  Artichoke, anchovy & gruyère gratin 537
  Braised artichoke, egg, olive & watercress
    salad 538
  Braised artichoke, fennel & broad bean
    salad with orange glaze 536
  Braised artichokes with garlic, bay & white
    wine glaze 534
  Braised chicken & artichokes with couscous
    537
  Braised lamb, artichokes, lemon &
    cinnamon with couscous 537
  Green olive, artichoke & kale tapenade 590
  Lamb, artichoke & mint ragù 535
  Mezzanotte paste 588
  Roman-style fried artichokes 539
  Shaved fennel, artichoke & almond salad
    535–6
  Soft polenta with crab, artichoke &
    poached egg 352
  Veal, artichoke & mint ragù 535
asafoetida 6
Asian greens 398–400
  see also amaranth, bok choy, choy sum,
    gai choy (mustard greens), gai lan,
    kang kong
asparagus 404–6
  Asparagus soup 407
  Asparagus with bagna cauda 406
  Asparagus with poached egg & prosciutto
    406
  *Broad bean salad with bagna cauda &
    spring vegetables* 431
  Cheesy buttered greens 430
  Crumbed asparagus spears 407
  Grilled asparagus & haloumi salad with
    fennel, walnuts & pomegranate 406–7
  Lobster salad à la russe 200
  Porcini & asparagus risotto 151
  Sautéed wild asparagus with tarragon &
    brown butter 406
  *Shaved fennel & artichoke salad with
    vegetables* 536
  Spring minestrone 531
  Spring vegetable risotto 149
  *White asparagus with walnut & rye
    skordalia* 600
aubergines *see* eggplant
avocado 408–10
  American-style ranch salad 557
  avocado mousse 413
  Broad bean & avocado dip 431
  Chicken & corn koftas with avocado &
    coriander 249
  Chocolate & avocado ganache 412
  Coconut & raspberry cake with chocolate
    ganache 746
  Crab with avocado mousse, mint, chilli &
    sweet pickled cucumber 413
  Daikon, edamame & avocado salad, with
    sesame, apple & soy dressing 640–1
  Fried corn cakes with chilli jam & smashed
    avocado 498
  Guacamole no. 2 413

  Lime leaf & white pepper guacamole 412
  Prawn cocktail 413
  Simple guacamole 412
  Soba noodles with avocado, sprouts,
    umeboshi & sesame 410
  Tuna poké bowl with avocado, shiitake,
    sesame, wakame & cucumber 415
avocado oil 22

B

baba ghanoush
  Baba ghanoush 519
  Zucchini baba ghanoush 669
babka, Chocolate, with hazelnuts 762–3
bacon 326
  Grilled gem lettuce & bagna cauda 556
  Grilled oysters with bacon 210
  *Pumpkin & taleggio risotto with cured
    meat* 632
  Shoyu ramen broth 58–9
  Spiced creamed tomato soup with bacon
    665
  Vinaigrette potatoes with meat 624–5
  XO sauce 98
Bagna cauda 83
Baharat 6
baking powder (baking soda) 6
baking soda (bicarbonate of soda) 8
baking
  equipment 34–41
  savoury baking 836–7
  sweet baking 728–30
Bamies (Greek-style braised okra) 580
bananas
  Banana & blueberry slab cake 760
  Banana custard 801
  Mashed banana & coconut muffins 732
  Odette's best banana bread 760
bánh mì
  Bánh mì with roast chicken 333
  Bánh mì with roast pork belly 332–3
  Salt & pepper tofu for bánh mì 332
bao
  Seared duck breast with roasted plum &
    hoisin sauce for pancakes or bao 263
  Spicy pork bao 333
barberries 7
  Byzantine salad 379
  Coconut, cherry & pistachio slice 761
  Toasted muesli 394
barley 7, 368
  Barley 'risotto' with mushrooms & speck
    572
  black barley salad 246–7
  Braised lamb neck & barley broth 308–9
  Byzantine salad 379
  Charred broccolini with tuna mayonnaise,
    black barley, egg & anchovy dust 442–3
  cooking 371

Harira 461
Kingfish kibbeh nayyeh 166
Left-over chicken, barley & vegetable soup 252
Pea & ham soup 334
Pearled barley, parsley & toasted pepita salad 378
Roast chicken & black barley salad 246–7
Roasted cauliflower, barley & parsley salad with scorched almonds & feta 477
Smoked ham hock & borlotti bean soup 425–6
Vegetarian baked haloumi-stuffed eggplant 521

basil 7
Anchovy, tomato & basil topping for focaccia 844
Basil & tomato topping for focaccia 844
basil oil 662
Bruschetta 655
Capsicum & eggplant salad 464
Crustacean stock with herbs 52
Genovese salad 624
Grilled zucchini salad 668
Insalata caprese 662
Lasagne 136
Maltagliata of beef with rocket, fine kale & ricotta 288
Melanzane sotto aceto with banana peppers, basil & chilli 523
Mussels with garlic & tomato 214
Panzanella with buffalo mozzarella 658
Pasta alla Norma 521
Pasta with fresh tomato sauce 658
Pea & mozzarella salad 611
Pesto 90
Rocket & basil pesto 531
Sauce vierge with herbs 82
Summer vegetable lasagne 136
Zucchini & pesto pasta 674
see also Thai basil

batter
rice flour batter 237
tempura beer batter 187

bass grouper
Fish & mussels en papillote 178
Salt-baked fish 175

bay leaves 7
Abbacchio al forno 315–6
Braised artichokes with garlic, bay & white wine glaze 534
Chicken bone broth 53
Classic white vegetable stock 51
Crunchy lacto-fermented vegetables 508
Garam masala 15
Golden chicken stock 54
Hasselback potatoes with paprika & bay leaves 626
Herb oil for fish 165
Lardo 326
Persian roast chicken on buttered rice with quince paste & bay leaves 250
Petit salé aux lentilles 334
Porchetta 338

Preserved lemons with bay & cinnamon 695
Preserved lemons with bay & star anise 695
red-wine poaching liquid 710
Roasted pears with honey, verjuice, rosemary & bay leaves 711
Roasted rack of pork with fennel 343
Rosemary & bay salt 26
Slow-cooked robust ragù of pork & beef 336
Slow-roasted quince with honey, cinnamon & cloves 714
thyme & oregano rub 424
verjuice poaching liquid 711
Whole snapper baked with cumin, lemon, bay & green harissa 181
Whole snapper pan-fried with bay & garlic 181

beans 7–8, 368–9
food safety concerns 372
see also adzuki beans, black beans, borlotti (cranberry) beans, broad beans, butterbeans, cannellini beans, fava beans, gigante beans, great northern beans, green beans, haricot (navy) beans, kidney beans, lima beans, mung beans, romano beans, snake beans
Béarnaise sauce 79
Béchamel 70–1

beef 272–7
A nod to Harry's Bar original carpaccio 280
A quick Bordelaise sauce with bone marrow & roasted shallots 68
Asian brisket with vinegared blood plums 291
Baked stuffed eggplant 520–1
Beef & pork loaf with haloumi, pistachio & pomegranate molasses 288–9
Beef carpaccio 280
Beef pho 57
Beef rendang 292–3
Bistecca alla fiorentina 278
Borscht 418
Boeuf bourguignon cobbler 284
Boeuf bourguignon pie 284
Brown beef glacé 55
Brown beef stock 55
Casarecce with osso buco 121
Cevapcici with wild fennel 529
Chow mein-style beef with wombok 292
Classic roasted eye fillet 286
cooking the perfect steak 277
Corned beef 289
Corned beef with herb & mustard sauce 289
Cured beef with black onion spice & parmesan 281
Grilled minute steak with soy & sesame mushrooms 281
Italian-style braised beef 285
Koftas baked with tomato & smoky eggplant, with pine nuts & parsley 309–10

Korean sesame grilled beef with sake, ginger & soy marinade 293
Lasagne 136
Left-over corned beef, egg & cabbage salad with smoked salt 289
Maltagliata of beef with rocket, fine kale & ricotta 288
Martini family stuffed capsicums 464–5
Olives ascolana 587
Oxtail consommé 56
Oxtail risotto 148
Pedro Ximénez–braised beef cheeks with celeriac & parsnip purée & persillade 285–6
Pho broth 57–8
Ragù alla bolognese 283
Risotto alla milanese 148
Roast meat tortellini 114–5
Roasted eye fillet with Japanese seasonings 286
Roasted scotch fillet 283
Roasted standing rib rack 288
Seared beef with bean thread noodles, beans, wood ear fungus & gochujang 292
Slow dry-roasted spiced asado ribs 290
Slow-cooked robust ragù of pork & beef 336
Slow-roasted eye fillet 285
Traditional French steak tartare 279
Vinaigrette potatoes with cornichons, dill, caperberries, crème fraîche & fried egg 624–5
Vinaigrette potatoes with meat 624–5
Vine leaf beef & bone marrow pie 287

beer
Beer-battered flathead & twice-cooked potato cakes 187
Lamb ribs braised with treacle & dark ale 304

beetroot 416–8
Beetroot jelly 421
Beetroot tabouleh with currants & sunflower seeds 419
Beetroot, carrot & pomegranate salad 420
Borscht 418
Jamón, fig, beetroot, goat's curd, watercress & mint salad 702
Kohlrabi, cabbage & beetroot slaw 548–9
Pickled turnip torshi 639
Potato rösti with ocean trout 623
Raw quick pickled beetroot 419
Roasted beetroot, cinnamon & pomegranate dip 420
Waldorf salad with more vegetables 490
bell peppers *see* capsicum
beluga (black) lentils *see* lentils

berries 686–8
Berries & cream sponge cake filling 748
Berry & almond burnt butter torte 722
Berry & chocolate muffins 732
Berry & ginger clafoutis 721
Berry crumble 688
Berry, coconut & mint smoothie 688

Berry, toasted almond & chocolate muffins 732

Berry turnovers 688

Cream- or jam-filled doughnuts 773

Smashed berry sauce 687

Summer berry & chia pudding loaf 689

see also barberries, blackberries, blueberries, raspberries, strawberries

biber salçasi 8

bicarbonate of soda (baking soda) 8

bircher, Coconut 393

biscuits

Anzac biscuits 757

Cat's tongue biscuits (Lengua de gato) 755

Cheesecake-flavoured biscuit turnovers 825

Chocolate biscuit sandwiches with sesame cream 754-5

Dark chocolate & hazelnut biscuits 754

No-bake nutty biscuit base 738

Salted nut & choc chip biscuits 755

Sugared butter custard biscuits 759

Vanilla butter biscuits 754

biscotti

Almond & pistachio biscotti 758

Amaretti biscotti 758-9

bisque, Quick creamy seafood sauce or 67

black barley *see* barley

black beans 7

Black bean & ginger sauce 100

Black bean, quinoa & cherry tomato salad 380

Black turtle bean, pork belly & morcilla braise (frijoles negros) 340

Corn, black bean & pomegranate salad 503

Mapo-style tofu with beans & pork 436

blackberries

Apple, blueberry & blackberry galette 818

Blackberry & coconut cheesecake muffins 732

Blackberry or raspberry icing 802

Cherry, semolina, almond & yoghurt cake 753

Jam crostata 826

red-wine poaching liquid 710

Ricotta & blackberry hotcakes 768-9

Spiced red wine pears 710-1

blind-baking pastry shells 811

blinis

Buckwheat blinis 377

Potato blinis 621

Blintzes 771

blue cheese *see* gorgonzola, Roquefort

blue-eye trevalla 49

Bouillabaisse-style stew 214-5

Fish & mussels en papillote 178

Fish cakes with parsley 190-1

Fish stock 52-3

Fragrant seafood soup with bok choy 402

Fried fish with tomato & fig 705

Fish with Thai caramel sauce & herbs 172

Sour fish & mussel curry with celery hearts & kang kong 488-9

Sour fish curry with okra & celery heart 581

blueberries

Apple, blueberry & blackberry galette 818

Banana & blueberry slab cake 760

Friands 734-5

Ricotta & blueberry hotcakes 768-9

Smashed blueberry glaze 774

bocconcini

Lasagne 136

Spinach, ricotta & feta cannelloni with mint passata sauce 133

Summer vegetable lasagne 136

Bo ssäm 341-2

Bois Boudran sauce 88

bok choy 398

Fragrant chicken soup with bok choy 401-2

Stir-fried greens & shiitake with XO sauce 401

Udon noodles with chicken, shiitake, bok choy, miso & kimchi 402

bolognese

Ragù alla bolognese 283

Vegetable bolognese 576

Bombe Alaska 807

bonito flakes *see* katsuobushi

Böreks with cheese 831

borlotti (cranberry) beans 7, 422-4

Borlotti bean salad with mustard fruits 426

Borlotti beans with herbs & freekeh 427

Braised fresh borlotti beans in lemon & cumin stock 426

Braised pork shoulder with borlotti beans & taleggio 424

Chilli con pollo with chorizo & beans 232

Smoked ham hock & borlotti bean soup 425-6

Spiced bean & vegetable braise 425

Borscht 418

bottarga 8

Octopus braised in rosé & tomato with radicchio & bottarga 219-20

Roasted & raw fennel salad with preserved fish 527

Shaved fennel, artichoke & walnut salad with cured fish 536

Tagliatelle with lemon cream 123-4

Boeuf bourguignon 284

Bouillabaisse-style stew 214-5

bouquet garni 8

brains, Crispy lamb's, pancetta & feta, with curly endive & mint 308

Brazil nuts

Lime & coconut cheesecake 738

No-bake nutty biscuit base 738

bread 836-7

Almond bread 758

bread improver 8

Carrot, chervil & gruyère loaf 472-3

Classic dinner knot rolls 846

croûtes 174

Lebanese talami bread topped with za'atar 852

Lebanese talami bread with spiced tomato topping 852

maintaining sourdough starter 849

Moroccan semolina flat breads 852

Naan 855

Potato bread 844

Pretzels 841

Simit/koulouri 842-3

Sourdough bread 847-51

Super seed loaf 376

white country sourdough loaf 850-1

wholemeal & rye sourdough loaf 850-1

see also focaccia, pitta

bread & butter pudding, Deluxe 778

bread improver 8

Bread sauce 70

bresaola

Duck bresaola 267

Fennel & buffalo mozzarella salad with cured meat 530

Seared radicchio with burrata & cured meat 566

brik pastry 8

brittle, Sesame 786

broad beans 428-30

Beef carpaccio with broad beans 280

Braised artichoke, fennel & broad bean salad with orange glaze 536

Broad bean & avocado dip 431

broad bean & pea paste 432-3

Broad bean & pea salad with nasturtium leaves, goat's cheese & bagna cauda 431

Cheesy buttered broad beans & peas 430

Falafel with broad beans & tahini yoghurt 432

Fennel & buffalo mozzarella salad with broad beans, mint & green sultanas 530

Grilled lamb cutlets with smashed broad beans & hot feta dressing 432-3

Linguine with prawns & broad beans 433

Malloreddus with prawns, fennel & broad beans 526

Mapo-style tofu with beans & pork 436

Raw Jerusalem artichoke salad with broad beans & cheese 544

Shaved fennel & artichoke salad with vegetables 536

Spaghetti aglio e olio with mint & broad beans 123

Spring minestrone 531

broccoli 440-2

Broccoli stems with chilli & garlic 443

Broccoli with lemon, chilli, fennel seeds & pecorino 444

Charred broccoli, ramen & nori salad 444-5

Cheesy lunchbox muffins 858

Frittata 355

Orecchiette with broccoli & cime di rape 444

Smashed broccoli with preserved lemon 442

Well-cooked broccoli with anchovies & pine nuts 442
see also gai lan (Chinese broccoli)

broccolini 440-2
Baked polenta with stracchino & greens 382
Broccolini with speck, shallot & garlic 442
Charred broccolini with tuna mayonnaise, black barley, egg & anchovy dust 442-3

broths 58
Braised lamb neck & barley broth 308-9
Chicken bone broth 53
chicken broth 502
Chicken noodle broth with porcini polpette 253
Pho broth 57-8
Shoyu ramen broth 58-9
see also stocks

brown lentils *see* lentils

brownies
Mocha brownies 762
Odette's chewy triple chocolate brownies 762
Rum & chocolate brownies 762

bruschetta
Bruschetta 655
Bruschetta of prawns, cannellini beans & truffle 203
Celeriac, fennel & rice brodo with ricotta bruschetta 483

brussels sprouts 446-8
Roasted brussels sprouts with honey & dukkah 453
Shaved brussels sprouts with roasted king brown mushrooms, manchego & maple dressing 453

Bucatini amatriciana 121

buckwheat 8, 368
Buckwheat blinis 377
Japanese mixed rice & grains 382
Nutty granola 377
Nutty, salty, sweet & seedy crunch mix 377

buffalo mozzarella *see* mozzarella

bulgur 8, 368
Beetroot tabouleh with currants & sunflower seeds 419
Kingfish kibbeh nayyeh 166
Tabouleh 87

bullhorn peppers 458

burrata
Broad bean & pea salad with cheese 431
Green aglio e olio with cheese 122
Seared radicchio with burrata, balsamic-pickled cherries & scorched almonds 566

butter 8, 730
Baby turnips with butter glaze 643
Baked buttered rice 384
Beurre blanc 69
Beurre rouge 69
Blintzes 771
Brown butter & lemon sauce for crepes & blintzes 771

Burnt butter sauce with lemon, capers & parsley 73
Burnt butter sauce with lemon, sage & toasted walnuts 73
butter cream 807
Butter-poached Moreton Bay bugs 203
Butter-poached prawns 202-3
Buttery minted peas 610
Cafe de Paris butter 72
cardamom butter filling 766
Carrots with butter, honey & thyme glaze 469
Cheesy buttered broad beans & peas 430
Clarified butter 360
Classic puff pastry 822
Compressed puff pastry 822
Cream cheese shortcrust pastry 830
Frangipane 796
Golden syrup butter caramel sauce 793
Maple syrup, brown sugar & cinnamon icing 804
Nasturtium & miso butter 72
Parsley & lemon butter 73
Persian roast chicken on buttered rice with quince paste & bay leaves 250
Pommes anna 624
Risotto bianco with brown butter, hazelnuts, lemon & ricotta 148
Roast chicken with butter & dill 250
Rough puff pastry 823
Salted butter 361
Salted caramel sauce 794
Sautéed wild asparagus with tarragon & brown butter 406
Simple butter cake 736-7
Simple duck sauce 262
Spinach, lentil & yoghurt salad with brown butter 558
Sugared butter custard biscuits 759
Swordfish with beurre rouge 183
Turnip & shiitake braised in soy dashi & brown butter sauce 642
Vanilla butter biscuits 754
Vanilla frosting 803

Butter chicken 248-9

butter cream 807
Italian meringue & Italian meringue butter cream 807

butter lettuce 553
Bo ssäm 341-2
Daikon, edamame & avocado salad with sesame, apple & soy dressing 640
Traditional French steak tartare with lettuce 279
Watercress & potato soup 558

butterbeans 371
Clams with jamón, garlic & butterbeans 211

buttermilk
American-style ranch salad with buttermilk dressing 557
Apple, fennel & witlof slaw with buttermilk dressing 680
Buttermilk 361
Buttermilk dressing 361

Pear, fennel & witlof slaw with buttermilk dressing 680
Simple fried buttermilk chicken 230-1

Byzantine salad 379

C

cabbage 446-8
Cabbage rolls with lamb, rice, pine nuts & dill 451
Classic cabbage slaw 448
Gado gado with kimchi 478
Gado gado with roasted vegetables 478
Grace's braised cabbage 450
Italian-style coleslaw 448
Kimchi pancakes with a tamari & sesame dipping sauce 457
Kohlrabi, cabbage & beetroot slaw 548-9
Korean sesame grilled beef with sake, ginger & soy marinade 293
Left-over corned beef, egg & cabbage salad with smoked salt 289
Left-over pork sandwich 344
Pickled spring vegetables 470-1
Quick apple & witlof salad 680
Sauerkraut 454-5
Savoy cabbage slaw with apple, sour cream, caraway & fennel seed 449
Simple dressed white cabbage 449
Simple soused cabbage 340
Soft-boiled eggs with green mango salad & citrus & chilli relish 358
Tunisian vegetable couscous royale with rosewater labneh 386-7
Udon noodles with chicken, shiitake, bok choy, miso & kimchi 402
Veal & pork polpette with savoy cabbage, taleggio & truffled pecorino 337
White cabbage & pea slaw 448-9
see also choy sum, wombok

Cacio e pepe 120

cakes
Apricot, semolina, almond & yoghurt cake 753
Banana & blueberry slab cake 760
Basque cheesecake 738-9
Brown sugar dark chocolate loaf cake 747
Carrot cake 742
Cherry, semolina, almond & yoghurt cake 753
Classic poppy seed loaf 752
Classic sponge cake 748
Coconut & raspberry cake with chocolate ganache 746
Coconut butter pandan cake 744-5
Deluxe chocolate galette cake 746-7
Friands 734-5
Hazelnut plum streusel cake 741
Heavenly sponge filled with cream & strawberries 689
Italian blood orange breakfast cake 740

Lamingtons 749
Lemon cheesecake 698
Lime & coconut cheesecake 738
Lime coconut butter pandan cake 745
Madeleines 736
Marble cake 737
Mazaresi cakes 732
Odette's best banana bread 760
Orange & almond cake with glacé orange
  744
Plain coconut cake 745
Sicilian cassata-style ricotta cake 752–3
Simple butter cake 736–7
Spiced earl grey tea & honey cake 740
Spiced pineapple & walnut cake 742
Spiced pumpkin & olive oil loaf cake 742–3
Spiced zucchini & walnut cake 674
Sticky chocolate ginger cake 745
Torta caprese all'arancia e cioccolato
  (Dark chocolate & almond torte) 751
Torta caprese bianco cioccolato 751
*Zucchini, coconut & macadamia loaf with
  lime cream cheese icing* 734
see also cupcakes, muffins

calamari
Blanched calamari with tuna sauce &
  olives 220
Calamari fritti 223
Grilled calamari with smoky tomato
  dressing 223
camembert: Dauphinoise with camembert
  627
canapés, Smoked salmon & cucumber 513
cannellini beans 7–8
*Bruschetta of prawns, cannellini beans &
  truffle* 203
Chilli con pollo with chorizo & beans 232
Prawns with cannellini beans & truffle 203
Spring minestrone 531
Winter minestrone with roasted root
  vegetables 607
cannoli 820
capers and caperberries 8–9
Anchoïade 78
Blanched calamari with tuna sauce &
  olives 220
Braised fennel with tomato & olives 529
Burnt butter sauce with lemon, capers &
  parsley 73
Caponata bianco with toasted walnuts 489
celery & olive salad 188
Celery salad with fennel, capers & dill 491
Fish & mussels en papillote 178
Mezzanotte paste 588
Orecchiette with eggplant, oregano,
  balsamic & ricotta 132–3
Pissaladière 599
Pizza 'number 1' 856
Pizza diavolo 857
puttanesca sauce 117
Queen green tapenade 590
Rustic salsa verde with potato 86
Salsa verde 86
Sauce gribiche 78

Spaghetti puttanesca 117
Tagliatelle with lemon cream & capers 124
tomato, mint & anchovy sauce 132
tonnato sauce 297
Traditional French steak tartare 279
Tuna niçoise 438–9
Vinaigrette potatoes with cornichons, dill,
  caperberries, crème fraîche & fried egg
  624–5
Vitello tonnato 297
Caponata bianco with toasted walnuts 489
Capretto 316
capsicum 458–60
Bouillabaisse-style stew 214–5
Braised lamb chump chops with potato,
  jalapeño & oregano 314
Butter chicken 248–9
Capsicum & eggplant salad 464
Chilli con pollo with chorizo & beans 232
Corn, black bean & pomegranate salad 503
Fish soup with spiced rouille & croûtes
  174–5
Gazpacho 657
Harira 461
Harissa 92
Harissa roast capsicum salad with goat's
  cheese 462
Lebanese skewered chicken with cumin,
  lemon, black pepper & garlic 247
Martini family stuffed capsicums 464–5
ñora peppers 85
orange & black olive salsa 345
Piperade 465
Provençale tomato-stuffed peppers with
  olives & anchovies 662
Ratatouille 672
Roasted charred capsicums 463
Rouille 80
Salsa romesco 84
Shakshuka with capsicum 463
Spiced bean & vegetable braise 425
*Spiced corn & manchego loaf with
  capsicum & red onion* 858
Summer vegetable lasagne 136
Sweet & sour sauce with pineapple 100
The simplest roasted capsicum salad 462
Tunisian green capsicum & pumpkin salad
  460
Tunisian vegetable couscous royale with
  rosewater labneh 386–7
see also peppers
caramel
Dulce de leche 795
Easy vanilla crème caramel 781
Golden syrup butter caramel sauce 793
Peach caramel sauce 721
Salted caramel & almond popcorn 788
Salted caramel sauce 794
Salted coconut caramel 794
Salted macadamia & almond caramels 790
Thai caramel sauce for fish 105
Toffeed figs 705
caraway seeds 9

cardamom 9
Baharat 6
Black dal 389
*Blood orange & Campari marmalade with
  cardamom* 699
cardamom dough 766
Chocolate babka with hazelnuts 762–3
Cinnamon & cardamom buns 766–7
Crème fraîche glaze with cardamom 804
Dal fry 388
fennel, sumac & yoghurt marinade 311
Garam masala 15
Honey & white wine poaching syrup for
  stone fruit 723–4
Iraqi chicken with tomato 0& cardamom
  rice 242
Lamb rogan josh 317–8
Pumpkin, chickpea, cashew & coconut
  curry 633
Ras el hanout 25–6
Spiced muffins 732
Spiced pumpkin & olive oil loaf cake 742–3
Sweet spice mix for baked goods 792
Tunisian dukkah 13
Yoghurt with spices 365
Za'atar 33
Zhoug 87
carpaccio
A nod to Harry's Bar original carpaccio 280
Beef carpaccio 280
carrots 466–8
Bánh mì with roast pork belly 332–3
Barbecued Dutch carrot & leek salad
  468–9
Beetroot, carrot & pomegranate salad 420
Borscht 418
Braised lamb neck & barley broth 308–9
Braised pork shoulder with borlotti beans
  & taleggio 424
Brown beef stock 55
Carrot cake 742
Carrot paste salad with lemon, caraway &
  nigella seeds 473
carrot top dressing 469
Carrot, chervil & gruyère loaf 472–3
*Carrot, cinnamon, pecan & cream cheese
  muffins* 732
Carrots with butter, honey & thyme glaze
  469
Cassoulet 391
Charred fennel salad with vegetables 528
Chicken bone broth 53
Corned beef 289
Crunchy lacto-fermented vegetables 508
Duck, celeriac & verjuice ragù 259
Gigantes plaki 380–1
Golden chicken stock 54
Ham hock & leek terrine 328
Italian sausage ragù 335
Italian-style braised beef 285
Italian-style coleslaw 448
Kohlrabi, cabbage & beetroot slaw 548–9
Lamb navarin 643

Left-over chicken, barley & vegetable soup 252

Left-over lamb roast shepherd's pie 319

Lobster salad à la russe 200

Moroccan carrot, date & green chilli salad 471

Pasties 469–70

Pea & ham soup 334

Pedro Ximénez–braised beef cheeks with celeriac & parsnip purée & persillade 285–6

Petit salé aux lentilles 334

Pickled spring vegetables 470–1

Quick-pickled carrots 472

Roast carrot & root vegetable soup with cinnamon & ginger 472

Roast chicken & black barley salad 246–7

Roasted carrots with harissa & goat's curd 468

Roasted rack of pork with fennel 343

Robust vegetable fumet 51

Shiitake, tofu & cashew san choy bau 555

Shoyu ramen broth 58–9

Simple duck sauce 262

Slow-cooked robust ragù of pork & beef 336

Smoked ham hock & borlotti bean soup 425–6

Spiced bean & vegetable braise 425

Spring minestrone 531

Tunisian vegetable couscous royale with rosewater labneh 386–7

Veal osso buco with white wine & gremolata 296

Vegetable bolognese 576

Winter minestrone with roasted root vegetables 607

cashew nuts

Apricot & sesame oat bars 392

Egg, tomato & spinach curry with ginger & turmeric 359

Fried rice with wood ear fungus & cashews 402

Nut yoghurt 394

Pumpkin, chickpea, cashew & coconut curry 633

Shiitake & cashew san choy bau 555

cassia bark 9

Black dal 389

Glazed red pork with cassia, star anise, black vinegar & wood ear fungus 341

Lamb rogan josh 317–8

Pho broth 57

Spiced tea eggs 356

see also cinnamon

Cassoulet 391

Cat's tongue biscuits (Lengua de gato) 755

cauliflower 474–6

Cauliflower cheese 478

Cauliflower purée 476

Cauliflower rice 478

Cauliflower salad (roasted & raw) 478–9

Cauliflower steaks 477

Cheesy lunchbox muffins 858

Crunchy lacto-fermented vegetables 508

Gado gado with roasted cauliflower, cucumber & eggs 478

Kohlrabi, cauliflower & fenugreek soup 548

Orecchiette with cauliflower 444

Pickled spring vegetables 470–1

Pizza bianco with sausage, roasted cauliflower, chilli & cherry tomatoes 857

Roasted cauliflower & turmeric soup with yoghurt & poached egg 476

Roasted cauliflower, barley & parsley salad with scorched almonds & feta 477

Roasted whole cauliflower 476

cavatelli 131

see also pasta

caviar see fish roe

cavolo nero 550–5

Maltagliata of beef with rocket, fine kale & ricotta 288

Orecchiette with cavolo nero 444

cayenne pepper 9

celeriac 480–2

Bistecca alla fiorentina 278

Borscht 418

Braised red lentils with turmeric, curry leaves, fried garlic & haloumi 387

Celeriac & mustard condiment for steak 485

celeriac & parsnip purée 286

Celeriac remoulade 484

Celeriac, apple & kale slaw with anchovy 484–5

Celeriac, fennel & rice brodo with ricotta bruschetta 483

Duck, celeriac & verjuice ragù 259

Harira 461

Italian-style coleslaw 448

Lobster salad à la russe 200

Pedro Ximénez–braised beef cheeks with celeriac & parsnip purée & persillade 285–6

Petit salé aux lentilles 334

Pommes anna with vegetables 624

Roasted celeriac, parsnip, potato & fennel with ras el hanout 485

Roasted rack of pork with fennel 343

Roasted whole celeriac – several ways 483

Tunisian vegetable couscous royale with rosewater labneh 386–7

Vegetarian braised celeriac & artichokes with couscous 537

Vine leaf beef & bone marrow pie 287

Waldorf salad with more vegetables 490

Warm celeriac salad with yoghurt, aleppo chilli, pine nuts & sultanas 482

celery 486–8

Asian brisket with vinegared blood plums 291

Baked beans with mustard seeds, vinegar & tomato 390

Basic vinaigrette lentils 385

Black turtle bean, pork belly & morcilla braise (frijoles negros) 340

Braised fresh borlotti beans in lemon & cumin stock 426

Braised lamb neck & barley broth 308–9

Braised pork shoulder with borlotti beans & taleggio 424

Brined lamb shoulder 307

Brown beef stock 55

Caponata bianco with toasted walnuts 489

Cassoulet 391

Celeriac remoulade 484

celery & olive salad 188

Celery, lemon & parsley salad with a fried garlic & fennel seed dressing 491

Celery, lemon, orange & parsley salad 491

Celery salt 9

Chicken bone broth 53

Chicken, corn & noodle soup 502–3

Chilli con pollo with chorizo & beans 232

Classic white vegetable stock 51

Corned beef 289

Crustacean stock 52

cucumber, celery heart & herb salad 240

Deep-fried red mullet with celery & olive salad 188

Fish soup with spiced rouille & croûtes 174–5

Fish stock 52–3

French onion soup 596

Gado gado with roasted cauliflower, cucumber & eggs 478

Gigantes plaki 380–1

Golden chicken stock 54

Ham hock & leek terrine 328

Harira 461

Italian sausage ragù 335

Italian-style braised beef 285

Lamb navarin 643

Lamb, artichoke & mint ragù 535

Lamb, spinach, pomegranate & date salad with crisp pitta 314

Left-over chicken, barley & vegetable soup 252

Left-over lamb roast shepherd's pie 319

Lobster salad à la russe 200

Nero vinaigrette 89

Pan con tomate with soft-boiled eggs & celery salt 656

Panzanella with buffalo mozzarella 658

Pea & ham soup 334

Pear, fennel, celery heart, Roquefort & poppy seed salad 710

Pedro Ximénez–braised beef cheeks with celeriac & parsnip purée & persillade 285–6

Petit salé aux lentilles 334

Pickled spring vegetables 470–1

Prawn & poached chicken vermicelli salad 240

Prawns with cannellini beans & truffle 203

Quick & simple duck stock 266

Ragù alla bolognese 283

Raw turnip with walnut oil, celery leaves & parsley 642

Roast duck & pan sauce 258–9

Robust vegetable fumet 51

Shiitake, tofu & cashew san choy bau 555
Simple duck sauce 262
Slow-cooked robust ragù of pork & beef 336
Smoked ham hock & borlotti bean soup 425–6
Sour fish & mussel curry with celery hearts & kang kong 488–9
Sour fish curry with okra & celery heart 581
Spaghetti with sardines, currants & pine nuts 124
Spiced bean & vegetable braise 425
Spiced Chinese pickles 640
Spring minestrone 531
Traditional French steak tartare 279
Tunisian vegetable couscous royale with rosewater labneh 386–7
Veal osso buco with white wine & gremolata 296
Vegetable bolognese 576
Velouté 64
Waldorf salad with roast chicken wrapped in iceberg 490
White chicken stock 54
Winter minestrone with roasted root vegetables 607
celery seeds 9
cephalopods 216–7
see also cuttlefish, octopus, squid
Cevapcici with wild fennel 529
champignons 568
Boeuf bourguignon 284
Champignons with garlic, wine & cream 575
Mushroom risotto 151
Velouté 64
Chantilly (basic whipped cream) 799
chard
Grilled gem lettuce & bagna cauda 556
Rainbow chard & chickpea salad 556
Winter minestrone with roasted root vegetables 607
see also silverbeet
Chawanmushi 356
cheddar 9
American-style ranch salad with cheese & croutons 557
Béchamel with cheese 70–1
Cauliflower cheese 478
Charred corn & cheddar fritters 498–9
Cheddar & feta scones with mixed seeds 859
Cheesy lunchbox muffins 858
Corn chowder with potato & dill 502
Fluffy goat's cheese & gruyère omelette 355
Fluffy prawn & crab omelette with prawn essence & watercress 355
Greens, potato & cheese pie with olive oil pastry 828
Gruyère & confit garlic tarts 828
Left-over pork sandwich 344

Mac & cheese 120
Pasties 469–70
Savoury scones 772
Spinach & cheddar omelette 353
Vegetarian mac & cheese 120
Zucchini, ham & pea slice with feta 672–3
cheese
for pasta 111
for risotto 147
Labneh 362
Ricotta 362
see also bocconcini, camembert, cheddar, cream cheese, feta, fior di latte, fontina, goat's cheese, gorgonzola, Grana Padano, gruyère, haloumi, kefalograviera, kefalotyri cheese, labneh, manchego, mascarpone, mizithra, mozzarella, Parmigiano Reggiano, pecorino, provolone, ricotta, Roquefort, scarmorza, stracchino, stracciatella, taleggio
cheesecakes
Basque cheesecake 738–9
Cheesecake-flavoured biscuit turnovers 825
Lemon cheesecake 698
Lime & coconut cheesecake 738
Chermoula 90
cherries 718–9
Apple & cherry turnovers 681
Apple & berry galette with cherries 818
Cherry & almond burnt butter torte 722
Cherry & ginger clafoutis 721
Cherry compote with brioche & crème fraîche 723
Cherry puff pastry tart 824–5
Cherry, raspberry & vanilla jam 723
Cherry, semolina, almond & yoghurt cake 753
Cherry, vanilla & balsamic compote 722
Chocolate panforte with almonds, figs & sour cherries 760–1
Christmas pudding 778–9
Coconut, cherry & pistachio slice 761
French shortcake with crème pâtissière & cherries 819
Lemon cream & cherry possets 696
Mazaresi cakes 732
Poppy seed, sour cherry & vanilla scrolls 764
Seared radicchio with burrata, balsamic-pickled cherries & scorched almonds 566
Sicilian cassata-style ricotta cake 752–3
Tomato & cherry gazpacho 657
chervil 9
An exquisite herb salad 17
Asparagus with poached egg & prosciutto 406
Baby chard & curly endive salad with soft-boiled egg dressing & honey bacon 557
Basic vinaigrette lentils 385
Bois Boudran sauce 88
Carrot, chervil & gruyère loaf 472–3

Corned beef with herb & mustard sauce 289
Crumbed zucchini flowers with crab mayonnaise & peas 669
Cucumber, grape & herb salad with shallot dressing 508
Oxtail risotto 148
Sauce gribiche 78
Sauce viege with herbs 82
Savoury crepes 771
Spaghettini with crab, lemon, herbs & chilli 125
chestnuts
chestnut flour 14
Roasted quince & chestnuts 716
see also water chestnuts
chia seeds 9, 369
Apricot & sesame oat bars 392
Cheddar & feta scones with mixed seeds 859
Chia pudding 393
Date, sesame, coconut & macadamia nut balls 393
Gluten-free shortcrust pastry for a tart base 812
No-bake seed bars 392
Toasted muesli 394
Summer berry & chia pudding loaf 689
Super seed loaf 376
chicken 226–9
A simple roast chicken 229
Balinese-style chicken skewers 104
Balsamic pepper strawberry & chicken sandwiches 689
Bánh mì with roast chicken 333
Braised chicken & artichokes with couscous 537
Brined roast chicken, Greek-style, with magic smashed potatoes 245
Butter chicken 248–9
Chargrilled poussins with a lemon, chilli, herb & golden sultana salad 236
Chawanmushi 356
Chicken & corn koftas with avocado & coriander 249
Chicken & ginger wontons with peanuts 231
Chicken bone broth 53
Chicken chops with wild rice salad 379
Chicken coconut curry with makrut lime leaf, lemongrass & turmeric 238
Chicken fricassee with Dutch creams, speck & tarragon 239
Chicken liver parfait 233
Chicken livers with witlof & radicchio fatoush salad, currants & sumac 234
Chicken noodle broth with porcini polpette 253
Chicken poké bowl with avocado, shiitake, sesame, wakame & cucumber 415
chicken stock from a left-over roast 49
chicken stock from raw bones 49
Chicken, corn & noodle soup 502–3

Chicken, corn & shiitake pot-sticker
dumplings 500
Chicken, leek & mushroom pie 603
Chilli con pollo with chorizo & beans 232
Chinese chicken stock 54
Chinese-style roasted chicken 243
Chow mein-style chicken with wombok 292
Congee 383
Corn chowder with potato & chicken 502
Crispy sweet-chilli chicken with wombok,
Thai basil & peanuts 242
Double chicken stock 54
Dry-fried chicken 245
Golden chicken stock 54
Iraqi chicken with tomato & cardamom
rice 242-3
Japanese-style chicken meatballs 251
Korean-style fried chicken 237
Lebanese skewered chicken with cumin,
lemon, black pepper & garlic 247
Left-over chicken, barley & vegetable soup
252
Mapo-style tofu with beans 436
Moorish chicken skewers 345
Oven-baked poussins with tomato, sherry,
fennel & olives 590-1
Pâté de campagne 327
Persian roast chicken on buttered rice with
quince paste & bay leaves 250
Prawn & poached chicken vermicelli salad
240
Prawn, corn & shiitake pot-sticker
dumplings 500
Pumpkin & chicken coconut curry 633
Ragù alla bolognese 283
Roast chicken & black barley salad 246-7
Roast chicken with butter & dill 250
Roast chicken with coriander seeds, thyme
& tomato 243
Roast chicken with spiced yoghurt crust
253
Roast meat tortellini 114-5
Roasted lemongrass & turmeric chicken
steaks 246
Sauce diable 65
Schnitzel 345
Scotch quail eggs 360
Shiitake & chicken san choy bau 555
Shoyu ramen broth 58-9
Silverbeet & haloumi pies with chicken 563
Simple fried buttermilk chicken 230-1
Simple honey, soy & ginger drumettes 237
Spinach, mint & rice salad with chicken
560
Stir-fried chicken thighs with kecap manis,
curry leaves & black pepper 234
Sweet & spicy Thai chicken drumettes
236-7
Syrian chicken with ginger, lemon &
saffron 248
Udon noodles with chicken, shiitake, bok
choy, miso & kimchi 402
Waldorf salad & roast chicken wraps 490
Waldorf salad with roast chicken wrapped
in iceberg 490

White chicken stock 54
White-poached chicken 230
chickpeas 9, 369
chickpea flour (gram/besan) 14
Chickpea, garlic & turmeric salad with
witlof 386
Chickpeas with mushrooms, red-wine
vinaigrette & tarragon 574
Clams with jamón, garlic & chickpeas 211
Falafel with broad beans & tahini yoghurt
432
Harira 461
Hummus 374
Plain falafel 432
Pumpkin, chickpea, cashew & coconut
curry 633
Rainbow chard & chickpea salad 556
Raw silverbeet, sorrel & hazelnut salad
560-1
Roasted brussels sprouts with honey &
dukkah 453
Tunisian vegetable couscous royale with
rosewater labneh 386-7
chicory 550-5
Apple, fennel & witlof slaw with buttermilk
dressing 680
Braised witlof with ginger 554
Chickpea, garlic & turmeric salad with
witlof 386
Horta 552-3
Lobster salad à la russe 200
Prawns with cannellini beans & truffle 203
Quick apple & witlof salad 680
Roasted & raw Jerusalem artichoke salad
544
Traditional French steak tartare with
lettuce 279
Waldorf salad with roast chicken wrapped
in iceberg 490
Witlof, rocket & macadamia salad with
pork & fennel sausage, mustard & honey
554
chilli sauce 9-10
Barbecued prawns with gochujang, sesame
& lime 202
Bo ssäm 341-2
Chilli crab 199-200
chilli cucumber dipping sauce 192
chilli, lime & brown sugar dressing 499
Chopped egg tartare 351
Cognac dijon dressing 279
Crisp sweet potato chips with chilli sauce
620
Devilled eggs 356
Fermented cooked chilli sauce 97
Ginger, soy & gochujang sauce 95
Gochujang chilli sauce 97
Harissa 92
Korean-style fried chicken 237
Left-over pork sandwich 344
Lime leaf & white pepper guacamole 412
Marie Rose sauce (cocktail sauce) 77
sichuan pepper dipping sauce 342
Speedy pork belly with gochujang 341

Spiced sesame & peanut dressing 94
Simple guacamole 412
Spicy aïoli 76
Spicy pork bao 333
Stir-fried kang kong & wombok with tofu &
fermented chilli 400
Stir-fried pea shoots with shrimp paste &
chilli 400-1
Teriyaki sauce 101
Whole pickled chillies & a simple
fermented chilli sauce 494-5
see also chillies, gochujang
chillies 10, 492-4
A quick pantry snack 512
American-style ranch salad 557
An inspiration from ajo blanco 513
Anchoïade 78
Asian brisket with vinegared blood plums
291
Bánh mì with roast pork belly 332-3
Beef rendang 292-3
Black dal 389
Blanched calamari with tuna sauce &
olives 220
Braised lamb chump chops with potato,
jalapeño & oregano 314
Broccoli stems with chilli & garlic 443
Broccoli with lemon, chilli, fennel seeds &
pecorino 444
Caponata bianco with toasted walnuts 489
Chicken coconut curry with makrut lime
leaf, lemongrass & turmeric 238
Chilli & ginger dumpling dipping sauce
103
Chilli crab 199-200
chilli cucumber dipping sauce 192
chilli garlic dressing 527
chilli paste 610
Chow mein-style beef with wombok 292
citrus & chilli relish 358
Corn & pineapple salsa 499
Corn with chilli & lime glaze 502
Corn, black bean & pomegranate salad 503
Crab with avocado mousse, mint, chilli &
sweet pickled cucumber 413
Crab, pea & potato samosas 611
Crisp-fried eggs, corn, smoked trout &
herb salad with tangy oyster sauce
dressing 358
Crispy sweet-chilli chicken with wombok,
Thai basil & peanuts 242
cucumber, celery heart & herb salad 240
Dal fry 388
dried 10
Dried chilli flakes, chilli powder & chilli
salt 495
Egg, tomato & spinach curry with ginger &
turmeric 359
Eggplant purée with chilli oil & walnuts
516
Fermented cooked chilli sauce 97
Fermented red cooked chilli paste 494
Fragrant chicken soup with bok choy
401-2

Fried corn cakes with chilli jam & smashed avocado 498
golden garlic, sichuan pepper & ginger dressing 614
Green harissa 92
Green tomato salsa with dill & mint 664
Grilled eggplant with tahini & yoghurt dressing, pomegranate, chilli & mint 516
Grilled minute steak with soy & sesame mushrooms 281
Guacamole no. 2 413
Harissa 92
Herb & chilli oil 86
Kimchi 455-6
Kingfish crudo with chilli, ginger & coriander 164
Kohlrabi, cabbage & beetroot slaw 548-9
Lamb & eggplant karahi curry 318
Lamb rogan josh 317-8
lemongrass & ginger marinade 237
lemongrass & turmeric marinade 246
Mango, ginger & chilli relish 495
Melanzane sotto aceto with banana peppers, basil & chilli 523
Mezzanotte paste 588
Moroccan carrot, date & green chilli salad 471
Mussels with chorizo, tomato & white wine 213
Nuoc cham 93
orange & black olive salsa 345
Oyster shooters with cucumber, ginger vinegar & white pepper jelly 510-1
Oysters with fire ice 208
Pickled spring vegetables 470-1
Pizza bianco with sausage, roasted cauliflower, chilli & cherry tomatoes 857
Pizza diavolo 857
Prawn & poached chicken vermicelli salad 240
Queen green tapenade 590
red curry paste 266
Red duck curry with lychee & fried basil salad 266-7
red kimchi paste 456
rendang paste 293
Roasted blood plum relish 725
Roasted chillies 495
Roasted pumpkin with cinnamon, chilli, pickled onion, yoghurt & feta 631
Roasted pumpkin with tahini & yoghurt dressing, pomegranate, chilli & mint 516
Roasted zucchini with anchovy, oregano & chilli 672
Rustic salsa verde with potato 86
Satay sauce 104
Seared squid & pea salad with tomato & chilli 612
Shiitake, tofu & cashew san choy bau 555
Sichuan pepper & chilli dressing 93
Sliced pickled jalapeños 494
Snapper crudo with finger lime, fennel, chilli & a burnt butter dressing 165

Soft-boiled eggs with green mango salad & citrus & chilli relish 358
Sour fish curry with okra & celery heart 581
Spaghetti aglio e olio 123
Spaghettini with crab, lemon, herbs & chilli 125
Spiced bean & vegetable braise 425
Spiced Chinese pickles 640
Spiced corn & manchego loaf 858
Spicy fried quail with sichuan pepper salt 269
Spicy malt plum sauce 725
Sticky spiced honey lamb shanks 305
Stir-fried pea shoots with shrimp paste & chilli 400-1
Sweet & spicy Thai chicken drumettes 236-7
Sweet Zuni-style pickles 668
tamari & sesame dipping sauce 457
Thai caramel sauce for fish 105
Thai green papaya salad 438
Thai-style chilli jam 96
togarashi 31
Tom yum goong 201
Tomato & pomegranate dressing with chilli 82
Tunisian vegetable couscous royale with rosewater labneh 386-7
Vinaigrette potatoes with cornichons, dill, caperberries, crème fraîche & fried egg 624-5
Watermelon & prawn salad citrus & chilli relish 201
white kimchi paste 456
Whole pickled chillies & a simple fermented chilli sauce 494-5
XO sauce 98
Zhoug 87
see also aleppo pepper, chilli sauce, gochujang, gochugaru, harissa
Chimichurri 85
Chinese broccoli see gai lan
Chinese cabbage see wombok
Chinese five-spice 10
Chinese five-spice salt 10
Chinese flowering cabbage see choy sum
chips
Eggplant chips 518
Fennel chips 531
Kale chips 551
Parsnip chips 606
Polenta chips 383
Zucchini 'chips' 667
chives 10
Asparagus with poached egg & prosciutto 406
Basic vinaigrette lentils 385
Bois Boudran sauce 88
Chilled cucumber & sesame salad with shiso & garlic chives 507
Crumbed zucchini flowers with crab mayonnaise & peas 669
Cucumber sandwiches 511

Fluffy goat's cheese & gruyère omelette 355
garlic chives 10
Herbed velouté 64
Lobster salad à la russe 200
Omelette with goat's curd & chives 353
Omelette with smoked salmon, chives & crème fraiche 353
Pea & mozzarella salad 611
Potato blinis 621
Potato rösti with ocean trout 623
Prawns with cannellini beans & truffle 203
Roasted & raw Jerusalem artichoke salad 544
Savoury crepes 771
Smoked salmon & cucumber canapés 513
Spaghettini with crab, lemon, herbs & chilli 125
Stir-fried cucumber with wood ear fungus & snow peas 510
chocolate 10, 730
Berry & chocolate muffins 732
Berry, toasted almond & chocolate muffins 732
Brown sugar dark chocolate loaf cake 747
cannoli 820
Cat's tongue biscuits (Lengua de gato) 755
Chocolate & avocado ganache 412
Chocolate & honey sauce 793
Chocolate babka with hazelnuts 762-3
Chocolate biscuit sandwiches with sesame cream 754-5
Chocolate crème pâtissière 798-9
Chocolate fudge icing 805
Chocolate ganache 806
Chocolate ginger icing 805
chocolate glaze 749
Chocolate gravel 783
chocolate hazelnut filling 763
Chocolate hot cross buns 765
Chocolate mille-feuille 824
Chocolate mousse 782
Chocolate panforte with almonds, figs & sour cherries 760-1
chocolate ricotta cake filling 752
Chocolate sweet shortcrust 812
Chocolate tart 817
Churros 775
Coconut & raspberry cake with chocolate ganache 746
Coconut, cherry & pistachio slice 761
Dark chocolate & hazelnut biscuits 754
Dark chocolate truffles with nutty praline 791
Date, sesame, coconut & macadamia nut balls 393
Deluxe bread & butter pudding 778
Deluxe chocolate galette cake 746-7
éclairs 821
Frangipane crostata 826
Lamingtons 749
Mille-feuille 824
No-bake seed bars 392
Nutella icing 805

Odette's chewy triple chocolate brownies 762

Pâte à choux for éclairs & profiteroles 821

profiteroles 821

Red velvet cupcakes with Italian meringue icing 731

Roasted peaches stuffed with ricotta & chocolate, with crushed biscotti 720

Rum & chocolate brownies 762

Salted nut & choc chip biscuits 755

Self-saucing chocolate pudding 782-3

Sicilian cassata-style ricotta cake 752-3

Sticky chocolate ginger cake 745

Thick real hot chocolate 775

Tiramisu 776-7

Torta caprese all'arancia e cioccolato 751

Torta caprese bianco cioccolato 751

Whipped white chocolate ganache 806

White chocolate & strawberry mille-feuille 824

chorizo

Baked beans with chorizo 390

Black aïoli with cured meat 76

Black turtle bean, pork belly & morcilla braise (frijoles negros) 340

Chilli con pollo with chorizo & beans 232

Mussels with chorizo, tomato & white wine 213

Seared scallops with chorizo & apple 210-1

Choron 79

choux dough 821

Chow mein-style beef with wombok 292

chowder, Corn, with potato & dill 502

choy sum 398

Fried rice with wood ear fungus & cashews 402

Pork & prawn wontons with choy sum & kale 342

Stir-fried choy sum & gai lan with oyster sauce 401

Stir-fried greens & shiitake with XO sauce 401

Christmas

Chocolate panforte with almonds, figs & sour cherries 760-1

Christmas pudding 778-9

Christmas pudding semifreddo 779

Cucumber & lime granita with gin jelly, yoghurt sorbet & minted cucumber 511

Gingerbread Christmas cookies 757-8

Lemon cream & cherry possets 696

Pavlova 784

Summer berry & chia pudding loaf 689

Tiramisu 776-7

Torta caprese all'arancia e cioccolato 751

Churros 775

chutney, Roasted rhubarb, blood plum & ginger 646

cilantro *see* coriander

cime di rape 440-2

Horta 552-3

Orecchiette with broccoli & cime di rape 444

Risotto with ricotta, spinach & verjuice-braised leek 149

cinnamon 10

Baharat 6

Baked buttered rice with spices 384

Braised lamb, artichokes, lemon & cinnamon with couscous 537

Carrot, cinnamon, pecan & cream cheese muffins 732

Chinese five-spice 10

Chocolate babka with hazelnuts 762-3

Cinnamon & cardamom buns 766-7

Cinnamon buns 767

cinnamon crumble 688

Cinnamon panna cotta 781

cinnamon sugar 685, 773, 775

Coconut bircher 393

Cream- or jam-filled doughnuts 773

Crème fraîche glaze with cinnamon & lemon 804

Date, sesame, coconut & macadamia nut balls 393

Doughnuts in honey & orange blossom syrup with ricotta & pistachios 773

Garam masala 15

Gingerbread Christmas cookies 757

Honey & orange blossom syrup 792

Honey & white wine poaching syrup for stone fruit 723

Jerusalem artichoke pickle 545

Lemon, date & orange-blossom marmalade 699

Maple syrup, brown sugar & cinnamon icing 804

Martini family stuffed capsicums 464-5

Mini cinnamon-bomb doughnuts 773

No-bake seed bars 392

Nutty, salty, sweet & seedy crunch mix 377

Orange & anise doughnuts 773

Pedro Ximénez–braised beef cheeks with celeriac & parsnip purée & persillade 285-6

Poppy seed, sour cherry & vanilla scrolls 764

Preserved lemons with bay & cinnamon 695

Quatre épices 24

Quick quince & apple relish 716

Rainbow chard & chickpea salad 556

Ras el hanout 25-6

Rizogalo 395

Roast carrot & root vegetable soup with cinnamon & ginger 472

Roasted beetroot, cinnamon & pomegranate dip 420

Roasted parsnip & purple sweet potato with cinnamon, nutmeg & garlic 606-7

Roasted pears with earl grey tea, marsala, cinnamon & orange 711

Roasted pumpkin with cinnamon, chilli, pickled onion, yoghurt & feta 631

Slow-roasted quince with honey, cinnamon & cloves 714

Spiced earl grey tea & honey cake 740

Spiced lamb shanks with rhubarb, honey & fried vine leaves 647

Spiced pumpkin & olive oil loaf cake 742

Spiced pumpkin, date, almond & moghrabieh salad 635

Spiced red wine pears 710-1

Spiced zucchini & walnut cake 674

Sticky spiced honey lamb shanks 305

Sweet spice mix for baked goods 792

Toasted muesli 394

Viennese strudel 684-5

Yoghurt with spices 365

see also cassia bark

citric acid powder 10

citrus 694

citrus & chilli relish 358

Citrus curd 797

citrus cure 169

Citrus delicious pudding 698-9

Citrus nori tartare for fish 187

Citrus-cured gravlax 169

Citrus-cured sardines 168

Soft-boiled eggs with green mango salad & citrus & chilli relish 358

supreming (segmenting) citrus 694

Watermelon & prawn salad citrus & chilli relish 201

see also finger limes, grapefruits, lemons, limes, mandarins, oranges, pomelos, tangelos

clafoutis, Roasted apricot & ginger 721

clams 205

Bouillabaisse-style stew 214-5

Clams in white-wine sauce 211

Clams with jamón, garlic & butterbeans 211

Linguine vongole 127

Sour seafood curry with more seafood 581

Stir-fried clams with XO sauce 211

Clarified butter 360

Clotted cream 800

cloves 11

Apple, blueberry & blackberry galette 818

Baked whole apples with verjuice & a clove crumb 684

Borscht 418

Bread sauce with cloves and nutmeg 70

Chocolate panforte with almonds, figs & sour cherries 760-1

Christmas pudding 778

Free-form stone fruit tart 814

Friands 734-5

Garam masala 15

Hazelnut plum streusel cake 741

Lamb rogan josh 317

Melanzane sotto aceto with banana peppers, basil & chilli 523

Pickled shallots & currants with parsley & cornichons 596

Preserved lemons with bay & cinnamon 695

Quatre épices 24

Quick kohlrabi pickle 548

Roasted pears with earl grey tea, marsala, cinnamon & orange 711
Slow-roasted quince with honey, cinnamon & cloves 714
Spiced red wine pears 710-1
Spiced zucchini & walnut cake 674
Spiced-yoghurt leg of lamb 311
Sticky chocolate ginger cake 745
Sugared butter custard biscuits 759
Sweet spice mix for baked goods 792
Vitello tonnato 297
Yoghurt with spices 365
cobbler, Boeuf bourguignon 284
Cocktail sauce (Marie Rose sauce) 77
cocoa powder 11

coconut 11
Anzac biscuits 757
Baked buttered rice with coconut & lemon 384
Banana custard 801
Beef rendang 292-3
Blackberry & coconut cheesecake muffins 732
Coconut & pandan jasmine rice 384
Coconut & raspberry cake with chocolate ganache 746
Coconut bircher 393
Coconut butter pandan cake 744-5
Coconut, cherry & pistachio slice 761
coconut flakes 11
Date, sesame, coconut & macadamia nut balls 393
desiccated coconut 11
Lamingtons 749
Lime & coconut cheesecake 738
lime & coconut filling 738
Mango with salted caramel, ginger & lime 794
Mashed banana & coconut muffins 732
No-bake nutty biscuit base 738
Nutty granola 377
Plain coconut cake 745
powdered coconut 11
Super seed loaf 376
Toasted muesli 394
Zucchini, coconut & macadamia muffins with lime cream cheese icing 734

coconut cream 11
Beef rendang 292-3
Caramelised barbecued prawns 202
Chicken coconut curry with makrut lime leaf, lemongrass & turmeric 238
Chilled coconut & lime leaf rice pudding 395
Coconut butter pandan cake 744-5
Coconut hoisin dipping sauce 96
Coconut panna cotta with coconut jelly, black sesame tuiles, mango & lime leaf 783
Lime & coconut cheesecake 738
lime & coconut filling 738
Pumpkin, chickpea, cashew & coconut curry 633

Red duck curry with lychee & fried basil salad 266-7
Salted coconut caramel 794
Tapioca pearls in coconut with tropical salad & caramel sauce 780-1

coconut milk 11
Amber's yoghurt mango lassi 365
Coconut & pandan jasmine rice 384
Kohlrabi, cauliflower & fenugreek soup 548
Red duck curry with lychee & fried basil salad 266-7
Satay sauce 104
Simple coconut soup-style sauce for steamed fish 162

coconut water
Berry, coconut & mint smoothie 688
coconut jelly 783
Coconut panna cotta with coconut jelly, black sesame tuiles, mango & lime leaf 783
coconut oil 22

cod 158, 160-3
Bouillabaisse-style stew 214-5
Salt-baked fish 175
Steamed whole fish with spring onion, ginger & sesame 177

coffee
Coffee cupcakes 731
Coffee granita 780
Coffee icing 804
Coffee mascarpone cream 800
coffee syrup 776
French shortbread sandwiches with mascarpone cream, almonds & praline 813
Mocha brownies 762
red wine, orange & coffee sauce 720
Tiramisu 776-7
Twice-roasted duck with salted orange, cocoa nibs & coffee 264-5
coleslaw, Italian-style 448

compotes
Cherry compote with brioche & crème fraîche 723
Cherry, vanilla & balsamic compote 722

condensed milk
Brown sugar dark chocolate loaf cake 747
Crème fraîche glaze with salted dulce de leche 804
Dulce de leche 795
Lime & coconut cheesecake 738
No-churn dulce de leche ice cream 795

condiment salads
Beetroot, carrot & pomegranate salad 420
Celeriac & mustard condiment for steak 485
Celeriac remoulade 484
Celery, lemon & parsley salad with a fried garlic & fennel seed dressing 491
Corn, black bean & pomegranate salad 503
Kohlrabi & cucumber salad with lemon yoghurt dressing 549

Raita 98
Rustic salsa verde with potato 86
Yoghurt, cucumber & mint salad/dip 508
Zaalouk 518-9
Congee 383
consommé, Oxtail 56
cookies, Gingerbread Christmas 757-8
cookware 34-41

coriander 11
Bánh mì with roast pork belly 332-3
Beef pho 57
Beef rendang 292-3
Black bean, quinoa & cherry tomato salad 380
Bo ssäm 341-2
Braised zucchini with fresh tomato & herbs 671
Butter chicken 248-9
Chargrilled poussins with a lemon, chilli, herb & golden sultana salad 236
Charred broccoli, ramen & nori salad 444-5
Chermoula 90
Chicken & corn koftas with avocado & coriander 249
Chilled cucumber & sesame salad with shiso & garlic chives 507
Chilli crab 199-200
Coriander & black pepper salt 11
Coriander, onion & citrus sauce 11
Corn & pineapple salsa 499
Crab, pea & potato samosas 611
Crisp-fried eggs, corn, smoked trout & herb salad with tangy oyster sauce dressing 358
Crispy pork belly salad with sesame spiced dressing, cucumber & coriander 331
Crispy sweet-chilli chicken with wombok, Thai basil & peanuts 242
Dal fry 388
Egg, tomato & spinach curry with ginger & turmeric 359
Fragrant chicken soup with bok choy 401-2
Fried corn cakes with chilli jam & smashed avocado 498
Fried rice with wood ear fungus & cashews 402
Green harissa 92
Grilled asparagus & haloumi salad with fennel, walnuts & pomegranate 406-7
Grilled pork fillet, wombok & crispy egg 341
Guacamole no. 2 413
Harira 461
Kimchi pancakes with a tamari & sesame dipping sauce 457
Kingfish crudo with chilli, ginger & coriander 164
lemon & coriander coating 168
lychee & fried basil salad 266-7
Mapo-style tofu with beans & pork 436
Moroccan carrot, date & green chilli salad 471

Moules frites meets South-East Asia 204
Pea salad with a golden garlic, sichuan pepper & ginger dressing 614–5
Pork roll 333
Pumpkin, chickpea, cashew & coconut curry 633
Quick-cured ocean trout with finger lime & coriander 168
Quick herb salad 267
Raita 98
red curry paste 266
Seared duck breast with roasted plum & hoisin sauce for pancakes or bao 263
Shiitake, tofu & cashew san choy bau 555
Skinless merguez-style sausages 308
Sour fish curry with okra & celery heart 581
Spiced green soup 381
Stir-fried kang kong & wombok with tofu & fermented chilli 400
Sweet & spicy Thai chicken drumettes 236–7
Syrian chicken with ginger, lemon & saffron 248
Tuna & sweet potato sesame patties with pickled arame salad 622
Tunisian vegetable couscous royale with rosewater labneh 386–7
Wild rice, herb, almond & currant salad 378
Zaalouk 518–9
Zhoug 87
coriander seeds 11

corn 496–8
Barbecued whole corn 498
Charred corn & cheddar fritters 498–9
Cheesy lunchbox muffins 858
Chicken & corn koftas with avocado & coriander 249
Chicken, corn & noodle soup 502–3
Corn & pineapple salsa 499
Corn chowder with potato & dill 502
Corn with chilli & lime glaze 502
Corn, black bean & pomegranate salad 503
Crisp-fried eggs, corn, smoked trout & herb salad with tangy oyster sauce dressing 358
Fried corn cakes with chilli jam & smashed avocado 498
Pork & prawn wontons with chilli & sichuan pepper dipping sauce 342
Prawn, corn & shiitake pot-sticker dumplings 500
Pure corn purée 499
Salted caramel & almond popcorn 788
Spiced corn & manchego loaf 858
corn salad *see* mâche
Corned beef 289
cornflour (cornstarch) 11

cornichons
Grilled gem lettuce & bagna cauda 556
Ham hock & leek terrine 328
Italian tartare 77

Pickled shallots & currants with parsley & cornichons 596
Rustic salsa verde with potato 86
Sauce gribiche 78
Traditional French steak tartare 279
Vinaigrette potatoes with cornichons, dill, caperberries, crème fraîche & fried egg 624–5
cornstarch *see* cornflour

cos (romaine) lettuce 550, 553–4
Buttery minted peas 610
Grilled gem lettuce & bagna cauda 556
Prawn cocktail 413
Roast chicken & black barley salad 246–7
Seared ocean trout with grilled lettuce, peas & pea tendrils 561–2
Watercress & potato soup 558

cotechino 326
Cassoulet 391
Petit salé aux lentilles 334–5
coulis, Raspberry toffee 689

couscous 12, 368, 537
Braised chicken & artichokes with couscous 537
Braised lamb, artichokes, lemon & cinnamon with couscous 537
moghrabieh (pearl couscous) 20
Mussels with chorizo, tomato & white wine 213
Spiced pumpkin, date, almond & moghrabieh salad 635
Tunisian vegetable couscous royale with rosewater labneh 386–7
see also moghrabieh

crabs 198
An inspiration from ajo blanco with crab 513
Bouillabaisse-style stew 214–5
Chilli crab 199–200
Corn chowder with crab, potato & dill 502
crab & ricotta cannelloni filling 135
Crab cakes 199
Crab cannelloni with crustacean dressing 135
Crab with avocado mousse, mint, chilli & sweet pickled cucumber 413
Crab, corn & shiitake pot-sticker dumplings 500
Crab, pea & potato samosas 611
Crab, prawn or bug tail risotto 149
Crumbed zucchini flowers with crab mayonnaise & peas 669
Crustacean essence 52
Crustacean stock 52
Crustacean vinaigrette 52
Fluffy prawn & crab omelette with prawn essence & watercress 355
Crab omelette with oyster sauce 353
Roast duck, crab & tapioca soup 265
Roast pumpkin & shellfish soup with Thai flavours 634
Soft polenta with crab, artichoke & poached egg 352

Spaghettini with crab, lemon, herbs & chilli 125
Vietnamese spring roll with crab, prawn & shiitake 575

crackers
Grissini 856
Lavoche-style olive oil crackers 840
Oatcake crackers 840–1
Rye crackers 838
Spiced seed crackers 839
Taralli 842
cranberries 12–3
cranberry beans *see* borlotti beans

cream 12, 730
Baked custard tart 817
Basic whipped cream 799
Basque cheesecake 738–9
Béchamel 70–1
Berries & cream sponge cake filling 748
Braised witlof with ginger & cream 554
Champignons with garlic, wine & cream 575
Chicken fricassee with cream 239
Chocolate & honey sauce 793
Chocolate biscuit sandwiches with sesame cream 754–5
Chocolate ganache 806
Chocolate mousse 782
Classic puff pastry 822
Clotted cream 800
Coffee mascarpone cream 800
Cream cheese shortcrust pastry 830
Cream of mushroom soup 574–5
Cream- or jam-filled doughnuts 773
Creamed mustard kipfler potatoes 622
Crema fresca 364
Crème brûlée 780
Cured kingfish with crema fresca, lime & spiced seed crackers 168
Dark chocolate truffles with nutty praline 791
Dauphinoise potatoes 627
Easy vanilla crème caramel 781
eggless custard 815
Gnocchi with leek & gorgonzola 602
Golden syrup butter caramel sauce 793
Grilled oysters with horseradish 210
Heavenly sponge filled with cream & strawberries 689
honey sabayon cream 703
Horseradish cream dressing 70
Jerusalem artichoke soup 544
Lemon cream & cherry possets 696
Lemon tart 814–5
No-churn dulce de leche ice cream 795
Nutella icing 805
Pâte à choux for éclairs & profiteroles 821
Pavlova 784
Piperade tart 829
profiteroles 821
Quick creamy seafood sauce or bisque 67
Rhubarb tartlets 649
Ricotta 362
Roasted garlic jus with tarragon 66

Salted butter 361
Salted caramel sauce 794
Salted macadamia & almond caramels 790
Scorched honey & yoghurt parfait 785
Sicilian cassata-style ricotta cake 752–3
Simple custard tarts 815
Spiced creamed tomato soup with bacon 665
Strawberries romanoff 688
Tagliatelle with egg, truffle & Parmigiano Reggiano 119
Tagliatelle with lemon cream 123–4
Thick vanilla custard 801
Tiramisu 776–7
Twice-baked cheese soufflé 357
Vanilla & fig leaf panna cotta with scorched lemon syrup 707
Vanilla crème anglaise 800–1
Vanilla crème pâtissière 798
vanilla custard 817
Velouté 64
Watercress & potato soup 558
Whipped white chocolate ganache 806
Yoghurt panna cotta 781
Zucchini & cream soup with cumin 673
see also coconut cream

cream cheese
Artichoke, anchovy & gruyère gratin 537
Basque cheesecake 738–9
Blackberry & coconut cheesecake muffins 732
Blintzes 771
Böreks with cheese 831
Carrot cake 742
Carrot, cinnamon, pecan & cream cheese muffins 732
Cheesecake-flavoured biscuit turnovers 825
Chocolate biscuit sandwiches with sesame cream 754–5
Cream cheese & ricotta filling 799
Cream cheese icing 803
Cream cheese shortcrust pastry 830
Frangipane crostata 826
Lemon cheesecake 698
Lime & coconut cheesecake 738
lime & coconut filling 738
Maple syrup, brown sugar & cinnamon icing 804
Quick olive dip 587
Smoked salmon & cucumber canapés 513
Vanilla frosting 803
Zucchini, coconut & macadamia muffins with lime cream cheese icing 734
cream of tartar 12
Crema fresca 364
Crème brûlée 780
crème caramel, Easy vanilla 781
crème fraîche 12
Bread sauce 70
Cherry compote with brioche & crème fraîche 723
creamy mustard dressing 484
Crème fraîche glaze 804

Cured kingfish with crema fresca, lime & spiced seed crackers 168
Fish & mussels en papillote 178
French onion soup with an indulgent French finish 596
French-inspired scramble 351
Frittata 355
Jerusalem artichoke soup with egg, crème fraîche & caviar 544
lemony tahini yoghurt 432
Mazaresi cakes 732
Omelette with smoked salmon, chives & crème fraîche 353
Roasted & raw Jerusalem artichoke salad 544
Roasted Jerusalem artichoke salad with horseradish & salmon roe 542
Salted butter 361
Vinaigrette potatoes with cornichons, dill, caperberries, crème fraîche & fried egg 624–5

crepes
Crepes 771
Crepes suzette 771
Savoury crepes 771

cress
Roast duck, crab & tapioca soup 265
see also kang kong (Siamese watercress), mustard cress, watercress
Croquetas with smoked eel & manchego 190

crostata
Crostata filled with ricotta & quince 826
Frangipane crostata 826
Jam crostata 826
crostoli 820
croûtes 174

crudo
Kingfish crudo with caviar, cucumber & mustard cress 510
Kingfish crudo with chilli, ginger & coriander 164
Snapper crudo with a lemon emulsion & horseradish 164
Snapper crudo with finger lime, fennel, chilli & a burnt butter dressing 165
crumble, Berry 688
Crumpets 769

crustaceans 194–8
see also crab, lobster, prawns

cucumber 504–6
A quick pantry snack 512
An inspiration from ajo blanco 513
Bánh mì with roast pork belly 332–3
Bo ssäm 341–2
Celery, lemon & parsley salad with a fried garlic & fennel seed dressing 491
Chilled cucumber & sesame salad with shiso & garlic chives 507
chilli cucumber dipping sauce 192
Crab with avocado mousse, mint, chilli & sweet pickled cucumber 413

Crispy pork belly salad with sesame spiced dressing, cucumber & coriander 331
Crunchy lacto-fermented dill pickles 505
Cucumber & lime granita with gin jelly, yoghurt sorbet & minted cucumber 511
cucumber & wakame salad 415
Cucumber kimchi 456
Cucumber sandwiches 511
cucumber, celery heart & herb salad 240
Cucumber, grape & herb salad with shallot dressing 508
Gado gado with roasted cauliflower, cucumber & eggs 478
Gazpacho 657
Greek salad 512
Japanese quick-pickled cucumber & wakame salad 506
Kingfish crudo with caviar, cucumber & mustard cress 510
Kohlrabi & cucumber salad with lemon yoghurt dressing 549
Oyster shooters with cucumber, ginger vinegar & white pepper jelly 510–1
pickled arame salad 622
Pickled Lebanese cucumbers 506
Pickled spring vegetables 470–1
Prawn & poached chicken vermicelli salad 240
Rockling with Thai caramel sauce & herbs 172
Seared duck breast with roasted plum & hoisin sauce for pancakes or bao 263
Sesame saganaki with quick-pickled cucumber 510
Smoked salmon & cucumber canapés 513
Spiced Chinese pickles 640
Spicy pork bao 333
Stir-fried cucumber with wood ear fungus & snow peas 510
sweet pickled cucumber 413
Tom yum goong 201
Tuna poké bowl with avocado, shiitake, sesame, wakame & cucumber 415
Tzatziki 507
Yoghurt, cucumber & mint salad/dip 508
cumin 12

cupcakes
Coffee cupcakes 731
Red velvet cupcakes with Italian meringue icing 731
Vanilla cupcakes 731
curd, Lemon, lime or passionfruit 797
cured meat *see* bacon, bresaola, chorizo, guanciale, jamón, lardo, morcilla, mortadella, pancetta, pastrami, prosciutto, salami, sausages

currants
Barbecued Dutch carrot & leek salad 468–9
Beetroot tabouleh with currants & sunflower seeds 419
Blintzes 771
Borlotti beans with herbs & freekeh 427

Broad bean & pea salad with nasturtium leaves, goat's cheese & bagna cauda 431

Cheese, silverbeet & hazelnut filling for sambouseks 833

Chicken chops with wild rice salad 379

Chicken livers with witlof & radicchio fatoush salad, currants & sumac 234

Christmas pudding 778–9

Classic hot cross buns 765

Dolmades with rice, pine nuts, currants & lemon 375

Fennel & mandarin salad with olives, currants & chilli 531

Leek with walnut & rye skordalia 600

Pickled shallots & currants with parsley & cornichons 596

Roasted carrots with harissa & goat's curd 468

Spaghetti with sardines, currants & pine nuts 124

Syrian chicken with ginger, lemon & saffron 248

Vegan & vegetarian baked tomatoes 663

Viennese strudel 684–5

Vine leaf beef & bone marrow pie 287

Wild rice, herb, almond & currant salad 378

curries

Beef rendang 292–3

Butter chicken 248–9

Chicken coconut curry with makrut lime leaf, lemongrass & turmeric 238

Egg, tomato & spinach curry with ginger & turmeric 359

Lamb & eggplant karahi curry 318

Lamb rogan josh 317–8

Pumpkin, chickpea, cashew & coconut curry 633

Red duck curry with lychee & fried basil salad 266–7

Sour fish & mussel curry with celery hearts & kang kong 488–9

Sour fish curry with okra & celery heart 581

curry leaves 12

Braised red lentils with turmeric, curry leaves, fried garlic & haloumi 387

Herb oil for fish 165

Lamb & eggplant karahi curry 318

Mango, ginger & chilli relish 495

Pumpkin, chickpea, cashew & coconut curry 633

Rockling with Thai caramel sauce & herbs 172

Sour fish curry with okra & celery heart 581

Spiced okra with curry leaves 582

Stir-fried chicken thighs with kecap manis, curry leaves & black pepper 234

curry powder 12

custards

Baked custard tart 817

Banana custard 801

custard 356

eggless custard 815

Thick vanilla custard 801

vanilla custard 817

cuttlefish 216–7

Risotto nero with cuttlefish 149–50

D

daikon 636–9

Daikon & shiitake braised in soy dashi & brown butter sauce 642

Daikon, edamame & avocado salad, with sesame, apple & soy dressing 640–1

Fish marinated with white miso 184

Kimchi 455–6

Pickled daikon & mint salad 304

Spiced Chinese pickles 640

Tempura dipping sauce 98

Tuna poké bowl with avocado, shiitake, sesame, wakame & cucumber 415

Vietnamese spring roll with crab, prawn & shiitake 575

Wombok, daikon, shiitake & tofu salad 450

dairy 348–50, 730

see also butter, cream, crème fraîche, fromage frais, milk, sour cream, yoghurt

dal

Black dal 389

Dal fry 388

Dashi 53

dashi powder 12

dates

date paste 314

Date, sesame, coconut & macadamia nut balls 393

Lamb, spinach, pomegranate & date salad with crisp pitta 314

Lemon, date & orange-blossom marmalade 699

Moroccan carrot, date & green chilli salad 471

Saffron scones with lemon, date & orange-blossom marmalade & labneh 772

Sticky date pudding 778

Dauphinoise potatoes 627

Dauphinoise with camembert 627

Devilled eggs 356

dill 12

Beetroot tabouleh with currants & sunflower seeds 419

Böreks with cheese & greens 831

Braised artichoke, fennel & broad bean salad with orange glaze 536

Byzantine salad 379

Cabbage rolls with lamb, rice, pine nuts & dill 451

Cauliflower salad (roasted & raw) 478–9

Celery salad with fennel, capers & dill 491

Chargrilled poussins with a lemon, chilli, herb & golden sultana salad 236

Chicken, leek & mushroom pie 603

Chopped egg tartare 351

Citrus-cured gravlax 169

Corn chowder with potato & dill 502

Crunchy lacto-fermented dill pickles 505

Cucumber, grape & herb salad with shallot dressing 508

Frittata 355

Green tomato salsa with dill & mint 664

Greens & cheese pie 564–5

Italian tartare 77

Kohlrabi & cucumber salad with lemon yoghurt dressing 549

Omelette with blackened roma tomatoes, dill & marinated feta 353

Pan-seared tomatoes on toast with feta & dill 663

Quick herb salad 267

Roast chicken with butter & dill 250

Salad of lentils & smoked trout with dill & horseradish cream dressing 385

Spinach, lentil & yoghurt salad with brown butter 558

Vinaigrette potatoes with cornichons, dill, caperberries, crème fraîche & fried egg 624–5

Wild rice, herb, almond & currant salad 378

Wombok, daikon, shiitake & tofu salad 450

dill seeds 12

dipping sauces

Chilli & ginger dumpling dipping sauce 103

chilli cucumber dipping sauce 192

Coconut hoisin dipping sauce 96

Fresh ponzu 101

sichuan pepper dipping sauce 342

soy, sesame & ginger dipping sauce 500

tamari & sesame dipping sauce 457

Tempura dipping sauce 98

dips

Bagna cauda 83

Black aïoli 76

Black aïoli with cured meat 76

Broad bean & avocado dip 431

Fava 373

Hummus 374

Quick olive dip 587

Roasted beetroot, cinnamon & pomegranate dip 420

Simple guacamole 412

Spicy aïoli 76

Tahini dip/sauce 71

Taramasalata 182

Turkish-style roast pumpkin & walnut dip 632–3

Tzatziki 507

Yoghurt, cucumber & mint salad/dip 508

Zaalouk 518–9

see also dipping sauces, mayonnaise, sauces, skordalia

dolmades 375

Domatokeftedes 664

dough
  cardamom dough 766
  choux dough 821
  Coeliac pizza bases 857
  Egg pasta dough 111–3
  Galani dough for crostoli & cannoli 820
  Pizza base 856
  samosa dough 611
  Semolina dough for orecchiette, pici & gnocchi sardi 131
  sourdough mother/starter 849
  yeasted Babka dough 763

doughnuts
  Classic doughnuts 774
  Cream- or jam-filled doughnuts 773
  Doughnuts in honey & orange-blossom syrup with ricotta & pistachios 773
  Mini cinnamon-bomb doughnuts 773
  Orange & anise doughnuts 773

dressings 62–3
  black sesame dressing 561
  Buttermilk dressing 361
  carrot top dressing 469
  chilli garlic dressing 527
  chilli, lime & brown sugar dressing 499
  Cognac dijon dressing 279
  creamy mustard dressing 484
  Crispy garlic & soy vinegar dressing 94
  cumin & garlic dressing 419
  cumin & vinegar dressing 379
  feta dressing 432–3
  Fresh ponzu 101
  ginger & sesame dressing 450
  ginger, lime & olive oil dressing 510
  golden garlic, sichuan pepper & ginger dressing 614
  Goma dare (sesame dressing) 102
  Green goddess dressing 89
  hazelnut vinegar dressing 560
  Horseradish cream dressing 70
  lemon & oregano dressing 218
  lemon garlic dressing 407
  lemon mustard dressing 490
  lemon yoghurt dressing 549
  lime & pomegranate dressing 503
  maple dressing 453
  Mignonette dressing for oysters 207
  mint & lemon dressing 427
  orange & tarragon dressing 528
  paprika vinegar dressing 462
  Peanut & ginger dressing 95
  pomegranate dressing 262
  pomegranate dressing 314
  Prawn dressing 67
  Salmoriglio 83
  sesame & lime dressing 507
  sesame & mirin dressing 582
  Sesame dressing 94
  sesame, apple & soy dressing 640
  shallot dressing 508
  sherry vinegar dressing 710
  Sichuan pepper & chilli dressing 93
  Smoky tomato dressing 84
  soft-boiled egg dressing 557
  sour cream dressing 449
  sour cream roast garlic dressing 484
  spiced lemon dressing 477
  Spiced sesame & peanut dressing 94
  tahini & yoghurt dressing 478–9
  tahini dressing 518
  tamari sesame dressing 415
  tangy oyster sauce dressing 358
  Toasted sesame & miso dressing 102
  Tomato, pomegranate & sumac dressing 82
  truffle dressing 203
  umeboshi & sesame dressing 410
  Wholegrain mustard & maple dressing 87
  yoghurt dressing 560
  see also vinaigrettes
dried scallops (conpoy) 13

duck 256–8
  Cassoulet 391
  Duck bresaola 267
  duck fat 13
  Duck leg confit 260
  Duck rillettes with sherry 330
  Duck, celeriac & verjuice ragù 259
  Liver parfait 233
  Pan-seared duck breasts 263
  Quick & simple duck stock 266
  quick duck stock 50
  Red duck curry with lychee & fried basil salad 266–7
  Roast duck & pan sauce 258–9
  Roast duck, crab & tapioca soup 265
  Roasted potatoes with thyme 626
  Scorched honey & thyme gastrique for duck 265
  Seared duck breast with roasted plum & hoisin sauce for pancakes or bao 263
  Shiitake, duck & cashew san choy bau 555
  Simple duck sauce 262
  Slow-roasted duck with baharat & pomegranate molasses 265
  Spiced duck with pickled watermelon 262
  Take a Chinese barbecued duck and … 258
  Twice-roasted duck 264
  Twice-roasted duck with salted orange, cocoa nibs & coffee 264–5

dukkah 13
  Tunisian dukkah 13
Dulce de leche 795
dulce de leche, No-churn, ice cream 795

dumplings
  Chicken & ginger wontons with peanuts 231
  Pork & prawn wontons with chilli & sichuan pepper dipping sauce 342
  Pork & prawn wontons with choy sum & kale 342
  Pork, wombok & ginger dumplings 500
  Prawn, corn & shiitake pot-sticker dumplings 500

E

éclairs 821
edamame 13
  Daikon, edamame & avocado salad, with sesame, apple & soy dressing 640–1
eel
  Crisp-fried eggs, corn & herb salad with eel 358
  Croquetas with smoked eel & manchego 190
  Jerusalem artichoke soup with seafood 544
  Vinaigrette potatoes with seafood 624–5
eggplant 514–6
  Baba ghanoush 519
  Caponata bianco with toasted walnuts 489
  Capsicum & eggplant salad 464
  Crispy eggplant with spiced caramel & fried Thai basil 522–3
  Deluxe eggplant parmigiana with anchovies 522
  Eggplant & tomato kasundi 520
  Eggplant chips 518
  Eggplant purée with chilli oil & walnuts 516
  Eggplant with miso glaze & spring onions 521
  Eggplant, sesame, egg, olive & radish salad 518
  Grilled eggplant with tahini & yoghurt dressing, pomegranate, chilli & mint 516
  Lamb & eggplant karahi curry 318
  Lamb koftas baked with tomato & smoky eggplant, with pine nuts & parsley 309–10
  Melanzane sotto aceto with banana peppers, basil & chilli 523
  Moussaka 310–1
  Orecchiette with eggplant, oregano, balsamic & ricotta 132–3
  Pasta alla Norma 521
  Ratatouille 672
  Red duck curry with lychee & fried basil salad 266–7
  Smoked eggplant soup with kefalograviera 519
  Summer vegetable lasagne 136
  Vegetarian baked haloumi-stuffed eggplant 521
  Zaalouk 518–9
eggs 13, 348–51, 730
  63°C (145°F) egg 351
  A simple frangipane fruit tart 796
  Aïoli 76
  Asparagus with poached egg & prosciutto 406
  Baked custard tart 817
  Banana custard 801
  Black aïoli 76
  Boiled egg on toast with anchovies, onion & paprika 352

Braised artichoke, egg, olive & watercress salad 538
Charred broccolini with tuna mayonnaise, black barley, egg & anchovy dust 442–3
Chawanmushi 356
Chicken, corn & noodle soup 502–3
Chocolate crème pâtissière 798–9
Chopped egg tartare 351
Crème brûlée 780
Crisp-fried eggs, corn, smoked trout & herb salad with tangy oyster sauce dressing 358
Devilled eggs 356
Egg pasta 111–3
Egg, tomato & spinach curry with ginger & turmeric 359
Eggplant, sesame, egg, olive & radish salad 518
Eggs en cocotte with wilted spinach & parmesan 359
Fennel, egg, lemon & rice brodo with & ricotta bruschetta 483
Fluffy goat's cheese & gruyère omelette 355
Fluffy prawn & crab omelette with prawn essence & watercress 355
French onion soup with an indulgent French finish 596
French-inspired scramble 351
Fried rice with peas, prawns & egg 610
Frittata 355
Gado gado with roasted cauliflower, cucumber & eggs 478
Giant meringues 784
Hollandaise 79
honey sabayon cream 703
Italian meringue 807
Jerusalem artichoke soup with egg, crème fraîche & caviar 544
Kingfish kibbeh with egg 166
Left-over corned beef, egg & cabbage salad with smoked salt 289
Lemon meringue pie 806
Lemon tart 814–5
Lemon, lime or passionfruit curd 797
Lime & coconut cheesecake with meringue 738
Lobster salad à la russe 200
Mascarpone citrus curd icing 803
Master olive oil mayonnaise 74
Omelette with pecorino & parsley 352–3
Pan con tomate with soft-boiled eggs & celery salt 656
Pavlova 784
Piperade tart 829
Red velvet cupcakes with Italian meringue icing 731
Roasted & raw fennel salad with mint & egg yolk 527
Roasted apricot & ginger clafoutis 721
Rouille 80
Sauce gribiche 78
Scotch quail eggs 360
Shakshuka with capsicum 463
Simple Thai-style hard-boiled eggs 356

soft-boiled egg dressing 557
Soft-boiled eggs with green mango salad & citrus & chilli relish 358
Spaghetti carbonara 119–20
Spiced tea eggs 356
Squid ink pasta 128
Stracciatella soup 55
Tagliatelle with egg, truffle & Parmigiano Reggiano 119
Thick vanilla custard 801
tonnato sauce 297
Tortilla de patata 623
Truffled eggs 357
Truffled eggs en cocotte 357
Tuna niçoise 438–9
Twice-baked cheese soufflé 357
Vanilla crème anglaise 800–1
Vanilla crème pâtissière 798
vanilla custard 817
Vegetarian waldorf salad 490
Vinaigrette potatoes with cornichons, dill, caperberries, crème fraîche & fried egg 624–5
Vitello tonnato 297
Whole-egg mayonnaise 75
zabaglione 776
emulsion, Lemon 80
endive see chicory

endive, curly (frisée) 550–5
A nod to Harry's Bar original carpaccio 280
Crispy lamb's brains, pancetta & feta, with curly endive & mint 308
Grilled gem lettuce & bagna cauda 556
Maltagliata of beef with rocket, fine kale & ricotta 288
Quail saltimbocca with caramelised pears 268–9
Spaghettini with crab, lemon, herbs & chilli 125
energy balls: Date, sesame, coconut & macadamia nut balls 393

enoki mushrooms 568
Grilled minute steak with soy & sesame mushrooms 281
Tom yum goong 201
extract, Pandan 744

F

falafels
Falafel with broad beans & tahini yoghurt 432
Plain falafel 432
farro 13, 368
Braised lamb neck broth with grains 309
Roasted cauliflower, barley & parsley salad with scorched almonds & feta 477
Fava 373
fava beans 8
Spiced bean & vegetable braise 425

fennel 13, 524–6
A simple roast chicken 229
Apple, fennel & witlof slaw with buttermilk dressing 680
Baked fennel & leek with provolone sauce 528–9
Black turtle bean, pork belly & morcilla braise (frijoles negros) 340
Bouillabaisse-style stew 214–5
Braised artichoke, fennel & broad bean salad with orange glaze 536
Braised fennel with tomato & olives 529
Caramelised fennel 525
Celeriac, fennel & rice brodo with ricotta bruschetta 483
Celery salad with fennel, capers & dill 491
Cevapcici with wild fennel 529
charred fennel salad 176
Charred fennel salad with tarragon 528
Classic white vegetable stock 51
Crunchy lacto-fermented vegetables 508
Crustacean stock 52
Cured kingfish with crema fresca, lime & spiced seed crackers 168
Fennel & buffalo mozzarella salad with broad beans, mint & green sultanas 530
Fennel & mandarin salad with olives, currants & chilli 531
Fennel & orange salad with olives, currants & chilli 530
Fennel chips 531
Fennel, egg & rice brodo with bruschetta 483
Fennel gratin 528
Fennel, potato & sausage tray bake 530
Fish & mussels en papillote 178
Fish pie 188–9
Fish soup with spiced rouille & croûtes 174–5
Fish stock 52–3
Greek salad 512
Grilled asparagus & haloumi salad with fennel, walnuts & pomegranate 406–7
Herb oil for fish 165
Left-over chicken, barley & vegetable soup 252
Malloreddus with prawns & fennel 526
Oven-baked poussins with tomato, sherry, fennel & olives 590–1
Pea & ham soup 334
Pear, fennel & witlof slaw with buttermilk dressing 680
Pear, fennel, celery heart, Roquefort & poppy seed salad 710
Pickled spring vegetables 470–1
Pork chops with orange & fennel glaze 343–4
Prawns with cannellini beans & truffle 203
Roasted & raw fennel salad with mint & egg yolk 527
Roasted celeriac, parsnip, potato & fennel with ras el hanout 485
Roasted flounder with charred fennel 176
Roasted rack of pork with fennel 343
Robust vegetable fumet 51

Sauce vierge 82
Shaved fennel, artichoke & almond salad
    535–6
Skinless merguez-style sausages 308
Snapper crudo with finger lime, fennel,
    chilli & a burnt butter dressing 165
Spiced Chinese pickles 640
Spiced-yoghurt leg of lamb 311–2
Spring minestrone 531
Sweet pickled fennel 531
treacle, fennel & pepper cure 171
Tunisian vegetable couscous royale with
    rosewater labneh 386–7
*Waldorf salad with roast chicken & more
    vegetables* 490
Winter minestrone with roasted root
    vegetables 607

fennel seeds 13
Celery, lemon & parsley salad with a fried
    garlic & fennel seed dressing 491
Cured kingfish with fennel, paprika &
    pepper 171
Fennel, black pepper & garlic paste 529
fennel, sumac & yoghurt marinade 311
Gravlax with treacle, fennel & pepper 171
Mussels with garlic, black pepper & fennel
    seeds 213
Taralli 842

fenugreek 13
Black dal 389
celery & olive salad 188
Fried sardines with tomato & fig 705
Kingfish kibbeh nayyeh 166
Kohlrabi, cauliflower & fenugreek soup
    548
seeds 14
Sour fish curry with okra & celery heart
    581
Spiced bean & vegetable braise 425

feta 14
Baked tomatoes stuffed with rice, feta &
    pine nuts 663
*Baked zucchini stuffed with rice, feta & pine
    nuts* 663
Böreks with cheese 831
Cheddar & feta scones with mixed seeds
    859
Cheese, silverbeet & hazelnut filling for
    sambouseks 833
Cheese-filled lebanese talami bread 852
Crispy lamb's brains, pancetta & feta, with
    curly endive & mint 308
feta dressing 432–3
Greek salad 512
Greens & cheese pie 564–5
Grilled lamb cutlets with smashed broad
    beans & hot feta dressing 432–3
Grilled pumpkin salad with pumpkin oil
    dressing, pickled grapes & goat's cheese
    630
Lamb koftas baked with tomato & smoky
    eggplant, with pine nuts & parsley
    309–10
Lebanese talami bread with cheese & greens
    852

Lemonia's pumpkin & feta pie with olive oil
    pastry 631
*Omelette with blackened roma tomatoes,
    dill & marinated feta* 353
Pan-seared tomatoes on toast with feta &
    dill 663
Piperade tart 829
Ricotta & goat's cheese ravioli 117
Roasted beetroot, cinnamon &
    pomegranate dip 420
Roasted cauliflower, barley & parsley salad
    with scorched almonds & feta 477
Roasted pumpkin with cinnamon, chilli,
    pickled onion, yoghurt & feta 631
Roasted tomatoes with sumac & cumin 30
Savoury scones 772
Silverbeet or zucchini & feta omelette 353
Slow-roasted red onion frittata 598
Smashed broccoli with preserved lemon
    442
Smoked eggplant soup with tahini & feta
    519
Spinach, ricotta & feta cannelloni with
    mint passata sauce 133
Zucchini, ham & pea slice with feta 672–3

fettucine 112
Fettuccine alfredo 119

field mushrooms 568, 571
Barley 'risotto' with mushrooms & speck
    572
Chickpeas with mushrooms, red-wine
    vinaigrette & tarragon 574
Cream of mushroom soup 574–5
Grilled minute steak with soy & sesame
    mushrooms 281
Grilled mushrooms 575
Mushroom ragù 576–7
Mushroom tortellini 115
Omelette with mushroom & taleggio 353
Risotto funghi 149
Vegetable bolognese 576

figs 700–1
A simple frangipane fruit tart 796
Brûléed figs 707
Chocolate panforte with almonds, figs &
    sour cherries 760–1
Even simpler frangipane tarts 797
Fig & filo honey stack 703
Fig & ginger jam 706
Figs poached in syrup 703
Fried sardines with tomato & fig 705
Gorgonzola, fig & walnut pizza 857
Jamón, fig, beetroot, goat's curd, watercress
    & mint salad 702
Toffeed figs 705
Vanilla & fig leaf panna cotta with scorched
    lemon syrup 707
Veal saltimbocca with fresh figs 702–3
filo pastry 564

finger limes
*Cured kingfish with crema fresca, finger
    lime & spiced seed crackers* 168
Kingfish crudo with caviar, cucumber &
    mustard cress 510

Quick-cured ocean trout with finger lime &
    coriander 168
Snapper crudo with finger lime, fennel,
    chilli & a burnt butter dressing 165
Tuna poké bowl with avocado, shiitake,
    sesame, wakame & cucumber 415
fior di latte: Insalata caprese 662

fish 154–63
buying 154–7
Corn chowder with smoked fish 502
Fish & mussels en papillote 178
Fish cakes with parsley 190–1
Fish marinated with white miso 184
Fish soup with spiced rouille & croûtes
    174–5
Fish stock 52–3
preparing 157–63
*Roasted & raw fennel salad with preserved
    fish* 527
Roasted flounder with charred fennel 176
Rockling with Thai caramel sauce & herbs
    172
Salt-baked fish 175
Simple seafood pie sauce 71
Sour fish & mussel curry with celery hearts
    & kang kong 488–9
Sour fish curry with okra & celery heart
    581
Steamed whole fish with spring onion,
    ginger & sesame 177
Swordfish with beurre rouge 183
Thai fish cakes 192–3
see also anchovies, bass grouper, blue-eye
    trevalla, bottarga, cod, fish roe, flathead,
    gurnard, hapuka, katsuobushi (bonito
    flakes), kingfish, mackerel, mullet,
    salmon, sardines, snapper, trout, tuna,
    whiting

fish roe
Barbecued prawns with taramasalata &
    salmon roe 202
Crab with avocado mousse, mint, chilli &
    sweet pickled cucumber 413
Devilled eggs with shellfish 356
*Jerusalem artichoke soup with egg, crème
    fraiche & caviar* 544
Kingfish crudo with caviar, cucumber &
    mustard cress 510
Kingfish kibbeh nayyeh 166
Oyster shooters with cucumber, ginger
    vinegar & white pepper jelly 510–1
Quick-cured ocean trout with finger lime &
    coriander 168
Slow-roasted Jerusalem artichokes with
    roe & pan-fried scallops 542
Smoked salmon & cucumber canapés 513
Roasted Jerusalem artichoke salad with
    horseradish & salmon roe 542
Tagliatelle with lemon cream & caviar 124
Taramasalata 182
wasabi tobiko 32
fish sauce 14
Flatbread-style focaccia 845

flathead
    Beer-battered flathead & twice-cooked potato cakes 187
    Classic fish & potato cakes 187
    Fish cakes with parsley 190–1
    Fish pie 188–9
    Fish stock 52–3
    Fried fish with tomato & fig 705
flax seeds *see* linseeds
flours 730
    for pasta 108
    types of 14
focaccia
    Anchovy, tomato & basil topping for focaccia 844
    Basil & tomato topping for focaccia 844
    Flatbread-style focaccia 845
    focaccia Pugliese (Potato bread) 844
    Schiacciata con l'uva 845
    Slow-rise focaccia 845
fontina 14
    Artichoke, anchovy & gruyère gratin 537
    Baked polenta with gorgonzola, radicchio, walnuts & balsamic 382
    Deluxe eggplant parmigiana with anchovies 522
    Greens, potato & cheese pie with olive oil pastry 828
    Jerusalem artichoke soup with cheese toast 544
Frangipane 796
Frangipane crostata 826
freekeh 14, 368
    Borlotti beans with herbs & freekeh 427
    Byzantine salad 379
    cooking 371
    Kingfish kibbeh nayyeh 166
    Roasted cauliflower, barley & parsley salad with scorched almonds & feta 477
Friands 734–5
fricassee, Chicken, with Dutch creams, speck & tarragon 239
frisée *see* endive, curly
frittatas
    Frittata 355
    Slow-roasted red onion frittata 598
fritters
    Charred corn & cheddar fritters 498–9
    Lamb, pea & mint pancake fritters 319
    Sweet potato fritters 625
    Zucchini & haloumi fritters with burnt honey sauce 673–4
fromage frais
    Braised artichoke, egg, olive & watercress salad 538
    Fromage frais or yoghurt panna cotta 781
    Lemon cheesecake 698
frosting *see* icing
fudge icing, Chocolate 805
fumet, Robust vegetable 51
furikake 15

G

Gado gado with roasted cauliflower, cucumber & eggs 478
gai choy (mustard greens) 398, 553
gai lan 398
    Fried rice with wood ear fungus & cashews 402
    Stir-fried choy sum & gai lan with oyster sauce 401
galangal 15
    Fragrant chicken soup with bok choy 401–2
    Moules frites meets South-East Asia 204
    red curry paste 266
    rendang paste 293
    Satay sauce 104
    Tom yum goong 201
Galani dough for crostoli & cannoli 820
galettes
    Apple, blueberry & blackberry galette 818
    Deluxe chocolate galette cake 746–7
    Rhubarb galette 650
    Sweet galette pastry 813
ganache
    Chocolate & avocado ganache 412
    Chocolate ganache 806
    Whipped white chocolate ganache 806
Garam masala 15
garlic 15
    Abbacchio al forno 315–6
    Aïoli 76
    Anchoïade 78
    Black aïoli 76
    Braised artichokes with garlic, bay & white wine glaze 534
    Braised red lentils with turmeric, curry leaves, fried garlic & haloumi 387
    Braised silverbeet with garlic & lemon 555
    Brined roast chicken, Greek-style, with magic smashed potatoes 245
    Broccoli stems with chilli & garlic 443
    Broccolini with speck, shallot & garlic 442
    Celery, lemon & parsley salad with a fried garlic & fennel seed dressing 491
    Chickpea, garlic & turmeric salad with witlof 386
    chilli garlic dressing 527
    Clams with jamón, garlic & butterbeans 211
    Crispy garlic & soy vinegar dressing 94
    cumin & garlic dressing 419
    Duck leg confit 260
    Fennel, black pepper & garlic paste 529
    Garlicky green olive tapenade 590
    Gruyère & confit garlic tarts 828
    Ham hock & leek terrine 328
    lemon garlic dressing 407
    lemon garlic mayonnaise 200
    Mezzanotte paste 588
    Mussels with garlic & tomato 214

    Mussels with garlic, black pepper & fennel seeds 213
    Pea salad with a golden garlic, sichuan pepper & ginger dressing 614–5
    Pedro Ximénez–braised beef cheeks with celeriac & parsnip purée & persillade 285–6
    Pho broth 57–8
    Pulled slow-cooked pork shoulder with cider 333
    Roasted garlic jus with tarragon 66
    Roasted parsnip & purple sweet potato with cinnamon, nutmeg & garlic 606–7
    Rosemary, garlic & parmesan oil 26
    Simply roasted leg of lamb with rosemary & garlic 315
    sour cream roast garlic dressing 484
    truffle dressing 203
    Veal scallopini with guanciale, oyster mushrooms & fermented garlic 295
    Whole snapper pan-fried with bay & garlic 181
    XO sauce 98
    yoghurt & garlic sauce 312
garlic chives *see* chives
garlic powder 15
gastrique, Scorched honey & thyme, for duck 265
Gazpacho 657
gelatine 15
gem lettuce
    Grilled gem lettuce & bagna cauda 556
    Watercress & potato soup 558
ghee 159
gigante beans 8
    Gigantes plaki 380–1
ginger 15–6
    Asian brisket with vinegared blood plums 291
    Beetroot jelly 421
    Berry & ginger clafoutis 721
    Black bean & ginger sauce 100
    Black dal 389
    Braised witlof with ginger 554
    Charred broccoli, ramen & nori salad 444–5
    Cherry & ginger clafoutis 721
    Chicken & ginger wontons with peanuts 231
    Chicken, corn & noodle soup 502
    Chilli & ginger dumpling dipping sauce 103
    Chocolate ginger icing 805
    Chocolate hot cross buns 765
    Chow mein-style beef with wombok 292
    Congee 383
    Cream cheese icing with ginger 803
    Daikon & shiitake braised in soy dashi & brown butter sauce 642
    Dal fry 388
    Egg, tomato & spinach curry with ginger & turmeric 359
    fennel, sumac & yoghurt marinade 311
    Fig & ginger jam 706

Fish marinated with white miso 184
Fried rice with wood ear fungus & cashews 402
ginger & sesame dressing 450
Ginger & spring onion sauce 95
ginger, lime & olive oil dressing 510
Ginger, soy & gochujang sauce 95
Gingerbread Christmas cookies 757–8
Glazed red pork with cassia, star anise, black vinegar & wood ear fungus 341
Gochujang chilli sauce 97
golden garlic, sichuan pepper & ginger dressing 614
Grilled minute steak with soy & sesame mushrooms 281
Japanese-style chicken meatballs 251
Kimchi 455–6
Kingfish crudo with chilli, ginger & coriander 164
Korean sesame grilled beef with sake, ginger & soy marinade 293
Lamb & eggplant karahi curry 318
Lamb rogan josh 317–8
lemongrass & ginger marinade 237
Mango with salted caramel, ginger & lime 794
Mango, ginger & chilli relish 495
Mapo-style tofu with beans & pork 436
Oyster shooters with cucumber, ginger vinegar & white pepper jelly 510–1
Peanut & ginger dressing 95
Pho broth 57–8
Pork & prawn wontons with chilli & sichuan pepper dipping sauce 342
Pork & prawn wontons with choy sum & kale 342
Pork, wombok & ginger dumplings 500
Prawn, corn & shiitake pot-sticker dumplings 500
Preserved Meyer lemons with ginger & star anise 696–7
Pumpkin, chickpea, cashew & coconut curry 633
Raita 98
Red duck curry with lychee & fried basil salad 266–7
rendang paste 293
Roast carrot & root vegetable soup with cinnamon & ginger 472
Roasted apricot & ginger clafoutis 721
Roasted blood plum relish 725
Roasted eye fillet with Japanese seasonings 286
roasted plum & hoisin sauce 263
Roasted rhubarb, blood plum & ginger chutney 646
Satay sauce 104
sesame & mirin dressing 582
sesame, apple & soy dressing 640
Shiitake, tofu & cashew san choy bau 555
Shoyu ramen broth 58–9
Simple coconut soup-style sauce for steamed fish 162
Simple honey, soy & ginger drumettes 237
soy, sesame & ginger dipping sauce 500

Spiced Chinese pickles 640
Spiced red wine pears 710–1
Spicy malt plum sauce 725
Spring onion oil 103
Steamed whole fish with spring onion, ginger & sesame 177
Sticky chocolate ginger cake 745
Stir-fried choy sum & gai lan with oyster sauce 401
Stir-fried green beans with sesame, ginger & oyster sauce 437
Stir-fried kang kong & wombok with tofu & fermented chilli 400
Sweet & sour sauce with pineapple 100
Syrian chicken with ginger, lemon & saffron 248
Teriyaki sauce 101
White-poached chicken 230
XO sauce 98

glazes
  Baby turnips with butter glaze 643
  Braised artichokes with garlic, bay & white wine glaze 534
  chocolate glaze 749
  Corn with chilli & lime glaze 502
  Crème fraîche glaze 804
  maple glaze 331
  Miso doughnut glaze with sesame 774
  miso glaze 521
  orange glaze 536
  rich soy glaze 840
  Sherry vinegar–glazed shallots & taleggio on toast 596
  Sichuan pepper & honey glaze 331
  Smashed blueberry glaze 774
globe artichoke see artichokes
glucose 16
gnocchi
  Classic potato gnocchi 137–8
  Gnocchi alla romana 138
  gnocchi sardi 131
  Gnocchi with leek & gorgonzola 602
  Gnocchi with prawns & fennel 526
  Pan-seared potato gnocchi with scallops, mushrooms & lemon 140
  preparing 136–7
  Ricotta & semolina gnocchi 141
gnudi, Ricotta & spinach 141
goat: Capretto 316
goat's cheese & curd
  Basque cheesecake 738–9
  Broad bean & pea salad with nasturtium leaves, goat's cheese & bagna cauda 431
  Bruschetta with cheese 655
  Fluffy goat's cheese & gruyère omelette 355
  Frittata 355
  goat's curd 16
  Grilled pumpkin salad with pumpkin oil dressing, pickled grapes & goat's cheese 630
  Harissa roast capsicum salad with goat's cheese 462

  Jerusalem artichoke soup with cheese toast 544
  Lemon cheesecake 698
  Omelette with goat's curd & chives 353
  Piperade tart 829
  Raw Jerusalem artichoke salad with broad beans & cheese 544
  Ricotta & goat's cheese ravioli 117
  Roasted carrots with harissa & goat's curd 468
  Roasted cauliflower, barley & parsley salad with scorched almonds & feta 477
  Shaved fennel & artichoke salad with goat's cheese 536
  Smoked eggplant soup with goat's cheese 519
  Spiced corn & manchego loaf 858
  Tomato tarte tatin with manchego, thyme & dried olives 660
  Twice-baked cheese soufflé 357
gochugaru 16
  Kimchi 455–6
  red kimchi paste 456
gochujang 16
  Barbecued prawns with gochujang, sesame & lime 202
  Bo ssäm 341–2
  Ginger, soy & gochujang sauce 95
  Gochujang chilli sauce 97
  Korean-style fried chicken 237
  Seared beef with bean thread noodles, beans, wood ear fungus & gochujang 292
  Speedy pork belly with gochujang 341
  Spicy pork bao 333
goji berries 13
Goma dare (sesame dressing) 102
Gomashio 16
gorgonzola
  Apple, fennel & witlof slaw with cheese 680
  Baked polenta with gorgonzola, radicchio, walnuts & balsamic 382
  Gnocchi with leek & gorgonzola 602
  Gorgonzola with port-steeped muscatels & oatcakes 841
  Gorgonzola, fig & walnut pizza 857
  Pear, fennel, celery heart, Roquefort & poppy seed salad 710
grains 368–9
  cooking 371–2
  see also amaranth, barley, buckwheat, bulgur, couscous, farro, freekeh, polenta, quinoa, rice, rye, spelt
Grana Padano 24, 111
  Abbacchio al forno 315–6
  Artichoke, anchovy & gruyère gratin 537
  Baked lamb-stuffed eggplant 520–1
  Barley 'risotto' with mushrooms & speck 572
  Béchamel 70–1
  Braised pork shoulder with borlotti beans & taleggio 424
  Broccoli with lemon, chilli, fennel seeds & pecorino 444

Broccolini with speck, shallot & garlic 442
Bucatini amatriciana 121
Casarecce with osso buco 121
Cheesy buttered broad beans & peas 430
Crumbed asparagus spears 407
Deluxe eggplant parmigiana with anchovies 522
Gnocchi alla romana 138
Gnocchi with leek & gorgonzola 602
Italian sausage ragù 335
Italian-style coleslaw 448
Lasagne 136
Left-over corned beef, egg & cabbage salad with smoked salt 289
Lemonia's pumpkin & feta pie with olive oil pastry 631
Mac & cheese 120
Mortadella agnolotti 114
Orecchiette with eggplant, oregano, balsamic & ricotta 132–3
Pesto 90
Polenta 383
Pork polpette & potato al forno 337
Pumpkin, rosemary & taleggio risotto 632
Risi e bisi 613
Risotto nero with cuttlefish 149–50
Roast meat tortellini 114–5
Silverbeet & haloumi pies 563
Spaghetti puttanesca 117
Spinach, ricotta & feta cannelloni with mint passata sauce 133
Stuffed zucchini flowers 668–9
Summer vegetable lasagne 136
Tagliatelle with lemon cream 123–4
Thyme-crumbed onions 598
Vegetarian mac & cheese 120
White cabbage & pea slaw 448–9
Zucchini, ham & pea slice with feta 672–3

granitas
Chianti & raspberry granita with ice cream 784–5
Coffee granita 780
Cucumber & lime granita with gin jelly, yoghurt sorbet & minted cucumber 511
granola, Nutty 377
grapefruits 691–4
citrus & chilli relish 358
Fresh ponzu 101
Soft-boiled eggs with green mango salad & citrus & chilli relish 358
Watermelon & prawn salad citrus & chilli relish 201

grapes
An inspiration from ajo blanco 513
Baked olives, grapes & ricotta 588
Borlotti beans with herbs & freekeh 427
Cucumber, grape & herb salad with shallot dressing 508
Grilled pumpkin salad with pumpkin oil dressing, pickled grapes & goat's cheese 630
Roasted pork scotch with burnt honey & thyme, scorched grapes & grilled peaches 344

Schiacciata con l'uva 845
see also muscatels
gratins
Artichoke, anchovy & gruyère gratin 537
Dauphinoise potatoes 627
Fennel gratin 528
great northern beans 8
Baked beans with mustard seeds, vinegar & tomato 390
Cassoulet 391
Greek (rigani) oregano 23
Greek basil 7
green beans 434–6
Chow mein-style beef with wombok 292
Crunchy lacto-fermented vegetables 508
Gado gado with roasted vegetables 478
Genovese salad 624
Left-over chicken, barley & vegetable soup 252
Mapo-style tofu with beans & pork 436
Seared beef with bean thread noodles, beans, wood ear fungus & gochujang 292
Shiitake, tofu & cashew san choy bau 555
Spring minestrone 531
Stir-fried green beans with sesame, ginger & oyster sauce 437
Tuna niçoise 438–9
Tuna, brown rice & green bean salad with sumac 437
Vegetarian brown rice & green bean salad 437
Winter minestrone with roasted root vegetables 607
Green goddess dressing 89
green lentils *see* lentils
Gremolata 16
Grissini 856
gruyère 16
American-style ranch salad with cheese & croutons 557
Artichoke, anchovy & gruyère gratin 537
Béchamel with cheese 70–1
Braised witlof with ginger, ham & cheese 554
Carrot, chervil & gruyère loaf 472–3
Cauliflower cheese 478
Fluffy goat's cheese & gruyère omelette 355
Fluffy prawn & crab omelette with prawn essence & watercress 355
Gruyère & confit garlic tarts 828
Jerusalem artichoke soup with cheese toast 544
Mac & cheese 120
Piperade tart 829
Roasted & raw Jerusalem artichoke salad 544
Roasted carrots with Champagne vinegar & maple dressing 469
Roasted parsnip with anise, maple syrup & gruyère 606
Savoury crepes 771
Stuffed zucchini flowers 668–9

Twice-baked cheese soufflé 357
Vegetarian mac & cheese 120
guacamole 412–3
guanciale
Abbacchio al forno 315–6
Bucatini amatriciana 121
Chicken fricassee with Dutch creams, speck & tarragon 239
Crab cannelloni with crustacean dressing 135
Pumpkin & taleggio risotto with cured meat 632
Risi e bisi 613
Spaghetti carbonara 119–20
Spiced creamed tomato soup with bacon 665
Veal scallopini with guanciale, oyster mushrooms & thyme 295
gurnard
Fish cakes with parsley 190–1
Fish soup with spiced rouille & croûtes 174–5

H

haloumi 16
Beef & pork loaf with haloumi, pistachio & pomegranate molasses 288–9
Beetroot tabouleh with haloumi 419
Böreks with cheese 831
Braised red lentils with turmeric, curry leaves, fried garlic & haloumi 387
Charred fennel salad with fried haloumi 528
Cheese-filled lebanese talami bread 852
Fried haloumi with vine leaves, pistachios, za'atar & pomegranate molasses 363
Grilled asparagus & haloumi salad with fennel, walnuts & pomegranate 406–7
Lebanese skewered chicken with cumin, lemon, black pepper & garlic 247
Lebanese talami bread with cheese & greens 852
Pan-seared tomatoes on toast with feta & dill 663
Silverbeet & haloumi pies 563
Vegetarian baked haloumi-stuffed eggplant 521
Zucchini & haloumi fritters with burnt honey sauce 673–4
ham
Braised witlof with ginger, ham & cheese 554
Cheesy lunchbox muffins 858
Ham hock & leek terrine 328
Ham hock & pea risotto 148
Ham hock, rosemary & taleggio risotto 148
Pea & ham soup 334
Savoury crepes 771
Slow-roasted red onion quiche 598
Smoked ham hock & borlotti bean soup 425–6

Smoked ham hock & pea soup 426
Zucchini, ham & pea slice with feta 672-3
see also jamón

hapuka
Bouillabaisse-style stew 214-5
Fish & mussels en papillote 178
Sour fish & mussel curry with celery hearts
& kang kong 488-9

haricot (navy) beans 8
Winter minestrone with roasted root
vegetables 607
Harira 461

harissa 16
*Braised lamb & artichokes with couscous,
olives and harissa 537*
Green harissa 92
Harissa 92
Harissa roast capsicum salad with goat's
cheese 462
Roasted carrots with harissa & goat's curd
468
Skinless merguez-style sausages 308
Whole snapper pan-fried with cumin,
lemon, bay & green harissa 181
Zaalouk 518-9
Hasselback potatoes with paprika & bay leaves
626

hazelnuts 368
Almond & pistachio biscotti 758
Berry turnovers 688
black barley salad 246-7
Celeriac remoulade with nuts 484
Cheese, silverbeet & hazelnut filling for
sambouseks 833
Chocolate babka with hazelnuts 762-3
chocolate hazelnut filling 763
Chocolate panforte with almonds, figs &
sour cherries 760-1
Dark chocolate & hazelnut biscuits 754
Gnocchi with leek, gorgonzola & nuts 602
hazelnut base 650
Hazelnut plum streusel cake 741
Hazelnut streusel muffins 732
hazelnut vinegar dressing 560
*Lamb ribs braised with toasted hazelnuts
304*
Nutella icing 805
Raw silverbeet, sorrel & hazelnut salad
560-1
Rhubarb galette 650
*Risotto bianco with brown butter,
hazelnuts, lemon & ricotta 148*
Roast chicken & black barley salad 246-7
Roasted & raw Jerusalem artichoke salad
544
Salsa romesco 84

herbs 16-7
An exquisite herb salad 17
bouquet garni 8
Herb oil for fish 165
herb-based sauces 82-92
Herbed velouté 64
Quick herb salad 267

see also basil, chervil, chives, coriander,
dill, lemon myrtle, marjoram, mint,
oregano, parsley, rosemary, sage,
savoury, tarragon, Thai basil, thyme,
Vietnamese mint, watercress
hoisin sauce 17
Hollandaise 79
holy basil 7

honey 17
Almond & pistachio biscotti 758
Apple & cherry turnovers 681
Apricot & sesame oat bars 392
Baby chard & curly endive salad with soft-
boiled egg dressing & honey bacon 557
burnt honey & thyme sauce 344
burnt honey sauce 673-4
Carrots with butter, honey & thyme glaze
469
Chocolate & honey sauce 793
Chocolate panforte with almonds, figs &
sour cherries 760-1
Coconut bircher 393
Date, sesame, coconut & macadamia nut
balls 393
Doughnuts in honey & orange blossom
syrup with ricotta & pistachios 773
Fig & filo honey stack 703
Figs poached in syrup 703
Honey & orange-blossom syrup 792
Honey & white wine poaching syrup for
stone fruit 723-4
honey filo crisps 703
Honey panna cotta 781
honey sabayon cream 703
Madeleines 736
No-bake seed bars 392
Raw turnip with walnut oil, celery leaves &
parsley 642
Roasted brussels sprouts with honey &
dukkah 453
Roasted pears with honey, verjuice,
rosemary & bay leaves 711
Roasted pork scotch with burnt honey
& thyme, scorched grapes & grilled
peaches 344
Roasted quince & chestnuts 716
Salted caramel & almond popcorn 788
Salted macadamia & almond caramels 790
Scorched honey & thyme gastrique for
duck 265
Scorched honey & yoghurt parfait 785
Sichuan pepper & honey glaze 331
Simple honey, soy & ginger drumettes
236-7
Slow-roasted quince with honey,
cinnamon & cloves 714
Spiced earl grey tea & honey cake 740
Spiced lamb shanks with rhubarb, honey &
fried vine leaves 647
Sticky spiced honey lamb shanks 305
Syrian chicken with ginger, lemon &
saffron 248
Witlof, rocket & macadamia salad with
pork & fennel sausage, mustard &
honey 554

Honeycomb 789
Horenso gomaae (Pressed spinach with
sesame) 561
horseradish 17
Bread sauce 70
Celeriac & mustard condiment for steak
485
Crunchy lacto-fermented vegetables 508
Grilled oysters with horseradish 210
*Grilled scallops with horseradish &
Parmigiano Reggiano 210*
Horseradish cream dressing 70
Mustard sauce 66
Roasted Jerusalem artichoke salad with
horseradish & salmon roe 542
Salad of lentils & smoked trout with dill &
horseradish cream dressing 385
Slow-roasted Jerusalem artichokes with
roe & pan-fried scallops 542
Smoked salmon & cucumber canapés 513
Snapper crudo with a lemon emulsion &
horseradish 164
*Traditional French steak tartare with
horseradish 279*
Watercress & potato soup 558
Horta 552-3
hot cross buns
Chocolate hot cross buns 765
Classic hot cross buns 765
hot sauce *see* chilli sauce
hotcakes, Ricotta & blueberry 768-9
Hummus 374

I

ice cream
Bombe Alaska 807
No-churn dulce de leche ice cream 795
iceberg lettuce 553
Bánh mì with roast pork belly 332-3
Easy souvlaki 312
Kimchi pancakes with a tamari & sesame
dipping sauce 457
Maltagliata of beef with rocket, fine kale &
ricotta 288
Prawn cocktail 413
Sesame-crumbed ocean trout with nori
mayo in a brioche bun 191-2
Shiitake, tofu & cashew san choy bau 555
Vietnamese spring roll with crab, prawn &
shiitake 575
Waldorf salad with roast chicken wrapped
in iceberg 490
icing
Basic sugar icing 802
Blackberry or raspberry icing 802
Chocolate fudge icing 805
Chocolate ginger icing 805
Coffee icing 804
Cream cheese icing 803
Lemon, lime or passionfruit icing 802

Maple syrup, brown sugar & cinnamon icing 804
Mascarpone citrus curd icing 803
Nutella icing 805
pistachio & almond marzipan icing 752
Vanilla frosting 803
Insalata caprese 662
invert sugar 31

J

Jam crostata 826
Jam tarts 826
jams
    Cherry, raspberry & vanilla jam 723
    Fig & ginger jam 706
    Super-simple roasted raspberry jam 687
    Thai-style chilli jam 96
see also marmalade
jamón 17, 323, 325
    Asparagus with poached egg & prosciutto 406
    Clams with jamón, garlic & butterbeans 211
    Fennel & buffalo mozzarella salad with cured meat 530
    Jamón, fig, beetroot, goat's curd, watercress & mint salad 702
    Shaved fennel & artichoke salad with cured meat 535–6
jasmine rice 26
jellies
    Beetroot jelly 421
    coconut jelly 783
    gin jelly 511
    Quince jelly 717
    White peach & rosewater jelly 724
    white pepper jelly 510
Jerusalem artichoke 540–2
    Beef carpaccio with Jerusalem artichokes 280
    Jerusalem artichoke pickle 545
    Jerusalem artichoke soup 544
    Raw Jerusalem artichoke salad with broad beans & cheese 544
    Roasted & raw Jerusalem artichoke salad 544
    Roasted Jerusalem artichoke salad with horseradish & salmon roe 542
    Slow-roasted Jerusalem artichokes with roe & pan-fried scallops 542
juniper berries 17
jus, Roasted garlic, with tarragon 66

K

kaffir lime leaves *see* makrut lime leaves
kale 550–5
    Celeriac, apple & kale slaw with anchovy 484–5
    Green olive, artichoke & kale tapenade 590
    Kale chips 551
    Maltagliata of beef with rocket, fine kale & ricotta 288
    Pork & prawn wontons with choy sum & kale 342
    Raw parsnip salad 607
    Roasted & raw Jerusalem artichoke salad 544
    Spiced bean & vegetable braise 425
    Warm celeriac salad with yoghurt, aleppo chilli, pine nuts & sultanas 482
    see also cavolo nero
kang kong (water spinach, Siamese watercress) 398
    Sour fish & mussel curry with celery hearts & kang kong 488
    Stir-fried kang kong & wombok with tofu & fermented chilli 400
    Stir-fried pea shoots with shrimp paste & chilli 400–1
kasundi, Eggplant & tomato 520
katsuobushi (bonito flakes) 17
    black sesame dressing 561
    Dashi 53
    Enhanced soy sauce 101
    Fresh ponzu 101
    Mac & cheese 120
    Shoyu ramen broth 58–9
    Tempura dipping sauce 98
kecap manis 18
kefalograviera 18
    Baked lamb-stuffed eggplant 520–1
    Sesame saganaki with quick-pickled cucumber 510
    Smoked eggplant soup with kefalograviera 519
kefalotyri cheese: Moussaka 310–1
kelp *see* arame, kombu, nori, wakame
kenchur 18
kidney beans 8
    Black dal 389
    Chilli con pollo with chorizo & beans 232
Kimchi 455–6
king brown mushrooms 568–70
    Barley 'risotto' with mushrooms & speck 572
    Pan-seared potato gnocchi with scallops, mushrooms & lemon 140
    Shaved brussels sprouts with roasted king brown mushrooms, manchego & maple dressing 453
    Veal scallopini with guanciale, oyster mushrooms & thyme 295

kingfish
    Cured kingfish with crema fresca, lime & spiced seed crackers 168
    Cured kingfish with fennel, paprika & pepper 171
    Fish marinated with white miso 184
    Kingfish crudo with caviar, cucumber & mustard cress 510
    Kingfish crudo with chilli, ginger & coriander 164
    Kingfish kibbeh nayyeh 166
    Quick-cured fish with finger lime & coriander 168
koftas
    Chicken & corn koftas with avocado & coriander 249
    Lamb koftas baked with tomato & smoky eggplant, with pine nuts & parsley 309–10
kohlrabi 546–8
    Kohlrabi & cucumber salad with lemon yoghurt dressing 549
    Kohlrabi, cabbage & beetroot slaw 548–9
    Kohlrabi, cauliflower & fenugreek soup 548
    Quick kohlrabi pickle 548
koji 18
kombu 18
    Dashi 53
    Fresh ponzu 101
    Shoyu ramen broth 58–9
    Tempura dipping sauce 98
Koulouri/simit 842–3

L

labneh
    Grilled pumpkin salad with pumpkin oil dressing, pickled grapes & goat's cheese 630
    Labneh 362
    Orange-blossom labneh 363
    Roasted pumpkin with cinnamon, chilli, pickled onion, yoghurt & feta 631
    rosewater labneh 386
    Saffron scones with lemon, date & orange-blossom marmalade & labneh 772
lamb 300–303
    Abbacchio al forno 315–6
    Baked lamb-stuffed eggplant 520–1
    Barbecued lamb leg with oregano & lemon 312
    Braised lamb chump chops with potato, jalapeño & oregano 314
    Braised lamb neck & barley broth 308–9
    Braised lamb neck with white wine, tomato & oregano 316
    Braised lamb shank & barley broth 309
    Braised lamb, artichokes, lemon & cinnamon with couscous 537
    Brined lamb shoulder 307

Cabbage rolls with lamb, rice, pine nuts & dill 451
Capretto 316
Cevapcici with wild fennel 529
Crispy lamb's brains, pancetta & feta, with curly endive & mint 308
Crumbed lamb cutlets 310
Dolmades with lamb 375
Easy souvlaki 312
Grilled lamb cutlets with smashed broad beans & hot feta dressing 432-3
Harira 461
Lamb & eggplant karahi curry 318
Lamb & pine nut filling for sambouseks 833
Lamb koftas baked with tomato & smoky eggplant, with pine nuts & parsley 309-10
Lamb navarin 643
Lamb ribs braised with treacle & dark ale 304
Lamb rogan josh 317-8
Lamb, artichoke & mint ragù 535
Lamb, pea & mint pancake fritters 319
Lamb, spinach, pomegranate & date salad with crisp pitta 314
Lebanese peas with lamb 614
Left-over lamb roast shepherd's pie 319
Moussaka 310-1
Pasties 469-70
Roast meat tortellini 114-5
Roasted lamb rack 305
Simply roasted leg of lamb with rosemary & garlic 315
Skinless merguez-style sausages 308
Slow-roasted boned lamb shoulder 304
Spiced lamb shanks with rhubarb, honey & fried vine leaves 647
Spiced-yoghurt leg of lamb 311-2
Sticky spiced honey lamb shanks 305
Vine leaf beef & bone marrow pie 287
lamb's lettuce *see* mâche
Lamingtons 749

lardo 325
Lardo 326
Pâté de campagne 327
Seared ocean trout with grilled lettuce, peas & pea tendrils 561-2
Lasagne 136
lasagne, Summer vegetable 136
lassi, Amber's yoghurt mango 365

leafy vegetables 550-4
see also cavolo nero, chard, chicory, kale, radicchio, silverbeet, spinach

leeks 592-5
Baked fennel & leek with provolone sauce 528-9
Barbecued Dutch carrot & leek salad 468-9
Braised lamb neck & barley broth 308-9
Brown beef stock 55
Chicken, leek & mushroom pie 603
Classic white vegetable stock 51
Corn chowder with potato & dill 502

Croquetas with smoked eel & manchego 190
Crustacean stock 52
Duck, celeriac & verjuice ragù 259
Fish soup with spiced rouille & croûtes 174-5
Gnocchi with leek & gorgonzola 602
Ham hock & leek terrine 328
Jerusalem artichoke soup 544
Leek with walnut & rye skordalia 600
Left-over chicken, barley & vegetable soup 252
Lemonia's pumpkin & feta pie with olive oil pastry 631
Pedro Ximénez-braised beef cheeks with celeriac & parsnip purée & persillade 285-6
Quick & simple duck stock 266
Risotto with ricotta, spinach & verjuice-braised leek 149
Roasted cauliflower & turmeric soup with yoghurt & poached egg 476
Robust vegetable fumet 51
Spiced bean & vegetable braise 425
Watercress & potato soup 558
legumes, tinned 18
lemon myrtle 18
lemon thyme *see* thyme
lemon verbena 18

lemongrass 18
Balinese-style chicken skewers 104
Beef rendang 292-3
Chicken coconut curry with makrut lime leaf, lemongrass & turmeric 238
Fragrant chicken soup with bok choy 401-2
lemongrass & ginger marinade 237
lemongrass & turmeric marinade 246
Moules frites meets South-East Asia 204
Nuoc cham 93
Pumpkin, chickpea, cashew & coconut curry 633
Red duck curry with lychee & fried basil salad 266
Roasted lemongrass & turmeric chicken steaks 246
Satay sauce 104
Simple coconut soup-style sauce for steamed fish 162
Thai caramel sauce for fish 105
Thai fish cakes 192-3
Tom yum goong 201

lemons 690-3
A simple poaching liquid for stone fruit 724
Baked buttered rice with coconut & lemon 384
Barbecued lamb leg with oregano & lemon 312
Blood orange & Campari marmalade 699
Braised chicken, artichokes, lemon & cinnamon with couscous 537
Braised fresh borlotti beans in lemon & cumin stock 426

Braised lamb, artichokes, lemon & cinnamon with couscous 537
Braised silverbeet with garlic & lemon 555
Broccoli with lemon, chilli, fennel seeds & pecorino 444
Brown butter & lemon sauce for crepes & blintzes 771
Burnt butter sauce with lemon, capers & parsley 73
Burnt butter sauce with lemon, sage & toasted walnuts 73
Buttermilk 7
Candied orange & lemon peel 790
Carrot paste salad with lemon, caraway & nigella seeds 473
Celery, lemon & parsley salad with a fried garlic & fennel seed dressing 491
Celery, lemon, orange & parsley salad 491
Chargrilled poussins with a lemon, chilli, herb & golden sultana salad 236
citrus cure 169
Citrus delicious pudding 698-9
Citrus nori tartare for fish 187
Citrus-cured gravlax 169
Citrus-cured sardines 168
Coriander, onion & citrus sauce 11
Cream cheese icing 803
Crema fresca 364
Crème fraîche glaze with cinnamon & lemon 804
cumin & lemon marinade 247
Cured kingfish with fennel, paprika & pepper 171
dijon, cumin & lemon marinade 236
Dolmades with rice, pine nuts, currants & lemon 375
Easy preserved lemons 694-5
Fennel, egg, lemon & rice brodo with & ricotta bruschetta 483
French-style vinaigrette 88
Fresh ponzu 101
Friands 734-5
Gravlax with treacle, fennel & pepper 171
Greek-style lemon & oregano potatoes 626
gremolata 296
Horseradish cream dressing 70
Lebanese skewered chicken with cumin, lemon, black pepper & garlic 247
lemon & coriander coating 168
lemon & oregano dressing 218
lemon & peppercorn cure 171
Lemon cheesecake 698
Lemon cheesecake with lemon sherbet 698
lemon cream 696
Lemon cream & cherry possets 696
Lemon emulsion 80
lemon garlic dressing 407
lemon garlic mayonnaise 200
lemon mustard dressing 490
Lemon tart 814-5
lemon yoghurt dressing 549
Lemon, date & orange-blossom marmalade 699
Lemon, lime or passionfruit curd 797
Lemon, lime or passionfruit icing 802

lemony tahini yoghurt 432
Mascarpone citrus curd icing 803
mint & lemon dressing 427
Moroccan carrot, date & green chilli salad 471
Pan-seared potato gnocchi with scallops, mushrooms & lemon 140
Parsley & lemon butter 73
parsley & lemon paste 191
Prawn dressing 67
Preserved lemon paste 695
Preserved lemons with bay & cinnamon 695
Preserved lemons with bay & star anise 695
Preserved Meyer lemons with ginger & star anise 696–7
Quince jelly 717
Quince paste 717
Risotto bianco with brown butter, hazelnuts, lemon & ricotta 148
Salmoriglio 83
scorched lemon syrup 707
Smashed broccoli with preserved lemon 442
Snapper crudo with a lemon emulsion & horseradish 164
sour cream dressing 449
sour cream roast garlic dressing 484
Spaghetti with spinach, lemon & pangrattato 124
Spaghettini with crab, lemon, herbs & chilli 125
spiced lemon dressing 477
Syrian chicken with ginger, lemon & saffron 248
Tagliatelle with lemon cream 123–4
Tahini dip/sauce 71
tahini dressing 518
Taramasalata 182
treacle, fennel & pepper cure 171
Vanilla & fig leaf panna cotta with scorched lemon syrup 707
white wine & lemon marinade 218
Whole snapper baked with cumin, lemon, bay & green harissa 181
yoghurt & garlic sauce 312
yoghurt & lemon sauce 181
Lengua de gato (Cat's tongue biscuits) 755
lentils 18–9, 369
Basic vinaigrette lentils 385
Black dal 389
Braised red lentils with turmeric, curry leaves, fried garlic & haloumi 387
Byzantine salad 379
Dal fry 388
Harira 461
Mejadra 385
Petit salé aux lentilles 334
Salad of lentils & smoked trout with dill & horseradish cream dressing 385
Spiced green soup 381
Spinach, lentil & yoghurt salad with brown butter 558

Vegetarian baked haloumi-stuffed eggplant 521
Zucchini flower, wild rice, lentil & yoghurt salad 671
lettuce 550–4
see also butter lettuce, cos lettuce, cress, endive (curly), gem lettuce, mâche (lamb's lettuce/corn salad), mustard cress, rocket, sorrel, watercress
levain 849–50
lima beans 370
Gigantes plaki 380–1
lime leaves *see* makrut lime leaves
limes 690–3
Citrus delicious pudding 698–9
Barbecued prawns with gochujang, sesame & lime 202
chilli cucumber dipping sauce 192
chilli, lime & brown sugar dressing 499
citrus & chilli relish 358
Citrus delicious pudding 698–9
Citrus nori tartare for fish 187
Coriander, onion & citrus sauce 11
Corn with chilli & lime glaze 502
Cucumber & lime granita with gin jelly, yoghurt sorbet & minted cucumber 511
cucumber, celery heart & herb salad 240
Cured kingfish with crema fresca, lime & spiced seed crackers 168
Fresh ponzu 101
ginger, lime & olive oil dressing 510
Lemon, lime or passionfruit curd 797
Lemon, lime or passionfruit icing 802
Lime & coconut cheesecake 738
lime & coconut filling 738
lime & pomegranate dressing 503
Lime coconut butter pandan cake 745
Lime leaf & white pepper guacamole 412
Mango with salted caramel, ginger & lime 794
Mango, ginger & chilli relish with fish sauce & lime 495
Nuoc cham 93
pomegranate dressing 262
Prawn & poached chicken vermicelli salad 240
sesame & lime dressing 507
Soft-boiled eggs with green mango salad & citrus & chilli relish 358
Spiced duck with pickled watermelon 262
Spiced sesame & peanut dressing 94
tangy oyster sauce dressing 358
Thai caramel sauce for fish 105
Watermelon & prawn salad citrus & chilli relish 201
Zucchini, coconut & macadamia muffins with lime cream cheese icing 734
see also finger limes
linguine 112
linseeds 369
Cheddar & feta scones with mixed seeds 859
No-bake seed bars 392

Spiced seed crackers 839
Super seed loaf 376
lion's mane mushrooms 571
Barley 'risotto' with mushrooms & speck 572
lobster 196–7
An inspiration from ajo blanco with seafood 513
Lobster salad à la russe 200
lychees
coconut jelly 783
Coconut panna cotta with coconut jelly, black sesame tuilles, mango & lime leaf 783
lychee & fried basil salad 266–7
Red duck curry with lychee & fried basil salad 266–7

M

Mac & cheese 120
macadamia nuts 368
Anzac biscuits with macadamia nuts 757
Date, sesame, coconut & macadamia nut balls 393
Deluxe chocolate galette cake 746–7
Salted macadamia & almond caramels 790
Witlof, rocket & macadamia salad with pork & fennel sausage, mustard & honey 554
Zucchini, coconut & macadamia muffins with lime cream cheese icing 734
mace 19
mâche (lamb's lettuce/corn salad) 553
Kingfish kibbeh nayyeh 166
Pickled daikon & mint salad 304
Witlof, rocket & macadamia salad with pork & fennel sausage, mustard & honey 554
mackerel
Fish marinated with white miso 184
Kingfish crudo with chilli, ginger & coriander 164
Quick-cured ocean trout with finger lime & coriander 168
Madeleines 736
mahleb seeds 19
makrut lime leaves 19
Beef rendang 292–3
Chicken coconut curry with makrut lime leaf, lemongrass & turmeric 238
Chilled coconut & lime leaf rice pudding 395
Chilli crab 199–200
Citrus delicious pudding with makrut lime leaf 398–9
Coconut panna cotta with coconut jelly, black sesame tuilles, mango & lime leaf 783

Crisp-fried eggs, corn, smoked trout & herb
salad with tangy oyster sauce dressing
358
curry paste 238
Fragrant chicken soup with bok choy
401–2
Gado gado with roasted cauliflower,
cucumber & eggs 478
Grilled pork fillet, wombok & crispy egg
341
Herb oil for fish 165
lemongrass & ginger marinade 237
Lime leaf & white pepper guacamole 412
lychee & fried basil salad 266–7
mango & pineapple salad 780
Moules frites meets South-East Asia 204
Pumpkin, chickpea, cashew & coconut
curry 633
red curry paste 266
Red duck curry with lychee & fried basil
salad 266–7
Simple coconut soup-style sauce for
steamed fish 162
Simple Thai-style hard-boiled eggs 356
Snapper crudo with finger lime, fennel,
chilli & a burnt butter dressing 165
Sour fish & mussel curry with celery hearts
& kang kong 488–9
Stir-fried clams with XO sauce 211
Thai caramel sauce for fish 105
Thai fish cakes 192–3
Tom yum goong 201

manchego
Cheesy buttered broad beans & peas 430
Croquetas with smoked eel & manchego
190
Shaved brussels sprouts with roasted king
brown mushrooms, manchego & maple
dressing 453
Spiced corn & manchego loaf 858
Stuffed zucchini flowers 668–9
Tomato tarte tatin with manchego, thyme
& dried olives 660
*Vegetarian roasted Jerusalem artichoke
salad with horseradish & cheese* 542

mandarins 690–4
citrus & chilli relish 358
Citrus delicious pudding with mandarin
398–9
*Fennel & mandarin salad with olives,
currants & chilli* 531
Sichuan pepper & mandarin salt 29
Soft-boiled eggs with green mango salad &
citrus & chilli relish 358
Watermelon & prawn salad citrus & chilli
relish 201
mangetout *see* snow peas

mangoes
Amber's yoghurt mango lassi 365
amchur 6
Coconut panna cotta with coconut jelly,
black sesame tuiles, mango & lime
leaf 783
mango & pineapple salad 780

Mango with salted caramel, ginger & lime
794
Mango, ginger & chilli relish 495
Prawn & poached chicken vermicelli salad
240
Soft-boiled eggs with green mango salad &
citrus & chilli relish 358
Tapioca pearls in coconut with tropical
salad & caramel sauce 780–1
mantecatura 147

maple syrup 19
Banana & blueberry slab cake 760
Chia pudding 393
Chocolate & avocado ganache 412
Gochujang chilli sauce 97
maple dressing 453
maple glaze 331
Maple syrup, brown sugar & cinnamon
icing 804
Nutty, salty, sweet & seedy crunch mix 377
Pork spare ribs with maple glaze 331
Roasted carrots with Champagne vinegar &
maple dressing 469
Roasted parsnip with anise, maple syrup &
gruyère 606
Sliced pears roasted with maple syrup,
thyme & white pepper 709
Slow dry-roasted spiced asado ribs 290
Super seed loaf 376
Toasted muesli 394
Tofu 'mayonnaise' 75
Wholegrain mustard & maple dressing 87
Marie Rose sauce (cocktail sauce) 77

marinades
cumin & lemon marinade 247
dijon, cumin & lemon marinade 236
fennel, sumac & yoghurt marinade 311
Fresh ponzu 101
Korean sesame grilled beef with sake,
ginger & soy marinade 293
lemon & coriander coating 168
lemongrass & ginger marinade 237
lemongrass & turmeric marinade 246
white miso marinade 184
white wine & lemon marinade 218

marjoram 19
Charred fennel salad with tarragon 528
Grilled zucchini salad 668
Salmoriglio 83

marmalades
Blood orange & Campari marmalade 699
Lemon, date & orange-blossom
marmalade 699
see also jams
marshmallows, Raspberry sherbet 791

mascarpone
Coffee mascarpone cream 800
Deluxe eggplant parmigiana with
anchovies 522
French shortbread sandwiches with
mascarpone cream, almonds & praline
813
Lemon cheesecake 698
Mascarpone citrus curd icing 803

Pennette with tuna, tomatoes &
mascarpone 125
Tiramisu 776–7

mash
Classic potato mash 625
Mustard mash 625
Taleggio mash 625

mayonnaise 19, 63
lemon garlic mayonnaise 200
Master olive oil mayonnaise 74
miso & nori mayonnaise 191
Oat milk mayonnaise 74
Saffron mayonnaise 75
Sesame mayonnaise 75
Tofu 'mayonnaise' 75
tuna mayo 442–3
Tuna mayonnaise 74
Whole-egg mayonnaise 75
Mazaresi cakes 732

meatballs
Chicken noodle broth with porcini
polpette 253
Japanese-style chicken meatballs 251
Pork polpette & potato al forno 337
Veal & pork polpette with savoy cabbage,
taleggio & truffled pecorino 337
Mejadra 385

meringue
Bombe Alaska 807
Italian meringue 807
Italian meringue & Italian meringue butter
cream 807
Lemon meringue pie 806

milk 19
Béchamel 70–1
Bread sauce 70
Buttermilk 361
Cauliflower cheese 478
Clams in white-wine sauce 211
Polenta 383
provolone sauce 528
Ricotta 362
Rizogalo 395
Thick real hot chocolate 775
Thick vanilla custard 801
Vanilla crème anglaise 800–1
Vanilla crème pâtissière 798
Yoghurt 365
see also buttermilk, coconut milk,
condensed milk
Mille-feuille 824

mint 20
An exquisite herb salad 17
Barbecued prawns with salsa verde 202
Beetroot tabouleh with currants &
sunflower seeds 419
Berry, coconut & mint smoothie 688
Blanched calamari with tuna sauce &
olives 220
Borlotti bean salad with mustard fruits 426
Borlotti beans with herbs & freekeh 427
Braised artichoke, egg, olive & watercress
salad 538

Braised artichoke, fennel & broad bean salad with orange glaze 536
Braised zucchini with fresh tomato & herbs 671
broad bean & pea paste 432–3
Broad bean & pea salad with nasturtium leaves, goat's cheese & bagna cauda 431
Buttery minted peas 610
Byzantine salad 379
Cheesy buttered broad beans & peas 430
Crab with avocado mousse, mint, chilli & sweet pickled cucumber 413
Crispy lamb's brains, pancetta & feta, with curly endive & mint 308
Cucumber & lime granita with gin jelly, yoghurt sorbet & minted cucumber 511
Cucumber, grape & herb salad with shallot dressing 508
Domatokeftedes 664
Eggplant purée with chilli oil & walnuts 516
Fennel & buffalo mozzarella salad with broad beans, mint & green sultanas 530
Fresh mint sauce 82
Green goddess dressing 89
Green tomato salsa with dill & mint 664
Grilled asparagus & haloumi salad with fennel, walnuts & pomegranate 406–7
Grilled eggplant with tahini & yoghurt dressing, pomegranate, chilli & mint 516
Grilled pumpkin salad with pumpkin oil dressing, pickled grapes & goat's cheese 630
Herb & chilli oil 86
Jamón, fig, beetroot, goat's curd, watercress & mint salad 702
Kohlrabi & cucumber salad with lemon yoghurt dressing 549
Kohlrabi, cabbage & beetroot slaw 548–9
Lamb, artichoke & mint ragù 535
Lamb, pea & mint pancake fritters 319
Lamb, spinach, pomegranate & date salad with crisp pitta 314
Lebanese peas with lamb 614
mint & lemon dressing 427
mint passata sauce 133
Moorish pork skewers with orange & black olive salsa 345
New potatoes with green goddess dressing 89
Orecchiette with tomato, mint & anchovy sauce 132
Paloise sauce 79
Pickled daikon & mint salad 304
Raw silverbeet, mint & pistachio salad 561
Raw turnip with walnut oil, celery leaves & parsley 642
Risi e bisi 613
Roasted & raw fennel salad with mint & egg yolk 527
Roasted pumpkin with tahini & yoghurt dressing, pomegranate, chilli & mint 516
Rockling with Thai caramel sauce & herbs 172

Rustic salsa verde with potato 86
Salsa verde 86
Shaved brussels sprouts with roasted king brown mushrooms, manchego & maple dressing 453
Side of salmon with walnuts, tahini, mint & pomegranate molasses 172
Smashed broccoli with preserved lemon 442
Southern Italian fried zucchini 671
Spaghetti aglio e olio with mint & broad beans 123
Spiced duck with pickled watermelon 262
Spinach, lentil & yoghurt salad with brown butter 558
Spinach, mint & rice salad with yoghurt dressing 560
Spinach, ricotta & feta cannelloni with mint passata sauce 133
tomato, mint & anchovy sauce 132
Tzatziki 507
Veal, artichoke & mint ragù 535
Wombok, daikon, shiitake & tofu salad 450
Yoghurt, cucumber & mint salad/dip 508
Zaalouk 518–9
Zucchini & haloumi fritters with burnt honey sauce 673–4
Zucchini flower, wild rice, lentil & yoghurt salad 671
see also Vietnamese mint
mirin 20
miso 20
Eggplant with miso glaze & spring onions 521
Fish marinated with white miso 184
Fish soup with spiced rouille & croûtes 174–5
Gochujang chilli sauce 97
Japanese-style chicken meatballs 251
Lamb ribs braised with treacle & dark ale 304
miso & nori mayonnaise 191
Miso doughnut glaze with sesame 774
miso glaze 521
Nasturtium & miso butter 72
Roasted eye fillet with Japanese seasonings 286
Toasted sesame & miso dressing 102
Udon noodles with chicken, shiitake, bok choy, miso & kimchi 402
white miso marinade 184
mizithra 20
Baked lamb-stuffed eggplant 520–1
Baked tomatoes stuffed with rice, feta & pine nuts 663
mizuna 553
Daikon, edamame & avocado salad, with sesame, apple & soy dressing 640–1
Kingfish kibbeh nayyeh 166
Mocha brownies 762
moghrabieh 20
Spiced pumpkin, date, almond & moghrabieh salad 635

morcilla 325
Black turtle bean, pork belly & morcilla braise (frijoles negros) 340
Moreton Bay bugs
Butter-poached Moreton Bay bugs 203
note on 203
mortadella
Mortadella agnolotti 114
Seared radicchio with burrata & cured meat 566
mosto cotto 27
Moules frites 204
mousakka
Béchamel for moussaka 70–1
Moussaka 310–1
mousse
avocado mousse 413
Chocolate mousse 782
Crab with avocado mousse, mint, chilli & sweet pickled cucumber 413
mozzarella 20
American-style ranch salad with cheese & croutons 557
Broad bean & pea salad with nasturtium leaves, fresh mozzarella & bagna cauda 431
Deluxe eggplant parmigiana with anchovies 522
Fennel & buffalo mozzarella salad with broad beans, mint & green sultanas 530
Greens, potato & cheese pie with olive oil pastry 828
Insalata caprese 662
Lasagne 136
Left-over pork sandwich 344
Panzanella with buffalo mozzarella 658
Pea & mozzarella salad 611
Pizza 'number 1' 856
Pizza margherita 857
Pumpkin, anchovy & ricotta pizza 857
Raw Jerusalem artichoke salad with broad beans & cheese 544
Seared radicchio with burrata, balsamic-pickled cherries & scorched almonds 566
Spinach, ricotta & feta cannelloni with mint passata sauce 133
Summer vegetable lasagne 136
see also stracciatella
muesli, Toasted 394
muffins
Cheesy lunchbox muffins 858
Classic muffins 732
Zucchini, coconut & macadamia muffins with lime cream cheese icing 734
mullet
Deep-fried red mullet with celery & olive salad 188
Fish soup with spiced rouille & croûtes 174–5
mung beans 8
Japanese mixed rice & grains 382

muscatels
Schiacciata con l'uva 845
Gorgonzola with port-steeped muscatels & oatcakes 841
mushrooms 568–72
Barley 'risotto' with mushrooms & speck 572
Classic white vegetable stock 51
Cream of mushroom soup 574–5
Mushroom ragù 576–7
Mushroom risotto 151
Mushroom tortellini 115
Savoury crepes 771
Simple fried mushrooms 576
Vegetarian fragrant soup with bok choy 402
see also abalone mushrooms, champignons, enoki mushrooms, field mushrooms, king brown mushrooms, lion's mane mushrooms, oyster mushrooms, pine mushrooms, porcini mushrooms, portobello mushrooms, shiitake mushrooms, slippery jack mushrooms, Swiss brown mushrooms, truffles, wood ear fungus
mussels 204–5
Bouillabaisse-style stew 214–5
Devilled eggs with shellfish 356
Fish & mussels en papillote 178
Moules frites 204
Moules frites meets South-East Asia 204
Mussels with chorizo, tomato & white wine 213
Mussels with garlic & tomato 214
Mussels with garlic, black pepper & fennel seeds 213
Sour fish & mussel curry with celery hearts & kang kong 488–9
Sour fish curry with seafood 581
mustard 21
Béchamel with mustard & parsley 70–1
Celeriac & mustard condiment for steak 485
Celeriac remoulade 484
Citrus-cured gravlax 169
Corned beef with herb & mustard sauce 289
Creamed mustard kipfler potatoes 622
Devilled eggs 356
dijon, cumin & lemon marinade 236
French-style vinaigrette 88
Gravlax with treacle, fennel & pepper 171
lemon mustard dressing 490
Mac & cheese 120
Master olive oil mayonnaise 74
Mustard mash 625
Mustard sauce 66
Nori tartare 77
red wine vinaigrette 574
Roasted scotch fillet 283
Sauce gribiche 78
Slow-roasted eye fillet 285
Tofu 'mayonnaise' 75
Traditional French steak tartare 279
Whole-egg mayonnaise 75

Wholegrain mustard 21
Wholegrain mustard & maple dressing 87
Witlof, rocket & macadamia salad with pork & fennel sausage, mustard & honey 554
see also mustard seeds
mustard cress 552
Kingfish crudo with caviar, cucumber & mustard cress 510
Roasted & raw Jerusalem artichoke salad 544
Salad of lentils & smoked trout with dill & horseradish cream dressing 85
Warm celeriac salad with yoghurt, aleppo chilli, pine nuts & sultanas 482
mustard greens *see* gai choy, mizuna
mustard seeds 21
Baked beans with mustard seeds, vinegar & tomato 390
Cauliflower cheese 479
Crab, pea & potato samosas 611
Crunchy lacto-fermented dill pickles 505
Egg, tomato & spinach curry with ginger & turmeric 359
Jerusalem artichoke pickle 545
Lamb & eggplant karahi curry 318
Mango, ginger & chilli relish 495
pickled arame salad 622
Pickled spring vegetables 470–1
Quick quince & apple relish 716
Sour fish curry with okra & celery heart 581
Spiced okra with curry leaves 582
Spicy malt plum sauce 725
Sweet pickled fennel 531
Sweet pickled onions 597
Sweet Zuni-style pickles 668
Wholegrain mustard 21

N

Naan 855
Napoli (Simple tomato sugo) 116
nasturtium 552
An exquisite herb salad 17
Broad bean & pea salad with nasturtium leaves, goat's cheese & bagna cauda 431
Nasturtium & miso butter 72
navarin, Lamb 643
nduja: *Black aïoli with cured meat* 76
nectarines 718–20
A simple frangipane fruit tart 796
Cherry, semolina, almond & yoghurt cake 753
Grilled peaches or nectarines 722
Honey & white wine poaching syrup for stone fruit 723–4
Puff pastry tart with fruit 824–5
Roasted stone fruit 720
Roasted stone fruit & ginger clafoutis 721
niçoise, Tuna 438–9

nigella seeds 21
noodles 21
Beef pho 57
Charred broccoli, ramen & nori salad 444–5
Chicken noodle broth with porcini polpette 253
Chow mein-style beef with vermicelli 292
Chow mein-style beef with wombok 292
Harira 461
Prawn & poached chicken vermicelli salad 240
Ramen 59
Seared beef with bean thread noodles, beans, wood ear fungus & gochujang 292
Soba noodles with avocado, sprouts, umeboshi & sesame 410
Udon noodles with chicken, shiitake, bok choy, miso & kimchi 402
ñora peppers 85
nori sheets 21
Charred broccoli, ramen & nori salad 444–5
Citrus nori tartare for fish 187
Japanese-style chicken meatballs 251
miso & nori mayonnaise 191
nori salt 187
Nori tartare 77
Ramen 59
Nuoc cham 93
nut meal 21
nut oil 22
nutmeg 21
nuts 21, 368–71
Crispy eggplant with spiced caramel & fried Thai basil 522–3
Free-form stone fruit tart 814
Nutty praline 786
Salted nut & choc chip biscuits 755
see also almonds, Brazil nuts, cashew nuts, chestnuts, hazelnuts, macadamia nuts, peanuts, pecans, pine nuts, pistachios, walnuts, water chestnuts

O

oats 21
Anzac biscuits 757
Apricot & sesame oat bars 392
Banana & blueberry slab cake 760
Berry crumble 688
cinnamon crumble 688
Coconut bircher 393
Gorgonzola with port-steeped muscatels & oatcakes 841
No-bake muesli bars 392
No-bake nutty biscuit base 738
Nutty granola 377
Oat milk mayonnaise 74
Oatcake crackers 840–1

Toasted muesli 394
Vegan parsnip & potato purée 606
Vegan potato skordalia 621
ocean trout *see* trout

octopus 217
Braised baby octopus with red wine, oregano, paprika & cherry tomatoes 219
Chargrilled octopus 218
Octopus braised in rosé & tomato with radicchio & bottarga 219–20

oils 62
basil oil 662
Herb & chilli oil 86
Herb oil for fish 165
Rosemary, garlic & parmesan oil 26
spice oil 386
Spring onion oil 103
types of 22–3

okra 578–80
Greek-style braised okra (bamies) 580
Okra with shiso, soy & toasted sesame seeds 582
Sour fish curry with okra & celery heart 581
Spiced okra with curry leaves 582
Tempura okra 580
olive oil 22
olive oil pastry 469

olives 23, 584–7
Anchovy, tomato & basil topping for focaccia 844
Baked olives, grapes & ricotta 588
Blanched calamari with tuna sauce & olives 220
Braised artichoke, egg, olive & watercress salad 538
Braised fennel with tomato & olives 529
Braised lamb & artichokes with couscous, olives & harissa 537
Caponata bianco with toasted walnuts 489
celery & olive salad 188
Deep-fried red mullet with celery & olive salad 188
Eggplant, sesame, egg, olive & radish salad 518
Fennel & mandarin salad with olives, currants & chilli 531
Garlicky green olive tapenade 590
Greek salad 512
Green olive, artichoke & kale tapenade 590
lye-cured olives, note on 586
Marinated olives 591
Mezzanotte paste 588
Moorish chicken skewers with orange & black olive salsa 345
Moorish pork skewers with orange & black olive salsa 345
Olives ascolana 587
orange & black olive salsa 345
Oven-baked poussins with tomato, sherry, fennel & olives 590–1
Pissaladière 599
Pissaladière with green olive paste 599
Pizza 'number 1' 856

Pizza diavolo 857
Pizza napolitana 857
Potato bread 844
Provençale tomato-stuffed peppers with olives & anchovies 662
puttanesca sauce 117
Queen green tapenade 590
Quick olive dip 587
Quick olive tapenade 587
Simple cured olives 586–7
Spaghetti puttanesca 117
Tomato tarte tatin with manchego, thyme & dried olives 660
Tuna niçoise 438–9
Vitello tonnato 297

omelettes 352
Fluffy goat's cheese & gruyère omelette 355
Fluffy prawn & crab omelette with prawn essence & watercress 355
Omelette with blackened roma tomatoes, dill & marinated feta 353
Omelette with goat's curd & chives 353
Omelette with mushroom & taleggio 353
Omelette with pecorino & parsley 352–3
Omelette with smoked salmon, chives & crème fraiche 353
Prawn or crab omelette with oyster sauce 353
Spinach & cheddar omelette 353
Silverbeet or zucchini & feta omelette 353

onions 592–5
Boiled egg on toast with anchovies, onion & paprika 352
Borlotti bean salad with mustard fruits 426
Bread sauce with onion 70
Coriander, onion & citrus sauce 11
French onion soup 596
Fried onion rings 594
Mejadra 385
Onion sauce 599
Pearl onions à la grecque 597
Potato & slow-roasted red onion salad 598
Quick-pickled onions 594
Roasted pumpkin with cinnamon, chilli, pickled onion, yoghurt & feta 631
Simple caramelised onions 598
Slow-roasted red onion frittata 598
Slow-roasted red onion quiche 598
Slow-roasted red onions 598
Sour sherry onions 599
Spiced corn, manchego, capsicum & red onion loaf 858
Sweet pickled onions 597
Thyme-crumbed onions 598
see also shallots, spring onions

orange-blossom water 23
Doughnuts in honey & orange-blossom syrup with ricotta & pistachios 773
Honey & orange-blossom syrup 792
honey sabayon cream 703
Lemon, date & orange-blossom marmalade 699
Orange-blossom labneh 363

Roasted apricot & orange-blossom clafoutis 721
Saffron scones with orange-blossom marmalade 772

oranges 690–4
Blood orange & Campari marmalade 699
Blood orange marmalade 699
Braised artichoke, fennel & broad bean salad with orange glaze 536
Candied orange & lemon peel 790
Celery, lemon, orange & parsley salad 491
Chargrilled poussins with a orange, chilli, herb & golden sultana salad 236
Charred fennel salad with tarragon & orange 528
Chocolate hot cross buns 765
citrus & chilli relish 358
citrus cure 169
Citrus-cured gravlax 169
Cream cheese icing with orange 803
Crème fraiche glaze with cardamom & orange 804
Crepes suzette 771
Fresh ponzu 101
Glacé orange 790
Italian blood orange breakfast cake 740
Maltaise sauce 79
Moorish chicken skewers with orange & black olive salsa 345
Moorish pork skewers with orange & black olive salsa 345
Orange & almond cake with glacé orange 744
Orange & anise doughnuts 773
orange & black olive salsa 345
orange & tarragon dressing 528
Orange-blossom labneh 363
orange glaze 536
orange syrup 740
Pork chops with orange & fennel glaze 343–4
red wine, orange & coffee sauce 720
red-wine poaching liquid 710
Rhubarb tartlets 649
Roasted pears with earl grey tea, marsala, cinnamon & orange 711
Roasted stone fruit 720
Seasoned pistachio dust 376
Smashed blueberry glaze 774
Teriyaki sauce 101
Twice-roasted duck with salted orange, cocoa nibs & coffee 264–5
Watermelon & prawn salad citrus & chilli relish 201
orecchiette 131
see also pasta

oregano 23
Baked olives, grapes & ricotta 588
Barbecued lamb leg with oregano & lemon 312
Beef & pork loaf with haloumi, pistachio & pomegranate molasses 288–9
Braised baby octopus with red wine, oregano, paprika & cherry tomatoes 219

Braised lamb chump chops with potato,
jalapeño & oregano 314
Braised lamb neck with white wine, tomato
& oregano 316
Braised pork shoulder with borlotti beans
& taleggio 424
Caponata bianco with toasted walnuts 489
Chimichurri 85
Golden chicken stock 54
Greek-style lemon & oregano potatoes 626
lemon & oregano dressing 218
Pasta with fresh tomato sauce 658
Pommes anna with oregano 624
Porchetta 338
Roasted potatoes with thyme 626
Roasted zucchini with anchovy, oregano &
chilli 672
thyme & oregano rub 424
Tomato confit 656

osso buco
Casarecce with osso buco 121
Veal osso buco with white wine &
gremolata 296

oxtail *see* beef

oyster mushrooms
Tom yum goong 201
Veal scallopini with guanciale, oyster
mushrooms & thyme 295

oyster sauce 23

oysters 206–8
Bo ssäm 341–2
Devilled eggs with shellfish 356
Grilled oysters with horseradish 210
Jerusalem artichoke soup with seafood 544
Oyster shooters with cucumber, ginger
vinegar & white pepper jelly 510–1
Oysters with fire ice 208
shucking 208

P

pancakes
American-style pancakes 768
Crepes 771
Kimchi pancakes with a tamari & sesame
dipping sauce 457

pancetta
Barley 'risotto' with mushrooms & speck
572
Bucatini amatriciana 121
Celeriac, fennel & rice brodo with pancetta
483
Chicken fricassee with Dutch creams,
speck & tarragon 239
Crispy lamb's brains, pancetta & feta, with
curly endive & mint 308
Italian sausage ragù 335
Italian-style braised beef 285
Pâté de campagne 327
*Pumpkin & taleggio risotto with cured
meat* 632

Ragù alla bolognese 283
Risi e bisi 613
Spaghetti carbonara 119–20
Veal osso buco with white wine &
gremolata 296
Veal scallopini with guanciale, oyster
mushrooms & thyme 295
Winter minestrone with roasted root
vegetables 607

pandan leaves 23
Coconut & pandan jasmine rice 384
Coconut butter pandan cake 744–5
Pandan extract 744
panforte, Chocolate, with almonds, figs & sour
cherries 760–1
Pangrattato 123
panko 23

panna cotta
Cinnamon panna cotta 781
Classic panna cotta 781
Coconut panna cotta with coconut jelly,
black sesame tuilles, mango & lime
leaf 783
Honey panna cotta 781
Vanilla & fig leaf panna cotta with scorched
lemon syrup 707
Yoghurt panna cotta 781
Panzanella with buffalo mozzarella 658
papaya: Thai green papaya salad 438
paprika 23

parfait
Chicken liver parfait 233
Scorched honey & yoghurt parfait 785

parmesan
Apple, fennel & witlof slaw with cheese 680
Baked polenta with gorgonzola, radicchio,
walnuts & balsamic 382
Baked tomatoes stuffed with rice, feta &
pine nuts 663
Cassoulet 391
Cheddar & feta scones with mixed seeds
859
cheese sauce for Moussaka 310–1
crab & ricotta cannelloni filling 135
Crab cannelloni with crustacean dressing
135
Crumbed lamb cutlets 310
Cured beef with black onion spice &
parmesan 281
Eggs en cocotte with wilted spinach &
parmesan 359
Fennel gratin 528
Fine parmesan crisps 359
Genovese salad 624
Gorgonzola, fig & walnut pizza 857
Lamb, artichoke & mint ragù 535
Moussaka 310–1
Omelette with pecorino & parsley 352–3
Pasta alla Norma 521
Pasta with fresh tomato sauce 658
Pizza 'number 1' 856
Pizza bianco with prosciutto & rocket 857
*Pizza bianco with sausage, roasted
cauliflower, chilli & cherry tomatoes* 857

Pizza diavolo 857
polpette 253
Pumpkin, anchovy & ricotta pizza 857
Ricotta & spinach gnudi 141
Roasted carrots with Champagne vinegar &
maple dressing 469
Rosemary, garlic & parmesan oil 26
Spaghetti with spinach, lemon &
pangrattato 124
Stracciatella soup 55
Taleggio mash 625
*Warm celeriac salad with potato &
parmesan* 482
Winter minestrone with roasted root
vegetables 607

parmigiana
Deluxe eggplant parmigiana with
anchovies 522
Vegetarian eggplant parmigiana 522

Parmigiano Reggiano 24, 111
A nod to Harry's Bar original carpaccio 280
Asparagus with bagna cauda 406
Asparagus with poached egg & prosciutto
406
Beef carpaccio 280
Braised artichoke, fennel & broad bean
salad with orange glaze 536
Cacio e pepe 120
Cured beef with black onion spice &
parmesan 281
Fettuccine alfredo 119
Green aglio e olio 122
Grilled oysters with horseradish 210
*Grilled scallops with horseradish &
Parmigiano Reggiano* 210
Orecchiette with broccoli & cime di rape
444
Orecchiette with tomato, mint & anchovy
sauce 132
Panzanella with buffalo mozzarella 658
Raw silverbeet, sorrel & hazelnut salad
560–1
Roasted & raw Jerusalem artichoke salad
544
Ricotta & spinach ravioli 116
Risotto bianco 148
Scotch quail eggs 360
Shaved brussels sprouts with roasted king
brown mushrooms, manchego & maple
dressing 453
Shaved fennel, artichoke & almond salad
535–6
Simple porcini risotto 150
Spaghetti carbonara 119–20
Tagliatelle with egg, truffle & Parmigiano
Reggiano 119
*Vegetarian roasted Jerusalem artichoke
salad* 542

parsley 24
Beetroot tabouleh with currants &
sunflower seeds 419
Borlotti bean salad with mustard fruits 426
Borlotti beans with herbs & freekeh 427

Braised artichoke, egg, olive & watercress salad 538
Burnt butter sauce with lemon, capers & parsley 73
Cabbage rolls with lamb, rice, pine nuts & dill 451
Cafe de Paris butter 72
Caponata bianco with toasted walnuts 489
carrot top dressing 469
Celery, lemon & parsley salad with a fried garlic & fennel seed dressing 491
Celery, lemon, orange & parsley salad 491
Chermoula 90
Chimichurri 85
Corn chowder with potato & parsley 502
Corned beef 289
Corned beef with herb & mustard sauce 289
Falafel with broad beans & tahini yoghurt 432
Fish cakes with parsley 190-1
Frittata 355
Gigantes plaki 380-1
Green aglio e olio 122
Green goddess dressing 89
Greens & cheese pie 564-5
gremolata 296
Ham hock & leek terrine 328
Herb & chilli oil 86
Herbed velouté 64
Italian tartare 77
Lamb koftas baked with tomato & smoky eggplant, with pine nuts & parsley 309-10
Linguine vongole 127
Martini family stuffed capsicums 464-5
Mussels with chorizo, tomato & white wine 213
Omelette with pecorino & parsley 352-3
Orecchiette with broccoli & cime di rape 444
Oxtail risotto 148
Parsley & lemon butter 73
parsley & lemon paste 191
Pâté de campagne 327
Pearled barley, parsley & toasted pepita salad 378
Pedro Ximénez-braised beef cheeks with celeriac & parsnip purée & persillade 285-6
Pennette with tuna, tomatoes & mascarpone 125
Persillade 86
Petit salé aux lentilles 334
Pickled shallots & currants with parsley & cornichons 596
Porchetta 338
Pork polpette & potato al forno 337
Queen green tapenade 590
Quick herb salad 267
Quick olive tapenade 587
Quick prawn essence 67
Rainbow chard & chickpea salad 556

Raw turnip with walnut oil, celery leaves & parsley 642
Roasted cauliflower, barley & parsley salad with scorched almonds & feta 477
Rustic salsa verde with potato 86
Salad of lentils & smoked trout with dill & horseradish cream dressing 385
Salmoriglio 83
Salsa verde 86
Sauce gribiche 78
Sauce vierge 82
Spaghetti with spinach, lemon & pangrattato 124
Spinach, lentil & yoghurt salad with brown butter 558
Spring minestrone 531
Tabouleh 87
Traditional French steak tartare 279
Tunisian grilled smashed sardines on toast 183
Veal osso buco with white wine & gremolata 296
Zhoug 87

parsnips 604-6
Barley 'risotto' with parsnip chips 572
Borscht 418
celeriac & parsnip purée 286
Confit parsnip salad 606
Parsnip & potato purée 606
Parsnip chips 606
Pasties 469-70
Pedro Ximénez-braised beef cheeks with celeriac & parsnip purée & persillade 285-6
Pommes anna with vegetables 624
Raw parsnip salad 607
Roast carrot & root vegetable soup with cinnamon & ginger 472
Roasted celeriac, parsnip, potato & fennel with ras el hanout 485
Roasted parsnip & purple sweet potato with cinnamon, nutmeg & garlic 606-7
Roasted parsnip with anise, maple syrup & gruyère 606
Tunisian vegetable couscous royale with rosewater labneh 386-7
Winter minestrone with roasted root vegetables 607

passata (puréed tomatoes) 24
Roasted tomato passata 660-1

passionfruit
Lemon, lime or passionfruit curd 797
Lemon, lime or passionfruit icing 802
Pavlova 784
Raspberry sherbet marshmallows 791

pasta 108-13
Agnolotti del plin 115
Bouillabaisse-style stew 214-5
Bucatini amatriciana 121
Cacio e pepe 120
Casarecce with osso buco 121
Chicken noodle broth with porcini polpette 253

Chicken, corn & noodle soup 502-3
cooking 110, 113
Crab cannelloni with crustacean dressing 135
dried 24, 109-10, 112-3
Egg pasta 111-3, 128
Fettuccine alfredo 119
fresh 108, 110
Genovese salad 624
Green aglio e olio 122
Lasagne 136
Linguine vongole 127
Linguine with prawns & broad beans 433
Mac & cheese 120
Malloreddus with prawns & fennel 526
Mortadella agnolotti 114
Mushroom tortellini 115
Mussels with chorizo, tomato & white wine 213
Orecchiette with broccoli & cime di rape 444
Orecchiette with eggplant, oregano, balsamic & ricotta 132-3
Orecchiette with tomato, mint & anchovy sauce 132
Pasta alla Norma 521
Pasta with fresh tomato sauce 658
Pennette with tuna, tomatoes & mascarpone 125
preparing 110
Ricotta & spinach gnudi 141
Ricotta & spinach ravioli 116
Roast meat tortellini 114-5
scraps 110
Sea urchin linguini with roasted tomato passata & butter 128
Semolina dough for orecchiette, pici & gnocchi sardi 131
shapes 109, 112-3
Spaghetti aglio e olio 123
Spaghetti carbonara 119-20
Spaghetti puttanesca 117
Spaghetti with sardines, currants & pine nuts 124
Spaghetti with spinach, lemon & pangrattato 124
Spaghettini with crab, lemon, herbs & chilli 125
Spinach, ricotta & feta cannelloni with mint passata sauce 133
Squid ink pasta 128
Summer vegetable lasagne 136
Tagliatelle with egg, truffle & Parmigiano Reggiano 119
Tagliatelle with lemon cream 123-4
Tortelloni with pumpkin, sage & mustard fruits, with burnt butter sauce 114
Vegetarian mac & cheese 120
Winter minestrone with roasted root vegetables 607
Zucchini & pesto pasta 674
see also gnocchi
Pasta frolla (Italian sweet pastry) 825

pastes
broad bean & pea paste 432–3
chilli paste 610
curry paste 488–9
date paste 314
Fennel, black pepper & garlic paste 529
Fermented red cooked chilli paste 494
Mezzanotte paste 588
parsley & lemon paste 191
Preserved lemon paste 695
Quince paste 717
red kimchi paste 456
white kimchi paste 456
Pasties 469–70
pastrami: *Vinaigrette potatoes with meat* 624–5

pastry 810–1
blind-baking pastry shells 811
brik pastry 8
choux dough 821
Classic puff pastry 822
Compressed puff pastry 822
Cream cheese shortcrust pastry 830
filo pastry 564
Galani dough for crostoli & cannoli 820
Gluten-free shortcrust pastry for a tart base 812
olive oil pastry 469
Pasta frolla (Italian sweet pastry) 825
pastry essentials 810–1
Pâte à choux for éclairs & profiteroles 821
Pâte brisée (shortcrust pastry) 829
Pâte sablée (French shortbread) 813
Pâte sucrée (Sweet shortcrust) 812
Rough puff pastry 823
sablé breton 819
Sambouseks 832
Short olive oil pastry 828
sour cream shortcrust pastry 599
strudel/pastry 685
Sweet galette pastry 813
sweet pastry for tartlets 649
patties, Tuna & sweet potato sesame, with pickled salsa 622
Pavlova 784

peaches 718–20
A simple peach dessert 721
Cherry, semolina, almond & yoghurt cake 753
Fruit-spiked apple & peach turnovers 681
Grilled peaches or nectarines 722
Honey & white wine poaching syrup for stone fruit 723–4
Peach caramel sauce 721
Roasted peaches stuffed with ricotta & chocolate, with crushed biscotti 720
Roasted pork scotch with burnt honey & thyme, scorched grapes & grilled peaches 344
Roasted stone fruit 720
Roasted stone fruit & ginger clafoutis 721
White peach & rosewater jelly 724
peanut oil 22

peanuts 368
Bánh mì with roast pork belly 332–3
Beef rendang 292–3
Chia pudding 393
Chicken & ginger wontons with peanuts 231
Crispy pork belly salad with sesame spiced dressing, cucumber & coriander 331
Crispy sweet-chilli chicken with wombok, Thai basil & peanuts 242
Gado gado with roasted cauliflower, cucumber & eggs 478
Kohlrabi, cabbage & beetroot slaw 548–9
Peanut & ginger dressing 95
Prawn & poached chicken vermicelli salad 240
Salted caramel popcorn with nuts 788
Satay sauce 104
Simple Thai-style hard-boiled eggs 356
Soft-boiled eggs with green mango salad & citrus & chilli relish 358
Spiced sesame & peanut dressing 94
Thai green papaya salad 438
Tofu 'mayonnaise' 75
pearled barley *see* barley
pearl couscous *see* moghrabieh

pears 708–9
Baked whole pears with verjuice & a clove crumb 684
Celeriac remoulade with pear 484
Even simpler frangipane tarts 797
Pear, fennel & witlof slaw with buttermilk dressing 680
Pear, fennel, celery heart, Roquefort & poppy seed salad 710
Quail saltimbocca with caramelised pears 268–9
Roasted pears with earl grey tea, marsala, cinnamon & orange 711
Roasted pears with honey, verjuice, rosemary & bay leaves 711
Saffron-poached pears 724
Sliced pears roasted with maple syrup, thyme & white pepper 709
Spiced red wine pears 710–1

peas 608–10
broad bean & pea paste 432–3
Broad bean & pea salad with nasturtium leaves, goat's cheese & bagna cauda 431
Buttery minted peas 610
Cheesy buttered broad beans & peas 430
Chicken noodle broth with greens 253
Chow mein-style beef with wombok 292
Crab, pea & potato samosas 611
Crumbed zucchini flowers with crab mayonnaise & peas 669
Fried rice with peas, prawns & egg 610
Frugal pea supper 612
Genovese salad 624
Grilled lamb cutlets with smashed broad beans & hot feta dressing 432–3
Ham hock & pea risotto 148
Lamb, pea & mint pancake fritters 319
Lebanese peas with lamb 614

Left-over lamb roast shepherd's pie 319
Lobster salad à la russe 200
Martini family stuffed capsicums with peas 464–5
Pasties 469–70
Pea & mozzarella salad 611
Pea & potato samosas 611
Pea salad with a golden garlic, sichuan pepper & ginger dressing 614–5
Quick rice & peas 375
Risi e bisi 613
Seared ocean trout with grilled lettuce, peas & pea tendrils 561–2
Seared squid & pea salad with tomato & chilli 612
Simple seafood pie sauce 71
Slow-roasted red onion frittata 598
Spinach, mint & rice salad with yoghurt dressing 560
Spring minestrone 531
White cabbage & pea slaw 448–9
Zucchini & haloumi fritters with burnt honey sauce 673–4
Zucchini, ham & pea slice with feta 672–3
see also snow peas, split peas, sugar-snap peas
pecans: *Carrot, cinnamon, pecan & cream cheese muffins* 732

pecorino 24, 111
Broccoli with lemon, chilli, fennel seeds & pecorino 444
Bucatini amatriciana 121
Cacio e pepe 120
Green aglio e olio 122
Lamb, artichoke & mint ragù 535
Omelette with pecorino & parsley 352–3
Orecchiette with broccoli & cime di rape 444
Orecchiette with tomato, mint & anchovy sauce 132
Veal & pork polpette with savoy cabbage, taleggio & truffled pecorino 337

pepitas 369
Byzantine salad 379
Cheddar & feta scones with mixed seeds 859
Date, sesame, coconut & macadamia nut balls 393
Grilled pumpkin salad with pumpkin oil dressing, pickled grapes & goat's cheese 630
No-bake seed bars 392
Nutty, salty, sweet & seedy crunch mix 377
Pearled barley, parsley & toasted pepita salad 378
Roast carrot & root vegetable soup with cinnamon & ginger 472
Spiced seed crackers 839
Super seed loaf 376
Toasted muesli 394
Zucchini, ham & pea slice with feta 672–3
pepita oil 22

peppers
  Melanzane sotto aceto with banana peppers, basil & chilli 523
  see also aleppo pepper, capsicums, chillies

peppercorns 24
  sansho pepper 28
  sichuan pepper 28

perilla *see* shiso
Persillade 86

pesto
  Pesto 90
  Rocket & basil pesto 531
  Zucchini & pesto pasta 674

pho
  Beef pho 57
  Pho broth 57-8

pici 131
  see also pasta

pickles 25
  Crunchy lacto-fermented dill pickles 505
  Emma's pickled rhubarb 648
  Jerusalem artichoke pickle 545
  pickled arame salad 622
  Pickled daikon & mint salad 304
  pickled ginger 16
  pickled grapes 630
  Pickled Lebanese cucumbers 506
  Pickled radishes 639
  Pickled shallots & currants with parsley & cornichons 596
  Pickled spring vegetables 470-1
  Pickled turnip torshi 639
  Quick kohlrabi pickle 548
  Quick-pickled carrots 472
  Quick-pickled onions 594
  Quick-pickled turnips with soy & rice vinegar 640
  Raw quick pickled beetroot 419
  Sliced pickled jalapeños 494
  Spiced Chinese pickles 640
  sweet pickled cucumber 413
  Sweet pickled fennel 531
  Sweet pickled onions 597
  Sweet Zuni-style pickles 668
  Whole pickled chillies & a simple fermented chilli sauce 494-5
  see also capers, cornichons

pies
  Boeuf bourguignon pie 284
  Chicken, leek & mushroom pie 603
  Deep-dish apple pie 818
  Fish pie 188-9
  Greens & cheese pie 564-5
  Greens, potato & cheese pie with olive oil pastry 828
  Left-over lamb roast shepherd's pie 319
  Lemon meringue pie 806
  Lemonia's pumpkin & feta pie with olive oil pastry 631
  Silverbeet & haloumi pies 563
  Sugar-crusted apple pie 818
  Vine leaf beef & bone marrow pie 287

pine mushrooms 568, 571
  Barley 'risotto' with mushrooms & speck 572
  Carrot, mushroom & gruyère loaf with mushroom 472-3
  Mushroom ragù 576-7
  Mushroom risotto 151
  Mushroom tortellini 115
  Omelette with mushroom & taleggio 353
  Risotto funghi 149

pine nuts 368
  Almond & pistachio biscotti 758
  Baked tomatoes stuffed with rice, feta & pine nuts 663
  Baked zucchini stuffed with rice, feta & pine nuts 663
  Cabbage rolls with lamb, rice, pine nuts & dill 451
  Dolmades with rice, pine nuts, currants & lemon 375
  Eggplant, sesame, egg, olive & radish salad 518
  Fennel & orange salad with pine nuts 530
  Gnocchi with leek, gorgonzola & nuts 602
  Green aglio e olio with crunch 122
  Lamb & pine nut filling for sambouseks 833
  Lamb koftas baked with tomato & smoky eggplant, with pine nuts & parsley 309-10
  Maltagliata of beef with rocket, fine kale & ricotta 288
  Mejadra 385
  Pesto 90
  Pork polpette & potato al forno with pine nuts 337
  Spaghetti with sardines, currants & pine nuts 124
  Tuna, brown rice & green bean salad with sumac 437
  Vine leaf beef & bone marrow pie 287
  Warm celeriac salad with yoghurt, aleppo chilli, pine nuts & sultanas 482
  Well-cooked broccoli with anchovies & pine nuts 442

pineapple
  Corn & pineapple salsa 499
  Grilled pineapple with pink peppercorns for pavlova 784
  mango & pineapple salad 780
  Spiced pineapple & walnut cake 742
  Sweet & sour sauce with pineapple 100
  Tapioca pearls in coconut with tropical salad & caramel sauce 780-1
Piperade 465
Piperade tart 829

pipis 205
  Bouillabaisse-style stew 214-5
  Linguine vongole 127
Pissaladière 599

pistachio 368-9
  Almond & pistachio biscotti 758
  Beef & pork loaf with haloumi, pistachio & pomegranate molasses 288-9
  Chocolate panforte with almonds, figs & sour cherries 760-1
  Coconut, cherry & pistachio slice 761
  Cured beef with black onion spice & parmesan 281
  Dark chocolate truffles with nutty praline 791
  Doughnuts in honey & orange-blossom syrup with ricotta & pistachios 773
  Fried haloumi with vine leaves, pistachios, za'atar & pomegranate molasses 363
  Mazaresi cakes 732
  Nutty granola 377
  Nutty, salty, sweet & seedy crunch mix 377
  Pâté de campagne 327
  pistachio & almond marzipan icing 752
  Raw silverbeet, mint & pistachio salad 561
  Seasoned pistachio dust 376
  Sicilian cassata-style ricotta cake 752-3
  Spiced duck with pickled watermelon 262
  Tunisian dukkah 13

pitta
  fried pitta 314
  Puffed pitta pockets 854-5
  Soft pitta bread for wraps, souvlaki or dips 854

pizza
  Coeliac pizza bases 857
  Gorgonzola, fig & walnut pizza 857
  Napolitana 857
  Pizza 'number 1' 856
  Pizza base 856
  Pizza bianco with prosciutto & rocket 857
  Pizza bianco with sausage, roasted cauliflower, chilli & cherry tomatoes 857
  Pizza diavolo 857
  Pizza margherita 857
  Pumpkin, anchovy & ricotta pizza 857
  Salami pizza 857

plums 718-20
  A simple frangipane fruit tart 796
  Asian brisket with vinegared blood plums 291
  Cherry, semolina, almond & yoghurt cake 753
  Hazelnut plum streusel cake 741
  Honey & white wine poaching syrup for stone fruit 723-4
  Puff pastry tart with fruit 824-5
  Roasted blood plum relish 725
  roasted plum & hoisin sauce 263
  Roasted rhubarb, blood plum & ginger chutney 646
  Roasted stone fruit 720
  Roasted stone fruit & ginger clafoutis 721
  Seared duck breast with roasted plum & hoisin sauce for pancakes or bao 263
  Spicy malt plum sauce 725
  see also prunes, umeboshi

poaching liquid
 A simple poaching liquid for stone fruit 724
 Honey & white wine poaching syrup for stone fruit 723–4
 poaching bath for pretzels 841
 poaching stock for meat 297, 308
 red-wine poaching liquid 710
 verjuice poaching liquid 711
poké, Tuna, bowl with avocado, shiitake, sesame, wakame & cucumber 415

polenta 25
 Baked polenta with gorgonzola, radicchio, walnuts & balsamic 382
 Cheesecake-flavoured biscuit turnovers 825
 Pasta frolla (Italian sweet pastry) 825
 Polenta 383
 Polenta chips 383
 Soft polenta with crab, artichoke & poached egg 352
 Spiced corn & manchego loaf 858
polpette *see* meatballs

pomegranate molasses 25
 Beef & pork loaf with haloumi, pistachio & pomegranate molasses 288–9
 Beetroot, carrot & pomegranate salad 420
 Cheese, silverbeet & hazelnut filling for sambouseks 833
 Chicken livers with witlof & radicchio fatoush salad, currants & sumac 234
 Fried haloumi with vine leaves, pistachios, za'atar & pomegranate molasses 363
 Grilled asparagus & haloumi salad with fennel, walnuts & pomegranate 406–7
 Kohlrabi & cucumber salad with pomegranate molasses 549
 Lamb & pine nut filling for sambouseks 833
 pomegranate dressing 262, 314
 Roasted beetroot, cinnamon & pomegranate dip 420
 Side of salmon with walnuts, tahini, mint & pomegranate molasses 172
 Slow-roasted duck with baharat & pomegranate molasses 265
 Tomato, pomegranate & sumac dressing 82
 Turkish-style roast pumpkin & walnut dip 632–3

pomegranates 25
 Beetroot, carrot & pomegranate salad 420
 Corn, black bean & pomegranate salad 503
 Grilled asparagus & haloumi salad with fennel, walnuts & pomegranate 406–7
 Grilled eggplant with tahini & yoghurt dressing, pomegranate, chilli & mint 516
 Kohlrabi & cucumber salad with lemon yoghurt dressing 549
 Lamb, spinach, pomegranate & date salad with crisp pitta 314
 lime & pomegranate dressing 503

 Roasted beetroot, cinnamon & pomegranate dip 420
 Roasted cauliflower, barley & parsley salad with scorched almonds & feta 477
 Roasted pumpkin with tahini & yoghurt dressing, pomegranate, chilli & mint 516
 Side of salmon with walnuts, tahini, mint & pomegranate molasses 172
 Spiced duck with pickled watermelon 262
 Spinach, mint & rice salad with yoghurt dressing 560
 Tomato, pomegranate & sumac dressing 82

pomelos 690–2
 citrus & chilli relish 358
 Soft-boiled eggs with green mango salad & citrus & chilli relish 358
 Watermelon & prawn salad citrus & chilli relish 201
Pommes anna 624
ponzu 25
popcorn, Salted caramel & almond 788
poppy seeds 25
Porchetta 338

porcini 25, 570
 Chicken fricassee with porcini mushrooms 239
 Chicken noodle broth with porcini polpette 253
 Cream of mushroom soup 574–5
 Enhanced soy sauce 101
 Mushroom risotto 151
 Mushroom tortellini 115
 Porcini & asparagus risotto 151
 Porcini powder 570
 Porcini, rosemary & taleggio risotto 151
 Simple porcini risotto 150
 Slow-cooked robust ragù of pork & beef 336
 Vegetable bolognese with porcini mushroom 576

pork 322–6
 Baked stuffed eggplant 520–1
 Bánh mì with roast pork belly 332–3
 Beef & pork loaf with haloumi, pistachio & pomegranate molasses 288–9
 Bo ssäm 341–2
 Braised pork shoulder with borlotti beans & taleggio 424
 Cabbage rolls with lamb, rice, pine nuts & dill 451
 Cassoulet 391
 Cevapcici with wild fennel 529
 Chow mein-style pork with wombok 292
 Crispy pork belly salad with sesame spiced dressing, cucumber & coriander 331
 Crispy roasted pork belly 332
 Glazed red pork with cassia, star anise, black vinegar & wood ear fungus 341
 Grilled pork fillet, wombok & crispy egg 341
 Lardo 326
 Left-over pork sandwich 344
 Mapo-style tofu with beans & pork 436

 Moorish pork skewers with orange & black olive salsa 345
 Mortadella agnolotti 114
 Olives ascolana 587
 Pâté de campagne 327
 Petit salé aux lentilles 334
 Porchetta 338
 Pork & prawn wontons with chilli & sichuan pepper dipping sauce 342
 Pork & prawn wontons with choy sum & kale 342
 Pork bolognese 576
 Pork chops with orange & fennel glaze 343–4
 Pork polpette & potato al forno 337
 Pork rillettes with sherry 330
 Pork roll 333
 Pork spare ribs with maple glaze 331
 Pork pot-sticker dumplings 500
 Pork, wombok & ginger dumplings 500
 Pulled slow-cooked pork shoulder with cider 333
 Ragù alla bolognese 283
 Ramen 59
 Roast meat tortellini 114–5
 Roasted lemongrass & turmeric pork steaks 246
 Roasted pork scotch with burnt honey & thyme, scorched grapes & grilled peaches 344
 Roasted rack of pork with fennel 343
 Sage & rosemary pork chops 344
 Schnitzel 345
 Shoyu ramen broth 58–9
 Sichuan pepper & honey glaze 331
 Slow-cooked robust ragù of pork & beef 336
 Speedy pork belly with gochujang 341
 Spicy pork bao 333
 Teriyaki pork belly wrapped with shiitake, spring onion & togarashi 343
 Veal & pork polpette with savoy cabbage, taleggio & truffled pecorino 337
 see also bacon, bresaola, chorizo, cotechino, guanciale, ham, jamón, lardo, morcilla, mortadella, nduja, pancetta, pastrami, prosciutto, salami, sausages, speck

portobello mushrooms 568
 Cream of mushroom soup 574–5
 Grilled minute steak with soy & sesame mushrooms 281
 Grilled mushrooms 575
 Mushroom risotto 151
possets, Lemon cream & cherry 696
pot-sticker dumplings, Prawn, corn & shiitake 500
potato starch 25

potatoes 616–20
 Abbacchio al forno 315–6
 Asparagus soup 407
 Baby chard & curly endive salad with soft-boiled egg dressing & honey bacon 557

Beer-battered flathead & twice-cooked potato cakes 187
Borscht 418
Braised fennel with tomato & olives 529
Braised lamb chump chops with potato, jalapeño & oregano 314
Braised lamb neck with white wine, tomato & oregano 316
Brined roast chicken, Greek-style, with magic smashed potatoes 245
Carrot paste salad with lemon, caraway & nigella seeds 473
Cauliflower purée 476
Chicken fricassee with Dutch creams, speck & tarragon 239
Classic fish & potato cakes 187
Classic potato gnocchi 137-8
Classic potato mash 625
Corn chowder with potato & dill 502
Crab, pea & potato samosas 611
Cream of mushroom soup 574-5
Creamed mustard kipfler potatoes 622
Dauphinoise potatoes 627
Dauphinoise with camembert 627
Fennel, potato & sausage tray bake 530
Fish & mussels en papillote 178
Fish cakes with parsley 190-1
Fish pie 188-9
Gado gado with roasted vegetables 478
Genovese salad 624
Greek-style lemon & oregano potatoes 626
Greens, potato & cheese pie with olive oil pastry 828
Hasselback potatoes with paprika & bay leaves 626
Jerusalem artichoke soup 544
Lamb navarin 643
Left-over lamb roast shepherd's pie 319
Lobster salad à la russe 200
Moules frites 204
Moussaka 310-1
Mustard mash 625
New potatoes with green goddess dressing 89
Pan-seared potato gnocchi with scallops, mushrooms & lemon 140
Parsnip & potato purée 606
Pasties 469-70
Pea & potato samosas 611
Petit salé aux lentilles 334
Pommes anna 624
Pork polpette & potato al forno 337
Potato & slow-roasted red onion salad 598
Potato blinis 621
Potato bread 844
potato cakes 187
Potato rösti with ocean trout 623
Potato skordalia 621
Roasted cauliflower & turmeric soup with yoghurt & poached egg 476
Roasted celeriac, parsnip, potato & fennel with ras el hanout 485
Roasted potatoes with thyme 626

Rustic salsa verde with potato 86
Salad of lentils & smoked trout with dill & horseradish cream dressing 385
Simple seafood pie sauce 71
Smoked eggplant soup with kefalograviera 519
Taleggio mash 625
Tortilla de patata 623
Traditional French steak tartare with chips 279
Tuna & sweet potato sesame patties with pickled arame salad 622
Tuna niçoise 438-9
Vegetarian roasted Jerusalem artichoke salad 542
Vegetarian vinaigrette potatoes 624-5
Vinaigrette potatoes with cornichons, dill, caperberries, crème fraîche & fried egg 624-5
Warm celeriac salad with potato & parmesan 482
Watercress & potato soup 558
Zucchini & cream soup with cumin 673
poussins *see* chicken
praline, Nutty 786
prawns 194-5
An inspiration from ajo blanco 513
Barbecued prawns 202
Bouillabaisse-style stew 214-5
Bruschetta of prawns, cannellini beans & truffle 203
Butter-poached prawns 202-3
Caramelised barbecued prawns 202
Chawanmushi 356
Crustacean essence 52
Crustacean stock 52
Crustacean vinaigrette 52
Fish pie 188-9
Fish soup with spiced rouille & croûtes 174-5
Fluffy prawn & crab omelette with prawn essence & watercress 355
Fried rice with peas, prawns & egg 610
Linguine with prawns & broad beans 433
Malloreddus with prawns & fennel 526
Pork & prawn wontons with chilli & sichuan pepper dipping sauce 342
Pork & prawn wontons with choy sum & kale 342
Prawn & poached chicken vermicelli salad 240
Prawn cocktail 413
Prawn dressing 67
Prawn head dust 195
Prawn omelette with oyster sauce 353
Prawn risotto 149
Prawn velouté 64
Prawn, corn & shiitake pot-sticker dumplings 500
Prawns a la plancha 194
Prawns with cannellini beans & truffle 203
Quick creamy seafood sauce or bisque 67
quick prawn (shrimp) stock 50
Quick prawn essence 67

Roast pumpkin & shellfish soup with Thai flavours 634
Simple seafood pie sauce 71
Sour fish curry with seafood 581
Spaghetti aglio e olio with prawns 123
Thai fish cakes 192-3
Tom yum goong 201
Vietnamese spring roll with crab, prawn & shiitake 575
Watermelon & prawn salad citrus & chilli relish 201
see also shrimp
preserved lemons
Easy preserved lemons 694-5
Preserved lemon paste 695
Preserved lemons with bay & cinnamon 695
Preserved lemons with bay & star anise 695
Preserved Meyer lemons with ginger & star anise 696-7
Pretzels 841
profiteroles 821
prosciutto 25
Asparagus with poached egg & prosciutto 406
Fennel & buffalo mozzarella salad with cured meat 530
Pizza bianco with prosciutto & rocket 857
Quail saltimbocca with caramelised pears 268-9
Shaved fennel & artichoke salad with cured meat 535-6
Veal saltimbocca with fresh figs 702-3
provolone 25
Baked fennel & leek with provolone sauce 528-9
provolone sauce 528
prunes
Christmas pudding 778-9
Roasted rack of pork with fennel 343
spiced prunes 343
Wholesome hoisin sauce 96
puddings
Chia pudding 393
Chilled coconut & lime leaf rice pudding 395
Christmas pudding 778-9
Christmas pudding semifreddo 779
Citrus delicious pudding 698-9
Deluxe bread & butter pudding 778
Self-saucing chocolate pudding 782-3
Sticky date pudding 778
Summer berry & chia pudding loaf 689
puff pastry *see* pastry
pulses 368-9
cooking 371
see also beans, chickpeas, lentils, peas
pumpkin 628-30
Grilled pumpkin salad with pumpkin oil dressing, pickled grapes & goat's cheese 630
Lemonia's pumpkin & feta pie with olive oil pastry 631
Pommes anna with vegetables 624

Pumpkin, anchovy & ricotta pizza 857
Pumpkin, chickpea, cashew & coconut
   curry 633
Pumpkin, rosemary & taleggio risotto 632
Roast carrot & root vegetable soup with
   cinnamon & ginger 472
Roasted pumpkin with cinnamon, chilli,
   pickled onion, yoghurt & feta 631
*Roasted pumpkin with tahini & yoghurt
   dressing* 516
Roasted pumpkin with skordalia 600
Spiced pumpkin & olive oil loaf cake 742–3
Tortelloni with pumpkin, sage & mustard
   fruits, with burnt butter sauce 114
Tunisian green capsicum & pumpkin salad
   460
Tunisian vegetable couscous royale with
   rosewater labneh 386–7
Turkish-style roast pumpkin & walnut dip
   632–3
pumpkin seed (pepita) oil 22
pumpkin seeds *see* pepitas
purée
   Cauliflower purée 476
   celeriac & parsnip purée 286
   Eggplant purée with chilli oil & walnuts
   516
   Parsnip & potato purée 606
   Pure corn purée 499
puttanesca sauce 117

Q

quail 268
   Quail rillettes with sherry 330
   Quail saltimbocca with caramelised pears
   268–9
   Roasted lemongrass & turmeric quail steaks
   246
   Spicy fried quail with sichuan pepper salt
   269
Quatre épices 24
quiche, Slow-roasted red onion 598
quinces 712–4
   Even simpler frangipane tarts 797
   Frangipane crostata 826
   Persian roast chicken on buttered rice with
   quince paste & bay leaves 250
   Poached quince 714
   Quick quince & apple relish 716
   Quince jelly 717
   Quince paste 717
   Roasted quince & chestnuts 716
   Roasted stone fruit & ginger clafoutis 721
   Slow-roasted quince with honey,
   cinnamon & cloves 714
quinoa 25, 368
   Beetroot tabouleh with currants &
   sunflower seeds 419
   Black bean, quinoa & cherry tomato salad
   380
   Super seed loaf 376

R

rabbit: *Rabbit rillettes with sherry* 330
radicchio 553
   Baked polenta with gorgonzola, radicchio,
   walnuts & balsamic 382
   Chicken livers with witlof & radicchio
   fatoush salad, currants & sumac 234
   Fennel & orange salad with radicchio 530
   Maltagliata of beef with rocket, fine kale &
   ricotta 288
   Octopus braised in rosé & tomato with
   radicchio & bottarga 219–20
   *Pear & fennel salad with radicchio &
   walnut* 710
   Pennette with tuna, tomatoes &
   mascarpone 125
   Seared radicchio with burrata, balsamic-
   pickled cherries & scorched almonds
   566
radishes 636–9
   Broad bean & pea salad with nasturtium
   leaves, goat's cheese & bagna cauda 431
   Crispy pork belly salad with sesame spiced
   dressing, cucumber & coriander 331
   Eggplant, sesame, egg, olive & radish salad
   518
   Italian-style coleslaw 448
   Kingfish kibbeh nayyeh 166
   Lamb ribs braised with treacle & dark ale
   304
   Maltagliata of beef with rocket, fine kale &
   ricotta 288
   pickled arame salad 622
   Pickled radishes 639
   Roasted radishes with thyme 643
   Spiced Chinese pickles 640
   Waldorf salad with roast chicken wrapped
   in iceberg 490
   White cabbage & pea slaw 448–9
ragùs
   Duck, celeriac & verjuice ragù 259
   Italian sausage ragù 335
   Lamb, artichoke & mint ragù 535
   Mushroom ragù 576–7
   Ragù alla bolognese 283
   Slow-cooked robust ragù of pork & beef
   336
   Veal, artichoke & mint ragù 535
rainbow chard *see* chard
Raita 98
Ramen 59
Ras el hanout 25–6
raspberries
   Berries & cream sponge cake filling 748
   Berry turnovers 688
   Blackberry or raspberry icing 802
   Cherry, raspberry & vanilla jam 723
   Chianti & raspberry granita with ice cream
   784–5
   Coconut & raspberry cake with chocolate
   ganache 746

*French shortcake with crème pâtissière &
   raspberries* 819
   Friands 734–5
   Lamingtons 749
   Lemon cream & cherry possets 696
   Raspberry sherbet marshmallows 791
   Raspberry toffee coulis 689
   Rhubarb tartlets 649
   Super-simple roasted raspberry jam 687
   *White chocolate and strawberry mille-
   feuille* 824
Ratatouille 672
ravioli 113
red lentils *see* lentils
Red velvet cupcakes with Italian meringue
   icing 731
relishes
   Mango, ginger & chilli relish 495
   Quick quince & apple relish 716
   Roasted blood plum relish 725
remoulade, Celeriac 484
rendang paste 293
rhubarb 644–6
   Emma's pickled rhubarb 648
   Rhubarb galette 650
   Rhubarb muffins 732
   Rhubarb tartlets 649
   Roasted rhubarb & strawberries with rose
   geranium 648
   Roasted rhubarb, blood plum & ginger
   chutney 646
   Spiced lamb shanks with rhubarb, honey &
   fried vine leaves 647
rice 26, 144, 368, 371–2
   absorption method 372
   Arancini 148
   Baked buttered rice 384
   Baked tomatoes stuffed with rice, feta &
   pine nuts 663
   *Baked zucchini stuffed with rice, feta & pine
   nuts* 663
   black rice, wholegrain 372
   Braised lamb neck & grain broth 309
   Cabbage rolls with lamb, rice, pine nuts &
   dill 451
   Cauliflower rice 478
   Celeriac, fennel & rice brodo with ricotta
   bruschetta 483
   Charred broccolini with tuna mayonnaise,
   black barley, egg & anchovy dust 442–3
   Chicken chops with wild rice salad 379
   Chilled coconut & lime leaf rice pudding
   395
   Coconut & pandan jasmine rice 384
   Congee 383
   Croquetas with smoked eel & manchego
   190
   Dolmades with rice, pine nuts, currants &
   lemon 375
   food safety concerns 372
   Fried rice with peas, prawns & egg 610
   Fried rice with wood ear fungus & cashews
   402
   Frugal pea supper 612

Iraqi chicken with tomato & cardamom rice 242-3
Japanese mixed rice & grains 382
Martini family stuffed capsicums 464-5
Mejadra 385
Persian roast chicken on buttered rice with quince paste & bay leaves 250
Quick rice & peas 375
Risi e bisi 613
Rizogalo 395
Spinach, mint & rice salad with yoghurt dressing 560
Toasted glutinous rice powder 384
Tuna poké bowl with avocado, shiitake, sesame, wakame & cucumber 415
Tuna, brown rice & green bean salad with sumac 437
types of 26
Vegetarian brown rice & green bean salad 437
Vine leaf beef & bone marrow pie 287
Wild rice, herb, almond & currant salad 378
Zucchini flower, wild rice, lentil & yoghurt salad 671
see also risotto
rice flour 14
rice wine *see* sake, shaoxing rice wine
ricotta
Baked olives, grapes & ricotta 588
Blintzes 771
Böreks with cheese 831
Bruschetta with cheese 655
Casarecce with osso buco 121
Celeriac, fennel & rice brodo with ricotta bruschetta 483
Cheese-filled lebanese talami bread 852
Cheesecake-flavoured biscuit turnovers 825
Cheesy lunchbox muffins 858
chocolate ricotta cake filling 752
Crab cannelloni with crustacean dressing 135
Cream cheese & ricotta filling 799
Deluxe bread & butter pudding 778
Doughnuts in honey & orange-blossom syrup with ricotta & pistachios 773
Frangipane crostata 826
French strawberry shortcake with whipped ricotta 819
Frittata 355
Green aglio e olio with cheese 122
Greens & cheese pie 564-5
Lasagne 136
Lebanese talami bread with cheese & greens 852
Lemon cheesecake 698
Maltagliata of beef with rocket, fine kale & ricotta 288
Mazaresi cakes 732
Orecchiette with eggplant, oregano, balsamic & ricotta 132-3
Orecchiette with tomato, mint & anchovy sauce 132

Pasta alla Norma 521
Pizza 'number 1' 856
Pumpkin, anchovy & ricotta pizza 857
Raw Jerusalem artichoke salad with broad beans & cheese 544
Ricotta 362
Ricotta & apple compote hotcakes 768-9
Ricotta & blackberry hotcakes 768-9
Ricotta & blueberry hotcakes 768-9
Ricotta & goat's cheese ravioli 117
Ricotta & semolina gnocchi 141
Ricotta & spinach gnudi 141
Ricotta & spinach ravioli 116
Risotto bianco with brown butter, hazelnuts, lemon & ricotta 148
Risotto with ricotta, spinach & verjuice-braised leek 149
Roasted peaches stuffed with ricotta & chocolate, with crushed biscotti 720
Shaved fennel, artichoke & almond salad 535-6
Sicilian cassata-style ricotta cake 752-3
Spinach, ricotta & feta cannelloni with mint passata sauce 133
Stuffed zucchini flowers 668-9
Summer vegetable lasagne 136
Whipped vanilla ricotta filling 799
rillettes
Ocean trout & smoked trout rillettes 174
Pork rillettes with sherry 330
Risi e bisi 613
risotto 144-7
Arancini 148
Barley 'risotto' with mushrooms & speck 572
cooking 146-7
Crab, prawn or bug tail risotto 149
Ham hock & pea risotto 148
Ham hock, rosemary & taleggio risotto 148
mantecatura 147
Mushroom risotto 151
Oxtail risotto 148
Porcini & asparagus risotto 151
Porcini, rosemary & taleggio risotto 151
Pumpkin, rosemary & taleggio risotto 632
rice for 26, 144
Risi e bisi 613
Risotto alla milanese 148
Risotto bianco 148
Risotto bianco with brown butter, hazelnuts, lemon & ricotta 148
Risotto funghi 149
Risotto nero with cuttlefish 149-50
Risotto with ricotta, spinach & verjuice-braised leek 149
Sausage & sage risotto 149
Simple porcini risotto 150
Spring vegetable risotto 149
Rizogalo 395
rocket 550-5
A nod to Harry's Bar original carpaccio 280
An exquisite herb salad 17
Grilled gem lettuce & bagna cauda 556
celery & olive salad 188

Cured beef with black onion spice & parmesan 281
Maltagliata of beef with rocket, fine kale & ricotta 288
Pizza 'number 1' 856
Pizza bianco with prosciutto & rocket 857
Quail saltimbocca with caramelised pears 268-9
Raw parsnip salad 607
Rocket & basil pesto 531
Vitello tonnato 297
Witlof, rocket & macadamia salad with pork & fennel sausage, mustard & honey 554
rogan josh, Lamb 317-8
romaine lettuce *see* cos lettuce
romano beans: Braised romano beans 438
romanoff, Strawberries 688
Roquefort
Pear, fennel, celery heart, Roquefort & poppy seed salad 710
Roasted & raw Jerusalem artichoke salad 544
rose geranium: Roasted rhubarb & strawberries with rose geranium 648
rosemary 26
Blood orange & rosemary marmalade 699
Grilled mushrooms 575
Ham hock, rosemary & taleggio risotto 148
Herb oil for fish 165
Italian-style braised beef 285
Lardo 326
Porchetta 338
Porcini, rosemary & taleggio risotto 151
Pumpkin, rosemary & taleggio risotto 632
Roasted pears with honey, verjuice, rosemary & bay leaves 711
Roasted potatoes with thyme 626
Roasted scotch fillet 283
Rosemary & bay salt 26
Rosemary, garlic & parmesan oil 26
Sage & rosemary pork chops 344
Schiacciata con l'uva 845
Simply roasted leg of lamb with rosemary & garlic 315
Slow-roasted eye fillet 285
Slow-roasted red onions 598
Veal osso buco with white wine & gremolata 296
rosewater 27
rosewater labneh 386
Tomato & pomegranate dressing with rosewater 82
Tunisian vegetable couscous royale with rosewater labneh 386-7
Yoghurt with spices 365
White peach & rosewater jelly 724
rösti, Potato, with ocean trout 623
Rouille 80
rye
flour 14
Rye crackers 838
rye sourdough loaf 850-1
walnut & rye skordalia 600

S

saba, vincotto and mosto cotto 27
saffron 27
saganaki *see* kefalograviera
sage 27
  Barley 'risotto' with mushrooms, speck &
    crispy sage 572
  Burnt butter sauce with lemon, sage &
    toasted walnuts 73
  Duck bresaola 267
  Italian sausage ragù 335
  Italian-style braised beef 285
  Pâté de campagne 327
  Pumpkin, rosemary & taleggio risotto with
    crispy sage 632
  Quail saltimbocca with caramelised pears
    268–9
  Ragù alla bolognese 283
  Sage & rosemary pork chops 344
  Sausage & sage risotto 149
  Slow-cooked robust ragù of pork & beef
    336
  Tortelloni with pumpkin, sage & mustard
    fruits, with burnt butter sauce 114
  Veal osso buco with white wine &
    gremolata 296
  Veal saltimbocca with fresh figs 702–3
sake 27
  Chawanmushi 356
  Enhanced soy sauce 101
  Goma dare (sesame dressing) 102
  Korean sesame grilled beef with sake,
    ginger & soy marinade 293
  Teriyaki sauce 101
  white miso marinade 184
salads
  American-style ranch salad 557
  An exquisite herb salad 17
  Barbecued Dutch carrot & leek salad
    468–9
  Beetroot, carrot & pomegranate salad 420
  black barley salad 246–7
  Black bean, quinoa & cherry tomato salad
    380
  Borlotti bean salad with mustard fruits 426
  Braised artichoke, egg, olive & watercress
    salad 538
  Braised artichoke, fennel & broad bean
    salad with orange glaze 536
  Broad bean & pea salad with nasturtium
    leaves, goat's cheese & bagna cauda 431
  Capsicum & eggplant salad 464
  Carrot paste salad with lemon, caraway &
    nigella seeds 473
  Cauliflower salad (roasted & raw) 478–9
  celery & olive salad 188
  Celery, lemon & parsley salad with a fried
    garlic & fennel seed dressing 491
  Celery, lemon, orange & parsley salad 491
  Chargrilled poussins with a lemon, chilli,
    herb & golden sultana salad 236
  charred fennel salad 176

Charred fennel salad with tarragon 528
Chicken livers with witlof & radicchio
  fatoush salad, currants & sumac 234
Chickpea, garlic & turmeric salad with
  witlof 386
Chilled cucumber & sesame salad with
  shiso & garlic chives 507
Confit parsnip salad 606
Corn, black bean & pomegranate salad 503
Crispy pork belly salad with sesame spiced
  dressing, cucumber & coriander 331
cucumber & wakame salad 415
cucumber, celery heart & herb salad 240
Cucumber, grape & herb salad with shallot
  dressing 508
Daikon, edamame & avocado salad, with
  sesame, apple & soy dressing 640–1
Eggplant, sesame, egg, olive & radish salad
  518
Fennel & buffalo mozzarella salad with
  broad beans, mint & green sultanas 530
Fennel & mandarin salad with olives,
  currants & chilli 531
Genovese salad 624
Greek salad 512
Grilled asparagus & haloumi salad with
  fennel, walnuts & pomegranate 406–7
Grilled pumpkin salad with pumpkin oil
  dressing, pickled grapes & goat's cheese
  630
Grilled zucchini salad 668
Harissa roast capsicum salad with goat's
  cheese 462
Insalata caprese 662
Jamón, fig, beetroot, goat's curd, watercress
  & mint salad 702
Japanese quick-pickled cucumber &
  wakame salad 506
Kohlrabi & cucumber salad with lemon
  yoghurt dressing 549
Left-over corned beef, egg & cabbage salad
  with smoked salt 289
mango & pineapple salad 780
Moroccan carrot, date & green chilli salad
  471
Panzanella with buffalo mozzarella 658
Pea & mozzarella salad 611
Pea salad with a golden garlic, sichuan
  pepper & ginger dressing 614–5
Pear, fennel, celery heart, Roquefort &
  poppy seed salad 710
Pearled barley, parsley & toasted pepita
  salad 378
pickled arame salad 622
Pickled daikon & mint salad 304
Potato & slow-roasted red onion salad 598
Prawn & poached chicken vermicelli salad
  240
Quick apple & witlof salad 680
Quick herb salad 267
Rainbow chard & chickpea salad 556
Raw Jerusalem artichoke salad with broad
  beans & cheese 544
Raw parsnip salad 607

Raw silverbeet, sorrel & hazelnut salad
  560–1
Roasted & raw fennel salad with mint & egg
  yolk 527
Roasted & raw Jerusalem artichoke salad
  544
Roasted cauliflower, barley & parsley salad
  with scorched almonds & feta 477
Salad of lentils & smoked trout with dill &
  horseradish cream dressing 385
Seared squid & pea salad with tomato &
  chilli 612
Shaved fennel, artichoke & almond salad
  535–6
Soft-boiled eggs with green mango salad &
  citrus & chilli relish 358
Spinach, lentil & yoghurt salad with brown
  butter 558
Spinach, mint & rice salad with yoghurt
  dressing 560
The simplest roasted capsicum salad 462
Tuna, brown rice & green bean salad with
  sumac 437
Tunisian green capsicum & pumpkin salad
  460
Vegetarian brown rice & green bean salad
  with sumac 437
Waldorf salad with roast chicken wrapped
  in iceberg 490
Warm celeriac salad with yoghurt, aleppo
  chilli, pine nuts & sultanas 482
Watermelon & prawn salad citrus & chilli
  relish 201
Wild rice, herb, almond & currant salad
  378
Witlof, rocket & macadamia salad with
  pork & fennel sausage, mustard & honey
  554
Wombok, daikon, shiitake & tofu salad 450
Yoghurt, cucumber & mint salad/dip 508
Zaalouk 518–9
Zucchini flower, wild rice, lentil & yoghurt
  salad 671
see also condiment salads, slaws, tabouleh
salami 325
  Fennel & buffalo mozzarella salad with
    cured meat 530
  Olives ascolana 587
  Salami pizza 857
salmon 154–60
  Citrus-cured gravlax 169
  Crudo with caviar, cucumber & mustard
    cress 510
  Fish marinated with white miso 184
  Fragrant seafood soup with bok choy 402
  Gravlax with treacle, fennel & pepper 171
  Kingfish kibbeh nayyeh 166
  Omelette with smoked salmon, chives &
    crème fraiche 353
  Quick-cured ocean trout with finger lime &
    coriander 168
  Salt-baked fish 175
  Sesame-crumbed ocean trout with nori
    mayo in a brioche bun 191–2

Side of salmon with walnuts, tahini, mint & pomegranate molasses 172
Smoked salmon & cucumber canapés 513
Vinaigrette potatoes with meat or seafood 624-5
see also fish roe
Salmoriglio 83

salsas
Corn & pineapple salsa 499
Green tomato salsa with dill & mint 664
orange & black olive salsa 345
Rustic salsa verde with potato 86
Salsa romesco 84
Salsa verde 86

salt 27
aleppo chilli salt 6
celery salt 9
Chinese five-spice salt 10
Coriander & black pepper salt 11
nori salt 187
Rosemary & bay salt 26
Sichuan pepper & mandarin salt 29
Sichuan pepper salt 29
salted caramel *see* caramel

sambouseks
Cheese, silverbeet & hazelnut filling for sambouseks 833
Lamb & pine nut filling for sambouseks 833
Sambouseks 832
samosas, Crab, pea & potato samosas 611
san choy bau 555

sandwiches
Balsamic pepper strawberry & chicken sandwiches 689
Bánh mì with roast pork belly 332-3
Cucumber sandwiches 511
French shortbread sandwiches with mascarpone cream, almonds & praline 813
Left-over pork sandwich 344
Pork roll 333
Sesame-crumbed ocean trout with nori mayo in a brioche bun 191-2
sansho pepper 28

sardines
Citrus-cured sardines 168
Dashi 53
Fried sardines with tomato & fig 705
Spaghetti with sardines, currants & pine nuts 124
tinned 28
Tunisian grilled smashed sardines on toast 183
Satay sauce 104

sauces 62-3
A quick Bordelaise sauce with bone marrow & roasted shallots 68
Aïoli 76
Anchoïade 78
Bagna cauda 83
Béarnaise sauce 79
Béchamel 70-1
Beurre blanc 69

Beurre rouge 69
Black aïoli 76
Black bean & ginger sauce 100
Bois Boudran sauce 88
Bread sauce 70
Brown butter & lemon sauce for crepes & blintzes 771
Burnt butter sauce with lemon, capers & parsley 73
Burnt butter sauce with lemon, sage & toasted walnuts 73
burnt honey & thyme sauce 344
burnt honey sauce 673
cheese sauce for Moussaka 310-1
Chimichurri 85
Chocolate & honey sauce 793
Choron 79
Coriander, onion & citrus sauce 11
Enhanced soy sauce 101
Fast red-wine sauce for meat 65
Fermented cooked chilli sauce 97
Fresh mint sauce 82
Fresh ponzu 101
Gochujang chilli sauce 97
Golden syrup butter caramel sauce 793
Green harissa 92
Green peppercorn sauce for steak 84
gremolata 296
Harissa 92
Hollandaise 79
Italian tartare 77
Lemon emulsion 80
Maltaise sauce 79
Marie Rose sauce (cocktail sauce) 77
meat sauce for Moussaka 310-1
mint passata sauce 133
Mustard sauce 66
Nori tartare 77
Nuoc cham 93
Onion sauce 599
Paloise sauce 79
Parsley & lemon butter 73
Peach caramel sauce 721
Persillade 86
provolone sauce 528
puttanesca sauce 117
Quick apple sauce for roast duck or pork 684
Quick creamy seafood sauce or bisque 67
Quick prawn essence 67
red wine, orange & coffee sauce 720
Roasted garlic jus with tarragon 66
roasted plum & hoisin sauce 263
Rouille 80
Salted caramel sauce 794
Salted coconut caramel 794
Satay sauce 104
Sauce diable 65
Sauce gribiche 78
Sauce vierge 82
Scorched honey & thyme gastrique for duck 265
Simple coconut soup-style sauce for steamed fish 162

Simple duck sauce 262
Simple seafood pie sauce 71
Simple tomato sugo 116
Smashed berry sauce 687
Spicy malt plum sauce 725
Sweet & sour sauce with pineapple 100
Sweet & sour tamarind sauce 611
Tahini dip/sauce 71
tare 58
Teriyaki sauce 101
Thai caramel sauce for fish 105
Tomato essence 85
tomato, mint & anchovy sauce 132
Velouté 64
Whole pickled chillies & a simple fermented chilli sauce 494-5
XO sauce 98
yoghurt & garlic sauce 312
yoghurt & lemon sauce 181
Zhoug 87
see also chutney, dipping sauces, mayonnaise, pesto, salsas
Sauerkraut 454-5

sausages
Black aïoli with cured meat 76
Böreks with cheese & fried sausage 831
Fennel & buffalo mozzarella salad with cured meat 530
Fennel, potato & sausage tray bake 530
Italian sausage ragù 335
Mortadella agnolotti 114
Pizza bianco with sausage, roasted cauliflower, chilli & cherry tomatoes 857
Pork polpette & potato al forno 337
Salami pizza 857
Sausage & sage risotto 149
Scotch quail eggs 360
Seared radicchio with burrata & cured meat 566
Silverbeet & haloumi pies with sausages 563
Skinless merguez-style sausages 308
Slow-cooked robust ragù of pork & beef 336
Witlof, rocket & macadamia salad with pork & fennel sausage, mustard & honey 554
see also chorizo, cotechino, morcilla, mortadella, nduja, salami
savoury 28
savoury baking 836-7
scallions *see* spring onions

scallops 206
An inspiration from ajo blanco with seafood 513
Bouillabaisse-style stew 214-5
Crumbed scallops 210
dried scallops (conpoy) 13
Grilled scallops 210
Jerusalem artichoke soup with seafood 544
Pan-seared potato gnocchi with scallops, mushrooms & lemon 140
Seared scallops with chorizo & apple 210-1

Slow-roasted Jerusalem artichokes with roe & pan-fried scallops 542
XO sauce 98
scamorza 28
Deluxe eggplant parmigiana with anchovies 522
Lasagne 136
Summer vegetable lasagne 136
Schiacciata con l'uva 845
Schnitzel 345
scones
Cheddar & feta scones with mixed seeds 859
Classic scones 772
Saffron scones 772
Scotch fillet steak 277
Scotch quail eggs 360
scramble, French-inspired 351
scrambling eggs 351
scrolls, Poppy seed, sour cherry & vanilla 764
sea urchin: Sea urchin linguini with roasted tomato passata & butter 128
seafood 152
see also clams, crabs, cuttlefish, eel, fish, mussels, octopus, oysters, pipis, prawns, scallops, shrimp, squid
seaweed see arame, kombu, nori, wakame
seed oils 22–3
seeds 368–9
see also chia seeds, linseeds, pepitas, sesame, sunflower seeds
semifreddo, Christmas pudding 779
sesame 28, 369
Apricot & sesame oat bars 392
Barbecued prawns with gochujang, sesame & lime 202
black sesame dressing 561
Böreks with cheese 831
Charred broccoli, ramen & nori salad 444–5
Chilled cucumber & sesame salad with shiso & garlic chives 507
Chocolate biscuit sandwiches with sesame cream 754–5
Classic dinner knot rolls 846
Coconut bircher 393
Coconut panna cotta with coconut jelly, black sesame tuiles, mango & lime leaf 783
Crispy pork belly salad with sesame spiced dressing, cucumber & coriander 331
Daikon, edamame & avocado salad with sesame, apple & soy dressing 640
Date, sesame, coconut & macadamia nut balls 393
Eggplant with miso glaze & spring onions 521
Eggplant, sesame, egg, olive & radish salad 518
Falafel with broad beans & tahini yoghurt 432
Fish marinated with white miso 184
Fried rice with wood ear fungus & cashews 402

ginger & sesame dressing 450
Gochujang chilli sauce 97
Goma dare (sesame dressing) 102
Gomashio 16
Grilled minute steak with soy & sesame mushrooms 281
Japanese mixed rice & grains 382
Japanese-style chicken meatballs 251
Kimchi pancakes with a tamari & sesame dipping sauce 457
Korean sesame grilled beef with sake, ginger & soy marinade 293
Korean-style fried chicken 237–8
Lebanese talami bread topped with za'atar 853
Lebanese talami bread with spiced tomato topping 853
Mapo-style tofu with beans & pork 436
Miso doughnut glaze with sesame 774
No-bake seed bars 392
Nutty, salty, sweet & seedy crunch mix 377
Okra with shiso, soy & toasted sesame seeds 582
Pea salad with a golden garlic, sichuan pepper & ginger dressing 614
Prawn or crab omelette with oyster sauce 353
Pressed spinach with sesame (Horenso gomaae) 561
Pretzels 841
sesame & lime dressing 507
sesame & mirin dressing 582
Sesame brittle 786
Sesame dressing 94
sesame dressing (Goma dare) 102
Sesame mayonnaise 75
sesame oil 22
Sesame saganaki with quick-pickled cucumber 510
sesame seeds 28, 369
Sesame tuilles 788
Sesame-crumbed ocean trout with nori mayo in a brioche bun 191–2
sesame, apple & soy dressing 640–1
Silverbeet & haloumi pies 563
Simit/koulouri 842–3
Simple honey, soy & ginger drumettes 237
Soba noodles with avocado, sprouts, umeboshi & sesame 410
Soy, sesame & apple vinaigrette 102
soy, sesame & ginger dipping sauce 500
Spiced seed crackers 839
Spiced sesame & peanut dressing 94
Spiced tea eggs 356
Spicy pork bao 333
Steamed whole fish with spring onion, ginger & sesame 177
Stir-fried green beans with sesame, ginger & oyster sauce 437
Super seed loaf 376
Sweet & spicy Thai chicken drumettes 236–7
tamari & sesame dipping sauce 457
tamari sesame dressing 415
Toasted muesli 394

Toasted sesame & miso dressing 102
Tuna & sweet potato sesame patties with pickled arame salad 622
Tuna poké bowl with avocado, shiitake, sesame, wakame & cucumber 415
Tunisian dukkah 13
Turkish tomato & sesame topping 853
umeboshi & sesame dressing 410
Wild rice, herb, almond & currant salad 378
Wombok, daikon, shiitake & tofu salad 450
Za'atar 33
Zucchini 'chips' 667
see also tahini
Shakshuka with capsicum 463
shallots
A quick Bordelaise sauce with bone marrow & roasted shallots 68
Broccolini with speck, shallot & garlic 442
Celeriac remoulade with shallots & pickles 484
Crisp fried shallots 600
fried 14
Onion sauce 599
Pickled shallots & currants with parsley & cornichons 596
Pissaladière 599
Quick-pickled onions 594
Salt-roasted shallots 595
shallot dressing 508
Sherry vinegar–glazed shallots & taleggio on toast 596
Sweet pickled onions 597
shaoxing cooking wine 28
Black bean & ginger sauce 100
Chicken & ginger wontons with peanuts 231
Glazed red pork with cassia, star anise, black vinegar & wood ear fungus 341
Pork & prawn wontons with chilli & sichuan pepper dipping sauce 342
Pork & prawn wontons with choy sum & kale 342
Shiitake, tofu & cashew san choy bau 555
Simple honey, soy & ginger drumettes 237
Steamed whole fish with spring onion, ginger & sesame 177
Stir-fried clams with XO sauce 211
Stir-fried kang kong & wombok with tofu & fermented chilli 400
Sweet & sour sauce with pineapple 100
XO sauce 98
shellfish 204–8
see also clams, mussels, oysters, pipis, scallops
sherbet, Raspberry, marshmallows 791
shiitake mushrooms 28, 568–70
Chawanmushi 356
Chicken noodle broth with porcini polpette 253
Daikon & shiitake braised in soy dashi & brown butter sauce 642
Enhanced soy sauce 101

Fish & shiitake mushrooms marinated with white miso 184
Fragrant chicken soup with bok choy 401–2
Fried rice with wood ear fungus & cashews 402
Glazed red pork with cassia, star anise, black vinegar & wood ear fungus 341
Japanese-style chicken meatballs 251
Prawn, corn & shiitake pot-sticker dumplings 500
Ramen 59
Roast duck, crab & tapioca soup 265
Seared beef with bean thread noodles, beans, wood ear fungus & gochujang 292
Shaved brussels sprouts with roasted king brown mushrooms, manchego & maple dressing 453
Shiitake, tofu & cashew san choy bau 555
Shoyu ramen broth 58–9
soy shitake mushrooms 415
Stir-fried greens & shiitake with XO sauce 401
Teriyaki pork belly wrapped with shiitake, spring onion & togarashi 343
Tuna poké bowl with avocado, shiitake, sesame, wakame & cucumber 415
Turnip & shiitake braised in soy dashi & brown butter sauce 642
Udon noodles with chicken, shiitake, bok choy, miso & kimchi 402
Vietnamese spring roll with crab, prawn & shiitake 575
Wombok, daikon, shiitake & tofu salad 450
shiso (perilla) 28

shortbreads
Breton shortbreads with almonds & demerara 819
French shortbread (Pâte sablée) 813
French shortbread sandwiches with mascarpone cream, almonds & praline 813
French strawberry shortcake with crème pâtissière 819
shortcrust pastry see pastry
shoyu 28

shrimp 28
Beef rendang 292–3
citrus & chilli relish 358
Crispy eggplant with spiced caramel & fried Thai basil 522–3
Fried rice with peas, prawns & egg 610
red curry paste 266
red kimchi paste 456
Thai caramel sauce for fish 105
Thai green papaya salad 438
Thai-style chilli jam 96
XO sauce 98
see also prawns
Siamese watercress see kang kong

sichuan pepper 28–9
Asian brisket with vinegared blood plums 291

Chinese five-spice 10
golden garlic, sichuan pepper & ginger dressing 614
Mapo-style tofu with beans & pork 436
Roasted blood plum relish 725
Sichuan pepper & chilli dressing 93
Sichuan pepper & honey glaze 331
Sichuan pepper & mandarin salt 29
sichuan pepper dipping sauce 342
Sichuan pepper salt 29
Spiced Chinese pickles 640
Spicy fried quail with sichuan pepper salt 269

silverbeet 550–5
Böreks with cheese & greens 831
Braised lamb neck & barley broth 308–9
Braised lamb, artichokes, lemon & cinnamon with couscous 537
Braised silverbeet with garlic & lemon 555
Cheese, silverbeet & hazelnut filling for sambouseks 833
Cheesy buttered greens 430
Green aglio e olio 122
Greens & cheese pie 564–5
Greens, potato & cheese pie with olive oil pastry 828
Lebanese talami bread with cheese & greens 852
Left-over chicken, barley & vegetable soup 252
Raw silverbeet, mint & pistachio salad 561
Raw silverbeet, sorrel & hazelnut salad 560–1
Silverbeet & haloumi pies 563
Silverbeet or zucchini & feta omelette 353
Spiced green soup 381
Winter minestrone with roasted root vegetables 607
see also chard
Simit/koulouri 842–3

skewers
Balinese-style chicken skewers 104
Lebanese skewered chicken with cumin, lemon, black pepper & garlic 247
Moorish pork skewers with orange & black olive salsa 345

skordalia
Almond skordalia 373
Potato skordalia 621
walnut & rye skordalia 600

slaws
Apple, fennel & witlof slaw with buttermilk dressing 680
Celeriac, apple & kale slaw with anchovy 484–5
Classic cabbage slaw 448
Italian-style coleslaw 448
Kohlrabi, cabbage & beetroot slaw 548–9
Pear, fennel & witlof slaw with buttermilk dressing 680
White cabbage & pea slaw 448–9

slippery jack mushrooms 568–70
Barley 'risotto' with mushrooms & speck 572

Carrot, mushroom & gruyère loaf with mushroom 472–3
Mushroom risotto 151
smoothie, Berry, coconut & mint 688

snake beans
Gado gado with roasted vegetables 478
Thai fish cakes 192–3
Thai green papaya salad 438

snapper
Fish cakes with parsley 190–1
Fish stock 52–3
Fish with Thai caramel sauce & herbs 172
Salt-baked fish 175
Snapper crudo with a lemon emulsion & horseradish 164
Snapper crudo with finger lime, fennel, chilli & a burnt butter dressing 165
Snapper en papillote 178
Thai fish cakes 192–3
Whole snapper baked with cumin, lemon, bay & green harissa 181
Whole snapper pan-fried with bay & garlic 181

snow peas 608–10
Pea salad with a golden garlic, sichuan pepper & ginger dressing 614–5
Prawn & poached chicken vermicelli salad 240
Stir-fried cucumber with wood ear fungus & snow peas 510
soba noodles see noodles
sorbet, Strawberry or watermelon 784

sorrel 29, 551–2
foraging 551
Greens & cheese pie 564
Herbed velouté 64
Raw silverbeet, sorrel & hazelnut salad 560–1
Spinach, mint & rice salad with yoghurt dressing 560
Witlof, rocket & macadamia salad with pork & fennel sausage, mustard & honey 555
soufflé, Twice-baked cheese 357

soups
Asparagus soup 407
Braised fresh borlotti beans in lemon & cumin stock 426
Braised lamb neck & barley broth 308–9
Chicken noodle broth with porcini polpette 253
Chicken, corn & noodle soup 502–3
Corn chowder with potato & dill 502
Cream of mushroom soup 574–5
Fish soup with spiced rouille & croûtes 174–5
Fragrant chicken soup with bok choy 401–2
Fragrant seafood soup with bok choy 402
French onion soup 596
Gazpacho 657
Harira 461
Jerusalem artichoke soup 544

Kohlrabi, cauliflower & fenugreek soup
548
Left-over chicken, barley & vegetable soup
252
Pea & ham soup 334
Roast duck, crab & tapioca soup 265
Roasted cauliflower & turmeric soup with
yoghurt & poached egg 476
Smoked eggplant soup with kefalograviera
519
Smoked ham hock & borlotti bean soup
425–6
Smoked ham hock & pea soup 426
Spiced creamed tomato soup with bacon
665
Spiced green soup 381
Spring minestrone 531
Stracciatella soup 55
Tom yum goong 201
Tomato & cherry gazpacho 657
Vegan inspiration from ajo blanco 513
Vegetarian fragrant soup with bok choy 402
Watercress & potato soup 558
Winter minestrone with roasted root
vegetables 607
Zucchini & cream soup with cumin 673

sour cream
Balsamic pepper strawberry & chicken
sandwiches 689
creamy mustard dressing 484
Fried corn cakes with chilli jam & smashed
avocado 498
Hazelnut plum streusel cake 741
Miso doughnut glaze with sesame 774
sour cream dressing 449
sour cream roast garlic dressing 484
sour cream shortcrust pastry 599
Spiced sesame & peanut dressing 94
Sourdough bread 847–51
sourdough mother/starter, making 849
souvlaki, Easy 312
spatchcocking 229

speck 325
Barley 'risotto' with mushrooms & speck
572
Broccolini with speck, shallot & garlic 442
Chicken fricassee with Dutch creams,
speck & tarragon 239
Spiced creamed tomato soup with bacon
665
XO sauce 98
spelt: *Vegetarian baked haloumi-stuffed
eggplant* 521

spice mixes
Baharat 6
black onion spice 281
Chinese five-spice 10
cinnamon sugar 685
dry marinade spices 290
Garam masala 15
Gomashio 16
Greek spice mix 16
moorish spice mix 345
Nutty, salty, sweet & seedy crunch mix 377

Quatre épices 24
Ras el hanout 25–6
Seasoned pistachio dust 376
seasoning powder 290
spice coating 269
spice oil 386
sweet smoky spice mix 331
Sweet spice mix for baked goods 792
thyme & oregano rub 424
Tunisian dukkah 13
Za'atar 33
see also pastes, salt

spinach 550–5
Böreks with cheese & greens 831
Chicken noodle broth with greens 253
Congee 383
Egg, tomato & spinach curry with ginger &
turmeric 359
Eggs en cocotte with wilted spinach &
parmesan 359
Fragrant chicken soup with bok choy
401–2
Frittata 355
Green aglio e olio 122
Green goddess dressing 89
Green harissa 92
Greens & cheese pie 564–5
Greens, potato & cheese pie with olive oil
pastry 828
Lamb, pea & mint pancake fritters 319
Lamb, spinach, pomegranate & date salad
with crisp pitta 314
Lebanese talami bread with cheese & greens
852
New potatoes with green goddess dressing
89
Pressed spinach with sesame (Horenso
gomaae) 561
Quick herb salad 267
Ricotta & spinach gnudi 141
Ricotta & spinach ravioli 116
*Risotto with ricotta, spinach & verjuice-
braised leek* 149
Savoury crepes 771
Spaghetti with spinach, lemon &
pangrattato 124
Spiced green soup 381
Spinach & cheddar omelette 353
Spinach, lentil & yoghurt salad with brown
butter 558
Spinach, mint & rice salad with yoghurt
dressing 560
Spinach, ricotta & feta cannelloni with
mint passata sauce 133
spinach, ricotta & feta cannelloni filling
133
Tagliatelle with lemon cream 123–4
see also kang kong (water spinach, Siamese
watercress)

split peas 29, 608
Fava 373
Pea & ham soup 334
Smoked ham hock & pea soup 426

sponge cake
Berries & cream sponge cake filling 748
Classic sponge cake 748
Heavenly sponge filled with cream &
strawberries 689

spring onions 592, 594–5
Barbecued prawns with gochujang, sesame
& lime 202
Beef pho 57
Black bean & ginger sauce 100
black onion spice 281
Charred broccoli, ramen & nori salad
444–5
Charred fennel salad with vegetables 528
Chicken & ginger wontons with peanuts
231
Chimichurri 85
Chow mein-style beef with wombok 292
Crab cakes 199
Crisp-fried eggs, corn, smoked trout & herb
salad with tangy oyster sauce dressing
358–9
Crispy pork belly salad with sesame spiced
dressing, cucumber & coriander 331
Cured beef with black onion spice &
parmesan 281
Domatokeftedes 664
Eggplant with miso glaze & spring onions
521
Fish pie 188–9
Fried rice with wood ear fungus & cashews
402
Ginger & spring onion sauce 95
Glazed red pork with cassia, star anise,
black vinegar & wood ear fungus 341
*Gnocchi with leek, gorgonzola & spring
onion 'ash'* 602
Grilled minute steak with soy & sesame
mushrooms 281
Kimchi 455–6
Kimchi pancakes with a tamari & sesame
dipping sauce 457
Kingfish crudo with caviar, cucumber &
mustard cress 510
Kohlrabi, cabbage & beetroot slaw 548–9
Nori tartare 77
Peanut & ginger dressing 95
Seared duck breast with roasted plum &
hoisin sauce for pancakes or bao 263
Spicy fried quail with sichuan pepper salt
269
Spring onion 'ash' 602
Spring onion oil 103
Steamed whole fish with spring onion,
ginger & sesame 177
Teriyaki pork belly wrapped with shiitake,
spring onion & togarashi 343
Vietnamese spring roll with crab, prawn &
shiitake 575
white kimchi paste 456
White-poached chicken 230
spring roll, Vietnamese, with crab, prawn &
shiitake 575

squid 216–7

Blanched calamari with tuna sauce & olives 220

Bouillabaisse-style stew 214–5

Calamari fritti 223

Grilled calamari with smoky tomato dressing 223

Seared squid & pea salad with tomato & chilli 612

squid ink 29

sriracha 29

star anise 29

steak, Cauliflower 477

sterilising jars 40

stew, Bouillabaisse-style 214–5

stocks 44–50

beef stock 49

Braised fresh borlotti beans in lemon & cumin stock 426

Brown beef glacé 55

Brown beef stock 55

chicken stock from a left-over roast 49

chicken stock from raw bones 49

Chinese chicken stock 54

Classic white vegetable stock 51

Crustacean stock 52

Dashi 53

Double chicken stock 54

essentials 48–50

Fish stock 52–3

Golden chicken stock 54

poaching stock for meat 297

Quick & simple duck stock 266

quick duck stock 50

Robust vegetable fumet 51

soy stock 230

stock cubes/powder 29

stock reductions 64–8

White chicken stock 54

see also broths

stone fruit 718–20

A simple poaching liquid for stone fruit 724

Free-form stone fruit tart 814

Roasted stone fruit 720

Roasted stone fruit & ginger clafoutis 721

see also apricots, cherries, nectarines, peaches, plums, quince

stracchino

Baked polenta with gorgonzola, radicchio, walnuts & balsamic 382

Baked polenta with stracchino & greens 382

Fluffy prawn & crab omelette with prawn essence & watercress 355

Greens, potato & cheese pie with olive oil pastry 828

Savoury crepes 771

stracciatella

Green aglio e olio with cheese 122

Raw Jerusalem artichoke salad with broad beans & cheese 544

Stracciatella soup 55

strawberries

A simple frangipane fruit tart 796

Balsamic pepper strawberry & chicken sandwiches 689

Berries & cream sponge cake filling 748

French strawberry shortcake with crème pâtissière 819

Heavenly sponge filled with cream & strawberries 689

Puff pastry tart with fruit 824–5

Roasted rhubarb & strawberries with rose geranium 648

Strawberries romanoff 688

Strawberry or watermelon sorbet 784

White chocolate & strawberry mille-feuille 824

streusel cake, Hazelnut plum 741

strozzapreti 131

see also pasta

strudel, Viennese 684–5

sugar-snap peas 608–10

Broad bean & pea salad with nasturtium leaves, goat's cheese & bagna cauda 431

Pea salad with a golden garlic, sichuan pepper & ginger dressing 614–5

Risi e bisi 613

sugars

cinnamon sugar 685, 773, 775

dusting sugar 791

types of 29–30

sumac 30

sunflower seeds 369

Beetroot tabouleh with currants & sunflower seeds 419

Byzantine salad 379

Cheddar & feta scones with mixed seeds 859

No-bake seed bars 392

Nutty, salty, sweet & seedy crunch mix 377

roasting 371

Super seed loaf 376

Toasted muesli 394

Zucchini, ham & pea slice with feta 672–3

swedes: Pasties 469–70

sweet basil 7

sweet potato 616–20

Crisp sweet potato chips with paprika mayo 620

Pommes anna with vegetables 624

Roast carrot & root vegetable soup with cinnamon & ginger 472

Roasted parsnip & purple sweet potato with cinnamon, nutmeg & garlic 606–7

Sweet potato fritters 625

Winter minestrone with roasted root vegetables 607

Swiss brown mushrooms 568

Barley 'risotto' with mushrooms & speck 572

Chicken, leek & mushroom pie 603

Chickpeas with mushrooms, red-wine vinaigrette & tarragon 574

Mushroom risotto 151

Swiss chard *see* silverbeet

syrups

Basic sugar syrup 793

coffee syrup 776

Honey & orange-blossom syrup 792

Honey & white wine poaching syrup for stone fruit 723–4

orange syrup 740

scorched lemon syrup 707

T

tabouleh

Beetroot tabouleh with currants & sunflower seeds 419

Tabouleh 87

tagliatelle 112–3

tahini 30

Apple, blueberry & blackberry galette 818

Apricot & sesame oat bars 392

Baba ghanoush 519

Cauliflower salad (roasted & raw) 478–9

Chocolate biscuit sandwiches with sesame cream 754–5

Date, sesame, coconut & macadamia nut balls 393

Falafel with broad beans & tahini yoghurt 432

Goma dare (sesame dressing) 102

Grilled eggplant with tahini & yoghurt dressing, pomegranate, chilli & mint 516

Hummus 374

lemony tahini yoghurt 432

No-bake seed bars 392

Pressed spinach with sesame (Horenso gomaae) 561

Roasted cauliflower & barley salad with tahini dressing 477

Roasted pumpkin with tahini & yoghurt dressing, pomegranate, chilli & mint 516

Sesame tuiles 788

Side of salmon with walnuts, tahini, mint & pomegranate molasses 172

Smoked eggplant soup with tahini & feta 519

Spiced sesame & peanut dressing 94

tahini & yoghurt dressing 478–9

Tahini dip/sauce 71

tahini dressing 518

Turkish-style pumpkin & walnut dip 632–3

yoghurt dressing 560

Zucchini baba ghanoush 669

talami, Lebanese, bread with spiced tomato topping 852

taleggio 30

Baked polenta with stracchino and greens 382

Braised pork shoulder with borlotti beans & taleggio 424

Ham hock, rosemary & taleggio risotto 148

Omelette with mushroom & taleggio 353

Porcini, rosemary & taleggio risotto 151

Pumpkin, rosemary & taleggio risotto 632
Sherry vinegar–glazed shallots & taleggio on toast 596
Taleggio mash 625
Veal & pork polpette with savoy cabbage, taleggio & truffled pecorino 337

tangelos
citrus & chilli relish 358
Soft-boiled eggs with green mango salad & citrus & chilli relish 358
Watermelon & prawn salad citrus & chilli relish 201

tapenades
Queen green tapenade 590
Garlicky green olive tapenade 590
Green olive, artichoke & kale tapenade 590
Quick olive tapenade 587

tapioca 31
Roast duck, crab & tapioca soup 265
Tapioca pearls in coconut with tropical salad & caramel sauce 780–1
Taralli 842
Taramasalata 182
tare 58

tarragon 31
An exquisite herb salad 17
Anchoïade 78
Asparagus soup 407
Barbecued prawns with salsa verde 202
Basic vinaigrette lentils 385
Béarnaise sauce 79
Bois Boudran sauce 88
Cafe de Paris butter 72
Champignons with garlic, wine & cream 575
Charred fennel salad with tarragon 528
Chicken fricassee with Dutch creams, speck & tarragon 239
Chicken, leek & mushroom pie 603
Chickpeas with mushrooms, red-wine vinaigrette & tarragon 574
Confit parsnip salad 606
Corned beef with herb & mustard sauce 289
Crustacean stock with herbs 52
Ham hock & leek terrine 328
Herbed velouté 64
Kohlrabi & cucumber salad with lemon yoghurt dressing 549
orange & tarragon dressing 528
Pea & mozzarella salad 611
red-wine vinaigrette 574
Roasted garlic jus with tarragon 66
Rustic salsa verde with potato 86
Salsa verde 86
Sauce gribiche 78
Sauce viege with herbs 82
Sautéed wild asparagus with tarragon & brown butter 406
Spinach, lentil & yoghurt salad with brown butter 558
Tomato essence 85
Traditional French steak tartare with tarragon 279
Tuna niçoise 438–9

tartare
Chopped egg tartare 351
Citrus nori tartare for fish 187
Italian tartare 77
Nori tartare 77
tartare, Traditional French steak 279

tarts
A simple frangipane fruit tart 796
Baked custard tart 817
Cherry & almond burnt butter torte 722
Cherry puff pastry tart 824–5
Chocolate tart 817
Crostata filled with ricotta & quince 826
Even simpler frangipane tarts 797
Frangipane crostata 826
Free-form stone fruit tart 814
Gluten-free shortcrust pastry for a tart base 812
Gruyère & confit garlic tarts 828
Jam crostata 826
Jam tarts 826
Lemon tart 814–5
Piperade tart 829
Rhubarb tartlets 649
Simple custard tarts 815
Tarte tatin 682
Tomato tarte tatin, with manchego, thyme & dried olives 660
tempura beer batter 187
Tempura dipping sauce 98
Tempura okra 580
Teriyaki pork belly wrapped with shiitake, spring onion & togarashi 343
Teriyaki sauce 101
terrine, Ham hock & leek 328

Thai basil 7
Beef pho 57
Chilli crab 199–200
Crisp-fried eggs, corn, smoked trout & herb salad with tangy oyster sauce dressing 358
Crispy eggplant with spiced caramel & fried Thai basil 522–3
Crispy sweet-chilli chicken with wombok, Thai basil & peanuts 242
cucumber, celery heart & herb salad 240
Fragrant chicken soup with bok choy 401–2
Kohlrabi, cabbage & beetroot slaw 548–9
lychee & fried basil salad 266–7
Moules frites meets South-East Asia 204
Pork roll 333
Rockling with Thai caramel sauce & herbs 172
Sour fish & mussel curry with celery hearts & kang kong 488–9
Stir-fried kang kong & wombok with tofu & fermented chilli 400
Tom yum goong 201
Vietnamese spring roll with crab, prawn & shiitake 575
Wombok, daikon, shiitake & tofu salad 450

thyme 31
burnt honey & thyme sauce 344
Carrots with butter, honey & thyme glaze 469
Cassoulet 391
Chicken bone broth 53
Classic white vegetable stock 51
Crustacean stock 52
Dauphinoise potatoes 627
Duck bresaola 267
Duck, celeriac & verjuice ragù 259
Duck leg confit 260
Golden chicken stock 54
Herb oil for fish 165
lemon thyme 31
Pedro Ximénez–braised beef cheeks with celeriac & parsnip purée & persillade 285–6
Petit salé aux lentilles 334
Roast chicken with coriander seeds, thyme & tomato 243
Roasted pork scotch with burnt honey & thyme, scorched grapes & grilled peaches 344
Roasted potatoes with thyme 626
Roasted quince & chestnuts 716
Roasted radishes with thyme 643
Roasted rhubarb, blood plum & ginger chutney 646
Roasted scotch fillet 283
Roasted tomato passata 660–1
Salt-roasted shallots 595
Scorched honey & thyme gastrique for duck 265
Simple caramelised onions 598
Sliced pears roasted with maple syrup, thyme & white pepper 709
Slow-roasted eye fillet 285
Slow-roasted red onions 598
thyme & oregano rub 424
Thyme-crumbed onions 598
Tomato confit 656
Tomato tarte tatin with manchego, thyme & dried olives 660
Veal scallopini with guanciale, oyster mushrooms & thyme 295
Tiramisu 776–7
toffee, Raspberry, coulis 689

tofu 31
Chow mein-style tofu with wombok 292
Gado gado with tofu 478
Mapo-style tofu with beans & pork 436
Salt & pepper tofu for bánh mì 332
Shiitake, tofu & cashew san choy bau 555
Stir-fried kang kong & wombok with tofu & fermented chilli 400
Tofu 'mayonnaise' 75
Udon noodles with chicken, shiitake, bok choy, miso & kimchi 402
Vegan bánh mì 333
Vegan chow mein-style tofu with wombok 292
Vegetarian bánh mì 333
Vegetarian fragrant soup with bok choy 402
Wombok, daikon, shiitake & tofu salad 450

togarashi 31
tom yum paste 31
Tom yum goong 201
tomatoes 652–5
  Abbacchio al forno 315–6
  American-style ranch salad 557
  Anchovy, tomato & basil topping for
    focaccia 844
  Asian brisket with vinegared blood plums
    291
  Baked beans with mustard seeds, vinegar
    & tomato 390
  Baked tomatoes stuffed with rice, feta &
    pine nuts 663
  Barbecued prawns with smoky tomato
    dressing 202
  Basil & tomato topping for focaccia 844
  Black bean, quinoa & cherry tomato salad
    380
  Black dal 389
  Black turtle bean, pork belly & morcilla
    braise (frijoles negros) 340
  Bois Boudran sauce 88
  Bouillabaisse-style stew 214–5
  Braised baby octopus with red wine,
    oregano, paprika & cherry tomatoes 219
  Braised fennel with tomato & olives 529
  Braised lamb neck with white wine, tomato
    & oregano 316
  Braised romano beans 438
  Braised zucchini with fresh tomato & herbs
    671
  Bruschetta 655
  Bucatini amatriciana 121
  Butter chicken 248–9
  Cabbage rolls with lamb, rice, pine nuts &
    dill 451
  Caponata bianco with toasted walnuts 489
  Capsicum & eggplant salad 464
  Cassoulet 391
  Chicken coconut curry with makrut lime
    leaf, lemongrass & turmeric 238
  Chilli con pollo with chorizo & beans 232
  Choron 79
  Corn, black bean & pomegranate salad 503
  Crustacean vinaigrette 52
  Deluxe eggplant parmigiana with
    anchovies 522
  Domatokeftedes 664
  Egg, tomato & spinach curry with ginger &
    turmeric 359
  Eggplant & tomato kasundi 520
  Fish soup with spiced rouille & croûtes
    174–5
  Fried green tomatoes 662
  Fried sardines with tomato & fig 705
  Gazpacho 657
  Gigantes plaki 380–1
  Greek salad 512
  Greek-style braised okra (bamies) 580
  Green tomato salsa with dill & mint 664
  Grilled calamari with smoky tomato
    dressing 223
  Harira 461

Harissa 92
Insalata caprese 662
Iraqi chicken with tomato & cardamom
  rice 242–3
Italian sausage ragù 335
Lamb & eggplant karahi curry 318
Lamb koftas baked with tomato & smoky
  eggplant, with pine nuts & parsley
  309–10
Lamb navarin 643
Lamb rogan josh 317–8
Lebanese peas with lamb 614
Lebanese talami bread with spiced tomato
  topping 852
Left-over lamb roast shepherd's pie 319
Malloreddus with prawns & fennel 526
Martini family stuffed capsicums 464–5
mint passata sauce 133
Moussaka 310–1
Mussels with chorizo, tomato & white
  wine 213
Mussels with garlic & tomato 214
Nero vinaigrette 89
Octopus braised in rosé & tomato with
  radicchio & bottarga 219–20
*Omelette with blackened roma tomatoes,
  dill & marinated feta* 353
Orecchiette with tomato, mint & anchovy
  sauce 132
Oven-baked poussins with tomato, sherry,
  fennel & olives 590–1
Oysters with fire ice 208
Pan con tomate with soft-boiled eggs &
  celery salt 656
Pan-seared tomatoes on toast with feta &
  dill 663
Panzanella with buffalo mozzarella 658
passata (puréed tomatoes) 24
Pasta alla Norma 521
Pasta with fresh tomato sauce 658
Pea & ham soup 334
Pea & mozzarella salad 611
Pearl onions à la grecque 597
Pennette with tuna, tomatoes &
  mascarpone 125
Petit salé aux lentilles 334
*Pizza bianco with sausage, roasted
  cauliflower, chilli & cherry tomatoes* 857
Pizza margherita 857
Potato bread 844
Provençale tomato-stuffed peppers with
  olives & anchovies 662
puttanesca sauce 117
Ragù alla bolognese 283
Ratatouille 672
Roast chicken with coriander seeds, thyme
  & tomato 243
Roasted tomato passata 660–1
Roasted tomatoes with sumac & cumin 30
Salsa romesco 84
Sauce vierge 82
Sea urchin linguini with roasted tomato
  passata & butter 128
Seared squid & pea salad with tomato &
  chilli 612

Shakshuka with capsicum 463
Simple tomato sugo (Napoli) 116
Slow-cooked robust ragù of pork & beef
  336
Smoked ham hock & borlotti bean soup
  425–6
Smoky tomato dressing 84
Sour fish & mussel curry with celery hearts
  & kang kong 488–9
Sour fish curry with okra & celery heart
  581
Spaghetti puttanesca 117
Spiced bean & vegetable braise 425
Spiced creamed tomato soup with bacon
  665
Spiced duck with pickled watermelon 262
Summer vegetable lasagne 136
Sweet & sour sauce with pineapple 100
Syrian chicken with ginger, lemon &
  saffron 248
Tabouleh 87
Thai caramel sauce for fish 105
Thai green papaya salad 438
tinned 31
Tom yum goong 201
Tomato & cherry gazpacho 657
*Tomato & pomegranate dressing with
  chilli* 82
*Tomato & pomegranate dressing with
  rosewater* 82
Tomato confit 656
Tomato essence 85
tomato paste (concentrated purée) 31
tomato, mint & anchovy sauce 132
Tomato, pomegranate & sumac dressing
  82
Tomato tarte tatin with manchego, thyme
  & dried olives 660
Tuna niçoise 438–9
Tuna poké bowl with avocado, shiitake,
  sesame, wakame & cucumber 415
Tunisian vegetable couscous royale with
  rosewater labneh 386–7
Turkish tomato & sesame topping 852
Vegetable bolognese 576
Vine leaf beef & bone marrow pie 287
Wholesome hoisin sauce 96
Zaalouk 518–9
tonnato sauce 297
tortellini 113
  Tortelloni with pumpkin, sage & mustard
    fruits, with burnt butter sauce 114
Tortilla de patata 623
treacle, fennel & pepper cure 171
trevalla *see* blue-eye trevalla
trimoline/invert sugar 31
trout
  Citrus-cured gravlax 169
  Crisp-fried eggs, corn, smoked trout & herb
    salad with tangy oyster sauce dressing
    358
  Crudo with caviar, cucumber & mustard
    cress 510
  Fish marinated with white miso 184

Fish pie 188–9
Gravlax with treacle, fennel & pepper 171
Kingfish kibbeh nayyeh 166
Ocean trout & smoked trout rillettes 174
Potato rösti with ocean trout 623
Quick-cured ocean trout with finger lime &
  coriander 168
Salad of lentils & smoked trout with dill &
  horseradish cream dressing 385
Salt-baked fish 175
Seared ocean trout with grilled lettuce,
  peas & pea tendrils 561–2
Sesame-crumbed ocean trout with nori
  mayo in a brioche bun 191–2
Side of fish with walnuts, tahini, mint &
  pomegranate molasses 172
Sour fish & mussel curry with celery hearts
  & kang kong 488–9
Spinach, mint & rice salad with trout 560
Steamed whole fish with spring onion,
  ginger & sesame 177
Vinaigrette potatoes with seafood 624–5
truffles 571
Beef carpaccio with truffle 280
*Bruschetta of prawns, cannellini beans &
  truffle* 203
Jerusalem artichoke soup with truffle 544
Prawns with cannellini beans & truffle 203
Tagliatelle with egg, truffle & Parmigiano
  Reggiano 119
*Traditional French steak tartare with
  truffles* 279
truffle dressing 203
Truffled eggs 357
Truffled eggs en cocotte 357
truffles, Dark chocolate, with nutty praline 791
tuilles, Sesame 788
tuna
Blanched calamari with tuna sauce &
  olives 220
Charred broccolini with tuna mayonnaise,
  black barley, egg & anchovy dust 442–3
Crudo with a lemon emulsion &
  horseradish 164
Crudo with chilli, ginger & coriander 164
Fish with beurre rouge 183
lightly cured tuna 415
Pennette with tuna, tomatoes &
  mascarpone 125
*Roasted & raw fennel salad with preserved
  fish* 527
tinned/jarred 32
tonnato sauce 297
Tuna & sweet potato sesame patties with
  pickled arame salad 622
Tuna, brown rice & green bean salad with
  sumac 437
tuna mayo 442–3
Tuna mayonnaise 74
Tuna niçoise 438–9
Tuna poké bowl with avocado, shiitake,
  sesame, wakame & cucumber 415
Vitello tonnato 297

turmeric 31
Beef rendang 292–3
Black dal 389
Braised red lentils with turmeric, curry
  leaves, fried garlic & haloumi 387
Chermoula 90
Chicken coconut curry with makrut lime
  leaf, lemongrass & turmeric 238
Chickpea, garlic & turmeric salad with
  witlof 386
Fragrant chicken soup with bok choy
  401–2
Jerusalem artichoke pickle 545
lemongrass & turmeric marinade 246
Roasted cauliflower & turmeric soup with
  yoghurt & poached egg 476
Roasted lemongrass & turmeric chicken
  steaks 246
turnips 636–9
Baby turnips with butter glaze 643
Borscht 418
Lamb navarin 643
Lobster salad à la russe 200
Pickled turnip torshi 639
Quick-pickled turnips with soy & rice
  vinegar 640
Raw turnip with walnut oil, celery leaves &
  parsley 642
Tunisian vegetable couscous royale with
  rosewater labneh 386–7
*Turnip & shiitake braised in soy dashi &
  brown butter sauce* 642
turnovers
Apple & cherry turnovers 681
Berry turnovers 688
Cheesecake-flavoured biscuit turnovers
  825
Fruit-spiked apple & peach turnovers 681
turtle beans *see* black beans
Tzatziki 507

U

Udon noodles with chicken, shiitake, bok
  choy, miso & kimchi 402
umeboshi 32
Nori tartare 77
umeboshi & sesame dressing 410

V

vanilla 32
Amaretti biscotti 758–9
Baked custard tart 817
Banana & blueberry slab cake 760
Banana custard 801
Basic whipped cream 799
cannoli 820

Cat's tongue biscuits (Lengua de gato) 755
Cheesecake-flavoured biscuit turnovers
  825
Cherry & almond burnt butter torte 722
Cherry compote with brioche & crème
  fraîche 723
Cherry, raspberry & vanilla jam 723
Cherry, vanilla & balsamic compote 722
Chilled coconut & lime leaf rice pudding
  395
Chocolate & avocado ganache 412
Chocolate & honey sauce 793
Chocolate fudge icing 805
Classic muffins 732
Classic poppy seed loaf 752
Clotted cream 800
Coconut & raspberry cake with chocolate
  ganache 746
Coffee mascarpone cream 800
Cream cheese & ricotta filling 799
Cream- or jam-filled doughnuts 773
Crème brûlée 780
Deluxe bread & butter pudding 778
Deluxe chocolate galette cake 746–7
Easy vanilla crème caramel 781
Fig & ginger jam 706
French strawberry shortcake with crème
  pâtissière 819
*French strawberry shortcake with whipped
  ricotta* 819
Yoghurt panna cotta 781
Glacé orange 790
Hazelnut plum streusel cake 741
Heavenly sponge filled with cream &
  strawberries 689
Honey & white wine poaching syrup for
  stone fruit 723
Italian meringue & Italian meringue butter
  cream 807
Lemon cheesecake 698
Lemon cream & cherry possets 696
Pasta frolla (Italian sweet pastry) 825
Poached quince 714
Poppy seed, sour cherry & vanilla scrolls
  764
Quick quince & apple relish 716
Quince paste 717
Red velvet cupcakes with Italian meringue
  icing 731
Rhubarb galette 650
Rizogalo 395
Roasted pears with honey, verjuice,
  rosemary & bay leaves 711
Salted caramel & almond popcorn 788
Salted nut & choc chip biscuits 755
Sicilian cassata-style ricotta cake 752–3
Simple butter cake 736–7
Simple custard tarts 815
Simply cooked apples with spices 681
Spiced zucchini & walnut cake 674
Sticky date pudding 778
Strawberries romanoff 688
Sugared butter custard biscuits 759
Tarte tatin 682
Thick real hot chocolate 775

Thick vanilla custard 801
Vanilla & fig leaf panna cotta with scorched lemon syrup 707
Vanilla butter biscuits 754
Vanilla crème anglaise 800–1
Vanilla crème pâtissière 798
Vanilla cupcakes 731
vanilla custard 817
Vanilla frosting 803
Whipped vanilla ricotta filling 799
Yoghurt panna cotta 781
Yoghurt with spices 365

veal 270, 294
Brown beef stock 55
Mortadella agnolotti 114
Olives ascolana 587
Veal & pork polpette with savoy cabbage, taleggio & truffled pecorino 337
Veal osso buco with white wine & gremolata 296
Veal saltimbocca with fresh figs 702–3
Veal scallopini with guanciale, oyster mushrooms & thyme 295
veal stock 49
Veal, artichoke & mint ragù 535
Vitello tonnato 297
vegetable oils 23
Velouté 64
verjuice/verjus 32
Vietnamese mint 20
Beef pho 57
Moules frites meets South-East Asia 204
Pork roll 333
Prawn & poached chicken vermicelli salad 240
Vietnamese spring roll with crab, prawn & shiitake 575
vinaigrettes 63, 82
Crustacean vinaigrette 52
French-style vinaigrette 88
Nero vinaigrette 89
red-wine vinaigrette 574
Soy, sesame & apple vinaigrette 102
Soy vinaigrette 103
Tamari-boosted all-round vinaigrette 103
vincotto 27
vine leaves 32
vinegars 32, 62
Vitello tonnato 297
vongole *see* clams, pipis

W

wakame 32
cucumber & wakame salad 415
Daikon & shiitake braised in soy dashi & brown butter sauce 642
Japanese quick-pickled cucumber & wakame salad 506
Tuna poké bowl with avocado, shiitake, sesame, wakame & cucumber 415

Waldorf salad with roast chicken wrapped in iceberg 490
walnuts 368
Baked polenta with gorgonzola, radicchio, walnuts & balsamic 382
Burnt butter sauce with lemon, sage & toasted walnuts 73
Caponata bianco with toasted walnuts 489
Carrot cake 742
Celeriac remoulade with nuts 484
Eggplant purée with chilli oil & walnuts 516
Deluxe chocolate galette cake 746–7
Gnocchi with leek, gorgonzola & nuts 602
Gorgonzola, fig & walnut pizza 857
Green aglio e olio with crunch 122
Grilled asparagus & haloumi salad with fennel, walnuts & pomegranate 406–7
Leek with walnut & rye skordalia 600
Lemonia's pumpkin & feta pie with olive oil pastry 631
Odette's chewy triple chocolate brownies 762
Pear, fennel & celery salad with radicchio & walnut 710
Raw turnip with walnut oil, celery leaves & parsley 642
Roasted pumpkin with walnut & rye skordalia 600
Shaved fennel, fried artichoke & walnut salad 353–6
Side of salmon with walnuts, tahini, mint & pomegranate molasses 172
Spiced pineapple & walnut cake 742
Spiced zucchini & walnut cake 674
Turkish-style roast pumpkin & walnut dip 632–3
Waldorf salad with roast chicken wrapped in iceberg 490
walnut & rye skordalia 600
White asparagus with walnut & rye skordalia 600
warrigal greens 550–5
wasabi 32
wasabi tobiko *see* fish roe
water chestnuts 33
Pork & prawn wontons with choy sum & kale 342
Vietnamese spring roll with crab, prawn & shiitake 575
water
acidulated water 6
see also orange-blossom water, rosewater
water spinach *see* kang kong (Siamese watercress)
watercress 552
Braised artichoke, egg, olive & watercress salad 538
Carrots with butter, honey & thyme glaze 469
Corned beef with herb & mustard sauce 289
Cucumber sandwiches 511
Cured beef with black onion spice & parmesan 281

Eggplant, sesame, egg, olive & radish salad 518
Fluffy prawn & crab omelette with prawn essence & watercress 355
Green goddess dressing 89
Herbed velouté 64
Jamón, fig, beetroot, goat's curd, watercress & mint salad 702
Kingfish kibbeh nayyeh 166
Nasturtium & miso butter 72
New potatoes with green goddess dressing 89
Vitello tonnato 297
Warm celeriac salad with yoghurt, aleppo chilli, pine nuts & sultanas 482
Watercress & potato soup 558
see also kang kong (Siamese watercress)
watermelon
Spiced duck with pickled watermelon 262
Strawberry or watermelon sorbet 784
Watermelon & prawn salad citrus & chilli relish 201
whipped cream, Basic 799
white anchovies 33
whiting
Deep-fried fish with celery & olive salad 188
Fried fish with tomato & fig 705
wholegrains *see* grains
wild rice 26
wine 33
witlof *see* chicory
wombok
Chow mein-style beef with wombok 292
Crispy sweet-chilli chicken with wombok, Thai basil & peanuts 242
Grilled pork fillet, wombok & crispy egg 341
Kimchi 455–6
Pork, wombok & ginger dumpling filling 500
Pork, wombok & ginger dumplings 500
Shiitake, tofu & cashew san choy bau 555
Spiced Chinese pickles 640
Stir-fried kang kong & wombok with tofu & fermented chilli 400
Wombok, daikon, shiitake & tofu salad 450
wontons
Chicken & ginger wontons with peanuts 231
Pork & prawn wontons with chilli & sichuan pepper dipping sauce 342
Pork & prawn wontons with choy sum & kale 342
Pork, wombok & ginger dumplings 500
Prawn, corn & shiitake pot-sticker dumplings 500
wood ear fungus 568
Fried rice with wood ear fungus & cashews 402
Glazed red pork with cassia, star anise, black vinegar & wood ear fungus 341
Roast duck, crab & tapioca soup 265

Seared beef with bean thread noodles, beans, wood ear fungus & gochujang 292

Stir-fried cucumber with wood ear fungus & snow peas 510

wraps, Waldorf salad & roast chicken 490

yoghurt & lemon sauce 181
Yoghurt, cucumber & mint salad/dip 508
yoghurt dressing 560
Yoghurt panna cotta 781
Yoghurt with spices 365
Zucchini flower, wild rice, lentil & yoghurt salad 671

X

xanthan gum 33
XO sauce 98

Y

yeast 33

yoghurt 33, 365

Amber's yoghurt mango lassi 365
Apricot, semolina, almond & yoghurt cake 753
Balsamic pepper strawberry & chicken sandwiches 689
Cherry, semolina, almond & yoghurt cake 753
Coconut bircher 393
Cucumber & lime granita with gin jelly, yoghurt sorbet & minted cucumber 511
fennel, sumac & yoghurt marinade 311
Grilled eggplant with tahini & yoghurt dressing, pomegranate, chilli & mint 516
Labneh 362
lemon garlic mayonnaise 200
lemon yoghurt dressing 549
lemony tahini yoghurt 432
Nut yoghurt 394
Orange-blossom labneh 363
Raita 98
Roast chicken with spiced yoghurt crust 253
Roasted cauliflower & turmeric soup with yoghurt & poached egg 476
Roasted pumpkin with cinnamon, chilli, pickled onion, yoghurt & feta 631
Roasted pumpkin with tahini & yoghurt dressing, pomegranate, chilli & mint 516
rosewater labneh 386
Scorched honey & yoghurt parfait 785
Spinach, lentil & yoghurt salad with brown butter 558
Spinach, mint & rice salad with yoghurt dressing 560
tahini & yoghurt dressing 478-9
Tahini dip/sauce 71
Tzatziki 507
Warm celeriac salad with yoghurt, aleppo chilli, pine nuts & sultanas 482
Yoghurt 365
yoghurt & garlic sauce 312

Z

Za'atar 33
Zaalouk 518-9
zabaglione 776
Zhoug 87

zucchini 666-8

Baked zucchini stuffed with rice, feta & pine nuts 663
Braised zucchini with fresh tomato & herbs 671
Grilled zucchini salad 668
Left-over chicken, barley & vegetable soup 252
Ratatouille 672
Roasted zucchini with anchovy, oregano & chilli 672
Silverbeet or zucchini & feta omelette 353
Southern Italian fried zucchini 671
Spiced zucchini & walnut cake 674
Spring minestrone 531
Spring vegetable risotto 149
Spring vegetable salad with bagna cauda 431
Summer vegetable lasagne 136
Sweet Zuni-style pickles 668
Tunisian vegetable couscous royale with rosewater labneh 386-7
Vegetable bolognese 576
Zucchini 'chips' 667
Zucchini & cream soup with cumin 673
Zucchini & haloumi fritters with burnt honey sauce 673-4
Zucchini & pesto pasta 674
Zucchini baba ghanoush 669
Zucchini, coconut & macadamia muffins with lime cream cheese icing 734
Zucchini, ham & pea slice with feta 672-3
Zucchini, wild rice, lentil & yoghurt salad 671

zucchini flowers

Asparagus with bagna cauda 406
Crumbed zucchini flowers with crab mayonnaise & peas 669
Spring vegetable risotto 149
Spring vegetable salad with bagna cauda 431
Stuffed zucchini flowers 668-9
Zucchini flower, wild rice, lentil & yoghurt salad 671

Acknowledgements

It's been something of a life's journey for me to this book, and it has definitely been a constant companion for the past five years. It has been a great privilege to write, and it feels like it comes with a huge responsibility.

My hope was to create modern Australian cookbook for today and for generations to come. A book to grow up with and to give to someone you cherish. A help to shop and cook well and a guide to enjoy, appreciate and respect the food on our tables.

To tell the truth, an understanding of the enormity of the project didn't really happen until we stepped deep into the planning stage, all ten of us around the table … and so it began.

I had plenty of ideas of where I wanted to take things, combining recipes old and new with opinions and tricks of the craft to share through my filter, but I really wanted to take the opportunity dig out the deep reflection and my personal viewpoint to add the richness I wanted. This of course required a lot of help!

I am indebted to a great group of collaborators who helped me expand on the depth I was seeking or to add detail and instructions, pointing out the sometimes obvious steps skipped for the novice.

First and foremost, 'genius' Marcus Ellis. A great creator of the written word, especially when it comes to the culinary space. Your impeccable ability to turn my sometimes awkward cook's prose and vision into something very special, eloquent and richly entertaining – along with your meticulous research, planning and writing – is unique and wonderful. Writing this book with you has been the best, most reflective and rich experience. It was enormous but, from conception to completion, I was in the best hands. The introduction and chapter introductions read beautifully and are totally engaging and informative yet still very approachable. I am deeply indebted and simply cannot thank you enough. This book would not have been possible with anyone else but you in this role. I treasure our very long food journey and friendship, and look forward to celebrating the successes of this book with you.

Fiona and Sandy. Hardie Grant's investment and encouragement on such a vast project was both brave and beautiful.

In particular, Jane Willson's vision, enthusiasm and true interest gave us all great confidence. In a very competitive industry, her clarity of vision, a feeling for exactly who needs this book and why, and an uncanny knack to see the finished beauty combined with the grit and belief that anything was possible, steered us to print … after a deadline shift or three!

The Hardie Grant team one and all … Julie Pinkham, Roxy Ryan, editors Anna Collett and Elena Callcott, and the wider team Katri Hilden, Megan Ellis, Andrea O'Connor and Helena Holmgren … a massive thanks to you all for hours of time spent finessing this massive project. Creating a perfect and brilliantly useful cookbook needs so many experienced eyes.

To Loran McDougall, who managed to stay on top of an ever-shifting target and files of constant new ideas, thousands of images from many photo sessions and endless shot lists. In a sea of endless content, her presence was always calm and reassuring, holding the tiller firm.

Vaughan Mossop … your art direction on such a massive project was brilliant and focused. Thanks for your eye. The clean and precise design detail set the bar high and was instrumental in helping the book to find its groove, in particular early on.

Alice Oehr, after admiring your work from a distance for a long time and watching your career blossom, it's a wonderful opportunity to have you illustrate my book. Your distinct bright and colourful style is addictive and fun, your love of food shines through and resonates with me, and people naturally gravitate towards your energetic, playful drawings and colourways. Thank you for the outstanding cover you have created. I love it.

Kirstin Thomas, welcomed aboard late in the process but integrally important. Thank you for your fresh eyes and enthusiasm for this enormous book, finessing and fussing the internal layout and the cover with a super-experienced eye. Thank you.

Cathy Baker, my very special friend for life. True sounding board of all my creativity no matter how crazy, there at any hour with lots of laughs and enthusiasm, and sound and sometimes sensible professional advice. Thanks for the hand to hold and shoulder to cry on during the writing and testing of this book. We all needed it at times. And for effortlessly keeping all involved on track and for communicating through the tough times of the pandemic.

Lucy Hogarth and Claire McLennan for all the special little bits of magic and encouragement along the way.

My food is brought to life by the very talented photographer Mark Chew. Unflappable and patient, Mark would walk in and seamlessly pick up where he left off sometimes a year before. The set is quite an organic environment and at times I am evolving or changing dishes as we go. His ability to capture this cook's view is a delicate and precious commodity. Your shots are beautiful and truthful, and I am grateful for our work together.

Karina van de Pol, I am so happy you were part of this crack team we pulled together for this book. It was bigger than imagined and I had great confidence in your vision, and your contribution was effortlessly in sync. It was quite a journey at times, so thanks for enduring the ride, being so grounded and for sharing lots of fun and laughs along the way.

Emma Warren, a very talented cook and author with the most beautiful palate, a natural affinity for produce and a wicked turn of phrase, and such a deep understanding of seasonality and growing produce. The other half of hundreds of conversations about food, and how we eat and prepare. You have unique understanding of my vision, but more importantly you are one in a million. I love you, Guapa.

To chef Josh Reekie, a special thank you for all the help, advice and last-minute cameos on the shoots and testing. I am most appreciative of your calm and unflappable presence.

To chef José Santiago for helping out with gusto on the last shoot, which was a challenge and rather chaotic – but a job extremely well done. Thank you. And to Ava Wraight, for two days of random recipe testing with me – thank you.

Odette Martini, my darling little sister. I am so proud of you and I thank you for your recipes and contribution to this book. Your expertise, precision, love and appreciation of food is never ending, as is your ability and willingness to help me at any hour. Thanks for organising me at the drop of a hat, and for your sound advice on all things, especially baking. Flexible and multi-talented, your abilities are next level. This book wouldn't be quite the same or possibly even finished without your help. Special thank you, little sis.

And special thanks and gratitude to Tony Dench on bread-baking advice and recipes.

To my sister Justine for endless advice and love, I really miss you being nearby – so many taste-testing appointments to catch up on. Thank you for your enthusiasm in testing many things randomly for me over the years, you are always a massive help and your feedback has been invaluable. Thank you, Justine.

Judy Webb, all is good and organised when you're on a shoot and sending humorous and positive vibes out daily, like little rays of sunshine that bounce off us all. I am sure this is reflected in the pages. I am so appreciative of your time and dedication, and I treasure our friendship.

My parents Monica and Pierre have always nurtured my talents and given full encouragement to a somewhat headstrong daughter. They supported an early entry to a cooking career, and their consistent support is a great comfort. The emphasis on our family sharing meals and lively discussion are treasured and invaluable. I love you.

Michael Gerbran, you are the most supportive of this book and you haven't even seen it yet! I am privileged to have you as a friend and business partner. I am deeply appreciative of your encouragement and belief in this book and me. I look forward to the adventure of life and business ahead. Much gratitude and love to you.

Marnie Engerlander Rowe. A heap of gratitude for your true friendship and support through thick and thin. Thanks for background research and recipes supplied, endless laughs and conversations on food and life, travels and adventures that sometimes leads us to the strangest places, doing the most mundane and extraordinary things at the same time! You are very special to me and I truly thank you for all your support during the time its taken me to write this volume.

Sushil Jung Rana, thanks for your total support and hard work over many years and your dedication to cooking my food. I am extremely appreciative, as you have contributed in making this book possible in many ways.

Philippa Sibley, thank you for your insight, wise palate and many food discussions. Your kitchen prowess is welcome anytime and it's been a delight to reignite and continue our long friendship and work together.

We are all learning and in a great collective of evolving ideas. Many chefs and food writers have contributed to satisfying my curiosity and given me things to think about, in no particular order ... Alain Ducasse, Claudia Roden, Anthony Bourdain, Kylie Kwong, Damien Pignolet, Andrew McConnell, David Thompson, Martin Boetz, Tony Tan, Stephanie Alexander, Greg Malouf, Maggie Beer, Dan Hunter, Thomas Keller, Yotam Ottolenghi, Alice Waters, Charmaine Solomon, Neil Perry, Rick Stein, Giorgio Locatelli, Diana Henry, Simon Hopkinson, Tansy Good, Jeremy Strode, Guy Grossi, Liz Egan, David Chang, Fergus Henderson and Daniel Chirico.

Michael ... my inspiration for love and life and all things fine. You keep me grounded and motivated, supported and focused all at once with a funny side shining through at all times. Thank you, mi amore ... this book wouldn't exist without you right by my side (and the dirty dishes would be out of control by now).

And to our very special girls, Stella and Amber. I'm pretty sure you are as happy as I am to see this book come fruition. You have all been there all the way, allowing me to concentrate and test for hours. Along with that came endless meals and desserts and cakes and breads, sometimes randomly presented at odd times.

The three of you are my constant inspiration and nothing makes me happier than cooking for you. Your willingness to taste and offer sometimes (but not always!) amusing opinions was always very valuable and very special.

To all staff past and present that have helped in many small ways. Thank you.

And thanks to Rudi the vizsla, involved in shooting and testing all the way but who recently passed away. We all miss you.

To all my supplier friends over the years ... very special thanks to Gary McBean from Gary's Meats, George Kaparos and Con Andronis from Clamms Seafood, Mark, Sam and John Narduzzo from Pino's Fine Produce, and Anthony Femia from Maker and Monger, for your personal contributions and support directly on this book.

Suppliers

Baker Bleu
bakerbleu.com.au

Baker D. Chirico
bakerdchirico.com.au

Calendar Cheese Company
calendarcheese.com.au

Clamms Seafood
clamms.com.au

Claringbold's Quality Seafood
(03) 9826 8381

Damien Pike, Mushroom Man
0411 438 465

Dench Bakers
denchbakers.com.au

Dobson's Potatoes
(03) 5772 1521

Friend and Burrell
friendandburrell.com.au

Glenora Heritage Produce
glenoraheritageproduce.com

Gary's Quality Meats
garysqualitymeats.com.au

Grange Meat Company
(03) 9417 2689

Great Ocean Ducks
greatoceanducks.com

Hagen's Organics
hagensorganics.com.au

Holy Goat Cheese
holygoatcheese.com.au

In the Pantry
(03) 9827 1999

John Cesters
gamemeatandvenison.com.au

Maker and Monger
makerandmonger.com.au

Market Lane Coffee
marketlane.com.au

Mount Zero Olives
mountzeroolives.com

Northside Fruit & Veg
northsidefv.com

Pino's Fine Produce
pinosfineproduce.com

Prahran Seafoods
(03) 9827 0528

Royal Nut Company
royalnutcompany.com.au

Savour and Grace
savourandgrace.com.au

Scicluna's Real Food Merchants
sciclunas.com.au

Simon Johnson
simonjohnson.com

That's Amore Cheese
thatsamorecheese.com.au

The Essential Ingredient
essentialingredient.com.au

The Fermentary
thefermentary.com.au

Toscano's
toscanos.com.au

Vic's Meat
vicsmeat.com.au

Western Plains Pork
westernplainspork.com

Will Studd
willstudd.com

Yarra Valley Caviar
yarravalleycaviar.com.au

About the author

It's no overstatement to say that Karen Martini is one of Australia's most beloved chefs and food communicators – someone who taught a generation about bold, simple, joyful flavours, and someone who reached a broad and loyal audience through television, books, newspapers and her own Melbourne restaurants.

Karen's food message is drawn from her long professional cooking career, her Tunisian-Italian heritage and from the challenges of feeding nutritious and stimulating food to her young family. Her acclaimed career includes two-hatted stints as executive chef and owner at Melbourne Wine Room and as founding executive chef at Sydney's Icebergs Dining Room and Bar, as well as her own ventures with partner Michael Sapountsis – St Kilda pizzeria mr. wolf and the ambitious Hero, in Melbourne's iconic ACMI building, where she is a founding partner and creative food director.

Karen has had a TV presence for nearly two decades, including as resident chef on Australia's longest-running lifestyle television series, *Better Homes and Gardens*. She is a weekly columnist for the Nine newspaper magazine supplement *Good Weekend*, she is in-demand as a host and participant at events and festivals, and she is the author of eight cookbooks.

karenmartini.com   [◉] karen_martini

About Marcus Ellis

Marcus Ellis is a Melbourne-based food and wine writer and wine professional. He has worked with Karen for more than twenty years, both at the coalface in restaurants, and across several of her books and food columns, editing, researching and evolving content. He has also worked as an editor on a number of successful cookbooks, while also developing wine content and working as a fine-wine consultant.

Published in 2022 by Hardie Grant Books,
an imprint of Hardie Grant Publishing

Hardie Grant Books (Melbourne)
Wurundjeri Country
Building 1, 658 Church Street
Richmond, Victoria 3121

Hardie Grant Books (London)
5th & 6th Floors
52–54 Southwark Street
London SE1 1UN

hardiegrantbooks.com

Hardie Grant acknowledges the Traditional Owners of the country on which
we work, the Wurundjeri people of the Kulin nation and the Gadigal people
of the Eora nation, and recognises their continuing connection to the land,
waters and culture. We pay our respects to their Elders past and present.

A catalogue record for this
book is available from the
National Library of Australia

NATIONAL
LIBRARY
OF AUSTRALIA

Cook
ISBN 978 1 74379 449 4
ISBN 978 1 74379 897 3

10 9 8 7 6 5 4 3 2 1

Publisher: Jane Willson and Roxy Ryan
Project Editor: Loran McDougall
Writer: Marcus Ellis
Editor: Katri Hilden
Editorial Assistant: Elena Callcott
Design Manager: Kristin Thomas
Designer: Vaughan Mossop
Typesetter: Megan Ellis
Illustrator: Alice Oehr
Photographer: Mark Chew
Stylist: Karina van de Pol
Home Economist: Emma Warren
Production Manager: Todd Rechner

Colour reproduction by Splitting Image Colour Studio
Printed in China by 1010 Printing International Limited